A Treatise on Stock and Stockholders, Bonds, Mortgages and General Corporation Law

A TREATISE

ON

STOCK AND STOCKHOLDERS,

BONDS, MORTGAGES,

AND

GENERAL CORPORATION LAW,

AS APPLICABLE TO

RAILROAD, BANKING INSURANCE, MANUFACTURING, MINING,
TELEGRAPH, TELEPHONE EXPRESS, GAS, WATER-WORKS,
COMMERCIAL, TURNPIKE, BRIDGE, CANAL, STEAM-
SHIP, AND OTHER PRIVATE CORPORATIONS

BY

WILLIAM W. COOK,

OF THE NEW YORK BAR.

THIRD EDITION.

VOL. I.

CHICAGO:
CALLAGHAN AND COMPANY.
1894

STATE JOURNAL PRINTING COMPANY,
PRINTERS AND STEREOTYPERS,
MADISON, WIS

TO

THE HONORABLE

THOMAS M COOLEY, LL.D.,

PROFESSOR, AUTHOR AND JUDGE,

WHOSE PRE-EMINENT ABILITY, UNTIRING RESEARCH,

PROFOUND LEARNING AND EXALTED CHARACTER

HAVE SECURED FOR HIM AN

IMPERISHABLE FAME AS A JURIST,

UNDER WHOSE INSTRUCTION THE AUTHOR ACQUIRED A DESIRE TO SEARCH OUT

AND MASTER THE PRINCIPLES OF THE LAW,

THIS WORK

IS

RESPECTFULLY DEDICATED.

PREFACE TO THIRD EDITION.

This edition contains double the amount of material found in the second edition, and has increased the size of the work to two volumes

The subjects covered by the additional material are important and extensive Bonds, mortgages, deeds of trust, foreclosures, receivers and reorganizations are treated in several chapters in detail and with full notes New chapters on the law peculiar to steam railroads, street railroads, gas, telegraph, telephone, electric light, plank-road, and other corporations owing a duty to the public, have been added In addition thereto a comprehensive synopsis of the constitutional and statutory provisions of the various states so far as they affect corporations is contained in this edition.

Several chapters of the second edition have been rewritten, notably the chapters on corporate meetings, corporate elections, dividends, preferred stock and "watered" stock Moreover, the numerous cases and new principles of law that have arisen on the subject of corporations during the past four years have been embodied in this third edition

The large sales of the second as well as first editions indicate that the original plan of the work — a statement of general principles in the text and an exhaustive analysis of the cases in the notes — is satisfactory to the profession In this belief the author has pursued the same mode of treatment in the expansion of the work and the inclusion of new subjects

WILLIAM W COOK

New York, January 9, 1894.

PREFACE TO SECOND EDITION.

The second edition of this work is a treatise on the law of corporations as approached from the stand-point of stock and stockholders

The first edition has been revised, enlarged, extended, and in large part rewritten No substantial part of it has been omitted, and the general arrangement, order and section numbers have been retained. But the notes have been enlarged by all the recent cases, the text has been compressed into brief forms of expression, and many chapters have been entirely remodeled

In addition to this a large number of new subjects and principles are given, so as to make the book a complete work on corporation law. Among these new subjects may be mentioned the power of a corporation to hold land; to make mortgages; to borrow money; to loan money; to issue bills and notes; to issue debentures; to issue bonds secured by mortgages; to assign for the benefit of creditors; to give preferences; to exercise the power of eminent domain; to sell all its property, to consolidate, merge, amalgamate, absorb and lease; to enter into pools; to limit its liability; to make traffic arrangements, to make discriminations; to maintain monopolies and exclusive privileges, to become a partner in a copartnership; to guaranty the bonds or stocks of another corporation; to be an accommodation indorser, to undertake a new business; to be an executor or trustee; to pay for lobbying, and various other acts. A detailed statement of the law is made as to the power of the directors, executive committee, president, secretary, treasurer, cashier, general manager, superintendent and other agents to act and contract for the company. The proper method of executing corporate contracts and the liability of officers on irregularly-executed contracts, the character and use of the corporate seal; the law as to notice and admissions, the liability of the corporation for torts; and the rules, regulations and complications of directors' acts and meetings, are fully explained Irregular incorporations, lapses of charters, misfeasances, malfeasances and non-feasances; and dissolutions of corporations, with all the interests and complicated questions connected therewith, are examined

"Trusts," the recent combinations in trade, are explained and their legality considered. This edition also treats of foreign corporations, with their various rights, disabilities and liabilities, and of the process, pleadings, procedure and service in suits by and against foreign and domestic corporations.

The author believes that the law of stock and stockholders leads naturally up to and includes the whole law of corporations. He believes that the difficulty in understanding corporation law is due largely to the method of studying the subject. That legal fiction, that intangible existence, that imaginary body called the corporation, is not easily understood, and is not always dealt with intelligently. It is believed, however, that he who understands the rights, duties, powers and liabilities of stock and stockholders will have little difficulty in understanding the nature of corporations, the powers of corporations, the *status* of corporate creditors, and the various peculiarities of corporation law. A complete exposition of the law of stock and stockholders is a complete exposition of the law of corporations.

The remarkably rapid growth of corporations during the past twenty-five years has created a body of law which is fast becoming a system of jurisprudence in itself. In the days of Angell and Ames, corporation law was just arising, and in their great work it was impossible to give the infinite detail and subdivision of principle which now exist. In these latter days, however, a text-book on corporation law must give more than general principles and undigested citations of cases. It must explain the applications of the general principles; subdivide the topics, evolve rules from frequently-recurring facts, point out the difficulties, rights and remedies in the separate cases as they have arisen, and give the gist of the decisions themselves.

The writer has sought to make a clear, practical and complete presentation of the subject for the every-day use of the bench and bar. The subdivisions, the chapter subjects and the section headings are made so as to aid in finding, without delay, the point of law in which any one may be interested. These divisions and headings have been built up from the cases themselves, and from a study of the subjects which arise most frequently in the courts and in business transactions. The writer has carefully avoided all theories, long discussions, and, as far as possible, the use of technical language. He has not hesitated to express his opinion when the occasion seemed to warrant it, but his sole object has been to give a complete and concise statement of the law governing the subject.

The plan of the work is original and this volume is the result of a long and conscientious study of the sources of authority — the cases themselves These have been systematically examined and collected, and made the groundwork of the subdivisions of the book

A special effort has been made to develop fully those subjects which are litigated most often in the courts, and which occasion doubt, difficulty, danger and lawsuits to corporations and stock holders The number and complexity of the decisions have caused some confusion and doubt even in the mind of the bench itself Out of the chaos of material which lay scattered throughout many thousands of reports, the writer has sought to construct a treatise that will be a practical guide on all subjects relative to stocks and corporation law A special effort has been made to explain fully those principles which are of importance and constant interest and use to lawyers, investors, directors, stockholders, corporations and the general public

Copious notes are given for the purpose of illustrating, fortifying and explaining the text By this method it is believed that the thread of the subject is preserved in the text, and the mind of the reader not distracted by a mass of details On the other hand, by the notes the subject is still further developed, and the application of the principles to particular facts fully set forth.

The dates of the cases are given in the notes It is believed that thereby the relative importance of a given case can be more easily ascertained and determined It is also worthy of note that the dates of the cases become of great use when there is a conflict of authority By the dates also the important facts are brought out that the law of stock and stockholders and of corporations is of very recent origin; that most of the cases have arisen within the past fifty years, that the law relative to stockholders' actions against directors has arisen within thirty years, and that we are as yet only on the threshold of that new jurisprudence which, though now in a formative state, is for the future to regulate the great subject of corporations having a capital stock

In the composition of this work the author has been burdened with an abundance rather than a paucity of material The law of corporations, when explored in all its branches and details, is a vast subject There are over twelve thousand cases cited in this volume Although it is difficult to exhaust in a single volume the law contained in so great a number of cases, yet a conscientious effort has been made to do so

The generous reception, given to the first edition, which was double the number usually printed, is appreciated by the author The mode of treatment appears to have been satisfactory, and it has been retained in the present enlargement of the work to the whole field of corporation law. If an equally favorable judgment is passed upon the second edition, it will be a reward commensurate with the labor and thought involved in a work of this magnitude.

WILLIAM W. COOK.

NEW YORK, *November 4, 1889.*

CONTENTS.

PART I.

ISSUE OF AND LIABILITY ON STOCK.

CHAPTER VIII.

CHAPTER IX.

CHAPTER X.

CHAPTER XI.

CHAPTER XII.

CHAPTER XIII.

CHAPTER XIV.

CHAPTER XV.

CHAPTER XVI

CHAPTER XVII.

PART II.

TRANSFERS OF STOCK.

CHAPTER XVIII.

CHAPTER XIX.

CHAPTER XX.

CHAPTER XXI

CHAPTER XXII.

CHAPTER XXIII.

CHAPTER XXIV.

PART III

MISCELLANEOUS RIGHTS OF STOCKHOLDERS.

CHAPTER XXXV.

CHAPTER XXXVI.

CHAPTER XXXVII.

CHAPTER XXXVIII.

PART IV.

FRAUDS — ULTRA VIRES ACTS — INTRA VIRES ACTS — NEGLIGENCE
AND IRREGULAR CONTRACTS OF DIRECTORS, STOCKHOLDERS,
PROMOTERS AND AGENTS

CHAPTER XXXIX.

CHAPTER XL.

CHAPTER XLI

CHAPTER XLII.

CHAPTER XLIII

CHAPTER XLIV

CHAPTER XLV.

PART V.

BONDS, MORTGAGES, FORECLOSURES, RECEIVERS AND REORGANI-
ZATIONS

CHAPTER XLVI.

CHAPTER XLVII.

CHAPTER XLVIII

CHAPTER XLIX.

CHAPTER L.

CHAPTER LI.

CHAPTER LII.

PART VI.

CHAPTER LIII.

CHAPTER LIV.

CHAPTER LV.

PART VII.

CHAPTER LVI.

B

CHAPTER LVII.

CHAPTER LVIII.

TABLE OF CASES.

[The references are to the foot paging.]

[The references are to the foot pag. 19.]

[The references are to the foot paging]

[The references are to the foot paging]

[The references are to the foot-paging]

[The references are to the foot paging]

[*The references are to the foot-paging.*]

[The references are to the foot paging]

[The references are to the foot-paging.]

[The references are to the foot paging]

[*The references are to the foot-paging.*]

[The references are to the foot paging]

D

[The references are to the foot-paging.]

[The references are to the foot paging]

[The references are to the foot-paging.]

[*The references are to the foot-paging.*]

lxii   TABLE OF CASES.

[The references are to the foot paging]

E

[*The references are to the foot-paging*]

[*The references are to the foot-paging.*]

E.

[The references are to the foot-paging]

[The references are to the foot paging]

[*The references are to the foot-paging.*]

[The references are to the foot-paging.]

F

[*The references are to the foot-paging.*]

[*The references are to the foot-paging.*]

[*The references are to the foot-paging.*]

[The references are to the foot paging]

[The references are to the foot paging]

[The references are to the foot paging]

[*The references are to the foot-paging.*]

[The references are to the foot-paging.]

[*The references are to the foot-paging.*]

H

[The references are to the foot-paging]

[The references are to the foot-paging.]

l

[The references are to the foot paging]

[*The references are to the foot paging*]

[*The references are to the foot-paging.*]

[The references are to the foot-paging]

[The references are to the foot paging]

[The references are to the foot paging]

[*The references are to the foot-paging*]

TABLE OF CASES.

[The references are to the foot paging]

[The references are to the foot paging]

[The references are to the foot paging]

[The references are to the foot-paging.]

[*The references are to the foot-paging*]

[*The references are to the foot-paging.*]

L

[*The references are to the foot-paging.*]

[The references are to the foot-paging.]

[*The references are to the foot paging.*]

[The references are to the foot-paging.]

V.

[The references are to the foot-paging]

[The references are to the foot paging]

[*The references are to the foot-paging*]

[The references are to the foot-paging]

7

[*The references are to the foot-paging*]

STOCK AND STOCKHOLDERS, BONDS, MORTGAGES,

AND

GENERAL CORPORATION LAW.

PART I.

ISSUE OF AND LIABILITY ON STOCK.

CHAPTER I.

DEFINITIONS AND SCOPE OF THE WORK.

§ 1. *Definition of corporation* — A corporation is an artificial person like the state. It is a distinct existence — an existence separate from that of its stockholders and directors   Chief Justice Marshall, in the Dartmouth College Case,[1] defined a corporation as

---

[1] Dartmouth College v. Woodward, 4 Wheat, 518. 636 (1819)

The supreme court of the United States has said that "An incorporated company is an association of individuals, acting as a single person and by their corporate name," and again "Private corporations are but associations of individuals united for some common purpose, and permitted by the law

"an artificial being, invisible, intangible, and existing only in contemplation of law."

A corporation can be created by or under legislative enactment, and by that alone.[1]

§ 2. *Definition of charters, general and special* — A charter is the instrument which creates the corporation. It formerly was granted by the king. Later it was granted by an act of the legislature — a separate act being passed for each charter   At present the constitutions of many of the states require that in all possible cases the

to use a common name, and to change its members without a dissolution of the association " United States *v* Trinidad Coal Co, 137 U S, 160 (1890).

The following cases give definitions of a corporation   Ohio Ins Co *v* Nunnemacher, 15 Ind, 295 (1860), Ohio, etc, R. R. Co *v.* Wheeler, 1 Black (U. S.), 286, 295 (1861), per Taney, C J , Board, etc, Tippecanoe Co *v* Lafayette, etc., R R. Co., 50 Ind, 85, 108 (1875), Railroad Commissioners *v* Portland, etc., R R. Co., 63 Me, 269, 277 (1872), Thompson *v* Waters, 25 Mich, 214, 223 (1872), Baltimore, etc, R. R Co *v* Fifth Bap Church, 108 U S, 317, 330 (1882), People *v* Assessors of Watertown, 1 Hill, 616, 620 (1841), Thomas *v* Dakin, 22 Wend, 9, 70, 104 (1839), Warner *v.* Beers, 23 Wend, 103, 123, 124 (1840), Head *v* Providence Ins. Co, 2 Cranch (U S S C), 127, 167 (1804), Bank of U S *v* Deveaux, 5 Cranch, 61, 88 (1809), per Marshall, C J ; Louisville, etc , R R. Co *v* Letson, 2 How, 497, 552 (1844); 2 Kent, Com., 268, State *v* Milwaukee, etc , R'y Co, 45 Wis., 579, 592 (1878).

In Tippling *v.* Pexall, 2 Bulst, 233 (1613), "The opinion of Manhood, chief baron, was this, as touching corporations that they are invisible, immortal, and have no soul. A corporation is a body aggregate, none can create souls but God, but the king creates them, and therefore they have no souls "

The domicile of a corporation is entirely distinct from the domicile of its officers or stockholders. Perry *v* Round, etc., Assoc., 22 Hun, 293 (1880). See, also, cases in ch. XLV, *infra*, where the

jurisdiction of the federal courts was at issue.

It is well to state here that a joint-stock corporation and a joint-stock association are essentially different   Both have a capital stock, and both are managed by boards of officers and meetings of the stockholders. But a joint-stock company is unincorporated and is but a partnership. See ch XXIX.

[1] Franklin Bridge Co. *v.* Wood, 14 Ga, 80 (1853), United States Trust Co *v.* Brady, 20 Barb 119 (1855), Penn R. R. Co *v* Canal Com'rs, 21 Pa. St , 9 (1852), Stowe *v* Flagg, 72 Ill , 397 (1874), Hoadley *v.* County, etc., Essex, 105 Mass., 519 (1870): State *v* Bradford, 32 Vt , 50 (1859), McKim *v* Odom, 3 Bland's Ch. (Md), 407, 417 (1829).

In England certain colleges have power to create corporations. No such power exists in this country   Medical Inst. *v* Patterson, 1 Denio, 61 (1845)

Congress has constitutional power to incorporate a bank. McCullough *v.* State of Md , 4 Wheat., 316 (1819) Congress may incorporate interstate railroads. California *v* Pacific R R. Co, 127 U. S., 1, 39 (1888).

No particular form of words is requisite to create a corporation   Denton *v* Jackson, 2 John. Ch , 320 (1817)   Yet a statute which seems to create a corporation may be construed not to have that effect. See Walsh *v* Trustees, etc., 96 N. Y., 427 (1884), holding that the trustees of the Brooklyn bridge are not a corporation, but that the property belongs to the two cities of New York and Brooklyn.

legislature shall pass general acts whereby, by the simple filing of a prescribed instrument, persons may form a corporation without applying to the legislature at all.   These general acts specify the contents of the instrument to be filed, and specify also the powers of the corporation   A charter is special where a special act of the legislature creates the corporation   A charter is under the general act when it consists of a certificate of incorporation filed with the public authorities in accordance with a general act of the legislature allowing corporations to be formed in that manner   The general laws of the state apply to a corporation organized under a special act so far only as the former are consistent with the latter [1]

[1] The provisions of the general statutes relative to corporations are not applicable to a special charter so far as the provisions of the special charter seem to be inconsistent with those of the general statutes   See State v Bowen, 30 Barb, 24, affirmed on other points, 21 N Y, 517, also Hollis v Drew, etc, Seminary, 95 N Y, 166, 173, Lefevre v Lefevre, 59 N Y, 434, Clarkson v Hudson River R R Co, 12 N Y, 304, Johnson v Hudson River R R Co, 49 N Y, 455; Burroughs v Burroughs, 68 N Y, 259.

A general statute reserving the power to amend or repeal charters is a part of all special charters passed subsequently Griffin v. Kentucky Ins. Co, 3 Bush (Ky) 592; approved in Louisville Water Co v Clark, 143 U. S. 1 (1892).

The charter of a company formed under the general law consists not only of its articles of association, but also of the general statutes of the state under which the organization takes place People v Chicago Gas T. Co, 22 N E Rep, 798 (Ill, 1889)

"Corporations organized under the general law are vested with the powers conferred by the general act, and those contemplated by the certificate, and such incidental powers with respect to the general and special powers as are necessary in the sense of convenient, reasonable and proper" Ellerman v Chicago Junction, etc., Co. et al, 23 Atl Rep., 287 (N J, 1891).

Special powers may be given to an old corporation although a new constitution prohibits special charters Wallace v Loomis, 97 U S, 146 (1877)

Although a constitutional provision requires incorporations under general acts if at all, yet an old charter existing prior to the constitutional provision may be amended by the legislature after such constitutional provision Farnsworth v Lime Rock, etc R. R, 22 Atl Rep 373 (Me, 1891)

An old special charter may be amended although a new constitution forbids the grant of special charters St Joseph, etc, R R v Shambaugh, 17 S W Rep, 581 (Mo, 1891).

Concerning the abuses which grow out of the granting of special charters, see Cook on The Corporation Problem, pp 110-113.

In New York the legislature is to decide whether a special or general incorporation law shall be enacted People v Bowen, 21 N Y, 516 (1860), Gilbert El. R. R. Co, 70 N Y, 361 (1877)

A charter cannot be sold, mortgaged or assigned, although the property and power to operate the property may be See Part VI, infra

In the case Citizens' Bank v. Board of Assessors, 54 Fed Rep, 73 (1893), the court held that the acceptance by the corporation of an act which compelled the corporation to accept the terms of a new constitution did not have that effect.

In the case Citizens' St. R. Co. v Memphis, 53 Fed. Rep., 715 (1893), the court

The state creates the corporation upon the application of individuals, who are called incorporators. The incorporators then organize the corporation. The functions of the incorporators thereupon cease and stockholders proceed to contribute the capital and elect directors. The directors then start and continue to keep in operation the powers of the corporation

§ 3 *Definition of powers, express and implied* —The powers of the corporation are given by the charter, and these powers are express or implied.

The express powers are those which are expressly specified in the charter or the statutes under which the corporation was incorporated

The implied powers of a corporation are those which naturally arise from the nature of the business. Thus a corporation has implied power to buy, hold and sell necessary real estate and other property in its corporate name; to sue and be sued in that name; to do business in its corporate name without rendering its stockholders liable as partners for its debts; to govern its officers, agents and business by by-laws, to issue transferable shares of stock to its stockholders to have its business managed by directors instead of by the stockholders as in a partnership, to continue business although its stockholders die or sell their stock, to borrow money and give bills, notes and acceptances; to issue negotiable bonds; to assign for the benefit of creditors; and, except in *quasi*-public corporations, such as railroads, to give a mortgage.[1]

held that a charter granted without the reserved right to amend or repeal did not become subject to the right to amend or repeal although it had entered into a consolidation after a constitutional provision was passed reserving this right in all cases The consolidation was held not to have dissolved the old corporation.

[1] The definition of a corporation throws some light upon its nature, but a still clearer idea is obtained by considering the inherent powers of corporation. 1 Blackstone's Com, 475, says that the inseparable incidents or powers of all corporations aggregate are (1) To have perpetual succession. (2) To sue and be sued, and grant and receive in the corporate name (3) To purchase and hold lands and chattels (4) To have a common seal (5) To make by-laws. Chancellor Kent, in II Com.,

278, n., adds (6) The power to expel members 1 Kyd on Corp, 13, 69. 70, has a different summary of incidents

The greatest and most vital features of modern corporations, however,— features that have become prominent since those authors wrote,— and the features that have rendered possible the universal use and great achievements of corporations, are two in number: (1) The limited liability conferred, by implication, by the granting of a charter (2) The right of the corporation to issue shares of stock and the right of the members to transfer them.

A corporate franchise may mean either the power to act as a corporation, or may mean the right which a corporation has to operate a franchise, such as a railroad's right of way The former is not property. It is not an element of value in estimating the value

The theory of a corporation is that it has no powers except those expressly given or necessarily implied But this theory is no longer strictly applied to private corporations A private corporation may exercise many extraordinary powers, provided all of its stockholders assent and none of its creditors are injured There is no one to complain except the state, and the business being entirely private the state does not interfere Thus fifty years ago the courts would summarily have declared it illegal for a business corporation to become an accommodation indorser of commercial paper But to-day if all the stockholders assent thereto and creditors are not injured, such an act is held to be legal [1]

Again the old theory of a corporation was that it could not give away its assets But the modern view is that a private corporation may do so if all its stockholders assent and it creditors are paid Public policy does not require business corporations to confine themselves strictly to their express and implied powers [2]

In the case of railroad corporations, however, public policy does intervene and does limit the implied powers A railroad company has no *implied* power to sell, lease or mortgage its road, or to charge such rates for service as it sees fit, or to charge one man more than another for the same service.[3]

---

of the majority of the stock. Johnson v Kirby, 65 Cal , 482 (1884) It is not an asset A bank franchise does not pass to its assignee for the benefit of creditors, and the court will deny his application to sell it Fretsam v Hav, 13 N E. Rep , 501 (Ill , 1887) For various definitions of franchise, see Wait on Insolvent Corporations, § 12

It has been said that the essence of a corporation consists of a capacity (1) to have perpetual succession under a special name and in an artificial form, (2) to take and grant property, contract obligations, sue and be sued, by its corporate name as an individual , and (3) to receive and enjoy in common grants of privileges and immunities Thomas v Dakin, 22 Wend , 1 The supreme court of Illinois, speaking of the above, says "The first two describe the franchises which belong to the incorporators, the last those which belong to the corporation " Snell v Chicago, 24 N E Rep , 532 (Ill , 1890)

[1] See § 774, *infra*

[2] The New York court of appeals said in the case Kent v Quicksilver Mining Co , 78 N Y 159, 186 " A bank has no authority from the state to engage in benevolent enterprises , and a subscription, though formally made, for a charitable object would be out of its powers, but it would not be otherwise an illegal act , yet if every stockholder did expressly assent to such an application of the corporate funds, though it would still be in one sense *ultra vires* no wrong would be done, no public interest harmed , and no stockholder could object, or claim that there was an infringement of his rights, and have redress or protection Such an act, though beyond the power given by the charter unless expressly prohibited if confirmed by the stockholders could not be avoided by any of them to the harm of third persons This arises from the principle that the trust for stockholders is not of a public nature' See also § 774.

[3] See Part VI, *infra.*

"Every public grant of property or of privileges or franchises, if ambiguous, is to be construed against the grantee and in favor of the public," and especially so as regards corporations organized under general laws.[1]

§ 4 *The certificate of incorporation under the general act cannot legally contain any powers, restrictions or provisions except those called for by the statute.*— Frequently the incorporators desire to obtain more powers than the statute specifies, or to restrict unalterably some of the powers possessed by the corporations, or to regulate in some unalterable way the business of the company. For the purpose of doing so they insert in the certificate of incorporation under the general act special provisions not called for by the act which authorizes the incorporation.

The law is clear that the articles of association of a corporation organized under a general act are allowed to contain only those matters and statements which are required by the statute itself The incorporators are not at liberty to insert additional provisions and regulations If such additional provisions and regulations are inserted they are void. The law does not recognize them. They do not constitute a part of the charter, but are rejected as surplusage and extraneous matter. If the articles of association contain the matters required by the statute and also contain additional matters, the former are sufficient to sustain the charter, and the additional matter does not vitiate the legitimate part of the articles, but the additional matter is disregarded by the law as though it had not been written All of the decisions hold that any statements of restrictions inserted in the articles of association, outside of the statements required by the general act allowing the incorporation, are unauthorized and void.[2]

In New York, New Jersey and under the National Banking Act

---

[1] Central Trans. Co v Pullman's Car Co, 139 U S, 24, 49 (1891)

[2] Eastern Plank Road Co v Vaughan, 14 N Y, 546 (1856); Oregon R'y Co. v Oregonian R'y Co., 130 U. S. 1, 25 (1889), Albright v Lafayette, etc, Association, 102 Pa St, 411 (1883), Becket v. Uniontown, etc, Assoc, 88 id, 211 Grangers', etc, Ins Co v Kamper, 73 Ala, 325, Thomas v Railroad Co, 101 U S, 71 (1879), Penn R R Co v St Louis, etc, R R Co, 118 U S, 290, 307 (1886), Bigelow v Gregory, 73 Ill, 197, Rochester Ins Co v Martin, 13 Minn, 54; Western U T Co. v U P R'y, 1 Mc-

Crary, 418 (1880); Ancient Club v Miller, 7 Lansing, 412, People v. Utica Ins. Co, 15 Johns, 358 (1818)

A provision cannot be included in a charter under the general act, whereby stockholders are to vote according to their stock Commonwealth v. Nickerson, 10 Phil, 55 (1873).

For many decisions on this subject see ch XIII, §§ 231-234, notes.

The by-laws cannot modify the articles of incorporaton in any of the particulars required by statute to be stated in the articles of incorporation Guinness v Land Corp., L. R., 22 Ch. D, 349 (1882)

such special provisions are allowed,[1] and a broad public policy favors the allowance of them, but under the usual general incorporating act they are void

The certificate of incorporation may, however, provide that the business shall be two or more of the kinds of business which are authorized by the statute[2]

§ 5 *Mistakes, irregularities and illegalities in becoming incorporated* — Often it happens that mistakes are made in organizing a corporation The certificate of incorporation may be defective, or it may not be filed or published as required by the statutes, or the corporation itself may be irregularly organized thereafter. Complicated questions then arise as to the rights and liabilities of the various parties. Stockholders cannot set up such irregularities as a defense to an action by the corporation to enforce their subscriptions to stock.[3] Corporate creditors cannot hold the stockholders liable as partners by reason of the irregular incorporation[4] Indeed, the general rule now is, with few exceptions, that no one can question

Concerning the advisability of allowing the incorporators to insert provisions in the articles of incorporation restricting and regulating the powers of the corporation or directors or stockholders, see Cook on the Corporation Problem, pp. 90 91

In incorporating under the general act no powers can be placed in the articles of incorporation except such powers as the general act authorizes People v Chicago Gas L. Co , 22 N E Rep , 798 (Ill , 1889).

Where a land company is incorporated under the general act, and the general act does not provide for any statement in the articles of association as regards the amount of debts which the corporation may incur, a provision inserted in the articles of association that "the indebtedness of the company shall not exceed $500 at any time" is not a part of the charter The provision is at the most merely a by-law The court said "We think that the limitation of $500 in the charter of the corporation cannot be regarded of any more force than a by-law" Sherman, etc , Co v Morris, 23 Pac Rep , 569 (Kan 1890)

A provision in the charter that the stock shall be divided in a certain way

is binding upon the corporation so far as it is concerned, and upon the parties thereto, but may be contradicted by other evidence of what the agreement really was Bates v Wilson, 24 Pac Rep , 99 (Colo , 1890)

Provisions for internal management should not appear in a charter In re The Stevedores' Beneficial Association 14 Phila. Rep , 130 , Re M E Patterson Memorial Church, 41 Leg Int , 233, Re St Luke's Church, id 74; Re Central Democratic Ass'n. 46 Leg Int , 380 , Boos' Appeal, 109 Pa St , 596

[1] See Part VI, *infra*, also, Society, etc , v Meyer, 52 Pa. St., 125

[2] Bird v Daggett, 97 Mass , 494 (1867)

A statement in the articles of incorporation that the company may carry on such business as it thinks to be for the benefit of the stockholders is void Re Crown, etc., Bank, 62 L. T. Rep , 823 (1890)

Charters for enumerated objects "and other purposes" will be rejected In re Journalists' Fund, 8 Phila Rep., 272 So as to mining for "minerals." Re Glenwood Co , 6 Pa Co Ct. Rep , 575.

[3] See § 183, *infra*

[4] See §§ 231-239, *infra.*

the regularity of the incorporation except the state, where the
statutes allow incorporation and the company has endeavored to
incorporate and is acting as a corporation.[1] But where the purpose for which the corporation is organized is illegal or not specified in the act authorizing the incorporation, then the rule is different.[2]

§ 6 *A corporation is not a partnership; but where the corporation is a mere "dummy," its existence is sometimes disregarded
and its acts held to be the acts of its officers and stockholders.*— A
corporation is an entity and existence separate from its officers and
stockholders. And the inclination of some writers to assimilate a
corporation as nearly as possible to a partnership and to apply
to the former the rules applicable to the latter leads only to confusion and is contrary to the law.[3]

The difference between a corporation and a partnership and the
advantages of a corporation over a partnership as a means of doing
business are very marked and should not be limited by construction.[4]

[1] See § 637, *infra*.

[2] See chapter XIII, *infra*

The organization of a company to
carry on the lottery business in foreign
countries was held legal in Macuee *v*
Persian, etc, Corp, 62 L T Rep, 894
(1890)

[3] The house of lords in England has
pointed out the fact that there is no real
analogy between an ordinary partnership and a corporation. Birch *v* Cropper, 61 L T Rep, 621 (1889), refusing
to apply the analogy and saying that to
apply it would in the case before it
"work inequality and injustice and not
equity"

A trading corporation is governed by
the ordinary rules of partnership, except so far as special conditions may be
inserted into their constitution by the
legislature or by their own articles of
association Oakes *v* Turquand, L R,
2 H L, 325, as referred to in Whiting *v*
Hovey, 13 Ont. App Cas, 7 (1886)

In speaking of the fact that decisions
concerning municipal corporations and
the powers of their officers are not at
all applicable to private corporations,
Chief Justice Ruger, in Wallace *v*
Walsh, 125 N. Y., 26, 36 (1890), said :

"It is manifest that no analogy exists
between the action of a body of men
invested with the exercise of political
power under special conditions, and the
action of the trustees of a private corporation in the conduct of its ordinary
business operations The one relates to
the execution of powers, and the other
to the performance of duties and the enjoyment of privileges The one is controlled by the principles governing the
relations of principal and agent, and the
other to the general rules regulating the
consequences following a neglect or dis-
obedience of the requirements of statutes affecting private relations. In the
one case the question as to what is a
good execution of a power is involved,
and in the other as to what may be considered an adequate performance of a
duty These questions are manifestly
controlled by different rules, and that
which is required in one is not an
authority for the requirements of the
other"

[4] In his work on The Corporation Problem, pp 2, 3, the author describes these
differences as follows

"The partnership has been found to
be clumsy, dangerous and insufficient.

8

A corporation is an entity, an existence, irrespective of the persons who own all its stock   The fact that one person owns all the stock does not make him and the corporation one and the same person.[1]   Although one railroad corporation owns all the stock of another railroad corporation, yet the separate existence of the two corporations continues and they are not thereby merged [2]

If unsuccessful it brings ruin upon all of its members, because each partner is liable absolutely for all debts   Any member may bind the firm by his contract and each one has an equal voice in deciding its policy   Its capital and credit, and consequently its amount of business, are limited necessarily by the capital and credit of a very few men — the members themselves.   The death of a member or the transfer of his interest dissolves the firm   Any member may arbitrarily cause a dissolution at any time, and the insolvency of a member renders the partnership property subject to levy of execution for his debt. Upon the death of a partner the surviving partners have the sole charge of winding up the business, and the executor of the deceased partner is not allowed to come in   A partner may withdraw his money only at a sacrifice, or by long and expensive proceedings.   He cannot conveniently sell his interest or borrow money upon it.   New partners cannot readily or safely be admitted

"The partnership is restricted in its capital, dangerous in its liabilities, narrow in its exclusion of new members, too free in its mode of making contracts, and too contracted in its opportunities for withdrawal.   It is becoming obsolete as a mode of doing business on a large scale.

"In a corporation all this is changed The members are not liable for the debts   The amount already invested may be lost, but the private fortunes of the stockholders are not involved   The business is done and contracts made not by all, but by a select few, called directors.   A large capital is created by the union of funds from many sources.   A person may safely invest in many enterprises and yet not take part in the management nor watch the business of any one of them   The leading spirit in an enterprise may hold a majority of the stock and may admit associates, employees or strangers as holders of a minority of the stock, and yet he will retain the management as though he were the single owner of the concern Persons may easily buy into or retire from the enterprise   Dissolution is not brought about by the death or withdrawal or dissatisfaction of a stockholder   The insolvency of a stockholder does not affect the business of the corporation   Upon the death of a stockholder his executor votes his stock and has a voice in the continuation of the business   A stockholder may sell or pledge his interest readily and intelligibly by reason of the reports, dividends and market quotations of his stock The corporation is a protection in that the liability is limited, it is capable in that it renders possible the collection of a great capital, it is efficient because the directors and they alone govern its policy and its contracts, and it is convenient because it is easy to sell or buy or pledge, or bequeath one's interest in the concern "

[1] § 709, infra.

[2] Although one railroad owns or controls all the stock of another railroad, yet the former is not personally liable for the negligence, debts. etc. of the latter   Atchison etc. R R z Cochran, 23 Pac. Rep, 151 (Kan, 1890)

A railroad company owning all the stock and bonds of another company does not own the property of the latter and cannot sue on a cause of action be-

9

Not only is the identity of the corporation preserved as distinct from its stockholders, but it is also distinct from its promoters, incorporators and antecedents. It is not liable on the contracts and obligations of its promoters.[1] Nor is it liable for the debts of a prior corporation to whose property it succeeds by foreclosure sale [2] Where a partnership or a corporation is merged into another corporation, the creditors of the former may pursue the property but they cannot hold the corporation liable for the debt,[3] unless the latter took with such notice that it may be held to account.[4]

But there are occasions where the courts will ignore the corporate existence and will hold that its acts are the acts of its stockholders and *vice versa* the same as in a partnership Thus where an individual organizes a corporation to violate a contract which

longing to the latter Fitzgerald v Missouri P R'y, 45 Fed Rep, 812 (1891).

Where one corporation owns all the stock of another corporation, the property of the latter is not subject to a mortgage given by the former, but an independent first mortgage may be given by the latter company Central T Co v Kneeland, 138 U S., 414 (1891).

A bridge owned by a bridge corporation is not to be taxed as railroad property, even though its stock is owned by the stockholders in a railroad corporation, and the stock has been pledged to such railroad corporation and the bridge itself leased to the latter St. Louis, etc., R'y v Williams, 13 S. W. Rep., 796 (Ark., 1890).

Although a new railroad corporation is clearly a "dummy" corporation, its incorporators and officers being officers in another railroad corporation and its expenses being paid by the latter company, still it is a legal corporation Southern Kan etc., R. R. v Towner, 21 Pac Rep, 221 (Kan, 1889), 23 id, 151

The fact that one corporation owns a large amount of stock in another corporation does not affect the identity of the two. *Ex parte* Fisher, 20 S C, 179 (1882)

As to the power of one corporation to buy the stock of other corporations, see §§ 315–317, *infra* Concerning the liability, see, also, § 643, *infra*.

But in Nebraska a "dummy" domestic corporation cannot condemn land for a foreign corporation Koenig v. Chicago, etc, R. R, 43 N. W Rep., 433 (Neb., 1889)

A railroad company owning practically all the stock of another company may lease the line of the latter company to another company Chicago, etc., R'y v Union Pac. R'y, 47 Fed Rep, 15 (1891).

Where a railroad company causes a telegraph company to be incorporated and subscribes to all its stock and appoints all its officers and holds it out as the future owner of a telegraph system which the railroad owns, and then sells that system to someone else, a person contracting with the telegraph company on the faith of the scheme being carried out may hold the railroad company liable on the contract on the principle of a principal being liable on the contracts of its agent. Interstate Tel Co v Balt. & O. T. Co, 51 Fed. Rep, 49 (1892)

A domestic corporation cannot obtain a patent to a mining claim under the federal statutes, unless all of its stockholders are citizens of the United States, and are severally and individually qualified and competent to make the location Thomas v Chisholm, 21 Pac Rep., 1019 (Colo, 1889) See, also, chs. 13, 38, 39, 43.

[1] See § 707, *infra*
[2] See § 643, *infra*
[3] See § 667, *infra*, and ch. II
[4] See § 727, *infra*

he himself would not be allowed to violate, the court will enjoin the corporation as though it were the person himself[1] So, also, where a director causes the corporation to give a valuable contract to a corporation in which he is secretly interested, this is the same as though he were interested in a firm which received that contract[2]

This same principle applies to trade combinations of corporations called "Trusts"[3] The corporate existence will be disregarded and the acts and contracts of the persons holding all the stock will be considered the acts and contracts of the corporation itself where the effect is the same as though the corporation had acted or contracted as a corporation. Hence where all the stock is combined with all the stock of other combinations in order to form a combination which is illegal, the state will forfeit the charter of the corporation, although technically it is not a party to the agreement[4]

§ 7. *Classes of corporations and the class considered herein* — For the better understanding of the law of corporations, and for the treatment of special branches of that law, the early writers, like Kyd, Blackstone, Kent, Angell and Ames, and many subsequent authors, subdivided corporations into distinct classes. These subdivisions have been made on various principles of classification When divided with respect to the members of corporations they are aggregate and sole. As regards their functions they are public, such as cities and towns, *quasi*-public, such as counties and school districts; and private, and again private corporations are divided into ecclesiastical and lay, and still further, lay corporations are divided into eleemosynary or charitable, and civil, the latter of which include all private corporations that are created for temporal purposes, such as banking, insurance, trading railroad, manufacturing, turnpike, bridge and canal corporations, and certain educational institutions[5]

[1] See ch. XXXIX, *infra.*

[2] Id.

[3] See ch XXIX, *infra*

[4] Id., also, State *v* Standard Oil Co, 30 N. E Rep, 279 (Ohio, 1892).

[5] Concerning the question of whether a railroad company is a private corporation, the court said in Pierce *v* Commonwealth, 104 Pa. St, 155 (1883)

"Railroad and canal companies are private corporations This we have decided in point twice within the last two years, once in the case of Timlow *v* The Philadelphia & Reading Railroad

Co, 3 Out., 284, and again in the case of The Pittsburgh & Lake Erie Railroad Co *v* Bruce, 6 Out, 23 . . So in the case of The Trustees of the Presbyterian Society *v* The Auburn & Rochester Railroad Co, 3 Hill, 567, it is said that a railroad company is not public nor does it stand in the place of the public, it is but a private corporation over whose rails the public may travel if they choose to ride in its cars. Indeed, we regard it as a misnomer to attach even the name 'quasi-public corporation' to a railroad company, for it

11

A domestic corporation is one that has been organized under the laws of the state referred to A foreign corporation is one that has been organized under the laws of another state or of a foreign government An alien corporation is one that has been organized under the laws of a foreign government.[1]

At an early day private corporations for business purposes were few in number and of little importance in the law. Chancellor Bland states that no instance of such a corporation in the colonial times of America can be found[2] In England, also, at that time, private corporations for profit were of small consequence. But the past seventy-five years have completely reversed the relative importance of the different classes of corporations, and, at the present time, private corporations for temporal purposes have completely overshadowed all other kinds.

With this change there is a decided tendency to re-classify the subject, and the modern treatises on corporation law have recognized the fact that old classifications are to be disregarded, and that corporations are to be divided into joint-stock corporations, or those having a capital stock, and corporations without a capital stock. Indeed, the modern text-books on corporations treat very little of the older classes of corporations and the principles which govern them, but fully and explicitly of corporations having a capital stock.

This change is due largely to the remarkable growth of the law regulating the one prominent difference between the two classes. That feature is that corporations with a capital stock have stock and stockholders, while corporations without a capital stock have none, and are governed largely by principles of law that have changed little since the days of Blackstone, Kyd and Kent. It is with this feature of modern corporations, that of stock and stockholders, as distinguished from the characteristics of the early corporations, which have sunk into comparative unimportance,[3] that the present work is concerned

has none of the features of such corporations, if we except its qualified right of eminent domain, and this it has because of the right reserved to the public to use its way for travel and transportation Its officers are not public officers, and its business transactions are as private as those of a banking house. Its road may be called a *quasi*-public highway, but the company itself is a private corporation and nothing more "

A mining and manufacturing corporation is a private corporation Wolffe v Underwood, 8 S Rep , 774 (Ala 1891)

[1] An English corporation is an alien corporation. Eureka, etc., Co. v. Richmond, etc , Co , 2 Fed. Rep., 829 (1880)

The residence of a corporation is the town or city specified in its articles of incorporation Rossie Iron Works v. Westbrook, 50 Hun, 345 (1891). '

[2] McKim v Odom, 3 Bland's Ch. (Md), 407, 418 (1828) For a list of the first incorporated business companies in America, see Harvard Law Review, Nov 1888, p 165

[3] The subject of municipal corporations would seem to form an exception

§ 8. *Corporations having a capital stock* — The questions which arise in connection with corporations having a capital stock may be divided into two groups The first includes those principles of law which affect all corporations, whether they have a capital stock or not. Of such a kind are the old questions of how a corporation shall contract, whether a seal be necessary, whether and how it may act through an agent, the right to sue and be sued in various courts, and to hold and dispose of property. These questions, capacities and incidents, for the most part, have become so well settled as to give rise to comparatively little litigation at the present day.[1]

On the other hand, it is believed that the modern law of corporations, as regards its litigated questions, its unsettled principles, its new problems and its rapidly crystallizing results, is the law of stock and stockholders. This law involves the issue of stock and the rights, duties, liabilities and miscellaneous incidents of stockholdership. Indeed, it may be said that the law of stock and stockholders is the proper standpoint from which to treat of general corporation law It is upon this theory that the present edition of this work has been written [2]

§ 9. *Definition of capital stock* — Capital stock is the sum fixed by the corporate charter as the amount paid in or to be paid in by the stockholders for the prosecution of the business of the corporation and for the benefit of corporate creditors [3] The capital stock is to be clearly distinguished from the amount of property pos-

to this statement, were it not that the great and deservedly successful work of Judge Dillon on Municipal Corporations has clearly stated, and thereby settled, most of the difficult subjects connected with that branch of the law

[1] The first edition of this treatise did not include these subjects The present edition, however, has been extended so as to include all subjects of corporation law

[2] See the preface for an explanation of the author's ideas on this subject.

[3] For various definitions see Barry v Merchants' Ex Co, 1 Sand Ch, 280, 305 (1844), Christensen v Eno, 106 N Y, 97, 100 (1887); Hightower z Thornton, 8 Ga., 486, 500 (1850), Hannibal & St. Joseph R. R. Co. v Shacklett, 30 Mo, 551, 558 (1860); St. Louis, Iron M, etc, R R. Co. v Loftin, 30 Ark, 693, 709 (1875), Bent v. Hart. 10 Mo. App.,

143, 146 (1881), Mutual Ins Co v. Supervisors, etc, 4 N Y., 442 (1851), Bailey v Clark, 21 Wall, 284 (1874), where Field, J, says "it applies only to the property or means contributed by the stockholders as the fund or basis for the business or enterprise for which the corporation or association was formed ' Jones v Davis, 35 O St. 474, 476 (1880), Burrall v Bushwick R R Co, 75 N. Y. 211 (1878), where Folger, J defines it as "that money or property which is put in a single corporate fund by those who, by subscription therefor, become members of a corporate body " Williams z Western Union Tel Co, 93 N Y, 162, 188 (1883), where Earl, J , tersely says it is "the property of the corporation contributed by its stockholders or otherwise obtained by it, to the extent required by its charter." Sanger v. Upton, 91 U. S, 56, 60 (1875), State v.

13

sessed by the corporation   Occasionally it happens that, under the terms of statutes relating to taxation which have been drawn without regard to the technical meaning of words, the courts will construe the capital stock to mean all the actual property of the corporation.[1] But this is for the purpose of carrying out the intent of the statute, and is not the real meaning of the term. At common law the capital stock does not vary, but remains fixed, although the actual property of the corporation may fluctuate widely in value and may be diminished by losses or increased by gains. The term "stock"[2] has been used at times to indicate the same thing as capital stock. Generally, however, it means shares of stock, and in this sense it is used in this treatise.

§ 10 *Definitions of corporator, subscriber, shareholder and stockholder* — A corporator is one of those to whom a charter is granted, or of those who file a certificate of incorporation under a general incorporating statute.[3] A subscriber is one who has agreed to

Morristown Fire Ass'n, 23 N J L, 195, State *v* Cheraw & C R. R. Co, 16 S. C., 524 (1881). A savings bank corporation may be formed without any capital stock, the profits going to depositors. Huntington *v* Sav. Bank, 96 U. S, 388 (1877) Such is the statute law of New York.

The word "capital" has been defined as "the property or means contributed by the stockholders as the fund or basis for the business or enterprise for which the corporation was formed" Iron R'y *v* Lawrence, etc., Co, 30 N E Rep, 616 (Ohio, 1892)

Definition of capital stock People *v.* Coleman, 126 N Y, 433 (1891)

"Capital stock of a corporation is a different thing from shares of stock. The capital stock represents the property and assets of the company, which may consist in whole or in part of real estate. The certificates or shares of stock are the evidence of an interest which the holder has in the corporation, and it is well settled that this interest is personal property." Wilkes Barre, etc., Bank *v.* City of Wilkes Barre, 24 Atl Rep., 111 (Pa., 1892)

Where the charter prescribes that the debts shall not exceed one-half of the capital stock, capital stock means the

paid-in capital stock and not the capital stock as stated in the charter. Lehigh, etc, R'y Co.'s Appeal, 18 Atl Rep., 498 (Pa, 1889)

[1] Ohio & M R. R. Co *v* Weber, 96 Ill, 443 (1880), City of Philadelphia *v* Ridge Ave R. R. Co., 102 Penn St., 190 (1880); Security Co. *z* Hartford, 23 Atl. Rep, 699 (Conn, 1891)

[2] Burr *v* Wilcox, 22 N Y., 551, 555 (1860), People *v* Commissioners, etc., 23 N. Y., 192, 220 (1861), Bailey *v* Railroad Co., 22 Wall, 604, 637 (1874) Formerly government bonds were called "stock," both in England and in this country. Bank of Commerce *v* New York, 2 Black, 620 (1862); Weston *v.* City of Charleston, 2 Pet., 449 (1829); Cavanagh's Law of Money Securities (2d ed.), 488–494. This use of the term still prevails in England, but is generally obsolete in this country, although the securities of the city of New York are still called "stock."

In tax statutes, "stock" may be defined to mean shares of stock Lockport *v* Weston, 23 Atl Rep, 9 (Conn, 1891).

[3] Chase *v.* Lord, 77 N Y., 1–11 (1879), the court saying· "Corporators exist before stockholders, and do not exist with them. When stockholders come

take stock from the corporation on the original issue of such stock [1] A shareholder in this country means the same thing as a stockholder, and the terms are used interchangeably to indicate one who owns stock in a corporation and has been accepted as a stockholder by the corporation [2] A stockholder does not stand in the attitude of a partner towards the corporation

§ 11. *Relation of stockholders towards the corporation* — A corporation may contract with its stockholders to the same extent and in the same manner that it may with any other persons [3]

in, corporators cease to be " *Cf* Lady Bryan's Case, 1 Saw, 349 In Pennsylvania, under a peculiar statute, it has been held that the incorporators thereof need not be subscribers See Densmore Oil Co *v* Densmore, 64 Penn St, 43, 51 (1870)

It has frequently been held that where a statute authorizes persons to form a corporation, although the statute does not, in express terms, say that they must be of full age, yet it is implied that they shall be of full age Matter of Globe, etc , Assoc, 63 Hun, 263 (1892) *Cf.* 67 L. T Rep. 85.

A married woman is not at common law qualified to act as an incorporator nor as treasurer. 9 Ry & Corp L J, 107

A corporation is legally organized although the incorporators are not shareholders as required by statute Welch *v* Importers', etc , Bank, 122 N Y, 177 (1890)

[1] Busey *v* Hooper, 35 Md, 15, Spear *v* Crawford, 14 Wend, 20, 23 In The Thames Tunnel Company *v* Sheldon, 6 Barn & C, 341 (1827), the word "subscriber" is elaborately defined, and it is held to mean only such persons as have entered into an express contract to take up a certain definite number of shares. See, also, a definition at some length by Cooley, J , in Peninsular, etc . R. R. Co *v* Duncan, 28 Mich, 130 (1878)

Subscribers are stockholders, although no certificates have been issued to them and no payments made McComb *v* Barcelona, etc , Assoc , 10 N Y Supp, 546 (1890).

' It is the payment which makes the subscriber a stockholder ' Bates *v* Great Western Tel Co, 25 N E Rep, 521 (Ill 1890)

A "subscription" for stock is different from a sale ' A "subscription" applies to an original issue. Bates *v* Great Western Tel Co, 25 N E. Rep, 521 (Ill, 1890)

[2] See Roosevelt *v* Brown, 11 N. Y 148, 150 (1854), State *v* Ferris, 42 Conn, 560 (1875), Adderly *v* Storm, 6 Hill, 624 (1844), Worrall *v* Judson, 5 Barb, 210 (1849) Where the registered holder is merely a nominal holder he will not be entitled to special privileges, such as free admission to a place of amusement Appeal of American Acad, etc 108 Pa. St., 510 (1885)

A person is held to be a stockholder, although no certificate has been issued to him See § 192, *infra* Moreover, he may be held to be a stockholder, although he has sold and transferred his certificate of stock, if such transfer has not been recorded on the corporate stockbook See chapter XV *infra*

[3] Hartford & N H R. R. Co *v* Kennedy, 12 Conn , 499, 509 (1838), Gordon *v* Preston, 1 Watts, 385 (1833), Central R R, etc , Co *v* Claghorn, 1 Speers' Eq (S C), 545, 562 (1844)

Thus, where one subscribed for stock and paid for it by mortgages payable at times mutually agreed upon between the parties, 'this was merely a mode of payment " "He stands in two capacities, one as debtor to the association, one as stockholder in it. These capacities are independent of each

A stockholder, as a creditor of the corporation, may obtain security for his debt in exclusion of other creditors.[1]

A stockholder has no legal title to the property or profits of the corporation until a dividend is declared, or a division made on the dissolution of the corporation[2] He may sue the corporation or be sued by it, both at law and in equity.[3] However, he has a direct interest in the corporation, and at times may take the part of the corporation in prosecuting or defending its suits.[4]

The stockholder is not liable for the debts of the corporation.[5]

The admissions or declarations of stockholders do not bind the corporation,[6] nor do the admissions of one stockholder bind another stockholder[7]

Notice to individual stockholders is not notice to the corporation,

other " Ely v Sprague, 1 Clark's Ch. (N Y), 351 (1840); Longley v Stage Line Co, 23 Me, 39 (1843), holding that where a creditor consented, as a stockholder, to the re-organization of the company which had become indebted to him under the former organization, he had not thereby forfeited his right to recover from the newly-organized corporation, to which he had become a subscriber, American Bank v. Baker, 4 Met (Mass.), 164, 176 (1842), holding that a corporation vote to compromise certain securities to the detriment of a member who was also a creditor could not be regarded as consented to by him in his absence

[1] Reichwald v Commercial Hotel Co., 106 Ill, 439 (1883)

[2] Hyatt v Allen, 56 N Y, 553 (1874); Jones v Terre Haute, etc, R. R. 57 N Y, 196 (1874); Brundage v Brundage, 1 N Y Supr. (T & C), 82 (1873); Goodwin v Hardy, 57 Me, 143 (1869), Minot v Paine, 99 Mass., 101 (1868); Granger v Bassett, 98 Mass, 462 (1868); Phelps v Farmers', etc., Bank, 26 Conn, 269 (1857), Burroughs v N C R. R. Co., 67 N C., 376 (1872), Curry v Woodward, 44 Ala, 305 (1870); Lockhart v Van Alstyne, 31 Mich, 76, 78 (1875). See, also, ch XXXII, on Dividends.

[3] Waring v. Cahawba Co., 2 Bay (S. C.), 109 (1797), where this right of a stockholder was the question directly

in litigation, Rogers v. Danby Univ. Soc, 19 Vt., 187 (1847), Culberston v. Wabash Nav Co, 4 McLean, 544 (1849), Pence v. Partridge, 44 Mass, 44 (1841); Barnstead v. Empire Min Co., 5 Cal. 299 (1855), Ex parte Booker, 18 Ark., 338 (1857), Sanborn v. Lefferts, 58 N. Y, 179 (1874), Cary v Schoharie, etc, Co, 2 Hun, 110 (1874); Wausau, etc, Co. v Plummer, 35 Wis, 274; Sawyer v. Methodist Ep Soc, 18 Vt., 405 (1846): Dunstan v Imperial, etc, Co, 3 B & Ad, 125 (1822); Gifford v New Jersey, etc., Co., 2 Stock. Ch., 171 (1854), Samuel v. Holladay, 1 Woolw., 400, 418 (1869). A stockholder may collect his debt the same as other creditors. Lang v Dougherty, 12 S. W. Rep, 29 (Tex, 1889). See, also, 30 Pac. Rep, 882

A stockholder who is also a director may nevertheless sue to compel his corporation to abate a nuisance. Leonard v Spencer. 108 N Y., 338 (1888).

[4] Part IV is on this subject. It is, however, a general rule that a stockholder cannot usually come in as a party and defend a suit in which the corporation is the defendant, even though the corporation is unable or unwilling to defend See § 659, infra.

[5] See chapter XIII.

[6] See § 726, infra.

[7] Simmons v. Sisson, 26 N. Y., 264 (1863).

and their knowledge of facts is not notice of those facts to the corporation[1] Service of process on a stockholder is not service on the corporation[2]

A stockholder in an insurance company has the same rights that a stockholder in any other corporation has[3]

The stockholder is an individual, distinct from the corporation in its contracts and transaction of business The mere fact that he is a stockholder does not make him an agent to contract for it or bind it by his acts[4]

One person may own all the stock, and yet the existence, relations and business methods of the corporation continue[5]

The stockholders, assembled together in a corporate meeting, have the powers to elect officers make by-laws, increase or reduce the capital stock, if the statute permits, authorize auxiliary or fundamental changes in the charter, if constitutional and perform a few other acts for and in behalf of the corporation But there their powers cease. The forming of corporate contracts, the management of corporate business, the employment and direction of agents, the bringing or defending of suits, and all the infinite details of corporate management, are under the control of the directors and their agents. The stockholders have no power herein, either individually or in meeting assembled[6]

A stockholder is chargeable with notice of entries made upon the corporate books, if they were made in his presence and he presumably assented thereto[7]

---

[1] See § 727, *infra*.

[2] See § 752, *infra*

[3] Thus, a shareholder in an insurance company, conducted on both the stock and the mutual-insurance plan, is entitled to all the rights in the guaranty accumulations that a stockholder in any other corporation has in the corporate assets Traders', etc, Ins Co v Brown, 8 N E Rep, 134 (Mass, 1886)

[4] See §§ 708, etc., *infra*.

Where the law permits punishment or confiscation of property, but not both, the conviction of a stockholder for violation of the internal revenue law prevents a confiscation of the corporation property United States v Distillery, 43 Fed Rep, 846 (1890)

Damages may be recovered by a corporation for a fraud practiced upon it, even though an agent of the corporation, who aided in the perpetration of the fraud, was a stockholder in the corporation Grand Rapids, etc, Co v Cincinnati, etc, Co, 45 Fed Rep, 671 (1891)

[5] See §§ 708 etc

[6] See § 712 *infra*.

"The property of a corporation is not subject to the control of individual members, whether acting separately or jointly They can neither incumber nor transfer that property, nor authorize others to do so The corporation — the artificial being created — holds the property, and alone can mortgage or transfer it, and the corporation acts only through its officers, subject to the conditions prescribed by law ' Humphreys v McKissock, 140 U. S., 304 (1891).

[7] See § 727, *infra*.

A shareholder in a corporation which does not properly insure
its property has such an insurable interest in that property that he
may recover upon a policy thereon taken in his own name, for an
amount which, added to the company's insurance, would cover his
interest [1]

At common law the stockholder, on account of his interest in
the corporation, was not a competent witness for the corporation in
a suit in which the corporation was a party.[2] In some states, how-

[1] Warren r Davenport Fire Ins Co,
31 Iowa, 464 (1871), distinguishing Phillips z Knox County Ins Co, 20 Ohio,
174 (1851) Cf Seaman v Enterprise
Fire, etc, Ins. Co., 18 Fed Rep, 250,
S C., 5 McCrary, 558 (1883) Contra,
Riggs v Commercial, etc., Ins Co., 51
N Y Super Ct, 466 (1884). See Greenhood on Public Policy, 255, Angell on
Fire & Life Insurance, ch XI, and cases
cited

A stockholder has an insurable inter-
est in the property of the corporation
Riggs v Commercial, etc., Ins. Co., 125
N Y, 7 (1890).

[2] Potter r Bank of Rutland. 19 Vt,
410 (1847), McAuley v The York, etc, 6
Cal, 80 (1854). See cases in next note
In Pierce z Kearney, 5 Hill, 82 (1843),
a shareholder was held incompetent to
testify that the defendant, in an action
to enforce a statutory liability of stockholders, was a stockholder

Compare, however, In the Matter of
Kip, 1 Paige, 601 (1829), involving the
testimony of a corporator and pew-
holder in a church corporation; Mokelumne, etc., r Woodbury, 14 Cal, 265,
in which, in deciding upon the competency of a stockholder as a witness, the
court held that "members of a corporation who are answerable personally
for the corporate debts and liabilities
stand in the same position in relation
to the creditors of the corporation as if
they were conducting their business as
a common partnership" To same effect, Mitchell z Beckman, 64 Cal, 117
(1883)

The president, though a stockholder,
is a competent witness for the company

if he is willing to testify, since his private interest is greater than his stockholder interest Church v. Sterling, 16
Conn, 388 (1844)

A stockholder in a company which is
a creditor of a party to a suit may testify in behalf of the latter Simons v
Vulcan etc, Co 61 Pa St, 202 (1869)

The purchase by a bank of its own
stock, in order to enable the stockholder
to testify for it, was upheld, though its
charter prohibited it from purchasing
goods, etc Farmers', etc, Bank v
Champlain Trans. Co, 18 Vt, 131 (1846)

Washington Bank v Palmer, 2 Sandf.
Super Ct, 686 (1850), and New York,
etc, R R Co v. Cook, id., 732 (1850),
are both to the effect that a stockholder
is not a party to the action, nor a person for whose immediate benefit it is
prosecuted, within meaning of the code.
He is therefore a competent witness

A stockholder need not testify against
his corporation. Bank of Oldtown v.
Houlton, 21 Me, 501 (1842)

A stockholder, under the New York
statute, cannot testify to a personal communication between the corporation
and a deceased person Keller v. West,
etc., Co., 39 Hun, 348 (1886).

A witness who is agent of a corporation, the latter being a party to the suit,
is entitled to the same privilege as to
libelous statements made by him as
witness that a party has. Nissen v.
Cramer, 10 S. E Rep, 676 (N. C., 1890)

The plaintiff in a suit against a corporation may offer a stockholder as a witness Hart v New Orleans, etc., R. R.,
1 Amer. St. R'y Dec, 4 (La, 1841).

ever, this rule has been changed by statute, and in others it is easily evaded by a formal transfer of the certificate of stock to another person [1] A stockholder is incompetent to serve as a judge [2] or juror [3] in a case where the corporation is a party A stockholder or director of an insolvent corporation is competent and qualified to act as its receiver or assignee [4] A director need not necessarily

[1] That a transfer will render the transferrer competent see Ill Ins Co v Marseilles Mfg Co, 6 Ill, 236 (1844), Union Bank v Owen, 1 Humph (Tenn), 338 (1843), Bell v Hull, 6 M & W 699 (1840), 1 Greenleaf's Evidence § 429 He is competent though the transfer has not been registered Bank of Utica v Smalley, 2 Cow, 770 (1824), Gilbert v Manchester Iron Mfg Co 11 Wend, 627 (1834), Delaware, etc, R R Co v Irick, 23 N J Law, 321 (1852), and although he expects to buy it back, but there must be no agreement expressly to that effect Utica Ins Co v Cadwell, 3 Wend, 296 (1829), State v Catskill Bank, 18 Wend, 466 (1837) Contra Carver v Braintree Mfg Co 2 Story, 432 (1843).

[2] Dimus v Prop of Grand Junction Canal, 3 H L Cases 759 (1852), where the lord chancellor was a stockholder in the defendant company, and had affirmed a decree by the vice-chancellor in the case The house of lords reversed the decision on this ground Cooley on Constitutional Limitations §§ 410, 411, Washington Ins Co v Price 1 Hopk Ch (N Y), 1 (1823) Chancellor Sandford therein refusing to follow Chancellor Kent in Stuart v Mechanics' & Farmers' Bank, 19 Johns, 496, 501 (1822) In Peninsular R y Co v Howard, 20 Mich, 18 (1870), the court say "It is not a matter of discretion with the judge or other person acting in a judicial capacity, nor is it left to his own sense of propriety or decency, but the principle forbids him to act in such capacity at all when he is thus interested, or when he may possibly be subject to the temptation " In New York the statute now prevents an interested judge from sitting N. Y Code of Civil Procedure §§ 828, 839 See Cregin v Brooklyn etc, R R Co 19 Hun, 349 (1879) Being related to a stockholder does not disqualify. Searsburgh T Co v Cutter, 6 Vt, 315 (1834)

A judge is not disqualified merely because he formerly owned stock Nicholson v Showalter, 18 S W Rep, 326 (Tex, 1892)

[3] Page v Contocook Valley R R Co, 21 N H, 438 (1850) Peninsular R R Co v Howard 20 Mich 18 (1870) Fleeson v Savage S M Co, 3 Nev, 157 (1867), Silver v Ely 3 Watts & S (Penn), 420 (1842). Cf Williams v Smith, 6 Cow, 166 (1826) The incompetency extends to the son of a stockholder Georgia R R Co v Hart 60 Ala 550 (1878) A person donating to the railroad is incompetent to serve in condemnation proceedings Michigan Air Line R y Co v Barnes, 40 Mich, 383 (1879) But the fact that the corporation is interested in a subsequent case on the same facts does not render the stockholder incompetent Commonwealth v Boston etc, R R Co 57 Mass 25 (1849)

Objection to competency must be raised at the trial It cannot be raised for first time by motion for new trial Williams v Great Western R y Co 3 H & N, 869 (1859)

The fact that a juror and plaintiff are both stockholders in the same corporation is no cause for challenge in a suit not involving the corporation Brittain v Allen, 2 Dev Eq (N C), 120 (1829).

A juror is qualified although his wife is related to a stockholder Butler v Glens, etc, R R, 121 N Y, 112 (1890).

[4] Covert v Rogers, 38 Mich, 363 (1878), Re Eagle Iron Works, 8 Paige, 385

be a stockholder, unless a statute or the charter expressly so provides.[1]

§ 12   *Shares of stock defined — What law governs.*— A share of stock may be defined as a right which its owner has in the management, profits and ultimate assets of the corporation   By the court of appeals of New York it is said that "the right which a shareholder in a corporation has, by reason of his ownership of shares, is a right to participate according to the amount of his stock in the surplus profits of the corporation on a division, and ultimately on its dissolution, in the assets remaining after payment of its debts "[2]

(1840), modifying S. C, 3 Edw Ch., 385 (1840), Bowery Bank Case, 16 How Pr, 56 (1857)   *Cf* Attorney-General *v* Bank of Columbia, 1 Paige, 511 (1829), § 2420, N. Y Code of C. P, expressly authorizing such appointments

In Atkins *v* Wabash, etc., R. Co, 29 Fed Rep, 161 (1886), however, the court removed the receivers, and said " Receivers should be impartial between the parties in interest, and stockholders and directors of insolvent corporations should not be appointed unless the case is exceptional and urgent, and then only on consent of the parties whose interests are to be intrusted to their charge"   See, also, chapter LI, *infra*.

In New Jersey a corporate officer is held to be ineligible to the position of receiver   Freeholders *v*. State Bank, 28 N. J Eq, 166 (1877); McCullough *v* Merchants', etc, Co, 29 N J Eq, 217 (1878).

The court will not appoint as counsel for the receiver the counsel for the party who obtained the receivership. Emmons *v* Davis, etc, Co, 16 Atl Rep, 157 (N J, 1888)

[1] Wight *v* Springfield, etc., R. R Co, 117 Mass, 226 (1875), *Re* St. Lawrence Steamboat Co, 44 N. J. L, 529, 541 (1882), State *v* McDaniel, 22 Ohio St., 354 (1872).   *Cf* Bartholomew *v* Bentley, 1 Ohio St, 37 (1852), Despatch Line *v* Bellamy Mfg Co., 12 N. H, 205, 223 (1841), Cumming *v* Prescott, 2 Younge & C., 488 (1837), Stack's Case, 33 L. J. (Ch.), 731 (1864)

[2] Plimpton *v* Bigelow, 93 N. Y., 592,

599 (1883).   To same effect see Burrall *v* Bushwick R. R. Co., 75 N. Y., 211, 216 (1878), Kent *v* Quicksilver Mining Co. 78 N Y, 159 (1879), Jermain *v.* Lake Shore, etc. R. R. Co, 91 N Y, 483, 492 (1883) Field *v* Pierce, 102 Mass, 253, 261 (1869), Jones *v* Davis, 35 Ohio St. 474, 477 (1880), Bradley *v.* Bauder, 36 id, 28, 35 (1880); Bent *v.* Hart, 10 Mo. App., 143 (1881); Harrison *v.* Vines, 46 Tex, 15, 21 (1876), Brightwell *v.* Mallory, 10 Yerg (Tenn), 196 (1836); Barksdale *v* Finney, 14 Gratt, 338, 357 (1858); Van Allen *v* Assessors, 3 Wall., 573, 585 (1865), Union Nat'l Bank *v* Byram, 22 N E Rep., 842 (Ill, 1889)

"The interest of each stockholder consists in the right to a proportionate part of the profits whenever dividends are declared by the corporation during its existence under its charter, and to a like proportion of the property remaining upon the termination or dissolution of the corporation, after payment of its debts."   Gibbons *v* Mahon, 132 U. S, 549 (1890)

Chief Justice Shaw, by way of a definition of a share of stock, says · "The right is, strictly speaking, a right to participate, in a certain proportion, in the immunities and benefits of the corporation, to vote in the choice of their officers, and the management of their concerns, to share in the dividends of profits, and to receive an aliquot part of the proceeds of the capital on winding up and terminating the active existence and operations of the corporation."

It is said that the rights which a share of stock secures to its owner are the rights "to meet at stockholders' meetings, to participate in the profits of the business, and to require that the corporate property shall not be diverted from the original purpose "[1]

In England a share means the same as it does in this country; but the word "stock" there signifies a number of paid-up shares, so united that the owner may divide it and transfer it in large or small quantities, irrespective of the number and par value of the shares which have been thus merged into "stock."[2]

Hence a share of stock may be defined as a proportional part of certain rights in the management and profits of the corporation during its existence, and in the assets upon dissolution.[3]

It has been well settled that shares of stock are personalty and not realty A share of stock is not real estate, has nothing to give it the character of real estate, is not land, nor an hereditament, nor an interest in either of them.[4]

Fisher t The Essex Bank, 5 Gray 373, 378 (1855) Cf Arnold r Ruggles, 1 R. I., 165 (1837)

[1] Forbes t Memphis etc, R. R. Co, 2 Woods, 323, 331 (1872) Cf Payne t Elliott, 54 Cal, 339 (1880) Mr Justice Sharswood says ' A share of stock is an incorporeal intangible thing It is a right to a certain proportion of the capital stock of a corporation — never realized except upon the dissolution and winding up of the corporation — with the right to receive in the meantime such profits as may be made and declared in the shape of dividends ' Neiler r Kelley, 69 Penn St, 403, 407 (1871). See, also, Bridgman t City of Keokuk, 33 N W Rep, 255 (Iowa, 1887).

[2] Norrice r Aylmer, L R, 7 H L, 717, says "Shares are not necessarily converted into stock as soon as they are paid up, they may exist either as paid-up shares or as not paid-up shares. But, as regards stock, that can only exist in the paid-up state   There is a certain extent of change as well as consolidation in these paid-up shares They are changed from ordinary shares in this respect, that they are no longer incapable of being subdivided "

Stock "is a fund or capital which is capable of being divided into and held

in any irregular amount. Thus, the ordinary government funds (consols now thrices, etc) are called stocks, because a person can buy them in any amount (such as £99 19s 11d as well as £100). A share or debenture on the other hand, is of a fixed amount (such as £10 £50 £100), and is incapable of subdivision or consolidation." Rapalje & Lawrence's Law Dic, p. 1224 Shares may be converted by the company into stock, so as to enable their holders to dispose of them in small or irregular amounts Hurrell & Hyde on Joint-Stock Companies, 47

[3] Oakbank Oil Co, t Crum, L R, 8 App Cas, 65 (1882)

[4] Bligh t Brent, 2 Younge & C. (Exch), 268 (1836) Edwards t Hall, 6 De G, M & G 74 (1855) Bradley r Holdsworth, 3 Mees & W, 422 (1838) Ex parte Lancaster Canal Navigation Co, 1 Dea. & Ch 411 (1832), Watson t Spratley 28 Eng Law & Eq, 507 (1854) In Allen t Pegram 16 Iowa, 163, 173 (1864) Mr Justice Dillon says Mr Williams treats of shares in corporations as 'incorporeal, personal property'— a very neat and accurate designation Wms on Pers Prop 155 ' See, also, Johns t Johns, 1 Ohio St, 350 (1853), Thurman, J, Arnold t Ruggles, 1 R L,

In some of the earlier cases, upon the theory, perhaps, that the shareholders had a direct interest in the tangible property of the corporation, shares were held to be real estate where the corporate property consisted wholly or chiefly of realty [1]

But as a result of all the authorities it is clearly settled that shares of stock are to be regarded as personalty,[2] a view which has frequently found expression in declaratory statutes both in England [3] and the various states of the Union [4]

Stock, though personalty, is not a chattel; [5] it is rather a chose in action, or, as some older authorities declare, property in the nature of a chose in action [6]

It is, moreover, of such a nature that it cannot ordinarily, either

165 (1837), Dyer v Osborne, 11 id, 321, 325 (1876) Tippets v Walker, 4 Mass, 595. 596 (1808), Parsons, C J , Sargent t Franklin Ins Co, 8 Pick, 90 (1829), Weyer v Second National Bank, 57 Ind 198 (1877) Manns v Brookville National Bank, 73 id, 243 (1881), Seward t City of Rising Sun 79 id., 351 (1881), Southwestern R R Co v Thomason, 40 Ga, 408 (1869) Cf Wheelock t Moulton 15 Vt, 519 (1843), Russell v Temple (Mass, 1798). 3 Dane's Abr, 108, 109

[1] Price t Price, 6 Dana (Ky), 107 (1838), Copeland v Copeland, 7 Bush, 349 (1870) But as soon as this latter decision was handed down, the legislature passed an act declaring shares of stock in Kentucky to be personal property, thus bringing the courts of that state into line with other common-law courts upon this question In Meason s Estate, 4 Watts, 341 (1835), there is to be found a tendency to hold shares in a toll-bridge, real estate Turnpike stock was held realty in Welles v Cowles, 2 Com, 567 (1818), S. P, Knapp t Williams, 4 Ves Jr, 430, note (1798) So of canal shares. Tomlinson v Tomlinson, 9 Bear, 459 (1826) Cf Buckeridge v Ingram, 2 Ves, 652 (1795), Drybutter v Bartholomew, 2 P Wms, 127 (1723), The King t Winstanley, 8 Price, 180 (1820) Contra, Walker t Milne, 11 Bear, 507 (1849) See, also. Sparling v Parker, 9 id, 450 (1846), Myers v Perrigal, 18 L. J. (Chan), 185 (1849),

S C., 21 L J (C P), 217 (1852), Ashton t Langdale, 4 Eng L & Eq, 80 (1851); S C, 20 L. J. (Chan), 234, and an interesting discussion of the question in 3 Dane's Abridgment, 108 et seq

[2] See cases cited supra Also, an essay on Stock, its Nature and Transfer, 7 Southern Law Review (N. S), 430 (1881).

[3] 41 Geo III, ch 3, Watson v Spratley, 28 Eng Law & Eq, 507 (1854), Ex parte Vallance, 2 Deacon, 354 (1837); Ex parte Lancaster Canal Navigation Co., 1 Dea & Ch, 411 (1832)

[4] 1 Rev Laws of New York, 247, New York Laws of 1848, ch 40, § 8, New York Laws of 1850, ch 140, § 8, Laws of New Jersey, 1830, p 83, § 17; Code of Virginia, p 550, § 21.

[5] King v. Copper, 5 Price (Eng Exch), 217 (1870).

[6] Wildman v Wildman, 9 Ves., 174 (1803), How v Starkweather, 17 Mass., 240 243 (1821), Hutchins v. State Bank, 12 Metc, 421, 426 (1847), Union Bank of Tennessee v The State, 9 Yerg (Tenn), 490, 500 (1836), Allen v Pegram, 16 Iowa, 163, 173 (1864), Arnold v. Ruggles, 1 R I, 165 (1837), Slaymaker v Bank of Gettysburg, 10 Penn. St., 373 (1849); Denton t Livingston, 9 Johns, 96 (1812); Chesapeake, etc, R. R. Co. v Paine, 29 Gratt, 502, 506 (1877), Barksdale v Finney, 14 id, 338, 357 (1858); Fisher v. Essex Bank, 5 Gray, 373, 377 (1855); People's Bank v. Kurtz, 99 Penn St, 344, 349 (1882): Humble v. Mitchell, 11

by act of the law or act of its owner, be taken into tangible possession, although, of course, its representative — the certificate of stock — may be [1]

It is an English doctrine that shares of stock are not "goods, wares or merchandise," as those terms are to be understood in construing that section of the statute of frauds which requires delivery, payment or memorandum in writing of a sale thereof [2] In this country, however, the courts have taken the opposite view [4] Furthermore, it is said that shares are not money, [4] nor are they security for money, [5] nor a credit [6]

Shares of stock, being in the nature of a chose in action, are, at common law, not subject to attachment or levy of execution [7] but most of the states have enacted statutes which have changed this rule   This species of property may be made subject to taxation, [8] and for purposes of taxation it exists apart from the corporation, the corporate property, the corporate franchises and the capital stock   In most of the states, and in the federal courts, trover lies for the conversion of stock   In Pennsylvania, however, a contrary rule prevails, although conversion is held to be in reference to certificates of stock [9]

Justice Story, in his Conflict of Laws, says that questions relating to shares of stock are to be determined by the law of the state of the corporation [10] For purposes of attachment and execution levied upon stock this is undoubtedly true, since it is only at the domicile of the corporation that such an attachment or execution can be levied [11] As regards the taxation of stock, however, the stock follows the domicile of the stockholder, and may be taxed in ac-

Adol & El, 205, 208 (1839). *Cf* Kellogg *v* Stockwell, 75 Ill 68 (1874); *In re* Jackson L. R., 12 Eq, 354 (1871)

[1] Jermain *v* Lake Shore, etc, R. R. Co, 91 N Y, 483, 492 (1883); Neiler *v* Kelley, 69 Penn St, 403, 407 (1871), Payne *v* Elliot, 54 Cal., 339, 341 (1880)

[2] See §§ 339, 340, *infra.*

[3] Id

[4] Nightingal *v* Devisme, 5 Burr, 2589, S C 2 Wm Black, 684 (1770), Jones *v* Brinley, 1 East, 1 (1800), Douglas *v* Congreve, 1 Keen, 410 (1836).

[5] Ogle *v* Knipe, 38 L J (Chan) 692 (1869), Gosden *v* Dotterill, 1 Mylne & K 56 (1832)? Lowe *v* Thomas, 5 De G, M & G, 315 (1854), Hotham *v* Sutton 15 Ves, 320 (1808), Atkins *v* Gamble, 42 Cal, 86 (1871), Wilson *v* Little, 2 N Y.,

443 (1849)   Mechanics' Bank *v* New York, etc, R. R. Co, 13 N Y, 599, 626 (1856).

[6] New Orleans National Banking Association *v* Wiltz, 10 Fed Rep, 330 (1881), S C, 4 Woods, 44   See, also, Smith *v* Crescent City, etc, Slaughterhouse Co 30 La Ann, 1378 (1878)

[7] See chapter XXVII

[8] See chapter XXXIV

[9] See chapter XXXV

[10] Story on Conflict of Laws (8th ed), § 383   And see the discussion of this subject in Black *v* Zacharie, 3 How, 483 (1844)   As to the *situs* of stock see article in 45 Alb. L. J, 330, 147 U. S., 360, 135 id, 533, 7 S. Rep, 90.

[11] See chapter XXVII

cordance with the law of the domicile of such stockholder[1] In reference to transfers of stock, the law of the forum governs.[2] Legal proceedings against the stock may be initiated at the domicile of the corporation[3]

In regard to shares of stock owned by married women, the payment of dividends is governed by the law of the domicile of the corporation,[4] but the legality of transfers is governed by the law of her domicile[5]

A guardian's sale of stock is governed by the law of the state of the guardianship[6]

A certificate of stock is not necessary to the complete ownership of the stock,[7] nor is payment of the subscription necessary thereto.[8] But the corporation is bound, upon demand, to issue a certificate of stock to one who is entitled to it,[9] and, if it refuses, the stockholder may bring suit in equity to compel its issuance,[10] or he may sue it in an action at law for damages[11]

As regards the common-law and statutory liability of a stockholder on his stock, the law of the domicile of the corporation determines the extent of the liability, while the law of the *forum* determines the method of enforcing that liability[12]

§ 13 *Classes of stock* — The capital stock of a corporation may be either common or preferred. By *common stock* is meant that stock which entitles the owners of it to an equal *pro rata* division of profits, if any there be, one shareholder or class of shareholders having no advantage, priority or preference over any other shareholder or class of shareholders in the division. By *preferred stock* is meant stock which entitles its owners to dividends out of the

---

[1] See chapter XXXIV.

The case of Glenn *v* Clabaugh, 3 Atl Rep, 902 (1886), holds that the insolvent laws of Maryland cannot discharge a Maryland subscriber to a Virginia corporation The validity of a contract to sell stock under the statute of frauds is determined by the *lex loci contractus* Tisdale *v* Harris, 37 Mass, 9 (1838).

[2] See chapter XXII

[3] See chapter XXVII, and §§ 361, 362, *infra*, and, in general, see Noyes *v* Spaulding, 27 Vt, 420 (1853), Richmondville Mfg Co *v* Prall, 9 Conn, 487 (1833); Black *v* Zacharie, 3 How, 483 (1845) As regards national banks, see Scott *v.* Pequonnock Nat'l Bank, 15 Fed Rep, 494 (1883), Continental Nat'l Bank *v* Eliot Nat'l Bank, 12 Rep., 35;

Dickinson *v* Central Nat'l Bank, 129 Mass, 279, Sibley *v* Quinsigamund Nat'l Bank, 133 Mass., 515 (1882), State *v* First Nat'l Bank, etc, 89 Ind, 302 (1883), Holbrook *v* New Jersey, etc, Co, 57 N Y, 616 (1874).

[4] See § 542, *infra.*

[5] See § 319, *infra.*

[6] See § 328, *infra.*

[7] Wheeler *v* Millar, 90 N Y., 353 (1882), Burr *v* Wilcox, 22 N Y, 551, 555 (1860), Thorp *v* Woodhull, 1 Sand. Ch, 411 (1844).

[8] Wheeler *v* Millar, *supra.*

[9] See § 192, *infra*

[10] Id.

[11] Id.

[12] See chapters XI and XII.

net profits before or in preference to the holders of the common stock   Common stock entitles the owner to a *pro rata* of dividends equally with all other holders of the stock except preferred stockholders, while preferred stock entitles the owner to a priority in dividends

By *watered* or *fictitious stock* is meant stock which is issued as fully paid up, when, in fact, the whole amount of the par value thereof has not been paid in   If any amount less than the whole face value of the stock has not been paid, and the stock has been issued as full paid, then the stock is watered to the extent of the deficit   Watered stock is, accordingly, stock which purports to represent, but does not represent, in good faith, money paid in to the treasury of the company, or money's worth actually contributed to the working capital of the concern   The issue of such stock may be lawful, but sometimes it is in fraud of the rights of some interested party, as, *e. g*, creditors of the corporation, certain shareholders or classes of shareholders [1]

By *deferred stock* or *bonds* is meant stock or bonds the payment of dividends or *interest* upon which is expressly postponed until some other class of shareholders are paid a dividend, or until some certain obligation or liability of the corporation is satisfied.[2]

By *overissued* or *spurious stock* is meant stock issued in excess of the full amount of capital stock authorized by the charter of the corporation.[3]   Such stock is void even though issued in good faith.

In Massachusetts some classes of corporations issue what is there known as *special stock*   This is a peculiar kind of stock, essentially local in character, provided for by statute, and unknown before the year 1855   Its characteristics are that it is limited in amount to two-fifths of the actual capital, it is subject to redemption by the corporation at par after a fixed time, to be specified in the certificate, the corporation is bound to pay a fixed half-yearly sum or dividend upon it as a debt, the holders of it are in no event liable for the debts of the corporation beyond the amount of their stock, and the issue of special stock makes all the general stockholders liable for all debts and contracts of the corporation until the special stock is fully redeemed.[4]

§ 14   *Certificates of stock* — A certificate of stock is from one point of view a mere muniment of title, like a title deed   It is not the stock itself, but evidence of the ownership of the stock, that is to say, it is a written acknowledgment by the corporation of the interest of the shareholder in the corporate property and franchises; it operates to transfer nothing from the corporation to the

---

[1] See chapter III.

[2] See § 762, *infra*, and chapter III.

[3] See §§ 291, 298.

[4] See chapter XVI, *infra.*

shareholder, but merely affords to the latter evidence of his rights. It should be clearly apprehended that the certificate is not the stock, but merely written evidence of the ownership of shares.[1] Accordingly it follows that shares have no "ear-marks" — that one share cannot be distinguished from another share — but that it is only the certificates which are distinguishable one from the other by their numbers and in other ways[2] The certificate, therefore, has value in itself only as evidence, and, apart from the shares which it represents, it is utterly worthless.[3] And even as evidence it is not in every case essential, it is merely a convenient voucher, which the shareholder has a right to receive if he asks for it[4] One element of its value to the shareholder is that it is *prima facie* evidence of his title.[5]

The right of every shareholder to demand and receive from the company a certificate is generally conceded.[6] When certificates are executed by a part only of the officers required by law to sign them, they may be void.[7] But a certificate issued to an officer of the corporation who is a shareholder, although the certificate is

[1] Hawley v Brumagim, 33 Cal, 394 (1867), Campbell v Morgan, 4 Bradw, 100 (1879), Peoples Bank v. Kurtz, 99 Penn St., 344 (1882), Hubbell v Drexel, 11 Fed Rep, 115 (1882), Van Allen v. Assessors, 3 Wall, 573, 593 (1865), Burr v Wilcox, 22 N Y 531 (1860), Birmingham Nat'l Bank v Roden, 11 S. Rep., 883 (Ala, 1892) "Stock is one thing, and certificates another The former is the substance, and the latter is the evidence of it.' Hawley v. Brumagim, supra.

[2] Hubbell v Drexel, supra

[3] Payne v. Elliot, 54 Cal, 339

[4] Johnson v Albany, etc, R R Co, 40 How. Prac., 193 (1870). Cf Arnold v. Suffolk Bank, 27 Barb, 424 (1857), a case in which the distinction between a refusal on the part of a corporation to issue a certificate in a certain form and a refusal to recognize the owner of shares as owner — a denial of his property in the stock — is clearly drawn The supreme court of Indiana have noted the distinction to the effect that a certificate is not the title, but only evidence of the title, to shares. The court say "The certificate did not constitute the title to the stock. . . In legal contemplation the certificate was merely an additional and convenient evidence of the ownership of the stock " Cincinnati, etc, R R Co. v Pearce, 28 Ind, 502 (1867).

[5] Broadway Bank v. McEliath, 13 N. J Eq, 24 (1860), Courtright v. Deeds, 37 Iowa, 503 (1873), Walker v Detroit Transit etc, Co, 47 Mich, 338 (1882)

[6] Buffalo, etc, R R Co v Dudley, 14 N Y, 336, 347 (1856), National Bank v Watsontown Bank, 105 U S, 217 (1881) A valid certificate may be issued out of the state in which the corporation exists Courtright v Deeds, 37 Iowa, 503 (1873) See § 61
The failure of the corporation to issue a certificate is no defense to an action to collect the subscription. See § 192, infra
The certificate of stock need not be under seal. Halstead v Dodge, 51 N. Y. Super Ct, 169 (1884). There is no common-law rule requiring certificates of stock to have the corporate seal placed upon them Coddington v. Railroad, 103 U S, 409 (1880), dictum.

[7] Holbrook v Farquier, etc, Co, 3 Cranch, C C, 425 (1829). See § 363

signed by that officer, is valid.[1]   It is not, however, essential to the
existence of the corporation that certificates of stock shall be issued.[2]
Without a certificate the shareholder has a complete power to
transfer his stock,[3] to receive dividends,[4] and to vote,[5] and he is individually liable as a stockholder.[6]   A certificate of stock may be
a valid subject of a *donatio causa mortis*, of a legacy, a contract of
sale, a pledge, or a gift.[7]   Under the English statute an issue of
stock by a corporation has reference only to the issue of the certificates, and means an original putting out of the shares.[8]   In New
York, making out and mailing the certificates has been held to constitute a due issuing thereof.[9]   And in Maryland, the stub of a
book from which certificates have been detached is evidence of
their regular issue.[10]

Certificates of stock are not negotiable instruments   They have
sometimes been said to have a *quasi*-negotiability, but this phraseology throws little light upon the real character of the transferability of stock.   It may be said in general that by the operation
of the law of estoppel the purchaser of a certificate of stock, in
good faith and for value, may take it free from many claims of
previous holders which would be allowed to come in, in the case of
a sale of an ordinary chose in action.[11]

§ 15. *Definition of bond, mortgage, deed of trust, debenture, articles of association, memoranda of association, scrip, certificate book,
transfer book, stock ledger, underwriting, founders' shares — A
bond* of a corporation is an instrument executed under the seal of
the corporation, acknowledging the loan and agreeing to repay the
same upon terms set forth therein   A coupon bond is one that has
coupons attached, usually in the form of promissory notes to pay
an amount of money equal to the annual or semi-annual interest on
the bond   A registered bond is one whose negotiability is temporarily withdrawn by a writing on the bond that it belongs to a
specified person, and by a registry to that effect at an office specified by the company

[1] Titus v President, etc, of the G W.
Turnpike Road, 61 N Y, 237 (1874)

[2] Chester Glass Co v Dewey, 16 Mass.
94 (1819), Burr v. Wilcox, 22 N Y, 551
(1860)

[3] First National Bank v Gifford, 47
Iowa, 575 (1877), National Bank v Wat-
sontown Bank, 105 U S, 217 (1881) *Cf*
Brigham v Mead 10 Allen 245 (1865)

[4] Ellis v Proprietors of Essex Merrimack Bridge, 2 Pick, 243 (1824).

[5] Beckett v. Houston, 32 Ind, 393
(1869)

[6] Agricultural Bank v Wilson, 24 Me,
273 (1844), Mitchell v Beckman, 64 Cal,
117 (1883)

[7] See chapter XVIII

[8] East Gloucestershire R'y Co v Bartholomew, L. R. 3 Exch., 15 (1867),
Bush's Case, L. R. 9 Chan, 554 (1874)

[9] Jones v Terre Haute, etc, R. R. Co.,
17 How Pr, 529 (1859).

[10] Weber v Fickey, 47 Md., 196 (1877).

[11] See chapter XXIV.

A *mortgage* given by a corporation may be similar to the ordinary mortgage given by an individual.

But usually a corporate mortgage is made in the form of a *mortgage deed of trust* Such a deed of trust is a mortgage, the mortgagee, however, being a trustee for bondholders, and the bonds being secured by the mortgage deed of trust. The trustee may be an individual but generally is a trust company. Where the mortgage is to secure a large number of bonds, it is almost necessary that a deed of trust be used. Otherwise the mortgage would run to the bondholders, who are constantly changing, and many of whom are soon unknown to the corporation mortgagor. Moreover in foreclosing such a mortgage serious difficulties would arise. Hence where a corporation gives a mortgage to secure bonds, this mortgage is made in the form of a deed of trust.

The word "*debenture*" has no definite legal meaning. It may be applied to any promise or security of the company to pay money. It may be a mere promise to pay, or a covenant under seal to pay, or a mortgage or charge under the seal of the company.

"*Debenture stock*" is an English term and means borrowed money consolidated into one mass for the sake of convenience. Instead of each lender having a separate bond or mortgage, he has a certificate entitling him to a certain sum, being a portion of one large loan.[1] In this country the same thing is done by issuing to a bond-holder a certificate entitling him, and him alone, to a specified sum and interest in exchange for bonds to the same amount which he delivers to the company at the time when he receives the certificate.

Articles of association are similar to by-laws, and are for the regulation and management of the corporation.

Memoranda of association are the same as the American articles of incorporation required to be filed under general statutes for incorporations.[2]

In England *scrip* is a written acknowledgment by a corporation that the holder will be entitled to certain shares of stock and a certificate therefor when the unpaid instalments on such shares are all paid in. They are negotiable instruments.[3]

[1] Lindley on Company Law, p. 195.

[2] Deed of settlement is a term that was used in England, prior to 1862, to indicate the same as the modern articles of association and memoranda of association See Burrows *v.* Smith, 10 N Y., 550, 555 (1853), Rapalje & Lawrence's Law. Dic., 361; London Financial Association *v.* Kelk, L. R., 26 Ch. D., 107;

Guiness *v.* Land Corporation of Ireland, L. R., 22 Ch D., 369.

[3] Goodwin *v.* Robarts, L. R., 1 App. Cas., 476 (1876), Rumball *v.* Metropolitan Bank, L. R., 2 Q B. Div., 194 (1877).

In this country scrip generally means a kind of dividend. *e. g.,* land scrip dividend entitling the holder to take so much land, and a scrip dividend en-

The *certificate book* of a corporation contains the printed, lithographed or engraved certificates of stock, which are filled out and signed by the proper officers and then delivered to the stockholders A stub in the book, opposite each certificate, states the name, amount, date, etc , of the certificate which is issued   When the certificate is returned, upon a transfer to a new person, it is canceled and attached to the old stub   On the back of the certificate a blank form for a transfer of the stock represented by it is given

The *transfer book* is for the purpose of keeping a record of transfers of stock   The entries in it correspond to the transfers on the backs of the canceled certificates of stock   The entries in the transfer book are generally made by a clerk as attorney in fact for the transferrer. The form of transfer on the back of the certificate contains such a power of attorney

The *stock ledger* contains a statement of how much stock the past and present stockholders have owned or now own

Underwriting means an agreement, made before the shares are brought before the public, that in the event of the public not taking all the shares or the number mentioned in the agreement, the underwriter will take the shares which the public do not take [1]

Founders' shares are shares which take the profits after certain dividends are paid on the other shares   They are a sort of deferred stock. They are issued to the founders or promoters of the enterprise   They are unknown in America. In England they often acquire a great value

So enormous have been the profits of some of the trust and investment companies that their founders' shares, which divide the surplus after payment of a moderate maximum dividend on the ordinary shares, are worth almost fabulous sums of money. The Trustees, Executors and Securities Insurance Company is the most remarkable illustration, with its founders' shares quoted on the market at something like seven thousand five hundred per cent. Founders' shares in the Foreign and Colonial Debenture, the Imperial Bank of Persia, the London Produce Clearing, the United States Debenture. and the North of England Trustee Debenture and Assets all command an extraordinary premium

Founders' shares are often given as a gift to eminent persons who consent to act as directors and to be held out to the public as such.

---

titling the holder to future dividends the same as stock receives, but without the voting privilege of stock. See chapter XXXII, *infra*.

[1] The underwriter is liable on the stock *Re* Licensed, etc., Ass'n, 60 L. T. Rep , 684 (1889).

CHAPTER II.

STOCK MAY BE ISSUED LEGALLY FOR MONEY OR PROPERTY, OR BY A STOCK DIVIDEND

§ 16 *Methods of issuing stock.*— There are in general three methods of issuing stock It may be issued, first, by means of subscriptions, payable in cash, the subscription being made in writing, or by acts equivalent thereto [1] Second, the issue may be by means of subscriptions. payable in labor, property, or both. Third, the issue may be by a stock dividend

§ 17. *First method: Issue by money subscription.*— An issue of stock by means of a subscription, payable in cash, is the most simple and safe method of issuing stock In the absence of any agreement to the contrary, an ordinary subscription for stock is deemed a cash subscription, and payment in money may be enforced. The subscription contract is generally made by a writing duly signed by the subscriber The writing itself is contained in books opened by the corporation or by commissioners appointed in conformity with a statute, or it is made without formality on subscription lists or separate sheets of paper

A subscription, payable in cash, may arise also from the mere acts or declarations of a party. A person having assumed the position of a subscriber or stockholder is frequently held to be bound as such. Any act or declaration, sufficient to indicate an intent on the part of the person to be a subscriber, and an acceptance by the corporation of the person as such, is equivalent to a written subscription, and the person is bound as a subscriber [2]

§ 18. *Second method: Issue for property, labor or construction work.*— The issue of stock for labor, property, contract work, or

---

[1] See chapter IV. [2] Id.

any valuable consideration other than money, has given rise to much controversy and litigation   In England a long line of decisions, under the Companies Act, has established the principle that stock need not necessarily be paid for in cash, but that it may be paid for in money's worth [1] Such, also, was the rule at common law [2] The well-established rule now is that a subscription for stock, payable by its terms in property or labor, or both, is a good and legal subscription. If the property is taken at a valuation made without fraud, the payment is as effectual and valid as though made in cash to the same amount. An issue of stock for property is one which finds support, not only in the decisions, but in the daily transactions of corporations,[3] and the law does not compel the corporation and the subscriber to go through the useless form of a payment by the corporation to the subscriber of the value of the

---

[1] See many cases in chapter III Stacy v Little Rock, etc, R R Co 5 Dill, 348, 376 (1876)

[2] Woodhall's Case, 3 De G & Sm, 63 (1849), Burkinshaw v Nichols, L R, 3 App. Cas, 1004, 1012 (1878), where, payment having been made in property, the court said "If there had been no statutory enactment forbidding a transaction of that kind, it is a transaction which might be properly valid" Cf dictum in Sanger v Upton, 91 U S, 56, 60 (1875) "It is not now questioned that a corporation may issue its stock by way of payment in the purchase of property. This is on the principle that there is no need for the roundabout process of first issuing the stock for money, and then paying the money for the property But it is necessary that the property so taken be considered reasonably worth the par value of the stock paid for it ' Chouteau v Dean, 7 Mo App, 210 (1879), Wyman v Amer Powder Co, 62 Mass, 168 (1851), Reichwald v Commercial Hotel Co, 106 Ill, 439 (1883), Haydon v Atlanta Cotton Factory, 61 Ga, 234 (1878) "Whatever may have been formerly held, it is now established that subscriptions to corporate stock need not, in the absence of statutory provisions requiring it, be paid for in cash. The principle is now gen-

erally accepted, both in England and America, that any property which the corporation is authorized to purchase, or which is necessary for the purposes of its legitimate business, may be received in payment for its stock Any payment, whether it be in money or money's worth, so that it be in good faith, will give the shares so paid for the *status* of paid-up stock In the language of Lord Justice Gifford, in Drummond's Case 4 Ch App, 772 'If a man contracts to take shares he must pay for them, to use a homely phrase, in meal or in malt, he must either pay in money or money's worth, if he pays in one or the other that will be a satisfaction '   The contract to receive in payment the latters patent, plows, material and other assets of its predecessor, Unthank & Coffin, was therefore not *ultra vires* " Coffin v Ransdall, 11 N E Rep, 20 (Ind 1887) holding, also, that payment for stock by transferring to the corporation the property and assets of a partnership was legal, provided that a fair valuation was placed upon the property so conveyed If such property is overvalued, the dangers incurred thereby are various See ch III 20 S W Rep, 965

[3] Foreman z. Bigelow, 4 Cliff, 308, 544 (1878).

property, and an immediate repayment of the same money by the subscriber to the corporation on his subscription.[1]

There is some doubt as to whether an oral agreement of the corporate agents that a subscription may be paid in property is binding upon the corporation   Under the well-established rule that parol evidence will not be allowed to add to or vary a written agreement, it has been held that such an oral agreement with the agent cannot be admitted in evidence.[2]　When, however the parol agreement is made subsequently to the act of subscribing, and is supported by a sufficient consideration, it is valid and enforceable [3]

§ 19　*When such subscriptions are not legal* — A subscription payable by its terms in labor or property is in the nature of a conditional subscription   Accordingly, in certain states, where a percentage or fixed amount of the capital stock must be subscribed for before a charter can be obtained, and where, by the decisions of the courts, such preliminary subscriptions must be absolute and unconditional, a subscription payable by its terms in labor or property, being conditional to that extent, cannot form a part of the preliminary subscription [4]　In such states, however, subscriptions to the remainder of the capital stock, the part subscribed after the charter has been or may be obtained, may be conditional, and may, by their terms, be payable in property or labor [5]　On the ground that subscriptions payable in property or labor are conditional, it has been held also that a subscription payable in labor or property is not to be counted in ascertaining whether the full capital stock has been subscribed,[6] in order to enforce subscriptions for stock

---

[1] Seawright r Payne, 6 Lea (Tenn), 283 (1880), Blant t Enlen, 59 Md, 1 (1882), Spargos Case, L R , 8 Ch App. 412 (1873), Boot & Shoe Co. v Hart, 56 N H., 548 (18.6)   Payment in property by subscribers was held not allowable in Neuse River Nav Co v Com'rs of Newbern, 7 Jones' Law (N C), 275 (1859), also Henry v Vermillion & Ashland R R Co, 17 Ohio, 187 (1813), although the latter case seems to involve an oral agreement to allow such payment, and to have been decided on that ground. There is a long line of cases sustaining the validity of an issue of stock for money's worth instead of money itself. They are given in this and the following chapter. So well established has this

principle of law become that the few cases holding to the contrary can no longer be considered good law   "That in the absence of fraud an agreement may ordinarily be made by which stockholders could be allowed to pay for their shares in patents, mines or other property, to which it is not easy to assign a determinate value, would appear to be well settled"   New Haven, etc., Co v Linden Spring Co., 142 Mass., 349 (1886)

[2] See § 137, *infra.*

[3] Id

[4] See §§ 79 180, *infra.*

[5] See § 82, *infra.*

[6] See § 180, *infra.*

§ 20. *What property may be received* — A corporation may receive in payment of its shares of stock any property which it may lawfully purchase,[1] and, in general, may receive any consideration which is suitable and applicable to the purposes for which the corporation was organized[2] A railroad corporation may receive payment in contract work, in right of way, or in any kind of material or labor applicable to its construction[3] A manufacturing corpo-

---

[1] Brant *v.* Ehlen, 59 Md, 1 (1882), The American Silk Works *v* Salomau, 4 Hun, 135 (1875)

In Louisiana the general act for incorporation prescribes that the articles of incorporation shall state the time when and the manner in which "the stock shall be paid for" See New Orleans, etc, R. R. Co *v* Frank, 1 South Rep., 310 (La., 1887)

[2] See Green's Brice's Ultra Vires (2d ed.), 145; Angell & Ames (11th ed), § 517 "Payment of stock subscriptions need not be in cash, but may be in whatever, considering the situation of the corporation, represents to that corporation a fair, just, lawful and needed equivalent for the money subscribed" Liebke *v* Knapp, 79 Mo 22 (1883) Payment in newspaper advertising of the enterprise upheld in this case The subscription may, by its terms, be payable in plank for a plank-road company, and the subscriber is a stockholder before payment is completed. Haywood, etc, Co *v* Bryan, 6 Jones' Law (N C), 82 (1858) Payment in Confederate bonds redeemable in cotton upheld Schroder's Case, L R, 11 Eq Cas, 131 (1870) So, also, payment in stock in a coal corporation carrying on a supplementary business East, etc, R R. Co *v* Lighthouse, 6 Rob. (N. Y), 407 (1868) Payment by a patent-right has been upheld. Edwards *v.* Bringier Sugar Extracting Co, 27 La. Ann, 118 (1875); and in another case, under a statute not upheld Tasker *v* Wallace, 6 Daly, 364 (1876) Payment may be by canceling a debt of the company past due Carr *v.* Le Fevre, 27 Pa. St, 413 (1856); Reed *v* Hayt, 51 N Y. Super Ct., 121 (1884). Or

not yet due Appleyards Case, 49 L. J (Ch), 290 (1880) Payment, however, to a bank in its own currency was not upheld, it being statutory that only specie could be received King *v* Elliott, 13 Miss, 428 (1845) Payment by check cannot be objected to by another subscriber Thorp *v* Woodhull, 1 Sandf. Ch, 411 (1844) Stock may be issued to the president in payment of past salary and debts Reed *v* Hayt, 4 Ry & Corp. L J, 135 (N Y, 1888)

[3] "We can see no objection whatever to a railroad company issuing stock and taking in payment materials or labor or lands necessary for its road" Clark *v.* Farrington, 11 Wis, 306 (1860) As to payment in stock for construction work, see, also, Wood on R ys, § 282. "The corporation had a right to accept payment of stock in labor or materials, in damages which the company were liable to pay, or in any other liability of the company, provided these transactions were entered into and carried out in good faith" Phil & West Chester R. R. Co *v* Hickman, 28 Pa St, 318 (1857), Bedford County *v* Nashville, C & St Louis R. R Co, 14 Lea (Tenn), 525 (1884), holding, also, that thirty years delay in demanding the stock is no bar to the right To same effect, payment being in services, Kobogum *v.* Jackson Iron Co, 43 N. W Rep, 602 (Mich, 1889). Payment may be in cross-ties Ohio, Ind & Ill R. R. Co *v* Cramer, 23 Ind, 490 (1864) Or in real estate and services Cin, Ind & Chicago R. R. Co *v* Clarkson, 7 Ind, 595 (1856) Or in services and materials Phillips *v.* Covington & Cin Bridge Co, 2 Metc (Ky), 219 (1859) Or by construction of the road.

ration may receive payment in the good-will of a business or the stock in trade.[1] Land may be taken in payment when the corporation would be allowed to purchase the same.[2] Promissory notes may also be taken, under the corporate power, to give credit and extend the time of payment of debts [3]

§ 21. *Payment in property as a favor, not as a contract right.*— There is an important distinction to be made between payments in

See § 17. One railroad having power to consolidate with another may, in payment therefor, issue stock to the contractors who are constructing the latter Branch *v* Jesup, 106 U S., 468 (1882) A corporation may agree to give $5,000 of stock to one who will borrow $15,000 for it. Arapahoe, etc , Co. *v.* Stevens, 22 Pac Rep , 823 (Colo., 1889). A contract that subscriptions shall be payable in land is illegal by statute in Alabama, but after subscription payment in land may be allowed. Knox *v.* Childersburg L Co., 5 South Rep , 579 (Ala., 1889).

[1] Pell's Case, L. R., 5 Ch., 11 (1869).

[2] Goodin *v* Evans, 18 Ohio St., 150 (1868), Cin , Ind & Chicago R. R. Co *v.* Clarkson, 7 Ind., 595 (1856), Peck *v* Coalfield Coal Co , 11 Bradw (Ill). 88 (1882); Brant *v* Ehlen, 59 Md , 1 (1882); Jones' Case, L R., 6 Ch App., 48 (1870); Maynard's Case, 23 W. R., 119 In Foreman *v* Bigelow, 4 Cliff , 508, 544 (1878), the court say "Argument to show that the transaction of issuing the stock in payment for the mineral land would have been valid . . . is scarcely necessary." In Indiana formal acceptance by the directors is necessary. State *v.* Bailey, 16 Ind , 46 (1861); Junction R. R Co *v* Reeve, 15 Ind , 236 (1861); Dayton, etc , R. R Co. *v.* Hatch, 1 Disney, 84 (1855), Carr *v.* Le Fevre, 27 Penn. St., 413 (1856), Johnson *v.* N. Y. & Erie R. R. Co , 2 Sand . 39 (1848) A corporation receiving a deed of land in payment of stock subscription is protected in its title to the land the same as any other *bona fide* purchaser of it would be against a former vendor's lien for the purchase-money Frenkel *v* Hudson, 2 South. Rep., 758 (Ala., 1887).

[3] Stoddard *v* Shetucket Foundry Co , 34 Conn , 542 (1868), Ogdensburgh, etc., R. R. Co *v* Wooley, 3 Abb. Ct. of App. Dec , 398 (1864), Magee *v.* Badger, 30 Barb , 246 (1859), Goodrich *v* Reynolds, 31 Ill , 490 (1863); Vermont Central R. R. Co. *v.* Clayes, 21 Vt., 30 (1848); Hardy *v* Merriweather, 14 Ind , 203 (1860); Pacific Trust Co *v.* Dorsey, 72 Cal., 55 (1887). In Wisconsin a corporation may accept in payment of stock a note secured by a mortgage on real estate. Clark *v* Farrington, 11 Wis., 306 (1860); Blunt *v* Walker, 11 Wis., 234 (1860); Cornell *t* Hichens, 11 Wis., 353 (1860); Lyon *v* Ewings, 17 id , 61 (1863), Andrews *v* Hart, id., 297; Western Bank of Scotland *v* Tallman, 17 Wis, 530 (1863) In Tennessee payment in notes is not upheld, but the subscriber is to be credited with the amount collected on such notes. Moses *v.* Ocoee Bank, 1 Lea (Tenn), 398 (1878). In New York the payment of a subscription by one's own note is prohibited by statute. 1 R. S, ch. 18, title 4, § 2 Payment by bond and mortgage was upheld in Valk *v.* Crandall, 1 Sandf. Ch., 179 (1843), and in Leavett *v* Pell, 27 Barb , 322 (1858) Also in Pennsylvania, Leighty *v.* Susquehanna & Waterford T. Co., 14 S. & R. (Pa), 434 (1826), although the payment was contrary to statute; also, People *v.* Stockton, etc., R. R. Co , 45 Cal , 306 (1873). But a worthless note is not payment Bouton *v* Dament, 123 Ill , 142 (1887). A company authorized by statute to sell stock for cash may sell it for the bonds of the vendee, and may enforce the bonds. Southern Life Ins. Co *v.* Lanier, 5 Fla., 110 (1853).

property, where the subscription itself, by its terms, allows such payment, and a payment in property, which is allowed, as a matter of favor, by the corporation, the subscription itself being silent as to the mode of payment[1] The latter class of transactions have been uniformly upheld, except when positively prohibited by statute, and payment has even been held to be valid, although the statute required it to be in money or in cash[2]

§ 22 *Sale of stock for property.*— The issue of stock for property, labor or contract work need not necessarily be accompanied with the formality of a subscription.[3] Frequently the issue is spoken of as a sale of the stock for the property received in pay-

---

[1] Many of the cases which apparently are cases of subscriptions wherein the subscriber has expressly stipulated that he may pay in property or labor, will be found, on close examination, to be absolute subscriptions payable in cash. Afterwards the corporation, although not obliged so to do, accepts property or labor instead of the cash This kind of transaction is almost universally upheld by the courts when entered into and carried out in good faith Such payment is upheld even in opposition to the express terms of a statute requiring payment in cash See § 23 Many of the American cases, also, are plainly cases in which payment in property was allowed by the corporation, not as a right but as a matter of favor. The courts uphold such agreements because they are similar to offsets of accounts, and the delays, uncertainties, special privileges, and other objections to subscriptions payable in terms in property and labor are obviated See Boot & Shoe Co v Hoit, 56 N H, 543 (1876), Stoddard v. Shetucket Foundry Co, 34 Conn, 542 (1868), where the court say, "that the defendant could have insisted upon the plaintiff's payment for his stock in cash is unquestionable" See, also, Vermont Central R R Co v Clayes, 21 Vt, 30 (1848), Boston, etc, R R Co v Wellington, 113 Mass, 79 (1873). A subscription may be made and then by another contract be paid up by a lease of a railroad Coe v East, etc, R R, 52 Fed Rep, 531 (1892) In New York rail-

road corporations must require payment in cash of a certain percentage of the subscription at the time of subscribing Laws 1850, ch 140, §§ 2, 4 Ninety per cent. may be paid in such manner as the directors may require Id, § 7 Even here, however the courts hold that the ten per cent. may be paid by property actually received Beach v Smith, 30 N Y, 116 (1864), where payment was by services rendered The court said "Was it necessary, for any purpose, that the ceremony of paying money by the company to the defendant, and by the defendant of the same money back again, should be gone through with? It seems to me not.'

[2] See p 36, note 4

[3] A charter provision authorizing the opening of stock subscription books does not amount to a prohibition against any other mode of becoming a stockholder "If a railroad could sell its stock for the right of way, for lands for depot purposes, for iron, or anything essential to the accomplishment of its purpose, it might do so ' It is a legal issue of stock without subscription Western Bank of Scotland v Tallman 17 Wis, 530 (1863) See, also, Clark v Farrington, 11 Wis, 306 (1860), Reed v Hayt, 51 N. Y Super Ct, 121 (1884) In Jackson v Traer, 20 N W Rep 704 (1884), stock having been issued in payment of contract work, the court say We have seen no case which recognizes a difference between those stockholders who become such in pur-

ment   Sometimes the issue is by means of a contract, whereby,
upon the completion of certain work, the party is to be entitled to
the stock. The New York court of appeals stated the law clearly
when it said, in respect to such issues, that "the right of the officers of a railroad corporation to enter into an agreement to build
its road and pay for the construction of the same in stock or bonds
cannot be seriously questioned, and contracts of this description
are frequently made for such a purpose."[1]

It is doubtful, however, whether any clearness of ideas is obtained, under any circumstances, by calling an original issue of
stock a sale of stock   Such a transaction is not a sale of stock. A
sale of stock means a transfer of stock after the stock has been
issued, or an agreement to transfer the same. Such original issues
of stock as are occasionally spoken of as being sales of stock might
better be considered as informal subscriptions arising by the acts
or declarations of the parties, and payable in property by the terms
of the contract[2]

§ 23   *English statutes on issues of stock for property* — In England the payment for stock in property, labor or contract work is
regulated largely by act of parliament. The statute requires that
payment shall be in cash, unless the contract allowing payment in
property is registered at a specified public registry.[3] Nevertheless,
even where no registry is made, the courts have held that a payment in property is equivalent to a payment in cash, where the
property has been actually delivered[4] Such a payment in prop-

suance of a written agreement and
those who become such by the mere acceptance of stock issued to them "

[1] Van Cott *v.* Van Brunt, 82 N. Y,
535 (1880). See, also, Eppes *v* Miss.,
Gainesville & Tuskaloosa R. R. Co, 35
Ala. 33 (1859), Brady *v* Rutland &
Burlington R. R. Co, 3 Blatch, 25;
S C, 21 Vt, 660, Troy & Greenfield
R. R Co. *v* Newton, 8 Gray, 596 (1857),
McMahon *v* N Y, etc. R. R. Co, 20
N Y, 463 (1859), construing such a con-
tract

[2] See Weiss *v* Mauch Chunk Iron Co.,
58 Penn St., 295 (1868), St. Paul, etc.,
R. R Co *v* Robbins, 23 Minn, 440
(1877), Clark *v* Continental Improvement Co., 57 Ind, 135 (1877)

[3] Companies Act, Amendment 1867,
30 and 31 Vic, ch 131, § 25

[4] Under this statute three classes of
cases of unregistered contracts arise

First, where payment is actually made
in property, if fairly made, it is upheld,
under the principles laid down in sec-
tion 16   See Jones' Case, L. R., 6 Ch.
App., 48 (1880), Maynard's Case, 22 W.
R., 119 (1877), payment by colliery, *Re*
Boylan Hull Colliery Co., L. R., 5 Ch.
App., 346 (1870), Drummond's Case,
L. R., 4 Ch App., 772 (1869), Schroder's
Case, L R, 11 Eq Cas., 131 (1870); Pell's
Case, L. R, 5 Ch, 11 (1869), by services,
Ex parte Clarke, L. R., 7 Eq, 550. The
amounts on each side must be payable
presently and in cash   Fothergill's Case,
L. R., 8 Ch App, 270 (1873), so that the
transaction is in the nature of a set-off.
Forbes' Case, L. R, 5 Ch. App., 270 (1870);
64 L T Rep, 61   Conveyance of a lease
held to be a good payment. Spargo's
Case, L. R, 8 Ch App., 407 (1873)   A
second class of unregistered agreements
to take pay in property turn upon the

erty, however, is as a matter of favor, and not as a matter of right [1] It is to be distinguished from the payment in property which the subscriber may not yet have made, but has a right to make in the future The one is an executed contract. The other may still be an executory contract.

§ 24 *Performance of contract of payment in property — Obligation of the corporation to issue the stock.*— Subscriptions payable in property are not subject to calls, and a demand for the property must be made by the corporation [2] Upon failure of the subscriber to furnish the property, or upon insolvency of the corporation, such subscriptions become payable in cash [3] A payment of part of the subscription in cash does not waive the right of the subscriber to pay the balance in property [4]

The stock may be issued to a contractor before his work in payment therefor has been completed.[5] If the corporation prevents the completion of the contract or refuses to fulfill, the contractor may hold it liable for damages or may have specific performance.

question whether the agreement that payment shall be in property is a condition precedent or subsequent to the subscription If the condition is precedent, and must be performed before the subscription can be enforced, none of the parties are bound, even though the corporation becomes insolvent. Pellatt's Case, L. R., 2 Ch., 527 (1867); Stace's Case, L. R., 4 Ch. App., 682 (1869) The third class is where the contract to pay in property is construed to be a condition subsequent. The condition being subsequent the party must pay, and if the corporation becomes insolvent, he must pay in cash Elkington's Case, L. R., 2 Ch App, 527 (1867), Simpson's Case, L. R., 4 Ch App., 184 (1868), Bridger's Case, L. R., 5 Ch App, 305 (1870), Thomson's Case, 34 L J (Ch), 525 (1865), Fisher's Case, 53 Law Times Rep, 832 (1886), Sherrington's Case, 34 Weekly Rep, 49 (1865). See, also, §§ 47, 78.

[1] See § 16
[2] See § 89, *infra.*
[3] See § 89, *infra.*
[4] Id.
[5] Pendleton, etc., Co. v. Mahan, 18 Pac. Rep., 563 (Oreg, 1888) If a corporation accepts an absolute order upon it by the

contractor to deliver to a third person certain stock, it cannot afterwards decline to issue the stock on the ground that the contractor has not performed his work Appeal of Hite, etc, Co, 12 Atl Rep, 267 (Pa, 1887)

The courts of Massachusetts will not, at the suit of a foreign construction company, enjoin a foreign railroad company and a resident from the issue by the railroad company to the resident of bonds and stock which the railroad company has contracted to deliver to the construction company The suit should be at the residence of the railroad company Kansas Con Co v Topeka, etc, R. R, 135 Mass, 34 (1883)

Where property is deeded to trustees to deed to a corporation for part of the stock, the remaining stock to be for working capital, the *cestui que trust* are entitled to the stock before the rest is sold The statute of limitations does not run. Philes v Hickies, 18 Pac Rep., 595 (Ariz, 1888)

If the corporation prevents the completion of the contract the contractor may recover as damages the value of the work already done and also the profits lost Mayers v York & Cumberland R. R. Co, 2 Curtis, 28 (1854). If

§ 25. *Third method of issue: By stock dividend.*—The third method of issuing stock is by a stock dividend. It is allowable when an amount of cash or property equal to the amount of the par value of the stock so divided is added permanently to the capital stock of the corporation   A stock dividend can be made only when the whole of the capital stock has not been issued, or when it may be increased. It can never increase the capital stock beyond the amount as limited by legislative enactment. An issue of stock by a stock dividend is prohibited by constitutional or legislative enactment in some states. In England it has been a question of doubt whether stockholders can be compelled to accept a dividend of stock   These questions, however, are discussed elsewhere.[1]

§ 26. *Pledge of stock by a corporation.*—It is now settled that a corporation may pledge its unissued stock to secure the debts of the corporation [2]   It is also clear that, for non-payment of the debt so secured, the pledgee may sell the stock;[3] and such sale is legal even though the stock does not sell for its full par value [4]

§ 27 *Issue of stock for partnership property or the property of another corporation* — A copartnership may, of course, sell its stock to a corporation and take shares of stock in payment. But if the partnership is in a failing condition at the time of the transfer, the creditors of the firm may disregard the sale and levy an execution on the property itself.[5] The same rules apply to a sale by one company to another.[6]

the corporation refuse to issue the stock according to contract the contractor may recover as damages the *market* value of the stock   Porter v Buckfield Branch R. R. Co, 32 Me, 539 (1851), Barker v Rutland & Washington R. R. Co, 27 Vt, 766 (1855). If the contract provides for payment to the contractor in stock, without stating that the stock is to be taken at its par value, the contractor may demand the stock at its market value, and if it is worthless, he may then demand money in lieu thereof. Hart v Lauman, 29 Barb, 410 The contractor cannot, however, complain because the capital stock has been increased, nor is a tender of the stock to

him necessary   Moore v. Hudson River R. R. Co, 12 Barb, 156 (1851).

If in organizing and issuing the stock the amount to be issued for the property is not what the contract calls for, the vendor may compel a specific performance. Bailey v. Champlain, etc., Co, 46 N W. Rep., 539 (Wis., 1890). See, also, §§ 61, 335.

[1] See § 51, ch XXXII.

[2] See § 465, *infra*.

[3] See § 476, *infra*.

[4] See § 465, note.

[5] This subject and the numerous complicated questions connected with it are considered in chapter XL, *infra*, also § 6.

[6] Id.

CHAPTER III.

"WATERED" STOCK.—STOCK ISSUED ILLEGALLY FOR MONEY, PROPERTY, OR BY A STOCK DIVIDEND IT IS THEN CALLED "WATERED" OR FICTITIOUSLY PAID-UP STOCK.

A. NATURE OF WATERED STOCK.

§ 28. *Object of issuing fictitiously paid-up stock* — The issue of shares of stock as "paid up," when in fact they are not paid up, gives rise to some of the most complicated questions connected with the law of corporations.

A share of stock is supposed, in theory, to represent its par value in money or money's worth, paid in or to be paid in to the corporation. Accordingly, when it is issued as paid up, it is bought and sold in open market on the supposition that the corporation has received its full par value.[1] Upon this basis, transactions in paid-up

[1] The reasons why the par value of the stock is required by the law to be turned in to the corporation are stated by the supreme court of the United States, in

39

stock, involving many millions of dollars, are of daily occurrence
in the commercial centers of the country. The facilities which exist for the sale of properly issued stock are equally available for
the sale of fictitiously paid-up stock, until it has become well understood and expected that railroad and business corporations will
make these issues of stock.[1] The issue is generally to the organizers or other co-operators, in ostensible payment for property or
construction work. It is no unusual thing for a newly-organized
railroad corporation to issue to a construction company bonds and
stock whose par value is many times the value of the construction
work done.[2] These bonds and the stock are then sold to the public at a profit, large or small, according to the prospects of the enterprise and the skill of the parties who are manipulating the corporation Soon, however default is made in the payment of the
interest on the bonds, and this is followed by corporate insolvency,

Handley *v.* Stutz, 139 U S, 417, 428
(1891), as follows:

"The stock of a corporation is supposed to stand in the place of actual
property of substantial value, and as
being a convenient method of representing the interest of each stockholder
in such property, and to the extent to
which it fails to represent such value it
is either a deception and fraud upon the
public, or an evidence that the original
value of the corporate property has become depreciated. . . . If it be
once admitted that a corporation may
issue stock without receiving a consideration therefor, and where it does not
represent actual or substituted value in
corporate assets, there is apparently no
limit to the extent to which the original
stock may be 'watered,' except the
caprice of the stockholders." Concerning the subject of watered stock, see,
also, Cook on The Corporation Problem,
pp. 24-33.

[1] "According to the estimate of the
most widely acknowledged statistical
authorities upon railways, through the
methods of sale or hypothecation,
$3,700,000,000 of purely paper values
have been sold to the public" Hudson
on The Railways and The Republic, 274
(1886), a book that deals with the railway problems of the day from an anti-

railway point of view. See, also, Preface
to Poor's Manual for 1884.

[2] Jeans on Railway Problems, 311
(1887), says "In 1872 the difference between the total cost of American railways and their equipment, and the total
capital of the system, was $85,250,000.
In 1884 this sum had been increased to
upwards of $162,000,000. In 1872 the
watered capital amounted to an average
of about $1,800 per mile, but in 1884 the
average of such capital was only $1,343
per mile. At the end of 1884 fully ten
per cent. of the total capital embarked
in American lines was additional to the
actual cost of the railways and their
equipment, and the greater part of it
may be regarded as representing 'watered' stock"

Atkinson on the Distribution of Products (2d ed , 1886), page 259, says: "The
elimination of what has been called
'watered stock and bonds' against
which the silly crusade of the so-called
anti-monopolists has been directed, is
therefore in process of accomplishment
by methods far more potent than any
possible legislative acts, namely, by the
triple competition of water-ways Second The competition of one railway
with another. Third The competition
of product with product in the greater
markets of the world."

foreclosure, receivership and re-organization   The issue of fictitiously paid-up stock is the favorite device of corporate promoters, organizers and manipulators in carrying out their plans of realizing enormous gains from small investments, and in accumulating great fortunes at the expense of the public   Occasionally, too, the issue is made for the purpose of concealing large and unreasonable profits, which, if known, might cause the public to regulate and diminish the source of income   In such cases a stock dividend is generally resorted to.

§ 29. *Methods of issuing "watered" stock — Forfeited stock.*— All stock which has been issued as paid-up stock, but whose full par value has not been paid in to the corporation in money or money's worth, is watered to the extent that the par value exceeds the value actually paid in   There are three different ways in which watered stock is issued   It is done by issue of certificates of stock for an amount of *money* less than the par value of the stock, the certificates asserting on their face that the full value has been paid in, or for *property* or *construction work* taken at a fraudulent overvaluation,[1] or by a *stock dividend*, the equivalent par value of which has not

---

[1] Mr Simon Stern, in the Cyclopædia of Political Science, Political Economy and United States History, vol III, p. 527, describes this method of issuing "watered" stocks and bonds as follows

"A line from one point to another, say a distance of one hundred miles, is surveyed. It is ascertained that it will cost about $15,000 a mile to build, including acquisition of land, and about $5,000 a mile to equip, a total of $20,000 a mile. Application is then made for town and county aid, which aid is generally represented by investment in the stock of the road   The first purpose is to give as little as possible in the way of value in return for such money aid, and it is therefore necessary to interpose between the stock and the property a sufficient number of mortgages to make prospective value of the stock of little or no value. A construction company is then organized, which takes the town and county aid as part of its capital and the railway corporation, instead of making its contract on the basis of cash, issues to the construction company, say first-mortgage bonds of $20,000 a mile, or possibly $25,000 a mile, second-mortgage bonds of $20,000 a mile, and stock of an equal value — making a total capitalization of $65,000 a mile, instead of $20,000 at which the road could be constructed   The construction company is composed generally, directly or indirectly, of the officers of the road and their friends, who build the road upon the basis of cash obtained by negotiating through bankers the securities represented by the bond issues of the railroad company, they acquire the stock for little or nothing, and also frequently a large proportion, if not the whole, of the second mortgage, and in prosperous times they may succeed in building and equipping the road on the issue of the bonds secured by the first mortgage alone   By this system the road comes into existence laboring under the necessity to earn, over and above operating expenses, interest on a funded debt about double the cost of the enterprise, and, if possible, to earn dividends on the stock beyond that sum "

been permanently added to the capital stock. Each of these three methods, as was shown in the preceding chapter, may be the means of issuing stock which had been paid up in good faith. Each, also, is available for the issue of "watered" stock. The second method particularly — that of taking property at an overvaluation — is well calculated to conceal the fictitious character of the issue, and to accomplish the purposes of the participants.

Where, however, a corporation has acquired shares of its own capital stock, either by purchase or by forfeiture for non-payment of calls, it may re-issue and sell the same at market prices.[1]

§ 30 *Dicta in regard to such issues* — There are various opinions, generally *dicta*, contained in the cases, as to the character of stock issued as paid up, when in fact it has not been paid for. The customary expression is that such an issue is a fraud upon the law and upon the public and upon the stockholders; or that it is against public policy; or is a fraud on subsequent purchasers of the stock so issued [2] Other cases, however, and cases of high authority, hold that an issue of stock as full paid-up stock, under an agreement that the full par value shall not be paid, is not necessarily a fraudulent transaction, but that as between the parties thereto it is a legal and valid agreement, and violates no principle of public policy [3]

[1] Ramwell's Case, 50 L. J (Ch), 827 (1881), where the stock had been forfeited See, also, to same effect, *dictum* in Otter v. Brevoort, etc., Co, 50 Barb, 247 (1867), People v Albany, etc, R. R, 55 Barb, 344, 371 (1869).

But where a subscription is not paid, and the stock is transferred to the corporation as "treasury stock" and then sold below par, the purchaser is liable for the unpaid par value Alling v. Ward, 24 N E Rep., 551 (Ill, 1890).

It is not necessary that treasury stock be placed in the names of trustees for the benefit of the company. See §§ 309–314.

[2] In Barnes v. Brown, 80 N Y 527, 534 (1880), the court said in a *dictum* "It is not claimed, and could not be claimed, that the corporation or its directors could create any valid stock by issuing the same without any consideration The directors assuming to issue stock in that way would perpetrate a wrong upon the corporation and its stockholders, and a fraud upon every person who took such stock as full-paid stock, relying upon the appearances, and deceived thereby " In the case of Sturges v Stetson, 1 Biss, 246 (1858), the court said "The subscription of stock by plaintiff, for less than the price of the shares fixed in the charter, was void, as against law and the power of the directors." See, also, *Ex parte* Daniell, 1 De G & J, 372 (1857), Oliphant v. Woodhaven, etc., Co, 63 Iowa, 332 (1884); Tobey v Robinson, 99 Ill., 222, 228 (1881); Osgood v King, 42 Iowa, 478 (1876)

[3] In Scoville v. Thayer, 105 U. S, 143 (1881), the court say: "It is conceded to have been the contract between him and the company that he should never be called upon to pay any further assessments upon it [the stock] The same contract was made with all the other shareholders, and the fact was known to all As between them and the company this was a perfectly valid

The explanation of this is, as will be shown hereafter, that such issues are open to attack in some cases and in other cases they are not It depends altogether on who complains of the issue and against whom complaint is made. The issue may be fraudulent as to one party while it is free from fraud as to another party.

The general statement of law that watered stock is illegal throws little light upon the important questions of the rights, risks and liabilities growing out of such issues of stock. The stockholder and the practitioner wish to know whether such stock is void or is voidable, or is valid. They wish to know, also, what are the rights and remedies of the various parties involved. If the stock is valid, then the question arises whether any one is liable for that part of the par value which has not been paid, and also who may bring suit to enforce that liability.

It is well settled that watered stock is not illegal and void *per se*, unless it is declared to be void by constitutional or statutory pro-

agreement It was not forbidden by the charter or by any law or public policy " In the case of *In re* Ambrose, etc , Co., L. R., 14 Ch Div , 390, 394-5, where paid-up stock was issued for property taken at a gross overvaluation, the court said " It seems to me impossible to say that, however wrong the transaction was in respect to other persons, there was anything wrong as between the company and the vendors " In Flinn *v* Bagley, 7 Fed Rep , 785 (1881), the court held that it was only as a fraud upon future creditors that exception could be taken to an issue of stock at a discount In Lorillard *v* Clyde, 86 N Y , 384 (1881), the court held it legal for the parties, as between themselves, to issue paid-up stock for property taken at a valuation agreed upon between themselves The court said " If it had appeared that the organization of the corporation in this way was a device to defraud the public, by putting valueless stock on the market, having an apparent basis only, a different question would be presented " See, also, Otter *v* Brevoort Co , 50 Barb , 247-256 (1867), *dictum*, Spring Co *v* Knowlton, 103 U. S , 49-58 (1880), *dictum*.

There have also been various *dicta* in

the cases and text-books that the issue of " watered " stock by mining companies is a customary, and hence legal, issue. There is no reason, however, why stock issued for a mine should be issued more recklessly than stock issued for a patent-right

The case generally cited as holding that mining companies may legally issue watered stock is *Re* South Mountain Consol Min Co , 7 Saw , 30 (1881), S C , 4 Fed Rep , 403. In this case, however, it is stated that corporate creditors were protected " by the personal liability of each shareholder for his *pro rata* share of the indebtedness of the corporation." Aff'd, 14 Fed Rep., 347 (1882).

Under the Minnesota statute authorizing mining corporations to sell their unissued stock as the corporation may see fit, and providing that if it is issued thus, as paid up, no further liability shall exist, the sale of shares of a par value of $2 for six cents exempts the purchaser from further liability to any one, including corporate creditors Ro s *v* Silver, etc , Co , 29 N W Rep , 591 (Minn , 1886), Ross *v* Silver, etc , Co , 31 N W. Rep , 219 (Minn , 1887) See, in general, Kimberly *v*. Arms, 129 U. S , 512, 530 (1889)

visions. Nearly all the cases assume this to be the rule, and do not discuss it. Even when a constitution or statute declares such stock to be void, it is rarely possible to apply the statutory law A few cases speak of such stock as being void; but, inasmuch as the remedies given in those cases were remedies for the rescission of contracts for fraud, they do not establish the proposition that the issue was void absolutely [1]

§ 31. *Fictitious stock may be voidable* — Is stock voidable when fraudulently issued as paid up? There are few cases on this question, but the tendency of the courts is to hold that such issues of stock may be avoided by a withdrawal of the issue and a cancellation of the certificates Thus a court of equity, on the application of a dissenting stockholder, has decreed that stock falsely issued as paid-up stock should be delivered up to the corporation for cancellation [2] Where, however, the stock has passed into the hands of *bona fide* purchasers for value, such purchasers are entitled to retain the stock. Some cases intimate that the stock fictitiously issued may be canceled, except a part whose par value would equal the amount actually paid in by the persons receiving it [3] Many cases hold also that the transaction is in the nature of a fraudulent contract, and that it may be rescinded for fraud; in which case the stock would have to be returned to the corporation.

So far as the right of the corporation to issue stock below par is concerned, the courts have frequently held that the issue is an *ultra vires* act.[4] But an *ultra vires* act is not always void abso-

[1] Sturges *r* Stetson, 1 Biss , 246 (1858); Fosdick *v* Sturges, 1 Biss , 255 (1858); Gilman, etc , R R Co. *v* Kelly, 77 Ill , 426 (1875), Campbell *v* Morgan, 4 Bradw. (Ill.), 100 (1879) See, also, § 47

[2] Gilman, etc , R R. Co. *r* Kelly, 77 Ill , 426 (1875) In this case it was admitted that the stock was issued gratuitously and for the purpose of enabling the construction company to own a majority of the stock, thereby controlling the corporation

[3] Sturges *v* Stetson, 1 Biss , 246, 254 (1858) The court said, in a *dictum*, that stock taken at less than par, with knowledge, is subject to the right of other stockholders, being such at the time of its issue, "to have it reduced to the charter value of the shares. This would take from him nearly one-third of his shares" In Fosdick *v* Sturges, 1 Biss , 255 (1858), the court say there can

be no question that this remedy is available.

[4] Fisk *v.* Chicago, etc , R. R. Co , 53 Barb., 513 (1868), where the court says "It is not a question of good faith, or of honest intention, or of wise policy, or skilful or discreet management on the part of the directors. It is a question of power." In West, etc., R. *v.* Mowatt, 12 Jur , pt. 1, 407 (1848), the court sustained a demurrer to a bill for specific performance of a contract to take shares from the corporation at a discount, the court holding that the contract was *ultra vires* In *Ex parte* Daniell, 1 De G & J., 372, the court says "It was very properly admitted . . . that the directors of the company had no power to pass the resolution" issuing the stock for less than its par value. In Brown's Case, 2 De G , F & J , 275. 295 (1860), it is held to be "beyond the

lutely, and it is voidable only at the instance of persons standing in a certain relation towards the act. Who can avoid the act will be explained hereafter.

B WATERED STOCK ISSUED FOR CASH.

§ 32 *First method of issue: By discount in cash* — As already stated, paid-up stock may be improperly issued in three different methods· by part cash payment; by taking property at an over-valuation, by an invalid stock dividend

An issue of paid-up stock for cash, upon payment of only part of the par value of the stock. is not often made, inasmuch as the real nature of the transaction is readily discovered and easily remedied Sometimes the corporation makes the issue under a contract with those receiving it that no more than a certain percentage of the par value will be called for. Again, a release is sometimes made by a resolution of the directors or stockholders, after subscriptions have been made and partly paid, discharging the subscribers from any further liability on such subscriptions The proceedings are generally spread upon the corporate records, certificates are issued, asserting on their face that they are paid up, and all inquiries at the corporate office are answered by a substantiation of that assertion.

§ 33 *Dangers attending this method* — There are various dangers and liabilities growing out of such a transaction The stock is liable to be canceled.[1] The person to whom it was issued,[2] or his transferee with notice,[3] or the corporate officers participating in the act,[4] may, under certain circumstances, each be held liable personally for the unpaid par value of the stock. They may be liable to the corporation itself,[5] or to the corporate creditors,[6] or to *bona fide* transferees of the stock [7]

A *bona fide* transferee of such stock, however, is not liable [8] But it has been held that the corporation may refuse to allow a transfer on the corporate transfer book of stock so issued [9]

§ 34. In England there has been great doubt on this subject [10] It formerly was held that, where a contract for the issue of stock for cash at a discount is regularly registered with the public registrar, as provided by statute, then the person to whom the

functions and in excess of the powers" of the directors

[1] See § 31
[2] See §§ 46, 47, 167.
[3] See § 49.
[4] See § 48.
[5] See § 38.
[6] See §§ 42, 43
[7] See § 40
[8] See § 50
[9] People v Sterling Mfg Co, 82 Ill. 457 (1876)
[10] See § 43

stock was thus issued by contract as paid-up stock was not liable to the corporation, nor corporate creditors, nor any other person, for the unpaid par value of the stock, and his transferee was likewise protected [1]

The latest authority in England, however, is in accord with the American rule, and holds that stock cannot be issued for cash at a discount [2]

---

[1] *Re* Ince Hall Rolling Mills Co , 30 W R , 945 (1882); S C, L R , 23 Ch D, 545 The court refused to hold liable the person receiving the stock, but in a *dictum* said "Assuming that the contract was *ultra vires*, what would be the result? If it is *ultra vires* it must be set aside *in toto*, the consequence being that these gentlemen would be entitled to be relieved of their shares and receive back the money paid upon them ' In the case of Guest *v* Worcester R R Co L R , 4 C P , 9 (1868), where stock had been issued as paid-up stock to a corporate creditor as security for his debt, nothing having been paid on such stock, the court said it did " not entertain a shadow of a doubt," and that the holder was not liable thereon. In Baron De Beville's Case, L R , 7 Eq. Cas . 9 (1868), " paid-up " shares had been issued to De Beville who had subscribed for " paid-up " shares, but had paid no part of the par value thereof The court held him not liable. In this case the corporation had authority to issue ordinary shares for cash, and " paid-up " shares for property or services. See, also, Gold Co, L R , 11 Ch. D , 701; James *v* Eve, 6 H. L. Cas , 335 , Plaskgnaston Tube Co , L. R , 23 Ch. D , 542 *Ex parte* Daniell, 1 De Gex & Jones, 372 (1857), is not strictly in accordance with the preceding authorities, but in Daniell's case the issue was to a director who was acting in a fiduciary capacity. The case is so distinguished in Carling's Case, L R , 1 Ch D , 115 (1875)

In *Re* Dronfield Silkstone Coal Co , L. R., 17 Ch. Div., 76 (1880), on page 97, the court says: "If the company could not question it, neither can a creditor ; for he can obtain nothing but what the company can get from the shareholders" See, also, *Re* Ambrose Lake T. & C. Min Co , L R . 14 Ch. D , 390 (1880); *Re* Ince Hall Rolling Mills Co , 30 W. R , 945 (1882), where the court said the same as in the preceding case. In Waterhouse *v.* Jamieson, L R , 2 H. L. (Sc.), 29, the court said, page 37 "I take it to be quite settled that the rights of creditors against the shareholders of a company, when enforced by a liquidator, must be enforced by him in right of the company , what is to be paid by the shareholders is to be recovered in that right." *Cf.* remarks of the lord chancellor, page 32

[2] *Re* Addlestone, etc , Co., 58 L. T. Rep., 428 (1887) In *Ex parte* Stephenson, 15 L. R., Ir , 51 (1885), it was held that, upon dissolution of the corporation, the stockholders are entitled to the remaining assets in proportion to the amounts paid by them, without regard to the " water " in the stock.

An issue of stock in England for cash at less than par is invalid, even though the contract is duly registered under the Companies Act. The holders are liable for the unpaid par value *Re* London, etc., Co., 59 L. T. Rep., 109 (1888)

In England an issue of stock for cash at a discount is illegal, and a holder may sue to rescind the issue to him and for repayment of the money paid. *Re* Almado, etc., Co , 59 L. T Rep , 159 (1888), overruling *Re* Ince, etc , Co., 23 Ch. D , 545, n , and *Re* Plaskgnaston, etc , Co , id , 542

A person subscribing for and taking stock for cash at less than par cannot repudiate the same and cancel the sub-

C. WATERED STOCK ISSUED FOR PROPERTY OR CONSTRUCTION WORK WHICH IS OVERVALUED

§ 35. *Second method: Issue of stock for property taken at an overvaluation.*— A second method of issuing stock as paid up, when it is not actually paid up, is by its issue for property taken at an overvaluation. This method is the most frequently employed, the most difficult to prove, and the least easy to remedy. A large amount of litigation and confusion has been experienced and gone through with in determining the principles of law which should govern such transactions. The questions which have perplexed the courts were, first, what constituted an overvaluation sufficient to invalidate the contract; second, what remedy should be applied when the contract was invalidated.

It is now well settled that in order to invalidate an issue of stock which is issued for property taken at an overvaluation, it must be shown not only that there was an overvaluation, but also that such overvaluation was intentional and consequently fraudulent [1]

The property is not to be considered as overvalued merely because, subsequently, it turns out to be so. The various circumstances under which the valuation was made should be considered in determining the *bona fides* of the transaction [2]

---

scription on the ground that he supposed that the issue was legal. *Re* Railway, etc., Pub. Co., 61 L. T. Rep., 94 (1889). *Cf. Re* Zoedone Co., 60 id. (1889); *Re* Midland, etc., Co., 60 id., 666 (1889)

An agreement of the company that stock may be issued at a certain figure below par is not such a "contract" as upon being duly filed authorizes such an issue. *Re* New Eberhardt Co., 62 L. T. Rep., 301 (1889).

[1] Brant *v.* Ehlen, 59 Md., 1 (1882) In this case the court said "So long as the transaction stands unimpeached for fraud, courts will treat as a payment that which the parties themselves have agreed shall be a payment, and this, too, in cases where the rights of creditors are involved" New Haven, etc., Co *v* Linden Spring Co., 142 Mass. 319 (1886).

Where the plaintiff does not allege fraud in the valuation the action fails. An action framed on the theory of unpaid subscriptions is ineffectual as a remedy. Coffin *v* Ransdell, 11 N. E. Rep., 20 (Ind., 1887).

In Phelan *v* Hazard, 3 Dill 45 (1878), Judge Dillon thoroughly reviews the authorities and says "The contract is valid and binding upon the corporation and the original shareholders unless it is rescinded or set aside for fraud, and . . . while the contract stands unimpeached the courts, even where the rights of creditors are involved, will treat *that* as a payment which the parties have agreed should be payment" See, also, Brant *v* Ehlen, *supra*, fully explaining the meaning of the term trust fund as applied herein Crawford *v* Rohrer, 59 Md., 599 (1882)

[2] Schenck *v* Andrews, 57 N. Y., 133 (1874) In Coit *v* North Car Gold Amal Co., 14 Fed Rep., 12 (1882), the court said corporators ' ought not to be made liable individually for the debts of the company at the instance of creditors, because, at a later day, the estimate

47

D WHO MAY COMPLAIN AND AGAINST WHOM COMPLAINT MAY BE MADE.

§ 36 *Liability on "watered" stock, and who may enforce it* — When it has been established that the overvaluation of the property taken in payment for stock was intentional and fraudulent, the questions then arise, what liability has been incurred, who is liable, and what is the remedy? The clearest method of investigating and presenting the law in answer to these questions is by considering, first, who may complain of the transactions — who may be the party plaintiff or complainant; second, who is liable in such a transaction — who is to be made the defendant. Incidentally also there arise questions as to the extent of that liability, and the remedy to be applied.

§ 37 *Who may complain of an issue of stock as "paid up," when it has not been fully paid?*— *The state.*— As already indicated, the issue of stock as paid-up, when not actually paid up, is an act *ultra vires* of the corporation. The commission of *ultra vires* acts by a corporation, to the detriment of the public, renders its charter liable to forfeiture, at the instance of the state.

The issue of fictitiously paid up stock, with a view to defrauding the public, might constitute a misuse of the corporate rights and privileges In such a case, however, it has been held that the state would not forfeit the charter of the corporation. But a very palpable case of fraud will justify the forfeiture.[1]

---

fairly put upon the property at that time has become modified by subsequent events, and will not amount to the value which they set upon it."

On appeal the court, in affirming the judgment below (see 119 U S, 343) (1886), said " Where full-paid stock is issued for property received, there must be actual fraud in the transaction to enable creditors of the corporation to call the stockholders to account.' To same effect, Mege's Case, 10 W N (Eng), 203 (1875)

In Carr *v* Le Fevre, 27 Pa. St, 413 (1856), the court said that if the directors 'took lands at a prospective value, never realized, it is nothing more than many individuals and corporations have done before. Such an error in management or in their judgment of the value of a purchase, made without fraud, forms no ground for rescinding the con-

tract." See, also, Schroder's Case, L. R., 11 Eq Cas, 131 (1870).

Where a mine is turned in at a large valuation for stock, no fraud is proved by the mere fact that the mine subsequently turns out to have been worth only one-fifth of that amount. Fraud exists only when intentional overvaluation, "or such reckless conduct in the placing of this value, without regard to its real worth, as would indicate, without explanation, an intent to defraud." Young *v* Erie Iron Co, 31 N. W. Rep., 814 (Mich, 1887)

[1] *Quo warranto* does not lie against a corporation merely because it issues its stock below par State *v.* Minn, etc., Co, 41 N W Rep., 1020 (Minn, 1889).

In Holman *v* State, etc., 5 N. E. Rep., 556, 702 (Ind , 1886), the state caused a charter to be forfeited because the subscribers for stock were insolvent at the

Moreover, when a corporation is guilty of an *ultra vires* act, and such act is detrimental to the interests of the public, it is possible that the attorney-general may file an information for the purpose of enjoining or setting aside such act [1] Such a proceeding, however, would be difficult to maintain.

§ 38. *Right of the corporation itself to complain* — The corporation itself, after issuing its stock as paid-up stock, and declaring it so to be, cannot subsequently repudiate that declaration and agreement and proceed to collect, either from the person receiving the stock or his transferee, the unpaid part of the par value. It is estopped from so doing.[2]

time of subscribing, thereby perpetrating a fraud on the public. See, also. State *v* Atchison, etc, R R., 38 N W Rep, 43 (Neb, 1888) The case Jersey City G L Co *v.* Dwight, 29 N J Eq 242, was overruled by Railroad *v* Railroad, 32 N J. Eq, 755, according to Elizabethtown G. L. Co *v* Green, 18 Atl Rep, 844 (N J, 1890), affirmed, 24 id, 560

The state may bring an action to forfeit a charter where the corporation commences business before the full capital stock is subscribed People *v* Natl. Sav. Bank, 11 N E. Rep., 170 (Ill 1887)

The state cannot enjoin private parties from dealing in "watered" stock State *v.* American Cotton Oil Trust, 3 S Rep, 409 (La, 1888), People *v* Natl Sav Bank, 11 N. E. Rep. 170 (Ill 1887), affirmed on rehearing, 22 id, 288 (1889). See, also, Columbus etc, R R *v* Burke, 20 Week. L. Bull, 287

Quo warranto failed in Commonwealth *v.* Central P R'y, 52 Pa St 506 (1866), where a large amount of "watered" stock was issued *Contra,* 12 S Rep, 377.

[1] See § 635, *infra.*

The state will not be allowed to intervene in a foreclosure suit for the purpose of preventing it on the ground that the bonds are illegal and void, and that on a re-organization a greater issue will be made State *v* Farmers', etc, Co, 17 S W Rep. 60 (Tex, 1891).

Concerning the power of the state to object to an *ultra vires* act of a private corporation by any proceeding other than *quo warranto,* see People *v.* Ballard, 134 N Y 269 (1892)

[2] In the case of Scoville *v* Thayer, 105 U S, 143 (1880), the court said, in a *dictum* "No call could have been made by the company under its agreement with the shareholders unless to pay its creditors. . . The shares were issued as paid up, on a fair understanding, and that bound the company " The issue had been at a discount.

See, also, Union etc, Co. *v* Frear, etc, Co., 97 Ill, 537 (1881), *dictum* In the case of Granite Roofing, etc, Co. *v* Michael, 54 Md, 65 (1880), stock was issued as paid up for cash although not actually paid The corporation passed under the control of purchasers of the stock, who caused the corporation to sue the original subscribers for the unpaid par value of the stock. The court said "While the law may reject, as illegal and fraudulent, that which the parties have agreed upon. . . it will not arbitrarily incorporate, in lieu thereof, terms in the contract to which the parties have never assented." In the case of *Re* Ambrose, etc, L R., 14 Ch Div, 390 (1880), where all the stockholders acquiesced and there were no creditors' rights involved, the court held that the corporation could not hold the directors liable for the profits made by them In Zirkel *v* Joliet Opera House Co, 79 Ill, 331 (1875), the corporation had released the subscriber after the subscription had been made The release being without consideration, and

Where, however, actual fraud enters into the transaction, then the corporation is not estopped from having the agreement set aside The person receiving the stock can then be compelled to return the stock or its market value, and take back that which he gave to the corporation for it But the corporation cannot hold him liable for the par value of the stock.[1]

not a contract, was held void, and the corporation was allowed to recover The case of The Society of Prac Knowl v Abbott, 3 Beav, 559 (1840), was distinguished in Re British S P B Co, L R, 17 Ch D, 467 (1881), the latter case holding that no one is liable on fictitiously paid up stock where all acquiesced and there was no intent to bring in new stockholders This is held to be the rule even though new stockholders were subsequently brought in

In the case of Harrison v Union Pac. R'y Co, 13 Fed. Rep, 522 (1882), where plaintiff sued to recover on bonds guarantied by the defendant, the court said "The intention of the Arkansaw Valley Railway Company was to sell the stock to Harrison for less than its par value, i e., to give him $15,000 in stock (twenty bonds of the company), guarantied by the Kansas Pacific Company, and the Clay county bonds, all for $15,000 in cash There is nothing in the statutes of Colorado, where the corporation was created, to forbid the sale of stock at less than par, nor was Harrison forbidden to purchase the stock by reason of the fact that he was already a stockholder and director in the Kansas Pacific Railway Company The transaction was therefore valid as between the corporation and Harrison, whatever the right of the creditors of the corporation as against Harrison may be" See, also, Harrison v Arkansas, etc, R. R., 8 South. L R, 182 (U. S. C. C., 1882)

In St. Louis, etc, R. R. Co v Tiernan, 15 Pac Rep, 544 (Kan, 1887), it was held that an issue of $3,600,000 of stock and the payment of $200,000 to directors for an old road-bed which had cost them

$15,000, was legal, since all the stockholders and directors, except a few nominal holders of stock, were fully informed of the facts, and no other stockholders came in until several months subsequently The corporation was held incompetent to complain See, also, Flinn v Bagley, 7 Fed Rep., 785 (1881); Re Glen Iron Works, 17 Fed Rep., 24 (1883) Cf People v Sterling Mfg Co., 82 Ill, 457 (1876) As to receivers, see 20 S. W. Rep., 1015

Where all the stockholders unite in the issue of watered stock to the president for his own use, and assent to a contract between him and the company, the corporation itself cannot subsequently complain Arkansas, etc., Co v Farmers', etc, Co, 22 Pac Rep, 954 (Colo 1889)

The corporation itself cannot complain First Nat'l Bank v Gustin, etc, Co, 44 N W Rep, 198 (Minn, 1890).

The city court of New York in Zelaya Min Co. v Meyer, 8 N Y. Supp, 487 (1890), held that where a corporation agrees to and does issue its stock below par, the corporation itself cannot levy assessments for the unpaid par value.

[1] See § 47 It is to be noticed, however, that there are few well-defined cases on this principle of law. Most of the cases on the liability of the director herein involved the additional fact that the director received some of the stock himself In the case of Continental Tel. Co. v Nelson, 49 N Y. Super. Ct., 197 (1883), the president was sued by the corporation itself for issuing stock in payment of labor, the par value of the stock being worth over twice the value of the labor. The court held that he was liable only for the actual market value of the

The corporation has also a remedy herein against its directors who issued the stock either fraudulently or in an *ultra vires* manner.[1] This liability is similar to their general liability to the corporation for fraudulent, negligent or *ultra vires* acts on their part.[2] The measure of their liability herein is not the par value of the stock, less the value actually received therefor by the corporation, but it is the actual or market value of the stock, less the property or cash actually received by the corporation on the stock so issued. It has also been held that the corporation cannot, in a court of equity, compel a person, who agreed to take stock at a discount, to carry out the contract, inasmuch as it is *ultra vires*.[3]

Where the corporation contracts to issue stock to a contractor for work to be done in the future, and such work is not completed, various complications arise. This subject, however, is considered elsewhere.[4]

§ 39. *Stockholders participating in the act cannot complain.*— Stockholders in a corporation, who participate or aid in the issue of paid-up stock, upon payment of less than its par value, or who have knowledge of the act and acquiesce therein, cannot afterwards complain of the transaction, either in their own behalf or in behalf of the corporation. They are bound by estoppel or acquiescence.[5]

---

stock in excess of the value of the labor, and submitted the question to the jury.

A corporation cannot refuse to transfer stock on the ground that the vendor fraudulently induced the company to issue the stock to him where the company has been guilty of laches in not seeking a remedy before the transfer. The vendee in this case was a director. American, etc., Co. *v* Bayless, 15 S. W. Rep., 10 (Ky., 1891).

Although the incorporators of a New Jersey company have contracted to issue sixty per cent of its stock to a person for two patents, yet the board of directors after the company is organized may refuse to carry out the agreement, one patent being worthless and the other not having been perfected. The court said: "To justify a corporation in issuing stock under our act for property purchased, there should be an approximation, at least, in true value of the thing purchased to the amount of the stock which it is supposed it represents."

Edgerton *v* Electric, etc., Co., 24 Atl. Rep., 540 (N. J., 1892).

[1] See § 48
[2] See Part IV.
[3] West R. R. Co *v* Mowatt, 12 Jur., pt. I, 407 (1848)
[4] See ch. XLVI and § 24
[5] In *Re* Gold Co. L. R., 2 Ch. Div., 701, 712, the court says: "It could not be a fraud upon, or a wrong to, the existing stockholders, because every one of them was a party to the transaction." See, also, Scoville *v* Thayer, 105 U. S., 143 (1881), Lorillard *v* Clyde, 86 N. Y., 384 (1881), Hall *v*. Brooklyn El. R. R., N. Y. L. J. April 30, 1892. But in the case of Knowlton *v* Congress, etc., Co., 14 Blatch., 364, 368 (1877), the court said in a *dictum* "Can there be any doubt that, up to the time of the abandonment of the scheme by the defendant the plaintiff could have resorted to a court of equity and restrained further proceedings and vacated the proceedings already taken? The cases are nu-

The cases are in conflict on the question whether the party receiving stock at a partial discount of its par value may repudiate the transaction and recover from the corporation the money he

merous where courts of equity have interfered to prevent the consummation of a wrong, upon the motion of a party who was instrumental in its inception" Affirmed, 103 U S, 49 The issue of stock in that case was held to be absolutely void by statute.

A participating stockholder cannot complain, even though he or his assignee is a corporate creditor Callanan v. Windsor, 42 N W. Rep, 652 (Iowa, 1889), Lewis v N Y, etc., Iron Co., N Y L. J, April 30, 1890

A purchaser of stock that has voted for an issue of "watered" bonds and stock is estopped from complaining, even though the issue was prohibited by the constitution of the state (Pennsylvania) Wood v Corry, etc., Co, 44 Fed Rep., 146 (1890).

A participating stockholder cannot as a corporate creditor enforce the liability. Callanan v Windsor, 42 N. W. Rep., 652 (Iowa, 1889)

A purchaser of stock who voted in favor of a re-organization scheme cannot object to the scheme as being ultra vires, there being nothing illegal per se. in it. Hollins v St. Paul, etc, R. R., 9 N. Y Supp, 909 (1889)

In the case of Skinner v. Smith, 134 N. Y, 240 (1892), $10,000 of stock was issued for letters patent. Afterwards, with the consent of all the stockholders, the transaction was rescinded, the stock being returned and the patents retransferred A license to manufacture under the patents was then transferred to the company for $350,000 in stock. The court found that the transaction was in good faith and with no intent to defraud future stockholders, and that the license was an adequate consideration for the stock The court held that there was nothing illegal in the transaction.

A stockholder cannot have a receiver appointed and mortgages set aside where all the stock is "water," even though the controlling party has made the mortgages to himself and is about to sell the assets of the company to another company controlled by himself, and has levied an assessment on the stock of the old company in order to sell out the stock. Robinson v Dolores, etc., Co, 29 Pac. Rep., 750 (Colo., 1892)

A person to whom watered stock has been issued as full-paid stock is not such a bona fide stockholder as may compel a creditor to return bonds which were illegally issued. The stock is void under the Wisconsin statutes. Hinckley v. Pfister, 53 N W Rep., 21 (Wis., 1892)

A conditional sale of stock, the condition being that the sale shall be complete for fifty cents on the dollar, when the stock is worth par, is valid Until the stock is worth par, no further sum is recoverable by a creditor who as a stockholder participated Callanan v Windsor, 42 N. W. Rep., 652 (Iowa, 1889).

A person who buys stock in a company, knowing that the stock was issued without consideration, cannot compel another stockholder to return his stock to the company for cancellation or to account for dividends Clark v. American Coal Co., 53 N. W Rep, 291 (Iowa, 1892).

Where three persons own all the stock of a company, two of them may buy the stock of the third and give the company's notes in partial payment for the same The transaction is legal inasmuch as none is injured and all consent. Neither subsequent purchasers of the stock, nor those who become stockholders after the notes are paid, nor stockholders who consent to the arrangement, can complain of it. Schilling, etc., Co., et al v Schneider et al, 19 S. W Rep. 67 (Mo., 1892).

Where about one-half of the capital stock is issued as full-paid stock for property, the real value of which is one-

has already paid thereon[1] It is certain, however, that where the stockholders participating in the issue use the stock to rob a railroad and bribe a judge, and then disagree among themselves, the courts will not render aid to one as against the others[2]

§ 40. *Transferees of participating stockholders cannot complain* Not only the participating and acquiescing stockholders, but also their transferees, are bound by the participation or acquiescence. The transferee cannot claim to have greater rights than his transferrer, as regards a general remedy invalidating the whole transaction. He cannot bring suit in behalf of the corporation and other stockholders against the party or parties participating in the issue, inasmuch as his own title is tainted with the same fraud[3]

---

quarter of the par value of the stock, and then subsequently the remaining stock is sold for cash at one-quarter of its par value, as between the stockholders and the corporation, the remaining seventy-five cents on the dollar cannot be collected from the parties to whom the stock was issued for cash, it having been agreed at the time of the issue that the stock should be full-paid and non-assessable Green *v* Abietine, etc., Co, 31 Pac Rep, 100 (Cal, 1892)

[1] The case of Clarke *v* Lincoln Lumber Co., 49 Wis, 655 (1884). holds that a participating subscriber cannot withdraw and recover back sums already paid. See, also, Goff *v* Hawkeye, etc, Co., 62 Iowa, 691 (1883) Knowlton *v.* Congress & Empire Spring Co, 57 N Y, 518, 537 (1874), holds the same, the court saying. ' Such parties are left in the position they have placed themselves." The latter case was decided otherwise in the federal courts (14 Blatch, 364, and 103 U S, 49), it being there held that a recovery might be had where others are repaid A person to whom stock is issued for cash at a discount may sue to have his subscription canceled *Re* Goedone Co., 60 L T Rep, 383 (1889).

Mandamus will not issue to compel the issue of stock at a discount, in performance of a resolution by the stockholders that such issue shall be made Equity will not aid the fraud State *v.* Timken, 23 N J. Law, 87 (1886).

[2] Tobey *v* Robinson, 99 Ill, 202 (1881) The courts will not aid a stockholder as against directors' breaches of trust. where the business is illegal and the stock fictitious and "watered ' Le Warne *t* Meyer, 38 Fed Rep, 191 (1889).

[3] Parsons *v* Hays, 14 Abb N C, 419 (Super Ct., 1883), Nott *v* Clews, 14 Abb New Cases (N Y), 437, Ffooks *t* Southwestern R'y, 1 Sm & G, 142 (1853), *Re* British, etc, Co, L R, 17 Ch D, 467 (1881), Flagler Co *v* Flagler, 19 Fed Rep, 468 (1884, Circ Ct Mass); S C, 14 Abb. New Cases (N Y), 135; *In re* Syracuse, etc, R R Co, 91 N Y, 1 (1883), Kent *v* Quicksilver, etc, Co, 78 N Y, 159, 188 (1879) The purchaser of stock which was issued to directors cannot complain that the directors were guilty of fraud in the issue Barr *v* N. Y, etc, R R, 125 N Y, 263 (1891) See, also Langdon *v* Fogg, 18 Fed Rep, 5 (1883) *Contra*, Parson *v* Joseph, 8 S Rep, 768 (Ala, 1891) In the late case of Foster *v* Seymour, 23 Fed Rep, 65 (1885, U S Circ Ct., Wallace, J), an issue of stock for property at an over-valuation is distinctly held to be no fraud upon the corporation, nor upon the stockholders, all of whom participated "A purchaser of the stock would not be injured by the transaction unless he paid more for it than it was worth, and every purchaser would stand upon the particular circumstances of his purchase " A suit against the

Nor can he bring an action against the corporation[1] But the transferee is by no means without a remedy. He may bring an action for damages against those who, knowing the facts, induced him to purchase, or those who made it possible for the fraud to be practiced, or who actually assisted in perpetrating the fraud upon him[2]

The transferee has other remedies If the transfer to him was from one of the participants, he may rescind the transfer and recover back the price paid by him,[3] or, if the contract of purchase is not yet completed, he may refuse to take the stock.[4]

guilty parties, who were the directors, to compel them to account for a fraudulent disposition of corporate property, will not lie. The fraud is not corporate; it is personal. See, also. § 733

[1] In Re Gold Co, L. R., 11 Ch D, 701 (1879), the court said "It was not a wrong done by the company or to the company.' In Re Ambrose Lake T & C Min Co, L R, 14 Ch D, 390, 397 (1880), the court says "There would be no liability on the part of the company, as such"

[2] The leading case on this principle of law is Cross v Sackett, 6 Abb. Pr R., 247 (1858), argued by eminent counsel and decided by learned judges A bona fide purchaser in open market, from an innocent holder of stock issued as paid up for property taken at an overvaluation, sued a director, being also an original stockholder, for damages The court in its decision said "When a party projects and publicly promulgates the scheme of a joint-stock company, when he causes the usual books to be opened, and allows or causes the inscription of a person as an owner of an interest to a definite amount and value therein, which is false within his own knowledge, when he embodies such false statements in a certificate of this right directly issued and of the same effect as if signed by himself, when he accompanies that certificate by a written power authorizing a transfer at large by the party to whom he has given the certificate, when that representation induces an innocent person to

advance his money,— the defendant's own individual act has created the privity of contract, . . . and he must be held responsible to any one who has been deceived "

The plaintiff must prove that a representation was made that the stock was paid up, and that he relied thereon, and that the representation was false and fraudulent. McAleer v McMurray, 58 Penn St, 126 (1868), Priest v. White, 1 S W Rep, 361 (Mo, 1886)

The court, in In re Ambrose Lake Tin & Cop. Min Co, L R, 14 Ch D., 390, 397 (1880), said that the transferee has a remedy against the person who, in any way, made the misrepresentations to him. Re Gold Co, L R, 11 Ch. D, 701, pp. 713, 714, is to the same effect. In Barnes v Brown, 80 N Y., 527 (1880), the plaintiff, being under contract to receive paid-up stock from defendants, received such, and afterwards discovered that its par value had not been paid in to the corporation The court held that he could recover damages from the defendant for the fraud.

[3] Fosdick v Sturges, 1 Biss, 255 (1858). In this case the certificate was brought into court to be disposed of as the court should direct

[4] Sturges v Stetson, 1 Biss., 246, 253 (1858), the court holding that an action for the price of such stock is in the nature of a bill in equity for the specific performance of a contract, and the defendant may defeat it by avoiding the contract altogether, although the certificates have been transferred to him

§ 41. *Stockholders dissenting at the time of the issue may com
plain.*—Stockholders, being such when an issue of paid-up stock is
improperly made, and not assenting to or acquiescing in it, may
bring suit in a court of equity to annul and set aside the whole
transaction[1]　It has been held that the issue may be canceled[2]
The dissenting stockholders' rights and remedies herein, in their
scope and details, are similar to the rights and remedies of stockholders in other cases of *ultra vires* acts or fraud to the injury of
the corporation — a subject fully treated in the fourth part of this
work.[3]

§ 42. *Corporate creditors as complainants where the issue is for
money.*— According to well-established rules of law in America,

To same effect, Coolidge v Goddard, 77
Me, 579

[1] In Fisk v Chicago & Rock Isl R R.
Co, 53 Barb, 513 (1868), the court enjoined any transfer of the stock, and
appointed a receiver to receive what
the corporation had realized from the
stock, and to use the funds in returning
the stock and paying damages caused
thereby　In Sturges v Stetson, 1 Biss.,
246, 254 (1858) and Fosdick v Sturges,
1 Biss, 255, 259 (1858), the court in *dicta*
said that the issue could be withdrawn,
leaving with the guilty parties so much
stock as the money paid by them would
equal the par value of.

Stockholders may restrain the issue
of deferred "bonds," i. e, irredeemable
bonds entitling the holder to interest
after a certain dividend is paid to the
stockholders, it being merely a scheme
to issue stock below par　Taylor v Phil,
etc, R. R. Co., 7 Fed. Rep, 386 (1881).
Compare ch 46, *infra.*

In New York, by statute, income bonds
with voting privileges may be issued.

Laches on the part of the dissenting
stockholder will bar his remedy. Taylor
v South, etc, R. R. Co, 13 Fed Rep 152
(1882)

[2] Campbell v. Morgan, 4 Bradw (Ill),
100 (1879); Gilman, Peoria & Spring
R. R. Co v Kelly, 77 Ill, 426 (1875)

A dissenting stockholder may cause
an issue of stock to be canceled where
it was issued for land at five times its

real value, and then the capital stock
was doubled and the increase issued for
nothing　Parson v. Joseph, 8 S. Rep.,
788 (Ala, 1891)

A dissenting stockholder may cause
to be canceled certain stock which was
issued without consideration to a construction company in which the directors are interested　Gilman, etc, R. R.
v Kelly, 77 Ill, 426 (1875)

Where the president, in order to get
control of the corporation, causes a
meeting of the board of directors to vote
stock in payment for services and property whose value is much less than the
par value of the stock, the stock being
voted to outside parties, but thereafter
secretly transferred to the president, a
stockholder may compel him to return
the stock to the corporation for cancellation　Such an issue is also illegal by
the statutory law of the state　Perry v.
Tuscaloosa, etc. Co., 9 South Rep., 217
(Ala., 1891)

The issue of new stock by the corporation cannot be enjoined where neither
the corporation nor any of its directors
are parties to the action. White v Wood,
129 N Y, 527 (1892).

[3] They cannot have the corporation
wound up therefor　*In re* Gold Co,
L R., 11 Ch D 701. Morrison v. Globe
Panorama Co., 28 Fed Rep., 817 (1886)
See, also, § 701, *infra*, 68 L T Rep., 103
(1893)

corporate creditors may object to certain transactions, which, as between the corporation and its stockholders and third persons, may be valid and binding   This right of corporate creditors is an essentially American doctrine.   It is based on the principle, first enunciated by Judge Story, that the capital stock of the corporation is a trust fund, to be preserved for the benefit of corporate creditors.   That principle of law, when applied to a transaction whereby stock is issued as paid up, when it is in fact not paid up, enables corporate creditors to object to the act, and, in certain cases, to undo what has been done, and, in other cases, to compel payment of the actually unpaid part of the par value of the stock Where the issue of stock was for cash, under an agreement that only part of the par value need be paid, corporate creditors may compel the persons receiving the stock to pay the unpaid full par value.[1]

A resolution by a corporation that upon the stockholders paying

[1] The leading case on this point is Sagory v Dubois 3 Sandf Ch Rep, 466, 499 (1846), where the court said "The defendant being liable by force of his subscription for the stock, the resolution of the directors   .   not to make any further calls upon the shares was unavailing to discharge his liability in respect of the association and its creditors." In Scoville v Thayer, 105 U S, 143 (1881), the court said that a contract whereby stockholders are to pay but part of the par value of their stock to the corporation, ' though binding on the company, is a fraud in law on its creditors. which they can set aside when their rights intervene and their claims are to be satisfied the stockholders can be required to pay their stock in full " Upton v Tribilcock, 91 U S., 45 (1875), is the first of a series of cases growing out of the failure of the Great Western Insurance Company of Illinois   The other cases are Sanger v Upton, 91 U S, 56 (1875), Webster v Upton, 91 U S, 65 (1875), Chubb v Upton, 95 U S, 666 (1877), Pullman v. Upton, 96 U S., 328 (1877); Hawley v Upton, 102 U S., 314 (1880) Upton v Burnham, 3 Biss, 431 (1873), S C, 3 Biss, 520, and Upton v. Hansbrough, 3 Biss, 417 (1873), Great Western Tel Co v Gray, 14 N E. Rep, 214

(Ill 1887)   This series of cases established for the federal courts the rule given above See, also, Flinn v Bagley, 7 Fed Rep., 785 (1881), giving full review of the American and English doctrine herein, In re Glen Iron Works, 17 Fed Rep., 374 (1883), Union M. L. Ins Co. v Frear Stone Mfg Co, 97 Ill, 537 (1881), also reviewing the doctrine; Hickling v Wilson, 104 Ill., 54 (1882), Northrop v Bushnell, 38 Conn., 498 (1871) Fisher v Seligman, 7 Mo. App., 383 (1879), Eyerman v Krieckhaus, 7 Mo App, 455 (1879), Skrainka v. Allen, 7 Mo App, 434 (1879), Pickering v. Templeton, 2 Mo App., 424 (1876), Christensen v Eno, 21 Weekly Dig, 202 (1885), Mann v Cooke, 20 Conn, 178 (1850); Myers v Seeley, 10 Natl. Bank Reg, 411, 20 S. W Rep, 1015

Where the directors of an insurance company issue to themselves all the stock at one-third of its par value, and upon an increase of the capital vote to themselves, for services in selling the increase, one share for every two shares sold, they are liable upon corporate insolvency for the unpaid par value of the first issue, and the par value of the stock received as compensation Their transferee with notice was held not liable Freeman's Assignee v. Stine, 15 Phil, 37 (1881)

in a portion of the par value of the stock the capital shall be deemed to be fully paid is wholly ineffectual as against the creditors of the company.[1]

In order to enforce a liability where stock is issued as full-paid stock for cash at less than the par value, it is not necessary to prove that fraud entered into transaction, where the issue was for cash, since there is no possibility of mistaken judgment in the value of the thing received in payment.[2]

It has been held that the custom of the country will exempt stockholders from liability on stock issued as paid up when it was not paid up. Such a decision, however, is inconsistent with the great weight of authority, and must be considered poor law[3]

[1] "It is the settled doctrine of this court that the trust arising in favor of creditors by subscriptions to the stock of a corporation cannot be defeated by a simulated payment of such subscription, nor by any device short of an actual payment in good faith. And while any settlement or satisfaction of such subscription may be good as between the corporation and the stockholders it is unavailing as against the claims of the creditors. Nothing that was said in the recent cases of Clark v Bever, 139 U S, 96; Fogg v Blair, 139 U S, 118, or Handley v Stutz, 139 U S, 417, was intended to overrule or qualify in any way the wholesome principle adopted by this court in the earlier cases, especially as applied to the original subscribers to stock. The later cases were only intended to draw a line beyond which the court was unwilling to go in affixing a liability upon those who had purchased stock of the corporation, or had taken it in good faith in satisfaction of their demands." Camden v Stuart, 144 U S, 104 (1892), 20 S W. Rep., 1015

Persons taking stock from the corporation for cash at forty cents on the dollar cannot avoid liability to corporate creditors for the remaining sixty cents by setting up that unknown to them the stock had previously been issued to a contractor for work to be done, and that he appointed the corporation his agent to sell the stock at forty cents on the dollar. Their subscription to the stock was an original subscription and bound them. Bates v Great Western Tel Co, 25 N E Rep, 521 (Ill, 1890)

Where property is sold to the company for stock and cash, the cash may be credited on other subscriptions. Re Jones, etc, Co, Lim, 61 L T Rep, 219 (1889)

[2] Flinn v. Bagley, 7 Fed Rep, 785 (1881)

[3] Re South Mountain Consol Min Co, 7 Sawyer 30 (1881) In this case it is stated that corporate creditors were protected "by the personal liability of each shareholder for his pro rata share of the indebtedness of the corporation" See comments on this case, supra, § 30 The English rule is now the same as the American See § 34, supra

Stock, however, which is purchased by the corporation, after its original issue, may be sold by the corporation at a discount. The corporation may then sell the same as an individual stockholder. Otter v Brevoort, etc. Co, 50 Barb, 247 (1867) Ramwells Case, 50 L J (Ch), 827 (1881), where the stock came to the corporation by forfeiture See, also, § 29, supra. In many cases stock is issued to a patentee for his patent, and he then donates and turns back to the corporation a part of this stock to be sold at a reduced price for the benefit of the corporate treasury Lake Superior Iron Co v Drexel, 90 N Y, 87 This transaction is legal, and it is not at all necessary that the stock so donated

But the amount collected must be to the extent and for the purpose of paying corporate creditors' claims only.[1] A resolution discharging stockholders from all liability on stock after thirty per cent of the par value has been paid, and then suffering a forfeiture of the stock, is void so far as corporate creditors are concerned.[2]

It is legal for the company to pay a cash commission to a person who procures subscriptions, even though that commission is deducted from the subscription price[3]

Where a railroad corporation is in financial straits, and its stock worth nothing, it is legal for the corporation to settle with one of its creditors by issuing stock to him at twenty cents on the dollar. Other corporate creditors cannot afterwards hold him liable for the remaining eighty cents on the dollar.[4]

be placed in the names of trustees for the benefit of the corporation It may be transferred to the corporation direct. In Stribling v Bank of the Valley. 5 Rand (Va), 132, where the bank took a note for its own stock at a price in excess of the market value of the stock, the court held the note to be usurious

It is a question for the jury whether fraud exists in sale of stock, represented to be paid up, when part of the payments had been by dividends from the corporation. Kruger v Andrews, 35 N W Rep, 245 (Mich , 1887).

But where the corporation has an accumulated profit, and that profit is by agreement with the stockholders applied to unpaid subscriptions, such stock is then paid up Kenton etc , Co v McAlpin, 5 Fed Rep , 737 (1880).

Where the capital stock is reduced, and subscribers cancel unpaid subscriptions and take paid-up stock to the extent of their payments on the old stock, old corporate creditors may hold them liable on the former In re State Ins Co. 14 Fed Rep , 28 (1882).

The presumption is that a corporate creditor did not know and acquiesce in the issue of "watered" stock Stutz v Handley, 11 Fed Rep., 531 (1890)

As affecting corporate creditors herein, the statute of limitations does not commence to run until judgment is recovered by the corporate creditors against

the corporation Christensen v Quintard, 36 Hun, 334 (1885).

For other cases on the right of corporate creditors to sue, see § 735, infra

[1] Scoville v. Thayer, 105 U S , 143, 155, (1881)

[2] Slee v Bloom, 19 Johns. Rep , 456 (1822).

[3] Re Licensed, etc , Assoc., 60 L. T. Rep , 684 (1889).

A corporation may agree to give $5,000 of stock to one who will borrow $15,000 for it. Arapahoe, etc , Co v. Stevens, 22 Pac Rep , 823 (Colo , 1889).

A commission of fifteen per cent. may be paid by the company to those who agree to take all the stock not subscribed for by the public. Re Licensed, etc , Assoc , supra

[4] Clark v Bever, 139 U. S., 96 (1891). After deciding that nothing in the Iowa statutes forbids the issue of stock below par, the court says

"If the legislature had intended that the acquisition of stock at less than its face value should be conclusive evidence in every case that the stock, as between creditors and stockholders, is 'unpaid,' it would have been easy to so declare, as has been done in some of the states. If such a rule be demanded by considerations of public policy, the remedy is with the legislative department of the government creating the corporation. A rule so explicit and unbending could

Where stock is given by the company gratuitously as a "bonus" to persons who are induced thereby to purchase the bonds of the company, it has been held that such persons are liable to corporate creditors for the par value of such stock [1]

But in New York a different rule prevails and the stockholder is not liable [2]

In the federal courts it is the law that an embarrassed corporation may, upon an increase of its stock, put such stock upon the market and sell it for the best price that can be obtained, and that the corporation may throw in as a bonus a certain amount of full-paid stock to the purchaser of its bonds, and there will be no liability on the stock.[3]

be enforced without injustice to any one, for all would have notice from the statute of the will of the legislature"

A limitation on the extent of this case is laid down in that the stockholders are liable, "unless it appears that they acquired the stock under circumstances that did not give creditors and other stockholders just ground for complaint." Affirming 31 Fed. Rep., 670 (1887) To same effect, Morrow v Iron, etc., Co, 87 Tenn., 262, 276 (1889)

[1] A "bonus" of paid-up stock to a director who loans money to the company and takes its notes and bonds as collateral is not legal, the issue of the stock being the original issue The court, in a *dictum*, stated that the director was liable for the full par value of the stock Richardson v Green, 133 U S, 30 (1890)

Persons purchasing bonds from a company and taking stock as a "bonus," the stock being unissued until that time, are liable for the par value of the stock. Stutz v Handley, 41 Fed Rep 531 (1890), reversed on other grounds, 139 U. S, 417, Haldeman v Ainslie, 82 Ky, 395. Where the stockholders increase the stock and distribute part of it among themselves as full-paid stock, but give nothing for it, they may be held liable by corporate creditors for the par value thereof Handley v Stutz, 139 U S, 417 (1891), Skramka v Allen, 76 Mo, 384.

In a suit for contribution in the federal court by a Missouri stockholder, who has been compelled by the Missouri courts to pay for stock issued to him as a "bonus," the court will follow the Missouri decision rather than a New York decision holding that the same "bonus" created no liability Allen v Fairbanks, 45 Fed. Rep., 445 (1891)

A distribution gratis of stock among the stockholders has been held to be an unauthorized reduction of the capital stock, and it will be ordered to be returned Holmes v Newcastle, etc, Co, 45 L. J (Ch.) 383 (1875)

[2] In New York it is held that unissued shares of stock may be issued gratuitously to stockholders, also bonds of the company, and they are not liable for the par value or any part thereof to the corporation or corporate creditors, unless they agree to pay therefor or the statute requires payment. A subscription is otherwise, since it is a contract Even though the stockholder has sold such stock and bonds, he is not liable to corporate creditors for the amount received from the sale He has received nothing from the corporation except a promise to pay (Skramka v Allen, 7 Mo., 434, S C, 76 id, 384, not followed) Christensen v Eno, 106 N Y, 97 (1887) Christensen v Quintard, 8 N Y Supp, 400 (1890)

[3] Handley v Stutz, 139 U S., 417 (1891) The court said 'To say that a cor-

Where the capital stock of the corporation is increased, the increase is not a trust fund for the benefit of corporate creditors who were such before the increase was made [1]

In Minnesota the doctrine is clearly and boldly announced that the issue of stock for cash at less than par is legal and that nothing more can be collected on such stock, except by corporate creditors who have relied, or can fairly be presumed to have relied, on the representation that the capital stock is as stated; in other words, that it was paid in full. [2]

Inasmuch as a corporation may pledge its unissued stock to a corporate creditor, the pledgee cannot be held liable thereon on the ground that the stock was " watered." [3]

§ 43 *Corporate creditors as complainants where the issue is for property or construction work.*— The rights of corporate creditors where stock has been issued for property taken at an overvaluation are considered elsewhere. [4]

§ 44 *Who is liable, and the character of the liability—Liability of the corporation* — The corporation itself, it has been intimated, is not liable to any person by reason of the issue of its stock as

poration may not, under the circumstances above indicated, put its stock upon the market and sell it to the highest bidder, is practically to declare that a corporation can never increase its capital by a sale of shares, if the original stock has fallen below par   . The liability of a subscriber for the par value of increased stock taken by him may depend somewhat upon the circumstances under which, and the purposes for which, such increase was made. If it be merely for the purpose of adding to the original capital stock of the corporation, and enabling it to do a larger and more profitable business, such subscriber would stand practically upon the same basis as a subscriber to the original capital   But we think that an active corporation may, for the purpose of paying its debts, and obtaining money for the successful prosecution of its business, issue its stock and dispose of it for the best price that can be obtained "

[1] Coit v North Car Gold Amal Co, 14 Fed Rep, 12 (1882), aff'd, 119 U S, 343 (1886)

Only those who become corporate creditors after an increase of stock is voted can hold liable the subscribers to such increase which was issued without value received   Handley v Stutz, 139 U. S, 417 (1891).

[2] The basis of the creditor's suit is not contract, but fraud. Creditors who were such before the watered stock was issued cannot complain of it. Nor can a subsequent creditor complain if he knew of the issue of watered stock. Nor will one who purchased claims after the corporation became insolvent and a receiver was appointed be allowed to complain   Hospes v. Northwestern, etc, Co, 50 N. W. Rep, 1117 (Minn, 1892).

[3] See § 465, *infra*.

Unissued stock may be issued by the corporation as a pledge to secure a loan, and the corporation cannot set up that it was issued at less than par in violation of the constitution   The issue is good in the hands of the pledgee to the extent of the loan   Gasquet v Crescent City B Co, 49 Hun, 496 (1892)

[4] See §§ 46, 47, *infra*

60

full-paid stock, when, as a matter of fact, it has not been fully paid.[1] It is very certain that the stockholder has no remedy herein against the corporation, since his remedy is against the corporate officers, as in other cases of breach of trust by them. As regards corporate creditors, they cannot complain provided the corporation remain solvent and able to pay its debts. If, on the other hand, it becomes insolvent, it would be no object to them to bring suit against the corporation.

§ 45. *Liability of persons to whom stock is issued for cash at less than par.*—Where stock is issued for cash at less than par, the parties taking it are liable to corporate creditors for the unpaid par value thereof,[2] unless the issue was subsequent to the commencement of business and the real value of the stock was paid in to the corporation in order to enable it to go on with its business instead of becoming insolvent.[3] A representation of the corporate agents to the person receiving the stock, that full payment will not be required, is immaterial. and constitutes no defense.[4]

§ 46. *Liability of persons to whom stock is issued for property taken by the corporation at an overvaluation.*— A dissenting stockholder may object to such an issue, inasmuch as it decreases the value of his stock. He may have the transaction set aside, and the person receiving the stock compelled to return it or pay over its actual market value, less the value of property given for it[5]. The person receiving stock at a discount is liable also to a *bona fide* transferee of that stock[6]

Corporate creditors, however, are the persons who generally complain. The company becomes bankrupt and they are not paid. They then find that the capital stock did not represent cash, it was paid for by property taken by the corporation at a valuation much greater than its real value. The company being insolvent and its property gone, the corporate creditors seek to hold the stockholders liable. They seek to hold the stockholders liable for the par value of the stock, less the real value of the property which was turned into the corporation. During the past ten years there

[1] In the case of *In re* Ambrose L T & Cop. Min. Co, L. R., 14 Ch D., 390, 397 (1880), the court says: "There would be no liability on the part of the company as such." In *Re* Gold Co., L. R., 11 Ch D., 701 (1879), where the proceeding was to compel a winding up of the company on account of an improper issue of paid-up stock, the court refused to support the proceeding, and said, pp. 713, 714, "it was not a wrong done by the company or to the company." See, also, Lewis *v* Meier, 14 Fed. Rep, 311 (1882). *Cf.* § 157, *infra*

[2] See § 42

[3] See § 42.

[4] Upton *v* Tribilcock, 91 U. S, 45 (1875), Ogilvie *v* Knox Ins Co.. 22 How , 380 (1859)

[5] See § 41.

[6] See § 40, and Fisher *v.* Seligman, 7 Mo. App., 863 (1879)

has been a vast amount of litigation on this subject. The courts still disagree in their conclusions, but a careful study of the cases will show that upon authority as well as principle the stockholders cannot be held liable in such a case, unless the property was of so trifling a character that it practically had no value whatever. This class of cases has arisen under two aspects; first, at common law; and second, under statutes

At common law it is well settled that corporate creditors cannot hold stockholders liable on stock which has been issued for property, even though the property was turned over to the corporation at an agreed valuation which was largely in excess of the real value of the property, provided the property had some substantial value. There have been cases which refuse to follow this rule, but it is clearly established by the great weight of authority. The reason of the rule is that if the payment by property was fraudulent, then the contract is to be treated like other fraudulent contracts. It is to be adopted *in toto*, or rescinded *in toto*, and set aside. Both parties are to be restored as nearly as possible to their original positions The property or its value is to be returned to the person receiving the stock, and he must return the stock or its real value. Another reason for the rule is that the stock had no value when it was issued for property. "If, when disposed of by the railroad company, it was without value, no wrong was done to creditors." Such is the language of the supreme court of the United States.[1]

---

[1] The leading case on this subject, perhaps, is Van Cott v. Van Brunt, 82 N. Y., 535 (1880), a case that has been severely criticised, but which is not only in accordance with general principles of law governing the rescission of contracts, but is in strict accordance with the authorities and cases on the subject of paid-up stock

The most important case, however, is the recent one of Fogg v Blair, 139 U. S, 118 (1891), holding that where all the stock and a large quantity of bonds are issued by a railroad corporation to its contractor in payment for the construction of the road, the contractor is not liable to corporate creditors on the stock, even though the bonds were a sufficient consideration for building the road, unless the corporate creditors prove that the stock at the time of its issue had a real or market value The court said· "If, when disposed of by

the railroad company, it was without value, no wrong was done to creditors." Even the Missouri constitution and statutes do not change this rule.

It is legal for a railroad company to issue bonds and stock in payment for the construction of its road If all the parties assent no one can complain. "As the stock was issued as a part of the consideration for construction, it cannot be said that it was taken without value given" The par value is immaterial "The fact that they were created for an expenditure less than the par value of the aggregate issues of capital stock and bonds does not affect the question at all" Barr v. N. Y., etc, R. R., 125 N Y, 263 (1891)

Stockholders cannot be held liable for the difference between the par value of their stock and the actual value of property turned in to the corporation in payment of the stock, unless fraud is

There is nothing sacred about the par value of stock. Moreover, in business circles it has become customary to capitalize property at a reasonably high figure   This is due to the fact that it is easier to sell stock at less than par than at par, and also to the fact that,

proved   "If the transaction was an honest one, the difference in value between the property constituting the consideration of the sale and the stock had no legal significance .   The valuation of property in making the exchange, either on the one side or the other, cannot be supervised or controlled by a court of chancery , for in the absence of deceit, or some other corrupt constituent, the bargain between the parties cannot be disturbed "   Bickley v Schlag, 20 Atl Rep , 250 (N J , 1890).

Where stock is issued for construction work the persons receiving the stock cannot be held liable on the theory of the stock not having been paid up, unless fraud is charged and proved The statements of one of the officers to tax commissioners are not admissible as evidence of the cost of the work   The act of the company in crediting each of the directors with one thousand dollars on their subscriptions in payment of services rendered and money advanced was upheld   Clow v Brown, 31 N E Rep , 361 (Ind , 1892)

Where a corporation issues its stock, as full paid, in payment for coal lands, and the stock is sold to a purchaser for value, the purchaser is not liable to creditors of the corporation on the stock on the ground that it is not full-paid stock, even though the land was taken at a great overvaluation, there being no actual fraud in the transaction   The text as stated above was quoted with approval   Du Pont v Tilden, 42 Fed Rep , 87 (1890)

In Coffin v. Ransdell, 1 Corp. & L J , 326 (Ind , 1887), the court sustained the rule given in the text, and said   "Suppose it to be true that, in consummating the arrangement, the property of Unthank & Coffin was turned into the corporation at an overvaluation, and

that the defendant and the other corporators participated in the alleged wrong   The transaction was the result of an agreement which the parties had the right, as between themselves, to make   Shall he be capriciously punished by being made liable ex contractu upon a contract which he never made ? If the defendant has participated in a fraud whereby creditors of the corporation who exercised ordinary business sagacity had suffered damages, whatever redress such creditors may now obtain while their representative retains the defendant's property must be sought by an action ex delicto "   See, also, Continental Telegraph Co v. Nelson, 18 Weekly Dig , 48 (1883), S C., 49 N Y Super Ct , 197, Crawford v Rohrer. 59 Md , 599 (1882), Brant v Ehlen, 59 Md , 1 (1882), Morrison v Globe Panorama Co , 28 Fed Rep , 817 (1886) Judge Dillon, in Phelan v Hazard, 5 Dill , 45, reviewed the authorities and sustained the principles enunciated herein   Before any recovery can be had in this class of cases the transaction must be set aside.   Scoville v Thayer, 105 U S , 143, 156 (1881); Wood s Claim, 9 W R., 366 (1861)

In Anderson's Case, L. R. 7 Ch D , 75, stock was issued to a promoter for property taken at an overvaluation This action was to render him liable for the par value of the stock, less the real value of the property   The court said pp. 94, 95, 104   "I am not going to alter men's contracts unless the provisions of an act of parliament compel me to do so . . .   You cannot alter the contract to such an extent as to say, though you have bargained for paid-up shares, we will change that into a bargain to take shares not paid up, and put you on the list of contributories on that ground. . . .   If you set aside

by a large capitalization, dividends are kept low enough to avoid the cupidity of possible competitors and the interference of legislatures   To such an extent is this practice carried of issuing stock for property at an overvaluation, that the investing public and

this allotment of shares, you must set it aside altogether, and then you cannot make them a contributory, and if you do not set it aside altogether you must adopt it, and the utmost you can do is, as I said before, that you can take away any profit from the person who has improperly made it." In Curries Case, 3 De G, J & S., 367 (1863), the court said that the transaction "was either valid or invalid If valid, it is clear that neither he [the person receiving the stock] nor his alienees can be called upon to contribute in respect of those shares If invalid, I cannot see my way to hold that either a court of law or a court of equity could do more than treat the purchase as void, and undo the transaction altogether It could not, as I apprehend, be competent either to a court of law or to a court of equity to alter the terms of the purchase, or treat as shares not paid up shares which were given as paid-up shares in part consideration of the purchase.   Fraud — assuming there was fraud — would of course warrant the court in treating the purchase as void, or in undoing it, but it could not, I conceive, authorize any court to substitute other terms" See, also, Barnett's Case, L R 18 Eq, 507 (1874), where the issue had been canceled by the corporation. In Van Cott v Van Brunt, cited *supra*, a case very similar in its facts to those of the preceding case, the court said: ' The conclusion of law was erroneous that the scheme was fraudulent as against the company and against the creditors, and that the defendants were only entitled to credit for the actual outlay, paid or incurred, and were liable for the amount unpaid on the stock. The result must be that the defendant was not liable to pay the par value of the stock received

by him under the contract for building and equipping a portion of the road " Page 542 This case has been severely criticised as being contrary to established principles of law.

In Phelan v. Hazard, *supra* (1878), Judge Dillon thoroughly reviews the authorities, and says "The contract is valid and binding upon the corporation and the original shareholders unless it is rescinded or set aside for fraud; and

. while the contract stands unimpeached, the courts, even where the rights of creditors are involved, will treat *that* as a payment which the parties have agreed should be payment." See, also, Brant v Ehlen, 59 Md., 1 (1882), fully explaining the meaning of the term trust fund as applied herein Crawford v Rohrer, 59 Md., 599 (1882).

In Coit v. Gold Amal. Co, 119 U S., 343 (1886, affirming 14 Fed. Rep., 12), where this question clearly arose, the court said that the creditors could not hold the stockholders liable unless there was an intentional and fraudulent overvaluation. The court said that "where full-paid stock is issued for property received, there must be actual fraud in the transaction to enable creditors of the corporation to call the stockholders to account, a gross and obvious overvaluation of property would be strong evidence of fraud." The court held that although a machine and a license to use a patent were put into the company in payment for $100,000 of stock, yet there was no fraud

To same effect, Mege's Case, 10 W. N. (Eng.), 208 (1875).

In Carr v. Le Fevre, 27 Pa. St., 413 (1856), the court said that if the directors "took lands at a prospective value, never realized, it is nothing more than many individuals and corporations have done before. Such an error in manage-

persons who give credit to corporations rather expect it, and they no longer rely upon the nominal capitalization of the company   Experience has taught them that they must investigate the real financial condition of the company, and invest or give credit upon that alone

ment or in their judgment of the value of a purchase, made without fraud, forms no ground for rescinding the contract." See, also, Schroder's Case, L. R., 11 Eq Cas, 131 (1870)

The doctrine laid down in Van Cott v- Van Brunt, *supra*, was approved in Coe v East, etc , R. R., 52 Fed Rep., 531 (1892),

In the case Stewart v St. Louis, etc., R. R. Co, 41 Fed Rep, 738, where a railroad road-bed worth $2,000 was turned in to a corporation for $200,000 of its notes and $3,000,000 of its stock, the court held that the notes were good and could be collected

The corporate creditor's bill may be by one, but must be in behalf of all   Cleveland, etc , Co. v Texas, etc , R'y Co , 27 Fed. Rep., 250 (1886).

In passing upon the legality of an issue of $500,000 of stock for a road that had just been sold under a mortgage for $100,000, the court said in Commonwealth v. Central Pass R'y, 52 Pa. St., 506, 515 (1886): "In all such cases the determination of the amount of stock must be an arbitrary adjustment.   As we have said, the cost of the property is no fair measure of what the stock represents, and if the real value be adopted as the standard, it is no standard at all   It varies with the estimates of witnesses, and the franchises are incapable of valuation . . .   If that was a sum greater than the actual value of the company's franchises and property, as it was greater than the cost, we are unable to see how the public was affected by the exaggerated estimate."

A few cases seem to be in conflict with the above authorities.   Thus, in Wetherbee v Baker, 35 N. J Eq, 501 (1882), the defendant neither owned nor conveyed to the corporation the property which he alleged constituted pay-

ment.   Savage v. Ball, 17 N J Eq , 142 (1864), held that the validity of an election is not affected by the question whether the stock voted was issued for value or not

In North Carolina it has been held that the value of the property turned in in payment for the stock may be ascertained by the court, and the stockholders held liable for the par value of the stock less the real value of the property, if such property was fraudulently overvalued   Clayton v Ore, etc., Co, 14 S E Rep, 36 (N C, 1891)

In the case First Nat'l Bank v Gustin, etc , Co, 44 N W Rep, 198 (Minn , 1890), there is a *dictum* to the effect that in certain cases *bona fide* creditors may enforce payment of the difference between par value of the stock and the real value of the property turned in as payment for it in full

It has been held that the person receiving the stock becomes liable for profits made thereby   Four Mile V R. R. Co. v Bailey, 18 Ohio St , 208 (1868)

Where a railroad worth $112,000 is sold to a new corporation for $1,120,000 of bonds and all its capital stock, the transaction is fraudulent.   The bondholders may obtain judgment against the company on their bonds and then compel the stockholders to pay the full par value of their stock   Preston v Cincinnati, etc , R. R. Co , 36 Fed. Rep , 54 (1888)   See Lloyd v Preston on p 67, *sub*

In Osgood v King, 42 Iowa, 478 (1876), where stock was issued for land grossly overvalued, the court held the vendor liable for the par value of the stock less the actual value of the land   The person receiving the stock was a director at the time

In Jackson v Traer, 64 Iowa, 469 (1884), overruling S C, 16 N W. Rep,

(5)

The fact that the person to whom the stock is issued returns a part of it as a gift to the corporation or to trustees for the corporation to sell the same below par and put the proceeds in the corporate treasury for a working capital does not necessarily prove that the property was overvalued   The person receiving the stock may have been willing to sacrifice a part of his stock and property in order to make the rest more valuable.[1]

In no case can a corporate creditor complain where, at the time when he contracted with the company, he knew that the stock had been issued for property taken at an overvaluation.[2]

120 (1884), the stock was not issued to the construction company for the purpose of constructing the corporate works, but was issued after the construction was finished, and a cash debt was due them, which was paid by an issue of the stock to pay that debt already due

The supreme court of the United States, in Clark v Bever, 139 U. S, 96 (1891), refused to follow the decision in Jackson v Traer, 64 Iowa, 469

In Chisholm Bros v. Forney, 65 Iowa, 140 (1884), where full-paid stock was issued for a patent-right, in good faith, but the patent-right subsequently turned out to be worthless, the stockholders were held liable to corporate creditors as though no payment had been made.

Where $100,000 of stock was issued for patents worth $16,000, and $50,000 of the stock was transferred by the patentees to a trustee for all the stockholders, a subscriber for $1,500 of stock, who pays the company therefor $500, is liable to corporate creditors for $1,000, even though the $1,500 of stock was a part of the $50,000 of stock that the inventors retained and directed the company to issue to defendant. The defendant was not a *bona fide* subscriber or transferee, but was one of the promoters and was president of the company Fraud cannot be alleged in defense Boulton Carbon Co v. Mills, 43 N W Rep , 290 (Iowa, 1889)

In the following case a very peculiar device was successful Stock was issued conditionally that its issue be complete and binding when it became worth par, and that the price then to be paid for it to the company should be fifty cents on the dollar The stock was issued and partly paid for, but never reached par in value   Held, that a participating stockholder, who was also a creditor could not, nor could his assignee, enforce any liability. Callanan v. Windsor, 42 N W Rep , 652 (Iowa, 1889).

[1] Lake Superior Iron Co. v Drexel, 90 N. Y , 87 (1882), Williams v. Taylor, 120 N Y , 244 (1890)

The person to whom stock has been issued in payment for property may donate a part of it as a bonus to go with bonds sold at par directly from the corporation to the person taking the bonus. The value of the property in this case was not proved. Davis v Montgomery, etc , Co, 8 S Rep , 496 (Ala., 1890). In the case of Van Gestel v The Van Gestel Electric Street Car Co (N. Y L J , July 3, 1890), the court enjoined a company from disposing of such stock contrary to the contract.

[2] Bank of Fort Madison v. Alden, 129 U S , 373 (1889)

A corporate creditor who took the note of the corporation in payment of an antecedent debt, and took with full knowledge of the facts as to the issue of the stock for property, cannot complain A corporate creditor cannot complain as to stock issued subsequently to the debt. First Nat'l Bank v. Gustin, etc , Co , 44 N. W. Rep , 198 (Minn , 1890).

An issue of stock for an old franchise and uncompleted road-bed of a railroad

There is a limit, however, beyond which the courts will not go in sustaining the issue of stock for property taken at an overvaluation. If the property which is turned in is practically worthless, or is unsubstantial and shadowy in its nature, the courts will hold that there has been no payment at all, and that the stockholders are liable on the stock.[1]

is valid although the par value of the stock is much more than the value of the property All the stockholders having assented thereto, and there being no creditors, the transaction is valid A holder of bonds issued long subsequently, and who purchased with knowledge of the facts, cannot complain and hold the stockholders liable Walburn v Chenault, 23 Pac. Rep., 657 (Kan, 1890) See 20 S. W Rep, 1015

A stockholder who is also a creditor, and who became such with full knowledge that the stock was paid for by property at an overvaluation, cannot as a creditor compel other stockholders to make payments on their stock as being partly unpaid Whitehall z Jacobs, 44 N W Rep, 630 (Wis, 1890)

A person who buys an old railroad bed for $2,000, which is all it is worth, and then forms a corporation of which he is a director, and sells the road-bed to the company for $200,000 in company notes and $3,600,000 of its stock, may collect the notes if all parties at the time knew all the facts and consented thereto Stewart v St. Louis, etc, R. R., 41 Fed Rep, 736 (1887)

[1] The supreme court of the United States, in the case of Camden v Stuart, 144 U. S, 104 (1892), held liable for unpaid subscriptions the subscribers to $150,000 of stock who had turned in therefor a *contract* for real estate and a health resort which a year prior thereto they had taken The court did not allow any value for the contract and threw out the good-will, and said (p 115) "The experience and good will of the partners, which it is claimed were transferred to the corporation, are of too unsubstantial and shadowy a nature to be

capable of pecuniary estimation in this connection It is not denied that the good-will of a business may be the subject of barter and sale as between the parties to it, but in a case of this kind there is no proper basis for ascertaining its value, and the claim is evidently an afterthought The same remark may be made with regard to the contract of January 30, and the loss of time and trouble to which the parties were subjected, which are now claimed to be elements of value in the property contributed to the corporation, but of which no account was made at the time "

In the case of Lloyd v Preston, 146 U S, 630 (1892), affirming 36 Fed Rep, 54 (1888), where the owner of a railroad sold it to a newly-organized corporation for stock and bonds, the par value of which were fifty times the real value of the railroad, the court held that the bondholders and other creditors who had obtained judgment against the corporation, the execution being returned and satisfied, might hold the party receiving the stock liable thereon on the ground that the subscription price of such stock has never been paid The court said "The entire organization was grossly fraudulent from first to last, without a single honest incident or redeeming trait." The court also said · It having been found, on convincing evidence, that the overvaluation of the property transferred to the railway company by Harper, in pretended payment of the subscriptions to the capital stock, was so gross and obvious as, in connection with the other facts in the case, to clearly establish a case of fraud, and to entitle *bona fide* creditors to enforce actual payment by the subscribers, it

The remedy of the corporate creditor is in equity An action at law for fraud or for conspiracy is difficult to maintain [1]

§ 47. The preceding section contains the common law on the liability of persons who pay for stock in property taken at an overvaluation The common law sustains the transaction and hence renders easy the issue of watered stock Now in former days watered stock did much harm. It deceived people and induced them to buy the stock or bonds, or to extend credit to the company, on the supposition that the capital stock had really been paid for at actual par value Hence, when it became clear that the common law did not prevent the issue of watered stock, but compelled the public to rely, not upon statements of the capital stock, but on an investigation of the actual condition of the company, a demand arose for statutes and constitutional provisions to protect the people from watered stock

This demand gave rise to certain constitutional provisions which have been enacted in several states. These provisions are very similar in their wording, and are substantially as follows: "No corporation shall issue stocks or bonds except for money. labor done or money or property actually received, and all fictitious increase of stock or indebtedness shall be void" [2]

It is now over twenty years since the first of these provisions was enacted, and yet it may be said that these constitutional provisions have decidedly failed to remedy the evil which they were expected to cure They are so sweeping in their effects, and so disastrous to innocent holders of corporate securities, that the courts are reluctant to declare void the stock and bonds which have passed into *bona fide* hands. The provision is held to be applicable and effective only when the issue is entirely fictitious It does not interfere

---

only remains to consider the effect of the defenses set up" See, also, Garrett v. Kansas, etc, Co, 20 S. W. Rep, 965 (Mo , 1892)

Where an insolvent partnership transfers its assets to a newly-created corporation in payment for its shares of stock, and the corporation *assumes all the debts* of the partnership, the payment for the stock is fraudulent *per se* A corporate creditor may hold the stockholders liable on the subscription as though no payment had been attempted Sayler, Assignee, v Simpson, 4 Ry & Corp. L. J , 195 (Ohio, 1888).

[1] The corporate creditor's remedy herein is not by an action at law for

fraud and deceit. Priest v. White, 1 S. W. Rep., 361 (Mo , 1886).

It is difficult for a corporate creditor to seek collection by making out a conspiracy. Brackett v Griswold, 13 N. Y. Supp , 192 (1891)

[2] See Constitution of Ill (1870), art. XI, § 13, Neb. (1875), art. XI, § 5, Mo. (1875), art. XII, § 8, Penn (1873), art. XVI, § 7, Texas (1876), art. XII, § 6, Colorado (1876), art. XV, § 9, Arkansas, art XII, § 8, Alabama, art. XIV, § 6; Louisiana (1879), art. 238. In the last state any corporation issuing such stock shall forfeit its charter See, also, Part VII, *infra.*

with the customary methods of starting the corporate enterprise by the issue of stock and bonds in payment for the construction of the corporate works, and, except in Alabama, it may be said that the courts have construed away the language and purpose of the provision.[1]

[1] Peoria, etc, R. R. Co. v Thompson, 103 Ill., 187 (1882) In this case bonds and cash were given to the contractors in payment for the construction of the road The transaction was upheld In California the supreme court in Stein v Howard, 65 Cal., 616 (1884) has held that the constitutional prohibition does not prevent the issue of stock at less than its par value. The meaning of "fictitious" is defined to be that given in Webster's Dictionary The court said · "Of the shares proposed to be issued *there is no one share* upon which a person can place his finger and say, that share is or will be feigned, imaginary, not real; counterfeit, false, not genuine " An injunction to restrain such an issue of new increased stock was refused In New Castle R R Co v Simpson, 21 Fed Rep, 535 (1884), the court, in passing on the provision in the Pennsylvania constitution, held that a contract giving a construction company $300 000 of stock and $300,000 of bonds for work worth but $180 000 will be set aside, although $40,000 of work has been done The construction company will be repaid the $40,000 in cash See S C, 23 Fed Rep., 214 (1885), holding that the contractor may recover back not only this, but also a reasonable compensation and interest.

Receiving the subscriber's note in payment for stock does not render the stock void, under this constitutional provision Pacific Trust Co v Dorsey, 13 Pac Rep, 148 (Cal, 1887), Pacific Trust Co v Dorsey, 12 Pac Rep, 49 (Cal., 1886)

The supreme court of the United States in Memphis, etc., R R Co v Dow, 120 U S, 287 (1887), held that this provision did not invalidate a transaction upon the reorganization of a company after a foreclosure of its property,

and a purchase of the property by a committee for the bondholders, whereby they took in payment of such property the bonds and stock of the new corporation, even though the stock alone of the new company thus taken was, at its par value, equal to the value of the property involved

If the tangible property of the corporation is actually in excess of the par value of the capital stock, then a stock dividend to the extent of that excess would be legal, but the proceedings to declare the stock dividend must show these facts or the dividend will be enjoined Fitzpatrick v Dispatch, etc, Co, 83 Ala 604 (1887) The court very judiciously changed the reasoning of its opinion as reported in 2 S Rep, 727

Where all the stock and a large quantity of bonds are issued by a railroad corporation to its contractor in payment for the construction of the road, the contractor is not liable to corporate creditors on the stock, even though the bonds were a sufficient consideration for building the road unless the corporate creditors prove that the stock at the time of its issue had a real or market value "If when disposed of by the railroad company it was without value, no wrong was done to creditors " Even the Missouri constitution and statutes do not change this rule. Fogg v Blair, 139 U S, 118 (1891)

A contract calling for "original ground floor or treasury stock " means any of the stock that is issued where the statutes prohibit fictitious stock All the stock is then presumed to be "ground floor " stock and to represent at par the actual value received Williams v Searcy, 10 S Rep, 632 (Ala, 1891)

Land may be turned in in payment for stock even at an overvaluation where

The trouble with such remedies is, that they attempt to cure the evil after it has been consummated, instead of attempting to prevent its occurrence

the valuation is set forth in the incorporation papers under the Pennsylvania act   Cock i Bailey, 23 Atl Rep, 370 (Pa , 1892)

Stock issued as full paid for no consideration whatsoever is void under the constitutional provision that stock shall be issued only " for labor done, services performed, or money or property actually received " The original holder of such stock cannot institute a suit to remedy a wrong done to the corporation by its president. Arkansas, etc, Co v Farmers', etc, Co., 22 Pac. Rep, 954 (Colo., 1889).

A contract by a corporation that it will issue its stock for one-fifth of its par value is void under the Alabama constitutional prohibition   The subscriber having sold his contract to another person cannot collect on such sale   Williams v. Evans, 6 S Rep, 702 (Ala, 1889) See, also, concerning the rule in Alabama, Knox v Childersberg, etc, Co., 5 S Rep, 579 (Ala, 1889)

The person to whom stock has been issued in payment for property may donate a part of it as a bonus to go with bonds sold at par directly from the corporation to the person taking the bonus   The value of the property in this case was not proved   Davis i Montgomery, etc, Co, 8 S Rep, 496 (Ala, 1890)

Where parties pay $5 000 on a $55,000 contract to buy land and then organize a corporation and turn this contract into the corporation for $250,000 of stock issued as full paid, the company agreeing to pay the other $50,000, they are liable to corporate creditors for the difference between $250,000 and the value of the property   The constitution and statute of Alabama forbid such a transaction   Elyton, etc, Co v Birmingham, etc., Co, 9 S Rep, 129 (Ala, 1891).

In the case of Coe v East, etc, R. R.,

52 Fed Rep., 531 (1892), the court held that the above provision in Alabama against watered stock and bonds did not invalidate bonds, although $10,000 of bonds and $10,000 of stock were issued for every mile of road constructed, even though it cost much less than $20,000 cash per mile

Where $100,000 of bonds and $125,000 of stock are issued in payment of construction work of the value of $121,000, the bonds are valid and may be enforced by *bona fide* purchasers. Wood v Corry, etc., Co, 44 Fed Rep., 146 (1890). This last case held also that only the state could object to an issue of " watered " stock and bonds as being in violation of this constitutional provision

The constitutional provision in Alabama forbidding the issue of stock or bonds except for value, and the statutory provision requiring subscriptions to railroad stock to be paid in money, labor or property at their money value, does not prevent one railroad company selling its property to another railroad company for bonds and stock of the latter and the value placed upon the property may be its net earning power and the cost of rebuilding it   It is immaterial that the original cost was much less   Grant v East, etc, Co of Ala., 54 Fed Rep, 569 (1893).

Although the statutes authorize the directors to dispose of the capital stock at any time remaining unpaid in such manner as the by-laws may prescribe, yet this does not authorize the issue of stock for cash at less than par   Mathis v Pridham, 20 S W Rep, 1015 (Tex, 1892)

Where stock is issued as full paid for labor done and the good faith is not questioned and the consideration was performed, the stockholders cannot be held liable on the stock as not being paid up in full   Holly Mfg Co v. New

Statutes are found in some of the states on this subject   There have been a large number of decisions under these various statutes, and those decisions have been confused with the cases which were decided on the common law alone.   The following are some of these statutes:

In New York directors in manufacturing corporations are made personally liable for all corporate debts, if, in the reports which they are required to file, they misstate facts   Accordingly, if they state the capital stock to have been paid up, when in fact it was paid for by property taken at a fraudulent overvaluation, then the penalty applies.   Most of the New York cases on watered stock have arisen under this statute.   Under this statute the court of appeals were at first in doubt whether proof of a mere overvaluation of the property was sufficient to set aside the payment as a full payment, or whether it was necessary for the plaintiff to prove

Chester, etc., Co, 48 Fed. Rep, 879 (1891).

The issue of stock in violation of this provision of the constitution renders the charter liable to forfeiture by the state. State v Atchison, etc, R. R., 38 N. W. Rep, 43 (Neb, 1888)

A contractor who receives bonds in payment of construction work and sells them cannot claim that they are void as contrary to the statute prohibiting "watered" bonds   Reed's Appeal, 16 Atl Rep, 100 (Pa, 1888).

Where a consolidated company of New York and Pennsylvania issues bonds in New York, fictitiously, such bonds cannot be enforced in Pennsylvania, since they are void by its constitution.   A foreclosure in New York of the mortgage securing the bonds may be set aside and the bonds declared void   Pittsburgh, etc. R. R. Co's Appeal, 4 Atl. Rep, 385 (Penn, 1886)

The fact that a contractor received stock and bonds four times in par value the value of the work is not fatal, where no fraud is alleged and the actual cost of the work is not alleged.   But where the contractor then entered into a contract whereby the mortgage was to be foreclosed, and he was to participate in the property purchased at the sale, all for the purpose of cutting off

other creditors, he is liable to them. Cleveland, etc, Co. v Crawford, 9 R'y & Corp L. J, 171 (Chicago, 1891)

In regard to the constitutional provision against the issue of fictitious bonds and stock, the supreme court of Alabama has said "The constitutional provision, standing by itself, does not require that the amount of money, or the value of the labor or property, for which stock or bonds are issued, shall correspond with the face value of the stock or bonds for which it is issued " Hence the court held that bonds might be issued at less than their par value, provided that some substantial value was paid for them, such value to be fair and reasonable, and "not a mere trick or device to evade the law ' Nelson v. Hubbard, 11 S Rep, 413 (Ala, 1892)

It is legal for a company to issue $67 000 of bonds and $67,000 of full-paid stock even to one of its directors for $67,000 in cash, if this was all that the whole $134,000 of securities were worth and if all the directors and stockholders knew of it and agreed to it.   The provision in the California constitution relative to watered stock and bonds does not invalidate them   Union, etc, Co v. Southern, etc, Co., 51 Fed. Rep, 840 (1892)

also that the overvaluation was intentional and fraudulent [1] Later
cases, however, have firmly established the principle that not only
must proof be given that there was an overvaluation of the property or services rendered, but proof also must be given that such
overvaluation was intentional and consequently fraudulent.[2]

The property is not to be considered as overvalued merely because, subsequently, it turns out to be so   The various circumstances under which the valuation was made should be considered
in determining the *bona fides* of the transaction [3] The questions
as to whether there was an overvaluation of the property, and
whether that overvaluation was intentional and fraudulent, are
generally questions of fact to be submitted to the jury.[4] Where,
however, the overvaluation is so great as to bear evidence upon its
face that it was intentional and fraudulent, the court will hold that,
unless the transaction is reasonably explained, there is no question
of fact for the jury, but that, as a matter of law, the overvaluation
was fraudulent.   Various cases which have arisen under this statute are given in the notes below.[5]

[1] Boynton *v* Hatch, 47 N Y, 225
(1872) Three of the judges held that
proof of fraud was necessary, and three
that it was not necessary   All con-
curred in holding that proof of overvaluation was competent and necessary

[2] Douglas *v* Ireland, 73 N Y, 100
(1878), Schenck v Andrews, 57 N Y,
133 (1874), Boynton *v* Andrews, 63 N
Y, 93 (1875), Lake Superior Iron Co *v.*
Drexel, 90 N. Y, 87 (1882).

[3] Schenck *v* Andrews, 57 N Y, 133
(1874) In Coit *v* North Car Gold
Amal Co, 14 Fed Rep., 12 (1882), the
court said corporators "ought not to be
made liable individually for the debts
of the company at the instance of creditors, because, at a later day, the estimate fairly put upon the property at
that time has become modified by subsequent events and will not amount to
the value which they set upon it." Affirmed, 119 U S, 343 (1886)

[4] Boynton *v* Hatch, 47 N. Y. 225
(1872), Lake Superior Iron Co *v* Drexel,
90 N Y, 87 (1882)

[5] Thus, where stock for $900,000 was
issued for property which the jury
found to be worth $64 000, the court

held, as a presumption of law, that the
transaction was fraudulent   Douglas *v*
Ireland, 73 N. Y., 100 (1878) In another
case, involving the same facts, the trial
court submitted the question to the
jury. Brockway *v* Ireland, 61 How.
Pr, 372 (1880).

In another case, where stock for
$100,000 was issued for property worth
not more than $50,000, the court held
that, in the absence of evidence to explain the presumption of fraud, there
was no question for the jury, and that
the transaction was fraudulent upon its
face. Boynton *v* Andrews, 63 N Y, 93
(1875). An issue of $190,000 of stock
for property worth $27,500 was held to
be a fraudulent overvaluation, as a matter of law   Osgood *v* King, 42 Iowa,
478 (1876) The case of Lake Superior
Iron Co *v* Drexel, 90 N Y, 87, tends to
make the valuation of the property a
question for the jury exclusively. In
that case stock for $2,500,000 was issued
for property in a patent; $900,000 of
the stock was returned to the corporation as a gift The court held that the
question of fraud was for the jury
This case was followed in Draper *v*
Beadle, 16 Weekly Dig, 475 (1883),

Under the New York statute stockholders also are liable in certain companies to double the amount of their stock until a certificate is filed to the effect that the capital stock is all paid in [1]

Supm Ct. N Y, Gen T. In Bolz v Ridder, 19 Weekly Dig, 463 (1884). N Y Com Pl, the remarkable rise in value of a patent-right from $1,000 to $100,000, when sold for stock issued in payment therefor, was held to be only presumptively fraudulent and may be explained sufficiently to raise a question for the jury The directors in estimating the value of property may take the opinion of experts and rely thereon Brockway v Ireland, 61 How Pr, 372 (1880) See, also, Knowles v Duffy, 40 Hun, 485 (1886) Cf Thurston v Duffy 38 Hun 327 (1885)

Under the New York statute where patents worth $75,000 are transferred to the corporation in payment for $300,000 of stock, and $100 000 of the stock is at once donated to the company by the inventor, and other stock is at once sold by him for about one-third of the par value, the only fraudulent intent that need be proved is that the directors knew that the patents were not worth $300,000 National Tube, etc, Co v Gilfillan, 124 N Y, 302 (1890)

In determining whether property is worth the par value of stock which is issued for it, the intrinsic or market value is the test, but the jury may consider also "its value for the use to which it was to be put, and the adaptability of it to any specific purpose, and any peculiar advantages it then had" Huntington v. Attrill, 118 N Y, 365 (1890) The evidence of experts as to the value of similar property is not admissible Id

Under the New York statute, where property worth but $60,000 is turned in for $1,000,000 of stock and $200,000 of bonds, the act is fraudulent Blake v. Griswold, 103 N Y 429 (1886), sustaining a finding of the special term to that effect See, also, Hatch v Attrill, id, 383 (1890)

In the case Chittenden v Thaunhauser, 47 Fed Rep, 410 (1891) the court held the directors liable under the statute for a false report, where $1 500,000 of stock was issued for mines and property which was offered for sale at about the same time for $150,000

In Ferguson v Gill, 64 Hun, 284 (1892), $100,000 of stock was issued for a patent which turned out to be worthless The statute made the directors liable if they knew this fact. The court held that the officers were entitled to prove the conversation at which the value was fixed upon

In Thurber v Thompson, 21 Hun, 472 (1880), the court said the jury should have before them "evidence of the probable enhanced value growing out of the contemplated improvements made and to be made by the company, and of the public improvements which were expected to add largely to the value of the land for the new objects and purposes to which it was to be devoted It would be extremely unjust to such a company as this to hold that farming lands upon which the site of a city or town is about to be established and

[1] It has been held that an issue of $300,000 of full-paid stock for a right to apply for patents, if found by the jury to be an intentional overvaluation of that right subjects a transferee of any of the shares, taking with notice of all the facts, to this statutory liability in New York to an amount equal to the par value of the stock National, etc Co v Gilfillan, 46 Hun, 248 (1887)

Under the statute creating a double liability until the stock is fully paid, a creditor may show that property was taken at an overvaluation knowingly and fraudulently and may then enforce the liability Goodrich v. Dorman, 14 N Y Supp, 879 (1891).

In Ohio, by statute, an issue of stock to a director, directly or indirectly, for less than the par value thereof, is void.[1]

In Maine the statutes are construed so as to render stockholders liable to corporate creditors where property is taken in payment at an overvaluation.[2] So also in Wisconsin [3]

which are brought for that purpose, and mapped, platted and subdivided into city or village lots, are to be viewed, upon a question of overvaluation, merely as agricultural land"

See, also, Huntington v Attrill, 42 Hun, 459 (1886), (aff'd, see supra), where land costing $80,000 was turned in for $700,000 of stock The finding of the jury that the act was fraudulent was sustained on appeal And where property worth but $60,000 is turned in for $1,000,000 of stock and $200,000 of bonds, the act is fraudulent as a matter of law Blake v Griswold, 103 N Y , 429 (1886)

In New York, under the statute allowing the incorporation of manufacturing companies, it has been assumed that an issue of stock as paid up for cash, at less than its par value, is void Spring Co v Knowlton, 103 U S, 49 (1880), Knowlton v Congress and Empire Spring Co, 14 Blatch , 364 (1877), Knowlton v Congress, etc , Co, 57 N Y , 518 (1874) These three decisions arise from the litigation of a single case After being reversed in the New York court, it was removed into the federal court In all three decisions the invalidity of the stock was conceded by both parties. The federal courts differed from the state courts, and held that a person partly paying for such illegal stock may recover back such payment, although he had allowed the stock to be forfeited for non-payment of further calls.

Under the New York Manufacturing Company Act providing for the issue of stock for property "to the amount of the value thereof," the value of the property must equal the par value of the stock. Gamble v Queens, etc , Co , 123 N Y., 91 (1870), the court referring

to and affirming Van Cott v. Van Brunt, 82 N Y , 535, as being a decision sustaining the common-law right to issue stock below par.

In estimating the value of property turned in to a corporation in payment of stock a fair profit to the contractor is to be allowed Id.

[1] Section 3313 of the Revised Statutes of Ohio sets forth that "all capital stocks, bonds, notes or other securities of a company purchased of a company by a director thereof, either directly or indirectly, for less than the par value thereof, shall be null and void." In Zabriskie v Cleveland, C. & C R. R. Co , 23 How , 381 (1859), this provision was held not to affect the liability of a guarantor of such bonds

But in Union Trust Co. v N Y., etc , R. R. Co 1 R'y & Corp. L J , 50 (Ohio Com Pl , 1887), the court, in applying this statute, held that, where fifty millions of paid-up stock and fifteen million of bonds are given to a syndicate, of which a director is a member, for eighteen millions of money, the stock and bonds and the mortgage securing the bonds are void

[2] In Maine it is held that where property purchased by individuals for $6,667 67 is turned in to the corporation for $240,000 of full-paid stock, the stockholders are liable on the stock as though the subscription price had not been paid. This decision is made under the statute that property shall be taken "at a bona fide and fair valuation thereof." In this case a part of the stock was turned back as treasury stock and sold at a small figure The court expressly stated that its decision was based on the statute and that alone Libby v Tobey, 19 Atl. Rep., 904 (Me , 1890).

[3] In Wisconsin under the statutes and

A statute prohibiting the sale of stock below par does not prevent the corporation from pledging it, and a sale of the stock by the pledgee below its par value is legal [1]

There have been decisions under the Missouri statutes in addition to those under the constitutional provision referred to above And various other states have statutes on this subject [3]

also under the common law as understood by the courts of that state, stockholders who paid for their stock by turning in mining property known to them to be worth only one-tenth of the par value of the stock are liable for the remaining nine-tenths of the par value to corporate creditors The question of whether the creditors knew all the facts is a matter to be set up in defense. Gogebic Inv. Co v Iron, etc, Co, 47 N. W Rep, 726 (Wis, 1891)

[1] Peterborough, etc, R. R. Co. v Nashua, etc, R. R. Co, 59 N H, 385 (1879)

[3] In Missouri a contractor who was paid in bonds and stock was held liable to corporate creditors for the par value of the stock over and above the market price of all the bonds and stock so given, where such value was greater than a reasonable price for the contract work The court said 'that where an agreement is entered into between a contractor and a corporation, whereby the former is to perform work for, or furnish material to, the latter, and to take unpaid stock in part or in full payment, that such contractor, whether for labor or material, can only charge therefor the reasonable market value for such labor or material thus given in exchange, and that all agreements by the corporation to pay more than such reasonable compensation will be disregarded and held for naught by the courts, where the rights of creditors intervene, and this is the case even though no fraud be proven" Shickle v Watts, 7 S W. Rep, 276 (Mo, 1888).

Where all the stock and a large quantity of bonds are issued by a railroad corporation to its contractor in payment

for the construction of the road, the contractor is not liable to corporate creditors on the stock, even though the bonds were a sufficient consideration for building the road, unless the corporate creditors prove that the stock at the time of its issue had a real or market value. "If, when disposed of by the railroad company, it was without value, no wrong was done to creditors" Even the Missouri constitution and statutes do not change this rule Fogg v Blair, 139 U S, 118 (1891).

In the case of Northwestern, etc., Ins Co v Cotton, etc, Co, 46 Fed Rep, 22 (1891), the court held that where property worth $157 000 is turned into a corporation for $200,000, payable in $125 000 of stock and $75,000 of bonds, the creditors of the company might hold the parties liable on the stock, as though it were unpaid stock, and the creditor is presumed not to have known of the transaction when he contracted the debt

[3] See part VII, infra

In the case Brown v Duluth, etc, Ry, 53 Fed Rep, 889 (1893), the court refused to enjoin an issue of stock and refused to cancel stock already issued although $900,000 of bonds and $915 000 of stock were issued for construction work which cost $580,000 The court so held although the statute required the stock to be fully paid, and prohibited issues except for property actually received The plaintiff, however, was a holder who purchased with full knowledge of the facts The court said "This statute was not intended to prevent or interfere with the usual method of raising money to build railroads or for any legitimate corporate purpose It is not to be construed as obstructive

In England, in 1863, the Companies Clauses Consolidation Act[1] prohibited the issue of new stock for a price less than its par value An amendment thereto in 1869[2] struck out this prohibition, and gave power to the directors to issue stock on such terms and conditions as they saw fit   The Railway Companies Act[3] of 1867 is to the same effect.

In England the issue of stock for property or services is largely regulated by statute   On account of the many frauds perpetrated upon the public by the issue of stock for property taken at a gross overvaluation, parliament, in 1867, passed an act requiring all contracts whereby stock was issued for property or services to be publicly registered, under penalty of the payment being void.[4] Difficulty then arose as to what was the *status* and liability of a person receiving stock for property, in case the contract therefor was not publicly registered, as required by act of parliament.   The courts finally decided that, if the sums due reciprocally were expressly offset, then that the stock was to be deemed paid for, notwithstanding the statute.[5]   But a mere general understanding that

to the extent of restricting and hampering corporations in their internal management, and embarrass them in procuring means to carry out the legitimate purposes of the corporation, and unless it appears that, under the guise of building its road, bonds and stock of the defendant company are to be issued and put upon the market fraudulently that do not and are not intended to represent money and property, this corporation is not prohibited from entering into a real transaction based upon a present consideration, and having reference to legitimate corporate purposes "   The court also said that "such a provision does not necessarily indicate a purpose to make the validity of every issue of stock or bonds by a corporation depend upon the inquiry whether the money, property or labor actually received therefor was of equal value in the market with the stock or bonds so issued "

[1] See 26 & 27 Vict, ch 118, § 21

[2] See 32 & 33 Vict., ch 48, § 5.

[3] See 30 & 31 Vict, ch 127, § 27

[4] 30 & 31 Vict., ch 131, § 25   "Every share in any company shall be deemed and taken to have been issued and to be held subject to the payment of the

whole amount thereof in cash, unless the same shall have been otherwise determined by a contract duly made, in writing, and filed with the registrar of joint-stock companies at or before the issue of such shares "   Where the stockholders apply long after incorporation for leave to file with the public register the contract whereby stock is issued for property, the court will require them first to provide for existing debts. Re Darlington, etc, Co, 56 L. T. Rep., 627 (1887).

A mere vote of stock to a director in compensation for his services does not render him liable thereon for failure to register the contract, unless he knows of the entry of his name as holder of the shares or accepts certificates for the same   Arnot's Case, 57 L. T. Rep., 353 (1887).

[5] Pell s Case, L. R., 5 Ch. App., 11 (1869), Ex parte Clarke, L. R., 7 Eq. Cas, 550 (1869), Nicoll's Case, L. R., 7 Ch Div, 533 (1878). See, also, § 23. In Spargo s Case, L. R., 8 Ch. App, 407 (1873), the court said   "If the parties account with each other, and sums are stated to be due on one side, and sums to an equal amount due on the other

the property is payment for the stock is insufficient   The prohibition in the statute then applies, and payment in cash will have to be made upon a winding up[1] The point decided by these cases seems to have been misapprehended in a few American cases[2]

Frequently actions herein are against corporate officers who directly or indirectly received the stock.[3] This class of cases is considered in the next section

§ 48. *Liability of the officers of the corporation.*—There is great difficulty in defining clearly and accurately the liability of the corporate officers herein. This is because the officers may have committed an *ultra vires* or fraudulent act, or may have participated in the profits as promoters, or may have received a gift of part of the stock from the parties to whom they issued it

There are few cases holding a director liable for loss to the corporation where an issue of its stock for money or property less in value than the par value of the stock has been made   Such an action would be similar in its character to the numerous cases against directors for their frauds and *ultra vires* acts.[4]

In a suit of this character, however, against an officer of the corporation, he is liable not for the par value of the stock, less the value of the property or labor received therefor, but at the most

---

side on that account, and those accounts are settled by both parties, it is exactly the same thing as if the sums due on both sides had been paid " See, also, Maynard's Case, 22 Week R., 119, *Re* Vulcan Iron Works, Law Times, May, 1885, p. 61.

[1] Dent's Case, L R., 15 Eq Cas., 407 (1873); Fothergill s Case, L. R., 8 Ch. App, 270 (1873), Crickmer's Case, L. R, 10 Ch App, 614 (1875), Rowland's Case, 42 L. T. (N S.), 785 (1880). Person taking stock at a discount for property overvalued may withdraw. *Re* Midland, etc, Co., 60 L. T. Rep, 666 (1889)

[2] See Wetherbee *v.* Baker, 35 N. J Eq, 501 (1882)

[3] A statement filed with the state commissioner as required by statute, in regard to the amount of the paid-up stock, is not such a representation as will sustain an action for damages for fraudulent representations inducing a person to take the notes of the company   Hun-

newell *v* Duxbury, 28 N E Rep, 267 (Mass, 1891).

In an action by a treasurer for pay for his services it is no defense that the corporation with a capital fixed at $1,000,000 had $50,000 paid in in cash to comply with the statute, and then the remaining capital stock, $950,000, together with the cash so paid in, were issued for two patents, and that the treasurer checked out therefor the said $50,000, being the part unexpended at that time   Sears *v* Kings County El R'y Co, 31 N E Rep, 490 (Mass, 1892)

The fact that the corporate officers have filed a false statement as to the amount of paid-up capital stock will not sustain an action for damages for fraud in inducing a party to take the notes of the corporation   Representations as to the credit of a corporation must be in writing in order to be actionable under the Massachusetts statute   Hunnewell *v* Duxbury *et al*, 31 N E Rep, 700 (Mass, 1892)

[4] See Part IV.

he can be held liable only for the market value of the stock, less the value of the labor or property received by the corporation.[1]

Where, however, the directors receive a part of the stock themselves, either by its issue directly to themselves, or by being secret partners with those to whom it is issued, or by a gift to them from the parties to whom it is issued, then the directors may be compelled to account to the corporation for the stock actually received by themselves. In such a case, however, the directors, as such, cannot be made liable on the watered stock issued to third persons and still retained by them. The directors are liable only to the extent that they themselves received stock. This liability arises from the principle of law that a director must account to his corporation for any secret gift that may be made to him by persons contracting with the corporation; and must account also for profits made by his secret participation in contracts between the corporation and third persons.[2] In such cases the director is liable to the corporation or its creditors, not for the par value of the stock received by him, but for the actual value of the stock, or for the profit or price which he received therefor.[3]

[1] Continental Tel Co. v Nelson, 49 N. Y Super Ct, 197 (1883), where the question as to what was the market value was submitted to the jury. See, also, Nott v Clews, 14 Abb N. C (N. Y.), 437, overruling a demurrer In this case, however, the directors had received part of the stock as a gift See, also, Osgood v King, 42 Iowa, 478 (1876); but see Flagler, etc., Co. v Flagler, 19 Fed. Rep, 468 (1884), Langdon v Fogg, 18 Fed Rep, 5 (1883), S. C, in state court, 14 Abb. N. C (N Y), 435

[2] See §§ 649, 650, and cases in notes thereto.

[3] In Carling's Case, L R, 1 Ch. D, 115 (1875) where the person receiving stock for property taken at an overvaluation gave part of it to a corporate director, the court held that the corporation could demand of the director either the stock, or the profit realized by him, or the profits thereby lost by the corporation, but could not compel him to pay the full par value of the stock In De Ruvigne's Case, L R, 5 Ch D, 316 (1876), where shares of stock were issued as paid up to a person for services palpably overvalued, and he transferred a part of the stock to a director, De Ruvigne, the court said: "If the company attempt to make the appellant [director] a contributor, and they allege fraud in the original agreement by which he was to take the shares, they must either throw over the agreement altogether, or they must take it altogether, they cannot adopt it as to one part and reject it as to the rest." The court said the director could be held liable for breach of trust and be made to pay to the corporation the selling value of the shares, and since some of the stock was sold at par, he was chargeable with the par value of the stock so received by him.

In Anderson's Case, L. R., 7 Ch. D, 75, 94, the court held that, if shares were improperly issued to a director at a discount, the contract might be set aside and the consideration returned, or the profits realized by him might be recovered In Currie's Case, 3 De Gex, J & S, 367 (1863), where shares were taken both directly and indirectly by the corporate officers for property and services grossly overvalued, the court held that the transaction might be un-

There is still another class of cases, in which a director acts also as a promoter of the company and receives stock for his services He then is liable to account to the corporation therefor, not only as a director, but also as a promoter.[1]

Another class of cases may exist where the directors vote stock to themselves in payment for their services to the company.[2]

Whether the directors are liable herein to purchasers of stock or to corporate creditors in an action for deceit is an open question [3]

done altogether for fraud, but there was no liability on their part to contribute anything on the shares The only remedy is to set aside the transaction and recover the profits thereof. Langdon v. Fogg, 18 Fed Rep, 5 (1883); S. C., 14 Abb N C (N. Y.), 435, holding that the directors are not liable to the corporation for the par value of stock issued to their dummy for property and then transferred to themselves See, also, § 650, *infra*, and cases in notes

In the case of *Re* Ambrose Lake T. & C. Minn. Co, L. R., 14 Ch D, 390 (1880), it was held that where all the stockholders acquiesced, and there were no creditors' rights involved, the corporation cannot recover from its directors profits realized by them from shares issued to them as paid up in consideration of property taken at a gross overvaluation The corporation was held to be in no position to complain In Van Cott v. Van Brunt, 82 N Y, 535 (1880), where the facts were very much the same as in the preceding case, the court said: "If the defendant [director and president] had realized a sum beyond the amount actually expended, there might have been, perhaps, some ground for claiming that the arrangement would inure to and for the benefit of the company." Page 541

[1] See the important case of Chandler v. Bacon, 30 Fed Rep., 538 (1887), also, § 651, *infra*, and cases cited In Iowa where "watered" stock is given as a gift by the patentees to a promoter, who afterwards became the first president of the company, he is liable to corporate creditors for all the "water" there is in

the stock Boulton Carbon Co v Mills, 43 N W. Rep, 290 (Iowa, 1889)

[2] See § 657, *infra*

[3] See §§ 157, 158, 355

A sale or pledge of stock stamped "non-assessable," when in fact it was not legally paid paid up, renders liable for false representations the president and secretary who made such sale or pledge and who knew that it was not paid-up stock Windham v French 24 N E. Rep, 914 (Mass, 1890)

In Bartholomew v Bentley 15 Ohio, 659 (1846), certain persons incorporated a bank, incurred large debts, then sold their stock to the bank and left the creditors nothing A creditor brought an action on the case for fraud The court sustained the action, and said "If the defendants, with the design to defraud the public generally, have knowingly combined together and held forth false and deceptive colors, and done acts which were wrong, and have thereby injured the plaintiff, they must make him whole by refunding to the full extent of that injury, and they cannot place between him and justice with any success, the charter of the German Bank of Wooster whether it be valid or void, forfeited or *in esse* Neither a good nor a bad thing may be falsely used for purposes of deception, and made a scapegoat for responsibility Nor is it material that there should have been an intention to defraud the plaintiff in particular If there was a general design to defraud all such as could be defrauded by taking their paper issues, it is sufficient, and the plaintiff may maintain his suit, provided he has

The officers of the corporation who participate in the issue of stock as paid up, when it has not been fully paid, are liable to persons purchasing such stock for damage thereby suffered.[1] In Massachusetts, by statute, corporate officers are made liable for corporate debts, if they issue stock for property at an unfair valuation of the latter[2]

§ 49 *Liability of the persons purchasing the stock with notice.*— It seems to be generally assumed, as a matter of course, that persons purchasing stock, with notice that it had not been paid up, although in fact it had been issued as paid up, are liable on such stock to the same extent that their transferrers were liable.[3]

§ 50 *Liability of the bona fide transferees without notice.*— A *bona fide* purchaser for value and without notice of stock issued by a corporation as paid up cannot be held liable on such stock in any way, either to the corporation, corporate creditors, or other persons, even though the stock was not actually paid up as represented. Such a purchaser has a right to rely on the representations of the corporation that the stock is paid up. Difficulty sometimes arises in determining what will constitute a sufficient representation that the stock is paid up. A representation by the corporate agents that the full par value will not be required is insufficient.[4] The word "non-assessable," stamped or printed or written on the face of the certificate, is not a sufficient representation that the stock is paid up, so as to protect a *bona fide* purchaser thereof, where the certificate also shows that only twenty per cent. has been paid thereon[5]

---

taken the paper and suffers from the fraud . . . The act incorporating the president and directors of the German Bank of Wooster, admitting it to be in force, conferred no authority upon any person to hold out false colors to deceive the public, no authority to issue bills without the means of redeeming them, and those who combined to use it for the purposes of swindling acted for themselves rather than as agents of the bank."

Creditors of a corporation cannot hold the directors liable for fraud, deceit, etc., in forming a sham corporation, when no misrepresentations can be traced to them. Mere statements as to the amount of capital stock are insufficient. Brackett v. Griswold, 112 N. Y., 451 (1889).

[1] Cross v Sackett, 6 Abb. Pr., 247 (1858); Re Gold Co., 11 Ch. D, 701 (1878). See, also, § 47, *supra.*

[2] Statutes of Mass., Acts of 1875, ch. 177, § 2

[3] Upton v Tribilcock, 91 U. S., 45 (1875) But they are not liable if any prior owner was *bona fide* and without notice Barrow's Case, L. R., 14 Ch. D, 432 (1880). A transferee of "watered" stock taking with notice is liable the same as his transferrer Boulton Carbon Co v. Mills, 43 N. W. Rep, 290 (Iowa, 1889)

[4] Webster v. Upton, 91 U. S, 65 (1875); Upton v. Tribilcock, 91 U. S, 45 (1875).

[5] Webster v Upton, 91 U. S, 65, 71 (1875), Sanger v. Upton, id., 56 (1875).

Where, however, a statement is made on the face of the certificate that it is paid-up stock, the *bona fide* purchaser of the certificate need not inquire further, but may rely on that representation, and is protected thereby against liability[1]

A purchaser of stock is entitled to rely on statements in the corporate books that the stock is paid up[2] The law goes still further, and holds that where a person in open market, in good faith and without notice, purchases certificates, such stock is to be deemed "paid up" in his hands, and he is protected as a *bona fide* purchaser, even though there is nothing on the face of the certificates stating that they are paid up[3] This can now be laid down as the

[1] This principle of law was clearly laid down, explained and sustained in the recent case of Young *v* Erie Iron Co, 31 N W. Rep, 814 (Mich 1887). In Waterhouse *v* Jamieson, L. R., 2 H L. (Sc), 29, where the stock was purchased in open market, the court said " Here the appellant is a *bona fide* holder of shares upon which, no doubt, there was a false statement made by the company, of which he had no knowledge, and as to which he was under no obligation to inquire, and therefore he cannot be subjected to liability by having imputed to him a knowledge of the falsehood " In Brant *v* Ehlen, 59 Md, 1 (1882) the court said " Where shares are issued by the company to the subscriber as full-paid shares, and are sold by the subscriber as such, there is no ground on which a promise can be implied, on the part of the purchaser without notice, to be answerable either to the company or its creditors, should the representations on the faith of which he purchased prove to be false He could not be held liable on the ground of contract, because he never agreed to purchase any other shares than full-paid shares, and if it be said that the shares were fraudulently issued, he could not be held liable on the ground of fraud, because he was in no sense a party to the fraud " In Steacy *v* Little Rock & Ft. Smith R. R. Co, 5 Dill, 348 (1879), Judge Dillon examined, at considerable length, the reasons of the rule protecting *bona fide* purchasers of stock issued

as paid up, and sustained the rule itself See, also, Burkinshaw *v* Nichols, L. R. 3 App Cas. 1004 (1878). One case, Myers *v* Seeley, 10 Nat'l Bankr Reg, 411, lays down a different doctrine The court says " The assignee of shares can be in no better condition t'ran the assignor . The question is simply whether the stock has been really paid in full to the corporation The assignee may have paid for it to the assignors, and may have relied on the representations of the latter and of officers of the company, that the shares bought were fully paid, yet creditors are not bound thereby, and if the stock was not fully paid, the holder is liable to creditors for the amount remaining unpaid." This case must be considered poor law See 68 L T Rep 15

[2] Erskine *v* Loewenstein, 11 Mo App, 595 (1884)

[3] Keystone Bridge Co *v* McCheney, 8 Mo App 496 (1880), Foreman *v* Bigelow, 4 Cliff 508 (1879). as explained in 8 Mo App, 496, Johnson *v* Sullivan, 15 Mo App, 55 (1884) where the court says " If any presumption of fact arises from the face of a stock certificate in customary form, as was the one in this case, it is that the stock . is fully paid up ' See, also, Erskine *v* Loewenstein, 82 Mo, 301 (1884), Cleveland, etc, Co *v*. Texas, etc, R'y Co, 27 Fed Rep 250 (1886).

If a certificate of stock is silent on its face as to whether it is full paid or not, a *bona fide* purchaser is protected in considering it full-paid stock. West

established rule. It is based on sound public policy, favoring, as it does, the transfer of personal property, and the *quasi*-negotiability of stock, and discountenancing secret liens and constructive notice

A purchaser in open market of stock represented to be paid up by a statement to that effect on the certificate is presumed to be a *bona fide* purchaser. Hence there has arisen the well-established rule, both in America and England, that a *bona fide* purchaser for value, and without notice, of stock issued as paid up, is not liable for any part of the par value which may not have been paid.[1]

Nashville, etc, Co. *v* Nashville Sav Bank, 6 S. W Rep, 340 (Tenn., 1888) *Cf* Burkinshaw *v* Nichols, L. R., 3 App Cas, 1004, 1017 (1878) In Brant *v* Ehlen, 59 Md, 1 (1882), the court say " The purchaser is not bound to suspect fraud when everything seems fair . Any other doctrine would virtually destroy the transferable nature of such shares, and paralyze the whole of the dealings in the stock of the corporations "

A party purchasing a certificate of stock which does not state whether it is paid up or not may assume that it is paid up, and will be protected in that assumption Du Pont v. Tilden, 42 Fed Rep, 87 (1890)

An inquiry by a purchaser of stock of corporate officers, as to whether it was full-paid stock, must be made to officers having authority to speak for the corporation. Browning *v* Hinkle, 51 N. W, Rep, 605 (Minn, 1892)

[1] In *Re* British Farmers' Pure Linseed Cake Co, L. R, 7 Ch D, 533 (1878), aff'd, L. R, 3 App. Cas, 1004 ('880), the court held that, if the *bona fide* purchaser were not protected, " no person buying shares in the market, as paid-up shares would be safe, for he would get nothing more than a certificate to show they are paid up . Obviously such a construction would destroy the transferable nature of shares altogether." See, also, Foreman *v* Bigelow, 4 Cliff, 508 (1878), McCracken *v.* McIntyre, 1 Duv. (Can.), 479, Stacey *v* Little Rock & Ft S. R. R. Co., 5 Dill, 348 (1878); Jackson *v.* Slido, etc, Co., 1 Lea (Tenn), 210, Brant *v* Ehlen, 59 Md, 1 (1883); Waterhouse *v* Jamieson, L. R., 2 H. L. (Sc.), 29. *Cf* Crickmer's Case, L. R., 10 Ch App, 614 *Contra*, Myers *v* Seeley, 10 Nat'l Bank, Reg, 411 It is immaterial that the payment in stock issued as paid up turns out to have been valueless. The *bona fide* purchaser is protected, and the corporation must allow registry by him Protection Life Ins. Co. *v* Osgood, 93 Ill, 69 (1879) In the case of Wintringham *v* Rosenthal, 25 Hun, 580 (1881), the court held that a *bona fide* purchaser of stock, which he purchased supposing it to be paid up, is not liable for the unpaid par value. The stock was issued by a bank, evidently on a cash subscription. This case practically overrules Mann *v* Currie, 2 Barb., 294 (1848). The general railroad act of New York (Laws 1850, ch 140, § 10) prescribes that each stockholder shall be liable " to an amount equal to the amount unpaid on the stock held by him" In the case of Tasker *v* Wallace, 6 Daly, 364, 374 (1876), the court held that under this statute, " as between a stockholder and a creditor, it is wholly immaterial whether he was a *bona fide* and innocent purchaser of stock which the vendor assured him had been paid." This remark was, it seems, a *dictum*, and being by an inferior court is doubtful as an authority The representation moreover, was not on the face of the certificate, nor was it made by the corporation. In the case

Where a subscriber who has not yet taken out his certificate of stock instructs the corporation to issue the certificates to a designated transferee, the latter has been held to be the original allottee of that stock, and, if the stock was irregularly issued as paid-up stock, he cannot claim to be a *bona fide* transferee without notice [1]

A contrary rule has been laid down in other cases, however, and would seem to be more in accordance with justice [2]

E ISSUE OF WATERED STOCK BY A STOCK DIVIDEND.

§ 51. *Third method: Issue by stock dividends* — The third method of issuing fictitiously paid up stock is by a wrongful use of the power to issue stock dividends It seems to be generally conceded that if the capital stock and the actual property of the corporation is not permanently increased to the extent of the par value of the stock distributed as a dividend, then that the issue of stock by such dividend is irregular, and under certain circumstances fraudulent.[3]

In some of the states stock dividends are prohibited by constitutional or statutory provisions [4]

of Hubbell *v* Meigs, 50 N Y 480, 489 (1872), where the purchaser of Wisconsin railroad stock sued his vendor for damages for deceit on the ground, among others, that the stock had been issued fictitiously as paid up, the court said ' It is unnecessary to determine whether the corporation was authorized by its charter to sell its stock at less than par, or whether, in so selling, its officers did not violate their duty The plaintiff was a *bona fide* purchaser, and, being such, acquired a valid title to the stock transferred to him "

[1] Rowland's Case 42 L T (N S), 785 (1880), Potter's Appeal, Weekly Notes, 1878, p. 81, *Re* Vulcan Iron Works, Law Times, 1885, p 61

[2] Young *v* Erie Iron Co., 31 N W. Rep, 814 (Mich, 1887), Carling's Case, L R., 1 Ch D, 115 (1875) See, also, § 62, *infra*.

[3] In Williams *v* Western Union Tel Co., 93 N Y., 189 (1883), the court said that a stock dividend "could be declared by a corporation without violating its letter, its spirit or its purpose   . There is no public policy which, in all

cases, condemns such dividends . . No harm is done to any person, provided the dividend is not a mere inflation of the stock of the company, with no corresponding values to answer to the stock distributed   . So long as every dollar of stock issued by a corporation is represented by a dollar of property, no harm can result to individuals or the public from distributing the stock to the stockholders ' Howell *v* Chicago & Northw R'y Co, 51 Barb. 378 (1868) is to the same effect. In Bailey *v* Railroad Co, 22 Wall, 604, the court said that net earnings however expended or invested, "belong to the stockholders, and may be distributed as they may direct, in dividends of stock or by a sale of property " See, also, ch 32 Where the company is under obligations to issue stock to represent interest or subscriptions until dividends are declared, a stock dividend does not stop the interest. Hardin County *v* Louisville, etc, R. R., 17 S. W Rep, 860 (Ky, 1891).

[4] Ill Const, art. XI, § 13 In Wisconsin by statute. R S 1878, § 1753, amended by ch. 93, Laws 1881 In Mas-

The decided tendency of the law, however, is to sustain and even encourage stock dividends, where they are regularly and legally made by adding to the property representing the capital stock further property to represent the stock dividend   By such an act the

sachusetts railway corporations are by statute prohibited from declaring a stock dividend except by authority of the general court. Pub Stat. of Mass, ch 112, § 61   It has been held not a violation of this statute for a railway company to distribute among its shareholders, without the assent of the general court, shares of its own stock which it had purchased from the commonwealth, when it had legislative authority for such purchase and distribution Commonwealth *v* Boston & Albany R. R. Co, 142 Mass, 146 (1886). See § 287

If the tangible property of the corporation is actually in excess of the par value of the capital stock then a stock dividend to the extent of that excess would be legal, but the proceedings to declare the stock dividend must show these facts or the dividend will be enjoined   Fitzpatrick *v* Dispatch, etc, Co, 83 Ala., 604 (1887). The court very properly changed the reasoning of its opinion as reported in 2 S. Rep., 727

In one point of view stock dividends are objectionable   They are issued to represent the increased value of the corporate property as it stands. In the case of railroads, this increase of value arises very largely from the increased value of the eminent domain franchises which the corporation is using   These franchises belong to the people, and the people are entitled to the increased value of them   Such an increased value could be readily secured to the people by a reduction of railroad charges   But by stock dividends, based on this increased value of the franchise, the railroad is able, by increasing its stock, to divide all profits and yet not declare more than a six or eight per cent dividend   The smallness of the dividend prevents a legislative reduction of rates

If, however, no stock dividend were allowed, and the increased earning capacity of the railroad gave large profits, such profits would have to be employed in improving the property or in making extravagant dividends, which would justify a reduction of railroad rates. It is urged, in reply to this view, that about three out of four railroad enterprises are the cause of total loss to their projectors, and that the fourth should be made to pay more largely, by reason of the risk incurred, also that large capital and great ability in managing enterprises of such magnitude should be more fully compensated.

Mr Swan, in Investors' Notes on American Railroads (1886), p. 42, presents an ingenious argument on this question when he says   "The assertion by a state of a right to fix rates and limit dividends by *ex post facto* legislation, without regard to existing charters and without compensation or indemnity, is, in fact, the barely disguised assertion of a right to confiscate to a greater or less extent the increment of value legitimately accruing to a going concern   In connection with a railroad the increment of value cannot with any semblance of propriety be described as an 'unearned' increment. In a vast number of instances an American railroad may be said to create the settlement of population which is destined to furnish passengers and to produce freight   Reflex activities are of course stimulated, and contribute in their turn to the development of traffic; but in many instances the railroad itself primarily constitutes the determining condition of settlement in a particular place, and of the transportation of passengers and merchandise through a particular channel   Subject to the restraints of equitable regulation, the

responsibility of the corporation is increased, creditors are more secure, inasmuch as there is more property to respond to their claims, and the stockholders have increased their investment by adding the profits to the capital stock instead of distributing them by a cash dividend

right of a constructing company to the increasing benefit of the business which it builds up by its outlay and its skill is no less real than that of the founder of a purely commercial or professional business to the increasing benefit of his capital or ability"

Alexander on Railway Practice (1887), p 37, says with some force "It is asserted that much of the stock of our railroads is not legitimate, but is water Such an argument may apply against any particular railroad that earns exorbitant dividends, but against the system as a whole it does not For it would be easy to show that for every dollar of water in existing stocks two dollars of the money of railroad investors has been lost like water spilt in the sand. Much of it was lost, doubtless, by bad judgment, but the fact remains that our existing system of railroads, as a whole, has cost fully as much as it is capitalized at. Scarcely one of them was originally built as it stands to-day. The earlier ones have been rebuilt and re-equipped three or four times, as experience pointed out necessary improvements. Many of them, too, were built before the business really demanded them, and the loss from this source has been enormous . . . If the State would guaranty the interest upon money legitimately invested in railroad construction, investors would readily furnish all that might be desired, and railroads could and would be built without watered stock But the state very properly refuses to assume any risk and leaves it to be borne entirely by the investor The latter, then, having all the risk naturally demands to have also all the chances of profit if the road turns out a success He discounts the future, and takes watered stock to represent what he hopes will be his earnings That is the only way that communities wanting railroads can induce investors to supply the funds But I record my conviction that the practice of stock-watering should be prohibited, without much hope of ever seeing it done and more on the ground that it is against public policy to make it easy for men to build railroads, or float any enterprises with other people's money, than from the fear of railroads being enabled to practice extortion by the possession of watered stock."

CHAPTER IV.

METHOD OF SUBSCRIBING — PARTIES TO SUBSCRIPTIONS — ACTION TO ENFORCE SUBSCRIPTIONS.

A. METHODS OF SUBSCRIBING.

§ 52. *Generally no formalities necessary.*— The contract of subscription for shares of stock in an incorporated company may be entered into in various ways. Whenever an intent to become a subscriber is manifested, the courts incline, without particular reference to formality, to hold that the contract of subscription subsists It is, as in the case of other contracts, very much a question of intent Formal rules are for the most part disregarded. And in general a contract of subscription may be made in any way in which other contracts may be made [1] Any agreement by which a person shows an intention to become a stockholder is sufficient to

---

[1] Blunt v Walker, 11 Wis, 334, 349 (1860).

bind both him and the corporation[1] When one accepts or assumes the position and duties, and claims the rights and privileges and emoluments, of a stockholder, and the corporation accepts or acquiesces therein, such person is estopped to deny that he is a subscriber, even though there may have been something irregular or defective in the form or manner of his subscription, or there may have been no formal subscription at all[2]

Merely accepting and holding a certificate of stock is sufficient to constitute one a stockholder[3]

There have been various *dicta* to the effect that a subscription cannot be entered into by parol,[4] but the later and better opinion is that such a subscription is valid and binding

[1] Fry z Lexington, etc, R. R. Co, 2 Metc (Ky), 314 (1859) Wellersburg, etc, Co. v Young, 12 Md, 476 (1858), Gill v Kentucky, etc, Co, 7 Bush, 635 (1870), Oler v Baltimore, etc, R R. Co, 41 Md, 583 (1874); Schaeffer v Missouri, etc, Co., 46 Mo, 248 (1870)

[2] Sanger v Upton, 91 U S, 56 (1875), Upton v Tribilcock, 91 id 45 (1875), Wheeler v. Millar, 90 N Y. 353 (1882), Hamilton, etc, Co v Rice, 7 Barb, 159 (1849), Dorris z French, 4 Hun, 293 (1875) Boston, etc R R Co v Wellington, 113 Mass. 79 (1873), *Ex parte* Besley, 2 Mac. & G, 176 (1850), Clark v Farrington, 11 Wis, 306 (1860), Jewell v Rock River, etc, Co, 101 Ill, 57 (1881), Haynes v Brown. 36 N H, 545 (1858), Chaffin v. Cummings, 37 Me, 76 (1853), Chester, etc., Co. v Dewey, 16 Mass, 94 (1819), Griswold v Seligman, 72 Mo, 110 (1880), Boggs v Olcott, 40 Ill., 303 (1866), Musgrave v Morrison, 54 Md., 161 (1880), Phoenix, etc, Co v Badger, 67 N Y, 294 (1876), S. C, 6 Hun, 293 (1875), Palmer v. Lawrence, 3 Sandf, 161 (1849), Phila., etc, R R. Co. v Cowell, 28 Penn St., 329 (1857), Cheltenham, etc, R'y Co. v. Daniel, 2 Q. B, 281, West Cornwall v Moffatt, 15 Q B., 521 (1850). And see the dissenting opinion of Lord St Leonards in Spackman v Evans, L. R., 3 H of L Cas., 171, 197 (1868); Harrison v Heathorn, 6 Man & G, 81 (1843), Ness v Angas, 3 Exch, 805 (1849), Ness v. Armstrong, 4 id, 21 (1849), Moss v. Steam

Gondola Co, 17 C B, 180 (1855), Bailey v Universal Provident Life Association, 1 C. B (N S.), 557 (1857).

"Underwriting means an agreement before the shares are brought before the public, that in the event of the public not taking the whole or the number mentioned in the agreement, the underwriter will apply for the allotment of and take the shares which the public do not take' The underwriter is liable on the stock Re Licensed, etc, Assoc, 60 L. T Rep., 684 (1889).

[3] Upton v Tribilcock, 91 U S., 45 (1875), McLaughlin z Detroit, etc, R. R. Co, 8 Mich, 100 (1860), Stutz z Haldeman, 41 Fed Rep., 531 (1890). See also, McHose v Wheeler, 45 Pa St 32 (1863), Clark v. Continental, etc, Co 57 Ind, 135 Person taking stock from a corporation on its original issue is liable without subscription Shickle v Watts, 7 S W Rep, 274 (Mo, 1888)

[4] Pittsburgh, etc, R. R. Co. v Gazzam, 32 Pa St 340 (1858). In this case an attempt was made to make defendant liable upon his signature to a paper by which the signers agreed to subscribe for stock in a railroad company, but the signatures were shown to have been copies and not originals. Vreeland v N J Stone Co, 29 N J Eq, 188. The decision was on the question of fraud in inducing defendant to take the stock. Thames Tunnel, etc, v Sheldon, 6 Barn & C, 341, holding that one who had subscribed a preliminary paper and had

It has been held that, where a director is required to be a stockholder, the act of serving as a director is an implied subscription for stock to the amount required in order to be a director [1]   But a contrary rule now exists [2]

A subscription in a small pocket memorandum book has been

paid the sum required in advance, but who had not signed the contract referred to in an act of parliament. was not a subscriber within the meaning of that act.

Fanning v Insurance Co, 37 Ohio St., 339 (1881), a suit upon a note secured by a mortgage claimed to have been given in payment for stock   The proof showed that defendant verbally agreed with a canvasser to take the stock, but did not sign any subscription book or other contract, and never received certificates of stock   Held, that there was no subscription and no sufficient consideration for t ie note.

Galveston Hotel v Bolton, 46 Tex, 633 (1877)   In this case defendant had signed an informal paper as a subscription for stock, and had offered excuses for not paying the first call, asking for time, etc   The informal paper was lost, and defendant's name did not appear on the company's books in any capacity. After the organization of the company he acknowledged to its secretary his obligation to pay the call   Held, that he was not a stockholder liable to calls

In Iowa it is denied that parol subscriptions are void   Hence, where a person present at a corporate meeting directed the secretary to subscribe certain stock, and the secretary did so on a loose sheet of paper, the court held the subscriber bound, also that the corporate records reciting the facts were competent to show acceptance, though recorded subsequently   Colfax Hotel Co v Lyon, 29 N W Rep, 780 (Iowa, 1886) A verbal subscription suffices   The statute of frauds does not apply   Bullock v Falmouth, etc, Co, 3 S. W Rep, 129 (Ky, 1887)   Where a person orally tells a director that he will subscribe a speci-

fied amount of stock, and gives a check in part payment he is liable as a stockholder   Cookney's Case, 3 De G & J, 170 (1858).   And see, also, various cases in the notes herein, involving somewhat similar facts.

[1] See Harwood's Case, L. R., 13 Eq, 30 (1871); Stephenson's Case, 45 L. J. (Ch), 488, In re British & American Telegraph Co, L R., 14 Eq, 316 (1872), In re Empire Assurance Co., L R., 6 Chan, 469 (1871)

Where one accepts the office of director without owning the required number of shares of stock and is in consequence under obligation to qualify himself by taking stock, he is not obliged to t ke the stock from the company, but may purchase or procure the shares as he is able in the open market or at private sale   Brown's Case, L R, 9 Chan, 102 (1873), Karuth's Case, L R, 20 Eq 506

[2] Onslow's Case, 55 L T Rep, 612 (1881), and cases cited   And see summary in Healey's Company Law and Practice, 135, 139

The common-law rule that a director is not liable to the amount of qualification shares which he is required by statute to have, but which he does not have, is not applicable to directors in national banks   Finn v. Brown, 142 U. S, 56 (1891)

Hawley's Case, L. R. 6 Ch. D, 705 (1877), holds that a director who was not qualified did not by acting render himself liable to creditors to the amount of qualification stock.   The court, in a dictum, said   "He never was a director, and he never will be a director, as far as that election is concerned," although of course his acts as director may bind the company as to third persons.   See,

held sufficient to bind the subscriber[1] So, a subscription on a single sheet of paper may be binding,[2] even though the charter provides for the opening of books.[3] A signature to the certificate required by statute to be filed in order to obtain the charter of incorporation, with the number of shares placed opposite to the signature, is a sufficient subscription to bind both the corporation and the subscriber[4]

§ 53. *Informalities, irregularities and mistakes in subscriptions.* But a subscription to an incomplete copy of the articles of association will not bind the subscriber,[5] and again, a subscription paper in which the names of directors were left blank has been held not enforceable against a subscriber after the blank has been filled without his consent or concurrence.[6] Equity will not, how-

also, *Ex parte* Stock, 33 L J (Ch), 731 (1864).

Resignation releases the liability. *In re* Self-Acting, etc, Co., 34 L T Rep, 676; Marquis of Abercorns Case, 4 De G, F & J, 78 (1862), *Ex parte* Jobling, 58 L T. Rep, 823 (1888) See, also, ch 37.

"Can a director part with his qualification shares?" See on this subject 8 Ry. & Corp L J

[1] Buffalo, etc, R. R. Co v Gifford, 87 N. Y., 294 (1882), Brownlee v Ohio, etc, R. R. Co., 18 Ind, 69 (1862) *Contra.* McClelland v Whiteley, 11 Biss, 444 (1883); S C. 15 Fed Rep, 322 The full christian name need not be subscribed. State v Beck, 81 Ind, 501 (1882)

[2] Iowa, etc, R. R. Co v. Perkins, 28 Iowa, 281 (1869), Hamilton, etc, v Rice, 7 Barb, 157 (1849) *Cf.* Bucher v. Dillsburg, etc., R. R. Co, 76 Penn St, 306 (1874), Hawley v Upton, 102 U S, 314 (1880)

[3] Mexican Gulf, etc, R R. Co. v. Viavant, 6 Rob (La), 305 (1843); Ashtabula, etc., R. R. Co v Smith, 15 Ohio St., 328 (1864).

[4] Phœnix, etc, Co v Badger, 67 N Y, 294 (1876), S C, 6 Hun, 295, Nulton v Clayton, 54 Iowa, 425 (1880), Herries v Wesley, 13 Hun, 492 (1878)

Where the statute provides that the persons signing the articles of incorporation shall set opposite their names the amount of their subscription, a subscriber who complies therewith but does not acknowledge the articles as required by the statute is not bound by his subscription so far at least as the articles are concerned Coppage v Hutton, 24 N E. Rep, 112 (Ind, 1890)

[5] Dutchess, etc, R R Co. v Mabbett, 58 N Y, 397 (1874).

[6] Dutchess, etc, R. R. Co. v Mabbett, 58 N Y, 397 (1874), the court saying "A signature to an incomplete paper, wanting in any substantial particular, when no delegation of authority is conferred to supply the defect, does not bind the signer without further assent on his part to the completion of the instrument" To same effect, Consol's Ins Co. v Newall, 3 Foster & F, 130 (1862), where the number of shares was left in blank. See, also, Eakright v. Logansport, etc., 13 Ind, 404 (1859) In this case the charter required that directors should be named in the articles of association The adoption of the articles at the time of electing directors was held to be a substantial compliance with the charter, the requirement being considered as only directory

But where an actual subscription is made, with a view of influencing other subscriptions, but the number of shares to be taken is left blank, so that the subscription itself might be subsequently withdrawn, it was held that

ever, in the absence of fraud, relieve a subscriber merely upon the ground that he by mistake subscribed for more stock than he intended, in a case where he suffered the corporation to act upon the faith of his subscription.[1] But if one signs an agreement to subscribe, on a subscription paper, entirely misunderstanding the nature of the contract he is entering into, his subscription must, on general principles, be treated as null and void for want of mutual consent Cases of this nature may arise without involving the question of fraud [2]

If the business of the incorporation is illegal, the subscription, of course, cannot be enforced [3]

Many cases are given in the notes which will throw some light on the various principles of law as applicable to the facts in actions to collect subscriptions.[4]

the corporate agents might fill up the blank, and thereby bind the subscriber. Jewell v Rock River, etc., Co., 101 Ill, 57 (1881)

The case of Clark v Continental, etc, Co, 57 Ind, 135 (1877), held that an agreement to pay in instalments a certain sum to a contractor as the work progressed, in consideration of stocks to be delivered by the corporation, after full payment has been made in this way, was not a subscription to capital stock, and that the maker of such an agreement was not a subscriber

[1] Diman v Providence, etc, R. R. Co., 5 R. I, 130 (1858)

[2] Jackson v Hayner, 12 Johns, 469 (1815), Thoroughgood's Case, 2 Rep, 9, Foster v Mackinnon L R., 4 C P., 704 (1869), Rockford, etc, R. R. Co v. Schunick, 65 Ill, 223 (1872) — not stock cases, but sustaining the general principle

Reed v Richmond, etc., 50 Ind, 342 (1875) In this case the statute authorizing the organization of street railway companies required that the articles of association should, among other things, state the number of directors and their names Neither of these requirements was observed, and in an action to recover a subscription the court held the subscription void, saying. "If one of these requirements can be dispensed

with, or held to be directory merely, we do not see where we are to stop The case of Eakright v The Logansport, etc, R. R. Co., supra, went as far in this direction as we are willing to go "

[3] See ch XIII.

Notes given in the purchase of stock in a corporation whose sole business is to carry on an infringing telephone business are without consideration and void Clemshire v Boone, etc, Bank, 14 S W. Rep, 901 (Ark, 1890).

[4] Boggs v Olcott, 40 Ill, 303 (1866), holding that the payment of calls by one whose name appears to a subscription to the stock of a corporation is an admission that his signature and subscription were authorized and binding upon him Musgrave v Morrison, 54 Md, 161 (1880), to same effect. A promise to subscribe for a certain amount of stock, for the purpose of inducing the company to adopt a certain route, is enforceable, though no formal subscription ever was made Rhey v Evensburg, etc., Co. 27 Pa St, 261 (1856), Hawley v. Upton, 102 U S., 314 (1880). Where the paper issued was a bond in consideration of shares received, but which were in fact never issued, the signer was held to be a stockholder Cayuga, etc, v Kyle, 64 N Y, 185 (1876) Where the articles of association were defective in not distinctly stating the termini of

§ 54 *Various defenses to subscriptions* — There are various defenses to the validity and enforceability of a subscription which have been treated of elsewhere Thus, a subscriber to the capital stock of an incorporated company is, in general, bound to know

the road nor the counties through which it passed, it being held that such defect could not avail the defendant in an action for a balance of an unpaid subscription, the person agreeing to place stock is not liable as stockholder Gorrissen's Case, L. R., 8 Ch, 507 (1873), Boston, etc, *v* Wellington, 113 Mass, 79 (1873), in which the railroad was not divided into sections as contemplated by the subscription paper, the change, however, being a merely formal irregularity In an old case in Massachusetts it was held that a statement, made at a public meeting of the corporation, by one of the stockholders, that he would spend half his estate, or enough of it to make the enterprise undertaken by the corporation a success, did not render him liable for a failure to do so. Andover, etc, Co *v.* Hay, 7 Mass., 102 (1810).

The validity of a subscription depends upon the law of the state creating the corporation, unless payment is to be made elsewhere Penobscot, etc, Co. *v* Bartlett, 73 Mass, 244 (1858)

Burlington, etc., *v* Palmer, 42 Iowa, 222, was an action upon a subscription note to a railroad, which, by agreement, was not to be delivered until a right of way had been secured, when a contract should be executed by the railroad to construct an extension upon certain conditions *Held*, that the fact that the contract last referred to did not contain one of the conditions, which had, however, been complied with, did not constitute a defense to the action

Lane *v* Brainerd, 30 Conn, 565 (1862), where one who had subscribed in an irregular way, but had acted as a stockholder and accepted the office of director, was held to have waived all objection to the form of his subscription To same effect, Danbury & Nor-

walk Railroad Co *v* Wilson, 22 Conn, 435 (1853)

Where the name of an individual appears upon the stock book of a corporation as a stockholder, the presumption is that he is regularly and lawfully the holder and owner of the stock, and, in the absence of evidence that the stock has come to him by transfer, that he was regularly a subscriber Turnbull *v* Payson, 95 U. S, 148 (1877), Pittsburgh, etc, R. R Co *v* Applegate, 21 W Va, 172 (1882), McHose *v* Wheeler, 45 Pa St, 32 (1863), and many cases in § 55 *infra*

The fact that a subscription paper does not correctly designate the *terminus* of a railroad already built is no defense to a subscriber Boston, etc, R R. Co. *v* Wellington, *supra* The legislature cannot make a person a subscriber in opposition to his will Richmond, etc, Co *v* Clarke, 61 Me, 351 (1873)

One who never subscribes in writing for stock, nor assumes the position or rights of a stockholder, but gives a bond to repay the subscription price, which is loaned to him, is not liable on the bond Butler University *v* Sconover, 16 N E Rep, 642 (1888)

It is a question of fact and of contract whether a party loaned money to the company or was a subscriber to the stock McComb *v* Barcelona, etc, Assoc, 134 N Y. 598 (1892).

Where the corporation contracts with the subscriber to give him indefinite time in which to pay for his stock the subscription is void McComb *v* Credit Mobilier, etc, Co, 13 Phila, 468 (1879), Van Allen *v* Illinois etc, R. R. Co, 7 Bosw, 515 (1861) It is otherwise when only a reasonable credit is given Mitchell *v* Beckman, 64 Cal, 117

The fact that the subscriptions to various subscription lists of the same

the legal effect of his subscription; and false and even fraudulent representations made to him at the time of taking his subscription, as to the legal effect of his contract of subscription, are not suf-

character are cut off from the headings and pasted under one heading does not release the subscribers It is not a mutilation. Sodus Bay, etc., R. R. Co. v. Hamlin, 24 Hun, 390 (1881).

Charlotte, etc , v Blakely, 3 Strobh , 245 (1848) In this case one who subscribed a paper agreeing to take certain railroad stock " provided the road comes to Columbia," but did not sign the subscription books when opened, was held not to be a stockholder

Erie, etc , R. R. Co. v. Owen, 32 Barb , 616 (1860) In this case it is said that there are two modes in which a person, under the general railroad act of the state of New York, may become a stockholder in a railroad corporation, viz by subscribing the articles of association, and becoming a member of the corporation as the act provides (§§ 1 and 2), or by subscribing to the capital stock, in the book opened by the directors, after the corporation is in existence, and that no one who has only signed the articles of association, before the corporation came into being, is a corporator or member of the corporation, unless the articles so signed by him have been duly filed in the office of the secretary of state, as required by the statute. It is doubtful whether this can be considered good law. This case is distinguished in Buffalo, etc., R. R. Co. v Clark, 22 Hun, 359, 362, and Sodus, etc R. R. Co v Hamlin, 24 Hun, 390, 394.

Although the statute provides for subscription books, yet a subscription on a subscription paper will be valid People v Stockton, etc , R. R. Co., 45 Cal , 306 (1873), Ashtabula, etc , R. R. Co. v Smith, 15 Ohio St., 328 (1864), Brownlee v Ohio, etc., R. R. Co, 18 Ind , 68 (1862) Buffalo, etc., R. R. Co v Gifford, 87 N Y, 294 (1882); Hamilton, etc., Co v Rice, 7 Barb., 157 (1849); Stuart v Valley R. R.

Co, 32 Gratt., 146 (1879). Especially where the loose sheets are subsequently bound up into a volume and make part of the records of the corporation. Woodruff v. McDonald, 33 Ark., 97 (1878).

Ex parte Besley, 2 Mac. & G , 176, in which the defendant was liable to be a subscriber and liable to creditors of a railway although he had not signed any subscription paper or book, but had attended meetings of the provisional committee as a member thereof, and had paid small assessments ordered by it

Carlisle v Saginaw, etc , 27 Mich , 315 (1873) Where the law required subscriptions to be made "in the manner to be provided by its by-laws," a subscription made before such by-laws were adopted was declared to be void.

New Brunswick, etc , v Muggeridge, 4 Hurl. & N , 160 (1859). Defendant had agreed in writing to accept shares he desired to subscribe for, and had paid the sum required in advance, but he did not sign the articles of association subsequently sent to him for his signature. In an action for calls he was held not to be a shareholder although his name had been placed as such upon the company's register The decision rested upon a clause in the Joint-Stock Companies Act, 1856, to the effect that no person shall be deemed to have accepted any share unless his acceptance be in writing.

Tilsonburg, etc , Co. v. Goodrich, 8 Ontario Rep , 565 (1885), which was an action for calls on shares "The defendant" (although one of the projectors and original subscribers) "was not a party to the petition, and he is not by the terms of the [general] statute a member of the company, and he has done nothing since the patent, by attending meetings or otherwise, which can have relation to his agreement to

ficient to release him.[1] Parol conditions or agreements in reference to subscriptions which are absolute on their face are generally not sustained.[2] The right of a stockholder to withdraw from his subscription is also discussed elsewhere in this volume.[3] And many other defenses which have been raised to defeat actions for the collection of subscriptions are considered elsewhere.[4]

§ 55. *Proof of subscription.*—It is presumptive evidence that one is a subscriber or stockholder when his name appears on the books of the company in either of these capacities.[5] And so also it is said that the commissioners' books are *prima facie* evidence of the subscriptions found in them,[6] and likewise as to the original subscription paper.[7] And again, entries in the proper books by

take stock." The court with regret held that he was not a stockholder.

As to enforceability of subscriptions, not for stock, but as a gift to enterprises, see Smith *v* Sowles, 10 Atl Rep 536 (Vt., 1887), McCabe *v* O Connor, 28 N W Rep 573 (Iowa, 1886), Broadbent *v* Johnson, 13 Pac Rep. 83 (Idaho, 1882), where subscription was to a railroad; Gaus *v* Reimensnyder, 2 Atl Rep, 425 (Pa), note, Grand Lodge *v* Farnham, 11 Pac Rep, 592 (Cal, 1886); Roberts *v* Cobb, 9 N E Rep., 500 (N Y), note (1886), Utica etc, R R Co *v* Brinkerhoff, 21 Wend, 139 (1839); Watkins *v* Evans, 63 Mass, 537 (1852). See, also, 117 id, 456 (1875), Presbyterian Church *v.* Cooper, 20 N E. Rep, 352 (N Y, 1889), Cottage, etc, Church *v.* Kendall, 121 Mass, 529, Livingston *v* Rogers, 1 Caines, 585 (1804), Trustees, etc, *v* Stewart, 1 N Y., 581 (1848), Amherst Academy *v* Cowls, 23 Mass, 427 (1828).

A subscriber or donator of money to a factory cannot prevent its moving away if it is a losing enterprise Ayres *v* Dutton, 49 N. W. Rep., 897 (Mich, 1891).

[1] See § 196, *infra*

[2] See ch. IX A defendant, it is said, however, who is sued on a subscription absolute, may show that he agreed orally to subscribe conditionally, and placed his name on blank paper, and that the secretary of the corporation subsequently, without his knowledge, subscribed the name unconditionally to a subscription paper See § 137, *infra.* And it is held that when a corporation invites and accepts subscriptions as a loan, to be repaid in full and the subscription canceled it cannot repudiate such a contract and treat the subscription so induced as absolute. See § 247, n, *infra*

[3] See §§ 167–170, *infra*

[4] See ch X.

[5] Hoagland *v* Bell, 36 Barb, 57 (1861), Turnbull *v* Payson, 95 U S 418 (1877), Hamilton, etc, Co *v* Rice, 7 Barb, 157; Pittsburg, etc, R R Co *v* Applegate, 21 West Va, 172 (1882); Taylor *v* Hughes, 2 Jones & Lat (Irish Chan), 24, 55 (1844); McHose *v* Wheeler, 45 Penn St, 32 (1863) *Cf* Coffin *v* Collins, 17 Me., 440 (1840); Whitman *v* Proprietors, etc, 24 id, 236 (1844), Rockville, etc, Co *v* Van Ness, 2 Cranch, C C, 449 (1824) Mudgett *v* Horrell, 33 Cal., 25 (1867) Or when a certificate has been issued to him, which he produces. Boardman *v* Lake Shore, etc, R R Co, 84 N Y., 157 (1881); Agricultural Bank *v* Burr, 24 Me., 256; Vanderwirken *v* Glenn, 6 S E Rep., 806 (Va., 1888); Lewis, Adm'r, *v* Glenn, 6 S E Rep., 866 (Va, 1888)

[6] Rockville, etc, Co *v.* Van Ness, 2 Cranch, C C, 449 (1824); Wood *v.* Coosa, etc, R R Co., 32 Ga 273 (1861)

[7] Partridge *v,* Badger, 25 Barb., 146 (1857).

commissioners duly appointed to take subscriptions are evidence against the subscribers.[1] So corporate books to which a subscription has been transferred by authority of the subscriber are evidence of the subscription,[2] and also the books that contain the original subscriptions[3]

Entries on the stock ledger and corporate books are competent evidence of an issue of stock to a person.[4] But the presumption that one is a stockholder, arising from the fact of his name being found in the stock and transfer book, may be met by proof to the contrary[5] When, however, the books of the corporation have been destroyed or lost, a certified copy of the recorded list of the

[1] Wood v Coosa, etc, R. R. Co, 32 Ga., 273 (1861)

[2] Iowa etc R R Co v. Perkins. 28 Iowa, 281 (1869), Hawley v Upton. 102 U S., 314 (1880) Cf Whitman v Proprietors, etc, 24 Me 236 (1844)

[3] Marlborough, etc, R R Co v Arnold, 9 Gray, 159 (1858) Cf Mudgett v Horrell, 33 Cal, 25 (1867).

The subscription books are *prima facie* evidence of stockholdership Semple v Glenn, 9 S. Rep, 265 (Ala, 1891)

In enforcing a subscription, stockholdership is proven by showing the name on the subscription list and proving payment of several assessments Glenn v McAllister's Ex'rs, 46 Fed Rep., 883 (1891).

The stock book and a subscription list are sufficient to prove stockholdership in the absence of rebuttal testimony Glenn v Liggett. 47 Fed Rep, 472 (1891) But entries in the cash book are not admissible, nor the report of the treasurer of the corporation Id.

Stockholdership may be proved by admissions of the stockholder, and the testimony of the treasurer, and by the record book purporting to contain copies of the original minutes The stock book could not be found Congdon v. Winsor, 21 Atl Rep, 540 (R. I., 1891).

[4] Chapman v Porter, 69 N Y, 276 (1877)

[5] Mudgett v. Horrell, 33 Cal, 25 (1867) Cf. Brewers', etc., Ins Co. v. Burger, 10 Hun, 56 (1877).

The stock books are sufficient to prove stockholdership, if the name contained therein is the same as defendant's and was entered as his name Liggett v Glenn, 51 Fed Rep, 381 (1892)

The corporate books are not admissible to prove stockholdership Howard v Glenn, 11 S E Rep, 610 (Ga, 1890).

The books of the corporation are *prima facie* evidence of stockholdership Lehman v Glenn, 6 S Rep., 44 (Ala, 1889), Lehman v Semple, 6 S Rep, 44 (Ala, 1889)

A mistake in entering the name of the subscriber on the corporate books may be fatal to proving stockholdership by the books Where the subscription is denied, the best evidence is the subscription itself and until it is accounted for, the stock ledger is inadmissible in evidence If the action is on the written subscription, recovery can be on that alone Taussig v Glenn, 51 Fed. Rep., 409 (1892).

Where there is no law authorizing a paper containing the subscriptions to the capital stock of a corporation to be filed in the office of the secretary of state, a copy thereof, certified under the seal of the secretary of state, is not admissible as evidence, in a suit by the corporation, to charge the defendant as stockholder. Troy, etc., R R Co. v Kurr, 17 Barb., 581, 600 (1854), Tilsonburg, etc, Co v. Goodrich, 8 Ontario (Q B Div) 565 (1885). Cf. Bouchaud v Dias, 3 Denio, 238 (1846), Dick v. Balch, 8 Peters, 30 (1834).

names of shareholders, required by statute to be filed in the office of the register of deeds, is *prima facie* evidence as to the fact of subscription and ownership of the shares [1] So it is said that the stock book of a corporation is not admissible in evidence in an action by a creditor of the corporation against one alleged to be a stockholder for the purpose of proving that he is such stockholder [2] In order to let in secondary evidence of a subscription, there must be proof of an original subscription and of the loss of the book or paper, or the absence of the original paper satisfactorily accounted for.[3] But parol evidence is admissible to show that a certificate has been issued to one by a wrong Christian name [4] The mere erasure of a subscription will not of itself prevent a recovery upon it [5] Various other principles of evidence relative to proving one to be a subscriber are given in the notes below [6]

[1] Cleveland v Burnham, 55 Wis, 598 (1885) A corporation may, by suit, compel its agents to deliver up subscription lists, or in lieu thereof be liable themselves on the subscriptions People's etc., Co v Babinger, 4 S. Rep, 82 (La, 1888).

[2] Mudgett v Horrell, 33 Cal, 25 (1867)

[3] Pittsburgh, etc, R R Co v Gazzam, 32 Penn St, 340 (1858), Graff v Pittsburgh etc, R R Co., 31 id, 489 (1858), Hays v Pittsburgh, etc, R R Co, 38 Penn St, 81 (1860)

[4] Cleveland v Burnham, 55 Wis, 598

[5] Johnson v Wabash, etc, Co, 16 Ind, 399 (1861) And where one took a book for subscriptions from an agent of the corporation, and subscribed himself and persuaded others to subscribe, and kept the book some months but finally, because of a difference with the agent about the payment for his services, cut his name out of the book and returned it to the company, it was held, in an action by the company for the amount of his subscription, that he was bound thereon just as though he had left his name on the list of subscribers Greer v Chartiers R R Co 96 Penn St, 391 (1880), Railroad Co. v White, 10 S C., 155 (1878).

It has been held, however, in New York, that where the statutory certificate required by law to be filed in order to obtain incorporation remains in the hands of a subscriber, or either of them, a subscriber may erase or modify his subscription as he sees fit, even though he had previously induced others to subscribe Butt v Farrar, 24 Barb, 518 (1857)

[6] See cases in notes to the preceding sections of this chapter, also the following cases

Galveston Hotel Co v Bolton, 46 Tex, 633 (1877), where the original subscription paper was lost and the name of the defendant did not appear on the books of the company, and he had not paid the stipulated advance, nor participated in any action of the company, but had acknowledged verbally to the secretary his obligation to pay *Held*, that the evidence was not sufficient to meet the proof that he was a legal subscriber

Pittsburgh, etc, v Applegate, 21 W Va, 172 (1882) where, in the absence of the subscription list, the company's stock book was held to be admissible in evidence as tending to show that defendants were stockholders Citing cases.

Iowa, etc, v Perkins, 28 Iowa, 281 (1869) Defendant attended a township meeting called to obtain subscriptions to a railroad company The names of subscribers were written by the *parties soliciting* upon a slip of paper, being authorized to do so by the subscribers The meeting then gave authority to an offi-

§ 56   *The English rule* — In England the contract of subscription for shares is entered into in a somewhat more technical or formal manner   An application, in the first instance, is made in writing for specified number of shares, which application is held to be a mere offer, open for acceptance by the corporation for only a limited time [1]   If the application be accepted, the corporation formally allots to the applicant the desired number of shares, and gives him a notice of the allotment.   The notice is of the essence of the contract.   An allotment without notice is not sufficient to bind the applicant as a contributory or a shareholder [2]   If the notice of allotment is sent by mail, the allottee becomes bound from the time of posting the letter, whether he received it or not [3]   And

cer of the company to transcribe the subscriptions into the company's book *Held*, that the book thus became the original contract of subscription, and was admissible in evidence without proof of loss of the ship

Haynes v Brown, 36 N H 545 (1859) The absence of records being sufficiently accounted for to make parol evidence admissible, defendant's attendance at meetings of the corporation and his acting as president were accounted competent proof of his being a stockholder

Corporate stock book, containing list of stockholders number of shares owned by each, amount paid and amount due, and containing defendant s name among others, is sufficient evidence of balance due on unpaid subscription   Glenn v Orr, 2 S E Rep, 538 (N C, 1887)

A contract between the defendant, who is sued as a stockholder, and his attorney relative to defending the action is inadmissible to prove stockholdership. Liggett t Glenn, 51 Fed. Rep., 381 (1892), Dorsheimer v Glenn, id, 404

[1] Ramsgate, etc, Co t Montefiore, L R, 1 Exch, 109 (1866), *In re* Bowron, · L. R., 3 Eq, 428 (1868), and the cases generally cited, *infra*, in this section

A subscriber may withdraw before allotment by a legally convened meeting of the directors   *Re* Portuguese, etc., Mines, 62 L. T. Rep., 88 (1889).   But not where the allotment is made irregularly before, but regularly confirmed after, the withdrawal.   Id., 179

[2] Hebbs' Case, L. R., 4 Eq. 9 (1867); Gunn's Case, L. R., 3 Chan, 40 (1867), *In re* Peruvian R v Co, L. R., 4 Chan, 322 (1869), Pellatt's Case, L. R., 2 Chan, 527 (1867)   Ward s Case, L. R., 10 Eq, 659 (1870), Harris Case, L. R., 7 Chan, 587 (1872), Household, etc, Co v Grant, L R., 4 Exch Div, 216 (1879)   The mere act of signing the memorandum of association does not make one a stockholder   Mackley's Case, L R, 1 Ch Div, 247 (1875)   A mere allotment without an entry of the name on the stock registry does not render the person liable as a stockholder.   Nicoll's Case, L. R., 29 Ch Div., 421 (1883)   Nor is one a stockholder unless he signs the deed of settlement.   Irish Peat Co. v Phillips, 1 Best & S., 598 (1861)   Nor will a certificate be issued till then Wilkinson v Anglo, etc, G M Co., 18 Q B., 728 (1852)

Although an allotment of stock may be illegal by reason of notice not having been given of a directors' meeting, yet the allotment may be confirmed by a subsequent legally called meeting   *Re* Portuguese etc, Mines, Limited, 63 L T Rep., 423 (1890)

[3] Harris' Case, L R, 7 Chan, 587 (1872), Household, etc, Co v Grant, L R, 4 Exch Div, 216 (1879), Townsend's Case L R 13 Eq, 148, Hebbs' Case, L R, 4 Eq, 9 (1867)   *Contra*, British, etc, Telegraph Co v. Colson, L. R, 6 Exch., 108 (1871); *In re* Constantinople, etc, Co., 19 W. R., 219 (1870).

if the allottee knew of the fact of the allotment, and especially if he acted or suffered others to act upon the assumption that he was a shareholder, a formal notification may be unnecessary to bind him [1] The application being in the nature of an offer or a proposition may be withdrawn at any time before it has been regularly accepted, and it must be accepted within a reasonable time, or the party making it cannot be held bound,[2] and although the application should be in writing, the withdrawal of it may be oral [3] It seems to be well settled in England, that, in order to make the contract to take up shares completely binding, there must be the application in writing, the allotment of the shares to the applicant, and a communication to him of notice of the allotment [4]

§ 57. *Subscriptions taken by commissioners.* — Although the statute provides for subscription, either by an original subscription to the articles of association, or, after the incorporation, by a subscription in books to be opened by commissioners, nevertheless it has been held that a subscription in some other way is binding.[5] The

[1] Levita's Case, L. R., 3 Chan. 36 (1867); *In re* Peruvian R'y Co, L R , 4 Chan., 322 (1869), Richards *v* Home, etc., Assoc, L. R., 6 C P, 591 (1871); Pellatt's Case, L. R., 2 Chan, 527 (1867).

[2] Ward's Case, L. R., 10 Eq, 659 (1870), Best's Case, 2 De G , J & S, 650 (1865), Ramsgate, etc , Co *v* Montefiore, L R , 1 Exch, 109 (1866); Chapman's Case, L. R, 2 Eq, 567 (1866), Ritso's Case, L. R., 4 Chan. Div., 774 (1877), Wilson's Case, 20 L T (N S), 962 (1869)

[3] Wilson's Case, 20 L. T. (N S), 962 (1869).

[4] Adams' Case, L R , 13 Eq, 474, Hebbs' Case, L R , 4 Eq, 9 (1867), Pellatt's Case, L. R., 2 Chan . 527 (1867); Roger's Case, L R , 3 Chan , 637 (1868); Tucker's Case, 20 W. R., 89 (1871) *Cf.* Bloxam's Case, 33 Beav , 529, distinguished in Pellatt's Case, *supra*. But under the twenty-third section of the Companies Act of 1862, the decisions are uniform that whenever one signs the memorandum of association he becomes a share owner, and must be put on the list of contributories, although no shares may have been allotted to him. *In re* London etc., Co, L. R., 5 Chan. Div , 525 (1877), Evan's Case, L. R., 2 Chan ,

427 (1867), Sidney's Case, L R , 13 Eq , 228 (1871), Levick's Case, 40 L J (Chan), 180 (1870); Hall's Case, L R. 5 Chan , 707 (1870), distinguishing Snell's Case, L. R, 5 Chan , 22 (1869) An allotment to a person who has not applied for shares is not binding. *Re* The Northern, etc , Co , Limited, 63 L T Rep., 369 (1890)

[5] Buffalo, etc , R. R Co *v* Gifford, 87 N Y, 294 (1882), Stuart *v* Valley R R Co, 32 Gratt, 146 (1879) *Contra,* Troy etc , R R Co. *v.* Tibbits, 18 Barb , 297 (1854), Parker *v* Northern, etc , R R Co, 33 Mich., 23 (1875); Unity Insurance Co *v* Cram, 43 N H , 636 (1862), Schultz *v* Schoolcraft, etc , R Co , 9 Mich , 269 (1861) But when the statutes provide for commissioners, it is said they must all be present in order to the valid performance of the judicial duties assigned to them Crocker *v* Crane, 21 Wend , 211 (1839) It is said that in the taking of subscriptions the commissioners act ministerially, but in the distribution or allotment of shares they act judicially , and that a distribution of shares by commissioners not sufficient in number to constitute a legal board is void Crocker *v* Crane, *supra*

It has been held that the commission-

commissioners may themselves be subscribers to the stock,[1] but they can have no priority of right to subscribe over others, and no subscriptions can lawfully be taken with closed doors The books must be open, and the public must have an opportunity to subscribe.[2] The commissioners have only such general powers as are necessary to validate the subscriptions to the stock. Their authority and functions cease upon the organization of the corporation.[3]

§ 58. *Subscriptions in excess of the capital stock* — In general, after the full amount of stock provided for in the act of incorporation has been subscribed, any further subscriptions are void.[4] Where, by statute, the commissioners do not properly apportion stock, in cases involving an excess of subscriptions, an aggrieved subscriber may apply to a court of equity for relief.[5]

But, after the organization of the corporation, the duty to appor-

---

ers may limit the amount of stock which any one subscriber may take, and will, in a proper case, be sustained therein on grounds of public policy, although the power so to act is not specifically conferred upon them by the statute Brower *v.* Passenger R R. Co , 3 Phila , 161 (1858). And accordingly fictitious subscriptions for the purpose of evading such a limitation of the amount of stock to be taken by a single subscriber are illegal and void. Perkins *v* Savage, 15 Wend , 412 (1836) Commissioners to take subscriptions may refuse to allow one person to subscribe for half of the stock, and may refuse to accept a subscription from a person as trustee. Thomas *v.* Citizens', etc , R'y, 1 Amer St. R'y Dec , 299 (Pa , 1858)

[1] Walker *v.* Devereaux, 4 Paige, 229 (1833)

[2] Brower *v* Passenger R'y Co., 3 Phila., 161 (1858) When the amount of the subscription is not limited, the commissioners, in the absence of other express provision, may usually decide when enough stock has been subscribed, and their decision is practically conclusive as an exercise of discretion Saugatuck, etc , Co. *v* Westport, 39 Conn , 337, 348 (1872) Their failure to take the statutory oath will not invalidate the subscriptions taken by them, if they are in other essential respects regular Holl-

man *v.* Williamsport, etc., Co , 9 Gill & J , 462 (1838)

[3] James *v* Cincinnati, etc., R. R. Co. 2 Disney (Cin Super. Ct.), 261 (1868); Peninsular, etc , R R. Co *v* Duncan, 28 Mich , 130 (1873). Hardenburgh *v.* Farmers', etc , Bank, 3 N J. Eq , 68 (1834); Walker *v* Devereaux, 4 Paige, 229 (1833), Crocker *v* Crane, 21 Wend , 211 (1839), . Wellersburg, etc , Co *v* Hoffman, 9 Md , 559 (1834); Smith *v* Bangs, 15 Ill , 399 (1854), State *v* Lehre, 7 Rich. Law, 234 (1854)

The corporation may by suit set aside illegal subscriptions — the subscribers not being qualified. Union Bank *v.* McDonough, 5 La., 63 (1833)

[4] Lathrop *v* Kneeland, 46 Barb , 432 (1866), Machley's Case, L. R., 1 Chan Div , 247 (1875).

[5] Walker *v* Devereaux, 4 Paige, 229 (1833); Meads *v* Walker, Hopk. Ch , 587 (1825). *Cf.* Haight *v* Day, 1 John. Ch , 18 (1814)

Where an apportionment is provided for in the event of an excess of subscriptions, it is said that the contract of subscription is not complete until the apportionment is made; that there can be neither stockholders nor corporation prior to the apportionment. Walker *v* Devereaux, 4 Paige, 229 (1833); Crocker *v* Crane, 21 Wend 211 (1839). Burrows *v* Smith, 10 N Y., 550 (1853). *Cf* Buf-

tion the stock, if there has been an oversubscription, belongs to the corporation and not to the commissioners[1]   And, in the absence of statutory authority, the commissioners, even before organization, have no general power, if they receive excessive subscriptions, to reduce proportionally all the subscriptions and apportion the stock It is their only duty to take subscriptions up to the full amount of the prescribed capital, and to refuse anything beyond that[2]   Neither can the corporation, if it has issued the full amount of the stock, recover on subscriptions in excess. The subscriber acquires no title by such a subscription, and corporate creditors can enforce no liability thereon.[3]

§ 59. *Subscriptions and organization where there is a special charter and no commissioners are provided for* — This subject is considered elsewhere[4]

§ 60. *Subscriptions delivered in escrow* — Subscriptions for shares may be made and delivered in escrow to an agent of the corporation who is engaged in taking subscriptions,[5] or to a director of the corporation.[6]   But a delivery in escrow to a commissioner is bad, and a subscription so delivered is absolute[7]   Delivery of a

falo, etc, R R Co v Dudley. 14 N Y, 336, 346 (1856)

Where a resolution was passed by a board of directors, entitling a promoter to have a certain number of shares allotted to him, and the available shares had been disposed of before his bill for specific performance was filed. *held*, he had no ground for coming into equity. Ferguson v Wilson, L. R., 2 Ch. App., 77, 87 (1866).

[1] State v. Lehre, 7 Rich Law, 234 (1854), where an application for *mandamus* to compel commissioners to re-apportion stock agreeably to the charter of a company, and for *quo warranto* against officers claimed to have been illegally elected, was refused, the appellate court holding that the commissioners had no power to re-apportion stock after the subscribers had become a body corporate Smith v Bangs, 15 Ill, 399 (1854). In this case, after the commissioners had closed the subscription books and called a meeting, at which directors were chosen, they re-opened the books to receive further subscriptions. On the application of one of the

directors they were restrained by injunction, the court holding that their powers were at an end

[2] Van Dyke v. Stout, 8 N J Eq, 333 (1850)

[3] Burrows v Smith, 10 N Y., 550 (1853), Oler v Baltimore, etc , R R Co, 41 Md , 583 (1874)   When the corporation has accepted subscriptions in excess of the capital stock, corporate officers cannot buy in shares of the stock at a discount and then re-issue them to provide for the oversubscription, charging the corporation par for the stock bought in, and thereby realizing a profit to themselves individually on the transaction East New York, etc . R R Co. v. Elmore, 5 Hun, 214 (1875)

[4] See ch. XXXVI, *infra.*

[5] Cass v Pittsburgh, etc., R R Co , 80 Penn St., 31 (1875)

[6] Ottawa, etc , R R Co. v Hall, 1 Bradw (Ill), 612 (1878)

[7] Wight v Shelby R R Co, 16 B Mon , 4 (1855) It is the rule in Kentucky that, to become effectual as an escrow, the delivery must be to a third person. Wight v. Shelby R R Co.

subscription in escrow, to become absolute on performance of certain conditions by the corporation, differs from a conditional subscription in this that a subscription in escrow is, strictly speaking, no subscription As in the case of a deed delivered in escrow, no estate passes until the second delivery. So, in the case of a subscription delivered in escrow, there is no subscription until a second delivery, and the depositary can only deliver it up on performance of the condition [1] So, also, a subscriber may show by parol an agreement with an agent of the corporation that his subscription to blank paper should not be a subscription until he had seen and approved the heading of the subscription paper.[2]

§ 61 *Liability of the corporation for refusal to issue a certificate of stock* — The corporation is bound, upon demand, to deliver to a stockholder a certificate of stock representing his interest in the corporation.[3] If it refuses to issue the certificate the stockholder may bring suit in equity to compel its issuance,[4] or he may recover

---

supra. But in Pennsylvania it seems the rule is otherwise Cass *v* Pittsburgh, etc, R R. Co., *supra* And so in Illinois Ottawa, etc, R. R. Co *v* Hall, *supra* Cf Price *v* Pittsburgh, etc., R. R Co, 34 Ill, 13, 36 (1864)

[1] Ottawa, etc, R. R. Co. *v.* Hall, 1 Bradw (Ill), 612 (1878). It is competent to show by parol that a subscription was delivered in escrow The court of appeals of Illinois declares that a contrary rule is not sustained by any respectable authority Ottawa, etc., R. R. Co. *v.* Hall, *supra* Cf Tonic, etc, R. R. Co. *v.* Stein, 21 Ill, 96 (1859).

[2] Bucher *v* Dillsburg, etc., R. R. Co, 76 Penn St., 306 (1874) This, however, amounted to a parol condition — a subject fully treated in chapter IX, *infra*

[3] Fletcher *v* McGill, 10 N E. Rep, 651 (Ind, 1887).

The stockholder is entitled to a certificate of stock Rio Grande, etc, Co *v.* Burns, 17 S W. Rep, 1043 (Tex., 1891).

A statute authorizing the issue of certificates of stock when it is fully paid up does not prevent the issue of such certificates before it is fully paid up Green *v* Abietine, etc., Co, 31 Pac. Rep, 100 (Cal, 1892)

The subscriber for stock is not entitled to a certificate until he has paid for the stock in full Baltimore, etc., Co *v* Hambleton, 26 Atl. Rep., 279 (Md, 1893)

Where a prospective corporate officer issues certificates of stock in the prospective corporation, a person who loans money on such stock as collateral security may hold such officer liable for issuing the stock before the corporation was organized Merchants' Nat. Bank *v* Robison, 30 Pac Rep., 985 (Utah, 1892) The duty of the corporation to issue a certificate is considered also in §§ 192, 197

A subscriber for stock who has paid ten per cent. cannot sue a consolidated company, into which his company has been merged, for a certificate, even though the articles of consolidation provide for the issue of one share of the latter company for every two shares of the old company, unless he has first demanded the certificate and has offered to pay the remaining ninety per cent. or asks for a certificate of stock not paid up. Babcock *v* Schuylkill, etc., R. R, 133 N Y, 420 (1892).

[4] Appeal of Rowley, 9 Atl Rep., 329 (Pa, 1887), Chester Glass Co *v.* Dewey, 16 Mass., 94 (1819), Ferguson *v.* Wilson.

of the corporation in *assumpsit* the value of the shares at the time of the demand [1]

The fact that the corporation has not issued a certificate to a stockholder for thirty years and that he has not insisted on his right as such is no bar to his suit to establish his stockholdership.[2]

In case the full capital stock has been issued, then, of course, specific performance of an agreement to issue more shares cannot be had [3] The liability of a corporation to issue stock to the subscribers thereof does not necessarily devolve upon another corporation which succeeds to its debts, liabilities and franchises [4]

L. R., 2 Ch, 77 (1866) *Cf* Thorp *v* Woodhull, 1 Sand. Ch, 411 (1844)

A corporation cannot be compelled by the subscriber for stock to issue a certificate therefor before it has been fully paid up. the stock being a part of the increased capital stock Baltimore, etc, Co *v.* Hambleton 26 Atl Rep, 279 (Md, 1893)

If in organizing and issuing the stock the amount to be issued for the property is not what the contract calls for, the vendor may compel a specific performance. Bailey *v* Champlain, etc, Co, 46 N W. Rep, 539 (Wis, 1890) See, also § 24.

[1] "A subscriber for shares of stock, in case the contract of subscription was regularly entered into, may, if the corporation refuse to issue him a certificate, have his action in equity for specific performance, or he may recover of the corporation, in *assumpsit*, the value of the shares at the time of the demand " Birmingham Nat Bank *v* Roden, 11 S Rep, 883 (Ala, 1892), quoting the text.

Wyman *v* American Powder Co., 62 Mass., 168 (1851) But to entitle one to recover back money advanced to a corporation for shares, upon the ground of a failure to issue the certificate, the subscriber must, before suit, rescind the contract and demand the money Swazy *v* Choate, etc, Co, 48 N. H, 200 (1868) See, also, 141 U S, 227

[2] Bedford County *v.* Nashville, etc., R. R., 14 Lea (Tenn), 525 (1884); Kobogum *v* Jackson Iron Co., 43 N W. Rep, 602 (Mich 1889).

[3] Finley, etc, Co *v* Kurtz, 34 Mich,

89 (1876) Where a bank contracted to give a person a certain amount of stock if he would do business with it, and he did so, the bank is liable in damages for refusal to deliver the stock Rich *u.* State Nat'l Bank of Lincoln, 7 Neb, 231 For the refusal of the corporation to issue original stock to a subscriber, the measure of damages is the difference between the price contracted for and the market value on the day when the issue ought to have been made Van Allen *v.* Illinois, etc, R R. Co, 7 Bosw, 515 (1861) For another rule as to the measure of damages, and one more in favor of the plaintiff, see Baltimore, etc, R'y Co *v* Sewall, 35 Md, 238 (1871), and see, also, ch XXXV. In Louisiana the universal legatee may pay for, and demand, the certificate of stock subscribed for by his ancestor The executor has no power to cancel the subscription, and the stock cannot be appropriated by a subsequent subscriber, who subscribed for it by consent of the executor State *v* Crescent City, etc, Co, 24 La Ann, 318 (1872). *Cf* Wallace *v* Townsend, 43 Ohio, 537. If a mistake has been made by which the certificates and stock have been issued to the wrong person, a court of equity will remedy it. O'Meara *v* North Am Min Rev, 2 Nev, 112 (1866)

[4] Conant *v* National, etc, Co, 8 Jones & S (N Y Super Ct), 83 (1875)

In England it seems that directors are not individually liable to subscribers for the breach by the corporation of its agreement to issue stock. Ferguson *v.*

§ 62 *Substitution of stockholders before the incorporation —
Alteration of the subscription paper* — There has been some controversy as to the legality of one person being substituted for another as a subscriber before the incorporation and issue of the stock.
If the facts are such that a cancellation of the subscription is legal,
then doubtless the substitution is legal.[1] But where such is not the
case, then it would seem that the substitution is merely a transfer
of the stock, and the transferrer, in that case, should be held liable
to the same extent as in other cases of transfer of stock.[2]

In California it is held that no substitution of stockholders is
legal, but the weight of authority clearly sustains a contrary rule[3]
If the vendor afterwards obtains the certificates and sells them
again to others, he is liable to the first person to whom he sold his
interest,[4] and is liable also to the latter if the corporation is never
formed[5] If the corporation is duly formed, the vendor may compel the vendee to pay for the subscription transferred.[6]

Where articles are materially altered without the consent of all
the subscribers, after their subscription and before the complete
organization of the company, such articles are not binding upon the
non-consenting subscribers[7]

Wilson, L. R., 2 Chan, 77 (1866). But
see, also, Swift v. Jewsbury, L. R., 9
Q B, 301, Betts v De Vitre, L. R., 3
Chau, 429, 441 (1868); Henderson v
Lacon, L R., 5 Eq, 249 (1867), Eagles-
field v Marquis of Londonderry, 25
Week Rep, 190

[1] See §§ 167-170, *infra*, on cancellation See, also, *dictum*, in Ryder v Alton, etc., R R. Co, 13 Ill., 516, 521
(1851) *Cf* Selma, etc, R. R. Co v
Tipton, 5 Ala., 787 (1842), to the effect
that a subscriber cannot withdraw

[2] See ch XV.

[3] Baltimore City R'y Co v Sewell, 35
Md, 238 (1871), Tempist v Kilmer, 3
C. B, 249 (1816), Hunt v Gunn, 13 C.
B (N. S), 226 (1862), Merrimac, etc.,
Co. v Levy, 54 Penn St., 227 (1867).
Contra. Hawkins v Mansfield Gold
Mining Co., 52 Cal, 513 (1877), Mor-
rison v Gold Mountain G M. Co, 52
Cal, 906, Coleman v Spencer, 5 Blackf
(Ind). 197 (1839). See, also, Chater v
San Francisco S F Co, 19 Cal, 219
(1861)

A substitution of stockholders after

organization by canceling some subscriptions and filling in others is illegal
There should be a transfer Cartwright
v. Dickinson, 12 S W Rep, 1030 (Tenn,
1890)

An alteration of a subscription list by
a subscription being changed and another name substituted releases other
subscribers who signed before the alteration Texas Printing, etc, Co v. Smith,
14 S W. Rep, 1074 (Tex., 1889) See,
also, on this subject, § 169 and § 50

[4] Beckitt v Bilbraugh, 8 Hare, 188
(1850).

[5] Kempson v Saunders, 4 Bing, 5
(1826) But the latter is not liable to
take the shares nor to indemnify his
vendor   Jackson v. Cocker. 4 Beav.,
59 (1841)

[6] Mahan v Wood, 44 Cal, 462 (1872).
And may collect a note given in payment

[7] Burrows v Smith, 10 N Y, 550 (1853).
See, also, 16 S E Rep., 877, 17 id, 305.

An alteration of a subscription list by
a subscription being changed and another name substituted releases other

§ 63 *Right to recover back money advanced on shares upon a failure to organize the company* — Where one has advanced money in good faith to the promoters of a company, as a deposit or assessment upon shares subscribed for to be subsequently issued, and the enterprise contemplated by the proposed incorporation is abandoned, or the company for any reason fails to be incorporated, such subscriber may recover back the money so advanced [1] Nor is he obliged to submit to the deduction of any part thereof to be applied to the payment of the expenses incurred by the promoters in attempting the incorporation [2]

B WHO IS COMPETENT TO SUBSCRIBE FOR STOCK.

§ 64 *Corporations generally not.*— Upon general common-law principles any one who is competent to enter into ordinary contracts may make a valid subscription for stock in an incorporated company. A subscription for stock is a contract, and, in general, any one who can contract may subscribe. The corporation itself, however, cannot be a subscriber to its own stock [3] It is conclusively settled that municipal corporations may lawfully sub-

---

subscribers who signed before the alteration Texas Printing, etc , Co v Smith, 14 S W Rep , 1074 (Tex , 1889).

A change in the subscription by several of the subscribers does not release the others Gibbons v. Grinsel, 48 N W Rep , 255 (Wis , 1891) An increase in the capital upon incorporation does not release Id

[1] Nockels v Crosby, 3 Barn & C , 814 (1825); Ward v Lord Londesborough, 12 C. B , 252 (1854), Asphitel v Sercombe, 5 Exch , 147 (1850), Williams v. Salmond, 2 Kay & J , 463 (1856); Chaplin v Clarke, 4 Exch , 403 (1849) Cf. Vallams v Fletcher, 1 Exch , 20 (1847), Grand Trunk, etc., R'y Co. v Brodie, 9 Hare, 823 (1852), Kempson v Saunders, 4 Bing , 5, where a vendee recovered from his vendor money paid for stock in a company which was never organized. And see, also, Williams v Page, 24 Beav , 654 (1857). "A bill in equity lies to recover back money paid on a bubble" Colt v Woollaston, 2 P Wms , 154 (1723); Green v Barrett, 1 Sim , 45 (1826). See, also "the bubble act," 6 Geo I , ch. 18, also § 705, etc., *infra*

Where a subscriber for stock pays for the stock before the company is organized, he may recover back the money if the company is not organized Bradford v Harris, 26 Atl Rep , 186 (Md , 1893).

Where promoters agree to sell stock in a proposed corporation upon a tender of the price by a certain day, such tender need not be made if the company is not organized The proposed purchaser may recover back the consideration. Manistee, etc , Co v Union, etc , Bank, 32 N. E Rep , 449 (Ill , 1892)

[2] Nockels v Crosby, *supra* But see, *contra*, Williams v Salmond, *supra*.

[3] Thus, where a number of individuals attempted to organize a corporation with a capital stock of seventy-two thousand five hundred shares, of the par value of $100 each, and six different persons subscribe for one share each, and one person then subscribes for the corporation as follows "Oregon Central Railroad Company, by G L. Wood, Chairman, seventy thousand shares, seven million dollars,' it was held that this subscription was void, and that the corporation could not be created by

subscribe for the stock of private corporations, when authorized by
statute to do so.[1] It is not equally clear that one private corporation may subscribe for the stock in another such corporation On
the contrary, such subscriptions are *ultra vires* and void unless
clearly within the ordinary objects and business of the subscribing
corporation [2] A railroad corporation cannot subscribe for shares
of stock in another railroad company,[3] nor can a steamship company be held liable upon a subscription for stock in a dry-dock
company,[4] nor can a manufacturing company legally subscribe to
the stock of a bank for the purpose of carrying on the banking business [5] All such contracts are, in general, *ultra vires* and not en-

such subscriptions Holladay *v* Elliott,
8 Oregon, 84 (1879). See, also, § 251,
infra And again it has been held that
where the directors of a company, in
order to make up the required amount
of capital stock, subscribed as trustees
for the corporation itself, they are liable
for calls on the amount so subscribed
In the same case a bill by a member of
the corporation on behalf of himself
and all the other members except the
defendants, praying that this transaction, although it had been sanctioned
unanimously at a meeting of the company, might be declared fraudulent and
void, was sustained, although some of
the members. on behalf of whom the
bill was filed, had been present and
voted at that meeting. Preston *v* Grand
Collier, etc. Co., 11 Sim , 327 (1840)

Allibone *v* Hager, 46 Pa. St., 48 (1863),
where the court held it no defense to
an action by a creditor of a corporation
that defendants had subscribed for stock
in their own names, but really as agents
for the corporation itself

[1] Sharpless *v* The Mayor, 21 Penn St,
147 (1853), and the long train of decisions following. The matter of municipal subscriptions is fully considered in
chapter VI

[2] Thus, for example, a banking corporation cannot lawfully subscribe for
stock in a railway corporation. Nassau
Bank *v* Jones, 95 N Y, 115 (1884),
holding that the bank could not recover
the profits on such subscription which
was made in the name of its agent, nor

for stock in any other corporation, the
business of which is wholly other than
banking Franklin Co. *v* Lewiston
Bank, 68 Me, 43 (1877); Mechanics'
Bank *v* Meriden Agency, 24 Conn , 159
(1855); Talmage *v* Pell, 7 N. Y., 328
(1852) *Cf.* First National Bank *v.* National Exchange Bank, 92 U. S, 122
(1875), and see Royal Bank of India's
Case, L R., 4 Chan , 252 (1869), Joint-
stock, etc, Co *v* Brown, L R, 8 Eq , 381
(1869); Berry *v* Yates, 24 Barb., 189
(1857), holding that one insurance company cannot subscribe to another. For
a failure of proof to show that a corporation was a subscriber for stock, see
McMillan *v* Carson, etc, Co, 12 Phil,
404 (1878) An owner of land cannot
defeat its condemnation by showing
that a corporation subscribed to part of
the capital of the corporation seeking to
obtain the land *In re* Rochester, etc ,
R R, 110 N Y, 119 (1888); Union Hotel
v Herr, 79 N Y, 454 (1880). See, also,
§§ 315–317, *infra*

[3] Maunsell *v* Midland Great Western
R'y Co, 1 Hem & M, 130 (1863). One
railroad company has no implied power
to subscribe to the capital of another,
and cannot do so indirectly by having
individuals subscribe and then indemnifying the individuals. Logan *v* Earl of
Courtown, 13 Beav, 22 (1859), and see
ch XIX.

[4] New Orleans, etc, Steamship Co. *v.*
Dry Dock Co, 28 La. Ann , 173 (1876).

[5] Sumner *v.* Marcy, 3 Woodb. & M.,
105

forceable [1] A construction company, however, is presumed to have power to subscribe for the stock of a railroad which it is building [2] A railroad company has no power to donate its funds to a fair [3] A hotel company may subscribe to a military encampment enterprise.[4]

§ 65. *Commissioners, directors, partners, etc, as subscribers* — Commissioners may be subscribers to the capital stock.[5] So, also, may directors and corporate officers subscribe, and a director, in the absence of fraud or fraudulent intent, may subscribe for the whole of the unsubscribed stock in his own name and for his own benefit [6] A partner, if the act be within the scope of the partnership business, may bind his firm by a subscription in the firm name [7] But if it is not within the scope of the partnership business, the person so signing is liable personally; and whether or not the subscription was within the scope of the partnership business may be a question for the jury [8]

§ 66. *Married women as subscribers* — At common law a married woman could not subscribe for stock, and any person subscribing in her name was himself personally liable on the subscription.[9] But now, in England, and generally in the United States by statute, a married woman may bind her separate estate by such a subscription.[10] and when it appears that the contract was with the wife, having been made directly and solely with her, the husband is not bound [11]

---

[1] See Part IV, on *ultra vires* contracts in general.

[2] *In re* Rochester, etc, R'y Co, 45 Hun, 126 (1887).

[3] See ch XL, *infra*.

[4] Richelieu Hotel Co. *v* International, etc, Co, 29 N E Rep, 1044 (La., 1892)

[5] Walker *v*. Devereaux, 4 Paige, 229 (1833)

[6] Sims *v* Street Railroad Co, 37 Ohio St., 556 (1882) See, also, § 653. But neither the commissioners (Brower *v.* Passenger R'y Co, 3 Phila, 161), nor any original stockholder (Curry *v* Scott, 54 Penn St., 270 — 1867), have any priority of right over the other subscribers, or the public generally, in the matter of subscription for stock. Cf § 70

[7] Maltby *v.* Northwestern, etc., R. R. Co, 16 Md, 422 (1860); Ogdensburgh, etc., R. R. Co. *v* Frost, 21 Barb, 541 (1856), Union Hotel Co. *v* Hersee, 79 N. Y., 454 (1880) Otherwise if not within the partnership business. Liv-

ingston *v* Pittsburg, etc., R. R Co, 2 Grant's Cas, 219, State *v* Beck, 81 Ind, 501 (1882). Where partners are stockholders, and all stockholders join in sureties to notes to aid the corporation, one partner may bind the firm by signing its name also as surety Morse *v* Hagenah, 32 N W Rep, 634 (Wis, 1887).

[8] Id

[9] Pugh & Sharman's Case, L. R., 13 Eq, 566 (1872)

[10] Witters *v* Sowles, 32 Fed Rep, 767 (1887), Mrs Matthewman's Case, L. R., 3 Eq, 781 (1866), Luard's Case, 1 De G, F & J, 533 (1860), Pugh & Sharman's Case, *supra*, Butler *v* Cumpston, L. R., 7 Eq, 16 (1868), In the Matter of the Reciprocity Bank, 22 N. Y., 9 (1860). See §§ 250. 319

[11] Angas' Case, 1 De G & Sm, 560 (1849), Dalton *v* Midland, etc, R'y Co, 13 C B, 474 (1853), S. C, 22 L. J. (C P), 177, Luard s Case, *supra*, Ness *v* Angas, 3 Exch, 805 (1849)

The recourse of the corporation or the corporate creditors is, in such a case, to her separate estate only.[1]

In England a husband has been held liable on his wife's subscription to the capital stock of an incorporated company, the subscription having been made before marriage [2]

§ 67. *Infant as subscriber.*—A subscription for stock by an infant is a contract to be governed by the general rules of law that apply to the contracts of infants generally. In general, the subscriptions of infants are voidable rather than void. He may repudiate it at majority, and thereby entirely escape liability; or he may ratify it, and thereby become as fully bound as though the subscription had been made after majority [3] Accordingly it is a settled rule that, where one subscribes for shares in the name of an infant, he is lia-

---

[1] Biggart v City of Glasgow Bank, 6 Rettie (Scotch Ct. of Sessions Cases), 470 (1879) Mrs. Matthewman's Case, L. R., 3 Eq , 781 (1866).

[2] Burlington's Case, 3 De G. & Sm , 18 (1849), where the husband was held liable although he had not fulfilled the conditions of the deed of settlement entitling him to become a member, but had only received dividends on the wife's shares.

Luard's Case, 1 De G. F. & J , 533 (1860), holding that where a woman, being a registered owner of stocks before marriage, attempted to deed them in trust so as to exclude the husband, but the trustees did not accept, and they continued in her name until the liquidation of the company, the husband should be placed with the wife on the list of contributories

White's Case, 3 De G & Sm , 157 (1850), was decided on special facts under the terms of a deed of settlement which regulated the rights of the husband and wife as to shares in her name. In this case a restricted liability for a limited time was imposed upon the husband he having done some acts in relation to the shares, but not sufficient to constitute an entire acceptance

Sadler's Case, 3 De G & Sm , 36 (1849), holding the husband liable when the shares came to the wife by legacy before marriage, although neither she nor the husband paid the covenanted calls,

received any dividends, or otherwise acted as members.

Kluht's Case, id., 210 (1850), where the husband was held liable for losses during, but not for losses before and after, the coverture He had not complied with necessary preliminaries for becoming a member, although he had done some acts in relation to the shares of the wife

And also upon a legacy of stock to her during coverture, where it appeared that the stock had been transferred to her, and the transfer duly accepted by her and her husband, and that she only had signed the dividend warrants and drawn the dividends, the proceeds being applied to ordinary household expenses. Thomas v City of Glasgow Bank, 6 Rettie (Scotch Ct. of Sessions Cases), 607 (1879)

[3] Lumsden's Case, L. R , 4 Chan , 31 (1868), where an infant transferred shares after coming of age, and did not attempt to repudiate his remaining shares until four months after the winding-up order, being nine months after his majority He was held to have affirmed his holding

Ebbett's Case, L. R., 5 Chan , 302 (1870), where a holding for fourteen months after majority without repudiating the shares was held to be an acquiescence, though the shareholder had never acted as such.

Baker's Case, L. R , 7 Chan., 115

ble personally to the corporation or the corporate creditors on the subscription [1] An infant's subscription must be repudiated within a reasonable time after coming of age or he will be held to have ratified it [2]

§ 68 *Subscription by agent* — A valid subscription may, of course, be made through an agent.[3] The subscriptions of the orig-

(1871), where a company was in process of being wound up, when an infant, holding shares as trustee, attained his majority, and he promptly repudiated the shares when the notice of a call was sent him four months afterwards Subsequently he, by letter, authorized the official liquidator to use his name in proceedings against the *cestui que trust Held,* that by the letter he had not retracted his repudiation of the shares

Mitchell's Case, L R, 9 Eq, 363 (1870). An infant holding shares as trustee, who took no steps to repudiate them for two years after coming of age, was held to be a contributory

Wilson's Case, L R., 8 Eq. 240 (1869) An infant holding shares in a trust, who came of age after the winding-up order was made, was held not to be a contributory, though he had made no formal repudiation, but had not done any act of acquiescence, except that his solicitors, acting for him and others, had opposed an order for a call.

Hart's Case, L. R., 6 Eq, 512 (1868) Where notice of intention to put the name of a female infant upon the list of contributories of a corporation in process of being wound up was served during infancy, and more than two years after her majority a summons for a call was made, when she applied to have her name removed from the list, it was held she was not precluded by the delay

Pim's Case, 3 De G & Sm, 11 (1849), where a son who, after the death of his father, discovered that shares had been taken in his own name, was held not to be a contributory, although at the request of an officer of the company, he

had surrendered the shares for exchange for others.

See §§ 250, 318

[1] Weston's Case, L. R, 5 Chan, 611 (1870), Richardson's Case, L. R, 19 Eq, 588 (1875), Reaveley's Case, 1 De G. & Sm, 550 (1848), *Ex parte* Reavely, 1 Hall & Tw, 118 (1849), Capper's Case, L. R., 3 Chan., 458 (1868), Castelo's Case, L R., 8 Eq, 504 (1869), Symon's Case, L. R., 5 Chan, 298 (1870), Reid's Case, 24 Bear, 318 (1857), Curtis' Case, L. R., 6 Eq, 455 (1868)

[2] Dublin, etc, R'y Co *v* Black, 7 Railway & Canal Cas, 434 (1852), S C, 8 Exch, 181. Infancy is a personal defense Beardsley *v* Hotchkiss, 96 N Y, 201 (1884) Where an infant allows his name to remain on the register after he becomes of age, he thereby ratifies his subscription Cork, etc, R'y Co *v* Cazenove, 10 Q B, 935 (1847). A court will not presume that an infant subscriber has avoided his contract, and hence a defense of infancy, in an action on a subscription, without an allegation of avoidance, is ineffectual, and the plaintiff may have judgment Leeds, etc, R'y Co *v* Fearnley 4 Exch, 26 (1849). But it has been held that repudiation before coming of age avoids the contract of subscription *ab initio,* and hence a plea of infancy and of repudiation while an infant, and of notice to the company that the stock was at their disposal, is a good defense to an action on a subscription Newry, etc, R'y Co *v* Coombe, 3 Exch, 565 (1849), S C, 18 L J (Exch), 325, Parson's Case, L R 8 Eq, 656

[3] Musgrave *v* Morrison, 54 Mo, 161 (1880), Burr *v* Wilcox, 22 N Y, 551

inal incorporators may be made by an agent.[1] No person can be made a subscriber to the capital stock of a corporation, and be subjected to the liabilities of a subscriber, by a subscription in his name, made by another without authority, but assuming to act as

(1860); Rhey v. Evensburg, etc., 27 Pa. St., 261; *In re* N. Y., etc., Co., 35 Hun, 220 (1885). Where bonds are purchased by one for several, they are liable to contribute therefor. Musgrave v. Buckley, 114 N. Y., 506 (1889).

If both the principal and agent are incorporators, and the agent subscribes in his own name, the principal cannot claim the stock, inasmuch as he has sworn in the articles of incorporation that all the incorporators were *bona fide* subscribers. Appeal of Rowley, 9 Atl. Rep., 329 (Pa., 1887).

In re Whitely Partners, L. R., 32 Ch. D., 337. A subscription by one of several heirs in the name of the "estate" is not binding on any of the heirs where a statute requires such subscription to be several. Troy, etc., R. R. Co. v. Warren, 18 Barb., 310 (1854).

Davidson v. Grange, 4 Grant's Ch. (U. Can.), 377 (1854). In this case a subscription by an agent in his own name was held to constitute him a trustee for his principals.

State v. Lehre, 7 Rich. Law, 234 (1854), holding that a statute forbidding any person from subscribing for shares in the name of another person did not exclude a subscription by an agent for his principal.

Cox's Case, 4 De G., J. & S., 53 (1863), was decided under the Companies Act, but the court was inclined to think the result would have been the same independent of that statute. It was there held that where a subscriber, in addition to his own shares, had caused a large number to be registered in the names of mere nominees for him, in order to delude the public as to the number of members, he was rightly placed on the list of contributories for all the shares when the company was wound up. This case was distinguished in King's Case, L. R., 6 Ch. App., 196 (1871).

On this question of "dummies," see ch. XIV. See, also, brief in 15 Ohio St., 332.

If such subscriptions are prohibited by the corporate charter, the principal cannot recover back money which he has given to the agent to subscribe. Perkins v. Savage, 15 Wend., 412 (1836).

Mere authority to an agent to subscribe is not a subscription in itself. Granger, etc., Co. v. Vinson, 6 Oregon, 172 (1876). Also, New Brunswick, etc., Co. v. Muggeridge, 4 Hurl. & N., 160 (1859).

In New York it is a penal offense for a person to subscribe for another who does not intend to pay, or to subscribe in the name of a fictitious person. N. Y. Penal Code, § 590.

Where one subscribes for stock in his own name, in pursuance of a verbal agreement between himself and another that the stock should belong to them jointly, and that he should hold it on joint account, and, the company subsequently becoming insolvent, the stockholders are called on to contribute an amount equal to their stock, it was held, in New York, that the nominal owner of the stock might have contribution from the joint owner. Stover v. Flack, 30 N. Y., 64 (1864); Orr v. Bigelow, 14 N. Y., 556 (1856). The parties had covenanted that plaintiffs should subscribe for stock, pay ten per cent. thereon, and then assign it to defendant, who engaged to indemnify them from further liability. Defendant refused to take the shares, and the corporation recovered judgment against

---

[1] *In re* N. Y., etc., R'y Co., 99 N. Y., 12 (1885).

his agent.   Such a subscription is not binding on the principal[1] But such an unauthorized subscription may be adopted and ratified by the person in whose name it was made without warrant of authority, in such a way as to make it valid and binding[2]   A person

plaintiffs for the balance of the subscription   In this action plaintiffs had judgment against defendant upon the covenant, the measure of damages being held to be the balance paid by them, and not that sum less the market value of the stock   A state subscribing through its officers is bound by their acts as directors   State v. Jefferson T Co. 3 Humph (Tenn), 305 (1842), Colt v Clapp. 127 Mass, 476 (1879), where one who had verbally agreed to purchase stock for the joint benefit of himself and others refused to divide the stock, he was held accountable to the others for their respective shares of dividends paid thereon in actions for money had and received

[1] Ticonic, etc, Co v Lang, 63 Me, 480 (1874), Pim's Case, 3 De G & Sm, 11 (1849), Hennessey's Case, 3 id, 191 (1850), Ex parte Hall, 1 Macn & G, 307 (1849)

Drover v. Evans, 59 Ind, 454, holding that where an agent to make a subscription exceeds his authority the principal is not bound by it.

Cf Chapman & Barker's Case, L R, 3 Eq, 361 (1867)   And this is equally the rule when it is sought to charge one by such a subscription, not in his individual capacity, but only in the capacity of trustee for another   Ex parte Hall, supra

[2] Musgrave v. Morrison, 54 Md, 161 (1880), Mississippi, etc, R. R. Co. v Harris, 36 Miss, 17 (1858), where the defendant promised to pay, Jones v Milton, etc, Co, 7 Ind, 547 (1856), where the principal subscribed over again, Philadelphia, etc, R. R. Co v Cowell, 28 Penn St, 329 (1857), where the defendant acquiesced for seven years, Putnam v City of Albany, 4 Biss, 365 (1869), where the city ratified

What acts or omissions, short of express ratification, will in law suffice to bind one upon such a subscription, is,

in general, a question for the jury   Philadelphia, etc, R. R Co v Cowell, 28 Penn. St, 329 (1857)   Cf Fox v Clifton, 6 Bing, 776 (1830)   It is held that silence or failure to object to the subscription for a considerable time after knowledge of it is brought to the subscriber is evidence of a ratification   McHose v. Wheeler, 45 Pa St, 32 (1863), Thompson v Reno Savings Bank, 10 Am & Eng Corp Cas, 203 (1885), Sanger v Upton, 91 U S, 56 (1875)   Contra, Hume v. Commercial Bank, 9 Lea, 728 (1882)   And giving a proxy to vote the stock may be sufficient to ratify such a subscription   McCully v Pittsburgh, etc, R. R. Co, 32 Pa St, 25 (1858)   Contra, McClelland v Whiteley, 11 Biss, 444 (1883)   But a mere declaration to strangers, by the person in whose name the subscription had been made, that he had taken that amount of stock, is not a ratification of the subscription   Rutland, etc, R. R Co v Lincoln, 29 Vt, 206 (1857)   And even the fact that one whose name had been in this way put down as a subscriber was a director in the corporation was held not in se, to imply knowledge that his name was on the books as a subscriber   In re Wincham, etc, Co, L R. 9 Chan Div, 329 (1878)   Cf Fox v Clifton, 6 Bing 776 (1830)   But as a rule it is believed that accepting the office of a director would in this country, be held a sufficient ratification of such a subscription, in the absence of any other   This is expressly declared to be the rule in Tennessee and elsewhere   Moses v Ocoee Bank, 1 Lea, 398 (1878), Danbury, etc, R R Co v Wilson, 22 Conn, 435 (1853)   Cf. Five Lexington, etc, R R Co., 2 Metc (Ky), 314 (1859)   Contra, Hume v Commercial Bank, 9 Lea, 728 (1882)

But where an agent takes stock as agent, on condition that it is to be sub-

subscribing for shares as agent for another, and in that other's name, but without authority, thereby becomes himself a subscriber in place of the person whose name he signs, or his unauthorized subscription may subject him to an action of damages [1] .

§ 69 *Subscriptions taken by an unauthorized agent of the corporation.*— A subscription taken by a person who has no authority from the corporation to take subscriptions is not in general enforceable [2] But it has been held that such a subscription may, by acceptance and ratification on the part of the corporation, be validated, and the subscriber made liable as though the subscription had been regularly taken.[3]

§ 70. *Unissued or increased capital stock.— Right to subscribe therefor.*— Where the whole capital stock or a part of the authorized capital stock is offered for subscription and a part only of the amount so offered is subscribed for, the remainder may be taken by any person, even though that person is a director in the company [4] But where the part offered for subscription is not taken, or where a part of the authorized capital is offered and is all taken, and subsequently it is resolved to issue more of the authorized capital, or where the capital stock is increased under the statutes and the increase is about to be issued, then a different rule prevails Every existing stockholder then has the right to subscribe at par for such a proportion of the stock to be issued as his old holdings bear to the amount of stock then outstanding.[5] Any other rule would enable the parties in control to seize the new stock, in some cases for gain because the stock is worth more than par, and in other cases so as to acquire increased votes at a coming election. In either case this would work a fraud on the other stockholders.[6]

mitted to the principal, and, "if approved, to be taken out in the purchase of thread.' the principal is not bound where he declines to accept, even though he did not notify the corporation of his refusal Merrick, etc, Co. *v* Philadelphia, etc, Co, 8 Atl Rep., 794 (Pa., 1887).

[1] Salem, etc, Corp *v* Ropes, 9 Pick, 187 (1829) In some jurisdictions it is held that by such a subscription the subscriber makes himself personally liable as a subscriber Union Hotel Co *v* Hersee, 79 N Y, 454 (1880), State *v* Smith, 48 Vt., 266 (1876) See, also, Troy, etc, R R Co *v* Warren, 18 Barb, 310 (1854); Pugh & Sharman's Case, L. R., 13 Eq, 566 (1872), McHose *v* Wheeler, 45 Pa. St, 32; Thompson *v* Reno, etc.,

Bank, 10 Am & Eng Corp. Cas., 203 (Nev, 1885), § 249, *infra*

[2] Essex, etc, Co *v* Collins, 8 Mass., 292 (1811); Shurtz *v* Schoolcraft, etc, R R Co, 9 Mich, 269 (1861), Carlile *v.* Saginaw, etc, R R Co 27 id, 315 (1873). *Contra*, Northeastern R R Co *v* Rodriques, 10 Rich Law, 278 (1857).

[3] Walker *v.* Mobile, etc, R R Co, 34 Miss, 245 (1857), Mobile, etc., R R Co. *v* Yandal, 5 Sneed, 294 (1858); Judah *v* American, etc, Co., 4 Ind, 333

[4] Sims *v* Street R R, 37 Ohio St, 556 (1882) Also, § 65, *supra*.

[5] See ch XVII, § 286.

[6] Where a director issues to himself at par, stock belonging to the corpora-

C. AN ACTION LIES TO COLLECT SUBSCRIPTIONS

§ 71. *A subscription for shares implies a promise to pay for them, and this promise sustains an action to collect, without proof of any particular consideration* — This rule of law is sustained by the great weight of authority. The signing of the subscription paper is an implied promise to pay the subscription [1]

There have been various opinions of the courts as to the consideration supporting this implied promise which sustains an action to collect the subscription. It has been held that the right to membership in the proposed corporation, and the probable advantages to be derived from membership in the company, constitute the consideration. [2]

tion and which is worth more than par, the transaction is voidable, but if all the stockholders acquiesce therein for a long time, the acquiescence of the executors of a deceased stockholder binds the estate St. Croix L. Co. z Mittlestadt, 44 N W. Rep, 1079 (Minn 1890)

Where, long after the company has commenced to do business, it has disposed of its property and is ready to declare a five hundred per cent. dividend, the directors issue to themselves at par that part of the original capital stock which never had been issued, it is a fraud on the remaining stockholders Arkansas, etc, Soc v Eichholtz, 25 Pac Rep, 613 (Kan, 1891) See, also, 14 N J Eq, 380

[1] Upton v. Tribilcock, 91 U S, 45 (1875); Hawley v Upton. 102 U S, 314 (1880); Webster v. Upton, 91 id, 65 (1875); Buffalo, etc., R R Co v. Dudley, 14 N. Y, 336 (1856), Small v Herkimer, etc., Co, 2 N Y, 330 (1849), Lake Ontario, etc, R. R. Co v Mason, 16 id, 451 (1857); Dayton v Borst, 31 id, 435 (1865), Northern R R. Co v Miller, 10 Barb, 260, 268 (1851). Waukon, etc, R R. Co v. Dwyer, 49 Iowa, 121 (1878), Nulton v Clayton, 54 id, 425 (1880) Miller z Wild Cat, etc, Co, 52 Ind, 51 (1875), Mitchell v Beckman, 64 Cal, 117 (1883), Merrimac, etc, Co v Levy, 54 Penn St., 227 (1867), Beene v Cahawba, etc., R. R. Co, 3 Ala 660 (1842), Fry v. Lexington, etc, R. R. Co, 2 Metc. Ky), 314 (1859), Gill z Kentucky, etc,

Co, 7 Bush, 635 (1870), Mt Sterling, etc, Co v Little, 14 id, 429 (1879), Chase v. East Tenn R R Co, 5 Lea (Tenn), 415 (1880) Even though the corporation has the power to forfeit the shares for non-payment. Hughes z Antietam, etc, Co, 34 Md, 316 (1870), Dexter, etc, Co v Millerd, 3 Mich, 91 (1854)

[2] Lake Ontario etc, R R Co z Mason. 16 N. Y, 451 (1857), Fort Edward, etc Co v Payne, 17 Barb, 567 (1854), Hamilton, etc, Co v Rice, 7 id, 157 (1849), Schenectady, etc. R. R. Co v Thatcher, 11 N Y, 102, 108 (1854) Barnes z Perine 12 id, 18 (1854). Osborn z Crosby, 63 N H, 583 (1885) Bullock z Falmouth, etc, Co, 3 S W Rep, 129 (Ky, 1887) See, also, Stewart z Trustees of Hamilton College, 2 Denio, 43 (1845), Hamilton College z Stewart, 1 N Y, 581 (1848), Dutcher's Manuf g Co. v Davis, 14 Johns, 238. Whittlesey z Frantz 74 N Y, 456. "It is well settled," said Hand, J, in the case of Fort Edward, etc Co z Payne, 17 Barb 567 (1854), "that a subscription to the capital stock of any company, from the membership of which a shareholder may derive pecuniary advantage, gives to the subscriber such an interest, or will support a promise to pay for the shares Such an enterprise is a combination of means for mutual profit and is in no sense a gift or promise without consideration" And elsewhere it is-

It has been held, also, that the stock to be received and the probable dividends thereon constitute the consideration[1]

Again, the consideration has been said to be the mutual obligation of all the subscribers to take and pay for their stock[2]

And, again, it has been held that a consideration is conclusively implied from the fact of subscription itself, that it is implied by law, and that the law thereby creates a duty and liability to pay for the stock[3]

The particular motive of a subscriber inducing him to subscribe is immaterial. The consideration which exists in law cannot be allowed to be governed by the ideas of the subscriber.[4] The assignee of a subscription may enforce it[5]

§ 72 *This rule prevails in regard to subscriptions taken before incorporation as well as to those taken after incorporation.*—Such, undoubtedly, is the rule sustained by the great weight of authority.[6]

said that "the advantage to be derived from being a member of such a company, and of the consequent right to participate in the pecuniary dividends, is a positive benefit, and where the agreement secures that advantage to the subscriber, on the organization of the company, the objection of a want of consideration cannot be made with success" Hamilton, etc, Co v Rice, 7 Barb, 157 (1849), adopted by Brown, J, in Lake Ontario, etc, R. R. Co v Mason, 16 N Y, 451, 463 (1857)

[1]Schenectady, etc., R. R Co v Thatcher, 11 N Y, 102, 107 (1854), Bish v Bradford 17 Ind, 490 (1861), New Albany, etc, R. R. Co. v Fields, 10 id, 187 (1858), Fry v Lexington, etc., R. R. Co., 2 Metc (Ky), 314 (1859) That the interest acquired by subscribing for shares of the capital stock is a good consideration for the promise to pay for them Union, etc., Co v Jenkins, 1 Caines, 381 (1803); Selma, etc, R. R. Co v Tipton, 5 Ala, 787 (1843) — a full and learned opinion Cf Goshen, etc, Co v Hurtin, 9 Johns, 217 (1812), Danbury, etc, R. R. Co v Wilson, 22 Conn, 435 (1853); East Tennessee, etc, R. R. Co v Gammon, 5 Sneed, 567 And again, that the prior proceedings and acts of the parties are a legal basis for the promise to pay, also, that the partial

execution of the purpose designed by the charter is a sufficient consideration. Kennebec, etc, R. R. Co v. Palmer, 34 Me, 366 (1852), McAuley v. Billenger, 20 Johns, 89 (1822), Amherst Academy v Cowls, 23 Mass., 427 (1828), Ohio, etc., College v Higgins, 16 Ohio St., 20 (1864). Cf McCully v Pittsburgh, etc., R. R. Co., 32 Penn St., 25 (1858) In Minnesota the implied promise to issue the stock is declared to be the consideration for the promise to pay for it. St. Paul, etc., R. R. Co v Robbins, 23 Minn, 439 (1877). And in Kentucky it is held that the promise by each of the subscribers is a sufficient consideration for the promises of the others. Twin Creek, etc., Co. v. Lancaster, 79 Ky, 552.

[2]Spear v. Crawford, 14 Wend., 20 (1835); Cole v Ryan, 52 Barb, 168 (1868), Upton v Tribilcock, 91 U. S, 45 (1875); Northern, etc, R. R. Co. v. Miller, 10 Barb., 260 (1851).

[3]East Tenn., etc., R. R. Co. v. Gammon, 5 Sneed (Tenn), 567.

[4]Ill River R. R. Co. v Zimmer, 20 Ill, 654 (1858), Miller v. Wild Cat, etc., Co, 52 Ind, 51 64 (1875); Andover, etc., Co. v Gould, 6 Mass, 39, 44 (1809), Parker v Northern, etc, R. R. Co., 33 Mich, 23 (1875)

[5]See § 111.

[6]Richelieu Hotel Co. v Interna-

112

It has been held, also, that the corporation may bring an action at law for damages against a subscriber to a preliminary subscription

tional, etc, Co., 29 N E Rep, 1044 (Ill 1892), West v. Crawford, 21 Pac Rep, 1123 (Cal, 1889), Muysville, etc., Co v Johnson, 29 Pac Rep, 126 (Cal, 1892), San Joaquin, etc, Co v Beecher, 29 Pac Rep., 785 (Cal, 1892), McCormick v Great Bend, etc, Co., 29 Pac. Rep 1147 (Kan, 1892), Minneapolis, etc., Co. v Crevier, 40 N W Rep, 507 (Minn, 1888), Reformed, etc, Church v Brown, 17 How Pr, 287 (1859); Penobscot, etc., R. R Co v Dummer, 40 Me, 172 (1855), Athol, etc, Co. v. Carey, 116 Mass, 471 (1875), Ashuelot, etc., Co v Hoit, 56 N H, 548 (1876), Cross v Pinckneyville, etc, Co., 17 Ill. 54 (1855), Griswold v Trustees, etc, 26 id, 41 (1861), Stone v Great Western, etc., Co., 41 id, 85 (1866), Proprietors, etc, v Dickinson 6 Gray, 586 (1856), Heaston v Cincinnati, etc., R. R Co, 16 Ind, 275 (1861), Miller v Wild Cat, etc, Co, 52 Ind, 51 (1875); Eastern, etc, Co v Vaughan 14 N. Y., 546 (1856), Buffalo, etc, R. R. Co v Gifford, 87 id, 294 (1882), Same v Clark, 22 Hun, 359 (1880), Peninsular, etc, R. R Co v Duncan, 28 Mich, 130 (1873); Buffalo, etc. R R Co v Dudley, 14 N Y, 336 (1856), Dayton v Borst, 31 id, 435 (1865), Rensselaer, etc, Co v Barton, 16 id, 457 (1854) Lake Ontario, etc. R R Co v Mason, 16 id., 451 (1857); Essex, etc Co v Tuttle, 2 Vt, 393 (1830), Kirksey v Florida, etc, R R Co, 7 Fla, 23 (1857) Beene v Cahawba, etc, R. R. Co. 3 Ala, 660 (1842); Selma, etc, R. R. Co v Tipton, 5 id, 787 (1843), Hartford, etc., R. R. Co v Kennedy, 12 Conn, 499 (1838), Thigpen v Mississippi, etc, R. R. Co, 32 Miss., 347 (1856), Gill v Kentucky, etc, Co, 7 Bush (Ky), 635 (1870), Instone v Frankfort, etc, Co, 2 Bibb (Ky), 576 (1812), Cucullu v Union Ins Co. 2 Rob (La), 573 (1842) Union, etc, Co v Jenkins, 1 Caines, 381 (1803); Goshen, etc, Co, v Hurtin, 9 Johns, 217 (1812), Dutchess, etc, Co

v Davis, 14 id, 238 (1817), Spear v Crawford, 14 Wend, 20 (1835), Harlem, etc, Co v Seixas 2 Hall (N Y Super Ct), 504 (1829) Nulton v Clayton, 54 Iowa 425 (1880), Worcester, etc, Co v Willard, 5 Mass, 80 (1809) Stanton v Wilson, 2 Hill, 153 (1841) Sagory v. Dubois 3 Sandf Chan, 466 (1846), Palmer v Lawrence, 3 Sandf Super Ct, 161 (1819), Twin Creek, etc, Co v. Lancaster, 79 Ky, 552 (1881), Minn, etc. Co v Davis, 41 N W Rep, 1026 (Minn, 1889) Cf Thompson v Page, 1 Metc (Mass), 565 (1840), Ives v Sterling, 6 id, 310 (1843), Robinson v Edinboro' Academy, 3 Grant's Cas., 107 (1861), Edinboro' Academy v Robinson, 37 Penn St, 210 (1860), Hutchins v Smith, 46 Barb, 235 (1865), Valk v Crandall, 1 Sandf Chan, 179, People's, etc, Co v Balch 8 Gray 303 (1857), Chater v San Francisco, etc, Co, 19 Cal, 219 (1861), Highland, etc., Co v McKean, 11 Johns 98 (1814), Tar River, etc, Co v Neal, 3 Hawks (N C), 520 (1825) Klein v Alton, etc, R. R. Co, 13 Ill, 514 (1851), Danet v Same, 13 id., 501 (1851) Sanger v Upton, 91 U S, 56 (1875), Kidwilly, etc, Co v Roby, 2 Price (Eng.), 93 (1815), Weiss v Mauch Chunk etc, Co 58 Pa St 295 (1868). The bringing of a suit by the corporation to collect a subscription constitutes an acceptance of the subscription by the corporation Buffalo etc, R. R Co v Clark, 22 Hun, 359 (1880). A subscription to a corporation to be organized is enforceable by the corporation. Auburn, etc, Ass'n v Hill, 32 Pac. Rep, 587 (Cal, 1893) The corporation may collect a subscription to its stock obtained prior to the incorporation, the subscriber having attended meetings and acquiesced in expenditures International, etc, Assoc v Walker, 47 N W Rep, 338 (Mich, 1890). It has been held that a corporation can defeat a subscriber's action for stock by proving

list who refuses to take and pay for the stock,[1] and that the
measure of damages for such a breach of contract to subscribe for
stock is the difference between the par and market value of the
stock involved.[2]

§ 73 *In New York a contrary rule prevails* — It has been held
by the New York court of appeals that where the preliminary
subscription did not purport to run to the company, but was merely
an agreement among the signers to subscribe to its stock, the company could not enforce the agreement as a subscription.[3] In that
state there is no implied contract to pay for stock, not even though
it is given to stockholders as a bonus.[4] The liability on stock de-

that it never accepted his subscription
Starrett *v* Rockland, etc, R R. Co, 65
Me, 374 (1876) But no formal acceptance by the corporation is necessary in
order to enforce a subscription. Strasburg R. R. Co *v* Eichternacht 21 Pa.
St., 220 (1853), Miller *v* Wild Cat, etc,
Co, 52 Ind, 51 (1875); Thrasher *v* Pike
County, 25 Ill, 393, Mt Sterling, etc,
Co. *v* Little, 14 Bush, 429 (1879), California, etc., Co *v.* Schafer, 57 Cal, 396
(1881), Poughkeepsie, etc, Co *v* Griffin,
24 N Y, 150 (1860); Troy, etc., R. R Co.
v Tibbits, 18 Barb, 297, Charlotte, etc.,
R R. Co *v* Blakely, 3 Strobh L, 245
(1848), Pittsburgh, etc, R R Co *v.*
Gazzam, 32 Pa. St., 340 (1858), Wallingford, etc., Co. *v* Fox, 12 Vt., 304 (1840),
Stowe *v* Flagg, 72 Ill, 397 (1874), Goff
v Winchester College, 6 Bush, 443
(1869), Perkins *v* Union, etc, Co, 12
Allen, 273 (1866), Dayton, etc, Co *v*
Coy, 13 Ohio St, 84 (1861) See, also, various cases in the first part of this chapter, and Brownlee *v* Ohio, etc, R R,
18 Ind, 68 (1862), Kilner *v* Baxter, L
R, 2 C P., 174 (1866). A subscription before incorporation is enforceable, where
defendant paid for one or more shares
after incorporation Bell's Appeal, 8
Atl Rep., 177 (Penn, 1887). Where a
subscriber before incorporation is offered
the stock by the corporation on certain
conditions which he refuses, he is not
liable as a stockholder Medler *v.*
Albuquerque, etc., Co., 28 Pac. Rep, 551
(N. M, 1892). A subscription with an
express promise to pay to an agent speci-

fied upon the incorporation of the company is collectible by him. West *v*
Crawford, 21 Pac Rep., 1123 (Colo, 1889)

[1] Quick *v* Lemon, 105 Ill, 578 (1883)
Thrasher *v* Pike Co, etc, R R. Co., 25
id, 393 (1861), Rhey *v* Ebensburg, etc.,
R. R. Co., 27 Pa. St., 261 (1856), Mt.
Sterling, etc, R. R. Co. *v* Little, 14
Bush, 429 (1879)

[2] Thrasher *v.* Pike Co., etc., R. R. Co.,
25 Ill., 393 (1861) It seems, also, that
such an action of damages might be
brought by one of the signers of the preliminary agreement against any other
signer who refused to take and pay for
stock after the incorporation of the
company, and that the measure of damages in this case would be, not the
amount subscribed, but the damage
sustained by the person suing. Lake
Ontario etc., R R. Co *v.* Curtiss, 80 N
Y, 219 (1880) In Pennsylvania a statute
which authorized a corporation to transfer a subscription from one enterprise to
another has been held unconstitutional.
Pittsburgh, etc, R R. Co *v* Gazzam,
32 Pa. St., 340 (1858) It is elsewhere
said that a subscription preliminary to
organization is no contract, but merely
a means of bringing the parties together Poughkeepsie, etc., R R. Co. *v*
Griffin 24 N Y, 150 (1860).

[3] Lake Ontario, etc, R R. Co *v.* Curtiss, 80 N Y, 219 (1880). See, also, § 705,
etc., *infra*, on promoters' contracts generally

[4] See § 42, *supra.*

114

pends upon express contract only[1] Hence where the corporation is not in existence when the contract is made between the parties, it, not being a party to the contract, cannot enforce the subscription[2]

§ 74. *In New England a subscription for stock cannot be enforced unless the subscriber expressly promised to pay, or the charter expressly obligated him to do so* — Such is the rule in New England It grew out of the peculiar charters of the early turnpike companies, which had shares of stock not limited in amount, but indefinite, so that, as a result, if a subscriber were liable at all, he was liable for the whole capital stock, except so far as it had already been paid in by himself and others. Consequently, inasmuch as these charters gave to the corporation the right to forfeit stock for non-payment of subscriptions, the courts held that an action to collect did not lie, and that the remedy by forfeiture was the only remedy of the corporation.[3] This rule has become firmly established in the

[1] Liability on the subscription price of stock in New York depends on contract only Glenn *v* Garth, 133 N Y, 18 (1892).

[2] This difficulty was experienced in soliciting subscriptions for a proposed World's Fair corporation in October, 1889 The form of contract finally used was, in substance, as follows

"The undersigned, in consideration of the advantages which will result to us respectively from concert of action, and from other good causes and considerations, and the efforts to be made by Samuel Babcock [giving names], to procure the subscriptions hereinafter provided for, and the organization of a corporation to control and manage such exposition do agree each for himself to pay to the said Samuel D Babcock and his associates hereinabove named, or at their request, to said corporation, the respective amounts set opposite our names upon the following terms and conditions, to wit·

"Such subscription shall not be binding until such corporation shall be organized.

"No subscription shall be binding until the said Samuel D Babcock and his associates above named shall have succeeded in obtaining subscriptions

hereto in the amount of at least $5,000,000

"Such subscription shall be a preliminary or guarantee fund to be paid in in instalments of not more than one-quarter of their respective amounts at any one time upon calls for the same, made at intervals of not less than three months by the said Samuel D Babcock and his associates, or, if they shall so determine, by the said corporation

"Samuel D. Babcock and his associates hereinabove named having been thus contracted with by the subscribers because of their having been selected as a finance committee aforesaid in and of said exposition, it is hereby further agreed that all stipulations in the agreement made dependent upon the action of said Babcock and his associates, shall be considered as fully met by the action of the majority of them, and in case of vacancy by death, resignation, or otherwise, such vacancy shall be filled by these subscribers." See 74 N Y, 72, 44 id, 126.

[3] Worcester, etc, Turnpike Co *v.* Willard, 5 Mass., 80 (1809); Andover, etc., Turnpike Co. *v* Gould, 6 Mass, 40 (1809), New Bedford, etc., Turnpike Co *v.* Adams, 8 id, 138 (1811), Essex, etc., Co *v* Collins, 8 id, 292 (1811), Franklin, etc., Co. *v* White, 14 id., 286 (1817)

New England states, and still prevails in its application to all classes of corporations [1]

§ 75 *Professor Collin's rules on this subject* — Professor Collin, of the Cornell Law School, states the law on this subject as follows:

"The following propositions are given as the substantially harmonious net result of much confusion in cases and text-books. Rambling remarks may be found contrary to each proposition, but very few reported cases have been decided contrary to any one of these propositions upon the facts coming within it, and I believe every proposition can be sustained in any state or federal court:

"(a) A preliminary agreement to form a corporation and take stock therein is not a contract by the subscribers with each other, and cannot be enforced by one or more against any other, but only by the corporation

"(b) Such an agreement, not made as a step authorized by statute in the process of forming the corporation, is a mere offer to the corporation not yet in existence, and is revocable by any subscriber until the birth of the corporation, which operates as an acceptance of the offer, and thereafter the subscription, if not previously revoked, is irrevocable and may be enforced by the corporation.

"(c) Such an agreement, made as a step authorized by statute in the process of forming the corporation, is made valid by the statute,

---

[1] Kennebec, etc , R R. Co *v* Kendall, 31 Me , 470 (1850), Belfast, etc , R. R. Co. *v* Moore, 60 id , 561 (1871), New Hampshire, etc , R. R. Co. *i* Johnson, 30 N H , 390 (1855); White, etc , R. R. Co. *v* Eastman, 34 id , 124 (1856), Essex, etc , Co *i* Tuttle. 2 Vt , 393 (1830), Connecticut, etc., R. R. Co *v* Bailey, 24 id , 465, Atlantic, etc., Mills *v.* Abbott, 9 Cush , 423 (1852), Katama, etc., Co *v.* Jernegan, 125 id , 156 (1879), Boston, etc.. R R. Co *v* Wellington, 113 id , 79 (1873); Buckfield, etc., R. R. Co *v.* Irish, 39 id , 44 (1854), Russell *v* Bristol, 49 Conn , 251 (1881) *Cf* Odd Fellows, etc , Co *v* Glazier, 5 Harr (Del), 172 (1848), Stokes *v.* Lebanon, etc , Co., 6 Humph., 211 (1845), City Hotel *v* Dickinson. 6 Gray. 586 (1856) Belfast, etc , R. R. Co. *v.* Cottrell, 66 Me , 185 (1876), Katowa Land Co *v* Holley, 129 Mass , 540 (1880), Mechanics', etc , Co. *v* Hall. 121 id , 272 (1876). In Maine an agreement to "take and fill" a number of shares has been held equivalent to an express promise to pay for them Buckfield, etc., R. R. Co *v* Irish, 39 Me , 44 (1854); Penobscot, etc R. R. Co *v* Bartlett, 12 Gray, 244 (1858) See, also, Seymour *v* Sturgess, 26 N Y, 134 (1862), Fort Edward, etc., Co. *v.* Payne, 17 Barb, 567 (1854), Pittsburgh, etc , R. R. Co *v* Gazzam, 32 Pa. St., 340 (1858). It is to be noticed that this rule was established before the announcement of that great principle of American law, that the capital stock of a corporation is a trust fund for the benefit of its creditors.

When "neither the general laws nor the act by which the plaintiffs were incorporated, nor any by-laws of the company, created any forfeiture of the shares for the non-payment of the assessments, . . . the legal effect of his (defendant's) subscribing for the stock is to render him liable in *assumpsit* even where there is no express promise to pay" Essex, etc., Co. *v.* Tuttle, 2 Vt., 393 (1830)

and is binding upon each subscriber from the time of signing and is irrevocable thereafter, but can be enforced only by the corporation

"(d) An agreement to pay money to trustees, to be by them paid to a corporation thereafter to be created, the trustees to return to the subscribers stock in the corporation accordingly, is a valid contract between the subscribers and the trustees.

"(e) The distinction made between a present subscription and an agreement to subscribe to the stock of a corporation thereafter to be created is unsound in principle, and disappears as mere *dicta* upon a thorough sifting of the cases

"(f) The damages recoverable by the corporation upon a subscription is the amount of the subscription, and all discussion of any other measure of damages, such as difference between par and market value of stock subscribed, arises from a misconception of the situation, and disappears from the net result of the authorities "

§ 76. *Stockholders' agreements to guarantee company debts* — An agreement of stockholders to be responsible for future debts of the corporation can be enforced, but the corporation and all the parties are to be made parties defendant.[1]

A modification of the contract between the subscribers and a contractor does not release the former where they accept the work upon the completion of the contract [2]

---

[1] Farmers' Nat. Bank *v.* Hannon, 14 Fed Rep , 593 (1883) If the plaintiff is one of the parties to the agreement his remedy is in equity   Id , 4 id , 612

An agreement of stockholders to indemnify, protect and save harmless in proportion to their stock other stockholders who sign corporate notes construed and the remedy explained Taylor *v* Coon, 48 N W Rep , 123 (Wis , 1891), Taylor *v* North, id , 126

Stockholders who sign corporate notes are co-sureties and not guarantors. Southerland *v* Fremont, 12 S E Rep , 237 (N C , 1890).

An agreement of stockholders that if a creditor of the corporation will release certain security they will give other security or that the debt will be paid is a contract of guaranty and not an original undertaking Home Nat. Bank *v* Waterman, 25 N E Rep , 648 (Ill , 1890).

A subscription agreement prior to incorporation. in which the parties state the number of shares taken, and in

which they agree to pay the contractors who are parties to the contract a specified sum, is a joint undertaking on the subscribers' part   The contractors may hold them liable as partners, the agreement not limiting their liability to the number of shares taken by each   An immaterial alteration after a part have signed does not release any one The agreement of the contractors to hold each subscriber liable only on his subscription if he would pay that is without consideration and void Any subscriber could expressly limit his liability to his subscription Davis *v* Shafer, 50 Fed Rep , 764 (1892) See Doud *v* Bank, 54 id , 846 *Cf* Davis *v* Barber, 51 id , 148.

[2] Gibbons *v* Ellis, 53 N W Rep , 701 (Wis , 1892).

An agreement of stockholders that certain corporate notes will be paid is released by taking new notes from the corporation extending the debt. Home Nat. Bank *v* Waterman's Estate, 29 N. E. Rep , 503 (Ill., 1891).

CHAPTER V.

CONDITIONAL SUBSCRIPTIONS.

§ 77. *Definition of conditional subscription* — A conditional subscription is one on which payment can be enforced by the corporation only after the occurrence or after the performance by the corporation of certain things specified in the subscription itself.[1] Oral agreements made with the subscriber to the effect that payment will not be required except on certain events or contingencies are sometimes spoken of as conditions to the subscription, but more properly are mere variations of a written contract, and are treated elsewhere.[2]

§ 78 *Conditions precedent and conditions subsequent.*—A conditional subscription is also to be distinguished from a subscription on a condition subsequent. A subscription on a condition subsequent contains a contract between the corporation and the subscriber, whereby the corporation agrees to do some act. It thereby combines two contracts: one the contract of subscription, the other an ordinary contract of the corporation to perform the specified acts[3] The subscription is valid and enforceable whether the con-

---

[1] A conditional subscription has often been spoken of as "a continuing offer which is final and absolute when accepted" Taggart v Western Md R. R Co , 24 Md , 563 (1866); Ashtabula & New London R. R. Co. v Smith, 15 Ohio St., 328 (1864), Lowe v Edgefield & K R. R. Co , 1 Head (Tenn), 659 (1858)

[2] See ch IX, also § 81.

[3] Thus, adding to a subscription the words, ' to be expended between the Connecticut river and the east line of the state," has been held to form a contract to that effect, but not to make the subscription conditional Lane v. Brainerd, 30 Conn , 565 (1862; Henderson & Nashville R. R. Co v Leavell, 16 B. Monroe (Ky), 358 (1855). So, also, of words requiring a certain location or route to be adopted Henderson & Nashville R R. Co v. Leavell, *supra,* the court saying, however, that if the route is laid out otherwise, before payment, probably the subscriber would be discharged, if changed after payment, it

ditions are performed or not.[1] The condition subsequent is the same as a separate collateral contract between the corporation and the subscriber, for breach of which an action for damages is the remedy.[2] The distinction between such a contract and the or-

could be enjoined Laches will bar the right to such an injunction Chapman v Mad River & Lake Erie R R Co, 6 Ohio St., 119 (1856). A more frequent requirement is a certain location of the route, and also the construction of a part of the whole of the road The first requirement is construed to be a condition precedent, the second a condition subsequent, since the payment of the subscription itself is necessary to carry out the requirement. Chamberlain v. Painesville & Hudson R R Co, 15 Ohio St., 225 (1864) Belfast & Moosehead Lake R'y Co v Moore, 60 Me, 561, 576 (1871), North Mo R R Co v Winkler, 29 Mo, 318 Bucksport & Bangor R R Co v Inhabitants of Brewer, 67 Me, 295 (1877), McMillan v Maysville & Lexington R R Co, 15 B Monroe, 218 (1854), Swartout v Mich An Line R R Co., 24 Mich, 389 (1872), where Judge Cooley says " It is only reasonable to infer that they would have expressed that intent more clearly, and would have indicated with definiteness what stage the work should reach, before their liability should become fixed " So also in Miller v Pittsburgh & Connellsville R R Co, 40 Pa St, 237 (1861), where the court say ' It is a most extraordinary defense, for it presupposes that the company were to build their road without money, and to deliver it, a finished work, to the stock subscribers, who were then to pay their subscriptions " In Pittsburgh & Steubenville R R Co v Biggar, 34 Pa St, 455 (1859), a condition, "provided the road goes within half a mile of Florence," was held to be a condition subsequent A condition that alterations shall be ordered only by a vote of the directors is a condition subsequent Bucksport & Bangor R R Co v Buck, 68 Me, 81 (1878) So also of a condition that com-

missioners should be appointed to see that other conditions are complied with Shaffner v Jeffries, 18 Mo, 512 (1853) And a condition that the money subscribed shall be expended on a certain part of the road Lane v Brainerd, 30 Conn, 565 (1862) A condition that a depot shall be established at a certain place is a condition subsequent Paducah, etc, R R v Parks, 8 S W. Rep., 842 (Tenn, 1888) A condition that bonds will be issued as a ' bonus" to a stockholder is void It is a condition subsequent The subscription is enforceable Morrow v Nashville, etc, Co, 10 S. W Rep, 495 (Tenn, 1889). Condition construed subsequent. Johnson v. Georgia, etc, R R Co, 8 S E. Rep, 531 (Ga 1889) For the English cases on conditions precedent and subsequent to subscriptions for stock, see ch II, *supra*

[1] A condition subsequent "will not defeat an action for the recovery of the money, notwithstanding it had not been performed when the action was commenced " Belfast & Moosehead Lake R'y Co v Moore, 60 Me, 561, 576 (1871) ' A failure to perform an independent stipulation, not amounting to a condition precedent, though it subject the party failing to damages, does not excuse the party on the other side from the performance of all stipulations on his part " Mill Dam Foundry v. Hovey, 38 Mass, 417 437 (1839)

[2] The subscriber is left to the ordinary remedies for breaches of contracts.

A subscriber cannot avoid payment as against a corporate creditor although the subscription was on condition that if the subscription exceeded one-half the cost of a certain building, only so much of the subscription should be called for as would equal that half. The subscriber cannot forfeit what he has paid and re-

dinary conditional subscriptions — that is, subscriptions on conditions precedent — is sometimes difficult to determine. The supreme court of Maine has said that the question whether a condition in a subscription " be precedent or subsequent is a question purely of intent, and the intention must be determined by considering not only the words of the particular clause, but also the language of the whole contract, as well as the nature of the act required and the subject-matter to which it relates " [1] The courts, in accordance with well-established rules, favor conditions subsequent.[2]

§ 79 *Conditional subscriptions not allowed in subscriptions to obtain incorporation* — Conditional subscriptions made before the incorporation of a company, and taken for the purpose of securing such incorporation, as prescribed by statute, are of doubtful validity. The weight of authority holds that subscriptions taken for the purpose of complying with a statute which grants a charter only upon a certain amount of stock being subscribed cannot be conditional, but must be absolute [3] This is clearly the rule in New York and Pennsylvania, and is founded in justice.[4]

fuse to pay the remainder Mathis v Pridham, 20 S W Rep 1015 (Tex , 1892)

A condition that the subscriptions when collected shall be used to build factories which should be leased was enforced in Porter v Carpenter, 23 Atl. Rep., 523 (N. H., 1874).

See, also, § 97, *infra*

[1] Bucksport & B R R. Co v Inhabitants of Brewer, 67 Me , 295 (1877) "The situation and relation of the parties to each other, the object sought to be attained, and the subject-matter to which the agreement relates, are material . . and indispensable aids" in deciding whether the condition be precedent or subsequent. Chamberlain v Painesville & Hudson R. R. Co , 15 Ohio St , 225 (1864)

[2] Chamberlain v Painesville & Hudson R. R. Co , 15 Ohio St., 225 (1864), Swartout v. Mich An Line R. R Co , 24 Mich , 389 (1872)

[3] "A subscription to the stock of a public corporation, made before letters patent are issued and an organization effected, must be considered absolute and unqualified, and any condition attached thereto void Commissioners have no authority to receive conditional

subscriptions " Boyd v Peach Bottom R'y Co., 90 Pa. St., 169 (1879). "Any other rule would lead to the procurement from the commonwealth of valuable charters without any absolute capital for their support, and thus give rise to a system of speculation and fraud which would be intolerable " Caley v Phila & Chester County R R. Co., 80 Pa St., 363 (1876) See, also, Erie, etc., Co v Brown, 25 Pa. St., 156 (1855); Nippenose Mfg Co v Stadton, 68 Pa. St., 256 (1871), Pittsburgh, etc., R R. Co v Stewart, 41 Pa. St., 54 (1861); Troy & Boston R. R Co. v. Tibbits, 18 Barb , 297 (1854) That conditional subscriptions are not to be counted in ascertaining whether the whole capital stock has been subscribed, which must be shown before another absolute subscriber can be made liable, see § 180

[4] Some of the old cases uphold conditional subscriptions made previous to and for the purpose of incorporation Chamberlain v Painesville & Hudson R. R. Co , 15 Ohio St., 225 (1864). It is doubtful, however, whether any well-considered case, under the present general laws allowing the incorporation of railroads, would sustain such a sub-

§ 80. *In New York the subscription is void; in Pennsylvania the condition is void.*— The New York and Pennsylvania cases differ, however, in regard to the effect of a conditional subscription to stock before and for the purpose of incorporation. In New York the whole subscription is void absolutely. It is as though not made, and cannot be enforced either by the corporation or by the would-be subscriber[1] In Pennsylvania a different rule prevails. The condition is void, but the subscription itself is treated as an absolute unconditional subscription, and may be enforced by the corporation[2] The commissioners are held to have only limited statutory powers, of which the subscriber is bound to take notice, and the express powers do not give authority to the commissioners to take conditional subscriptions. They have no right to receive various kinds of subscriptions, and any conditions are held to be void as a fraud upon the state, upon corporate creditors, and upon other subscribers[3]

§ 81. *Oral conditions are void.*— Under the general rule of evidence that a written agreement cannot be varied or added to by parol, it is not competent for a subscriber to stock to allege that he is but a conditional subscriber[4] The condition must be inserted in the writing in order to be effectual. Where, however, the parol agreement or condition is made subsequently to the making of the contract, and upon a sufficient consideration, it has been upheld[5]

§ 82. *Conditional subscriptions after incorporation are valid.*— A conditional subscription to stock, taken and accepted by a corporation after its incorporation, is legal and valid by the common-law

scription. The weight of authority is decidedly in favor of absolute subscriptions.

[1] Troy & Boston R. R. Co. v. Tibbits, 18 Barb., 297 (1854), *In re* Rochester, etc., R. R. Co., 50 Hun, 29 (1888), where the subscription was to be paid in land

[2] "Where one subscribes to the stock of a public corporation, prior to the procurement of its charter, such subscription is to be regarded as absolute and unqualified, and any condition attached thereto is void" Caley v. Phila. & Chester Co. R. R. Co., 80 Pa St., 363 (1876). "The subscription is valid and binding, and the condition null and void" Boyd v. Peach Bottom R'y Co, 90 Pa. St., 169 (1879) To the same effect, see Bedford R. R. Co v Bowser, 48 Pa. St., 29 (1864), Barrington v. Pitts-

burgh & Steubenville R. R. Co, 44 Pa St., 358, Pittsburgh & Steubenville R. R. Co v Biggar, 34 Pa St., 455 (1859), Same v Woodrow, 3 Phil., 271 (1858) The subscription itself, however, is not binding if it is not reported by the commissioners and used to obtain the charter. Ligonier Valley R. R. Co v Williams, 35 Leg Intel, 40 (1878). In the federal courts, Burke v Smith, 16 Wall, 390, 396 (1872), favors the Pennsylvania rule, while Putnam v City of New Albany, 4 Biss, 365, 383 (1869), favors the New York rule In both cases the opinions are *dicta* See also, Ellison v Mobile & O. R. R. Co, 36 Miss, 572 (1858)

[3] Same cases.

[4] See §§ 137, 138.

[5] Id

of all the States. In Pennsylvania the legality of such conditional subscriptions is clearly declared and sustained.[1] In New York, also, conditional subscriptions have been upheld,[2] but not where the condition is one that affects the route of a turnpike or railroad company In other states the legality of such subscriptions is rarely questioned, but is generally assumed to be admitted[3]

§ 83. *What condition may be attached to a subscription.*— Any condition which can be legally performed or complied with by the corporation may be the condition to a subscription for stock.[4] The condition may be that payment shall be in labor or materials;[5] it

---

[1] " It is no longer to be doubted that an incorporated company, after it has obtained its letters patent and effected its organization, may receive conditional subscriptions to its stock " Pittsburgh & Connellsville R R. Co v Stewart, 41 Pa St., 54 (1861), Caley v Phila & Chester County R. R. Co., 80 Pa St., 363 (1876), Phila, etc, R. R Co. v Hickman, 28 Pa St., 318 (1857) After incorporation conditional subscriptions may be received, although the letters patent have not been issued and cannot be until ten per cent of the capital stock is subscribed The conditional subscription cannot, however, form any part of such percentage. Hanover Junction & Susquehanna R. R. Co. v Haldeman, 82 Pa. St., 36 (1876).

[2] Ordinary conditional subscriptions were treated as valid in Union Hotel Co v Hersee, 79 N Y 454 (1880), Burrows t Smith 10 N Y , 550 (1853), Morris Canal & Bkg. Co. v Nathan, 2 Hall, 239 (1892) But the condition that a particular location of the proposed road should be adopted has been held to be contrary to public policy, since improper means would thereby influence the question of location Butternuts & Oxford Turnpike Co. v North, 1 Hill, 518 (1841), Fort Edward, etc, Co v Payne, 15 N Y , 583 (1857) Macedon & Bristol Plank Road Co. v Snediker 18 Barb , 317 (1854), *dictum* in Dix v Shaver, 14 Hun, 392 (1878) However, in the case of Lake Ontario Shore R. R. Co v Curtiss, 80 N. Y., 219 (1880) a condition of this kind was involved, and

no objection was made to its validity. Subscriptions conditional, in that payment is to be permitted in property, labor or contract for construction, have been repeatedly passed upon in New York and upheld See ch. II.

[3] " Except in New York, conditional subscriptions, in the absence of a special prohibition, so far as we have observed, have been sustained as authorized and not in conflict with public policy " Ashtabula & New London R. R. Co. v Smith, 15 Ohio St., 328 (1864) See, also, § 97, *infra*, New Albany & Salem R. R. Co. v McCormick, 10 Ind , 499 (1858), McMillan v Maysville & Lexington R. R Co, 15 B Monroe, 218 (1854), Dayton, etc, R. R. Co. v Hatch, 1 Disney, 84 (1855) A conditional subscription to the stock of a railroad company is legal Baltimore. etc., R. R. Co. v. Pumphrey, 21 Atl Rep , 559 (Md , 1891). Conditional subscriptions may be received Armstrong v Karshner, 24 N. E. Rep., 897 (Ohio, 1890) If the condition is *ultra vires* of the corporation, the subscription is not enforceable, there having been no performance Pellatt's Case, L. R., 2 Ch , 527 (1867).

[4] The subscriber " may agree to take and pay for the stock absolutely or upon such condition as he may choose to incorporate into his subscription " Penobscot & Kennebec R. R. Co v. Dunn, 39 Me , 587 (1855), Mathis v Pridham, 20 S W Rep, 1015 (Tex , 1892)

[5] See ch II

may require the expenditure of the subscription on a particular part of the enterprise,[1] it may stipulate that a certain amount or the whole of the capital stock shall be subscribed before calls are made on the subscriptions;[2] or it may limit the time within which certain things specified therein must be done[3] In most states the condition to a subscription may require the route of a railroad to be located on a particular line.[4] In New York such a conditional subscription has been held to be void, on the ground of public policy, inasmuch as the discretion of the directors, in laying out the route, would thereby be influenced by considerations other than those of a purely public nature.[5]

In general, however, subscriptions to the capital stock of a corporation may be conditional as to the time, manner or means of payment, or in any other way not prohibited by statute, or the

---

[1] Milwaukee & Northern Ill R R. Co v. Field, 12 Wis., 340 (1860), Hanover Junction & Sus. R. R. Co v Haldeman, 82 Pa. St., 36 (1876)

[2] Phil & West Chester R R. Co. v. Hickman, 28 Pa St., 318, Penobscot & Kennebec R R Co. v Dunn, 39 Me, 587 (1855), Hanover Junction & Sus R. R. Co v Haldeman, *supra*, Union Hotel Co v. Hersee, 79 N Y., 454 (1880) Even though the charter allowed the commencement of business upon the subscription of a less sum. Ridgefield & N. Y. R. R. Co. v Brush, 43 Conn, 86 (1875)

[3] Ticonic Water-power Mfg. Co v. Lang, 63 Me, 480 (1874), holding also that time herein is of the essence of the contract. See, also, Morris Canal & Banking Co v. Nathan, 2 Hall (N Y), 239 (1829). See, also, § 87

[4] Fisher v Evansville, etc, R. R. Co. 7 Ind, 407 (1856), Conn & Passumpsic R. R. Co. v Baxtar, 32 Vt, 805 (1860), Cumberland Valley R. R. Co v Baab, 9 Watts, 458 (1840), Evansville etc, R. R. Co v Shearer, 10 Ind, 246 (1858), Jewett v Lawrenceburgh, etc., R. R. Co, 10 Ind, 539 (1858), Missouri Pacific R'y Co v Taggard, 84 Mo, 264 (1884), Wear v Jacksonville, etc, R. R. Co, 24 Ill, 595 (1860), Taggart v Western Md R. R. Co, 24 Md, 563 (1866), Racine County Bank v Ayers, 12 Wis., 512 (1860) See,

also, Caley v Phil & Chester County R R Co, 80 Pa St., 363 (1876) Location may be required to be subject to the approval of the subscriber Roberts Case, 3 De Gex & Sm, 205 (1850) aff'd 2 Mac & G, 196. See, also, Mansfield, etc, R R. Co v Brown, 26 Ohio St, 224 (1875), Same v Stout, 26 Ohio St, 241 (1875), Chamberlain v Painesville, etc, R. R. Co, 15 Ohio St., 225 (1864), North, etc, R R Co. v Winkler 29 Mo, 318 (1860), Spartanburgh, etc, R. R. Co v De Graffenried, 12 Rich L. 675 (1860), Des Moines, etc, R R Co v Graff, 27 Iowa 99 (1869) A subscription or note, not for stock, but absolutely as a gift to the corporation, in consideration of a particular route being adopted, has been upheld Stowell v Stowell, 45 Mich, 364, First Nat'l Bank v Hendrie, 49 Iowa, 402 (1878) A subscription or donation to a railroad, conditional on the location of a depot is enforceable by the company Berryman v Cincinnati S R y, 14 Bush (Ky), 755 (1879) See § 650 A construction company, under contract to construct a road by the shortest route, cannot collect a sum promised by a third person for a deflection of the route Woodstock Iron Co. v Extension Co., 129 U S, 612 (1889

[5] See § 82, n

123

rules of public policy, and not beyond the corporate powers of the corporation to comply with [1]

§ 84. *Acceptance by the corporation is necessary* — The acceptance by the corporation of a conditional subscription is necessary to the formation of the contract [2] Until such acceptance the conditional subscription is but a continuing offer. After acceptance the subscriber is bound, until performance of the condition by the corporation, to await such performance, he cannot withdraw the conditional subscription after it has been accepted. It seems, however, that if the performance of the condition is delayed unreasonably by the corporation, the conditional subscriber will be thereby released from his obligation [3]

[1] Conditions inconsistent with the charter are void Thigpen v Miss, etc, R. R. Co, 32 Miss., 347 (1856) The conditions which may be legally made to a subscription are practically limited only by the power of the corporation to contract. A few of the conditions which have been passed upon by the courts have been given Many minor ones are involved in the cases, and present a great variety of conditions, corresponding, as they do, to the wishes and motives of individuals subscribing to the stock of the different kinds of joint-stock corporations The condition of a subscription may be that the subscriber be made secretary Mogridge s Case, 58 L. T Rep, 801 (1888)

[2] Junction R. R. Co v. Reeve, 15 Ind, 236 (1860), where the subscription was payable in land See, also, Galt's Ex'rs v Swain, 9 Gratt. (Va), 633 (1853) "When the offer was accepted the minds of the parties met and the contract was complete . The acceptance by the plaintiff constituted a sufficient legal consideration for the engagement on the part of the defendants." Taggart v Western Md R. R. Co, 24 Md, 563 (1866) By the entry of the subscription on the corporate record an acceptance is implied New Albany & Salem R. R Co v McCormick, 10 Ind 499 (1858) Acceptance by the president of the corporation, and a subsequent ratification by the directors of all his acts, is sufficient Pitts-

burgh & Connellsville R R. Co. v. Stewart, 41 Pa. St, 54 (1861) The delivery and acceptance may be proved by parol. Mansfield & New Lisbon R. R. Co v. Smith, 15 Ohio St., 328 (1864) Where it is delivered in escrow to the agent of the corporation, there can be no acceptance of it by the corporation, so long as such delivery continues. Cass v Pittsburgh, Va. & Charleston R'y Co, 80 Pa St., 31 (1875). It may be revoked while still in the hands of a corporate agent. Lowe v Edgefield & K. R. R. Co., 1 Head (Tenn), 659 (1858). The subscribers cannot withdraw unless there is unreasonable delay Armstrong v. Karshner, 24 N E Rep, 897 (Ohio, 1890).

[3] Where, the condition not being performed, the subscriber notifies the secretary of his withdrawal from the subscription, he is released. Wood's Case, L. R, 15 Eq, 236 (1873) "The objection to a continuing offer, that it suspends indefinitely the liability of the conditional subscribers, is sufficiently answered by the consideration that all such offers are subject to retraction, and may be recalled if their acceptance is unreasonably deferred" Taggart v Western Md R. R. Co, 24 Md, 563 (1866) See query and briefs in Mansfield, Coldwater & Lake Mich R. R. Co v Stout, 26 Ohio St, 241 (1875), which holds that the question of acceptance is immaterial where performance of the condition has been completed by the corporation

§ 85. *Construction of conditional subscription* — Conditional subscriptions, like other contracts, are to be construed reasonably and according to the intent of the parties, as indicated by the language used in the contract.[1] The circumstances under which the subscription was made are also to be taken into consideration.[2] If two interpretations are possible, that which facilitates the enterprise is preferred to that which retards it.[3] If the meaning is ambiguous, it is for the jury to say what the interpretation is to be.[4]

§ 86. *Performance of the condition.* — A condition to a subscription for stock must be performed or complied with before the subscriber can be compelled to pay such subscription.[5] A substantial performance of the condition is sufficient.[6] A failure to perform is not excused by reason of unforeseen difficulties arising from

---

[1] The whole contract is to be taken together, and is "to have a reasonable construction according to the intent of the parties." People's Ferry Co *v* Balch, 74 Mass., 303 (1857) "The language was chosen by them to express their mutual intent, and such construction must be given thereto as will carry into effect that mutual understanding . . We are to ascertain what the parties understood and intended by this language, and may not deviate therefrom, whether that contract, as so interpreted, be wise or unwise for either party." Memphis, Kan & Col R. R Co *v* Thompson, 24 Kan, 170 (1880)

[2] "The contract must be interpreted by the light of the circumstances which existed at the time it was made, and not of those which arose afterwards" Monadnock R. R. *v* Felt, 52 N H, 379 (1872), Detroit, L. & L. M R. R. Co *v* Starnes, 38 Mich, 698 (1878)

[3] Ashtabula & New Lisbon R. R. Co *v* Smith, 15 Ohio St., 328 (1864)

[4] Connecticut R. R. Co. *v* Baxter, 32 Vt, 805 (1860)

[5] Porter *v.* Raymond, 53 N H, 519 (1873), Monadnock R. R. *v* Felt, 59 N. H., 379 (1872), Montpelier & Wells River R. R Co *v* Langdon, 46 Vt, 284 (1873); Ashtabula & New Lisbon R. R. Co *v* Smith, 15 Ohio St., 328 (1864), Phil & West Chester R. R. Co *v.* Hickman, 28 Pa. St., 318 (1857); Burrows *v.* Smith,

10 N Y, 550 Upon the performance of the condition by the promisee the contract is clothed with a valid consideration, which relates back, and the promise at once becomes obligatory" Des Moines Valley R. R. Co *v* Graff 27 Iowa, 99 (1869). Upon fulfillment of the condition that a certain amount be subscribed, the subscription may be collected. Security State Bank *v* Racine, 48 N W Rep., 262 (Neb., 1891) A contract of subscription to a railroad company when certain things are done by it is collectible when these things have been done Lesher *v* Karshner, 24 N E. Rep, 882 (Ohio, 1890) A conditional subscription may be enforced after the condition has been performed Webb *v.* Baltimore etc, Co, 26 Atl. Rep, 113 (Md, 1893)

[6] O'Neal *v* King, 3 Jones' L. (N C), 517 (1856) See, also, Virginia, etc. R. R. Co *v* County Comm'rs, etc, 8 Nev, 68 (1870), Springfield St R'y Co. *v* Sleeper, 121 Mass, 29 (1876), People *v* Holden, 82 Ill, 93 (1876) Performance must be within a reasonable time Stevens *v* Corbitt, 33 Mich, 458 (1876). Subscription on express condition that it shall be payable only in case the whole amount is subscribed cannot be collected, where the whole amount was made up by including the subscriptions of married women who had not paid. Appeal of Hahn, 7 Atl Rep., 482 (Pa.,

floods and natural causes.[1]　A conditional subscriber is not a stockholder or member of the corporation until after the condition is performed[2]　Whether or not the condition has been performed is a question of fact[3]　Performance may be proved by parol or by the records of the corporation[4]

§ 87. Where the condition is that the work shall be begun, contracted for or completed within a certain time, time is of the essence of the contract, and any failure to perform within the time so specified defeats the subscription.[5]　A condition that the road

1886). Condition that subscription shall be payable only when a sum deemed sufficient by the directors has been subscribed is not fulfilled when the directors fixed a sum, and then later reduced the sum to the amount subscribed. Only unconditional subscriptions are to be counted. Brand v Lawrenceville, etc. R. R. Co, 1 S. E Rep, 255 (Ga, 1887). If performance turns on a writing, question is for the court. Id. Reasonable performance is all that is required. Thus completion of a blast furnace, as a condition, is satisfied by completion by lessee. Appeal of Cornell, 6 Atl Rep, 258 (Pa., 1886) Condition that company shall construct a road from and to specified points is not fulfilled by construction of part of the way and running over another railroad for the remainder of the distance. Brown v Dibble, 32 N. W Rep, 656 (Mich, 1887) *Contra*, People v. Holden, 82 Ill, 93. In the case of Martin v Pensacola & Geo. R. R. Co., 8 Fla., 370, 390 (1859), it is stated, in a *dictum*, that a strict compliance is necessary. But see Branham v. Record, 42 Ind, 181 (1873). A subscription to an enterprise, conditional upon the performance of that enterprise by certain named parties and a conveyance of the results to a corporation, may be enforced by such parties upon due performance. Brewer v. Stone, 77 Mass, 228 (1859). A subscription to a railroad, conditional upon its completing the road, is not enforceable by a consolidated company which succeeds to and completes the road. Toledo, etc., R. R. v. Hinsdale, 15 N. E.

Rep, 665 (Ohio, 1888). Substantial compliance with condition is sufficient. Cravens v Eagle, etc., Co, 21 N. E. Rep., 981 (Ind, 1889).

[1] Memphis, Kan. & Col. R. R. Co. v Thompson, 24 Kan, 170 (1880).

[2] Chase v Sycamore & Courtland R. R. Co., 38 Ill, 215 (1865), Slipher v Earhart. Adm. 83 Ind, 173 (1882); Evansville, Ind & Cleveland S L. R. R. Co v. Shearer, 10 Ind, 244 (1858)

[3] Jewett v Lawrenceburgh & U. M. R. R Co, 10 Ind, 539 (1858). And is a question for the jury St Louis & Cedar Rapids R. R. Co. v Eakins, 30 Iowa, 279 1870).

[4] By parol St Louis & Cedar Rapids R. R Co. v Eakins, 30 Iowa, 279 (1870). By corporate records Penobscot & Kennebec R. R Co v Dunn, 39 Me, 587 (1855). *Contra*, Phil & West Chester R. R. Co v. Hickman, 28 Pa. St., 318 (1857) Performance must be alleged in the complaint or declaration. Trott v Sarchett, 10 Ohio St., 241 (1859); Roberts v Mobile & O R. R. Co., 32 Miss., 373 (1856), Henderson & Nashville R. R. Co. v Leavell, 16 B Monroe, 358 (1855).

[5] Burlington & Missouri River R. R. Co. v. Boestler, 15 Iowa 555 (1864), per Dillon, J ; Freeman v. Mack, 67 Ind, 99 (1879), Memphis, Kan & Col. R. R. Co v Thompson, 24 Kan, 170 (1880); Portland & Oxford Central R. R. Co. v. Inhabitants of Hartford, 58 Me, 23 (1870). An agreement to pay a corporation a certain sum if it built and started a factory within a certain time is not collectible if the contract is not fulfilled within that time. Bohn Manuf. Co v.

shall be "permanently" located on a specified route is satisfied by the adoption of that route by the directors.[1] Where the question of whether performance has been completed rests in the decision of the directors, their conclusion cannot be questioned, unless fraud or bad faith is proved[2] A condition that the subscription shall be applied to a particular portion of the road is satisfied by the completion of that portion[3] Any fraud on the part of the corporation in the performance of the condition may be shown by parol[4] All of several conditions must be performed before calls are made[5] But if one part of the subscription be free from condition, that part may be collected independently.[6] Where, after part payment by the conditional subscriber, the corporate plans are changed, so that the condition is not complied with, the money, it has been held, may be recovered.[7]

§ 88. *Waiver of the condition*—A conditional subscriber to the stock of a corporation may waive the condition and performance thereof, and thus become liable on his subscription, as though it had been originally an absolute one The waiver may be by an oral statement or agreement of the subscriber[8] Certain acts of the subscriber have been held to indicate an intent to waive a condition to the subscription, and to be equivalent to a direct waiver. Thus acting as a director,[9] or as president of the corpora-

---

Lewis, 47 N W. Rep 652 (Minn, 1891) If the directors certify that the condition was performed within the specified time, the subscriber may prove the falsity of their certificate Morris Canal & Bkg. Co. *v.* Nathan, 2 Hall (N Y), 239 (1829) Upon the failure of the corporation to comply with this condition the subscription ceases to have any vitality "by its own limitation" Ticonic Water-power & Mfg Co *v* Lang, 63 Me, 430 (1874) In the case, however, of Missouri Pacific R'y Co *v* Taggard, 84 Mo., 264 (1884), a completion of the road within a reasonable time after the time specified in the condition was held to be a substantial performance, and sufficient, the grading having been completed in the specified time See, also, Moore *v* Campbell, 12 N E Rep, 495 (Ind, 1887), where the condition was inserted in a promissory note

[1] Smith *v* Allison, 23 Ind, 366 (1864), and see cases in § 78. So also a condition that the road shall cross another at a certain point is satisfied by its being so located Wear *v* Jacksonville & Savannah R R. Co, 24 Ill, 593 (1860)

[2] Cass *v* Pittsburg, Va & Charleston R'y Co, 80 Pa. St, 31 (1875)

[3] Nichols *v* Burlington & Louisa County Plank-road Co, 4 Greene (Iowa), 42 (1853).

[4] New York Ex Co. *v* De Wolf, 31 N Y, 271 (1865)

[5] Porter *v* Raymond, 53 N H, 519 (1873)

[6] St Louis, etc., R. R. Co. *v* Eakins 30 Iowa, 279 (1870)

[7] Jewett *v* Lawrenceburgh & U M R R. Co, 10 Ind, 539 (1858)

[8] Hanover Junction & Sus R. R. Co *v* Haldeman, 82 Pa. St., 36 (1876). See, also, Woonsocket Union R. R. Co *v* Sherman, 8 R. I 564 (1867).

[9] Lane *v* Brainard, 30 Conn, 565 (1862)

Where a person subscribes for preferred stock, but no preferred stock is provided for, and he becomes a director

tion,[1] paying the whole of the subscription,[2] giving an absolute promissory note without conditions in payment of the subscription,[3] have each been held to constitute a waiver of the condition to a subscription. But mere silence is not a waiver,[4] nor payment of part of the subscription,[5] nor aid in the attempt to start the enterprise, by soliciting subscriptions and being elected to a corporate office.[6]

§ 89. *Notice of performance and calls* — There is some doubt as to whether, upon performance of the condition, the subscriber is entitled to notice of such performance. The better rule seems to be that he is entitled to such notice, and that a general "call" for the payment of part or all of the subscriptions for stock does not apply to conditional subscribers, unless the condition has been performed, and the fact of performance has been brought to the attention of the subscriber.[7]

and acts as such for several years, he is liable on such stock to corporate creditors, as though it were a subscription for common stock. Tama, etc, Co v. Hopkins, 44 N. W. Rep, 797 (Iowa 1890)

[1] Dayton & Cincinnati R R. Co v Hatch, 1 Disney (Ohio), 84 (1855)

[2] Parks v. Evansville, Ind & Cleveland S L R. R Co, 23 Ind, 567 (1864)

[3] Chamberlain v Painesville & Hudson R R Co., 15 Ohio St, 225 (1864), Shipher v Earhart, Adm, 83 Ind, 173 (1882), Evansville, etc, R R. Co. v Dunn, 17 Ind, 603 (1861), Keller v Johnson, 11 Ind, 337 (1858), O'Donald v Evansville, etc, R R. Co, 14 Ind, 259 (1860). But not where the note was given by reason of false representations that the condition had been complied with Parker v Thomas, 19 Ind, 213 (1862), Taylor v Fletcher, 15 Ind, 80 (1860)

[4] Burlington & Mo River R R. Co v Boestler, 15 Iowa, 555 (1864), Bucksport & Bangor R R. Co v. Inhabitants of Brewer, 67 Me, 295 (1877). In Oregon it is held that where the condition was the subscribing of a certain amount within a certain time, which was not done, but was performed soon after that time, the conditional subscriber is bound, where he did not cause his subscription to be stricken from the books

Lee v Granger, etc, Co., 11 Pac. Rep., 270 (1886). Subscribers obtaining stock on condition that a building contract be given to them cannot rescind for nonperformance by the company, where the subscribers have long delayed rescission, after such refusal of the company to perform Rankin v. Hop, etc., Co, 20 L. T Rep., 207 (1869). Failure of a subscriber conditionally, for a long time, to have his name taken off the list, renders him liable on the wind-up Wheatcroft s Case, 29 L. T. Rep, 324 (1873).

[5] Pittsburgh & Connellsville R. R. Co. v. Stewart, 41 Pa. St, 54 (1861); Robert's Case, 2 Mac. & G, 196 (1850); Jewett v Lawrenceburgh & U. M. R. R. Co, 10 Ind, 539 (1858) But see Appeal of Mack, 7 Atl Rep., 481 (Pa., 1886), where, however, a substantial performance had been made

[6] Ridgefield & N Y R R Co. v. Reynolds, 46 Conn, 375 (1878)

[7] Chase v Sycamore & Courtland R. R. Co, 38 Ill, 215 (1865); Trott v Sarchett, 10 Ohio St, 241 (1859). *Contra*, Nichols v Burlington & Louisa County Plank-road Co, 4 Greene (Iowa), 42 (1853), Spartanburg & Union R. R. Co. v De Graffenreid, 12 Rich L. (S C.), 675 (1860), holding that no "call" is necessary, and that interest runs from the time of performance

Subscriptions payable in property are not subject to calls, and a demand for the property must be made by the corporation [1] Upon failure of the subscriber to furnish the property, or upon insolvency of the corporation, such subscriptions become payable in cash.[2]

[1] Ohio, etc., R. R. Co v. Cramer, 23 Ind , 490 (1864)   Payment cannot be required in instalments. Id. But upon demand the subscriber must ascertain when and where the materials are to be delivered   McClure v People's R. R. Co , 90 Pa. St , 269 (1879)

[2] Haywood, etc , R. R. Co. v. Bryan, 6 Jones (N C), 82 (1858), Sperry v Johnson, 11 Ohio, 452 (1842). See § 18, n 3. In one case, however, it was held that the subscriber was liable only in damages to the extent of the market value of the stock. Dayton & Cin. R. R. Co v Hatch, 1 Disney, 84 (1855) Subscription on condition of being appointed secretary is not enforceable on wind-up, the appointment not having been made. Rogers' Case, L. R., 3 Ch , 633 (1868).

CHAPTER VI.

MUNICIPAL SUBSCRIPTIONS.

§ 90 *A municipal corporation has no implied power or authority to subscribe for stock in any other corporation* — A municipal corporation, being in its nature and purposes a very different legal institution from an ordinary private corporation, being indeed but a mode or department of government — "an investing the people of a place with the local government thereof," [1] — it is plain that the general rules of law applicable to private corporations having capital stock are, for the most part, applicable when the rights, duties, powers and liabilities of municipal corporations are sought to be accurately determined? [2]

It is proposed to consider the right of a municipality to enter into the contract of subscription to the capital stock of other corporations, and of the liabilities, rights and duties growing out of such a subscription The subject practically narrows itself to the right of municipal corporations to subscribe to the stock of railway corporations, inasmuch as this right, wherever it exists, is almost universally exercised in favor of these corporations, and the adjudicated cases almost all present phases of the question applying to them.

It is a well-settled rule of law that municipal corporations have

[1] Cuddon *v* Eastwick, 1 Salk, 183 (1704), Dillon on Munic Corp. §§ 19, 20

[2] People *v* Morris, 13 Wend, 325 (1835); People *v* Hurlbut, 24 Mich, 44

(1871), State *v* Leffingwell, 54 Mo, 458 (1873); Norton *v* Peck, 3 Wis, 714 (1854), Ottawa *v* Carey, 108 U S, 110 (1883).

130

no implied right or authority to subscribe for the stock of any other incorporated company [1] In order, therefore, to establish the validity of a municipal subscription to the stock of a railway company, an express grant of authority from the legislature must be shown [2] The right to subscribe is derived from the legislative enactment, and whether or not an enabling act is sufficient to validate a subscription is a question of law for the court, not for the jury [3]

Every holder of municipal bonds issued to raise money to pay such a subscription, whether he receives them directly from the town or county or from the railway company to which they may have been delivered, or takes them from some prior holder in the ordinary course of business, is chargeable with notice of the statutory provisions under which they were issued.[4]

The right to make a donation to a railroad or other work of

[1] "To become stockholders in private corporations," says Judge Dillon. "is manifestly foreign to the usual purposes intended to be subserved by the creation of corporate municipalities" Dillon on Munic Corp, § 161 Kelley v Milan, 127 U S., 139 (1888) See, also Kenicott v Supervisors, 16 Wall. 452 (1872), Thompson v Lee County, 3 id, 327 (1865), Bell v Railroad Co, 4 id, 598 (1866), Wells v Supervisors, 102 U S, 625 (1880) Lamoille, etc, R. R. Co. v Fairfield, 51 Vt, 257 (1878), Burnes v Lacon, 84 Ill, 461 (1877), holding that a vote of the people of a town to subscribe for stock without the authorization of law is not binding upon the town To same effect, Allen v Louisiana, 103 U S, 80 (1880) Pennsylvania R. R. Co v Philadelphia, 47 Penn St., 189 (1864), City of Jonesboro' v Cairo, etc, R. R. Co, 110 U S, 192 (1883), holding that a general power to borrow money and issue bonds therefor does not confer the right to subscribe for stock, even with the sanction of the voters at a general election Cf Gelpcke v Dubuque, 1 Wall 220 (1863), Campbell v Paris, etc, R. R. Co, 71 Ill, 611 (1874), East Oakland v Skinner, 94 U S, 255 (1876), City of Lynchburg v. Slaughter, 75 Va, 57 (1880); Brodie v. McCabe, 33 Ark, 690 (1878) A municipal corporation cannot enforce a penal bond, given to it by a plank-road company, conditioned that the latter will use to build its road certain bonds issued by the former, it appearing that the aid to the plank-road company was ultra vires of the municipality City Council, etc, v Montgomery, etc, Co, 31 Ala, 76 (1857) Attorney-general may restrain municipality from illegally issuing bonds to a railroad company State v Saline, etc, Court, 51 Mo, 350 (1873), reviewing the English and American cases

[2] Sharpless v The Mayor, 21 Penn St., 147 (1853), Leavenworth Co v Miller, 7 Kan, 479 (1871) Cf Welch v Post 99 Ill, 471 (1881), Marsh v Fulton Co 10 Wall, 676 (1870) holding that the power to subscribe to the stock of a railroad is not sufficient to authorize a subscription to a new incorporation of a part of it, La Fayette v Cox, 5 Ind, 38 (1854) Dillon on Munic Corp, § 161, Ottawa v Carey, 108 U S 110 (1883) Lewis v City of Shreveport. 108 id, 282 (1883).

[3] Post v Supervisors, 105 U S 667 (1881) Leavenworth Co v Miller supra

[4] Ogden v County of Daviess, 102 U S, 634 (1880), Lewis v City of Shreveport, 108 id 282 (1883) City of Ottawa v Carey 108 id 110 (1883) McClure v Township of Oxford, 94 id, 429 (1876) This is the settled rule of the supreme court of the United States on this point

internal improvement must equally be derived from the act of the legislature. Without such express authority of law, a donation or issue of bonds as a gift to a railroad company is invalid and void.[1]

§ 91 *The legislature may authorize municipal subscriptions to public but not to private enterprises.*— It was long a question whether the legislature had the constitutional right to authorize a municipality to subscribe money, or donate it, in furtherance of any enterprise not governmental in its nature. It has been contended with great ability and learning that such a right does not inhere in the legislative branch of the government in this country, and consequently that such assumed grants are unconstitutional and void [2] But it is now a well-settled rule that the legislature has the constitutional power to authorize a municipal corporation, by its charter or an express act, to subscribe to the stock of a railway or other *quasi*-public corporation, and to issue and sell its bonds for that purpose [3] The inclination of municipalities to repudiate

---

[1] Dixon County *v.* Field, 111 U. S., 83 (1884)

The power of the legislature to authorize a municipality to donate funds or bonds herein is absolutely denied in Hanson *v.* Vernon, 27 Iowa, 28, Sweet *v.* Hulbert, 51 Barb, 312 (1868) *Cf* Commissioners *v.* Miller, 7 Kan, 479 The railroad cannot collect, as a donation, money which was voted as a subscription. Crooks *v.* State, 4 N E. Rep., 589 (Ind, 1886)

A gift of bonds is invalid. So, also, of a subscription payable in bonds where part of the bonds are turned back for the stock Post *v* Pulaski County, 49 Fed Rep, 628 (1892).

[2] Cooley on Const. Lim, pp 261-266, Dillon on Munic. Corp, §§ 12, 117, 153. For the rule in Michigan, Iowa and New York, see next note

Concerning the public phases of municipal aid to railroads, see Cook on The Corporation Problem, pp. 99-101.

[3] So held by the supreme court of the United States Knox County *v.* Aspinwall, 21 How, 539 (1858), Zabriskie *v* Railroad Co, 23 id, 381 (1859), Amey *v* Mayor, 24 id, 364, 376 (1860), Curtis *v* Butler Co, 24 id, 435 (1860), Gelpcke *v.* Dubuque, 1 Wall, 175 (1863), Mercer

Co. *v* Hackett. 1 id, 83 (1863); Seybert *v* Pittsburgh. 1 id, 272 (1863); Van Hastrup *v* Madison, 1 id, 291 (1863); Havemeyer *v.* Iowa Co, 3 id, 294 (1865); Thompson *v* Lee County, 3 id, 327 (1865), Rogers *v* Burlington, 3 id, 654 (1865), holding that power "to borrow money for *any* public purpose" gives authority to borrow to aid a railroad company, Mitchell *v.* Burlington, 4 id, 270 (1866), Von Hoffman *v.* Quincy, 4 id, 535 (1866); Campbell *v.* Kenosha, 5 id, 194 (1866), holding that a subscription may be validated by subsequent legislation, and such validation may be by implication; holding that levy of tax and payment of interest validates bonds irregularly issued; Meyer *v.* Muscatine, 1 id, 384 (1863), Lee County *v.* Rogers, 7 id, 181 (1868); Beloit *v* Morgan, 7 id, 619 (1868), City of Kenosha *v* Lamson, 9 id, 477 (1869); Railroad Co. *v* County of Otoe 16 id, 667 (1872); S. C, 1 Dillon, 338, holding that, unless restrained by provisions of the constitution of a state, its legislature may authorize a county to issue bonds and *donate* them to the railroad company which will give it a valuable connection with some other region As to the legislative power, donations and sub-

their obligations after receiving the benefits of those obligations has been thwarted by the courts. And the result is a satisfactory one. Any other decision would have checked the growth of the country, unsettled investments, and brought upon American munic-

scriptions for stock stand on the same ground. Town of Queensbury v. Culver, 19 Wall, 83 (1873), Woods v. Lawrence Co., 1 Black, 380 (1861), holding that where, by statute the grand jury of a county is required to fix the amount of the subscription, their act in pursuance thereof cannot afterwards be questioned by the county as to such amount, and if payment is to be made as may be agreed upon, an issue of bonds for that purpose is binding upon the county, Gilman v Sheboygan, 2 Black, 510 (1862), holding that a statute authorizing a city to borrow money, and to tax property to pay it, does not constitute such a contract with the bondholders that the state cannot afterwards modify the taxation even by the exemption of portions of taxable property, Olcott v. Supervisors, 16 id, 678 (1872), Rock Creek v Strong, 96 U S, 271 (1877), Hickory v Ellery, 103 id, 423 (1880), Clay Co v. Society for Savings, 104 id, 579 (1881), Taylor v Ypsilanti, 105 id, 60 (1881), Lewis v Barbour Co, 105 id, 739 (1881), Amoskeag National Bank v. Ottawa, 105 id, 667 (1881), Woods v. Lawrence Co., 1 Black, 386, Gilman v. Sheboygan, 2 id, 510, Town of Scipio v Wright, 101 U S., 665 (1879) And in the circuit and district courts of the United States Long v New London, 9 Biss, 539 (1880), Sibley v Mobile, 3 Woods, 535 (1876), United States v New Orleans, 2 id, 230 (1876)

Alabama — Stein v Mayor, etc. 24 Ala, 591 (1854), Opelika v Daniel, 59 Ala, 211 (1877), Ex parte Selma, etc, R. R. Co., 45 id, 696 (1871), Gibbons v Mobile, etc, R. R. Co, 36 id, 410 (1860)

Arkansas — Mississippi, etc., R R Co v Camden, 23 Ark, 300 (1861), English v. Chicot Co, 26 id, 454 (1871), Jacksonport v Watson, 33 id, 704 (1878)

California — Robinson v Bidwell, 22

Cal, 379 (1863), People v Coon, 25 id, 635 (1864), Napa Valley R. R. Co v Napa County, 30 id, 435 (1866), Stockton, etc R. R. Co. v. Stockton, 41 id, 147 (1871)

Colorado — People v Pueblo Co, 2 Col, 360 (1874)

Connecticut — Bridgeport v Housatonic R. R. Co. 15 Conn, 475 (1843), holding that a subscription made by a city without authority may be made valid by subsequent legislative action in this case the validating statute was passed upon the application of the city making the subscription, Beardsley v Smith, 16 id, 368 (1844), Society, etc, v New London 29 id, 174 (1860), Douglass v. Chatham, 41 id, 211 (1874)

Florida — Cotton v Leon Co 6 Fla, 610 (1856).

Georgia — Winn v Macon 21 Ga 275 (1857) Powers v Inferior Court of Dougherty County, 23 id, 65 (1857)

Illinois — Shaw v Dennis, 5 Gilm, 405 (1849), Prettyman v. Tazewell Co., 19 Ill, 406 (1858) holding that an injunction on the ground of fraud at an election authorizing a subscription will not be granted to one who delays until others have acted upon the faith that the municipal corporation will aid an enterprise, Robertson v Rockford 21 id, 451 (1859), Supervisors of Schuyler Co v People, 25 id 181 (1860), Butler v Dunham 27 id, 474 (1861). Dunnovan v Green, 57 id 63 (1870), Madison Co. v People, 58 id 456 (1871), Chicago, etc, R. R. Co v Smith, 62 id, 268 (1871), Decker v Hughes, 68 id 33 (1873) Quincy, etc R R Co v Morris, 84 id, 410 (1877), Chicago, etc, R. R. Co. v Aurora, 99 id, 205 (1881), Olcott v Supervisors, 16 Wall, 678 (1872). But see Weightman v Clark, 103 U S., 256 (1880)

Indiana — City of Aurora v West, 9 Ind, 74 (1857), S C, 22 id, 88, Evans-

ipalities the disgrace and disastrous loss of credit which arise from repudiation

The act of the legislature authorizing a municipal subscription, however, will not avail to validate such a contract, unless it is duly

ville, etc, R R. Co. v Evansville, 15 id, 395 (1860), Board of Bartholomew Co. r Bright, 18 id, 93 (1862) Thompson v City of Peru, 29 id, 305 (1868), Lafayette, Muncie, etc, R. R. Co v Geiger, 34 id, 185 (1870), John v Cincinnati, etc, R R Co, 35 id, 539 (1871), Commissioners of Crawford Co v Louisville etc, R R. Co. 39 id 192 (1872), Mt Vernon i Hovey, 52 id, 563 (1876), Indiana, etc, R. R. Co v Attica, 56 id, 476 (1877), Williams v. Hall, 65 id, 129 (1879), Bittinger v Bell, 65 id, 415 (1879), Brocaw v Gibson Co., 73 id, 543 (1881), Peed v Millikan, 79 id 86 (1881).

Iowa —" In Iowa, up to 1858, it was held that such acts were constitutional, but from that time up to 1869 they were held to be unconstitutional, when the court seems to have undergone a radical change, and from that time to the present the constitutionality of such measures has been sustained " Wood on Railways p 261, citing Dubuque Co v Dubuque, etc, R R. Co, 4 Greene (Iowa), 1 (1853), State v Bissell, 4 id., 328 (1854), Clapp v Cedar Co., 5 Iowa, 15 (1857), McMillen i Lee Co, 6 id, 391 (1858). The above authorities, prior to 1858, hold these acts constitutional, as do the following, handed down since 1869 Stewart i Polk Co., 30 Iowa, 9 (1870) Bonnifield v Bidwell, 32 id 149, Jordan v Hayne, 36 id 9 (1872), Muscatine, etc, R R. Co v Horton, 38 id 33 (1873), Wapello i. B & M R. R. Co 44 id, 585 (1876), McMillen v Boyles, 6 Iowa, 304 (1858), Games i Robb. 8 id, 193 (1859), Chamberlain v Burlington, 19 id 395, holding that a charter authorizing a city to borrow money for any public purpose " does not confer power to aid in constructing a railroad particularly King v Wilson, 1 Dillon. 555 (1871), as to how far the federal courts will follow the state

courts as to the constitutionality of such statutes While the following cases. decided between 1858 and 1869, hold such acts unconstitutional and void Stokes v. Scott, 10 Iowa, 166 (1859), State v Wapello, 13 id, 388 (1862), Myers v Johnson, 14 id., 47 (1862). See, also, in general, Doon Township v Cummins, 142 U S. 366 (1892).

Kansas — City of Atchison v Butcher, 3 Kan, 104 (1865), Leavenworth Co v. Miller, 7 id, 479 (1871), Southern, etc, R R. Co v Towner, 21 Pac Rep., 220 (Kan, 1889), Morris v Morris Co, 7 id, 576 (1871), State v Nemaha Co., 7 id, 542 (1871), Barnes v Atchison, 2 id, 454 (1864), Leavenworth, etc, R R Co v Douglas Co, 18 id, 169 (1877), Turner v Commissioners, etc. 27 Kan, 314 (1882), holding that, where the amount of bonds voted to be issued was in excess of the amount which a township might legally issue, the vote was a nullity only as to the excess. Kansas City, etc, R. R. v Richmond T., 25 Pac. Rep, 595 (Kan, 1891). Hutchinson, etc, R. R. v Fox, 28 Pac. Rep, 1078 (Kan, 1892)

Kentucky — Talbot v Dent, 9 B. Mon, 526 (1849), Slack v Maysville, etc., R. R. Co., 13 id, 1 (1852), Maddox v Graham, 2 Metc, 56 (1859), Shelby Co Court v. Cumberland, etc, R. R Co, 8 Bush, 209 (1871), holding that a subscription not authorized by law may be validated by later legislation, Allison v Versailles, etc, R R. Co, 10 id, 1 (1873), Chaffee County v Potter, 142 U. S, 355 (1892); Christian, etc, Court v. Smith, 13 S. W. Rep, 276 (Ky, 1890). Christian Co. Court v Smith, 12 S W. Rep, 134 (Ky, 1889). A railroad cannot be taxed to aid in paying a municipal subscription to its construction Louisville, etc., R. R v Com'th, 12 S. W. Rep, 1064 (Ky, 1890)

Louisiana — Police Jury v. McDon-

passed in accordance with all the constitutional formalities,[1] and after a subscription is made, any act of the legislature restricting or abridging the taxing power so as to deprive the municipality of

ough 8 La Ann, 341 (1853), Parker v Scogin, 11 id, 629 (1856) Cf Wilson v Shreveport, 29 id, 673 (1877).

Maine — Augusta Bank v. Augusta, 49 Me, 507 (1860), Stevens v Anson, 73 id 489 (1882)

Massachusetts — Supervisors v Wisconsin, etc, R R Co, 121 Mass, 460 (1877), holding that the legislature of Wisconsin has power to authorize counties to subscribe for stock in aid of railroads and to issue bonds therefor

Michigan — In Michigan the courts hold that statutes authorizing municipal corporations to subscribe to the stock of a railroad or vote bonds to it are void, and the subscription and bonds are void People v Salem, 20 Mich, 452 (1870). Thomas v Port Hudson, 27 id, 320 (1873), Bay City v State Treasurer, 23 id, 499, People v Detroit, 28 id, 228 (1873) But see Talcott v Pine Grove, 1 Flippin (U S), 120 (1871), where the position taken by the court of Michigan was held to be so contrary to precedent and so unexpected as to operate as a surprise upon the community, S. C affirmed, sub nom Township of Pine Grove v Talcott. 19 Wall, 660 (1873), which was adhered to in Taylor v Ypsilanti, 105 U S, 60 (1881) See, also, Chickaming v Carpenter, 106 U S, 663 (1882)

Minnesota — Davidson v Ramsey Co., 18 Minn, 482 (1872), State v Clark, 23 Minn, 422 (1877), Kimball v Lakewood, 41 Fed Rep, 289 (1890)

Mississippi — Strickland v Railroad Co. 27 Miss., 209, New Orleans, etc, R. R. Co v McDonald, 53 Miss., 240 (1876), Wells v Supervisors, 102 U S, 625 (1880), Madison County v Priestly, 42 Fed Rep, 817 (1890)

Missouri — St. Louis v Alexander, 23 Mo, 483 (1856), St. Joseph, etc, R. R.

Co v Buchanan Co, 39 Mo, 485 (1867) State v Macon County Court 41 id 453 (1867), Chillicothe etc, R R Co v Brunswick 44 id 553 (1867) State v Linn Co, 44 id, 504 (1869), Same v Sullivan Co, 51 id, 522 (1873), Osage Valley, etc, R R Co v Morgan County 53 id, 156 (1873) Smith v Clark County, 54 id, 58 (1873) State v Greene County, 54 id, 540 (1874), State v Hannibal, etc, R. R., 13 S W Rep 505 (Mo, 1890)

Nebraska — Hallenbeck v Hahn, 2 Neb, 377 (1873), Reineman v Covington, etc. R. R. Co 7 id, 310 (1878) holding that, if a county votes aid to a railroad in excess of the sum allowed by the law, such act is void and will not authorize the issue of any bonds whatever, Railroad Company v County of Otoe, 16 Wall, 667 (1872)

Nevada — Gibson v Mason, 5 Nev 283 (1869), Dixon County v Field, 111 U S, 83 (1884), Lincoln County v Luning, 133 U S, 529 (1890)

New Hampshire — Perry v Keane, 56 N H, 514 (1876)

New Jersey — Bernards Township v Morrison, 133 U S 523 (1890)

New York — In New York the courts have unwillingly sustained the validity of such grants Clarke v Rochester 28 N Y, 605 (1864) Grant v Courter, 24 Barb, 232 (1857), Benson v Albany, 24 id, 248 (1857), People v Henshaw 61 id, 409 (1870), Ex parte Tax-payers of Kingston, 40 How Pr 444 (1870) Gould v Town of Oneonta, 71 N Y 298 (1877), Sweet v Hurlburt, 51 Barb, 312 (1868), denying the constitutionality of a donation of bonds Cf People v Batchellor 53 N Y 128 (1873), holding that a municipal corporation cannot be compelled by the legislature, against its consent and that of its tax-payers, to become a stockholder in a corporation

[1] Amoskeag Nat l Bank v Town of Ottawa, 105 U S., 667 (1881)

the power to pay the bonds is unconstitutional and void[1]　In California the courts go even to the extent of holding that the legislature may compel a municipality to subscribe to the stock of a

which is private in character (as here, a railroad) — a statute for such a purpose is void, Queensburg v Culver, 19 Wall, 82 (1873), in which the New York doctrine is denied by the supreme court of the United States

But the law is clear, in New York, that such statutes and subscriptions thereunder are constitutional.　Bank of Rome v Rome, 18 N Y, 38 (1858), Starin v Genoa, 23 N Y, 439 (1861), Town of Solon v Williamsburg Saving Bank, 21 N E Rep, 168 (N Y, 1889), Alvord v. Syracuse Sav Bank, 98 N Y, 599 (1885), holding that the legislature may give to the bonds a negotiability which is not given to them by the court, Craig v Town of Andes, 93 N Y, 405 (1883), holding that bonds, even in bona fide hands, are void where part of the consents thereto were conditional, even though the bond recites that all legal steps to comply with the law were taken, Town of Lyons v Chamberlain, 89 N Y, 578 (1882), where the person to whom illegal bonds were issued was held to account for them, Cagwin v Town of Hancock, 84 N Y, 532 (1881), holding that the town may set up that a majority did not vote for the issue of the bonds, that the federal decisions will not be followed, that an innocent holder is not protected, and that "the bonding acts are now regarded as hostile to a sound public policy," Town of Springfort v Teutonia Sav Bank, id, 403 (1881), also holding that the affidavit of assessors as to the vote is only prima facie evidence　To same effect see Dodge v County of Platte, 82 N Y, 218 (1880), declaring void certain Missouri municipal bonds, Duanesburgh v Jenkins, 57 N Y, 177 (1874), sustaining the constitutionality of bonding acts and

reviewing the New York cases; People v Mitchell, 35 id, 551 (1866), S. C., 45 Barb, 208; People v Spencer, 55 N. Y., 1 (1873), Williams v. Duanesburgh, 66 id, 129 (1876), Horton v. Thompson, 71 id, 513 (1878); affirmed, 101 U. S, 665. In New York an effectual remedy against the illegal bonding of a town in aid of a railroad is found in holding liable to the town the parties who promoted the aid, for all sums paid by the town to bona fide holders of the bonds. Farnham v Benedict, 107 N Y, 159 (1887).　A suit in equity to cancel illegal municipal bonds does not lie, except where the defendant fails to allege that there is a remedy at law.　Town of Mentz v Cook, 108 N Y, 504 (1888). Long delay may bar the right of a municipality to have such bonds canceled. Calhoun v Millard, 121 N Y., 69 (1890). See, also, in general, Town of Solon v. Williamsburgh, etc., Bank, 114 N. Y., 122 (1889), Brownell v Town of Greenwich, id, 518 (1889)

North Carolina — Taylor v Newberne, 2 Jones' Eq, 141 (1855), Caldwell v. Burke Co., 4 id, 323 (1858), Hill v. Commissioners of Forsyth Co., 67 N C, 367 (1870), Wood v Com'rs of Oxford, 2 S E Rep (N C., 1887), McDowell v. Rutherford, etc, Co., id, 351 (N C., 1887), Goforth v Same, id, 361 (id)

Ohio — Cincinnati, etc, R. R. Co. v. Clinton Co, 1 Ohio St., 77 (1852), Steubenville, etc, R R Co v North Township, 1 id, 105 (1852), Cass v. Dillon, 2 id, 607 (1853), Thompson v. Kelley, 2 id, 647 (1853), State v Union Township, 8 id, 394 (1858), State v Com'rs, etc., 11 Ohio St., 183 (1860). Commissioners of Knox Co v Nichols, 14 id, 260 (1863), Fosdick v Perrysburg, 14 id, 472 (1863), Same v Goshen, 14 id, 569 (1863);

---

[1] Wolff v. New Orleans, 103 U. S, 358 (1880).　Cf. Edwards v. Williamson, 70 　Ala, 145 (1881), Hays v Dowes, 75 Mo., 250 (1881).

railway company and to issue its bonds in payment thereof [1] But this extreme view is disapproved in New York [2] and in Illinois, [3] the courts in these states taking the better ground that, while it is competent for the legislature to authorize a municipal subscription in a proper case, there is no power anywhere to compel such a subscription or donation.

Walker v Cincinnati, 21 id., 14 (1871); S. C, *sub nom.* Cincinnati v Walker, 1 Cin, 121 (1871).

Pennsylvania — Commonwealth v McWilliams, 11 Penn St., 61 (1849), Brown v Commissioners, 21 Penn St, 37 (1853), Sharpless v Philadelphia, 21 id, 147 (1853), Moers v Reading, 21 id, 188 (1853), Commonwealth v Allegheny Co, 32 id, 218 (1858), Same v Pittsburgh, 34 id., 496 (1859). Same v Same, 41 id, 278 (1861), Same v Perkins, 43 id, 400, Pennsylvania R R Co v Philadelphia, 47 id, 189 (1864), Riddle v Philadelphia, etc, R R. Co, 1 Pittsb, 158 (1872), County v Brinton, 47 Pa. St., 367 (1864).

South Carolina — Copes v. Charleston, 10 Rich Law, 491, County of Lancaster v Cheraw, etc, R. R, 5 S E Rep, 338 (S C., 1888); State v Whitesides, 9 S E Rep, 661 (S C, 1889); Floyd v. Perun, 8 S E. Rep., 14 (S C, 1888).

Tennessee — Tax-payers of Milan v Tennessee, etc, R. R. Co., 11 Bax, 329; County of Wilson v National Bank, 103 U S, 770 (1880), Nichols v Nashville, 9 Humph, 252 (1848), Louisville, etc, R. R. Co. v. County Court, 1 Sneed, 637 (1854); Williams v Duck River, etc., R. R. Co, 9 Bax, 488 (1876), Clay v Hawkins, 5 Lea, 137 (1880), Lauderdale Co v Fargason, 7 id, 153 (1881), Winston v Tennessee, etc., R. R. Co., 57 Tenn (1 Bax), 60 (1873)

Texas — San Antonio v Jones, 28 Texas, 19 (1866), Same v Lane, 32 id, 405 (1869), Same v Gould, 34 id, 49 (1870)

Vermont — Bennington v Park, 50 Vt., 178 (1877), First National Bank of St. Johnsbury v Concord, 50 id., 257 (1877).

Virginia — Goddin v Crump 8 Leigh, 120 (1837), Board of Sup rs v Randolph, 16 S E Rep, 722 (Va, 1893). See, also, Goshorn v Ohio County, 1 West Va., 308 (1865)

Wisconsin — Clark v Janesville, 10 Wis, 136 (1860), Bushnell v Beloit, 10 id, 195 (1860), Foster v Kenosha, 12 Wis, 616, Veeder v Lima, 19 id, 280 (1865), Fisk v Kenosha, 26 id, 23 (1870), Phillips v Albany, 28 id, 340 (1871); Rogan v Watertown, 30 id, 259 (1872), Lawson v Milwaukee, etc, R R Co., 30 id, 597 (1872), Oleson v Green Bay, etc, 36 id, 383 (1874). *Cf* Whiting v Sheboygan, etc, R. R Co, 25 id, 167 (1870). Municipal gift of land to a railroad. Northern P R R. Co v Roberts, 42 Fed Rep, 734 (1890) A county cannot donate land to a railroad Ellis v Northern, etc., R. R., 45 N W Rep, 811 (Wis., 1890).

The leading cases upon the constitutionality of statutes authorizing municipal subscription to railroads are Goddin v Crump, 8 Leigh, 120 (1837) — which is said by Judge Dillon to be the first in the long series, Leavenworth County v Miller, 7 Kan, 479 (1871), Slack v Maysville & Lexington R. R. Co, 13 B Mon, 1 (1852), Knox Co. v Aspinwall, 21 How (U S), 539 (1858), Sharpless v. Mayor, 21 Penn St, 147 (1853)

[1] Napa Valley R R Co v Napa County, 30 Cal, 435 (1866)

[2] People v. Batchelor, 53 N Y, 128 (1873). *Cf.* Queensburg v Culver, 19 Wall (U S), 82 (1873)

[3] Cairo, etc, R. R. Co. v Sparta, 77 Ill, 505 (1875).

While it may be conceded that, from a constitutional standpoint as well as from that of public policy and expediency, there are grave objections to the existence or exercise of this power, which has plainly been monstrously abused,[1] it is clear that the courts, almost universally, as has been shown, have taken and will continue to hold the most liberal views as to the legislative prerogative in this respect   Such authority inhering in the legislature is generally conceded

A municipality which has not yet been incorporated cannot hold an election and vote a subscription for stock.   The subscription is void [2] But a *de facto* municipal corporation recognized by the legislature cannot defeat its bonds by alleging irregular incorporation.[3] It is no objection to the validity of the legislative act, or the municipal subscription, that the subscription is made to a railway company not yet in existence,[4] or to the company that first builds the road [5]

It must not be overlooked, however, that municipalities never have the power, by virtue of any of these legislative enactments, to tax themselves for the benefit of enterprises or objects which are private in their nature.   Municipal subscriptions can only be made to the stock of companies of an essentially public character. This is a rule conclusively settled and plainly salutary [6] Questions

---

[1] Dillon on Munic Corp, §§ 12, 117, 157, Cooley on Const Lim, § 261 *et seq*

[2] Clark v Janesville, 13 Wis, 414 (1861), S C. 10 id, 136, Rochester v Alfred, 13 id, 432 (1861), Berliner v Waterloo, 14 id 378 (1861) See Lewis v Clarendon, 5 Dillon, 329 (1878), to effect that, if authority is given "to any incorporated town or city" to subscribe for stock, it is not limited to such towns as are incorporated when the act was passed

[3] Comanche County v Lewis, 133 U. S. 198 (1890)

[4] In the County of Daviess v Huidekoper it is held that county bonds in the hands of a *bona fide* holder for value are not rendered void by the fact that, at the time the vote authorizing the subscription was taken, the company to be benefited was not created according to law 98 U. S, 98 (1878). To same effect. James v Milwaukee, 16 Wall, 159 (1872). See, also, Concord v Portsmouth Savings Bank, 92 U S., 625

(1875), Railroad Co v Falconer, 103 id, 821 (1880). *Contra.* Rubey v Shain, 54 Mo, 207 (1873), People v. Franklin, 5 Lans (N Y), 129 (1871)

[5] North v Platte County, 45 N. W. Rep, 692 (Neb., 1890).

[6] Loan Association v Topeka, 20 Wall, 655 (1874), Weismer v Village of Douglass, 64 N Y, 91 (1876), Bissell v Kankakee, 64 Ill, 249 (1872), Brewer Brick Co v Brewer, 62 Me, 62 (1873); Allen v Inhabitants of Jay, 60 id, 124 (1872), Lowell v Boston, 111 Mass, 463 (1873), State v Osawakee Township, 14 Kan, 418 (1875), McConnell v Hamm, 16 id, 228 (1876); Union Pacific R. R. Co v Smith, 23 id, 745 (1880), Clark v Des Moines, 19 Iowa, 199 (1865), Frederick v. Augusta, 5 Ga, 561 (1848) Commercial Bank v City of Iola, 2 Dillon, 353 (1873), Savings Assoc v. Topeka, 3 id, 376 (1874) *Cf.* Bloodgood v Mohawk, etc, R. R. Co, 18 Wend, 9, 65 (1837) [Compare with this case Chapman v. Gates, 54 N. Y., 132, 144

involving the distinction between public and private uses are constantly arising when the validity of municipal bonds is the issue, and the courts very consistently adhere to the rule that municipal aid can lawfully be extended only to railways, or other enterprises of a distinctly public or *quasi*-public character [1]

§ 92 *Constitutional provisions prohibiting municipal subscriptions* — The unchecked exercise of this power on the part of the state legislatures has entailed upon the people of the states such a burden of taxation [2] that in many states are found constitutional prohibitions rendering it unlawful for municipal corporations to make subscriptions or lend their credit to any incorporated com-

(1873)] Osborne *v* Adams Co, 109 U S 1 (1882), S C, 106 U S, 181, Ottawa *v* Carey, 108 U S, 110 (1883), Freeland *v* Hastings, 10 Allen, 570 (1865), Jenkins *v* Andover, 103 Mass, 94 (1869), People *v* Salem, 20 Mich, 452 (1870), Curtis *v* Whipple, 24 Wis, 350 (1869), Cook *v* Manufacturing Co, 1 Sneed (Tenn). 698 (1854), Cooley on Const. Lim, § 212

[1] A municipal donation to a private manufacturing concern is void Cole *v* La Grange, 113 U S, 1 (1884) Aid to bridge manufacturing and iron-works company held void Loan Assoc *v* Topeka, 20 Wall, 655 (1874). Same as to hydraulic works. Weismer *v* Douglass, 64 N Y, 91 (1876) Also to linen company Bissell *v* Kankakee, 64 Ill, 249 (1872). Also exempting manufacturing companies from taxes for ten years. Brewer Brick Co. *v.* Brewer, 62 Me, 62 (1873). Also loan of credit to saw-mill and box factory Allen *v* Inhabitants. 60 Me, 124 (1872) Also to loan to persons rebuilding after a fire Lowell *v* Boston, 111 Mass., 454 Or to relieve the destitute poor State *v.* Osawkee, etc., 14 Kan, 418 (1875) Or to aid in constructing a woolen mill McConnell *v* Hamm, 16 Kan, 228 (1876) Or to build a dam Union Pac. R. R. Co *v* Smith. 23 id, 745 (1880). Or to construct a toll-bridge Clark *v* Des Moines, 19 Iowa, 199 (1865). To aid a company which manufactures bridges, plows stoves, etc Commercial Bank *v* City of Iola, 2 Dill, 353 (1873), Sav-

ings Ass'n *v* Topeka, 3 Dill, 376 (1874). *Cf* Bloodgood *v.* Mohawk, etc, R R. Co, 18 Wend, 9, 65 (1837), Chapman *v* Gates, 54 N Y, 132, 144 (1873) Or to aid a steam-grist mill Osborne *v* Adams Co, 109 U.S, 1 (1883), S C, 106 U S, 181 Or to aid the development of a water-power Ottawa *v* Carey, 108 U S, 110 (1883) Or to repay to persons money paid by them for substitutes in the army Freeland *v* Hastings, 10 Allen, 570 As to tax for a school-house, see Jenkins *v* Andover, 103 Mass 94 (1869) As to payment of money on account of drafting of soldiers, see Thompson *v* Pittston, 59 Me, 545, Tyson *v* School Directors, 51 Pa. St., 9 (1865). Aid to a private school is void (Curtis' Adm'r *v* Whipple, 24 Wis, 350), or to a manufacturing company Cook *v* Manuf'g Co, 1 Sneed (Tenn), 698, Cooley on Const. Lim, § 212. A municipality has no power to invest in the stock of a steamship company (Penn, etc, *v* Philadelphia, 47 Pa St, 189), nor to operate free ferries (Jacksonport *v* Watson 33 Ark, 701), but a subscription to a turnpike company has been held legal Clark *v* Leathers, 5 S W Rep. 576 (Ky., 1887), City of Aurora *v* West, 9 Ind, 74, S C, 22 id, 88. And to obtain a water supply Frederick *v* Augusta, 5 Ga, 561 (1848)

[2] Dillon on Munic Corp, §§ 156, 160 The sum of municipal indebtedness in this country is said to exceed one thousand millions of dollars, and the amount is constantly increasing.

pany or enterprise, not strictly and exclusively governmental in its nature and constitution. This is the case in Pennsylvania,[1] Ohio,[2] Illinois,[3] New York,[4] Indiana,[5] Missouri,[6] Mississippi,[7] and in some other states.[8] In general it will be found that these constitutional provisions forbid in terms any subscription or lending of credit by any municipality in the state, or by the state itself, to any company, association or corporation whatsoever   Sometimes the prohibition is absolute, and at other times two-thirds or a majority of the qualified electors of the municipality must vote to render such aid   The constitutional or statutory provisions which prohibit municipal subscriptions are construed to be prospective only, unless they contain express words making them retroactive[9]   This

[1] Amend to Const 1857, § 7, art II; Pennsylvania R. R. Co. v. Philadelphia, 47 Penn. St., 189 (1864)

[2] Const., art. VIII, § 6, Walker v. Cincinnati, 21 Ohio St., 14 (1871), Cass v. Dillon, 2 id , 607 (1853), Fosdick v Perrysburg, 14 id , 472 (1863), Thompson v Kelly, 2 id , 647 (1853), Wyscaver v Atkinson, 37 id , 80 (1881)

[3] Const 1870, Concord v Portsmouth Savings Bank, 92 U S , 625 (1875), Louisville v Savings Bank, 104 U S , 469 (1881); Harter v. Kernochan, 103 U S., 562 (1880); Fairfield v County of Gallatin, 100 U S , 47 (1879); Chicago, etc , R R. Co. v. Pinckney, 74 Ill , 277 (1874), County of Moultrie v. Rockingham Ten Cent Savings Bank, 92 U. S , 631 (1875), Robertson v Rockford, 21 Ill , 451. The constitutional prohibition in Illinois against lending credit applies to the state only, and not to counties or cities

[4] Amend Const , Jan 1, 1875; People v Fort Edward, 70 N Y , 28 (1877), Dodge v County of Platte, 82 id , 218 (1880), reversing S. C., 16 Hun, 283

[5] Const . art X, § 10, Lafayette, etc., R. R. Co v Geiger, 34 Ind , 185 (1870); John v. Cincinnati, etc , R. R. Co., 35 id , 539 (1871), Aspinwall v Jo Daviess Co., 22 How (U S.), 364 (1859), Brocaw v. Board of Commissioners, 73 Ind , 543 (1881).

[6] Const , art. XI, § 14, County of Schuyler v. Thomas, 98 U S., 169 (1878); Smith v. County of Clark, 54 Mo., 58 (1873); County of Macon v. Shores, 97 U. S.,

272 (1877); County of Ray v Vansycle, 96 id , 675 (1877), County of Scotland v. Thomas, 94 id . 682 (1876)

[7] Const., art XII § 14; Supervisors v. Galbraith, 99 U. S., 214 (1878); Hayes v Holly Springs, 114 id , 120 (1885); Grenada Co v. Brogden, 112 id , 261 (1884). Cf State of Minnesota v Young, 29 Minn., 474 (1881)   Where municipal aid bonds were issued under an unconstitutional statute, but are enforced by the United States courts in favor of bona fide holders, the municipality may recover back from the railroad company or its successor the amounts so paid to such bona fide holders   Town of Plainview v. Winona, etc , R. R. Co., 32 N. W. Rep., 745 (Minn., 1887)   In the case of Walker v. Cincinnati, 21 Ohio St., 14 (1871), the building of the Cincinnati Southern Railway by the city of Cincinnati was held legal, notwithstanding the State constitution forbade the legislature from authorizing any city, etc., becoming "a stockholder in any joint-stock company, corporation or association whatever"

[8] Walker v Cincinnati, 21 Ohio St , 14 (1871), S. C., 8 Am Rep , 24, and 11 Am Law Reg (N S), 346, and the note by Judge Redfield   Where the statutes limit the amount of debt which a county may incur in aid of railroads, and aid is voted to the full amount, subsequent aid is void. Chicago, etc., R'y Co. v Freeman, 16 Pac Rep., 828 (Kan, 1888).

[9] County of Moultrie v. Rockingham

principle is frequently applied when the constitutional enactment is passed after a municipal subscription is voted but before it is actually completed.[1]

It has been held that a provision restricting the power of a state to make subscriptions in aid of railroads cannot be construed so as to prohibit the municipal subdivisions of the state from subscribing.[2] And a restriction as to the power of a county will not be held applicable to a city[3] School districts have no power to sub-

Ten Cent Savings Bank, 92 U S, 631 (1875), Grenada Co v. Brogden, 112 id, 261 (1884), Fairfield v County of Gallatin, 100 id, 47 (1879), County of Randolph v Post, 93 U S., 502 (1876), Ralls v. Douglass, 105 U S, 728 (1881), County, etc., v Nicolay, 95 U S, 619 (1877), holding that when authority had been granted to a county in Missouri to subscribe, the power was not subject to a constitutional amendment requiring the assent of two-thirds of the voters of the county, County, etc., v Gillett, 100 U S, 585, following and approving last case, County, etc., v Foster, 93 U S, 567 (1876), to same effect, same constitution, Louisiana v Taylor, 105 U. S., 454, to same effect, same constitution, Durkee v Board of Liquidation, 103 id., 646 (1886), Howard County v Paddock, 110 id, 384 (1884), Dallas County v McKensie, 110 id, 686 (1884) The legislature cannot, after the adoption of a constitutional amendment prohibiting municipalities from voting aid, remedy defects in votes taken before the amendment was adopted Katzenberger v Aberdeen, 121 U. S, 172 (1887), Decker v Hughes, 68 Ill, 33 (1873), holding that, where a new state constitution has been adopted, the old one governs as to bonds issued under its authority though not actually issued until after the adoption of the new one, County v. Moultrie, 105 U. S, 370 (1881), holding that where a donation in aid of a railroad had been voted by a county before the adoption of the new constitution of Illinois, bonds to pay it might be issued after its adoption In Louisville v Savings Bank, 104 U S, 469 (1881), it was held that the court

would even take cognizance of the fractions of a day in order to do justice in such a case Schall v Bowman, 62 Ill, 321 (1872), Richards v Donagho, 66 id, 73 (1872), Wright v Bishop, 88 id, 302 (1878). Contra, Jeffries v Lawrence, 42 Iowa, 498 (1876), Falconer v Buffalo, etc, R. R. Co 69 N. Y, 491 (1877), List v Wheeling, 7 West Va, 501 (1874) Cf. Hayes v Holly Springs, 114 U S, 120 (1885), Hendricks v Jackson Co, 2 McCrary, 615 (1880).

[1] For cases involving a construction of the Illinois constitution and its effects on previous donations, see Fairfield v Gallatin Co 100 U S, 47 (1879), Chicago, etc., R. R. Co v Pinckney, 74 Ill., 277 (1874), Lippincott v Pana, 92 id, 24 (1879) Middleport v Ætna Ins. Co, 82 id, 562 (1876) Cf County of Moultrie v Fairfield, 105 U S, 370 (1881), Enfield v. Jordan, 119 U. S., 680 (1887)

[2] Pattison v Supervisors, 13 Cal, 175 (1859), New Orleans v Graihle, 9 La Ann, 561 (1854), Slack v Maysville, etc, R. R. Co, 13 B Mon, 1 (1852), Leavenworth Co v Miller, 7 Kan, 479 (1871); Prettyman v Supervisors, 19 Ill, 406 (1858). The courts are inclined to hold that a limit on the rate of taxation that a city may levy does not apply to a tax in aid of municipal subscriptions to railroads Cf People v State Treasurer, 23 Mich, 499 (1871), Pitzman v Freeburgh, 92 Ill, 111 (1879)

[3] Thompson v City of Peru, 20 Ind, 305 (1868), City of Aurora v. West, 9 Ind, 74 Statute may prescribe that the aid voted shall not bind property outside of a town in the county, unless

scribe to the stock of a railway, and bonds issued to pay such a subscription are void [1]

§ 93. *Change in the state constitution or the general statutory law after the municipal corporation has voted to subscribe* — Constitutional provisions or general statutes prohibiting municipal corporations from subscribing to the stock of other corporations, or from lending their credit thereto, are, as we have seen,[2] prospective in their application

That which a corporation has the constitutional or statutory right to do, and which it has done in pursuance of that right or authority, cannot be affected or undone by subsequent constitutional change or amendment, or by the passage of general statutes. This is a fundamental rule of constitutional law [3] If it be held

the residents outside of the town vote in favor of it. Kentucky Union R'y Co. v. Bourbon Co, 2 S W Rep., 687 (Ky. 1887), Dillon on Munic. Corp, § 162, citing Butz v Muscatine, 8 Wall, 575 (1869); Learned v Burrington, 2 Am Law Reg (N S), 394, and note, Leavenworth v Norton, 1 Kan, 432 (1863) Barnes v Atchison, 2 id, 454 (1864) And see Commonwealth v. Pittsburgh, 34 Penn St, 496 (1859), Amey v Alleghany City, 24 How (U S), 364 Fosdick v Perry burg 14 Ohio St, 472 (1863), Cumberland v. Magruder, 34 Md, 381 (1871), Assessors v Commissioners, 3 Brewst (Pa.), 333 (1869) State v Guttenburg, 38 N J L, 419

[1] Weightman v. Clark, 103 U. S, 256 (1880).

[2] § 92.

[3] See, in regard to the Illinois constitution, County of Clay v Society for Savings, 104 U S, 579 (1881), People v Logan County, 63 Ill, 374 (1872), County of Moultrie v Savings Bank, 92 U S., 631 (1875), Louisville v. Savings Bank, 104 id 469 (1881), Nelson v Haywood County, 11 S W Rep, 885 (Tenn, 1889), Choissel v People, 29 N E Rep, 546 (Ill, 1892) An irregular vote to issue bonds before constitutional provision is enacted cannot be legalized by legislative act afterwards Williams v. People, 24 N E Rep, 647 (Ill, 1890) Where the original subscription was conditional the condition cannot be waived after

a constitutional provision prohibiting these subscriptions has been passed. Richison v People, 5 N E. Rep. 121 (Ill, 1886) To the same effect, with regard to the constitution of 1875 of Nebraska, see State v. Lancaster Co, 6 Neb 214 (1870), and as to constitution of Missouri of 1865, see Louisiana v Taylor, 105 U. S, 454 (1881), County of Cass v Gillett, 100 id, 585 (1879), County of Scotland v Thomas, 94 id, 682 (1876), County of Ray v Vansycle, 96 id, 675, County of Calloway v. Foster, 93 id, 567 (1876), County of Ralls v Douglass, 105 U S, 728 (1881), in which bonds issued under a city charter without a popular vote were held valid notwithstanding the provisions of a constitution adopted afterwards, but in force when the bonds were issued, required a submission of such matters to a vote; State v Macon Co, 41 Mo, 453 (1867), to the same effect, State v County Court, etc., 51 Mo, 522 (1873), to the same effect. Cf State v Dallas Co., etc., 72 Mo, 329 (1880), where a later statute was held to have taken away the power under a former one A statute passed subsequently to a constitutional prohibition may legalize irregular subscription before prohibition Bolles v Brimfield 120 U S., 759 (1887) The repeal of the act authorizing a tax for municipal aid before any money has been expended by the railroad, excepting a small sum for surveys prevents a lessee

that a popular vote does not give the company proposed to be benefited a vested right to the subscription by the municipality, and that until the subscription is actually made the contract is unexecuted, and therefore obligatory upon neither party, there is ground for holding that a constitutional prohibition, taking effect after the election, but before the subscription is made pursuant to authority conferred by the popular vote, will be sufficient to invalidate the subscription   This was the view taken by the supreme court of the United States in the case of Aspinwall v Commissioners of the County of Daviess [1] and affirmed in some later cases [2] There are cases of authority, however, in favor of the rule that, after the corporation has, by a popular vote at an election lawfully held, voted to subscribe for stock, subsequent changes of the constitution or the general statutes will not affect the right of the municipality to go on and complete the contract, to make the formal subscription, and to issue the bonds or levy the special tax to pay the calls [3]

§ 94. *Statutory formalities must be substantially complied with —* A substantial compliance with the formalities prescribed by a statute authorizing a municipal subscription to stock is all that the law requires, but such a compliance is requisite to the validity thereof [4]

of the railroad enforcing payment when the taxes were not assigned to the lessee Baittel v Meader, 33 N W Rep, 446 (Iowa, 1887)

[1] 22 How, 364 (1859)

[2] Norton v Brownsville, 129 U S, 479 (1889), Wadsworth v Supervisors 102 U S., 534 (1880) See, also, Railroad Co v Falconer, 103 id, 821 (1880), German Bank v Franklin County, 128 U S, 526 (1888), Eddy v People, 20 N E Rep, 83 (Ill, 1889).

[3] United States v Jefferson Co, 5 Dillon, 310 (1878), Maenhant v New Orleans, 3 Woods, 1 (1876), Sibley v Mobile, 3 id, 535 (1876) Nicolay v St Clair County, 3 Dillon, 163 (1874), Hundekoper v Dallas County, 3 id, 171 (1875) Cf Red Rock v Henry, 106 U S, 596 (1882), and cases in note 5, *supra*

[4] Bonds issued by municipalities to aid railroads are valid only when issued in compliance with the statute authorizing them   Young v Clarendon Township, 132 U. S., 340 (1889), Hoff v Jasper County, 110 U S., 53 (1884), following

the ruling in Anthony v Jasper County, 101 U S, 693 (1879), where it was held that a *bona fide* holder of bonds could not maintain an action on bonds not registered with the state auditor as required by statute Bissell v Spring Valley, etc, 110 U S, 162 (1884), holding that when a statute required bonds to be attested by the county clerk under the seal of the county, bonds issued without his signature were not valid, Hamlin v Meadville, 6 Neb, 227 (1877), holding that a vote authorizing a subscription gives no power to make a donation, Cairo etc, v Sparta 77 Ill 505 (1875), where bonds were authorized by a vote upon a proposition that they should run *twenty years*, when the statute submitted a proposition to be voted upon for bonds to run not exceeding *ten* years The court refused to compel the city to issue them, Mustard v Hoppers, 69 Ind 324 where an election and a tax voted and levied in pursuance of it, were held *not* invalidated on account of a canvass of the votes which was not

But not every failure to observe all the formalities prescribed by the statute is sufficient to invalidate a subscription. When the omission is a matter of form more than of substance, it will not invalidate the subscription.[1]

entirely regular, People v Dutcher, 56 Ill , 144 (1870), holding that when the statute does not prescribe a mode of election it should be held in accordance with the law of the organization of the municipality, People v. Logan County, 63 Ill , 374 (1872) This case was an application for *mandamus* to compel a subscription A demurrer to an answer alleging that the vote in favor of subscription was obtained by fraudulent votes with the knowledge of the corporation to be benefited was overruled; Pana v. Lippincott, 2 Bradw (Ill), 466 (1877), where a vote taken at a *special* town meeting, when the statute required it to be taken at a *regular* meeting, was held not to confer authority to subscribe; People, etc , v Smith, 45 N Y , 77 (1871), holding that, when the act requires a petition of tax-payers, the power is personal to them and cannot be exercised by an agent, Wetumpka v Wetumpka, 63 Ala , 611 (1879), holding that a judgment on bonds issued by a municipality is conclusive upon it as to the validity of the bonds and as to all defenses which might have been urged against it at law ; but in a bill in equity to enforce a statutory trust by which the property, etc., of the municipality was pledged to pay them, it may show that the bonds were issued in violation of the conditions of the statute, Munson v Lyons, 12 Blatch , 539 (1875), holding that an objection which would be good in a direct review of the proceedings — as here that the petition of tax-payers gave the authorities no jurisdiction — may be of no avail as against *bona fide* holders of bonds, Thompson v Perrine, 103 U S , 806 (1880); County of Jasper v Ballou, 103 U S , 745, and Mass, etc., Can, Co. v Cherokee, 42 Fed Rep , 750 (1890), holding that a subsequent statute may correct errors. See, also, Carroll County v.

Smith, 111 U S , 556 (1884); Hawley v Fairbanks, 108 U S , 543 (1883), Buchanan v. Litchfield, 102 U S , 278 (1880), People v. Hurlburt, 46 N. Y., 110 (1871). People v. Suffern, 68 N. Y., 321 (1877), Wilson v Cancadia, 15 Hun, 218 (1878); Angel v Hume, 17 Hun, 374 (1879); People v Hutton, 18 Hun, 116 (1879); People v Barrett, 18 Hun, 206 (1879), Wheatland v Taylor, 29 Hun, 70 (1883). Municipal subscription, authorized by statute, to corporation to construct locks and dams, and duly made, cannot be enforced to pay for repairing old locks and dams. Jessamine County v Swigert's Adm'r, 3 S. W Rep., 13 (Ky , 1887) Where judgment is taken by default the facts alleged cannot be disputed in the *mandamus* proceedings. Harshman v Knox County, 122 U. S, 306 (1887). Vote of municipal aid is void if grantee is in alternative. State v. Roggen, 33 N. W. Rep., 108 (Neb., 1887). In Kansas a tax-payer cannot enjoin the board from declaring the vote on municipal aid He must wait and enjoin the subscription State v County of Babaunsee, 12 Pac Rep., 942 (Kan , 1887); People v. Town of Santa Anna, 67 Ill , 57 (1873), where an election was held illegal because held without a registration of voters as required by law, People v. Town of Laena, 67 Ill., 65 (1873), a similar case, Chicago, etc , v. Mallory, 101 Ill., 583, where an election presided over by one moderator with one clerk, when the law required three judges and two clerks, was held void, conferring no authority upon a town to issue bonds Municipal bonds issued without the order of the grand jury as required by statute are not collectible by an owner who does not show he is a *bona fide* holder. Frick v Mercer County, 21 Atl. Rep., 6 (Pa , 1891).

[1] Pana v. Bowler, 107 U. S., 529 (1882),

Many of these defenses, however, are defeated by the fact that the municipality is estopped from setting up the illegality, there having been long delay, or the recitals on the bonds themselves having represented that the legal formalities were duly observed [1]

holding that the fact that an election was irregularly conducted could not avail as a defense to bonds in the hands of a *bona fide* holder, the court refusing to follow the ruling of the Illinois supreme court in Lippincott *v* Pana, 92 Ill, 24 (1879), which declared the bonds void, Commissioners, etc, *v.* Thayer, 94 U. S, 631 (1876), where the court said "Defects, irregularities or informalities which do not affect the result of the vote do not affect its validity," Belfast, etc *v* Brooke, 60 Me, 568 (1872), where a call for a town meeting "to see if the town will loan its credit to aid in the construction" of a railroad named was held to give reasonable notice that a proposition to subscribe for its stock would be acted upon, Draper *v.* Springport, 104 U S., 501 (1881), in which the absence of a seal was held not to affect the right of a *bona fide* holder to recover upon bonds issued in payment of a subscription, Clarke *v* Hancock Co, 27 Ill, 305 (1862), where the informality consisted in submitting two propositions by one vote, and it was held not to invalidate bonds in hands of *bona fide* holders, Supervisors *v* Schenck, 5 Wall, 772 (1866), where bonds issued under a vote ordered by a "county court," instead of by the "board of supervisors," were held valid because taxes had been levied and interest paid upon them by the proper authorities for nine years before the claim was made that they were void Cf County of Jasper *v* Ballou, 103 U. S., 745 (1880), Pana *v* Bowler, 107 U. S, 529 (1882), Johnson *v* Stark, 24 Ill, 75 (1860), Singer Manuf'g Co *v* Elizabeth, 42 N J. L., 219, New Haven, etc, *v* Chatham, 42 Conn, 465 (1875), where a vote which should have been by ballot was taken by division of the house,

and no objection was made thereto until a railroad had in good faith issued bonds which were to be guarantied by the town.

[1] Nugent *v* Supervisors, 19 Wall, 241 (1873), is the leading case. It holds that the delivery of the municipal bonds to the railroad in exchange for the stock, together with the levy of a tax to pay the interest on the bonds, and the act of the municipality in voting as a shareholder, estop it from denying the legality of the subscription. Menasha *v* Hazard, 102 U S, 81 (1880) where bonds were issued to be valid when it was certified on them that certain conditions had been performed Such a certificate was held to estop the town from denying their validity, Whiting *v* Town of Potter, 2 Fed Rep, 517 (1880), in which it was held that retaining railroad stock received for bonds, and paying interest on the bonds for a long time, estopped a municipality from questioning their validity, such acts being a direct ratification of the issue, Lamb *v* Burlington, etc, 39 Iowa, 333 (1874), holding that voting a tax in aid of a railroad, and remaining silent for a year, during which the road was completed upon the faith of the tax, and until the benefits accruing from the completion were realized, estopped a township from denying the validity of the tax, Leavenworth, etc, *v* Douglas Co, 18 Kan, 169 (1877), where the failure of a railroad to comply with the conditions of an agreement by which it was to receive bonds was a matter of public knowledge, and the county issuing the bonds made no objection, but paid interest on the bonds for years, these circumstances were considered a ratification of the acts of the county officers in issuing them,

The meeting must be duly called and by the proper officer;[1] the notice of the meeting must be duly posted for the full time provided in the act

Lyons v. Munson, 99 U S, 684 (1878), holding that where, under the act of New York, the county judge decides upon an application of tax-payers, his judgment recited in the bonds cannot be attacked by the town in an action on bonds by a *bona fide* holder, and the town is estopped to deny their validity on that account. Hackett v Ottawa, 99 U S, 86, holding that, when bonds purport on their face to have been issued to provide for a loan for municipal purposes, the city is estopped from setting up against an innocent purchaser for value that they were void because the proceeds were appropriated to other purposes — as for a donation to a private corporation. Pendleton Co. v Amy, 13 Wall, 297 (1871), holding that where the issue of bonds by county officers, without previous fulfillment of conditions, would be a misdemeanor, the presumption is that the conditions were fulfilled, and the receiving of stock in payment and holding it for seventeen years work an estoppel, First Nat l, etc., v Wolcott, 19 Blatch, 370 (1871), where the retaining of stock received for bonds, and paying interest on the bonds, was held, as against *bona fide* holders, to be a ratification of the act of commissioners in issuing them, the recital on them being that they were issued in pursuance of a certain statute, Block v Commissioners, 99 U. S, 686 (1878), in which a county was held estopped from asserting that a majority of the electors had not voted in favor of the issue of bonds, the bonds having been issued three years after the vote was declared and recorded, Carroll Co v Smith, 111 U. S., 556 (1883), holding that a recital in a bond that it is authorized by a particular statute does not estop the municipality from setting up that it was not authorized by

a proper majority of voters, — in this case two-thirds. See, also, Amey v. Allegheny, 24 How, 364, Cagwin v. Hancock, 84 N. Y, 532 (1881), rev'g S C, 22 Hun, 291; Orleans v Platt, 99 U. S, 676 (1878)

[1] Town of Windsor v Hallett, 97 Ill, 204 (1880); County of Richland v. People, 3 Bradw (Ill), 210 (1878), Jacksonville, etc, R R Co v. Virden, 104 Ill, 339 (1882), Bowling Green, etc., R. R. Co v Warren Co, 10 Bush (Ky.), 711 (1874). But see Sauerhering v. Iron Ridge, etc, R. R. Co., 25 Wis, 447 (1870); Commissioners v. Baltimore, etc., R. R. Co, 37 Ohio St., 205 (1881).

[2] McClure v. Township, etc., 94 U. S. 429, Harding v. Rockford, etc., 63 Ill., 90 (1872), where bonds were held invalid because the notice of election was posted less than thirty days, as required by law; Packard v Jefferson Co., 2 Col, 338 (1874), holding that a change in the proposition to vote bonds which is in effect a new proposition cannot be legally voted upon at an election already called, there not being sufficient time remaining before the election to give the required notice; McClure v. Township, etc, 94 U. S., 429 (1876), in which bonds were declared void because the election by which they were authorized was not held pursuant to a notice of thirty days, as required by the act, Anderson v Beal, 113 U. S, 227 (1884), holding that, if the bonds on their face recite that they were issued in pursuance of a vote held on a certain day, the statement is equivalent to one that the vote was regular in form as to prior notice, and the municipal corporation is estopped from showing that it was held without proper notice in an action by a *bona fide* holder; George v Oxford, etc, 16 Kan, 72 (1876), holding that when an election authorizing the

§ 95 *Submission to popular vote.*—While the legislature may authorize a municipality to make a subscription to the stock of a railway or other corporation without submitting the question to a vote of the people,[1] it has the power to direct that the question shall be so submitted Such an act does not amount to a delegation of legislative powers[2] When it is provided that a subscription can be made only upon the petition of a certain proportion of

issue of bonds was held upon insufficient notice, and the facts appeared upon the face of the bonds, the bonds were void, Williams v Roberts, 88 Ill, 11 (1878), where an election called by twelve voters instead of twenty, as required, upon a ten days' notice, where the statute required twenty days, was held a nullity See, also, Wells v. Pontiac Co, 102 U S, 625 (1880); Lincoln v. Cambria Iron Co, 103 U S, 412 (1880) But where the notice was required by the statute to be "posted by the town clerk or supervisors," it was held that this did not require a posting by these officers in person, but that it was sufficient if they procured others to post the notice Lawson v Milwaukee, etc, R R. Co, 30 Wis, 597 (1872), Phillips v Albany, 28 id, 340 (1871), Jones v. Hurlburt, 13 N W. Rep, 5 (1882).

[1] Otoe County v Baldwin, 111 U S, 1 (1883), Thompson v Lee County, 3 Wall, 327 (1865), County of Ralls v Douglass, 105 U S, 728 (1881), State v Macon County Court, 41 Mo, 453 (1867); State v County Court of Sullivan County, 51 id, 522 (1873). Cf State v. Dallas County, 72 id, 329 (1880), McCallie v. Chattanooga, 3 Head (Tenn), 317 (1859), Chicago, etc, R R. Co v Aurora, 99 Ill, 205 (1881); Burr v Chariton Co, 2 McCrary, 603 (1880) In this case a charter of a railroad authorized it to receive subscriptions from counties without a vote of the people Bonds so issued were held valid though a prior special act required a vote of tax-payers as a condition precedent to such subscriptions

[2] Starin v Town of Genoa, 23 N Y., 439 (1861), Gould v Town of Sterling,

23 id, 456 (1861), Bank of Rome v Village of Rome, 18 id, 38 (1858), S C, 19 id, 20 (1859), People v Batchellor, 53 id, 128, 138 (1873), Town of Dunesburgh v Jenkins, 57 id, 177, 192 (1874), Hobart v Supervisors 17 Cal 23 (1860) Slack v Maysville, etc, R R Co, 13 B Mon 1 (1852), Winter v City Council of Montgomery, 65 Ala 403 (1880) In Harrington v. Plainview 27 Minn, 224 (1880), it is held that, where a submission to the people is provided for it must be to the legal voters of the municipality, and cannot lawfully be confined to resident tax-payers, whether legal voters or not Cf Babcock v Helena, 34 Ark, 499 (1879), Walnut v Wade, 103 U S, 683 (1880) Again where a popular vote, taken in accordance with a statute, authorized a subscription to a designated railway, and the bonds were issued to a consolidated road including the first — these facts appearing on the face of the bond — the invalidity of the transaction was held to appear on the face of it County of Bates v Winters, 97 U S, 83 (1877) Cf Chicot Co v Lewis 103 id, 164 (1880), Schaeffer v Bonham, 95 Ill 368 (1880). But where a town is authorized to subscribe not exceeding a certain sum to a designated railroad several subscriptions made at different times and authorized by as many elections, the aggregate not exceeding the amount named in the act, are valid Empire v Darlington, 101 U S, 87 (1879) See, also, Hunt v Hamilton, 25 Kan, 76 (1881), Society for Savings v City of New London, 29 Conn, 174 (1860), First Nat Bank v Concord 50 Vt., 257

the legal voters,[1] there must be a substantial compliance with the spirit as well as the letter of the act.[2]

When the enabling act provides for municipal aid to railways and other *quasi*-public enterprises upon the assent of a majority or two-thirds of the legal voters of the town or county, this is construed universally to mean that the measure is to be approved by a majority or a two-thirds vote, as the case may be; that is to say, by a majority or two-thirds of the voters who vote at the election called for the purpose, and not two-thirds or a majority of all the qualified electors in the territory. Those who fail to vote against the measure are not considered nor counted as having the power to vote[3]

[1] *E q*, in New York. People *v.* Hulbert, 59 Barb, 446; People *v.* Peck, 62 id, 545, People *v* Oliver, 1 Thomp. & C, 570 (1873). People *v* Hughitt, 5 Laus, 89 (1871), People *v* Franklin, 5 id, 129 (1871), People *v* Smith, 45 N Y, 772 (1871), Wellsborough *v* New York, etc, R. R. Co, 76 id, 182 (1879) *Cf* St Joseph Township *v* Rogers, 16 Wall, 644 (1872), Syracuse Savings Bank *v* Seneca Falls, 21 Hun (N Y), 304 (1880); Faris *v* Reynolds, 70 Ind, 360 (1880)

[2] People *v* Smith, 45 N Y, 772 (1871), Craig *z* Andes, 93 N. Y, 405, People *v.* Oldtown, 88 Ill, 202 (1878) If the statute requires a written application by ten legal voters before the clerk should call an election, such application is necessary to the validity of the election, and without proof of it the municipality cannot be compelled to issue bonds Monadnock R. R. Co *v* Petersboro, etc 49 N H, 281 (1870), holding that a town cannot delegate its power to authorize subscriptions to a committee; and a statute requiring the vote of "two-thirds of the legal voters present and voting at" the meeting must be strictly obeyed. Mercer Co *z.* Pittsburgh etc., 27 Pa. St., 389 (1856), in which a statute designated the grand jury of a county to decide upon a subscription It was held that the grand jury could not delegate the power so conferred to county commissioners, and that the commissioners could only subscribe in accordance with

the decision of the grand jury. Where the municipal bonds recite that the vote was on an application of fifty voters, where the statute required that the application should be by voters and taxpayers, *held*, that the bonds were void, where the application was not by taxpayers. Gilson *v.* Dayton, 123 U. S., 59 (1887). Municipal bonds issued on a vote of a minority of the voters, instead of a majority, as required by the statute, in aid of a railroad, are void. Onstott *v* People, 15 N. E. Rep., 34 (Ill., 1888). In Prettyman *v* Supervisors, 19 Ill., 406, 414 (1858), a case of subscription by a county to railroad stock, a tax-payer waited four months before alleging fraud in the election *Held* equivalent to acquiescence, and too late. See, also, People *v* Van Valkenburg, 63 Barb, 105 (1872), Evansville, etc, R R Co. *v* Evansville, 15 Ind, 395 (1860), Chicago, etc, R. R. Co. *v* Mallory, 101 Ill., 583 (1882). For the manner in Indiana of contesting an election, see Goddard *v.* Stockman, 74 Ind, 400 (1881).

[3] County of Cass *v* Johnson, 95 U S, 360 (1877), Carroll Co *v* Smith, 111 U. S, 556 (1884), County of Cass *v* Jordan, 95 id, 373 (1877), Hawkins *v* Carroll Co, 50 Miss, 735 (1874), Louisville, etc, R. R. Co *v* Tennessee, 8 Heisk, 663 (1875); State *v* Brassfield, 67 Mo, 331 (1878). Webb *v* La Fayette Co, 67 id, 353 (1878), People *v.* Chapman, 66 Ill, 137 (1872), People *v.* Harp, 67 id, 62 (1873),

The legislature may render effective a prior vote of a municipality, taken without statutory authority, in aid of a railroad. If the state courts vary in their decisions on municipal aid to railroads the federal court will decide upon its own judgment [1]

§ 96 *What officer or agent of the municipality may make the contract of subscription* — In the absence of any express provision in the enabling act the proper persons to execute the contract of subscription for a municipal corporation are those whose duty it is to execute other contracts for and in the name of the municipality.

Dunnovan *v.* Green 57 Ill, 63, holding that a statute which authorizes a subscription, provided a majority of votes are in favor of it, means a majority of votes cast, not a majority of all voters, Culver *v* Fort Edward, 8 Hun, 310 (1876), holding that, if the statute requires a vote of the majority of taxable inhabitants, the consent of a majority who attended the meeting is not sufficient, Walnut *v* Wade, 103 U S, 683 (1879), holding that "inhabitants" as used in an enabling act, meant legal voters; St. Joseph *v* Rogers, 16 Wall, 644 (1872), where a law of Illinois, requiring a vote of "a majority of the legal voters of any township" in one section, and a majority "voting at such election," was construed to mean a majority of those voting at the election, People *v* Oliver, 1 T & C (N Y), 570 (1873), holding that "tax-payers" includes all persons whose names are on the assessment roll as such, though wrongfully taxed — as non-residents, Milner *v* Pensacola, 2 Woods, 632 (1875), where a statute required the "consent of a majority of the corporation comprising" the city. A defense to an action on the bonds by an innocent holder, that only a minority of citizens voted, was held not good, Melvin *v* Lisenby, 72 Ill, 63 (1874), holding that the presumption is that the vote cast at an election held according to law is the vote of the whole number of legal voters, Reiger *v* Beaufort, 70 N C, 319 (1874), where a majority of votes cast at an election was held sufficient under a statute requiring a majority of the voters qualified to vote, although a majority of all the voters of the town did not vote. If petition must be signed by a majority of freeholder, minors and married women, etc, are to be counted. State *v* City of Kokomo, 8 N E. Rep, 718 (Ind 1886) See, also, Cagwin *v* Hancock, 84 N Y, 532 (1881) And for a contrary rule, well argued out, see Harshman *v* Bates Co, 92 U S, 569 (1875) [overruled, however in County of Cass *v* Johnson, 95 U S, 360 (1877)], and the dissenting opinions of Miller and Bradley JJ, in County of Cass *v* Johnson, 95 U S, 360, 370 (1877) As to the right of a voter or signer to revoke his consent once granted, see Springport *v* Teutonia Savings Bank, 84 id, 403 (1881), People *v* Sawyer, 52 N Y., 296, People *v* Wagner, 1 Thomp & C. 221 (1873); People *v* Hatch, 1 id, 113 (1873). Cf First Nat Bank *v* Dorset, 16 Blatch, 62 (1879), Noble *v* Vincennes, 42 Ind, 125 (1873), and see Hannibal *v* Fountleroy, 105 U S, 408 (1881)

[1] Anderson *v* Township of Santa Anna, 116 U S, 356 (1886) Cf State *v* Holladay, 72 Mo, 499, Smith *v* City of Fond du Lac, 8 Fed Rep, 289, McCall *v* Town of Hancock, 10 id, 8 The fact that the proposition to vote aid is defeated at one election does not prevent the calling of another election to submit the question again Supervisors *v* Galbraith, 99 U S 214 (1879), Society, etc, *v* City, etc, 29 Conn, 174 Nor does a vote of aid to one railroad prevent a subsequent vote of aid to another railroad Chicot Co *v* Lewis, 103 U S, 164

A subscription is a contract, to be executed in general in the ordinary way in which any other contract may properly be made. But the act authorizing the subscription frequently provides by whom and in what manner the contract shall be executed When this is the case the provisions of the statute are to be strictly complied with [1]

It has been held that, in order to constitute a valid municipal subscription to the stock of a railway company, it is not necessary that there be an actual act of subscribing.[2]

[1] Walnut z. Wade, 103 U S, 683 (1880), Town of Douglass v Niantic Savings Bank, 97 Ill, 228 (1881), Town of Windsor v Hallett, 97 Ill, 201 (1880). The commissioners cannot bind the municipality by a modification of the subscription voted by it Bell v Railroad Co, 4 Wall, 598 (1866). A subscription for a municipality by officers in a supposed office which does not constitutionally exist is void Norton z Shelby County. 118 U. S, 425 (1886) So, for example, where the act provides for the appointment of a board of commissioners to make the subscription, they only are competent to make it, they are for this purpose the agents of the municipality for which they act, they may insert conditions into the contract which, unless repudiated by the corporation, are valid, and will bind all parties concerned, then powers are to be exercised jointly, and therein all must act — a majority not being sufficient by their act to bind the municipality, their acts when once fully performed, are final and binding and cannot be recalled or revoked Danville v Montpelier, etc, R. R. Co, 43 Vt., 144 (1870). Cf First Nat. Bank z. Arlington, 16 Blatch, 57 (1879), Bank v Concord, 50 Vt 257; People v. Hitchcock, 2 T & C (N Y), 134 (1873), State v Hancock County, 11 Ohio St, 183 (1860), S C, 12 id, 596 Cf Jackson County v Brush, 76 Ill, 59 (1875), Kankakee v Ætna Life Ins Co, 106 U S, 668 (1882), Bissell v Township of Spring Valley, 110 U. S. 162 (1884), In re Bradner, 87 N. Y, 171 (1881) If the officers or agents of a municipality have a discretion with reference to the subscription to make it or not, as they may think best under the circumstances, their exercise of that discretion is final, and cannot be reviewed or questioned. Mercer County v Pittsburgh, etc., R. R. Co., 27 Penn St, 389 (1856). Cf. Falconer v Buffalo, etc, R. R. Co, 69 N. Y, 491 (1877), First Nat. Bank v. Concord, 50 Vt, 257 (1877).

[2] Nugent v Supervisors. 19 Wall, 241 (1873), holding, also, that a resolution by a duly authorized board of agents, declaring a subscription made, is, upon the acceptance of the subscription in that shape by the railway company, and a notice to the municipality of the acceptance, a good and binding subscription, although there was no subscription made in the books of the company To same effect. see County of Moultrie z Rockingham Ten Cent Sav Bank, 92 U S, 631 (1875), County of Cass v Gillett, 100 id, 585 (1879). Cf State v Jennings, 4 Wis, 549 The board whose duty it is to make the subscription may do so through the county clerk Chicago, etc, R. R Co. v Putnam, 12 Pac Rep, 593 (Kan, 1887). The bonds, if signed on Sunday, will be invalid, although the signature is by the proper officer De Forth v. Wisconsin, etc, R. R. Co, 52 Wis, 320 (1881), Bank, etc, v Town, etc, 84 N C, 169 (1881), where an omission of commissioners to sign bonds was held not fatal, the requirement being directory.

But the vote of the tax-payers or inhabitants, as the case may be, is not a subscription, nor does it amount to a subscription, nor does it in general vest in the company for whose proposed benefit the vote was taken a right to have a subscription made [1]

It has been held that the officers authorized to make the subscription have a certain amount of discretion in fixing the terms of payment [2]

§ 97 *Municipal subscriptions may be conditional.*— A municipal corporation may annex to its subscription any condition that an individual subscriber might lawfully prescribe, and may, in consequence, make the payment of the subscription depend upon the performance thereof [3] Moreover, a municipal corporation is en-

---

[1] Cumberland, etc, R. R. Co v Barren Co, 10 Bush (Ky), 604 (1874), Bates Co. v Winters, 97 U S. 83 (1877) A mere vote of the municipality is not a subscription If the road is foreclosed before subscription, no suit lies to collect. Board of Comm'rs v Cottingham, 17 N. E Rep., 855 (Ind, 1888), County of Bates v Winters, 97 U S, 83 (1877), holding that where, after an election in favor of making a subscription, the county court made an order for a subscription, and its agent reported that the railroad company had no stock-books, for which, and other reasons, he did not make the subscription, it was held that these acts were not final and self-executing, and did not constitute a subscription; Wadsworth v St. Croix Co., 4 Fed Rep., 378 (1880)

[2] Syracuse, etc, v Seneca, etc., 86 N Y, 317 (1881), where it was held that after regular proceedings had been taken to bond a town, the commissioners, under the law, had a right to make the bonds payable at one time or at different times. Winter v City Council, etc, 65 Ala, 403 (1880), where a vote authorized the issue of bonds to an amount not exceeding $1,000,000, and it was held that the corporate authorities had discretionary power to issue them for a less amount

[3] Brocaw v Gibson Co, 73 Ind, 543 (1881), Portland, etc, R. R Co v Inhabitants of Hartford, 58 Me, 23 (1870)

A municipality authorized to vote a subscription to the stock of a railroad company may impose conditions that shops be built in the town Casey v. People, 24 N E Rep, 570 (Ill, 1890), Chicago, etc, R. R. Co v Aurora, 99 Ill 207 (1881), holding that if of two conditions one is legal and the other unauthorized, and they are severable, the illegal one may be rejected and the bonds issued held good as to the other, Noesen v. Port Washington, 37 Wis, 168 (1875), Perkins v Port Washington, 37 id, 177 (1875), Town of Platteville v Galena, etc., R R Co, 43 id, 193 (1878), holding that, where a town accepted a written proposition from a railroad company, the terms and construction of it were not allowed to be modified by reason of representations made by the company to the voters before the election Foote v Mount Pleasant, 1 McCrary, 101 (1878) In this case the proceeds of city bonds issued in payment of a subscription to a railroad were to be expended within the county limits. It was held that, as between the city and the road or its assignees with notice, the bonds could not be enforced if no part of the proceeds had been so expended Atchison, etc, R. R. Co v Phillips Co, 25 Kan, 261 (1881) Cf Memphis, etc, R R Co v Thompson 24 Kan, 170 (1880), Red Rock v Henry, 106 U S 596 (1882), Shurtleff v Wiscasset, 74 Me, 130 (1882), State v Hau-

titled to the benefit of any implied conditions to which an individual subscriber would be entitled [1]

Where a condition precedent has not been fulfilled the subscription is not enforceable, and bonds issued in payment will be invalid even in the hands of *bona fide* holders; as, for example, where the location of a railway in a certain place is the condition, and the location is not made as required by the condition.[2] But if it be a condition subsequent, as where a town subscribed for .stock in a railway company upon condition that the road should "be built through the town on the line as run by the engineer, with a suitable depot for the convenience of the public," a failure to perform is not a defense to an action to collect assessments.[3]

cock Co., 11 Ohio St, 183 (1860). In this case commissioners who were authorized to subscribe for stock in a railroad to run through their county and to issue bonds therefor, and who had subscribed for the stock, were allowed, as against a proceeding to compel them to issue bonds, to set up the defense that the road had not been located in their county A certificate of the municipal authorities that the condition has been complied with renders the bonds issued on that certificate valid and enforceable, though the certificate was a fraud on the municipality Oregon v Jennings, 119 U S , 74 (1886). People, etc , v. Holden, 82 Ill , 93 (1876) In this case completing a road, except about one mile, and operating its trains for that distance over another road so as to supply all the wants of the public, was held a substantial compliance with a condition requiring its completion Hodgman v St Paul, etc., 23 Minn , 153 (1876), holding that a condition calling for the completion of a road to a certain point did not require the building of a bridge across a river, other facilities for crossing it being provided See, also, on conditional subscriptions, Concord v. Portsmouth, etc , 92 U S , 625 (1875); Railroad Co v Falconer, 103 U S , 821 (1880), ch. V, *supra.* In the case of Madison County Court v Richmond, etc , R R Co , 80 Ky , 16 (1882), it is held that, while a county may make such conditions as may seem proper to it before submitting

the question of a subscription to a popular vote, the county court cannot, after the vote is taken, require other conditions, or alter those already imposed, or by a second election change the terms of the contract of subscription as originally made and entered into See, also, Carroll v Smith, 111 U. S , 556 (1884)

[1] Lamb v Anderson, 54 Iowa, 190 (1880).

[2] Mellen v. Town of Lansing, 19 Blatch , 512 (1871); Chicago, etc., R. R. Co v Marseilles, 84 Ill , 145 (1876); Bucksport, etc , R. R. Co v Brewer, 67 Me , 295 (1877)

[3] Belfast, etc , R. R. Co v Brooks, 60 Me , 568 (1872) *Cf* Chicago, etc., R. R. Co v. Schewe, 45 Iowa, 79 (1876). As to a subsequent breach of a condition attached to the subscription, see People v. Rome, etc , R. R. Co, 103 N Y., 95 (1886) A contract to keep certain shops, etc., permanently in a place, in consideration of local aid, may be disregarded by the railroad after many years, when its terminus changes, etc. Texas, etc., R'y v. Marshall, 132 U S., 393 (1890). Lessees of purchaser of railroad purchased at foreclosure sale are not bound by contract of first railroad company, made with municipalities voting aid in reference to depots. People v Louisville, etc , R. R. Co , 10 N E. Rep., 657 (Ill , 1887) See, also, People v. Holden, 82 Ill , 93 (1876), Hodgman v. St. Paul, etc , R. R Co , 23 Minn , 153 (1876); State v Town of Clark, 23 id , 422 (1877); State

§ 98. *When may a municipal subscription be paid in bonds instead of money?* — The express power of a municipality to subscribe for stock does not authorize it to issue negotiable bonds therefor.[1] But where a municipal corporation is authorized to subscribe to the stock of a railway or other corporation, or to lend its credit thereto, and to issue bonds to that end, it may, in the exercise of its proper discretion, instead of selling the bonds and applying the proceeds to the payment of the subscription, deliver the bonds themselves to the railway company in exchange for an equivalent amount of the stock.[2]

In New York a contrary view prevails, and there is force in the New York argument that only thus can the full par value of the bonds be realized for the purposes of the enterprise[3]

v Lime, 23 id., 521 (1877) See, also, § 78, *supra* In New York it is held that, where a town imposes as a condition precedent to its subscription that the road be located and constructed through the town, the commissioners have no power to accept any agreement from the company or any substitute in lieu of full compliance. Falconer v Buffalo, etc., R. R. Co, 69 N Y, 491 (1877). Where the agent of the railroad represented that a depot was to be constructed at a certain place, a failure to so construct is good ground for enjoining the issue of municipal aid bonds. Wullenwahm v Dunnigan, 47 N. W. Rep, 420 (Neb, 1890) *Cf* ch IX. As to the right to revoke a consent by popular vote, see § 94, *supra*.

[1] Norton v Dyersburg, 127 U. S., 160 (1888). Even though a municipal corporation be authorized by statute to subscribe to the stock of a railroad, yet it cannot issue its negotiable bonds to pay such subscription, there being no statutory authority for the issue of such bonds. Hill v Memphis, 134 U S, 198 (1890).

[2] Meyer v The City of Muscatine, 1 Wall, 384, 392 (1863); Seybert v Pittsburgh, 1 Wall, 272 (1863), Evansville, etc., R. R. Co. v City of Evansville, 15 Ind, 395 (1860); Curtis v County of Butler, 24 How (U. S) 435; Commonwealth v Pittsburgh, 41 Penn St, 278;

Town of Concord v Portsmouth Savings Bank, 92 U S, 625 (1871), Aspinwall v. Jo Daviess Co., 22 How, 364 (1852), where, before the authorized subscription was made, a new constitution was adopted making such subscript ons void unless paid in cash, *held*, that bonds issued to pay a subscription made after the new constitution was adopted were void Statutory authority to raise money by tax and appropriate it to aid of railroad does not authorize issue of bonds by the municipality therefor Concord v Robinson, 121 U S, 165 (1887). Where a town issues bonds instead of paying money, as required by statute, and the bonds are declared void, the holder is not subrogated to the right of the railroad to the money itself Ætna, etc., Ins Co v Middleport, 124 U S, 534 (1888)

[3] Starin v Genoa, 23 N Y, 439 (1861); Bank of Rome v Village of Rome 19 id., 20 (1859); Horton v Town of Thompson, 71 id, 513 (1863), holding that, if the bonds were turned over to the railroad, the latter would sell them for what they would bring which would generally be less than par For decisions to the effect that, at common law, a municipal corporation cannot sell its bonds at less than par, see Neuse River Nav Co v Com'rs 7 Jones (N C) 275, Dan Neg Instr (3d ed), § 1533, County of Armstrong v Brinton, 47 Pa. St, 367

§ 99 *A municipal corporation as a stockholder.* — When a municipal corporation subscribes to the stock of a railway company, it becomes a stockholder in just the same sense as any individual subscriber, is entitled to the same rights, privileges and emoluments, and is subject to the same burdens of duty and liability as other holders of the stock [1]

This doctrine is established as an unquestioned rule of law by the long line of cases, both in the state and federal courts, which involve the validity of municipal bonds issued in aid of railway or other corporations

§ 100 *A municipality may enforce delivery of stock to itself in a proper case* — Under the same circumstances and conditions, and to the same extent, as any other subscriber, a municipal corporation may compel a railway or other corporation to deliver to it stock to which the subscribers in general are entitled   Whatever would prevent an individual subscriber from enforcing such delivery will equally prevent a municipality in a like case.[2] A mu-

---

(1864) Gould i Town of Sterling, 23 N. Y., 456 460 (1861).

[1] Shipley i The City of Terre Haute, 74 Ind., 297 (1881), Kreiger i Shelby R. R Co (Ky, 1886), 25 Am & Eng R R Cas, 528 (1886), Gray v The State, 82 Ind, 567 (1880), 1 Dan Neg Instr, § 436, Murray v Charleston, 96 U S, 432 (1877) See, also, Curran i The State, 15 How, 304, Robinson v Bank of Darien, 18 Ga, 65 County of Morgan i Allen 103 U S, 498 (1880), United States i Planters' Bank, 9 Wheat, 904, Morgan County v Thomas, 76 Ill, 120 (1875), State i Holladay, 72 Mo, 499, Marshall i Western, etc, R R, 92 N C, 322 (1885), County of Morgan v Allen, 103 U S, 498 (1880), holding that the creditors of an insolvent corporation may enforce the liability of municipal corporations upon their bonds, Robinson v Bidwell, 22 Cal, 379, People i Coon, 25 Cal, 635, holding that the individual members of a municipal corporation have no such interest in stock in a railroad subscribed for by it as will disable the legislature from authorizing it to compromise with the railroad A foreclosure of the railroad on a mortgage closes out the stock which a municipality has therein Spur-

lock v Missouri Pac. R'y Co, 2 S. W. Rep, 219 (Mo., 1886) See, also, ch. XXXVIII A judgment creditor may reach a municipal subscription payable in bonds by *mandamus*, after acquiring the company's right thereto. Smith v. Bourbon County, 127 U S., 105 (1888) A municipality as a stockholder may assent to the sale of the railroad by the corporation to another reorganized corporation Foster v Chesapeake, etc, R'y, 47 Fed Rep, 269 (1891) A municipality's stock in a corporation cannot be reached by a judgment creditor of the municipality except by proving that the subscription was legal Hughes v. Com'rs 12 S E Rep, 465 (N. C, 1890) Where stock in a railroad is owned by a part of a county, that part becomes a municipality for the purpose of owning and voting the stock Hancock v. Louisville, etc, R R, 145 U S, 409 (1892) Execution or garnishee process cannot be levied on stock held by an individual as trustee where the debt is his individual debt, nor can it be levied on the dividends from such stock So held where stock was owned by a city in trust for the citizens Hitchcock v Galveston W. Co., 50 Fed Rep, 263 (1880)

[2] Wapello Co. v Burlington, etc, R.

154

nicipal corporation, as a subscriber, is in no better position than an individual subscriber in this respect [1]

§ 101 *Division of the municipality after the subscription* — We find a line of cases in the reports of some of the western states which deals with the questions which have grown out of the subdivision of towns and counties in those states, after a donation or subscription has been made to some railway or other corporation. and before the bonds have been issued, or before they have become due and payable

It is, of course, not competent for the legislature so to divide a municipality as to release all or any part of it from the obligation of any contract into which the whole had previously entered [2] When a town or county is divided, or some part of it annexed to some other town or county, after the undivided municipality has voted a subscription, and it is provided in the act by which the division is accomplished that each part shall remain liable for the previous municipal indebtedness, such provision is held to mean nothing more than that, as concerns the subscription voted, each part is liable for its proportion only of the debt according to the valuation of the property of the undivided municipality at the time the vote was taken [3] This rule, however, cannot affect the creditor's right to hold liable the whole of the old municipality

§§ 102, 103 *Consolidation of companies after the municipal aid is voted* — When the company proposed to be benefited unites or is consolidated with another company or companies of a similar character, after the aid of a municipality has been voted and before the subscription has been paid — the company having before the election the right to consolidate — the bonds may lawfully be issued to or sold for the benefit of the new or consolidated company [4] When,

---

R. Co, 44 Iowa, 585 (1876) In this case the stock was to be issued only when fully paid.

[1] Pittsburgh, etc, R. R. Co v Allegheny Co., 79 Pa St, 210 (1875). Cf State v Garoutte, 67 Mo, 445 (1878)

[2] Sedgwick County v Bailey, 11 Kan, 631 (1873) Cf State v Lake City, 25 Minn, 404 (1879), Marion County v Harvey County, 26 Kan, 181 (1881), Henderson v Jackson County, 12 Fed Rep, 676 (1881)

[3] Hunt v Hamilton, 25 Kan, 76 (1881) See, also, Eagle v Beard, 33 Ark, 497 (1878), holding that, in the absence of statutory provision, the detached part of a county is released from liability for the

debts of the county, but the legislature may apportion the debt between the old and the new counties, McBride v Hardin County, 58 Ia, 219 (1882), holding that a county is not responsible for expenses incurred by one of the townships comprising it in voting taxes in aid of a railroad

[4] Livingston County v Portsmouth Bank, 128 U S, 102 (1888), New Buffalo v Iron Company, 105 U S, 73 (1881), Bates County v Winters 97 U S, 83, County of Scotland v Thomas, 94 id, 682 (1876), Town of East Lincoln v Davenport, 94 id, 801 (1876), Wilson v Salamanca, 99 id, 499 (1878), Empire v Darlington, 101 id, 87 (1879), holding that where stock in a railroad had been

however, the consolidation works such a fundamental change in the constitution and purpose of the original corporation that individual subscribers are thereby released, a subscription by the municipality will be invalidated,[1] but otherwise not[2] It is accordingly said that municipal bonds voted and delivered to a corporation under a changed name are not by such change invalidated[3]

subscribed for by a township under statutory authority, an additional subscription after it was consolidated with another road and under a new name was valid; Menasha *v* Hazard, 102 id, 81 (1880); Harter *v* Kernochan, 103 id, 562 (1880), holding that where township records showed that bonds were directed to be issued and delivered to a consolidated company, although the act authorizing them and the vote under it contemplated the issue to one of the consolidated companies, the township was estopped to deny their validity, County of Tipton *v* Locomotive Works, 103 id , 523 (1880), State *v* Green County, 54 Mo, 540 (1874), Vernon *v* Hovey, 52 Ind , 563 (1876). See, also, Nugent *z* Supervisors, 19 Wall , 241 (1873), County of Henry *v* Nicolay, 95 U. S. 619 (1877). In this case a railroad company had, after the subscription, transferred its franchises to another company In a suit upon the bonds, paid for the stock, in hands of an innocent purchaser, the bonds were upheld County of Schuyler *v* Thomas, 98 id , 169 (1877) *Cf* Harshman *v* Bates County, 92 U. S , 569 (1875) A municipal aid cannot be enforced where the railroad company sells all its property to another company. Cantillon *z* Dubuque, etc., R. R. Co., 35 N. W. Rep., 620 (Iowa, 1887)

[1] Lynch *v* Eastern, etc , R. R. Co., 57 Wis, 430 (1883). Harshman *v* Bates County, *supra*, will hardly be followed It does not accord with the current decisions See Crooks *v.* State, 4 N E. Rep., 589 (Ind , 1886).

[2] Atchison, etc , R. R. Co *v* Phillips Co, 25 Kan , 261 (1881), Society, etc., *v* New London 29 Conn.. 174 (1860). In this last case the new company was substantially the same as the one to which

the subscription was made. The court held the issue of the bonds to the new company valid; Illinois, etc , *v* Barnett, 85 Ill , 313 (1861), holding that the legal purchase of another road will not invalidate subscriptions; Howard Co *v.* Booneville, etc , 108 U S, 314, holding that the defense, after paying interest for several years, that the road constructed was not the one to whose stock the subscription was authorized, was not good, it appearing that it was a branch of the road referred to in the act Commonwealth *v* Pittsburgh, 41 Penn St , 278 (1861), Lewis *v* Clarendon, 5 Dillon, 329 (1878); Chickaming *v.* Carpenter, 106 U S, 663 (1882).

[3] Town of Reading *v.* Wedder, 66 Ill , 80 (1872); Commonwealth *v* Pittsburgh, 41 Pa St , 278 In the case of Marsh *v.* Fulton Co , 10 Wall , 676 (1870), where the legislature so amended the charter of a railway company as to divide the road into three divisions, and each division was made a new company, so that there were three distinct corporations in place of the original corporation, it was held by the federal supreme court that a subscription of stock and issue of county bonds, authorized by a popular vote to be made to the original corporation, could not legally be made to one of the three new corporations. Consolidation with another railroad no defense to the county, where the statute authorizing it existed at time of county vote Chicago, etc , R. R. Co. *v* Putnam, 12 Pac. Rep , 593 (Kan , 1887); County, etc , *z.* Locomotive, etc , 103 U S , 523 (1880), holding that if a municipal corporation consents to a consolidation of roads it is estopped from denying the validity of its bonds in the hands of a *bona fide* holder.

CHAPTER VII.

CALLS.

§ 104 *Definition of call* — A "call" may be defined to be an official declaration, by the proper corporate authorities, that the whole
or a specified part of the subscriptions for stocks is required to be
paid.[1] The term, however, is used with different meanings, and
may refer to the resolution of the officials that a part or the whole
of the subscription must be paid, or to the resolution and notification thereof, or the combination of facts making the parties called
on liable to an action for the non-payment of the money called.[2]
An assessment is a term often used to designate the same thing
as a call, but sometimes refers to payments sought to be recovered
from the stockholders, above and in addition to the par value of
the stock. An instalment is one of the several part payments into
which a single call may be divided.

[1] Braddock v Phil, Marlton & Medford R. R Co, 45 N J L, 363 (1883),
holding also that a direction by the directors to the president to collect the
subscriptions is a call In the case of
Spangler v. Ind. & Ill Central R R Co
21 Ill, 276 (1859), a call or assessment is
rather vaguely defined as "a rating or
fixing of the proportion by the board of
directors, which every subscriber is to
pay of his subscription, when notified
of it and when called in" Newry &
Enniskillen R'y Co. v Edmunds, 2 Ex

Rep., 118 (1848) holds that a call is an
application to each shareholder for a
proportion of his share
[2] Queen v Londonderry & Coleraine
R'y Co, 13 Q B 998 In Ambergate,
N & B & E J Ry Co. v Mitchell 4
Ex Rep, 540 (1849), it is said 'the word
call is capable of three meanings it
may either mean the resolution or its
notification, or the time when it becomes payable It must mean either
one of these three."

§ 105 *Call is generally necessary* — As a general rule a call must be made in order to render a subscription or any part thereof due and payable to the corporation   A contract of subscription, unlike other contracts to pay money, is a promise to pay; but, by implication of law, the payment is to be only at such times, and in such part payments, as may be designated by the corporate authorities in a formal declaration known as a "call"[1]   In other words, the subscription is a debt payable at a future time.[2]   The time when it shall be paid is indefinite until fixed by a call.

[1] "No action can be maintained against a stockholder for an instalment on his subscription until the board has directed the call to be made" Banet v. Alton & Sangamon R. R. Co., 13 Ill., 504 (1851), Spangler v Ind & Ill Central R. R. Co, 21 Ill, 276 (1859); Braddock v Phil, Marlton & Medford R R Co, 45 N J L., 363 (1883) In the case of Grosse Isle Hotel Co. v L'Anson's Exrs, 42 N J L., 10 (1880), aff'd, 43 N J L, 442 (1881), the court said a subscription for stock "imports an agreement not to pay at once the whole sum representing the value of the shares subscribed for, but a stipulation to pay such sum when called for by the directors, in amounts duly assessed" And in Bank of South Australia v Abrahams, L R, 6 Privy Council App., 262 (1875), the court said "The company has no absolute right, and the shareholder is under no absolute liability, to pay The right only arises if, and when, calls are made by the directors.   .   .   .   The due making of the call by the resolution of a board of directors is an essential condition precedent.' To the same effect, see Wilbur v Stockholders of the Corpn, 18 Bankr Reg, 178. Where, by statute or charter, payment is to be in such manner and proportion and times as the directors may order, there can be no suit to collect until after a call Grissell's Case, L R, 1 Ch. App, 528, 535 (1866); Ala & Fla R. R. Co v Rowley, 9 Fla, 508 (1861). Even where the stock is fraudulently issued as paid up, in payment for property, and the transac-

tion is impeached for fraud, a call is necessary before the subscription can be enforced Granite Roofing Co. v Michael, 54 Md, 65 (1880). Where, however, for failure to furnish the property due on a subscription, a suit for damages is brought by the corporation, no call need precede such suit. An allegation of a general demand suffices Cheraw & Chester R. R. Co. v Garland, 14 S C, 63 (1879). Ohio, Ind & Ill R. R. Co v Cramer, 23 Ind, 490 (1864). A call is not applicable to stock which was subscribed for after the call was made Pike v Shore Line, 68 Me, 445 (1878). A subscription payable "in such instalments and at such times as may be decided by a majority of the stockholders or board of directors," etc. is not collectible until the instalments and times have been so fixed North, etc, Co. v. Spullock, 14 S E. Rep, 478 (Ga, 1892).

[2] The subscription "is a present debt, payable at a future day" Pittsburgh & Connellsville R R. Co v. Clark, 29 Pa. St., 146 (1857). The subscription "creates a debt. but the debt does not accrue due until a call is made," Grissell's Case, L. R., 1 Ch App, 528, 535 (1866). In *In re* China Steamship & Coal Co., 38 L. J (Ch), 512 (1869), the court say : "The moment a call is made it is a debt due in every respect," although it cannot be collected by suit until later. The bankruptcy act does not release an applicant thereunder from liability for calls made after his release in bankruptcy. Glenn v. Howard, 3 Atl Rep., 895 (1886).

§ 106. *When a call is unnecessary — Payment in advance —* If, however, a subscription contains a promise to pay upon a certain day, no call is necessary; but the subscriber is bound to pay, at all events, upon the day named[1] So, also, if by statute or the charter the subscription becomes payable at a certain specified time, a call is hereby dispensed with, and is not required[2] A stockholder, on the other hand, is not obliged to wait for a call even when entitled to it. He may pay at any time[3]

§ 107. *New York rule.*— In New York it seems that a different rule prevails. In that state there is a tendency to hold that no call is necessary before suit is brought on a subscription for stock. The subscriber's obligation to pay, and the time and manner of payment, must be sought for in the contract itself. Unless the contract provides for calls, the subscription is payable absolutely and at once, or as soon as the corporation is duly organized[4] Accordingly, in an

[1] Estell *v* Knightstown & Middletown Turnpike Co, 41 Ind, 174 (1872), New Albany & Salem R R. Co *v* Pickens, 5 Ind, 247 (1854), Ross *i* Lafayette & Indianapolis R. R. Co, 6 Ind, 297 (1853), Breedlove *i* Martinsville & F R R. Co, 12 Ind, 114 (1859), Waukon & M R. R Co *v* Dwyer, 49 Iowa, 121 (1878) Where a subscriber gives a note in payment of the subscription an indorsee may enforce the note, although no calls have been made on subscriptions. Ruse *v* Bromberg, 7 S. Rep, 384 (Ala, 1889)

[2] Phœnix Warehousing Co *v* Badger, 67 N. Y., 294 (1876)

[3] Marsh *v.* Burroughs, 1 Woods, 463 (1871), Pool's Case, L. R, 9 Ch D, 322 (1878). But if such payment is by the directors themselves, and it is immediately repaid to them for fees, the corporation being insolvent, the transaction will be set aside Syke's Case, L. R., 13 Eq Cas, 255 (1871) So, also, a payment in advance, on an agreement that such payment shall be only a loan if the corporation is successful, but shall be a payment of the subscription if the corporation becomes insolvent, is held to be a loan, though insolvency occurs Barge's Case, L R, 5 Eq Cas., 420 (1868) Frequently a subscription is paid, before a call, by applying to its payment money due the subscriber from the corporation Adamson's Case L. R, 18 Eq Cas, 670 (1874). A subscription for bonds, the amount being payable on call, may be paid at once and the bonds demanded Watjen *i* Green, 21 Atl Rep, 1028 (N J, 1891) Where the purchase price of stock is to be in ten equal payments and interest is to be allowed if payment is made in advance, the interest may be collected Porter *v* Beacon, etc, Co, 26 Atl Rep, 216 (Pa. 1893). A stockholder who offers to pay his subscription in full, which offer is declined by the corporation, is not thereby released from his obligation if he continues to act as a stockholder Potts *v* Wallace, 146 U S, 689 (1892)

[4] Lake Ontario, Auburn & N Y R R. Co *v* Mason, 16 N Y, 451 (1859), Phœnix Warehousing Co *v* Badger, 67 N. Y, 294, 300 (1876) In the former case, however, calls were made and notice given by advertisement in a newspaper In the latter case, by the terms of the charter, all subscriptions were due at the time when suit was commenced Hence in both cases, the statements in reference to calls have the appearance of *data* In Mann *i* Pentz, 3 N Y, 415 (1850), it was held that a receiver could not collect uncalled subscriptions since " the only condition upon which he (the subscriber) could

action brought to collect a subscription, it is not necessary to allege that a call has been made, unless the terms of the subscription or the provisions of the corporate charter expressly provide for calls. These rules, however, seem not to have been directly passed upon in New York, and it is doubtful whether they can be considered as clearly established in that state[1]

§ 108 *In case of corporate insolvency no call is necessary.*— When a corporation becomes insolvent, and there exist subscriptions which have not been fully paid in, the directors frequently neglect or refuse to make the calls necessary for the purpose of paying the corporate debts. In such cases a court of equity will disregard the formality of a call, and will order the unpaid subscriptions to be paid to a receiver for the benefit of the corporate creditors[2] The courts very properly hold that it is not discretion-

have been made liable to the corporation was by regular calls made in pursuance of the charter" See, also, Bauton *r* Dry Dock, etc, Co., 4 E D Smith, 420 (1855), Seymour *v* Sturgess, 26 N Y, 134 (1862), Savage *v.* Medbury, 19 N Y, 32 (1859), Williams *v* Meyer, 41 Hun, 545 (1886) See, also, Howland *v* Edwards, 24 N Y 307 (1862)

[1] These rules seem to be peculiar to New York The decisions in some of the other states hold, however, that no notice of calls is necessary. See § 117 Practically, such a rule is equivalent to requiring no call at all, since in both cases collection is made only by direction of the directors or other officers, and in both cases the subscriber need not be informed of such directions

[2] "It is well settled that when stock is subscribed to be paid upon call of the company, and the company refuses or neglects to make the call, a court of equity may itself make the call, if the interests of the creditors require it." Scoville *v* Thayer, 105 U S, 143 (1881), Glenn *v* Williams, 60 Md, 93, Glenn *v* Sample, 80 Ala, 159 (1885). "A company call is but a step in the process of collection, and a court of equity may pursue its own mode of collection, so that no injustice is done to the debtor" Hatch *v.* Dana, 101 U S, 205 (1879). No call is necessary before stockholders are

liable to creditors on their unpaid subscription, even though the charter provides for a call Hill *v.* Merchants' Ins. Co, 134 U S, 515 (1890). See, also, Myers *v* Seeley, 10 Natl. Bank. Reg., 411, Sanger *v* Upton, 91 U S, 56 (1875); Wilbur *v.* Stockholders, etc., 18 Bank. Reg, 178 Where the corporation, being indebted, has the power to call, and does not choose to exercise it, equity at the instance of creditors will exercise it. Marsh *v* Burroughs, 1 Woods, 463 (1871); Boeppler *v* Menown, 7 Mo. App., 447 (1885), Adler *v.* Milwaukee Pat. B. Mfg. Co, 13 Wis, 57 (1860); Glenn *v.* Dodge, 3 Cent Rep., 283 (1886); Great W. Tel. Co. *v* Gray, 14 N E Rep., 214 (Ill, 1887); Ward *v* Griswoldville Mfg Co., 16 Conn, 593 (1844), Miller's Case, 54 L J. (Ch.), 141 (1885), Henry *v* Vermilion & Ashland R. R., Co., 17 Ohio, 187 (1848); Ogilvie *v* Knox Ins. Co, 22 How, 380 (1859); Curry *v.* Woodward, 53 Ala., 371 (1875), Chandler *v.* Keith, 42 Iowa, 99 (1875); Shackley *v.* Fisher, 75 Mo., 498 (1882) The filing of the bill in the suit in equity is equivalent to a call Hatch *v* Dana, 101 U. S, 205 (1879); Thompson *v* Reno Sav Bank, 7 Pac. Rep, 68; 19 Nev, 103, 171, 242, 291, 293 (1886). See, also, Yeager *v* Scranton, etc, Bank, 14 Weekly N. Cas, 296 (1884). A late case holds that a decree in a chancery suit is equivalent to a call Glenn *v*

ary with the directors to say whether the company's debts shall be paid or not. And this is the rule even though the statute provides that calls shall be made by the directors [1]

There has been some doubt as to whether the writ of *mandamus* would lie to compel the directors to make the call,[2] but the authorities seem to hold that the writ will not lie for this purpose. The usual procedure to collect unpaid subscriptions is an order of a court of equity made in a suit brought by corporate creditors for the purpose of applying corporate assets to corporate debts [3]

Saxton, 68 Cal , 353 (1886) If the court orders that notice of the call be given the receiver cannot collect by suit unless such notice is given Franklin Savings Bank *v* Fatzinger, 4 Atl Rep , 912 (Pa., 1886) Where the whole of the unpaid subscriptions are needed to pay corporate debts, no assessment, even by the court, is necessary But, unless the evidence clearly shows such necessity, it is for the jury to say whether the whole unpaid subscription shall be paid Citizens', etc.. Co *v.* Gillispie, 9 Atl Rep . 73 (Pa , 1887, citing cases). Seo § 207. Where an assignment is made by the corporation for the benefit of creditors, the statute of limitations begins to run within a reasonable time, even if no call is made Glenn *v.* Dorsheimer, 24 Fed Rep., 536. *Cf.* § 193 In Missouri it has been held that there can be no garnishment of an unpaid subscription until after a call has been made Parks *v.* Heman, 7 Mo. App , 14 (1879) In New York there are a few *dicta* to the effect that calls by the directors are necessary before unpaid subscriptions can be enforced for the benefit of corporate creditors Seymour *v.* Sturgess, 26 N Y , 134 (1862), Mann *v* Pentz, 3 N Y , 415 (1850) But the prevailing rule is sustained in Sagory *v* Dubois, 3 Sandf Ch . 466 (1846), where the court say · "The articles, it is true, in effect require that calls should be made by the directors, and probably the association could not maintain an action at law until such calls were regularly made; but that does not impair the remedy in behalf of the receiver."

[1] Glenn *v* Saxton, *supra,* Crawford *v.* Rohrer, 59 Md , 599 (1882) *Contra,* Paper Co *v* Waples, 3 Woods, 34 (1877), where the charter prescribed that calls should be only by a three-fourths vote of the stockholders

[2] "A chancellor will compel the directors to make the calls required by the charter whenever his aid is invoked by creditors or the representatives of creditors" Germantown Passenger R'y Co. *v* Fitler, 60 Pa. St., 124 (1869) The three English cases usually cited on this point do not hold that a *mandamus* lies herein Queen *i* Victoria Park Co , 1 Ad & El (N S), 541 , Queen *v* Ledyard, id , 616 , King *v* Katharine Dock Co., 4 Barn & Ad , 360 (1832). In the case of Dalton & Morgantown R. R. Co *v* McDaniel, 56 Ga , 191 (1876), the court held that a *mandamus* was unnecessary on the ground that the remedy by bill was easier and more complete, and that justice would be better administered in this way by an account of all the corporate debts, and of all liabilities of solvent stockholders, taken by a master in chancery In Hatch *v* Dana, 101 U S , 205 (1879), the court say a *mandamus* "can avail only when there are directors The remedy in equity is more complete " In Ward *v* Griswoldville Mfg Co , 16 Conn , 593 (1844), the court refused a *mandamus* because it would enforce the collection of only a few debts whereas the remedy in equity would enforce all proportionately

[3] 'Under such circumstances, before there is any obligation upon the stock-

§ 109 *Who has authority to make calls* — A call, in order to be legal and enforceable, must be made by the proper corporate authorities. Generally, the power to make calls is vested in the directors or in the stockholders at large. Unless the charter or a statute makes provision therefor, the question as to who shall make calls is a question of internal arrangement. If no provision whatever is made for the exercise of the power it devolves upon the directors, on the general principle that they alone have power to manage and superintend the financial matters of the corporation and to exercise all corporate powers, except those required to be exercised at corporate meetings [1] Even though the statute authorizes calls by the stockholders, yet the directors also have the same power.[2]

§ 110 *Calls by directors* — Where the power to make calls is vested in the directors, a call made by those who are directors *de facto* will be upheld.[3] The directors, in whom the power to make

ho'ders to pay without an assessment and call by the company, there must be some order of a court of competent jurisdiction, or, at the very least, some authorized demand upon him for payment" Scoville *v.* Thayer, 105 U. S, 143 (1881). In bankruptcy, it seems, the assignee, by succeeding to all the rights of the corporation, may make a call and enforce it. Hatch *v* Dana, 101 U. S, 205 (1879). See, also, §§ 202, 207, *infra.* At common law a court of equity could not make calls for benefit of corporate creditors *Dictum,* Grain's Case, L. R., 1 Ch D, 307, 323 (1875).

[1] Budd *t* Multnomah St. R'y Co., 15 Pac Rep, 659 (Oreg, 1887) The directors may make calls "as they may do all things, except such as are to be done by the shareholders at a general meeting" Ambergate, N & B & E. J. R'y Co. *v.* Mitchell, 4 Ex Rep, 540 (1849).

[2] Id In *Ex parte* Winsor, 3 Story, C C, 411 (1844), it was held, however, that where the charter gave to the corporation the power to assess stock it must be exercised exclusively by the stockholders in meeting assembled On the other hand, in Rives *v* Montgomery S P R. Co, 30 Ala, 92 (1857), the court held that stockholders who by charter have power to make calls may delegate

that power to the directors. See, also, Healey, Law and Pr. of Companies, 109

[3] 'An illegal election of directors cannot be set up in resistance of the payment of stock, but would be a case for a *quo warranto* to oust the illegally elected directors." Eakright *v.* Logansport & N Ind R. R. Co., 13 Ill, 404 (1859), Johnson *v* Crawfordsville R. R. Co., 11 Ind, 280 (1858), Fairfield C. T. Co. *v* Thorp, 13 Conn, 173 (1839); Steinmetz *v* Versailles R. R. Co, 57 Ind, 457 (1877), Macon R. R. Co. *v* Vason, 57 Ga, 314 (1876); Atherton *v* Sugar, etc, Co, 67 Ind, 334 (1879) In the case, however, of People's Mut. Ins. Co *v.* Westcott, 80 Mass., 440 (1860), a call by directors elected at a meeting held without notice was declared invalid and not enforceable A call may be enjoined on the ground that the directors were illegally elected Moses *v* Tompkins, 4 S. Rep, 763 (Ala, 1888). 'In England the courts will inquire into the right of directors to their office, in cases involving the validity of calls. Swansea Dock Co. *v* Lewien, 20 L. J (Ex), 447 (1851). If the directors were not legally elected, their calls and forfeitures of stock based thereon will be set aside Garden Gully, etc., Co *v* McLister, L. R, 1 App. Cas. 39 (1875). See Healey on Companies

calls is vested, cannot delegate their authority[1] It is a power the exercise of which involves a discretion which cannot be exercised by others A call by a minority meeting of the directors, no quorum being present, is void[2]

§ 111. *Assignment of subscription by corporation before or after call.*— The unpaid and uncalled subscriptions for stock cannot be mortgaged or sold by the corporation If the transfer by the directors were allowed, "the consequence would be that the discretion which they are bound to exercise would be wholly defeated and put an end to"[3] The power of making calls, being a discre-

---

110 If the corporate organization was not regular, and the directors were not legally elected, their call is not enforceable. Howbeach, etc, Co. v Teague, 5 H. & N, 151 (1860). Directors elected at a meeting called on thirteen days' notice instead of fourteen as required by statute may make calls, where their election has been confirmed by a subsequent annual general meeting Briton etc., Assoc v Jones, 61 L. T Rep., 384 (1889)

[1] Rutland & Burlington R. R. Co v Thrall, 35 Vt., 536 (1863), the court saying "Where the charter requires the directors to do some specific act, there seems to be a stronger reason why they should be held incapable of delegating such authority than when mere general powers are conferred on them" See, also, Banet v Alton & Sangamon R. R. Co, 13 Ill, 504 (1851), Pike v Shore Line, 68 Me, 445 (1878), Silver Hook Road v. Greene, 12 R. I, 164 (1878), where it was delegated to the treasurer, Mut. F. Ins Co v. Chase, 56 N H, 341 (1876), citing authorities, Monmouth Mut. F. Ins Co v Lowell, 59 Me, 504 (1871). But where the power is delegated and exercised, the call may be ratified by the directors, and will then be valid Read r Memphis Gayoso Gas Co., 8 Heisk (Tenn), 545 (1872), Rutland & B. R. R. Co. v Thrall, 35 Vt, 536 (1863). Although the directors cannot delegate the power to make a call, yet they may delegate the power "to determine the amount of some of the instalments and to designate the times

of payment." Banet r Alton & S R R. Co (1851), *supra* It is not necessary to allege that the directors were duly elected Miller v Wild Cat G Road Co., 52 Ind, 51 (1875), Steinmetz v Versailles & O T Co, 57 Ind, 457 (1887) But proof must be given that the proper authorities made the call N J Midland R'y Co v Strait, 35 N J L., 322 (1872).

[2] Price v Grand Rapids & Ind R. R. Co., 13 Ind, 58(1859), Hamilton v Same, 13 Ind, 347 (1859), Bottomley s Case, L R., 16 Ch D, 681 (1880) But may be confirmed by a quorum Phosphate of Lime Co, 24 L. T, 932

[3] *Ex parte* Stanley, 33 L. J (Ch), 535 (1864). To the same effect, see N J Midland R y Co v Strait, 35 N J L., 322 (1872); Wells v Rodgers, 50 Mich, 294 (1883), S C, 44 Mich, 411, 27 N W Rep, 671 (1886), involving the consolidation of two railroads See also Crooks v State, 4 N E Rep, 589 (Ind, 1886), Wallingford Mfg Co v Fox, 12 Vt., 304 (1840), Bank of South Australia v Abrahams, L R, 6 P C App, 262 (1875); Hurlbert v Root, 12 How Pr 511 (1855) Hill v Reid, 16 Barb, 280 (1853) · Hurlbert v Carter, 21 Barb, 221 (1855). Cf Smith v Hallett 34 Ind, 519 (1870), where the subscription was not for stock, but as a bonus The articles of incorporation of a company may authorize a mortgage on unpaid and uncalled subscriptions Re Pyle, etc Works, 62 L T Rep, 226 (1890) Affirmed, id, 887. The subscription may

tionary one, cannot be transferred to other parties. The transfer is void. The subscribers are bound to pay their subscriptions only when, in the opinion of the proper corporate authorities, or of a court of equity, the money is needed for corporate purposes. This power of ascertaining and determining the extent of the corporate needs, being a discretionary power, cannot be transferred or delegated to others. A different rule prevails, however, after a call has been made but not yet collected, and an assignment of the amount already called is legal and valid [1]

§ 112 *Interest runs from the time the call is due.*— A subscriber who has failed to pay for his shares according to the terms of his contract is properly chargeable with interest from the time of the default.[2] The company cannot be compelled to issue the stock until principal and interest are paid

§ 113 *Stockholders cannot question advisability of calls.*— The necessity or advisability of making a call is a matter which rests exclusively within the discretion of the corporate authorities who have power to make the call.[3] A stockholder, when sued upon an

be enforced by contractors to whom it has been assigned Darnall *v* Lyon, 19 S W Rep, 506 (Tex, 1892)

[1] Humber Iron-works Co., 16 Weekly Rep. 474, 667 (1868), Hills *v* Rodgers, 50 Mich, 291 (1883), Miller *v* Maloney, 3 B Mon (Ky), 105 (1842), where the call was assigned to the railroad contractor who owed the subscriber for work done Downie *v* Hoover, 12 Wis., 174 (1860), Morris *v* Cheney, 51 Ill, 451 (1869), where, however, it is not clear that a call had been made A call which has been determined upon, but not definitely made, may be transferred if it is afterwards duly made by the directors *Re* Sankey Brook Coal Co, L R., 9 Eq, 721 (1870) See L. R., 10 Eq. 381. As to the enforcement of a subscription by a subsequently created corporation formed by consolidation, see ch 53 A mortgage on all the land, property and effects of the corporation does not include uncalled subscriptions. Pickering *v* Ilfracombe R'y Co 37 L. J (C P). 118 (1868), Lishman's Claim, 23 L T Rep. (N S), 759 (1870), King *v* Marshall, 33 Beav, 565 (1864) *Cf Re* Marine M. Co, L R, 4 Eq, 601 (1867), British Prov L Ins. Co., *In re*, 4 De G,

J. & S., 407, Gardner *v.* London, etc., R'y Co., L R., 2 Ch, 201, 215. An assignee of unpaid subscriptions may assign to still another Rand *v.* Wiley, 29 N W Rep. 814 (Iowa, 1886). Right of one road built on line of abandoned road, to recover on private donation to latter, see Sickels *v* Anderson, 30 N. W. Rep., 78 (Mich, 1886)

[2] Gould *v* Oneonta, 71 N Y, 298 (1876), Rikhoff *v* Brown's Rotary, etc, Co, 68 Ind, 388 (1879), Casey *v* Galli, 94 U S, 673 (1876). See, also, Bull *v* Wilcox, 22 N Y, 551 (1860). *Cf* Stocken's Case, L. R., 5 Eq, 6 (1867), Cleveland *v* Burnham, 55 Wis., 598 (1886). In the case Glenn *v.* Liggett, 51 Fed. Rep., 381 (1892), interest was allowed only from the date of suit and not from the date of the call. 20 Atl Rep., 115

[3] The question of the necessity for the call "was a matter for the determination of the board of directors." Chouteau Ins. Co *v* Floyd, 74 Mo, 286 (1881). "The question whether these necessities demanded the payment of the money was for the directors." Judah *v* American L S Ins Co, 4 Ind, 333 (1853); Budd *v* Multnomah St. R'y Co., 15 Pac. Rep., 659 (Oreg, 1887).

unpaid call, cannot set up in defense that there was no occasion or use for the money. The call, however, must be for the *bona fide* purpose of raising money for corporate purposes It must not be for the purpose of enabling the stockholders to use the money to the detriment of the creditors of the failing corporation [1] Moreover, a court of equity will set aside calls and payments made and managed with a view to discharging the stockholders' liability, and preventing the proceeds from being applied to the general corporate debts. Equity, however, will not interfere with a call merely because the money received may be diverted by the directors to an act or enterprise beyond the powers of the corporation [2] The corporation cannot contract to postpone indefinitely a call.[3] To allow such postponement would be unjust to corporate creditors and other stockholders.

§ 114. *Calls must be impartial and uniform* — A call cannot be made so as to affect a part only of the subscribers It must be made on all alike, or it will be void.[4] The courts will not allow the directors of a company so to proceed as to require some stockholders to pay calls, and not to require others to do the same Any such attempt will be promptly set aside and rectified [5]

[1] Habertson's Case, L. R., 5 Eq. 286 (1868) Thus, where the amount paid in is immediately paid out to the directors for fees, the transaction is fraudulent, and is set aside Syke's Case, L R, 13 Eq Cas, 255 (1871). On the other hand, the directors cannot delay calls in order to enable themselves to transfer their stock and avoid liabilities Gilbert's Case, L. R., 5 Ch, 559 (1870), Preston v Grand Collier Dock Co, 11 Sim, 327 (1840).

[2] In the case of Bailey v Birkenhead, L & C J R'y Co, 12 Beav, 433 (1850), the court said: It is not within the jurisdiction of courts "to take the accounts and make the inquiries necessary for the purpose of ascertaining whether, under the circumstances to which the company is reduced, and in a continuing concern, it is proper, in the due management of the affairs of the company, to raise money by way of calls from the shareholders.' Corporate meetings are the places for such complaints See, also, Yetts v Norfolk R'y Co., 3 De G & Sm, 293 (1859)

[3] McComb v Credit Mobilier of America, etc. 13 Phil Rep, 168 (1878); Van Allen v Ill Central R R Co, 7 Bosw (N. Y) 515 (1861) — the last case holding, however, that this principle does not prevent the issue of bonds convertible into stock whenever the stockholder desires

[4] Pike v Bangor & Calais S L R R. Co, 68 Me, 445 (1878) Cannot object to call on ground that motives of directors were wrong Oglesby v Attrill, 105 U S, 605 (1881) A suit to collect thirty-five per cent. of a subscription fails where other subscribers have paid but two per cent Great Western Tel Co. v Burnham, 47 N W Rep, 373 (Wis 1890), Bowen v Kuehn, id, 374

[5] Preston v Grand Collier Dock Co, 11 Sim, 327 (1840) If directors use power to make calls oppressively they will be restrained Cannon v Trask L R, 20 Eq, 669 As where the object is to disqualify from voting those who cannot pay Anglo, etc., Bank v Baragnon, 45 L. T., 362.

§ 115. *Method of making call — No formality necessary.* — There are no prescribed or established rules stating how a call shall be made by the corporate authorities empowered to make it Any act or resolution which in a court of law would prove a clear official intent to render due and payable a part or all of the unpaid subscriptions seems to be sufficient [1] The call need not indicate when, or to whom, or where, payment is required to be made [2] These are to be stated in the notice of the call Mere irregularities are disregarded, and will not invalidate the call [3] The substantial fact must exist that the proper corporate officers voted or declared that payment be required. Hence the elements of a call seem to be that it shall be by the proper persons acting officially; and that a resolution, susceptible of legal proof,[4] be passed that a certain amount, either the whole or part,[5] of the subscriptions for stock shall be paid in.

[1] Budd v Multnomah St. R'y Co , 15 Pac Rep, 659 (Oregon, 1887), Citizens' Ins Co v. Sortwell, 10 Allen, 110, 112 (1865)

[2] Fox v Allensville, C S & V Turnpike Co , 46 Ind , 31 (1874), Andrew v Ohio & M R R. Co , 14 Ind , 169 (1860). In the case of Great North of Eng R'y Co v Biddulph, 7 M & W., 243 (1840), Baron Parke held that the resolution for a call need not state the place of payment nor the person to whom it was payable See, also Marsh v Burroughs, 1 Woods, 463 (1871), holding that the call need not specify either time or place See, also, Rutland & Burlington R. R Co v Thrall, 35 Vt , 356 (1863), that the place need not be stated Call made in a new name, legally assumed by the corporation is binding on subscribers who knew of the change of name. Shackleford v Dangerfield, L. R., 3 C P., 407 (1868).

[3] Irregularities are no defense The remedy is to revoke or set aside the call. "Call in fact made means that if made, and notice be given, . . . a party shall not wait to take advantage of any irregularity at the trial" Re British Sugar Ref Co , 3 K & J , 408 (1857), Southampton Dock Co v. Richards, 2 Railw. Cas , 215, 234 (1840), S. C , 1 Man. & Gr , 448. See, also, Shackleford v

Dangerfield, L R , 3 C P , 407 (1868). An error in the call may be corrected and cured by a subsequent call made after the first liability accrued but before suit. Phil & West Chester R. R. Co. v. Hickman, 28 Pa St , 318 (1857) A director who participated in making the call cannot set up informalities for the purpose of defeating it. Hays v Pittsburgh, etc., R R., 38 Pa St, 81 (1860) Payment and acquiescence in informality as to one call waives it as to another call Macon & Augusta R. R. Co v Vason, 57 Ga , 314 (1876)

[4] A call by the directors is valid although no entry of the resolution is made in the minutes of the directors' meeting Hays v Pittsburgh & S. R. R. Co. (1860), *supra* An entry of the resolution, made by the secretary in the book containing the minutes, is sufficient. Fox v Allensville C S. & V. T Co , 46 Ind , 31 (1874) An authorized subsequent call is competent proof of the validity of a previous call Barrington v Pittsburgh & S. R. R Co., 34 Pa. St , 358 (1859) The corporate books are competent to prove both the call and the mode of payment Barrington v. Pittsburgh, etc , R. R Co, *supra*, Comfort v. Leland, 3 Whart. (Penn.), 81 (1837).

[5] The call may be for the whole sub-

§ 116. *Time, place, amount and person to whom payable* — The time and place and person to whom calls are to be paid need not necessarily be designated or fixed by the persons authorized to make the call[1] These are duties which may be performed by other officers of the corporation, and frequently either the president or treasurer of the corporation performs this work The time of payment should be reasonable,[2] as also should be the place If no place or person to receive payment is designated, it is to be paid to the treasurer at his office.[3] The amount called need not be made payable in one sum at one time, but may be made due in instalments[4]

scription Fox *v* Allensville C S & V T Co , 46 Ind , 31 (1874). May be for the whole or for part. Hann *v* Mulberry & Jefferson G R Co , 33 Ind , 103 (1870), Stone *v* Great Western Oil Co , 41 Ill , 85 (1866), Spangler *v* Ind & Ill Central R. R. Co , 21 Ill , 276 (1859), Ross *v.* Lafayette & Indianapolis R R Co , 6 Ind , 297 (1855) Even though it be expressly provided that only a certain sum shall be assessed at one time, yet several assessments, each one not in excess of the stated sum, may be ordered by a single vote Penobscot R. R Co. *v.* Dummer, 40 Me , 172 (1856), Penobscot R. R. Co *v* Dunn, 39 Me , 587 (1855).

[1] See § 115, note 2 The directors themselves may fix the time, place and manner of payment, even at a meeting subsequent to the meeting ordering a call The call may be prospective The directors may order that on a certain date a call payable at a later date shall be made. Sheffield & Manchester R'y Co *v* Woodcock, 7 Mees & W , 574 (1840). The subscription itself may regulate the time of payment N J Midland R'y Co *v* Strait, 35 N J L , 322 (1872); Roberts *v* Mobile & O R. R. Co , 32 Miss , 373 (1856) Even though the statute provides otherwise Iowa & Minn R. R Co *v* Perkins, 28 Iowa, 281 (1869)

[2] Fairfield County Turnpike Co. *v* Thorp, 13 Conn , 173 (1839) The time between payments of instalments is entirely within the discretion of the directors, there being no provision regulating the subject. Hall *v* United States Ins Co., 4 Gill (Md), 484 (1860).

[3] A resolution of the directors that the instalments should be paid in at the times therein designated "imports that payments should be made to the treasurer, who is the proper and only officer to receive and keep the moneys of the corporation" Danbury & Norfolk R R. Co *v* Wilson, 22 Conn , 435 (1853). As to a tender to the president, see Mitchell *v* Vermont, etc , Co., 67 N Y , 280 (1876).

[4] London & North West R y Co *v* McMichael, 6 Ex , 273 (1851), Birkenhead L & C R'y Co *v* Webster, id , 461 (1851), Ambergate R'y Co *v* Norcliff, id , 461 (1851), not following Stratford & M R'y Co *v* Stratton, 2 B & Ad , 519 (1831) In Birkenhead L & E R'y Co *v* Webster, as reported in 6 Ex , 277, the court say "We are unanimously of opinion that a call payable by instalments is good, although debt will not lie for one instalment until all the instalments are due and payable" In Hays *v* Pittsburgh & Steubenville R. R. Co. 38 Pa St., 81 (1860), the court held that the directors by one resolution could call in the balance of the subscriptions, making the call payable in instalments, due at different times. To the same effect see Rutland & Burlington R. R. Co *v* Thrall, 35 Vt., 536 (1863), Lewis' Case, 28 L T (N S), 396, holding that several assessments, payable at different times, may be made by one vote, where the call was by the court.

§ 117. *Notice of calls — Cases holding it not necessary* — There is a wide and irreconcilable difference of opinion among the authorities on the question whether notice of a call must be given to a stockholder before suit can be brought for the collection of a call.

Frequently either the charter, or a statute, or the by-laws of the corporation, require notice to be given, and in such cases notice is, of course, necessary, in order to sustain suit [1] But where there is no provision in the charter, or statute, or by-laws, or subscription itself, prescribing that notice of calls shall be given to the stockholders, the weight of authority holds that no notice is necessary, and that an action to collect the call may be maintained without averring or proving such a notice [2]

§ 118. *Notice of calls — Cases holding it necessary* — There is, however, strong authority for the rule that notice of calls must be given before suit is brought for their collection [3] The reason for

---

[1] In many of the states there exist statutes, very similar in their terms, that notice shall be given of calls, and that in case of non-payment the stock may be forfeited These statutes have received different interpretations in different states The usual construction is that the notice required therein refers only to the forfeiture proceedings, and does not necessitate notice before bringing a suit at law for the collection of the call Smith *v* Indiana & Ill R'y Co, 12 Ind, 61 (1859); Lake Ontario, Auburn & N Y R R Co. *v.* Mason, 16 N Y., 451, 464 (1857). In other states such a statute is construed to require notice before suit. Hughes *v* Antietam Mfg Co, 34 Md, 316 (1870); Granite Roofing Co *v* Michaels, 54 Md, 65 (1880), Dexter & Mason P R Co *v* Millerd, 3 Mich, 91 (1854) Illinois River R R Co *v* Zimmer, 20 Ill, 654 (1858), holds that a statute regulating notice of calls does not release the stockholder

[2] Wilson *v* Wills Valley R R. Co, 33 Ga, 466 (1863), Eppes *v* Mississippi. Gainesville & Tuscaloosa R R Co, 35 Ala, 33 (1859) Grubb *v* Mahoning Nav Co, 14 Pa St, 302 (1850), Gray *v* Monongahela Nav Co, 2 W & S (Pa), 156 (1841), Grubbe *v* Vicksburg & Brunswick R R Co, 50 Ala, 398 (1873), Eakright *v* Logansport & Northern Ind R

R Co, 13 Ind, 404 (1859), Johnson *v.* Crawfordsville R. R. Co, 11 Ind, 280 (1858); New Albany & Salem R R. Co. *v* McCormick, 10 Ind, 499 (1858), Fisher *v* Evansville & C. R. R. Co, 7 Ind, 407 (1856); Ross *v* Lafayette & Indianapolis R R Co, 6 Ind, 297 (1855); Hill *v* Nisbit, 100 Ind, 341 (1884); Smith *v* Indiana & Ill R'y Co, 12 Ind, 61 (1859). In the last case the court says "These decisions rest upon the ground that the contract to pay by instalments is in effect a promise to pay on demand, and the demand involved in the suit itself was alone sufficient." Notice of calls is required by the Pennsylvania railroad act. McCarty *v* Selinsgrove, etc., R R, 35 Leg Intel, 410 (1878). In New York, since no call is necessary, no notice is necessary Cf Macon & Augusta R R. Co. *v* Vason, 57 Ga., 314 (1876)

[3] Wear *v* Jacksonville & Savannah R R. Co, 24 Ill, 593 (1860); Spangler *v* Ind & Ill Central R. R. Co., 21 Ill, 276 (1859) Cf Peake *v* Wabash R R. Co., 18 Ill, 88 (1856), holding that notice is unnecessary In the case of Carlisle *v.* Cahawba & Marion R. R. Co, 4 Ala. (N S), 70 (1842), the court say that notice must be given, since "the times, amount of instalments and manner of payment were all to be prescribed by the president and directors of the corporation,

this rule seems to accord with sound legal principles and with business expediency   It is a well-established principle of law that, when the facts or circumstances upon which the performance of a contract depends lie more particularly in the knowledge of the promisee than the promisor, the former must give the latter notice   Hence it would seem that since a subscription is not due absolutely, but only on call, and the time, place and amount of the call is fixed by persons other than the subscribers, the better and more reasonable rule would be that notice of the call should be required and must be given.

§ 119   *Methods of serving notice of calls* —The manner and mode of giving notice has given rise to some controversy   Unless provision is expressly otherwise, the notice must be given by handing to the subscriber a written notice, or by informing him orally that the call has been made, giving the amount, time, place and person to whom payment is to be made [1]   Where the notice is served, not personally, but by mail, the notice is effective only in case it is actually received.[2]   Whether it was so received is a question for the jury [3]   A publication of a notice in a newspaper is not binding and

depended upon their volition and action, and consequently were more properly within their knowledge" See, also, Scarlet v Academy of Music, 43 Md, 203 (1875), Essex Bridge Co. v Tuttle, 2 Vt, 393 (1830), Rutland & Burlington R. R. Co. v. Thrall, 35 Vt., 536 (1863), Miles v Bough, 3 Q B., 845 (1842), Edinburgh, etc, Ry v Hibblewhite, 6 M & W. 707 (1840); Alabama & Florida R. R Co v Rowley, 9 Fla., 508 (1861)   In Hughes v Antietam Manuf Co., 34 Md, 316 (1870), the court say. "To say that it [notice] is unnecessary, because the subscribers, who may be living in different parts of the county, and perhaps the state, are presumed in law to know all that is done by the directors, seems to us to be raising a presumption against the truth itself"

[1] The notice need not be written   Verbal notification suffices   Smith v Tallahassee Plank-road Co, 30 Ala, 650, 666 (1857). Notice to pay to the treasurer sufficiently indicates the place of payment. It is understood to be at his office   Muskingum Valley T Co v Ward, 13 Ohio, 120 (1844)   *Contra*, Dex-

ter & Mason P R. Co v Millerd, 3 Mich, 91 (1854). It must be proved to have been sent by authorized persons   Miles v. Bough, 3 Q B, 845 (1842)   Notice to various parties in the neighborhood is not sufficient   New Jersey Midland Ry Co v Strait, 35 N J L, 322 (1872)   No particular form of notice is necessary. The only question is "whether the notice gives the shareholder to understand that a call has been made, and that he is required to pay the amount on a given day"   Shackleford v Dangerfield, L. R., 3 C P, 407 (1868)

[2] "Constructive notice by mail is not a personal notice, although in some cases, by express statutory provision, it is sufficient to bind parties"   Hughes v Antietam Manuf Co, 34 Md, 316 (1870)

[3] A notice of a call may be by mail. If the subscriber denies that he received it, the question is for the jury   Braddock v Phil, Marlton & Medford R R. Co, 45 N J Law Rep, 363 (1883)   Only the person actually mailing the notice can testify to that fact. Jones v Sisson, 72 Mass, 288 (1856).

effectual unless it be proved that the subscriber who is sued actually read the notice as published.[1] A personal notice is sufficient, although the charter, statute or by-laws provide for notice by publication.[2] An express promise of the subscriber to pay a call which has been already made is presumptive evidence that he had notice of that call.[3] Notice by publication, given under the authority of

[1] In Alabama & Fla R. R Co v. Rowley, 9 Fla , 508 (1861), the court say such a mode of notice "might be attended with irreparable injury to innocent parties." See, also, *dictum* in Lake Ontario, Auburn & N Y R R Co v. Mason, 16 N Y, 451 (1857). In the case of Schenectady & S P R R. Co. v Thatcher, 11 N Y , 102 (1854), where the charter prescribed notice by publication or by mail, a director who aided in giving the notices was held to have had personal notice and to be bound " Personal service of due notice is clearly more advantageous to the defendant than either an advertisement in a newspaper or a notice sent by mail " See, also, Lexington & West Cambridge R. R. Co v Chandler, 13 Metc, 311 (1847) See, also, § 130 Notice in a newspaper is not good notice unless the statute so prescribes People's, etc , Assoc v Furey, 20 Atl Rep , 890 (N J , 1890)

In the case of Lincoln v Wright, 23 Pa St , 76 (1854) not a corporation case, Judge Jeremiah Black said that a notice by publication in a newspaper was no notice unless actually read by the person charged with the notice "It must be proved that he read it, otherwise it is no stronger than proof that the fact was orally and publicly uttered at a place where he was not present. . . . Where the law requires notice to be given to a party before a liability can be fixed upon him, and the mode of giving such notice is left undetermined, it should be given personally and in fact, and so proved " On the other hand, in Hall v U S. Ins Co, 4 Gill (Md), 484 (1847), notice of a call by newspaper was held sufficient. The court said : "There

is no proportionate object attained by the great inconvenience, labor and expenses incident to personal notice. The substitution of such newspaper publication in lieu of personal notice has so long been an universal usage, and of a notoriety equal to that of a publication of newspapers themselves, that the custom of doing so has become a part of the law of the land " See. also, Louisville & E T R. R. Co v Meriwether, 5 B. Mont (Ky), 13 (1844), to the same effect, and *dictum* in Danbury & Norfolk R. R. Co v Wilson, 22 Conn , 435 (1853), and §§ 130, 131, *infra*

[2] In the case of Miss, etc , R. R. Co v. Gaster, 20 Ark , 455 (1859), the statute prescribed sixty days' notice by publication Actual personal notice was given, and no publication was had The court sustained the notice and said "One of the criterions by which to determine whether the requirements of a statute are imperative or merely directory is that those acts which are of the essence of the thing required to be done are imperative, while those which are not of the essence are directory . . . The giving of sixty days' notice is imperative and must be strictly complied with, because it is of the essence of the thing required to be done, the mode of doing so is directory. because not of the essence, and may be either by publication in the manner prescribed by the charter or by actual personal notice " *Cf., semble,* in Tomlin v Tonica & Petersburg R. R. Co, 23 Ill , 429 (1860).

[3] Miles v Bough, 3 Q. B., 845 (1842); Fairfield County Turnpike Co v. Thorp, 13 Conn , 173 (1839).

a statute, charter or by-law, must strictly comply with the provis-ions prescribed as to the time and formalities.[1]

§ 120 *Demand, waiver, pleadings, etc* — After notice has been given, no demand is necessary before bringing a suit to collect the subscription.[2] The subscriber may, by his acts or express agree-ment, waive the call itself, or informalities in its making, or notice thereof.[3] It is immaterial that other shareholders have had no notice of the call.[4] The proof of calls and of notice, when required, must be clear and complete.[5] The pleadings in an action on calls must allege the various facts which complete the obligation of the subscriber to pay.[6]

[1] Where twenty days' notice was re-quired, proof of sending notice is insuffi-cient. Must prove the time of sending Cole v Joliet Opera House Co, 79 Ill, 96 (1875) Notice by publication "at least sixty days" is satisfied by *one* pub-lication sixty days or more before the time of payment. Muskingum Valley T Co v Weid, 13 Ohio, 120 (1844), Marsh v Burroughs, 1 Woods, 463 (1871) Fox v Allensville Co, 46 Ind, 31 (1871) Fifty-nine days is insufficient where sixty days is prescribed Macon & Au-gusta R. R. Co v Vason, 57 Ga, 314 (1876). The printed notice must be put in evidence Rutland & Burlington R. R. Co v Thrall, 35 Vt, 586 (1863) Proof of several insertions is by copy of first insertion and the testimony of the pub-lisher that the others were made Un-thank v Henry County T Co 6 Ind, 125 (1855) The secretary of the corpo-ration cannot, by a certificate, prove publication of notice Tomlin v Tonica & P R R Co 23 Ill, 429 (1860).

[2] Penobscot R R Co v Dummer, 40 Me, 172 (1856), Goodrich v Reynolds, 31 Ill, 491 (1863), Winters v Muscogee R. R Co, 11 Ga, 438 (1852) *Cf* Spang-ler v Ind & Ill Central R R. Co, 21 Ill, 276 (1859), holding that one demand made for several assessments suffices

[3] Macon & A R. R. Co v Vason, 57 Ga, 314 (1876) Payment of part of subscription is no waiver of right to have a call made for the balance before payment. Grosse Isle Hotel Co v Ex'rs of L'Anson, 43 N J L. 442 (1881)

The vote of a city to pay a call is no waiver of its invalidity Pike v Bangor & Calais Shore Line R. R Co, 68 Me, 445 (1878) The waiver must be clearly proved Rutland & B. R. R. Co v Thrall, 35 Vt, 536 (1863) Director par-ticipating in call cannot object thereto. York Tramways v Willows L R, 8 Q B. D, 685 Where a subscriber, upon receiving notice of a call, denies that he is a stockholder, he thereby waives fur-ther notice Cass v Pittsburg, etc, R'y, 80 Pa St, 31 (1875)

[4] Newry & Enniskillen R y Co v Ed-munds, 2 Ex Rep, 118 (1848), Shackle-ford v Dangerfield, L. R, 3 C P, 407 (1868)

[5] Scarlett v Academy of Music, 43 Md, 203 (1875). This case holds also that calls may be proved by reading ex-tracts from the minutes of the directors' meetings, without putting the books in evidence

[6] Must allege that the instalments are all due and payable, where several are sued on Bethel & Hanover T Co v Bean, 58 Me, 89 (1870) At common law the count set out in the declaration should be not on the contract of sub-scription, but in *indebitatus assump-sit* for calls or instalments due Peake v Wabash R. R Co, 18 Ill, 88 (1856). For the customary averments, see Spangler v Ind & Ill Central R. R. Co, 21 Ill, 276 (1859) For the defendants' pleading, see South Eastern R'y v Hib-blewhite, 12 A & E, 497 (1840).

CHAPTER VIII.

FORFEITURE OF SHARES FOR NON-PAYMENT.

§ 121 *The various remedies* — When a subscriber fails or refuses to pay for the shares of stock for which he has subscribed, the corporation generally has several methods of enforcing the contract. First, there is the common-law action to collect the subscription as a debt This remedy always exists, except in a few states where it is available only when the subscription itself or the charter creates a liability to pay [1] Second, the corporation may sue on the subscription, obtain judgment, and then proceed to sell the stock under an execution levied to collect the judgment.[2] Third, the corporation may bring an action at law for breach of contract, the measure of damages being the difference between the value of the stock at the price which the subscriber was to pay and the market value at the date of the refusal to pay [3] A fourth and very important remedy is that of forfeiture. It is the subject of this chapter It is effected in one of two ways: the forfeiture may be by a strict foreclosure of the stockholder's stock — that is, the taking of his stock by the corporation itself; or it may be by a public sale of the stock for non-payment of the subscription

§§ 122-123 *The remedy by public sale of stock is by statutory authority only.*— In addition to the remedy of an action at law to compel payment of a subscription for stock, there frequently is given to the corporation the right to sell the subscriber's stock for non-payment of his subscription and apply the proceeds to the payment of that subscription. This is what is generally known as a

---

[1] See § 74, *supra*

[2] Chase v East Tenn, etc, R. R. Co, 40 N H, 79 (1860).

5 Lea, 415 (1880)

[3] Rand v White Mountains R. R. Co.,

forfeiture of the stock   It is not a common-law remedy, and, consequently, can be resorted to by the corporation only when power to make the sale is given to the corporation by statute or by the act of incorporation [1] The right to forfeit may, however, be created by the consent of the stockholders, and be indorsed on the certificates of stock.[2]

The authority to forfeit shares for non-payment of the subscription cannot be created by a by-law [3] Such a forfeiture would be wholly void, and transfers based thereon would confer no rights upon the transferee [4]

§ 124 *The remedy by forfeiture is cumulative* — Frequently, when a corporation is authorized by statute to forfeit shares for non-payment of the subscription, the question arises whether the statutory remedy of forfeiture is exclusive, thereby preventing a resort to the common-law remedy of an action of *assumpsit* on the

---

[1] Westcott v. Minnesota, etc , Co, 23 Mich 145 (1871), Minnehaha, etc , Ass n of Minneapolis v Legg, 52 N W Rep, 898 (Minn , 1892), Budd v Multnomah St R'y Co, 15 Pac Rep, 659 (Oreg , 1887) In the last case the statute gave the corporation power to make by-laws for forfeiture of stock There being no by-law, a forfeiture was attempted by a resolution of the board of directors *Held*, this could not be done Barton's Case, 4 De G & J , 46 (1859), is similar and stronger, as public notices and advertisements were made of the threatened forfeiture Perrin v Granger, 30 Vt., 595 (1858); Clarke v Hart, 6 H of L Cases, 633 (1858), Stanhope's Case, L. R , 1 Chan 161 (1865) In Kelk's Case, L. R., 9 Eq 107 (1869), the forfeiture was provided for in deed of settlement, and hence regular If the corporation purchases at forfeiture sale, as it may by statute in California, execution against the corporation cannot be levied on such stock Robinson v. Spaulding etc , Co, 72 Cal , 32 (1887) A building association cannot provide that it will discount a subscriber's stock, loan him the amount thus discounted, and forfeit the whole if he does not pay. It is usury Henderson, etc , Assoc v Johnson, 10 S. W Rep , 787 (Ky , 1889).

[2] Weeks v Silver, etc , Co, 55 J & S (N Y), 1 (1887).

[3] Matter of the Long Island R R Co, 19 Wend , 37 (1837), S C, 32 Am Dec , 429 Kirk v Nowill, 1 Term Rep., 118 (1786) *Cf.* Kennebec, etc , R R. Co v Kendall, 31 Me , 470 (1850), Rosenback v Salt Springs National Bank, 53 Barb , 495, 506 (1868)

[4] Matter of the Long Island R R. Co, *supra* Yet where such a power was conferred by a by-law adopted at a meeting of the stockholders, a stockholder whose stock had been declared forfeited under the by-law, and who is shown to have assented to the by-law, will not be heard to question the validity of the forfeiture He is estopped Lesseps v Architects' Co, 4 La Ann. 316 (1849) The corporation cannot, by a by-law, forfeit shares temporarily until penalties or fines shall have been paid Adley v Reeves, 2 Maule & S 53 (1813), by Lord Ellenborough *Cf.* Cartan v Father Mathew, etc , Society, 3 Daly, 20 (1869), Pentz v Citizens Fire etc , Co, 35 Md , 73 (1871) But only the stockholder can object to a forfeiture on the ground that it is by by-law Detweiler v Breckenkamp, 83 Mo , 45 (1884) *Cf* §§ 131, 134 As to the effect of acquiescence or waiver by the stockholder, see §§ 129, 134, *infra*

contract   It is the well-established rule that it does not.   A grant
of the power to declare a forfeiture of the shares of a subscriber
for non-payment of calls does not, by implication, deprive the corporation of its option of remedies; and the corporate agents may,
in their discretion, upon the failure of the subscriber to pay for
his stock, either proceed against him by suit to collect the unpaid
calls, or may forfeit his shares of stock   The corporation, by such
a statute, is given its choice of remedies, and may pursue either.
The remedy by forfeiture is additional.[1]

[1] Delaware, etc, Co. v Sansom, 1
Binn 70 (1803), Instone v Frankfort
Bridge Co, 2 Bibb, 576 (1812); Rens-
selaer, etc, T. Co v Barton, 16 N Y.,
457 (1851), Lake Ontario, etc, R R Co.
v Mason, 16 id , 451 (1857), Buffalo. etc,
R R Co. v Dudley, 14 id, 336 (1856);
Tutweiler v Tuscaloosa, etc., Co, 7 S.
Rep. 398 (Ala, 1890); Harlem, etc,
Canal Co v Seixas, 2 Hall (N. Y Super.
Ct), 504 (1829), Fort Edward, etc. Co.
v Payne. 17 Barb, 567 (1854), Rens-
selaer. etc. R R Co. v Wetsel, 21 id,
56 (1855) Sagory v Dubois, 3 Sandf
Chan , 466 (1846), Troy, etc. R R Co.
v McChesney. 21 Wend, 296 (1839),
Herkimer, etc, Co. v Small, 21 id , 273
(1839), Ogdensburgh etc, R R Co v
Frost, 21 Barb, 541 (1856); Northern
R R Co v Miller, 10 id, 260 (1851);
Troy, etc, R R Co v Tibbits, 18 id,
297 (1854), Troy, etc, v Kerr, 17 id,
581 (1854), Union Turnpike Co. v
Jenkins, 1 Caines' Cas, 86, 95 (1804);
Goshen, etc., Co. v Hurtin. 9 Johns,
217 (1812), McDonough v Phelps, 15
How Prac , 372 (1856), Freeman v Win-
chester, 18 Miss., 577 (1848), Hartford,
etc, R R Co v. Kennedy. 12 Conn,
499 (1838), Mann v Cooke, 20 id., 178
(1850), Connecticut. etc, R R Co v
Bailey, 24 Vt, 465 (1852), Rutland, etc.,
R R Co v Thrall 35 id, 536 (1863);
New Hampshire, etc. R R Co v Johnson, 30 N H, 390 (1855), White Mountains R R Co v Eastman, 34 id, 124,
147 (1856); Piscataqua Ferry Co v
Jones, 39 id, 491 (1859), Hightower v
Thornton, 8 Ga 486, 502 (1850), Hughes
v Antietam, etc, Co, 34 Md., 316 (1870),
Beene v. Cahawba, etc., R. R. Co, 3
Ala., 660 (1842); Selma, etc., R. R. Co.
v Tipton, 5 id, 787 (1843); Gratz v.
Redd, 4 B. Mon (Ky), 178 (1843), Bos-
ton, etc.. R. R. Co. v Wellington, 113
Mass., 79 (1873) [Compare with this case
Worcester, etc, Co v Willard, 5 Mass,
80 (1809). Andover, etc., Co. v Gould, 6
id. 40 (1809) New Bedford, etc, Co v
Adams, 8 id., 138 (1811), City Hotel v
Dickinson, 72 Mass., 586 (1856); Mechanics', etc, Co v Hall, 121 Mass, 272
(1876).] Mexican Gulf, etc. R. R. Co v.
Viavant, 6 Rob (La), 305 (1843) New
Orleans, etc , Co v Briggs, 27 La. Ann,
318 (1875), Greenville, etc., R R. Co. v.
Cathcart, 4 Rich. Law, 89 (1850); Klein
v Alton etc, R. R. Co., 13 Ill, 514
(1851), Peoria, etc, R. R. Co. v. Elting,
17 id, 429 (1856), Kirksey v. Florida.
etc, Co, 7 Fla, 23 (1857); Tar River,
etc, Co v Neal, 3 Hawks (N. C), 520
(1825), Stokes v Lebanon, etc, Co., 6
Humph, 241 (1845), South Bay, etc,
Co. v. Gray, 30 Me, 547 (1849); Franklin Glass Co. v Alexander, 2 N. H, 380
(1821); S C, 9 Am. Dec, 92, and the
note at pp. 96-104. A subscriber for
stock cannot avoid liability to the corporation by setting up that the corporation has a lien on the stock therefor
and may enforce it. Lankershine, etc.
Co v Herberger, 23 Pac. Rep., 134 (Cal.,
1890) The corporation may sue for the
whole subscription and need not sue
merely for the deficiency that would
result from selling the stock. International, etc. Ass'n v. Walker, 47 N W
Rep, 338 (Mich, 1890). For a learned discussion of the general question how far

It is to be borne in mind, however, that in the New England states the right to forfeit stock for non-payment of assessments does not imply a right in the corporation to sue for such assessments. The latter right does not exist at all unless it is given by statute or by the express promise of the subscriber[1] But where both remedies exist, the corporation has its election which remedy to pursue.[2]

§§ 125, 126 *When one remedy is exhausted the corporation cannot resort to another.* — Although a corporation having the right to declare a forfeiture of shares for non-payment of calls may generally, at its option, either forfeit the stock or bring an action to collect the amount due, it does not follow that it can forfeit the stock and then bring an action for the unpaid calls, or any part thereof that may remain unsatisfied by the forfeiture The corporation when a shareholder is in default, may pursue either the one remedy or the other in its discretion; but it cannot forfeit the stock and afterwards sue at law. The first remedy excludes the second[3] In order, however, to bar the remedy of an action on the contract, the forfeiture must be complete and actual Consequently, a mere

the jurisdiction of a court of equity may be affected by statutes conferring similar jurisdiction upon the courts of law — an inquiry germane to the matter of the present section — see the note to the case of Payne *v* Bullard, 23 Miss., 88 (1851), in 55 Am Dec, 74, 77

[1] See § 74

[2] See §§ 125, 126

[3] Small *v* Herkimer, etc, Co, 2 N. Y, 330 (1849), reversing Herkimer, etc, Co *v* Small, 21 Wend, 273 (1839); S C, 2 Hill, 127 (1841). Northern R R. Co. *v.* Miller, 10 Barb, 260, 271 (1851); Ogdensburgh, etc, R. R. Co *v* Frost, 21 id, 541 (1856); Mills *v* Stewart, 41 N Y, 384 (1869); Macauly *v* Robinson, 18 La. Ann., 619 (1866), Allen *v* Montgomery, etc., Co, 11 Ala, 437 (1847), Athol, etc., R. R. Co *v.* Inhabitants of Prescott, 110 Mass, 213 (1872), Mechanics', etc., Co. *v* Hall, 121 id, 272 (1876) With these later Massachusetts cases compare Andover, etc, Co *v* Gould, 6 Mass, 40 (1809); Franklin, etc, Co. *v* White, 14 id, 286 (1817), Rutland, etc, R R. Co *v.* Thrall, 35 Vt, 536 (1863); Macon, etc, R R. Co. *v* Vason, 57 Ga, 314 (1876), Ashton *v* Burbank, 2 Dill, 435 (1873).

Such, also, seems to be the rule in England King's Case, L R, 2 Chan, 714 (1867), Knight's Case, id, 321 (1867), Snell's Case, L R, 5 Chan, 22 (1869) By statute in England the right to forfeit and the right to sue may be exercised together, and shares may be forfeited for non-payment of calls, whether those calls have been sued for or not. Great North, etc, R'y Co *v* Kennedy, 4 Ex, 417 (1849), Inglis *v* Great North R'y Co, 1 Macq, 112 (1852) But there is a line of cases in England where, by the terms of the deeds of settlement, only an option is given to sue or to forfeit, and it is then held that the corporation is concluded by its election Inglis *v* Great North R'y Co, 1 Macq (Scotch Ap), 112 (1852), where, notwithstanding the forfeiture and cancellation of shares and the issue of new ones, the right to recover in an action for calls was held to remain unimpaired in the company See, also, Birmingham, etc R'y Co *v* Locke, 1 Q B 256 (1841); Edinburgh, etc, R'y Co *v.* Hebblewhite 6 M & W, 707 (1840), London, etc., R'y Co. *v* Fairclough, 2 Man & Gr, 674 (1841)

threat that a forfeiture will be made if the call be not paid on or before a day named, or an unsuccessful attempt to sell the shares, will not be sufficient to bar the action [1] So long as the stockholder's right to the shares and to the immunities and emoluments attached thereto remain, his obligation to pay is not extinguished [2]

There is, however, a line of cases in which a contrary rule is sustained In these cases it is held that the forfeiture of shares of stock is like the foreclosure of a mortgage, and that, just as a mortgagee may have judgment against the mortgagor for a deficiency, so may a corporation have its action of *assumpsit* against a subscriber whose stock, having been forfeited, has failed to sell for enough to pay his entire indebtedness to the corporation on the subscription [3] This rule is held to apply equally to original subscribers or their transferees, and any stockholder is liable, under this rule, for the balance due upon assessments, after deducting the amount realized at the forfeiture sale [4]

§§ 127, 128. *Forfeiture relieves the shareholder whose shares are forfeited from liability to corporate creditors* — In the absence of fraud and collusion it is a settled rule that, where a corporation has authority to declare a forfeiture of shares for non-payment of calls, and a forfeiture is regularly declared, such formal declaration

[1] Macon, etc , R R Co *v.* Vason, 57 Ga., 314 (1876) See. also, cases cited *supra* and *infra* § 131

[2] Instone *v* Frankfort Bridge Co , 2 Bibb, 576, 581 (1812) *Cf* Buffalo, etc , R. R Co *v* Dudley, 14 N Y., 336, 347 (1856) It has been held. also, that an action to collect a subscription, when prosecuted to judgment, is a bar to the remedy by forfeiture Giles *v* Hutt, 3 Ex , 18 (1848)

[3] Carson *v* Arctic Mining Co 5 Mich , 288 (1858); Danbury, etc., R R Co *v.* Wilson, 22 Conn , 435 (1853); Great Northern R'y Co *v* Kennedy, 4 Exch , 417, 425 (1849)

[4] Merrimac Mining Co *v* Bagley, 14 Mich , 501 (1866) *Cf* Hartford, etc , R R. Co. *v* Kennedy, 12 Conn , 499 (1838); Brockenbrough *v* James River, etc , Co , 1 Patton & H (Va). 94 (1855), Mann *v* Currie, 2 Barb , 294 (1848) It is sometimes so provided expressly by statute or by the charter of the company. Brockenbrough *v* James River. etc , Co , 1 Patton & H , 94 (1855), Danbury,

etc., R. R. Co. *v* Wilson, 22 Conn., 435. 456 (1853), Great Northern R'y Co. *v.* Kennedy, 4 Exch , 417 (1849); Mann *v.* Cooke. 20 Conn , 178 (1849). But see Athol. etc R. R Co *v.* Inhabitants of Prescott, 110 Mass., 213 (1872); Kennebec, etc , R. R Co *v* Kendall, 31 Me , 470 (1850), Allen *v* Montgomery R. R. Co , 11 Ala , 437 (1847), Stokes *v* Lebanon, etc , Co., 6 Humph. (Tenn), 241 (1845), Mills *v* Stewart, 41 N. Y., 384 (1869) Or that any shareholder whose shares shall have been forfeited for non-payment of assessments shall nevertheless be liable to pay to the company all calls owing on such shares at the time of the forfeiture This seems to be a common provision in the articles of association of English companies Creyke's Case, L R , 5 Chan , 63 (1869), Stocken's Case, L. R., 5 Eq , 6 (1867) But in such a case interest is not collectible. Stocken's Case *supra* It is otherwise in ordinary defaults Gould *v* Oneonta, 71 N Y , 298 (1877), Rikhoff *v* Brown, etc , Co , 68 Ind , 388 (1879)

puts an end to the liability of the shareholder, and corporate creditors cannot subsequently hold such an expelled or released shareholder liable [1] This is the rule even though the debt was contracted
by the company before the stock was forfeited [2] The same principle of law that prevents the corporation from suing on a subscription after the stock has been forfeited prevents the corporate
creditors also from doing the same But, on the other hand, inasmuch as fraud vitiates all acts into which it enters, a forfeiture of
shares by collusion between a shareholder and the board of directors of the corporation will not release him from liability to contribute in the event of the insolvency of the company [3] In such
a case the creditors may invoke the interposition of a court of
equity to prevent the consummation of an inchoate forfeiture, or
to set aside one already accomplished [4] Hence, it is well settled
that the power of forfeiture cannot lawfully be exercised for the
purpose of enabling members to escape from their liability on their
stock, either to the corporation or its creditors [5] A stockholder,

[1] Allen v Montgomery R. R. Co., 11
Ala, 437, 450 (1847), Macauly v Robinson, 18 La. Ann, 619 (1866). Mills v
Stewart, 41 N Y, 384 (1869) Woollaston's Case, 4 De G & J, 437 (1859), Ex
parte Beresford, 2 Macn & G, 197
(1850); Kelk's Case, L. R. 9 Eq. 107
(1869); Dawes' Case, L R, 6 Eq 232
(1868), Snell's Case, L R, 5 Chan, 22
(1869). Nor, on the other hand can the
stockholder claim, after the forfeiture,
any of the rights of stockholdership
St. Louis, etc Co v. Sandoval, etc, Co,
116 Ill, 170 (1886)

[2] Mills v. Stewart, supra

[3] Slee v. Bloom, 19 Johns 456 (1822),
Burke v Smith, 16 Wall, 390 (1872),
Mills v. Stewart, 41 N Y, 384 (1869),
Walters' Second Case, 3 De G & Sm,
244 (1850); Richmond's Case, 4 Kay &
J., 305 (1858), Spackman's Case, 11 Jur
(N. S.), 207 (1865), Stanhope's Case, L R,
1 Chan, 161 (1866), Stewart's Case, L. R.,
1 Chan, 511 (1866), Gower's Case, L. R
6 Eq, 77 (1868)

[4] Germantown, etc., R'y Co v Fitler,
60 Pa. St., 124 (1869). See, also, Grand
Rapids Savings Bank v Warren 52
Mich, 557 (1884). The fact that the corporation might have forfeited the stock

but in fact did not, is no defense as
against the corporate creditors If a
transaction between a shareholder and
the directors is irregular, but is alleged
to have been acquiesced in, it is incumbent upon the stockholder to support
such allegation by showing that the
transaction was fully made known to
the general body of the shareholders.
Spackman's Case, 11 Jur (N S), 207
(1865) A stockholder whose stock is
forfeited in a building association for
non-payment of dues, as authorized by
the charter, cannot recover back the
money paid by him Freeman v Ottawa, etc, Assoc, 28 N E Rep., 611
(Ill., 1885).

[5] Spackman v Evans, L. R., 3 H of L.,
171 (1868), Stanhope's Case, L. R., 1 Ch,
161 (1866), Richmond's Case, 4 Kay & J,
305 (1858), Manisty's Case, 17 Solicitor's
Jour, 745, Gower's Case, L. R, 6 Eq,
77 (1868), Ex parte Jones, 27 L J, Chan,
666 (1858), Hall's Case, L. R, 5 Chan,
707 (1870), Mills v Stewart, 41 N Y,
384 (1869) Cf. Dixon v Evans, L. R., 5
H of L., 606 (1872), Lord Belhaven's
Case, 11 Jur (N S), 572 (1865), S. C., 12
L. T (N S), 595 (1867), Clarke v Hart,
6 House of Lords Cases, 633 (1858), Gar-

(12)

by mere abandonment of his shares, cannot forfeit them himself, and thus, by his own act, discharge himself from his obligation on the subscription [1]

§ 129 *Statutory formalities and general method of forfeiture.*— The general method of forfeiting shares for non-payment of calls is usually prescribed in detail by the statute authorizing the forfeiture. In the earlier cases there may be observed some tendency to hold that a substantial, in distinction from a strict, compliance with the requirements of the statute is all that is necessary to a valid forfeiture.[2] But in later cases, English [3] and American,[4] it is plainly declared, and it may be taken as a settled rule, that the validity of the forfeiture and sale of the shares of a subscriber in arrears depends upon a strict and formal compliance with the requirements of the enabling statute [5]

Thus a sale of the shares at private sale, when a sale by public auction was prescribed, has been held to invalidate the forfeiture.[6]

den Gully, etc , Co. v. McLister, L. R , 1 App Cas , 39 (1875), Sweny v Smith, L. R., 7 Eq , 324 (1869); Chouteau v Dean, 7 Mo App., 211 (1879). Cf Bedford R. R. Co v Bowser, 48 Pa St., 29 (1864).

[1] Rockville, etc., Turnpike Co. v Maxwell, 2 Cranch, C C., 451 (1824). For sundry illustrations of what will or will not justify a forfeiture, see, particularly, Sweny v Smith, L. R., 7 Eq , 324 (1869); Stocken's Case, L R , 3 Chan , 412 (1867), Count Palen's Case, L. R., 9 Eq , 107 (1869), Thomas' Case, L. R , 13 Eq , 437 No defense that defendant supposed he could pay balance of subscription or have a forfeiture of stock Ross v Bank, etc , 19 Pac Rep , 243 (Nev , 1888).

[2] Catchpole v Ambergate, etc , R y Co., 1 Ellis & B , 111 (1852), Nolan v Arabella, etc , Co , 6 W W & A B (Australian), 38. Cf. Woollaston's Case, 4 De G & J , 437 (1859), Knight's Case, L. R., 2 Ch , 321 (1867)

[3] Clarke v. Hart, 6 House of Lords Cases, 633 (1858), Johnson v. Lyttle's Iron Agency, 46 L J (Chan), 786 (1877). Cf. Knight's Case, L R , 2 Chan , 321 (1867), Garden Gully. etc , Co v McLister, L. R., 1 App. Cas , 39 (1875), London & B. R'y Co. v. Fairclough, 2 Mann

& G , 674 (1841). In England a forfeiture may be made after a call, and before the call is due The call is "owing" from the time when it is made. Faure, etc , Co. v Phillapart, 58 L T Rep , 525 (1888), where the forfeiture was made on two calls, one past due and one not yet due

[4] Portland, etc., R R Co. v Graham, 52 Mass , 1 (by Shaw, C. J , 1846); Germantown, etc , R'y Co v Fitler, 60 Penn St , 124 (1869). Eastern, etc , Plank-road Co v Vaughan, 20 Barb , 155 (1855), York, etc., R. R. Co. v. Ritchie, 40 Me , 425 (1855), Leweys Island R. R Co v Bolton, 48 id , 451 (1860), Downing v. Potts, 23 N. J Law, 66 (1851), Matter of the Long Island R. R. Co, 19 Wend , 37 (1837), Mitchell v Vermont Copper Mining Co , 40 N. Y. Super. Ct., 406 (1876); Occidental, etc , Assoc. v. Sullivan, 62 Cal , 394 (1882). Cf. Johnson v. Albany, etc . R. R Co , 40 How. Prac., 193 (1870); Rutland, etc., R. R. Co. v Thrall, 35 Vt , 536 (1863); Perrin v Granger, 30 id , 595 (1858).

[5] Garden Gully, etc , Co. v McLister, L. R., 1 App. Cas., 39 (1875), Germantown, etc., R'y Co v Fitler, 60 Penn St., 124 (1869).

[6] Lewey's Island R. R. Co. v Bolton,

There must be a properly constituted board of directors to declare a forfeiture of shares [1] It is held, in general, that, in the absence of statutory provisions as to order or details, the mode of forfeiture must be reasonable and just [2] The forfeiture may be regularly effected by a resolution of the board of directors, ordering a sale of all stock on which assessments shall remain unpaid at a day named in the future [3]

It is a well-established rule, also, that a forfeiture of shares, where the forfeiture was irregular or defective in its form, is not void, but voidable, and that, by subsequent knowledge and acquiescence, the shareholder and the company are alike estopped to

48 Me, 451 (1860). As to what is, in general, sufficient to satisfy the requirements of the rule that powers of forfeiture are to be construed strictly and exercised or pursued strictly, see Giles v Hutt, 3 Exch, 18 (1848), Catchpole v Ambergate, etc, R'y Co., 1 Ellis & B., 11 (1852); Birmingham, etc, R'y Co i Locke, 1 Q. B, 256 (1841), Graham v Van Diemen's Land Co., 1 Hurl & N, 541 (1856), Sweny v Smith, L. R., 7 Eq, 324 (1869), Stockton's Case I. R., 3 Chan, 412 (1867); Count Phalen's Case, L. R, 9 Eq, 107 (1869), Thomas' Case, L. R., 13 Eq, 437, Gower's Case, L. R., 6 Eq, 77 (1868). It has, however, been held in an English case — In re North Hallenbeagle Mining Co, Knight's Case, L. R., 2 Chan, 321 (1867) S. C, 15 L. T (N S), 546 (1869), — that, when it is a matter of mere form rather than of substance that has not been strictly followed, in proceedings to forfeit shares, the forfeiture will not necessarily be thereby invalidated.

[1] Garden Gully, etc, Co. v. McLister L. R., 1 App Cases, 39, 55 (1875) A stockholder may enjoin a forfeiture on the ground that the directors were illegally elected. Moses v Tompkins, 4 S. Rep, 763 (Ala, 1888)

[2] Rutland, etc, R. R. Co v. Thrall, 35 Vt, 536 (1863), Mitchell v Vermont Copper Mining Co, 67 N. Y., 280 (1876).

[3] Rutland, etc., R. R. Co v Thrall, 35 Vt., 536 (1863). See, also, Woollaston s Case, 4 De G. & J, 437 (1859). Under such a resolution a sale of the stock is not necessary to complete the forfeiture where the effect of the forfeiture is to release the stockholder from any future liability, and where he is not entitled to the surplus, if any there be, after sale Rutland, etc, R R. Co v Thrall, supra It is, however, said elsewhere that a general resolution, not specifying the stock which is forfeited but merely assuming to forfeit any and all stock whose owners are in arrears, does not effect a valid forfeiture Johnson v Albany, etc. R. R. Co 40 How Prac, 193 (1870) When, after default made in the payment of assessments, notice is given by the corporation that the shares of owners in arrears will be forfeited unless full payment of what is due be made by a day named, there is a presumption that the subsequent proceedings of the company looking to perfecting the forfeiture are valid and regular Knight's Case, 15 L T (N S), 546 (1867). holding that where, by the articles of association, provision is made for forfeiture by resolution with notice upon default, the court will assume that the requisite steps have been taken to make a valid forfeiture, even though it does not appear that such resolution was passed or that notice was sent. The notice is a notice that the forfeiture has already been declared, not that it will be made on further default. That notice is a condition precedent.

deny its validity.[1] Under the California code a corporation may by suit foreclose a lien which it has on its stock.[2]

§ 130 *Notice in cases of forfeiture.*— A notice to the delinquent subscriber that his shares will be forfeited at a day named is generally requisite to effect a forfeiture The subscriber is entitled to full knowledge of the fact that, unless he pays up within a specified time, he will lose his stock. The requirements of the statute or charter, with respect to the contents of the notice. and the length of time which is to elapse between the notice and the forfeiture,

---

[1] King's Case, L R., 2 Ch, 714, 731 (1867), Woollaston's Case, 4 De G & J, 437 (1859), Webster's Case, 32 L J, Ch, 135 (1862), Knight's Case, L R., 2 Ch., 321 (1867), Kelk's Case, L R, 9 Eq, 107 (1869), Austin's Case, 24 L T (N. S), 932 (1871), Prendergast *v.* Turton, 1 Y. & C (Ch), 98 (1841) *Cf* Lyster's Case, L R., 4 Eq, 233 (1867), Teasdale's Case, L R, 9 Ch, 54 (1873), Phosphate, etc., Co. *v.* Green, L R, 7 C P., 43 (1871) Here the company had power to forfeit shares for non-payment and to compromise debts, but were prohibited from purchasing their own shares The transaction in issue was held to be such a purchase, and hence *ultra vires.* but the members were estopped by knowledge and acquiescence In this case it was also said that, to show assent and acquiescence in such a case, it is not necessary or possible to prove the acquiescence of each individual shareholder It is enough to show circumstances which are reasonably calculated to satisfy the court or a jury that the thing to be ratified came to the knowledge of all who chose to inquire, all having full opportunity and means of inquiry Houldsworth *v* Evans, L R, 3 H. of L, 263 (1868), Spackman *v* Evans, L R, 3 H of L, 171 (1868) Here the terms of the withdrawal were not in accordance with the deed of settlement, and it was held after years that the party was still liable as a contributor Evans *v* Smallcombe, id, 249, where a member withdrawing under a like arrangement was held not liable on the double ground of lapse of time and a clear presumption of knowledge and acquiescence Houldsworth *v.* Evans, id, 263, where an irregularity in the condition of withdrawal was held substantial and the transaction *ultra vires.* (One lord dissented, that years of acquiescence retrospectively sanctioned it) Brotherhood's Case, 31 Beav., 365 (1862). Dissentient members were allowed to withdraw, by resolution, upon terms which were certainly *ultra vires.* The master of the rolls said that the transaction might have been set aside at the time, but all parties having had full knowledge, and having acquiesced for more than twelve years, the court would not, after such a lapse of time, touch the transaction. In Lesseps *v.* Architects' Co , 4 La. Ann., 316 (1849), the court regarded a general acquiescence in a by-law for a forfeiture, itself *ultra vires,* as a matter of contract, and refused equitable relief *Cf.* Lindley on Partnership, p 750, saying · "If there is power to forfeit, and the shares intended to be forfeited are treated by the company and the shareholders as forfeited, the company will be precluded from afterwards insisting that no forfeiture ever took place " Garden Gully, etc., Co *v* McLister, L R., 1 App Cas , 39, 55 (1875), holding that mere laches does not, of itself, disentitle the holder of shares to equitable relief against an invalid declaration of forfeiture

[2] Mechanics', etc., Assoc. *v.* King, 23 Pac. Rep., 376 (Cal., 1890).

must all be strictly complied with.[1] It is accordingly held that the notice must state correctly the amount due for non-payment of which the stock is to be forfeited.[2] The time, also, within which payment is to be made must be accurately stated,[3] and also the place where the sale is to be made.[4] The mode of giving notice of a contemplated forfeiture of stock is generally specified in the statute authorizing the forfeiture.[5]

[1] Heaston v. Cincinnati, etc., R. R. Co., 16 Ind., 275 (1861), Lewey's Island R. R. Co. v. Bolton, 48 Me., 451 (1860), Rutland, etc., R. R. Co. v. Thrall, 35 Vt., 536, 546 (1863); Lake Ontario, etc., R. R. Co. v. Mason, 16 N. Y., 451 (1854); Sands v. Sanders, 26 id., 239 (1863), Mississippi, etc., R. R. Co. v. Gaster, 20 Ark., 455 (1859), Hughes v. Antietam, etc., Co., 34 Md., 317 (1870); Johnson v. Lyttle's Iron Agency, 46 L. J. (Chan.), 786 (1877), Cockerell v. Van Diemen's Land Co., 26 L. J. (C. P.), 203 (1857), Watson v. Eales, 23 Beav., 294 (1856). Cf. Eppes v. Mississippi, etc., R. R. Co., 35 Ala., 33 (1859), Schenectady, etc., R. R. Co. v. Thatcher, 11 id., 102 (1854), Harlaem, etc., Co. v. Seixas, 2 Hall (N. Y. Super. Ct.), 504 (1829), Mitchell v. Vermont Copper Mining Co., 40 N. Y. Super. Ct., 406 (1876), New Albany, etc., R. R. Co. v. McCormick, 10 Ind., 499 (1858). Cf. Lexington, etc., R. R. Co. v. Chandler, 54 Mass., 311 (1847), where notice, provided for by a by-law, was held not a condition precedent, but only directory, and substantial compliance was sufficient. Knight's Case, supra, is sometimes wrongly cited, for the reason that there are two notices provided for (1) notice that forfeiture will be made on default at future time, and (2) notice after forfeiture that it has been made. The former is essential, the latter not.

[2] So where the notice stated that unless the amount of a certain call, together with lawful interest from the date of the call, was paid on or before a certain day the shares would be liable to forfeiture, it was held that, as interest was only payable from the day fixed for payment, and not from the date of the call, the notice was irregular, and that a forfeiture founded on a non-compliance with such a notice was bad. Johnson v. Lyttle's Iron Agency, 46 L. J. (Ch.), 786 (1877).

[3] A notice that the stock will be forfeited "on Monday, the 9th," when in point of fact the 9th comes on Friday, is not a sufficient notice. Watson v. Eales, 23 Beav., 294 (1856).

[4] Accordingly, a notice in all other respects regular, which does not state the place of sale, is insufficient, although it name the day of sale, and the auctioneer, who was and had long been an auctioneer in the place at which the notice was dated. Lexington, etc., R. R. Co. v. Staples, 71 Mass., 520 (1855). In the absence of a statutory provision as to time, it is said that three days' notice of the time and place of the sale of shares for non-payment of assessments is too short and unreasonable, where the owner of the shares lives at a distance in another state. Lexington, etc., R. R. Co. v. Staples, supra. In Rutland etc., R. R. Co. v. Thrall, 35 Vt., 536 (1863), a thirty days' notice is said to be sufficient and reasonable. And where the charter provided that notice of an assessment should be given to the subscriber thirty days before the order of the directors to sell the shares, a notice thirty days before the sale was held insufficient. Lewey's Island R. R. Co. v. Bolton, 48 Me., 451 (1860), Louisville, etc., Turnpike Co. v. Meriwether, 5 B. Mon., 13 (1844). A printed notice in designated newspapers, published in cities where the subscribers reside, is good notice of a call. Louisville, etc., Turnpike Co. v. Meriwether, supra.

[5] In Mississippi (Ouachita & Red

§ 131. *Notice is not the same thing as forfeiture* — A notice of a probable or certain forfeiture in the future, or a threat of forfeiture, is not forfeiture, and does not become forfeiture merely by non-payment of the call or assessment within the time specified in the notice.[1] A forfeiture is void if declared for the non-payment of assessments, when all or any one of the assessments were illegal or unauthorized.[2]

§ 132 *Tender, by stockholder, before forfeiture* — Where the amount due on a subscription for non-payment of which a forfeiture is about to take place is tendered to the proper officer of the corporation at any time before the sale actually takes place,[3] the

River R. R. Co. *v* Gaster, 20 Ark 455 — 1859) it is said that the mode of giving a notice in these cases is directory rather that mandatory, and that, where the charter provided that notice be given in certain newspapers, a personal notice would be sufficient See, also, Knight's Case, L. R., 2 Chan, 321 (1867) So where a by-law provided for notice by letter, it was held that personal notice sufficed Lexington, etc, R. R. Co. *v* Chandler, 54 Mass, 311 (1847) But see Lewey's Island R. R. Co *v.* Bolton, 48 Me, 451 (1860) In general, as to the effect of a notice left at one's residence or place of business, but which never reaches the person for whom it is intended, see Cockerell *v* Van Diemen's Land Co, 26 L. J. (C P), 203 (1857), 1 C B (N S.), 732. *Cf* Birmingham, etc, Ry Co *v* Locke, 1 Q B., 256 (1841), Graham *v* The Van Diemen's Land Co, 1 Hurl & N, 541 (1856) See, also, South Staffordshire Ry Co. *v* Burnside, 5 Exch, 129 (1850), and § 119

[1] Macon, etc, R. R. Co. *v* Vason, 57 Ga, 314 (1876), Bigg's Case, L. R., 1 Eq, 309 (1865), Cockerell *v* Van Diemen's Land Co, 26 L. R. (C P), 203 (1857); Water Valley Manuf Co *v* Seaman, 53 Miss, 655 (1876). where only a threat was made *Cf* § 125 But see Knight's Case, L. R., 2 Chan, 321 (1867) In Knight's Case it was further provided that the declaration of forfeiture should be at once entered in the register. Entry was duly made of the

date of the forfeiture, but not of the declaration itself All essentials being regular, and there being no strict requirement of a written resolution, the court held the forfeiture valid because the entry of forfeiture could not have been properly made without a resolution of the directors, which would hence be assumed. In Austin's Case, 24 L. T. (N S), 932 (1871), it is said that a corporation, after forfeiting shares, cannot set the forfeiture aside, and hold the owner liable as a subscriber, on the ground that the notice given him was irregular. It is for the subscriber alone to raise that objection to the validity of the forfeiture. *Cf* § 123, Birmingham, etc, R'y Co *v.* Locke, 1 Q. B., 256 (1841). A mere declaration of forfeiture is not sufficient to effect it, and is no bar to an action on the subscription Minnehaha, etc., Ass'n of Minneapolis *v* Legg, 52 N W Rep, 898. A resolution of forfeiture does not constitute forfeiture, and is no bar to an action Hayes *v* Franklin, etc., Co., 53 N. W. Rep, 381 (Neb, 1892)

[2] Stoneham, etc, R. R. Co. *v* Gould, 68 Mass, 277 (1854), Lewey's Island R R Co *v* Bolton, 48 Me, 451 (1860).

[3] Mitchell *v* Vermont Copper Mining Co, 67 N Y., 280 (1876), Sweny *v.* Smith, L. R., 7 Eq, 324 (1869). In Sweny *v* Smith a bill was filed to annul the forfeiture, which was made because the tender (although in time and place) was accompanied by a protest. *Held*, the protest did not vitiate

forfeiture is not valid. This rule is based in justice, and, while protecting the corporation and the public, it relieves the stockholder from the hardship of a harsh and summary remedy

§ 133 *Surplus, after valid forfeiture, belongs to the corporation.* Upon a sale of the stock forfeited, if the amount realized is more than the debt due the corporation, the surplus belongs to the corporation [1] The purchaser at the forfeiture sale, if the stock has been only partially paid for, must pay the instalments due and to come due, and if he fail to make these payments the stock must be sold again [2]

§ 134. *Equity will relieve a shareholder from an unauthorized forfeiture — Action at law for damages* — The share-owner himself, as well as a corporate creditor, may, in a proper case, invoke the aid of a court of chancery when his shares have been forfeited in an unauthorized or unlawful manner. Usually, in such a case, the shareholder may, by bill in equity, obtain a decree annulling the forfeiture [3] Where an illegal assessment has been made, and

the tender   Walker v Ogden, 1 Biss, 287 (Ill, 1859), where the articles of a private joint-stock company provided for a forfeiture, but in no express mode, and a forfeiture was declared of certain shares which thereafter remained undistributed No rights of third parties were vested in consequence; and the court of equity, never favoring forfeitures, decreed that upon payment of the whole amount due, principal and interest, the complainant should be allowed to redeem his stock The court did not *rule*, but was "inclined to the opinion," that "the mere declaration of the trustees" could not "have the effect to foreclose all Walker's interest," and "that a judicial decree of foreclosure upon a bill filed by the trustee was necessary in order to bar his right to redeem his stock "

[1] Small v Herkimer, etc. Co 2 N Y, 330 (1849), and see Sturges v Stetson, 1 Biss. 246 (1858), Gt North R'y Co v Kennedy, 4 Eq, 417, 426 (1849), by Rolfe, B (ruling on the language of a special act) "The company are not to sell more of the shares than will be sufficient, as nearly as can be ascertained, to pay arrears of calls, together

with interest and expenses, and, if there be any surplus, it is to be paid to the defaulter, who has a right to redeem at the last moment before sale That shows that the forfeited shares are a security only until payment." "It is clear that the declaration of forfeiture is in the nature of a mortgage" *Cf* Freeman v Harwood, 49 Me, 195, 198 (1859). *dictum*

[2] Sturges v. Stetson, 1 Biss, 246, 251 (1858)

[3] Sweny v Smith, L R., 7 Eq, 324 (1869), Mitchell v Vermont, etc, Co, 67 N Y, 280 (1876), Adley v Whitstable Co, 17 Ves 315 (1810, by Lord Eldon), Sloman v Bank of England, 14 Sim, 475 (1845), Norman v Mitchell, 5 De G, M & G, 648 (1854) Thus, a forfeiture of shares for non-payment of calls declared at a meeting held out of the state in which the company was incorporated, the meeting being in consequence an unlawful meeting, may be set aside upon a proper application to a court of chancery at any time within the period prescribed by the statute of limitations for bringing an action for conversion Ormsby v Vermont, etc., Co, 56 N Y, 623 (1874) Injunction not granted to

the stock is about to be sold, a stockholder may enjoin the sale and cause the assessment to be set aside[1]

So, also, equity will sometimes set aside a forfeiture upon purely equitable grounds; as, for example, where a forfeiture was declared for non-payment of calls, which, it was shown, were not paid because the shareholder had died, and no administrator had been appointed before the time for payment had fully elapsed[2] But it seems that the weight of authority is to the effect that a forfeiture of shares, lawful and regular, for non-payment of assessments, is one of those forfeitures from which equity will not afford relief except in very exceptional cases.[3] When the shareholder has lost his shares by an irregular or unlawful forfeiture, his suit should be for the recovery of his shares, and not for an undivided interest in the property of the company[4] Acquiescence or delay, as we have seen, on the part of the shareholder, will usually bar his right

restrain sale of stock for non-payment of assessments, though notice thereof was illegal, where the plaintiff does not offer to pay the calls Burnham v San F & Co., 17 Pac Rep., 939 (Cal , 1888). See, also, Same v Same, id , 940 (Cal , 1888) Forfeiture may be enjoined Moore v N. J , etc , Co., 5 N Y. Supp., 192 (1889) The forfeiture will not be set aside if the organization meeting of the company was illegal, having been held out of the state Smith v Silver, etc , Co., 30 Atl Rep., 1032 (Md 1885).

[1] Green v. Abietine, etc , Co , 31 Pac. Rep , 100 (Cal , 1892).

[2] Glass v. Hope, 16 Grant (Up. Can Chan), 420 (1869). Cf Walker v. Ogden, 1 Biss . 287 (1859).

[3] Sparks v The Company of Proprietors of the Liverpool Water-works, 13 Ves , 428 (1807), Prendergast v. Turton, 1 Y & C (Ch), 98 (1841), Germantown etc , R'y Co v Fitler, 60 Penn St., 124 (1869), Clark v Barnard, 108 U S , 436, 456 (1882) Equity will not relieve where, on the re-organization of a company, old stockholders fail to use their options for securing new shares before the expiration of a fixed time limit. Vatable v N Y , L E. & W R. R., 96 N Y., 49, 57 (1884) Equity will not relieve from such forfeiture, because to

do so would it is said, be in contravention of the direct expression of the legislative will Small v. Herkimer, etc., Co , 2 N Y , 330, 340 (1849). Neither can a share-owner have a forfeiture set aside merely because the calls which he refused to pay were for the purpose of paying debts which the company would not have owed but for the previous misappropriation of the corporate funds of the trustees Marshall v. Golden Fleece, etc , Co., 16 Nev., 156, 179 (1881), Weeks v Silver, etc., Co , 55 J & S (N. Y), 1 (1887); Taylor v. North. etc., Co , 21 Pac. Rep., 753 (Cal., 1889)

[4] Smith v Maine Boys Tunnel Co., 18 Cal , 111 (1861). The suit to set aside the forfeiture must be brought in the state where the corporation is incorporated North State, etc , Co v Field, 64 Md., 151 (1885), Sudlow v Dutch R. R. Co, 21 Beav , 43 (1855). See Wilkins v Thorne, 60 Md , 253 (1883) The courts of Maryland will not issue a *mandamus* to compel a foreign corporation to annul a forfeiture of stock This is a matter to be litigated in the courts of the state creating the corporation North State, etc , Co v Field, 20 Atl. Rep , 1039 (Md., 1885).

in a court of equity to have the forfeiture set aside[1] If the forfeiture is irregular the party deprived of his stock may collect
damages.[2]

[1] *Vide* § 129, *supra* It will, moreover, sometimes be found that a general
statute, or the charter of the corporation, fixes or limits the time within
which a shareholder will be allowed to
make such an application to a court of
chancery. Thus, in California, such an
application must be made within six
months Civ. Code, § 347.

[2] *Re* New Chile, etc., Co, Limited, 63
L. T. Rep 344 (1890). A corporation is
liable in damages for selling the stock of
a stockholder for non-payment of dues
where such sale was irregular and illegal,
being contrary to the requirements of the
by-laws, even though the corporation
buys the stock itself at such sale. The
fact that a surplus realized at the sale is
sent to the stockholder by check and is
received by him does not bar his remedy,
being in ignorance of the illegality Allen
v American Building, etc, Ass'n *et al*, 52
N. W. Rep, 144 (Minn, 1892)

CHAPTER IX.

DEFENSE OF PAROL AGREEMENTS AND FRAUDULENT REPRESENTATIONS INDUCING SUBSCRIPTIONS FOR STOCK.

§ 135. *The subject* — Parol agreements and fraudulent representations inducing subscriptions to stock have been a prolific source of litigation both in this country and in England. As a defense to actions brought for the collection of subscriptions, and as the basis of suits in equity to set aside subscriptions and compel a repayment of money already paid on such subscriptions, the agreements and representations made to induce persons to subscribe for stock have given rise to intricate principles of law peculiar to this subject

§ 136. *Definitions* — A parol agreement includes all representations and stipulations made before or at the time of subscribing, but not included in the written subscription, whereby the corporation is to do something or refrain from doing something in the future. A fraudulent representation, on the other hand, is a statement as to past acts or existing facts, or the omission of such a statement, which amount to a fraud on one who, relying thereon, subscribes to the stock of the company. Difficulty sometimes arises in determining whether a statement by a corporate agent inducing a subscription is merely a parol agreement or is a fraudulent representation. This question is one which must be decided first of all,

186

since the rules of law applicable to parol agreements, as a defense to an action on a subscription, differ greatly from those applicable to fraudulent representations

§ 137. *Oral agreements and executory contracts* — Where a subscription contract is absolute on its face, it is well settled, both in equity and at law, that parol evidence of previous or contemporaneous negotiations, stipulations, terms or agreements is not admissible to vary or add to the contract, except for the purpose of proving that the parties, at the time of consummating the agreement, intended and understood that such terms and stipulations would be incorporated in the contract, but omitted the same by accident, fraud or mistake [1] This rule, forbidding the introduction

[1] Piscataqua Ferry Co v Jones, 39 N. H, 491 (1859), Kennebec & Portland R. R. Co v Waters, 34 Me, 369 (1852) Cincinnati, Union & Ft Wayne R R Co v Pearce, 28 Ind, 502 (1867), Scarlett v Academy of Music, 46 Md, 132 (1876), Dill v Wabash Valley R R. Co., 21 Ill, 91 (1859), East Tenn & Va R R Co v. Gammon, 5 Sneed (Tenn), 567 (1858), Corwith v Culver, 69 Ill, 502 (1873), Jack v Naher, 15 Iowa, 450 (1863); Thornburgh v Newcastle & D R. R. Co., 14 Ind, 499 (1860), Gelpcke v. Blake, 15 Iowa, 387 (1863), holding that it is immaterial that the agent acted in good faith, Johnson v Pensacola & Ga. R. R. Co, 9 Fla, 299 (1860), Miss, O & R R R. Co v Cross, 20 Ark, 443 (1859), Ridgefield & N Y R R Co v Brush, 43 Conn, 86 (1875), Phœnix Warehousing Co v Badger, 6 Hun, 293 (1875); affirmed, 67 N Y, 294, Whitehall & P R R Co v Myers 16 Abb. Pr (N S), 34 (1872). But see Brewers' Fire Ins. Co. v. Burger, 10 Hun, 56 (1877), holding that where the original subscription contract is verbal and complete, and a part only of it is afterwards reduced to writing, it is competent to prove the whole agreement See, also, Hendrix v Academy of Music (Ga, 1885). *Cf.* Eighmie v Taylor, 98 N Y, 288 (1885). An oral condition to a subscription cannot be set up Masonic, etc, Assoc v Channell, 43 N W Rep, 716 (Minn, 1890) An oral statement that the subscriptions would be col-

lected only after connection had been made with a certain place is no defense Anderson v. Middle, etc, R. R., 17 S W Rep, 803 (Tenn, 1891)

In Georgia, under section 3803 of the code, where the subscription does not purport to contain the whole contract, parol evidence is admissible Hendrix v Academy of Music, 73 Ga, 437 (1884)

In Pennsylvania the case of McClure v People's Freight R'y Co, 90 Pa St. 269 (1879), sustains the general rule, and excludes a parol agreement or condition allowing payment in property But Rinesmith v People's Freight R'y Co, 90 Pa. St, 262 (1879)· Caley v Phil & Chester R R Co, 80 Pa St 363 (1876), Miller v Hanover June & Sus R. R Co, 87 Pa St, 95 (1878), and McCarty v Selinsgrove & N B. R R Co, 87 Pa St, 332 (1878), allow parol evidence to contradict the subscription contract where it is shown that but for the parol agreement the subscription would not have been made, the last two cases saying, however, that the evidence is inadmissible if other stockholders are interested in opposition to such parol agreement This unusual rule probably has its origin in an old English case (Pulsford v Richards, 17 Beav, 87, 1853), which holds that a representation is to be considered *fraudulent* when, ' if the real truth had been stated, it is reasonable to believe the plaintiff would not have entered into the contract." Thus a parol agreement

of parol evidence to explain, contradict or vary a written instrument, applies to a subscription contract for stock in a corporation. Neither party is permitted to prove a different contract from that expressed in the written instrument. Under the rule, not even a separate written contemporaneous contract is admissible to change the subscription contract [1]

§ 138. Thus, an agreement that a certain location will be adopted,[2] or that payment may be made in a certain way or at a certain time,[3] or that the subscription shall be merely nominal, for the purpose of inducing others to subscribe,[4] or that the subscription shall

that part payment in contract labor should be allowed was held to be void, inasmuch as it varied the terms of a written agreement. Ridgefield & N Y. R. R. Co v Brush, 43 Conn, 86 (1875). Contra, Louisville & Nash. R. R. Co v Thompson, 18 B. Mon, 735 (1857); McConahy i Centre & Kish Turnpike R Co. 1 Penn & W, 426 (1830), followed in Swatara R. R. t Brune, 6 Gill, 41 (1847), overruled by Nippenose Mfg Co. v. Stadon, 68 Pa. St, 256 (1871) See, also, Weber v Fickey, 52 Md, 501; Leibke t Knapp, 79 Mo, 22 (1883) Parol condition that others were to sign is not admissible. Minn etc., Co t Davis, 41 N W. Rep., 1026 (Minn, 1889). But it has been held that a parol agreement herein, made after the subscription, and on a new consideration, is valid Pittsburgh & Connellsville R. R. Co. v. Stewart, 41 Pa St., 54 (1861). See, also, Tonica, etc., R. R. Co. v Stein, 21 Ill, 96 (1859) Cf Bucher v Dillsburg, etc, R. R. Co. 76 Penn St 306 (1874), Brewers', etc, Ins Co v Burger, 10 Hun, 56 (1877), Eighmie v. Taylor, 98 N Y, 288 (1885).

The subscriber's remedy is against the person who made the agreement which has not been kept Felgate's Case, 2 D⁳ G J & S. 456 (1865). An action for damages for breach of contract lies against the corporation if the agreement amounts to a condition subsequent. See ch V

[1] Brownlee t O, Ind & Ill R. R Co, 18 Ind, 68 (1862). White Mts R. R. Co v. Eastman, 34 N. H, 124 (1856).

[2] North Car. R. R. Co. v Leach, 4 Jones' Law (N. C), 340 (1857), Wight v Shelby R R. Co, 16 B Monr, 4 (1855); Ellison v Mobile & O R R. Co. 36 Miss., 572 (1858), Miss. O & R. R. R. Co v Cross, 20 Ark, 443 (1859), Evansville, Indianapolis & C. S R. R. Co v. Posey, 12 Ind, 363 (1859), Eakright v Logansport & N Ind. R. R. Co, 13 Ind, 404 (1859); Carlisle v. Evansville, Ind. & C. S. R R. Co., 13 Ind, 477 (1859), Miller v. Wild Cat Gravel Road Co., 52 Ind, 51 (1875), S. C, 57 id, 241, Miller v Hanover June & Sus. R. R. Co, 87 Pa. St., 95 (1878), Gelpcke v. Blake, 15 Iowa, 387 (1863), Braddock v Phil, M & M. R. R. Co, 45 N J Law Rep, 363 (1883); Killer v Johnson. 11 Ind, 337 (1858), holding it immaterial that fraud was actually intended Contra, Rives v. Montgomery S. P R Co, 30 Ala, 92 (1857). Representations of an agent that the road will be built between the termini laid down in the charter are representations relative to the future and are not fraudulent though not carried out. Armstrong v Karshner, 24 N. E Rep., 897 (Ohio, 1890).

[3] Noble v Collender, 20 Ohio St, 199 (1870), Henry v Vermilion & A. R. R. Co, 17 Ohio, 187 (1848), Stewards of M E Church v Town, 49 Vt., 29 (1876), Ridgefield & N Y R. R. Co. v Brush, 43 Conn, 86 (1875), Thigpen v. Miss. Central R R. Co, 32 Miss, 347 (1856).

[4] Downie v White, 12 Wis, 176 (1860); Wetherbee v Baker, 35 N. J Eq, 501 (1882) Kishacoquillas & Centre T. R. Co. v McConahy, 16 S. & R. (Pa), 140

be in fact only a pledge of stock by the corporation to the sub scriber, or that the stock may be surrendered,[1] or that certain property would be purchased by the corporation,[2] or that the subscriber might keep his stock, but should not be liable for the full par value thereof,[3] or that payment would not be demanded until certain work had been completed,[4] or that the money would be applied to a particular part of the road,[5] or that a certain part of the road would be completed within a certain time,[6] or that the road will be extended to a certain point,[7] or other parol conditions,[8] or execu-

(1827), Phœnix W. Co v Badger, 6 Hun, 293 (1875), aff'd, 67 N. Y., 294, Psychaud v Hood, 23 La. Ann, 732 (1871), Cleveland Iron Co v Ennor, 12 Am & Eng Corp Cases, 88 (Ill, 1886), Robinson v Pittsburgh & C R. R. Co., 32 Pa St, 334 (1858), Graff v Pittsburgh & S R. R. Co., 31 Pa. St, 489 (1858), Mann v Cooke, 20 Conn, 178 (1849), Conn. & Pass Rivers R. R. v Bailey, 24 Vt., 465; Davidson's Case, 3 De G & S., 21 (1849), holding it to be a fraud on other subscribers, without requiring proof that there were such· Bridge's Case, L R., 9 Eq Cas, 74 (1869), New Albany & Salem R R. Co. v Slaughter, 10 Ind, 218 (1858); Blodgett v Morrill, 20 Vt, 509 (1848); Minor v Mechanics' Bank of Alexandria, 1 Peters, 46 (1828), Bates v Lewis, 3 Ohio St., 459 (1854), Litchfield Bank v. Church, 29 Conn, 137 (1860), Mangles v Grand Collier Dock Co, 10 Sim, 519 (1840); Preston v. Grand Collier Dock Co., 2 Rail Cas, 335 (1840); Chouteau Co v. Floyd, 74 Mo, 286 (1881). These cases hold that parol agreements are void as a fraud on corporate creditors and on other subscribers, and that the subscription is enforceable absolutely. It is no defense that there was a prior or contemporaneous oral agreement that the stock was not to be issued and the subscriber not to be held liable Wurtzbarger v Anniston, etc, Mills, 10 S. Rep., 129 (Ala, 1891) It is no defense that another party had promised the stockholder that the former would pay for the stock. Williams v. Benet, 13 S. E Rep., 97 (S C., 1891). A person sued as

a subscriber cannot set up that he subscribed at the solicitation of another person who agreed to take the subscription off his hands at once. Stutz v Handley, 41 Fed. Rep, 531 (1890)

[1] Melvin v. Lamar Ins Co, 80 Ill, 446 (1875), White Mts R R. Co v Eastman, 34 N H. 124 (1856) Cf §§ 247, 465, infra Or that the subscriber be released Gill v Balis, 72 Mo, 424 (1880)

[2] Kelsey v Northern Light Oil Co, 45 N Y, 505 (1871)

[3] Custar t Titusville Gas & Water Co, 63 Pa St 381 (1869), Union Ins Co v Frear S Manuf. Co., 97 Ill, 537 (1881), Upton t. Tribilcock, 91 U S, 45 (1875)

[4] La Grange & M P R. Co t. Mays, 29 Mo, 64 (1859), Clem v. Newcastle & D R. R. Co, 9 Ind, 488 (1857), holding that such a promise is contradictory of the legal effect of the subscription; Cincinnati U & Ft Wayne R. R. Co. v Pearce, 28 Ind, 502 (1867)

[5] Smith v Tallahassee Branch of C P R Co, 30 Ala, 650 (1857). An action to rescind the purchase of stock lies where the money paid therefor was to be applied to a certain purpose but was not so applied, but the receiver will not be directed to give up the money Moore v Robertson, 25 Abb N C, 173 (1890)

[6] Blair v Buttolph, 33 N. W Rep, 349 (Iowa, 1887).

[7] Low v Studebaker, 10 N. E. Rep, 301 (Ind, 1887)

[8] Topeka, etc, v Hale, 17 Pac. Rep, 601 (Kan, 1888), Marshall, etc, Co v Kellian, 6 S E Rep, 680 (N C, 1888) Parol cannot add to a condition of a conditional

tory contracts,— are held to be no defense to an action to collect
the subscription [1] Where, for the purpose of obtaining a subscription, a promise was made in behalf of the corporation that a branch
road would be built, it was held that this promise was but an expression of an existing intention which was liable to be changed,
and was no defense.[2] It was also held that a promise which, if
carried out, would necessitate an *ultra vires* act by the corporation,
is not binding, and is no defense [3]

§ 139 *Corporations chargeable with the fraudulent representations of their agents* — At an early day in England it was held in
a number of cases that corporations were not bound by the frauds
of their agents in obtaining subscriptions to stock [4] This doctrine
rested on the theory that the corporation gave the agent no power
or authority to commit a fraud, and that, consequently, the fraud
rendered the agent liable personally, but did not release or affect
the subscription.

subscription   Miller *v* Preston, 17 Pac
Rep. 565 (N M, 1888). An oral agreement
to take stock in payment of a note is no
defense to the note. The corporation
must pay it. Tuscaloosa, etc., Co. *v.*
Perry, 4 S Rep, 635 (Ala, 1888). Where
the agent of the railroad represented
that a depot would be constructed at a
certain place, a failure to so construct
is good ground for enjoining the issue
of municipal-aid bonds. Wullenwaber
v Dunnigan, 47 N. W Rep, 420 (Neb,
1890). An oral contract that the subscriber was to be allowed to pay in
property is good as against other stockholders who assented thereto, but such
contract must be clearly proven. Knoop
v Bohmrich, 23 Atl. Rep., 118 (N J.,
1891).

[1] Piscataqua Ferry Co. *v.* Jones, 39
N H, 491 (1859), Crossman *v* Penrose
Ferry Bridge Co., 26 Pa. St., 69 (1856);
New Albany & Salem R. R. Co. *v*
Fields, 10 Ind, 187 (1858); East Tenn &
Va R. R. Co *v* Gammon, 5 Sneed
(Tenn.), 567 (1858), Saffold *v* Barnes,
39 Miss, 399 (1860); Payson *v* Withers,
5 Biss., 269 (1873), Goff *v* Hawkeye
Pump & W M. Co, 62 Iowa, 691 (1884),
Corwith *v.* Culver, 69 Ill, 502 (1873)
Contra, Mahan *v* Wood, 44 Cal, 462

(1872) where the par value of the shares
was not what was promised

[2] McAllister *v* Indianapolis & Cin
R. R. Co, 15 Ind, 11 (1860). No defense that the subscribers were told
that branches would be established and
that they had not been Guarantee,
etc, Co. *v* Weil, 21 Atl Rep, 665 (Penn,
1891).

[3] Johnson *v* Crawfordsville, F. K. &
Ft. W R. R. Co, 11 Ind, 280 (1858),
where aid from another railroad was
promised, Peters *v* Lincoln & N W. R.
Co., 14 Fed Rep., 319 (1882), where an
ultra vires lease was promised: Baile *v.*
Calvert C E. Soc., 47 Md, 117 (1877).

[4] Dodgson's Case, 3 De G & Sm, 85
(1849); Bernard's Case, 5 De G & Sm.,
283 (1852); Gibson's Case, 2 De G & J.,
275 (1858); Holt's Case, 22 Beav, 48
(1856); Felgate's Case 2 De G, J. & S.,
456 (1865); Mixer's Case, 4 De G. & J.,
575, where a prospectus was issued by
the directors, Ayres' Case, 25 Beav, 513
(1858), the court holding that the corporation is bound by the misrepresentation only where it expressly authorized
the particular statement made. *Cf.*
Barry *v.* Craskey, 2 Johns. & Hem, 1
(1861).

§ 140   The modern doctrine, however, both in this country and in England, has completely exploded the theory that corporations are not chargeable with the frauds of their agents in taking subscriptions   The well-established rule now is that a corporation cannot claim or retain the benefit of a subscription which has been obtained through the fraud of its agents   The misrepresentations are not regarded as having actually been made by the corporation, but the corporation is not allowed to retain the benefit of the contract growing out of them, being liable to the extent that it has profited by such misrepresentations [1]   The question of the authority of the agent taking the subscription is immaterial herein   It matters not whether he had any authority, or exceeded his authority, or concealed its limitations [2]   The corporation cannot claim the benefits of his fraud without assuming also the representations which procured those benefits.   Parol evidence is admissible to show the fraud, since it does not vary or contradict the contract, but shows that no contract was properly formed [3]

§ 141   *The misrepresentations must be by authorized agents* — False representations by persons who do not act as intermediaries between the corporation and the subscriber in forming the contract cannot bind the corporation nor affect the subscription   They are statements of outside parties.[4]   The subscriber may have his

[1] Western Bank of Scotland *v* Addie, L R., 1 Sc App. Cas, 145 (1867); Nat'l Exchange Co *v* Drew, 32 Eng L & Eq, 1 (1853), Henderson *v* Lacon, L. R., 5 Eq Cas. 249 (1867); *Ex parte* Linger, 5 Irish Ch Rep. (N S.), 174, Montgomery S R y Co *v* Matthews, 77 Ala, 357 (1884) The principles governing these contracts are the same as the principles governing contracts between private individuals Directors, etc., of Central R'y *v* Kisch, L. R., 2 H L App Cas, 99 (1870), Anderson *v* Newcastle & Richmond R. R Co., 12 Ind, 376 (1859), Vreeland *v* N J Stone Co, 29 N. J Eq, 188 (1878), Ranger *v* Great W. R'y, 5 H L C, 72 (1859), Mackay *v* Com Bank, 5 P C., 394   As regards representations in reference to bonds secured by mortgage and the right of a purchaser of bonds to complain, see Van Weel *v* Winston, 115 U S, 228 (1885).

[2] Crumb *v.* U S. Min Co, 7 Gratt. (Va.), 353 (1851).   Provided, of course, that the misrepresentations were made

by persons legally connected with the taking of the subscription   An agent to obtain subscriptions may use the ordinary means of accomplishing the object of his appointment, such as representing the location and quality of the lands, and the like   Sandford *v* Handy, 23 Wend, 260 (1849)   See, also, Nelson *v* Cowing. 6 Hill, 336 (1844)

[3] N Y Exchange Co. *v* De Wolf, 31 N Y, 271 (1865), Jewett *v* Valley R'y Co, 34 Ohio St, 601 (1878)   In Pennsylvania the peculiar rule prevails that the agent's misrepresentations affect the subscription, and are a defense only when the agent actually had or reasonably appeared to have authority to make representations   This was the ancient English doctrine, long since abandoned Custar *v* Titusville Gas & Water Co, 63 Pa St., 381 (1869)

[4] Cunningham *v* Edgefield & Ky R R Co., 2 Head, 23 (1858)   The representations made to him by other subscribers or outsiders are immaterial

action for damages against such persons for deceit, but he cannot
charge the corporation with their misrepresentations   Sometimes,
also, the misrepresentations even of persons connected with the
corporation do not bind the corporation, inasmuch as their powers
are purely statutory, or have nothing to do with the taking of subscriptions. Thus, while there has been considerable controversy in
this country over the question of fraudulent representations by
commissioners having statutory powers to take subscriptions, it is
quite well settled that the subscriber is bound to know that the
commissioners have no power to make representations, and that
the corporation is not bound thereby [1] So, also, it has been held
that the representations by the president of the corporation do not
bind it where he had no authority to take subscriptions.[2] In Indiana it is held that an agent taking subscriptions before the incorporation of the company cannot bind it by his misrepresentations.[3]
If there is conflicting testimony as to the authority and *status* of
the agent, the question is to be submitted to the jury [4]

§ 142 *Corporation not bound by misrepresentations of officers at
a public meeting* — There is a difference of opinion among the authorities as to whether fraudulent representations made by one or
more of the company's officers, at a public meeting called to promote the procuring of subscriptions, are chargeable against the corporation where such representations were not expressly authorized
by the corporation. In New York, Iowa, Alabama and Louisiana
such misrepresentations do not bind the corporation.[5] In Georgia
and Wisconsin, on the other hand, such fraudulent representations

herein. His remedy is against them
personally.   Duranty's Case, 26 Beav,
268 (1858), *Ex parte* Frowd, 30 L. J.
(Ch). 322 (1860)

[1] Nippenose Mfg Co. v Stadon 68 Pa.
St. 256 (1871), Barington v Pittsburgh
& Steubenville R. R. Co. 34 Pa St., 358
(1859), Wight v Shelby R. R. Co, 16 B
Monr, 4 (1855); Rutz v Esler & R. Mfg
Co, 3 Bradw, 81 (1878)· Syracuse, P &
O R. R. Co v Gere, 4 Hun, 392 (1875),
North Car. R. R. Co. v Leach, 4 Jones'
L. (N. C), 340 (1857).

[2] Crump v U S. Mining Co., 7 Gratt.
(Va), 353 (1851), Rives v. Montgomery
South Plank R. Co, 30 Ala., 92 (1857).
In all such cases, however, if the corporation accepts a subscription taken by
an unauthorized agent, it cannot retain
the subscription and repudiate the rep-

resentations It must assume both or
neither

[3] Miller v. Wild Cat Gravel Road Co.,
57 Ind , 241 (1875).

[4] Kelsey v Northern Light Oil Co., 45
N. Y, 505 (1871); Crump v U. S Mining
Co., 7 Gratt. (Va.), 353 (1851).

[5] Buffalo & N. Y. City R. R. Co. v.
Dudley, 14 N. Y, 336 (1856), First Nat.
Bank v. Huiford, 29 Iowa, 579 (1870),
Smith v Tallahassee Branch of C. P. R.
R. Co, 30 Ala., 650 (1857), on the ground
of a want of authority, which the subscriber is bound to know, Vicksburg,
S & T R. R. v McKean, 12 La. Ann.,
638 (1857), on the ground that, if the
rule were otherwise, "there will be very
little security to those who loan money
or render assistance to institutions of
this kind.

are held to be admissible in evidence [1] The former rule seems to accord most with the modern tendency of the decisions, which go very far towards the enforcement of subscriptions after corporate creditors and other subscribers have become interested in the enprise

§ 143 *The misrepresentations may arise by prospectuses* — A prospectus issued by the authority of the directors or the stockholders of a corporation may be relied upon by a person in subscribing for stock, and if the prospectus contains a false representation, and the subscription is made by reason thereof, such representation is binding upon the corporation [2] In this class of corporate instruments, however, it is held that some high coloring and even exaggeration is allowable "In an advertisement of this description some allowance must always be made for the sanguine expectations of the promotors of the adventure, and no prudent man will accept the prospects which are always held out by the originators of every

---

[1] Atlanta & West Point R. R. Co v. Hodnett, 36 Ga, 669 (1867), McClellan v. Scott, 24 Wis, 81 (1869) The question of representations at a public meeting was submitted to the jury in Weems v. Georgia, etc, R. R., 14 S. E Rep, 583 (Ga, 1892)

[2] Oakes v. Turquand, L. R. 2 H L. App. Cas, 325 (1867), Ross v. Estates Investment Co., L. R., 3 Ch App, 682 (1868), Reese River Silver Min Co v. Smith, L. R, 4 H L 64 (1869) Blakes Case, 34 Beav, 639 (1865), Henderson v. Lacon, L. R, 5 Eq Cas, 249 (1867) In England it is enacted, by section 38 of the Companies Act, 1867 "Every prospectus of a company, and every notice inviting persons to subscribe for shares in any joint-stock company, shall specify the dates and names of the parties to any contract entered into by the company, or the promoters, directors or trustees thereof, before the issue of such prospectus or notice, whether subject to adoption by the directors or the company or otherwise, and any prospectus or notice not specifying the same shall be deemed fraudulent on the part of the promoters, directors and officers of the company knowingly issuing the same, as regards any person taking shares in the company on the faith of

such prospectus, unless he shall have had notice of such contract" For the application of this very important and commendable statute, see Cornell v. Hay, 8 C. P. 328 (1873), Gover's Case, L. R., 20 Eq, 114 (1875) Davidson v. Tulloch, 1 Macq, 783 (1860), Arkright v. Newbold, L. R, 17 Ch D, 311 (1880), Twycross v. Grant, L. R, 2 C P D, 469 (1877), Emma Min Co v. Lewis, L. R. 4 C P D, 396 (1879), Bagnall v. Carlton L R 6 Ch D, 371 (1877) Plympton Min Co v. Wilkins, 1882, W. N p 69, Sullivan v. Metcalf, L. R. 5 C P Div 455 (1880) But a prospectus containing statements based upon a report of the vendor of property to the corporation, which report is appended to the prospectus is no ground for rescission, even though the report is totally false All the stockholders and the company relied equally thereon Ex parte Vickers, 56 L. T Rep., 815 (1887) Several subscribers who have been induced by the same misrepresentations contained in a prospectus to subscribe for stock may join in a suit in equity for the benefit of themselves and others similarly deceived, to set aside their subscriptions. Bosher v. Richmond, etc, Co, 16 S. E. Rep., 360 (Va, 1892 See 66 L. T Rep., 700, reversing id, 191.

new scheme without considerable abatement "[1]   So, also, if the language used in the prospectus admits of two meanings, the subscriber relying on it must ascertain which meaning is intended[2] Unless the representation distinctly refers to what is actually existing at the time, it must be taken to represent what will result when the enterprise is carried out, and will then be merely an expression of opinion   Nevertheless a subscriber may have rescission where the prospectus is not an honest, candid, straightforward document, but suggests that which is untrue and is in a high degree misleading[3]

§ 144.   *Or by reports* — So, also, a report made by the corporate officers to the stockholders may be relied on by one who contemplates subscribing for stock.[4]   The corporation cannot say that such reports were intended for the stockholders alone   The law holds that the report is known. and is intended to be known, to all persons who contemplate becoming stockholders, and is the same as though published to the world.[5]

§ 145 *Misrepresentations amounting to fraudulent representations* — Any false statement by the authorized agents of a corporation in regard to the past or present *status* of the corporate enterprise or material matters connected therewith, whereby subscriptions are obtained, is a fraudulent representation.

Thus, a false statement that a certain amount of stock had been subscribed for,[6] or that certain property had been purchased;[7] that

[1] Directors, etc., of Central R'y Co. v Kisch. L. R., 2 H L App. Cas, 99 (1870)

[2] Smith v Chadwick, L. R., 9 H. L, 187 Hallows ι Fennie, L. R., 3 Ch App., 467 (1868), where the court say "If they may be construed in a different manner by different minds, it will be impossible to test the truth of any one man's assertion that he understood them in the sense in which they involved a misrepresentation " See, also, §§ 352, 353.

[3] Scott v The Snyder, etc., Co., 67 L T Rep., 104 (1892).

[4] Western Bank of Scotland v Addie, L R, 1 Sc App Cas., 145, New Brunswick & C R'y Co v Conybeare, 9 H L Cas., 711 (1862)

[5] National Exchange Co. v Drew, 32 Eng L & Eq. 1 (1855), Scott v. Dixon, 29 L J (Ex), 62, n , explained and adopted in L R., 6 H L, 377

[6] Ross v. Estates Investment Co, L

R., 3 Ch , 682 (1868), Henderson v Lacon, L R , 5 Eq , 249 (1867)   A statement that £200,000 had been subscribed. when in fact owners of property had contracted to convey the same to the company for £200,000 of stock. is a material misrepresentation.   Arnison v Smith, 59 L T Rep, 627 (1888). It is fraud to state that a certain person had subscribed for stock when in fact his stock was given to him   It is not fraudulent that the mine whose stock is sold would not pay for mining   A bill in equity lies to cancel a conveyance of land to pay for the stock.   Coles v. Kennedy, 46 N W Rep , 1088 (Iowa, 1890).

[7] Also that the property contained valuable mines, in full operation, and with large daily returns   Reese River Silver Min Co ι Smith, L R, 4 H. L, 64 (1869), Waldo v Chicago, St. P. & F. D L. R. R. Co , 14 Wis , 575 (1861); Ross v Estates Investment Co, *supra*.   Repre-

the corporate property is unincumbered · [1] that the corporation is solvent and prosperous, [2] that the directors have subscribed for stock, [3] that certain individuals are directors, [4] or as to the nature of the business to be undertaken, [5] or, in England, where the memoranda or articles of the association are different from the prospectus; [6] or that work on the enterprise had reached a certain stage of completion, [7] or that a certain price had been paid for property when in fact a large part of the price went to promoters, [8] or that

sentation that a certain patent-right owned by the company had been tested and found to be valuable, held not a misrepresentation, although it turns out to be worthless Denton v Macneil. L. R., 2 Eq, 352 (1866) Representation in good faith that title to land was good when in fact it was bad is not a misrepresentation New Brunswick & C R y Co v. Conybeare, 9 H L Cas 711 (1862) But misrepresentation that a government guaranty had been obtained is material Kisch v Central R y of Venezuela. 34 L J (Ch), 545

[1] McClellan v Scott, 24 Wis, 81 (1869), Water Valley Mfg Co v Seaman, 53 Miss, 655

[2] Tyler v Savage, 143 U S, 79 (1892), Bell's Case, 22 Beav, 35 (1856), Melendy v Keen, 89 Ill, 395 (1878), Western Bank of Scotland v Addie, L R., 1 Sc App. Cas., 145 (1877) Not so, however, where the directors honestly figured in debts which afterwards turned out to be bad. Jackson v Turquand, L R., 4 H L, 305 (1869) Directors held liable to depositors for fraudulent representations as to the bank's solvency Seale v Baker, 7 S W Rep, 742 (Texas, 1888).

[3] Henderson v Lacon, L R., 5 Eq Cas , 249 (1867)

[4] Blake's Case, 34 Beav , 639 (1865), Meuster's Case, 14 W R, 957 (1866) Persons who have accepted are directors, although without the qualification shares Hallows v Fernie L R 3 Ch App , 467 (1868) A misrepresentation as to the directors is ground for repudiating the subscription Re Metropolitan, etc , Ass'n, 64 L. T. Rep., 561 (1891), id ,

429 A misrepresentation as to who are the members of the council of administration is material and a rescission may be had Re Metropolitan, etc , Ass'n, 62 L T Rep , 30 (1889)

[5] Blackburn's Case, 3 Drew, 409 (1856) A person who has agreed to turn in property for stock may have the contract annulled on the ground that fraudulent representations were made about the process of manufacture by the corporation Kelley v Owens et al, 30 Pac. Rep , 596 (Cal , 1892)

[6] Downes v Ship L R, 3 H L, 343 (1868), Ex parte Briggs, L R , 1 Eq Cas, 483 (1866)

[7] Peel's Case, L R, 2 Ch App , 674 (1867), Ogilvie v Currie, 37 L J (Ch), 541 (1868), Lawrence's Case, L R, 2 Ch App , 412 (1867), Kincaid's Case, id (1867), Wilkinson's Case, L R, 2 Ch App , 536 (1867), Ashley's Case, L R, 9 Eq Cas, 263 (1870) Stewart's Case, L R, 1 Ch. App., 574 Whitehouse's Case, L R, 3 Eq, 790 (1867), Taite's Case, L R, 3 Eq, 795 (1867), Upton v Hansbraugh, 3 Biss , 417 (1873), Re Cachar Co , 36 L J (Ch), 490 (1867), Ship v Cresskill L R, 10 Eq Cas, 73 (1870) Cf Ex parte Briggs, L R , 1 Eq Cas , 483 (1866), Stewart's Case, L R, 1 Ch., 574 (1866). False representation that sufficient funds were at hand to build a specified part of the road, being a different part from that which the defendant required by his subscription to be completed before payment, is immaterial Blau v Buttolph, 33 N W, Rep , 349 (Iowa, 1887)

[8] Capel v Sims, etc , Co. 58 L T Rep , (1888) See, also, ch. XXXIX.

steam could be used where only horse-power was allowed,[1] or that the objects of the enterprise set forth in the subscription contract were of a certain nature, the subscriber not reading or hearing, and not being able to read, the contract,[2] or other material mis-statements of fact,[3] have been held to constitute a fraudulent representation, entitling the subscriber induced thereby to subscribe to the remedies provided for him by law in such cases In all these cases, however, the distinction between statements relative to the prospects and capabilities of the enterprise, and statements specifically specifying what does or does not exist, must be carefully borne in mind. The former are matters of opinion; the latter are material representations, and are fraudulent if false.[4]

§ 146. *Statements as to questions of law.*—Where a subscription is obtained by a false representation as to the legal effect of the subscription contract, or of corporate rights or liabilities, the subscriber has no remedy He is bound to take notice of the law.[5] Thus, a misrepresentation as to the extent to which the subscriber would be liable on his stock,[6] or that he may allow his stock to be

[1] Peek v Derry, 59 L. T. Rep., 78 (1888).

[2] West v Crawfordsville & A. T. Co., 19 Ind, 242 (1862)

[3] See ch XX, § 350 A representation that only $3 000 of stock and $12,000 bonds per mile would be issued is fraudulent where $12,000 of stock and $15,000 of bonds per mile have already been issued Weems v Georgia, etc., R R, 11 S. E Rep, 503 (Ga., 1890) Where an apartment-house corporation induces by prospectus subscriptions on representations that certain subscriptions entitle the holder to a perpetual leasehold in the apartments selected by the subscriber, he cannot afterwards be evicted on the ground that the building cost more than was expected and further rent must be paid. Compton v Chelsea, 8 N Y Supp., 622 (1890) A statement of assets that include not only separate items for moving, exhibiting, etc., the aggregate value of the buildings being given also, but also outstanding accounts with no deductions for bad debts, accrued interest with no allowance for interest on liabilities, expenses of perfecting a machine, the latter not yet being a success; and money paid for ex-

penses, it being also included in the value of the property,—is a false statement and sustains an action. Hubbard v Weare, 44 N. W. Rep., 914 (Iowa, 1890)

[4] Whether the statement refers to a "possibility or a contingency, or an intention," or to an existing fact, is a question sometimes for the jury, sometimes for the judge, generally the latter. Edgington v Fitzmaurice, L. R., 29 Ch D, 459 (1885). All the statements, together with the circumstances and history of the matter, are to be considered in deciding whether a misrepresentation was made. It is sufficient if the subscriber relied partly on the misrepresentation. He need not have relied on it exclusively. Id. See, also, Nicol's Case, 3 De G. & J, 420 (1858). The subscriber may, by contract, waive his right to rely on a representation Brownlee v Campbell, L. R., 5 App. Cas, 925 (1880)

[5] Parker v Thomas, 19 Ind, 213 (1862).

[6] Upton v Tribilcock, 91 U. S, 45 (1875), where the representation was that only a certain percentage could be called for. In Upton v Englehart, 3 Dill., 496 (1874), this representation was

forfeited,[1] or that payment would not be demanded until the enterprise was partly or wholly completed,[2] is a statement as to the law. It states that something can be done which the law prohibits from being done

§ 147 *Misrepresentation may be by suppression of the truth* — The misrepresentation entitling the subscriber to his remedies may consist in the suppression of what is true as well as in the assertion of what is false[3] Where any statement is made at all, it must be a fair and full statement of all the material facts. The corporate authorities, in issuing a prospectus, are " bound to state everything with strict and scrupulous accuracy, and not only to abstain from stating as fact that which is not so, but to omit no one fact within their knowledge, the existence of which might, in any degree, affect the nature or extent or quality of the privileges and advantages which the prospectus holds out as inducements to take shares."[4] Thus, an omission to state that a very large sum had been paid for property, the merits of which were fully set forth, has been held to be equivalent to a fraudulent representation[5] On the other hand, a failure to state that large sums were paid to the directors to induce them to act as such was held not to be a fraudulent omission[6]

§ 148 *Misrepresentation may be by statements made without knowledge of their falsity.* — Statements need not be intentionally false in order to amount to a fraudulent representation.[7] A false

held to be a defense, where it was made in one state with reference to the laws of another state See, also, Accidental Insurance Co v Davis, 15 L T, 182 (1866), where it was represented that further calls were not contemplated

[1] N E R R Co v Rodriques, 10 Rich. (S C), 278 (1857).

[2] Clem v Newcastle & Danville R R Co., 9 Ind, 488 (1857), New Albany, etc, R R. v Fields, 10 id, 187 (1858) For representation as to the route, see Ellison v Mobile, etc, R R Co, 36 Miss, 572 (1858), Wight v. Shelby R R Co, 16 B Mon, 4 (1855).

[3] "No misstatement or concealment of any material facts or circumstances ought to be permitted . . The suppression of a fact will often amount to a misrepresentation" Directors, etc, of Central R'y v Kisch, L R, 2 H L App. Cas, 99 (1867) In Oakes v Turquand, L. R., 2 H L Cas 325 (1867), the

court say the prospectus is objectionable, "not that it does not state the truth as far as it goes, but that it conceals most material facts with which the public ought to have been made acquainted, the very concealment of which gives to the truth which is told the character of falsehood "

[4] New Brunswick & Con R'y Co v Muggeridge, 1 Dr & Sm, 363, 381 (1860)

[5] Directors, etc, of Central R'y Co v. Kisch, *supra* In Gover's Case, L R, 1 Ch D, 182 (1875), under different circumstances, the contrary was held

[6] Heymann v. European Central Ry Co L R, 7 Eq Cas, 154 (1868) Statement need not be made that stock had been given to the directors and promoters in payment for services Pulsford v Richards, 17 Beav, 87 (1853) Not as to the amount of stock already subscribed Vane v Cobbald 1 Ex, 798 (1848)

[7] Corporate agents making represen-

statement, made in good faith but in ignorance, is, in a legal point of view, the same as an assertion which the party knew to be untrue[1] Thus, a prospectus issued by the directors, representing the corporate property as containing valuable mines, all of which was in good faith, but false, is the same as though the statements were made with knowledge of their falsity. Where, however, the statement in good faith was that the corporation had a government contract, which, upon litigation, was found to be untrue, the representation was held not to be fraudulent[2]

§ 149 *Misrepresentations that are insufficient.*— It is not every misrepresentation that enables a subscriber to set up that he was induced to subscribe by fraud[3] Thus, an honest mistake of judg-

tations in order to obtain subscriptions, are bound to know the truth or falsity of such statements Reese River Co *v.* Smith, L R, 4 H L, 64 (1869), affirming L. R., 2 Eq, 264, Glamorganshire Iron, etc, Co *v* Irvine, 4 F & F, 947 (1866), applying the same rule at law The English case of Kennedy *v* Panama, N Z & A R M Co, L. R. 2 Q B, 580 (1867), holds, however, that "where there has been an innocent misrepresentation or misapprehension, it does not authorize a rescission, unless it is such as to show that there is a complete difference in substance between what was supposed to be and what was taken, so as to constitute a failure of consideration," and that to hold otherwise would be to make a warranty out of the representation In the recent case of Edgington *v* Fitzmaurice, L R, 29 Ch D, 459 (1885), the court say that a statement of fact, which the person making does not know the truth of, is, "in the eye of the law, a fraudulent statement as much as if the parties making it had known it to be false" In this country the cases seem to favor a different rule The party making the representations must be proven ' to have had a fraudulent purpose in contemplation, or at least to have known that the statements were untrue" Nugent *v* Cincinnati, Harrison & Indianapolis S L. R. R. Co, 2 Disney, 302 (1858), Selma, M & M R R Co. *v* Anderson, 51 Miss, 829 (1876), Cunningham *v.* Edgefield & Ky. R. R

Co, 2 Head, 23 (1858). See, also, Chitty on Contracts, 682, and Montgomery etc, R'y Co *v* Matthews, 77 Ala, 357 (1884) The vigorous case of Henderson *v* Railroad Co, 17 Tex, 560 (1856), however, effectively presents the opposite view, and see § 356, *infra* See, also, 1 Story. Eq Juris, § 193, Story on Agency, §§ 127, 135, 137, 452

[1] Reese River Co *v.* Smith, L R, 4 H. L, 64 (1869)

[2] Kennedy *v* Panama, N Z. & O. R M Co., L R, 2 Q. B., 580 (1867).

[3] Mere matters of opinion as to whether the enterprise can be completed, or when it will be completed, or the prospects of profits, cannot be misrepresentations. The subscriber is bound to know that these are all matters of mere conjecture Brownlee *v* O, Ind & Ill. R R Co, 18 Ind, 68 (1862), Pickering *v* Templeton, 2 Mo App, 424 (1876), Hughes *v* Antietam Mfg Co, 34 Md, 316 (1870), Hardy *v* Merriweather, 14 Ind, 203 (1860); Andrews *v* O & Miss R. R. Co., 14 Ind, 169 (1860), Bish *v* Bradford, 17 Ind, 490 (1861), Walker *v* Mobile R. R. Co, 34 Miss, 245 (1857), Coil *v.* Pittsburgh College, 40 Pa. St, 439 (1861) Statements as to when the road would be completed are not such representations as will avoid a subscription for stock Jefferson *v.* Hewitt, 30 Pac. Rep., 772 (Cal, 1892) The fact that statements as to the affairs of the company are not filed as required by statute does not

ment, on the part of the directors, as to the collectibility of certain debts, whereby a company represented to be solvent turns out to be insolvent, is not a fraudulent representation So, also, of a representation as to the value of a patent-right, which, it was stated, would be tested further. On the other hand, a statement made with the intent to defraud the subscriber, but without that effect is immaterial, mere intent without damage is insufficient [1] A misstatement as to the contents of the subscription contract which the subscriber signs is immaterial, where he can read but does not [2] And where false representations are made, but before the subscription is completed the representations are made good by intervening events, the subscribers cannot complain [3] Frauds of the directors which are not the subject of a representation are not to be remedied by the principle of law governing the subject of false representation [4]

§ 150 *Subscriber is not bound to investigate the truth of representations* — If a subscriber has used reasonable caution and judgment in accepting the statements of corporate agents, it is no answer to his claim that he was induced to subscribe by fraudulent representations, to say that by proper inquiry he might have learned the truth, or by more vigilance he might have discovered the de-

---

amount to fraud in the sale of stock, nor do representations that the stock will pay twenty per cent dividends amount to fraud The question as to validity of stock, having once been litigated, cannot be again raised in an action for deceit in the sale of the stock The mere act of conspiracy is not sufficient to sustain the action unless damage is shown Robinson *v* Parks *et al*, 24 Atl Rep, 411 (Md, 1892) Representations that the stock would be a good investment and pay dividends, etc, constitute no defense Weston *v* Columbus Southern R'y Co, 15 S E Rep, 773 (Ga, 1892) In the cases, however, of Gerhard *v* Bates, 17 Jur 1097 (1853), and Taylor *v* Ashton, 11 M & W 401 (1843), it was held that a false guaranty of the promoters that a certain dividend would result from the enterprise constituted a false representation *In re* Nat'l, etc., Fuel Co, *Ex parte* North, 4 Drew, 529 (1859), held that one sued as contributory cannot plead fraudulent misrepresentation on part of company

because it was arranged between directors and shareholders that certain shares (of which these were a part) should have a preference. A statement as to the purpose for which the proceeds of bonds will be used by the company is immaterial The bondholder cannot rescind Banque, etc, *v* Brown, 34 Fed Rep, 145, 198 (1888) Stock may be issued before payment by machinery is made An action by another stockholder for cancellation of the stock on the ground of fraud fails unless there is clear proof that the person agreed that the machinery would succeed Pendleton Mfg Co *v* Mahanna, 18 Pac. Rep, 563 (Oreg 1888) See 21 N E. Rep., 12 (Ill, 1889)

[1] Killer *v* Johnson, 11 Ind, 337 (1858), Cunningham *v* Edgefield & Ky. R. R. Co, 2 Head, 23 (1858)

[2] Thornburgh *v* Newcastle & Danville R. R. Co, 14 Ind, 499 (1860)

[3] Ship *v* Cresskill, L R, 10 Eq Cas 73 (1870)

[4] Hornaday *v* Ind & Ill Central R R

ception [1]   Where the representations are by a prospectus, he is not obliged to examine documents referred to, even though such examination would have shown the falsity of the representations.[2] It is not incumbent upon him to institute inquiries, and to suspect fraud when all seems fair   But where the means of information are open equally to both parties, the subscriber has no right to rely upon the representations of the corporate agent, unless the latter dissuades the subscriber from investigation [3]   So, also, where the subscriber reads several documents, he cannot rely on representations in one which are corrected and limited by statements in the others, even though he claims to have overlooked such corrections [4]

§ 151. *Subscriptions induced by fraudulent representations are not void, but only voidable* — The principle of law that fraud vitiates all contracts applies to a contract of subscription; but this principle means, not that the contract is void *per se* from the formation of the contract, but that the contract is voidable at the option or election of the person defrauded [5]   Until such election is exercised, the contract is enforceable by both or either of the parties   Hence a subscription to stock, obtained by fraudulent representations, is not void from the time when it was made, nor is it void until it is ratified and confirmed by the defrauded subscriber, but it is valid until it is expressly rescinded and repudiated by the subscriber [6]   This principle is important in determining the method

9 Ind, 263 (1857), Heymann v European Central R'y Co, L R, 7 Eq Cas., 154 (1868)

[1] New Brunswick & Can R'y Co. v Muggeridge, 1 Di & Sm, 363 (1860), Upton v Englehart, 3 Dill., 496 (1874), Directors, etc, of Central R'y v Kisch, L R, 2 H. L. App. Cas, 99 (1870), *Ex parte* West. 56 L T Rep, 622 (1887) *Cf* Hallows v Fernie, L R, 3 Ch App, 467 (1868)   The subscriber is not bound to investigate the truth of statements which the other party with full knowledge of the facts makes   McClellan v Scott, 24 Wis, 81 (1869)   False statements as to who are the other subscribers are no defense where the subscriber has opportunity to ascertain.   Haskell v Worthington, 7 S W Rep. 481 (Mo, 1888).

[2] Kisch v Central R'y, 34 L J (Ch), 545 (1865), S C *supra*   In New York the general principle of law governing cases of misrepresentation is clearly

stated to be that "every contracting person has an absolute right to rely on the express statement of an existing fact, the truth of which is known to the opposite party, and unknown to him, as a basis of a mutual engagement; and he is under no obligation to investigate and verify statements, to the truth of which the other party to the contract, with full means of knowledge, has deliberately pledged his faith"   Mead v. Bunn, 32 N Y., 274 (1865).

[3] Jennings v Braughton, 22 L J. (Ch), 583 (1853), Walker v Mobile & O R R. Co, 34 Miss., 245 (1857)

[4] Scholey v Central R'y Co, L R, 9 Eq Cas, 766, n. (1870).

[5] Oakes v Turquand, L R, 2 H L. App Cas, 325 (1867), Upton v Englehart. 3 Dill, 496 (1874), Reese River Min Co v Smith, L R, 4 H L, 64 (1869)

[6] Tennant v City of Glasgow Bank, L R, 4 App Cas., 615 (1879).

of rescission, and particularly the time within which a rescission must be made

§ 152 *Remedies of a subscriber induced to subscribe by fraudulent representations* — There are, in general, five different remedies which are open to a subscriber induced to subscribe by fraud He may, upon discovering the fraud, rescind the subscription by notification to the corporate authorities, without taking legal proceedings; or he may wait until sued upon the subscription, and then set up the fraud as a defense to the action at law ; or he may file a bill in equity to restrain such suits at law, and to set aside the subscription contract, and also, if he wishes, to recover back payments already made on the subscription, or he may bring an action at law against the parties fraudulently inducing the subscription, and recover damages for the deceit, or he may sue for money had and received.

§ 153. *Rescission without legal proceedings.*— It is the duty and the right of directors, without waiting for a bill in equity or other legal proceedings, to revoke a subscription contract, and remove from the stockholders' list the name of a subscriber who reasonably proves that he was induced to subscribe by fraudulent representations chargeable to the corporation, and who requests a rescission of the subscription [1] The directors are not bound to make a hopeless defense. It is an ordinary business act within the powers of the directors, and their discretion is not to be controlled unless unreasonably exercised. Where, however, upon such a demand being made by the subscriber, the directors refuse to dissolve the subscription contract, the subscriber must resort to a bill in equity to have the contract set aside for fraud [2] A mere notification to the corporation is insufficient.

§ 154 *False representation as a defense to an action at law for calls* — The most common remedy of a subscriber induced by fraud to subscribe is to wait until the corporation brings suit to collect the subscriptions, and then to set up the fraud as a defense. Nearly all of the cases in this country are cases where this remedy has been adopted.[3] It is subject, however, to the danger that the cor-

---

[1] Wright's Case, L. R., 2 Eq , 331 , S C., L R., 7 Ch , 55 (1871), Blake's Case, 34 Beav , 639 (1865), Reese River Co. v Smith, L R., 4 H L., 64 (1869), affirming L R., 2 Eq , 264 , Ætna Ins Co v Shields, L R , 7 Eq , 264 , Bath s Case, 8 Ch Div , 334 (1878) See, also, Fox's Case, L R , 5 Eq , 118 (1868) *Contra*, Steel's Case, 49 L J (Ch), 176 (1879)

[2] Mere repudiation, not followed by

anything more, is insufficient. *Re* Scottish Petroleum Co , L R., 23 Ch Div , 413 (1882), where the directors refused to allow the rescission See, also, Hare's Case L R., 4 Ch , 503 (1869).

[3] " It is a good answer at common law to an action for calls that the defendant was induced to become the holder of the shares by the fraud of the plaintiffs " Bwlch-y-plwm Lead M Co v

poration may become insolvent, and thereby bar the defense.   The decided tendency of the law to preserve the rights of third persons will probably and properly tend to defeat this defense in all cases where the subscriber has not filed a bill in equity promptly upon discovering the fraud, but has waited to be sued by the corporation. The intervening rights of stockholders and corporate creditors call for prompt action on the part of a subscriber who seeks to avoid his liability on the ground of fraud

§ 155. *Remedy by bill in equity* — This is the fairest, safest and most complete remedy that the subscriber has   It is a decisive notice to the corporation and all third parties not to rely upon the subscription in question   It avoids the risk of future corporate insolvency   It enables the subscriber to set aside the contract, to enjoin actions at law for calls, and to recover back payments made before discovery of the fraud [1]   It is the customary, and it seems favorite, remedy in England, and has been clearly upheld in this country.[2]

§ 156   The complainant in a bill in equity to set aside a subscription obtained by fraud cannot sue in behalf of himself and others

Baynes, 36 L. J (Ex), 183 (1867) Deposit Life A. Co v Ayscough, 6 E. & B, 761 (1856), Sandford v Handy, 23 Wend, 260 (1840) *Cf.* 21 N W Rep., 304 (Cal , 1889).

[1] But the injunction to restrain the action at law will not be granted if the subscriber delays until the case is about to be tried   Thorpe v Hughes, 3 Myl & Cr , 742 (1838)   And where the stock has been fully paid and no injury can come from the delay, equity will not sustain the subscriber's bill to compel repayment, but will send him to a court of law, where a jury may pass upon the question of fraud   Askew's Case. L. R., 9 Ch , 664 (1874)   Equity, however, unquestionably has concurrent jurisdiction if it cares to exercise it.   Hill v Lane, L R., 11 Eq , 215 (1870), criticising Ogilvie v Currie, 37 L J , 541 (1867)   See, also, § 356. *infra*   And will enjoin the collection of the subscription pending the suit.   Walsh v Seager, 1886 (N Y Sup Ct)   And the equitable action will not be enjoined merely because the corporation subsequently becomes insolvent and a receiver is appointed   Id

[2] Where a person is induced to subscribe for stock on the fraudulent representations of the president that the company is in a prosperous condition, the person may file a bill in equity to recover back the money; and equity has jurisdiction on the grounds of discovery, account fraud, misrepresentation and concealment   Both the company and the president individually were made defendants and held liable.   Tyler v Savage 143 U S, 79 (1892).   A person induced by fraud to subscribe for stock may bring an equitable action to procure a rescission of the contract, a cancellation of her subscription, and the removal of the name from the stock books.   The statute of limitations does not begin to run until the fraud is discovered   Bosley v National, etc, Co, 123 N Y, 550 (1890); S C., 6 N Y Supp, 4, Banque, etc. v Brown, 34 Fed Rep, 115, 198 (1888), Waldo v Chicago, St. Paul, etc, R R. Co, 14 Wis., 575 (1861), Henderson v. Railroad Co, 17 Tex, 560 (1856), Rawlins v Wickham, 3 De G & J , 304 (1858)   And see the various English cases in this chapter

who may wish to come in   But several subscribers, defrauded in the same way, may join in the bill as co-complainants[1] The corporation is to be a defendant, and if merely a cancellation of the subscription and an injunction against suits at law are sought, the corporation, it seems, may be the sole defendant.[2] A court of equity in these actions will give complete relief by decreeing that the directors guilty of the fraud shall refund to the subscriber payments made by him before discovering the fraud[3] This relief dispenses with an action at law for damages for deceit, and when sought for in the bill in equity the guilty directors must be made parties. The bill is not multifarious by reason of its blending prayers for these various kinds of relief.[4]

§ 157. *Remedy by an action at law for deceit.*— An action at law for damages for deceit lies at the instance of a subscriber for stock, fraudulently induced to subscribe, against the persons guilty of the fraud.[5] The fraudulent representation, however, which must be

---

[1] Several subscribers who have been induced by the same misrepresentations contained in a prospectus to subscribe for stock may join in a suit in equity for the benefit of themselves and others similarly deceived to set aside their subscriptions. Bosher v Richmond, etc, Co, 16 S E Rep, 360 (Va., 1892) Several stockholders may join in filing a bill to rescind a subscription for stock on the ground that they were induced to subscribe by false representations that the corporation had a certain amount of paid-up capital, was out of debt and doing a profitable business, and that the subscribers would be employed The corporation may be enjoined from transferring its assets in the meantime and may be compelled to pay back the money paid by complainants. Sherman v American Stove Co, 48 N W. Rep., 537 (Mich, 1891) A plaintiff may upon the trial be compelled to elect whether he sues to hold the promoters liable for fraud or whether he sues in behalf of all stockholders and for the benefit of the corporation Brewster v. Hatch, 122 N Y, 349 (1890).

[2] Smith v Reese River, etc, Co., L. R., 4 H L, 64 (1869), Hallows v Fernie, L R, 3 Ch App, 467 (1868) A transferee of the shares cannot bring the suit The fraud is personal to the original subscriber. Duranty's Case, 26 Beav, 268 (1858)

[3] Vreland v N J Stone Co, 29 N J Eq R, 188 (1878), Reese River Silver Min Co v Smith, L. R., 4 H L 64 (1869). Where subscribers bring suit to set aside subscriptions and for repayment thereof, for fraud, and join the directors as co-defendants, the directors are not nominal parties Seddon v Virginia, etc, Co, 36 Fed Rep, 6 (1888) If the suit is in equity for damages intent must be shown Hubbard v Weare, 44 N W Rep, 914 (Iowa, 1890)

[4] Nor is it multifarious because it joins such a suit with one by the corporation to compel the directors to account to the corporation for the same fraud Ashmead v Colby, 26 Conn, 287 (1857)

[5] Clarke v Dickson, 6 C B (N S) 453 (1859), Miller v Barber, 66 N. Y. 558 (1876), Paddock v Fletcher, 42 Vt, 389 (1869) In England the liability of the directors herein is enforced generally in connection with a suit in equity and as a part of the equitable decree This is under a statute Western Bank of Scotland v Addie, L R, 1 Sc App Cas. 145 A false affirmation, made by the defendant with intent to defraud

proved to sustain this action must be a more intentional fraud than the one which suffices to rescind the contract. The subscriber must prove that a material false representation was made by the defendant, that the defendant recklessly made it or knew the representation to be false; that the plaintiff subscribed by reason, partially at least, of that representation, and that he was thereby injured [1]

the plaintiff, whereby the plaintiff receives damage, is the ground of an action upon the case in the nature of deceit. In such an action it is not necessary that the defendant should be benefited by the deceit, or that he should collude with the person thus benefited 1 Smith's Leading Cases (8th Eng ed), 66-94, as applicable to misrepresentations inducing subscriptions Brewster v Hatch 10 Abb N C, 400 (1881), aff'd 122 N Y, 349 (1890), sustains an action by subscribers for stock, for damages, for false representations by promoters as to the real cost of property purchased by the latter for the corporation See, a'so, ch XXXIX. There is no remedy at law or in equity against the estate of a deceased director herein except for property received by him Peek v Gurney, 6 H of L, 377 (1873) Subscribers to debentures may recover back the difference between the actual value of the debentures and the price paid Arnison v Smith, 59 L T Rep, 627 (1888).

[1] In the important case Derry v Peek, 61 L. T. Rep, 265 (1889), the house of lords decided that in order to sustain an action of deceit there must be proof of fraud, and nothing short of that will suffice Fraud is proved when it is shown that a false statement has been made (1) knowingly, (2) without belief in its truth, (3) recklessly But if a man make a false statement honestly believing it to be true, it is not sufficient to support an action of deceit to show that he had no reasonable grounds for his belief The directors of a tramway company issued a prospectus in which they stated that they were authorized to use steam power, and that by this

means a great saving in working would be effected. At the time of making this statement they had not in fact obtained authority to use steam power, but they honestly believed that they would obtain it as a matter of course. *Held* (reversing the judgment of the court below), that they were not liable in an action of deceit brought by a shareholder who had been induced to apply for shares by the statement in the prospectus. In an action for deceit by a misrepresentation in a prospectus as to the net profit on the capital employed, the action being against one who was a promoter, and also one of the vendors, and whose name appeared in the prospectus, and who became a director, the plaintiff must prove (1) that the defendant's statement was untrue; (2) that it was dishonest, (3) that he believed it to be untrue Glasier t Rolls, 62 L T Rep., 132 (1889), reversing 60 id , 591, and following the house of lords in Derry v Peek, 61 id , 265 See, also, Ship v. Cresskill, L R , 10 Eq Cas , 73 (1870) To sustain the action for deceit the plaintiff must show "that the defendants intended that people should act on the statements, that the statements are untrue in fact, and that the defendants knew them to be untrue, or made them under such circumstances that the court must conclude that they were careless whether they were true or not," also that the statement were relied upon, acted on, and damage sustained Edgington v Fitzmaurice, L R, 29 Ch D, 459 (1885) When the prospectus stated that the company were authorized to use steam for propelling street cars, when in fact it could only use horses, a subscriber relying thereon may hold the

The gist of the action is fraudulent intent[1] It cannot be maintained against the corporation, because the corporation, though liable to refund fraudulently acquired property, is not capable of a fraudulent intent.[2]

§ 158 The directors are not liable to an action for deceit by reason of the frauds of their agents,[3] nor is an innocent director liable

directors who issued the prospectus liable for deceit, upon proof that they knew the statement was false or were reckless in making it. Peek v Derry, 59 L. T Rep., 78 (1888) Must show reliance on the misrepresentations Priest ι. White, 1 S. W Rep, 361 (Mo, 1886).

[1] *Scienter* is fixed on the directors, making them liable in damages upon proof of incorrect representations, known to them to be incorrect, knowingly stated by them, and acted on by the plaintiff subscriber. Henderson v Lacon, L R., 5 Eq Cas., 249 (1867), Cargill v Bower, L. R., 10 Ch D, 502 (1878) See, also, Bale v. Cleland, 4 F & F., 113 (1864)· and see p. 79, n 3, *supra* Must allege knowledge and intent to deceive on their part "Falsely and fraudulently represented" does not properly plead the *scienter* Mahey v. Adams, 3 Bosw., 346 (1858) In case the representations are not fraudulent as against the corporation, they are not sufficient to entitle the subscriber to recover from the directors Heymann v European Central R'y Co, L R., 7 Eq Cas., 154 (1868). A subscriber for stock may hold the president liable for false representations made by the latter to other persons with an intent that the plaintiff be induced to act upon them The representations of the president that a dividend had been earned bind him, and are false where he paid close attention to its affairs, and where such dividend was made on an improper and untrue statement of assets and liabilities. It must be proven that the defendant president knew that the representations were false, but this may be proven by inference. A stockholder who is induced to make still further subscriptions

by reason of misrepresentations of an officer may hold him liable Hubbard v Weare. 44 N W Rep, 914 (Iowa, 1890) The directors are personally liable in an action for deceit where a prospectus falsely states that guarantied dividends were secured by a deposit of certain securities, and a person subscribes for stock relying upon such statements Knox v Hayman, 67 L. T. Rep, 137 (1892)

[2] Mixer's Case, 4 De G. & J, 575, Duranty's Case, 26 Beav., 268 (1858); Western Bank of Scotland v Addie, L. R., 1 Sc App Cas 145, Abrath v Northeastern R'y Co, 55 L. T. R. (N S), 63 (1886), Houldsworth v City of Glasgow Bank, L. R., 5 App Cas, 317, Benjamin on Sales (4th Am. ed), § 467σ *Contra*, Peebles v Patapsco Guano Co, 77 N C 233 (1877), Barwick v English Joint stock Bank. L R., 2 Ex, 259 (1867), Mackay v Com Bank of New Brunswick, L R, 5 P C, 394, not stock cases, but distinctly holding that a corporation is liable to an action for damages for deceit Where, however, the old corporation organizes a new corporation, and has the latter build a competing road on a new line, a stockholder of the old, who contributed lands, etc, may have an action for damages against it Chapman v Railroad Co, 6 Ohio St, 119 (1856) See, also, article in 1 R'y & Corp L. J, 122, Lubricating Oil Co. v Standard Oil Co, 42 Hun, 153 (1886); also, § 45

[3] Weir ι Burnett, 26 Week Rep, 147 (1877), Weir v Bell, L R, 3 Ex Div, 238 (1878), Eaglesfield v Marquis of Londonderry (H L), 26 W R., 540 (1878) See, also, Cargill v. Bower, L. R., 10 Ch D, 502 (1878), Watson ι. Earl Charle-

for the fraudulent representations of his co-directors — not even though the evidences of their fraud were entered on the corporate books, there being no ground for suspicion on his part [1]

A director cannot be held liable for false representations contained in the articles of association, which were made before he became a director.[2] But a director who stands by and allows a co-director to make the false representations is equally chargeable with the injury done thereby [3] The false representations supporting an action for deceit may have been by corporate reports or prospectuses, or by personal statements

§ 159. *Remedy by action for money had and received* — Where a subscriber pays his subscription in part or wholly, and afterwards discovers that the representations whereby he was induced to subscribe were fraudulent, he may bring an action at law for money had and received, and recover back from the corporation the money so received [4] If the money has not yet passed into the hands of the corporation he may recover it from the person who has it If, however, he would be barred from suing in a court of equity by reason of his laches or corporate insolvency, he would fail equally in this remedy at law [5]

§ 160. *Ratification as a bar to the subscriber's remedies.*— A subscription contract obtained by fraudulent representations may cease to be voidable and may become absolutely binding by acts of ratification. Any act of the subscriber, inconsistent with an intention to disaffirm the contract, will constitute a ratification of the subscription and a waiver of the right to avoid it by reason of fraud, provided the subscriber knew of the fraud at the time of such ratifying act. Thus, where the subscriber, after knowledge of the fraud, receives dividends, sells part of the stock,[6] instructs

mont, 12 Q B., 856 (1848): Arthur *v.* Griswold, 55 N Y, 400 (1874)

[1] *Re* Denham & Co., L R., 25 Ch. Div, 752 (1883).

[2] Mahey *v.* Adams, 3 Bosw , 346 (1858).

[3] Vreeland *v* N J Stone Co., 29 N. J. Eq , 188 (1878).

[4] Grangers' Ins Co. *v.* Turner, 61 Ga , 561 (1878); Hamilton *v* Grangers' L & H. Ins Co., 67 Ga , 145 (1881). But the subscriber cannot retain the stock and also sue Houldsworth *v.* City of Glasgow Bank L R., 5 App Cas , 317 (1880). See Jarrett *v* Kennedy, 6 C. B., 319 (1848). *Assumpsit* for money had and received, brought against the directors to compel them to repay money paid on

a subscription obtained by fraud, was sustained, without involving the question of a fraudulent intent. See Bruce *v* Nickerson, 5 N E. Rep., 647 (Mass, 1886). The action for money had and received cannot be brought against other stockholders for the fraud of a promoter. Perry *v.* Hale, 143 Mass., 540 (1887).

[5] Scholey *v.* Central R'y Co., L R., 9 Eq , 266, n (1870) Ayres' Case, 25 Beav , 513 (1858), Mixer s Case, 4 De G. & J., 575.

[6] Ayres' Case, 25 Beav , 513 (1858). But a sale of a part of the stock before the subscriber discovers the fraud is no bar to a rescission as to the rest. *Ex*

his broker to sell,[1] participates in the meetings,[2] pays calls,[3] or, in general, accepts any corporate benefit or continues to act as a stockholder,[4] he will be held to have waived all objections to the fraud, and to have ratified the subscription contract   But mere attendance at a stockholders' meeting,[5] or demanding a dividend,[6] or voting his shares by proxy,[7] is insufficient

§ 161   *Laches as a bar to the subscriber's remedies* — Where a subscriber for stock, who was induced to subscribe by fraud, neglects for an unreasonable time after the discovery of the fraud to have his subscription canceled, and, in the meantime, the interests of third persons become involved, and would be injured by the cancellation of such subscription, the subscriber's laches is a bar to relief, and a court of equity will refuse to set aside the subscription [8] Equity does not allow the subscriber to say. " I will abide by the company if successful, and I will leave the company if it fails "[9] Immediately upon receiving information of the fraud, it is his duty to decide whether he will rescind the contract or waive the fraud [10] Nevertheless delay is not fatal, unless circumstances and third parties' rights have so changed or been acquired that the re-

parte West, 56 L T Rep , 622 (1887)   A subscriber to stock cannot rescind for fraud, when he has had the stock transferred to his infant children, unless their right thereto is also tendered back Francis *v* New York, etc , R. R., 108 N Y , 93 (1888)

[1] *Ex parte* Briggs, L R, 1 Eq , 483 (1866).

[2] Harrison *v* Heathorn, 6 Man & G , 84 (1843), Chaffin *v* Cummings 36 Me., 76 (1853). A subscriber who acts as director and manager, and purchases lots from the company, cannot rescind his subscription on the ground that certain newspaper articles prepared by himself and others contain misrepresentations Raymond *v* San Gabriel, 53 Fed Rep., 883 (1893).

[3] Scholey *v* Central R'y Co. L. R., 9 Eq , 266, n (1870)

[4] Ogilvie *v* Knox Ins. Co , 22 How, 380 (1859) , Chubb *v* Upton, 95 U S , 665 (1877) , Litchfield Bank *v*. Church. 29 Conn , 137 (1860) Kishacoquillas Centre Co *v* McCanahy. 16 S. & R., 140 (1827). Waiver of one misrepresentation is not a waiver of others. *Ex parte* Hale, 55 L T Rep., 670 (1886).

[5] Stewart's Case, L R , 1 Ch App , 574 (1866), Woutner *v* Sharp, 4 C B , 404 (1847), *Re* Metropolitan, etc , Ass'n, 64 L T Rep , 561 (1891)

[6] Philadelphia R. R. Co. *v* Cowell, 28 Pa. St , 329 (1857)

[7] McCully *v* Pittsburgh, etc., R. R. Co , 32 Pa St , 25 (1858), Greenville, etc , R R Co *v* Coleman, 5 Rich L., 118 (1851)

[8] City Bank of Macon *v* Bartlett, 71 Ga , 797 (1883)   As a bar in an action at law Schwanck *v* Morris, 7 Rob (N Y), 658 (1868)   But it is no bar that other subscribers may have been induced to subscribe by reason of this subscription Western Bank of Scotland *v* Addie, L R , 1 Scotch App Cas . 145   *Cf* Parbury's Case 3 DeG & Sm . 43 (1849)

[9] *Re* London & Staffordshire Fire Ins Co , L R , 24 Ch Div , 149 (1883), Ashley's Case. L R , 9 Eq Cas. 263 (1870)

[10] Heymann *v* European Central R'y Co , L R , 7 Eq Cas. 154 (1868), Peek *v* Gurney, L R , 6 H L , 377 (1873). The last case overrules Bagshaw *v* Seymour, 18 C B , 903 (1856), and Bedford *v*. Bagshaw, 4 H & N , 538 (1859).

scission would be inequitable. Consequently, the decision of each case depends largely on the facts of the case Thus it has been held that a delay of one,[1] two,[2] three,[3] four[4] or six months,[5] or of two[6] or six ̄ years, was fatal under the circumstances of the case, while, under different facts, a delay of two months,[8] or even seven years,[9] was held not to be a bar. In the remedies by actions at law the statute of limitations governs, and, by analogy, courts of equity are inclined to follow the same period, unless there be an equitable reason to the contrary.

§ 162 The date from which laches begins to run is the time when the subscriber is first chargeable with notice that a fraud has been perpetrated upon him   Mere suspicions or random statements heard in public or in stockholders' meetings do not necessarily constitute notice [10] But after a subscriber's suspicions are reasonably aroused, it is his duty to investigate at once.[11] The corporation has the burden of proof in asserting that the subscriber had notice and was guilty of laches [12]

§ 163. *Corporate insolvency as a bar to the subscriber's remedies.* In England the principle has become well established that, after the statutory proceedings for winding up a corporation by reason of corporate insolvency have been commenced, a subscriber cannot rescind his subscription on account of fraud.[13] He is too late. It

---

[1] Taite s Case, L. R., 3 Eq Cas., 795 (1867), the delay evidently being to see which course would be most profitable. Peel's Case, L. R., 2 Ch App. 674 (1867). Kincaid's Case, L R. 2 Ch, 412 (1867)

[2] Wilkinson's Case, L. R, 2 Ch App., 536 (1867)

[3] Heymann v European Central R'y Co L. R, 7 Eq Cas, 154 (1869).

[4] Ex parte Lawrence. 36 L J (Ch), 490 (1867).

[5] Whitehouse's Case, L. R., 3 Eq Cas. 790 (1867)

[6] Farrar v Walker, 3 Dill, 506, n (1874), Ashley's Case, L R. 9 Eq. Cas., 263 (1870) Three years State v. Jefferson Turnpike Co, 3 Humph. (Tenn.), 305 (1842)

[7] Denton v Macneil, L. R., 2 Eq. 352 (1866) Four years' delay in complaining of the fraud inducing the purchase, after knowledge thereof, is fatal. Cedar, etc, Ins Co v Butler, 48 N. W. Rep. 1026 (Iowa, 1891). Where one stock-

holder who has been fraudulently induced to subscribe for stock awaits the result of an action by another stockholder brought to rescind his subscription on the same ground, the delay being nearly three years, and then commences suit for the same purpose only after a meeting has been called for a winding up, he is guilty of laches, and his remedy is barred Re Snyder, etc, Co, 63 L. T. Rep., 210 (1893).

[8] Directors, etc, of Central R'y v. Kisch, L. R, 2 H L App. Cas., 99 (1870)

[9] McClellan v Scott, 24 Wis., 81 (1869)

[10] Directors, etc, of Central R'y Co. v. Kisch, L. R., 2 H L App. Cas., 99 (1870).

[11] Ogilvie v Currie, 37 L. J (Ch.), 541 (1867), Ashley's Case, L. R, 9 Eq Cas, 263 (1870), Bosley v National, etc., Co., 123 N Y, 550 (1890).

[12] Re London & S F. Ins Co., L. R., 24 Ch Div, 149 (1883).

[13] Wright's Case, L. R, 12 Eq. Cas,

matters not that he did not discover the fraud until after the winding up has commenced The rights of corporate creditors prevail, then, over the equities of the subscriber[1] If, however, he instituted proceedings to rescind the contract before the winding up was commenced, he may be released, although the proceedings are not completed until after such winding up[2] So, also, where there are several similar cases, and by agreement with the corporate solicitors all the cases are to follow a test case, this agreement prevails, although a winding up is commenced before the test case is fully decided[3] The highest court in England in one case goes further, and intimates that corporate insolvency is a bar to rescission of a subscription for fraud, even though a winding up has not been commenced[4]

§ 164. In this country the effect of corporate insolvency upon the right of a subscriber to rescind his contract for fraud has not been passed upon so often as in England The decisions, however, clearly hold that corporate insolvency is a bar to such rescission[5]

331, Kent v Freehold, L. & B. M. Co, L R, 3 Ch App., 493 (1868), Henderson v Royal British Bank, 7 El & Bl, 356 (1857), Powis v Harding, 1 C B (N S), 533 (1857), Daniell v Off Managers of Bank, 1 H & N, 681 (1857), Oakes v Turquand, L. R., 2 H L App Cas, 325 (1867), Mixer's Case, 4 De G & J, 575, Clarke v Dickson 27 L J (Q B), 223 (1858) So, also, where there is a voluntary winding up by reason of corporate insolvency Stone v City & County Bank, L R, 3 C. P Div, 282 (1877), Collins v Same, id But not if the proceedings for rescission were commenced in good faith and in ignorance of the winding-up proceedings Hall v Old T L Min Co, L. R., 3 Ch D, 749 (1876).

[1] Turner v Grangers' L. & H Ins Co, 65 Ga, 649 (1880)

[2] Reese River Co v Smith, L R, 4 H L, 64 (1869), affirming S C., L. R, 2 Ch, 604, L R, 2 Eq, 264, reversing S. C, H L, 36 L J (Ch), 385 A subscriber is liable on a winding up although he had repudiated the subscription long before on the ground of fraud and understood that his name had been dropped Re Lennox etc, Co, 62 L T Rep, 791 (1890) If the party institutes legal proceedings to cancel his subscription on the ground of fraud prior to the commencement of the winding-up proceedings the insolvency of the company is no bar Cocksedge v Metropolitan, etc, Ass'n 64 L T Rep, 826 (1891)

[3] Pawle's Case, L R, 4 Ch, 497, McMill's Case, L R, 10 Eq, 503 (1870) But mere attendance at the meeting where such stipulation is made is insufficient The subscriber must plainly indicate an intention to abide by the test case Ashley's Case, L R, 9 Eq Cas, 263 (1870)

[4] Tennent v City of Glasgow Bank, L R 4 App Cas, 615 See, also, Burgess Case, L R 15 Ch D, 507 But the fact that the company is unable to meet its engagements at the time of rescission is no bar if the subscriber is ignorant thereof Ex parte Carhug, 56 L T Rep 115 (1887)

[5] Ruggles v Brock 6 Hun, 164 (1875) Saffold v Barnes, 39 Miss, 399 (1860) After the corporation becomes insolvent a subscriber cannot repudiate for fraud Duffield v Barnum, etc., Works, 31 N W Rep, 310 (Mich, 1887) In Chubb v Upton, 95 U S, 665, 667 (1877), the court say it has often been held that the defense of false and

In the bankruptcy courts also, under the late bankruptcy law, such a rule was upheld [1]

§ 165. *Essential allegations in legal proceedings to remedy a fraud inducing subscription.*— The essential allegations, especially in a suit in equity, necessarily vary according to the peculiar facts of each case Yet there are certain elements common to all the cases. It is necessary to allege that a material misrepresentation of a question of fact was made, setting out fully the fact misrepresented, that the person making the misrepresentation thereby bound the corporation, and that, upon discovery of the fraud, he immediately disaffirmed the contract [2] That the representation was false cannot be proved by statements made by the directors in stockholders' meetings.[3] The burden of proving that the representation was false, and that the subscriber relied thereon, is upon the subscriber [4]

---

fraudulent representations will not prevail against a receiver, especially where there has not been a prompt discovery of the fraud, followed by a repudiation , citing Upton *v* Tribilcock, 91 U S, 45 (1875), Webster *v* Upton, id 65 (1875), Sanger *v* Upton, id , 56 (1875); Ogilvie *v* Knox Ins Co, 22 Hun, 380 (1859) *Cf* Litchfield Bank *v.* Peck, 29 Conn , 384 (1860) Fraud is no defense as against creditors Mathis *v* Pridham, 20 S W Rep , 1015 (Tex , 1892) Fraud is no defense as against creditors. McDowall *v* Sheehan, 13 N Y Supp., 386 (1891) Fraud no defense after insolvency, etc. Howard *v* Glenn, 11 S. E. Rep., 610 (Ga., 1890) An action to rescind the purchase of stock lies where the money paid therefor was to be applied to a certain purpose but was not so applied, but the receiver will not be directed to give up the money Moore *v* Robertson, 25 Abb N C, 173 (1890)

[1] Farrar *v* Walker, 13 Nat. Bankr Reg 82 (1876), Michener *v* Payson, id 49 (1876)

[2] Quoted and approved in Armstrong *v* Karshner, 24 N E. Rep , 897 (Ohio, 1890), Bwlch-y-plwm L M Co *v* Baynes, 36 L J (Ex), 183 (1867); Deposit Life A Co. *v* Ayscough, 6 E & B., 761 (1856), Upton *v.* Englehart, 3 Dill , 496

(1871), Hallows *v.* Fernie, L. R., 3 Ch App , 467 (1868), Selma, M & M R R. Co *v* Anderson, 51 Miss, 829 (1876) — the last case holding it necessary to allege also that the f ct misrepresented was not a charter matter Carey *v.* Cin & Chicago R R. Co, 5 Iowa, 357 (1857), indicates that an allegation that the certificates are brought into court for disposal is proper See, also, Oregon Central R R. Co *v* Scoggin 3 Oreg , 161 (1869), Gilfillan *v* Mawhinney, 21 N E Rep , 299 (Mass., 1889).

[3] *In re* Devala Prov G. M Co., L R , 22 Ch Div , 593 (1883) *Cf* Phil , W & B R R Co *v.* Quigley, 21 How , 202 (1858) *Contra*, Jarrett *v.* Kennedy, 6 C B , 319 (1848)

[4] Jennings *v* Broughton, 22 L. J (Ch), 585 (1853) A subscription will not be decreed to be canceled unless the proof of fraudulent representations is very clear, especially where the subscription contained special terms in writing Western etc , Co. *v.* Purnell, 23 Atl Rep , 134 (Md , 1891). In New York, proof of other similar contemporaneous frauds is admissible Miller *v* Barber, 66 N. Y , 558 (1876). In Alabama it is not admissible Montgomery S R'y Co. *v* Matthews, 77 Ala , 357 (1884).

CHAPTER X.

MISCELLANEOUS DEFENSES TO SUBSCRIPTIONS FOR CAPITAL STOCK

§ 166. *Defenses to subscriptions not favored by the courts.*— It is a common saying and a well-recognized fact that the subscribers to certain corporate enterprises, especially railroads, rarely realize a profit from their investment, but, on the contrary, lose the whole amount of the subscription which they have made   These subscriptions are generally not called in until after corporate insolvency has occurred.   Then the reluctance of the subscriber to pay a subscription from which there is no hope of a return leads him to search out and build up all possible defenses to defeat any action for the collection of the amount due from him   Some of these defenses are just, and have been sustained, but most of them have not been allowed.   On the theory that, having taken the chances of large gains, the subscriber takes also the risk of total loss, and that the hardship of the subscriber is not equal to the superior equities and rights of corporate creditors the courts have uniformly discountenanced such defenses, and have rigidly enforced the subscriber's liability.

§ 167. *Release, withdrawal, surrender, cancellation or rescission.* These terms are frequently used as synonymous, although technically they have different meanings.   The term release, especially, has led to considerable confusion.   It has been applied to cases where the subscriber withdraws his offer to subscribe, the contract not yet having been closed,[1] second, to cases where the subscriber retains his stock, but is not required to pay the full par value thereof, third, to cases where the subscription contract is dissolved

---

[1] For this class of cases see ch. III.

211

by mutual agreement   The last class of cases forms the subject of this section   The term rescission is more properly applied to the defense of fraudulent representations [1]   Probably the term cancellation describes most accurately the dissolution of a subscription contract by the mutual consent of all parties concerned [2]

§ 168. A subscription contract, like any other contract, may be waived, canceled or dissolved by the mutual consent of all the parties interested.   The interested parties are the subscriber himself, the other stockholders, and the corporate creditors existing at the time of the cancellation   Frequently the directors of the corporation attempt to usurp this right and power of the general stockholders   The well-established rule, however, is that corporate directors have no power to agree with a subscriber that his subscription shall be canceled, unless such power is given to them by charter or statute or the by-laws of the corporation.[3]   The cancel-

---

[1] See ch IX.

[2] For a definition of the words "surrender ' and "cancellation," see Green's Brice's Ultra Vires (2d ed), 181, 189   *Re* Dronfield Silkstone Coal Co, L. R. 17 Ch D. 76 (1880), Colville's Case, 48 L J (Ch) 633 (1879)   Cancellation cannot be objected to on the ground that it reduces the capital stock   It no more reduces the capital stock than a forfeiture does.   *Re* Dronfield Silkstone Coal Co, *supra*

[3] In the case of Bedford R R Co *v* Bowser, 48 Pa St, 29, where, just before the expiration of their office, the directors fraudulently released part of the subscribers, the court said "It is an abuse of their trust wholly unauthorized, and at war with the designs of the charter, to single out some of the stock subscribers and release them from their liability   No such authority in them has ever been recognized "   The directors have no power to release a subscriber not to allow him to make additional conditions to his subscription   La Fayette, etc., Corp *v* Ryland, 49 N W Rep, 157 (Wis, 1891).   To the same effect, Rider *v* Morrison, 54 Md, 429 (1880)   Hughes *v* Antietam Mfg Co, 34 Md, 316 (1870)   Ryder *v* Alton, etc, R R Co, 13 Ill, 516 (1851), Tuckerman *v* Brown, 33 N Y, 297 (1865), Esparto

Trading Co   L. R., 12 Ch D, 191 (1879 ; Hall's Case, L. R, 5 Ch, 707, *Re* London & Prov Consol Coal Co., L. R., 5 Ch D, 525 (1877)   *Re* Argyle C. & C Co.   *Ex parte* Watson, Law Times, April 17, 1886, *Ex parte* Fletcher, 37 L J (Ch). 49 (1867), Addison's Case, L. R., 5 Ch, 294, Spackman *v* Evans L R, 3 H L, 171 (1868), Thomas' Case, L. R. 13 Eq, 437 (1872), where the directors had power to "enter into, alter, rescind or abandon contracts," Richmond's Case, 4 K & J 305 (1858), holding that power to forfeit does not give power to cancel   Adam's Case, L. R, 13 Eq 474 (1872), holding that power to compromise gives no power to cancel. " It would be putting into the hands of directors an almost unlimited power. .   . It might happen in cases where it would be impossible to fix fraud on them "   A cancellation of shares is void, and the subscriber is liable, though ten years have elapsed   *Ex parte* Watson. 54 L. T, 233 (1885)   *Cf* Plate Glass Ins. Co *v* Sunley, 8 El & Bl, 47 (1857), Kollman's Carriage Co *v* Beresford, 2 M & G, 197 (1850), Lord Belhaven's Case, 34 L. J (Ch), 503: *Ex parte* Blake, 32 L J (Ch), 278, Fox's Case, L. R., 5 Eq, 118 (1868), Dixon's Case, L. R., 5 Ch, 79, rev'd on another point, L. R., 5 H. L, 606, Burt *v* Farrar, 24 Barb., 518

lation of a subscription differs little from a purchase by the corporation of shares of its own stock. The rules of law governing such a transaction are laid down elsewhere.[1]

(1857), Gregory v Lamb, 16 Neb, 205 (1884), Erskine v Peck, 83 Mo 465 (1884). See also, § 153. The directors may release a subscription payable in property, part of which has been delivered. Nettles v Marco, 11 S E Rep, 595 (S C, 1890). Before organization a subscriber probably can be released by the promoters and his subscription canceled, but after organization the officers have no power to release him and take other subscriptions in his stead. Nothing but a transfer is then available. The officers cannot repay to him the amount paid in by him. He is and remains liable. Cartwright v Dickinson 12 S W Rep, 1030 (Tenn, 1890). A subscription may be canceled by and with the consent of the directors when fraud is involved. Four years afterwards corporate creditors cannot attack it. McDermott v Harrison 9 N Y. Supp 184 (1890). The express power of the directors to do all things 'conducive to the attainment of the objects for which it was established" does not enable them to agree to a cancellation. Re Dronfield Silkstone Coal Co, L R, 17 Ch D, 76 (1880). Cannot be canceled by a corporate solicitor, although the work in which the subscription is due can no longer be done. Wheatcroft's Case, 29 L T, 324 (1873). Sometimes the directors agree in advance to release or cancel a part or all of the subscriber's contract. Such agreements are void, not only as ultra vires, but as frauds on other subscribers. Melvin v Lamar Ins Co, 80 Ill, 446 (1875), Robinson v Pittsburgh & Connellsville R R Co, 32 Pa St, 334 (1858), Minor v Bank of Alexandria, 1 Pet, 65 (1828), Jewett v Valley R'y Co, 34 Ohio St, 601 (1878). White Mountains R R Co v Eastman, 34 N H, 124 (1856). See, also, Pickering v Templeton, 2 Mo App., 425; Downie v. White 12 Wis, 176 (1860), Blodgett v Morrill, 20 Vt, 509

(1848), Davidson's Case, 3 De G & S., 21 Bridger's Case, L R., 9 Eq 74, Litchfield Bank v Church 29 Conn, 137 (1860). Where, however, the issue itself is ultra vires, being fictitious paid-up stock, the directors may agree to a cancellation. Barnett's Case L R, 18 Eq, 507 (1874). Or an ultra vires stock dividend. Hollingshead v Woodward, 35 Hun, 410 (1885). They may cancel it for mistake in registering the wrong man. Ex parte Knightley, W M (1874), 18, 47. See Hartley's Case, L R, 10 Ch, 157. The agreement of a stockholder to surrender his stock in liquidation of an unpaid assessment is without consideration and does not bind a purchaser of the certificate. Hill v Atoka, etc, Co, 21 S W Rep, 508 (Mo 1893). The secretary cannot accept a surrender and cancellation of the subscription. Minnehaha, etc, Ass'n v Legg, 52 N W Rep, 898 (Minn, 1892). In England an express power given by the articles of association of the corporation may authorize cancellation by the directors. Colville's Case, 48 L J (Ch) 633, Snell's Case, Wright's Case, L R, 12 Eq 334, reversed in L R, 7 Ch, 55 (1871), Teasdale's Case L R, 9 Ch, 54, Whiteley's Case, 60 L T Rep, 807 (1889). Healey on Companies Law & Practice (Eng) says 'There is no inherent power in directors to accept a surrender of shares, nor is the acceptance of a surrender a matter lying between the majority and minority. Every shareholder must expressly . . . or impliedly join in the release, though a company may be precluded by knowledge and acquiescence from disputing the validity of the surrender.' Citing many cases, and discussing what constitutes notice and acquiescence.

[1] See §§ 251 309, 310, etc, infra. A scheme whereby the corporation takes back the stock and issues certificates of

§ 169 A subscriber for stock in a corporation cannot obtain a cancellation of his subscription except by the unanimous consent of the other subscribers [1] Even a majority of the stockholders cannot withdraw and refuse to proceed [2] These rules are just, and based upon a sound public policy. A subscriber may, however, withdraw at any time prior to the filing of the articles of incorporation [3]

indebtedness for it is invalid as against creditors The latter are entitled to the assets in preference to the former Heggie v Building etc, Ass'n, 12 S E Rep., 275 (N C 1890)

[1] K dwelly Canal Co. v Raby, 2 Price, 93 (1816), Lake Ontario. etc, R R Co v Mason, 16 N Y, 451, 463 (1857), Hughes v Antietam Mfg Co, 34 Md, 316 (1870) Johnson v Wabash & Mt. Vernon P R Co 16 Ind, 389 (1861), United Soc v Eagle Bank, 7 Conn, 457 (1829), Bishops Fund v Eagle Bank. id, 476 Selma & Tenn R R Co. v Tipton, 5 Ala (N S), 787 (1843). The plea in defense need not allege that the other stockholders assented to the cancellation Gelpcke v Blake, 19 Iowa, 263 (1863) Where, however, by the articles of association, acts of the directors ratified at stockholders' meetings were to be valid, a cancellation so ratified is legal, and the unanimous consent is not necessary Marshall v Glamorgan Iron & Coal Co. L R, 7 Eq. 129 (1868) Corporation is bound by agreement of agent that a person taking stock in the corporation and giving note in payment may return the stock at any time and be released from payment. Bank of Lyons v Demmon, Hill & Denio Supp. (N Y), 398 (1844). In Pennsylvania a subscriber for stock may withdraw at any time before the charter is applied for Muncy, etc Co v De La Green, 13 Atl Rep, 747 (Pa 1888). It is legal for a corporation, by common consent, to issue to its stockholders full-paid stock to the amount of cash actually paid in on a larger subscription, the first subscription being canceled, such arrangement being made before debts

are incurred Hill v Silvey, 8 S E. Rep., 803 (Ga, 1889) Where property is sold to a corporation for stock, and other stockholders are dissatisfied, the bargain may be rescinded The stockholder will then no longer be liable. Morgan v Lewis. 17 N E. Rep, 558 (Ohio, 1888) Cancellation is a question of fact. If there is no record of it, and the stockholder continues to act, he is bound. Topeka, etc., Co v Hale, 17 Pac. Rep, 601 (Kan, 1888). An offer or agreement to subscribe is revoked by death where it has not yet been accepted by the corporation Wallace v Townsend, 43 Ohio St., 537 (1885), Sedalia, W & S R'y Co. v Wilkinson 83 Mo, 235 (1884) The company may be compelled to issue a certificate to one who acquires his interest by the death of the original subscriber State v Crescent City, etc, Co., 24 La Ann, 318 (1872) Although the directors cannot. yet the stockholders by unanimous consent may allow subscriptions to be reduced one-half by cancellation of one-half, creditors' rights not intervening Glenn v. Hatchett, 8 S. Rep, 656 (Ala, 1890).

[2] Busey v Hooper, 35 Md, 15 (1871).

[3] Auburn, etc, Works v Schultz 22 Atl Rep, 904 (Pa., 1891). Up to the time of incorporation a subscriber for stock may withdraw Hudson, etc, Co. v. Tower, 30 N E. Rep, 465 (Mass., 1892). Prior to incorporation a subscriber may withdraw, especially if his subscription was informal and was merely to see what could be done. Planks. etc, Co. v. Burkhard. 49 N. W Rep., 562 (Mich, 1891), Garrett v Dillsburg, etc, R R. Co, 78 Penn St. 465 (1875), holding that at any time before the filing of the arti-

The consent of all the other stockholders, however, need not be express If the means of notice are sufficient, so as to raise a clear presumption of knowledge and acquiescence, and the arrangement is left unimpeached by any one for many years, no objection can be made The stockholders are bound by the cancellation [1] But where a subscription has been canceled, and calls already paid are refunded without the consent of the other stockholders, any stockholder may, by a bill in equity, have the money refunded to the corporation, and the subscriber made liable upon his canceled subscription [2] Moreover, the directors are personally liable to the corporation for loss occasioned by their improper cancellation of subscriptions [3] When, however, a subscriber fails to pay his subscription or exercise his rights, it has been held that the corporation may take his subscription as abandoned and allow others to fill it.[4] An alteration, however, of the subscription list by substitution of different stockholders may release dissenting stockholders [5] Where a subscription is not paid, and the stock is transferred to the corporation as "treasury stock" and then sold below par, the purchaser is liable for the unpaid par value [6] Where a subscription for stock is paid, the stockholder is entitled to his stock and past dividends although for thirty years he sleeps on his rights [7]

cles a subscriber may withdraw Cook v Chittenden, 25 Fed Rep, 514 (1885), allowing a withdrawal where no others have subscribed in reliance thereon, nor creditors' debts incurred Gulf, C, etc, R'y Co. v Neely, 64 Texas, 344 (1885), holding that there can be no withdrawal after an acceptance by the corporation Cf Tilsonburg, etc, Co. v Goodrich, 8 Ontario (Q B Div), 565 (1885), Ross v San Antonio, etc, R R Co, 31 Tex, 49 (1868) See, also, Goff v Flesher, 33 Ohio St., 107 (1877)

[1] Evans v Smallcombe, L R, 3 H L, 249 (1868). So, also, where the corporation retains the benefits of a cancellation, no objection can be made Miller v Second J B Ass'n, 50 Pa St., 32 (1865) Proof of cancellation need not necessarily be by the corporate records May be proved by evidence that the subscriber was not regarded "by himself or by the company as a stockholder" Stuart v Valley R. R. Co, 32 Gratt, 146 (1879)

[2] Melvin v Lamar Ins Co, 80 Ill, 446 (1875)

[3] Hodgkinson v Natl Co, 26 Beav, 473 (1859), Bank of St Mary's v St John, 25 Ala., 566 (1882) The subscriber also, may set up this defense Southern Hotel Co v Newman, 30 Mo 118 (1860)

[4] Perkins v Union B H & E M Co, 12 Allen, 273 (1866) Cancellation may be by the substitution of another person for the subscriber at the latter's request This occurs where regular transfer is not yet possible The signature of the first subscriber must be erased and that of his substitute inserted Otherwise the substitution fails Ryder v Alton & S R R. Co, 13 Ill 516 (1851). And see § 62

[5] See §§ 53, 62, supra

[6] Alling v Ward, 21 N E. Rep., 551 (Ill, 1890)

[7] Where, in 1845, an Indian chief disclosed an iron mine under promise of being compensated, and the officers of the unincorporated company gave him

§ 170 A cancellation of a subscription, to the detriment of corporate creditors, may be impeached by the latter and set aside [1] Especially is this the rule when the cancellation is made after the

a paper recognizing his right to twelve thirty-one one-hundredths interest, and after incorporation in 1848 eighteen full-paid shares of stock were set aside for the Indians, and twelve of such shares corresponded to the twelve thirty-one one-hundredths interest, the descendants of the chief are entitled to the stock although neither he nor they made any claim thereto until 1877 Back profits may also be recovered The statute of limitations is no bar A new corporation assuming the property and liabilities of the old one is liable Kobogum v Jackson Iron Co, 43 N W Rep, 602 (Mich 1889) To same effect, Bedford County v Nashville, etc, R R, 14 Lea (Tenn), 525 (1884)

[1] One who is a corporate creditor before the cancellation is made may object to it Vick v La Rochelle, 57 Miss, 602 (1880), Appeal of Miller, 1 Pa Sup Ct, 120, in which stock in an insurance company was subscribed for in order to enable the company to undergo an examination by the commissioner, a dividend being paid on it during their holding, and the notes given in payment being published as assets It was held that, although after the emergency had passed the stock was taken back by the company and the notes canceled, the subscribers were liable to its creditors, the transaction being looked upon as a fraud upon them Cancellation by withdrawal is not legal as against corporate creditors existing at the time of the withdrawal, even though all the stockholders assent thereto Farnsworth v Robbins, 31 N W Rep, 349 (Minn, 1887) Where a corporation takes land in payment for stock, then rescinds and eighteen months afterwards becomes insolvent, rescission is binding Sanderson v Ætna, etc, Co, 8 Cent L J, 266 (Ohio, 1879) So, also, if the debt was

incurred after the cancellation Johnson v Sullivan, 15 Mo. App., 55, Erskine v Peck 13 Mo App, 280, 21 N E Rep, 514 (Ill, 1889) The plea in defense, it has been held, need not allege that there were no corporate creditors at the time of the cancellation. Gelpcke v Blake, 19 Iowa 263 (1863) In England a different rule prevails. "If the company could not question it, neither can a creditor for he can obtain nothing but what the company can get from the shareholders" Re Dronfield Silkstone Coal Co. L R, 17 Ch D, 76 (1880). A bona fide cancellation of a subscription is valid and corporate creditors cannot have it set aside Waugencu v Aspell, 21 N E Rep 405 (Ohio, 1890) Where the directors rescind a subscription at the request of the subscriber he cannot be made liable five years later Re West London, etc, Bank, 60 L T Rep, 807 (1889) Subscribers whose stock is taken back by the corporation are not liable thereon either at common law or by statute relative to transfers. Alling v. Ward, 24 N. E Rep, 551 (Ill, 1890). A fraudulent release by a corporation of an unpaid subscription to an increase in the capital stock of a corporation is void even against a debt arising before the increase Carter v Union Printing Co et al, 15 S W Rep, 579 (Ark, 1891) This case holds also that a corporate creditor may object to the corporation releasing a stockholder from his stock and repaying to him the subscription which he has paid in The transaction may be set aside It is legal for the corporation to make an agreement with stockholders whereby the latter surrender their stock upon which they have paid twenty per cent, and receive full-paid stock to the amount of twenty per cent of the stock surrendered A receiver cannot attack this agreement even in behalf of credit-

216

corporation has become insolvent [1] In the United States courts it
is established that the governing officers of a corporation cannot,
by agreement or other transaction with the stockholder release the
latter from his obligation to pay, to the prejudice of its creditors,
except by fair and honest dealing, and for a valuable consideration [2]

§ 171 *Compromise* — A compromise differs from a cancellation
in that the subscriber pays to the corporation a part of the subscription price in order to be released from the balance   The stock is
delivered back to the corporation   The corporate authorities — generally the directors — have power to compromise any corporate debt,
and if, in the collection of subscriptions, there is reasonable doubt
as to the liability of the subscriber,[3] or if the subscriber is insolvent, the corporation may compromise the liability, and release a
part for the purpose of securing the residue   All that is required
is good faith [4] A receiver, however, cannot compromise a subscription, nor can a court of equity give him power so to do, unless all
the stockholders are parties to the equitable suit in connection with
which the receiver is appointed [5] A compromise is not binding if
there is no controversy.[6]

ors   Republic Life Ins Co, v Swigert,
25 N E Rep, 680 (Ill, 1890)   The " trust
fund " theory is denied in Hospes v
Northwestern, etc, Co, 50 N W Rep,
1117 (Minn, 1892)

[1] Chouteau Ins Co v Floyd, 74 Mo,
286   Gill v Balis, 72 Mo, 424, holding,
also, that it is immaterial that enough
subscriptions remain to pay the corporate debts

[2] " The governing officers of a corporation cannot, by agreement or other
transaction with the stockholder, release the latter from his obligation to
pay, to the prejudice of its creditors,
except by fair and honest dealing and
for a valuable consideration '   Potts v
Wallace, 146 U S, 689 (1892)   Burke v
Smith, 16 Wall, 390 (1872), New Albany
v Burke, 11 Wall 96 (1870)   So also,
in Illinois   See Zirkel v Joliet Opera
House Co, 79 Ill, 334 (1875)

[3] Bath's Case, L R, 8 Ch D, 334
(1878), Lord Belhaven's Case, 3 De G,
J & S, 41 (1865)   An unaccepted offer
of compromise is no defense, and com-
promises with other stockholders are no

defense   Howard v Glenn, 11 S E
Rep, 610 (Ga, 1890)

[4] Phil & W C R R Co v Hickman
28 Pa St, 318 (1857)   Power may be
given by statute   Pearson's Case, L
R, 7 Ch, 309, holding that, under the
English statute, the court may allow
but cannot compel, a receiver to compromise   Where a stockholder denies
his liability, and the directors compromise with him by reducing the amount
of his subscription, the compromise is
binding on all parties   Whitaker v.
Grummond, 36 N W Rep, 62 (Mich,
1888)

[5] Chandler v Brown 77 Ill, 333 (1875)
The fact that the court authorized the
receiver to compromise with some of
the stockholders is no defense to others
Hambleton v Glenn, 20 Atl Rep, 115
(Md, 1890)

[6] Phosphate, etc, Co v Green L R, 7
C P, 43 (1871), Spackman v Evans, L R,
3 H L, 171, 188, 231 (1868)   In Dixon v
Evans, L R, 5 H L, 606 (1872), the subscription was made upon a condition,
which remaining unfulfilled a com-

§ 172 *Non-payment of a percentage required by statute.*— The charter or statute governing a corporation often prescribes that each subscriber to the capital stock shall, at the time of subscribing, pay to the corporation a fixed sum or a specified proportion of the subscription. These statutes vary somewhat in their provisions, some declaring the subscription to be void unless the percentage is paid, others merely prescribing that it shall be paid.

In the actual taking of the subscriptions, it frequently happens that the subscriber has not the ready money requisite, and is allowed to subscribe without paying the same. When an attempt is made to collect such a subscription, the subscriber, if the enterprise has resulted disastrously, sets up the defense that he did not pay the statutory percentage, and that the subscription is void and not enforceable. A long list of cases, dating from the early litigation over railroads, has turned upon this defense. In some of the states the defense has been held insufficient, in others a contrary rule prevails, and in still others, first one rule and then the other has been adopted.

§ 173. The decided weight of authority and the most carefully considered cases hold that a subscriber for stock cannot escape the responsibilities of a stockholder by showing that he never paid the percentage or fixed amount required by the charter or statute to be paid at the time of subscribing[1] He will not thus be permitted to

promise was made permitting the withdrawal of the subscriber *Held,* after two appeals, that directors had power to enter into such a compromise, and the subscriber was not held in the winding up

[1] Webb z Baltimore. etc, Co, 26 Atl. Rep, 113 (Md, 1893), Illinois River R. R Co v Zimmer, 20 Ill, 654 (1858), holding that the commissioners may waive payment. The court say: "This indulgence is a most ungracious defense, which should not be allowed unless it is strictly required by some inflexible rule of law" Haywood & P~P R. Co. v. Bryan, 6 Jones' L (N C), 82 (1858), the court saying "It would be a strange rule which would allow him to take advantage of the other stockholders' forbearance and his own neglect ' Pittsburgh, W & K R R Co. v Applegate, 21 W Va, 172 (1882) On the theory that the statute is "to insure good faith, and to avoid shams in enterprises that

so vitally affect the public," but not to change the liability of stockholders to corporations Minnesota & St. L. R'y Co v Bassett, 20 Minn, 535 (1874), where the court said of the statute "While it confers upon plaintiff the right to insist upon the payment, it does not make the successful exercise of this right indispensable to the validity of the subscription" Water Valley Manuf. Co. v. Seaman, 53 Miss, 655 (1876), where the requirement was provided for in the subscription itself Barrington v. Miss. C. R. R. Co, 32 Miss, 370 (1856), where payment was made before the subscription See, also, Vicksburg, S & T R R. Co. v McKean, 12 La Ann, 638 (1857), Wright v Shelby R. R Co, 16 B. Monr. (Ky.), 4 (1855), Smith v Plank-road Co., 30 Ala, 650 (1857), Mitchell v. Rome R. R. Co., 17 Ga, 574 (1855), Henry v. Vermillion & A R. R. Co, 17 Ohio, 191 (1848); Chamberlain v Painesville & H. R. R. Co., 15 Ohio St., 225 (1864); Napier

take advantage of his own wrong and default to the prejudice of others. In some instances the percentage was paid in notes[1] or checks[2] instead of cash, in others, payment in cash was made at some period subsequent to the act of subscribing,[3] in still others, no payment at all was made on the subscription, and suit was

v Poe, 12 Ga., 170 (1852), Fiser v Miss. & Tenn R. R. Co, 32 Miss, 359 (1856), Ryder v Alton & S R R. Co, 13 Ill, 516 (1851) where the subscriber was one of the commissioners, Klein v Alton & S R. R. Co., 13 Ill, 514 (1851), where payment was made before the subscription books were closed Stuart v Valley R. R. Co, 32 Gratt. (Va), 146 (1879), Southern L. Ins Co v Lanier, 5 Fla, 110 (1853), Selma & Tenn R. R. Co v Roundtree, 7 Ala (N S), 670 (1845), Spartanburg & A R R Co v Ezell, 14 S C, 281 (1880), where a few subscribers paid in more than their percentage, and enough to make up for those not paying, Oler v Baltimore R R Co, 41 Md, 583 (1874), where the percentage was "payable," the court saying that this merely made it "due and collectible," like a call To the same effect, Ashtabula & N L R R Co v Smith, 15 Ohio St, 328 (1864). Payment by the subscriber's agent is sufficient. Litchfield Bank v Church, 29 Conn, 137 (1860) The following cases hold that non-payment of the required percentage is a good defense Charlotte & S C. R R Co v Blakeley, 3 Strobh Eq (S C), 245 (1848), State Ins. Co. v. Redmond, 1 McCrary, 308 (1880) The requirement herein was by by-law People v Chambers 42 Cal, 201 (1871), holding a check to be insufficient, Farmers & M. Bank v Nelson, 12 Md, 35 (1857), Taggart v Western Md R. R. Co., 24 Md, 588 (1866), Wood v Coosa & C. R R. Co, 32 Ga, 273 (1861), the statute prescribing that the subscription should be "void" A provision that only ten per cent. of the stock shall be paid up until certain contingencies arise is strictly construed by the courts City of Burlington v. Burlington Water Co., 53

N W Rep, 246 (Ia, 1892) Although the statute requires that a certain percentage of subscriptions shall be paid upon incorporation, yet one subscriber may pay the proportion of others Beattys v Town of Solon, 64 Hun, 120 (1892) It is no defense that the corporation commenced business before twenty-five per cent of its capital stock had been paid in as required by the charter Naugatuck, etc, Co v Nichols 20 Atl Rep, 315 (Conn, 1890).

[1] Vt. Central R. R Co v Clayes, 21 Vt., 30 (1848). A bond so given is collectible, as it would be if given to carry out a parol contract for the sale of land void by statute of frauds McRea v Russell, 12 Ired (N C), 224 (1851), the court saying that the statute 'was meant to protect stockholders from men of straw It was, moreover, meant to protect men from the consequences of making such subscriptions under the influence of momentary excitement, which they could not fulfill" The statute made the subscription void In the case of Home Stock Ins Co v Sherwood, 72 Mo, 461 (1880), payment by note and mortgage was sustained Hayne v Beauchamp, 13 Miss., 515 (1846), holds that the payment by note amounted to an informal subscription, the statutory subscription being void Pine River Bank v Hadsdon, 46 N H., 114 (1865)

[2] People v Stockton & V R R Co, 45 Cal, 306 (1873) there being funds in the bank to meet it

[3] Payment of a judgment, in an action for one call, estops the subscriber from setting up this defense. Hall v Selma & Tenn R. R Co, 6 Ala. (N S), 741 (1844).

brought for the whole amount.[1] Where the directors commence business before ten per cent of the capital is paid in as required by statute, the directors are personally liable as agents transacting business without authority from the principal[2] In England a failure to pay such a percentage is held not to affect the liability of the subscriber, but to restrict his right of transferring his stock[3]

§ 174 In New York there has been doubt and a strong tendency to change the rule laid down at an early day by the court The case of Jenkins *v* The Union Turnpike Company, in 1804,[4] decided that a failure by the subscriber to pay a required percentage at the time of subscribing was a good defense to an action on the subscription This decision has been distinguished, questioned and doubted by the courts.[5] The latest authority, however, in New

---

[1] In the case of Piscataqua Ferry Co *v.* Jones, 39 N H 491 (1859), the requirement was by by-law, not by charter. The subscription was to be void for non-payment The court thought otherwise The effect of non-payment is that "it is due and liable to be called for at any time — payable on demand, whenever needed by the corporation" Greenville & C R. R. Co *v* Woodsides, 5 Rich L. (S C), 145 (1851), where the subscriber also voted the stock

[2] Farmers', etc. Co. *v* Floyd, 26 N E Rep , 110 (Ohio, 1890)

[3] East Gloucestershire R'y Co *v.* Bartholomew, L R., 3 Ex , 15 (1867), Purdy's Case, 16 W R., 660 (1868), McEwen *v* West, L W & W Co , L. R., 6 Ch 655 (1871) — the statute stating that the stock should not "issue" or "vest" until one-fifth should be paid See, also, Morton s Case, L. R., 16 Eq , 104 (1873)

[4] 1 Caines Cases in Error, 86, reversing Union Turnpike Co *v* Jenkins, 1 Caines' Rep , 381

[5] Highland Turnpike Co *v* McKean, 11 Johns , 98 (1814), the court saying "It is a little difficult to ascertain the point upon which the court of errors grounded their decision" A subscriber, who is also the commissioner, need not pay the required percentage to himself In Crocker *v* Crane, 21 Wend , 211 (1839), payment in checks was held not

to be good, they evidently not having been given in good faith The court say 'Receiving an occasional check might have been a fair substitute " Thorp *v* Woodhull, 1 Sandf Ch , 411 (1844), sustains the validity of a bond and mortgage in payment of a subscription in which the percentage had been paid by a worthless check Eastern Plank-road Co *v* Vaughan, 14 N Y , 546 (1856), holds it not to be necessary "that each subscriber should pay five per cent upon his subscription, but only that five per cent. on the amount of the stock subscribed should be actually paid by some one " To the same effect, Lake Ontario, A & N. Y R R. Co. *v* Mason, 16 N Y, 451 (1857), the court saying that the object was "to insure the organization of real substantial companies in good faith, animated by an honest purpose, and having some degree of ability at least to undertake the proposed improvement." In the case of Rensselaer & W P R. Co. *v* Barton, 16 N Y, 457, n (1857), the court, in speaking of the decision in Jenkins *v* Union T Co , say "It may well be doubted whether the reasoning upon which it was based is sound, and whether, were the question to be again directly presented, this court would feel bound to follow it " Black River & Union R R Co *v* Clarke, 25 N. Y 208 (1862), holds that "the subscription

York, undoubtedly holds that if the subscriber merely signs the subscription contract and does not pay the percentage, he may thereby defeat his liability on such subscription [1]

§ 175. In Pennsylvania a similar state of doubt has existed. The case of Hibernia Turnpike Co v Henderson,[2] in 1822, decided that a failure by the commissioners taking subscriptions to stock to require payment of the statutory percentage made the subscription void and not enforceable. Later decisions do not overthrow the rigid rule, but distinguish and practically destroy it by holding that this defense is barred by a subsequent statute curing the defect,[3] or by a waiver in attending corporate meetings and voting,[4] or by transferring the shares,[5] or that the provision applies only to subscriptions taken by the commissioners,[6] or, under the act of 1868, that the percentage must be paid on subscriptions after, but not on those before, incorporation,[7] or that the requirement does not apply to a conditional subscription,[8] or that it is waived by any acts indicating an intent to be bound as a stockholder.[9]

one day, with payment the next would satisfy the statute, and so would actual payment at any period after subscription with intent to effectuate and complete the subscription See, also, Beach v Hazard, as stated in 30 N Y, 118 Ogdensburgh C & R R R Co. v Wooley, 3 Abb. Ct of App, 398 (1864), holds that the requisite percentage for all may be paid by a few subscribers and that a promissory note is good payment. Beach v Smith, 30 N. Y, 116 (1864), affirming S C, 28 Barb, 254, holds that payment in services performed under a contract with the company suffices Excelsior G B Co. v Stayner, 25 Hun, 91 (1881), holds that payment by check, on which payment is stopped, is insufficient Syracuse, P. & O R R. Co v Gere, 4 Hun, 392 (1875), sustains a suit by the corporation to collect such a check See, also, Ogdensburgh R. & C. R. R Co v Frost, 21 Barb, 541 (1856) Certified check is good payment. Re Staten I. R T. R. R. Co, 37 Hun, 422 (1885), 38 Hun, 381

[1] New York & O M R. R. Co. v Van Horn, 57 N Y, 473 (1874), holding also that a subsequent statute cannot cure such omission to pay, and thereby render the subscriber liable See, also, Perry v Hoadley, N Y Daily Reg May 6, 1887

[2] 8 S & R, 219 See, also Leighty v Pres of S & W. T Co, 14 S & R, 434

[3] Clark v Monongahela Nav Co, 10 Watts, 364 (1840)

[4] Erie & W P R. Co v Brown, 25 Pa. St., 156 (1855), the court saying "There is no merit in such a defense. The subscriber himself is under the highest moral obligations faithfully to perform the promise he has distinctly made In the case of Cam v Westchester R R. Co, 3 Grants Cas, 200 (1855), the court held that failure to pay the percentage did not render the charter forfeitable

[5] Everhart v Westchester & Phil R. R Co, 28 Pa St, 339 (1857)

[6] Phil. & W C R R Co v Hickman, 28 Pa. St 318 (1857) Contra under the act of 1868 See Butcher v Dillsburg & M R R Co, 76 Pa St, 306 (1874)

[7] Garrett v Dillburg & M R. R. Co, 78 Pa St, 465 (1875)

[8] Hanover J & S R R. Co v Haldeman, 82 Pa St, 36 (1876).

[9] Boyd v Peach B R'y Co, 90 Pa. St., 169 (1879), holding, however, that

§ 176. *Failure of the corporation to obtain subscriptions to the extent of the full capital stock.*— It is an implied part of a contract of subscription that the contract is to be binding and enforceable against the subscriber only after the full capital stock of the corporation has been subscribed. This condition precedent to the liability of the subscriber need not be expressed in the corporate charter nor the subscription itself. It arises by implication from the just and reasonable understanding of a subscriber that he is to be aided by other subscriptions. This rule is supported also by public policy, in that corporate creditors have a right to rely upon a belief that the full capital stock of the corporation has been subscribed.[1] If the corporation commences business before the full

payment cannot be by promissory note, although a demand note

[1] The leading case on this defense is Salem Mill-dam Corporation v Ropes, 23 Mass., 23 (1827), and 26 Mass, 187 (1829) In the case of Livesey v Omaha Hotel, 5 Neb, 50 (1876), Judge Redfield in the brief says "This rule has been held inflexible in all cases, both for the security of the public and also of the subscribers." Shurtz v Schoolcraft & T R R Co. 9 Mich 269 (1861), New York, H & N R. R. Co v Hunt, 39 Conn, 75 (1872), Hale v Sanborn, 16 Neb, 1 (1884), Haskell v Worthington, 7 S W Rep 481 (Mo, 1888), Halsey, etc., Co v Donovan, 57 Mich, 318 (1885), Peoria & R. I R. R. Co. v Preston, 35 Iowa, 118 (1872), the court saying that this is the rule, "unless a contrary intention appears, expressly or by implication, either in the charter or the contract of subscriptions;" Stoneham Branch R. R. Co. v Gould, 68 Mass., 277 (1854), the court saying: "This is no arbitrary rule, it is founded on a plain *dictate* of justice and the strict principles regulating the obligation of contracts," Bray v Farwell, 81 N Y, 600, 608 (1880) where the court say the directors "had no authority to go on with insufficient means, and thus wreck the company;" Selma, M & M R. R. Co v Anderson, 51 Miss, 829 (1876), Hughes v Antietam Manuf Co., 34 Md, 318, 332 (1870); Topeka Bridge Co. v. Cummings, 3 Kan, 55 (1864),

Allman v. Havana R. & E. R. R. Co, 88 Ill, 521 (1878), Temple v. Lemon, 112 Ill, 51 (1884) Littleton Manuf. Co v. Parker, 14 N H, 543 (1844), Hendrix v Academy of Music, 73 Ga, 437 (1884), Contoocook Valley R. R. Co. v Barker, 32 N H, 363 (1855); Prop. of N. Bridge v Story, 6 Pick, 45 (1827), Belfast & M. L. R. R. Co v Cottrell, 66 Me 185 (1875), Rockland, etc, Co v Sewall, 14 Atl Rep, 939 (Me, 1888); Memphis Branch R. R. Co. v Sullivan, 57 Ga, 240, Fox v Allensville, C S & V. T Co, 46 Ind, 31 (1874), Ham v North W G R. Co., 41 Ind, 196 (1872), holding also that the corporation in suing must aver that the full capital stock has been subscribed Central Turnpike Co v Valentine, 10 Pick, 142 (1830), holding also that the corporation has the burden of proving subscriptions for the full capital stock, Warwick R. R. Co. v Cady, 11 R I, 131 (1877), where the charter said that the capital stock should not exceed a specified sum, Fry's Ex'rs v Lexington & B S R. R. Co, 2 Met. (Ky), 314 (1859), holding also that the corporation must aver full subscription, Lewey's Island R. R. Co. v. Bolton, 48 Me 451 (1860); Lail v. Mt. Sterling C R. Co, 13 Bush (Ky), 34 (1877) holding that the corporation need not aver full subscriptions. *Cf.* Monroe v Fort W., J. & S. R. R. Co., 28 Mich 272 (1973). Where also, the corporation is incorporated with a less capital stock than was proposed when

capital stock is subscribed, the state may bring an action for the forfeiture of its charter[1] The subscriber, however, is liable for his proportion of the necessary expenses, preliminary to the incorporation and organization of the company[2]

§ 177. The act of incorporation may, of course, vary this rule Thus, it is well established that, where the charter authorizes the organization of the company, and the commencement of corporate

the defendant subscribed, he is not bound by the subscription Santa Cruz R. R. Co v Schurtz, 53 Cal, 106 (1878) A few cases seem to hold a contrary doctrine New Castle & A T Co v Bell, 8 Blackf (Ind), 584 (1847), Oregon Central R R. Co v Scoggin, 3 Oreg, 161 (1869), York & C R. R. Co v Pratt, 40 Me, 447 (1855) Cheraw & C R R Co v White, 10 S C, 155 (1878) See, also Chubb v Upton, 95 U S, 665 668 (1877) probably a *dictum* In the case of Skowhegan & A R R. Co v Kinsman, 77 Me, 370 (1885), the court seem to hold that, where there is in the subscription an express promise to pay, it is enforceable even though the whole capital stock is not subscribed If such a condition is expected, the court says it must be inserted in the subscription It has been held that where a subscription is made before incorporation, on a paper not fixing the capital stock, a failure to secure full subscription to the capital stock as fixed in the charter is no defense Belton, etc, Co v Sanders 6 S W Rep, 134 (Tex, 1887) Subscribers are not liable until the whole amount is subscribed They may recover back what they have paid Winters v Armstrong, 37 Fed Rep, 508 (1889) See, also, 42 N W Rep., 226 (Wis, 1889) A full subscription is not necessary if the subscriptions are payable to an agent and nothing is said about full subscription West v Crawford, 21 Pac Rep, 1123 (Colo., 1889) A stockholder may defend on the ground that the amount required by the subscription list to be subscribed shall be subscribed before he is held liable, especially where misrepresentations are made as to the amount which had been subscribed when the defendant subscribed The question is one for the jury Spelher, etc, Co v Leedom, 24 Atl Rep, 197 (Pa, 1892) When the capital is increased after the defendant subscribed he cannot insist on the subscription of the capital stock as increased Port Edwards, etc, R'y v Arpin 49 N W Rep 828 (Wis, 1891) Cf § 288 Full capital necessary Exposition, etc, R'y v Canal, etc, R y 7 S Rep, 627 (La, 1890). The question must be clearly raised by the findings, otherwise it will not be considered on appeal Arthur v Clarke, 49 N W Rep, 252 (Minn, 1891) Where stockholders proceed to business before the minimum capital prescribed by statute is subscribed and before the requisite amount is subscribed, they are liable to corporate creditors for such minimum capital. The creditors may sue them and the corporation in the same action Burns v Beck, 10 S E Rep, 121 (Ga, 1889) The defense of non-full subscriptions is available against creditors of the corporation Exposition, etc, R'y v Canal, etc, R'y 7 S Rep 627 (La 1890) The text above was approved in Portland, etc Co v Spillman, 32 Pac Rep, 688 (Ore, 1893), and Denny, etc, Co v Schram, 32 Pac Rep, 1002 (Wash, 1893) No defense that the full capital stock was not subscribed where creditor sues Hamilton v Clarion, etc, R. R., 23 Atl Rep, 53 (Pa, 1891)

[1] People v Nat Sav Bank, 11 N E, Rep, 170 (Ill, 1887), affirmed, 22 id, 288

[2] Salem Mill-dam Corp v Ropes, 23 Mass, 23 (1827).

work after a certain amount of the capital stock has been subscribed, such a charter provision is equivalent to an express authority to the corporation to call in the subscriptions as soon as this organization is effected[1] Subscriptions to the full amount of the capital stock are held not to be necessary The defense is not good

§ 178 Where the subscription itself specifies how much of the capital stock must be subscribed before payment may be enforced, such specifications are legal and effective, and until they are fully complied with the subscriber is not liable.[2] A subscription of this

---

[1] Schenectady & S P R R Co v. Thatcher, 11 N Y, 102 (1851), Rensselaer & W P R. Co v Wetsel, 21 Barb, 56 (1855), Hamilton & D P R Co v Rice, 7 Barb, 166 (1849), Sedalia, Warsaw etc, R'y Co v Abell 17 Mo App, 645 (1885), Perkins v Saunders 56 Miss, 733 (1879) Hunt v Kansas & M B Co, 11 Kan, 412 (1873), the court saying that otherwise there would be no propriety in allowing the organization before the full capital was subscribed Hoagland v Cin & F W R R Co, 18 Ind, 452 (1862) Hanover J & S R R Co v Haldeman, 82 Pa St, 36 (1876), Penobscot & K R R Co v Bartlett, 12 Gray, 244 (1858), holding so, even though no contracts for building the road were to be made until a larger subscription was obtained, Boston, B & G R R Co v Wellington, 113 Mass., 79 (1873), Minor v Mechanics Bank, 1 Peters, 46. New Haven & D R. R Co v Chapman 38 Conn, 65 (1871), Illinois River R. R Co v Zimmer, 20 Ill, 654 (1858), Lexington & W C R R Co v Chandler, 51 Mass, 311, Willamette F Co v Stannus, 4 Oreg, 261 (1872), Jewett v Valley R'y Co. 34 Ohio St., 601 (1878) A vigorous case to the contrary is Galveston Hotel Co v Balton, 46 Tex, 633 (1877). The court says ' There were good reasons for organizing the company to be found in the increased facility of thereby raising the subscriptions to the amount fixed for the capital stock and of other preliminary preparations for the execution of the work, when the subscription should reach that amount." A contrary

rule " would render nugatory the most important provision of the charter, which is the amount of its capital stock " When the capital stock is to be fixed by the corporation between two limits, the subscription of the full amount as fixed is a subscription of the full capital stock Kennebec & P R R Co v Jarvis, 34 Me, 360 (1852) There need not be a full subscription where the statutes authorize an organization as soon as one-half is subscribed Astoria, etc, R. R v Neill, 25 Pac. Rep, 379 (Oreg, 1890). The statutes may allow the corporation to proceed with business and collect subscriptions before the full capital stock is subscribed Schloss v Montgomery, etc, Co, 6 S. Rep 360 (Ala, 1889)

[2] Where, by its terms, it is not to be binding until a certain amount is subscribed, it is enforceable when that amount is secured, although less than the full capital stock Bucksport & B. R R Co. v Buck, 65 Me, 536 (1876). See, also, Iowa & Minn R. R Co v. Perkins, 28 Iowa, 281 (1869) Organization authorized where "250 to any one mile ' has been subscribed is satisfied by a $250 subscription in general. Fitch v. Poplar, etc Co, 13 S. W. Rep, 791 (Ky, 1890) Where the subscription list or articles of association signed by defendant expressly provide for the commencement of business before the full capital is subscribed, the defense is waived, Arkadelphia, etc., Mills v. Trimble, 15 S. W. Rep., 776 (Ark., 1891)

kind is a conditional subscription.[1] A condition that the subscription shall be payable only when sufficient subscriptions for the corporate purpose have been secured has been held to require funds sufficient to put the enterprise in full operation[2] On the other hand, a subscription to pay "when required" renders the subscribers liable before the full capital stock is subscribed[3]

§ 179. In England statutory provisions have almost entirely displaced the common-law rule The principle that a subscriber is not liable until the full capital stock has been subscribed is recognized as having been the original rule at law A few cases, however, seem to favor an opposite rule. Yet an eminent English authority says that, in all the cases in which the subscribers were held bound, they "had entered into a contract which precluded them from maintaining that the subscription of the whole of the originally proposed capital was an express or implied condition to their becoming shareholders" The English courts seem to have no clearly defined rule in this matter, but allow each case to turn largely on its own facts, releasing the subscriber if the discrepancy in the subscriptions is very large, and holding him liable if it is small, or if he in any way has aided the company in beginning business.[4]

[1] See ch. V.

[2] People's Ferry Co v. Balch, 74 Mass, 203 (1857), the court holding that funds for the land, structures and boats must be in hand before the defendant becomes liable

[3] Cheraw & C R. R. Co v Garland, 14 S. C., 63 (1880)

[4] Norwich & L Navigation v Theobold, 1 Moody & M, 151 (1828), required full subscription in accordance with a statute Fox v. Clifton, 6 Bing, 776 (1830), the earliest common-law English case on this subject, holds that the subscriber is not liable to corporate creditors unless the full capital stock has been subscribed Pitchford v Davis, 5 Mees. & W, 2 (1839), also fully agrees with the rule that prevails in this country Wontner v Shairp, 4 C. B, 404 (1847) sustained a recovery back of amounts paid on a subscription, under misrepresentations that the whole stock had been subscribed Waterford, W W & B R'y Co v Dalbiac, 4 Eng L & Eq, 452 (1850), refused to allow the

defense, since the charter allowed the corporation to purchase land before the full capital stock was subscribed Watts v Salter, 10 C B, 447 (1858), holds the same, the subscriber having aided in the incorporation, and given the directors power to proceed. Galvanized Iron Co v Westoby, 21 L J (Ex), 302 (1852), per B. Parke, says that at common law the subscriber is not liable unless the full capital stock is subscribed Contra, Lyons' Case, 35 Beav, 646 (1866) Johnston v Goslett, 3 C B (N S), 569 (1857) makes the directors liable to the subscriber for his deposit when they so proceed London & C Ins Co v Redgrave, 4 C B (N S), 524 (1858), holds the subscriber liable, he having aided in the incorporation Ornamental P W Co v Browne, 2 Hurl & C 63 (1863), holds the subscriber liable, under the statute of 19 and 20 Vic, ch 47, similar to the American statutes See, also, McDougall v Jersey I H Co, 10 Jur (N S), 1043 (1864) Peirce v Jersey W Co, L R, 5 Ex, 209 (1870) required a cer-

§ 180 Some difficulty has been experienced in determining what subscriptions shall be counted in ascertaining whether the full capital stock has been subscribed   Conditional subscriptions, the condition to which has not yet been performed by the corporation, are clearly not to be counted among the rest, since such subscriptions may never become enforceable.[1] This rule, if strictly insisted upon, would probably occasion great inconvenience to the corporation in enforcing the subscriptions for stock

The subscriptions of married women, infants or persons of unsound mind are to be excluded from the count [2] So, also, the subscriptions of insolvents are excluded, unless at the time of subscribing they were apparently able to pay the subscription [3] Considerable

tain amount to be subscribed, the charter itself so prescribing Elder v New Zealand L I Co, 30 L T (N S), 285 (1875), the most important case on this subject, holds that, where the directors are about to proceed with only one-fourteenth of the capital stock subscribed, a subscriber may apply to the court and have his name removed from the subscribers' list The court say that the case of McDougall v Jersey I H Co, supra, would have been decided otherwise had not two-thirds of the stock in that case been subscribed See, also, Howbeach Coal Co v Teague, 5 H & N, 151 (1860), dictum in Re Jennings, 1 Irish (Ch), 634 (1851).

[1] Troy & G R R Co v Newton, 74 Mass, 596 (1857), the condition being that the subscriber be allowed to pay in construction work, Oskaloosa Agricultural Works t Parkhust, 54 Iowa, 357 (1880), Brand v Lawrenceville, etc, R R Co, 1 S E Rep, 255 (Ga, 1887); New York, etc, R R Co v Hunt, 39 Conn, 75 (1872), Cabot & W S B v Chapin, 60 Mass, 50 (1850), where a subscription payable in other stock at par, when the market value was less, was not counted, Ticonic Co v Lang, 63 Me, 480 (1874) Subscriptions payable in property are not to be counted in ascertaining whether the full capital stock is subscribed California, etc, Co v Russell, 26 Pac. Rep, 105 (1891), holding, also, that an agent's unauthorized subscription is not to be counted even though

subsequently ratified by the principal. Conditional subscriptions, the condition of which cannot be fulfilled until after incorporation, are not to be counted in ascertaining whether the requisite capital stock has been subscribed Portland, etc, Co t Spillman, 32 Pac. Rep., 688 (Ore, 1893) Subscription on condition that interest shall be paid is counted Rutland & B R R. Co v. Thrall, 35 Vt, 536 (1863) Cf Greenville & C R R Co v Coleman, 5 Rich (S.C), 118 (1851) Invalid subscriptions are not counted Belfast & M L R R Co v. Cottrell, 66 Me, 185 (1875) Cf. Swartwout v Michigan Air Line R R Co, 24 Mich, 389 (1872), § 79, supra.

[2] Phillips v Covington & Cin Bridge Co, 2 Metc (Ky), 219 (1859), holding that subscriptions of infants, married women or insolvents are not to be counted unless already paid in. Fictitious paid-up stock, and stock convertible into corporate bonds, counted See, also, Appeal of Hahn, 7 Atl Rep, 482 (Pa, 1886), excluding subscriptions of married women Cf Litchfield Bank v Church, supra Payment of part with knowledge that married woman's subscription was counted is a waiver Appeal of Cornell, 6 Atl Rep, 258 (Pa., 1886). Ultra vires subscriptions of other corporations are not counted Berry v. Yates, 24 Barb, 199 (1857).

[3] Lewey's Island R R. Co v. Bolton. 48 Me, 451 (1860), Belfast, etc R'y Co. v. Inhabitants of Brooks, 60 Me., 568

difference of opinion exists as to whether subscriptions payable by their terms in labor or materials or contract work are to be included in the count [1] The better rule seems to be that the necessity of employing this method of carrying out many modern corporate enterprises requires that such subscriptions should be counted if the contract is made in good faith and the contractors are reasonably responsible men [2] The weight of authority, however, holds otherwise. The records of the corporation are sufficient and competent evidence that the full capital stock has been subscribed [3]

The directors and stockholders are not liable for corporate debts merely because they commence business before the capital stock was subscribed The incorporation was legal without it [4]

§ 181 A subscriber may waive the defense that the full capital stock of the corporation has not been subscribed This waiver may be either express or implied from the acts or declarations of

(1872), 32 Pac Rep, 1002 The subsequent failure of some of the subscribers is immaterial. Salem M D Corporation v Ropes, 26 Mass , 187 (1829).

[1] Not counted where the contractor failed to complete the work New York, H & N R R Co v Hunt, 39 Conn , 75 (1872), Troy & G R R Co v Newton, 74 Mass., 596 (1857), the court saying "The receipt of the stock by them depended entirely upon a contingency, as the contractors might fail to do the work and so no stock be earned," Oldtown & Lincoln R R Co v Veazie, 39 Me , 571 (1855), where the contract work was not completed In the case of Ridgefield & N Y R R Co. v Brush, 43 Conn , 86 (1875), such subscriptions were counted, the contract for payment in work being parol, and not allowed to vary the apparently absolute subscription

[2] Phillips v Covington & Cin. Bridge Co , 2 Metc (Ky), 219 (1859)

[3] Penobscot R R Co v Dummer, 40 Me , 172 (1855), Same v White, 41 Me , 512 (1856). Unless proof be introduced to destroy their effect. A call is notice that the full amount has been subscribed Harlem Canal Co v Seixas, 2 Hall (N Y), 504 (1829), Same v Spear, 2 Hall, 510, Litchfield Bank v Church, 29 Conn , 137 (1860), holding that the cer-

tificate of the commissioners that the full stock had been subscribed would not be questioned, even though they had counted married women's subscriptions. To same effect, see Lane v Brainerd, 30 Conn , 565 (1862), Marlborough Branch R R Co v Arnold 9 Gray, 159 (1857) If the corporate records are destroyed or lost there should be other clear evidence Central Turnpike Co v Valentine, 10 Pick , 142 (1830).

[4] National Bank v. Texas, etc , Co , 12 S W Rep, 101 (Tex 1889) It is not actionable negligence in directors to proceed to business because only a small part of the capital is subscribed Re Liverpool, etc , Ass'n, 62 L T Rep, 873 (1890) Paying in half of the subscription with a view to incorporation and then abandonment of incorporation does not render a subscriber liable as a partner Hendson v Spaulding 6 N Y Supp , 877 (1889) Where stockholders proceed to business before the minimum capital prescribed by statute is subscribed and before the requisite amount is subscribed, they are liable to corporate creditors for such minimum capital The creditors may sue them and the corporation in the same action Burns v Beck, 10 S E Rep, 121 (Ga, 1889) Cf. § 213

the subscriber[1] Many different facts have been passed upon by the courts, and held either to constitute or not to constitute a waiver of this defense   Thus, it has been held to amount to a waiver for the subscriber to act as a director, attend meetings and contract corporate debts,[2] or to pay assessments for several years, with full knowledge of all the facts,[3] or to write to the directors, requiring them to call a meeting,[4] or to participate as a stockholder and committee man for several months,[5] or to act as president of the corporation[6] But a subscriber does not waive this defense by paying a deposit;[7] or by attending a meeting;[8] or by participating in preliminary work and paying a statutory percent-

[1] Emmitt v Springfield J & P R. R. Co., 31 Ohio St. 23 (1876), Hager v Cleveland, 36 Md, 476 (1872), Masonic, etc Assoc v Channell, 43 N W Rep, 716 (Minn 1890). In Anderson v Middle etc, R. R, 17 S W Rep, 803 (Tenn, 1891) a special agreement was held to be a waiver of the full capital being subscribed, but not as to those who had not signed the agreement A subscriber by paying calls may waive objections to the full capital stock being subscribed California, etc, Hotel Co. v Callender, 29 Pac Rep, 859 (Cal, 1892) The whole capital stock must be subscribed before subscriptions are enforced, unless the subscription contract provides otherwise A subscriber may waive this, and the question of waiver is for the jury Hards v Platte, etc, Co, 53 N W Rep, 73 (Neb, 1892). Where the subscribers have induced a contractor to proceed on the theory that the full capital has been subscribed, it is no defense that one subscription was invalid Gibbons v. Ellis, 53 N. W Rep, 701 (Wis., 1892)

[2] Hager v Cleveland, supra A defendant waives the defense that the full capital stock was not subscribed where he serves as a director is present when calls are made, votes in favor of buying a building lot, serves on committees, prepares plans, etc Ass n v Hill, 32 Pac Rep, 587 (Cal, 1893).

[3] Morrison v Dorsey, 48 Md, 461 (1877).

[4] Tredwen v Bourne, 6 Mees & W,

461 (1840), holding it to be evidence of waiver

[5] Sharpley v. Louth & E. C. R'y Co, L R.. 2 Ch Div, 663 (1876). A stockholder who receives and retains a certificate for increased stock cannot, after corporate insolvency, set up that the full increased capital was not subscribed. Butler v Aspinwall, 33 Fed Rep, 217 (1887) By organizing and proceeding, stockholders waive the defense that the full capital stock was not subscribed. Dallemand v Odd Fellows', etc, Bank, 16 Pac Rep, 497 (Cal 1888)

[6] Corwith v Culver, 69 Ill, 502 (1873).

[7] Pitchford v Davis, 5 Mees. & W, 2 (1839).

[8] Woutner v Sharp, 4 C. B., 404 (1847); New H Central R. R. Co v Johnson, 30 N H, 390 (1855), Orynski v Loustannau, 15 S. W. Rep, 674 (Tex, 1890), holding that this defense is not waived by attending a corporate meeting, the subscriber not knowing all the facts; nor is it waived by paying part of the subscription. Power in the directors to make calls when they see fit does not destroy this defense A subscriber who attends meetings and participates in the organization waives the defense that the full capital stock has not been subscribed, but if he does so without knowledge of the fact that the full capital stock has not been subscribed he does not waive such defense Portland, etc, Co v Spillman, 32 Pac Rep, 688 (Ore, 1893), International, etc, Assoc. v Walker, 49 N W Rep, 1086 (Mich.,

age required to be paid at the time of subscribing,[1] or by paying assessments for surveys[2]

§ 182 *Failure to fix definitely the capital stock, where the amount is left in the discretion of the corporation* — Sometimes corporate charters, especially in the New England states are granted without specifying the exact amount of the capital stock, but either fixing the outside limit or allowing the corporate authorities to fix it between certain specified limits   Where the charter leaves the amount of the capital stock indefinite, it is the duty of the proper corporate authorities to determine what it shall be   and no subscriber can be held liable on his subscription until such determination is made.[3] After the capital stock is once fixed, there seems to be no rule preventing its being varied subsequently, provided the specified charter limits are observed[4] It has been held that even subscriptions to the amount of the lowest limit allowed by the charter are insufficient, unless that limit has been designated by the corporate authorities as the amount of the capital stock[5]

After the capital stock is so determined, the full amount thereof must be subscribed before any subscriber is liable[6] It is not necessary that the amount of the capital stock be fixed by formal

1891), holding that attendance at a meeting and voting are not necessarily a waiver

[1] Livesey v Omaha Hotel, 5 Neb, 50 (1876), Oldtown & L R R. Co. v Venzie, 39 Me, 571 (1855), where as an officer the subscriber aided in preliminary work. This case goes further and holds that there can be no waiver under any state of facts Full capital stock necessary. Acts and facts prior to the signing of the subscription do not constitute a waiver Curry Hotel Co v Mullins, 53 N W Rep, 300 (Mich, 1892)

[2] Mempais Branch R. R. Co v Sullivan, 57 Ga, 240 (1876) Atlantic Cotton Mills v Abbott, 63 Mass, 423 (1852), holds that paying assessments and attempting to transfer is not a waiver May v Memphis B R. R. Co, 48 Ga, 109 (1873), holds that paying an assessment with notice of this defense is no waiver of it.

[3] Worcester & N R. R. Co v Hinds, 62 Mass, 110 (1851); Troy & G R. R. Co v Newton, 74 Mass., 596 (1857) Pike v Shore Line 68 Me, 445 (1878); Somerset R. R. Co v Clarke, 61 Me, 381 (1871)

Contra, Warwick R R Co v Cady 11 R I, 131 (1875), City Hotel v Dickinson 72 Mass, 586 (1862) In the case of Kirksey v Florida & G P R Co 7 Fla, 23 (1857), it was held that the corporate charter need not mention any capital stock or shares of stock, and yet subscriptions may be taken and enforced In the case of Ward v Griswoldville Mfg Co, 16 Conn, 593 (1844), where the charter allowed the capital stock to vary from $5,000 to $50,000 it was assumed that the subscriptions were enforceable, although no fixed capital stock had been settled upon In the case of White Mts R R Co v Eastman, 34 N H 124 (1856), the charter allowed assessments when the lower limit of the capital stock was reached

[4] Somerset & K R R Co v Cushing, 45 Me, 524 (1858), Troy & G R R Co v Newton, 74 Mass, 596 (1857) — *dicta,* however, in both of these cases

[5] Pike v Shore Line, 68 Me 445 (1878).

[6] Somerset & K. R R Co v Cushing, 45 Me 524 (1858), Kennebec, etc, R. R. Co v Jarvis, 34 Me, 360 (1852).

declaration of the corporate authorities. It may be done by acts equivalent thereto Thus, a resolution to close the books on a given day,[1] or limiting the time of subscription and then closing the subscription books,[2] or voting that a certain amount of stock in addition to existing subscriptions shall be issued,[3] are the same as, and are equivalent to, an express resolution that the capital stock shall be the amount of subscriptions thus taken

§ 183 *Irregular incorporation of the company.*— Under the laws of most of the states, charters of incorporation are obtained by complying with the provisions of what are called general incorporating acts Usually these acts provide that a specified number of persons, by filing at a public registry a certificate setting out certain facts, may thereby form a corporation for the purposes named in such certificate The various steps to be taken, and the contents of each certificate, are prescribed by the statute It frequently happens, however, that in the formation of a corporation under the statute some part of the proceeding, through inadvertence or mistake, is not strictly complied with. The same thing happens, also, under a special act incorporating a certain company, and requiring it to perform specified things in order to render the incorporation complete. These defects may render the corporate charter forfeitable at the instance of the state. Accordingly the question has arisen whether such defects in the process of becoming incorporated are a good and sufficient defense to an action by the corporation to collect subscriptions to its stock.

§ 184 When an action is brought to collect a subscription, either directly or indirectly for the benefit of corporate creditors, it is well established that the subscribers cannot defeat such action by the defense that the corporation was not an incorporation, by reason of its not having fully complied with the terms of the statute providing for such an incorporation.[4] Not only is the subscriber

[1] Lexington & W C R R Co. v. Chandler, 54 Mass , 311 (1847).

[2] Bucksport & B R R Co v Buck, 65 Me , 536 (1876).

[3] Penobscot & K. R R Co v Bartlett, 78 Mass , 211 (1858)

[4] Hickling v Wilson, 104 Ill , 54 (1882), Wheelock v Kost, 77 Ill , 296 (1875), Casey i Galli, 94 U S , 673, Upton i Hansbrough, 3 Biss , 317 (1873), the court saying "I understand the rule to be well settled that, where papers having color of compliance with the statutes have been filed with the proper state officers and meet their approval, but are

in fact so defective as to be incapable of supporting the corporation as against the state, they are, as against a subscriber to its capital, held sufficient to constitute a corporation *de facto*, if supported by proof of user," Clark v Thomas. Rec. etc , 34 Ohio St , 46 (1874), Voorhees v Receiver of Bank, etc , 18 Ohio, 464 (1850), Ossippee Co. v. Canney, 64 N H , 295 (1874), McCune Min Co v Adams, 10 Pac. Rep., 468 (Kan , 1886), Hamilton v Clarion, etc, R R , 23 Atl Rep , 53 (Pa , 1891). Thompson v. Reno Sav Bank, 7 Pac. Rep , 68 (Nev., 1885), says "The certifi-

estopped, by the act of subscribing, from setting up this defense, but he is bound also by the rule that the existence of a corporation cannot be inquired into except by a direct proceeding in behalf of the state It is sufficient that the corporation exists *de facto*. If there is no authority of law for such a corporation, the members are liable as partners.[1]

§ 185. As between the corporation itself and the subscribers there is more difficulty and doubt in determining the rule The great weight of authority lays down the broad rule that "where there is a corporation *de facto*, with no want of legislative power to its due and legal existence, where it is proceeding in the performance of corporate functions, and the public are dealing with it on the supposition that it is what it professes to be; and the questions suggested are only whether there has been exact regularity and strict compliance with the provisions of the law relating to incorporations,— it is plainly a dictate alike of justice and of public policy, that, in controversy between the *de facto* corporation and those who have entered into contract relations with it, as corporators or otherwise, such questions should not be suffered to be raised"[2] This, doubtless, is the law of the land, although a

cate is made for the benefit of the public, not for the corporation or its stockholders. Those who participated in the incorporation of this bank, and, by a certificate made in pursuance of the statute, announced the amount of its capital stock, cannot, as against the creditors of the corporation, contradict their own certificate" The creditors of the consolidated company may enforce subscriptions to the stock of the constituent companies, and the irregularity of the incorporation of the consolidated company is no defense Hamilton v. Clauon, etc, R. R., 23 Atl. Rep, 53 (Pa., 1891) See, also, ch XIII

[1] See ch XIII

[2] Cooley, J, in Swartwout v Mich Air Line R. R Co, 24 Mich, 389 (1872) An important case on this subject is Tar River Nav Co v Neal, 3 Hawks (N. C.), 520 (1825), where the court say that "even where it is shown that such charter has been granted upon a condition precedent, and persons are found in the quiet possession and exercise of those corporate rights as against all but the sovereign, the precedent condi-

tion shall be taken as performed ' In this case the subscriber had participated in corporate meetings Wilmington C. & R. R. R. Co v Thompson 7 Jones' L. (N C), 387 (1860), Brookville & G. T Co v McCarthy, 8 Ind, 392 (1856), holding also that the subscriber cannot set up that the corporation had forfeited its charter for misuser and nonuser Central A & M Ass'n v Alabama G L. Ins Co, 70 Ala, 120 (1881), where the court say "Whoever contracts with a corporation having a *de facto* existence, the reputation of a legal corporation, in the actual exercise of corporate powers and franchises, is estopped from denying the legality of the existence of the corporation, or inquiring into irregularities attending its formation, to defeat the contract, or to avoid the liability he has voluntarily and deliberately incurred" It also holds that a subsequent statute curing the defect is constitutional and effective Appleton Mut. Fire Ins. Co v Jesser, 87 Mass, 446 (1862), the court saying that where "persons were found with the consent and under the author-

carefully-considered case in Missouri held to the contrary, and allowed a subscriber who had not done more than merely subscribe to set up this defense against the corporation, no creditor's rights being involved, and the court declared that all the cases denying

ity of the designated corporators, and without objection on the part of the sovereign power, actually exercising the corporate powers and claiming and using the franchise, they constituted a corporation *de facto*, and the lawfulness of their organization cannot be impeached collaterally in an action to recover an assessment ' McCarthy *v* Lavasche, 89 Ill, 270 (1878), holding that the defense is not allowable, even though the statute creating the corporation be unconstitutional See St Louis Ass'n *v* Hennessey, 11 Mo App, 555 Slocum *v.* Prov S & G P Co, 10 R. I, 112 (1871), McHose *v* Wheeler, 45 Pa St, 32 (1863), Tarbell *v* Page, 24 Ill, 48 (1860), where no certificate was filed, Wallworth *v* Brackett, 98 Mass, 98 (1867), Hanover J & S. R. R. Co *v* Haldeman 82 Pa St, 36 (1876), holding that non-user rendering the charter forfeitable is no defense, Rowland *v* Meadei Furniture Co, 38 Ohio St, 269 (1882), holding that actual judgment of forfeiture is no defense; Meadow *t* Gray, 30 Me, 547 (1849), Danbury & N R. R Co *v* Wilson, 22 Conn, 435 (1853), where the subscriber acted as a director, Central Pi. Co. *v* Clements, 16 Mo, 359 (1852), Maltby *v* Northwestern Va R R. Co, 16 Md, 422 (1860), where the subscriber had already paid calls, Crawford R. R. Co *v* Lacey, 3 Y. & J, 80 (1829), where incorporation was obtained by a false representation to parliament, Rockville & W T Co *v* Van Ness, 2 Cranch, C C, 449 (1824), where the subscriber had taken part in an election, Monroe *v* Fort W, J. & S. R. Co, 28 Mich, 272 (1873), where only three instead of five signed the certificate Rice *v.* Rock I & A R R. Co., 21 Ill, 93 (1859), Hunt *v* Kansas & M Bridge Co, 11 Kan, 412 (1873), where the subscriber acted as director, Home

Stock Ins. Co *v* Sherwood, 72 Mo., 460 (1880), Evansville. etc, Co. *v.* Evansville, 15 Ind, 395 (1860); Stoops *v.* Greensburgh, etc., Co, 10 Ind, 47 (1857), Kishacoquillas, etc., Co *v* McConahy, 16 S & R., 140 (1827), and cases in ch XXXVIII on this subject. Gill *v* Ky & C. G & S Min. Co, 7 Bush, 635 (1870); Wood *v* Coosa & C. R. R Co, 32 Ga, 273 (1861), Hagei *t* Bassett, 36 Md, 476 (1872), East P Hotel Co. *v.* West, 13 La. Ann, 545 (1858). See, also, Oregon, etc, *v* Scoggin 3 Oreg, 161, holding, under a statute, that the subscription may be sued on before the organization is completed. It is no defense that the corporation was organized on a fourteen-day notice instead of fifteen days Ossipee, etc, Co *v* Canney, 54 N H, 295 (1874) Stockholders, when sued on their statutory liability, cannot impeach the organization of the company. Aultman *v* Waddle, 19 Pac Rep, 730 (Kan, 1888) The subscriber cannot set up that the charter was unconstitutional Dows *v* Napier, 91 Ill, 44 (1878). In New York the first case is Dutchess Cotton Manufactory *t* Davis, 14 Johns, 238 (1817), then came Schenectady & S P R Co *v* Thatcher, 11 N Y, 102 (1854); Eaton *v* Aspinwall, 19 N Y, 119 (1859), Methodist E. U. Ch *v.* Pickett, 19 N Y, 482 (1859), the court saying it is sufficient for the corporation to be *de facto* "Two things are necessary in order to establish the existence of a corporation *de facto*, viz . (1) The existence of a chaiter, or some law under which a corporation with the powers assumed might lawfully be created; and (2) a user, by the party to the suit, of the rights claimed to be conferred by such charter or law. The rule established by law as well as by reason is, that parties recognizing the existence of corporations by dealing with them have

the defense were cases where the subscriber had acquiesced, "either
by the payment of part of the subscription or by becoming a director, or by attending meetings of stockholders, or by any other
act indicating an acquiescence in the validity of his subscription"[1]

§ 186. There is a different class of cases in which a subscriber
for stock is allowed to make the defense that the corporation has
not been regularly and legally incorporated Where the subscriber
made his contract of subscription previous to and in anticipation
of the incorporation, and does not, by his subsequent acts, acquiesce
in the mode of incorporation, he may set up that the corporation
has not been incorporated, and that he is not liable The rule that

no right to object to any irregularity in
their organization" Block R. & U R.
R. Co v Clarke, 25 N Y, 208 (1862),
Leonardsville Bank v Willard, 25 N Y,
574 (1862), Buffalo & Allegany R R.
Co v Cary, 26 N Y 75 (1852), Aspinwall v Sacchi 57 N Y, 331 (1874), Dorris v French, 4 Hun 292 (1875) Not,
however, where, at the time of signing
the articles, the names of the directors,
required to be inserted, were not inserted Dutchess & C C R R Co v
Mabbett, 58 N Y, 397 (1874), Cayuga
Lake R. R. Co v Kyle, 64 N Y, 185
(1876), Phœnix Warehousing Co. v
Badger, 67 N Y, 294 (1876), De Witt v.
Hastings, 69 N Y, 518 (1877), admitting
the defense on the ground that there
was no user of a corporate franchise;
Ruggles v Brock, 6 Hun, 164 (1875),
Mead v Keeler, 24 Barb, 20 (1857), Ab-
bott v Aspinwall 26 Barb, 202 (1857);
Childs v Smith, 55 Barb, 45 (1869), and
see Childs v Smith, 46 N Y, 34 (1871),
McFareon v Triton, 4 Denio, 392 (1847)
This is also the rule in the federal courts.
Webster v Upton, 91 U. S, 65 (1875);
Chubb v Upton, 95 U S. 665 (1877)
Contra, Thompson v Guion, 5 Jones'
Eq (N C), 113 (1859). *Cf* Katama
Land Co. v Holly, 129 Mass, 540 (1880)
The lapse of the charter, by limitation
of time within which work must be
commenced, is good defense McCully
v Pittsburgh & C. R. R. Co, 32 Pa. St.,
25 (1858) Subscribers to increased capital stock cannot escape liability therefor by setting up that the notice of increase was not published as required by
statute Handley v Stutz, 139 U S,
417 (1891) A subscriber to stock in a
West Virginia corporation doing all its
business in Minnesota cannot set up that
the company was not legally incorporated, and cannot set up that the plaintiff is not a corporation he having participated in its incorporation Minn,
etc, Co v Denslow, 48 N W Rep, 771
(Minn, 1891) It is no defense that the
charter was not registered in all the
counties through which the road runs
Anderson v Middle, etc, R. R., 17 S W
Rep, 803 (Tenn, 1891) Concerning the
question of who can complain of mistakes, irregularities and illegalities in
the corporation, see § 5 Where the
general railroad act provides that unless
work is commenced within two years
the charter shall be void, a subscriber
for stock prior to incorporation may set
up the defense that two years have
elapsed and the charter is void Bywaters v Paris, etc, R'y, 11 S. W Rep,
856 (Tex, 1889) Cannot deny incorporation when sued on a note given to it.
Columbia Electric Co v Dixon, 49 N
W. Rep, 244 (Minn, 1891) A note given
to be applied in payment of a subscription in a company to be formed has
been held to be good even though the
corporation was not legally formed, an
attempt at incorporation having been
made Smith v Gillen, 12 S. W Rep,
1073 (Ark, 1890)

[1] Kansas City Hotel Co. v Hunt, 57
Mo, 126 (1874)

a person contracting with a corporation recognizes thereby its capacity to contract, and cannot afterwards deny it in that transaction, does not apply to one who subscribes before incorporation. He may insist upon the organization of a regular and legal corporation [1]

§ 187 *Ultra vires acts of the directors of the corporation* — A subscriber for stock in a corporation cannot defeat an action to collect such subscription by the defense that the directors or the corporation itself have done corporate acts which are beyond the corporate powers.[2] There are other remedies open to the subscriber He may either enjoin such *ultra vires* acts, or may have them set aside if already accomplished [3] This defense is clearly

[1] Dorris *v* Sweeney, 60 N Y, 463 (1875), Rikhoff *v* Browne R. S S. M Co, 68 Ind, 388 (1879), Indianapolis F & Min Co *v* Herkimer, 46 Ind, 142 (1874), Nelson *v* Blakey, 47 Ind, 38 (1874), McIntyre *v* McLane D Ass n, 40 Ind, 104 (1872), Richmond Factory Ass'n *v* Clarke, 61 Me, 351 (1873), Reed *v* Richmond Street R. R Co, 50 Ind, 342 (1875), Taggart *v* Western Md R. R. Co, 24 Md, 563 (1866) the court saying "The preponderance of authority in favor of a strict compliance with the provisions of the charter, in cases of subscriptions prior to the organization of the company, is such as is not to be disregarded" *Cf* Buffalo, etc, *v* Hatch, 20 N Y, 157 (1859). The "records, books and minutes" of a corporation are sufficient evidence of its incorporation Glenn *v* Orr, 2 S E Rep, 538 (N C, 1887). A subscriber may deny that a consolidated company which succeeds his own was legally incorporated Mansfield, etc, R. R. *v.* Stout, 26 Ohio St, 241 (1875) Brown *v* Dibble, 32 N W Rep, 565 (Mich, 1887). In suing on an original subscription the corporation must allege that it has been duly incorporated The payment of part of the subscription is no waiver of the defense Schloss *v* Montgomery, etc, Co, 6 S Rep, 360 (Ala, 1889) Indefiniteness in the statement of the objects of incorporation is no defense Owenton, etc, Co. *v* Smith, 13 S. W. Rep, 426 (Ky, 1890)

[2] Cravens *v* Eagle, etc, Co., 21 N. E. Rep, 981 (Ind, 1889); First Municipality of N O *v* Orleans Theater Co., 2 Rob. (La.), 209 (1842), Hannibal R. C. & P. P. R Co *v* Menifee, 25 Mo, 547 (1857); Vicksburg, S & T R R. Co *v* McKean, 12 La Ann, 638 (1857); Smith *v* Tallahassee. etc, Plank-road Co, 30 Ala, 650 (1857), Prop of City Hotel *v.* Dickinson, 72 Mass, 586 (1856), Courtright *v* Deeds, 37 Iowa, 503 (1873); Ill. Grand T R. R. Co *v* Cook, 29 Ill, 237 (1862), Hammett *v* Little Rock & N. R. R. Co, 20 Ark, 204 (1859). In the case, however, of Macedon & B P R. Co *v* Lapham, 18 Barb., 315 (1854), an *ultra vires* extension of the line was held to be a good defense Subscriber cannot set up that corporation has not complied with charter Toledo, etc, R. R. Co. *v.* Johnson, 49 Mich, 148 (1882). *Ultra vires* acts and no notice of meetings are not good defenses. Cartwright *v.* Dickinson, 12 S W. Rep, 1030 (Tenn, 1890). If a manufacturing corporation does not locate its works in the place prescribed by its articles of incorporation, a subscriber to stock may withdraw his subscription Auburn, etc., Works *v.* Schultz, 22 Atl. Rep, 904 (Pa., 1891).

[3] "The stockholder has his remedy by injunction not to enjoin the collection of calls due upon his stock, but to restrain the corporation from the particular violation or abuse of its charter complained of" Miss., O. & Red R. R. R. Co. *v* Cross, 20 Ark., 443 (1859).

distinguishable from the common defense of amendments to the
charter, by the fact that the acts here complained of have no sanction from the legislative authorities[1] Thus, it has been held that
a subscriber cannot defeat an action to collect his subscription by
showing that the corporation has, without authority of law, and
in excess of its powers, executed a lease or sale of the road,[2] or
illegally issued its bonds,[3] or purchased shares of its own stock,[4]
or the stock of another corporation,[5] or changed the location or
route of the road[6] The last instance, especially, has been a frequent defense, but it has been uniformly discountenanced by the
courts where the change in the route was made, not by an amendment to the charter, but by the arbitrary, unauthorized act of the
corporate authorities

§ 188 *Frauds and mismanagement of directors.*— This defense
is very similar to the preceding one, and is governed by the same
rules of law A stockholder cannot defeat an action to collect his
subscription by the defense that the corporate affairs have been
managed fraudulently or recklessly or negligently[7] The stock-

In *Ex parte* Booker, 18 Ark, 338 (1857),
an application for an injunction to restrain the corporation from enforcing
the payment of a subscription, on the
ground that the corporation had committed *ultra vires* acts, was refused
And see, also, ch 52, *infra*

[1] Caley v Phil & C. C. R. R. Co, 80
Pa St, 363 (1876) A change in the law
between the time of making a subscription and the obtaining of the charter
may release or render illegal the subscriptions. Knox v. Childerburg Land
Co, 5 S Rep 578 (Ala, 1889) Where
the statutes under which the company
is organized allow the objects of the
company to be changed on a vote of
the stockholders, a dissenting stockholder
is not released from his subscription by
such change Mercantile Statement
Co v Kneal, 53 N W, Rep, 632 (Minn,
1892) For the principles of law herein
relative to amendments to the charter,
see § 502, etc

[2] Hays v Ottawa, O & F R V R. R.
Co., 61 Ill, 423 (1871), Ottawa, O & F
R V R. R. Co. v. Black 79 Ill, 262
(1875), Chicago, B & Q R. R. Co v
McGinnis, 79 Ill, 269 (1875), Ill Mid
R y Co v Supervisors, etc, 85 Ill 313

(1877), South Ga & Fla R R Co v.
Ayres 56 Ga, 230 (1876) See, also,
Tuttle v Mich Air Line R R Co, 35
Mich 247, Troy & Rutland R R Co v
Kerr, 17 Barb, 581 (1854) Or the whole
of a business Plate Glass Ins. Co v
Sunley, 8 El & Bl, 47 (1857)

[3] Merrill v Reaver, 50 Iowa, 404 (1879)

[4] *Re* Republic Ins Co, 3 Biss, 452
(1873)

[5] Cheltain v Republic Life Ins Co,
86 Ill, 220 (1877)

[6] Central P R Co. v Clemens, 16 Mo,
359 (1852), Miss, O & Red R R R Co
v Cross, 20 Ark, 443 (1859), Rives v
Montgomery, South P R. Co, 30 Ala, 92
(1857) Where, however, the terminus
was made two thousand feet away from
the location designated by charter, this
fact was held to constitute *prima facie*
a good defense Charters R R. Co v
Hodgens, 77 Pa St. 187 See, also § 82,
supra A change in the route under
statutes existing before the incorporation
does not release subscribers Armstrong
v Karshner, 24 N E. Rep, 897 (Ohio,
1890)

[7] People v Barnett, 91 Ill, 422 (1879),
Cheltain v Republic Life Ins Co, 86
Ill 220 (1877), Merrill v Reaver, 50

holder's remedies for such evils are of a different nature. For fraud, he may bring the guilty parties to an accounting;[1] for mismanagement, his only remedy is the corporate elections In no case has he been allowed to escape liability on his subscription by reason thereof. Thus, it is no defense that the corporate authorities fraudulently placed an overvaluation on property purchased by them for the corporation;[2] nor that they have made a fraudulent contract with a construction company[3]

§ 189 *Delay and abandonment of the enterprise.*— As a general rule, it is no defense to an action on a subscription to allege that the enterprise has been unduly delayed[4] The defense frequently is that there has been a non-user of the corporate franchises.[5] It is, however, a well-established principle that non-user of corporate franchises can be complained of only by the state or in the name of the state A subscriber has been held not to be discharged by the fact that the corporation was engaged thirteen years in completing the enterprise — a turnpike[6] Nor does a temporary abandonment of the work release the subscriber[7] But when the corporate work was not commenced for nine years, and in the meantime the subscriber had acted on the supposition of an abandonment and had sold property which the road was expected to benefit, he

Iowa, 404 (1879). Depreciation of the stock, by reason of mismanagement, no defense People *v* Barnett, 91 Ill, 422 (1879)

[1] See ch XXXIX. In the case of Hodgkinson *v* Nat. Live Stock Ins Co, 26 Beav, 473 (1859), equity restrained the enforcement of calls already made, by reason of the fraud of the directors; but it was conceded in this case that the subscriber was still liable on his subscription

[2] Hornaday *v* Ind & Ill Central R. R Co, 9 Ind, 263 (1857); Dorris *v* French, 4 Hun, 292 (1875), where a patent-right was purchased by the directors from themselves, for the corporation, at an exorbitant price.

[3] People *v* Logan County, 63 Ill, 374, 387 (1872)

[4] Pickering *v* Templeton, 2 Mo. App, 424 (1876) Miller *v* Pittsburgh & C R. R. Co, 40 Pa St., 237 (1861), where there was a delay of two and one-half years, the court saying "Until it can be shown how railroads can be built with-

out money, no such defense as is here set up can prevail" First Nat'l Bank *v* Hurford, 29 Iowa, 579 (1870), where there was a delay in the performance of a condition subsequent to the subscription See, also, Union Hotel Co *v.* Hursee, 79 N. Y, 454 (1880); reversing 15 Hun, 371. Boyle's Case, 54 L J (Ch), 550 (1885), holds that after a winding-up has commenced there can be no withdrawal; but the court in a *dictum* clearly says that an unreasonable delay in organizing will authorize a withdrawal by the subscriber. But where the charter has lapsed by reason of not complying with its terms, the stockholder is not liable. Sodus Bay, etc, R. R. Co *v* Lapham, 43 Hun, 314 (1887).

[5] Ouachita & Red R. R. Co. *v* Cross, 20 Ark, 443 (1855), Hammett *v* Little Rock & N R. R. Co, 20 Ark, 204 (1859).

[6] Gibson *v* Columbia & N R, T. & B Co, 18 Ohio St, 396 (1868)

[7] McMullen *v* Maysville & Lex R. R. Co, 15 B Monr (Ky), 218 (1854).

was held not liable on the subscription [1] An abandonment of part of the enterprise, however, is no defense [2]

A subscriber cannot defeat the subscription by the fact that the corporation has not completed, and has no intention of completing, the road in its entirety, [3] nor by the fact that the road has been sold under foreclosure [4] In Pennsylvania a failure on the part of the corporation to make a call for the subscription within six years, the statutory time of limitations on the collection of parol debts, is held to constitute an abandonment of the subscription, and to be a good defense [5] If the corporation is insolvent, and the subscription is needed to pay corporate creditors, abandonment cannot be set up.[6]

§ 190 *Failure of the corporate enterprise.*— The entire failure of the enterprise and the insolvency of the corporation constitute no defense to an action on calls [7] This defense would seem on the face of it to be frivolous, and yet is occasionally set up. Under the American doctrine a subscription is enforceable most of all when it is needed to pay corporate creditors This defense is closely allied to those that precede, and differs in little from the defense of abandonment of the enterprise.

[1] Fountain Ferry T. R Co v Jewell, 8 B Mon (Ky), 147 (1848) A note in payment of a subscription, payable by its terms after the road had been partially completed, is not enforceable where the enterprise was abandoned and fourteen years afterwards was revived and the road built Blake v Brown, 44 N W Rep, 751 (Iowa, 1890)

[2] Dorman v Jacksonville & A P R Co, 7 Fla, 265 (1857) No defense that the company had abandoned a part of its business nor that the company was organized for the sole benefit of the charter members Dallas, etc, Mills v Clancy, 15 S W Rep, 194 (Tex, 1891)

[3] Buffalo & J. R R Co v Gifford, 87 N Y., 294 (1882) affirming 22 Hun, 359 No defense that road not fully completed Armstrong v Karshner, 24 N E Rep, 897 (Ohio, 1890), Lesher v Karshner, id, 882

[4] Id

[5] Pittsburgh & C R M Co v Byers, 32 Pa. St, 22 (1858). The same rule is stated less broadly in McCully v Pittsburgh, etc, J R R Co, 32 Pa St, 25

(1858), where the court say, "if the delay was not satisfactorily accounted for, subscribers would be at liberty after that lapse of time to consider the enterprise abandoned" In this case an actual abandonment and return of subscription money to other subscribers was held to release all the subscribers In Delaware etc, R R. Co v Rowland, 9 Atl Rep, 929 (Penn, 1887), it was submitted to the jury whether the subscriber had been released by an abandonment of the enterprise See, also, § 195 *infra*

[6] Phœnix Warehousing Co v Badger, 67 N Y, 294 (1876), Smith v Gower, 2 Duv (Ky), 17 (1865), Hardy v Merriwether, 14 Ind, 203, and see the defense in § 190

[7] Bish v Bradford, 17 Ind, 190 (1861) Morgan County v Thomas, 76 Ill, 120 141 (1875), Four-mile V R R Co v Bailey, 18 Ohio St 208 (1868) Assessments are collectible though the work is not completed Red W Hotel Co v Friedrich 26 Minn, 112 (1879) See Buffalo, etc, R R Co v Gifford, *supra*

§ 191. *Subscriptions of other subscribers released or canceled, or given on special terms* — It is no defense for one subscriber, when sued upon his subscription, to allege that the subscriptions of others have been canceled, or that secret and more favorable terms were given to them than to him   If there has been a legal cancellation of other subscriptions the defendant cannot complain.[1] If he has the same right to a cancellation he may obtain it by a suit for that purpose[2] Moreover, a secret agreement of the corporation with certain subscribers to stock, whereby they are to be released from payment, or to have some other advantage not common to all the subscribers, is no defense to a subscriber who was not promised the same advantages[3] All such secret agreements are void, and the subscribers receiving them are liable on their subscriptions absolutely, as though no special advantages had been promised   Being so, a subscriber, though he did not participate therein, cannot complain   The fact that the corporation has forfeited the stock of other subscribers, and has compromised with still others, is no defense to a subscriber sued for calls.[4] So, also, the failure of another subscriber to pay the percentage required by statute is not a defense[5]

§ 192 *Failure of the corporation to tender a certificate* — It is no defense to an action on a subscription to allege that the corporation has not delivered nor tendered to the defendant the certificate

[1] Rensselaer & W. P R Co *v* Wetsel, 21 Barb, 56 (1855) If, however, the cancellation is on account of an abandonment of the enterprise, any other subscriber, when sued subsequently on his subscription, may set up such abandonment and cancellation, and thereby defeat the action   McCully *v* Pittsburgh & Erie R. R. Co, 32 Pa St, 25 (1858)

[2] County of Crawford *v* Pittsburgh & Erie R R. Co, 32 Pa St, 141 (1858)

[3] Anderson *v* Newcastle & R. R. R. Co, 12 Ind, 376 (1859), Jewett *v* Valley R y Co, 34 Ohio St. 601; Agu C Ins Co. *v* Fitzgerald, 15 Jur, 489 (1850), Memphis Branch R. R Co *v* Sullivan, 57 Ga, 240 (1876), Hall *v* Selma R. R. Co, 6 Ala 71, Conn, etc, R R. Co *v* Bailey, 24 Vt, 465, Jewell *v* Rock R P Co., 101 Ill, 57 (1881). In the case of Galena Iron Co *v* Ennor, 116 Ill, 55 (1886), the court said   "Such secret agreement was fraudulent as to the other subscribers, and was void and of no avail, and the subscription is to be regarded as a valid one for the amount subscribed"   See, also, Thompson *v* Reno Sav Bank, 19 Nev, 103, 171, 242, 291, 293 (1885)   The subscriber has the burden of proof that other subscriptions are colorable and fictitious   Hayden *v.* Atlanta Cotton Factory, 61 Ga, 233 (1878)   The case of Rutz *v* Ester & R. Mfg Co, 3 Bradw (Ill), 83 (1878), is contrary to the general rule   The case of New York Exchange Co *v.* De Wolf, 31 N Y, 270 (1865), reversing 5 Bosw, 593, holds that a subscriber may defeat an action on his subscription by showing that other subscriptions were unauthorized and not enforceable See, also, Berry *v* Yates, 24 Barb, 199, Nickerson *v* English, 142 Mass, 267 (1886)

[4] Dorman *v* Jacksonville & A P. R. Co 7 Fla 265 (1857)

[5] Swartwout *v* Mich An Line R. R. Co, 24 Mich, 389 (1872)

of stock to which he is entitled[1] The certificate is merely the stockholder's evidence of title to his stock It is not the stock itself, but only a convenient representative of it He would be a full stockholder, with all the rights of one, even if the certificates were

[1] Burr v Wilcox, 22 N Y 551 (1860), affirming 6 Bos, 198, Chandler v Northern Cross R R Co, 18 Ill, 190 (1856), Miller v Wild Cat G R Co, 52 Ind, 51 (1875), New Albany & S R R Co v McCormick, 10 Ind, 499 (1858), Slipher v. Earhart, 83 Ind, 173 (1882), Paducah, etc., Bank v Parks S S W Rep, 842 (Tenn, 1888), Heaston v Cincinnati & Ft W R R Co, 16 Ind, 275 (1861), Kennebec, etc, R R Co v Jarvis, 34 Me, 360, Chaffin v Cummings, 37 Me, 76 (1853). In behalf of corporate creditors, where the corporation is insolvent, a person is often held to be a stockholder although no certificate has been issued to him, and the ordinary *indicia* of stockholdership do not indicate that he is a stockholder Sanger v Upton, 91 U S, 56 (1875), Upton v Tribilcock, 91 U S, 45 (1875), Slee v. Bloom, 13 Johns, 456 (1822), Dorris v. French, 4 Hun, 292 (1875), Hamilton, etc, R R Co v. Rice, 7 Barb, 157–167 (1849), Clark v Farrington, 11 Wis, 306, 327 (1860); Haynes v Brown, 36 N H, 545–563 (1858), Chesley v Cummings, 37 Me, 76–83 (1853), Griswold v Seligman, 72 Mo, 110, Boggs v Olcott, 40 Ill, 303 (1866); Re South Mountain, etc, 7 Sawy, 20 (1881), Upton v Burnham, 3 Biss, 431 (1873), Johnson v Albany etc R R Co, 40 How Pr 193, Payne v Elliot, 54 Cal, 339 (1880). The subscriber may stipulate otherwise in his subscription Summers v Sleath, 48 Ind, 598 (1874), Schaeffer v Mo Home Ins Co, 46 Mo, 248 (1870), South Ga & Fla R R Co v Ayers, 56 Ga, 231 (1876), Vawter v Ohio & Miss R R Co, 14 Ind, 174 (1860). Spear v Crawford, 14 Wend, 20 (1835), Chester Glass Co v Dewey, 16 Mass, 94 (1819), Fulgam v Macon & B R R Co, 44 Ga, 597 (1872), Minnesota Harvester Works v Libby, 24 Minn, 327 (1877), Blyth's Case, L R, 4 Ch Div 140 (1876), Agricultural Bank v Burr, 24 Me, 256 (1844), Hawley v Upton 102 U S 314 (1880), Wheeler v Miller, 90 N Y 353 (1882). affirming 24 Hun 541 Wemple v St Louis etc, R R Co, 11 N E Rep, 906 (Ill 1887). The case of Clark v Continental Imp Co, 57 Ind, 135 (1877), holds that, where the action is for the whole subscription or the last instalments, a tender of the certificate, on condition of payment is necessary St Paul, etc, R R Co v Robbins 23 Minn 440 (1877), holds that a tender is necessary where the issue is of preferred stock, after the whole original capital stock has been issued Where a subscriber has tendered his subscription and demanded a certificate and is refused, a receiver cannot, upon insolvency of the company, hold him liable Potts v Wallace, 32 Fed Rep 272 (1887) A certificate of stock need not be tendered before suit is brought Webb v Baltimore etc, Co, 26 Atl Rep, 113 (Md, 1893), Astoria, etc R R v Hill, 25 Pac Rep, 379 (Ore 1890), California etc, Hotel Co v Callender, 29 Pac Rep 859 (Cal, 1892), Columbia Elec Co v Dixon, 49 N W Rep, 244 (Minn, 1891) Dallas etc Mills v Clancy, 15 S W Rep, 194 (Tex 1891), Maison v Deither, 52 N W Rep, 98 (Minn, 1892) A subscriber to the increased capital stock who has actually paid part of the price cannot recover back the money upon the corporate insolvency on the ground that no certificate was issued Pacific Nat Bank v. Eaton, 141 U S, 227 (1891). Thayer v Butler, id, 234 Butler v Eaton, id, 240 A consolidated company claiming a subscription made to one of the constituent companies must prove a tender of the stock Pope v Board of Com'rs, 51 Fed Rep, 769 (1892) A corporation

never issued at all.[1] Consequently, since it is for him to demand the certificate when he wishes it, and not for the corporation to tender it, it is no defense for him to allege that he has never received the paper representative of his stock. The corporation must, however, be in a position to issue such certificate[2] If certificates for the whole capital stock have already been issued, the defendant subscriber, by this fact, may defeat the action to collect his subscription[3] It has also been held that the plaintiff corporation must aver a readiness and willingness to deliver the certificate of stock.[4] The duty of a corporation to issue certificates of stock is considered elsewhere[5]

§ 193 *Set-off and counter-claim.*—It seems to be well established that, when a corporation has become insolvent, and the subscriptions for stock are being enforced for the benefit of corporate creditors, a subscriber cannot, in the suit brought to collect his subscription, set up a counter-claim or set-off[6] This rule is founded in equity

cannot be compelled by the subscriber for stock to issue a certificate therefor before it has been fully paid up, the stock being a part of the increased capital stock. Baltimore, etc, Co *v.* Hambleton, 26 Atl Rep, 279 (Md, 1893) The issue of certificates of stock is not necessary to render the subscriber liable Mathis *v.* Pridham, 20 S W Rep, 1015 (Tex, 1892).

[1] Fulgam *v* Macon, etc, R R. Co, 44 Ga, 597 (1872) The issuing of a certificate is not necessary to constitute stockholdership. Cartwright *v* Dickinson, 12 S. W Rep, 1030 (Tenn, 1890).

[2] McCord *v* Ohio & Miss R. R. Co., 13 Ind, 229 (1859) The subscriber may compel the corporation to issue a certificate to him. Buffalo, etc, R. R. Co. *v.* Dudley, 14 N Y, 336, 347 (1856), Mitchell *v* Beckman, 64 Cal, 117 (1883)

[3] Burrows *v* Smith, 10 N. Y, 550 (1853)

[4] James *v* Cincinnati, H & D. R. R. Co, 2 Disney, 261 (1858)

[5] See § 61.

[6] Handley *v* Stutz, 139 U S, 417 (1891), Sawyer *v* Hoag, 17 Wall, 610 (1873), Shickle *v* Watts, 7 S W. Rep, 274 (Mo, 1888), Government S Ins Co *v* Dempsey, 50 L J (Q B), 199 (1881). The leading case in England on this subject is Grissell's Case, L. R., 1 Ch, 528 (1866), where the court say, "if a set-off were attained against a call, it would have the effect of withdrawing altogether from the creditor's part of the funds applicable to the payment of debts." See, also, Black's Case, L. R., 8 Ch., 254 (1872), Mudford's Case, L. R., 14 Ch. D, 634 (1880), spoken of in Government S. I Co *v* Dempsey, *supra*, as holding that no counter-claim is to be allowed; Gill's Case, L. R., 12 Ch. Div, 755 (1879); Calisher's Case, L. R, 5 Eq, 214 (1868); Barnett's Case, L. R., 19 Eq, 449 (1875), *Re* Whitehouse & Co, L. R., 9 Ch. Div, 595 (1878), disapproving Brighton Arcade Co *v.* Dowling, L. R., 3 C. P., 175. See, also, Matthews *v* Albert, 24 Md, 527 (1866) Garnett & M G. Min. Co. *v.* Sutton, 3 B. & S., 321, allowing set-off, was based on a statute repealed by Companies Act, 1862 See Hiller *v.* Allegheny Mutual Ins. Co., 3 Pa St., 470 (1846), Long *v* Penn. Ins. Co, 6 Pa. St., 421 (1847) *Cf* Scammon *v.* Kimball, 92 U S, 362 (1875), Osgood *v.* Ogden, 4 Keyes, 70 (1868), Lawrence *v* Nelson, 21 N Y, 158 (1860). A subscriber cannot set off against his unpaid subscription a judgment lien where there are prior liens which would take the money due on his subscription if he should first pay

and wise public policy The stockholder is not deprived of his remedy for the debt due him from the corporation, but he is obliged to proceed in the same manner, and is allowed to participate in the final corporate assets to the same extent and at the same time as other creditors [1]

Where, however, payment of a subscription is demanded or enforced for the benefit of the corporation itself, and not for corporate creditors, it is competent for the subscriber to set up, in defense of the action, a set-off or counter-claim [2]

it in Not, on the other hand, if there are other debts of the company, will the obligation of the company to the stockholders be canceled by the company's offsetting the subscription against the debt unless the subscriber is insolvent. Gilchrist v Helena, etc. R R, 49 Fed Rep, 519 (1892), Boulton Carbon Co v Mills, 43 N W Rep, 290 (Iowa. 1889) In this case the learned court refers to § 227d (1st ed) of this work and dissents from the statement of law laid down herein It will be noticed, however, that § 227d stated the law as to set-off in cases of *statutory* liability of stockholders The right of set-off in cases of *subscription* liability of stockholders is stated in this work in § 193, *supra*, and the law as there laid down agrees with the decision in the above case — a case of subscription liability Where set-off is a good defense to the action of a creditor who is also a stockholder and is liable, it is a good defense as against the assignee of his claim Callanan v Windsor, 42 N W Rep. 663 (Iowa, 1889) Unpaid salaries voted to its officers by an insolvent corporation which has never made any profits cannot be offset as against the stockholders' liability to creditors Burns v Beck, 10 S E. Rep., 121 (Ga, 1889) A set-off is not allowed Hoby & Co, Lam, v Birch, 62 L T Rep, 404 (1890), reviewing the various contradictory decisions approved, Mathis v. Pridham, 20 S W Rep., 1015 (Tex, 1892). No set-off allowed as regards subscription liability, Tama, etc. Co v Hopkins, 44 N W Rep., 797 (Iowa. 1890) In a suit in equity by a receiver against all the stockholders, individual stockholders cannot plead in set-off debts due from the corporation Mathis v Pridham, 20 S. W Rep, 1015 (Tex, 1892) In Scovill v Thayer, 105 U S, 143, 152 (1881), the say " It is a general rule that a holder of claims against an insolvent corporation cannot set them off against his liability for an assessment on his stock in the corporation in a suit by an assignee in bankruptcy." To same effect, Thebus v Smiley, 110 Ill, 316 (1884), Williams v Traphagen, 38 N J Eq, 57 (1884). Payment of subscriptions in advance of calls, by turning in a debt thereon, is not payment upon corporate insolvency and winding-up Ex parte Kent, 58 L T Rep, 372 (1888), 59 id, 419 (1888) Cf. Healey on Law & Pr of Companies, 117, 729, 560, 599 Creditors who are stockholders cannot claim any part of the assets until their unpaid subscription is paid, but may claim their part before it is certain that any of the statutory liability will be required Appeal of Sahlendecker, 14 Atl Rep, 229 (Pa, 1888) A counter-claim which the company had, but which has been adjudicated against it, cannot be set up by stockholders when they are sued on their subscriptions Stutz v Handley, 41 Fed Rep, 531 (1890) A subscriber sued on his subscription may set off a debt due from the company to him Appleton v Turnbull, 24 Atl Rep 592 (Me, 1891) Concerning set-off as against the *statutory* liability of stockholders, see § 225, *infra*

[1] Grissell's Case, *supra* Cf Lang v Penn Ins Co, *supra.*

[2] Barnett's Case, *supra.*

§ 194 In New York it has recently been established that, where a corporate creditor brings an action at law to enforce an unpaid subscription, the subscriber may set up, in defense to the action, a set-off or counter-claim consisting of a debt due from the corporation to him, but that such a defense is not allowable in a suit in equity[1] The distinction is based on the fact that a general accounting of all corporate debts and assets is possible by the latter remedy, but is impossible in the action at law.[2]

§ 195 *Statute of limitations* — After a call has been made, and the subscription or a part of the subscription is thereby rendered due and payable, the statute of limitations begins to run. Difficulty, however, arises in determining whether the statute begins to run before the call is made In Pennsylvania there formerly was an inclination to hold that the call must be made before six years have elapsed after the call is possible, otherwise the right of collection is barred[3] But the better rule, and the one supported by the weight of authority, is that the statute of limitations begins to run on a subscription for stock only after a call has been made and

---

[1] Richards z Kinsley, N Y. Daily Reg , Dec 27, 1887 (Com Pl, Gen Term), where the rule is clearly laid down, also, Christensen v Colby, 43 Hun, 362 (1887) In both of these cases the rule is based on analogous decisions in regard to the stockholder's statutory liabilities See § 225 *infra.*

[2] Tallmadge v Fishkill Iron Co, 4 Barb , 382 (1848). In the case of Wheeler v Millar, 90 N Y , 353 (1882), the stockholder's subscription and statutory liability combined were sufficient to pay his own and the other debts involved in the case

See Sacketts Harbor R R Co v Blake, 3 Rich Eq , 225 (1851), Grose v Hilt 36 Me , 22 (1853), Whitman v Porter, 107 Mass , 522 (1871), a joint-stock company case , Poole s Case, L R., 9 Ch. Div , 322 Cf Eastman v. Crosby 90 Mass , 206 (1864).

[3] McCully v Pittsburgh & C R R. Co., 32 Pa. St , 25 (1858), Pittsburgh & C R. R. Co v Byers, 32 id , 22 (1858); Same v Graham, 36 id 77 (1859), Shackamason Bank v Disston, 2 R'y & Corp L J., 62 (Pa , 1887) Cf Pittsburgh & C R. R. Co v Plummer, 37 Pa St , 413 (1860) A contrary rule seems to have been fol-

lowed in Appeal of Mack, 7 Atl. Rep., 481 (1886) And it is now held in Pennsylvania that the statute of limitations runs against an unpaid subscription from the date of the assignment by the corporation for the benefit of creditors, and not from the time of a call. Franklin Sav Bank v. Bridges, 8 Atl. Rep., 611 (Pa , 1887) Cf Allibone v. Hagar, 46 Pa. St., 48, where a plea of the statute of limitations in a suit for unpaid subscriptions was not allowed, because by statute the liability of stockholders continued until the whole capital was paid in. In Shackamason Bank v. Dougherty, 20 Weekly Notes Cas., 297, it was held that a mere delay of six years in making calls barred all recovery, and obviously the bar of the statute was applied when no action was brought for six years after assessment made, or six years after the corporation assigned for the benefit of its creditors The statute of limitations begins to run when the subscription is made even though a call is not made until long afterwards Great Western T. Co v. Purdy, 50 N. W Rep., 45 (Iowa, 1891). See, also, § 189, *supra.*

is due [1] It has been held that where the statute is a bar against the corporation, it is a bar against corporate creditors [2] But a more just rule prevails in New York, to the effect that, inasmuch as the corporate creditor's right to enforce the unpaid subscription ac-

[1] The statute of limitations runs only from the time of a call Glenn v Marbury, 145 U. S., 449 (1892), Hawkins v Glenn, 131 U S, 319 (1889), Glenn v Liggett, 135 id, 533 (1890), Semple v Glenn, 9 S Rep, 265 (Ala 1891), Semple v Glenn, 6 S Rep, 46 (Ala, 1889); Lehman v Semple, 6 S Rep, 44 (Ala, 1889), Glenn v Priest, 48 Fed Rep, 19 (1891), Priest v. Glenn, 51 Fed Rep, 405 (1892). Where by statute the assignor is liable, the statute of limitations does not commence to run until there has been a call Priest v Glenn 51 Fed Rep, 400 (1892), Taggart v Western Md R R. Co, 24 Md, 563 (1866) Western R. R. Co v Avery, 64 N C, 489 (1870), Glenn v Williams 60 Md, 93 (1882), Baltimore, etc, Turnpike Co v Barnes, 6 H & J (Md), 57 (1823) Salisbury v Black's Adm'r, id, 293. Curry v Woodward, 53 Ala, 376 (1875), Glenn v. Soule, 22 Fed Rep, 417 (1884), Glenn v Foote, 36 id., 824 (1888), Great Western Tel Co v Gray, 14 N E Rep, 214 (Ill, 1887). Cf § 227, infra, Glenn v. Howard, 8 S E Rep, 636 (Ga, 1889) If a subscription is conditional, the statute of limitations runs only from the time of performance Appeal of Cornell, 6 Atl Rep, 258 (Pa, 1886) In New York, since no call is necessary, but subscriptions are due at once without it, the statute of limitations begins to run from the time of subscription, even against corporate creditors Williams v Meyer, 41 Hun, 545 (1886). Merely authorizing a receiver to collect subscriptions held not a call sufficient to set the statute of limitations running Glenn v Macon, 32 Fed Rep., 7 (1887). The statute of limitations begins to run on unpaid subscriptions from the dissolution of the corporation. Garesche v Lewis, 6 S W. Rep, 54 (Mo, 1887) Statute of limitations runs against unpaid subscriptions

only from the time of a call by the court, not from the time of an assignment to a trustee Vanderwerken v Glenn, 6 S E. Rep, 806 (Va 1888), Lewis. Adm'r, v Glenn, 6 S E. Rep, 866 (Va 1888). The state statute of limitations as to executors and estates will be applied by the federal courts to suits by a receiver for the enforcement of a stockholder's liability in a national bank Butler v Poole, 44 Fed Rep 586 (1890) Although the statute of limitations bars the action by the creditor against the corporation, yet if a lien exists by trust deed, the debt may be enforced against unpaid subscriptions Hambleton v Glenn, 9 S E Rep., 129 (Va, 1889) If the stockholder is a non-resident the statute of limitations does not run Tama etc, Co v Hopkins 44 N W Rep, 797 (Iowa, 1890) The statute of limitations is no bar Lehman v Glenn. 6 S Rep, 44 (Ala., 1889) The statute of limitations begins to run in favor of stockholders against the creditor's debt at the same time it commences to run in favor of the company, even though the company is sued before the statute is a bar as to it The statute runs against the liability of subscribers from the time of the subscription, where no call is made before the statute becomes a bar Hamilton v Clarion, etc, R. R, 23 Atl Rep, 53 (Pa, 1891) The statute of limitations does not begin to run as against creditors until they have exhausted their remedy against the company, and have established the amount due from the stockholders and necessary to pay the debt. Mathis v Pridham. 20 S W Rep., 1015 (Tex, 1892)

[2] Stelphen v Ware, 45 Cal, 110 (1872), Davidson v Rankin, 34 Cal, 503 (1868), in probate matters, Thompson v Reno Sav. Bank, 19 Nev., 103, 171, 242, 291, 293 (1885); South Car. Manuf. Co v

crues only after judgment against the corporation is obtained, the
statute of limitations runs only from the date of such judgment.[1]
Courts of equity will generally apply the same period of limitation,
unless there be special and equitable reasons for doing otherwise.[2]
Where a subscriber defeats even a part of the action on his subscription by setting up the statute of limitations, he cannot claim
the stock, at least unless he pays the part which was barred by the
statute[3]

§ 196 *Ignorance or mistake* — It is no defense to an action for
a subscription that the subscriber at the time of subscribing was

Bank of S C, 6 Rich. Eq (S C.), 227
(1851), First Nat. Bank *v* Greene, 17
N W. Rep, 86 (Iowa. 1883), affirmed on
rehearing, 20 id, 754 (1884) The statute
applicable to written contracts applies,
although the subscription is partly in
writing. Falmouth, etc, Co *v.* Shaw-
han, 5 N E Rep, 408 (Ind, 1886) It is
well to suggest here that the creditor,
before enforcing this liability, must first
obtain judgment against the corporation (See § 200, *infra*) The corporation
can defeat the action against it by setting up the statute of limitations, if sufficient time has elapsed If the corporation fails to set up that defense, the
stockholder may set it up in behalf of
the corporation when he is sued Such,
at least, is the rule in some jurisdictions
(See § 209, *infra*) The statute of limitations, by commencing to run against
one call, does not thereby commence to
run against the whole subscription.
Dorsheimer *v* Glenn, 51 Fed Rep, 400
(1892), Priest *v* Glenn, id, 405

[1] Christensen *v* Quintard, 36 Hun, 334
(1885), Christensen *v* Colby, 43 Hun, 362
(1887) See, also, § 225, *infra*, notes.

[2] Bank of United States *v.* Dallam, 4
Dana (Ky), 574 (1836). In the cases,
however, of Payne *v* Ballard, 23 Miss,
88 (1851), and Hightower *v* Thornton, 8
Ga, 486 (1850), it was held that the statute of limitations has no application by
analogy to the equitable actions to collect subscriptions. In Terry *v* Bank of
Cape Fear, 20 Fed. Rep., 777 (1884), the
court said, in a similar case: "In adjusting equitable rights, courts of equity

will never allow the statute of limitations to have a manifestly inequitable
and unjust operation. In Scovill *v*
Thayer, 105 U S, 143, 155 (1881), a case
in equity, the court say "Before there
is any obligation upon the stockholder
to pay without an assessment and call
by the company, there must be some
order of a court of competent jurisdiction, or, at the very least, some authorized demand upon him for payment.
And it is clear the statute of limitations .
does not begin to run in his favor until
such order or demand," citing cases. A
decree of a court of equity that the subscription be paid is equivalent to a call,
and the statute commences to run
Glenn *v* Saxton, 68 Cal, 353 (1886). An
assignment by the corporation for the
benefit of creditors starts the statute
within a reasonable time thereafter.
Glenn *v* Dorsheimer, 24 Fed Rep, 536
(1885); Glenn *v.* Priest, 28 Fed Rep, 907
(1886) For an explanation of the origin
of the Glenn cases, see Baltimore, etc,
R. R. Co *v* Glenn, 28 Md, 287 (1867)
Where a decree is made assessing the
stockholders on their subscriptions, the
statute of limitations begins to run from
the entry of the decree Glenn *v.* Mc-
Allister's Ex'rs, 46 Fed. Rep, 883 (1891).

[3] Johnson *v* Albany & Susquehanna
R R. Co, 54 N Y, 416, 426 (1873), where
the court say "The claim of the plaintiff is not supported by any principle
that should give it any consideration in
either a court of law or equity The
statute of limitations never paid a debt,
although it barred a remedy."

ignorant of the actual condition of the corporation.[1] Nor is it a defense that he was ignorant of the legal effect of the subscription contract which he signed [2]

§ 197 *Miscellaneous defenses.*— A subscriber cannot defeat an action for the collection of his subscription by alleging that the charter was obtained in bad faith,[3] or that, where a corporate creditor is enforcing payment, such creditor is also a director of the corporation,[4] or that other subscribers have paid their subscriptions in Confederate money,[5] or that he has paid the subscription by note instead of by cash, as required by the charter,[6] or that the promoters sold to the corporation a patent-right at an overvaluation;[7] or that the officers were illegally elected [8] or that an illegal by-law prevents his voting until calls are paid,[9] or that, by the charter, the whole capital stock should have been paid in before the commencement of business, which was not done,[10] or that the corporation has been ousted from its franchises [11] A material alteration, however, in a subscription contract is a good defense, unless the corporation proves it to have been made without its knowledge or procurement [12] The defense that the corporate charter has been amended by the legislature without the consent of the defendant subscriber is considered elsewhere,[13] as also the right of an assignee of the corporation to collect subscriptions [14] and the defense that the stockholder did not know the legal effect of his subscription [15] Various other defenses are referred to in the notes below.[16]

§ 198. *Waiver of defenses* — A subscriber to stock in a corporation may waive any defense he may have to the subscription The

[1] Payson v. Withers, 5 Biss, 269 (1873)

[2] New Albany & S R R Co v Fields, 10 Ind, 187 (1858), Clear v Newcastle & D R R Co, 9 Ind, 488 (1857) See, also, cases in § 146

[3] Peychaud v. Love, 24 La. Ann, 401 (1872), Garrett v Dillsburg & M R R. Co., 78 Pa St, 465 (1875), Smith v Heindecker, 39 Mo, 157 (1866)

[4] Chouteau Ins Co v Floyd, 74 Mo, 286 (1881)

[5] Mason & Augusta R R Co v Vason, 57 Ga, 314 (1876)

[6] Little v O'Brien, 9 Mass, 423 (1812)

[7] Dorris v French, 4 Hun, 292 (1875) See, also, ch III and notes

[8] Trustees of Vernon v Hills, 6 Cowen, 23 (1826). See, also, § 110, *supra* No

defense that the directors were not stockholders, as required by statute Ross v. Bank, etc, 19 Pac Rep, 243 (Nev 1888).

[9] Chandler v Northern Cross R R Co, 18 Ill, 190 (1856)

[10] McDermott v. Dongan, 44 Mo, 85 (1869)

[11] Gaff v Flesher, 33 Ohio St., 107, Rowland v Meader Furniture Co, 38 Ohio St., 269 (1882)

[12] Bery v Marietta, etc, R R Co, 26 Ohio St., 673 (1875) Cf Ellison v Mobile & O R R Co, 36 Miss, 572 (1858) See, also, § 53 *supra*

[13] See ch XXVIII

[14] See § 111 and ch LII

[15] See § 116. *supra*.

[16] Change of name is no defense. How-

waiver may be express, or it may arise by implication from the
acts and declarations of the subscriber.   Thus a payment of a call,
with full knowledge of the defense, is held to be a waiver;[1] and
any act indicating a clear intent to abide by or accept or pass over
an objection which the subscriber might make will be held to be a
waiver.[2]

ard v Glenn, 11 S. E. Rep., 610 (Ga., 1890).
A change of name during organization
is no defense.   Priest v Glenn, 51 Fed
Rep., 400 (1892) A slight change in the
name as incorporated is no defense
Joseph v Davis, 10 S. Rep., 830 (Ala., 1892)
A slight change in the name is no defense where the subscriber has already
paid assessments McCormick, etc., Co., 29
Pac Rep., 1147 (Kan., 1892) An increase
of the capital stock as allowed by the
charter does not release subscribers
Port Edwards, etc., R'y v Arpin, 49 N.
W. Rep 828 (Wis., 1891). It is no defense to a subscription that the subscriber did not read the paper Stutz v
Handley, 41 Fed Rep., 531 (1890). Although a corporation has taken more
subscriptions than its capital stock and
has issued certificates therefor, yet this
does not release subscribers up to the
correct amount. Cartright v Dickinson, 12 S W Rep., 1030 (Tenn., 1890) It
is no defense that a greater capital
stock is provided for in the charter than
in the preliminary agreement, nor that
the subscriptions have not all been paid
in, where the defendant acquiesced in
all this by attending meetings and voting International, etc., Ass'n v Walker,

47 N W. Rep., 338 (Mich., 1890). A subscription to stock is enforceable severally
although signed by several A change
in it by several of the subscribers does
not release the others. An increase in
the capital upon incorporation does not
release Gibbons v. Grinsel, 48 N. W
Rep., 255 (Wis., 1891) Sale under statutes existing at time of subscription is
valid and does not release subscriber
Armstrong v Karshner, 24 N. E. Rep.,
697 (Ohio, 1890) A person who has
been discharged under the bankrupt act
is not liable on subscriptions made
previous to his application in bankruptcy Glenn v Abell, 39 Fed. Rep.,
10 (1889); but see Sayre v. Glenn, 6 S.
Rep., 45 (Ala., 1889)

[1] Miss & Tenn R. R. Co v. Harris, 36
Miss., 17 (1858), Inter Mountain P. Co
v Jack, 6 Pac Rep., 20 (Montana, 1885);
Hamilton v Grangers' Life & H. Ins.
Co., 67 Ga., 145 (1881).

[2] See May v. Memphis Branch R. R.
Co., 48 Ga., 109 (1873); Middlesex Turn-
pike Co v Seman, 10 Mass., 385 (1813),
McCully v Pittsburgh & C R. R. Co., 32
Pa. St., 25 (1858) See, also, §§ 160, 161,
and ch. XLIV.

CHAPTER XI.

THE STOCKHOLDERS' LIABILITY TO CORPORATE CREDITORS UPON UNPAID SUBSCRIPTIONS.

§ 199 *Unpaid subscriptions a trust fund for the benefit of creditors* — The capital or capital stock of a corporation is the aggregate of the par value of all the shares into which the capital is divided upon the incorporation, it is the fund or resource with which the corporation is enabled to act and transact its business, and upon the faith of which persons give credit to the corporation and become corporate creditors The public, in dealing with a corporation, has the right to assume that its actual capital, in money or money's worth, is equal to the capital stock which it purports to have, unless it has been impaired by business losses The public has a right also to assume that the capital stock has been or will be fully paid up, if it be necessary, in order to meet corporate liabilities. Accordingly, the American courts go very far to protect corporate creditors, and in this country it is a well-settled doctrine that capital stock, and especially unpaid subscriptions to the capital stock, constitute a trust fund for the benefit of the creditors of the corporation.[1] There are three methods by which stockholders

---

[1] "Though it be a doctrine of modern date," says Mr Justice Miller in Sawyer *v* Hong, 17 Wall, 610, 620 (1873) "we think it now well established that the capital stock of a corporation, especially its unpaid subscriptions, is a trust fund for the benefit of the general creditors of the corporation. And when we consider the rapid development of corporations as instrumentalities of the commercial and business world in the last few years, with the corresponding necessity of adapting legal principles to the new and varying exigencies of this business, it is no solid objection to such a principle that it is modern, for the occasion for it could

247

seek to avoid their liability to corporate creditors first, by a cancellation or withdrawal from the contract, [1] second, by a release from their obligation to pay the full par value of the stock; [2] third, by a transfer of the stock [3] In each of these cases, however, a court of equity does its utmost to protect the corporate creditors, and a rigid scrutiny will be made in the interest of creditors into every transaction of such a nature [4]

not sooner have arisen " This seems to be a distinctively American doctrine It is not known to the English law, and was first clearly announced by Mr Justice Story in Wood v Dummer, 3 Mason, 308 (1824) See, also, the cases of Hightower v Thornton, 8 Ga , 486 (by Lumpkin, J , 1850), Germantown, etc , R'y Co v Fitler, 60 Penn St., 124 (1869), Crawford v Rohrer, 59 Md , 599 (1882), Lewis v Robertson, 21 Miss , 558 (1850), Bunn's Appeal, 105 Penn. St. 49 (1884), Curran v Arkansas, 15 How , 304 (1853), Mumma v Potomac Co , 8 Peters, 281 (1834), Sanger v Upton 91 U S., 56 (1875), County of Morgan v Allen, 103 id , 498 (1880), Osgood v Laytin, 3 Keyes (N Y), 521, S. C , 5 Abb Pr (N S), 1 (1867) Cf Vose v Grant, 15 Mass , 505 (1819), Spear v Grant, 16 id , 9 (1819), Baker v Atlas Bank, 9 Metc , 182 (1845), Osgood v King, 42 Iowa, 478 (1876), Chisholm v Forny, 65 id , 333; Jackson v Traer, 64 id , 469 (1884) In New York many decisions to this point have been rendered, especially in actions under the General Manufacturing Act (§ 10, ch 40, Laws of 1848) They are fully cited and considered in the chapter, infra, on Statutory Liability, q v See Gillet v Moody, 5 Barb., 184 189 (1849), Mills v Stewart, 41 N Y , 384 389 (1869); Morgan v. New York, etc , R R Co , 10 Paige. Chan , 290 (1843) To the same effect, see Salmon v The Hamborough Company, 1 Cases in Chan , 204 (1671); Nevitt v Bank of Port Gibson, 6 Smed & M., 513 (1846)

County of Morgan v Allen, 103 U. S , 498 (1880), Chouteau v Dean, 7 Mo App , 211 (1879), Gill v. Balis, 72 Mo , 424 (1880), Putnam v City of New Albany, 4 Biss , 365 (Ind , 1869), Re South Mountain. etc , Mining Co. 7 Sawyer, 30 (Cal , 1881), Union Ins Co v Frear Stone Manuf'g Co , 97 Ill , 537 (1881), Singer v Given, 61 Iowa, 93 (1883), Jackson v Traer, 64 Iowa, 469 (1884), Mathis v Pridham 20 S. W Rep., 1015 (Tex , 1892) In one case it is said that it is not within the ingenuity of man to devise a scheme to prevent courts of equity from enforcing the payment of unpaid subscriptions to capital stock for the benefit of corporate creditors. Upton v Hansbrough, 3 Biss., 417, 425 (1873) Cf Chisholm v Forny, 65 Iowa, 333 (1884) Unfortunately this cannot be said to be always the result of corporate creditors' suits to enforce such liability Generally, however, the courts are able to give relief Thus an arrangement entered into between the corporation and its stockholders, for the purpose of defeating the claims of creditors, in pursuance of which the stockholders are allowed, after it is ascertained that the corporation is insolvent, to buy in depreciated and repudiated claims against the company, and thus to extinguish their indebtedness for stock subscribed, is held fraudulent and void Goodwin v McGehee, 15 Ala , 232 (1849), Thompson v Meisser, 108 Ill , 359 (1884) And a payment in full for stock, followed by an immediate loan of part or all of the purchase price by the corporation back to the subscriber, is a fraud as to creditors and the public, and will be set aside Sawyer v Hoag, 17 Wall, 610 (1873) A fraudulent device by which

[1] See §§ 167-170.
[2] Id , also ch III
[3] See ch XV.
[4] Sawyer v. Hoag, 17 Wall , 610 (1873),

§ 200 *Can be reached only after judgment against the corporation and execution returned unsatisfied* — Although it may be considered settled law, at least in the United States, that unpaid subscriptions to the capital stock of corporations constitute a trust fund for the benefit of corporate creditors, yet such unpaid balances of subscription are not the primary or regular fund for the payment of corporate debts Persons transacting business with the corporation look to the corporation itself for the payment of their debts Credit is given to the corporation, not to the stockholders; and it is the natural order of business that the creditors of the corporation are to be paid by the corporation from funds in the corporate treasury Ordinarily, corporate creditors have no knowledge or concern about the subscription list, and unpaid or partially paid subscriptions are a matter entirely between the corporation and the subscribers So long as the corporation meets its obligations in the ordinary course of business, corporate creditors have no need to concern themselves about unpaid subscriptions to the stock But when the corporation is in default and embarrassed, or for any reason fails to pay its debts, then its creditors have rights with reference to such unpaid subscriptions They then have the right to know whether all the subscriptions for stock have been fully paid in, and, if not, they have the right to compel such payment.

It accordingly becomes important to know at what point, in their efforts to collect what is due them, corporate creditors may cease to pursue the corporation and proceed directly against its delinquent members. The well-established rule upon this point is that a corporate creditor's suit to enforce payment of unpaid subscriptions can be properly brought only after a judgment at law has

a stockholder pays his subscription by a note, and subsequently obtains the note at a large discount, may be valid as against the company, but will be set aside as regards corporate creditors Bouton v Dement, 14 N W Rep, 62 (Ill, 1887) A subscriber cannot pay for his stock by purchasing full-paid stock and having this substituted for his subscription Marshall etc., Co v Killian, 6 S. E Rep., 680 (N C, 1888) The stockholder's liability in this respect is not confined in general to the original capital stock, but it attaches upon an authorized increase of the capital, to such increase. Chubb v Upton, 95 U S, 665 (1877). See, also, Veeder v Mudgett, 95 N Y, 295 (1884), Pacific National Bank Cases, 118 U S, 635 The filing of the statutory certificate declaring that the whole amount of the capital stock has been paid in is not conclusive of the fact, and will not prevent proof to the contrary Barre National Bank v Hingham Manuf g Co, 127 Mass 563 (1879), Wheeler v Millar, 90 N Y, 353 (1882), Veeder v Mudgett, 95 id, 295 (1884), Thompson v Reno Sav Bank (Nev, 1885) The question whether a stockholder may limit or entirely do away with his liability, by an express contract to that effect with corporate creditors, is considered elsewhere See § 216

been obtained against the corporation, and an execution returned unsatisfied[1] This rule is of such importance that, by statute, in many of the states, a creditor's right to proceed against a stockholder on his unpaid subscription is allowed only after the remedy against the corporation itself has been exhausted[2] By this is meant that judgment shall have been duly recovered against the corporation, and execution issued and regularly returned unsatisfied. Nothing short of that exhausts the remedy against the corporation.[3]

[1] Bank of the United States v Dallam, 4 Dana, 574 (1836), Walser t Seligman, 21 Blatch, 130 (1882), Wetherbee v Baker, 35 N J Eq, 501 (1882), Cutright t Stanford 81 Ill, 240 (1876), Baxter v Moses, 77 Me, 465 (1885), Terry v. Anderson, 95 U S, 628 636 (1877), Cleveland v Burnham, 55 Wis, 598 (1882), Freeland v McCullough, 1 Denio, 414 (1845) The suit is to be brought for this purpose in the courts of the state where the corporation exists. Barclay t Tallman, 4 Edw Chan, 123 (1842), Murray v Vanderbilt, 39 Barb, 140, 147 (1863), Bank of Virginia t Adams, 1 Pars Eq, 534 (1850), Patterson v Lynde, 112 Ill, 196 (1884), Harris v Pullman, 84 id, 20, 25 (1876), Bayliss v Swift, 40 Iowa, 648 (1875) See, also, § 219, infra Cf Claflin v McDermott. 12 Fed Rep, 375 (1882)

[2] Thornton t Lane, 11 Ga, 459 (1852), Lane v Harris, 16 id, 217 (1851), McClaren t Franciscus, 43 Mo, 452 (1869), New England, etc, Bank v Newport Steam Factory, 6 R I, 154 (1859), Priest v Essex Manuf g Co, 115 Mass. 380 (1874), Cambridge Water-works v Somerville Dyeing, etc, Co., 4 Allen, 239 (1862), Lindsley v Simonds, 2 Abb Prac (N S), 69 (1866), Blake t Hinkle, 10 Yerg, 218 (1836), Shellington v Howland, 53 N Y, 371 (1873); Wehrman v Reakirt, 1 Cin Super Ct, 230 (1871), Dauchy v Brown, 24 Vt, 197 (1852), Drinkwater v Portland Marine R y, 18 Me, 35 (1841), Handy v Draper, 89 N Y, 334 (1882), Richards v Coe, N Y Daily Reg, August 2, 1887; and Richards t Beach, id, December 12, 1887, Burch v Taylor, 24 Pac Rep, 438 (Wash, 1890), Baines v Babcock, 27

Pac Rep, 674 (Cal, 1891) Cf. Perkins v Church, 31 Barb, 84 (1859).

[3] Rocky Mountain National Bank v Bliss, 89 N Y, 338 (1882) In this case it is held that a proceeding in rem. affecting only the property of the corporation attached, and execution against that property, is not what the rule requires, and again, that the recovery of a judgment and issue of execution in another state is not a compliance with the rule, but that a judgment in and execution issued out of a court of the state where the statute is in force is necessary To the same effect see Brice v Munro, 5 Canadian Law Times, 130, Ontario high court of justice, queen's bench division (1885), in which case it is held that an execution issued and returned in Quebec is not sufficient as against a company incorporated and existing in Ontario Contra, Shickle v. Watts, 7 S W Rep, 274 (Mo, 1888). See note 1, p 253

In England a scire facias is a necessary preliminary, unless there is some statutory enactment to the contrary. 2 Lindley on Partnership, 520, Bartlett v. Pentland, 1 Barn & Ad, 704 (1831); Clowes v. Brettell, 10 Mees. & W, 506 (1842), Winfield v Barton, 2 Dowl. (N S.), 355 (1872), Wingfield v Peel, 12 L J. (N S, Q B.), 102 (1842). In a suit by a corporate creditor against a corporation to obtain judgment before suing stockholders on their liability, the stockholders are not allowed to come in as parties Hambleton v Glenn, 9 S. E Rep, 129 (Va, 1889). Proof that a creditor has exhausted his legal remedy against the corporation is shown by the

This rule is founded in reason and a wise public policy relative to the transaction of business, since the corporate funds are the corporate creditors' primary resource, even where the liability of the individual shareholder is declared to be primary, like that of an original contractor or partner.[1] Where, however, the corporation has been adjudged a bankrupt, and a dissolution has in this way been brought about, the remedy against the corporation need not first be exhausted [2] Such, also, has been held to be the rule where the corporation is notoriously insolvent,[3] or is formally dissolved [4]

judgment and an execution thereon returned unsatisfied Evidence that the company owns a large amount of personal property besides its road and franchise is inadmissible Barnes z Babcock et al, 27 Pac Rep, 674 (Cal, 1891)

[1] Stone v Wiggin, 5 Metc 316 (1842), Stedman v Eveleth 6 id. 111 (1843)

[2] State Savings Association i Kellogg 52 Mo, 583 (1873), Dryden v Kellogg 2 Mo App., 87 (1876), Shellington i Howland, 53 N Y, 371 (1873) Cf Ansonia Brass & Copper Co v New Lamp Chimney Co, 53 N Y, 123 (1873) S C, 91 U S., 656, Walser v Seligman, 21 Blatch, 130 (1882) See § 219 And see, contra, Birmingham National Bank v Moses, 14 Hun, 605 (1878), Fourth Nat'l Bank v Francklyn, 120 U S, 747 (1887).

[3] Hodges v Silver Hill Mining Co., 9 Oreg. 200 (1881), Terry v Tubman, 92 U. S., 156 (1875), Camden v Doremus, 3 How, 515, 533 (1845), Stutz i Handley, 41 Fed Rep, 531 (1890) It has been held that the right of action accrues to the creditor whenever it is clear that the corporation has no property from which the claim can be paid A judgment is not necessary for the beginning of an action against the stockholder, though it may be necessary as evidence in such action to determine the measure of damages First Nat. Bank of Garrettsville i Greene, 64 Iowa, 445 (1884) Cf Cleveland i Marine Bank, 17 Wis., 545 (1863) A creditor of an insolvent corporation may bring a creditor's bill against the assignee for the benefit of creditors of a subscriber, even though no judgment against the corporation

had been obtained, and no other stockholders are made co-defendants Samainego v. Stiles, 20 Pac Rep, 607 (Ariz 1889)

[4] Kincaid v Dwinelle, 59 N Y, 548 (1875). Cf Hollingshead v Woodward, 35 Hun, 410 (1887) As to what is sufficient to dissolve a corporation for this purpose, see Kincaid i Dwinelle, supra Under a statute requiring dissolution of the corporation before corporate creditors can reach unpaid subscriptions, the corporation is deemed to be dissolved when it has ceased to exercise its proper functions, is without funds and is indebted Penniman v Briggs, 1 Hopk Chan (N Y), 300 (1821), Slee v Bloom, 19 Johns, 456 (1822), Bank of Poughkeepsie v Ibbotson, 24 Wend, 473 479 (1840) Cf Terry v Anderson, 95 U S 628 (1877) Remington v. Samana Bay Co, 140 Mass, 494 (1886), holds that the judgment herein against the corporation is void if the corporation has been dissolved It has been said that corporate creditors need not await the collection by the corporation of doubtful claims, but may compel the payment of their claims by the shareholders and let the latter take the risk and delay "Creditors," say the supreme court of Tennessee, "will not be required to await the collection of doubtful claims or claims in litigation The stockholders must pay promptly and take upon themselves the onus of delay and risk as to all such cases." Moses v Ocoee Bank, 1 Lea, 398, 413 (1878). See, also, Stark i Burk 9 La Ann, 341, 343 (1854) General creditors may also reach un-

A corporate creditor must obtain judgment against the corporation in the state where he brings his action to enforce the stockholder's subscription. or he must show that it was impossible to obtain one [1]

§ 201 *The remedy by garnishment or attachment or by notice to the stockholder* — There are various remedies which corporate creditors may employ to enforce the payment of partially paid up subscriptions Among these is that of garnishment. Thus, where a subscription has been called in, in part or wholly, and has not been paid by the subscriber, it is, at least to the extent of such calls, an asset of the corporation, and, like other assets, is subject to garnishment at the instance of a corporate creditor.[2]

When, therefore, a stockholder is in default for instalments of stock for which calls have been made, he stands in the attitude of any other debtor to the corporation, and may be garnished in the usual way, upon the theory of the authorities just cited, for the purpose of collecting the debt due from the corporation. But this remedy is not available to reach that part of the unpaid subscription for which calls have not been made [3]

Still another remedy is often given by statute. The statute may

paid subscriptions, although another corporate creditor has a mortgage lien on the corporate property, rights, privileges and franchises. Dean v Biggs, 25 Hun, 122 (1881). See, also, § 631

[1] National, etc, Co v Ballou, 146 U S 517 (1892), S C , 42 Fed Rep. 749 See, also, § 219, and note 3, p. 250

[2] Kern v Chicago, etc , Ass'n 29 N E. Rep , 1035 (Ill., 1892), Joseph z Davis, 10 S Rep , 830 (Ala , 1892), Meints v East St. Louis, etc., Co, 89 Ill , 48 (1878), Hannah v The Moberly Bank, 67 Mo , 678 (1878), Simpson v Reynolds 71 id., 594 (1880), Faull v Alaska etc , Mining Co , 8 Sawyer, 420 (1882), Curry v Woodward, 53 Ala , 371 (1875); Bingham v Rushing, 5 Ala , 403 (1843), Hays v Lycoming. etc , Co , 99 Pa. St., 621 (1882). Cf Rand v White Mountains R. R. Co., 40 N H , 79 (1860), Brown v Union Insurance Co 3 La Ann , 177 (1848), Angell and Ames on Corp , § 517 See Dean v Biggs, 25 Hun, 122 (1881) An attachment of unpaid subscriptions due to a foreign corporation will be stayed where sequestration proceedings are commenced, but the priority of the at-

tachment creditor will be preserved. *Re* Queensland, etc , Co , 58 L. T. Rep., 878 (1888).

[3] Bingham v Rushing, 5 Ala , 403 (1843), Brown v Union Insurance Co., 3 La. Ann , 177 (1848); Bunn's Appeal, 105 Pa St , 49 (1884). See also, Coalfield Coal Co v Peck, 98 Ill , 139 (1881). In Nevada the right of garnishment in a case where calls had not been made was expressly denied McKelvey v. Crockett, 18 Nev , 238 (1884). Cf Meints v East St. Louis, etc , Co., 89 Ill., 48 (1878) Hughes v Oregonian R'y Co., 11 Ore , 158 (1883), Peterson v Sinclair, 83 Pa St. 250 (1877), Langford v. Ottumwa Water-power Co., 59 Ia., 283 (1882) Chandler v Siddle, 10 N. B. R., 236 (1874) In New York there is no process of garnishment, but instead thereof an attachment is allowed. Under an attachment against a foreign corporation not chartered by the United States, the sheriff may levy upon the sums remaining unpaid upon a subscription to the capital stock of the corporation, the subscriber being within the county and having property therein,

provide that after the remedy is exhausted against the corporation, the stockholders may by summons be brought into that same suit and compelled to pay.[1]

"or upon one or more shares of stock therein held by such a person, or transferred by him for the purpose of avoiding payment thereof" New York Code of Civil Procedure, § 646 It has also been held that a corporate creditor, by an execution against the corporation, may reach an unpaid subscription though no call has been made *In re Glen Iron Works,* 17 Fed Rep., 324 (1883); S. C, 20 id, 674 (1884), Cucullu *v Union Insurance Co,* 2 Rob (La.), 571 (1842). *Cf* Bunn's Appeal, 14 Week Notes Cases, 190, and see Hannah *v. The Moberly Bank,* 67 Mo, 678 (1878) But this is a somewhat questionable rule, and the remedy proposed by it is probably very seldom invoked For the remedy in Pennsylvania, where by statute, after execution returned unsatisfied against the corporation, on order of the court, execution arises against the stockholders, see Lander *v. Tillia,* 11 Atl Rep., 86 (Pa., 1887). *Bank of Virginia v Adams,* 1 Par. Sel Eq Cas, 534 (1850), holding that a court of equity in Pennsylvania has no jurisdiction to compel stockholders of a foreign corporation residing there to pay a subscription to its stock on the application of its creditors. A judgment against a nonresident stockholder served outside of the jurisdiction is not enforceable. *Wilson v Seligman,* 36 Fed Rep., 154 (1888). As regards the statutory remedy of a creditor in enforcing an unpaid subscription in Maine, see *Libby v Tobey,* 19 Atl Rep, 904 (Me., 1890).

In the case of *Ogilvie v. Knox Ins. Co.,* 22 How, 380 (1859), the court said. "The creditors of the corporation are seeking satisfaction out of the assets of the company to which the defendants are debtors If the debts attached are sufficient to pay their demands the creditors need look no further. They are not bound to settle up all the affairs

of this corporation, and the equity between its various stockholders or partners, corporators or debtors"

[1] A state statute may provide that a judgment creditor of a corporation may summon in a stockholder who has not paid his subscription and compel him to pay such subscription to such judgment creditor *Hill v Merchants' Insurance Co,* 134 U S 515 (1890) Where the stockholder's liability attaches upon a notice served upon him, the creditor who first serves the notice acquires a prior right to collect. *Wells v Robb,* 23 Pac Rep, 148 (Kan, 1890) Although the stockholder's subscription liability may be enforced by levy of execution against his property on a judgment against the corporation, "after sufficient notice," yet notice to a nonresident stockholder by publication is not sufficient *Wilson v St Louis, etc, R. R.,* 18 S W Rep, 286 (Mo., 1891). Where the statutory mode of collecting subscriptions is by motion based on a judgment against the corporation notice of the motion being given to the stockholder, such notice is not good when served out of the state on a non-resident. A judgment based on such notice is not good *Wilson v. Seligman,* 144 U S, 41 (1892). In Missouri it is held that a "proceeding by motion for execution against a stockholder of an insolvent corporation is in no sense the institution of an independent suit, but a mere supplementary proceeding in aid of the execution against the corporation" *Kohn v Lucas,* 17 Mo App, 29 (1885), *Paxson v Talmage,* 2 West Rep., 105 (Mo., 1885)

The statutory remedy of issuing execution against stockholders for their unpaid subscriptions on a judgment against the corporation ceases when a receiver is appointed *Showalter v Laredo, etc, Co,* 18 S W. Rep, 491 (Tex., 1892). In England this plan has

§ 202 *The remedy by mandamus.*— It is doubtful whether corporate creditors can, in this country, have recourse to the writ of *mandamus* to compel the officers of the corporation to make a call for the purpose of raising money to meet corporate obligations [1]

In the English courts a *mandamus* is sometimes awarded in these cases.[2] But in this country the question of calls is not usually of much importance in such cases The corporation is generally insolvent; a bill is filed in a court of equity to collect and distribute all the assets, and calls on the subscriptions are made by the court itself.[3]

§ 203. *The remedy by action at law* — Another remedy is by an action at law. It has been held that unpaid subscriptions, after call, may be enforced by an action at law brought directly by the creditor against the delinquent subscriber, and that in such an action each subscriber is liable, not for his proportionate share, but to the full extent of his unpaid subscription.[4]

been tried and was unsatisfactory Creditors, when they could not obtain satisfaction from companies, singled out some unfortunate shareholder, and compelled him to pay the whole amount for which judgment had been recovered. This course was in the highest degree cruel: and parliament was induced, when legislating on joint-stock companies, in 1856, to leave out all those clauses, found in the preceding acts, enabling creditors to execute judgments against individual shareholders, and to provide, instead, that creditors should have the power, upon non-payment of the debts due to them from the company, to cause it to be wound up. The same view prevailed when the acts relating to joint-stock companies were remodeled in 1862 Consequently, a creditor of a company registered under the Companies Act, 1862, can only execute a judgment obtained against the company by proceeding against the corporate property, and, if necessary, by having recourse to a petition for winding up the company. In Lowry v. Inman, 46 N. Y., 119, a charter permitting the property of stockholders to be taken upon execution on a judgment against the corporation, and providing that such stockholders may use the same powers against

others to enforce contribution, was held not to create such a general individual liability as would sustain a personal action.

[1] Dalton, etc. R. R. Co v. McDaniel, 56 Ga., 191 (1876), Hatch v. Dana, 101 U S, 205, 215 (1879) *Cf.* Cucullu v. Union Insurance Co., 2 Rob. (La), 571, 573 (1842), Allen v Montgomery, etc, R. R Co, 11 Ala, 437 (1847)

[2] Queen v Victoria Park Co., 1 Ad & El (N S), 288 (1841), Queen v. Ledgard, id, 616, The King v Katherine Dock Co., 4 Barn & Ad., 360 (1832),

[3] See § 108, *supra*

[4] Bank of the United States v Dallam, 4 Dana, 574 (1836), Allen v. Montgomery, etc, R. R. Co, 11 Ala, 437 (1847); Persch v. Simmons, 3 N Y Supp, 783 (1889). An action to recover unpaid subscriptions may be at law. Faull v Alaska, etc., Mining Co, 8 Sawyer, 420 (1883); Tama, etc. Co v Hopkins, 44 N. W. Rep, 797 (Iowa, 1890); Wilbur v. Stockholders, 18 Bank Reg, 178 (1879); White v Blum, 4 Neb, 555 (1876), McCarthy v Lavasche. 89 Ill, 270 (1878); Freeman v Winchester, 18 Miss, 577 (1848). *Contra*, Griffith v Mangam, 73 N Y, 611 (1878). *Cf* Glenn v Lancaster, 109 N. Y, 641 (1888) Concerning the pleadings in suit at law to collect subscriptions, see Glenn v Sumner, 132

The tendency of the law, however, is to do away with this remedy, and to compel the creditor in all cases to seek his remedy in a court of equity This tendency is in accord with the best interests of corporate creditors and stockholders and the prevention of a multiplicity of suits, and is to be emphatically commended [1]

§ 204. *The remedy by bill in equity.*— The remedy most usually adopted by corporate creditors to obtain the payment of their claims against the corporation from the unpaid balances of subscriptions due the corporation by the subscribers to the capital stock is by a bill in equity. This is in the nature of a creditor's bill, reaching the equitable assets of the principal debtor It is the most effectual, simple and just remedy, and is not only the favorite remedy of the courts, but is generally resorted to by the corporate creditors themselves [2] Some of the courts have even gone to the

---

U S, 152 (1889) 'The legislature may modify a summary remedy to collect subscriptions *Ex parte* Northeast, etc , R. R. Co, 37 Ala, 679 (1861). Howard *v* Kentucky, etc, Ins Co, 13 B Mon (Ky.), 282 (1852) See, also, cases in § 208 A statutory remedy of one state is not available in another state   Christensen *v* Eno, 106 N Y, 97 (1887)

See, also, § 223, n , *infra* A corporate creditor may bring a common-law action to collect a subscription to a foreign corporation. Savings Assoc *v* O'Brien, 51 Hun, 45 (1889) A subscription paper, "We agree to pay," is several and not joint A suit against all the subscribers will fail Davis, etc , Co *v* Barber, 51 Fed Rep 148 (1892)

[1] See § 204

[2] Pfohl *v* Simpson, 74 N Y, 137 (1878), Mathez *v* Neidig, 72 id, 100 (1878), Dayton *v* Borst, 31 id, 435 (1865), Mann *v* Pentz, 3 id, 415 (1850), Stephens *v* Fox, 83 id, 313 (1881), S. C, 17 Hun, 435, Griffith *v* Mangam, 73 N Y, 611 (1878), Christensen *v* Eno, 106 id, 97, 100 (1887), Ward *v* Griswoldville Manuf'g Co, 16 Conn, 593 (1844), Bank of the United States *v* Dallam, 4 Dana, 574 (1836), Shickle *v*. Watts, 7 S. W Rep, 274 (Mo , 1888), Crawford *v* Rohrer 59 Md, 599 (1882), Hightower *v* Thornton, 8 Ga, 486 (1850), Hightower *v* Mustian, 8 id, 506

(1850), Dalton, etc , R R Co. *v* McDaniel, 56 id , 191 (1876), Germantown, etc , R'y Co. *v* Fitler, 60 Penn St, 124 (1869), Adler *v* Milwaukee, etc , Co, 13 Wis, 57 (1860), Curry *v* Woodward, 53 Ala, 371 (1875), Allen *v* Montgomery, etc , R. R. Co, 11 id 437 (1847), Wincock *v* Turpin, 96 Ill , 135 (1880), Hickling *v* Wilson, 104 Ill , 54 (1882), Henry *v* Vermillion, etc , Turnpike Co, 17 Ohio, 187 (1848); Miers *v* Zanesville and Maysville Turnpike Co , 11 id , 273 (1842), Judson *v* Rossie Galena Co., 9 Paige, 598 (1842), Van Pelt *v* U S, etc , Co , 13 Abb Prac (N S), 331 (1872) [Compare with this case Sherwood *v* Buffalo, etc., R R Co, 12 How Prac, 137 (1855), and Hammond *v* Hudson River, etc Co, 11 id , 33 (1854)] Marsh *v* Burroughs, 1 Woods, 463 (1871), Louisiana Paper Co *v* Waples 3 id , 34 (1877), Faull *v* Alaska Mining, etc , Co , 8 Sawyer, 420 (1883), Holmes *v* Sherwood, 3 McCrary, 405 (1881), S C, 16 Fed Rep, 725, Chandler *v* Siddle, 10 Bank Reg, 236, Myers *v* Seeley, 10 id 411 (1874), Wilbur *v* Stockholders, 18 id, 178 (1878), Harmon *v* Page, 62 Cal, 448 (1882), Ogilvie *v* Knox Insurance Co, 22 How, 380 (1859); Sanger *v* Upton, 91 U S, 56, 60 (1875), Hatch *v* Dana 101 id, 205 (1879), Salmon *v* Hamborough Co, 1 Cas. in Chan (Eng), 204 (1671), Patterson *v*. Lynde,

extent of holding a bill in equity to be the exclusive remedy for the corporate creditor in these cases.[1] Occasionally, also, statutes are enacted prescribing that a creditor who seeks to apply such assets to the payment of his claim can do so only by a suit in equity.[2] The right to proceed by a suit in equity herein has been held to exist, even where the general equitable remedy by creditor's bill has been abolished by statute.[3]

106 U S, 519 (1882), saying that "no one creditor can assume that he alone is entitled to what any stockholder owes, and sue at law so as to appropriate it exclusively to himself " A bill in equity may be filed in the federal courts to collect unpaid subscriptions and apply them to the payment of claims of complainants who are corporate creditors If the sums due the original complainants amount to more than $2,000, the court has jurisdiction If the aggregate collections are more than $5,000 an appeal lies. Handley v Stutz, 137 U S 366 (1890) It seems to be well settled that, in the United States courts, unpaid subscriptions can be reached by a corporate creditor in a court of equity only. Brown v Fisk, 23 Fed Rep, 228 (1885) In Ohio it was held that an action for unpaid assessments on subscription for stock might be joined in an action on the statutory liability of stockholders Warner v Callender, 20 Ohio St., 190 (1870) A bill in equity is the proper remedy Johnston v Markle Paper Co, 25 Atl Rep., 560 (Pa, 1893); Barnes v Babcock, 27 Pac Rep, 674 (Cal. 1891) The remedy is in equity alone Hamilton v Clarion, etc., R R., 23 Atl Rep, 53 (Pa., 1891), Burcle v Taylor, 24 Pac Rep, 438 (Wash, 1890); Universal, etc., Co v. Tabor, 27 Pac Rep, 890 (Colo., 1891) A bill may be filed by a judgment creditor whose execution has been returned unsatisfied to enjoin executions, have a receiver appointed, have subscriptions collected, etc Ballin v. J, etc., Imp Co., 47 N. W Rep, 516 (Wis., 1890). A corporate creditor, where the corporate property has been exhausted, may file a bill in the nature of a credit-

or's bill to collect unpaid subscriptions The suit may be against one subscriber. But the bill must be so framed that other creditors may come in Gilchrist v Helena, etc, R. R., 49 Fed. Rep., 519 (1892) The fund realized from the suit in equity is distributed ratably among all the creditors Mathis v Pridham, 20 S. W Rep, 1015 (Tex, 1892).

[1] Jones v Jarman, 34 Ark., 323 (1879), Harris v First Parish in Dorchester, 23 Pick., 112 (1839); Knowlton v Ackley, 8 Cush, 93 (1851), Erickson v. Nesmith, 15 Gray, 221 (1860), Smith v. Huckabee, 53 Ala., 191 (1875), Umsted v Buskirk, 17 Ohio St., 113, Pollard v Bailey, 20 Wall, 520 (1874), Terry v. Little, 101 U. S, 216 (1879) Cf. Spear p Grant, 16 Mass, 9 (1819), Hodges v Silver Hill Mining Co, 9 Oreg, 200 (1881). In Bunn's Appeal and Lane's Appeal, 14 Weekly Notes, 192 (Pa, 1884), the supreme court of Pennsylvania clearly held that upon corporate insolvency no creditor can sue at law for the application of unpaid subscriptions to his debt. His remedy is in equity alone As to discovering the names of stockholders, see Hipple v Fire, etc., Co., 8 Central Rep, 462 (N. J, 1886), also, §§ 519, 520, infra

[2] Hadley v Russell, 40 N. H, 109 (1860).

[3] Adler v. Milwaukee, etc., Manuf'g Co, 13 Wis, 57 (1860) The equitable jurisdiction herein seems to have been based on various grounds See Wilbur v The Stockholders, 18 Bank. Reg., 178. In one case the bill in equity has been held to be in the nature of an equitable attachment in which the subscribers are in effect called on to answer as garnishee of the principal debtor. Ogilvie

§ 205. *Parties to the bill in equity — Parties plaintiff* — A corporate creditor who seeks in this way to obtain payment of his claim from the unpaid subscriptions to the capital stock of the corporation should file his bill on behalf of himself and such other creditors as may wish to come in [1] The general rule is that such a suit is and should be for the benefit of any or all creditors who elect to come in as parties complainant and establish their debts according to the course and practice of a court of chancery [2] While the bill must be so framed as to permit other creditors if they elect, to come in and be made parties to the suit it is in no way necessary to join them as parties. The other creditors are proper but not necessary parties [3] Several creditors, however,

---

t Knox Insurance Co 22 How 380 (1859). In practice a receiver is usually appointed the amount of the corporate debts and the amount necessary to be contributed by the holders of shares not paid up is ascertained by proof or through a referee and master's report, and then there is a final decree affording, so far as the assets admit adequate relief, and, in any event, proportional relief to all parties. Dalton etc. R. R. Co v McDaniel, 56 Ga., 191 1876 Wilbur t The Stockholders, 18 Bank Reg 178; Ogilvie t Knox Insurance Co 22 How., 380 (1859).

[1] Handley r Stutz 137 U S, 366 (1890), Crease t Babcock 51 Mass 525 (1846), Holmes t Sherwood 3 McCrary, 405 (1881) Sawyer t Hoag 17 Wall 610 (1873), Mills r Scott, 99 U S, 25 (1878) Patterson r Lynde 106 id., 519 (1882) A creditor's suit to collect unpaid subscriptions must not only be in equity but must be for the benefit of all creditors. Bickley t Schlag, 20 Atl Rep 250 (N J 1890).

[2] Wetherbee t Baker 35 N J Eq 501 (1882), Coleman t White 14 Wis 700 (1862), Carpenter t Marine Bank 14 id, 705, n (1862), Morgan t New York, etc R. R. Co. 10 Paige 299 (1843), Masters t Rossie Lead Mining Co, 2 Sandf Chan 301 (1845) Mann t Pentz 3 N Y 415 (1850) Umsted t Buskirk, 17 Ohio St 113 (1866) Crease t Babcock 51 Mass 525 (1846) Pollard r Bailey 20 Wall 520 (1874), Terry t

Little 101 U S 216 (1879). Any creditor has a right to come in establish his claim and share pro rata in the distribution of the assets even though the bill was not filed for the benefit of such as should choose to come in and share the expense Turnball r Prentiss Lumber Co 55 Mich 387 1884 See also Tallmadge t Fishkill Iron Co 4 Barb 383 (1848) Walker t Crain 17 id 191 (1853). In consequence thereof no one creditor can by superior diligence in filing a bill obtain a preference over other creditors in respect of the unpaid balances of subscriptions. See the cases in preceding note There is, however, an earlier case in the Ohio reports which seems to recognize such a preference Miers t Zanesville & Maysville Turnpike Co. 13 Ohio 197 1844. See Adler r Milwaukee etc Co. 13 Wis, 57 1860 Wright t McCormack, 17 Ohio St. 86 (1860). There must be an account taken of the amount of debts, assets and unpaid capital and a decree for an assessment of the amount due by each stockholder Bell's Appeal, 8 Atl Rep. 177 Penn 1887. Otherwise it is for the jury to say whether the whole of the unpaid subscriptions are needed to pay corporate debts. Citizens, etc, Co t Gillespie 9 Atl Rep. 73 Pa 1887 The pleadings may be of such a nature that the trial must be at law Glenn t Lancaster 109 N Y 641 (1888).

[3] Marsh t Burroughs 1 Woods 463 (1871), Crease t Babcock 51 Mass 525

cannot bring separate suits of this nature   They must all join
in one proceeding.[1]   The stockholders need not wait to be made
parties defendant to a creditors' bill before moving for contribution, but may, in a proper case, before a suit in the nature of a
creditors' bill is filed against them by creditors of the corporation,
file a bill in equity upon their own account, making the corporation a party, to enforce the payment of unpaid balances of subscription, for the payment of corporate indebtedness, and for
contribution.[2]

§ 206. *Parties defendant* — The defendants to such a suit should
be the corporation itself,[3] and all from whom an unpaid subscrip-

(1846), Hatch v Dana, 101 U S, 205
(1879)   Cf Adler v Milwaukee, etc,
Co, 13 Wis., 57 (1860).   Corporate creditor suing need not join all the corporate creditors as co-complainants nor all
the stockholders liable as defendants
Appeal of Cornell, 6 Atl. Rep, 258 (Pa,
1886).   Other creditors may come in on
a bill by a creditor to collect unpaid
subscriptions   Bailey v Pittsburg, etc.,
Co, 21 Atl Rep., 72 (1891)

[1] Crease v Babcock, 51 Mass, 525
(1846)   But see Perry v Turner, 55 Mo,
418 (1874)   And an action to compel
the payment of an unpaid subscription
may be joined by a creditor with an
action to enforce a statutory liability.
Warner v Callender, 20 Ohio St, 190
(1870).   Accordingly, where a bill is
filed, on behalf of all the creditors who
chose to come in, against all the stockholders in default, the courts will enjoin a separate creditor's suit.   Pierce v
Milwaukee Construction Co, 38 Wis.,
253 (1875)   Cf. Coleman v. White, 14
id   700 (1862); Carpenter v Marine
Bank, id, 705, n (1862); Ballston Spa
Bank v Marine Bank, 18 id, 490 (1864).
A stockholder who is also a creditor
may file a bill as a creditor to reach unpaid subscriptions.   He must, however,
pay his own subscription in full.   Bickley v Schlag, 20 Atl Rep, 250 (N' J,
1890), Bissit v Kentucky River Navigation Co, 15 Fed Rep, 353 (1882) and the
valuable note, Thompson v Reno Savings Bank (Nev, 1885).   Cf Hogg's Appeal. 88 Penn St., 195 (1878), Calhoun

v The Steam Ferry Boat, etc., 27 Int.
Rev Rec, 273 (1881), in which case it
is held he cannot sue the corporation.
But see Milvain v Mathei, 5 Exch, 55
(1850). in which it is held that a corporation sued by a stockholder may set
off any amount due by him on calls.
Cf Ex parte Windsor, 3 Story's C.C,
411 (1844); Weber v Fickey, 47 Md,
196 (1877), holding that a stockholder
who is also a creditor and who has not
fully paid his subscription cannot recover from another stockholder the full
amount of his claim   Emmert v Smith,
40 id, 123, to same effect.   In distributing the proceeds of sale of the property of a corporation the claims of such
creditors as are stockholders should be
reduced by the amount unpaid upon
their stock

[2] Fiery v Emmert, 36 Md, 464 (1872).

[3] The corporation is ordinarily a necessary party   Mann v. Pentz, 3 N. Y,
415 (1850), Walsh v Memphis, etc, R.
R. Co, 2 McCrary, 156 (1881); S C, 19
Fed Rep, 152, Wilbur v The Stockholders, 18 Bank Reg, 178 (1846);
Wetherbee v Baker 35 N J Eq, 501
(1882), First Nat. Bank v Smith, 6 Fed.
Rep., 215 (1879), Brinkerhoff v. Brown,
7 Johns Chan, 217 (1823).   But see,
contra, Walser v Seligman, 21 Blatch,
130 (1882), a well-considered case, and
Wellman v Howland Coal & Iron
Works, 19 Fed Rep, 51 (1884).   In the
former of these cases the court say "Sufficient reason for not making it (the
corporation) a party is found in the

tion is due, except such as are unknown or insolvent, or beyond the jurisdiction [1]

The stockholders against whom the bill is filed may, however, it seems, when all are not made parties, file a cross-bill, obtain a dis-

fact that it is beyond the jurisdiction of this court, and also in the fact that it is practically defunct." In the case last cited it was held that, where a corporation is without property or officers or place of business, it need not be made a party of record

[1] Vick v Lane 56 Miss 681 (1879), Walsh v Memphis, etc R. R. Co, 2 McCrary, 156 (1881), Hadley v. Russell, 40 N H, 109 (1860), Erickson v Nesmith, 46 id, 371 (1860), Pierce v Milwaukee, etc, Co, 38 Wis, 253 (1875); Coleman v White, 14 id, 700 (1862), Carpenter v Marine Bank, 14 id, 705, n (1862), Umsted v. Buskirk, 17 Ohio St., 113 (1866), Mann v Pentz, 3 N Y, 415 (1850) Cf Young v New York & Liverpool Steamship Co, 10 Abb Prac, 229 (1860), holding that judgment creditors are not proper parties defendant without showing why they were not made parties plaintiff The bill should contain an appropriate allegation as to the shareholders unknown, insolvent, or out of the jurisdiction, and a prayer that, upon discovery they be made parties when possible Bogardus v Rosendale Manufacturing Co, 7 N Y, 147 (1852) "Where the attempt is to reach the liability of the shareholders on their subscription to capital stock, all the solvent stockholders within the jurisdiction must be joined except where this will be excused upon an allegation that the number is too great." Chalmers, J, in Vick v Lane, 56 Miss, 681, 684 (1879) Cf Bonewitz v Van Wert Co. Bank, 41 Ohio St. 78 (1884) But on the other hand, with respect to the matter of joining all the solvent shareholders who are in arrears as parties defendant to the bill, provided they are within the jurisdiction, we find a line of authorities in support of the proposition that all such stockholders are not

always necessary parties to the bill, that such a suit may properly be brought against one, or any, of the delinquent stockholders as well as against all, and that a bill will not be held defective merely because it fails to include all the delinquent stockholders as parties defendant. Ogilvie v Knox Insurance Co, 22 How, 380 (1859), Hatch v Dana, 101 U. S, 205 (1879), Marsh v Burroughs, 1 Woods, 463 (1871), Holmes v Sherwood, 3 McCrary, 105 (1881), Glenn v Williams, 60 Md, 93 (1882), Bartlett v Drew, 57 N Y, 587 (1874), Griffith v Mangam, 73 id, 611 (1878), Brundage v Monumental, etc, Mining Co 12 Oregon, 322 (1885) Cf Von Schmidt v Huntington, 1 Cal, 55 (1855), Lamar Insurance Co. v. Gulick, 102 Ill, 11 (1882). Any other rule would place upon the creditor a burden which would be unjust and perhaps destructive of the remedy itself In Hatch v Dana supra, there was a bill to compel payment of a debt out of the unpaid subscription of a single stockholder. It was not sought to wind up the company It being urged that a creditor of an insolvent corporation is not at liberty to proceed against one or more delinquent subscribers to recover the amount of his debt, without an account being taken of other indebtedness, and without bringing in all the stockholders for contribution, the court by Mr Justice Strong, said: "The liability of a subscriber for the capital stock of a company is several and not joint By his subscription each becomes a several debtor to the company, as much so as if he had given his promissory note for the amount of his subscription At law, certainly, his subscription may be enforced against him without joinder of other subscribers, and in equity his liability does not cease to be several A

covery of the remaining delinquent stockholders, bring them in as parties, and thus enforce contribution.[1] If all the parties who are liable have not been brought before the court, it has been held that those who are defendants of record cannot be charged with liability which should fall upon those who are absent, unless it be shown that the absentees are insolvent or beyond the jurisdiction of the court.[2] There is doubt, however, as to the soundness of this rule

creditor's bill merely subrogates the creditor to the place of the debtor, and garnishes the debt due to the indebted corporation It does not change the character of the debt attached or garnished It may be that, if the object of the bill is to wind up the affairs of this company, all the shareholders, at least so far as they can be ascertained, should be made parties, that complete justice may be done by equalizing the burdens, and in order to prevent a multiplicity of suits But this is no such case The most that can be said is that the presence of all the stockholders might be convenient, not that it is necessary When the only object of a bill is to obtain payment of a judgment against a corporation out of its credits or intangible property, that is, out of its unpaid stock, there is not the same reason for requiring all the stockholders to be made defendants" See, also, Bonewitz v Van Wert Co Bank, 41 Ohio St, 78 (1884), where it was held error to give judgment against the defendants properly before the court, when the return of the summons was entirely silent as to two of the defendants As to when bills brought by creditors in these cases are and are not multifarious, see Allen v Montgomery R. R. Co. 11 Ala, 437 (1847) Cambridge, etc, Co. v Somerville, etc, Co, 14 Gray, 193 (1860), where the liability of some of the defendants was as directors and of others as stockholders, and the bill was held to be multifarious Barre National Bank v Hingham Manuf Co, 127 Mass, 563 (1879); Pope v Leonard, 115 id, 286 (1874), Deaderick v Wilson, 8 Baxter, 108 (1874), Holmes v Sherwood, infra

Executors of a deceased stockholder may be joined with other stockholders as defendants where the suit is in equity. Hamilton v Clarion, etc, R R., 23 Atl Rep, 53 (Pa, 1891). A creditor's bill filed to collect the unpaid subscriptions of stockholders will be dismissed where only a few of the stockholders are made party defendants and no allegation is made showing clearly and in detail that the other stockholders cannot be reached and brought in Dunston v Hoptonie Co, 47 N W Rep, 322 (Mich, 1890). An insolvent stockholder is not necessarily a party to a suit by corporate creditors to collect subscriptions. Wilson v. California, etc, Co, 54 N W Rep, 643 (Mich., 1893). All the stockholders need not be joined as defendants Baines v. Babcock, 30 Pac. Rep, 776 (Cal, 1892); Gibbons v Trussel, 48 N W Rep., 255 (Wis, 1891) A stockholder may be held liable on a subscription, although the corporation is not made a party defendant and other stockholders are not joined A court of equity has jurisdiction Potter v Dear, 30 Pac Rep, 777 (Cal, 1892).

[1] Hatch v Dana, 101 U S, 205 (1879). In the original bill itself there may properly be a prayer, when some of the delinquent shareholders are unknown, for a discovery, in order that such unknown stockholders may be made parties by amendment Hipple v Five, etc., Imp Co, 3 Atl Rep., 682 (N J, 1886), Bogardus v Rosendale Manuf Co., 7 N Y, 147 (1852), Morgan v New York, etc, R. R. Co, 10 Paige, 290.

[2] Wood v Dummer, 3 Mason, 308 (1824), But see Marsh v. Burroughs, 1 Woods, 463 (1871) Cf. Erickson v. Nesmith, 46 N. H, 371 (1866) Contra,

§ 207 *A court of equity may make a call* — It is well settled that, when stock is subscribed to be paid in upon call by the corporate authorities, and the company neglects or refuses to make such calls as are necessary to raise funds to meet the just corporate obligations, a court of equity will itself make the necessary calls if the interests of the creditors require it [1] The court will, in behalf of the creditors, do what it is the duty of the corporation to do in respect of calls [2] And the court may make the call although the statute says calls shall be made by the trustees, directors or managers [3] The question of whether interest on the call may be collected is considered elsewhere [4]

§ 208 *Receivers and assignees in bankruptcy for the benefit of creditors — Their duties, powers and liabilities as to unpaid subscriptions* — When a corporation becomes insolvent, with corporate

Appeal of Cornell, 6 Atl Rep. 258 (Pa, 1886), citing Strong's Appeal, 10 W N Cases, 409 When there are delinquent stockholders beyond the jurisdiction, the stockholders who have been sued and compelled to pay more than their due proportion must look to them for contribution Holmes *v* Sherwood, 3 McCrary, 405 (1881)

[1] See § 108, *supra*

[2] Scovill *t* Thayer, 105 U S, 143, 155 (1881); Hatch *v* Dana, 101 id, 205, 214 (1879), Curry *v* Woodward, 53 Ala, 371 (1875), Wilbur *v* Stockholders, 18 Bank Reg, 178 (1878), Marsh *t* Burroughs, 1 Woods, 463 (1871) Myers *v* Seeley, 10 Bank Reg, 411 (1874); Henry *v* Vermillion, etc, R. R. Co, 17 Ohio, 187 (1848), Robinson *v* Bank of Darien, 18 Ga, 65 (1855), Ward *v* Griswoldsville Mfg Co, 16 Conn, 593 (1844), Sanger *v* Upton, 91 U S, 56 (1875); Chubb *v.* Upton, 95 id, 665 (1877), Glenn *v* Williams, 60 Md, 93 (1882). *Cf* Germantown, etc, R'y Co *t* Fitler, 60 Pa St., 124 (1869), Chandler *t* Keith, 42 Iowa, 99 (1875), Mann *v* Pentz, 3 N Y, 415 (1850), Ogilvie *v* Knox Insurance Co, 22 How, 380 (1859), Adler *v* Milwaukee Mfg Co., 13 Wis, 57 (1860) And see Seymour *v* Sturgess, 26 N Y., 134 (1862), Wheeler *v* Millar, 90 id, 353 (1882) The court itself may make a call Marson *v* Deither, 52 N

W Rep, 38 (Minn 1892). A call is necessary, or the equivalent, where the receiver sues Chandler *v* Siddle, 3 Dill, 477 (1874) No call is necessary where creditors file a bill to reach unpaid subscriptions Hamilton *v* Clarion, etc, R. R., 23 Atl Rep, 53 (Pa 1891). Non-resident stockholders are bound by the decree of the court levying the assessment. Howard *v* Glenn, 11 S E Rep, 610 (Ga, 1890) Where the statute requires twenty days' notice to stockholders before calls are made, creditors must give this notice before claiming and collecting the unpaid subscription Universal, etc, Co *v.* Tabor, 27 Pac Rep, 890 (Colo, 1891)

[3] Crawford *v* Rohrer, 59 Md, 599 (1882) *Cf.* Glenn *t* Saxton, 68 Cal, 353 (1886) A call may be made in behalf of corporate creditors although the company had contracted with the stockholders not to call in the subscriptions until a later date *Re* Cordova, etc, Co, 64 L T Rep, 772 (1891) Where, however, it was provided by the charter of the corporation that all calls are to be made only upon a three-fourths vote of the stockholders, it was held that a call by the court was irregular Trustees of the Louisiana Paper Co *v* Waples, 3 Woods, 34 (1877).

[4] See § 112.

creditors on the one hand pressing their claims, and subscriptions to the capital stock wholly or partially uncollected on the other hand, it is usual to place the assets of the company, including the claims against delinquent share-owners, in the hands of a third person for the benefit of all concerned. Such a person may be an assignee under state insolvent laws, a receiver, or an assignee for the benefit of creditors. A receiver in such a case may be defined to be a third person appointed by a court of equity to act as the representative alike of creditors and stockholders for the purpose of collecting the corporate assets and paying the corporate debts.[1] It is the right and duty of such a receiver to collect the unpaid subscriptions, so far as may be necessary, for the purpose of paying the corporate debts in full.[2]

[1] Johnson v. Laflin, 5 Dill, 65 (1878), High on Receivers (2d ed), 1

[2] Dayton v. Borst, 31 N Y, 435 (1865), Nathan v. Whitlock, 9 Paige, 152 (1841), Mein's Appeal, 85 Pa St, 75 (1877), Dorris v. French, 4 Hun, 292 (1875), Van Wagenen v. Clark, 22 id, 497 (1880), Frank v. Morrison, 58 Md, 423 (1882), Chandler v. Brown, 77 Ill, 333 (1875), Calkins v. Atkinson, 2 Lans, 12 (1870). Cf. Tucker v. Gilman, 45 Hun, 193 (1887). Assignee for benefit of creditors of an insolvent corporation may enforce unpaid subscriptions. Chamberlain v. Bromberg, 3 S. Rep, 434 (Ala, 1888), Tobey v. Russell, 9 R. I, 58 (1868), Stewart v. Lay, 45 Iowa, 604 (1877), Clark v. Thomas, 34 Ohio St, 46 (1877), Phœnix, etc. Co. v. Badger, 67 N Y, 294 (1876). As incidental to the receiver's power to collect unpaid balances of subscription, it is held that he may, as an officer of the court, make calls for the amount due. Hall v. United States Ins Co, 5 Gill (Md), 484 (1847), Rankine v. Elliott, 16 N Y., 377 (1857). Lionberger v. Broadway, etc., 10 Mo App, 499 (1881), holds that an assignee for benefit of creditors may, by a bill in equity, compel the directors of the insolvent corporation to make an assessment upon the capital stock, payable to him, such a suit is not affected by the fact that certain creditors are proceeding against the stockholders by motion

under the statute, since the proceeding by motion is cumulative merely and not exclusive. Chandler v. Keith, 42 Iowa, 99 (1875), holds that a stockholder who had paid all regular assessments could not be called upon by the receiver, in an action at law, to pay the remainder of his subscription until a general call is made upon the stockholders for the amount assessed upon their shares, and this call should be preceded by the fact that losses have been sustained by the corporation, showing a necessity for an assessment and call upon the stockholders. Under the English Railway Companies Act of 1867, a receiver has no such power. In re Birmingham, etc., R'y Co, L. R., 18 Chan Div, 155 (1881). In New York, by statute, the receiver may sue. See Dayton v. Borst, 31 N Y, 434 (1865), and see, previous to the statute, Mann v. Pentz, 3 N Y, 415 (1850), reversing 2 Sandf Ch, 257. The receiver cannot enforce the subscription where the defendant had transferred his stock and been discharged by the corporation. Cutting v. Damerel, 88 N Y, 410 (1882). It may be remarked here that the receiver has no power to enforce statutory liability, this liability not being an asset of the corporation. See Fairnsworth v. Wood, 91 N Y, 308 (1883), and the chapter on Statutory Liability, infra. The receiver of a foreign corporation,

As long as the authority of the receiver exists, a creditor cannot directly bring suit against delinquent shareholders, but the receiver may be compelled to act in the matter at the instance of creditors [1]

An assignee for the benefit of the creditors of a corporation, like a receiver, represents both the corporation and the creditors, and should collect unpaid subscriptions, [2] and, in like manner, an as-

duly empowered to sue at home, may sue resident stockholders for the balances due the company, provided the corporation itself could have done so if it had remained solvent. Dayton v. Borst, 31 N. Y., 435 (1865), a case where a receiver appointed by the court of chancery in New Jersey was held competent to maintain a suit of this nature in New York against a citizen thereof. Mann v Cook, 20 Conn, 178 (1850), McDonough v Phelps. 15 How Prac, 372 (1856), Seymour v Sturges, 26 N. Y., 134 (1862) It has been held that a receiver may collect unpaid balances due on subscriptions, although the other corporate assets have not been collected and the amount of the liabilities is undetermined Starke v. Burke, 9 La Ann, 341 (1854) And that if, on the final settlement, there is a surplus, it is to be returned *pro rata* to the shareholders. Pentz v Hawley, 1 Barb Chan (N Y), 122 (1845) But the more modern and better rule is that a receiver has no authority to call upon a subscriber for his unpaid balance until the court have determined the amount of the corporate indebtedness and fixed definitely the liability of each share of the stock. Chandler v Keith, 42 Iowa, 99 (1875). See, also, Mills v. Scott, 99 U S, 25 (1878) After a transfer, the transferrer is not liable to the receiver any more than he would have been to the corporation Billings v Robinson, 94 N. Y., 415 (1884); affirming 28 Hun, 122. The court cannot give a receiver power to compromise claims upon unpaid subscriptions Chandler v Brown, 77 Ill, 333 (1875). See §§ 167-171, 210 It has been held that the assignee can-

not sue to set aside a fraudulent device by which a stockholder has escaped payment of his subscription Bouton v. Dement, 14 N E Rep, 62 (Ill, 1887) Receiver cannot enforce subscriptions which the corporation could not enforce. Winters v. Armstrong, 37 Fed Rep, 508 (1889) The receiver may sell the subscription at auction and the subscriber may buy it Dean v Biggs, 25 Hun, 122 (1881).

[1] It is the receiver's duty to act promptly and vigilantly in the collection of the assets, and to compel payment of balances due by subscribers on unpaid stock, if such a course is necessary to meet the demands of creditors. If the receiver fails to do his duty in this respect the creditors may compel him to act, inasmuch as they cannot act directly themselves Gas Light Co. v. Haynes, 7 La Ann, 114 (1852), New Orleans Gas Light Co v Bennett, 6 id., 457 (1851), Starke v Burke, 9 id, 341 (1854), Atwood v Rhode Island Agric. Bank, 1 R. I, 376 (1850). Rankine v Elliott, 16 N Y, 377, holding that when a receiver of an insolvent railroad is appointed in an action in behalf of all its creditors, the right to proceed for the collection of unpaid subscriptions vests in him, and a judgment creditor will be enjoined from proceeding against a stockholder in an action begun after the order was made but before the appointment is perfected While the receiver is in charge, a corporate creditor cannot sue to enforce a stockholder's liability on an unpaid subscription Merchants', etc, Bank v Northwestern, etc, Co, 51 N W Rep, 119 (Minn, 1892).

[2] Shockley v Fisher, 75 Mo, 498 (1882).

signee in bankruptcy could recover the amounts due by stockholders on account of their subscriptions, and his proper remedy was

Vanderwerker v Glenn, 6 S. E Rep., 806 (Va, 1888). Cf. Germantown, etc, R'y Co v Fitler, 60 Pa. St. 124 (1869). Eppright v Nickerson, 78 Mo, 482 (1883), holding that an insolvent corporation may include in an assignment for the benefit of its creditors the liability of its stockholders for unpaid stock for which no call has been made. An action at common law on subscriptions must be in the company's name and not in the name of the assignee of the company. Glenn v Marbury, 145 U S, 499 (1892). An assignee of the corporation for the benefit of creditors may sue. Cartright v Dickinson, 12 S. W. Rep., 1030 (Tenn, 1890). An assignment for the benefit of creditors made by order of a directors' meeting at which three directors were present and the other two were not notified is invalid and no bar to a creditor's action to collect unpaid subscriptions. Dorubecher v Columbia, etc, Co, 28 Pac Rep, 899 (Oreg, 1892). In Indiana a creditor of a manufacturing corporation can collect his debt from unpaid subscriptions through a receiver, and in that way only. Wheeler v Thayer, 22 N E Rep, 972 (Ind, 1889). The United States district court has jurisdiction of an action by the receiver of an insolvent national bank to collect assessments on stock. Stephens v Bernays, 44 Fed Rep, 642 (1890). A receiver may cause to be assessed and may collect assessments on parties liable therefor to pay insurance losses. McDonald v Ross-Lewin, 29 Hun, 87 (1883). Where a receiver is appointed to take charge of the "whole property" he may sue to collect unpaid subscriptions. Showalter v Laredo, etc, Co, 18 S W. Rep, 491 (Tex, 1892). In a judgment creditor's suit for sequestration and a receiver, both the corporation and a stockholder liable on his subscription being made parties, the receiver may have judgment against the stockholder

Spooner v. Bay, etc., 50 N W Rep, 601 (Minn, 1891). Although some fraudulent claims have been allowed in the court which appointed the receiver and made the calls, yet a stockholder who is sued in another state cannot enjoin the collection of the judgment on that ground. Foote v. Glenn, 52 Fed Rep, 529 (1892). Although the statute of limitations is a bar, unless the court allows creditors to be substituted in place of a receiver, who has brought suits to enforce the liability of stockholders and is held not to have had authority to do so, yet such substitution will not be granted. Fairbanks v Farwell, 30 N E Rep., 1056 (Ill, 1892). The position of the receiver as regards the collection of subscriptions is thus stated in Republic Life Ins. Co v Swigert, 25 N E Rep., 680 (Ill, 1890). "We understand the rule to be that, where a receiver is appointed for the purpose of taking charge of the property and assets of a corporation, he is, for the purpose of determining the nature and extent of his title, regarded as representing only the corporate body itself, and not its creditors or shareholders, being vested by law with the estate of the corporation and deriving his own title under and through it; and that, for purposes of litigation, he takes only the rights of the corporation, such as could be asserted in his own name; and that upon that basis only can he litigate for the benefit of either stockholders or creditors . . . Almost all of the causes cited by defendants in error fall in one or another of the four classes following: Where the receiver by force of some statute can act for the creditors; where the act complained of was ultra vires and not binding upon the corporation; where the receiver was appointed in a proceeding prosecuted by creditors, which was supplemental to execution, and the receiver had the rights of the

by bill in equity, making all the delinquent shareholders parties to
the bill [1]

§ 209. *The judgment against the corporation impeachable only
for fraud or want of jurisdiction.*— That a judgment conclusively
settles all matters of controversy involved in the suit, so far as parties or their privies are concerned, excepting where it may be impeached for fraud or want of jurisdiction, is well-established law
When, therefore, a corporate creditor has obtained judgment against
the corporation, and execution is returned unsatisfied, and he then
proceeds to enforce his remedy against the holders of stock not
paid up, the question arises whether the stockholders may set up in
defense matters which the corporation might have set up or did set
up to defeat the creditor's claim against the corporation

It has been strenuously insisted that he might   This was Chancellor Kent's famous contention in the case of Slee *v* Bloom,[2] but
the authorities have firmly established the rule that, in the absence
of fraud and collusion, judgments against the corporation, if the
court had jurisdiction, are conclusive against the stockholders as to
the validity and amount of the creditor's claim.[3] Thus, it is held

creditors at whose instance, and to secure whose claims, he was appointed,
and where the receiver was suing for
property or assets that belonged to the
debtor. . . . We think the decided
weight of authority sustains the rule
in respect to the powers of receivers,
where there has been no enlargement of
their powers by legislative enactment,
that they have such rights of action
only as were possessed by the persons
or corporations upon whose estates they
administer " The court referred to and
considered many authorities   "The receiver represents the creditors as well
as all other parties interested in the
corporation " A subscriber sued by
him on the subscription cannot set up
fraudulent representations inducing him
to subscribe   Ruggles *v* Brock, 6 Hun,
164 (1875). Where the bonds are invalid
a receiver appointed in the foreclosure
suit has no power to collect subscriptions. Farmers' L. & T Co *v* San
Diego, etc, St Car Co, 49 Fed Rep., 188
(1892) A receiver may collect the unpaid par value of stock issued for cash
at less than par, even though the corporation agreed with the stockholders

that no more than the amount already
paid should ever be required Such an
agreement does not bind the receiver
in so far as it is necessary for him to collect the money to pay creditors Mathis
v Pridham, 20 S W. Rep, 1015 (Tex,
1892).

[1] Sawyer *v* Hoag, 17 Wall, 610, 621
(1873), Upton *v* Tribilcock, 91 U S, 45
(1875), Sanger *v* Upton, id, 56, Webster *v* Upton, id, 65, Chubb *v* Upton,
95 id, 665 (1877), Payson *v* Stoever, 2
Dill, 427 (1873), Upton *v* Hansbrough,
3 Biss, 417 (1873) Cf County of Morgan *v* Allen, 103 U. S 498 (1880) The
principles of equity applicable to actions
by a receiver in cases of this nature
will, in general, unless some statute has
changed the law, be found applicable to
these actions when brought by assignees
at common law or in bankruptcy

[2] 5 Johns Chan 366 (1820), reversed
by 19 Johns, 456, 473 (1822), by Spencer,
C. J

[3] Slee *v*. Bloom, 20 Johns, 669 (1822),
Hawkins *v*. Glenn, 131 U S., 319 (1889),
Henry *v* Vermillion, etc, R. R Co, 17
Ohio, 187 (1848), Hampson *v* Weare,
4 Iowa, 13 (1856); Millikin *v* White-

that the stockholder cannot take advantage, in the suit against him, of a defect in the service of process upon the corporation in the original suit His remedy in such a case is by a direct proceeding[1] In New York the conclusiveness of the judgment in these cases has been much questioned.[2]

house, 49 Me, 527 (1860), Wilson v Pittsburgh, etc, Coal Co, 43 Pa St., 424 (1862), Bank of Wooster v Stevens, 1 Ohio St., 233 (1853), Stevens v. Fox, 83 N Y, 313 (1881); Marsh v Burroughs, 1 Woods, 463 (1871), Grund v Tucker, 5 Kan, 70 (1869), Bissit v Kentucky River Navigation Co, 15 Fed Rep, 353, and the note, p 360 (1882), Hawes v Petroleum Co, 101 Mass, 385 (1869). So, also, in actions to enforce statutory liability of stockholders, a judgment against the corporation is equally conclusive Donworth v Coolbaugh, 5 Iowa, 300 (1857), Came v Brigham, 39 Me, 35 (1854), Hawes v Anglo-Saxon Petroleum Co., 101 Mass, 385 (1869), holding that a judgment by default is prima facie conclusive, Stephens v Fox, 83 N Y, 313 (1881), Holyoke Bank v Goodman Paper Mfg Co 63 Mass, 576 (1852), holding that a judgment by default is conclusive, Bigelow on Estoppel, 129. 4th ed ; Freeman on Judgments, § 177, 3d ed The stockholder may, of course, set up that he is not a stockholder, and other similar defenses, such as are specified in chapter X See infra, §§ 210, 224 See, also, Merrill v Suffolk Bank, 31 Me, 57 (1849), Johnson v Somerville, etc, Co, 81 Mass, 216 (1860), Glenn v Springs, 26 Fed Rep, 494, Powell v. Oregonian R'y, 38 Fed Rep, 187 (1889); Barton v Paine, 22 Atl Rep, 218 (Me, 1891) The decree of the court where the corporation is located is conclusive as to whether service was properly made on the corporation, such service being on two directors and the cashier The decree is also conclusive that no laches existed in bringing suit, that the statute of limitations was no bar to the decree, that the court had authority to make an assessment; that

the change in the corporate name did not discharge the stockholders' liability ; and that the trustee, Glenn, might sue the stockholders Lehman v. Glenn, 6 S. Rep., 44 (Ala., 1889). Nor can he set up that the creditors' rights are based on purchases made ultra vires by the corporate officers. Sumner v. Marcy, 3 Woodb. & M, 105 (1847). The judgment against the corporation is conclusive, and it cannot be shown that it arose on a contract which was ultra vires Barnes v Babcock, 30 Pac. Rep, 776 (Cal, 1892). Cannot attack the debts upon which the judgment was obtained Hambleton v. Glenn, 20 Atl. Rep., 121 (Md, 1890) No defense that the judgment against the corporation was obtained by collusion with one of the directors. Id.

[1] Came v Brigham, 39 Me., 35 (1854) The stockholder sued on his subscription may set up that the judgment against the corporation was obtained by service on one who had ceased to be an officer Beardsley v Johnson, 121 N. Y., 224 (1890) Cf Wheeler v Millar, 24 Hun, 541 (1881) In Chesnut v Pennell, 92 Ill, 55 (1879), it was held that a decree against the corporation is not admissible in evidence against a stockholder who was not a party to the bill or decree, actually or constructively, and that in such a case proof of the liability of the corporation to the creditor should be given

[2] New York is practically the only state where this question presents any difficulty, and the confusion which there reigns is largely due to the failure to distinguish between cases of liability for unpaid subscriptions and liabilities created by statute. In some of the cases the meaning of the court is not clear, and often the question did not

Where the stockholders are liable only on a particular class of corporate debts, or to certain classes of creditors only, the court will not, of course, reject evidence tending to show either that the debt recovered belongs or does not belong to the class on which the shareholder is liable [1]

§ 210. *Defenses available against corporate creditors in actions to compel payment of balances of subscriptions* — There are, of course, certain defenses which subscribers may set up when actions are brought against them on behalf of corporate creditors. These defenses are the same as those which may be set up to defeat an action by the corporation to enforce the subscription.[2] But both in England and in this country the courts do not favor such de-

come up directly for decision The general rule was originally stated essentially as in the text, by Spencer, C J, in Slee v. Bloom, 20 Johns, 669 (1822), reversing S C, 5 Johns Ch, 366 (1821) This was followed by Moss v Oakley, 2 Hill, 265 (1842) Moss v McCullough, 5 Hill, 131 (1843), started a new theory, that the case was the ordinary one of principal and surety, and hence a judgment against the corporation was not even *prima facie* evidence against the stockholder Although this ruling was overturned on the final determination, S C, 7 Barb, 279 (1849), it was followed in Strong v Wheaton, 38 Barb, 616 (1861) In Belmont v Coleman, 21 N Y, 96 (1860), on appeal from 1 Bosw, 188, three justices affirmed the ruling below that the judgment was *prima facie* evidence, while the other four refused to commit themselves to that doctrine Conklin v Furman 8 Abb Pr (N S), 161 (1865), accepts the original rule as stated by Spencer, C J Then follow two later cases, Miller v White, 50 N Y, 137 (1872), and McMahon v Macy, 51 id, 155, which reject that rule in strong terms But both these cases are easily distinguishable on the principle stated *supra* They were suits to enforce a statutory penalty against trustees for failure to file a certain report It may be said, then, that after all the New York rule in the cases really covered by the language of the text differs com-

paratively little from the general law. The courts, under the influence of some of the earlier decisions hesitate to accept the rule of conclusiveness, but the latest case in the court of appeals, Rapallo, J, uses this language "The creditor thus claims through the corporation, and to entitle him to this statutory subrogation or transfer he need only show that he is a creditor If he shows this fact by evidence which is binding and conclusive against the corporation, such evidence should be competent against the stockholder to establish the title of the creditor to succeed to the rights of the corporation A judgment against the corporation, being the highest evidence against it, should be as effectual to pass its title to the fund in question as a deed or any other form of transfer" Stephens v Fox, 83 N Y, 313, 317 (1881) *Cf* Wheeler v Millar, *supra* See, also, Grund v Tucker, 5 Kan, 70 (1869), Merchants' Bank v Chandler, 19 Wis, 434 (1865)

[1] Wilson v The Stockholders, 43 Pa St, 421 (1862) Conant v Van Schaick, 24 Barb, 87 (1857), Larrabee v Baldwin, 35 Cal 155 (1868) *Cf.* Hudson v Carman, 41 Me, 84 (1856), holding that the judgment obtained may not be conclusive evidence of the organization and existence of the corporation, and if denied they must be proved

[2] See ch X.

fenses, especially after the corporation has become insolvent. Moreover, there are many defenses which might defeat an action by the corporation, but which do not prevent the corporate creditor from enforcing the subscription [1]

§ 211. *Contribution* — Corporate creditors compelling stockholders to pay their subscriptions are under no obligation to see that the payments made by the subscribers are proportionally equal [2] A court of chancery will compel subscribers to pay in full the amount of their unpaid subscriptions if the corporate indebtedness make it necessary, leaving them to seek contribution from the other shareholders [3] The rule, moreover, is well settled that a

[1] Such as fraud on the part of the corporation, inducing a subscription See §§ 163, 164, *supra* So, also, fraud and mismanagement on the part of the directors and corporate officers is not a valid defense herein *In re* Republic Insurance Co, 3 Biss, 452 (1873). The stockholder may set up that the corporation had no stock to offer him Lathrop *v* Kneeland, 46 Barb, 432 (1866). *Cf* Mackley's Case, L R, 1 Chan Div, 247 (1875) Acts that estop the subscriber as against the corporation estop him as to corporate creditors Griswold *v* Seligman, 72 Mo, 110 (1880) But mere entries in corporate books are not admissible in evidence to prove the creditor's claim, Neilson *v* Crawford, 52 Cal, 248 (1877)

Where a firm or partnership becomes a subscriber in the copartnership name, corporate creditors may have execution against any one of the partners The partnership subscription is not a defense of which any single partner can avail himself to escape liability Bray's Adm'r *v* Seligman's Adm r, 75 Mo., 31 (1881). It is no defense that judgment against the defendant stockholder for the full amount of his liability has been recovered by other creditors, and that he settled the same at a discount Kunkelman *v* Reutchler, 15 Brad (Ill), 271 (1884). Prominent among these defenses is the defense that the corporation contracted with the defendant that his stock should be deemed fully paid-up stock, although in fact the full

par value had never been paid. See ch III

The unpaid subscription may be collected in payment of damages for a tort the same as for a contract debt. Powell *v* Oregonian R'y, 36 Fed Rep, 726 (1888), 38 id, 187 In Maine this rule is declared by statute Grindle *v*. Stone, 4 East. Rep., 623 (1886). For many other defenses, see ch. XII, where defenses were set up to defeat the statutory liability

[2] Peutz *v* Hawley, 1 Barb. Chan , 122 (1845).

[3] Peutz *v* Hawley, *supra* (1845), Evans *v* Coventry, 25 L J , Chan , 489 (1856); Marsh *v* Burroughs, 1 Woods, 463 (1871) As to whether solvent stockholders are required to make up, for the benefit of creditors, the deficiency of defaulting or insolvent subscribers to the full amount of the formers own unpaid subscriptions, see South C Mfg. Co *v.* Bank of S C., 6 Rich (Eq), 227 (1854). But actual subscribers are not liable for that part of the capital stock which was never subscribed Evans *v.* Coventry, 25 L J , Chan., 489 (1856) It is no defense to show that notes were given in payment of subscriptions, or that notes by insolvent persons were procured to be given, when it appears that nothing was ever realized from the notes. Nathan *v*. Whitlock, 9 Paige. Chan , 152 (1841). When it is made to appear by proof that some of the stockholders are insolvent, the solvent must pay the proportion of the insolvent,

shareholder who has been compelled to pay more than his proportion of the debts of the company may maintain an action against his co-stockholders for contribution[1]

Contribution may properly be enforced in the corporate creditor's suit. It is largely for this purpose that all the delinquent shareholders may be and should be made parties defendant[2]

---

to be apportioned among them according to and up to the amount of their stock subscribed and unpaid. Such is the rule in Oregon. Hodges v Silver, etc., Co., 9 Oregon, 200 (1881). Cf. § 213. All of the stockholders who are defendants will have judgment entered against them for their full liability, and they must seek contribution themselves. Hamilton v Clarion, etc., R. R., 23 Atl Rep., 53 (Pa., 1891).

[1] Wincock v Turpin, 96 Ill, 135 (1880), Millaudon v New Orleans, etc., R R Co, 3 Rob (La), 488 (1843), Marsh v Burroughs, 1 Woods, 463 (1871), Holmes v Sherwood, 3 McCrary, 405 (1881), Umsted v Buskirk, 17 Ohio St 113 (1866), Matthews v Albert, 24 Md, 527 (1866), Stewart v Lay, 45 Iowa, 604 (1877), Handley v Russell, 40 N H, 109 (1860), Erickson v Nesmith, 46 id, 371 (1866), Masters v Rossie Lead Mining Co. 2 Sandf Chan, 301 (1845), Aspinwall v Torrence, 1 Lans, 391 (1870); Stover v Flack, 30 N. Y., 64 (1864), Farrow v Bivings, 13 Rich (Eq), 25 (1866), Brinham v Wellersburg Coal Co., 47 Pa. St., 43 (1864) Cf Andrews v Callender, 30 Mass, 484 (1833), Gray v. Coffin, 63 Mass, 192 (1852), Sutton's Case, 3 De G. & Sm., 262 (1850). In

Pennsylvania the right to contribution is said to be purely statutory. Brinham v Wellersburg Coal Co, supra, Allen v Fairbanks, 45 Fed Rep, 415 (1891). A liability for contribution on subscriptions does not cease upon the death of the stockholders. Allen v Fairbanks, 40 Fed Rep, 188 (1889). The remedy of one stockholder against another for contribution is in equity and not at law. Koons v Martin, 66 Hun, 554 (1893).

[2] N Y Code of Civil Procedure, §§ 1791–1794, Masters v Rossie Lead Mining Co, 2 Sandf Chan, 301 (1845), Holmes v Sherwood, 3 McCrary, 405 (1881), Hadley v Russell, 40 N H, 109 (1860), Umsted v Buskirk, 17 Ohio St, 113 (1866), Hodges v Silver Hill Mining Co, 9 Oregon, 200 (1881). Where the articles of incorporation provide that the indebtedness shall not exceed a certain sum, but debts are contracted in excess of the limit, and, the corporation being insolvent, the officer who contracted the debt pays it off out of his own individual funds, he cannot claim contribution unless the debt in excess of the limit was contracted by the unanimous assent of the stockholders. Haldeman v Ainslie, 82 Ky., 395 (1884).

CHAPTER XII.

STATUTORY LIABILITY OF STOCKHOLDERS TO CORPORATE CREDITORS.

A. EXTENT OF THE LIABILITY.

§ 212, 213. *Statutory liability in general* — Probably the most characteristic feature of a corporate existence is the fact that, by being a corporation, its stockholders are liable only for the par value of the stock held by them, and when that is once paid in money or property there is no further liability This exemption from liability need not be declared in the charter, but arises from the very fact of incorporation. For this reason legislatures are very ˙careful, in giving joint-stock companies special powers, to distinctly declare that the company shall not thereby become a corporation The very fact of incorporation by itself releases subscribers for stock from all liability for corporate debts, except to the extent of their unpaid subscriptions It has been deemed wise, however, by the state legislatures, in many instances, to increase the liability of stockholders to corporate creditors Accordingly, statutes are passed expressly declaring that the stockholders shall be liable for a specified sum, in addition to their unpaid subscriptions. This is called the statutory liability of stockholders. It

270

rarely exists as regards stockholders in railroad corporations, but frequently exists in the case of manufacturing and various other corporations,[1] and nearly always exists as against the stockholders in banks.

This additional liability may be imposed by the state constitution, or by the charter, or by a general statute   Where this liability is imposed by a provision existing at the time of the creation of the corporation, there is no doubt of its constitutionality.   But where the liability is created by a statute or constitutional provision enacted after the corporation was incorporated, then there arise difficult questions of constitutional validity   A full discussion, however, of the constitutionality of such a statute is considered elsewhere [2]

§ 214   *This liability is strictly construed and limited* — Inasmuch as all statutes creating an additional liability on the part of stockholders are in derogation of the common law, they are to be strictly construed.   They are a wide departure from established rules, and, though founded on considerations of public policy and general convenience, are not to be extended beyond the plain intent of the words of the statute.[3]

§ 215. *Particular statutes construed.*— The character, nature and extent of the liability imposed by constitutional provisions or by statute upon stockholders, in addition to their common-law liability, vary, of course, widely, and the extent of the liability created by each statute will depend entirely upon the particular words of

---

[1] A complete statement of the liability of stockholders in various corporations in all the states and territories is given in Part VII, *infra*

[2] See § 497, *infra*. It is constitutional for the legislature at the time of enacting a general incorporating act to provide for an extra liability of directors who make false reports   Huntington v Attrill, 118 N Y, 365 (1890).

[3] Gray v Coffin, 9 Cush, 192 (1852). O'Reilly v Baid, 105 Pa St, 569 (1884), Chase z Lord, 77 N Y, 1 (1879), Mean's Appeal, 85 Pa St, 75 (1877), Dane v Dane Mfg Co, 14 Gray, 489 (1859), Chamberlin v Huguenot Mfg Co, 118 Mass, 532 (1875), Grose v Hilt, 36 Me, 22 (1853), Coffin z Rich, 45 id, 511, Windham Provident Institution, etc, z Sprague, 43 Vt, 502 (1871), Dauchy z Brown, 24 id, 197, Moyer v Pennsylvania Slate Co, 71 Pa St,

293 (1872), Youghiogheny Shaft Co. z Evans, 72 id, 331 (1872), Diven z Lee, 36 N Y., 302 (1867), Lowry z Inman, 46 id, 119 (1871), Salt Lake City National Bank v Hendrickson, 40 N J Law, 52   Cf Priest v Essex Hat Mfg Co, 115 Mass, 380 (1874), Ripley v Sampson, 10 Pick, 371 (1830), Knowlton v Ackley, 8 Cush, 93 (1851)   Bassett v St Albans Hotel Co, 47 Vt, 313 (1875), Davidson v Rankin, 34 Cal, 503 (1868), Mokelumne Hill, etc, Co z Woodbury, 14 id, 265 (1859), Dewey z St Albans Trust Co, 57 Vt, 332 (1885)   A contrary rule seems to have been adopted in Carver z Braintree Mfg Co 2 Story, 432 (1843) where liability for debts contracted during membership was held to include "dues owing"   Also in Rider v Tritchey, 30 N E Rep, 692 (Ohio, 1892). Freeland v McCullough, 1 Denio, 414 (1845).

the enactment.[1] Occasionally, however, a provision imposing additional liability is found to be substantially repeated in the statutes
of many states   Such is the case with the provision that stockholders shall be liable "to an amount equal to their stock." This
is construed to impose a double liability [2] When it has been enforced, each subscriber will have paid double for his stock — once
on the subscription and once on the statutory liability.

Stockholders in national banks are subject to this double liability.   Not only that, but if at any time the capital stock of the bank

[1] Root ι Simnock 11 N E Rep., 339
(Ill. 1887), citing many cases, Wheeler
v Millar, 90 N Y, 353, 359 (1882) Matter of the Empire City Bank, 18 N Y,
199, 218 (1858), Ohio Life Ins Co v.
Merchants' Ins Co, 11 Humph (Tenn),
1, 23 (1850), Lewis v St. Charles Co., 5
Mo App, 225 (1878) Cf Briggs v.
Penniman, 8 Cow, 387 (1826) Bank of
Poughkeepsie v Ibbotson, 24 Wend, 473
(1840)

[2] A liability "to an amount equal to
the amount of stock held by them respectively " has been construed to create
the double liability Booth v Campbell, 37 Md, 522 (1872), Matthews v
Albert, 24 id, 527 (1866), Morris v Johnson, 34 id, 485 (1871), Hager v Cleveland, 36 id, 476, 491 (1872). The former
constitutional provision in Alabama that
stockholders were 'liable to the extent
of their stock" meant a double liability McDonnell v Alabama, etc, Ins
Co, 5 S Rep, 120 (Ala., 1888). A liability of stockholders for "double" the
amount of their stock means a liability
once for the unpaid subscriptions and
then an additional liability of twice the
par value of the stock, making a triple
liability altogether Parrish's Appeal,
19 Atl Rep, 569 (Pa., 1890) A liability
"equally and ratably to the extent of
their respective shares of stock" does
not authorize a judgment against one
for any more than his proportion
Buenz v Cook, 24 Pac Rep, 679 (Col,
1890) The constitution of Missouri
formerly contained a provision, now repealed, imposing a double liability. See
Perry v. Turner, 55 Mo, 418 (1877). By
the constitution of 1875, a provision
taken from amendment of 1870 provides,
'in no case shall any stockholder be individually liable in any amount over
and above the amount of stock owned
by him or her." Construed in Schricker
v Ridings, 65 Mo, 208, to limit liability
to unpaid subscriptions Prov. Sav.
Inst ι Jackson, etc, 52 Mo, 552 (1873);
Miller v Marion, 50 id, 55 (1872); Perry
v Turner, 55 id, 418 (1874). See, also,
Ochiltree v Railroad Co, 21 Wall., 249
(1874) A statute imposing a liability to
the amount of the stock has been held
in Texas to be merely declaratory of the
subscription liability Walker v. Lewis,
49 Tex, 123 A liability " to the amount
of what remains unpaid upon his subscription to the capital stock " is declaratory and creates no liability beyond the
subscription price. Burch v. Taylor, 24
Pac. Rep, 438 (Wash, 1890). In Massachusetts, by statute, stockholders in
manufacturing corporations are liable
as tenants in common to creditors to
the extent of the capital stock, until it
has been divided into shares. Hawes v.
Anglo-Saxon Petroleum Co., 101 Mass,
385 (1869), Same v Same, 111 id, 200
(1872). Cf Burnape v Haskins Steam-
engine Co, 127 Mass, 586 (1879) Cf
Hager v Cleveland, supra, Morris v
Johnson, supra But where some of
the stock is held by the corporation itself, this will not compel the other shareholders to bear the statutory liability as
to the stock so held by the corporation
Crease v. Babcock, 10 Metc., 525, 556
(1846).

becomes diminished by losses, the comptroller of the currency may compel the stockholders to discontinue business or to assess themselves to replace the loss.[1]

A very common statutory liability is that which makes stockholders liable for debts due from the corporation to its servants or laborers   There has been difficulty in determining what persons are to be classed as servants, but the courts are not inclined to give a broad application to the word[2]

[1] See R. S. of U S, § 5205

[2] It may be stated as the rule, that only those who perform menial or manual services are within the class contemplated in the statute, "that he who performs them must be of a class whose members usually look to the reward of a day's labor or service for immediate or present support, from whom the company does not expect credit, and to whom its future ability to pay is of no consequence" Wakefield v Fargo, 90 N Y, 213, 217 (1882)   Cf. Adams v Goodrich, 55 Ga, 233 (1875)   This overrules some of the earlier New York cases, e g, Vincent v Bramford, 1 Jones & Sp. 506; S C, 12 Abb Prac (N S), 252 which held an engineer and foreman, who sometimes also acted as superintendent, to be a servant within the meaning of the rule, Harris v Norvell, 1 Abb. N C. 127 (1876), which held a reporter employed by a newspaper company, and a city or assistant editor, if not an officer of the company, to be a servant, Hovey v. Ten Broeck, 3 Robertson, 316 (1865) holding an overseer and book-keeper within the protection of the act.   A master mechanic and superintendent of works is a servant or laborer   Sleeper v Goodwin, 31 N W. Rep, 335 (Wis, 1887)   A superintendent of laborers is a "laborer" himself   Pendergast v Yandes, 24 N E Rep, 724 (Ind., 1890)   An expert employed to adjust and start the machinery is entitled to the statutory lien for "labor"   In re Black, 47 N W Rep, 312 (Mich, 1890)   A traveling salesman is a "clerk" within the meaning of the statute rendering stockholders liable for debts to

'clerks,' etc   Hand v. Cole, 12 S. W Rep. 922 (Tenn, 1890).

The following employees have been held not servants or laborers within the protection of the rule   The secretary of a manufacturing company.   Coffin v Reynolds 37 N Y, 640 (1868), overruling Richardson v Abendroth, 43 Barb, 163, and perhaps Williamson v Wadsworth, 49 id, 294 (1867), which is the case of a civil engineer and traveling agent at a fixed salary   A civil engineer   Pennsylvania, etc, R. R. Co. v Leuffer, 84 Pa St., 168 (1877)   Contra, Conant v Van Schaick, 24 Barb, 87.   Cf Williamson v Wadsworth, 49 Barb, 294 (1861)   A consulting engineer   Ericsson v Brown, 38 Barb, 390 (1862)   An assistant chief engineer   Brockway v Innes, 39 Mich, 47 (1878)   Cf Peck v Miller, 39 Mich, 594 (1878)   An overseer on a plantation   Whitaker v Smith, 84 N. C, 340 (1879)   Contra, Hovey v Ten Broeck, 3 Robertson (N Y Super Ct) 316 (1865)   A contractor   Boutwell v Townsend, 37 Barb 205 (1860), Aikin v Wasson, 24 N Y, 182 (1862), Balch v New York, etc, R. R. Co, 46 id, 521 (1871), Atcherson v Troy, etc, R R Co, 6 Abb Prac (N S), 329   Cf Kent v New York, etc, R R. Co, 12 N Y 628 (1855), McCluskey v Cromwell 11 id, 593   An agent of a mining corporation employed to take charge of its mines in a foreign country. Hill v Spencer, 61 N Y, 274 (1874), Dean v De Wolf, 16 Hun, 186 (1878), Krause v Ruckel, 17 id, 463 (1879)   A book-keeper and general manager   Wakefield v Fargo, 90 N Y, 213 (1882)   A superintendent.   Kincaid v Dwinelle,

Many of the states have statutes rendering stockholders or directors liable to creditors unless certain reports or certificates are filed.[1] Directors are sometimes made personally liable for making

59 N. Y., 548 (1875) *Cf* Gordon *v* Jennings, L. R, 9 Q B Div, 45 (1882). And compare, also, Gurney *v* Atlantic, etc, R y Co., 58 N Y, 358 (1874). Counsel is not an "employee" Louisville. etc, R. R. *v* Wilson, 138 U S, 501 (1891). A contractor is not an employee under the Indiana statute Vane *v.* Newcombe, 132 U S, 220 (1889) A statutory preference to servants and employees gives no preference to the secretary Wells *v* Southern, etc, R'y, 1 Fed Rep, 270 (1880). In general only manual or menial laborers are protected by the statute Adams *v* Goodrich, 55 Ga, 335; People *v.* Remington, 45 Hun, 329 (1887) *Cf.* Heebner *v* Chave, 5 Pa St, 115 (1847); Harrod *v* Hamer, 32 Wis, 162 (1873) Under the mechanics' lien laws of the several states, a wider meaning has been given to the word "laborers" These cases are frequently confused with the statutes considered herein Stryker *v* Cassidy, 76 N Y, 50 (1879); Mutual Benefit Ins Co. *v* Rowood, 26 N J Eq, 389 (1875), Bank of Pennsylvania *v.* Gries, 35 Pa St, 123 (1860); Arnoldi *v* Gonin, 22 Grant's Chan (Up. Can), 314 (1875), Mulligan *v* Mulligan, 18 La. Ann, 21 (1866), Knight *v* Norris, 13 Minn, 475 (1868) Raeder *v* Bensberg, 6 Mo App, 445 (1878), Foushee, *v.* Grigsby, 12 Bush, 75 (1876); Smallhouse *v.* Kentucky, etc, Co., 2 Mont, 443 (1876), Capron *v.* Stout, 11 Nev., 304 (1881) The mere fact that one does some manual labor incidental to his position as manager or foreman or superintendent will not constitute him a laborer within the intent of these statutes. Krauser *v* Ruckel, 17 Hun, 463 (1879), Ericsson *v* Brown, 38 Barb, 390 (1862) *Cf* Wakefield *v* Fargo, 90 N Y, 213 (1882) But where a foreman did so much manual labor that it was not a mere incident of his foremanship, it was held that he might recover as a laborer

Short *v* Medberry, 29 Hun, 39 (1883) See, also, Poor on N. Y. Mfg Act, p. 70. In construction of the Pennsylvania liability for labor and supplies, see Weiss *v* Mauch Chunk Iron Co, 58 Pa St, 295 (1868); Reading Industrial Manuf'g Co. *v* Graeff, 64 id, 395 (1870); Moyer *v* Pennsylvania, etc, 71 Pa St. 293 (1872), where a statute imposing liability for debts due workmen, etc, and materials furnished was construed not to include debts for hauling, repairing wagons, lumber for erecting machinery, powder for blasting, etc.; Weigley *v.* Coal Oil Co, 5 Phila, 67 (1862). A claim against stockholders on their statutory liability to laborers is assignable Day *v* Vinson, 47 N W Rep, 269 (Wis, 1890).

[1] As to whether this liability is a penal liability, see § 223, *infra* Cases on statutes of this character are given throughout this chapter The following recent cases may also aid in giving an idea of this kind of liability: Under a statute rendering the stockholders liable to corporate creditors to the extent of the unpaid portion of the par value of their stock unless a true statement of the affairs of the company is made annually, the stockholders are so liable if the statement which is filed is a false statement Condon *v* Winsor, 21 Atl Rep., 510 (R. I. 1891), refusing to follow Stedman *v* Eveleth, 6 Metc, 114 Directors are not liable by statute requiring an annual report, where such report is filed, even though it be false If the statute makes them liable for knowingly making a false report, knowledge must be averred Matthews *v* Patterson, 26 Pac. Rep, 812 (Colo., 1891). This statutory liability of directors for failure to file reports is not avoided by the fact that the company is insolvent and has gone out of business Gans *v.* Switzer, 24 Pac Rep, 18 (Mont, 1890 A statutory liability of officers for a

loans in excess of the capital stock [1] A liability imposed by a constitution may or may not be self-executing without any statutory provision, according to the wording of the provision itself [2] An increase or reduction of the capital stock leads often to complications in addition to the usual ones incident to the statutory liability.[3] Various decisions on the liability of stockholders and directors under particular statutes are given in the notes below [4]

It remains to add that this class of statutes, except in the case of banks, have on the whole proved lamentable failures. They drive corporations from a state, are rarely relied upon by creditors, and are productive of incessant litigation

false report applies only to debts created after the false report is made Torbett v Godwin, 62 Hun, 407 (1891)

[1] Where directors are liable for corporate debts in excess of the subscribed capital stock, the capital stock includes that paid for by property as well as in cash Moore v Lent 22 Pac Rep 875 (Cal, 1889). In enforcing a liability of directors for debts in excess of the capital a creditor must sue for the benefit of all, and can recover only a proportion of the excess over such capital stock Anderson v Speers, 21 Hun, 568 (1880) A director cannot enforce a statutory liability of the directors for debts contracted by the corporation in excess of the capital stock, the directors being liable "jointly and severally" by statute, but such debt due to the director is counted Thacher v King, 31 N E Rep, 618 (Mass, 1892). The statutory liability of stockholders for a failure to file a certificate that the capital stock has been fully paid, and the statutory liability of directors for debts in excess of the capital stock, do not apply to a judgment in an action of tort Leighton v Campbell, 26 Atl Rep, 14 (R I, 1890) Liability of director in national bank for loans in excess of amount allowed by law. Witters v Sowles, 43 Fed Rep 405 (1890) Stephens v Overstolz, 43 Fed Rep, 771 (1890)

[2] A constitutional liability may not be enforceable where no statute has been passed to enforce it, as for example, the provision that "dues from corpora-

tions shall be secured by individual liability of the stockholders to an additional amount equal to the stock owned by each stockholder, and such other means as shall be provided by law " Morley v Thayer, 3 Fed Rep, 737 (1880) Under the Ohio constitutional provision imposing a liability on stockholders, a general act authorizing incorporations must contain a provision to that effect or the act will be void. State v Sherman, 22 Ohio St, 411 (1872) A constitutional provision that stockholders shall be liable to the extent of their stock is self-executing and applies to all corporations It renders them liable to the extent of the par value of their stock in addition to the liability on subscriptions A release to the corporation does not release this statutory liability Willis v St Paul, etc, Co, 50 N W Rep, 1110 (Minn, 1892)

[3] See §§ 288, 289, concerning this subject

[4] Under the Iowa statutes the stockholders are liable as partners where the certificate of incorporation failed to state the highest amount of indebtedness which the company might incur Heuer v Carmichael, 47 N W Rep, 1034 (Iowa, 1891) "Dues" include insurance policies McDonnell v Ala, etc, Co, 5 S Rep 120 (Ala 1889). The constitutional liability of stockholders applies if a part of the business as set forth in the charter consists of mercantile business The objection that all stockholders and creditors are not joined

§ 216 *Waiver by corporate creditors of their statutory rights against shareholders* — A corporate creditor may, by express contract, when the debt is incurred, waive his right to collect from the stockholder debts which the corporation fails to pay.[1] And the corporation in its contracts with third persons may, it is held in England, lawfully stipulate for the exemption of its members from the liability imposed upon them by statute in the event of the insolvency of the corporation [2]

It has been held to be competent for any one dealing with the company to contract to hold the shareholders responsible to only a limited extent, to no extent at all, or to any specified extent mutually agreed upon.[3]

must be raised by answer Densmore *v* Red Wing, etc., Co, 48 N W Rep., 528 (Minn., 1891) The case of Austin *v* Berlin, 22 Pac Rep., 433 (Colo, 1889), holds that new directors are not liable for the statutory delinquencies of the old Policy-holders' claims come within the meaning of the words "debts due," for which stockholders are held liable McDonnell *v* Ala, etc, Ins. Co, 5 S Rep, 120 (Ala., 1888) A debt contracted in the midst of acts for which directors are liable by statute is contracted "after such violation" Patterson *v.* Minn, etc., Co, 42 N. W Rep, 926 (Minn, 1889) In Maine by statute stockholders are liable as subscribers if their stock is paid for by property taken at an over-valuation Libby *v* Tobey, 19 Atl Rep, 904 (Me, 1890) Under the Iowa statute rendering officers, etc, liable for diversion of funds, a policy-holder may recover, where a consolidation with another company has been made and plaintiff was excluded from the new company Grayson *i* Willoughby, 42 N W Rep, 591 (Iowa, 1889) A complaint to enforce a stockholder's liability for labor done in the construction of the road is not good if it omits the allegation as to the construction of the road Toner *v* Fulkerson, 25 N E Rep, 218 (Ind, 1890) Where stockholders are liable for debts other than mortgage debts, an agreement of the company to pay another company's mortgage debt is not a mortgage debt Barron *v* Paine,

22 Atl Rep., 218 (Me, 1891) Where stockholders in manufacturing corporations are not liable, but in other companies are liable, under a statute, yet, if the charter authorizes other business than manufacturing, they are liable although only the manufacturing business is pursued Arthur *v* Willius, 46 N W. Rep, 851 (Minn, 1890)

[1] Robinson *v* Bidwell, 22 Cal, 379 (1863), French *v* Teschemaker, 24 id, 518 (1864), Basshor *v* Forbes, 36 Md., 154 (1872), Brown *v* Eastern Slate Co., 134 Mass, 590 (1883), where the waiver was oral

[2] *Re* Athenæum, etc., Society, 3 De G. & J, 660 (1859), Halket *v* Merchant Traders', etc, Association, 13 Q B, 960 (1849), Durham's Case, 4 Kay & J, 517 (1858) *Cf* Shelford on Joint-stock Companies (2d London edition), 4 Although the subscribers themselves may stipulate with each other for such a restricted liability, nothing is more clear than that, as to the rest of the world, each shareholder is liable for the whole amount of the debts of the company. Nor will notice that a stipulation of this kind has been entered into between the shareholders prevent a creditor from holding each of them liable to the full extent of his demand See Greenwood's Case, 3 De G, M & G, 459, The State Fire Ins Co, Meredith's Case, and Conver's Case, 1 N R., 510, V C. W

[3] *In re* State Fire Insurance Co., 1 Hem. & M, 457 (1863), S. C, 1 De G,

§ 217 *Statutory liability not enforceable to pay damages recovered against the corporation in tort* — The statutory liability imposed upon the shareholders in corporations is a liability exclusively for debts and demands accruing against the corporation by reason of its contracts   It cannot, therefore, be enforced to pay damages recovered against the corporation in an action in tort [1]

J & J, 634, 35 L J Chan, 834, 34 id, 436, Hassell r Merchant Traders' Association, 4 Exch, 525   Lord Talbot's Case, 5 De G & Sm 386 (1852) S C 21 L J Chan, 816   See also, Reid r Allan, 4 Exch, 326 (1849), S C, 19 L J, Exch, 39   And compare *In re* Independent Assurance Co, *Ex parte* Cope, 1 Sim (N S), 54, Sunderland Marine Insurance Co r Kearney, 16 Q B, 925 (1851), S C 20 L J (Q B) 417, Pedell r Gwynn, 1 Hurl & N, 590 (1857), S C, 26 L J, Exch, 199, Gordon r Sea, Fire and Life Assurance Society, 1 Hurl & N, 599 (1857) S. C, 29 L J, Exch, 202   And see Hess r Werts, 4 Serg & R, 361 (1818)   King r Accumulation, etc, Assurance Co, 3 C. B (N S) 151 (1857)   *Cf* Hallett r Dowdall, 18 Q B D (1852)   The mere fact that the articles of association of an unincorporated company provide against personal liability is no defense even though the contracts say that they are subject to the provisions in such articles   Sullivan r Campbell 2 Hall (N Y), 271 (1829), Hess r Wirts, 4 Serg & R. (Pa), 356 (1818), Greenwood's Case, 3 De G, M & G, 459 (1854)   The same rule prevails in an ordinary copartnership   Bromley r Elliot, 38 N H, 287 (1859)   Directors are bound to know of the restriction and have no recourse to the stockholders, nor does a firm in which a director is a member   *In re* Worcester, etc, Co, 3 De G, M & G, 180 (1853)   Contract that promoters shall not be liable binds an engineer   Lardman r Entwistle, 7 Ex, 632 (1852)   Where promoters stipulate that they shall not be liable the party who tacitly assents to that condition is bound   Giles r Smith, 11 Jur

334 (1847)   See also, ch XLIII, *infra*, Kent's Com, vol III, p 27, Story on Partn § 164   A contrary doctrine seems to have prevailed in Davis r Beverly, 2 Cranch, C C (U S), 35 (1811), Riggs r Swann, 3 id, 183 (1827), reversed on another point by Mandeville r Riggs, 2 Pet, 482   The exemption from liability must be clearly proved   Skinner r Dayton, 19 John 513, 537 (1822)   A stipulation against holding stockholders liable has been held to refer to statutory liability and not the subscription liability   Preston r Cincinnati, etc, R R 36 Fed Rep 54 (1888)   A provision in an insurance policy that the directors shall not be liable, although the statute makes them liable, is not good   Greene r Walton, 13 N Y Supp 147 (1891)   See 28 N E Rep, 874

[1] Heacock r Sherman, 14 Wend, 59 (1835)   In this case the stockholders in a company which owned a bridge and against which a judgment had been recovered for damages because the bridge was out of repair, were held not to be liable upon such a demand, since the act imposing a personal liability upon them contemplated a liability only for demands arising *ex contractu*   In general the word "debt," as used in statutes imposing a personal liability upon stockholders, is construed to include only liabilities arising *ex contractu* and not to include liability for damages recovered against the corporation in actions sounding in tort   Child r Boston, etc, Iron Works, 137 Mass 516 (1884)   S C, 50 Am Rep, 328, where a judgment for infringement of patent was not enforced   Leighton r Campbell 20 Atl Rep, 14 (R I, 1890), Mill Dam Foundry Co r Hovey, 21 Pick, 417, 455

D. THE ENFORCEMENT OF THE LIABILITY.

§ 218 *The statutory liability can be enforced by corporate cred-*
itors only — Stockholders and directors as creditors.— The statutory liability of the stockholder is created exclusively for the benefit
of corporate creditors It is not to be numbered among the assets
of the corporation, and the corporation has no right or interest in
it It cannot enforce it by an assessment upon the shareholders.[1]
Nor can the corporation upon the insolvency assign it to a trustee
for the benefit of creditors[2] It is a liability running directly and
immediately from the shareholders to the corporate creditors.[3]
Accordingly, a receiver of an insolvent corporation, invested with
"all the estate, property and equitable interests" of the concern,
has no power to enforce such a liability as this.[4] The action to

(1839). sustaining an unliquidated claim
for damages. Dryden v Kellogg, 2 Mo
App., 87 (1876), enforcing a judgment
for breach of warranty of title, Doolit-
tle v Marsh, 11 Neb, 243, Esmond v
Bullard, 16 Hun, 65 (1878), S C affirmed,
sub nom Losee v Bullard, 79 N Y, 101
(1880), Archer v Rose, 3 Brewster
(Pa). 261 (1871), Cable v McCune, 26
Mo, 371 (1858), defeating a judgment for
damages for loss of a steamboat, Bohn
v Brown, 33 Mich, 257, 263 (1876) *Cf*
Stanton v Wilkeson, 8 Ben, 357, refusing to enforce herein a judgment against
a common carrier for negligence, Chase
v Curtis, 113 U S, 452 (1884). *Cf* Carver v Braintree Mfg Co, 2 Story, 432,
448; Wyman v American Powder Co.
8 Cush, 168, 182. Zimmer v Schleehauf,
115 Mass, 52 But the stockholders'
subscription liability may be enforced
to pay damages arising from torts.
Powell v Oregonian R'y, 36 Fed Rep,
726 (1888), 33 id, 187 The word "dues,"
as contained in the Ohio constitution,
rendering stockholders individually liable, renders them liable not only in contracts of the corporation but on torts
committed by the corporation Rider
v Fritchey, 30 N E Rep, 692 (Ohio,
1892)

[1] Umsted v Buskirk, 17 Ohio St., 113
(1866), Liberty Female College Association v Watkins, 70 Mo, 13 (1879)

[2] Wright v McCormick, 17 Ohio St,

86, 95 (1866), Dutcher v Marine National
Bank, 12 Blatch, 435 (1875). See, also,
Cuykendall v Corning, 88 N Y, 129
(1882)

[3] Bristol v Sanford, 12 Blatch, 341
(1874), Lane v. Morris, 8 Ga, 468 (1850);
Arenz v Weir, 89 Ill, 25. This was an
action by a judgment creditor against
a stockholder after a distribution of corporate assets by a receiver The creditor was held to stand "on an independent platform, above that of a receiver,
having no concern with the corporation,
and the stockholder is bound under the
law to answer to him" Breese, J

[4] Billings v Robinson, 94 N Y, 415
(1884), Farnsworth v Wood, 91 N. Y,
308 (1883), Jacobson v Allen, 12 Fed
Rep., 454 (1882), Cuykendall v. Corning,
88 N Y, 129 (1882), Arenz v Weir, 89
Ill, 25. Jacobson v Allen, 29 Blatch,
525 (1882), Cutting v Damerel, 88 N Y.,
410 (1882) *Cf* Davis v Gray, 16 Wall,
203 (1872), Attorney-General v. Guardian Mutual, etc, Ins Co, 77 N. Y, 272
(1879). Receivership of corporation
does not prevent creditors enforcing directors' liability Patterson v Minn,
etc, Co, 42 N W Rep, 926 (Minn, 1889).
Doubtful whether corporate creditors
may sue to enforce directors' statutory
liability after a receiver has gone in
Minn, etc, Mfg Co v Langdon 46 N
W Rep, 310 (Minn, 1890) The receiver
of a national bank may sue a stock-

enforce can be maintained only by the creditors themselves, in their own right and for their own benefit[1]

It has been held that statutory liability of stockholders cannot be enforced by the directors as "creditors"[2]

It is uncertain whether a stockholder, who is also a creditor of the corporation, can bring an action at law against his co-stockholders to enforce a statutory liability.   In Massachusetts,[3] Illinois[4] and New York[5] the rule is settled that such an action cannot be maintained   In those jurisdictions the only remedy for such a creditor in such a case is by a bill in equity for contribution[6]   But in Pennsylvania[7] and in Maine[8] the rule is otherwise, and it is no objection to the creditor's action that he is himself also a shareholder.[9]

§ 219 *Judgment and execution must be obtained against the corporation before the stockholder's statutory liability can be enforced.* Even when not expressly provided by statute, it is the rule, accord-

holder in the state courts to recover an assessment. Peters ι Foster, 56 Hun, 607 (1890) The creditor may proceed to judgment though a receiver has been appointed   Mason ι N Y., etc., Mfg Co, 27 Hun, 307 (1882)

[1] Farnsworth ι Wood, 91 N Y, 308 (1883) See, also, Mason ι New York Silk, etc, Co, 27 Hun, 307 (1882), Billings ι Trask, 30 id, 314 (1883) See, also, Walker ι Crain, 17 Barb, 128 (1853); Story ι Furman, 25 N Y, 215 (1862) Cuykendall ι Corning, 88 N. Y, 129 (1882), Herkimer Co Bank ι Furman, 17 Barb, 116 (1853), Hurd ι Tallman, 60 id, 272 (1871)

[2] McDowall ι Sheehan, 129 N Y, 200 (1891) A director who is a creditor cannot in certain cases share with the other creditors and prove a claim due to him from the corporation. Neither can such claim be proved where it belongs to a firm or company of which the director was a member, or to the assignee of such firm or company   Thacher ι King, 31 N. E. Rep., 648 (Mass., 1892).

[3] Thayer ι Union Tool Co, 4 Gray, 75 (1855)

[4] Meisser ι Thompson 9 Brad (Ill), 368, 108 Ill, 359

[5] Mathez ι Neidig, 72 N Y, 100 (1878), Clark v. Myers, 11 Hun, 608 (1877).

Bailey ι Bancker, 3 Hill, 188 (1842) (overruling upon this point Simonson v. Spencer, 15 Wend, 548 — 1836) Beers v Waterbury, 8 Bosw., 396 (1861), Richardson v. Abendroth, 43 Barb, 162 (1864), Deming ι Puleston, 33 Super Ct, 231. *Cf.* Sanborn ι Lefferts, 58 N Y, 179 (1874), Garrison ι Howe, 17 N Y, 458 (1858) To same effect, Perkins ι Sanders, 56 Miss, 733 (1879) *Cf* Slee v. Bloom, 5 Johns Ch, 366 382 (1821)

[6] But see Potter ι Stevens Machine Co, 127 Mass., 592 (1879) and Sav Ass'n v O Brien, 51 Hun, 46 (1889)

[7] Bingham ι Wellersburg Coal Co., 47 Pa St., 43 (1864)

[8] Fowler ι Robinson, 31 Me, 189 (1850).

[9] In a suit in equity to enforce stockholders' statutory liability, a plea that the decedent of one of the complainants was also a stockholder and no offer to pay his liability had been made is not a good plea Newbury ι. Robinson, 41 Fed Rep, 458 (1890) In New York it seems that the assignee of a judgment may bring the suit to enforce statutory liability, though the assignee be a stockholder. Woodruff & Beach Iron Works v. Chittenden, 4 Bosw 406 (1859). See, also, Garrett ι Sayles, 1 Fed Rep, 371 (1880), aff'd 110 U S, 288, Potter v Stevens Machine Co, 127 Mass, 592 (1879).

ing to the weight of authority, that corporate creditors, before they can proceed against the shareholders upon their statutory liability, must first exhaust their remedy against the corporation and its assets[1] This rule arises from the fact that the liability of the stockholders is not the usual fund for the payment of corporate debts, but that the corporate treasury is the primary resource. Accordingly, the statutory liability of the stockholders is not to be resorted to, if the assets of the corporation, including the unpaid subscriptions for stock, will suffice to pay the debts[2]

[1] Means' Appeal, 85 Pa St, 75 (1877), Fourth Nat Bank v Francklyn, 120 U S, 747 (1887). Bayliss v Swift. 40 Iowa, 648 (1875), McClaren v Franciscus. 43 Mo, 452 (1869), Wright v McCormack. 17 Ohio St, 86 (1866), Wehrman v Reakirt. 1 Cinn Super. Ct, 230 (1871), Lane v Harris, 16 Ga, 217 (1854), Drinkwater v Portland, etc, Ry, 18 Me, 35 (1841), Dauchy v Brown, 24 Vt, 197 (1852), Cambridge Water-works v Somerville Dyeing Co, 4 Allen, 239 (1862), Toucey v Bowen, 1 Biss, 81 (1855) Cf Patterson v Wyomissing Manuf Co, 40 Pa St., 117 (1861), Harper v Union Manuf Co., 100 Ill, 225 (1881), Hatch v Burroughs, 1 Woods, 439 (1870). In Colorado stockholders liable by statute may be joined as party defendants in the original suit against the corporation Tabor v Goss, etc, Co., 18 Pac. Rep, 537 (Colo, 1888) Judgment against the corporation is first necessary Where some of the creditors are proceeding against the stockholders without first obtaining judgment against the corporation, but one creditor has procured a judgment and exhausted his remedy against the corporation, the latter may enjoin the other creditors from pursuing their remedy Hoyt v Bunker, 32 Pac Rep, 126 (Kan, 1893) If no judgment has been obtained, the stockholders can set up such defenses as would have been available to the company Railroad Co v Smith, 31 N E Rep., 743 (Ohio, 1891) In an action by a judgment creditor to enforce a statutory liability, claims by himself and others not yet reduced to judgment may be proved Thacher v. King, 31 N E. Rep., 648 (Mass., 1892)

[2] Stewart v Lay, 45 Iowa, 604 (1877); Wright v McCormack, 17 Ohio St, 86 (1866) There is, however, a line of authorities in support of the proposition that a judgment against the corporation is not a prerequisite to the enforcement of the shareholders' statutory liability Perkins v Church, 31 Barb, 84 (1859), Southmayd v Russ, 3 Conn, 52 (1819), Culver v Third National Bank, 64 Ill, 528 (1871); Davidson v Rankin, 34 Cal, 503 (1868), Young v Rosenbaum, 39 id, 646 (1870), Morrow v Superior Court, 64 Cal, 383 (1883); Bird v Calvert, 22 S C, 292 (1884) No previous judgment against the corporation is necessary in enforcing directors' statutory liability Patterson v. Minn, etc., Co, 42 N W. Rep, 926 (Minn, 1889) In Alabama the remedy against the corporation need not be first exhausted unless the statutes expressly require it. McDonnell v. Alabama, etc, Ins. Co., 5 S. Rep, 120 (Ala, 1888) Cf. § 200, supra In these cases it is held in general that the shareholder's liability under the statute is unconditional, original and immediate, not dependent on the insufficiency of the corporate assets, and not collateral to that of the corporation upon the event of its insolvency. Thus, in the case of Manufacturing Company v Bradley, 105 U S, 175 (1881), it was held that, upon a bill being filed against the corporation for the collection of a debt the shareholders might

Frequently the statutes which impose this extraordinary or *extra* common-law liability upon shareholders provide that a creditor shall obtain judgment against the corporation, and that an execution duly levied thereunder shall have been returned wholly or partially unsatisfied, before the creditor has a right to proceed against the stockholders individually [1] But, in general, proceedings against the corporation are not to be required when they would be nugatory or impossible [2]

properly be made parties in order to avoid a multiplicity of suits and upon the ground that the shareholders were immediately liable under that provision of their charter which made "members of the company . . jointly and severally liable for all debts and contracts made by the company until the whole amount of the capital stock fixed and limited by the corporation' is paid in Under the New York act of 1875 a stockholder may be sued before judgment against the corporation, but cannot be held liable until after such judgment. Walton *v* Coe, 110 N Y, 109 (1888)

[1] See Laws of 1848, New York ch 40, § 24, commonly known as "The General Manufacturing Act' Handy *v* Draper 89 N Y, 334 (1882) But a contrary rule prevailed under the Business Corporation Act of 1875 See Walton *v* Coe, 110 N Y, 109 (1888). See, also, Rocky Mountains National Bank *v* Bliss, 89 N Y, 338 (1882), Dean *v* Mace, 19 Hun, 391 (1879) Sometimes the statute provides that a specific demand shall have been made Haynes *v* Brown, 36 N H, 545 (1858) In Wisconsin, by statute, there need be no precedent judgment against the corporation Sleeper *v* Goodwin, 31 N W Rep 335 (Wis, 1887) The case of Patterson *v* Lynde, 112 Ill, 196 (1884), holds that the judgment must be obtained in the state where enforcement is sought and that not even a judgment in the federal circuit court for that district will suffice *Cf.* § 200, *supra*

[2] *Cf* Shellington *v* Howland, 53 N Y, 371 (1873), where proceedings required

as conditions precedent to liability were rendered impossible by the operation of United States bankruptcy law See also State Sav Ass'n *v* Kellogg, 52 Mo 583 (1873), Dryden *v* Kellogg 2 Mo App, 87 *Cf* Ansonia Brass & Copper Co *v* New Lamp Chimney Co, 53 N Y, 123 (1873), S C affirmed, 91 U S 656 (1875), Fourth Nat'l Bank *v* Francklyn 120 U S, 747 (1887) Paine *v* Stewart, 33 Conn, 516 (1866), where under a statute providing that the property of stockholders could not be levied upon while corporate property could be found to satisfy the debt it was held that evidence that the corporate property was in the hands of a receiver was sufficient to prove the condition Chamberlain *v* Huguenot etc, 118 Mass, 532 (1875), holding that proceedings in bankruptcy do not in Massachusetts, prevent recovering judgment against the bankrupt corporation for the purpose of perfecting the liability of stockholders It has been held in New Hampshire, that before suit is brought against the stockholder, he should be given notice of the default of the corporation, and a demand should be made Hecks *v* Burns, 38 N H, 141 (1839) Even where the statute requires it, a suit to enforce a statutory liability need not be delayed until the corporate property has all been applied to the payment of debts if it be clear that such property will be insufficient to pay everything Munger *v* Jacobson, 99 Ill 349 (1881) Or where the corporation is clearly insolvent, and it would be idle to wait the return of the execution Flash *v* Connecticut, 109 U S, 371 (1883) Kincaid *v* Dwinelle, 59 N Y, 548 (1875)

A judgment must be obtained and execution issued and returned in the state where suit is brought, or good reason must be shown why they are not.[1]

Where the statutes provide for an enforcement of the shareholder's statutory liability only upon the dissolution of the corporation, it is held that a dissolution, in the sense in which that term is here used, takes place when the corporation comes into the condition of having debts and no assets, or has ceased to act and exercise its corporate functions, or has suffered acts to be done which end the object for which it was created.[2]

§ 220. *Difficulties in determining whether the creditor's remedy is at law or in equity.*— Perhaps the most difficult, unsettled and unsatisfactory question concerning the statutory liability of stockholders is the question whether that liability must be enforced at law or must be in equity, or may be in either a court of law or of equity. After determining this point there arises the further difficulty of ascertaining who shall be parties plaintiff and parties defendant — whether one corporate creditor may sue, or all must join, whether one stockholder may be pursued as a single defendant, or all the stockholders must be brought in. The law on

Cf Toucey v Bowen, 1 Biss, 81 (1855), Munger t Jacobson, *supra* Or the corporation is dissolved Patterson v Lynde, 112 Ill , 196 (1884) A judgment against the corporation is not necessary to enforce the stockholder's liability when the corporation is insolvent, has ceased to do business, and has made an assignment for the benefit of creditors. Morgan v Lewis, 17 N E Rep., 558 (Ohio, 1888) Judgment against the corporation need not first be obtained if the corporation has been dissolved Hardman v Sage, 124 N Y , 25 (1890). The issue and return of an execution unsatisfied against the corporation is necessary where the corporation is a going concern, but not where it is insolvent and has assigned for the benefit of its creditors Barrick v Gifford, 24 N E Rep , 259 (Ohio, 1890).

[1] See § 223.

[2] Bank of Poughkeepsie v Ibbotson, 24 Wend , 473 (1840); Slee v Bloom 19 Johns , 456 (1822), Penniman v. Briggs. Hopkins' Chan , 300 (1825); S C, *sub nom.* Briggs v Penniman, 8 Cowen, 387

(1826), State Savings Association v Kellogg, 52 Mo , 583 (1873), Dryden v. Kellogg, 2 Mo App , 87 (1876); Perry v. Turner, 55 Mo., 418 (1874); Central Agric , etc , Association v Alabama, etc , Ins Co., 70 Ala , 120 (1881); McDonnell v Ala , etc , Ins. Co., 5 S. Rep , 120 (Ala , 1888). *Cf* Morley v Thayer, 3 Fed Rep., 737 (1880), holding that bankruptcy of the corporation is not a dissolution of a corporation within the meaning of the statute of Massachusetts imposing liability upon stockholders. In Florida upon dissolution the stockholders are liable "to an extent equal in amount to the amount of stock by him owned, together with any amount unpaid thereon " The dissolution need not be a judicial decree to that effect It is sufficient if there are debts and no assets, and the corporation has ceased to act and exercise its corporate functions, or has suffered acts to be done which end the object for which it was created Suit against the corporation first is not necessary in such a case. Gibbs v Davis, 8 S. Rep., 633 (Fla , 1891).

these points is in a transition stage   The question is largely one of practice, and from experience the courts will doubtless evolve that rule which is most just and convenient   At present, however, not only must the decisions of the state in which the action is brought be examined, but it is necessary also to note carefully the wording of the statute creating the liability.   Where the statute prescribes expressly the form of the remedy, it is the well-established rule that that remedy was intended by the legislature to exclude every other, and it must be strictly pursued [1]

§ 221   *The remedy at law.*— In New York the shareholder's liability, imposed by the statute relative to miscellaneous corporations, is held to be such that any creditor who has recovered a judgment against the company, and sued out an execution thereon, which has been returned unsatisfied, may sue any stockholder and recover to the extent provided by the statute in an action at law [2]

[1] Lowry v Inman, 46 N Y, 119, 127 (1871), Morley v Thayer, 3 Fed Rep, 737, 741 (1880), Haskins v Harding, 2 Dillon, 99 (1873), Allen v Walsh, 25 Minn, 543 (1879)   Windham Provident Savings Institution v Sprague, 43 Vt, 502 (1871), Dauchy v Brown, 24 Vt, 197, Bassett v St Albans Hotel Co, 47 id, 313 (1875), Pollard v Bailey, 20 Wall 520 (1874), Knowlton v Ackley, 8 Cush, 93, 98 (1851), Erickson v Nesmith, 15 Gray, 221 (1860), Brinham v Wellersburg Coal Co, 47 Pa St, 43 (1864), Hoard v Wilcox, 47 id, 51, Youghiogheny Shaft Co v Evans, 72 id, 331 (1872)   Cf Andrews v Callender, 13 Pick, 484 (1833), Potter v Stevens Machine Co, 127 Mass, 592 (1879), Grose v Hilt 36 Me, 22 (1853), Diven v Lee, 36 N Y, 302 (1867), Wehrman v Reakirt, 1 Cinn Super Ct, 230

[2] Abbott v Aspinwall, 26 Barb, 202 (1857), Wiles v Suydam, 64 N Y, 173 (1876), Shellington v Howland, 53 id, 371 (1873)   Handy v Draper, 89 id, 334 (1882), Rocky Mountain National Bank v Bliss, id, 338 (1882), Mathez v Neidig, 72 id, 100 (1878), Flash v Conn, 109 U S, 371, 380 (1883), Weeks v Love, 50 N Y, 568 (1872)   And this was the rule, also, under the earlier statute of March 22, 1811, R S, 7th ed, p 1726   Bank of Poughkeepsie v Ibbotson, 24

Wend, 473 (1840)   Cf Van Hook v Whitlock, 3 Paige, 409 (1832), Simonson v Spencer, 15 Wend, 548 (1836), Richards v Coe, N Y, Daily Reg, Aug 2, 1887   But when the action is to enforce the statutory liability to employees, "laborers, servants and apprentices," in New York, it has been held that all the shareholders should be made parties   Strong v Wheaton, 38 Barb, 616 (1861)   The creditor must sue one or all   Dean v Whiton, 16 Hun 203 (1878)   In Illinois, under the charter provision that ' each stockholder shall be liable to double the amount of stock " owned, it was held that the stockholders were severally and individually liable, that is, that an action at law against one or all of them would lie   McCarthy v Lavasche, 89 Ill, 270 (1878), Hull v Burtis, 90 id, 213 (1878), Fuller v Ledden, 87 id, 310 (1877)   In Pennsylvania, under the statute relating to the incorporation of manufacturing companies, the corporate creditor proceeds against the shareholders in an action at law upon the original contract, making the corporation and all the shareholders parties defendant   Brinham v Wellersburg Coal Co, 47 Pa St, 43 (1864), Mansfield Iron Works v Willcox, 52 id, 377 (1866), Hoard v Wilcox, 47 id, 51 (1864)   McHose v Wheeler, 45 id, 32

So, also, when it is provided by statute that the shareholders "shall, to the amount of the stock by them held, be jointly and severally liable for all the debts and responsibilities of such company," it is held that an action at law may be maintained on the individual liability by any corporate creditor against any individual shareholder[1]

Where an action at law can be maintained, and the shareholder's liability is limited and several, each shareholder being made liable for a sum certain, a separate action will lie against each one[2] And unless the remedy at law has been enlarged by statute, so as to allow judgment separately against each one of several defendants before the court in the same proceeding, each creditor must sue each shareholder, or each creditor must sue some one or more shareholders separately[3]

(1863) See Patterson v Wyomissing Manuf'g Co., 40 Pa St , 117 (1861) And to same effect, Thompson v Jewell, 43 Mich , 240 (1880), Pope v Leonard, 115 Mass 286 (1871) Under a Georgia statute by the provisions of which each shareholder in banking corporations in that state is made liable to redeem his proportionate share of the outstanding circulation, a single creditor may have his action at law against any individual shareholder Lane v Harris, 16 Ga , 217 (1854) Lane v Morris, 8 Ga , 468 (1850) Branch v Baker, 53 id, 562 (1874), Hatch v Burroughs, 1 Woods, 439 (1870) Cf Bank of Poughkeepsie v Ibbotson, 24 Wend , 473 (1840)

[1] Grund v Tucker, 5 Kan , 70 (1869) Norris v Johnson, 34 Md , 485 (1871). See Bullard v Bell, 1 Mason, 243 (1817, by Story, J) Cf Matthews v Albert, 24 Md , 527 (1866), Culver v Third National Bank, 64 Ill, 528 (1871), Bond v Appleton, 8 Mass 472 The Missouri statute may be enforced at law Savings Assoc v O'Brien 51 Hun, 45 (1889). By statute in California the remedy may be at law Borland v Haven, 37 Fed Rep , 394 (1888)

[2] Bank of Poughkeepsie v Ibbotson, 24 Wend , 473 (1840), Perry v Turner, 55 Mo , 418 (1874), Boyd v Hall, 56 Ga , 563 (1876), where the liability was *pro rata*, Paine v Stewart, 33 Conn , 516

(1866), Culver v Third National Bank, 64 Ill , 528 (1871), Abbott v. Aspinwall, 26 Barb , 202 (1857), Garrison v Howe, 17 N Y , 458 (1858), Terry v Little, 101 U S, 216 (1879)

[3] Abbott v Aspinwall, 26 Barb , 202 (1857), Paine v Stewart, 33 Conn, 516 (1866), Matter of the Hollister Bank, 27 N Y , 393 (1863), Perry v Turner, 55 Mo , 418 (1874), Bank of Poughkeepsie v Ibbotson 24 Wend , 473 Cf Milroy v Spur Mountain Iron Mining Co , 43 Mich , 231 (1880) Where the shareholder's liability is held to be like that of a partner, then all must be joined as defendants, and the omission of any one is ground for a plea in abatement. Allen v Sewall, 2 Wend , 327 (1829), but holding that it cannot be taken advantage of on the trial, Strong v Wheaton, 38 Barb., 616 (1861), holding that, under the New York code, defect of parties herein must be objected to by demurrer or answer, Reynolds v. Feliciana Steamboat Co , 17 La. Rep., 397 (1841), Dean v Whitory, 16 Hun, 205 (1878), Bonewitz v Bank, 41 Ohio St , 78, holding that the sheriff's return showing clearly that other stockholders are out of the jurisdiction must be in proof Cf Dodge v Minnesota, etc , Slate Roofing Co , 16 Minn , 368 (1871), Culver v Third National Bank, 64 Ill 528 (1871), Branson v Oregonian R'y Co.,

Under a statute providing that " each shareholder shall be individually and personally liable for his proportion of all the debts and liabilities of the company contracted or incurred,   for the recovery of which joint or several actions may be prosecuted," it has been held that the liability of the shareholders is substantially that of partners[1] So, also, a general joint and several liability for all the corporate debts makes the stockholders liable as partners as though there had been no incorporation[2] Under the provisions

10 Oregon, 278 (1882), Hoag v Lamont, 60 N Y, 96 (1875). Abbott v Aspinwall, 26 Barb, 202, 207 As to the joinder of parties in Pennsylvania, see Mansfield Iron Works v Willcox, 52 Pa St, 377 (1866), McHose v. Wheeler, 45 id, 32 (1863), Hoard v Wilcox, 47 id, 51 (1864) Creditor suing directors on a statutory liability need not join all creditors nor all directors Patterson v. Minn, etc, Co, 42 N W Rep, 926 (Minn, 1889). The corporation need not be joined as a party defendant The suit may be against the estate of a deceased stockholder It may be a separate suit from that against the corporation Nolan v. Hazen, 47 N W Rep, 155 (Minn, 1890). In Pennsylvania the corporation also should be made a party defendant Hoard v Wilcox 47 Pa St 51, Mansfield Iron Works v. Willcox, 52 Pa. St., 377 (1866) Cf Deming v Bull. 10 Conn, 409 (1835), Middletown Bank v. Magill, 5 id, 28 (1823) In Vermont a provision that shareholders "shall be personally holden" is held to create only a joint liability Windham Provident Savings Institution v Sprague. 43 Vt, 502 (1871). The suit may be at law and by one creditor against one stockholder The corporation need not be joined Gibbs v Davis, 8 S Rep, 633 (Fla, 1891) The liability of stockholders under the Kansas statute is several and not joint The creditors cannot join several stockholders in one suit. Each must be sued separately Abbey v W B, etc, Co, 24 Pac Rep, 426 (Kan, 1890)

[1] Davidson v Rankin, 34 Cal, 503 (1868) Cf Young v Rosenbaum, 39 id, 646 (1870), Larrabee v Baldwin, 35 id 155 (1868), McAuley v York Mining Co

6 id, 80 (1856), Adkins v Thornton 19 Ga, 326 (1856) [this case is frequently miscited, owing to a misprint in the original report as Dozier v Thornton] Branch v Baker, 53 Ga, 562 (1874) Dane v Young, 61 Me, 160 (1872), Castleman v Holmes, 4 J J Marsh 1 (1830). Cf Fuller v Ledden, 87 Ill, 312, Brown v Hitchcock, 36 Ohio St, 678. The constitutional and statutory liability of stockholders in California is a contract obligation, and may be enforced by attachment. Kennedy v California, etc, Bank 31 Pac Rep, 846 (Cal, 1892). The liability of a stockholder in a California bank for his proportion of a corporate debt was enforced at law in Barling v Bank of B N A, 50 Fed Rep 260 (1892)

[2] Planters Bank, etc, v Bivingsville, etc, Manuf Co, 10 Rich Law, 95 (1856), Southmayd v Russ 3 Conn, 52 (1819), Middletown Bank v Magill, 5 id, 28, 45 (1823), Deming v Bull 10 id 409 (1835), Conant v Van Schaick, 24 Barb., 87 (1857), Allen v Sewall, 2 Wend, 327 (1829), Moss v Oakley, 2 Hill, 265 (1842), Harger v McCullough 2 Denio, 119 (1846), McCullough v Moss, 5 id, 767 (1846), Corning v McCullough 1 N Y, 47 (1847), Moss v Averell, 10 id, 449 (1853), Wyles v Suydam, 64 id, 173, 176 (1876), Conklin v Furman, 8 Abb Pr (N S), 164, S C, 57 Barb 487 Abbott v Aspinwall, 26 Barb, 207, Erickson v Nesmith, 46 N H, 371 (1866), White v Blum 4 Neb 555 (1876) New England Commercial Bank v Newport Steam Factory, 6 R I. 154 (1859), Moies v Sprague, 9 id, 541 (1870), Witherhead v Allen, 28 Barb, 667, Chase v Lord, 77 N Y, 83.

of the constitution and statutes of Ohio, and of other states, it is held that while the undertaking of the shareholder is not primary, and is to be resorted to only in case of the insolvency of the corporation. still the liability, when it does properly arise, is essentially that of partners.[1] This class of cases holds that, unless the statute prescribes otherwise, the common-law rules as to the liability of partners, and the remedies for enforcing that liability, apply to the statutory liability of shareholders in incorporated companies [2]

[1] And that although the stated extent of the shareholder s liability, as provided by the statute, cannot be exceeded, still, up to the full measure of his liability, he may be charged, although it be shown that, if other solvent shareholders had contributed their full proportion, it would not be necessary for him to pay Wehrman v Reaknit, 1 Cinn Super Ct., 230 (1871) Brown v Hitchcock, 36 Ohio St., 678 Cf Stewart t Lay, 45 Iowa, 604 (1877), Crease v. Babcock, 10 Metc, 525 (Mass, 1846) In Wisconsin stockholders in banking corporations are liable by statute as original and principal debtors, substantially as though they were partners, except, as in Ohio, that the responsibility of each is limited to a sum equal to his shares of stock. Coleman v. White, 14 Wis, 700 (1862) Under the Wisconsin statute making stockholders liable for the debts where business is commenced before one-half the capital stock is subscribed and twenty per cent paid in, the statute allows suit without joining the corporation as a defendant. Flour City Nat. Bank t Wechselberg, 45 Fed Rep, 547 (1891)

[2] Story v Furman 25 N. Y., 214, 221, 222 (1862), New England Commercial Bank v Newport Steam Factory, 6 R I, 154, 189 (1859), Moies v Sprague, 9 id, 541 (1870) It is sometimes held that a general statutory liability means a liability on the part of the stockholder only in the proportion which his interest bears to the total indebtedness of the corporation Boyd v Hall, 56 Ga, 563 (1876), Reynolds v Feliciana Steamboat Co, 17 La Rep, 397 (1841) In such a

case, where the shareholders are jointly and severally personally liable for debts contracted by the corporation, which it cannot or does not pay, in proportion to the number of shares they own, it seems to be settled that they are to be held principal debtors, and not mere sureties for the corporation Harger v. McCullough, 2 Denio, 119 (1846), Corning v. McCullough, 1 N Y., 47 (1847), the court saying that the stockholders stand towards the creditors "on the same ground and under the same responsibility . . as they would, if unincorporated, have stood," Moss v Averell, 10 id, 450 (1853), Simonson v Spencer, 15 Wend, 548 (1836), sustaining the action for debt, Bailey v Bancker, 3 Hill, 188 (1842), holding, also, that a creditor must sue a stockholder upon the original demand and not upon the judgment against the company, Southmayd v Russ, 3 Conn, 52 (1819), holding that, since the liability is original, scire facias will not lie against a stockholder, but he must be sued as if there were no incorporation, Marcy v. Clark, 17 Mass, 330 (1821) In Michigan it is held that they are sureties Hanson v. Donkersley, 37 Mich, 184 (1877) Cf Grand Rapids Savings Bank v Warren, 52 id, 557 (1884). It has been held, also, that they are not sureties for each other Lane t. Harris 16 Ga, 217, 234 (1854), Crease v Babcock 10 Metc, 525 (1846). Cf. Larrabee v Baldwin, 35 Cal, 155 (1868) This seems to be the rule, in general, as to all statutory liability Young v Rosenbaum, 39 Cal, 646 (1870), Taylor on Corporations, §§ 714, 715, Erickson t Nesmith, 46 N H, 371 (1866); Thomp-

The liability of stockholders in national banks is fixed by an order of the comptroller of the currency [1]

§ 222. *The remedy in a court of equity* — The remedy in equity is the favorite remedy of the courts. It is just, certain, impartial and clear. It enforces once for all the liability of the stockholders, and at the same time provides for contribution. It distributes the assets equally and equitably among all the corporate creditors It prevents a multiplicity of suits, and avoids the difficult question as to whether a suit at law will lie. The only and great objection to the remedy in equity is that it is protracted, vexatious and expensive.[2]

Frequently the courts have held that an action at law to enforce a statutory liability is not a proper proceeding, but that the rights of all parties can be properly adjusted only in a court of equity, and that the latter remedy is exclusive of all others [3]

---

son *v* Meisser, 108 Ill , 359 (1884) It is obvious that the question whether the creditor, in pursuing his remedy against the shareholder, may sue one or any of the shareholders at his option, or must sue all, in a joint action, is of the highest importance. It goes to the very form and essence and content of his action; but it is a point upon which, as has been already intimated, a text-writer cannot deduce from the reported cases any clearly-settled rule of general application It is, in every case where the statute does not contain an explicit provision, a question of construction to be determined by the courts in expounding the words of the statute

[1] It is for him to determine whether and to what extent the statutory liability of the stockholders shall be enforced Casey *v* Galli, 94 U S, 673 (1876); Kennedy *v.* Gibson, 8 Wall , 498 (1869), Strong *v* Southworth, 8 Ben , 331, National Bank *v* Case, 99 U S, 628 (1879). A voluntary assessment of the stockholders by themselves does not affect or decrease this statutory liability 118 U S, 634 (1886). The United States district court has jurisdiction of an action by the receiver of an insolvent national bank to collect assessments on stock Stephens *v* Bernays, 44 Fed Rep, 642 (1890) The statutory liability of stock-

holders in a national bank may be enforced by an action at law and the assessment as made by the comptroller is conclusive Young *v* Wempe, 46 Fed Rep, 354 (1891) The liability of directors under the National Banking Act for loans to separate persons of amounts in excess of one-tenth of the capital stock can be enforced only in a court of equity Welles *v* Graves 41 Fed Rep 459 (1890), Peters *v* Foster, 56 Hun, 607 (1890) As regards the remedy under the National Bank Act, see Kennedy *v* Gibson, 8 Wall, 498 (1869), Casey *v* Galli, 94 U S, 673 (1876), and act of June 30, 1876, ch 44, Witters *v* Sowles, 32 Fed Rep, 767 (1887), Richmond *v* Irons, 121 U S, 27 (1887), as to joinder of causes of action

[2] Thus with reason the court said, in Mason *v* Alexander, 41 Ohio St , 318 · "By reason of the great number of stockholders, the frequent transfers of stock, the decease of parties, and of other causes, delays vexatious, expensive and almost interminable, seem to be inevitable in all such proceedings, so much so indeed that such liability has grown to be looked upon as furnishing next to no security at all for the debts of corporations "

[3] Thus under a charter provision that stockholders shall "be bound respect-

In many jurisdictions the rule prevails that creditors in these cases have a concurrent remedy, either at law or in equity. The action at law will lie upon the debt, while, on the other hand, the equitable jurisdiction arises from the power of a court of chancery to compel contribution among the shareholders and to effect an equitable distribution among the creditors [1]

In the courts of the United States it is the rule that, where a stockholder's statutory liability is by the terms of the statute a joint and several or several liability, the creditor may, after the remedy against the corporation has been exhausted, enforce his rights in an action at law, but, in all other cases of statutory liability, the remedy must be in equity, as in cases of unpaid subscriptions [2] In several of the state courts it is held that a creditor's

---

ively for all debts of the bank in proportion to their stock holden therein," it was held that an action at law by a single creditor against a single stockholder would not lie. Pollard v Bailey, 20 Wall, 520 (1874), Hatch v Dana, 101 U S, 205 (1879), Terry v Little, id, 216, Smith v. Huckabee, 53 Ala, 191 (1875), Jones v Jarman, 34 Ark, 323 (1879) Cf Wright v McCormack, 17 Ohio St, 86 (1866), Sands v. Kimbark, 37 Barb, 108, 120 (1863), Cushman v Shepard, 4 id, 113 (1848) Nor under a statute making the stockholders of a banking company "individually responsible to the amount of their respective share or shares of stock for all its indebtedness and liabilities of every kind" Coleman v. White, 14 Wis 700 (1862), Carpenter v. Marine Bank, id, 705, n (1862).

Also upon the ground that at law the indebtedness of the corporation and the several liabilities of the members could not be equitably adjusted Low v Buchanan, 94 Ill, 76 (1879), where the directors were held liable for an excess of indebtedness, Queenan v Palmer, 34 Alb L J, 117 (Ill, 1886), Stewart v. Lay. 45 Iowa, 604 (1877), Norris v Johnson, 34 Md, 485 (1871), Garrison v Howe, 17 N Y, 458 (1858), Story v Furman, 25 id, 214 (1862). Cf Flash v Conn, 109 U S, 371 (1883)

Where, in South Carolina, the charter of a bank provided that upon the failure

of the bank "each stockholder shall be liable and held bound . . . for any sum not exceeding twice the amount of . . . his . . shares," it was held by the supreme court of the United States that a suit in equity by or on behalf of all the creditors is the only appropriate mode of enforcing the liability incurred by such a failure. Terry v. Little, 101 U S, 216 (1879).

[1] Bank of the United States v. Dallam. 4 Dana, 574 (1836); Van Hook v. Whitlock, 3 Paige, 409 (1832), Bank of Poughkeepsie v Ibbotson, 24 Wend, 473 (1840); Masters v Rossie Lead Mining Co, 2 Sandf Chan, 301 (1845), Pfohl v. Simpson, 74 N Y, 137 (1878), Eames v. Doris, 102 Ill, 356 (1882), Culver v. Third National Bank, 64 id, 528 (1871), Perry v. Turner, 55 Mo., 418 (1874); Norris v. Johnson, 34 Md, 485, 489 (1871), Matthews v. Albert, 24 id, 527 (1866). Cf. Weeks v. Love, 50 N Y, 568 (1872), Garrison v Howe, 17 id, 458 (1858). And see the following New York cases, wherein it is held that a remedy in equity is preferable Morgan v. New York etc, R. R. Co, 10 Paige. 290 (1843); Sherwood v Buffalo, etc, R. R. Co., 12 How Prac, 136 (1855), Hinds v Canandaigua, etc., R R Co, 10 id, 487 (1855); Courtois v Harrison, 12 id, 359 (1856) — the last three cases relating to supplementary proceedings

[2] Pollard v Bailey, 20 Wall, 520 (1874);

remedy against a shareholder upon the statutory liability is in equity alone[1]   In New York and Illinois a stockholder sued at law for the enforcement of this liability may institute an equitable proceeding to bring in all the parties[2]

Terry v Little. 101 U S, 216 (1879)
Cf. Terry v Tubman, 92 U S, 156 (1875), Andrews v Bacon, 38 Fed Rep, 777 (1889); Cuykendall v Miles, 10 Fed Rep, 342 (1882), where the court said: "The supreme court hold that the mode in which a liability of this kind is to be enforced depends entirely upon the particular law governing the corporation If that law merely provides for a proportionate liability of all stockholders for all debts there should be a bill in equity for the benefit of all the creditors and against all the stockholders. (Citing cases) But if the law of the state authorizes an action by one creditor against one stockholder, that remedy may be pursued." Patterson v Lynde, 106 U. S, 519 (1882). As to joinder of parties, see R. S of U. S., § 737. An action at law lies in the federal courts, herein, when that remedy is appropriate Bullard v Bell, 1 Mason, 243 (1817). Or where the courts of the state creating the liability hold that an action at law will lie. Mills v Scott, 99 U. S, 25 (1878) In the federal courts a suit to enforce a director's statutory liability is in equity. Stone v Chisolm, 113 U S, 302 (1884)

[1] Harris v. First Parish, 40 Mass, 112 (1839), Coleman v White, 14 Wis, 700 (1862); Ladd v Cartwright, 7 Oreg, 329; Smith v Huckabee, 53 Ala., 191 (1875). See Patterson v Lynde, 106 U S, 519 (1882) In Illinois there was some doubt as to whether the bill in equity would lie, but the late case of Tunesma v Schuttler, 114 Ill., 156 (1885), holds that, in case the corporation is insolvent and the corporate creditors numerous, a bill in equity is the proper remedy. Under the Manufacturing Company's Act of Illinois, the creditor's remedy is held to be clearly in equity   Rounds v McCormick, 114 Ill, 252 (1885); Harper

v Union Mfg Co, 100 Ill, 225 (1881), Low v. Buchanan, 94 Ill, 76 (1879) See Pierce v Milwaukee, etc, Co, 38 Wis, 253 (1875) for the rule in that state Where under a creditor s bill a receiver is appointed and the assets administered, and then by a supplemental bill the stockholder's liability enforced, a creditor who received a dividend under the original bill cannot sue a stockholder at law   Tunesma v Schuttler, 28 N. E Rep, 605 (Ill, 1885)   The remedy is in equity alone, and non-joinder of any stockholders as defendants will render the bill demurrable   Friend v Powers, 9 S Rep, 392 (Ala., 1891)

[2] Pfohl v Simpson, 74 N Y, 137 (1878); Cochran v American Opera Co., N Y. Daily Reg, Jan 5, 1888   In Wisconsin a long line of decisions hold that the creditor's remedy against stockholders can be in equity only   Sleeper v Goodwin, 31 N. W. Rep, 335 (Wis., 1887), citing many cases, Garrison v Howe, 17 N Y, 458 (1858)   Semble, Thebus v. Smiley, 110 Ill, 316 (1884); Eames v. Doris, 102 Ill., 350 (1882)   All the stockholders should be made parties, but the defect may be waived. Arthur v Willius, 46 N W. Rep., 851 (Minn, 1890)   The liability of stockholders under the Ohio laws is several and to all creditors   Newbury v Robinson, 41 Fed Rep, 458 (1890)   When the equitable remedy is pursued, the corporation and all the solvent shareholders within the jurisdiction who are known must be made defendants   Contribution among the shareholders is of the essence of the proceeding, and that is best effected when all are made parties   Walsh v. Memphis, etc., R. R. Co, 2 McCrary, 156 (1881); S. C, 6 Fed. Rep, 797; Umsted v Buskirk, 17 Ohio St., 113 (1866), holding, also, that defendant stockholders may insist on joinder of co-stockholders. Erickson

A still different remedy from all these exists where the judgment creditor of the corporation, after execution returned unsatisfied, may issue execution against any stockholder without being obliged to institute a new action [1]

Another remedy still is to allow the plaintiff creditor to join stockholders as defendants in his original suit against the corporation [2]

§ 223 *Enforcement of the statutory liability in the courts of another state — Penal liabilities —* The stockholders of a corporation are generally widely scattered, and reside in many states Accordingly, when some or all of them are non residents of the state in which the corporation exists, the important question arises whether

r Nesmith, 46 N H , 371 (1866); Hadley r Russell. 40 N H , 109 (1860). The joinder of all the shareholders may be dispensed with in a case where it is shown to be impracticable Umsted r Busknk, 17 Ohio St., 113 (1866), Pettibone r McGraw, 6 Mich , 441 (1859), Pierce r Milwaukee Construction Co , 38 Wis , 253 (1875); Coleman *v.* White, 14 Wis , 700 (1862); Crease *v* Babcock, 10 Metc. 525 (1846); Brundage *v* Monumental, etc , Mining Co , 12 Oregon, 322 (1885), holding, also, that a defendant stockholder desiring to bring in other stockholders must do that by an appropriate cross-proceeding And an action to enforce statutory liability may be joined with an action to collect unpaid subscriptions Warner *v* Callender, 20 Ohio St., 190 (1870) But a claim against stockholders upon a liability imposed by statute cannot be joined in one bill in equity with a penal claim against the directors of the company Cambridge Water-works r Somerville Dyeing, etc , Co , 14 Gray, 193 (1859), Pope r Leonard, 115 Mass., 286 (1874), Nappier r Mortimer, 11 Abb Pr (N S.), 455 *Cf* Wiles r Suydam, 64 N Y , 173 (1876) The late case of Mason *v* Alexander, 13 Am. & Eng Corp Cas , 54 (Ohio, 1886), holds that the corporation is a necessary party to the creditor's suit in equity, that judgment against the stockholders is to be against them severally; and that interest is to be allowed from the commencement of the suit, "although the

amount of recovery may thereby exceed the stockholder's original liability." See, also, § 226, *infra*, to the effect that any creditor may enjoin the proceeding at law and bring all parties into a suit in equity. In a corporate creditor's action against a few stockholders, to enforce their liability and to obtain discovery of other stockholders, the discovery may be compelled Hipple r Fire, etc., Co , 3 Central Rep , 462 (N J , 1886) See, also, §§ 519, 520, *infra*. A married woman in Arkansas may own stock and be liable thereon. Her liability may be enforced in equity Bundy *v.* Cocke, 128 U S , 185 (1888) Proceedings to enforce the statutory liability are made elastic, and applications of creditors who come in may cure defects in the original papers. Arthur r Willius, 46 N. W. Rep , 851 (Minn , 1890)

[1] See § 201, *supra*.

[2] Milroy *v* The Spurr, etc., 43 Mich , 231, holding that, if the statute authorizes a suit against the corporation alone or jointly with one or more stockholders, a creditor who elects to sue it alone cannot afterwards proceed upon the same debt against the corporation and stockholders jointly One of the creditors who is a party to the sequestration proceedings may in those proceedings enforce the stockholder's statutory liability McKeesick r Seymour, etc.. Co , 50 N W. Rep., 1110 (Minn , 1892).

the courts of one state will enforce a stockholder's statutory liability created by the statutes of another state. If not, then non-resident stockholders practically escape the liability which they assumed when they became members of the corporation

The cases are uniform in holding that the extent of the stockholder's statutory liability and the character of that liability depend upon and are determined by the charter of the corporation or the statute of the state which created it [1]

In general, when the courts of one state are asked to enforce the statutory liability of stockholders in a corporation created by another state, two things are to be considered   First, is the statutory liability itself a contract liability or a mere penalty? Second, are the remedies provided by the laws of the state where suit is sought to be brought adequate to the just enforcement of the liability?

The law is clear that the courts of one state will not enforce penalties imposed by another state [2] But the usual statutory liability of stockholders is not a penalty. The courts are unanimous in holding that where by statute the stockholders in a corporation, instead of being relieved entirely from liability to corporate credit-

---

[1] Payson v. Withers, 5 Biss., 269 (1873). Seymour v. Sturgess, 26 N. Y., 134 (1862), McDonough v. Phelps, 15 How. Prac., 372 (1856), Ex parte Van Riper, 20 Wend. 614 (1839), Aultman's Appeal, 98 Pa. St., 505 Cf Hill v. Beach, 12 N. J. Eq., 31 (1858), Nabob of Carnatic v. East India Co., 1 Vesey, Jr., 371 (1791), Dutch West India Co. v. Henriquez, 1 Strange, 612 See, also, ch I, supra This principle applies, of course, only to corporations which were legally incorporated For the liability where the incorporation was not legal, see chapter XIII An administrator may enforce the statutory liability even in a foreign jurisdiction The United States courts take judicial notice of the statutes of the various states Newberry v. Robinson, 36 Fed. Rep., 841 (1888) In Bateman v. Service, L. R., 6 App. Cas., 386 (1881), the ground is taken that a liability created by statute remains the same wherever the corporation may transact its business, or wherever the shareholders may happen to live and that the fact of doing business in a foreign state does not subject the share-

holders of the corporation to the operation of laws which create statutory liability in such foreign state In accordance with this view it was held in Ohio, where a foreign corporation, without statutory liability of its stockholders, did business in Ohio, where the statutes prescribe a personal liability for stockholders in domestic corporations of similar character, that the shareholders of the foreign corporation are protected by the exemption they enjoy at home Second National Bank v. Hall, 35 Ohio St., 158 (1878) See, also, Jessup v. Carnegie, 80 N. Y., 441 (1880), and see § 243, infra

[2] Story on the Conflict of Laws, §§ 620, 621, Wharton on the Conflict of Laws, § 853 et seq., Rorer on Interstate Laws, 148, 149 See, also, Lowry v. Inman 46 N. Y., 119 (1871), Patterson v. Baker, 21 How. Prac., 180 (1867), Howell v. Manglesdorf, 33 Kan., 194 (1885) "Penal laws are strictly local, and cannot have any operation beyond the jurisdiction of the country where they were enacted" Scoville v. Canfield, 14 Johns., 338 (1817)

ors, are only partially relieved therefrom, the additional liability is a contract liability, and will be enforced by the courts of any state   In other words, the ordinary statutory liability of stockholders is a contract liability, and will be enforced as such by the courts of all the states [1]

[1] Corning v. McCullough, 1 N. Y, 47 (1847); S. C, 49 Am Dec., 287, Freeland v. McCullough, 1 Denio. 414 (1845), S C, 43 Am Dec, 685, Hodgson v Cheever, 8 Mo. App., 321 (1880), Manville v Edgar, 8 id, 321 (1880), Queenan v Palmer, 117 Ill, 619 (1886), Aultman's Appeal, 98 Pa St, 505 (1881), Sacketts Harbor Bank v Blake, 3 Rich Eq, 225; Woods v Wicks, 7 Lea (Tenn), 10 (1881); Ex parte Van Riper, 20 Wend, 614 (1839), McDonough v Phelps, 15 How. Prac, 372 (1856), Lowry v Inman, 46 N Y, 119 (1871) See, also, Paine v Stewart, 33 Conn, 516 (1866), Bond v Appleton, 8 Mass, 472 (1812), Hutchins v New England Coal Mining Co, 4 Allen, 580 (1862); Grand Rapids Bank v Warren, 52 Mich, 537 Cf Bateman v Service, L R, 6 App. Cas, 386 (1881); Norris v Wrenschall, 34 Md, 492 (1871), Terry v Calnan, 13 S. C, 220 (1879); Tinker v Van Dyke, 1 Flippin, 532 (1876) Cf Lowry v Inman, 46 N Y, 119, 127 (1871), Strong v. Wheaton, 38 Barb., 625 (1861), Brown v Hitchcock, 36 Ohio St, 678 (1879); Hatch v Burroughs, 1 Woods, 413 (1870), Flash v Conn, 109 U S, 371 (1883); Fourth Nat'l Bank v. Francklyn, 120 U. S., 747 (1887), Cuykendall v Miles, 10 Fed Rep, 342; Nimick v Mingo Iron Works. 25 West Va, 184 (1884). Cf. Woods v Wicks, 7 Lea (Tenn), 40 (1881); Lawler v. Burt, 7 Ohio St, 340 (1857). A Maryland case holds that the statutory liability of a stockholder in a New York manufacturing corporation is a penalty, and cannot be enforced in that state   Attrill v. Huntington, 70 Md, 191 (1889) But in the case of Huntington v Attrill, 146 U S, 657 (1892), the court reversed the court of appeals of Maryland (70 Md, 191), which refused to enforce in Maryland a judgment obtained in New York by a corporate creditor against an officer of the corporation, who, under the statutes of New York, was rendered liable to corporate creditors by reason of signing a false certificate as to the amount of the capital stock of the company   The supreme court of the United States held that such a liability was not penal in the international sense. And when the suit is maintainable, the construction placed upon the statute of the state in which the corporation exists, by the courts of that state, is, as a general rule, controlling, and will be followed by the courts of the state where the suit to enforce is brought. Jessup v. Carnegie, 80 N Y, 441 (1880); Chase v Curtis, 113 U S, 452 (1884); Sav Assoc. v. O'Brien, 51 Hun, 45 (1889)   In the case of New Haven, etc, Co v Linden Spring Co., 6 East. Rep., 663 (Mass, 1886), the court, in refusing to enforce a subscription made to a foreign corporation, without an express promise to pay, said: "That the statutes of a state do not operate extraterritorially, proprio vigore, will be conceded   How far they should be enforced beyond the limits of the state which has enacted them must depend on several considerations — as, whether any wrong or injury will be done to the citizens of the state in which they are sought to be enforced   whether the policy of its own laws will be contravened or impaired; and whether its courts are capable of doing complete justice to those liable to be affected by their decrees"   To same effect, Halsey v. McLean, 94 Mass, 438 (1866). The statutory liability of stockholders in California is a contract liability.   Dennis v Superior Court, 27 Pac. Rep, 1031 (Cal, 1891)   The statutory liability of stockholders in New York business corporations to the extent of their stock until a certifi-

A different rule prevails as to the statutory liability of corporate officers for failure to file reports, or give certain notices, or make certain contracts Such liability is generally construed to be penal, and will not be enforced by the courts of other States [1]

This question of whether the liability is a penalty arises often in ascertaining what particular statute of limitations applies [2] There

cate is filed that the whole capital stock is paid in is not a penal liability and it survives the death of a stockholder Cochran v Wiechers, 119 N. Y, 399 (1890).

[1] Derrickson v Smith, 27 N J Law, 166 (1858), First National Bank v Price, 33 Md, 487 (1870), where a statute of Pennsylvania imposing liability upon directors and officers contracting or assenting to an indebtedness in excess of the amount of capital was held to be penal (But see, *contra*, Field v Haines, 28 Fed. Rep., 919 — 1886) Halsey v McLean, 12 Allen, 438 (1866), Bird v Hayden, 1 Robertson (N Y Super Ct), 383 (1863); Union Iron Co v Pierce, 4 Biss, 327 (1869) The twelfth section of the New York Manufacturing Companies Act), to the effect that the corporate officers shall be liable for the debts of the corporation in case they fail to make an annual public report of the business of the corporation (Laws of 1848, ch 40), is universally held to be penal in its character. Chase v Curtis, 113 U S, 452 (1885); Stokes v Stickney, 96 N Y., 323 (1884); Pier v Hanmore, 86 id., 95 (1881); Pier v. George, 86 id, 613 (1881); Veeder v. Baker, 83 id, 156 (1880), Knox v. Baldwin, 80 id, 610 (1880), Easterly v. Barber, 65 id, 252 (1875), Wiles v. Suydam, 64 id, 173 (1876); Jones v Barlow, 62 N. Y. 202 (1875), Merchant's Bank of New Haven v Bliss, 35 id, 412 (1866), Gadsden v Woodward, 103 N Y, 244 In New York if the suit is commenced by summons only to recover a penalty, a reference must be made on the summons to the statute Nordell v Wahlstedt, N Y L J, Jan 16, 1890. A stockholder's liability for failure to file a certificate each year is a penal liability

and cannot be enforced in a foreign jurisdiction Sayles v Brown 40 Fed. Rep, 8 (1889) Foreign stockholders cannot be sued in their state for contributions towards a penal liability paid by domestic stockholders Id The liability of stockholders, for a failure to file a certificate to the effect that the capital stock is fully paid up is a penal liability. Sayles v Brown, 4 Fed Rep, 8, Howell v Roberts, 45 N W. Rep, 923, Halsey v McLean, 12 Allen, 438, Erickson v Nesmith, 4 Allen, 233, Mitchell v Hotchkiss, 48 Conn, 9, Steam Engine Co v Hubbard, 101 U S, 188, Savings Ins. Co. of St. Louis v O'Brien, 5 R'y & Corp L J, 318 The statutory liability of a director in a national bank is not a penal liability and it survives the death of the director who is liable. Stephens v Overstoltz, 43 Fed. Rep, 465 (1890) The statutory liability of trustees of clubs for all debts contracted during their term of office is a contract liability. Rogers v Decker, 131 N Y, 490 (1892).

[2] Gridley v Barnes, 103 Ill, 211, Diversey v. Smith, id, 378 (1882) See, also, Cable v McCune, 26 Mo, 380, Lawlor v. Burt, 7 Ohio St, 311 (1857), Cady v. Smith, 12 Neb, 628 (1882), Knox v Baldwin, 80 N Y, 610 (1880) Cf Duckworth v Roach, 81 N Y, 49 (1880), Wiles v. Suydam, 69 N Y, 173 The federal courts follow the state decisions Price v Yates, 7 Weekly Notes, 51 (U S C C, Pa, 1879) The three years' statute of limitations relative to penalties applies to an action to hold directors liable under a statute making them liable for all debts if they commit *ultra vires* acts which result in insolvency Merchants', etc, Bank v Northwestern, etc, Co, 51 N. W Rep, 117 (Minn, 1892). A statu-

can never be such a thing as a vested right to enforce a penalty.[1] Until judgment is obtained the legislature may relieve the parties from this penalty[2]

The second question is whether the courts of one state will enforce a statutory liability created by another state, when the legal procedure for enforcing that liability is prescribed by the latter state and is not feasible in the former state. As already stated, when the statute creating the liability prescribes the procedure for enforcing it, that procedure is exclusive of all other remedies[3] Hence, instances have occurred in which the enforcement of this statutory liability in another state has failed, by reason of difficulties attending the legal procedure to be used in enforcing that liability[4] The liability will be enforced only when it may be enforced by the procedure of the state wherein the enforcement is sought.[5]

tory liability of directors for failure to file reports is penal and subject to the statute of limitations on penalties A judgment need not be obtained against the corporation first. Larsen v James, 29 Pac Rep 183 (Colo, 1892) A penal liability of a director ends in case of his death, unless it is already merged into a judgment, in which case it survives Carr v Rischer, 119 N. Y, 117 (1890) The statutory liability of officers for corporate debts for failing to publish an annual notice is not a penalty and is not barred by the one year statute of limitations Coy v Jones 47 N W. Rep, 208 (Neb, 1890) The statutory liability of stockholders in case the articles are not published as required by statute is not such a penal liability as to be barred by the one year statute of limitations Howell v Roberts, 45 N W. Rep, 923 (Neb., 1890) The statutory provision in Illinois making officers liable for debts in excess of the capital stock is not a penal liability, and is not barred by the two year statute of limitations It may be enforced in equity Wolverton v. Taylor, 23 N E Rep, 1007 (Ill, 1890).

[1] Yeaton v United States, 5 Cranch, 281 (1809), Norris v Crocker, 13 How., 429 (1851).

[2] Id, also § 497, note

[3] See § 220, supra.

[4] Lowry v Inman, 46 N Y, 119 (1871).

where the remedy prescribed by the Georgia corporation was an execution levied on stockholders' property, and based on the judgment against the corporation only, Third Nat'l Bank v Gregory N Y L J, Dec 8, 1890, Nimick v Mingo Iron Works, 25 W. Va, 184 (1881) See, also, Sav Assoc v. O'Brien, 51 Hun 45 (1889) Where the statute provides that the creditor's remedy shall be by bill in equity, and that all stockholders shall be joined, the liability cannot be enforced in a state where this remedy is not possible Erickson v Nesmith, 4 Allen, 233 (1862), S C, 15 Gray, 221 (1860) Cf S C, 46 N H, 371 (1866)

[5] Lowry v Inman, supra, Drinkwater v Portland, etc, R R. Co., 18 Me, 35 (1841), Nimick v Mingo, etc, Works, supra, Christensen v Eno, 106 N Y, 97 (1887), Erickson v Nesmith, 15 Gray, 221 Cf Taft v Ward, 106 Mass., 518 (1871) The Illinois courts will not enforce the statutory liability of Illinois stockholders in a Michigan corporation where the Michigan courts have never construed the statute and no bill has been filed there to determine the debts, assets and various liabilities Young v. Farwell, 28 N E Rep, 845 (Ill, 1891). A Wisconsin court will not enforce the statutory liability of a resident stockholder in a Michigan mining company

Generally, the statute creating the liability must be pleaded where the action is in another state [1] The United States courts, however, take judicial notice of the statutes of all the states, and in those courts this part of the pleading may be omitted [2] The courts of one state will entertain a bill of discovery filed by corporate creditors to obtain the names of stockholders in a corporation in another state, with a view to enforcing their statutory liability in the latter state [3]

Before suit can be brought against a stockholder a judgment must be obtained and execution returned unsatisfied in the state where suit is brought unless it is impossible [4]

§ 224. *How far the judgment against the corporation is conclusive of the creditor's claim.* — In general, the judgment in these cases against the corporation is conclusive as to the amount and validity of the creditor's claim. Consequently, in most of the states, when suit is brought to enforce the stockholder's statutory liability, that judgment can be impeached by him only for fraud and collusion, or for want of jurisdiction [5]

for debts due to laborers where the Michigan statute gives, as a remedy for enforcing such liability, a joint action at law against both the corporation and the stockholder May v Block, 45 N W Rep., 940 (Wis, 1890) A resident of New York cannot bring suit in Massachusetts against a resident of California to hold him liable as a stockholder in a Kansas corporation under a statute making him liable when the remedy against the corporation has been exhausted, even though judgment against the latter was obtained in Kansas The courts of Massachusetts have uniformly refused to enforce the statutory liability in corporations organized in other states Bank of North Am v Rindge, 27 N E Rep., 1015 (Mass, 1891)

[1] Salt Lake, etc., v Hendrickson, 40 N J Law, 52, holding that the foreign statute, when pleaded, must be set forth in substance, and an averment "pursuant to the statute" is insufficient

[2] Fourth National Bank v Francklyn, 120 U S, 747 (1887), Newberry v Robinson, *supra* In New Hampshire it is held to be necessary to set out in the pleading the remedy provided by the laws of the state creating the corpora-

tion and the liability, and to show that this remedy can be employed in the court where suit is brought. Rice v. Merrimack Hosiery Co, 56 N H, 114 (1875)

[3] Post v. Toledo, etc, R R Co, 11 N E Rep, 540 (Mass, 1887)

[4] See § 200, also p 281, n 1 An action in New York, to enforce the statutory liability of a stockholder in a New York corporation, does not lie, where the only execution issued was in Colorado Rocky Mountain Bank v Bliss, 89 N Y, 338 (1882), Dean v Mace, 19 Hun, 391 (1879), Summer v Marcy, 3 Woodb & M, 105. See, also, § 219, *supra* If the execution is issued in the county of the chief place of business as required by statute it need not be issued in other counties to enforce stockholder's liability for labor debts Ripley v Evans, 49 N W Rep, 504 (Mich, 1891).

[5] Thayer v New England Lithographic Co, 108 Mass, 523 (1871), Borland v. Haven, 37 Fed Rep, 394 (1888), Came v. Brigham, 39 Me, 35 (1854); Millikin v Whitehouse, 49 id, 527 (1860), Wilson v The Stockholders, etc, 43 Pa St, 424 (1862), Donworth v Coolbaugh, 5 Iowa, 300 (1857), Farnum v Ballard, etc, Ma-

In some jurisdictions, however, this judgment against the corporation is only *prima facie* evidence of the validity and amount of the creditor's claim.[1] And in New York judgment against the corporation and the execution returned wholly or partially unsatisfied are evidence only that the corporation cannot pay its debts. They only serve to show that the creditor has taken the necessary precedent steps to collect his claim from the corporate assets. But he cannot rely upon the judgment obtained against the corporation to establish his right to recover against the shareholder. It is not even *prima facie* evidence either of the amount or validity of his claim. The stockholder may set up any defense that the corporation might have set up.[2] This means that the corporate

chine Shop, 12 Cush, 507 (1853), Handrahan *v* Cheshire Iron Works, 4 Allen, 396 (1862), Gaskill *v* Dudley, 6 Metc., 546; Hampson *v* Weare, 4 Iowa, 13 (1856), Bullock *v*, Kilgour, 39 Ohio St., 543 (1883). *Cf* Merrill *v* Suffolk Bank, 31 Me, 57 (1849); Holyoke Bank *v* Goodman, etc., Mfg Co, 9 Cush, 576 (1852), Bank of Australasia *v*. Nias, 16 Q B, 711, S. C, 20 L. J. (C. B), 284 (1851), and § 209, *supra*. Stockholders sued on their liability may show that the judgment was obtained by default, and that a valid defense exists to the original claim Irons *v* Mfrs Bank, 36 Fed Rep, 843 (1888) A stockholder cannot attack the debt on the ground of fraud where the debt was incurred in the adjustment of claims, and the statute of limitations is a bar to any fraud in the settlement. Railroad Co *v* Smith *et al*, 31 N E. Rep., 743 (Ohio, 1891). In the case of Schrader *v* Manuf'rs Bank, 133 U S., 67 (1890), the supreme court allowed stockholders, who had been sued on their statutory liability on national bank stock to go back of the judgment against the bank, such judgment having been rendered after the bank had gone into liquidation

[1] Grund *v* Tucker, 5 Kan, 70 (1869), Hawes *v* Anglo-Saxon, etc, Co., 101 Mass, 385 (1869), Grand Rapids Savings Bank *v*. Warren, 52 Mich, 557, Merchants' Bank *v* Chandler, 19 Wis., 435 (1865) And see Neilson *v*. Crawford, 52 Cal, 248 (1871), passing also on the admissibility of the books of the corporation to prove its indebtedness to a creditor in an action against a stockholder

[2] Moss *v* McCullough, 5 Hill, 131 (1843). [This case was reversed *upon another point* in McCullough *v* Moss, 5 Denio 567 (1846)] McMahon *v*. Macey, 51 N Y, 155 (1872), Miller *v*. White, 50 id., 137 (1872); Chase *v* Curtis 113 U S, 452 (1884); Esmond *v* Bullard, 16 Hun, 65 (1878); Conant *v* Van Schaick, 24 Barb, 87 (1857). But see Slee *v* Bloom, 20 Johns, 669 (1822); Belmont *v*. Coleman, 21 N. Y, 96 (1860); Hastings *v*. Drew, 76 id., 9 (1879), Lawler *v*. Rosebrook, 48 Hun, 453 (1888), Moss *v*. Oakley, 2 Hill, 265 (1842), Berridge *v*. Abernethy, 24 N Y. Week Dig, 513 (1886); Stephens *v* Fox, 83 id, 313 (1881), in which the ground is taken that the judgment in these cases is *prima facie* evidence or more, without, however, overruling the earlier cases; Trippe *v*. Huncheon, 82 Ind, 307 (1882), where a complaint founded on the judgment was held bad on demurrer because the liability of the stockholder was looked upon as being upon the original debt and not upon the judgment; Southmayd *v*. Russ, 3 Conn, 52 (1819), where, for the same reason, a proceeding by *scire facias* was not allowed to be maintained; Whitney Arms Company *v* Barlow, 63 N Y, 62 (1875). Practically the corporate creditor must bring his action anew against the shareholder upon his original demand. Bailey *v*.

creditor is obliged to prove his cause of action over again, and repeat what he has already proved in his action against the corporation. Such, also, seems to be the rule in Illinois[1]

In any jurisdiction where the stockholders are, by statute, made liable for only a certain class of the corporate indebtedness, it is plain that they cannot be charged upon a judgment recovered against the corporation, unless it be shown that the claim in controversy comes within the class upon which they are liable[2]

§ 225. *Stockholder's miscellaneous defenses against his statutory liability* — There are two classes of defenses that may occur to a stockholder to defeat his statutory liability. One class is of defenses that the corporation itself might have set up, or did set up, against the plaintiff when he sought to collect his debt from the corporation. As already explained herein, in some jurisdictions, particularly New York, the stockholder may set up these defenses, although the corporation has failed to establish them. In other and most jurisdictions he cannot.

A second class of defenses include those which are personal to

---

Bancker, 3 Hill, 188 (1842); Kincaid *v.* Dwinelle, 59 N Y, 548 (1875); Moss *v.* Averell, 10 id, 449 (1853), Witherhead *v* Allen, 4 Abb App Dec, 628 (1867) As to the effect of recitals in a decree against the corporation, see Chesnut *v.* Pennell, 92 Ill, 55 (1879). This judgment against the corporation is admissible only as evidence that the condition precedent to his right to recover from the shareholder has been complied with Wheeler *v* Miller, 24 Hun, 541 (1881); S. C., *sub nom* Wheeler *v* Millar, 90 N. Y., 353 (1882); Strong *v* Wheaton, 38 Barb, 616 (1861) But *cf.* Tyng *v.* Clarke, 9 Hun, 269 (1876). See, also, Bissit *v* Kentucky, etc, Navigation Co, 15 Fed Rep, 353 (1882), and the annotation; Union Bank *v.* Wando Mining, etc., Co., 17 S C., 339 (1881). The judgment may avail, however, in these cases to prevent the statute of limitations from barring the action. Van Cott *v* Van Brunt, 2 Abb N C., 283, 294 (1877); reversed on other points, 82 N. Y, 535 (1880)

[1] Chesnut *v.* Pennell, 92 Ill, 55 In Quick *v* Lemon, 105 Ill., 578 (1883), where the corporation had not pleaded a counter-claim against a creditor in a

suit at law, a stockholder was permitted to file a cross-bill in a chancery suit brought by judgment creditors against the corporation and certain stockholders The stockholder may set up that the plaintiff's claim grew out of business transacted by the corporation after it had been put into liquidation by the court. Richmond *v* Irons, 121 U. S, 27 (1887).

[2] Bohn *v.* Brown, 33 Mich, 257 (1876); Wilson *v* The Stockholders, etc 43 Pa St, 424 (1862); Conant *v* Van Schaick, 24 Barb, 87 (1857) *Cf* Larrabee *v* Baldwin, 35 Cal, 155 (1868), Farnsworth *v* Wood, 91 N Y, 308 (1883). Where stockholders are liable for corporate debts existing on a certain date, the existence of a corporate creditor's debt on that date may be found by evidence other than his judgment against the corporation Congdon *v* Winsor, 21 Atl Rep, 540 (R I, 1891). A statutory liability of directors for debts of the corporation does not render them liable on an accommodation indorsement by the corporation — the indorsement being non-enforceable Nat'l Park Bank *v.* Remsen, 43 Fed Rep., 226 (1890).

the particular stockholder, and not such as the corporation might have set up   They are largely such defenses as the stockholder might set up against the corporation to defeat his subscription. They do not refer to the validity of the creditor's debt, but they deny that that particular defendant is one of those who are liable for the corporate debts.   There are, in addition to the defenses specified in a previous chapter,[1] several defenses which are peculiar to this statutory liability.

(a) *Release or extension* — A release by the corporate creditor of one shareholder from his proportion of the corporate indebtedness will not operate to release the other shareholders[2]   Thus, where the shareholders are held to be severally and not jointly liable under the statute, one may be released without releasing the others.[3] But whether an extension given to the corporation by a creditor will not discharge a shareholder as to his liability by statute seems uncertain[4]

---

[1] Ch X, *supra*

[2] Herries *v* Platt, 21 Hun, 132 (1880). See, also, Prince *v* Lynch, 38 Cal, 528 (1869) holding that the other stockholders liable only proportionately are released only proportionately   The assumption of the corporate debt by a third party may be rescinded   Borland *v* Haven, 37 Fed Rep, 394 (1888).

[3] Bank of Poughkeepsie *v* Ibbotson, 5 Hill, 461 (1843)   *Cf.* Herries *v* Platt, 21 Hun, 132 (1880)

[4] In the case of Harger *v* McCullough, 2 Denio, 119 (1846), it was held that it would not, while in the later case of Parrott *v* Colby, 6 Hun, 55 (1875), S C. affirmed, 71 N Y, 597 (1877), without expressly overruling Harger *v* McCullough it is plainly declared, in making an application of the short statute of limitations provided by the General Manufacturing Act of New York (N Y Laws of 1848, ch 40, § 24), that the liability of shareholders in these cases cannot be revived or extended by any renewal or extension of the indebtedness which the creditors may make with the corporation   And in accordance with that view, where the effect of the extension granted by the creditor to the corporation had been to postpone the action against the shareholder beyond the time prescribed by the statute within which such an action is maintainable — that is one year from the time the corporate debt was first due — it was held that the shareholder was thereby discharged   Parrott *v* Colby, *supra*, Jagger Iron Co *v* Walker, 76 N. Y., 521 (1879), Hardman *v* Sage, 47 Hun, 230 (1888), Stilphen *v* Ware, 45 Cal, 110 (1872).   See, also, Jones *v.* Barlow, 62 N. Y, 202 (1875), Bolen *v* Crosby, 49 N Y., 183 (1872)   In Aultman's Appeal, 98 Pa. St., 505 (1881), it was held that, where the extension was granted at the request of the directors, the stockholders had assented, and there was no release.   A release of the corporation under an insolvency statute is a release of the stockholder's statutory liability   Mohr *v* Minn, etc, Co., 41 N W Rep., 1074 (Minn, 1889).   See, also, Hanson *v* Donkersley, 37 Mich, 184 (1877), ruling that the Michigan statute does not make stockholders primarily liable, and holding that the individual liability for corporate debts is discharged by an extension of time and the acceptance of a corporate note   A laborer's statutory right to collect from the stockholders is not waived by taking the corporate note. Jackson *v* Meek, 9 S. W. Rep., 225 (Tenn, 1888)   See § 225 (*f*) sub

(b) *Liability already paid* — It is a defense to the stockholder to prove that his full statutory liability has already been paid by him   A stockholder who has voluntarily paid corporate debts to the full extent of his corporate liability is entitled to set up that fact   And when such a payment was *bona fide* it is a bar to an action to collect any further amount [1]

(c) *Set-off* — Closely related to the defense of payment already made, there is the defense that the defendant stockholder has claims against the corporation, and that he is to be credited to that amount as a set-off [2]

It has been held that, where the statute creates a fund out of which the creditors are to be paid ratably, then the stockholder

[1] Garrison v Howe, 17 N Y, 458 (1858), Mathez v Neidig, 72 N Y, 100 (1878), Lane v Harris, 16 Ga, 217 (1854), Belcher v Willcox, 40 id, 391 (1869), Robinson v Bank of Darien 18 id., 65, 109 (1855), Woodruff & Beach Iron Works v Chittenden, 4 Bosw, 406 (1859), Boyd v Hall, 56 Ga, 563 (1876), San Jose Savings Bank v Pharis, 58 Cal, 380   Cf. Thebus v Smiley, 110 Ill, 316 (1884), where fraud was involved, Delano v Butler, 118 U S, 634 (1886)   Contra, Fowler v Robinson, 31 Me, 189 (1850), Grose v Hilt, 36 Me, 22   But when a creditor has actually commenced a suit to enforce the statutory liability of any individual shareholder, it is then too late for that shareholder to defeat the action by paying some other corporate creditor's claim Jones v Wiltberger, 42 Ga, 575 (1871). See, also, Lane v. Harris, 16 Ga, 217, Thebus v Smiley, 110 Ill, 316 (1884). A contrary conclusion was reached in Richards v Brice, 3 N Y Supp, 911 (Com Pl, 1889), but the plain injustice of allowing the stockholder to defeat an action by such a device will not commend this decision   Nor will a shareholder who has employed an agent to buy up claims at a discount, and then confessed judgment in favor of that agent, be permitted to plead such a judgment in bar of an action by other creditors   Manville v Karst, 16 Fed Rep, 173 (1883). A mortgage by an insolvent stockholder in an insolvent cor-

poration to one of the corporate creditors is a preference to the extent of the stockholder's liability for corporate debts   Gatch v Fitch, 34 Fed Rep, 566 (1888), Ingalls v Cole 47 Me, 530, 541, holding that the mere pendency of suits is not a defense for a stockholder in a later action, unless the prior claims have been legally established and his liability exhausted   Payment of the judgments at a discount is no exhaustion of the liability though the judgments at full value would have exhausted it   Kunkelman v Rentchler, 15 Bradw (Ill), 271 (1884)

[2] A shareholder cannot himself buy in claims at a discount, and then set them off at their face value in an action to enforce his statutory liability to creditors Gauch v Harrison, 12 Bradw (Ill), 457 (1883)   See, also, Thompson v Meisser, 108 Ill, 359 (1884), Diven v Phelps, 34 Barb, 224 (1861)   A stockholder can defeat his statutory liability by offsetting judgments against the corporation purchased by himself, but only to the extent that he paid for the judgments. Bulkey v Whitcomb, 49 Hun, 290 (1888), Laugle v National Ins Co, 45 Mo, 109 (1869), Holland v Heyman 60 Ga, 174 (1878)   Where a stockholder is liable by statute and is also a creditor of the insolvent corporation, the court will order a set-off   Sowles v Witters, 40 Fed Rep, 413 (1889)   Cf Id, 403   Cf Boulton Carbou Co v Mills, 43 N W Rep, 290 (Iowa, 1889)   See a criticism on this case in § 193, n, supra.

cannot set off an indebtedness of the corporation to him. He must pay in what the statute requires, and then prove his claim against the corporation like any other creditor.[1] But where the shareholder's liability by statute is immediate and personal and several, and any creditor may sue any shareholder, then the shareholder may set off a debt, owing to him from the corporation, when he is sued by a corporate creditor.[2]

(d) *Interest.* — In South Carolina,[3] Maine and Illinois,[4] the share-

[1] Matter of the Empire City Bank 18 N. Y., 199, 227 (1858): Matthews v Albert, 24 Md , 527 (1866); Briggs v Cornwell, 9 Daly, 436, Hobart v Gould, 8 Fed Rep., 57 (1881), Hillier v Allegheny Mutual Ins Co, 3 Pa. St., 470, Lawrence v Nelson, 21 N. Y , 153 (1860); Thebus v. Smiley, 110 Ill , 316 (1884), Witters v Sowles, 32 Fed Rep, 130 (1887) See, also, Clapp v. Wright, 21 Hun, 240 (1880); Buchanan v Meisser, 105 Ill , 638 (1883). A stockholder sued on his statutory liability cannot offset judgments which he has purchased against the corporation, except to the extent that he paid for them Bulkley v Whitcomb, 1 N Y. Supp., 748 (1888), aff'd, 121 N Y , 107 The stockholder cannot purchase claims against the corporation at a discount and set them off, but can set them off for the amount paid by him for them, even though they are purchased in an agent's name Abbey v. Long, 24 Pac. Rep., 1111 (Kan , 1890) A stockholder who is also a director and is sued on his statutory liability as a stockholder cannot set off a judgment against the insolvent company, which judgment he purchased for a nominal sum Bulkley v. Whitcomb, 121 N Y, 107 (1890) For cases where the stockholder brings action as a corporate creditor, see Terry v. Bank of Cape Fear, 20 Fed Rep, 777; Weber v. Fickey, 47 Md , 196 See, also, Emmert v. Smith, 40 id , 123, and §§ 193, 194, *supra,* Hollister v Hollister Bank, 2 Abb App Dec , 367 (1865) In this case stockholders of an insolvent bank, after paying the judgments had against them to enforce their individual liabilities,

turned around and asked to be made, to the extent of those judgments, creditors of the bank, and thus entitled to participate *pro rata* with other creditors. *Held,* nothing is to be repaid to the stockholders until all the debts of the bank are paid.

[2] Mathez v. Neidig, 72 N Y , 100 (1878); Agate v Sands, 73 id , 620 (1878); Wheeler v Millar, 90 id , 353, 362 (1882); Richards v Crocker, N. Y. Daily Reg., April 22, 1887 , Christensen v Colby, 43 Hun, 362 (1887), Tallmadge v. Fishkill, 4 Barb , 382 (1848); Boyd v Hall, 56 Ga., 563 (1876), Remington v. King, 11 Abb. Prac , 278 (1859) This defense is allowed by the courts of New York in actions to enforce the liability imposed by the statute of that state known as the Manufacturing Companies Act of 1848. N. Y. Laws of 1848, ch 40, §§ 10, 24. See Wheeler v. Millar, 90 N Y , 353 (1882), a case in which the right to set-off under this statute is fully considered. The shareholder's right to set off his claim against the corporation in defense to an action against him to enforce his statutory liability may sometimes be a matter of *bona fides* Boyd v Hall, 56 Ga., 563 (1876), Belcher v Willcox, 40 id , 391 (1869), Thompson v Meisser, 108 Ill , 359, Buchanan v. Same, 105 id , 638 (1883), Welles v Stout, 38 Fed Rep., 807 (1889).

[3] Sacketts Harbor Bank v. Blake, 3 Rich Eq , 225 (1849), Cole v Butler, 43 Me , 401 (1857). See Grand Rapids Savings Bank v Warren, 52 Mich., 557 (1884), Cleveland v Burnham, 64 Wis, 347 (1885); 20 S. W. Rep., 1015.

[4] Munger v. Jacobson, 99 Ill , 349 (1881).

holder is not liable for interest on the amount for which the statute makes him answerable, and when he pays the principal sum the whole liability is discharged. In New York interest is collectible from the time the suit to enforce is commenced, instead of beginning from the time when judgment is entered.[1]

(e) *Costs.*— Although it is a condition precedent to the action against the shareholder that a judgment be recovered against the corporation, it has been held no part of the shareholder's statutory liability to pay the costs of obtaining that judgment Accordingly a judgment against the shareholder was held not to include any part of the costs of the proceeding against the corporation, but there has been strong dissent from this doctrine[2]

(f) *Statute of limitations* — Where the liability of the shareholder is immediate and primary, and not contingent on the obtaining of a judgment against the corporation, it is clear that the statute of limitations begins to run in favor of the shareholder when the debt matures against the corporation.[3]

---

[1] Handy v Draper, 89 N Y, 334 (1882), Burr v Wilcox, 22 id, 551 (1860) Cf Casey v. Galli, 94 U S, 673 (1876); Richmond v. Irons, 121 U S, 27 (1887) Where a referee computed the interest on the plaintiff's claim from the date on which it became due from the company instead of from the day the suit against the shareholder was commenced, it appearing that the indebtedness was less than the amount of the shareholder's liability, and that the allowance of interest did not swell it beyond that limit, the court of appeals held such a computation no error. Wheeler v. Millar, 90 N Y, 353, 362 (1882) Interest on the judgment is allowed in suit to enforce a stockholder's liability. Shickle v. Watts, 7 S. W Rep, 274 (Mo., 1888). Interest is allowed from the day when the referee ascertains and reports the debts of the corporation. Nat'l Com Bank v. McDonnell, 9 S. Rep., 149 (Ala, 1891).

[2] Bailey v Bancker, 3 Hill, 188 (1842); Richmond v. Irons, 121 U. S., 27 (1887); Roike v Thomas, 56 N Y, 559, 565 (1874); Miller v White, 50 N Y, 137 (1872). Cf. Veeder v Mudgett, 27 Hun, 519 (1882) It is possible that the rule might be otherwise in a case where the judgment is held to be conclusive as against the shareholder So in Michigan Grand Rapids Savings Bank v Warren, 52 Mich, 557 (1884). A judgment for costs against a corporation may be enforced against the director s statutory liability Allen v Clark, 108 N Y, 269 (1888) Costs may be collected against stockholders in suits to enforce this liability. Irons v Manufacturers' Bank, 36 Fed Rep, 843 (1888), holding that a creditor enforcing the stockholder s liability in behalf of himself and other creditors may have his costs

[3] Davidson v. Rankin, 34 Cal, 503 (1868), Lindsay v Hyatt, 4 Edw Chan (N Y), 97 (1842), Godfrey v Terry, 97 U. S., 171 (1877), Conklin v Furman, 8 Abb. Pr (N S), 164 (1865) Schalucky v Field, 16 N E. Rep, 904 (Ill, 1888). Compare Carrol v. Green, 92 U S, 509 (1875), Terry v Tubman, 92 id, 156 (1875), Terry v. McLure, 103 id, 442 (1880), Corning v McCullough, 1 N Y, 47 (1847), Jagger Iron Co v Walker, 76 N Y, 522 (1879) See, also, Terry v Calnan, 13 S C, 220, Lawler v Burt, 7 Ohio St, 340, King v Duncan, 38 Hun, 461 (1886), Sulphen v Ware, 45 Cal, 110 (1872), holding that, under California statute of limitations, the three years

But when the creditor must first obtain a judgment against the corporation and sue out an execution, which must be duly returned wholly or partially unsatisfied before the cause of action arises against the shareholder of his statutory liability, then the statute of limitations commences to run upon the return of the execution.[1]

begin to run from the time the debt was due and is not extended by a judgment obtained against the corporation The stockholder's liability under the California statute being a liability as a principal debtor, the statute of limitations begins to run as soon as the creditor's right of action against the corporation commences An extension of the time as to the corporation by renewal notes does not stop the statute of limitations as regards the stockholder's liability Hyman t Coleman, 23 Pac. Rep, 62 (Cal, 1890) The statute of limitations begins to run against a bank stockholder's statutory liability from the closing of the doors of the bank It begins to run against the corporation and stockholders at the same time Mitchell t Beckman, 28 Pac Rep, 110 (Cal, 1883). The liability in California of stockholders by statute for corporate debts begins when the debt is contracted and cannot be extended by the corporation so as to extend this stockholder's liability Redington t Cornwall, 27 Pac Rep, 40 (Cal, 1891) The extension of a debt by taking a note does not delay the application of the statute of limitations so far as a stockholder's liability is concerned Hardman r Sage, 124 N Y, 25 (1890) The state statute of limitations as to executors and estates will be applied by the federal courts to suits by a receiver for the enforcement of a stockholder's liability in a national bank Butler r Poole, 44 Fed Rep, 586 (1890) The stockholder's statutory liability dates from and is based upon the original debt created by the corporation and not from or upon the judgment against the corporation Newberry v. Robinson, 41 Fed Rep, 458 (1890) An action based on the notes is not on the debt for which the notes

were given. Griffith v Green, 13 N Y. Supp, 470 (1891). The statute of limitations under the Ohio law begins to run against the stockholder's liability from the time when the corporation makes an assignment for the benefit of creditors, even though no judgment has been obtained by the creditor Barrick r Gifford, 24 N E Rep, 259 (Ohio, 1890) In a suit by one creditor for the benefit of all, other creditors may come in although the statute of limitations would be a bar against a separate suit by them Id See, also, § 225 (a) supra

[1] Handy r Draper, 89 N Y, 334 (1882), Merritt r Reid, 13 Week Dig. (N Y), 453 (1882) Longley v Little, 26 Me, 162 (1846) In Terry r Tubman, 92 U S, 156 (1875), where the charter of a bank contained a provision making the shareholders individually liable for the ultimate redemption of its bills, the liability of the shareholders was held to arise, and hence the statute of limitations to commence to run in their favor, upon the open and notorious insolvency of the bank So, likewise, where shareholders were made individually liable "upon the failure of the bank," it was held that, the liability arising upon the failure, the statute of limitations began to run at that time Carrol v Green, 92 U S, 509, 511 (1875). To the same effect is Baker v. Atlas Bank, 9 Metc, 182 (1845), Terry r McLure, 103 U. S. 412 (1880), Godfrey r Terry, 97 id, 171 (1877). The case of Terry r Anderson, 95 U S, 628 (1877), sustains the constitutionality of a statute shortening the statute of limitations herein The case In re Bank of Sing Sing, 32 Hun, 462 (1884), affirmed, 96 N Y, 672, held that twenty years' delay by receiver in making report bars any assessment on stockholders. A statute of limitations

It is a general rule of law that the statute of limitations applicable to any ordinary action to enforce a contract is the one applicable to the action to enforce the statutory liability of shareholders in incorporated companies [1]

Accordingly, the suit must usually be commenced within six years after the cause of action has accrued [2]

running from the time of dissolution of the company is not set running by corporate insolvency and cessation of business. Sleeper 𝑧 Goodwin, 31 N W. Rep., 335 (Wis 1887) Cf § 195 The statute of limitations begins to run only from the time when the creditor's right to sue the stockholders begins McDonald 𝑣 Alabama, etc, Ins Co, 5 S Rep, 120 (Ala, 1888), Powell 𝑧 Oregonian R'y, 38 Fed Rep, 187 (1889), 33 N E Rep. 233

[1] Green 𝑣 Beckman, 59 Cal, 545 (1881), Corning 𝑣 McCullough, 1 N Y, 47 (1847), Wiles 𝑣 Suydam, 64 id, 173, 176 (1876), Mappier 𝑣 Mortimer, 11 Abb. Prac (N S), 455 (1871), Baker 𝑧 The Atlas Bank, 9 Metc, 182 (1845), The Commonwealth 𝑧. The Cochituate Bank, 3 Allen, 42 (1861), N Y. Code of Civil Proc, § 382.

[2] The citations in the preceding note See, also, Phillips 𝑧 Therassou, 11 Hun, 141 (1877), holding that where by statute the capital must be paid in within two years upon pain of dissolution, and imposes liability upon stockholders for debts of the corporation until the capital is fully paid, the statute of limitations begins to run at the expiration of the two years allowed for paying the capital. Under the New York Manufacturing Act relative to the two-year statute of limitations to a stockholder's statutory liability, it begins to run upon the dissolution of the corporation The creditor must sue within that time Hollingshead 𝑣 Woodward, 107 N Y, 96 (1887), King 𝑧 Duncan, 38 Hun, 461 (1886), holding that under that statute the creditor is not required to delay his suit until the two years has expired, Knox 𝑣 Baldwin, 80 N Y, 610 (1880), Hawkins 𝑣 Furnace Co., 40 Oh o St, 507 (1884) In South Carolina, under the statute of limitations of 1712 in that state, this action must be begun within four years Carrol 𝑧 Green, 92 U S 509 (1875) Terry 𝑧 McLure 103 id, 442 (1880) And on the other extreme in some of the older cases, it is held that an obligation, such as this, to pay money, arising under a statute, is a debt by specialty, and accordingly that it is barred only by a lapse of twenty years Bullard 𝑧 Bell, 1 Mason, 243, 289 (1817, by Judge Story), Thornton 𝑧 Lane 11 Ga 459 (1852) Lane 𝑧 Morris, 10 id 162 (1851) But see this view condemned in Carrol 𝑧 Green, 92 U S 509, 515 (1875), in an opinion by Justice Swayne, construing the South Carolina statute of 1712 Cf Green 𝑧 Beckman, 59 Cal, 545 (1881), construing § 359, California Code of Civil Procedure 38 Fed Rep, 777 Sometimes there is a provision that the action must have been commenced by the creditor against the corporation within a given limited time after the maturity of the debt, in order to hold the share-owner on his statutory liability N Y Laws of 1848, ch 40, § 24, Shellington 𝑣 Howland, 53 N Y, 371 (1873), Birmingham National Bank 𝑧 Mosser, 14 Hun 605 (1878) Lindsley 𝑧 Simonds, 2 Abb Prac (N S), 69 (1866) Cf State Sav Ass'n 𝑧 Kellogg, 52 Mo, 583 (1873) See, also, Freeland 𝑧 McCullough, 1 Denio 414, 422 (1845), Merchants', etc, Co 𝑧 Bliss, 21 How Pr, 366, aff d 35 N Y, 414 (1860) Lewis 𝑣 Ryder 13 Abb Pr, 1, Kuykendall 𝑣 Draper 19 Hun, 577, Moore 𝑧 Boyd, 15 Pac Rep, 670 (Cal, 1887) Frequently, also, there is a limitation applicable particularly to transfers of stock Paine 𝑣 Stewart 33 Conn, 516 (1882) In this case a statute of Minnesota imposing

If a statutory liability be held to be a penalty, then of course it will be held to come within that provision of the statute of limitations which provides for actions to enforce penalties [1]

In general, whatever the statute be, it is the rule that a lapse of time sufficient to constitute a bar at law will in equity be given the same effect; in other words, in these cases there is the same statute of limitations both at law and in equity [2]

Other defenses — The cause of action against a stockholder, arising from his statutory liability, is not defeated by his death. The action may proceed against his estate [3] The liability of solvent stockholders is not extended beyond the limit fixed by statute, even though other stockholders are insolvent.[4] A petition in bankruptcy by a stockholder is no bar to the enforcement of his liability, unless the corporate creditor was a party to the bankruptcy proceeding.[5] The admissions of one stockholder cannot bind another stockholder herein.[6] Various other defenses are considered in the notes below.[7]

liability upon stockholders while they were such, and for one year thereafter, was held, in an action in Connecticut, not to be operative against one who had not been a stockholder for more than a year before the action was brought. In New York this limitation is two years. See Handy *v.* Draper, 89 N. Y, 334, and ch XV, *infra*

[1] See § 223, *supra*

[2] Bank of Poughkeepsie *v* Ibbotson, 24 Wend 473 (1840); Carrol *v* Green, 92 U S, 509 (1875), Baker *v.* The Atlas Bank, 9 Metc, 182 (1845), Lindsay *v.* Hyatt, 4 Edw Chan (N Y), 104 (1842), Van Hook *v* Whitlock, 3 Paige, 409 (1832), Commonwealth *v.* Cochituate, 3 Allen, 42 (1861); Terry *v.* McLure, 103 U. S, 442 (1880). When the statute prescribes the limitation, there is of course no controversy. Baker *v.* Bachus' Adm'r 32 Ill, 99.

[3] Richmond *v* Irons, 121 U. S., 27 (1887); Chase *v* Lord, 77 N. Y, 1. But see Dane *v* Dane Mfg Co., 80 Mass, 489 (1860)

[4] Crease *v* Babcock, 51 Mass, 525. See, also, under the National Bank Act, United States *v.* Knox, 102 U. S., 422 (1880).

[5] Birmingham Bank *v.* Mosser, 14 Hun, 605.

[6] Simmons *v.* Sisson, 26 N. Y., 264 (1863).

[7] The court will not authorize the receiver of a national bank to compromise with the stockholders on their liability, even though more can be realized thereby, the stockholders having fraudulently conveyed away their property in order to avoid liability. *In re* Certain Stockholders of Cal Nat'l Bank, 53 Fed. Rep, 38 (1892). Stockholders cannot set up that their corporation was not authorized by law. McDonnell *v.* Ala, etc, Ins. Co, 5 S. Rep, 120 (Ala, 1888); Nat'l Com. Bank *v.* McDonnell, 9 S. Rep., 149 (Ala, 1891). The defendant cannot set up that he intended his subscription as a gift, where he received and retained the certificate. McDowall *v.* Sheehan, 13 N. Y. Supp, 386 (1891). It is no defense that the corporation had committed an *ultra vires* act in buying out another corporation; nor that other stockholders had not paid for their stock in full, such unpaid portion being insufficient to pay the debts, nor that no certificates of stock had been issued. Mitchell *v* Beckman, 28 Pac. Rep., 110 (1883). A corporation is not liable on a contract of its promoters to pay for drawings, plans, etc Hence, although by statute stockholders are personally

§ 226 *Priority among creditors* — When the creditor is entitled to an action at law against an individual shareholder for an enforcement of a statutory liability, in order to collect a claim against the corporation it has been held that the creditor first suing any shareholder is entitled to priority in enforcing his claim as against that particular shareholder   The diligent creditor is entitled to the payment of his claim, although other creditors are thereby deprived of payment [1] The right to a priority, however, in these cases, is in general one of questionable propriety, and the courts are not inclined to favor it [2] And one creditor may, at the instance of the rest, be restrained from the prosecution of his individual suit where it is in prejudice of the equal rights of all the others [3]

§§ 227–229 *Contribution among shareholders* — Upon general principles of equity, where a shareholder has been held liable, under the provisions of a statute, for a debt of the corporation of which he is a member, he may maintain an action against his co-shareholders for contribution [4] Where the stockholders' statutory lia-

---

liable on corporate contracts, if the corporation commences business before one-half of its capital is subscribed and twenty per cent is paid in, they are not liable on such a contract   Buffington *v* Bardon 50 N W Rep , 776 (Wis , 1891) Under the California statute it seems that a mere subscriber for stock is not liable where he did not fulfill the subscription   Bank of Yolo *v* Weaver, 31 Pac Rep., 160 (Cal , 1892)

[1] Cole *v* Butler, 43 Me , 401 (1857), holding, also, that the rights of a creditor who moves first cannot be affected by the fact that another creditor, pursuing a shorter remedy, obtains judgment before him , Ingalls *v* Cole 47 id , 530, 541 (1860), Jones *v* Wiltberger 42 Ga., 575 (1871), Robinson *v* Bank of Darien, 18 id , 65, 108 (1855), Thebus *v* Smiley, 110 Ill , 316 (1884)   Cf. Weeks *v* Love, 50 N Y , 568 (1872), Miers *v* Zanesville, etc , Turnpike Co , 13 Ohio, 197 (1812)   See, also, § 225 (b)

[2] Wright *v* McCormack, 17 Ohio St., 86, holding that, if part of the creditors institute an action to enforce the liability of all, no creditor can acquire priority or institute a separate suit on his own behalf, Smith *v* Huckabee, 53

Ala 191 (1875), Chicago *v* Hall, 103 Ill , 342 (1882), holding that if a suit at law by a creditor against a stockholder be enjoined by other creditors who seek to enforce the liability for the benefit of all the creditors and the stockholders discharge their liability, the creditor so enjoined has no prior lien upon the fund

[3] Eames *v* Doris, 102 Ill 350 (1882), Pfohl *v* Simpson, 74 N Y , 137 (1878)   Cf Garrison *v* Howe, 17 N Y , 458 (1858).

[4] Aspinwall *v* Sacchi, 57 N Y 331 (1874), Stewart *v* Lay, 45 Iowa, 604 (1877), Umsted *v* Buskirk 17 Ohio St., 113 (1866), Matthews *v* Albert, 24 Md , 527 (1866) Hadley *v* Russell 40 N H , 109 112 (1860), Erickson *v* Nesmith, 46 id 371 (1866) Gray *v* Coffin, 9 Cush 192 (1852) Middletown Bank *v* Magill, 5 Conn , 61 (1823) Bunham *v* Wellersburg Coal Co , 47 Pa St , 43 (1864), Masters *v* Rossie Lead Mining Co , 2 Sandf, Chan , 301 (1845) Farrow *v* Billings, 13 Rich Eq , 25, Clark *v* Myers, 11 Hun, 608 (1877), holding that the action cannot be against one only , O Reilly *v* Bard, 105 Pa St , 569 (1884), holding that a stockholder who pays a judgment

bility is enforced by a suit in equity, contribution is of course enforced, in that suit, so far as the parties can be found within the jurisdiction [1]

against the corporation is confined to the remedy provided in the act, and in this case could not maintain *assumpsit* for contribution against other stockholders who were not parties to the judgment. As to the Pennsylvania statutory method of obtaining contribution, see also, Bunham *v* Wellersburg, etc. Co, 47 Pa St, 43 (1864). Stockholders seeking to enforce contribution from co-stockholder in foreign corporation must show that he, the plaintiff, is legally liable Eastman *v* Crosby, 8 Allen, 206 See. also, Ladd *v* Cartwright, 7 Oreg, 329, Patterson *v* Lynde, 106 U S, 519 (1882) A shareholder, it is said being also a creditor of the corporation may make use of whatever advantage his position as shareholder gives him to secure the payment of his claim. even to the exclusion of other creditors who are not shareholders Whitwell *v* Warner, 20 Vt, 425, 444, Reichwald *v* Commercial Hotel Co, 106 Ill, 439, holding that the securing of a large debt to a stockholder for money advanced, by means of a deed of real property, with agreement that it should be considered security. was not fraudulent See, also, Bristol Milling, etc, Co. *v* Probasco, 64 Ind., 406, Terry *v* Bank of Cape Fear, 20 Fed Rep, 777. See, also, § 226, *supra*, to the effect that a

stockholder sued at law may enjoin the suit and bring all parties into a suit in equity. Officer paying statutory liability may have contribution Nickerson *v* Wheeler, 118 Mass, 295. *Cf* Ray *v* Powers, 134 Mass, 22, Hartman *v* Ins. Co of Valley of Va, 32 Gratt. 242 (1879), Chandler *v* Brown, 77 Ill, 334 (1875), Bronson *v* Wilmington, etc., Ins Co. 85 N C, 411 (1881), Perry *v* Turner 55 Mo, 418 (1874), Lindley on Partnership, pp 1223–1474. A stockholder and director who pays his liability under the California statute may have contribution from other stockholders Redington *v* Cornwell, 27 Pac. Rep, 40 (Cal, 1891)

[1] Harpold *v* Stobart, 21 N E. Rep., 637 (Ohio 1889). This case holds also that a stockholder in Ohio "is liable to creditors of the corporation for such portion only of the debts existing while he held the stock and remaining due (not in excess of the amount of stock assigned) as will be equal to the proportion which the capital stock assigned by him bears to the entire capital stock held by solvent stockholders, liable in respect to the same debts, who are within the jurisdiction, to be ascertained at the time judgment is rendered."

CHAPTER XIII.

LIABILITY OF STOCKHOLDERS WHERE THE SUPPOSED INCORPORA-TION DOES NOT PROTECT THEM AND FOR ASSESSMENTS BEYOND THE PAR VALUE OF THE STOCK.

§ 230 *Different liabilities of a stockholder on his stock* — A stockholder may be said to be liable on his stock in three different ways First, he is liable to the corporation and corporate creditors until the full par value of his stock has been paid [1] Second, he may have an additional liability imposed upon him by statute [2] Third, it may happen that by some accident, mistake or neglect the supposed corporation was never duly incorporated, or for some other reason the members become liable as partners in a copartnership, or it may be within the power of the corporation to assess the stockholder for sums over and above and in addition to the par value of the stock This third kind of liability is unusual in its character, and is the subject of this chapter.

§ 231 *Liability as partners by reason of material defects in becoming incorporated.*— The statutes under which incorporations are generally made provide that a corporation may be formed by taking certain steps, usually the making and filing with the state, and also with the local authorities, a certificate signed by the corporators, and containing a statement of the business, of the capital stock, and other facts material to the organization of the corporation.

Occasionally, however, it happens that this certificate is not fully made out, as required by the statute, or is not filed, or some other step prescribed by law is not complied with The corporation is then not duly incorporated, and the state, by *quo warranto*, may oust it from its user of corporate franchises But it is a very different and difficult question to determine whether a private individual may take advantage of such facts, and claim that the supposed corporation is not a corporation, but only a partnership

[1] See chs XI and III 　　　　　[2] See ch XII.

307

§ 232 *When the regularity of acts in becoming incorporated cannot be questioned by a private individual* — As already explained,[1] a subscriber for stock in a corporation cannot, when sued for calls on his stock, set up that the corporation was not duly incorporated He is estopped from so doing   Nor can a stockholder, who has funds of the corporation in his hands, defeat an action by the corporation therefor by setting up that the corporation was not duly incorporated[2]   And, in general, a party contracting to pay money to a corporation, or to transfer property to it as a corporation, cannot avoid the obligation of that contract by alleging the fact that the corporation was not duly incorporated, provided that such corporations were allowed by law[3]   Nor, on the other hand, can the corporation itself avoid its contracts on such grounds[4]

§ 233. *Corporate creditors cannot hold stockholders liable as partners by reason of irregularities, mistakes or omissions in the incorporation of a de facto corporation* — There are many cases to the effect that a corporate creditor seeking to enforce the payment of his debt may ignore the existence of the corporation, and may proceed against the supposed stockholders as partners, by proving that the prescribed method of becoming incorporated was not complied with by the company in question.   For instance, it has been held that where the articles of association were signed, but not filed until some time subsequently, debts contracted in the *interim* might be collected from the stockholders as partners[5]   So, also, a total failure to file or record the certificate or articles of incorporation has been held to render the members liable as partners,[6] as also an omission of the members to sign and publish the

[1] See §§ 183-186 , Buffalo & A R. R. Co v Cary, 26 N Y , 75.

[2] Kiutz v Paola Town Co , 20 Kan , 397 (1878)

[3] See 19 Am Dec , 67, notes , Lessee of Frost t Frostburg Coal Co , 24 How , 278 (1860) where the grantor of land to a corporation claimed that no title passed , Pope v Capital Bank, 20 Kan , 440 (1878), where the plaintiff corporation sued the defendant on a promissory note , Fay v Noble, 7 Cush , 188, where a third person was not allowed to impeach a transfer of property by a corporation to another person setting up that the transfer was invalid owing to informalities in the corporation   See ch XXXVIII.   Under the California Code, § 358, the regular incorporation of a *de*

facto corporation cannot be questioned in an action by it for damages for an injury to property   Golden etc , Co. v Joshua, etc , Works, 23 Pac. Rep., 45 (Cal , 1890).   Concerning the question of who can complain of mistakes, irregularities and illegalities in the corporation, see, also. ch. I, *supra*.

[4] Holbrook v St Paul Fire & M. Ins. Co , 25 Minn , 229 (1878)

[5] Bigelow v Gregory, 73 Ill , 197 (1874); McVicker v Coue, 28 Pac. Rep., 76 (Oreg , 1891)   See, also, Bergen v Porpoise F Co , 13 Am & Eng Corp. Cas, 1 (N J , 1886)   *Contra*, Whitney t. Hyman, 101 U S , 392 (1879).   *Cf.* 17 Atl Rep., 840 (Vt. 1889)

[6] Field v Cooks. 16 La Ann., 153 (1861), Abbott v Omaha Smelting Co.,

articles of association,[1] or an indefinite statement of where the principal place of business of the corporation is to be?[2] In Iowa and Nebraska the statutory law makes the stockholders liable if the incorporation was irregular[3]

4 Neb., 416 (1876), Garnett v Richardson, 35 Ark, 144 (1879), Ferris v Thaw, 72 Mo, 449 (1880), Coleman v Coleman, 78 Ind, 344 (1881), Martin v Fewell, 79 Mo, 401, 410 (1883) In the case of Hurt v Salisbury, 55 Mo, 310 (1874), corporate officers were held personally liable on a promissory note signed by them as officers, where the certificate of incorporation was not filed as required In Richardson v Pitts, 71 Mo 128 (1879), the same officers were held to be entitled to contribution from other members of the supposed corporation Cf Blanchard v Kaull, 44 Cal, 440 (1872), Western, etc, T Co v U P Ry, 3 Fed Rep, 721, 729 (1880) In Garnett v Richardson, 35 Ark, 144, the court held stockholders liable as partners until the certificate was filed with the secretary of state. Cf Harrod v Hamer, 32 Wis., 162 (1873), where the statute effected an incorporation without filing, but prohibited organization until after the articles were filed. The filing of the certificate in the county clerk's office, as required by statute, is essential to incorporation Childs v Hurd, 9 S E. Rep., 362 (W. Va., 1889). In Bigelow v. Gregory, 73 Ill, 197 (1874) the court held that there was no corporation until the certificate was filed, and that a creditor might recover from a stockholder as a partner In Indianapolis Min Co v Herkimer, 46 Ind, 142 (1874) the court held that there was no corporation until the certificate was filed, and that a subscriber to the articles who had agreed to pay the corporation his dues when it was organized could successfully resist its suit until the certificate was filed In State v Cent. O Mut R Ass'n, 29 Ohio St., 399, the court ousted an association whose notice of acceptance to the state was indefinite and ambiguous.

[1] Unity Ins Co v Cram, 43 N H, 636 (1862), Kaiser v Lawrence S Bank 56 Iowa 104 (1881), where the articles were not properly signed and acknowledged This case also disapproves the decision in Humphrey v Mooney, 1 Col, 282 (1880) In enforcing this partnership liability, the assumed corporation is not to be made a party defendant with the members thereof Smith v Colorado Fire Ins Co, 14 Fed Rep, 399 (1882)

[2] Harris v McGregor, 29 Cal 124 (1865) The fact that the party contracted with them under a corporate name is immaterial, since, at common law, parties may carry on business under any name they may choose Lauferty v Wheeler, 11 Abb N C 223, Lindley on Partn, 182 (Callaghan & Co, 1881) The case of Chaffe v Ludeling 27 La Ann, 607 (1875), well says "Obligors are bound not by the style which they give to themselves, but by the consequences which they incur by reason of their acts It matters not what they choose to call themselves" See also, Nat'l Bank, etc, v Landon, 45 N Y, 410, 414 (1871), Ridenour v Mayo, 40 Ohio St 9 (1883) Cf Wentz v, Lowe, 3 Atl Rep, 878 (Pa, 1886) An individual may enforce a contract which he makes for himself but in the name 'The National Associated Press James H Goodsell, President " Goodsell v Western etc, Tel Co, 130 N Y 430 (1892) Corporate creditors may attack the validity of the corporate organization Empire Mills v Alston, etc, Co, 15 S W Rep, 505 (Tex, 1891). Insufficient statement in the papers to be filed as to the property which is turned in for stock renders the stockholders liable as partners Van Horn v Corcoran, 18 Atl Rep, 16 (Pa 1889)

[3] In Clegg v. Hamilton Co., 61 Iowa,

§ 234 During the past few years, however, the great weight of authority has clearly established the rule that where a supposed corporation is doing business as a *de facto* corporation, the stockholders cannot be held liable as partners, although there have been irregularities, omissions or mistakes in incorporating or organizing the company. The corporation is a *de facto* corporation where there is a law authorizing such a corporation and where the company has made an effort to organize under that law and is transacting business in a corporate name.[1] This rule applies to claims based on tort the same as to those based on contract[2]

It must be admitted that this conclusion of the law is reasonable

121, the court held that publishing the articles, which did not contain all the requirements of the statutory notice, was insufficient, and stockholders were liable as partners In Iowa stockholders are liable as partners, by statute, if the incorporation is not regular Eisfield v Kenworth, 50 Iowa, 389 (1879) In First Nat Bank v Davies, 43 Iowa, 424 (1876), the court held that, where the state waived notice by permitting the filing to be made with its secretary within ninety days, vested rights accrued which would not be affected by failure to file within that time See, also, Jessup v Carnegie, 80 N Y, 441 (1880) Under the Iowa statutes the stockholders are liable as partners where the certificate of incorporation failed to state the highest amount of indebtedness which the company might incur. Heuer v Carmichael, 47 N W Rep., 1034 (Iowa, 1891) Although the articles are not recorded as required by statute, yet as between themselves the parties are stockholders and not partners. Heald v Owen, 44 N W Rep, 210 (Iowa, 1890) Under the Iowa statutes an insufficient incorporation of the plaintiff foreign corporation is not put in issue by a denial of a corporation The deficiency must be specifically alleged Warden, etc, Co v Jack, 48 N W Rep., 729 (Iowa, 1891) In an action against individual stockholders to charge their property with a judgment rendered against the corporation, the plaintiff is not estopped to allege defects in its or-

ganization by reason of having recognized the corporation in dealing with it and in bringing suit against it as such Heuer v Carmichael (Iowa), 47 N W. Rep., 1034, followed Stivers v Carmichael, 49 N W Rep, 984 (Iowa, 1891) Failure to complete the publication as required by statute does not render the stockholders liable under the Iowa statute to a creditor who entered into his contract before the time allowed for publication had expired Thornton v. Balcom *et al*, 52 N. W. Rep, 190 (Iowa, 1892) Although the statute requires the articles to state the amount of indebtedness which may be incurred, the articles may fix the amount with the right to the stockholders to increase it up to the statutory limit Thornton v Balcom *et al* 52 N. W Rep., 190 (Iowa, 1892) The fact that the whole capital stock is not subscribed is not a failure to comply with the law relative to organizations so as to render the stockholders liable as partners under the Iowa statute Sweney *et al* v Talcott *et al*, 52 N W Rep., 106 (Iowa, 1892). Although the statute renders stockholders liable as partners unless there has been a substantial compliance with the statute relative to organization, yet the courts are not inclined to enforce such liability Porter v Sherman, etc, Co., 54 N. W Rep, 424 (Neb, 1893).

[1] See cases in notes below, also § 185, note

[2] Demarest v Flack, 32 N Y St. Rep., 675, affirmed, 128 N. Y., 205

and just. There is no reason why parties who have dealt with a corporation as a corporation should afterwards be allowed to claim more than they originally bargained for and to hold the stockholders personally liable Such a rule would be disastrous in the extreme The dangers to business, the hardship to innocent parties and the disinclination to invest in corporate enterprises would be such, if stockholders were subject to this unknown peril, that the courts have gradually departed from the old decisions on this subject and have wisely refused to hold the stockholders liable Recent cases have so settled the law beyond reasonable controversy.[1]

[1] Whitney v Wyman, 101 U S, 392. The members of a supposed corporation are not liable individually on a loan of money made to it, even though it was irregularly incorporated Larned v Beal, 23 Atl Rep, 149 (N H, 1889) "Where there is a statute authorizing the creation of a corporation, an attempt to comply with the statute, and an actual exercise of corporate functions, the existence of the corporation can only be destroyed by a direct proceeding" Crowder v Town of Sullivan, 28 N E Rep, 94 (Ind, 1891) Where the articles were filed with the county clerk on November 9, 1886, and goods were purchased of plaintiff soon after, and the articles were not filed with the secretary of state until August 17, 1887 the plaintiff cannot ignore the corporation and hold the parties liable as partners The plaintiff made the contract supposing he was dealing with a corporation Vannemare v Young, 20 Atl Rep, 53 (N J, 1890) Under the Colorado statute requiring the certificate to set forth by whom the corporate affairs shall be conducted, a provision that they shall be conducted by the president, vice-president and attorney, instead of providing for directors, is insufficient The corporation is only de facto, but an incorporator and a vendor of property to it cannot question the incorporation Bates v Wilson, 24 Pac Rep, 99 (Colo, 1890) Though the provision in the Kentucky statutes requiring publication of the charter is not complied with, yet

the corporation is valid and complete, except that the state may proceed to annul the charter No other party can raise the objection Stutz v Handley, 41 Fed Rep. 531 (1890), Walton v Riley, 85 Ky, 413, 421, overruling Heinig v Manufacturing Co, 81 Ky, 300 Failure to file the articles with the secretary of state is not fatal Portland, etc Co v Bobb, 10 S W Rep, 794 (Ky, 1889) In proving incorporation it is not necessary to prove publication as required by statute Brown v Corbin, 42 N W Rep, 481 (Minn, 1889). Although there are less stockholders and less directors than the statute or charter require, yet the acts of these are sufficient to sustain obligations incurred by the corporation with third persons Welch v Importers', etc, Bank, 122 N Y 177 (1890) The grantor of land cannot claim that the grantee was unincorporated and not qualified to hold land the incorporation being only partially completed Reinhard v Virginia, etc, Co, 18 S W Rep, 17 (Mo, 1891) The failure to specify the term of existence is not fatal where the general act limits the time Albright v Lafayette, etc, Ass'n, 102 Pa. St, 411, 423 (1883), Becket v Uniontown, etc, Ass n, 88 id, 211 (1878)

In the case Seacord v. Pendleton, 55 Hun, 579 (1890), there was no pretense of any attempt to incorporate the bank and yet the stockholders were held not liable See S C, sub nom Merchants' Nat'l Bank v Pendleton, 9 N Y Supp, 46 In Christian v Bowman, 51 N. W. Rep,

The mere assumption of corporate powers, without any attempt at incorporation, cannot, of course, exempt the members from full liability as partners [1]

The corporation itself cannot set up the defense that it was irregularly incorporated,[2] nor can a foreign corporation.[3]

663 (Minn, 1892), where there was a failure to file the proper affidavit of publication, the directors were held personally liable for debts, but the court stated that if the case had been properly tried a different conclusion might have been reached One who takes part in organizing the company cannot hold its members liable as partners on the ground that it was irregularly organized, Allegheny Nat'l Bank v Bailey, 23 Atl Rep , 439 (Pa, 1892). Nor can one to whom he assigns a leasehold Egbert v Kimberly, id , 436 Where a creditor of a bank sues the stockholders as partners the burden of proof is on him to prove that no corporation existed, it being shown that the bank always acted as such and held itself out as such and was supposed so to be by the stockholders. Hallstead v Curtis, 22 Atl Rep , 977 (Pa , 1891) Although a majority of the incorporators assume to be residents, but are not and the charter is forfeited, yet stockholders who become such after incorporation and without knowledge of the fraud cannot be held liable as partners American Salt Co. v Heidenheimer, 15 S. W Rep, 1038 (Tex , 1891) A stockholder cannot sustain a bill in equity to have the de facto going corporation wound up as a partnership by proving that the articles were not filed in the office of the recorder of deeds for the county, nor by proof that his subscription was not in good faith   'The general rule is that one who deals with a corporation as existing de facto is estopped to deny that as against it it has been legally organized " Bushnell v Consolidated, etc ,

Co, 27 N E Rep, 596 (Ill , 1891) A failure to organize does not render the stockholders liable as partners, business having been carried on without organization after the filing of the papers. Cory v Lee, 8 S. Rep , 694 (Ala , 1891). The failure to insert in the certificate a provision as to the residences of the persons does not render the stockholders liable as partners The defendant in this case alleged that it was a corporation de facto and that plaintiff sold goods to and contracted with defendant as a corporation, knowing that it was doing business as such The contract was made with it in its corporate name and capacity Sniders, etc , Co. v. Troy, 8 S Rep, 658 (Ala 1890)

In Alabama the stockholders are not liable for the debts, merely because the articles of incorporation do not specify the instalments by which the unpaid capital stock shall be paid in Bolling v Le Grand, 6 S. Rep. 332 (Ala , 1889) Where a corporation has been authorized by a judge as provided by statute, but no certificate has been issued, the corporation is sufficiently formed to defeat the plea of nul tiel corporation. Sparks v Woodstock, etc , Co, 6 S. Rep, 195 (Ala , 1889). If proof is given by plaintiff that a copartnership existed and the defense is that it was a corporation, the defendant must prove that fact   Although the company had a president and secretary, this in itself does not raise a presumption of a corporation Clark v Jones, 6 S Rep, 362 (Ala , 1889) Failure to file the articles of association with the county clerk, as required by statute, does not render the

<hr>

[1] Pettis v Atkins, 60 Ill , 454 (1871); Fuller v. Rowe, 57 N Y , 23 (1874).
[2] See § 637, infra

[3] Liter v Ozokerite Min, Co, 27 Pac. Rep., 690 (Utah, 1891)

§ 235 *Extent of the liability by reason of deficient incorporation.*— The mere fact that an attempted incorporation has failed does not necessarily render all the participants therein liable absolutely for the debts of the concern   At the most, each is liable

stockholders liable as partners Granby, etc. Co *v* Richards, 8 S W Rep, 216 (Mo, 1888)   Where the certificate or articles are to be filed both with the state and the local authorities, a failure as to the former does not render the stockholders liable as partners, provided the articles or certificate are filed with the local authorities Mokelumne Hill Min. Co *v*. Woodbury, 14 Cal, 424 (1859), Rusbeck *v* Oesterricher, 4 Abb N C, 411 (1878), Cross *v* Pinckneyville Mill Co, 17 Ill 54. The creditor cannot sue the directors for damages for a fraudulent conspiracy herein, especially when he was informed that the corporation had been irregularly incorporated   Nelson *v* Luling, 62 N Y, 645 (1875) Stating place of business suffices for principal place of business   *In re* Spring, etc, Works, 17 Cal, 132 (1860)   That a failure to file the certificate with the secretary of state does not invalidate the corporation, see Tarbell *v* Page, 24 Ill, 46 (1860). See, also, to same effect, Planters', etc, Bank *v* Padgett, 69 Ga, 159 (1882), Humphreys *v* Mooney, 5 Col, 282 (1880), Gartside Coal Co. *v* Maxwell, 22 Fed Rep, 197 (1884), Merriman *v* Magivennis, 12 Heisk (Tenn), 494 (1873), Merchants', etc, Bank *v* Stone, 38 Mich, 779 (1878) Jessup *v* Carnegie, 80 N. Y, 441 (1880), applying an Iowa decision to an Iowa case, First Nat. Bank *v* Davies, 43 Iowa, 424 (1876). In Holmes *v* Gilliland, 41 Barb, 568, the court held that failure to give notice to the community by publication does not make the stockholders partners In the case of De Witt *v* Hastings, 69 N Y, 518 (1877), where no certificate was filed owing to an abandonment of the enterprise, it was held that a subsequent filing of it could not render liable one of the original promoters who took no part in the filing of the articles of associa-

tion, although his name was attached thereto. In People *v* Selfridge, 52 Cal, 331, an action was brought on the ground that the certificate filed did not show, as required, that a majority of the stockholders were present at the meeting to organize The defendant offered to prove that a majority were in fact present, but the court refused to receive the evidence and rendered judgment of ouster Such facts, however, are no defense to subscriptions See §§ 183-186, *supra,* and § 637, *infra* See, also, ch XLI, relative to foreign corporations And see ch XXXVIII, as to who can attack the legality of a *de facto* corporation

A failure to notify each member of the meeting to organize is immaterial McClinch *v* Sturgis, 72 Me 288 (1881) See, also, Judah *v* America, etc, Co, 4 Ind, 333 (1853), Russell *v* McLellan, 31 Mass, 63 (1833), Newcomb *v* Reed, 12 Allen, 362. A failure to give the statutory notice of the first meeting is immaterial where all but one stockholder was present and he afterwards ratified all that was done Babbitt *v* East, etc, Co (N J, 1876), Stew Dig, p. 208, § 13 The omission of an immaterial part of the acknowledgment by an incorporator, and the omission of a certificate of notaryship, do not render the incorporators liable as partners Stout *v* Zulick, 7 Atl Rep, 363 (N J, 1886) A failure to commence the principal business does not invalidate the incorporation Trowbridge *v* Scudder, 66 Mass, 83 (1853) Nor does an *ultra vires* act or fraud of the corporation have that effect Laugan *v* Iowa & Minn Con Co, 49 Iowa, 317 (1878), Second Nat'l Bank of Cin *v* Hall, 35 Ohio St, 158 (1878) Where, however, an incorporated society used all its funds to contest a debt, the court compelled the

only in case he would be liable if the original plan had been to form a partnership. If he was not a member when the debt was contracted he cannot be held liable on that particular debt.[1] One case goes still further, and holds that one who becomes a member subsequently to the attempted incorporation, but takes no part in the organization or management of the company, cannot be held liable for its debts.[2]

§ 236 *Liability as partners by reason of fact that corporations cannot be organized for the business involved.*— The general incorporating acts common to most of the states usually specify the particular kinds of business for the prosecution of which corporations may be formed thereunder. It follows that no business can be carried on by persons, as a corporation, under the incorporating act, unless that particular business is specified therein. Many decisions on what kinds of business are included in the words used in various statutes of the different states are given in the notes below.[3]

members to replace the money so used Adm'r of Bigelow v Cong. Society of M, 11 Vt., 283 (1839) In the case of Medill v Collier, 16 Ohio St. 599, 613 (1866), the court said ' When the entire business carried on by persons in the name of a corporation is such as the corporation is prohibited by law from doing, they cannot interpose the corporate privileges between them and the liabilities which the law imposes upon individuals in the transaction of similar business without the use of the corporate name ' Where the articles of incorporation are signed and filed, but no organization ever had, a part of the subscribers are not liable for debts contracted by another part in the corporate name Rutherford v Hill, 29 Pac. Rep, 546 (Oreg, 1892). Although the corporation is apparently abandoned and an agreement as to contributions is signed, yet the courts are inclined to hold that the business is still that of the corporation Rio Grande, etc, Co v Burns, 17 S W Rep, 1043 (Tex, 1891). Stockholders cannot be held liable as partners on the ground of illegal incorporation where there is a law authorizing incorporation for that purpose, and an attempt was made to organize thereunder, and there was *user.* Finnegan

v Knights, etc, Ass n, 53 N. W Rep, 1150 (Minn, 1893). Although the statutes require the directors to be residents of the state, nevertheless, even though the directors are non-residents, the incorporation is valid and the corporation is not dissolved, nor are the stockholders liable as partners Demarest v Flack, 128 N Y, 205 (1891). Statutory provisions as to notice of the first meeting are directory They need not be observed if the stockholders acquiesce. Braintree, etc, v Braintree, 16 N. E. Rep, 420 (Mass, 1881)

[1] Fuller v. Rowe, 57 N. Y., 23 (1874). See, also § 508, *infra* In a suit against stockholders as partners, the defendants may require the joinder of their associates. De Witt v Hastings, 69 N. Y, 518 (1877).

[2] Stafford Bank v Palmer, 47 Conn, 443 (1880). *Cf* Richardson v. Pitts, 71 Mo, 128 (1879)

[3] Thus, where a rifle club attempted incorporation under the statute allowing incorporation for " literary, scientific and charitable purposes," the members were held individually liable for damages to the widow of a man who was killed by a bear which the club was keeping Vredenburg v. Behan, 33 La. Ann, 627 (1881). See, also, Glen v.

If a general incorporating act is unconstitutional, all supposed corporations formed thereunder are merely partnerships and the members are liable as partners[1] If the business itself, for which

Breard, 35 La. Ann, 875 (1883) Many business purposes may be specified in one charter Bird v Daggett, 97 Mass. 494 (1867) A bank cannot incorporate under act for ' any species of trade or commerce " Bank of California v Collins, 7 Hun, 336 (1876) A purchaser of stock from one of the supposed stockholders cannot recover back the purchase price from all of such stockholders His remedy is other than this. Perry v. Hale, 10 N E. Rep, 174 (Mass, 1887) Several objects may be included in the same articles of incorporation West v Crawford, 21 Pac Rep, 1123 (Colo., 1889) An application for a charter for " the mining for and manufacturing of oil and gas " is too general and indefinite to be granted An application should express singleness of purpose, but two pursuits may be combined when kindred and cognate. Op Atty.-Gen, Re Newton Hamilton Oil and Gas Co, 10 Pa Co Ct. Rep., 452 Under the words "or other lawful business," in the general incorporating statute, a company may be organized to buy and sell real estate Brown v Corbin, 42 N W. Rep. 481 (Minn, 1889) Indefiniteness in the statement of the objects of incorporation is no defense Owenton, etc, Co v. Smith 13 S W Rep., 426 (Ky, 1890) A company may incorporate to buy, use and deal 'in real estate, livestock, bonds, securities, and other properties of all kinds, on its own account and for commission, in the United States and elsewhere," under the Texas statute authorizing incorporation for purposes of " mutual profit or benefit." National Bank i Texas, etc, Co., 12 S W Rep, 101 (Tex, 1889) A constitutional prohibition against the incorporation of any church does not prevent the incorporation of the ' General Assembly of the Presbyterian Church in the United States." Guthrie v. Guthrie's Executor.

10 S. E Rep, 327 (Va, 1889) A corporation for mining and trading cannot come under an act for mining Isle, etc, Co v Sec y of State 43 N W Rep, 14 (Mich, 1889). A medical college cannot be incorporated under an act to incorporate benevolent, charitable scientific and missionary societies People i Gunn, 96 N Y, 317 (1884) A mutual reliance society cannot be incorporated under an act for incorporating benevolent, charitable, scientific and missionary societies. People i Nelson, 46 N Y, 477 (1871) Where the general act authorizes incorporation for manufacturing gas "or " manufacturing electricity, a company may be organized for both of these purposes People v Rice, 33 N E Rep, 816 (N Y, 1893) Express business is an " industrial pursuit,' as used in the federal statute allowing incorporation in territories Wells, etc. Co i Northern Pac R'y Co, 23 Fed Rep, 469 (1884) A mercantile enterprise may be incorporated under an act authorizing incorporation for any "industrial or productive industry " Carver, etc, Co v Hulme, 19 Pac. Rep., 213 (Mont, 1888) An elevator company cannot incorporate under a manufacturing company act. Mohr i Minn. etc, Co 41 N W Rep., 1074 (Minn 1889). Printing and publishing a newspaper is not a manufacturing business Press, etc, Co i State Board, 16 Atl Rep 173 (N J, 1888). Under an act authorizing incorporations for "trade,' an incorporation for buying and selling land is sustained Finnegan i Knights, etc. Ass'n, 53 N W. Rep, 1150 (Minn, 1893)

[1] Kennedy v. McLellan, 43 N W. Rep, 638 (Mich., 1889) There may be a question as to the validity of the law itself allowing the incorporation. Williams v. Bank of Michigan, 7 Wend, 540 (1831), State of Michigan v. Howard, 1

a corporation is attempted, is illegal the charter is no protection[1]
Frequently certain kinds of business are not mentioned in the act
for the reason that it is not deemed wise public policy to allow a
limited liability in that class of business, such as construction companies for the building of railroads.[2] Accordingly, where the business for which incorporation is sought is not within the classes of
business mentioned in the act itself, the attempted incorporation is
void and the participants are liable as copartners.

§ 237 *Liability as partners by reason of the fact that the corporation is incorporated in one state, but does all its business in another
state* — By the comity of states the rule has become well established

Mich., 512 (1846), Chenango Bridge Co
v Paige, 83 N Y, 178, 190 (1880). As to
a corporation incorporated by a state,
as a state, before it was admitted to the
Union, see Mayers v Manhattan Bank,
20 Ohio, 283 (1851) *Contra*, Scott v
Detroit, etc, Society, 1 Doug Rep.
(Mich), 119 (1843)

[1] Notes given in the purchase of stock
in a corporation whose sole business is
to carry on an infringing telephone
business are without consideration and
void Clemshire v Boone, etc, Bank,
14 S. W. Rep, 901 (Ark, 1890) Where
a lottery scheme is organized under the
act authorizing the organization of
benevolent and charitable institutions,
a court of equity will enjoin the continuance of business and will wind it
up, the officers being guilty of illegal
conduct. Peltz v Supreme, etc, Union,
19 Atl Rep., 668 (N. J, 1890). The organization of a company to carry on
the lottery business in foreign countries
was held legal in Macuee v. Persian,
etc, Corp, 62 L T Rep., 894 (1890).
Cf. Le Warne v Meyer, 38 Fed Rep,
191 (1889) The secretary of state will
not be compelled to accept articles of
incorporation for bookmaking, i e,
gambling on races, even though the
statute legalizes and regulates race
tracks *In re* New York Booking Co,
N Y. L. J, April 29, 1892 The courts
will refuse a charter to a company
whose business is to be " to promote the
business of such retail dealers as become members thereof and to protect

them," etc., the interest being to combine the retail coal dealers Matter of
Richmond Retail Coal Co, 9 R'y &
Corp L J, 31 (Phila., 1890). Persons
incorporated for the purpose of doing
a grain gambling business have been
held jointly and severally liable for
money obtained from a customer The
corporate character does not protect
them McGrew v City Produce Exchange, 4 S W Rep, 38 (Tenn, 1887).

[2] See Part VII, *infra*, concerning the
statutes It has been held, however,
that, under the general act for the incorporation of companies for constructing and operating a railroad, a company for the construction alone of the
road may be incorporated. "That there
can be a railroad company which does
nothing but construct the road, and a
railroad company which does nothing
but operate the constructed road, cannot be doubted. It is not essential to
the idea of a railroad company that it
should both construct and operate a railway." First National Bank of Davenport
v. Davies, 43 Iowa, 424 (1876), followed in
Jessup i Carnegie, 80 N Y, 441 (1880);
Langan v Iowa & Minn. Construction
Co, 49 Iowa, 317 (1878). Where the
general incorporating act does not provide for the incorporation of railroad
or banking corporations under it, a
corporation organized under it to buy
and sell railroad stock and bonds and to
lease railroads and operate and aid
them is void Clarke v Central R. R.,
etc 50 Fed. Rep., 338 (1892).

that a corporation organized under the laws of a state may transact business beyond the borders of that state[1]

A broad and liberal view of the comity of states and the interests of business was taken by the New York court of appeals in the cases of Demarest v Flack,[2] and Merrick v Van Santvoord,[3] where the court refused to hold the stockholders liable as partners, although the companies were clearly organized for the purpose of doing all of their business outside of the state wherein they took out their charters. This rule of law has been laid down by the courts of Ohio also, and is established by the great weight of authority[4]

---

[1] "It is very true that a corporation can have no legal existence out of the boundaries of the sovereignty by which it is created . . . But although it must live and have its being in that state only, yet it does not by any means follow that its existence there will not be recognized in other places, and its residence in one state creates no insuperable objection to its power of contracting in another" Ch J Marshall, in Bank of Augusta v Earle, 13 Pet, 521 (1839)

[2] It is legal for citizens of New York to take out a charter in West Virginia, even though all the corporate business is to be transacted in New York The stockholders are not liable as partners Demarest v Flack, 128 N Y, 205 (1891) The court said (p 217) "It in any particular case it is thought by those interested in the matter that the business can be done in our own state and by our own citizens with greater facility under the form of a foreign corporation than under that of a domestic one, there is no public policy which forbids its transaction under such form" Affirming 11 N Y Supp, 83

[3] Merrick v. Van Santvoord, 34 N Y., 207 (1866), reversing Merrick v Brainerd, 38 Barb., 574, where, although a Connecticut corporation did all its corporate business and performed all its corporate acts in New York excepting the holding of elections, yet the court, in a well-considered and ably-written opinion, held that the corporation did not thereby lose its corporate char-

acter, and that its members were not liable as partners, saying ' We think the recognition, in our state, of the rights hitherto conceded in our courts to foreign corporations is neither injurious to our interests, repugnant to our policy nor opposed to the spirit of our legislation . . It would be neither provident nor just to inaugurate a rule which would unsettle the security of corporate property and rights, and exclude others from the enjoyment here of privileges which have always been accorded to us abroad   A corporation is an artificial being, and has no dwelling, either in its office, its warehouses, its depots or its ships. . . The grant of franchises without restriction is equivalent to a specific authority to exercise them wherever the company might find it convenient or profitable, whether within or without the limits of the state of Connecticut.'

[4] Although parties incorporated in Kentucky, by reason of the greater liberality of the Kentucky corporation statutes, and although the corporation does all its business in Ohio, nevertheless its corporate charter is recognized, and the stockholders are not liable as partners on a corporate note Second Nat'l Bank v. Lovell, 2 Cin Rep, 397 (1873), Second Nat'l Bank of Cin v Hall, 35 Ohio St, 158 (1878), the court holding it to be no fraud on the Ohio laws for a corporation organized under the laws of Kentucky to do all its business in Ohio, even though thereby the stockholders escape a personal liability. See, also,

§ 238. There are, however, decisions to the contrary. In Massachusetts it has been held that where a citizen of Massachusetts incorporates a company in New Hampshire, and states in the certificate of incorporation that the chief place of business is in a city in New Hampshire, and that he and his associates are jointly interested, the corporation is fraudulent and void — it being proved, in fact, that all the business was carried on in Massachusetts, and that the associates were "dummies," having one share of stock each.[1]

Danforth v Penny, 3 Metc, 564 (1842) A subscriber to stock in a West Virginia corporation doing all its business in Minnesota cannot set up that the company was not legally incorporated, and cannot set up that the plaintiff is not a corporation, he having participated in its incorporation Minn, etc, Co v. Denslow, 18 N W Rep, 771 (Minn, 1891) In Wright v Lee, 51 N W Rep, 706 (S. D, 1892), it appears that a Minnesota corporation did all its business in South Dakota The court held this to be legal See, also, 35 Kan, 242-244 Concerning the legality, purpose and effect of persons incorporating in one state with the intention of doing all of the corporate business in another state, see Cook on The Corporation Problem, pp 107-110 See, also, article in 25 Am Law Rev, 352, criticising the law as laid down above and another article in 35 Am Law Rev, commending the law as laid down above Bateman v Service L R, 6 App, 386 (1881), Stevens v Phœnix Ins. Co., 41 N Y, 149 (1869). A party contracting with a foreign corporation to pay it in oil from land assigned by it to him cannot defeat the suit of the corporation by alleging that it was incorporated in another state to do all its business in the state, and thereby was guilty of a fraud Newburg Petroleum Co v Weare, 27 Ohio St, 343 (1875). A corporation of one state "lawfully may, as they often actually do, remove their officers, agents, offices and effects into another sovereignty, and there exercise their functions and franchises" Pa Co. v Sloan, 1 Bradw (Ill), 364 (1878) A Connecticut corporation may hold land in New Hampshire, although it does little or no business in Connecticut. New Hampshire Land Co v. Tilton, 19 Fed Rep, 73 (1884). A corporation may sell its products in any state and collect notes given in payment Hall v Tanner, etc, Co, 8 S Rep, 348 (Ala, 1890). "Comity between the states authorizes a corporation to exercise its charter powers within another state, but it does not permit the exercise of a power where the policy of that state, distinctly marked by legislative enactments or constitutional provision, forbids it." In this case the consolidation of competing lines of railway was involved Clarke v Central R. R., etc, 50 Fed Rep, 338 (1892). A limited partnership formed under the laws of Spain will be recognized and upheld by our courts King v Sarria, 69 N Y, 24 (1877), where the court discusses the comity of states 21 S W Rep, 488

[1] Montgomery v Forbes, 19 N E. Rep, 342 (Mass, 1889) In this case the holder of a note signed in the corporate name, and given for goods sold, sued a stockholder for the price of the goods. The court sustained the suit and said "The apparent corporation was not a corporation. . The defendant's pretended associates were associates only in name, he alone was interested in the enterprise The articles of agreement were recorded in Nashua, N. H, and stated that the business was to be carried on there, but it was not in fact carried on there, and was not intended to be. This is not a case where a corporate charter has been granted, but the organization of the corporation under the charter has been defective. . . . The business was his personal business, which he transacted

In New Jersey, at an early day, it was held that a corporation could not become incorporated under the laws of New York for the purpose of carrying on all its corporate transactions in the state of New Jersey [1] The stockholders were decided to be merely partners   Likewise it was held that where a corporation was incorporated to do business in a certain city in the state, but actually does all its business in another city of that state. the incorporation is a fraud upon the law, and the company is the same as though unincorporated [2]

In these days, however, when New Jersey is the favorite resort for the class of corporations now under consideration. the laws of that state having been framed especially for the purpose of attracting them, it is not at all probable that the old decisions in that state on this subject would be adhered to

In Texas it has been held that its citizens are liable as partners where they incorporate in another state to carry on a mercantile business in Texas. the legislature having substantially forbidden incorporation for that purpose [3]

---

under that name"   Cf Saltmarsh v Spaulding, 17 N E Rep, 316 (Mass, 1888)

[1] The corporation "cannot be recognized by any court in New Jersey as a legally constituted corporation. nor be dealt with as such   If it can be, what need is there of any general or special law in our state?   Individuals desirous of carrying on any manufacturing business may go into the city of New York, organize under the general laws of that state, erect all their manufacturing establishments here, and under their assumed name transact their business not only free from all personal responsibility, but under cover of a corporation not amenable to our laws"   Hill v Beach. 12 N J Eq Rep, 31 (1858).

[2] The corporation was incorporated to do business in Trenton, but actually transacted all its business in Jersey City   The court said   "The doctrine that the organization cannot be inquired into collaterally has no application as the case stands, because the charter does not fit this company and was not intended for it.' Booth v Wonderly, 36 N J L, 250 (1873)   This doctrine was followed in a New York case in an in-

ferior court, the facts being that a New Jersey corporation had no office or place of business in New Jersey, and did no business there, but transacted its business in New York   "It was not an existing corporation within the meaning of the statute of New Jersey. under which it purports to have been incorporated   . . It was a fraud upon the laws of New Jersey. and cannot screen defendants and its organizers from personal responsibility as partners for contracts made in New York under the assumed name " Kruse v Dusenbury, 19 Weekly Dig (N Y Com Pl), 201 (1884)   This last case seems to have been decided without noticing Merrick v Van Santvoord, supra, and the case certainly is not the law of New York   Chief Justice Beasley, in Erie Railway Co v State. 31 N J L, 544, says "A statute (and by parity of reason we might add a decision by the court) that should abolish the rule of comity and should refuse a recognition of foreign corporations. would. it is conceived, have this effect and no more, i e, to convert corporations, as to that state, into a partnership of individuals "

[3] Stockholders are liable as partners in

319

In Canada, also, at an early day, the same rule seems to have been laid down [1]

§§ 239-240 There certainly is a limit beyond which the courts will not go   In order that such contracts may be upheld and the corporate character be sustained, it is necessary that both the state creating the corporation and the corporation so created shall have acted in good faith in conferring and taking the corporate privileges. Thus, where a corporation was incorporated by the legislature of Pennsylvania, and authorized to do business anywhere but in that state, the court of Kansas refused to recognize its corporate character.[2] The comity of states does not prevail to that extent

§ 241 *Assessments by the corporation in excess of the par value of the stock — Stockholders are not liable therefor* — It is a principle of law, coeval with the existence of corporations having a capital

Texas on business done in Texas where they organized a corporation in Iowa to do a mercantile business the laws of Texas not authorizing incorporation for that purpose Empire Mills z Alston, etc Co, 15 S W Rep, 200 (Tex, 1891) It appeared in this case, however, that the legislature had expressly declared the policy of the state by repealing a statute that authorized incorporation for mercantile purposes See S C, 15 S W Rep, 505, on rehearing The fact that the company is doing all its business in another state does not release the company from its obligation to issue certificates of stock to its stockholders Rio Grande, etc, Co z Burns, 17 S W Rep, 1013 (Tex, 1891)

[1] In Canada it is held that no state can validly authorize a body corporate to transact business out of its own territory Bank of Montreal r Bathune, 4 Up Can, Q B 311, Genesee Mutual Ins Co z Westman 8 id, 487, Union Rubber Co r Hibbard, 6 Up Can. C. P, 77 If carefully examined, these cases decide that a corporation formed to carry on a particular business in one country exceeds its powers if it carries on a similar business out of that country At the same time the judges who decided those cases based their judgments on supposed grounds of international law The first

case mentioned above held that a bank chartered in Lower Canada has no power to discount a note in Upper Canada and sue upon the same, but may recover for money had and received. In the case of Genesee, etc, Mut. Ins. Co r Westman, 8 Up. Can, Q B, 487 (1852), the court held that a New York corporation had no right or power to enter into any contract at all or transact any business in a corporate capacity in that province In the case of Reynolds z. Gallihei, etc, Co, 7 R. & G, 466 (Can., 1886) it appears that a Massachusetts corporation owned a mine in Nova Scotia The decision was concerning an attachment, and the legality of the company's acts was not questioned

[2] Land Grant R'y & Trust Co v Coffey County, 6 Kan, 245 (1870), the court saying "No rule of comity will allow one state to spawn corporations, and send them forth into other states to be nurtured and do business there, when said first-mentioned state will not allow them to do business within its own boundaries.' And see opinion of Attorney-General of Texas (1887), 2 R'y & Corp L. J, 433, to the effect that a Scotch corporation, authorized to purchase l nd anywhere excepting at home, cannot hold lands in Texas.

stock, that, unless the corporate charter or a constitutional statute provides otherwise, a stockholder, the full par value of whose stock has been paid in, is not liable and cannot be made to pay any sums in addition thereto [1] The mere legislative act of creating a corpo-

[1] Great Falls & C R. R Co v Copp, 38 N H , 124 (1859), State v Morristown Fire Ass'n, 3 Zab, 195 (1851), Morley v Thayer, 3 Fed Rep , 737 (1880), Chase v Lord, 77 N Y, 1 (1879), Slee v Bloom, 19 Johns , 453, 473 (1822) Shaw v Boylan, 16 Ind , 384 . Coffin v Rich, 45 Me , 511 (1858), Gray v Coffin 63 Mass , 192, 199 (1852), French v Teschmaker 24 Cal , 518, 540 , Inhabitants of Norton v Hodges, 100 Mass , 241 (1868) "The creation of the corporation necessarily destroys the common-law liability of the individual members for its debts ' People v Coleman, 133 N Y , 279 (1892) " After the full par value of the stock subscribed for has been paid, the common-law liability of the stockholders, both as respects the corporation and its creditors, is at an end ' Toner v Fulkerson 25 N E Rep , 218 (Ind 1890) "Liability of stockholders in a corporation is undoubtedly a creature of statute It does not exist at common law " Buenz v. Cook, 24 Pac Rep , 679 (Col , 1890). The chief stockholders cannot be held liable for the corporate debts on the theory of a "general understanding" that they would be responsible The corporation alone is liable Circulars. bill-heads, letters, etc , used in the business and containing the corporation's name are admissible to show that the business was conducted in corporate name and on the corporate responsibility Butte Hardware Co v Wallace 22 Atl Rep , 330 (Conn , 1890) Stockholders are not liable for services rendered to the company, even though they induce the party to render such services Davidson v Westchester etc , Co, 99 N Y , 558 (1885) Oliver v Liverpool & L. L. & F. Ins Co. 100 Mass , 531, 539 (1868), holding that, in order to prevent this limited liability, the English parliament expressly declared joint-stock com-

panies not to be incorporations , Myers v Irwin, 2 Serg & R . 371 (1816), the court saying "The personal responsibility of the stockholder is inconsistent with the nature of a body corporate." Liverpool Ins Co v Massachusetts, 10 Wall , 566, 576 (1879) New Eng Bank v Stockholders of N S Factory, 6 R I , 188 (1859) Walker v Lewis 49 Texas 123 (1878) Green v Beckman, 59 Cal , 545 (1881) Jones v Jarman, 34 Ark , 323 (1879) Windham Prov Inst v Sprague, 43 Vt 502 (1871). Woods v Hicks, 7 Lea (Tenn), 40 on the ground that the corporate creditor contracts not with the stockholders but with the corporation , Terry v Little, 101 U S , 216 (1879), the court saying , "The individual liability of stockholders in a corporation is always a creature of statute It does not exist at common law , ' Smith v. Huckabee, 53 Ala . 191 (1875) where the court said " Immunity from such liability is one of the inducements which has led to multiplication of private corporations, and caused them to supersede, to a great extent, in hazardous enterprises, or enterprises requiring large capital, partnerships ," Spence v Iowa Valley Construction Co 36 Iowa, 407 (1873), the court saying ' It is one of the distinguishing features of incorporation that the individual property of its members may be exempt from liability for corporate debts Therein consists the great superiority of a corporation over a partnership or an unincorporated joint-stock company ," Salt Lake City Nat. Bank v Hendrickson, 40 N J L Rep 52 (1878), Van Sandau v Moore, 1 Russ Ch , 392, 408 (1826), Atwood v Rhode I Agri Bank. 1 R. I., 376 (1850) the court saying , "At common law the stockholders in a corporation are not liable individually for the corporate debts The capital stock

ration produces by implication this limited liability of its members. For this reason the statutes regulating joint-stock companies are frequently careful to state that nothing therein contained shall give such companies the character of corporations.[1] The older text-books and the earlier reports did not emphasize or probably appreciate the vitality of this principle of law. Of such importance is it that it would seem to be the great and distinguishing characteristic of corporations, and not a subsidiary or unimportant one. It seems to have been assumed rather than established by direct adjudication[2] In the early turnpike company cases of New England a contrary rule appears to have been assumed, and the subscriber appear to have been open to assessments indefinitely, except that he might forfeit his stock.[3] Such companies, however, had no fixed par value of their stock At present the rule of non-liability at common law, beyond the par value of the stock, is established beyond question, and forms the chief inducement in the formation of the many corporations of the day.

§ 242. Attempts have been made in various ways to authorize the assessment of stockholders for amounts after the par value of their stock has been paid in. Such efforts have generally failed It cannot be done by a majority vote of the stockholders, nor of the directors, nor by a by-law[4] The liability is sometimes created

---

is the fund to which alone the creditors must resort, unless in cases of fraud" 5 N. Y. Supp, 192 (1889). The case of Atlantic De Laine Co. v Mason, 5 R. I., 463 (1858), holds that the payment of one invalid assessment is no waiver of the right to object to another Cf Field v Pierce, 102 Mass., 253 (1869). If the stockholders voluntarily contribute to the corporate treasury in order to make it a success, such gifts are not corporate debts and cannot be recovered back Bidwell v Pittsburgh, etc., R'y Co, 6 Atl Rep, 729 (Pa, 1887); Leavitt v Oxford, etc., Co., 3 Utah, 265 (1883) In England "the liability of a shareholder in a corporate body is determined by the conditions of incorporation. Without express provision, no member of a corporate body is individually liable for the corporate debt. A company may be registered under the Companies Act, 1862, with limited or unlimited liability According to the nature of such registration a share-

holder will be liable to contribute, respectively, the unpaid amount on his shares, or to the extent of the company's guaranty, or indefinitely" Cavanagh's Law of Money Securities (2d ed), 494, citing Lion, etc., Ins Co v Tucker, L. R, 12 Q B. D, 176, In re Norwich Ins. Society, L R, 13 Ch D, 693; In re City, etc, Bank, L. R, 4 App Cas, 337 550, 567, 581, 583, 598, 607, 615, 624, 632, City, etc, Bank v Houldsworth, L R, 5 App Cas, 317

[1] Oliver v Liverpool, etc, Ins. Co, supra, Laws of N. Y. 1854, ch. 245, § 3 And see ch XXIX.

[2] In the case of Carr v Iglehart, 3 Ohio St, 457 (1854), the court took counsel to task for questioning this principle of law. For an opinion that at common law the stockholders were liable for all corporate debts, see Harvard Law Review, Nov. 1888, p 160

[3] Middlesex Turnpike Co. v. Swan, 10 Mass, 384

[4] Flint v. Pierce, 54 Mass., 539 (1868);

by statute.[1] Where the state has reserved the power to alter, repeal or amend the charter, it may authorize the corporation to levy assessments on its stockholders, in addition to the subscription of their stock. The reasoning of this rule is clear. The limited liability is a part of the corporate privileges conferred. A right to repeal the franchises includes the right to repeal in part or altogether the franchise or privilege of limited liability. On such grounds, laws of this character, however harsh in their operation, are upheld as constitutional.[2]

Kennebec & Portland R. R. Co. v. Kendall, 31 Me., 470 (1850), Trustees of Free School v. Flint, 54 Mass., 539 (1847); Reid v. Eatonton Mfg. Co., 40 Ala., 98 (1869). In the first-mentioned case the defendant subscribed to such a by-law, among other by-laws, when he subscribed for stock. Placing the words "individual property of stockholders liable" on the face of corporate liabilities has no effect in itself. Stockholders are liable only as prescribed by law. Lowry v. Inman, 46 N. Y., 119 (1871). An agreement of a vendee of stock with the vendor to pay the corporate debts is not enforceable by corporate creditors. Free Schools v. Flint, 54 Mass., 543 (1847). But the agreement is enforceable if made directly with creditors. Maxwell's Case, L. R., 20 Eq., 585 (1874). By consent of the stockholders each share may be subject to further assessment, and, when this agreement is printed on the certificates, the purchaser is bound by it. Weeks v. Silver, etc., Co., 55 J. & S. (N. Y.), 1 (1887). The case, however, of Hume v. Winyah & W. Canal Co., Carolina Law Journal, 217, held, at an early day, that where a corporation, not professing to have any fixed capital, made a by-law by which each of the corporators was bound to contribute equally or ratably to all expenses incurred, the corporators were liable personally. See 21 S. W. Rep., 556.

[1] In California, under sections 331, 333, of the Civil Code, a corporation may assess its members to any extent "for the purpose of paying expenses,

conducting business or paying debts. Santa Cruz R. R. Co. v. Spreckles, 65 Cal., 193 (1884). In California all shares of stock are assessable even though they have once been fully paid. Green v. Abietine, etc., Co., 31 Pac. Rep., 100 (Cal., 1892). A better construction of such a statute prevails in Vermont. Under a charter provision that "if at any time the stock paid into said corporation shall be impaired by loss or otherwise, the directors shall forthwith repair the same by assessment," a receiver was not allowed to assess, since the provision is only to prevent a continuance of business with an impaired capital. Dewey v. St. Albans Trust Co., 59 Vt., 332 (1886). In Pennsylvania it is held that, though the corporation has power to assess beyond the par value of the stock, yet such power may be restricted by by-law. Price's Appeal, 106 Pa. St., 421 (1884). In Texas it is possible to form a corporation wherein assessments may be made on members ratably to any amount for corporate purposes. Guadalupe, etc., Ass'n v. West, 7 S. W. Rep., 817 (1888) — a stock-protecting corporation. In Idaho it is held that the statutory provisions rendering stockholders jointly and severally liable for debts authorizes the directors to levy assessments to pay for improvements already made. Sparks v. Lower, etc., Ditch Co., 29 Pac. Rep., 134 (Idaho, 1892).

[2] Gardner v. Hope Ins. Co., 9 R. I., 194 (1869), Meadow Dam Co. v. Gray, 30 Me., 547 (1849). See, also, §§ 290, 497, infra.

§ 243. *Miscellaneous cases of liability or non-liability.*— It has been held, on grounds of public policy, that although a corporation is advertised as having a capital stock of a fixed amount, the shareholders and directors are not liable personally, even though subscriptions have not been taken to that amount. They are not liable either for the untaken stock, or on the ground of false representations, since the capital stock is understood to represent what the corporation hopes to obtain in subscriptions.[1] An oral promise to

[1] First Nat'l Bank v Almy, 117 Mass., 476 (1875), Wakeman v. Dalley, 51 N. Y, 27, 30; Evans v Coventry, 25 L. J. (Ch), 489 (1856), Crease v Babcock, 51 Mass, 525, 557 (1846). *Contra*, Haslett v. Wotherspoon, Strob Eq (S C), 209, 229 (1847) In Illinois there is a statutory liability in a case like this. Stat. of Ill, ch 32, § 18 Where, upon incorporation, the capital stock is fixed at $25,000, and is subscribed, but no part thereof is paid in, and business is commenced, the participators are liable as partners under the Pennsylvania statute It is a fraud on the law Hill, etc, Co v Stetler, 13 Atl Rep, 306 (Pa, 1888) A corporation may commence business before any stock is subscribed unless the charter forbids. Johnson v. Kessler, 41 N W Rep, 57 (Iowa, 1888) Where, by the charter, a certain amount of the capital stock must be paid in before business is commenced, it is sufficient that that amount was paid in by a few stockholders paying their subscriptions in full Lander v Logan, 16 Atl Rep, 44 (Pa, 1889) See, also, § 186 Subscribers for stock are not liable for such part of the capital stock as has not been subscribed for by any one, no fraud being involved Sweeney et al v Talcott et al 52 N. W. Rep., 106 (Iowa, 1892). Stockholders are not liable as partners merely because the whole capital stock has not been subscribed. Thornton v Balcom et al, 52 N. W. Rep, 190 (Iowa, 1892) The directors are not liable for corporate debts merely because they commence business before the capital stock was subscribed. The incorpo-

ration was legal without it. National Bank v. Texas, etc., Co., 12 S. W. Rep., 101 (Tex, 1889). Where the directors commence business before ten per cent. of the capital is paid in as required by statute, the directors are personally liable as agents transacting business without authority from the principal Farmers', etc., Co v Floyd, 26 N E Rep., 110 (Ohio, 1890). Paying in half of subscriptions with a view to incorporation, and then abandonment of incorporation, does not render a subscriber liable as a partner Hudson v Spaulding, 6 N Y. Supp., 877 (1889). Where stockholders proceed to business before the minimum capital prescribed by statute is subscribed and before the requisite amount is subscribed, they are liable to corporate creditors for such minimum capital. The creditors may sue them and the corporation in the same action. Burns v Beck, 10 S E. Rep, 121 (Ga, 1889). Where the alleged directors of an athletic association enter into contracts in its name after the charter is acknowledged and filed with the secretary of state, but no capital stock is subscribed and no steps taken to complete the organization or comply with the law, the directors are personally liable on such contracts Walton v. Oliver, 30 Pac. Rep, 172 (Kan, 1892) In the case Consolidated, etc, Co v. Kansas, etc., Co., 45 Fed Rep., 7 (1891), the court said : "It is true, as contended by counsel, that the statute did not require that this increment of stock should be actually paid up Yet the public deals with such concerns on the faith of such capi-

pay corporate debts is void by the statute of frauds[1] Partners, by becoming incorporated, do not thereby cease to be partners as to all the debts of the former partnership[2] A stockholder is not liable as a partner by reason of misrepresentations that the corporation is solvent, though probably he would be liable in damages for false representations[3] Upon the dissolution of the corporation the liability of the stockholder ceases If the business is carried on thereafter by the agents, no liability therefor attaches to the former stockholders,[4] unless they expressly authorize it[5] Persons who purchase a railroad at an execution sale thereof cannot continue to run it in the name of the old railroad corporation, and thereby be protected from liability as partners[6] They do not succeed to its corporate character, although they purchase its property. In all cases, however, in which the members of an association might have been held liable as partners, the right of the creditor to enforce that liability is barred by his bringing suit and obtaining judgment against the supposed corporation[7]

Although there are less stockholders and less directors than the statute or charter requires, yet the acts of these are sufficient to sustain obligations incurred by the corporation with third persons[8]

Questions relative to the mode of organizing under a special charter are considered elsewhere[9] Stockholders sometimes guaranty the liabilities of the company This class of contracts is considered elsewhere[10] Where a corporation is a mere "dummy," the courts will sometimes ignore its existence and reach the stockholders and officers This class of cases also is considered else-

---

tal *in esse*, and it is that which chiefly gives it credit. It is to be imputed to these directors and stockholders that they pretended and claimed all along that the stock subscribed by them was paid up."

[1] Trustees of Free School *v* Flint, 54 Mass, 539 (1868).

[2] Broyles *v* McCoy, 5 Sneed (Tenn), 602 (1858) The case of Martin *v* Fewell, 79 Mo., 401, 412 (1883), holds also that, "for the debts incurred after they become a corporation, then liability will depend upon the fact of actual notice of their incorporation to the plaintiffs at the time such debts were incurred"

[3] Searight *t* Payne, 2 Tenn Ch, 175

[4] Central City Sav Bank *v* Walker, 66 N. Y., 424 (1876), aff'g 5 Hun 34 A con-

tract made by the officers after the charter has been forfeited does not bind the stockholders Wilson *t*. Terson, 12 Ind, 285 (1859)

[5] Nat'l Union Bank of Watertown *t* London, 45 N Y, 410 (1871)

[6] Chaffe *r* Ludeling, 27 La Ann, 607 (1875).

[7] Cresswell *r* Oberly, 17 Brad (Ill), 281 (1885), Pochelu *t* Kemper, 14 La Ann, 308 (1859) The partners herein cannot bring an action at law against each other Their remedy is in equity Crow *r* Green. 17 W N C, 409 (Pa., 1886) See, also, ch XXIX, on Joint-stock Companies

[8] Welch *r* Importers', etc, Bank, 122 N Y, 177 (1890)

[9] See ch XXXVI.

[10] See ch. IV.

where.[1] Where stockholders are sued on a corporate liability they need not plead the incorporation   They may merely deny liability.[2]

[1] See § 6.

[2] Where suit is brought against stockholders to hold them liable as partners they may deny liability and need not set up the affirmative defense that the corporation alone is liable   Demarest v. Flack, 128 N. Y., 205 (1891). In an action for damages the defense that the defendant is merely a stockholder in the party who really is liable should be set up by the general issue and not by a plea.   Dade Coal Co v. Haslett, 10 S. E Rep, 435 (Ga., 1889).

326

CHAPTER XIV.

LIABILITY OF PLEDGEES, TRUSTEES, EXECUTORS, AGENTS, ETC

§ 244 *The subject* — Where the apparent owner of shares is not the real owner, the registered title to the stock being in one person and the equitable or real ownership being in another, various intricate questions have arisen involving the matter of liability for unpaid subscriptions and liability under the statute. The cases present every variety of ownership and every phase of liability, including many instances of transfer for the purpose of avoiding liability. The principles and rules of law governing this branch of the subject are somewhat numerous and complicated, nevertheless they are comparatively well settled

§§ 245-246. *The liability of trustees and cestui que trust* — A trustee of stock who is recorded on the corporate books as a stockholder is, at common law, liable on such stock as though he were the absolute owner of the same. This is the rule even though he is recorded on the corporate books not as an absolute owner, but as a trustee of the stock [1] And the liability of the trustee is not limited by the amount of the trust property. [2] Each trustee is liable not merely for his proportion, but for the whole amount due upon the stock. [3]

[1] Chapman & Barker's Case, L. R. 3 Eq, 361 (1866), Davis v Essex, etc, Soc, 44 Conn, 582, Bugg's Case, 2 Dr & Sm, 952, Muir v City of Glasgow Bank, L R, 4 App Cas, 337 (1879) See also, Sales v. Bates, 6 E Rep, 703 (R I, 1886), Holt's Case, 1 Sim (N S), 389 (1851), Mitchell's Case, L R. 9 Eq, 363 (1870), King's Case, L. R. 6 Ch, 196 (1871); Grew v Breed, 10 Met, 569 (1846) Leifchild's Case, L. R., 1 Eq, 231 (1865), Hemming v Maddick, L R., 9 Eq, 175 (1870), *Ex parte* Oriental, etc, L. R., 3 Ch, 791 (1868), Ind's Case, L R., 7 Ch, 485 (1872) *Cf.* Saunders' Case, 2 De G, J & S, 101

[2] Hoare's Case, 2 John & H, 229 (1862)

[3] Cunningham v City of Glasgow, L. R., 4 App. Cas, 607 (1879).

The *cestui que trust* is not liable on the stock held by the trustees. The corporation cannot hold him liable, neither can the corporate creditors   The *cestui que trust* cannot be held either on the unpaid subscription or on the statutory liability of the stock   He is a stranger to the corporation and its creditors [1]

But here the exemption of the *cestui que trust* ceases. He does not entirely escape liability. His exemption from liability to the creditors of the trust does not protect him from liability to the trustee. He is bound to indemnify the trustee and to repay to him any debts which the latter may have paid in the administration of the trust.[2]   The indemnity which the trustee may claim from him

---

[1] Mitchell's Case, L R, 9 Eq, 363, *Ex parte* Bugg, 2 Drew & Sm, 452 (1865), Williams' Case, L. R., 1 Ch Div, 576; King's Case, L R., 6 Ch App, 196 (1871), Fenwick's Case, 1 De G & Sm, 557 (1849), Newry, etc, Co *v* Moss, 14 Beav 64   Frequently, however, the statutes of the state creating the corporation change these rules   In New York, by statute, trustees holding stock in railroad or manufacturing corporations are released from liability   Laws of 1892, ch 688, sec 54.   By the statutes of the United States a similar provision applies to national banks   R. S., § 5152   But this exemption does not protect the trustee unless the stock registered in his name is registered to him as "trustee"   Davis *v* Essex, etc, Soc, 44 Conn, 582 (1877).   A trustee is not liable on national bank stock, his trusteeship appearing on the books   Welles *v* Larrabee 36 Fed Rep., 866 (1888)   These statutes, however, apply, of course, only to stock issued by corporations which have been incorporated by the government which enacted the statute.

[2] Butler *v* Cumpston, L. R., 7 Eq, 16 (1868), James *v* May, L. R, 6 H of L., 328 (1873), *Re* National Financial Co, L. R., 3 Ch, 791 (1868). Perry on Trusts, §§ 485, 486   In the case of Jervis *v* Wolferston, L. R., 18 Eq, 16 (1874), the court said, in enforcing indemnity to the trustees of stock   "I take it to be a general rule that where persons accept a trust at the request of another, and that other is a *cestui que trust*, he is personally liable to indemnify the trustees for any loss accruing in the due execution of the trust, and under that doctrine I shall hold that the estate of the testator becomes liable to indemnify the trustees against the payment of this large sum of money" Hemming *v* Maddick, L R., 7 Ch App, 395 (1872) where the court held also that the trustee might authorize the corporation to use the trustee's name and collect from the *cestui que trust*   In Hughes *v* India, etc, Co, L R, 22 Ch D, 561 (1882), it is held that the trustees cannot sue for indemnity before the corporation has demanded payment.   See, also, Phene *v* Gildan, 5 Hare, 11 (1845), where a mortgagor of stock was held liable to indemnify the mortgagee, who had been held liable on the stock.   The court said the mortgagor was liable the same as a 'trustee of leasehold property under covenants for the benefit of a *cestui que trust*"   In Balsh *v* Hyham, 2 P. Williams, 453 (1728), the lord chancellor said that "it is a rule that the *cestui que trust* ought to save the trustee harmless as to all damages relating to the trust," and consequently that the *cestui que trust* must repay to the trustee money borrowed by the latter and given to the *cestui que trust*, the trust consisting of stock which was pledged to secure the loan   Approved in *Ex parte* Chippendale, 4 De G, M. & G, 19, 54 (1854). Lindley on Partnership, pp. 758, 759, says 'The right of a trustee to indemnity .

cannot be denied on the ground that the trustee is irresponsible, and consequently that the corporation cannot get anything from him.[1] But until the trustee is actually called on by the corporation to pay, he cannot compel the *cestui que trust* to give indemnity[2]

This liability, however, of the *cestui que trust* may be avoided If the trustees are willing to provide in the trust instrument that the *cestui que trust* shall not be liable, such a provision is legal and effectual The *cestui que trust* then escapes liability absolutely and completely[3]

§ 247. *The liability of a pledgee of shares* — A pledgee of stock, that is, one to whom the stock has been transferred in pledge or as collateral security, and who has had the stock transferred into his own name on the corporate books, is liable to the creditors of the corporation as though he were the absolute owner of the stock[4]

from his *cestui que trust* very closely resembles the right of an agent to indemnity from his principal . . A trustee is clearly entitled to be indemnified out of the trust property against all costs, charges and expenses properly incurred, and against all losses sustained by him in the execution of his trust, and if the trust property is not sufficient for the purpose of indemnifying him in respect of such matters, his *cestui que trust*, if under no disability, is personally liable to indemnify him unless such liability is excluded by some special circumstance. . . If there is an express covenant to indemnify, the obligation will be limited by the covenant."

[1] *In re* National Financial Co., L. R., 3 Ch, 791 (1868), Cruse *v* Paine, L. R., 6 Eq, 641 (1868)

[2] Hughes-Hallett *v* Indian, etc., Co, L. R., 22 Ch D, 561 (1882)

[3] Thus, *Ex parte* Chippendale, 4 De G., M & G, 19, 52 (1854)   The court says, in a *dictum* "No doubt a company's deed, or any other deed, may be so formed as to deprive directors or trustees of the right to indemnity, and, if parties think proper to accept directorships or trusts under deeds so framed, they must abide by the consequences See, also, Gillan *v* Morrison, 1 De G & Sm, 421 (1847), holding that an express agreement that the *cestui que trust* shall be

liable to the trustee to a certain extent and no more is binding on the trustee

[4] Nat'l Com Bank *v* McDonnell, 9 S. Rep., 149 (Ala, 1891). Moore *v* Jones, 3 Woods, 53 (1877), Pullman *v* Upton. 96 U S, 328 (1877), Aultman's Appeal, 98 Pa St, 505 (1881), Crease *v* Babcock, 51 Mass, 525 (1846), Holyoke Bank *v* Burnham, 65 Mass, 183 (1853), Sleeper *v* Goodwin, 31 N W. Rep, 335 (Wis 1887), Roosevelt *v* Brown, 11 N Y, 148 (1854), Matter of The Empire Bank. 18 id, 199 (1858), Grew *v* Breed, 10 Metc, 569 (1846), Royal Bank of India's Case, L. R, 7 Eq, 91 (1868), *S. C, L. R., 4 Chan, 252 (1869), Weikersheim's Case, L. R, 8 Chan, 831 (1873), Price & Brown's Case, 3 De G & Sm, 146 (1850), in which the holders of shares taken as security, who had new shares issued in their own names in exchange for the old shares which had been called in were declared to be contributories, though the directors knew the nature of their holding, Richardson *v* Abendroth 43 Barb, 162 (1864)   And the pledgee is liable upon the stock even after his debt has been paid and the certificate handed back to the pledgor, if the retransfer is not properly entered on the corporate books   Bowdell *v* The Farmers' & Merchants National Bank of Baltimore, 25 Nat Bank Reg, 405 (1877), Johnson *v* Somerville Dyeing,

This rule has frequently been enforced in the case of a pledge of shares of stock in a national bank.[1] If, however, the stock has been recorded on the corporate books, not in the name of the pledgee, but in the name of a "dummy," the pledgee is not liable thereon.[2] A statute frequently relieves the pledgee[3]

etc., Co., 15 Gray, 216 (1860), Adderly v. Storm, 6 Hill, 624 (1844).

[1] Magruder v Colston, 44 Md, 349 (1875); Wheelock v. Kost, 77 Ill., 296 (1875), Hale v. Walker, 31 Iowa, 344 (1871), Barre National Bank v Hingham Manuf'g Co, 127 Mass, 563 (1879); National Bank v Case, 99 U S, 628 (1878)

[2] Heukle v Salem Mfg Co, 39 Ohio St, 547 (1883), Welles v Larrabee. 36 Fed Rep, 866 (1888) In the case of Anderson, Receiver, v. Philadelphia Warehouse Co, 111 U S, 479 (1883), it is held that a pledgee of shares of stock in a national bank, who takes the security for his benefit in the name of an irresponsible person, as trustee, for the avowed purpose of avoiding individual liability as a share-owner, incurs no liability which can be enforced by creditors of the bank in case of its failure To same effect Newry, etc., R'y Co v Moss, 14 Beav 64 (1851), § 470, infra A transfer of shares by one who holds them as collateral security, for the purpose of avoiding liability thereon, is not a conversion Hiatt v Griswold, 5 Fed. Rep., 573 (1881) Cf § 253.

[3] New York Laws of 1892, ch 688, § 54, also Part VII, infra See McMahon v Macy, 51 N Y, 155 (1872). A similar provision is found in the old New York Manufacturing Companies Act of 1818 (New York Laws of 1848, ch. 40, § 16) See Stover v Flack, 30 N Y, 64 (1864), S. C, 41 Barb., 162 Cf Case of the Reciprocity Bank, 22 N Y., 9, 17 (1860) And a similar provision has been enacted in Maryland Matthews v Albert, 24 Md, 527 (1866). Addison's Case, L R., 5 Chan 294 (1870). In Burgess v. Seligman 107 U S, 20 (1882), the supreme court of the United States construed the Missouri statute, and held.

that the pledgees were not liable to corporate creditors upon the shares so held by them, and such also is the rule now in Missouri Union Sav Ass'n v Seligman, 92 Mo, 635 (1884), overruling Griswold v Seligman, sub So, also, a pledgee of the corporation itself has been held not liable, especially where the statutes declared pledgees not liable and the creditor suing became such before the pledgee voted the stock held by him. Union Sav Assoc. v Seligman, 15 S. W. Rep., 630 (Mo, 1891), reversing 11 Mo App, 142, overruling Griswold v. Seligman, 72 Mo, 116, and following Burgess v. Seligman, 107 U S, 20 See, also Melvin v Lamar Ins Co., 80 Ill 446 (1875), §§ 138, 465. In England, Chapman's, etc, Case, L R., 3 Eq, 365, Re Anglesea Colliery Co, L R, 2 Eq, 379. Inds' Case, L R., 7 Ch, 485, were under the Companies Act. In the case Re City Terminus Hotel Co., L R, 14 Eq, 10 (1872), a hotel company borrowed £40,000 of a railroad company and gave its unissued shares as security, they being placed in the hands of a trustee, with power to sell, and thus reduce the debt. Afterwards the railway company bought the hotel, and the latter was wound up. Held, that the railway company were not stockholders, but creditors, and were entitled to deduct the amount of the loan from the purchase-money See, also, Manchester, etc, Case, 22 Week Rep., 41 (1875). Nellis v Coleman, 98 Pa St., 465 (1881), where the corporation received subscriptions as a loan, to be repaid It was held to be valid In a late Massachusetts case it is said that the pledgee is liable on the stock as owner only when the certificate fails to show that the shares are held merely as collateral Barre National Bank v Hingham Manuf'g Co, 127 Mass, 563 (1879);

A pledgee of stock who holds the certificates, but who does not appear on the corporate books as a stockholder, is not liable as a stockholder.[1]

§ 248 *The liability of an executor or administrator* — The estate of a deceased person is liable upon the stock held and owned by the decedent in the same way and to the same extent that the shareholder was liable in his life-time. Accordingly, an executor or administrator of the estate of a deceased shareholder is chargeable upon the shares of the decedent to the extent of the property that comes into his hands as the personal representative of the deceased[2] The executor or administrator becomes personally liable, however, upon the stock, if he pay away the assets of the estate in legacies without making provision to meet the liability on the stock.[3] When

S. P., Davis *v* Essex Baptist Society, 44 Conn., 582 (1877)

[1] Prouty *v* Prouty, etc , Co., 25 Atl Rep, 1001 (Pa, 1893) An unrecorded pledgee is, of course, not liable on statutory liability Henkle *v* Salem, etc, Co, 39 Ohio St, 547 (1883) See, also, § 258, *infra*

[2] Thomas' Case, 1 De G & Sm., 579 (1849), Baird's Case, L R, 5 Chan , 725 (1870), holding that the presumption is that executors of a deceased shareholder succeed to his full liability, Stewart's Trustee *v.* Evans, 9 Scotch Ct of Ses Cas (3d series), 810 (1871), Evans *v* Coventry, 25 L J , Chan , 489 (1856), holding the executor liable only to the extent of the estate funds To same effect, Blakeley's Case, 13 Beav , 133 (1850), *Ex parte* Gouthwaite, 3 Mac & G , 187 (1851), *Ex parte* Doyle, 2 Hall & Twell's (Eng Chan), 221 (1850); *Ex parte* Hall, 1 Mac & G., 307 (1849); Hamer's Devisee's Case, 2 De G, M & G , 366 (1852), Robinson's Executor's Case, 6 id , 572 (1856), Ness *v.* Armstrong, 3 De G & Sm , 38, note (1849); Straffars' Case, 1 De G , M & G , 576 , Bulmer's Case, 33 Beav , 435, Gouthwaite's Case, 3 De G & Sm , 258 (1850), Taylor *v* Taylor, L R , 10 Eq , 477 (1870), Alexander's Case, 15 Sol Jour , 788 (1871), Hamer's Case, 3 De G & Sm , 270 (1850); Grew *v* Breed, 10 Metc., 569 (1846), New England Commercial Bank *v* Stockholders of the Newport Steam Factory, 6 R I , 154

(1859), Crandall *v* Lincoln, 52 Conn , 73 (1884), Bailey *v* Hollister, 26 N Y , 112 (1862), Chase *v* Lord, 77 id , 1 (1879), Witters *v* Sowles, 25 Fed Rep., 168 (1885), S C , 32 id , 130 (1887), relative to the liability of an executor under the federal statute governing national banks, also Davis *v* Weed (U S D C), 44 Conn , 569, Schouler on Executors, § 380 , New York Laws of 1850, ch 110, § 11 , 1848, ch 40, § 13. An administrator is not liable on national bank stock even though he is the residuary distributee of the estate Matter of Bingham, 127 N Y , 296 (1891). Some of the earlier Massachusetts cases are in apparent conflict with the rule declared in the text Child *v* Coffin, 17 Mass , 64 (1820), Gray *v* Coffin, 9 Cush , 200 , Ripley *v* Sampson, 10 Pick 371 (1830); Andrews *v* Callender, 13 id , 484 (1836), Dane *v* Dane Manuf'g Co , 14 Gray, 489 (1860), Grew *v* Breed, 10 Metc 569 (1846) See, also *Re* Cheshire Banking Co , 54 L T Rep , 558 (1886).

[3] Taylor *v* Taylor, L. R., 10 Eq , 477 (1870), Jefferys *v* Jefferys, 24 L T Rep (N S). 177 (1871), Thomas' Case, *supra* In Stewart's Trustees *v* Evans, 9 Scotch Ct. Ses Cas (3d series), 810 (1871), it is held that, where executors pay away the estate *bona fide*, they are not, after a lapse of sixteen years, liable personally for a deficit on shares *Cf* Witters *v* Sowles, 25 Fed. Rep., 168 (1885)

the executors accept a transfer in their own names they make themselves personally liable on the stock [1] An executor who takes new shares for the estate is personally liable thereon.[2]

§ 249. *The liability of principal and agent on stock standing in the agent's name.*—Sometimes a subscription for stock is made by one person as the agent of another, and the stock is entered on the corporate books in the name of the agent. In such a case it is the rule that corporate creditors may hold either the principal or the agent responsible on the stock [3] But an agent who is compelled to assume and pay charges on the stock may recover from

[1] Alexander's Case, 15 Sol Jour, 788 (1871). In New York it is held that an action to charge an executor on the stock of the estate need not be joined with an action to enforce an individual subscription by the executor Erie, etc, R y Co. v Patrick, 2 Keyes, 256 (1865) A special statute of limitations applicable to executors will apply to an executor's liability on stock Sales v Bates, 6 East. Rep, 703 (R. I, 1886) In England an executor is liable personally on stock, if he transfers it to himself, otherwise not, the title to the stock being left in the name of the testator Healey s Company Law and Practice, p 90, Buchan's Case, L R, 4 App Cas, 549 (1879).

[2] Fearnside & Dean's Case, L R, 1 Chan, 231 (1866); Spence's Case, 17 Beav, 203 (1853), Jackson v Turquand, L. R, 4 H L, 305 (1866); Mallorie's Case, L R, 2 Chan, 181 (1867). Cf. Russell's Executor s Case, 15 Sol Jour, 790 (1871)

[3] Burr v Wilcox, 22 N Y, 551 (1860). See, also, §§ 68. 69, and § 253, infra. Cf Grangers' Market Co. v Vinson, 6 Oregon, 172 (1876), Barrett's Case, 4 De G, J & S, 416 (1864), where one who allowed another to use his name in registering stock as a favor, and under agreement that he should incur no liability, was held to be a contributory A broker who has the stock transferred into his own name is liable as though he were the full owner M'Kim v Glenn, 8 Atl Rep, 130 (Md, 1887). An unregistered transfer to one as agent to

sell does not render him liable for the unpaid subscription. Powell v. Willamette, etc, R. R. Co., 15 Pac Rep., 663 (Oreg, 1887) Mann v Currie, 2 Barb. 294 (1848), where one who held stock in his own name, but really as an agent or broker for its sale, was held to be a stockholder at the suit of creditors One to whom stock is issued, and in whose name it appears on the books of the corporation, is liable to the creditors of the corporation for the unpaid subscription, although he is not the owner of such stock Baines v Babcock et al, 27 Pac Rep., 674 (Cal, 1891) One who subscribes to corporate stock for his wife, in the wife's name, is not liable on the subscription, because a married woman cannot make such a subscription, but if the subscription is for himself, although in the wife's name, it is otherwise. The fact that the husband took part of the stock in his own name and participated in the business of the company tends to show that the subscription was for his benefit Shields v. Casey, 25 Atl Rep., 619 (Pa, 1893). Where a party subscribes for stock in the name of his son, even without the consent or knowledge of the son, the party so subscribing is not liable himself thereon Re Britannia, etc., Ass'n, Limited, 64 L T Rep, 184 (1890), reversing 63 L T Rep, 480 Where the husband subscribes for stock in his wife's name and she is incompetent to respond, he is liable on the stock Nat'l Com'l Bank v. McDonnell, 9 S Rep, 149 (Ala, 1891).

his principal the amount so paid [1] Where a transfer is made, not to the principal himself, but to an agent, the latter is but a nominal holder, and is subject to the rules applicable to such.

The transferee of an agent, when suit is brought by corporate creditors to enforce a demand against the stock, cannot set up that the agent had no power to transfer the stock to him. If he has received the certificates and appears as a stockholder on the books of the corporation, he is, as between himself and creditors of the corporation, a shareholder [2]

It is a serious question whether so-called "dummies"—that is, persons holding in their own names stock which belongs to others, in order to enable the latter to avoid liability thereon — are not to be regarded as agents rather than trustees. This question, however, is considered elsewhere [3]

§ 250. *Liability where stock is subscribed for or held by or in the names of infants and married women* — It has already been shown that an infant cannot be held liable upon a subscription to stock,[4] and any person subscribing for shares in the name of an infant renders himself personally liable thereon. So, likewise, when shares are assigned or transferred to infants as a contrivance to escape liability, the transferrer remains liable [5] And this is the rule as to an infant transferee, although the transfer was *bona fide*, and even in ignorance of the infancy of the transferee.[6] The infant may, however, upon attaining his majority, ratify or acquiesce in a trans-

---

[1] Orr v. Bigelow, 14 N. Y., 556 (1856); affirming S. C, 20 Barb, 21 (1851), Stover v Flack, 30 id , 64 (1864).

[2] Wakefield v Fargo, 90 N Y , 213 (1882). Upon the liability of agents or trustees in these cases, see Crandall v. Lincoln, 52 Conn , 73 (1884).

[3] See § 253, *infra.*

[4] See §§ 67 318

[5] Capper's Case, L R , 3 Chan., 458 (1868), Mann's Case, id., 459, note (1867); Weston's Case, L. R., 5 Chan , 614 (1870); Richardson's Case, L R , 19 Eq., 588 (1875), Roman v Fry, 5 J J. Marsh , 634 (1831), Castleman v Holmes, 4 id , 1 (1830). But see Parson's Case, L R , 8 Eq , 656, where the action of the company in continuing an infant's name, and not notifying his vendor of his infancy, was held to be such laches as to estop the official liquidator from substituting the vendor's name for that of the infant. Curtis' Case, L R , 6 Eq , 455

(1868); Reid's Case, 24 Beav., 318 (1857), and see cases in the succeeding notes herein.

[6] Weston's Case, L R , 5 Chan , 614 (1870) Thus, a broker purchasing shares for the account of an infant was held liable as holder of the stock, not even his broker s agency availing to protect him Ruchisky v De Haven, 97 Pa St. 202 (1881), Mann's Case, *supra* In Nickalls v Merry, L. R., 7 H L, 530 (1875), a stock jobber was held liable where, in a suit to recover calls on stock sold by him for the Stock Exchange, it turned out that the ultimate transferee of the shares was a minor, and his transferrer had, in consequence, been compelled to pay the calls If three persons buy fifteen shares and take title in an infant's name, each is liable on five shares and no more Brown v. Black, 29 L. T. Rep , 363 (1873).

fer of shares to him during his infancy, and thereby render himself liable on the stock[1] The plea of infancy in these cases must, however, allege repudiation within a reasonable time after attaining majority.[2]

What is a reasonable time within which the infant must repudiate the contract in order to escape chargeability is, in general, a question of law, and it will vary with the particular circumstances of each individual case In general it is the rule that the transferee, on coming of age, must disaffirm promptly. Laches will bar his right to repudiate[3]

---

[1] Lumsden's Case, L. R. 4 Chan, 31 (1868), where an infant held stock for six months Accordingly, where an infant, after becoming of age, permits his name to remain on the registry as a shareholder, he is held to have ratified the antecedent transfer to him during his minority Cork, etc, R'y Co v Cazenove, 10 Q B, 935 (1817) An infant may be an incorporator at least until he repudiates the transaction All rights acquired prior to such repudiation are protected Re W Laxon & Co., 67 L T Rep., 85 (1892).

[2] Dublin, etc, R'y Co. v Black, 8 Exch, 181 (1852). Cf Birkenhead, etc., R'y Co v Pilcher, 5 Exch, 24 (1850). Where an infant transferee became of age ten months before the winding up, he was held liable as a contributory by acquiescence Ebbett's Case, L. R., 5 Chan, 302 (1870), S C, 18 W R, 202 (1869). But in a case where the winding up came just before an infant transferee became of age, it was held that no affirmative repudiation was necessary, but that some distinct act of affirmation alone would avail to render him liable after majority Wilson's Case, L. R., 8 Eq, 240 (1869). Where the winding up occurs just before or just after the infant transferee becomes of age, it is said that he need not expressly repudiate in order to escape liability, "because he cannot tell whether the company intends to enforce their claim against him, and, therefore, he is not bound till some steps are taken to resist his being a shareholder in the company" Mitchell's

Case, L. R., 9 Eq, 363 (1870). It seems, also, that a repudiation during infancy may, under certain circumstances, avail to discharge an infant shareholder from liability to pay calls which are made after he attained the age of twenty-one years Newry & Enniskillen R'y Co. v. Coombe, 3 Exch, 565, 578 (1849) The court, in speaking to this point, said· "He became a shareholder by contract during infancy, and during infancy he disaffirmed the contract, therefore, in my opinion, he ceased to be a shareholder liable to be sued for calls. Where the infant transferee, coming of age after the winding up had been commenced, offered to affirm the contract, it was held that the liquidators might, in the interest of the creditors, refuse to accept the offer, and might instead hold the transferrer liable Symon's Case, L. R., 5 Chan, 298 (1870); Costello's Case, L. R., 8 Eq, 504.

[3] In one English case we find it held that two years' delay after coming of age is a ratification of the contract. Mitchell's Case, L R, 9 Eq, 363 (1870). And in another case ten months is held sufficient Ebbett's Case, L. R., 5 Chan, 302 (1870). While in a third case a lapse of three years was held not to amount to an affirmance of the contract. Hart's Case, L R. 6 Eq 512 (1868). In this case the infant shareholder came of age six months after the proceedings to wind up the company had been commenced He was served with notice of these proceedings shortly before his majority. Two years after, a list of share-

No general rule can be laid down as regards the effect of a transfer of stock to a married woman   By the law of most of the states she may contract as a *feme sole* in respect to her separate estate, and doubtless may become a transferee of stock [1]   In such cases

holders liable as contributors, which included his name, was filed, and a year later a notice of a call was served on him   He resisted the collection of the amount of that call, and, although his resistance was made three years after he came of age, the court held that he was liable   But after a repudiation of the contract on attaining majority it is held that rendering aid in holding the transferee liable is not a waiver by the infant of his formal repudiation of the transfer to him of which the corporate creditors can take advantage, when for any reason they fail to make their claim against the vendor of the infant. Baker's Case, L R, 7 Chan, 115 (1871). If a father transfers shares of stock to his minor son, though in good faith, he is, upon the winding up, liable upon the stock as though no transfer had been attempted, if the son repudiates the transaction. Litchfield's Case, 3 De G & Sm, 141 (1850), Weston's Case, L R, 5 Chan 614 (1870) *Cf.* Roman v Fry 5 J J Marsh, 634 (1831). And a director in an incorporated company, who induces his minor children to take stock in the company in their own names, is liable upon the winding up for a breach of trust, in case the children are still minors *Ex parte* Wilson, L. R., 8 Chan, 45 (1872) But if a father buy shares in the name and for the benefit of his son, who is a minor, and when the transfer is made informs the broker of the vendor of the minority of the transferee, the father, upon the winding up, is not liable on the stock, but, the transferee continuing a minor when the right of action accrues, the corporate creditors may look to the transferrer   Maitland's Case, 38 L J, Chan, 554 (1869)   So, also, where the vendor of shares allows the certificate to be made to the minor son of

his vendee, and the son upon attaining his majority repudiates the transaction, the vendor and not the vendee is liable upon the winding up   Hennessey's Case, 3 De G & Sm, 191 (1850)   But where a shareholder transferred to an infant, and this infant to another infant, who in his turn transferred to an adult capable of responding upon the stock, all the transfers having been duly registered, it was held that the last vendee was a contributory and that the immediate transfers could not be avoided   Gooch's Case, L R, 8 Chan, 266 (1872). After a winding up is commenced, a person in whose name, while an infant, stock had been placed, but who had, with knowledge, allowed the subscription to continue after he came of age, cannot repudiate   *Re* Yoeland, etc, 58 L T Rep, 922 (1888)   It seems, therefore that the act of the infant in transferring shares is valid and effectual to pass the title and to discharge himself from liability on the stock.

[1] See §§ 66, 319   A woman to whom stock is transferred in the corporate books is liable on the statutory liability if she approves or acquiesces in it in any way, as by signing an application to change the charter of the bank or by indorsing checks which are made out to her for dividends   She is estopped from denying that she knew what she was signing   It is immaterial whether new certificates were issued to her, and also whether the transfer to her was by the husband in order to conceal his property   A married woman may be a stockholder in a bank in the District of Columbia, and be liable on the statutory liability. The court refused to pass on the question as to what property might be reached as against her   Keyser v Hitz, 133 U S, 138 (1890)   See, also, Johnson v Gal-

she would also have power to transfer her stock without the consent of her husband

§ 251 *The liability of the corporation itself as a stockholder.*— When the corporation becomes the purchaser of its own stock, and the shares, as is generally the case, are transferred into the name of a trustee for the corporation, it is the rule, both here and in England, that the trustee is personally liable in respect of all the shares so standing in his name [2]

laghei, 3 De G., F & J, 491 (1861); Mrs Matthewmann's Case, L R., 3 Eq, 781, Luard's Case, 1 De G, F & J, 533; Queen v Carnatic R. Co, L. R, 8 Q B., 290 (1873). In Angus' Case, 1 De G & Sm, 560, the constitution of the corporation prevented such a transfer See, also, Matter of Reciprocity Bank, 22 N Y, 9 In England the husband is liable on stock owned by his wife when he married her Builinson's Case. 3 De G & Sm, 18 (1849), Sadler's Case, id., 36, White's Case, id, 157 But he is liable only for subsequent liabilities of the company Kluht's Case, id., 210 See, also, Butler v. Cumpston, L. R., 7 Eq, 16, where the wife was a *cestui que trust* A husband has been held liable on stock which was given to his wife after their marriage by way of legacy, and was accepted by her Thomas v City of Glasgow Bank, 6 Scotch Ct. of Sess (4th series), 607 (1879) A married woman is herself liable for the statutory liability on stock, where she has power to be a stockholder Sales v. Bates, 6 East Rep, 703 (R. I, 1886), Bundy v. Cocke. 128 U S., 185 (1888) So, also, as to national banks Witters v Sowles, 32 Fed Rep., 767 (1887), Ibid, 35 id, 640 (1888), 38 id., 700, Keyser t Hitz, 2 Mackey, 473 (U. S D C, 1883); Hobart v Johnson, 19 Blatch, 359 (1881) Anderson v Line, 14 Fed. Rep., 405 (1880). The case of Simmons t Dent, 16 Mo App, 288 (1884), holds that under a statute whereby a married woman may become a stockholder, a transfer of stock from the husband to the wife is valid, and relieves him from liability on the stock the same as though he had transferred

to any other person. A married woman may give away or pledge her stock Walker v. Joseph, etc, Co, 20 Atl Rep, 885 (N J, 1890) Married women are liable on the statutory liability Parish's Appeal, 19 Atl Rep, 569 (Pa, 1890) A married woman is not at common law qualified to act as an incorporator nor as treasurer 9 R'y & Corp L J, 197

[2] Matter of the Empire City Bank, 18 N Y, 199, 226 (1858), Allibone v Hager. 46 Pa St., 48 (1862); Crandall v Lincoln 52 Conn, 73 (1884) *Cf* Sanger v. Upton 91 U S, 56, 60 (1875) To the same effect are the English cases *In re* St. Marylebone Banking Co, 3 De G. & Sm, 21 (1849), *In re* National Financial Co, L R., 3 Chan, 791 (1868), in which one who held shares in one company as trustee for another company was declared to be a creditor of the company for which he held the shares to the amount of the calls made upon and paid by him on account of the other company Chapman & Barker's Case, L. R., 3 Eq, 361 (1866), holding, also, that the trustee might have a right to be indemnified by the company of which he was merely a trustee. The trustee for the corporation has recourse against it for calls paid by him. Goodson's Claim, 28 W R., 766 (1880), Ind's Case, L R., 7 Chan, 485 (1872); Eyre's Case, 31 Beav, 177; Munt's Case, 22 id, 55, Richmond's Case, 3 De G & Sm, 96, Walter's Case, id, 244. The last four cases are instances of attempted transfers to trustees for the benefit of the corporation being declared void as illegal and the original holders being

The transferrer, also, if he knew that the transferee took as trustee for the corporation, is liable upon the stock[1] But when this knowledge is not imputable to the transferrer, he is not liable[2] Nor, of course, is he liable when the corporation has power, by charter or otherwise, to deal in its own shares[3] Where the owner of stock transfers it directly to the corporation itself, without the intervention of a trustee, the transferrer is not released from his liability on the stock, but remains as fully chargeable as though no transfer had been attempted[4]

§ 252. *The liability of legatees, assignees in insolvency and joint owners.*— A legatee of shares of stock may, of course, if he thinks proper, decline to receive his testator's gift But if he accepts the legacy, it is well settled that, as specific legatee, he is bound to pay all calls made upon the stock after the death of the testator[5] He

---

declared liable Sec. also §§ 282, 314 Where the company issues its stock as collateral security to notes given to it by its subscribers in payment for such stock, and then sells the notes, the stock follows the notes and may be subjected to the payment of judgment on the notes If the corporation has issued the stock to others it must pay the judgments Houston, etc, R y z Bremond, 18 S W. Rep., 448 (Tex., 1886) Concerning a pledge of its own stock by a corporation, see § 465.

[1] Lawe's Case, 1 De G. M & G, 421 (1852), Walter's Second Case, 3 De G & Sm, 244 (1850); Daniell's Case, 22 Bear, 43 (1856) Cf Johnson v Laflin, 5 Dill, 65 (1878), S. C., Thompson Nat Bank Cases, 331, S C, 103 U S. 800 (1880), and particularly Crandall r Lincoln, 52 Conn 73 (1884) See, also, § 309

[2] Hollwey's Case, 1 De G & Sm, 777 (1849), Nicol's Case, 3 De G & J, 387 (1859), Johnson v Laflin, 103 U S, 800 (1880).

[3] Grady's Case, 1 De G, J & S, 488 (1863), Lane's Case, id, 504 (1863). Sometimes by agreement between discontented stockholders and the directors of the corporation, transfers are made by such shareholders as desire to be released from their obligation as shareholders to nominees of the direct-

ors, with the intent thereby to relieve themselves from liability upon the stock In such cases it is held that the action of the directors in permitting or sanctioning such a transfer was *ultra vires*, and that in consequence the transferrer is still liable Morgan's Case, 1 De G & Sm, 750 (1849), Bennett's Case, 5 De G, M & G, 284 (1854), *In re* Patent Paper Manuf'g Co, L R, 5 Chan, 294 (1870), Nathan r Whitlock, 9 Paige, 152 (1841) See also, §§ 253, 309, 310, *infra*

[4] Case of the Reciprocity Bank, 22 N Y, 9 (1860), Currier z Lebanon Slate Co, 56 N H. 262 (1875), Johnson z Laflin, 5 Dill, 65 (1878), S C, 6 Central Law Jour, 124, 103 U S, 800 (1880), Walter's Second Case 3 De G & Sm, 244 (1850), Glenn r Scott, 28 Fed Rep, 804 (1886) Compare Zulueta's Claim, L R, 5 Chan, 444 (1870), *In re* Patent Paper Manuf g Co, L R, 5 Chan, 294 (1870) Subscribers whose stock is taken back by the corporation are not liable thereon either at common law or by statute relative to transfers Alling r Ward, 24 N E Rep, 551 (Ill, 1890) See §§ 167–171

[5] Day z Day, 6 Jur (N. S.), 365 (1860). Cf Witters z. Sowles, 25 Fed. Rep, 168 (1885)

must also pav all calls voted before, but not due and payable in the regular course of business until after, the testator's death.[1]

It has been held that an assignee of the estate of a bankrupt is not liable, personally or as assignee, upon the bankrupt's share of stock. He is not bound, as assignee, to accept as part of the estate property of this nature, when it is of an onerous or unprofitable character.[2]

Upon the death of one who is joint owner with another or others of shares of stock, the liability thereon attaches only to the surviving owners, and the estate of the deceased owner cannot be charged.[3]

§ 253 *The use of " dummies " and transfers to nominal and fictitious persons —* Frequently it happens that persons purchasing or subscribing for stock do not wish to take the stock in their own names, inasmuch as they thereby incur liability, or make known to the public the fact that they are stockholders. Accordingly, it is the custom in such cases to have the stock taken or purchased in the names of other persons   These latter are called "dummies"[4] The law is well settled that such a "dummy" is liable on the stock to the corporation and corporate creditors to the same extent that he would be if he were the real owner of the stock.[5] And it is

---

[1] Addams *v* Ferick, 26 Beav, 384 (1859) For a more complete statement of the law relative to legacies of stock, see ch XVIII

[2] American File Co. *v* Garrett, 110 U S, 288 (1883). Amory *v* Lawrence, 3 Cliff., 523 (1872), and see Rugely & Harrison *v* Robinson, 19 Ala, 404 (1851); Streeter *v* Sumner, 31 N H, 542 (1855); *Ex parte* Davis, L R, 3 Chan Div, 463; Furdonjee's Case, id, 268, holding that the liability upon shares not being a debt provable in insolvency proceedings is not barred by the order of discharge And where a corporation itself assigned shares of its own stock to an assignee for the benefit of corporate creditors, it was held that the assignee was not liable, personally or as assignee, thereon. *In re* City Terminus Hotel Co, L R, 4 Eq, 10 (1872) It has been held otherwise, however, in a case where the assignment was absolute and the assignee was also a creditor Protection Life Insurance Co. *v* Osgood, 93 Ill, 69 It

has been held that one who makes an assignment for the benefit of creditors is thereby released from liability on stock, even though the transfer has not been recorded in the corporate books. Sales *v.* Bates, 6 East. Rep., 703 (R I, 1886)

[3] *Re* Maria Anna, etc, Coal & Coke Co., 44 L J, Chan, 423 (1875); Hill's Case, L R, 20 Eq, 585 (1874)

[4] The cases in this section refer to the use of "dummies" without the real owner appearing at all on the corporate books as a stockholder These cases differ from those where stock is transferred by a stockholder from himself to a "dummy" or irresponsible person. See §§ 263-266.

[5] Wakefield *v* Fargo, 90 N Y., 213 (1882); Case of Reciprocity Bank, 22 id, 9 (1860), Barrett's Case, 4 De G., J & S, 416 (1864), Bugg's Case, 2 Dr. & Sm., 952 *Cf.* Fox *v* Clifton, 6 Bing (Eng), 776 (1830) A transfer of stock on the books to a director renders him liable on the

established that the real owner of the stock is liable to repay to his "dummy" any sum of money which the latter has paid to the corporation or the corporate creditors [1] An attachment against the "dummy" may take the stock.[2]

But a more difficult question arises when an attempt is made to hold the real owner of the stock liable to the corporation or corporate creditors. Where the real owner was formerly the registered stockholder, but has transferred his stock to an irresponsible person, a class of cases is found which is considered elsewhere [3]

A different class of cases, however, is now under consideration, and in America it has been held, where a person purchased stock in a national bank, but had it transferred, not to himself, but to another person. a "dummy," that the real owner of the stock is liable thereon, although he never appeared on the corporate books as a stockholder [4]

statutory liability, even though the transfer was to render him eligible for office, and he was unaware of the transfer, and had paid the dividends to the transferrer As director he was bound to know Brown v Finn 34 Fed Rep, 124 (1888) When a director enters stock in his wife's name, but she knows nothing of it and he receives all dividends and votes it, she cannot be charged as a stockholder Longdale Iron Co v Pomeroy Iron Co, 34 Fed Rep, 448 (1888)

[1] This is the rule whether the relation of the real owner be considered that of a principal towards an agent (see § 249, supra), or that of cestui que trust towards a trustee (see § 245)

[2] White v Rankin, 8 S Rep, 118 (Ala, 1890)

[3] See §§ 263–266, infra

[4] Davis v Stevens, 17 Blatch, 259 (1879), where the question was, "Whether, in an action at law by a receiver of the bank, the real owner of stock in a national bank, standing by his procurement in the name of another, and never having been in his own name on the books, can be charged as a shareholder with the statutory liability for debts?" Held, that the real owner is liable "Every principal is responsible for the obligations of his agency The debt of the agent is the debt of the

principal, and always recoverable from the principal" See, also, to same effect, Case v Small, 10 Fed Rep, 722 (1881), Castleman v Holmes, 4 J J Marsh, 1 (1830) In England, under its statutes a different rule prevails See King's Case, L. R, 6 Ch App., 196 (1871), William's Case, L R, 1 Ch D, 576 Fenwick's Case, 1 De G & Sm, 557 (1819), Cox's Case, 4 De G, J & S, 53 (1863) The real owner of stock is likewise liable where he transfers it from his own name to that of an irresponsible person §§ 263–266, infra Cf cases in note 3, p 332, supra An undisclosed owner of stock, standing in the name of another as trustee, is liable on the statutory liability. Borland v Haven, 37 Fed Rep, 394 (1888), Castleman v Holmes, 4 J J Marsh, 1 (1830), holding that one who subscribed for stock in the name of an infant for the purpose of avoiding responsibility, and who enjoyed the benefits of the stock, was individually responsible as a stockholder for debts of the corporation Where the "dummy" dies, and his representatives claim the stock, and they pay the real owner a small sum in settlement, the compromise will be upheld Antoine v Smith 4 S Rep, 321 (La, 1888) Where the "dummy" dies and is insolvent, the stock cannot be reclaimed by the

In England a directly contrary rule prevails.[1]

In America the relation of the real owner to the "dummy" is held to be that of principal and agent, and the principal is held liable, on the ground that an undisclosed principal is liable on the contracts of his agent In England the real owner of the stock is looked upon as a *cestui que trust*, and hence is not liable [2] Under the Ohio statute the word "stockholders" applies to persons owning stock in the name of another, as well as to persons appearing on the corporate books as stockholders [3] ,

A transfer to a fictitious person is void, and leaves all parties as they were [4]

real owner Hirsch z Norton, 17 N E. Rep , 612 (Ind , 1888) Stock held in the name of a "dummy ' is subject to his debts, even though he notified the secretary of the company that he held it in trust *Ex parte* Ord, 2 Mont & A , 724 (1835), *Ex parte* Watkins, id 348 (1835), reversing 1 id , 693

[1] King's Case, L R, 6 Ch App , 196 (1871), where the court says it does not know upon what ground a court, setting aside a transaction as fraudulent, is able to make a new contract for persons which they had never made themselves Cox's Case, 4 De G , J & S , 53 (1863), is distinguished on the ground that Cox had agreed to take certain shares, and the decision was in the nature of specific performance In Cox's Case, also, he had, by the use of "dummies," entrapped the public into believing that many persons were investing In Williams' Case, L R , 1 Ch D , 571 (1875), where a purchaser of shares had them transferred to one of his employees, the real owner was held not liable thereon In the case *Ex parte* Bugg, 2 Drew & Sm , 452, a similar conclusion was arrived at, the court saying that the relation between the real owner and the "dummy" was that of *cestui que trust* and trustee Such, also, is the rule laid down in Fenwick's Case, 1 De G & Sm , 557 (1849), where

the purchaser had the stock transferred into the name of the "dummy" as "trustee" A person who subscribes for stock in a Canadian corporation in the name of another, a "dummy," is not liable for the unpaid subscription Molson's Bank z Boardman, 47 Hun, (N Y), 135 (1888) That a *cestui que trust* is not liable on stock held by his trustee, see §§ 245, 246 See, also, cases in note 2, p. 330, *supra*

[2] See *supra*

[3] Lloyd v Preston, 146 U S , 630 (1892).

[4] Arthur v Midland R'y Co., 3 Kay & J , 201 (1857). See Pugh & Sharman's Case L R., 13 Eq , 566 (1872), where the transfer was to a married woman, but the court treated it as a transfer to a fictitious person In Muskingum, etc , Co. z Ward, 13 Ohio, 120 (1844), where the transfer was made to a fictitious person, the court held that the transaction was a mere nullity, and that it could not be regarded as an abandonment of the stock So where one purchased, or assumed to purchase, shares for an infant, and took the certificate in the name of an imaginary person, it was held that by such a transaction the purchaser did not become liable upon the shares, nor was the vendor released Maitland's Case, 38 L J , Chan , 554 (1869) See, also, Richardson's Case, L R , 19 Eq , 588.

CHAPTER XV.

LIABILITY AS AFFECTED BY TRANSFERS.

§ 254. *The subject herein* — When shares of stock are transferred from one owner to another it at once becomes an important matter to determine who is liable upon unpaid subscriptions, and who must assume the liability imposed by statute   The difficulty is increased by the rule of law that no transfer is complete until it is duly entered or recorded in the transfer book of the corporation The complication is usually greatest in cases involving the question of statutory liability, since generally each case turns more or less upon the particular words of the statute by which the liability is imposed   There are, however, many rules which are general in their character and application, governing the liability of shareholders as affected by transfer, and these are the subject of this chapter

§ 255. *Liability of the transferrer on unpaid subscriptions after registry* — Transfers of shares may be made at any time after the contract of subscription is made, and before any part or after a part of the subscription price has been paid   The well-established and general rule of law is, that where a stockholder makes an absolute transfer of his stock in good faith, and the transfer is duly recorded in the corporate stock book, the transferrer is thereby wholly discharged from all further liability upon the uncalled subscription price of the stock.[1]

---

[1] Huddersfield Canal Co *v* Buckley, 7 Term Rep, 36 (1796, by Lord Kenyon), Executors of Gilmore *v* Bank of Cincinnati, 8 Ohio, 62, 71 (1837)   A transferrer is not liable on an unpaid subscription   "A transfer of stock made in good faith and at a time when the corporation is a going and solvent con-

341

This important rule is peculiar to corporation law. It is based
on public policy and an appreciation of the demands of trade. The
transferrer is released, although the corporate officers enter the

cern, and which is entered upon the
books, would certainly relieve the transferrer from all of the responsibilities
which attached to him as a stockholder "
Tucker t Gilman, 121 N Y, 189 (1890),
Billings v Robinson, 94 N Y, 415 (1884),
affirming S C, 28 Hun, 122 (1882),
Wakefield t Fargo, 90 N Y, 213 (1882),
Cowles v Cromwell, 25 Barb, 413
(1857), Cole v Ryan, 52 id, 168 (1868),
Isham v Buckingham, 49 N Y, 216
(1872), Stewart t Walla, etc, Co, 20
Pac Rep, 605 (Wash Ter, 1889), Miller
v Great Republic Ins Co, 50 Mo, 55
(1872) Allen v Montgomery R R Co,
11 Ala, 437, 451 (1847) Haynes v
Palmer, 13 La Ann, 240 (1858), Weston s Case L R, 4 Chan, 20 (1868), Mc-
Kenzie v Kittridge, 24 Upp Can, C P,
1 (1874) The mere fact that the transferrer, after the registry, paid a call
does not estop him from denying his
liability for subsequent calls Provincial Ins Co v Shaw, 19 U. C (Q. B),
533 (1860) It is not necessary to the
validity of the transfer that there should
be a consideration moving from transferee to transferrer, and so, where one
gives his share away absolutely and in
good faith, the same rule as to liability
prevails In re European Bank, Master's Case, 41 L J, Chan, 501 (1872)
Neither does it alter the rule that no
certificates of stock have been issued.
In such a case the transferee becomes
liable on the stock, and the transferrer's
liability is at an end Burke v. Smith,
16 Wall, 390 (1872), Brigham v. Mead,
10 Allen, 245 (1865) See, also, First
Nat'l Bank v Gifford, 47 Iowa, 575, 583,
Isham v Buckingham, 49 N. Y, 216
(1872). As regards the rule where the
transfer is made before the corporation
is organized, see § 61 The statutes of
the state may, of course, change this
rule Thus in Pennsylvania, see Brightley's Purdon's Digest, pp. 1420-1427,

and in Virginia, see Glenn v. Scott, 28
Fed Rep, 804 (1886), McKim v Glenn,
8 Atl. Rep, 130 (Md, 1887). In Pennsylvania and Virginia both the transferrer
and transferee are liable. Glenn v Foote,
36 Fed Rep, 824 (1888), Priest v Glenn,
51 Fed Rep, 400 (1892); Hambleton v
Glenn, 9 S E Rep, 124 (Va., 1889). Subscribers to stock are liable according to
the law of the state incorporating the
company and not according to the law
of the state where the subscribers reside A subscriber to stock in a Virginia corporation is liable by statute although he has transferred his stock
Morris v Glenn, 7 S Rep, 90 (Ala,
1888) In Pennsylvania, after considerable doubt and conflict, it has been
clearly stated by the supreme court that
the transferee of stock is liable on the
unpaid subscription Bell's Appeal, 8
Atl Rep, 177 (Pa, 1887), Citizens', etc.
Co. v Gillespie, 9 Atl Rep, 73 (1887),
where, however, the transferee directly
contracted to pay But compare West
Philadelphia Canal Co v Innes, 3 Wharton, 198 (1838), Aultman's Appeal, 98
Pa. St, 505 (1881), Bunn's Appeal, 105
id, 49 (1884), Palmer v Ridge Mining
Co, 34 id, 288, Pittsburgh Iron Co v
Otterson, 4 Week. Notes Cas, 545 (1878),
Delaware Canal Co t Sansom, 1 Binn.,
70 (1803) Merrimac Mining Co v Levy,
54 Pa St., 227 (1867). And, in general,
as regards the Pennsylvania General
Railroad Act of February 19, 1849, see
Pittsburgh, etc, R R Co v Clarke, 29
Pa St, 146 (1857), Graff t. Pittsburgh,
etc, R R Co, 31 id, 489 (1858). Cf.
Frank's Oil Co. v McCleary, 63 id, 317
(1869), holding that the transferee in a
mining company is not liable Messer-
smith v Sharon Savings Bank, 96 id,
440 (1880), to same effect, and see Aultman's Appeal, 98 id, 505 (1881), involving an Ohio corporation; Pittsburgh,
etc, Iron Co v Otterson, 4 Week Notes

transfer against the protest of the transferrer[1] The transferrer, however, is liable for calls payable before the transfer is made,[2] and in some cases for calls made before but payable after the transfer[3]

§ 256 *Liability of the transferee on unpaid subscriptions after registry.*—When a transfer of stock is made, and the transfer is duly recorded in the corporate stock book, the transferee thereupon becomes liable for any balance of the subscription price remaining unpaid at the time of the transfer The transfer releases the transferrer, and charges the transferee.[4]

Cas, 545 (1878); Miller *v* Peabody Bank, 15 Week Notes Cas., 76, Reimer Co *v* Rosenberger, 40 Leg Int, 383, Pittsburgh R R Co *v* Clarke, 29 Pa, 173 In Maryland, also, the ordinary statutory provision holding stockholders liable until the capital stock is fully paid in is held to render the shareholder liable, even though he has transferred his shares. Hager *v* Cleveland, 36 Md, 476 (1872) After a transfer and registry the stockholder is not liable on the subscription even under a statute. Libby *v* Tobey, 19 Atl Rep, 904 (Me, 1890). In New York no stock in either railroad or manufacturing corporations, created by the laws of that state, can be lawfully transferred while there are calls unpaid upon the shares N Y Session Laws, 1850, ch 140 § 8, N Y Session Laws, 1848, ch. 40, § 8 In California railroad stock cannot be issued until it is fully paid up Brewster *v* Hartley, 37 Cal, 15 (1869) In Tennessee it is held that, upon a valid transfer, the transferrer is released, not only upon his liability for unpaid subscriptions, but also as to all the existing debts of the corporation; and this is the general rule Jackson *v* Sligo Mfg Co., 1 Lea, 210 (1878) So in Alabama. Allen *v* Montgomery R R, 11 Ala, 437 (1847).

[1] London, etc, R y Co. *v.* Fairclough, 2 Man & G, 674, 706 (1841); Upton *v* Burnham, 3 Biss., 520 (1873), Webster *v* Upton, 91 U. S, 65 (1875). In a proceeding in equity a transferee will be compelled to pay calls made after transfer of the certificate and before registry of the same Webster *v* Upton, *supra*

[2] Vicksburg, etc, R. R. Co. *v* McKean, 14 La Ann, 724 (1859), and cases in this section generally, and § 258, *infra*

[3] North American Colonial Association *v* Bentley, 19 L J (Q B.), 427 (1850); Schenectady, etc, Plank-road Co *v.* Thatcher, 11 N. Y., 102, 113 (1854) *Contra*, West Philadelphia Canal Co *v* Innes, 3 Wharton, 198 (1838) But this case was decided on the ground that the transferee had not accepted the stock, and could not be held liable by the corporation Cf Aylesbury Railway Co *v.* Mount, 4 Man & G, 651, reversing 5 Scott's New Rep, 127 (1842), *In re* Hoylake R'y Co, L R, 9 Chan, 257 (1874).

[4] Webster *v* Upton, 91 U S, 65 (1875),
Pullman *v* Upton, 96 id, 328 (1877), Upton *v* Hansbrough, 3 Biss, 417 (1873), Hall *v* United States Ins Co. 5 Gill (Md), 484 (1847), Bond *v* Susquehanna Bridge Co, 6 Har & J, 128 (1825), Merrimac Mining Co *v* Bagley, 14 Mich, 501 (1866), Brigham *v* Mead, 10 Allen, 245 (1865), Hartford etc, R. R. Co *v.* Boorman, 12 Conn, 530 (1838), Moore *v.* Jones, 3 Woods, 53 (1877), Merrimac Mining Co. *v* Levy, 54 Pa St, 227 (1867); Huddersfield Canal Co *v* Buckley, 7 Term Rep, 36 (1796). In Gray's Case, L R., 1 Ch Div, 664, where an owner of iron-works sold them to an incorporation for its stock, and having guarantied that the net dividends should be not less than ten per cent. on the paid-up capital, for which purpose the shares given as consideration were vested in trustees, but were not to be registered in their names except by their own direction, it was held that they were not liable as

In Pennsylvania [1] and some other states, the liability of the transferee is regulated by statute   Where, by statute or a by-law of the corporation, no valid transfer can be made while there are calls due and unpaid, it is held that a transfer without such payment will not render the transferee liable thereon [2]

§ 257 *Knowledge that the shares are not fully paid up, how far imputable to a transferee* — The question whether the purchaser of shares is bound to take notice that the stock he purchases is not fully paid for is a serious and complicated one. The better opinion, and the one most in accord with the usages, analogies and demands of trade, is that, where one buys stock in open market, in good faith, and without notice that the subscription price thereof has not been paid up, such a purchaser cannot be held liable to pay the unpaid balance of subscription [3]

stockholders because they had not elected to be registered as stockholders. When a person takes shares of a company, he, as between himself and other shareholders, takes those shares with all the rights and liabilities attaching to them, so that his co-shareholders have a perfect right to insist upon his contributing with them towards the liquidation of debts contracted before he joined the company Taylor r Ifill, 1 N R , 566, V. C W , Cape's Executor's Case, 2 De G , M & G , 562, Mayhew's Case 5 id , 837 See, too Horsley z Bell, 1 Bro C C , 101, note Sanderson's Case 3 De G & S, 66, cannot be regarded as correct on this point. See Henderson r Sanderson, 3 H L C , 698

[1] See notes to the preceding section

[2] Watson r Eales, 23 Beav , 294 (1856); McCready r Rumsey, 6 Duer, 574 (New York Super Ct , 1857), was a case under a prohibition to transfer in articles of association of a bank, organized under the General Banking Act of 1838 of the state of New York, *In re* Bachman, 12 Nat Bank. Reg , 223 (1875), where the corporation had a lien on the stock

[3] Certificates of stock have become such important factors in trade and credit, and general investment by all classes, that the law is steadily tending towards the complete protection of a *bona fide* purchaser of them in open market, and without notice of facts which will decrease the apparent value of the stock   The constant tendency of the courts to increase the negotiability of certificates of stock will probably, at some time hereafter, not allow any liability on unpaid subscriptions to be enforced against a transferee unless such liability is stated on the face of the certificate itself   At present it is still a question whether a purchaser of the certificate is bound to inquire and know whether the stock is issued as paid-up stock or not See ch III Where a member has not paid for his stock in full and sells it as though it was full paid he must refund to the transferee the balance which the transferee is obliged to pay   Jamison r Harbert, 54 N W Rep , 75 (Iowa, 1893). But where a subscription is not paid, and the stock is transferred to the corporation as "treasury stock ' and then sold below par, the purchaser is liable for the unpaid par value   Alling r Ward, 24 N E. Rep. 551 (Ill , 1890). A contract by a corporation that it will issue its stock for one-fifth of its par value is void under the Alabama constitutional prohibition   The subscriber having sold his contract to another person cannot collect on such sale Williams v. Evans, 6 S Rep , 702 (Ala , 1889).

§ 258 *Liability on subscription after transfer but before registry — Irregular and attempted transfers* — Until a transfer is recorded in the transfer book of the corporation, the transferee, not being duly organized as a stockholder, is not chargeable either with corporate debts or unpaid balances of the subscription   He is bound to protect and indemnify his transferrer, but he is not liable to the corporation or corporate creditors or other stockholders [1]   The transferrer, however, is not released from liability until the transfer is duly registered in the corporate books [2]   This rule, however, has not been rigidly adhered to, and it is the law that, where the corporation accepts the transferee as a stockholder and pays dividends to him, or where, through the negligence or fault of the corporation, no transfer on the books is made, in such cases the transferrer is released, and the transferee only is liable on the stock [3]

---

[1] Marlborough Manuf g Co r Smith, 2 Conn, 579 (1818), Topeka etc, Co r Hale, 17 Pac Rep, 601 (Kan, 1888) Midland etc, R'y Co r Gordon 16 Mees & W, 804 (1847)   In Indiana it has been held that a statute will not be construed so as to make both transferrer and transferee liable directly for the same indebtedness   Williams r Hanna, 40 Ind, 535 (1872).

[2] Shellington r Howland, 53 N Y, 371 (1873), Worrall r Judson 5 Barb, 210 (1849), Louisiana Insurance Co r Gordon, 8 La Rep, 174 (1835), Dane r Young, 61 Me, 160 (1872), Fowler r Ludwig, 34 Me, 455 (1852), Davis r Essex, etc, Society, 44 Conn, 582 (1877), Kellogg r Stockwell, 75 Ill, 68, Bowdell r Farmers', etc, Nat Bank, U S, C C (D Md, 1877), Brown s N B, Cas, 147, London, etc R y Co, r Fairclough, 2 Man & G, 674 (1841), to the same effect, McEuen r West London Wharves, etc, Co, L R, 6 Chan, 655, in which it was held that the sale and transfer by delivery of scrip certificates, allotted and issued to a subscriber entitling the bearer to exchange them for share certificates, would not exonerate the vendor from liability for calls, even though the vendee had paid some calls, Midland, etc, r Gordon, 6 Mees & W 604 (1847), Sayles r Blane, 19 L J (Q

B) 19, S C, 6 Eng R'y Cases 79   See, also Hawkins r Glenn, 131 U S 319 (1889)   The registered stockholder is liable on the subscription Bines r Babcock, 30 Pac Rep, 776 (Cal 1892)   An original subscriber for stock is not released from his obligation although he sells and transfers the certificate of stock, such transfer not having been recorded on the corporate books Hood r McNaughton, 24 Atl Rep, 497 (N J, 1892)   A person sued as a subscriber cannot set up that he subscribed at the solicitation of another person who agreed to take the subscription off his hands at once Stutz r Handley, 41 Fed Rep, 531 (1890)

[3] Isham r. Buckingham 49 N Y, 216 (1872), Cutting r Damerel, 88 id, 410 (1882), Chambersburg Ins. Co r Smith 11 Pa St., 120 (1849), Murry r Bush, L R, 6 House of Lords, 37 (1873), Upham r. Burnham 3 Biss, 431 (1873), S C, id, 520   Where the transferrer signs the transfer on the back and delivers the same to his broker, who sells the stock and then presents the certificate to the corporation for transfer, and the corporation agrees so to do, but neglects to for a year, the transferrer is not liable on the stock Young r M Kay, 50 Fed Rep., 394 (1892)   The transferrer of stock in a national bank is released

It is immaterial that no certificate of stock is issued to the transferee   The registry is complete without it.[1]   When the transferrer

from liability when he goes with the transferrer to the bank, delivers the old certificate duly transferred and leaves the same for registry, even though no registry is made   Hayes v Shoemaker, 39 Fed Rep, 319 (1889).   A substitution of stockholders after organization by canceling some subscriptions and filling in others is illegal.   There should be a transfer   Cartwright v Dickinson, 12 S W Rep, 1030 (Tenn, 1890).   Where a party buys stock through a broker and the broker without authority causes the stock to be transferred on the books to the purchaser, but the latter upon receiving the certificates returns them and repudiates the transfer and orders a sale and transfer, and the company fails before such resale is made   the purchaser is not liable to corporate creditors on the subscription price of the stock   Glenn v Garth, 133 N Y, 18 (1892)   Where a person subscribes to the proposed increased capital stock, but the increase is not made, and the officers surreptitiously transfer some of their old stock to him, he is not liable on the statutory liability thereon, even though he accepted the stock, if he accepted in ignorance of the fraud practiced upon his   Stephens v Follett, 43 Fed Rep, 842 (1890).   A stockholder is liable by statute on stock where he has merely transferred the certificate, and no effort has been made to complete the

transfer on the corporate books   Where there is no transfer book, but certificates are merely canceled and new ones issued, this is sufficient to effect a transfer on the corporate books.   Plumb v Bank of Enterprise, 29 Pac. Rep, 699 (Kan, 1892).   Where a person agrees to accept a transfer of stock, and acts as director, he is liable on the unpaid subscription though no formal transfer is made   Weinman v Wilkinsburg, etc., R'y Co., 12 Atl Rep., 288 (Pa., 1888); Bernard's Case, 5 De G & Sm, 283 (1852) See, also, § 260, infra   Cf Ex parte Hall, 1 McC & G, 307 (1849), holding that an unregistered transferee is not liable merely because he accepts dividends; Shipman's Case, L R, 5 Eq, 219, in which a purchaser offered a name to which he wished the shares transferred on the register, but which was rejected by the directors   The vendor, in whose name they stood, was held liable for calls, and the court refused to remove his name. Sheffield, etc, v Woodcock, 7 Mees & W, 574, holding that where, by law, transfers of stock were to be made by deed, a transfer in blank, and stating the consideration untruly, made to a purchaser who afterwards signed and sent to the company a proxy, in which he described himself as the proprietor of the shares, constituted him a stockholder for the purpose of requiring him to respond to calls for assessments;

---

[1] First Nat'l Bank, etc., v Gifford, 47 Iowa, 575, 583, Brigham v Mead, 10 Allen, 245 (1865), Straffon's Executor's Case, 1 De G, M & G, 576 (1852) Chouteau Spring Co. v Harris, 20 Mo, 382 (1855), holding that an assignment upon the books of the company, without having a new certificate issued, is a sufficient transfer to exonerate the assignor from liability for assessments; and that any transfer in writing is valid against a company which, having notice, refuses to allow it to be made. The

shareholder cannot set up for defense, to an action by a corporate creditor, that some third person had contracted to purchase his shares, or a portion of them, but that with the consent of the corporate authorities it had been agreed that, until that third person had paid the notes given for the purchase price of the stock, the transfer should not be made on the corporate stock-book   Phœnix Warehousing Co. v Badger, 67 N. Y., 294 (1876), affirming S C., 6 Hun, 293 (1875)

has done all in his power to complete the transfer and is guilty of no laches, his liability to corporate creditors is thereby determined, and accordingly, he is discharged, as though the registry

Taylor v Hughes, 2 Jones & Lat. (Ir Ch), 24 in which the court refused to hold liable as a stockholder of a bank one who has transferred his stock seven years before, though not by a proper method and whose name had not appeared on the books during that time but had been re-entered by a committee after the failure of the bank Burnes v Pennell, 2 H. of L. Cas, 497, held that where certain forms were to be observed by a transferee of shares in a Scotch joint-stock company, the required acts were for the benefit of the company, and therefore the leaving of one of such acts unexecuted by a purchaser was not allowed to enable him to retire from his contract. Maguire's Case, 3 De G & Sm, 31 In this case a shareholder in a steam packet company transferred two shares to his son without his knowledge The son did not receive dividends nor do any act as proprietor, but, for the purpose of obtaining free passages upon the boats of the company, he obtained from the company certificates that he was a proprietor It was held that the son was a contributory in respect of the two shares. A receiver cannot apply to have a transferee's name put on the list of contributories on ground of undue delay of the company in registering the transfer Only the transferer can complain Sichell's Case L R, 3 Ch, 119 (1867). See Marlborough Mfg Co. v. Smith, 2 Conn, 579 (1818), holding that a mere entry on the corporate books that a transfer has been made is insufficient, and see, also, Lane v Young, 61 Me, 160, holding that the failure to have the registry properly witnessed invalidates it A person who buys stock at an execution sale, after it has already been pledged for its full value to others and a transfer to them made, is not liable for calls on the stock, even though such

pledgees transferred it to him without his knowledge Simmons v Hill, 10 S W Rep, 61 (Mo, 1888) A vendee of stock who is to be entitled to it only upon payment is not liable for the subscription price if he never pays for the stock and his name never appears on the books Cormac v Western, etc, Co, 41 N W Rep, 480 (Iowa 1889). For other cases holding the transferee liable, although all the formalities of registry were not complied with, see Ex parte Dixon, 1 De & Sm, 225 (1860), Gordon's Case, 3 De G & Sm, 249 (1850), Stafford's Case, 1 De G, M & G, 576 (1852), Walter's Case, 3 De G & Sm, 149 (1850), London, etc, R'y v Fairclough, 2 Man & G, 674 (1841), Loudon, etc, R'y v Freeman, 2 Man & G, 606 (1841), Birmingham, etc, R'y v Locke, 1 Q B, 256 (1841) For a case holding that the transferer is liable, see Keene's Case, 3 De G, M & G, 272 (1853) For cases to the effect that the transferrer is, in general, discharged only when the transfer is actually recorded, and duly recorded in the stock-book, and when all the prescribed conditions of a valid transfer have been duly complied with, Cartmell's Case, L. R., 9 Chan. 691 (1874), Heritage's Case, L R, 9 Eq, 5 (1869), Hennessy's Executor's Case, 3 De G & Sm, 191 (1850), Ex parte Henderson, 19 Beav, 107 (1854) Where the consent of the board of directors is necessary to a transfer, no transfer is complete without it, and the transferrer remains liable. Bosanquet v. Shortridge, 4 Ex, 699 (1850). But this case at law was enjoined by Bargate v Shortridge, 5 H L C, 297 (1855), in equity, and it was held that the transferrer was not liable To same effect, see Taylor v Hughes, 2 Jo & La (Irish), 24 (1844), where the registry was not regularly made, but the transferee was treated as a stockholder,

had been made.[1] The corporation cannot hold an unrecorded transferrer liable on the unpaid subscription for stock.[2]

Cf Murray ι Bush, L. R., 6 H. of L, 37 (1872), affirming L. R., 6 Ch, 246 In this case the deed of settlement, among other things, required a transferee to covenant by deed to abide by the rules of the company A director who failed to comply with that requirement was held to be a shareholder as to the shares, because he had been recognized as a shareholder by the directors at a meeting of shareholders and had been at that meeting elected a director The transferrer was held not liable Contra Keene's Ex'rs Case, 3 De G. M & G. 272 (1853), Mayhew's Case, 5 De G M & G, 837 (1851) where the parties went together to the proper officer of the company and deposited a transfer, but no notice in writing was given to the officer as required by the company's rules The transferee was held to be properly placed on the list of contributories See, also next note

[1] Whitney ι Butler, 118 U S, 655 (1886) See, also § 383 Ex parte Henderson, 19 Beav, 107 (1854), Shortridge v Bosanquet, 16 Beav, 84 (1852) overruling S. C, sub nom Bosanquet v Shortridge, 4 Exch., 699 (1850). In White's Case, L. R., 3 Eq, 86 (1866), a transferrer was held not discharged because of laches, Fyfe's Case, L. R., 4 Ch, 768 (1869) where there was an improper delay on the part of the company in registering a transfer, Lowe's Case, L. R, 9 Eq, 589 (1870), on similar facts and to same effect, Nation's Case, L R, 3 Eq, 77 (1866), in which the directors did not confirm a transfer at their next meeting after it was left for that purpose, thereby causing an unnecessary delay, Hill's Case, L. R 4 Ch, 769 (1869) note to same effect as Fyfe's Case, supra, Ward v Garbt's Case, L. R 4 Eq, 189, in which the court rectified the register by completing a transfer which was duly executed and left for

registry the day before the corporation stopped business, but was not registered on that account, Ward's Case, L R, 2 Eq, 226 (1867), in which the names of purchasers of shares had not been placed on the register in place of that of the vendor in consequence of disputes among themselves, Ex parte Hall, 5 R'y & Canal Cas., 624 (1849), holding that where a transferee whose name has not been actually entered on the registry has so acted — as being a trustee for his wife — and his acts have been so far adopted that a waiver of the necessary forms may be inferred, he will be held a contributory in winding-up proceedings. De Pass' Case, 4 De G & J, 544 (1859) In this case the certificates were transferable by delivery, and in winding-up proceedings the holders were adjudged to be contributories, though it appeared that as to some shares they were not delivered until after the winding-up order was made and, as to others, that they were delivered to a clerk for a nominal consideration in order to escape liability. Marino's Case. L R, 2 Ch, 596 (1867), in which the transferee, who lived in Smyrna, and had not sufficient time to execute and forward the deed required of him by the rules and usage of the company to effect a valid transfer, was held not to be a contributory; Skowhegan Bank v Cutler, 49 Me, 315 (1872), holding that, in order to hold a transferee liable, it must be shown that statutory provisions relating to transfer have been observed, Laing v Burley, 101 Ill, 591 (1882), holding that, where there was no transfer on the books of a national bank as required by law, but new certificates had been issued to the transferee, who was also recognized as a shareholder on the bank's ledger, the transferee was liable, Midland, etc, v. Gordon, 16 Mees & W, 804 (1847).

[2] Vale Mills v. Spalding, 62 N H, 605 (1883).

§ 259 *Does the statutory liability attach to him who is the registered stockholder when the corporate debt is contracted, or is due, or is sued upon?*— When the question of statutory liability is considered there is more difficulty, as between transferrer and transferee, in determining who is to be charged Frequently the statute itself prescribes when the liability is to attach The important question which arises herein is whether the corporate debt raises a liability against him who was the registered stockholder when the corporation entered into the contract leading to the debt, or against him who was the registered stockholder when the debt itself became due and payable to the corporate creditor, or against him who was the registered stockholder when suit is brought by the corporate creditor against the corporation to collect the debt, or against him who was the registered stockholder when suit is brought against the stockholder

Under certain statutes to that effect, those stockholders are liable who are such at the time when the execution against the corporation is returned *nulla bona* [1]

holding that a holder of scrip certificates for shares to be allotted at a future time having sold them in the market, was liable for calls until the name of the vendee was registered as the holder of them See, also, Harpold *v* Stobart, 21 N E. Rep, 637 (Ohio, 1889) That the failure to record the transfer is the fault of the corporation itself, or of the officer thereof whose duty it is to make the entries in the stock-book, is not sufficient to relieve the shareholder who, having transferred his shares fails to see to it that the proper entry is actually and duly made In *re* Bachman, 12 Nat Bank Reg, 223 (1875).

[1] Nixon *v* Green. 11 Exch, 550, affirmed, 25 L J, Exch . 209 (1856), Dodgson *v* Scott, 2 Exch, 457 (1849), Longley *v* Little, 26 Me, 162 (1846), Bond *v* Appleton 8 Mass., 472 (1812) In this case, under a statute making the original stockholders, their successors, assigns and the members of the corporation liable for the debts of the corporation, it was held that only such persons as were members at the time payment was refused were intended, McClaren *v* Franciscus, 43 Mo. 452 (1869), Douchy *v* Brown, 24 Vt, 197. *Cf* Deming *v*.

Bull, 10 Conn, 409 (1835) Under the provision of a charter that stockholders should ' at all times be liable for all debts due by said corporation," it was held that those who were members when the debt was contracted, but had transferred their stock absolutely and in good faith before the commencement of the suit against the corporation are not to be held liable under the statute Middletown Bank *v* Magill, 5 Conn, 28 (1823), following Bond *v* Appleton *supra*, Child *v* Coffin, 17 Mass, 64 (1820), holding that, where there is a statutory provision 'that a creditor, in a certain case, may levy his execution upon the body or estate of any member of the corporation, this must be understood of such as were members at the time of the commencement of the action, and of those only ' It does not authorize an execution upon the estate of a corporator who died before the commencement of the action

Under the statute making all the members of a company liable in certain cases for its debts, the liability extends to all who were members when it was sought to be enforced, and is not confined to such persons as were members

As to whether under the usual statute making the stockholders liable, to a greater or less extent, for the debts of the corporation, a registered stockholder is liable for debts contracted before he became such as well as for those contracted while he was such, although he subsequently transfers his stock, the words of the statute control, and decisions on various statutes are given in the notes below.[1]

when the debt was contracted   Curtis v Harlow, 12 Metc., 3 (1846)

[1] Chesley v Pierce, 32 N H, 388 (1855), holding that, under a statute making stockholders liable for the debts of a corporation, the individual stockholders are not liable for debts contracted before they became such; Castleman v Holmes, 4 J J Marsh, 1 (1839), but here a statute made them liable for debts, etc., contracted "during the time he or they held stock;" Mill-dam, etc., v Hovey, 21 Pick, 417, 453 (1834) where the question arose on an objection to a witness in a suit against a corporation on the ground that it was liable for its debts, Bank v Burnham, 11 Cush, 183 (1853), a case where, under a statute making liable "all members" of a corporation, a shareholder was held for all debts contracted while he was a member, although he ceased to be a member before they were payable, and not liable for debts contracted before he became a member if his membership expired before they became payable and action brought, Southmayd v Russ, 3 Conn, 52 (1819), holding that the judgment creditor cannot proceed against stockholders by scire facias, but must sue them upon their liability; Williams v Hanna, 40 Ind, 535 (1872), holding that owners of stock at the time corporate debts are contracted are intended in a statute making stockholders liable for all debts of the company, etc; Larrabee v Baldwin, 35 Cal, 155 (1868); Moss v Oakley, 2 Hill, 265 (1842); holding that a charter declaring stockholders jointly and severally liable for the debts of the company makes liable only such as were members when the debt was con-

tracted, and not those persons who became members afterwards   Judson v. Rossie, etc, 9 Paige, 598 (1842), to the same effect, McCullough v. Moss, 5 Denio, 567, 572, 585 (1846) to same effect; Adderly v Storm, 6 Hill, 624, holding that they are considered liable whose names appear on the books of the company as stockholders when the debt was contracted   But see McMaster v Davidson, 29 Hun, 512 (1883), varying this rule as applicable to New York manufacturing corporations; and cf. Tracy v. Yates, 18 Barb, 152 (1854); Phillips v Therasson, 11 Hun, 141 (1877); King v Duncan, 38 Hun, 461 (1886), Davidson v Rankin, 34 Cal, 503 (1868), holding that the cause of action against a stockholder of a mining corporation, under the laws of California, accrues at the same time as against the corporation   In Ohio those who own the stock at the time the corporate creditor commences his suit against stockholders to enforce their statutory liability are liable under the Ohio statute   It is immaterial that some of the stock was issued after the debt itself was incurred by the corporation   See, also, Barrick v Gifford, 24 N E Rep, 259 (Ohio, 1890)   Stockholders are liable under the Ohio statute for debts incurred before they became stockholders, but the equities between them and the transferers of the stock may be adjusted in the same suit.   Railroad Co v Smith, 31 N E Rep, 743 (Ohio, 1891)   Under the Ohio statute the transferees are liable for precedent debts   See Brown v Hitchcock, 36 Ohio St. 667 (1881)   See, also, Mason v Alexander, 44 Ohio St, 318 (1886), Wheeler v Faurot, 37 id, 26

§ 260 *Transferrer's statutory liability after transfer but before registry.*— The previous section treated of the statutory liability of a transferrer in cases where the transfer is recorded on the corporate books at the same time that the sale and transfer of the certificates

(1881); Brown *v* Hitchcock, *supra*, holding, also, that the liability is not discharged by a subsequent transfer of the stock, that in such cases there is an implied undertaking by the assignee to indemnify the assignor from the liability for debts contracted while he was a stockholder. Hager *v* Cleveland, etc., 36 Md., 476, holding that, by virtue of the statute of Maryland, the transfer of stock does not exonerate the transferrer from liability for a corporate debt contracted while he was a stockholder and before the capital stock was paid in. His liability is in the nature of a contract with the company, and is not affected by a transfer of his stock In Illinois suit may be brought against him who is a stockholder at the time suit is brought. ' The liability being because of the ownership of stock, it follows the stock, into whosesoever hands it may go, and whoever purchases it does so at the risk of this liability " Root *v* Sinnock, 11 N. E. Rep, 339 (Ill., 1887). Individual liability continues, even after the death of the stockholder, until a transfer is made Davis *v* Weed (U S D C), 44 Conn., 569 See, also, Witters *v* Sowles, 32 Fed Rep, 130 (1887), Phillips *v* Therasson, 11 Hun, 141 (1877), Tracy *v* Yates, 18 Barb., 152 (1854), holding that, under the New York statute of 1848, a stockholder is not liable for debts contracted before he was such But see McMaster *v* Davidson, 20 Hun 542 (1883) *Cf* Rosevelt *v* Brown, 11 N Y, 148 (1854), Cutting *v* Damerel, 88 id, 410 (1882) See, also, § 261, *infra* A stockholder does not, by transfer, avoid a statutory liability to creditors who were such at the time of the transfer Jackson *v* Meek, 9 S. W Rep, 225 (Tenn., 1888) It is not always clear precisely when a given indebtedness may be held

to have been "contracted " When a corporate note has been renewed, it is doubtful whether the renewal operates to create a new indebtedness or to continue and perpetuate that indebtedness for which the original note was given In Ohio it is held that a renewal which is a payment or extinguishment of the debt discharges the shareholders who were bound under the old note Wheeler *v* Faurot, 37 Ohio St, 26 (1881) And in Maine the date of the second or renewal note is taken as the time when the indebtedness accrued Milliken *v* Whitehouse, 49 Me, 527 (1860) While in Massachusetts the debt is said to be contracted when the corporation accepts a bill of exchange Byers *v* Franklin Coal Co, 106 Mass, 131 (1870) *Cf* Freeland *v*. McCullough, 1 Denio, 414, 426 (1845), holding that, in a suit upon a note given by the corporation for a debt on a simple contract the stockholders at the time the debt was contracted are the ones to be held liable See also, in New York, Parrott *v* Colby 6 Hun 55, affirmed, 71 N Y, 507 (1877), Jagger Iron Co *v* Walker, 76 N Y, 521 (1879) overruling Fisher *v* Marvin, 47 Barb, 159 Moss *v* Oakley, 2 Hill, 265 (1842), holding that, where stockholders at the time the debt was contracted are liable, a note given for a debt will be presumed to have been made when the debt was contracted It has been held that the debt does not accrue, as against the shareholder, at the time judgment thereon is recovered against the corporation Larrabee *v* Baldwin, 35 Cal, 155, 168 (1868) In this case Sawyer, C J, said " The claim of the respondent, that the judgment is itself a contract creating a new debt, within the meaning of the statute, for which all who were stockholders at the date of the rendition of the judgment are per-

are made   But frequently there is some delay in registering the transfer in the corporate books, and in such cases the further complication arises as to who is liable for corporate debts and liabilities incurred during that *interim*   The rule in such cases, however, is clear   The law is well settled that the transferrer of stock is liable to corporate creditors on his statutory liability, up to the time of a registry of the transfer, to the same extent that he would be if no sale and transfer of the certificate had been made until the date of the registry   Until registry is made, corporate creditors may hold the unregistered transferrer liable, as though he had not sold his stock   As to them the transfer will be deemed to have been made only at the date of the record thereof in the corporate stock-book [1]   Such, also, is the rule of the English courts [2]   The cor-

sonally liable, is too absurd to require argument to refute it "   Registered transferees are liable the same as their transferrers, even though before the transfer the statutory liability was decreased by statute   The liability to old creditors follows the stock   Nat'l Com Bank *z* McDonnell, 9 S Rep 149 (Ala, 1891), Tracy *r* Yates, 18 Barb, 152 (1854), holding that the transferee is not liable on prior debts, Cape's Executor s Case, 2 De G, M & G, 562, holding that the transferee is liable for debts incurred before as well as after the transfer, McMaster *z* Davidson, 29 Hun, 512 (1883), holding that the transferee is liable on debts contracted before he became such, but falling due after he became a stockholder   Under the Massachusetts Manufacturing Act, as re-enacted in Rhode Island, "the liability extends to all persons who were stockholders when the debt sought to be enforced was contracted, and also to all persons who are stockholders when the liability is sought to be enforced, although they may have become such

since the debt was contracted ; but it does not extend to persons who had become stockholders after the debt was contracted, and had ceased to be such before the debt became payable and action was brought."   Sales *v* Bates, 2 N E Rep, 633 (R I, 1886)   By the law of copartnership a new partner is not liable for old debts   See Lindley on Partnership, 205, 435, 208 (Callaghan & Co, 1888)

[1] Brown *v* Hitchcock, 36 Ohio St, 667 (1881) holding, also, that after the liability attaches to a stockholder it is not discharged by an assignment or transfer of the stock, but the subsequent holders of it impliedly undertake to indemnify the assignor from his liability, Wehrman *v.* Reakirt, 1 Cinn. Super. Ct, 230 (1871)   *Cf* Jackson *v.* Sligo Manuf'g, etc., Co, 1 Lea (Tenn.), 210 (1878)   In an action to charge a transferrer for corporate debts incurred between transfer and registry, the transferee is, in Ohio, a necessary party   Wheeler *z* Faurot, 37 Ohio St, 26 (1881), Richmond *z* Irons, 121 U S, 27 (1887),

[2] Musgrave & Hart's Case, L R, 5 Eq, 193 (1867), Walker's Case, L R, 6 Eq, 30 (1868), McEuen *z* West London Wharves, etc, Co, L R 6 Chan, 655 (1871), Gower's Case, L R, 6 Eq, 77 (1868), holding that, where shares had been forfeited by a resolution of the directors, but the names of their owners had not been removed from the register, they were contributories in winding-up proceedings instituted a year later   Humby's Case, 5 Jur (N. S), 215 (1859), Head's Case, L R, 3 Eq, 84 (1866), White's Case, L R, 3 Eq, 86 (1866)   Shepherd s Case L R, 2 Chan, 16 (1866)

porate creditor, in determining who are stockholders, need only show that the persons whom he sues appear as stockholders on the corporate stock-books [1]

A different question arises when an irregular registry of the transfer has been made, or the transferrer has done all in his power to effect a registry, or the corporation has accepted the unregistered transferee as a stockholder These questions, however, are considered elsewhere [2]

§ 261. *The transferee's statutory liability* — The transferee of stock whose name has been duly entered on the stock-book as a shareholder becomes thereupon liable on the stock to corporate creditors. The registry which operates to change the stockholder at the same time operates to charge the transferee [3] It is immaterial that no certificate has been issued to the transferee, or that the corporation has not issued certificates to any of the shareholders [4] Nor will the transferee be heard to allege, as defense against an action to enforce the statutory liability, that he was induced by fraudulent representations to purchase the shares [5] Whether the

Shellington v Howland, 53 N Y, 371 (1873), Johnson v Underhill, 52 id 203 (1873), Veiller v Brown 18 Hun 571 (1879), Richardson v Abernoth 43 Barb, 162 (1864), Worrall v Judson, 5 id, 210 (1849), Borland v Haven 37 Fed Rep, 394 (1888), Dane v Young 61 Maine, 100 (1872), Skowhegan Bank v Cutler, 49 id, 315 (1860) Fowler v Ludwig, 34 id, 455 (1852), Stanley v Stanley, 26 id, 191 (1846), holding that parol evidence is not admissible as against the books of a corporation to prove who were its stockholders in suits by creditors In support of the general rule see, also, Irons v Manufacturers' Nat Bank 27 Fed Rep 591 (1886), Price v Whitney 28 Fed Rep, 297 (1886), holding that the executors of one whose name appears on the books as a stockholder are liable for assessment, though deceased, in his life-time, had sold the stock Transferrer is liable on debts existing at time of registry of transfer Harford v Stobart, 21 N E Rep., 637 (Ohio, 1889)

[1] Magruder v Colston, 44 Md, 349, 356 (1875) Cf Fisher v Seligman, 75 Mo 13 (1881), Adderly v Storm, 6 Hill, 624 (1844), Crease v Babcock 10

Metc, 525 (1846), Matter of the Empire City Bank, 18 N Y, 200 224 (1858), Holyoke Bank v Burnham 11 Cush, 183, 187 (1853) A stockholder is presumed to be a stockholder until the contrary is shown Barron v Paine, 22 Atl Rep 218 (Me, 1891)

[2] See § 258, supra

[3] Webster v Upton, 91 U S, 65 (1875), De Pass' Case 4 De G & J, 544 (1859) Cape's Executors Case, 2 De G, M & G, 562 (1852), Briggs v Waldron 83 N Y, 582 (1881) Cf Chesley v Pierce, 32 N H, 388 (1875), Thebus v Smiley 110 Ill, 316 (1884), to the effect that there can be but one amount for which there is liability on account of the same stock, and the statutory double liability having been once met by an owner of the stock, his transferee takes it free from liability

[4] See § 258, supra

[5] Oakes v Turquand, L R., 2 House of Lords, 325 (1867), Houldsworth v City of Glasgow Bank, L R, 5 App. Cas., 317 (1880) Tennent v City of Glasgow Bank, L R, 4 App Cas., 615 (1872), and see ch IX Cf. Slater's Case, 35 Bear, 391 (1866)

statutory liability attaches to a shareholder, in respect of debts contracted before he became a member of the corporation, is a question turning upon the words of the statute.[1] Nevertheless, although the transferee may not be liable to others, he clearly is liable herein to his transferee for liabilities herein which fall upon the latter.[2] A purchaser of stock may be held liable to creditors upon the liability imposed by statute, although the transfer is not recorded.

§ 262 *Liability of transferee to transferrer herein* — A transfer of stock may be said to involve three distinct acts, all of which may take place at one and the same time, or each at a different time   There is, first, the agreement of sale, by which the right to the stock passes from the transferrer to the transferee; second, the formal transfer of the certificate of stock, third, a registry of the transfer, by an entry on the corporate transfer-book.   It frequently happens that the registry is not made until some time after the agreement of sale, and that during the *interim* calls on the subscription are made or corporate creditors' rights attach.   The law then holds liable the transferrer whose transfer has not been registered   But in reality his transferee ought to meet that liability.   Hence the rule that for liabilities arising after a sale of stock, but before a registry of the same on the corporate books, the vendee is liable to the vendor when such liabilities are paid by the latter [3]

[1] See § 259

[2] See § 262   An unrecorded transferee is liable on the statutory liability of stockholders.   McDowall *v* Sheehan, 129 N Y . 200 (1891)   A stockholder of record in a national bank cannot set up that the transfer was made without his knowledge or consent, where he was cashier of the bank and was bound by law to know about the stock book. Finn *v.* Brown, 142 U S., 56 (1891)   A person to whom stock is transferred on the corporate books is liable on the statutory liability, if he approves or acquiesces in it in any way as by signing an application to change the charter of the bank, or by indorsing checks which are made out to him for dividends.   He is estopped from denying that he knew what he was signing   It is immaterial whether a new certificate was issued to him or not.   Keyser *v* Heitz. 133 U S, 138 (1890)

[3] Lord *t* Hutzler, 3 Atl Rep., 891

(1886), Johnson *v.* Underhill, 52 N. Y, 203 (1873), Kellogg *v* Stockwell, 75 Ill, 68 (1874); Hutzler *v* Lord, 64 Md, 534 (1885)   Brigham *v* Mead, 10 Allen, 245 (1865), Walker *v* Bartlett 18 C. B., 845, overruling Humble *v* Langston, 7 Mees & W, 517, Gissell *v* Bristowe, L R., 3 C P, 112 (1868), Davis *v* Haycock, L R. 4 Exch 373 (1871), Bowring *v.* Shepherd, L R., 6 Q B, 309 (1869); Kellock *v* Enthoven. L R, 9 Q B. 241 (1874), S C, L R, 8 Q B. 458. The statute of limitations does not begin to run against the transferrer until the assessment is paid by him.   Hutzler *v.* Lord, *supra* So, also, when shares are sold for future delivery, but before the time for delivery the seller, in order to save the stock from forfeiture, is compelled to pay assessments duly levied upon it, the seller may refuse to deliver until he is repaid the amount of such assessments. Whitney *v* Page (N Y. Super Ct), Daily Register, March 31,

The transferrer in these cases may have recourse to the real and not the nominal transferee [1] In case of several successive transfers, the transferrer who has paid an assessment or corporate debt may look to his immediate transferee, although there be another one in the series who will ultimately be charged [2] Generally the transferrer who has paid seeks his remedy by a suit in equity for indemnity, and also to compel a registry of the transfer [3]

1885 A transferrer who seeks recourse to his transferee for calls paid by the former after the transfer does not prove the transfer by showing a registry of the same He must prove some act of purchase or acceptance by the transferee Tripp v Appleman, 35 Fed Rep., 19 (1888)

[1] Castellan v Hobson, L R 10 Eq. Cas, 47 (1870) But not to an intervening unregistered transferee Shaw v Fisher, 2 De G & Sm. 11 (1848), S C. 5 De G, M & G, 596 (1855) See, also, § 253, supra. An unrecorded transferee who has transferred the certificate to still another party is not liable to his transferrer for calls made after the transferee had transferred to the second transferee. Brinkly v Hambleton, 8 Atl Rep, 904 (Md, 1887) In Lessassier v Kennedy, 36 La Ann, 539 (1884), an unregistered vendee escaped liability of indemnity to his vendor, because the vendee sold to a person to whom the transfer direct from the first vendor was made on the corporate books, but without the knowledge of the vendor The dissenting opinions in this case are to be commended

[2] Nickalls v Eaton, 23 L T (N S), 689 (1871), Kellock v Enthoven, supra Or he may look to the final transferee, even though the call was made before the latter purchased Hawkins v Maltby, L R, 3 Ch, 188 (1867) See S C, L R, 6 Eq, 505 (1868)

[3] Wynne v Price, 3 De G & Sm, 310 (1849); Cheale v Kenward, 3 De G & J, 27 (1858), Morris v Cannan 4 De G, F & J, 581 (1862), Hawkins v Maltby, L R, 4 Chan, 200 (1868), holding, however, that the vendor cannot re-

cover from the vendee interest which he has had to pay to a liquidator by way of penalty for not having paid calls promptly, Butler v Cumpston L R, 7 Eq 16, Evans v Wood, L R., 5 Eq, 9 (1867), Paine v Hutchinson, L R., 23 Eq, 257, Cruse v Paine, L R, 6 id 611, S C, 4 id, 441 (1868), Shaw v Fisher, 2 De G & Sm, 11 (1848) James v May, L R. 6 House of Lords, 328 Allen v Graves, L R, 5 Q B, 479 (1870), holding that, where the purchaser did not offer as transferee the name of a person to whom no reasonable objection could be made he had not fulfilled the contract of sale and was liable for the amount of a call subsequently made, and interest, as damages, Shaw v Rowley, 16 Mees. & W, 810 (1847), sustaining an action for price of shares sold on which a previous call had not been paid, it being held that plaintiffs could recover because they could have paid the call and transferred the stock if defendants had furnished the name of the transferee when requested In Ohio, under the act creating statutory liability on the part of shareholders, transferees are liable, as between themselves and their vendors for all indebtedness of the corporation, whether incurred before or after the transfer, "as if they had owned the stock from the organization of the company" Wheeler v Faurot, 37 Ohio St, 26 (1881) Brown v Hitchcock, 36 id, 667 (1881), a case wherein the question of statutory liability is very fully and satisfactorily discussed To same effect Cape's Case, 2 De G, M & G, 562 (1852) That a transferrer may compel the transferee to register the transfer,

§§ 263-265 *A transfer to a "dummy" or to an insolvent to escape liability* [1] — In the United States a transfer of shares in a failing concern, made by the transferrer with the intention and for the purpose of escaping liability as a shareholder to a person who for any cause is incapable of responding in respect of such liability, is void both as to creditors of the company and as to other shareholders, and that, too, although as between the transferrer and transferee the transaction may have been absolute and no secret trust involved[2]. But, on the other hand, it has been held that if

see § 384. The court will determine the liability as between the transferrer and transferee, in connection with the corporate creditors' suit, brought to enforce the stockholder's liability. Mason v Alexander, 44 Ohio St., 318 (1886), Sayles v Blanc, 19 L. J. (Q. B.), 19 (1849), holding that a transferrer who continues to be the owner on the registry, and who has been compelled to pay calls made after the transfer, cannot recover the money so paid from the transferee upon the common count for money paid for his use.

[1] The cases in this section refer to instances where a person transfers stock from his own name to that of a "dummy." An entirely different class of cases exists where the person really interested buys stock or subscribes for stock in the name of a "dummy," and the name of the real owner never appears on the corporate books. The latter class of cases are treated of in § 253, *supra*.

[2] Nathan v Whitlock, 3 Edw. Chan (N. Y.), 215 (1838), S. C., 9 Paige, 152 (1841), Rider v Tritchey 30 N. E. Rep., 692 (Ohio, 1892). Transferee held liable herein though transfer of certificate was made long previous, but registered only shortly before insolvency, and though all parties acted in good faith. Richmond v Irons 121 U. S, 27 (1887), Veiller v Brown, 18 Hun, 571 (1879), McLaren v Franciscus, 43 Mo., 452 (1869); Miller v Great Republic Ins Co, 50 id., 55 (1872), holding, however, that if a sale and transfer be made honestly and without intent to defraud the creditors of

the corporation, the fact that the purchaser is insolvent will not render the vendor liable. Provident Savings Institution v Jackson Place Skating and Bathing Rink, 52 id, 557 (1873); Chouteau Spring Co. v Harris, 20 id, 382, Mandion v Fireman's Ins. Co., 11 Rob. (La.), 177 (1845), where the transfer was a gift, *In re* Bachman, 12 Nat. Bank Reg, 223 (1875), Marcy v Clark, 17 Mass, 330 (1821), Central Agricultural, etc Association v Alabama Gold Life, etc, Co, 70 Ala, 120 (1881), Gaff v Flesher, 33 Ohio St., 107 (1877); Douchy v Brown, 24 Vt., 197 (1852), Aultman's Appeal, 98 Pa St., 505 (1881). In the last case one who held stock as collateral security and surrendered it after the company's insolvency to the company, which issued a new certificate to the former owners, was held responsible to the creditors of the company. Everhart v West Chester, etc, R. R. Co, 28 id, 339 (1857), Rider v Morrison, 54 Md, 429 (1880), Paine v Stewart, 33 Conn., 516 (1866), Bowden v Santos, 1 Hughes (U. S.), 158 (1877), Wehrman v. Reakirt, 1 Cin Super. Ct., 230 (1871), Bowden v Johnson, 107 U. S, 251 (1882); Davis v Stevens, 17 Blatch., 259 (1879). *Cf* Allen v. Montgomery R. R. Co., 11 Ala, 457 (1847), Billings v Robinson, 28 Hun, 122 (1882); aff d. 94 N. Y., 415 (1884). It is also held that the owner of stock cannot escape liability by transferring it to his infant children, or by taking it originally in their name. Roman v. Fry, 5 J. J. Marsh, 634 (1831). It has been held, also, that no transfer made in anticipation of a judgment against the corpora-

the transfer is *bona fide*, and the transferrer is ignorant of the insolvency of the transferee, and the company is not insolvent, the transfer is effectual, and the transferrer is released from liability.[1] The creditor's remedy to enforce the liability of a shareholder who has in this way fraudulently assigned or transferred his stock is in a court of chancery.[2]

§ 266 *The rule in England.*— The rule in England is that a shareholder may transfer his shares, when the company is in a failing condition, to a man of straw for a nominal consideration, even although the sole purpose of such a transfer be to escape liability. If the transfer be out and out, and not merely colorable, and collusive with a secret trust attached, it is valid, and the transferrer is thereby released from liability, both as to corporate creditors and the other shareholders.[3] But if the transfer is merely color-

tion, and for the purpose of escaping liability, is valid, and shareholders who make such a transfer will be held liable McLaren *v* Franciscus, 43 Mo, 452 (1869) Macey *v* Clark, 17 Mass, 330 (1821)

[1] Miller *v* Great Republic Ins Co, 50 Mo, 55 (1872) See, also, Cole *v* Ryan, 52 Barb, 168 (1868) *Cf* Billings *v* Robinson, 94 N Y, 415 (1884), S C, 28 Hun, 122 (1882). A stockholder who promises a corporate creditor, at a time when the company's affairs are involved, that he will not transfer, thereby inducing him not to sue to collect his debt, is liable to such creditor in case he does transfer Paine *v* Stewart, 33 Conn, 516 (1866) But a transfer will be held valid, it seems, when it is made pursuant to an antecedent option agreement, although the final transfer is really made in order to avoid liability Holyoke Bank *v* Burnham, 65 Mass, 183 (1853), Magruder *v* Colston, 44 Md, 349 (1875) *Cf* Chapman *v* Shepherd, L R, 2 C P, 228 (1867), under the English statute

[2] Johnson *v.* Southwestern Railroad Bank, 3 Strobh Eq (S C), 263, 295 (1848).

[3] De Pass' Case, 4 De G & J, 544 (1859); Weston's Case, L R, 4 Chan, 20 (1868), Harrison's Case, L R 6 Chan, 286 (1871), Master's Case, L R 7 Chan, 292 (1872) Hahn's Case, L R, 7 Chan

266. n (1872), Bishop's Case, id (1872), Wilham's Case, L R, 1 Chan Div, 576 (1875) King's Case, L R, 6 Chan, 196 (1871), Chynoweth's Case, L R, 15 Chan Div, 13 (1880), Jessopp's Case, 2 De G & J 638 (1858), *In re* Taurine Co, L R, 25 Chan Div, 118 (1883), Moore *v* McLaren, 11 Up Can C P, 534 (1862) Batties' Case, 39 L J, Chan, 391 (1870). *Cf* Bunn's Case, 2 De G F & J, 275 (1860) Thus in De Pass' Case, 4 De G & J, 544 (1859), the facts were that De Pass, owning two hundred and fifty shares of stock in the Mexican & South American Company, for which he had paid £1,750, upon learning that the concern was involved, handed the certificate to his clerk, without having previously spoken to him of the matter, saying that he might have the stock for a sovereign, which the clerk instantly paid, and at the same time accepted the shares In about three weeks this clerk sold the shares to another person in the employ of De Pass Upon the winding up of the company, which was ordered within a few days after the sale by De Pass to his clerk although it was shown that the shares at the time of that sale were worth considerably more than a sovereign, still, inasmuch as the transaction appeared to have been absolute, although confessedly made to escape possible liability, it was held that the

able, and there exists a secret trust in favor of the transferrer, so that as between the parties there has been no *bona fide* transfer, but the object is to secure the shares to the transferrer in the event that the concern becomes prosperous, and to leave them to the transferee if there is a winding up, the transferrer's name will be put in the list of contributories, and the pretended transfer be wholly ignored [1]

The right to transfer shares in England seems to exist up to the time the company is ordered to be wound up and business is suspended [2] But after that time the right is gone, and it is the duty of the management to refuse to allow a transfer.[3] Any collusion between the stockholders and the directors to evade the rules governing transfers, for the purpose of evading liability, will invalidate the transfer.[4] Persons to whom shares have been transferred

transfer might stand, and that De Pass was not liable in respect to the shares after the date of the sale to the clerk But in Master's Case, L R, 7 Chan, 292 (1872), a transfer of two hundred and eighty shares of stock, on which £15 per share had been paid, for a nominal consideration to an irresponsible son-in-law of the transferrer, the transfer being made only for the purpose of escaping liability upon the shares, was held to discharge the transferrer A transfer by a director in a failing corporation to avoid liability is void *Re* South London, etc, Co, 59 L T Rep, 210 (1888).

[1] Budd's Case, 3 De G, F & J, 297 (1861), Payne's Case, L. R. 9 Eq, 223 (1869), Kintrea's Case, 39 L J, Chan, 193 (1869), S C, L R, 5 Chan 95, Chinnock's Case, Johns (Eng Chan), 714 (1860), Costello's Case, 2 De G, F & J, 302 (1860), Hyam's Case, 1 id 75 (1859), Lund's Case, 27 Bear, 465 (1859), *Ex parte* Bennett, 18 id, 339 (1853); Daniell's Case, 22 id, 43 (1856), Lyre's Case, 31 id, 177 (1862); Munt's Case, 22 id 55 (1856), Slater's Case, 35 id, 391 (1866), Bank of Michigan v Gray, 1 Up Can, Q B, 422 (1834), Cox s Case, 33 L J, Chan, 145 (1864), William s Case, L. R., 9 Eq, 225, n. (1869), Capper's Case, L R, 3 Chan, 458 (1868), Mann s Case, id, 459, n. (1868), Mitchell's Case,

L R, 9 Eq 363 (1870); *Ex parte* Hatton, 31 L. J, Chan, 310 (1862) Pugh & Sharman s Case, L R, 13 Eq, 566 (1872); Lankester's Case, L R, 6 Chan, 905, n. (1871), Gilbert's Case, L R, 5 Chan, 559 (1879) *Cf* Castellan v Hobson, L. R., 10 Eq, 47 (1870); Maynard v Eaton, L R, 9 Chan, 414 (1874), Colquhoun v Courtenay, 43 L J, Chan, 338 (1874), Richardson's Case, L. R., 10 Eq., 588 (1875)

[2] De Pass' Case, *supra*, and the cases generally in the preceding notes.

[3] Mitchell's Case, L R, 4 App. Cas, 548 (1879), Weston's Case, L R, 4 Chan, 20, 30 (1868), *Ex parte* Parker, L R, 2 Chan, 685 (1867), Chappell's Case, L R, 6 Chan, 902 (1871) In this country directors have in general no power to refuse or prevent transfers, such as inheres in the boards of management in English companies

[4] Eyre's Case, 31 Bear, 177 (1862), Bennett's Case, 5 De G, M & G, 284 (1851) Nor may a director make use of his position as director to transfer his stock, and thus escape chargeability upon it. Munt's Case, 22 Bear., 55 (1856) Nor will a stockholder be allowed to relieve himself when he learns of the probable insolvency of the concern by inducing the directors to postpone their application for an order to wind up until he have time to transfer

without their knowledge or assent are not estopped, when the knowledge is brought to them, from repudiating and denying the stockholdership [1] The present tendency in England is to give greater security to corporate creditors, and it is probable that the English rule in regard to transfers to insolvent persons will gradually be changed.

his shares to a pauper or other irresponsible person Ex parte Parker, L. R. 2 Chan, 685 (1867), Gilbert's Case, L. R., 5 Chan, 559 (1870), Allin's Case, 16 Eq, 449 (1873). And a director who transfers shares standing in his name to a person already holding all the shares any one person is allowed to hold will not thereby escape liability Ex parte Brown 19 Beav, 97 (1854). In general, moreover, a transferrer is not exempt from liability by reason of a transfer, unless the transferee has the present capacity to assume the liability Nickalls v Merry, L. R., 7 H L, 530 (1875), Browne v Black, L. R., 8 Chan, 939 (1873), Mann's Case L. R., 3 Chan, 459, n (1868) Cf Johnson v Laflin, 5 Dill, 65, 81 (1878), Case of the Reciprocity Bank, 22 N Y, 9 (1860) Accordingly a transfer to an infant for the purpose of escaping liability is futile Symon's Case, L R., 5 Chan, 298 (1870), Weston's Case, id, 614 (1870), Curtis' Case, L R, 6 Eq, 455 (1868); Castello's Case, L R, 8 Eq, 504 (1869),

Walsh v The Union Bank, 5 Quebec L. R., 289 (1879)

[1] Birch's Case, 2 De G & J, 10 (1857), Fox's Case, 3 De G, J & S, 465 (1863) Higg's Case, 2 Hem & M, 657 (1865) Somerville's Case, L R, 6 Chan, 266 (1870) Cf Bullock v Chapman, 2 De G & Sm, 211 (1848) And see, also, case of the Reciprocity Bank, 22 N Y, 9 (1860) A colorable transfer, as has appeared, will not operate to discharge the transferrer where shares were collusively assigned to a servant for the purpose of evading liability Hence when the servant, upon the concern becoming solvent attempted to claim the shares as though the transfer had been out and out, the court, having previously decided against the bona fides of the transaction, held the owner entitled to a declaration that the servant held the shares in trust for him Colquhoun v Courtney, 43 L J, Chan, 358 (1874) As to a transfer made in ignorance of the fact that a winding up has been commenced, see Emmerson's Case, L R, 1 Ch, 433 (1866).

CHAPTER XVI.

ISSUE OF PREFERRED STOCK AND STOCK UPON WHICH INTEREST IS GUARANTIED

§ 267 *What is preferred stock* — By preferred stock is to be understood stock which entitles the holder to receive dividends from the earnings of the company before the common stock can receive a dividend from such earnings [1] In other words, it is stock entitled to dividends from the income or earnings of the corporation before any other dividend can be paid [2] The relation of debtor and creditor does not exist between the preferred stockholders and the corporation, and the right to a preferred or guarantied dividend is not a debt until the dividend is declared A dividend is money paid out of profits by a corporation to its shareholders A preferred dividend is nothing more than that which is paid to one class of shareholders in priority to that to be paid to another class [3]

---

[1] Totten v Tison, 54 Ga., 139 (1875)

[2] Chaffee v Rutland R. R. Co., 55 Vt., 110 (1882).

[3] Belfast, etc, R. R. Co v Belfast, 77 Me., 445 (1885), Taft v Hartford, etc, R. R. Co, 8 R. I, 310, 333 (1866), Chaffee v Rutland, etc, R. R Co, 55 Vt, 110 (1882) A preferred dividend has also been defined as "substantially interest chargeable exclusively on profits" Henry v Great Northern R y Co, 1 De G & J, 606, 637 Crawford v North Eastern, etc R. R. Co, 3 Jur (N S), 1093 (1856) The preferred stockholder

is one who may say, " Nobody shall have any portion of the profits of the company until I have been paid my dividend " Henry v Great Northern R'y Co, 4 Kay & J, 1, 32 (1857) aff'd, 1 De G & J, 606. A preferred dividend is said to be 'a pledge of the funds legally applicable to the purposes of a dividend" Taft v Hartford, etc, R. R Co, 8 R. I, 310, 335 (1866) "Payment of dividends to preferred stockholders differs from such payment to the holders of common stock only in that they are entitled to dividends in priority

Guarantied stock is the same thing as preferred stock,[1] except of course where one corporation guaranties dividends on the stock of another corporation.[2]

§ 268 *When may a corporation issue preferred stock?* — Upon the incorporation of a company the incorporators and stockholders may agree that a part of the stock shall be preferred stock This is generally done by a by-law It is undoubtedly legal, since there is no rule of public policy that forbids it, and moreover it amounts only to a contract of the stockholders as to how they shall divide the profits among themselves.[3]

to any dividends upon the common stock" Miller v Ratterman, 24 N E. Rep., 496 (Ohio, 1890).

[1] Taft v Hartford, etc, R. R. Co, 8 R. I, 310, 333, 334, 335 (1866), Henry v Great Northern R'y Co. 4 Kay & J. 1, 12, 21 (1857), affirmed, 1 De G & J, 606, Lockhart v Van Alstine, 31 Mich, 76 (1875) A guarantied dividend differs in nothing from a preferred dividend. Miller v Ratterman, 24 N E Rep, 496 (Ohio, 1890) Cf Boardman v Lake Shore, etc., R'y, 84 N Y, 157, 174 (1881). holding that the word "guarantied" made the dividends cumulative See §§ 273, 274.

[2] See ch XLVI, *infra*

[3] The case *Re* South etc, Brewery Co. L R. 31 Ch D, 261 (1885), clearly holds that, although the charter and statutes are silent on the subject, yet that the by-laws may provide for the issue of preferred stock, and this provision being in the original by-laws, a stockholder cannot enjoin a subsequent issue of the stock, approving Harrison v Mexican R y, L R. 19 Eq Cas. 358 (1875) Judge Cooley, in the case Lockhart v Van Alstine, 31 Mich, 76, 81, 85 (1875), said, in reference to the issues of preferred stock, even though the issues are not provided for by charter or statute, ' there can be no reasonable objection to them if they are entered into with full knowledge on the part of all concerned . The guaranty properly construed is not void, but unobjectionable " In the case Kent v Quicksilver, etc., Co., 78 N Y, 159, affirming

17 Hun, 169, the court said " We know nothing in the constitution or the law that inhibits a corporation from beginning its corporate action by classifying the shares in its capital stock, with peculiar privileges to one share over another, and thus offering its stock to the public subscriptions thereto No rights are got until a subscription is made Each subscriber would know for what class of stock he put down his name and what right he got when he thus became a stockholder. There need be no deception or mistake, there would be no trenching upon rights previously acquired, no contract, express or implied, would be broken or impaired ' The same question has recently arisen in the United States courts, and the court there held that a stockholder, who is an officer of the company who is active in having preferred stock issued subscribes for it, takes his certificate therefor, votes upon it and induces others to take it, cannot after two years, when the corporation is insolvent, say that the statutes of the state authorize the issue of common stock only Banigan v Bard, 134 U S, 291 (1890), S C, 39 Fed Rep, 13. The highest authority in England, Lindley on Companies, p 396. says 'Shares conferring on their holders preferential or additional rights not enjoyed by the holders of other shares are called preference shares They can only be created when the authority to create them is given by statute or charter, or by agreement between all parties interested If, however, authority to

But after the corporation has been organized, with common stock only, and the stock issued in whole or in part, and business commenced and money invested in stock, it is then too late to make the unissued stock preferred stock, or to increase the capital stock and issue preferred stock, unless all the stockholders assent thereto. It would be a breach of contract to issue preferred stock then, inasmuch as the existing stockholders invested their money on the basis of common stock only. Hence a dissenting stockholder may enjoin the corporation, the directors and the majority of stockholders from issuing preferred stock in such a case [1]

issue them is given by a company's memorandum of association, or by its articles of association as originally named, preference shares may be issued." If all assent, the issue is legal. *Re* Bridgewater, etc, Co, 58 L T Rep, 476 (1888) affirmed, id. 866 In the case Bates *v* Androscoggin, etc, R. R., 49 Me, 491 (1860), preferred stock was issued by unanimous consent, but without express statutory authority Preferred stock was issued without statutory authority in Gordon's Ex rs *v* Richmond, etc, R. R., 78 Va, 501 (1884) In Sturge *v* Eastern Union R'y, 7 De G, M & G, 158 (1855), the court declined to pass upon the question whether, at common law, it was legal for a corporation to issue preferred stock In England a stock dividend of preferred stock may be enjoined by any stockholder, inasmuch as any stock dividend may be objected In America the rule is different. See ch XXXII, *infra* A person who participates in an issue of preferred stock, and also subscribes for part of it, cannot repudiate it upon the insolvency of the company. Bard *v* Banigan, 39 Fed Rep, 13 (1889) Where a person bought new preference stock of a railway company which both he and the directors *bona fide* believed they had power to issue, but which in truth, they had not, it was held that he had no remedy against them, for there was nothing more than a common mistake of law Eaglesfield *v* Marquis of Londonderry, 4 Ch D, 693 It is no defense to a subscription for stock that the com-

pany had secretly agreed with certain subscribers to give them a preferred dividend Such an agreement is void as regards another subscriber who did not assent thereto Ryder *v.* Alton, etc, R R, 13 Ill. 501 (1851).

[1] After a part of the stock has been issued, the majority stockholders and the directors cannot give a preference to the remaining stock where the minority object. Hutton *v* Scarborough, etc., Co., 4 De G, J & S, 672 (1865), S C, 2 Dr & Sm, 521, Kent *v.* Quicksilver, etc, Co. 78 N Y, 159 (1879). In the case of Moss *v* Syers, 32 L J, Ch, 711 (1863), the court at the instance of dissenting stockholders enjoined the issue of preferred stock which was not provided for by the charter or by the original agreement of the stockholders. A pledgee of a certificate of stock is not bound by a subsequent agreement of all the stockholders to surrender to the corporation a part of their stock, which part is then to be considered preferred stock and is to be sold by the corporation for the purpose of paying corporate debts Although all the other stock has had this agreement stamped on the certificates, yet the corporation cannot insist that the purchaser of the stock so pledged shall allow the same agreement to be stamped on the new certificate issued to such purchaser. The court will order a transfer free from the agreement Campbell *v* American, etc, Co., 122 N Y, 455 (1890) A preliminary injunction against the issue of preferred stock in order to raise capital for an old

So also a common stockholder may object where preferred and common stock are already issued and an attempt is made to issue second preferred [1]

But the dissenting stockholder must move quickly in the matter. If he delays in bringing his suit, so that the interested parties are justified in believing that he acquiesces in the issue, and the issue itself is made, his remedy is barred. His injunction suit will fail [2]. If, however, the statutes of the state authorize the issue, or if the by-laws contemplate a future issue of preferred stock, its issue will be legal, even though some of the stockholders object [3]

Where the articles of incorporation specify the amount of preferred and common stock, and also state that further stock may be issued, this increased stock must be common stock, and cannot be second preferred stock, even though the by-laws provide that it may be issued on such conditions as the corporation may determine [4]

Preferred stock may be issued subsequently to the issue of the

corporation was refused in Fielden v Lancashire, etc, Ry, 2 De G & Sm, 536 (1848), because only five stockholders dissented, but the court expressly refused to declare the issue a legal one

[1] Melhado v Hamilton, 28 L T (N S), 578 (1873) S C, 29 id, 364

[2] A stockholder who is an officer of the company, who is active in having preferred stock issued, subscribes for it, pays for it, takes his certificate therefor, votes upon it and induces others to take it, cannot after two years when the corporation is insolvent, say that the statutes of the state authorize the issue of common stock only. Banigan v Bard, 134 U S, 291 (1890), affirming 39 Fed Rep. 13. The court has refused relief where there was a delay of four years, Kent v Quicksilver Mining Co, 78 N Y, 159 (1879), or ten years. Taylor v South, etc., R. R. Co. 4 Woods, 575 (1882), S C, 13 Fed Rep, 152. Delays in raising the question of the validity of an issue of preferred stock, advantages having accrued in the meantime to the corporation and the shareholders, have been held such acquiescence as will bar the right of a stockholder to object. Acceptance of the preferred stock and dividends thereon also bars the right to

challenge the legality of the issue Branch v Jesup, 106 U S, 468 (1882). Preferred stock may by unanimous consent be issued although the statutes are silent concerning it. When issued after the first issue of stock has been made it may be prevented by a dissenting stockholder, yet delay on the part of the latter will bar his objection. Hazlehurst v Savannah, etc, R R, 43 Ga, 13 (1871). But see Moss v Syes, 32 L J, Ch, 711 (1863)

[3] If the by-laws provide that any increased capital may be made in such manner and with rules, regulations, privileges and conditions as a meeting of the stockholders might determine, preferred stock may be issued on an increase of the capital stock. Harrison v Mexican, etc, R'y, L. R., 19 Eq Cas. 358 (1875)

[4] Melhado v Hamilton, 28 L T Rep 578, affirmed, 29 id, 364 (1873), the court saying "If they could issue one share they could issue a thousand, and if at seven per cent. they might issue them at seventy per cent. and thus, at a general meeting, they might pass resolutions which would have the effect of utterly annihilating the interests of the ordinary shareholders"

common and against the dissent of the minority stockholders, where the legislature amends the charter and provides for the issue of preferred stock Such an amendment is considered incidental and is constitutional.[1]

A subscriber to preferred stock may be liable on the subscription, although no preferred stock can be issued,[2] and a person who loans money to be repaid in such stock may recover it back if the stock cannot be issued[3]

§ 269. *Rights of preferred stockholders — Amount of preference — Voting — Subsequent leases, consolidations, etc* — The rights, powers and privileges of preferred stockholders depend largely on the terms upon which it is issued Preferred stock takes a multiplicity of forms according to the desire and ingenuity of the stockholders and the necessities of the corporation itself. The percentage of preferred dividend is always fixed at the time of the issue. It is a matter of contract[4] The preferred dividends may be made

---

[1] Everhart v West Chester, etc , R R. Co., 28 Pa St., 339 (1857), holding that a charter amendment authorizing the issue was legal; Rutland, etc , R R Co v Thrall, 35 Vt., 536, 545 (1863), to same effect, and holding that a common stockholder could not defeat his subscription on this ground, Williston v Michigan, etc , R R. Co 95 id , 400 (1866); Curry v Scott, 54 Pa St , 270 (1867), Covington v Bridge Co , 10 Bush (Ky), 69 (1873), where the dissenting stockholder did not object until after the preferred stock had been issued and dividends laid upon it In Covington, etc., Bridge Co v. Sargent, 1 Cin Super Ct , 354 (1871), there is an intimation that such a statute is unconstitutional, and the court held that statutory power to issue a certain amount of preferred stock did not authorize an issue of partly preferred and partly common This decision may well be questioned. In England an act of parliament may authorize such an issue Stevens v South Devon R'y, 9 Hare 313 (1851). And in one case the legality of the issue of preferred stock under a statute was put upon the ground not of the right to borrow money, but upon the ground of a right to raise funds by sale of stock. Chaffee v Rutland, etc , R R Co, 55

Vt , 110 (1882) In the case of Eichbaum v City of Chicago Grain Elevators, 65 L T Rep , 704 (1891), the court held that the company upon increasing its capital stock might, by a majority vote of its stockholders, make such increased capital preferred stock, calling for a certain dividend with no rights in surplus profits beyond that dividend, and might give to common stockholders the right to exchange their common stock for such preferred

[2] Where a person subscribes for preferred stock but no preferred stock is provided for, and he becomes a director and acts as such for several years, he is liable on such stock to corporate creditors, as though it were a subscription for common stock Tama. etc., Co v Hopkins, 44 N W Rep , 797 (Iowa, 1890)

[3] Where a corporation borrows money and agrees to repay it in preferred stock but has no power to issue the preferred stock, the party paying the money may recover it back Anthony v. Household, etc , Co, 18 Atl Rep , 176 (R I 1889).

[4] The amount of preference, and whether cumulative or not, is all a matter of contract Smith v Cork, etc , R'y, Ir Rep , 3 Eq , 356 (1869) The amount of preference may be deter-

cumulative or not cumulative If nothing is specified in respect
to this, then the law makes the preferred dividends cumulative[1]
It seems that unless the contract expressly provides otherwise, preferred stockholders participate in the surplus profits remaining
after the proper dividend has been declared on the preferred and
an equal dividend on the common stock[2]

Where the preferred stockholders are entitled to participate in all
dividends paid after their preferred dividend is paid, they are entitled to participate in a dividend of scrip, similar to a stock dividend
and representing accumulated profits which have been used for betterments[3] The disposition of the surplus profits after the regular
dividends have been paid is a matter of contract[4]

After the preference has been fixed the company cannot alter it
by altering the amount of preference and providing for the redemption of shares out of the surplus profits.[5]

Preferred stockholders are entitled to vote at elections and to exercise the various rights of stockholders the same as common stockholders, unless this right is expressly withheld from them by the
terms under which the stock is issued.[6]

As already stated there are an infinite variety of provisions under
which preferred stock may legally be issued. These provisions are
to be found in the charter, the by-laws, the certificates of stock, the

mined by the by-laws, and the provisions of such a by-law constitute a contract. Belfast, etc, R. R. v. Belfast, 77
Me , 445 (1885).

[1] See §§ 273, 274, infra.

[2] Id

[3] Gordon's Ex'rs v Richmond, etc, R.
R., 78 Va., 501 (1884)

[4] Where the articles of incorporation
specify that after certain dividends
have been paid on both the preferred
and common stock, one-fifth of the surplus shall go to the preferred stock, the
company cannot devote such surplus to
redeeming of shares. Ashbury v Watson, L. R., 30 Ch D , 376 (1885)

[5] Ashbury v. Watson, L. R., 30 Ch D ,
376 (1885). If a stockholder, by accepting the benefits, assents to a change in
the privileges which pertain to his stock,
he cannot afterwards object thereto.
Compton v Chelsea, 13 N Y Supp., 722
(1891). A pledgee of a certificate of
stock is not bound by an agreement of
all the stockholders to surrender to the

corporation a part of their stock, which
part is to be then considered preferred
stock and is to be sold by the corporation for the purpose of paying corporate
debts. Although all the other stock
has had this agreement stamped on the
certificates, yet the corporation cannot
insist that the purchaser of the stock so
pledged shall allow the same agreement
to be stamped on the new certificate
issued to such purchaser The court
will order a transfer free from the
agreement. Campbell v American, etc ,
Co , 122 N Y., 455 (1890)

[6] Miller v. Ratterdam, 24 N E. Rep ,
496 (Ohio, 1890), where the right to vote
was expressly withheld. In the case Mc-
Intosh v Flint, etc , R. R., 34 Fed Rep ,
350 (1887), it appeared that the common
stockholders were by contract deprived
of their right to vote for a specified
time In the case Re Barrow, etc , Co.,
59 L. T Rep , 50 (1888), the right to vote
was withheld from preferred stockholders.

resolutions of the stockholders and directors, the minutes of corporate meetings, the reports of or to the company, and any contracts under which the stock was issued. The rights pertaining to the stock are matters of contract, and this contract is ascertained from the sources specified above.[1] Some of the various devices for raising money by issuing various kinds of preferred stock are referred to in the notes below[2]

§ 270. Where the corporation has power to lease its road, it may make a lease, although the rental is sufficient to pay a dividend on the preferred stock alone, leaving nothing for the common stockholders.[3]

[1] Boardman v Lake Shore, etc., R. R Co., 84 N Y, 157 (1881), Gordon v. Richmond, etc, R. R. Co., 78 Va. 501, 510 (1884), Baily v Hannibal, etc, R. R. Co., 1 Dill, 174 (1871); S C, 17 Wall, 96, St John v Erie R'y Co., 22 id, 136 (1874), Webb v Earle, L R, 20 Eq, 556 (1875); Matthews v Great Northern, etc, R'y Co, 28 L J, Chan, 375 (1859), construing a statute affecting the rights of holders of "guarantied" and "deferred" stock, Belfast, etc, R. R Co. v Belfast, 77 Me, 445 (1885), Stevens v South, etc, R'y Co, 9 Hare, 313 (1851), Sturge v Eastern, etc., R'y Co, 7 De G, M. & G, 158 (1857): Harrison v Mexican, etc., R'y Co, L R, 19 Eq. Cas, 358 (1875), Crawford v Northeastern, etc, R'y Co., 3 Jur (N S), 1093 (1856), Henry v Great Northern, etc, R'y Co, 1 De G & J, 606, 642, 646 (1857), Matthews v Same, 28 L J, Ch, 375 (1859). See, also, Coates v. Nottingham, etc, 30 Bear, 86 The agreement is ascertained from the contract, reports, resolutions, conveyances, etc Rogers v. New York, etc., Land Co, 134 N Y., 197 (1892).

[2] Under the powers conferred by the statute, 30 and 31 Vict., ch 127, various plans have been devised by English companies on the verge of insolvency to raise funds, and a favorite device is the issue of preferred shares of stock. Thus, in one case, there were five kinds of preference shares. Corry v Londonderry etc., R'y Co., 29 Bear., 263 (1860). See, also, by way of illustration as to these various methods in England of raising funds by the issue of preferred shares, Matthews v Great Northern, etc, R'y Co, 28 L J, Chan, 375 (1859), Re Cambrion R'y Co, L R, 3 Chan, 278 (1868); Re Potteries, etc., R'y Co., id, 67 (1867), Webb v Earl, L R, 20 Eq 556 (1875), Stevens v Midland, etc., R'y Co, L R, 8 Chan. 1064 (1873); Re Bristol, etc, R'y Co, L R, 6 Eq, 448 (1868), Re Devon, etc, R'y Co, id, 610 (1868), Munas v Isle of Wight R'y Co, L R, 8 Eq, 665 (1869;, Re East & West, etc, R'y Co, id, 87 (1869); London, etc, Association v Wrexham, etc., R'y Co, L R, 18 Eq, 566 (1874), Re Anglo-Danubian, etc, Co., L R, 20 Eq, 339 (1875), Midland R'y Co v Gordon 16 Mees & W, 804 (1847). For a scheme where the stock was divided into half shares, one-half of which were deferred to the other half, see Re Brighton, etc, R'y, 62 L T Rep., 353 (1890). In Phillips v Eastern R. R, 138 Mass., 122 (1884), a scheme appears by which under a statute the creditors elected two-thirds and the stockholders one-third of the directors

[3] Middletown v Boston, etc, R. R., 53 Conn, 351 (1885) In the case Re Buenos Ayres. etc, Co, 66 L T. Rep., 408 (1892), a sale of the company's enterprise to the government upon terms which paid something to the preferred stockholders but left nothing for the common stockholders was sustained

But in a contract of lease the rent must be applied to income bonds before it is applied to dividends and preferred stock [1]

Where a corporation, having issued preferred stock, is merged into a new corporation by consolidation, the preferred shareholders of the old corporation may prosecute a suit for dividends against the new corporation if the consolidated company has assumed all the obligations of the old company.[2]

A preferred stockholder is entitled to a certificate of stock which sets forth the fact of the preference [3]

Sometimes the right is given to exchange common for preferred stock or preferred for common, or bonds for stock. Concerning any such options, it is the settled rule that any time limited for the exercise thereof is of the essence of the offer.[4]

Dividends on the preferred stock must be on all of that class, even though some of it has been exchanged for preferred stock bearing a lower dividend.[5]

[1] In Phillips v Eastern R R, 138 Mass, 122, 135 (1884), preferred stock had been offered, under a statute, in exchange for indebtedness to be paid from income only. The company leased its property, and the lessee agreed to use the net profits to pay dividends on the preferred stock the same as the interest on such debts as had not been converted into preferred stock, and if the net profits were not sufficient, each was to get the same proportionately. The court held this to be illegal, inasmuch as it placed the preferred stockholders on the same basis as the income creditors.

[2] Boardman v Lake Shore, etc, R R Co, 84 N Y, 157 (1881), Chase v Vanderbilt, 62 id, 307 (1875). Cf Prouty v Lake Shore, etc, R. R. Co, 52 N Y, 363 (1873).

[3] Where by statute municipal aid bonds are to be paid for by preferred stock, the municipality may by mandamus compel the company to issue a certificate of stock setting forth the preference. State v Cheraw, etc, R R., 16 S C, 524 (1881).

[4] Where the corporation offers to exchange preferred for common stock, upon the payment of an additional sum of money, a stockholder who delays for thirty years to avail himself of

the privilege cannot claim the right thereto. The fact that the corporation had taken in some of the common stock on a new basis of exchange is immaterial. Holland v Cheshire R'y, 24 N E Rep, 206 (Mass, 1890). An extension of the time when a bond is to be paid does not extend the time within which it may be exchanged for stock of the company. Muhlenberg v Philadelphia, etc, R R, 17 Pa St., 16 (1864). Where an option was given to holders of the common stock to take a certain number of new preferred shares within a given time, it was held that a shareholder who lived abroad and had no notice of the option until the expiration of the specified time could not, upon learning of it afterwards, come in and demand the right to purchase the preferred shares. Pearson v London, etc, Ry Co, 14 Sim, 541 (1845). Such, also is the rule where there is an option within a fixed time to convert loan notes into common shares. Campbell v London, etc, Ry Co 5 Hare, 519 (1846). See, also, § 283.

[5] Although the preferred stock is partly taken back by the company and new preferred stock of the same amount, bearing a less dividend, is issued in exchange, yet this does not enable the

Preferred stockholders are subject to a statutory liability the same as common stockholders [1]

§ 271. *Preferred stockholders are not creditors — Dividends can be only from profits — Mortgages securing preferred stock.* — Formerly it was a matter of doubt and discussion whether or not a preferred stockholder had any rights as a creditor of the company or was confined to his rights as a stockholder. The law is now clearly settled that a preferred stockholder is not a corporate creditor [2]

The preferred shareholder is but a shareholder with a right to have his dividend paid before dividends on the common stock are paid, and he is not entitled to any dividend until the corporation has funds which are properly applicable to the payment of dividends. A contract that dividends shall be paid on the preferred

---

company to declare a dividend on the part not exchanged, and on that alone. It must declare on all. Coey v. Belfast, etc., R'y, Ir. Rep., 2 C L, 112 (1866). If part of the preferred stockholders surrender their stock for new common stock on a reorganization without foreclosure, such stock is canceled, and holders not so surrendering their stock are entitled to arrears of dividends out of the first net profits, without allowing such surrendered stock to participate therein. West Chester, etc., R. R. v. Jackson 77 Pa St., 321 (1875). In this case there was a special act providing for the issue of preferred stock, and afterwards another for the issue of consolidated stock. A dividend having been declared, a holder of the preferred stock, who had declined to accept the consolidated, was held "entitled to receive just what the company agreed to pay when the money was received." In the case Griffith v. Paget, L. R., 6 Ch D, 511 (1877), S C, 25 W. R., 523, it was held that where the company is dissolved by a consolidation with another company, under a statute, the stockholders of the old being entitled to exchange their stock for stock in the new, the preferred stock is not entitled to preferred stock in the new.

[1] Railroad Co. v. Smith, 31 N E Rep., 743 (Ohio, 1891).

[2] The House of Lords in England have clearly laid down the rule that preferred stockholders are not creditors. Birch v. Cropper, 61 L. T. Rep., 621 (1889); Belfast, etc., R. R. v. Belfast, 77 Me., 445 (1885). A very full, clear and learned discussion of the essential differences between a preferred stockholder and a creditor of a corporation is to be found in Miller v. Ratterman, 24 N. E. Rep., 496 (Ohio, 1890), a case wherein the preferred stockholder was secured by a mortgage and was deprived of the right to vote at corporate elections. Taft v. Hartford, etc., R. R. Co, 8 R. I., 310 (1866), Chaffee v. Rutland, etc., R. R. Co, 55 Vt, 110 (1882), the court saying "The claim is that he is also a creditor with all the rights pertaining to that relation. Against this claim are the terms of the charter, the presumption of law and the usual course of business." In this case certificates issued for "scrip dividends" or "guarantied preferred stock" were convertible into mortgage bonds. The company having refused to convert them it was held that general *assumpsit* for the amount of the certificates would lie, and that the suit could be brought in the name of the holder for value. St. John v. Erie R'y Co., 10 Blatch., 271 (1874); S. C., 23 Wall., 137.

stock whether any profits are made or not would be contrary to public policy and void. An agreement to pay dividends absolutely and at all events — from the profits when there are any, and from the capital when there are not — is an undertaking which is contrary to law, and is void. Public policy condemns with emphasis any such undertaking on the part of a corporation as to its preferred or guarantied shares. Dividends on preferred stock are payable only out of the net earnings of the company.[1] The ques-

[1] Taft v. Hartford, etc. R. R. Co., 8 R. I., 310 (1866), Lockhart v. Van Alstyne, 31 Mich., 76 (1875), Chaffee v. Rutland, etc. R. R. Co., 55 Vt., 110 (1882), Warren v. King, 108 U. S., 389 (1882). Under the statute in Connecticut it was held that dividends may be declared on preferred stock where the net earnings since the issue of the stock are sufficient, even though prior to such issue the capital stock had been impaired. Cotting v. N. Y., etc., R. R., 54 Conn., 156 (1886). As supporting the rule in the text, see, also, Lockhart v. Van Alstyne 31 Mich., 76 (1875), Crawford v. Northeastern etc., R'y Co., 3 Jur. (N S), 1093 (1856). In Mills v. Northern R'y Co., etc. L. R., 5 Ch. App., 621 (1870), where a corporation, being in arrears in the payment of preferred stock dividends and being at the same time largely indebted, proposed to appropriate a portion of its capital and to borrow further sums upon debentures for the purpose of paying such preferred dividends, it was held, in a suit by the creditors to prevent such action, that inasmuch as the appropriation of the capital was justified on the ground that an equivalent portion of the revenue had been used for capital purposes, and the proposed loan was within the company's borrowing power, an injunction could not be granted. See, also, Elkins v. Camden, etc., R. R. Co., 36 N J Eq, 233 (1882). Belfast, etc., R. R. Co. v. Belfast, 77 Me., 445 (1885), and the cases supra.

In the case Guinness v. Land Corporation, L. R. 22 Ch. D., 349 (1882), the court declared illegal a provision for the payment of preferred dividends out of the capital stock. Interest on debts, even those incurred after the preferred stock was issued, and rent on leases including those taken after such issue, must be paid before dividends are declared on the preferred stock. St. John v. Erie R'y., 22 Wall., 137, affirming 10 Blatch., 271 (1872), defining also the meaning of net profits. In the case Williston v. Michigan Southern, etc. R. R. 95 Mass., 400 (1866). the court held that preferred and guarantied stock in a Michigan and Indiana corporation was not entitled to dividends unless there were net profits. Preferred dividends may be paid out of the *gross* earnings where the statute evidently so intended. Gordon's Ex'rs v. Richmond, etc. R. R., 78 Va., 501 (1884). See, also, Ragland v. Broadnax 29 Gratt., 401 (1877), where the court upheld the charge of guarantied dividends on the gross receipts. That was the case of a debt converted into guarantied stock. The debt would have borne, if it had not been converted into stock, interest at the rate of six per cent. per annum, whether there were net earnings or not. The court held that the guaranty of three per cent. dividend on the whole stock, which formerly belonged to the state, was simply the six per cent. interest upon the debt which was converted into stock; and it also held that it was chargeable, in accordance with the plain provisions of the statute, upon the gross receipts. Guarantied dividends can be paid only from net profits. Miller v. Ratterman, 24 N. E. Rep., 496 (Ohio, 1890).

tion of what constitutes net earnings has been treated elsewhere.[1]

Occasionally, however, a mortgage is given by the corporation
to secure the payment of dividends on preferred stock and to give
it a preference in payment over subsequent debts of the corporation upon insolvency or dissolution It is difficult to see how such
a mortgage would be legal except where it is issued under express
statutory authority. It is difficult to see how stockholders can
contrive legally to obtain a preference over corporate creditors secured or unsecured, as they would do by such a mortgage. Certain
it is that the courts will not readily give the stockholders a preference over creditors, even though the preferred stock is by its terms
to be a first claim on the property.[2]

A mortgage to secure preferred stock and dividends thereon has
been upheld in a few cases[3] In other cases that which was called

[1] See ch XXXII

[2] Preferred stock which is "to be and
remain a first claim upon the property
of the corporation after its indebtedness" has no lien ahead of present or
future debts of the company King v.
Ohio & M R'y 2 Fed Rep, 36 (1880)
See, also, Warren v King. 108 U S, 389
(1882), the court holding that although
the certificates of preferred stock provided that it should "be and remain a
first claim upon the property of the
company after its indebtedness." etc,
and although in foreclosure proceedings
the preferred stockholders asked to have
their stock declared a lien prior to a
subsequent mortgage, yet the court refused the application, declaring that
they had priority over the common
stock only It has been held, however,
that where preferred stock is issued, reciting that it is a lien on all the property of the corporation after the first
mortgage, the lien will be upheld by the
court as against subsequent mortgages
and general creditors, although such
lien was not secured by any mortgage
The trustees in the subsequent deed of
trust knew of and acquiesced in the priority of the preferred-stock lien, and the
deed itself recognized it This bound
the bondholders. Skiddy v Atlantic.
etc., R. R, 3 Hughes, 320, 355 (1878)

Cf Westchester, etc, v Jackson. 77 Pa
St, 321 (1875) In this case the preferred
stock to be redeemed by payment of the
par value and a sum which, with dividends and interest already paid, should
amount to eight per cent. per annum
from the time of its purchase from the
company, was declared to be a contract
which entitled its holder to his dividends before dividends were paid on the
common stock

[3] Although the power of a railroad to
borrow be limited, yet preferred stock
may be issued secured by a mortgage,
where the power to mortgage has been
given, and such preferred stock may be
deprived of the power to vote. Miller v.
Ratterdam. 24 N, E Rep, 496 (Ohio,
1890) A deed of trust given by a corporation upon its lands to secure the
performance of an undertaking of the
company to pay dividends on preferred
stock which was about to be issued, and
also ultimately to pay for the stock itself,
is a mortgage Where the corporation's
equity of redemption has been sold the
receiver of the corporation takes nothing Fitch v Wetherbee, 110 Ill, 475
(1881) In the case Davis v Proprietors,
etc, 49 Mass 321 (1844), the stock was
by law entitled to redemption when the
holder moved from the town The
court upheld and enforced the contract.

preferred stock was nothing more than income bonds with a voting power.[1]

A preferred stockholder is in no better position to enjoin the corporation from giving a mortgage than a common stockholder.[2] Where bonds are deposited as collateral security for preferred stock, it has been held that the corporation may call in, redeem and cancel the stock in exchange for the bonds,[3] but this would seem to be an illegal reduction of the capital stock

§ 272 *What are net profits applicable to preferred dividends.— The preferred stockholder's remedy to enforce a dividend* — It is largely a matter of discretion with a board of directors as to whether they will use the net profits for a dividend or will use them in the business of the company. There is a limit to this discretion, and the courts will not allow the directors to use their power oppressively by refusing to declare a dividend where the net profits and the character and condition of the business clearly warrant it. This is the rule where all of the stock is common stock.[4] Such also is the rule is regard to dividends on preferred stock. The preferred stockholder is not entitled as a matter of right to

In the case Gordon's Ex'rs v. Richmond, etc., R. R., 78 Va., 501 (1884) a mortgage had been given to secure the payment of the par value and dividends of preferred stock. The case involved a distribution of profits and not a foreclosure of the mortgage, but the court said that the mortgage was legal

[1] Burt v. Rattle, 31 Ohio St., 116 (1876), turned upon a general 'Act to authorize manufacturing corporations to issue preferred stock.' Where such stock was issued certifying that the corporation guarantied the holders certain dividends not exceeding legal rates, and the final payment of the certificates at a specified time, it being provided that such preferred stock might be converted into common stock, and the corporation issued its bond and mortgage to a trustee to secure such certificates, it was held that holders of the so-called preferred stock did not become stockholders and members, but creditors of the corporation, so that, on the winding up of the company's affairs, they had a lien upon the mortgage property superior to that of general creditors and assignees. "A mortgage creditor, although denominated a 'preferred stockholder,' is a mortgage creditor nevertheless, and interest is not changed into a 'dividend' by calling it a dividend." It was a self-evident misnomer in the act. So also under a statute. See Pittsburgh etc. v. County of Allegheny, 63 Pa St. 126 (1875. Compare S. C., 79 id., 210. In the case Miller v Ratterdam, 24 N E Rep., 496 (Ohio, 1890), the court held that the fact that a mortgage had been given to secure the payment of preferred dividends does not prevent such stock from being considered stock instead of a debt

[2] Preferred stockholders cannot prevent the corporation giving a consolidated mortgage to secure past and future debts. "Holders of preferred stock have no special control over the corporation or its management

The corporation is in no sense the trustee for the holders of preferred stock Its duty is to each other alike according to the conditions attached to the stock of each." Thompson v Erie R'y 11 Abb Pr, U S, 188 (Supr Ct, 1871.

[3] Totten v Tison, 54 Ga, 139 (1875)

[4] See ch XXXII, *infra*

his dividend, even though there are net profits which might be used for that purpose If the directors are reasonable in the exercise of their discretion, and use the profits to improve the road, it is held by the supreme court of the United States that the discretion of the directors will not be interfered with.[1] This rule will work no injustice where the corporation is liable for arrears of preferred dividends. But if such arrears are not collectible under the terms upon which the stock is issued, then the rule laid down by the supreme court will result in numerous frauds by the corporation on the preferred stockholder, since no dividend would be given to the preferred stockholder unless the net profits were sufficient for a dividend on the common stock also. For instance, where there are enough profits for two annual dividends on the preferred stock and no more, it will be a temptation to the common stockholders to declare no dividend at all the first year, and to declare a dividend on both the common and preferred stock the second year.[2]

The question of what constitutes "net profits" is discussed elsewhere[3] This question has arisen a few times in connection with preferred stock, and the courts are inclined to scan closely a refusal to declare dividends where there are net profits and where the preferred stock is non-cumulative[4] In an action to compel the decla-

---

[1] New York, etc. R R. Co v Nickalls 119 U S . 296 (1886), reversing 15 Fed Rep, 575

[2] For an instance, see McIntosh v Flint, etc , R. R , 34 Fed Rep., 350 (1887), S. C., 32 id 350 For a valuable note by Judge Seymour on Dividends, see 22 Cent L J , 452

[3] See ch XXXII

[4] Non-cumulative preferred stock is entitled to a dividend where all the property is leased for $36,000 a year, there is no floating debt the property cost over $1,000,000 , the bonded debt of $150,000, coming due in three years, may be extended and all annual outlays are but $9,000 The court will order the payment of a dividend Hazeltine v Belfast, etc , R R , 79 Me , 411 (1887) Directors are not allowed to use their power illegally wantonly or oppressively in refusing to declare dividends, but where the company owes $88 000 floating debt , $150,000 debt due in five years, and $1,000,000 due in thirty-five years,

at which time its profits would probably be nothing, the court will not order a dividend even on the preferred stock, although the company has $37,000 on hand and an annual income of $36,000 from the lessee of its road Belfast, etc , R R v Belfast, 77 Me , 445 (1885). Profits available for a dividend are such as are left after all debts for rolling stock, rails, station-houses, etc., are paid, but not the money raised under the borrowing powers Corry v Londonderry, etc., R'y, 29 Beav , 263 (1860) In the case Stevens v South Devon R'y, 9 Hare, 313 (1851), the court refused to enjoin the payment of dividends on preferred stock, even though the floating and unsecured debt had not been paid or provided for. Where, by a re-organization plan, common stockholders are allowed to vote, etc , only after certain dividends are declared on preferred stock, the court will determine whether such dividends should have been declared McIntosh v. Flint, etc , R R., 34 Fed. Rep , 350

ration of a preferred dividend the common stockholders are proper but not necessary parties [1]

A stock dividend is legal in America but cannot be forced upon stockholders in England.[2]

A bond dividend is legal, and even if it results in impairing the capital stock the court will not interfere if no harm can come from it [3]

§ 273 *Arrears of preferred stock, to what extent payable subsequently — Remedies to enforce payment of arrears —* When preferred stock is issued it is generally specified whether it is "cumulative" or "non-cumulative" In the former case all arrears of dividends must be paid on the preferred stock before any dividend is paid on the common In the latter case the contrary is the rule Such are the rules where the question is expressly settled by the terms under which the stock was issued.

(1887). See, also, Smith *v* Cork, etc, R'y Co., Ir. Rep, 3 Eq, 356 (1869)

Hence, in Dent *v* London Tramways Company, L R, 16 Chan Div, 344 (1880), it was held that the owners of preference shares, the dividend on which was "dependent upon the profits of the particular year only," were entitled to a dividend out of the profits of any year after setting aside a proportionate amount sufficient for the maintenance and repair of the tramway for that year only, and that they were not to be deprived of that dividend in order to make good the sums which in previous years should have been set aside by the company for maintenance, but which had been improperly applied by them in paying dividends But preferred shareholders are not entitled to a redemption of their stock in accordance with a statute if it would work an injustice to creditors and the other stockholders by taking all the money from the treasury and thereby crippling or wrecking the enterprise Culver *v* Reno, etc, Co, 91 Pa St, 367 (1879)

[1] Thompson *v* Erie R Co, 45 N Y, 468 (1871) See, also, Chase *v* Vanderbilt, 62 id, 307 (1875), holding that the corporate officers are not necessary parties

[2] See ch XXXII, *infra*. In Harnell *v*

Chicago, etc, R R, 51 Barb, 378 (1868), where the rights of the preferred and common stockholders were clearly defined by the contract a stock dividend of preferred stock was made to the preferred stockholders and of common stock to the common stockholders In figuring the amount of dividend thus declared the court estimated the stock dividends at their market values In the case Wood *v* Lary, 124 N Y 83 (1890), the court sustained the court below in refusing to cancel a mortgage and bonds, the bonds having been issued as a bond dividend to preferred stockholders S C, 47 Hun, 550

[3] Where the company pays dividends on preferred stock by issuing certificates entitling the holder to bonds in exchange therefor the company cannot afterwards refuse to deliver the bonds on the ground that the dividend was illegal or that such an issue of bonds was *ultra vires*, many bonds having already been so issued Chaffee *v* Rutland R R, 55 Vt, 110 (1882) Although a dividend may be illegal, yet "equity even would not interfere with a dividend unless it appeared that somebody in particular was hurt or liable to be injured It would not interfere after all danger had passed, and for the sake of vindicating general principles." Id.

If preferred stock is issued without any mention of whether or not the dividends are cumulative, then the law makes them cumulative. As soon as there are net profits available for dividends, the corporation must pay the preferred dividends and all arrears thereon before a dividend is declared on the common stock This is the well-settled rule at common law in this country [1] and in England [2]

[1] Boardman v. Lake Shore, etc., R. R. Co., 84 N Y, 157. (1881); Prouty v Michigan. etc, R. R. Co, 1 Hun, 655 (1873). Elkins v. Camden, etc., R. R. Co, 36 N J Eq, 233 (1882) Taft v Hartford, etc.. R R, 8 R. I, 310 (1866), West Chester, etc. R. R v Jackson. 77 Pa. St., 321 (1875). Lockhart v Van Alstine, 31 Mich, 76 (1875) per Cooley, J, Bates v Androscoggin, etc. R. R, 49 Me, 491 (1860) There are cases. however, to the contrary, under peculiar provisions governing the dividends When the preferred dividends are "dependent upon the profits of the particular year only," they are not cumulative Dent v London. etc, Co, L R, 16 Ch. D, 344 (1880) Preferred stock under a provision that "should a surplus then remain of net earnings. after both of said dividends, in any one year, the same shall be divided pro rata on all the stock," is noncumulative Hazeltine v Belfast, etc, R R, 79 Me, 411 (1887). See, also dictum in Cotting v N Y, etc, R. R., 54 Conn, 156 (1886).

Speaking of preferred stock the court said in Belfast, etc, R. R. v Belfast, 77 Me 413 (1885). in a dictum and under a by-law in that case· ' It was not intended in the present instance to guarantee a dividend If a dividend is prevented in any one year by a deficit of earnings it cannot be made up from the earnings of succeeding years. ' The preferred stock may be made non-cumulative Bailey v Hannibal. etc, R. R., 1 Dill, 174 (1871). S C, 17 Wall, 96 Where there is a statutory provision that dividends on the preferred stock shall not exceed a certain rate per cent., then there is no carrying over of ar-

rears. Elkins v. Camden, etc, R. R. Co, 36 N J Eq, 233 (1882)

[2] Henry v Great Northern, etc, R'y Co., 1 De G. & J, 606 (1857), aff'g 4 K & J, 1. Crawford v Northeastern R'y Co, 3 Jur (N S), 1093, Sturge v Eastern, etc., R'y Co, 7 De G, M & G, 158 (1855), Stevens v South, etc, R'y Co, 9 Hare, 313 (1851), Matthews v. Great Northern, etc, R'y Co., 28 L J, Chan, 375 (1859), Corry v Londonderry, etc., R'y Co., 29 Beav, 263 (1860), Webb v Earle, L R, 20 Eq, 556 (1875), Coates v. Nottingham, etc, R'y Co, 30 Beav, 86 (1861), Smith v Cork, etc, R'y Co, Ir L R, 3 Eq, 356 (1869), S C, 5 id, 65 The Companies Clauses Act of 1863, 26 and 27 Vict, ch 16, § 14, provides that preference shares or stock shall be entitled to the preference dividend or interest assigned thereto out of the profits of each year in priority to the ordinary shares and stock of the company, but that if in any year there are not profits available for the payments of the full amount or the preferential dividend or interest for that year, no part of the deficiency shall be made good out of the profits of any subsequent year, or out of any other funds of the company In Henry v Great Northern R'y Co, supra, in which the matter of arrears in preferred dividends was elaborately considered, it was stated that the reason why such arrears ought to be held payable out of subsequent profits is that otherwise there would be a temptation to the corporation to set aside profits for improvements when the profits were too small for a dividend on both the common and the preferred shares, and

The right of the preferred stockholder to arrears of dividends is not deemed waived by delay, nor in any way except upon clear proof of intent to waive[1] The dividends on the common stock may be made cumulative also before the preferred stock shares in the surplus profits remaining after preferred dividends are paid[2]

§ 274 The remedy of a preferred stockholder when the company proposes to pay dividends on the common stock before paying the arrears of dividends on preferred stock is in a court of equity[3] But an action at law will lie if dividends have already been

not to set aside enough for improvements when the company made a dividend for both Where each share in a company was converted into two half shares one preferred, the other common or deferred, and the holders of the preferred half shares had, in a former year, acquiesced in the declaration of a dividend on the deferred half shares, while there was an arrearage of dividends on the preferred half shares, it was held that although they had precluded themselves from making any claim to those specific arrears, they had not waived their right to claim subsequent arrears Matthews v Great Northern, etc, R'y Co, 28 L. J, Chan, 375 (1859)

[1] Boardman v. Lake Shore, etc R R, *supra* In Smith v Cork, etc., R y Ir Rep, 3 Eq, 356 (1869), the court held under the facts of that case that the preferred stockholders had not waived their right to arrears, although they had forborne and had taken part in inducing new capital to come in

[2] When the preferred stock is entitled to participate in the surplus after the dividends are paid on the preferred and "a dividend of the same amount upon the whole amount of paid-up capital" has been paid, arrears of dividends on the common stock as well as on the preferred must be paid before there is any surplus Allen v Londonderry, etc, R y Co 25 Week Rep 524 (1877)

[3] A suit in equity to restrain the corporation from declaring dividends on the common stock and to compel an accounting and the payment of dividends

on the preferred stock is the proper remedy Boardman v Lake Shore etc R R, 84 N Y, 157 (1881), Williston v Michigan, etc, R R Co 95 Mass, 400 (1866) In this case the decision was that when a preferred stockholder is entitled to share *pro rata* with holders of common stock in dividends over and above the preference his remedy is not by an action at law against the corporation, but by suit in equity, and that there is no remedy against a *foreign corporation* in such case In an action by a preferred stockholder in behalf of himself and others to enjoin the payment of dividends to common stockholders before the arrears of preferred dividends are paid, he need not join all the common stockholders as parties defendant Smith v Cork, etc, R'v, Ir Rep, 3 Eq, 356 (1869), Prouty v Michigan etc, R R Co, 1 Hun, 655 (1874), where an injunction was granted to restrain the declaring of dividends or making other disposition of the funds of the corporation until arrears on preferred stock should be paid, Thompson v Erie, etc, R R Co 45 N Y, 468, involving an action to 'enforce the declaration and payment of a dividend," Barnard v Vermont, etc, 89 Mass, 572 (1863) holding that where certificates for an intended dividend had been issued payable at a future time when the company should be able to pay them, the final decision as to when the company is able to pay does not rest with the directors but with the court Where the common stockholders in a re-organized company claim that the preferred

declared and paid to the common stockholders in violation of the rights of the preferred stockholders.[1]

When the arrears and dividends of preferred stock are recoverable, the interest on such arrears may be recovered from the time when moneys sufficient to pay the arrears were unlawfully used to pay dividends on the common stock instead of being used to pay the arrears on the preferred stock.[2]

§ 275. *Rights of the assignee or transferee of preferred stock in arrears of dividends.*— The transferee or assignee of preferred stock stands, in respect to arrears of dividends, in the shoes of his assignor or transferrer. The undeclared arrears of dividends pass to him in the transfer of the stock, unless by the terms of the transfer the arrears are expressly separated from the stock itself and reserved to the transferrer.[3] An assignment of preferred stock carries with it all arrears of dividends, and a subsequent assignment of arrears by the transferrer conveys nothing.[4]

§ 276 *"Special stock" in Massachusetts* — In Massachusetts incorporated companies are permitted by statute[5] to issue a peculiar kind of stock, known as "special stock" It is something essentially different from preferred stock.[6] Its essential characteristics are that it is limited in amount to two-fifths of the actual capital; it is subject to redemption by the corporation at par after a fixed time, to be expressed in the certificate, the corporation is

stockholders are defrauding them, a preliminary injunction will not be ordered unless imminent danger is shown McIntosh *v* Flint, etc, R. R. Co, 32 Fed Rep., 350 (1887). The plaintiff by offering in evidence his certificate of stock and showing that no dividends have been paid, makes out a *prima facie* case entitling him to dividends and arrears Boardman *v* Lake Shore, etc, R R, 84 N Y, 157 (1881)

[1] If dividends are declared and paid on the common stock, before paying the arrears of dividends on the preferred stock, the holders of the latter may collect such arrears by an action at law in *assumpsit* West Chester, etc, R. R. *v* Jackson, 77 Pa St, 321 (1875) In the case Bates *v* Androscoggin, etc, R. R, 49 Me. 401 (1860) an action of debt for past due dividends was sustained, although such dividends had not been declared, they having been earned Coey *v* Belfast, etc, R'y Co., Ir Rep., 2

C L, 112 (1866), holding that an action at law will lie against a railway company for not giving to the plaintiff preferred stockholder the same dividend that it has given to others

[2] Boardman *v* Lake Shore, etc, R. R. Co, 84 N Y, 157 (1881), Prouty *v* Mich S., etc. R. R, 1 Hun, 655 (1874) See Adams *v* Fort, etc, Bank, 36 N Y, 255 (1867). *Contra*, Cony *v* Londonderry, etc, R y Co., 29 Beav, 263 (1860). *Cf* ch XXXII, *infra*

[3] Jermain *v* Lake Shore, etc, R R Co., 91 N Y, 483 (1883), Boardman *v* Same, 84 id, 157 (1881). Hyatt *v* Allen, 56 id, 553 (1874), Manning *v* Quicksilver, etc, Co, 24 Hun, 361 (1881).

[4] Manning *v* Quicksilver Mining Co, 24 Hun, 361 (1881)

[5] Stats 1855, ch 290; 1870, ch 224, §§ 25 39, cl 4, Pub Stats, ch 106, §§ 42, 61 cl 3

[6] American Tube Works *v* Boston, etc., Co, 139 Mass., 5 (1885).

bound to pay a fixed half-yearly sum, or dividend, upon it as a debt, the holders of it are in no event liable for the debts of the corporation beyond their stock, and the issue of this special stock makes all the general stockholders liable for all debts and contracts of the corporation until the special stock is fully redeemed [1] Special stock can be issued only by a vote of three-fourths of the general stockholders of the company at a meeting duly called for that purpose [2] The guaranty of dividends of special stock in Massachusetts is an absolute one, and not in any degree conditional upon the earning of sufficient profits by the corporation [3]

§ 277. *Interest-bearing stocks* — Occasionally, instead of issuing preferred stock, a corporation issues ordinary common stock, together with a promise that the corporation will pay interest thereon Such a promise is generally lawful, and may be enforced as a contract in the nature of an agreement to pay a dividend [4] It is a lawful contract, however, only when it is to be interpreted as requiring payment from profits alone [5] Any contract on the part of a corporation to pay interest or dividends to its shareholders, with-

[1] The statutes cited *supra*, American Tube Works *v* Boston, etc, Co, 139 Mass, 5 (1885)

[2] Stats 1870, ch 224, § 25 And the corporation must have a clerk, who is sworn, and who acts as recorder at such meeting Stats 1870, ch 224, §§ 15, 18, Pub Stats, ch 106, §§ 23 26 See also, Reed *i* Boston Machine Co, 141 Mass, 454 (1886) This special stock is declared to be "a peculiar kind of stock, distinctly provided for by statute," and it is important that the marked distinction between preferred stock, as usually understood, and special stock, as authorized by the statutes cited in the notes, be kept plainly in view American Tube Works *v* Boston, etc, Co, 139 Mass, 5 (1885)

It was held, in accordance with this view, in the case last cited, that a vote of a corporation to issue special stock, at a meeting called to consider whether the corporation will issue preferred stock, is invalid, that a vote to issue special stock is invalid if the record of the meeting fails to show that three-fourths of the general shareholders voted for such issue, that the court will not presume, because the record showed that

more than three-fourths of the shareholders were present at the meeting, that therefore three-fourths or more voted for the issue of special stock, and that a holder of special stock which is illegally issued cannot, by estoppel or otherwise, become a member of the corporation in respect of such shares

[3] Williams *v* Parker, 136 Mass, 204 (1884) See, also, Allen *v* Herrick, 81 id, 274 (1860)

[4] Barnard *i* Vermont, etc, R R Co, 89 Mass, 512 (1863)

[5] Richardson *v* Vermont, etc, R. R. Co., 44 Vt, 613 (1872), Miller *v* Pittsburgh etc, R R Co, 40 Pa St, 237 (1861), Cunningham *i* Same, 78 Mass, 441 (1859), City of Ohio *i* Cleveland, etc, R R Co 6 Ohio St, 489 (1856), Wright *v* Vermont, etc, R R Co, 66 Mass, 68 (1853), Waterman *v* Troy, etc, R R Co, 74 id, 433 (1857), Barnard *v* Vermont, etc, R R Co, 89 id, 512 (1863) In the case of Ohio College, etc, *v* Rosenthal, 12 N E Rep, 665 (Ohio, 1887), where certificates of stock bearing interest were issued by a corporation which merely owned real estate, which was not organized for profit, never made any profit, never expected

out reference to the ability of the company to pay them out of its earnings, is wholly illegal and void.' Moreover, the directors or corporate officers paying interest on stock out of the capital stock are jointly and severally liable to refund the amounts so paid out.[2] A railway company may lawfully receive subscriptions to its capital stock upon the condition to pay interest thereon as soon as the amount of the subscription shall have been paid in, and until the completion of the road, or of some part thereof, or until the road shall have been put in operation.[3] It has been held that stipulated interest on stock cannot become a debt payable absolutely.[4] The right of a subscriber drawing interest on his stock to participate in elections and general corporate meetings, and to exercise generally the rights of a shareholder, is the same as that of other stockholders [5]

§ 278 *Rights of preferred shareholders on dissolution and on a reduction of the capital stock.* — Upon the dissolution of a corporation, and the distribution of its assets among the shareholders after the payment of the corporate indebtedness, it is the settled rule of law that, in the absence of any provision in the statutes, by-laws

to, and had existed forty years, a suit by a stockholder to collect interest failed.

[1] Painesville, etc., R. R. Co. v. King, 17 Ohio St., 534 (1867), Pittsburgh, etc, R. R Co v County of Allegheny, 79 Pa St., 210 (1875), id, 63 Pa St., 126 (1869), Lockhart v Van Alstyne, 31 Mich, 76 (1875), Troy, etc, R. R Co. v. Tibbits, 18 Barb., 297 (1854), Salisbury v Metropolitan, etc, R'y Co, 38 L J (N S), Ch, 249 (1869), *In re* National, etc, Co, L R., 10 Ch Div, 118 (1878) *Cf* Bardwell v Sheffield, etc, Co, L R, 14 Eq. Cas, 517 (1872). In the case City of Ohio v Cleveland, etc., R R, 6 Ohio St, 489 (1856). interest payable by stock dividends was allowed by statute. A subscriber to stock which by its terms is to draw interest cannot defeat the subscription on the ground that the provision as to interest is illegal Evansville, etc, R R v Evansville, 15 Ind, 395 (1860) In the case McLaughlin v Detroit, etc, R R, 8 Mich, 100 (1860), a railroad company issued stock bearing interest. The court sustained it The stock called for interest instead of dividends Bonds were tendered to the

stockholder in payment of such "interest" He declined the tender and sued for the interest money. The court sustained his suit. No question was raised as to paying such "interest" irrespective of profits

[2] *Re* National, etc, Co, 10 L R, Chan Div, 118 (1878)

[3] Milwaukee, etc, R. R Co v Field, 12 Wis, 340 (1860), Racine County Bank v Ayers, 12 id, 512 (1860), Miller v Pittsburgh, etc, R. R. Co., 40 Pa St., 237 (1861); Waterman v Troy, etc., R. R Co., 74 Mass, 433 (1857). The only effect of an agreement by the corporation to pay such interest is to enable those stockholders with whom the agreement is made to claim a dividend and arrears of dividends before other stockholders receive anything This is nothing more nor less than a preferred dividend.

[4] Barnard v Vermont, etc, R. R. Co., 89 Mo., 512 (1863) Nevertheless, the relation of debtor and creditor is created to the extent of the interest stipulated for McLaughlin v Detroit, etc, R. R. Co, 8 Mich, 100 (1864).

[5] McLaughlin v. Detroit, etc., R. R. Co., *supra.*

or certificate to the contrary, preferred shareholders have no priority over common stockholders. Their stock was preferred in respect of dividends, and not in reference to the capital stock. The assets of the corporation are to be distributed as though no preferred shares had been issued. The preferred shareholder in the distribution becomes a common shareholder.[1] Where, however, a preference as to capital has been expressly contracted for,[2] or is given by a statute,[3] the rule is, of course, otherwise.

If the capital stock is reduced the preferred stock is reduced proportionately with the common unless the preferred stock is preferred as to assets as well as dividends.[4]

[1] The House of Lords has held that upon the dissolution of a corporation having preferred stock and common stock the surplus assets, after repayment of the paid-up capital, the common stock not having been paid up, is divisible among all the stockholders, common and preferred, in proportion to their holdings. Birch v. Cropper, 61 L. T. Rep., 621 (1889), reversing the court below. See, also, In re London India Rubber Co., L. R., 5 Eq., 519 (1864). Re Bridgewater Nav. Co., 58 L. T. Rep., 476 (1888), id., 866, a case where there was a large surplus. McGregor v. Home Ins. Co., 33 N. J. Eq., 181 (1880), a dictum, the court holding, however, that under the statutes of the state the preferred stockholders had a preference as to assets also, the statute providing for a division of the surplus after payment to preferred stockholders. Stock with guaranteed dividends is stated, in Gordon's Ex'rs v. Richmond, etc., R. R., 78 Va., 501 (1884), to give a preference as to dividends, but not of the stock on a winding up. In the case of Griffith v. Paget L. R., 6 Ch. D., 511 (1877) S. C., 25 W. R., 523, it was held that where the company is dissolved by a consolidation with another company under a statute, the stockholders of the old being entitled to exchange their stock for stock in the new, the preferred stock is not entitled to preferred stock in the new. On a winding up, if it turns out that the profits had been systematically

overestimated for a number of years, thereby depriving common stockholders of the dividends, an account would be taken and such dividends would be then paid. Re Bridgewater, etc., Co., 64 L. T. Rep., 576 (1891).

[2] Re Bangor, etc., Slate Co., L. R., 20 Eq., 59 (1875)

[3] McGregor v. Home Ins. Co., 33 N. J. Eq., 181 (1880)

[4] When the capital stock is reduced by decreasing the par value of the stock the preferred stock may be reduced equally with the rest. Re Barrow, etc., Co., 59 L. T. Rep., 500 (1888). Where in consequence of losses the capital stock is reduced, as allowed by the charter, by reducing the par value of the stock one-half, the preferred stock as well as the common is reduced one-half. Bannatyne v. Direct etc., Co., 55 L. T. Rep., 716 (1886). But not where the preferred stock is preferred as to assets as well as dividends, unless all the preferred stockholders assent thereto. Re Quebrada Ry. Co. Ld., 482 (1889). Where a company has not issued or has acquired some of its stock it may reduce its capital stock by canceling the part owned by it, although it is all preferred or all common or part of both. Re Gatling Gun, Lim., 62 L. T. Rep., 312 (1890). Where there is both common and preferred stock it is legal for the company to reduce the common stock without reducing the preferred. Re Agricultural, etc., Co., 63 L. T. Rep., 748 (1890).

CHAPTER XVII.

INCREASE AND REDUCTION OF THE CAPITAL STOCK AND OVER-ISSUED STOCK.

§ 279. *Introductory.*— The capital stock of all incorporated companies is generally fixed by the charters which give them an existence. Frequently, however, in the progress of the corporate enterprise, it happens that the capital stock is found to be too small or too large for the demands of the business, and there is a desire to change it. This change can be made lawfully only under certain conditions and limitations. These are the subject of this chapter.

A LEGAL INCREASE OR REDUCTION OF CAPITAL STOCK.

§ 280 *Power of the legislature to authorize an increase or reduction* — It is clearly constitutional for the legislature, upon granting a charter, to fix the capital stock and to authorize the corporation to increase or decrease that capital stock. But where the legislature did not authorize the corporation to vary its capital stock, it is a serious question whether, as against a dissenting stockholder, the capital stock may be subsequently changed, even under the authority of a legislative enactment   The better and prevailing opinion is that it may be, that the statute authorizing the change is constitutional, and that the increase or reduction is valid [1]

A different conclusion may be reached, however, as regards the rights of creditors of the corporation   It is clear that the legislature cannot constitutionally authorize a reduction of the capital stock in prejudice of their rights as to an existing corporate indebtedness [2]

§ 281. *Power of the corporation to increase or reduce the capital stock* — In the absence of express authority from the state, a corporation has no power whatsoever to increase or reduce the amount of its stock, and any attempt upon the part of the corporation, either by the corporate officers or by the stockholders, to do so is wholly illegal and void [3] Accordingly it is not competent for a corporation, having a fixed capital stock and being without legislative authority to change it, to reduce that capital to the amount actually paid in [4]

Where the attempted increase or reduction of the stock is not authorized by the charter, not even the unanimous assent and agreement of all the parties concerned will legalize it   It is void [5]

A different rule prevails, however, where the increase of capital stock is authorized by charter or statute, but is informally made   In such a case the increase is valid as against all parties excepting the state which created the corporation [6]

An authority to reduce the number of shares cannot be inferred from the authority to increase, and a reduction with no other warrant of authority than a right to increase will be held void [7]

If the charter of the corporation provides that the capital stock shall not be less than a specified sum, nor greater than another specified sum, the corporation may commence business with less

[1] See ch XXVIII on this subject.
[2] Id.
[3] Scovill v Thayer, 105 U. S, 143, 148 (1881), Sutherland v Olcott, 95 N Y, 93, 100 (1884), New York, etc, R R. Co v Schuyler, 34 id, 30 (1865), Mechanics' Bank v New York, etc., R R Co, 13 id, 599 (1856), Grangers' Life, etc, Insurance Co v Kamper, 73 Ala., 325 (1882); Moses v. Ocoee Bank, 1 Lea (Tenn), 398 (1878), Ferris v Ludlow, 7 Ind 517 (1856); Lathrop v Kneeland, 46 Barb., 432 (1866), Salem Mill-Dam Corporation v. Ropes, 6 Pick, 23 (1827) "If," says Parker, C J, in the case last cited, "a corporation is created with a fund limited by the act, it cannot enlarge or diminish that fund but by a license from the legislature"

[4] Droitwich Patent Salt Co v. Curzon, L. R., 3 Ex, 35, 42 (1867).

[5] See § 292, *infra*.

[6] See § 288, *infra*.

[7] Sutherland v. Olcott, 95 N Y, 93 (1884), Seignouret v. Home Ins Co, 24 Fed. Rep, 332 (1885).

than the latter sum, and afterwards increase the capital until the limit is reached [1]

An injunction is the proper remedy to prevent an illegal increase or reduction of the capital stock of a corporation. But an injunction against the issue of new stock by a foreign corporation will be dissolved where the courts of the state where the corporation was created decide such issue of stock to be legal [2]

§ 282 *Effect of purchase by a corporation of shares of its own stock* — If a corporation has power to reduce its capital stock it has been held that it may do so by purchasing and retiring a portion of its shares [3] Whether such a purchase by a corporation will operate to diminish the capital stock is a question of intention   If a reduction is authorized by charter or by statute, and the formalities of making the reduction have been complied with, and the proper corporate authorities purchase for the corporation shares of its own stock and consider the capital stock thereby reduced, the law holds that a reduction of the capital stock is thereby made But if any of these elements are wanting, then no reduction is effected, and the corporation may at any time sell and re-issue the stock. Hence a mere transfer of shares to the corporation, whether the corporation assumes to buy the stock or the stockholders simply to surrender it, will in no case constitute a reduction when the corporation lacks authority from the legislature to reduce its capital   Even if the shareholder is held to be released by such a transfer, still the stock survives and subsists   The corporation is merely the holder of it, and may sell and re-issue it at any time. [4]

---

[1] Gray *v* Portland Bank, 3 Mass, 364 (1807), Somerset, etc, R. R. Co. *v* Cushing, 45 Me, 524 (1858). In the case last cited it is held that where the number of shares is not fixed by charter the directors or shareholders must fix it before an assessment can be levied, and that then, if the number fixed is greater than the number taken, it may be reduced subsequently

[2] O Brien *v* Chicago. Rock Island & Pacific R. R. Co, 53 Barb., 568 (1868) An increase of the capital stock without warrant of authority is denominated an overissue of stock — a subject fully considered in the succeeding sections of this chapter *q v* The issue of new stock by the corporation cannot be enjoined where neither the corporation nor any of its directors are parties to the action. White *v*. Wood, 129 N Y, 527 (1892).

[3] State *v* Smith 48 Vt, 266 (1876) *dictum.* So, also, City Bank of Columbus *v* Bruce 17 N Y, 507 (1858). *Contra*, Currier *v* Lebanon Slate Co, 56 N. H , 262 (1875) Where a company has not issued or has acquired some of its stock it may reduce its capital stock by cancelling the part owned by it, although it is all preferred or all common or part of both *Re* Gatling Gun, Lim., 62 L. T. Rep, 312 (1890)

[4] The purchase by a corporation of its own stock does not necessarily decrease the capital stock   "It might or might not have that effect at the option of the company, and would require, I think, some manifestation of such an intent to produce that result" Such stock may be re-issued at any time. City Bank of Columbus *v* Bruce, 17 N Y, 507 (1858). See, also, § 314, *infra,*

§ 283. *The issue of bonds convertible into stock.* — Where the charter of a railway corporation authorizes the issue of bonds, convertible at the option of the holder into stock, such an issue may be made, even though, if the bonds were converted into stock, the capital stock would thereby be increased beyond the amount fixed by the charter. The statute or charter authorizing such an issue of bonds is held to thereby authorize, by necessary implication, the right to increase the capital stock to the extent required in the fulfillment of the contract to allow the bonds to be converted into stock.[1]

The issue of a bond convertible into stock has the same effect as issuing stock, and the sale of such a bond at a discount would probably be governed by the same rules that pertain to stock.[2] The holder of the bonds may demand stock therefor at any time, and even though the demand is made just before a dividend is declared he is entitled to the stock and dividend.[3]

and Hartridge v Rockwell, R. M. Charlton (Ga), 260 (1828). In an early case a transfer to the corporation seems to have been regarded as a reduction of the capital stock *pro tanto* Percy v. Millaudon 3 La 568, 587 (1832). It is important to note in this connection that the purchase of its own stock by a corporation is an act not permitted at all in England, and not permitted in this country when corporate creditors' rights would be prejudiced thereby. See §§ 309-312 *infra* It has been held in a recent case (New Eng., etc. Life Ins Co v Phillips, 6 N E Rep, 534, Mass, 1886) that a purchase by a corporation of certificates of indebtedness effects a cancellation even though the certificates have a voting power.

[1] Belmont v Erie R'y Co, 52 Barb, 637, 669 (1869), Ramsey v Erie R'y Co, 38 How Pr, 193, 216 (1869) When bonds are convertible by their terms into stock, but the company has no stock, specific performance will not be decreed but damages given Chaffee v Middlesex R. R, 16 N E Rep, 34 (Mass, 1888) Where the stock of a land corporation is convertible into land a stockholder may enforce the change by bill in equity Franco, etc, Co v Bousselet, 7 S. W. Rep, 761 (Texas, 1888)

The bonds may provide that the holder may take certain lots of land in satisfaction thereof Chicago, etc, Land Co v Peck, 112 Ill 408 (1885).

[2] See ch III concerning the issue of stock Where, however, a corporation has power to increase its capital stock it may issue bonds at fifty per cent of their par value, convertible into stock upon payment of the other fifty per cent. Van Allen v Ill Central R. R. Co, 7 Bosw (N Y), 515 (1861)

[3] Jones v Terre Haute, etc, R. R. Co, 57 N Y, 196 (1874) Where bonds are convertible into stock, a bondholder is entitled to stock equal in par value to the par value of his bonds, but is not entitled in addition thereto to past stock dividends declared on such stock Sutliff v Cleveland, etc, R R, 24 Ohio St, 147 (1873) In a suit by holders of bonds convertible into stock against the corporation for refusal to allow such conversion, the plaintiffs must allege that they still hold the bonds Denney v Cleveland, etc, R. R, 28 Ohio St, 108 (1875) A corporation with authority to increase its capital stock may lawfully issue new shares and receive in payment therefor the bonds of the corporation. Lohman v New York etc, R R. Co, 2 Sandf. Super Ct, 39 (1848), Reed v.

An option to convert stock into bonds must be exercised within a reasonable time if the option itself contains no limit [1]

Where bonds are convertible into stock the holder may demand conversion into the stock of a new consolidated corporation that has assumed all the claims and liabilities of the old.[2]

§ 234 *The power of a court to direct an increase or reduction.*— The courts have no power, by mandate or decree or in any other manner, to effect an increase or reduction of the capital stock of a corporation   Hence, where the whole capital stock has been issued, and the corporation, by reason of its misconduct or mistakes, is bound to issue new certificates to the owner of the stock or pay him damages, the court can give judgment for damages only   It cannot order the corporation to issue stock, since to do so would be to direct an overissue.[3]

In Massachusetts a later and better rule prevails, to the effect that the corporation in such a case may be compelled to issue the stock, but in order to prevent an illegal overissue it must purchase an equal amount of shares in the market.[4]

Hayt, 51 N Y Super Ct., 121 (1884) See in general § 273

[1] Cathn v Green, 120 N Y, 411 (1890)   Where the subscribers for stock have an option to exchange their stock for bonds of the company and fail to exercise that option for nine years, when the company has passed into the hands of a receiver and the stock becomes worthless, the right is gone   The option, not being limited in time, must be exercised within a reasonable time. Id

[2] Day v Worcester, etc , R R, 23 N E Rep., 824 (Mass, 1890)   When by statute the consolidated company is liable for the contracts of the old companies, it must issue stock in exchange for bonds of the old company which were convertible into stock   India Mut Ins. Co v Worcester etc , R. R. 25 N E Rep, 975 (Mass 1890)   Where a bondholder has a right to convert his bonds into stock, a consolidation cannot deprive him of that right until after he has been notified of the intended consolidation and given an opportunity to exercise his rights. Rosenkrans v Lafayette, etc , R. R, 18 Fed Rep, 513 (1883)

[3] "When a corporation has issued certificates of stock (which are valid and not void) to the full extent of all the shares which by law and the constitution of the company it may issue, no court can order the issuance of other shares, because in that respect the powers of the corporation have been exhausted"   Smith v North American Mining Co, 1 Nev, 423 (1865); Williams v Savage Manuf Co, 3 Md Chan, 418 (1851), Mechanics' Bank v. New York, etc, R R Co, 13 N. Y, 599 (1856). In an action for the conversion of shares, the question of an increase or reduction not being involved, it was said that "To require a new issue of stock might in cases like this, where shares have gone into the hands of innocent purchasers, involve an overissue of stock, which would be illegal"   Baker v Wasson, 59 Texas, 140 (1883), S C, 53 id, 150 (1880).

[4] This rule, with an equitable adjustment of the conflicting interests of all the parties, where an owner of stock was deprived of it by forgery, was established by the supreme judicial court of Massachusetts in the case of Machinists' National Bank v Field, 126 Mass, 345 (1879). See, also, Pratt v.

Where corporate officers enter into a contract to pay for services or property wholly or partially in stock of the corporation, a court will not, after the whole amount of the stock has been issued, decree a specific performance of the contract, but the aggrieved party is remitted to his action for damages[1]

§ 285. *Shareholders, not directors, should authorize the increase.* An increase or reduction of the capital stock of a corporation is such a fundamental change in its affairs that, although it has been duly authorized by act of the legislature or by the charter of incorporation, it cannot lawfully be effected merely by the act or assent of the board of directors,[2] but must be authorized by the shareholders at a corporate meeting Where, however, the directors have made the change, and the stockholders have acquiesced therein, they are as fully bound as though the increase or reduction had been expressly authorized at a corporate meeting The shareholders' assent to the change may be shown as conclusively by their conduct and acquiescence as by a formal vote[3] The power to increase the capital stock may be vested in the directors[4] Although the shareholders have regularly voted to increase the capital stock,

Machinists' National Bank, 123 id , 110, and Boston, etc , R. R. Co v Richardson, 135 id , 473, each of the three cases growing out of the same transaction

[1] Finley Shoe, etc , Co. v Kurtz, 34 Mich , 89 (1876) In this case the court say that where the capital stock may be increased by vote of the stockholders, " it certainly could not be within the implied powers of any corporate officer to obligate the corporation to any such increase, and thus indirectly do what the law permits to be done only by the body of corporators, specially convened for the purpose" In actions against corporations for conversion of stock, the relief demanded is usually in the alternative being either for an issue of a certificate of stock, or damages in lieu thereof

[2] Percy v. Millaudon, 3 La , 568, 585 (1832), Eidman v Bowman, 58 Ill , 444 (1871), Finley Shoe, etc., Co v Kurtz, 34 Mich , 89 (1876), Crandall v Lincoln, 52 Conn , 73, 99 (1884), People v Parker Vein Coal Co , 10 How Pr , 543 (1854) See, also Railway Company v Allerton, 18 Wall , 233 (1873) Cf City of Chicago v Jones, 60 Ill , 383 (1871), Matter of

Wheeler, 2 Abb Prac (N S), 361 (1866), People v Twaddell, 18 Hun, 427, 432 (1879), State v Merchant, 37 Ohio St., 251 (1881) See, also, § 708, etc

[3] Sewell's Case, L R , 3 Chan , 131 (1868); Lane's Case, 1 De G , J & S., 504 (1863), Payson v Stoever, 2 Dill , 428 (1873) See, also, ch XLVII, *infra*, relative to mortgages, but see § 288, *infra* An allegation of ratification must not be in general terms, but must set out specifically the facts constituting the ratification Eidman v Bowman, 58 Ill , 444 (1871) An amendment of the charter which allows the directors instead of the shareholders to authorize an increase of the capital is not such a fundamental change in the constitution of the corporation as will operate to release non-assenting shareholders from the obligation on their stock Payson v Withers, 5 Biss , 269 (1873), Payson v Stoever, *supra*

[4] Sutherland v Olcott, 95 N. Y , 93 (1884) Then resolution that "the capital stock of this company be and the same is hereby increased to ——" is sufficient to effect the increase

in pursuance of adequate legislative authority, still, inasmuch as the increase is not accomplished until the shares are actually issued, the vote may be reconsidered in a lawful manner at any time before the stock is finally issued [1]

§ 286   *Prior right of the old stockholder to buy the new stock* — When the capital stock of a corporation is increased by the issue of new shares, each holder of the original stock has a right to offer to subscribe for and to demand from the corporation such a proportion of the new stock as the number of shares already owned by him bears to the whole number of shares before the increase.   This pre emptive right of the shareholder in respect of new stock is well recognized [2]   But this applies only when the capital is actually increased, and not to a re-issue of any portion of the

---

[1] Terry *v* Eagle Lock Co, 47 Conn, 141 (1879)   In this case the court say "It cannot be said that the capital is actually increased until the new stock is subscribed for at least.   Until then there is an element of uncertainty about it. It may never be taken   It is very clear that the vote to increase is not *per se* an increase"

[2] Gray *v* Portland Bank, 3 Mass, 364 (1807), Eidman *v* Bowman, 58 Ill, 444 (1871), Reese *v*. Bank of Montgomery, 31 Pa St, 78 (1855); Jones *v* Morrison. 31 Minn, 140 (1883); Bank of Montgomery *v* Reese, 26 Pa St, 143 (1856). *Cf* Curry *v* Scott, 54 Pa. St., 270 (1867), Miller *v* Illinois, etc., R R Co, 24 Barb, 312 (1857), Wilson *v* Bank of Montgomery County, 29 Pa St., 537 (1857), Mason *v* Davol Mills, 132 Mass, 76 (1882)   A sale of shares of the original capital stock carries with it as an incident the right which the vendor had previously acquired by subscription to shares of increased capital stock. Baltimore, etc, Co. *v* Hambleton, 26 Atl Rep, 279 (Md, 1893), Biddle's Appeal, 99 Pa St, 278, in which the option to subscribe for new stock was sold by an executor, Pratt *v* American Bell Tel Co, 111 Mass 225 (1886), where one who held notes convertible into stock at a future time sought to establish his right as a stockholder to an equitable share of an increase of capital stock to which shareholders had a first right to sub-

scribe upon favorable terms.   The court held that the suit could not be maintained, on the ground that until he had converted the notes into stock he had no rights as a stockholder, Ohio Ins. Co *v* Nunnemacher, 15 Ind, 294 (1860), where the charter varied the rule; *Re* Wheeler, 2 Abb Pr (N S), 361, 363, in which it was said that if new stock is not apportioned among old stockholders it should be sold at public sale to the highest bidder, so that all may share in the gains arising from its sale; Miller *v* Illinois, etc, 24 Barb, 312 (1857), that a stockholder who holds a receipt from a corporation for money payable on demand in cash, or, at his option, in new stock when issued, has no interest in such stock as a shareholder until he has elected to take it instead of the cash   In Massachusetts this right is preserved in the statutes.   Ch 106, § 37, ch. 112, § 58   In Massachusetts increased capital, if worth more than par, must in certain cases, by statute, be sold at public auction   See Att'y-Gen'l *v* Boston, etc, R. R. Co., 109 Mass, 99 (1871)   In New York, in banking corporations, it is secured to the shareholder by statute. Session Laws 1878, ch 274, § 5   But the pledgee of stock who holds it merely as collateral security is not entitled to this right to take up new shares   The right belongs to the pledgor   Miller *v* Illinois Central R. R Co, 24 Barb, 312 (1857).

original stock.[1] It applies, however, to such part of the original capital stock as is issued long after business has been commenced by the company Especially is this the rule where the directors issue such new stock to themselves or their friends in order to control an election or make a profit.[2] The right must be exercised within a fixed or a reasonable time, and if the shareholder fails to avail himself of it, he is barred, by laches or acquiescence, of his right to contest a disposition of the stock to some one else[3] The corporation cannot compel the old stockholders, upon their subscription for new stock, to pay more than par value therefor They are entitled to it without extra burden or expense beyond the regular subscription price[4] An attempt to deprive the stockholder of

[1] State v Smith, 48 Vt., 266 (1876), Hartridge v Rockwell, R M Charlton (Ga), 260 (1828), Curry v Scott, 51 Pa St , 270 (1869), in which Reese v Bank was said to decide "nothing more than that untaken stock is held by the corporation in trust for the corporators, and must be disposed of for the benefit of all," and it was held that a stockholder has no greater right than a stranger to subscribe to original stock untaken Cf Eidman v Bowman 58 Ill , 444 (1871), Gray v Portland R R Co , 3 Mass , 364 (1807)

[2] Where, long after the company has commenced business it has disposed of its property and is ready to declare a five per cent dividend, the directors issue to themselves at par that part of the original capital stock which never had been issued, it is a fraud on the remaining stockholders Arkansas, etc , Soc v Eichholtz, 25 Pac Rep , 613 (Kan , 1891) Where a director issues to himself, at par, stock belonging to the corporation and which is worth more than par, the transaction is voidable , but if all the stockholders acquiesce therein for a long time, the acquiescence of the executors of a deceased stockholder binds the estate St Croix L Co v Mittlestadt, 44 N W Rep 1079 (Minn , 1890) In the case of Reese v Bank, etc , 31 Pa St , 78 (1855), the court held that where a part of the authorized capital stock remained untaken, and a resolution of the directors was carried into effect by

which the untaken portion of the stock was issued to those shareholders not in arrears upon shares previously taken, to the exclusion, as to the new shares of those in arrears upon the original issue it was held an invalid discrimination and an unlawful imposition of a penalty upon those in arrears. In regard to the right to subscribe for the unissued portion of the original capital stock, see also, §§ 70, 653 Where a corporation has an authorized capital of $5 000, but only $2,500 are directed by the stockholders to be issued, it is illegal and fraudulent to issue the remaining authorized capital without giving the existing stockholders a prior right to subscribe to such increased capital pro rata Directors elected by reason of such illegal issue will be enjoined from acting where they are about to change the whole policy of the company Humboldt, etc , Ass'n v Stevens et al , 52 N W Rep , 568 (Neb , 1892).

[3] Terry v Eagle Lock Co 47 Conn , 141 (1879), Hart v St. Charles St R R Co , 30 La Ann , 758 (1878), Brown v Florida Southern R'y Co., 19 Fla 472 (1882)

[4] Cunningham's Appeal, 108 Pa St , 546 (1885) Where the corporation in issuing new stock requires the old stockholders to pay a bonus in order to subscribe, a former stockholder may pay the bonus in order to get the stock, and may then recover back the bonus by a suit. Dawson v Insurance Co , 5 R'y & Corp L J , 154 (1888, Com Pl Phil)

this right will be enjoined in the absence of laches or acquiescence.[1] The courts go very far in protecting the right of stockholders to subscribe for new stock.   It is often a very important right.

When the newly-issued shares have all been distributed or sold to others, in violation of a shareholder's pre-emptive right, his only remedy is an action at law against the corporation for damages And the measure of damages has been declared to be the excess of the market value above the par value at the time of the issue of the shares, with legal interest on such excess.[2]

A mere verbal notice by the stockholder to the corporation that he will take his proportion of the new issue under an increase is held in Louisiana not to be sufficient to render the company liable in damages for selling the shares to some one else[3]   The corporation may, however, and usually does, limit the time within which the shareholders may signify their intention to take up the new shares, and may require a part payment upon the shares within that time.[4]   The stockholder, therefore, who brings his action against the corporation for damages for refusal to allow him to

If on offering increased capital stock to the old stockholders the company requires more than par, a stockholder who pays it, even under protest cannot recover it back   He should have tendered par and then sued for refusal of the corporation to accept it.   De La Cuesta v Insurance Co, 20 Atl Rep, 505 (Pa, 1890)   Where by its charter a terminal and union depot company is obliged to allow new roads to demand and pay for a proportional part of the former company's capital stock, the price is par even though it is worth more   St. Paul, etc. Co v Minn, etc, R. R, 19 N W. Rep, 616 (Minn, 1891)

[1] A stockholder's remedy, it is said, in such a case is clearly against the corporation, and he is not obliged to sue at law for damages.   "The effect of such an action [i. e., the action for damages] would be to convert part of his interest as a shareholder into a judgment for damages, in other words, to sell a portion of his stock to the corporation

The judgment to be effectual must be against the corporation itself, not against the directors personally, who may be changed from time to time"   Dousman v Wisconsin & Lake Superior, etc. Co., 40 Wis, 418 (1876). In this case it is also held that the shareholder, where the stock is not yet fully issued, may have a decree in a court of equity restraining the whole issue, or else that there be an equitable distribution, and, if the shares are already partially distributed, that the proper amount be issued to the party complainant.   Cf Eidman v Bowman, 58 Ill, 444   In Massachusetts, however, this is not the rule, and in that state it is held that the courts have no power to compel the corporation or the directors to issue the shares to the party aggrieved   Sewall v Eastern R. R. Co, 9 Cush, 5 (1851).   But an action will lie against the corporation for damages Gray v. Portland Bank, 3 Mass, 364 (1807)

[2] Eidman v. Bowman, 58 Ill, 444 (1871), Reese v Bank of Montgomery, 31 Pa St., 78 (1855), Gray v Portland Bank, 3 Mass., 364 (1807)

[3] Hart v St. Charles St. R'y Co, 30 La Ann, 758 (1878), holding, also, that a tender must be made

[4] Sewall v Eastern R. R. Co., 63 Mass., 5 (1851), Hart v St. Charles St. R'y Co, 30 La Ann, 758 (1878)

subscribe for the new shares, or for selling the shares to some one else, or for depriving him in any other way of them, must allege and prove that he demanded the shares and offered to subscribe and pay for them in the regular way, within the time fixed for such subscriptions [1] Other shareholders similarly aggrieved are not to be joined as parties complainant Each stockholder sues alone, inasmuch as the liability of the corporation in these cases is several and not joint [2]

§ 287 *Issue of new stock by a stock dividend* — A frequent method of issuing an increase of the capital stock is by a stock dividend. In England there is some doubt as to whether such dividends may be imposed upon stockholders who object thereto, and demand the money dividend in lieu of which the stock is issued [3] In this country such dividends are legal unless prohibited by constitutional or statutory provisions [4] But in all cases of a stock dividend, as a method of issuing an increase of the capital stock, there must be in the possession of the corporation an amount of property over and above its corporate debts equal to the whole capital stock, including the increase, and this amount cannot afterwards be used for any kind of a dividend

§ 288 *Liability of the shareholder upon an increase of the capital stock — Irregularities in increasing the stock* — A person subscribing for shares of stock upon an increase of the capital stock is liable thereon the same as a subscriber to the original capital stock In some respects he cannot set up defenses that an original subscriber

---

[1] Wilson v Bank of Montgomery County, 29 Pa St, 537 (1857)

[2] Dousman v Wisconsin & Lake Superior Mining & Smelting Co, 40 Wis, 418 (1876) In an early Indiana decision it is said to be the law that where, in the charter, directors are given full power to effect an increase of the capital stock, "on such terms and conditions and in such manner as to them shall seem best," they may authorize the increase without the consent of the shareholders, that as to each increase there is no pre-emptive right, and that, accordingly, the newly-issued shares may be disposed of as the directors determine. Ohio Insurance Co. v Nunnemacher, 15 Ind, 294 (1860) So, also, in New York it is said that the executory purchaser of shares of the original stock is not entitled to the proportionate amount of new stock on an

increase of the capital Miller v Illinois Central R R Co, 24 Barb 312 (1857) An incorporator is not entitled to the increased stock as a gratuity, he must pay for it Brown v Florida Southern R'y Co, 19 Fla, 472 (1882)

[3] See ch XXXII *infra*

[4] Id ; also § 51, *supra*. Howell v. Chicago, etc R R Co 51 Barb, 378 (1868). An increase of the capital stock, by the issue of new shares and the sale of them for less than their par value, is not such an issue of fictitious stock" as the California state constitution forbids (art XII § 11) Stein v Howard, 65 Cal, 616 (1884) Where the company is under obligations to issue stock to represent interest on subscriptions until dividends are declared, a stock dividend does not stop the interest Hardin County v Louisville, etc, R R, 17 S. W. Rep., 860 (Ky, 1891)

might have set up. Thus, a subscriber for increased stock cannot defeat an action to enforce his subscription by setting up the failure of the corporation to obtain subscriptions for the whole of the authorized increase [1]   In general, a subscriber to an increase of stock cannot interpose defenses to his subscription which subscribers to the original stock could not have raised — such, for example, as technical objections to the validity of his contract of subscription [2] Nor can the subscriber set up that the increase was irregularly effected   It is for the state alone to raise the question whether corporate capital stock has been lawfully and regularly increased [3] Especially it is the rule that, as against corporate creditors, stockholders who have subscribed for the increased stock, accepted the certificate, and received dividends thereon, are estopped from defeating an action on their subscription by setting up that the stock was increased in an irregular or unlawful manner [4]   Subscribers to

[1] Clarke ł Thomas, 34 Ohio St, 46 (1877), Nutter v Lexington, etc , R R. Co, 6 Gray, 85 (1856), Delano v Butler, 118 U S, 634 (1886), Aspinwall v Butler, 133 U S., 595 (1890)   A subscriber for increased stock is liable although the full amount is not subscribed. Avegne ł Citizens' Bank, etc , 5 S Rep., 537 (La , 1889)   But see Eaton v Pacific, etc. Bank, 10 N E Rep , 844 (Mass , 1887)

[2] Kansas City Hotel Co. v. Hunt, 57 Mo , 126 (1874)

[3] Pullman v Upton, 96 U S, 328 (1877). A party purchasing a certificate of stock not under seal nor signed by the president must take notice, and cannot afterwards complain that it was an irregular increase of stock. Byers v Rollins, 21 Pac Rep., 894 (Colo , 1889). Stockholder participating in irregular increase of stock cannot afterwards object to it   Poole ł West, etc , Ass'n, 30 Fed Rep , 513 (1887). Irregularities in the increase of the capital stock will be disregarded as between the stockholders who participate. Bailey v Champlain, etc , Co , 46 N W Rep , 539 (Wis , 1890), Bard v Banigan, 39 Fed. Rep., 13 (1889)

[4] Chubb v Upton, 95 U S., 665 (1877). In re Miller's Dale, etc , Co , L R., 31 Ch D., 211 (1886), in which a subscriber

to new shares was not permitted to plead, as against creditors, that the issue was irregular because only thirteen days had elapsed between the passing of the resolution to increase the capital and the confirming of it, when the law required fourteen days, Kansas City Hotel Co v. Harris, 51 Mo., 464 (1873); and see McCarthy v Lavasche, 89 Ill., 270 (1878), Veeder v Mudgett, 95 N. Y , 295 (1884) — the last case holding that a statute allowing increase to be made by stockholders in meeting assembled on a specified notice is invalid if the notice did not conform to the statute, but that the stockholders are liable nevertheless to corporate creditors on such stock. Sewell's Case, L. R., 3 Chan , 131 (1868); Upton ł Jackson, 1 Flippin, 413 (1874); Kansas City Hotel Co v Hunt, 57 Mo., 126 (1874). In such a case the state alone can properly raise the question whether the corporate stock had been regularly and lawfully increased   Pullman v. Upton, 96 U. S , 329 (1877)   See Clarke ł Thomas, 34 Ohio St , 46 (1874), Matter of the Reciprocity Bank, 22 N Y, 9 (1860), Byers v Rollins, 21 Pac. Rep., 894 (Colo., 1889)   See, also, Peckham v. Smith, 9 How. Prac , 436 (1854). See, also, the principles and cases in § 298, infra   Irregularity of notice of a meeting to increase the capital stock has

390

increased capital stock cannot escape liability therefor by setting up that the notice of increase was not published as required by statute [1]

But a contrary rule prevails as regards essential steps in the increase. If there is no vote of the stockholders as required by statute, they are not liable on the stock [2] Stockholders of the original capital stock are of course not liable for the defaults of subscribers to the increased capital stock.[3]

§ 289 *Rights and liabilities of the shareholders upon a reduction of the capital stock.*— Upon an authorized reduction of the capital stock of an incorporated company, regularly effected, the amount of corporate assets over and above the amount of the capital stock as reduced is equivalent to surplus profits, and may be treated as

---

been held to be fatal Matter of Wheeler, 2 Abb Pr (N S), 361 (1866) If the statute requires a publication of notice of the intended increase, such publication must be made It cannot be waived, even by unanimous consent of the stockholders The public are entitled to knowledge of the increase. State *v* McGrath, 86 Mo, 239 (1886), the court refusing to grant a *mandamus* to compel the secretary of state to file the certificate The invalidity or irregularity of an increase of stock may be set up by the subscribers therefor as against creditors who were stockholders and managers of the company Sayles *v* Brown, 40 Fed Rep, 8 (1889).

[1] Handley *v* Stutz, 139 U S, 417 (1891) Holders of increased capital stock cannot defeat their liability for the subscription price by alleging that the increase was made by a stockholders' meeting held out of the state, or that proper notice of the meeting was not given, or that the required statutory publication of the increase was not made Stutz *v* Handley, 41 Fed Rep, 531 (1890) If the stockholders have knowledge of the intention to increase the stock, the failure to give statutory notice cannot be taken advantage of by one not injured by such want of notice Columbia Bank's Appeal, 16 Weekly Notes Cas, 357, 42 Leg Int., 236. Concerning the failure to give the

requisite notice, see, also, chs XXXVI and XLVI Where a person subscribes to the proposed increased capital stock, and the officers surreptitiously transfer some of their own old stock to him, he is not liable on the statutory liability thereon, even though he accepted the stock, being ignorant of the fraud practiced upon him Stephens *v* Follett, 43 Fed Rep, 842 (1890).

[2] The receiver of a national bank cannot hold stockholders liable on increased stock where such increase was not authorized by a two-thirds vote of the stockholders. Winters *v* Armstrong, 37 Fed Rep, 508 (1889) In American Tube Works *v* Boston, etc, Co., 139 Mass, 5 (1885), it was held that a creditor who had taken irregularly issued stock in payment of his debt might over two years thereafter, and after the corporation became insolvent, repudiate the stock and again become a creditor

[3] Veeder *v* Mudgett, 95 N Y., 295 (1884) See, also, § 215, *supra* Stockholder not participating is not liable for fraud in increase of stock where the directors received pay therefor in notes which are worthless So held under Iowa statute Miller *v* Bradish, 28 N W Rep 594 (Iowa, 1886) See, also, Delano *v* Butler, 118 U S, 634 (1886). A statutory requirement that a certificate shall be filed when stock is fully paid does not render old stockholders

such by the corporation   It may be set aside as surplus, or it may be divided among the shareholders proportionally by a dividend, unless the rights of previous corporate creditors would thereby be injured [1]   But it is not the rule that the reduction of the capital

liable for failure to file as to increased stock   Sayles v Brown, 40 Fed Rep, 8 (1889)   A liability imposed until a specified certificate is filed is not revived by an increase of the capital stock Veeder v Mudgett, 95 N Y, 295 (1884). See, also Ochiltree v Railroad Co, 21 Wall, 249 (1874), as to liability on increase of capital stock   As to the liability on a reduction of the capital stock and the constitutionality thereof, see Daue v Young, 61 Me, 160 (1872)   also § 497, infra   Where a person subscribes to the proposed increased capital stock, but the increase is not made, and the officers surreptitiously transfer some of their own old stock to him, he is not liable on the statutory liability thereon, even though he accepted the stock being ignorant of the fraud practiced on him Stephens v Follett, 43 Fed Rep., 842 (1890)   In suing a stockholder on a statutory liability for failure to file a certificate upon an increase in the capital stock, only those who hold the increased capital stock are liable   Griffith v Green, 129 N Y, 517 (1892)

[1] Strong v Brooklyn Crosstown R R. Co, 93 N Y, 426 (1883), where a corporation whose capital had been reduced one-half issued certificates of indebtedness bearing interest to shareholders for the excess   The application of a dissenting holder to have them declared illegal, and to restrain the corporation from paying them, was refused, Seeley v New York National Exchange Bank of New York, 8 Daly, 400 (1878), S C, aff'd, 78 N Y, 608 (1879), McCann v First Nat Bank, 14 N E Rep., 251 (Ind, 1887), approving of the text herein, and holding that where by reason of bad debts the capital stock is reduced, a subsequent collection of such debts does not sustain an action by a stockholder for his proportion thereof   If increase

is afterwards cancelled, a corporate creditor who was such previous to the increase cannot complain   Colt v Gold Amal Co, 119 U. S, 343 (1886)   A subscriber to the increased stock may recover back the money paid thereon if the corporation afterwards reduces the proposed increase, so that it shall correspond to the amount actually subscribed for   The principle laid down in §§ 176-181, supra, applies   Eaton v Pacific Nat Bank, 10 N E. Rep., 844 (Mass, 1887)   Cf § 289   For the rules herein relative to life estates and remainder in stock, see § 559   A stockholder may enjoin the corporation from reducing its capital stock, as allowed by statute; calling in all certificates of stock, issuing new certificates proportionately, declaring a dividend of the surplus over the reduced capital stock, and, on account of the corporate property being invested, borrow money to pay that dividend   Coquard v St. Louis, etc., Co. 7 S W Rep, 176 (Mo, 1888)   Under the English statute a reduction of the capital stock reduces the preferred as well as the common stock.   Bannatyne v. Direct, etc, Co, 55 L T Rep, 716 (1886). And in general see, also, In re State Ins Co, 14 Fed Rep, 28 (1882); Excelsior Co v Lacey, 63 N Y, 422 (1875). By-law cannot compel a stockholder to sell his stock to the corporation for the purpose of retiring it   Bergman v. St. Paul, etc, Assoc, 29 Minn, 275 (1882). In England it is the rule that when the assets are already reduced by losses the corporation cannot effect a reduction of the capital stock so as to cover up the losses   In re Ebbw Vale Steel, Iron & Coal Co, L R, 4 Chan. Div, 827 (1876). And yet it should seem that a greater injury would be worked upon the public by continuing business with an impaired capital than to reduce it openly

stock of a corporation always authorizes the distribution among the stockholders of a sum equal to the difference between the original and the reduced amount of capital Such a distribution is lawful only when it appears that the original capital stock is unimpaired. The corporation can divide among its stockholders only such a sum as will leave with the corporation an amount equal to the reduced capital stock[1] Not only this, but corporate creditors who were such before the reduction may disregard the reduction and enforce payment of their debts from the original unpaid subscriptions as though no reduction had taken place[2] But creditors whose debts were contracted subsequently to the reduction can look only to the capital stock, as reduced, for security They will be held to have given credit upon the faith of that amount of stock alone[3]

A reduction of the capital stock is effected only when all statutory formalities have been complied with[4]

§ 290. *Change in the number or par value of the shares* — It is a principle of law closely related to those already set forth in this chapter, and well settled, that the number of shares into which the capital stock has been divided, and the par value of those shares, can neither be increased nor diminished, in number or in value, without express warrant of authority either from the legislature or

---

to what it actually is. *Cf In re Kirkstall Brewery Co.* L R, 5 Chan Div, 535 (1877) In England, by statute, a plan for reducing the capital stock must be presented to and approved by the courts *Re Direct, etc,* Co, 55 L T Rep, 804 (1866) And a distribution of part of the capital stock among the shareholders proportionally is an unauthorized reduction, and the stock will be ordered to be returned *Holmes v Newcastle-upon-Tyne Abattoir Co,* 45 L. J. (Chan), 383 (1875). Where the capital stock is reduced by reason of certain doubtful securities the securities should not be withdrawn from the assets of the bank and put into a trust *McCann v First Nat'l Bank,* 30 N E Rep, 893 (Ind, 1892)

[1] *Strong v Brooklyn Crosstown R R. Co,* 93 N Y 426 (1883)

[2] *In re State Insurance Co,* 11 Biss, 301 (1882), S C, 14 Fed Rep, 28 *Bedford R R Co v Bowser* 48 Pa St, 29 (1864) Shareholders have no power to avoid liability on their stock by reducing either the amount of it or the par value of the shares *Dane v Young,* 61 Me, 160 (1872) *Cf Bedford R R Co v. Bowser,* 48 Pa St, 29 (1864)

[3] *Hepburn v Exchange, etc,* Co 4 La Ann, 87 (1849), *Palfrey v Paulding,* 7 id, 363 (1852), *Cooper v Frederick,* 9 Ala, 742 (1846) *Cf In re State Ins Co,* 14 Fed Rep, 28 (1882), S C, 11 Biss, 301

[4] See *Moses v Ocoee Bank,* 1 Lea (Tenn), 398, holding that, where a corporation has power under its charter to reduce its capital stock, it must clearly appear that it has ordered the reduction to be made, neither equivocal acts nor inferences nor unauthorized acts of a president or director will be sufficient *Ferris v Ludlow,* 7 Ind, 517 (1856), holding that where the records of a company showed that propositions to reduce its stock had been made, but failed to show any acceptance, there was no reduction See, also, *Grangers' Life, etc, v Kamper,* 73 Ala, 325 (1882)

the charter of the company [1]   When, however, the charter does not
fix the number or amount of the shares, it devolves upon the shareholder or directors to fix them; and in such a case it seems that
the limit established might lawfully be changed without special
authority [2]

B. ILLEGAL INCREASE OF STOCK, BEING OVERISSUED STOCK.

§ 291   *Unauthorized increase of stock may amount to overissued
stock.* — Where the full capital stock of a corporation has been issued, and there is no statute or charter provision authorizing an
increase of the stock, it is clear that any issue of stock in excess of
the capital stock is not a legitimate increase of the capital stock.
It is unauthorized and illegal, and is termed in law an overissue of
stock. There is a clear distinction between overissued stock and an
irregular increase of stock   The former is where an increase of the
stock is made, although no increase is authorized by the charter or
by statute   The latter occurs when there is a statutory or charter
provision authorizing an increase of the stock, but the formalities
prescribed for making that increase have not been strictly complied with.   Overissued stock is void, while an irregular increase
of stock is merely voidable.

An overissue of stock often arises by forgery on the part of an

---

[1] Salem Mill-dam Corporation v
Ropes, 23 Mass., 23 (1827); *Re* Financial
Corporation (Holmes Case), L R, 2 Ch,
714, 733 (1867), Droitwich Salt Co v
Curzon, L. R., 3 Ex, 35, 42 (1867),
Smith v Goldsworthy, 4 Q B., 430
(1843) *Cf* Sewell's Case, L R., 3 Ch, 131
(1868) "A corporation with a fixed
capital, divided into a fixed number of
shares, can have no power of its own
volition, or by any act of its officers and
agents, to enlarge its capital or increase
the number of shares into which it is
divided   The supreme legislative power
of the state can alone confer that authority" It cannot be increased "by
the covert or fraudulent efforts of one
or more of the agents of the corporation" New York & New Haven R. R.
Co v Schuyler, 34 N Y, 30, 48 (1865).
Cf. Scovill v Thayer, 105 U S, 143 (1881).
In New York a statute allowing such a
change exists   New York Session Laws,
1866, ch 73   Where all the shares are

reduced in par value from $50 to $38 and
the $12 difference is paid to the stock-
holders in cash, this is a reduction of
capital stock and not a dividend and
cannot be taxed as a dividend   Commonwealth v. Central T. Co, 22 Atl
Rep., 209 (Pa., 1891)   A reduction of
the par value of the common stock and
not of the preferred is not allowed in
England   *Re* Union, etc, Co, Lim, 61
L. T. Rep., 327 (1889)

[2] Somerset, etc., R. R. Co v Cushing,
45 Me, 524 (1858); Ambergate, Nottingham & Boston & Eastern R'y Co. v.
Mitchell, 4 Exch, 540 (1849); S C, 6
Eng R'y Cases, 234; *In re* European
Central R'y Co, L R., 8 Eq, 438 (1859)
It has been held allowable, however, for
the company to allow the holders of
paid-up shares to return them and take
in exchange shares of double the par
value as half paid up, and *vice versa,*
both kinds of stock being authorized
Teasdale's Case, L. R., 9 Chan, 54 (1873)

officer of the corporation who forges the necessary names of the corporate officers to the certificate and puts it in circulation.[1]

§ 292   *Overissued stock is absolutely void.*— By overissued stock is to be understood stock issued in excess of the amount limited and prescribed by the act of incorporation   Certificates of stock issued in excess of the certificates that represent the full authorized capital stock of the corporation represent overissued stock   Such stock is spurious and wholly void.   This is the settled law, and it prevails equally whether the overissue is the result of accident or mistake, or want of knowledge of the law, or is due to fraud and intentional wrong-doing   The *animus* or intent of the parties to the overissue is not material   Overissued stock, no matter how overissued, represents nothing, and is wholly and entirely valueless and void.[2]   So rigid and well established is this rule that not even a *bona fide* holder of such stock can give to it any validity or vitality   Overissued or spurious stock may, however, it seems, be legalized by a subsequent legal increase of the capital stock[3]

§ 293.   *Liability of the corporation as to overissued stock*   — Although it is settled law that overissued stock is void and valueless, and that no action lies either to compel the corporation to recognize the holder as a stockholder, or to issue in place thereof a valid certificate, yet where overissued certificates of stock, signed or purporting to be signed by the corporate officers having the authority to issue stock, and actually issued by such officers, are purchased by any person, or are taken in any manner in good faith and for value, such *bona fide* holder may sue the corporation in tort and recover damages.[4]

---

[1] See § 293

[2] The great and leading case on this subject is New York. etc., R. R Co *v* Schuyler, 34 N Y, 30 (1865)   *Cf.* Mechanics' Bank *v* New York etc., R. R. Co, 13 id, 599 (1856)   See, also, as to the point that overissued stock is void even in the hands of *bona fide* holders, People's Bank *v* Kurtz, 99 Pa St, 344 (1882), Bruff *v.* Mali, 36 N Y, 200 (1867), People *v* Parker, etc, Co, 10 How Prac, 543 (1854), Sewell's Case, L. R., 3 Chan App, 131, 138 (1868), Wright's Appeal, 99 Pa St., 425 (1882). Scovill *t* Thayer, 105 U S, 143 (1881)

[3] Sewell's Case, L. R., 3 Chan App, 131 (1868), New York, etc, R R Co *v* Schuyler, 34 N Y, 30, 56, 57 (1865)

[4] New York, etc, R. R Co *v* Schuy-
ler, 34 N Y, 30, 49 60 (1865), Bruff *v* Mali, 36 id, 200 (1867), Titus *v* Great, etc, Road Co, 5 Lans, 250 (1872), S C, 61 N Y, 237 (1874)   Bank of Kentucky *v* Schuylkill Bank, Parsons' Select Cas, 180, 216 (1846)   This was a suit in equity by a bank against another bank which, acting as its transfer agent, had made a large overissue of its stock. Tome *v* Parkersburg, etc, R. R. Co, 39 Md, 36 (1873), Willis *v* Phila, etc, R R Co, 6 Week Notes Cas, 461 (1879), Willis *v* Fry, 13 Phila, 33 (1879), People's Bank *v* Kurtz, 99 Pa St, 344 (1882)   See, also, Daly *v* Thompson, 10 Mees & W, 309 (1842), *In re* Bahia etc, R R Co, L R, 3 Q B, 584, 595 (1868); Simm *v* Anglo etc., Co, L R, 5 Q B Div, 188 (1879)   Waterhouse *v* London,

This rule applies also to overissues of stock which are caused by the forgery on the part of one corporate officer of the names of other corporate officers.[1]

etc, R R. Co, 41 L T (N S.), 538 (1879), Mandelbaum v North, etc, R R. Co., 4 Mich, 465 (1857) Wright's Appeal, 99 Pa St, 425 (1882) In many of these cases the overissue was due to a mistake of the corporation in allowing a transfer of stock The failure to surrender an old certificate does not give a purchaser of stock, notice that an overissue is being made Allen v South Boston R. R, 22 N E Rep. 917 (Mass, 1889) A party who purchases overissued stock, but is not a purchaser in good faith for full value, cannot hold the company liable where the stock was issued by the executive committee without authority Ryder v Bushwick R. R, 134 N Y, 83 (1892).

[1] Where the secretary and treasurer of a corporation, who is also its agent for the transfer of stock, and authorized to countersign and issue stock when signed by the president, forges the name of the latter and fraudulently issues a certificate of stock, the corporation is liable to a bank which has accepted such certificate in good faith as security for a loan In this case the bank caused inquiry to be made at the office of the railroad company and was informed by the secretary and treasurer that the certificate was genuine The bank was allowed to recover although it had sold the forged stock, but had taken it back upon the forgery becoming known Fifth Avenue Bank v. Forty-second Street, etc, Co, 33 N. E. Rep, 378 (N Y, 1893). Where the treasurer is the proper agent to issue stock and the president intrusts him with certificates signed in blank, the corporation is liable for overissued stock issued and sold by the treasurer for his own benefit, even though no old certificate was surrendered Allen v South Boston R. R 22 N E. Rep, 917 (Mass, 1889). Where the secretary of the company

has made fraudulent transfers of stock and falsified the share register, and fraudulently induced two of the directors to affix the seal of the company to the certificates, the company is liable to a purchaser of the certificates. The measure of damages is the price paid by the purchaser for the certificate with interest thereon, the application for transfer having been made to the company on that same day Re The Ottos, etc, Mines, 68 L. T Rep, 138 (1892); Shaw v Port Philip & C. Gold Min Co, L. R, 13 Q B D, 103 (1885), where the corporation was held liable on a certificate signed and issued by the secretary of the corporation, but who had forged thereto the names of the other corporate officers whose signatures were necessary to the issue of a certificate of stock Cf. Duncan v Luntley, 2 McN. & G, 30 (1849) See, also, Manhattan Beach Co v Harned, 27 Fed Rep., 484 (1886), where, however, the issue was by fraud rather than forgery, Moores v. Citizens' National Bank, 111 U S, 157 (1883), Brooklyn, etc, R. R. v Strong, 75 N. Y., 591 (1878) See, also, §§ 294, 363, N. Y. L. J., Aug 5, 1889, 21 Pac. Rep, 894 (Colo, 1889). A person who takes a certificate of stock issued directly from the corporation to himself, and takes it from the officer issuing it, as collateral security for a personal obligation of such officer, is bound to inquire into the issue. If the stock is spurious such a holder is not a bona fide holder Farrington v. South Boston R. R., 23 N E. Rep., 109 (Mass., 1890) Where the transfer agent of a corporation makes out a certificate of stock and forges the name of a fictitious person to an assignment thereof, and issues a new certificate to such fictitious person and causes the proper officers to sign such certificate, and then signs the fictitious person's name thereto and

A corporation, like a natural person, is liable in damages for the torts and frauds of its agents when acting within the scope of their proper employment, and when fraudulent certificates are issued by its officers, and pass innocently into the hands of *bona fide* holders for value, the corporation is estopped to deny the authority of such agents, and cannot escape liability for damages so resulting

If an innocent holder of overissued stock brings an action in equity to compel the corporation to record the transfer, he will be denied that relief, but may have, in lieu thereof, damages at law [1] The better remedy in such a case, therefore, is an action at law, and the measure of damages is the market value of the stock at the time the transfer was demanded [2]

§ 294 *Defenses of the corporation to such actions* — It frequently happens that an overissue of stock is made without a strict compliance with the formalities of an issue of genuine stock   Generally, certificates of stock must, according to the by-laws of the corporation, be signed by certain specified corporate officers Often, however, nothing in the charter or by-laws of the corporation regulates the form or contents of a certificate of stock. Accordingly, when action is brought against a corporation on overissued stock, the defense is sometimes set up that the certificates were not signed by the proper officers, or were not issued with the usual formalities, and consequently that, the purchaser having had no-

---

sells it, the company is liable in damages to a purchaser of the certificate Jarvis *v* Manhattan Beach Co, 6 N Y Supp, 703 (1889), S C, 53 Hun, 362 Where the signature of the president and treasurer to certificates is required and the president issues fraudulent certificates to himself and forges the treasurer's name thereto, the corporation is not liable therefor, even to *bona fide* purchasers. Hill *t* Jewett etc, Co, 28 N E Rep, 142 (Mass, 1891) In the case of Swain *v* West Philadelphia, etc R'y (see 18 Atl Rep, 383), the supreme court of Pennsylvania held a corporation liable for a fraudulent, false, spurious and void issue of stock by its president. 'The liability of the railway company arises on the principle of estoppel, which the necessities of trade and commerce require Stock certificates issued by a corporation having power to issue is a continuing confirmation of the ownership of the

special amount of stock by the person designated therein, or his assignee, and the purchaser has a right to rely thereon and claim the benefit of an estoppel in his favor as against the corporation " See. also Appeal of Jeans 11 Atl Rep, 862, Paper Co s Appeal, 99 Pa St, 513.

[1] Willis *v* Phila, etc, R R Co, 6 Week Notes Cas, 461 (1879), People's Bank *v* Kurtz, 99 Pa St, 314 (1882)

[2] People's Bank *t* Kurtz 99 Pa St, 314 (1882), Willis *v* Phila, etc, R R Co, 6 Week Notes Cas, 461 (1879), Tome *v* Parkersburg, etc, R R Co, 39 Md, 36 (1873) It is, however, a condition precedent to maintaining such an action that the holder of the overissued stock discharge any lien upon it which would have properly attached to genuine stock under the same conditions Mt Holly Paper Co.'s Appeal, 99 Pa St, 513 (1882)

tice of the infirmity, the corporation is not liable. But such a defense is not favored by the courts[1] Where, however, the charter provided that certificates of stock should be signed by the president, directors and treasurer, fraudulent overissues signed by the president and treasurer alone were held not sufficient to charge the corporation[2]

§ 295 *Personal liability of the officers of the corporation on overissued stock* —The officers of a corporation who are authorized to issue certificates of stock to the stockholders are liable, in tort, both to the immediate purchasers from them of spurious stock, falsely and fraudulently certified by them, and also to any subsequent purchaser buying upon the faith of the false certificate, and sustaining damage thereby.[3] There may be a joint action against the corporation and the corporate agents issuing the stock, or a separate action against either[4] A corporation may sue in *assumpsit* its treasurer

[1] New York, etc, R. R Co v Schuyler, 34 N Y, 30 (1865). Thus, where an officer of a corporation fraudulently issued stock for his own use, controlled all the books relating to the stock, and countersigned all the certificates, the corporation was held liable for the spurious stock Tome v Parkersburg, etc, R. R Co, 39 Md, 36 (1873) So, also, where overissued stock is issued under the genuine seal of the corporation, the corporation is liable People's Bank v Kurtz, 99 Pa. St., 344 (1882) See, also, Manhattan Beach Co v Harned, 27 Fed. Rep., 484 (1886) The last case, however, was where the corporate officers issued stock, not in excess of the capital stock, but a part of the unissued original capital stock They issued it not for the corporation, but in fraud of it and for their own benefit See, also, § 293, *supra*

[2] Holbrook v Fauquier, etc, Turnpike Co, 3 Cranch, C. C, 425 (1829). And overissued stock issued by the president to his private debtor, in payment of his private debt, has been held not to confer on such debtor a right to hold the corporation responsible Wright's Appeal, 99 Pa St., 425 (1882) In this case the court assumes that the debtor could not be heard to claim *bona fides*

[3] Bruff t Mali, 36 N. Y, 200 (1867),

Seizer v Mali, 41 id, 619 (1869), reversing S C, 32 Barb., 76 (1860), 11 Abb Prac, 129, Cazeaux v Mali, 25 Barb, 578 (1857) And the holder of genuine stock has an action against them for the depreciation of its value by reason of the overissue Shotwell v Mali, 38 id, 415 (1862). A person receiving stock from the directors of a corporation, in pledge for a loan to it, they knowing that the stock was overissued, may sue the directors for damages in an action for deceit. Whitehaven, etc, Co v Reed, 54 L. T. Rep. 360 (1886), National Exchange Bank t Sibley, 71 Ga, 726 (1883) See, also, Daly v Thompson, 10 M & W, 309 (1812). By statute in many of the states such forgeries are made a special criminal offense Regina v Nash, 2 Denison's Crim C, 493 (1852), New York Penal Code, § 591 Concerning the requirements of an indictment for issuing fraudulent stock, see West v. People, 27 N E Rep, 34 (Ill., 1891).

[4] Bruff v Mali, 36 N Y, 200 (1867). And when the action is against the officers responsible for the fraudulent overissue, if the evidence shows that the entire capital stock of the company had been issued prior to the dates of the certificates purchased or held by the plaintiff, and if it appears that the defendants prior thereto had, as officers of

who has illegally issued excessive stock and converted the proceeds to his own use [1]

§ 296 *Liability of the vendor of overissued stock* — In the absence of fraud the purchaser of overissued and spurious stock cannot hold his vendor liable thereon. The *bona fide* vendor can be held to warrant only his own title to the shares, not the right of the corporation to issue them If he came by them honestly and sells them in good faith there is no recourse to him, even though they turn out to be spurious.[2]

§ 297. *Equity will enjoin voting, transferring or dividends on such stock, and will adjust the rights of all parties* — A court of equity will, upon a proper application, grant an injunction to prevent the transfer of illegally-issued stock, or the payment of dividends thereon, or the voting of the pretended owners of such stocks [3] The most effectual remedy in these cases is a suit in equity, instituted by the corporation, whereby, in one proceeding, the rights and liabilities of all persons concerned with the overissue of the stock are fully and finally determined and adjudicated, and the overissued stock itself is retired and destroyed Such a proceeding is in the nature of a bill to quiet title, or to remove a cloud from the title of the genuine stock Spurious or overissued stock, issued by corporate officers having the apparent authority, and outstanding in the hands of numerous holders, is a cloud upon the title to the genuine stock. It is a cloud which a court of equity will remove; and a suit to that end may be commenced, either by the corporation [4] or by the stockholders themselves in their own behalf,

---

the corporation, issued spurious certificates of stock, then there is a presumption of law that the certificates in controversy are false and fraudulent, and the burden is upon the defendants to show that these particular certificates were issued, either upon the surrender of certificates of genuine stock, or upon the transfer on the books of the company of such stock — facts peculiarly within the knowledge of the corporate officers. Shotwell *v.* Mali, 38 Barb, 445, 469 (1862), a well-considered case; Bruff *v* Mali, *supra*

[1] Rutland R R *v* Haven, 19 Atl Rep., 769 (Vt., 1890)

[2] State *v* North Louisiana, etc R R Co, 34 La Ann, 947 (1882), People's Bank *v* Kurtz, 99 Pa St., 344 (1882), Seizer *v.* Mali, 41 N Y, 619 (1869) As to the liability of brokers for the forgery of their employees in delivering spurious stock to a customer, see Andrews *v* Clark, 20 Atl Rep, 429 (Md, 1890) In the case Isham *v* Post N Y L J, April 18, 1893, a broker was held liable to his customer for whom he had purchased certificates of stock which turned out to be forgeries See, also ch XXV

[3] Kent *v.* Quicksilver Mining Co., 78 N Y., 159 And where a corporate officer issues illegal and unauthorized stock he may be enjoined from allowing a transfer of it if proof is given of its illegal character and of a proposed transfer Sherman *v* Clark 4 Nev, 138 (1869)

[4] New York, etc, R R Co *v* Schuyler, 17 N Y, 592 (1858) Stock purchased from the secretary, as secretary, is not

where the corporation fails or refuses to institute it.[1] Were it not for this remedy in equity a corporation whose officers have fraudulently issued spurious stock would soon be thrown into insolvency and a receivership by reason of the multitudinous suits at law which would be brought, attended as such suits are by attachments and heavy bills of costs In order to protect, preserve and administer the corporate assets in such cases. and in order to prevent a multiplicity of suits and remove a cloud from the title to the other stock, a court of equity will assume jurisdiction.

§ 298 *Subscriber's right to defeat a subscription to overissued stock, and to recover back money paid thereon* — In addition to the remedy in equity, the holder of overissued stock has the further right at law to defeat an action on his subscription therefor; and that, too, even though he knew it to be overissued at the time the subscription was made.   There can be no estoppel in such a case, and not even creditors can enforce any liability on spurious or overissued stocks.[2] Where also a subscriber has paid an instalment on his subscription, although he knew when he made the subscription and paid the money that it was an illegal and unauthorized issue, he may rescind, and recover back what he has paid.[3] In Iowa it has been held that payment of a note given for overissued stock cannot be enforced where the consideration was expressed in the note to be the stock of the corporation to which the note was given, and the directors subsequently made an illegal and unauthorized increase in the stock, the maker of the note having had notice that a large amount of illegal stock had been issued, and that the illegal

---

good if overissued, and if the secretary sold it for his own benefit, even though it was duly signed A bill in equity lies to cancel it Cincinnati, etc , R'y v Citizens' Nat'l Bank, 3 R'y & Corp L J, 459 (Cin Court, 1888)

[1] Dewing v Perdicaries, 96 U S., 193 (1877), Wood v Union, etc , Ass'n, 63 Wis , 9 (1885), Perdicaris v Charleston Gaslight Co , Chase's Dec , 435 (1869) Cf Taylor v South & North Ala. R. R Co., 4 Woods, 575 (1882), where the subscriber acquiesced ten years The court denied any relief. In an action to cancel illegally increased stock the plaintiff must offer to surrender the part held by himself Byers v Rollins, 21 Pac. Rep , 894 (Colo , 1889).

[2] Scovill v Thayer, 105 U S , 143 (1881), Page v. Austin, 10 Can Sup Ct , 132,

Clark v Turner, 73 Ga , 1 (1884). Although a corporation has taken more subscriptions than its capital stock and has issued certificates therefor, yet this does not release subscribers up to the correct amount Cartright v Dickinson, 12 S. E Rep , 1030 (Tenn , 1890)

[3] Knowlton v Congress, etc , Co, 14 Blatch , 364 (1877), aff'd, 103 U. S., 49 (1880), Reed v Boston Machine Co , 141 Mass , 454 (1886) And the dissenting opinion of Dwight, Com'r, in Knowlton v Congress, etc , Co, 57 N Y , 518, 540 (1874) This case, however, was not strictly a case of overissued stock. A different class of cases exists where an increase of capital stock is authorized, but is irregularly made A subscriber is then liable See § 289, *supra.*

and valid stock could not be distinguished [1] But it is held that one who subscribes for overissued stock, *bona fide*, upon discovering that the stock is spurious cannot have a receiver appointed, pending an inquiry into the legality of the stock, to the end that, in case the stock is judicially declared invalid, such subscriber may recover back from the corporation the money so paid for the spurious shares, where the money received by the company had not been kept separate from its general funds, and could not be traced and identified [2]

[1] Merrill *v.* Gamble, 46 Iowa, 615 (1877), Merrill *v.* Beaver, 46 id, 646 (1877); Merrill *v.* Beaver, 50 id, 404 (1879).

[2] Whelpley *v* Erie Railway Co, 6 Blatch, 271 (1868).

PART II.

TRANSFERS OF STOCK.

CHAPTER XVIII.

LEGACIES AND GIFTS OF STOCK.

§ 299 *Definitions of general, specific and demonstrative legacies of stock.* — A general legacy of stock is a legacy whereby it becomes the duty of the executor or administrator to give to or procure for the legatee a certain amount of stock, as indicated by the will, there being nothing in the will itself to indicate that the legacy is to be satisfied from stock actually owned by the testator   A specific legacy of stock arises when the testator, in his will, directs or clearly indicates that the legacy is to be satisfied from stock which he owns.   A demonstrative legacy of stock is the same as a general legacy, except that it is to be purchased from a particular fund of the estate.   Demonstrative legacies of stock are of little importance as compared with the other two kinds [1]

§ 300 *Importance of the difference between general and specific legacies* — It is frequently of the greatest importance whether a legacy be a general or a specific one.   A large number of decisions, running back for nearly two hundred years, have been made in endeavoring to lay down rules on this subject.   The complications,

---

[1] That a legacy of stock may be demonstrative, see Ives *v* Canby, 48 Fed Rep, 718 (1891)   That legacies of stock may be demonstrative has been assumed by the cases   In the case, however, of Eckfeld's Estate, W. N. C. (Penn), 19 (1879), the court says a legacy of stock "may be either specific or general, according to the circumstances   It is never demonstrative   A demonstrative legacy is always pecuniary — differing, however, from an ordinary legacy in being referred to a particular fund or source of payment."

402

contradictions, inconsistent decisions and doubt that have arisen from the inherent difficulties of the subject are frequently adverted to and deplored by successive generations of judges.

The importance of determining whether a legacy of stock is general or specific rests in the fact that if it is specific it is entitled to certain advantages, and, on the other hand, is exposed to certain perils, while, if it is general, it is without those advantages, but is also free from the perils The advantages of a specific legacy of stock are that debts of the estate are to be paid from other funds. the specific legacy passes, though other legacies fail partially or wholly by reason of deficiencies in the estate, and the specific legatee is entitled to all dividends declared after the testator's death, instead of losing the first year's dividends, as in case of a general legacy of stock. General legacies of stock have none of these advantages On the other hand, a specific legacy of stock is open to the great danger of being revoked by the acts of the testator, and frequently so when the testator has no intention of revoking the legacy.[1] This revocation, arising by implication from the acts of the testator — such as selling the stock bequeathed, or using it in any way inconsistent with the idea of its passing under the will — is a danger that does not exist if the legacy is a general one, since general legacies of stock may be carried out by the executor's purchasing the stock for the purpose of the legacy.

§ 301. If a specific legacy will apply equally to paid-up stock and to stock not paid up, the legatee may take the former[2] If

[1] Kenkel v Macgill, 56 Md , 120 (1880), the court saying   " If the legacy is to be considered specific, then, in the event of the testator's parting with the thing or property bequeathed, or if from any cause it should be lost or destroyed, the legacy fails. Then, again, such legacies are not liable to abatement with general legacies; nor are they liable to contribution towards the payment of debts" Where evidently the intent was to give specific bonds it was so decreed Davies v Fowler, L R., 16 Eq, 308 (1873), Walton v Walton. 7 Johns Ch , 257 (1823) , Jacques v Chambers, 2 Coll , 435 (1846), holding also that the legatee may select his stock from different classes, but that he must pay calls on the stock due at the time of the testator's death but not paid In the case of Mullins v Smith, 1 Dr & Sm , 204 (1860), the difference between a spe-

cific and demonstrative legacy is thus described

"The points of difference between specific and demonstrative legacies are these

" A specific legacy is not liable to abatement for the payment of debts but a demonstrative legacy is liable to abate when it becomes a general legacy by reason of the failure of the fund out of which it is payable A specific legacy is liable to ademption, but a demonstrative legacy is not   A specific legacy, if of stock, carries with it the dividends which accrue from the death of the testator, while a demonstrative legacy does not carry interest from the testator's death.'

[2] Millard v Bailey, L R., 1 Eq , 378 (1866), Jacques v. Chambers (1846), supra.

the testator has made payments on the stock before calls have
been made, the legatee is entitled to the benefit.[1] If there is both
a specific and a general legacy of the same stock, the specific is to
be first satisfied[2] The specific legatee takes all the income and
profits of the stock,[3] whereas the general legatee has no interest in
the stock until twelve months after the testator's death[4] The specific legatee takes the stock, although there will then be no property left to pay pecuniary legacies.[5] However, he can have only
so much stock of that kind as the testator dies possessed of,[6] and if
the latter dies possessed of none, the specific legatee takes none[7]
The specific legatee does not take dividends declared and due before the testator's death, although such dividends have not been
collected[8]

§ 302 *Legacies of stock are construed to be general if the language will permit* — It is the policy of courts of justice to uphold
and carry out a legacy, and implied revocations are not looked
upon with favor Accordingly, in order to avoid the danger of
ademption, to which specific legacies are subject, the rule has become established that general legacies are to be favored by the
courts; and, if there is doubt as to whether a legacy be specific or
general, it will be construed to be of the latter kind.[9]

Where, however, the intent of the testator clearly was to give
particular stock owned by him, the court will declare the legacy to
be a specific one Thus, where the testator gives the legacy of
stock by describing it as " my " stock, the legacy is a specific one[10]

[1] Tanner v Tanner, 11 Beav , 69 (1848)

[2] Barton v Cooke, 5 Ves , 461 (1805)

[3] Loring v. Woodward, 41 N H, 391
(1860), holding also that parol evidence
cannot show a contrary intent of the
testator.

[4] Webster v. Hale, 8 Ves., 410 (1803)

[5] Drinkwater v Falconer, 2 Ves Sr,
622 (1755).

[6] Gordon v Duff, 28 Beav , 519 (1860);
Ashton v Ashton, 3 P Wms., 384 (1735).

[7] Evans v Trip, 6 Mad , 91 (1821)

[8] Perry v Maxwell, 2 Dev Eq (N C),
487 (1834).

[9] Davies v. Fowler, L R., 16 Eq , 308
(1873), Tifft v. Porter, 8 N Y , 516, 520 ,
Eckfeld's Estate, 7 W. N. C. (Pa.), 19
(1879)

[10] Walton v Walton, 7 Johns Ch 257
(1823), Loring v. Woodward, 41 N H,
391 (1860), Shuttleworth v Greaves, 4
Mylne & Cr , 35 (1838); Miller v. Little,

2 Beav , 259 (1840); Hayes v Hayes, 1
Keen, 97 (1836), Brainerd v. Cowdrey,
16 Conn , 1 (1843) The omission of the
word ' my " does not necessarily make
the legacy a general one Avelyn v.
Ward, 1 Ves Sr, 420 (1749) The word
" my " does not, however, have the same
significance in its application to a legacy
of an annuity as it has to a legacy of
stock Kirby v. Potter, 4 Ves., 748
(1799). In the case of Parrott v. Worsfold, 1 Jac & Walker, 574 (1820), a legacy of " all my stock that I may be
possessed of at my decease " was held
to be general, since there was no " individual thing given " Bequests in different sums to different legatees of
" my " stocks and bonds at their par
value, not describing them particularly,
are general legacies. They are not void
for uncertainty In re Hadden's Will,
9 N. Y. Supp., 453 (1890).

So also where the phrase "standing in my name"[1] is used, or "which I hold,"[2] or a direction is given to make up the specified amount from the general fund if the testator does not hold enough,[3] or the testator describes the stock as "now lying in the three per cents ,"[4] or uses the word "such,"[5] or makes a legacy of stock out of a quantity of stock,[6] or in another part of the will speaks of the stock as that of which the testatrix may die possessed,[7] or where, after several legacies, all apparently general, the testator bequeaths the remaining stock "standing in my name,"— the effect of all these is that the legacies are specific[8] A legacy of all the dividends, interest and proceeds from stock is a specific legacy, even though the testator did not own such stock at the time he made the will[9] There has been some difference of opinion as to whether the fact that the testator, at the time of making the will, possessed an equal or greater amount of stock than that bequeathed, and of the same kind, is to be taken as evidencing an intent to

---

[1] Ludlam's Estate, 13 Pa St, 188 (1850), Gordon v Duff, 28 Beav, 519 (1860), Kampf v Jones, 2 Keen, 756 (1837) Where, however, other parts of the will indicate that the legacy was general, it was held to be general See Auther v Auther, 13 Sim, 422 (1843), holding also that though, by the delay of the executor beyond a year in purchasing the stock, it rises, the legatee is entitled to the same amount as if it had been bought at the right time Fidelity Trust Company's Appeal, 108 Pa St, 339 and 492 (1885)

[2] Blackstone v Blackstone, 3 Watts, 335 (1839)

[3] Townsend v. Martin 7 Hare, 471 (1849), holding that such a legacy is specific and not demonstrative The case, however, of McGuire v Evans, 5 Ired Eq (N C), 269 (1848) holds that a legacy of stock, to take effect in case other legacies do not absorb that stock, is demonstrative, also that in case of legacies of the same stock to two different persons, each takes a moiety The cases of Mulling v Smith, 1 Dr & Sm, 204 (1860), Fountaine v Tyler, 9 Price, Ex , 94 (1821), and Queen's College v Sutton, 12 Sim, 521 (1842), hold that such a legacy is specific if the testator

leaves stock enough, but is general if he does not leave enough

[4] Morely v Bird, 3 Ves, 628 (1800), holding that if the executor has sold the stock the legatees may hold him liable for its value one year after the testator's death

[5] Davies v Fowler L R, 16 Eq, 398 (1873), the court saying that a legacy is specific when a meting out or dividing is evidently intended

[6] Hasking v Nicholls, 1 Y & C Ch , 478 (1842) And if the administrator has paid the dividends to another, he is personally liable A legacy of "ten shares of the stock of the W & N R Co" is a specific legacy, where a subsequent clause bequeathes "the balance of my stock as per my stock book" Trustees. etc. v Tufts, 23 N E Rep, 1006 (Mass. 1890)

[7] Measure v Carleton, 30 Beav , 588 (1862) This case also holds that, if an exact partition of the stock is impossible, enough will be sold to render it possible

[8] Sleech v Thorington, 2 Ves Sr , 560 (1751) A legacy of all of several articles is specific Tomlinson v Bury, 14 N E Rep , 137 (Mass , 1887)

[9] Stephenson v Dawson, 3 Beav , 342 (1840) See, also, Fidelity Trust Company's Appeal, supra.

make the legacy specific　The weight of authority holds that such a fact is not to be taken into consideration, and that if the words of the legacy make it general, it cannot be construed to be specific simply because by an examination of the testator's effects he is found to have possessed stock similar to that described in the will.[1]

§ 303. The most common form of a general bequest of stock is where the testator merely bequeaths a specified number of shares of a specified kind to the legatees, without any further words indicating that he then held or expected to hold the stock bequeathed[2] A direction to the executors to invest a certain sum in specified stock for the benefit of the legatee is a general legacy.[3] So, also, where the executors are directed to transfer to the legatee certain stock[4] A legacy of the residue of the testator's stock has been held to be a general legacy[5] A legacy to be paid " out of the four per cents." is general[6] A codicil which is general in form is held

[1] Robinson v Addison, 2 Beav, 515 (1840), the court holding that the legacy was general, and saying the testator " in effect gave such an indefinite sum of money as would suffice to purchase so many shares as he had given," Davis z Cain's Ex'r, 1 Ired Eq (N C), 304 (1840), Bransdan v Winter, Ambl, 56 (1738) Simmons v Vallance 4 Brown's Ch, 346 (1793), Bishop of Petersborough v Mortlock, 1 Brown's Ch, 565 (1784); Boys v Williams, 2 Russ. & Myl, 689 (1831), Partridge v Partridge, Cases temp. Talbot, 226 (1736), Tifft v Porter, 8 N Y, 516 (1853), where the court say " The mere possession by the testator, at the date of his will, of stock of equal or larger amount than the legacy, will not of itself make the bequest specific," Osborne v McAlpine, 4 Redf (N Y Sur), 1 (1878), Eckfeld's Estate, 7 W. N C (Pa), 19 (1879), Sponsler's Appeal, 107 Pa. St, 95 (1884), where the court also held that a codicil repeating a general legacy of stock will entitle the legatee to both legacies In Massachusetts a doctrine contrary to that stated in the text prevails　See White v Winchester, 23 Mass, 48 (1827), Metcalf v First Parish, 128 Mass 370 (1880). To same effect, Cuthbert v Cuthbert, 3 Yeates (Pa), 486 (1803); Jeffreys v Jeffreys, 3 Atk, 120 (1744).

[2] Wilson v Brownsmith 9 Ves., 180 (1803), holding also that, if there is not enough of such stock among the testator's assets, the deficiency must be purchased for the legatee. Pearce v Billings, 10 R. I., 102 (1871), the court saying that the evident intent of the testator was "to have the stock mentioned purchased for the legatees by his executor, or to have the legatees furnished with the means to purchase the stock for themselves." The value of the stocks one year after the testator's death is the amount to be paid to the legatees. In the case of Purse v Snaplin, 1 Atk, 413 (1737), where two legacies of stock of 5,000l. each were given, and the testator had but 5,000l. of stock, the court held that the general estate must purchase 5,000l of the same stock.

[3] Raymond v Brodbelt, 5 Ves., 199 (1800)

[4] Lambert v. Lambert, 11 Ves, 607 (1805), Sibley v Perry, 7 Ves, 522 (1802), the court saying a legacy is not specific " without something marking the specific thing — the very corpus; without describing it as standing in his name, or by the expression 'my stock,' etc"

[5] Parrot v Worsfold, 1 Jac. & W, 574 (1820). Contra, Bethune v. Kennedy, 1 Myl & C, 114 (1835).

[6] Deane v Test, 9 Ves, 146 (1803).

to be such, although it is but an increase of a previous legacy
which is specific, and which is revoked by the codicil [1]

§ 304. *Amount of stock conveyed by certain legacies* — A legacy
of "one hundred pounds, long annuities," has been held to mean
not that the legatee is entitled to an annual income from the estate
of one hundred pounds, but that he was entitled to have that
amount invested for him [2] A will reciting the amount of stock
held by the testatrix, and bequeathing it, or so much as should be
standing in her name at her death, does not give to the legatee
stock acquired after the making of the will and before the death
of the testatrix.[3] A bequest of stock "that I possess" is held to
mean stock possessed by the testator at the time of making the
will [4]

§ 305　There has been some controversy and doubt as to whether
a legacy of the testator's "money" would give to the legatee the
testator's stock in a corporation　The decided weight as authority
holds that it does not [5]　Nor will shares of stock belong to a legatee

---

[1] Johnson *v* Johnson, 14 Sim, 313
(1844)

[2] Att'y-Gen *v* Grote, 2 Russ & Myl,
699 (1831), Fonnereau *v* Payntz 1
Bro. Ch, 412 (1785)　See Pearce *t* Billings, *supra　Contra*, Stafford *t*. Horton 1 Bro Ch, 421 (1785). See, also,
§ 560

[3] Hotham *v* Sutton, 15 Ves, 319 (1808)
So, also, of a legacy of "the whole of
my stock in the Housatonic Bank,
amounting to $6,000" The legatee does
not take stock subsequently acquired
Foote, Appellant, 39 Mass, 299 (1839),
Douglass *v* Douglass, Kay, 404 (1854)
The case of Fidelity Trust Company's
Appeal, *supra*, states that at common
law a specific legacy of stock spoke from
the death of the testator, and that the
English Wills Act of 1838, and the
Pennsylvania act of 1879, were but declaratory in that respect.　If the testator, in making a specified bequest of
stock, speaks of the stock as "now standing in my name," the statute does not
apply, and the bequest speaks from the
date of the will　In Miller *v* Miller, 2
Beav, 259 (1840), the testator gave "one
share to each child him surviving" He
then had eight shares and seven children At his death he had ten shares and

eleven children　Only the eight shares
were held to pass

[4] Cochran *v* Cochran, 14 Sim, 248
(1844) This rule is sometimes changed
by statute　See, in England, § 24, Wills
Act, applied in Trinder *t*. Trinder, L. R,
1 Eq, 695 (1866), and Goodlad *v* Burnett, 1 K & J, 341 (1855), Hepburn *t*
Skerving, 4 Jur (N S), 651 (1858), Wagstaff *t* Wagstaff, L. R, 8 Eq, 229 (1869)
Bothamley *t* Sherson, L. R., 20 Eq, 304
(1875) and preceding note　Legacy of
bank stock conveys all stock deposited
in bank, there being no shares of bank
stock owned by the testator　Tomlinson *v* Bury, 14 N E Rep., 137 (Mass,
1887)　A will may bequeath not only
the stock standing in the name of the
testatrix, but also certificates of stock
owned by her but standing in the name
of others　Angell *et al v* Springfield
Home for Aged Women, 31 N. E. Rep,
1064 (Mass., 1893)

[5] Mullins *v* Smith 1 Dr & Sm, 204
(1860), Hotham *v* Sutton, 15 Ves, 319
(1808); Lowe *t* Thomas Kay, 369 (1854),
affirming 5 De G, M & G 315 (1854),
Goshen *t* Dotterill, 1 Myl & K, 56
(1832), Huddleston *v* Gouldsbury, 10
Bear 547 (1847), Douglas *v* Congreve,
1 Keen, 410, 424 (1836), Willis *t* Plas-

to whom the testator has given, by a last will and testament, his "securities for money,"[1] or "furniture," and all claims and demands of whatever nature,[2] or "every other article,"[3] or "ready money,"[4] or goods,[5] or "money and effects,"[6] but they will pass under a bequest of the "personal estate,"[7] or "residue of money,"[8] or "chattels."[9] If the testator, in describing the stock bequeathed, has very clearly made a mistake in the description, the legacy will be held to apply to the stock intended to be bequeathed. Thus, where the testator has "City Bank" stock, but bequeaths "Mechanics' Bank" stock, and the intent was to bequeath the former, the court will render a decree to that effect[10] Where, subsequently to the making of the will, and before the death of the testator, the stock bequeathed is changed in its character by operation of law, the legatee will nevertheless be entitled to the stock in its new form[11]

In England, where "shares" corresponds to the American "stock," but "stock" is a term applicable to a paid-up interest,

kett, 4 Beav, 208 (1841), Ogle r Knipe, L R., 8 Eq. 436 (1869), Ommaney v Butcher, 1 Tur & R., 260, 272 (1823), holding also that a bequest of stock for an indefinite charity fails, Beck, Ex'r. r McGillis, 9 Barb, 35, 39 (1850) Contra Waite v Coombes, 5 De G & S., 676 (1852), Chapman r Reynolds, 28 Beav, 221 (1860) where the testator had no property but stock, Bescoby v Pack, 1 Sim & Stu, 500 (1823), holding that 'money" will pass the 'funds" but not stock in private corporations, Newman v Newman, 26 Beav, 218 (1858), where the legacy was of "surplus money," Jenkins v. Fowler, 63 N. H, 244 (1884)

[1] Turner v Turner, 21 L J (Ch) 843 (1852).

[2] Delamater's Estate, 1 Whart. (Pa), 362 (1836)

[3] Colher v Squire, 3 Russ, 467 (1827)

[4] May t Grave, 3 De G & Sm 462 (1849)

[5] Cowling r Cowling, 26 Beav, 449 (1859) Contra, Kendall r Kendall, 4 Russ Ch, 360 (1828). Stock passes under a legacy of "my property at K's bank," the certificates being there Re Prater's Estate, 58 L, T Rep., 784 (1888)

[6] Borton v Dunbar, 30 L. J. (Ch.), 8 (1861).

[7] Kermode v Macdonald, L R., 3 Ch., 584 (1868)

[8] Dawson v Gaskom, 2 Keen, 14 (1837); Fulkeron i Chitty, 4 Jones' Eq. (N C), 244 (1858)

[9] Kendall v Kendall, supra.

[10] Roman Catholic Orphan Asylum v. Emmons, 4 Redf (N Y), 144 (1855), Door v Geary, 1 Ves Sr, 255 (1749), holding that a bequest of "East India stock" will apply to bank stock, when the testator had the latter but none of the former See, also, Trinder v. Trinder, L R, 1 Eq, 695 (1866), where a legacy of 'Great Western Railway" stock was held to apply to the stock of a road absorbed by the Great Western Railway Oakes r Oakes, 9 Hare, 666 (1852), where a bequest of "shares" was held to apply to "stock," Gallini v. Noble, 3 Mer Ch, 690 (1810), Pentecost t Ley, J. & W, 207 (1820); Clark v. Atkins, 90 N. C, 629 (1884), where "bank stock" was held to pass bonds. A palpable mistake of the testator in describing a legacy of bonds will be corrected by the court Holt v. Jex, 48 Hun, 528 (1888)

[11] See § 306 note 9

which, like a bank deposit, may be used in large or small quantities, a bequest of "shares" does not pass "stock" if there be any "shares" to which the legacy may apply[1] The words "funds" or "public funds" will include long annuities,[2] and "foreign funds" means securities guarantied by foreign governments,[3] but "funds" will not include bank stock,[4] nor East India stock[5] An unconditional bequest of the dividends of stock is a bequest of the stock itself[6] But a bequest of a specific sum to be paid from stock does not bequeath the stock itself, although amounting to a charge upon it[7] A bequest of stock to a legatee "to draw the income arising therefrom during her life-time, and at her death to dispose of the same as she shall see fit," vests the title to the stock, when it is set apart, in the legatee, even though the executors are directed to collect and pay to her the dividends[8] A bequest of the "rest and residue after deducting" certain specific legacies of stock includes those legacies, if they have lapsed by reason of the death of the legatees.[9] A general bequest of stock applies to full-paid as well as partly-paid stock.[10] Legacies may be made of stock over which the testator has the power of appointment,[11] and a will

[1] Oakes v Oakes, 9 Hare, 666 (1852).

[2] Howard v. Kay, 27 L. J (Ch), 448 (1858)

[3] Ellis v Eden, 23 Beav. 543 (1857); Cadett v Earle, L R, 5 Ch D 710 (1877), properly holding that New York and Ohio are foreign governments Cf Longdale's Settlement Trusts, L R, 5 Ch D, 710 (1877), relative to French railway securities.

[4] Slingsby v Granger, 7 H L. Cases, 273 (1859)

[5] Brown v Brown, 4 K & J., 704 (1858).

[6] A bequest of dividends and income to an institution as a permanent fund is an absolute gift of the stock Angell v Springfield Home for Aged Women, 31 N. E. Rep, 1064 (Mass 1892), Collier v Collier, 3 Ohio St, 369 (1854), Haig v Swiney, 1 Sim & Stu, 487 (1823), Page v Leapingwell, 18 Ves, 463 (1812), Fox v Carr, 16 Hun, 566 (1879), involving a similar question Cf Blann v Bell, 2 De G, M & G, 775 (1852), holding that this rule applies only to the "funds," but not to stock in private corporations. A legacy of stock to A, "the dividends derived from the same to be paid to her

by B, whom I name as trustee for said stock and bonds, as said dividends may accrue from time to time." passes complete title to the legatee No trust exists Appeal of Arnold, 6 Atl Rep, 751 (Pa, 1886)

[7] Wilson v Maddison, 2 Y & C Ch, 372 (1843)

[8] Onondaga Trust & Deposit Co v Price, 87 N Y, 542 (1882)

[9] Carter v Taggart, 16 Sim, 423 (1848), Shuttleworth v Greaves, 4 Myl & Cr, 35 (1838), holding that a legacy of stock lapses as to those dying before the testator, though it is given to them, "their executors, administrators or assigns"

[10] Emery v Wason, 107 Mass 507 (1871) This case holds also that, where a call on the stock becomes due the day after the testator died, it was the duty of the executor to pay it from the general fund

[11] See Re David s Trusts, 1 Johns, 495 (1859), Innis v Sayer, 3 Mac & G, 606 (1851), Lawnds v Lawnds, 1 You & Jer, 445 (1827), Nannock v Horton, 7 Ves, 391 (1802), Re Gratwick's Trusts, L R, 1 Eq, 177 (1865), Warren v Postlewaite, 2 Coll. Ch, 116 (1815), Walker

may provide for an annuity to be derived from stock.[1] In all these cases the intention of the testator is the "pole star" of the courts.

§ 306. *Ademption or revocation of a legacy of stock, and abatement* — The ademption of a legacy is a revocation of that legacy in part or wholly, not by an express revocation in the will, but by the acts of the testator. Consequently, an ademption applies only to specific legacies.[2] An ademption of a specific legacy of stock generally arises by a sale of the stock by the testator If the specific stock bequeathed is not owned by the testator at the time of his death the legal conclusion is that the specific legacy is adeemed, and the legatee takes nothing.[3] A sale of the stock by the testator after the will is made revokes or adeems the legacy, and it is as if never made.[4] A codicil giving all the " personal estate " to another is a revocation of a bequest of stock in the original will.[5] Where the testator specifies the amount of his stock, the specific legatees of it abate proportionately with the residuary legatee, if upon his death it is insufficient.[6] The rule is otherwise if no mention is made of what amount of stock he owns.[7] If the general property of the testator is exhausted in the payment of the debts of the estate, specific legacies of stock abate proportionately with other

---

r Mackie, 4 Russ , 16 (1827), disapproved in Hughes v. Turner, 3 Myl & K., 697 (1834)

[1] As to the construction of different provisions in wills, where an annuity on stock is created, see Innes r Mitchell, 9 Ves , 212 (1803), Kerr r Middlesex Hospital 2 De G , M & G , 576 (1852), Ross z Borei, 2 Jo & H , 469 (1862), Yates v. Maddan, 3 Mac. & G , 532 (1857), Blewitt r Roberts, Cr & Ph, 274 (1841) Potter r Baker, 13 B , 273 (1851), Robinson r Hunt, 4 B , 450 (1841) Hedges r Harpur, 3 De G & J., 129 (1858), Evans r Jones, 2 Collyer, 516 (1846), Manseige v. Campbell, 3 De G & J , 232

[2] A bequest of $2,000 of certain bonds is demonstrative and not specific and not adeemed where the testator had $10,000 of such bonds and sold them Ives r Canby, 48 Fed Rep . 718 (1891)

[3] Ford v. Ford, 23 N H , 212 (1851), although not a stock case, says in regard to this branch of the law "It is now established in England that the

only question is whether the specific thing remains at the death of the testator, and that the intention to adeem will not be considered beyond the expressions in the will   . The weight of American authority is in favor of the English rule "

[4] Ashburner v Macguire, 2 Brown's Ch , 108 (1786), White r Winchester, 23 Mass.. 48 (1827) Humphreys v Humphreys, 2 Cox, 184 (1789), Hayes z Hayes 1 Keen, 97 (1836); Blackstone v Blackstone, 3 Watts, 335 (1839).

[5] Kermode r Macdonald, L R., 1 Eq , 457 (1866), affirmed, L R, 3 Ch , 584 (1868)

[6] Elwes r Causton, 30 Beav., 554 (1862), following Page v Leapingwell, 18 Ves 463 (1812)

[7] Petre v Petre, 14 Beav, 197 (1851); De Lisle r Hodges, L R, 17 Eq , 440 (1874), Vivian r Mortlock, 21 Beav , 252 (1855) The debts of the estate may be directed to be paid from the residue of the stock Choat v Yeates, 1 Jac. & Walk , 102 (1819)

specific legacies[1] A specific legacy of stock is not adeemed by a change in the stock produced by an act of the government Thus, where the government buys the stock, a specific legatee takes the compensation if it has not yet been collected by the testator,[2] but not if it has been collected and used by the latter[3] A change by law of the funds into funds bearing a lower rate of interest does not adeem a specific legacy of it,[4] even though the testator sells the former and buys the latter kind of funds[5] A specific legacy of stock by a *feme covert*, who had the power to bequeath it, is not adeemed by the fact that she had the stock transferred into her own name after the death of her husband[6] A specific legacy which has been adeemed is not revived by a republication of the will after the ademption[7]

§ 307 *Duty of executor or administrator as regards a specific or general legacy of stock* — Where a legacy of stock is made, it is the duty of the executor or administrator to carry into effect the wishes of the testator by turning over to the legatee the stock bequeathed if the legacy be specific, or, if the legacy be general, by either setting aside for the legatee the required amount of stock from the testator's effects, or purchasing the same for the legatee The specific legacy of stock vests in the legatee as soon as the executor is satisfied that the general fund will pay the debts of the estate and consents to such vesting When once given the consent of the executor is irrevocable, and only a court of chancery can reach the stock and subject it to the testator's debts[8] The liability of the legatee to pay calls on the stock is discussed elsewhere.[9]

---

[1] Sparks v Weedon, 21 Md , 156 (1863)
When general legacies of stock abate proportionately with other general legacies, the stock is estimated at its value twelve months after the testator's death Blackshaw v Rogers, cited in 4 Brown's Ch , 349

[2] Walton v Walton, 7 Johns Ch , 257 (1823)

[3] Ludlam's Estate, 13 Pa St , 188 (1850)

[4] Brown v McGuire, 1 Beat Ir Ch , 358 (1829) But a legacy of stock in an unincorporated company, which, after the making of the will, is incorporated and the value of the stock changed, which change the testator accepts, fails whether considered as a specific legacy adeemed, or a general legacy impossible

of fulfillment In re Grey, 67 L T. Rep , 134 (1887)

[5] Partridge v Partridge, Cases temp Talbot, 226 (1736) Roper on Legacies, p 331, 2d ed (1848), is inclined to the opinion that a specific legacy of stock is not revived by a purchase of similar stock after a sale of the stock bequeathed

[6] Dingwell v Askew, 1 Cox's Ch , 427 (1788)

[7] Trustees, etc , v Tufts, 23 N E Rep , 1006 (Mass , 1890)

[8] Onondaga Trust & Deposit Co. v. Price, 87 N Y , 542 (1882) Hill v Rockingham Bank 44 N H , 567 (1863) holding that the legatee should sue the corporation at law for refusing transfer where the parties interested in the will

---

[9] See § 560, *infra*.

§ 308 *Gifts of stock* — Shares of stock in a corporation may be the subject of a gift   No formal method of carrying out the gift is necessary   A formal instrument of transfer, duly delivered to an agent with directions to deliver to the donee, vests title in the donee, though no certificates are transferred [1]   A gift of stock, vested by a due transfer into the name of the donee, cannot be revoked by the donor [2]   In order to constitute a gift a perfectly clear intent so to do must be proved.[3]   Where the gift is made in gratitude for care to be bestowed on another, the gift will fail upon the death of the donee if it is proved that the stock had not been fully and finally delivered [4]   A gift of the dividend of stock is a gift of

assent, and in equity if both the corporation and such parties do not assent. A decree of a probate court that the legacy of stock shall be turned over to the legatee cannot be required by the corporation   Under the Vermont statute it is the duty of the executor to transfer stock to the residuary legatee. Witters v Sowles, 25 Fed Rep, 168 (1885).   As regards sales of stock by an executor, see § 329, *infra*   If stock specifically bequeathed is not given to legatee, but is used for other purposes, the other legatees must make good its value   Tomlinson v Bury, 14 N E. Rep, 137 (Mass, 1887)   Executors in New York are not entitled to commission on transfers of stock specifically bequeathed   Schenck v Dart, 22 N Y, 420 (1860).   A legacy may be paid by the stock of the decedent at a valuation thereby agreed upon   Chase v Burritt, 14 Atl Rep, 212 (Conn, 1888)

[1] De Caumont v Bogert, 36 Hun, 382 (1885), treating also a gift as an advancement   See S C, *Re* Morgan, 101 N Y, 74   In England, under the statutes, it is held that a gift of stock does not vest in the donee until registry on the corporate books   Nauney v. Morgan, 57 L T Rep, 48 (1887)

[2] Standing v Bowring, L. R., 27 Ch. D, 341 (1884), where the donor transferred into the joint names of donor and donee, and afterwards attempted to dispose of the whole stock   A gift of stock fully made and accepted cannot be retracted   Walker v Joseph, etc, Co., 20

Atl Rep., 885 (N J, 1890).   A father who takes stock in the name of a son in order to qualify him as a director, and takes back the certificates, does not thereby make a gift of the stock.   *Re* Gooch, 62 L T Rep, 384 (1890)

[3] Where, however, the stock is purchased by one in the name of another, parol evidence may show as against the creditors of the former that he intended the stock as a gift to the latter   Rider v Kidder, 10 Ves, 361 (1805).   A gift of stock to take effect only upon the death of the donor is not absolute and is subject to the payment of his debts existing at the time of his death   Sterling v Wilkinson, 3 S E. Rep, 533 (Va, 1887)   A gift of stock whereby the owner makes himself a trustee of it for his donee is complete, and a recognition of the trust in his will does not render the stock a part of his estate, subject to the dower right of his wife   Dickerson's Appeal, 8 Atl Rep, 64 (Pa, 1887), Stone v Hackett, 12 Gray. 227   Although a person buys stock as trustee, and charges the price on his books against his daughters and credits them with dividends, yet if he sold the stock and used the money the stock was not an advancement to them. Herkimer v McGregor 25 N. E. Rep, 145 (Ind, 1890)

[4] Jackson v Twenty-third St. R'y Co., 88 N Y, 520 (1882)   When a gift of stock is made in accordance with an agreement to compensate the donee for taking care of the donor, a delivery of

the stock itself [1]　A gift of stock by one legatee to another, in the belief that the testator so intended the stock to be disposed of, cannot be revoked after an unsealed instrument of transfer is signed and actual transfer made, even though it is afterwards found that the testator had no such intent [2]　A stockholder who has transferred his stock into the joint names of himself and his wife cannot dispose of his interest by a last will and testament　It passes to the wife as the survivor.[3]　A gift of stock, *donatio causa mortis*, may be made by a mere delivery of the certificate to the donee [4]　So, also, the delivery and acceptance of a gift of stock is held to be effectual where the donor had the stock transferred into the name of the donee and took out certificates in the donee's name, even though the donor died before the donee knew of the gift.[5]

the certificate without any transfer suffices　Reed *v.* Copeland. 50 Conn , 472 (1883)　But the contract to make the gift must not be in opposition to public policy, nor in fraud of the rights of other stockholders. Nickerson *v* English, 142 Mass , 267 (1886).

[1] See § 305

[2] Delamater's Estate, 1 Whart (Pa), 362 (1836)

[3] Dummer *v* Pitcher, 5 Sim , 35 (1831), affirmed, 2 M & K , 262 (1833)　A gift of stock direct from the husband to the wife is legal　She thereupon takes a sole and separate estate therein　Deming *v* Williams, 26 Conn , 226 (1857). The case of Francis *v* New York & B El. R. R. Co, 17 Abb N C, 1 (N. Y , 1885), holds that, when a gift of stock is made to a minor, it is complete and irrevocable, so far as the donor is concerned; but the minor may, upon attaining majority, either accept or refuse it.

[4] Grymes *v* Hone, Ex'r, 49 N Y , 17 (1872), Walsh *v* Sexton, 55 Barb , 251 (1869), Allerton *v* Lang, 10 Bosw , 362 (1863)　The last two cases hold that the certificates need not even be indorsed or transferred, but that a mere delivery without any writing is sufficient. *Cf* § 375. A delivery of a certificate of stock without written assignment is not a good gift *inter vivos*　Matthews *v.* Hoagland, 21 Atl Rep , 1054 (N J , 1891) No delivery of stock to a wife as a gift exists where after the husband's death the stock is found among his papers in her possession and not indorsed　Morse *v.* Weston, 24 N E Rep , 916 (Mass , 1890) Although no transfer is made of the certificate, yet if it is found among the papers of a deceased person it will be presumed to be his, though standing in the name of his sister who also is dead, the stock having been considered of little value by them. *In re* Mape's Estate, 12 N Y Supp , 9 (1890)　A *donatio causa mortis* of stock is revoked by the recovery of the donor, even though it is registered.　Stainland *v* Willott, 3 Mac & G , 664 (1850)　In England railway stock is not the subject of a *donatio causa mortis* by a delivery of the certificate, since the transfer can be by deed only　Moore *v* Moore, 43 L. J. (Ch.), 617 (1874)

[5] Robert's Appeal, 85 Pa. St., 84 (1877) In Maryland it is held that a mere transfer of the certificates of stock, without a registry on the corporate book, is incomplete as a gift, and cannot be enforced against the personal representatives of the deceased donor　Baltimore Retort, etc , Co *v* Mali, 66 Md , 53 (1886)　But a written memorandum left by a decedent to the effect that he thereby gives certain stock to a person, but retains the same during life in order that he, the donor, may have the dividends, is not a valid gift. *Re* Shield, 53 L. T. (N. S.), 5 (1885).

CHAPTER XIX.

WHO MAY BUY AND SELL STOCK.

§ 309 *Competency of a corporation to purchase shares of its own capital stock.* — In England a long line of decisions has established the rule that, at common law, a corporation cannot purchase shares of its own capital stock.[1] This rule is enounced clearly and decisively, and is closely adhered to.[2] The corporation may be given an express power for this purpose, but, unless so given, the purchase is held to be beyond the legal powers of the directors and of the whole body of stockholders.[3] The object of the rule is to pre-

---

[1] Trevor v Whitworth, 57 L T Rep., 457 (H of L., 1887), reviewing many cases, *Re* Marseilles Extension R'y Co, L. R., 7 Ch, 161 (1871), Evans v. Coventry, 25 L J (Ch), 489, 501 (1856); Cross' Case, 38 L J (Ch), 583 (1869); Morgan's Case, 1 De G. & Sm, 750 (1849); *Ex parte* Morgan, 1 Mac. & G, 225 (1849), Eyre's Case, 31 Beav., 177 (1862); 3 R'y & Corp. L J, 169. *Cf.* Taylor v. Hughes, 2 J & Lat (Irish Ch), 24 (1844), holding that a banking company at common law may buy its own stock the same as a copartnership may buy out a partner. Where a director buys merchandise of his corporation, and pays for it in stock of the corporation, and

the transaction is ratified in general meeting, the director, on a winding up, is not liable for the value of the merchandise. Weeks' Case, 17 L. R., Ir, 239 A purchase by a corporation of its own stock and payment by debentures is void, and a resale of the stock at a discount is void *Re* London, etc., Co., 59 L T Rep, 109 (1888).

[2] Zulueta's Claim, L R, 5 Ch, 444 (1879): Hope v. International Financial Soc, L R, 4 Ch Div, 327 (1876), holding also that a stockholder may enjoin the purchase, distinguishing Teasdale's Case, L. R., 9 Ch, 54.

[3] Zulueta's Claim, *supra;* Hope v. International Financial Soc, *supra.* See,

serve the rights of the corporate creditors, and also to confine the corporation within the express powers given it, and the implied powers necessary to its transaction of business[1] If the sale is completed, and the corporation afterwards become insolvent, the stockholder who sold the stock to the corporation is liable, on the winding up, as though he never had made such a sale[2] If, however, the stockholder sells to a person, not knowing that the latter is purchasing as a trustee for the corporation, the vendor is not liable on such stock[3] The directors authorizing or directing a purchase for the corporation of shares of its own capital stock are liable personally to the same extent that the selling stockholder would have been had the sale not taken place[4] Generally the

also, Lindley on Partnership, p 739 (Callaghan & Co, 1881). Under an express power to the directors to enter into any contract and engagement that seemed best for the company, such a purchase was upheld Singer's Case, W N (1869), 206; Cockburn s Case, 4 De G & Sm, 177 (1850) where power was given by the deed of settlement. See, however, Ward's Case, 29 W R., 768 (1881), where an express power to purchase its own stock was held not to authorize a trafficking in that stock — the buying and selling for purposes of gain Where a company has power to purchase its own stock and does purchase stock which has not been paid up, the liability on that stock cannot be included as among the debts of the company. Re The Sovereign, etc, Co, 67 L. T. Rep, 336 (1892). Having purchased its own stock from profits, a company may reduce its capital stock to that extent. Re York, etc, Co, 60 L T Rep, 744 (1889)

[1] Id Compare however, Ward's Case, 29 W R., 768 (1881), where the court says "If the company could not question it, neither can a creditor; for he can obtain nothing but what the company can get from the shareholders"

[2] Walter's 2d Case, 3 De G & Sm, 244 (1850), Richmond s Ex'rs Case, 3 De G & Sm 96 (1850), Munts' Case, 22 Beav, 55 (1856), where the stockholders disagreed and the corporation bought out one faction; Daniell's Case, 22

Beav, 43 (1856), Bennett's Case, 5 De G, M & G 284 (1854), where the stockholders disagreed concerning the validity of a lease, and the corporation bought out part If, however, the corporation, six years after the transfer, discovers that the transfer was invalid, and summarily retransfers to the vendor, the latter may apply to a court of equity to compel the corporation to keep the stock Gardiner ι Victoria Estates Co., 12 Ct of Ses (Sc 4th series), 1356 (1885) See, also, § 251, supra

[3] Nicol's Case, 3 De G & J 387 (1858), Grady s Case 1 De G, J & S, 488 (1863), where the vendee was managing agent of the corporation and the sale of the stock was to stop litigation Richmond's Case, 3 De G & Sm, 96 (1849), holds, however, that if the vendor's selling agent his solicitor, knew that the sale was for the benefit of the corporation, the stockholder himself is chargeable with knowledge See Re Orpen, 32 L. J (Ch) 633 (1863) holding that it is a question for the jury whether the vendee purchased for the corporation or for himself Johnson ι Laflin, 5 Dill, 65, 103 U S, 800 (1878) See, also, § 251

[4] Evans v Coventry, 25 L. J (Ch), 489, 501 (1856) To same effect, Land Credit Co of Ireland ι Fermoy, L. R., 8 Eq Cas, 7 (1869), Marzette s Case, 42 L. T (N S), 206 (1880) The directors may have contributions from each other for sums paid out by their authority for

415

transfer is made, not to the corporation directly, but to a trustee on behalf of or for the benefit of the corporation   This practice is not at all necessary,[1] and has no effect other than a transfer direct to the corporation itself, unless it be that the vendor of the stock may not know that his vendee purchases for the corporation, and thereby escapes liability on the winding up   If the contract is executory, the corporation may repudiate it and refuse to pay the purchase-money for the stock[2]   If, however, the sale is completed, the stock belongs to the corporation, and does not pass to the vendor's assignee in bankruptcy.[3]

§ 310. Where the transfer of stock to the corporation is made by one of the original subscribers for stock, it frequently becomes a difficult question to decide whether the transaction was a cancellation of the subscription *contract or was a sale of the stock* to the corporation. Each case turns largely on its own peculiar facts and circumstances. If the transaction is a cancellation, it is legal. In England, if it is a sale, it is illegal   The courts seem to favor a construction whereby the transaction is held to be a sale, and the stockholder made liable on the winding up[4]

§ 311. *Rule in the United States.*—In this country there has been a difference of opinion as to whether a corporation may purchase shares of its own stock. In Illinois, Massachusetts and other states such a purchase is legal and allowable.[5] And, indeed, if there is no statutory liability on stock, and if stockholders do not object,

---

such purchases, and for which one or more has been held liable to the corporation   Ashhurst *v* Mason, L. R., 20 Eq , 225 (1875)   The directors are not liable to the vendor of the stock for the failure of the corporation to complete their purchase for it of its own stock Abeles *v* Cochran, 22 Kan , 405 (1879).

[1] See ch III

[2] The corporation may even refuse to pay the price to the brokers employed by its directors to buy its stock. Zulueta's Claim, L R , 5 Ch , 444 (1879). This, of course, does not authorize the corporation to retain the stock so purchased.

[3] Great Eastern R'y Co. *v* Turner, 42 L. J. (Ch.), 83 (1873).

[4] Hall's Case, L. R., 5 Ch , 707 (1870), distinguishing Snell's Case, L. R., 5 Ch , 22. See, also, Thomas' Case, L. R., 13 Eq , 437 (1872), Teasdale's Case, L. R., 9 Ch 54 (1873), Duke's Case, L. R., 1 Ch.

Div , 622 (1876). See, also, §§ 167–170, *supra.*

[5] First Nat. Bank *v.* Salem, etc , Co., 39 Fed Rep., 89 (1889). In Illinois, in Chicago, P. & S R. R. *v.* President, etc., of Town of Marseilles, 84 Ill., 145 (1876), the court said "We entertain no doubt that a railroad company may, for legitimate purposes, purchase shares of stock which have been issued to individuals. Such is believed to have been the general custom of such bodies; nor have we known the power to have been questioned." A contract whereby the corporation agreed to take back the stock unless certain things were done within a certain time was sustained S. C , id., 643, where the court says, "the power of the directors of a company, when not prohibited by their charter, to purchase shares of stock of their company," is well recognized, Clapp *v* Peterson, 104 Ill., 25 (1882), Chetlain *v.* Republic Life Ins.

there is no reason why the *net profits* of a corporation should not be applied to purchasing its stock, instead of being used for a

Co, 86 Ill, 220 (1877), Fraser v. Ritchie, 8 Bradw, 554 (1881) where a perfectly solvent concern sold certain property and took its own stock in payment, Dupee v. Boston Water-power Co, 111 Mass, 37 (1873), holding that a stockholder could not enjoin the purchase, the court saying "In the absence of legislative provision to the contrary, a corporation may hold and sell its own stock, and may receive it in pledge or in payment in the lawful exercise of its corporate powers," Leland r Hayden, 102 Mass, 542 (1869), Crease z Babcock, 51 Mass, 525, 557 (1846), holding that the stockholders are not liable for the deficiency caused by part of the stock being owned by the corporation In Pennsylvania, in Eby v Guest 94 Pa St., 160 (1880), and Early & Lane's Appeal, 89 id, 411 (1879), it was held that "the assignment of the stock of a corporation to itself, as collateral security for a loan, divests the title of the assignor so far as to prevent a sale of it under a *fi. fa* against the assignor" But in Coleman v Columbia Oil Co, 51 Pa. St, 74 (1865), where a stockholder had accepted the benefit of the purchase and then objected to its legality, the court said "The employment of corporate funds to speculate in the stock of the company to which the funds belong is not a practice to be encouraged, but the present plaintiff is not in position to censure the practice" He "should have sought an injunction against the company to restrain the purchase, or to cancel it if done before he had knowledge of it, or if he would bring an action at law he should have declared for his share of the funds which he complains were misapplied in buying the shares" In Georgia, in the case of Hartridge r Rockwell, R M Charlton, 260 (1826), the court held "If from the course of business or the state of things the capital of the bank cannot be usefully employed in loans

there can, I think, be no objection against the purchase of its own stock " The legislature, however, thought differently, and by the Penal Code of 1833 made such purchases a penal offense See Robinson r Beale, 26 Ga, 17 (1859) where the purchase was held to be authorized under a power to purchase goods, etc See, also, as supporting the doctrine Farmers' & Mechanics' Bank v Champlain Transportation Co, 18 Vt., 131, 139 (1846), Iowa Lumber Co r Foster, 49 Iowa, 25 (1878), under a power to purchase "property that may be deemed desirable in the transaction of its business " A corporation which has agreed to pay a person a certain sum for his stock in the corporation, if he will transfer it to a corporate creditor in payment of the corporate debt, is liable for that sum to the stockholder Snyder r Tunitas, etc, Co, 13 Pac Rep, 479 (Cal, 1887) "A corporation may, if it acts in good faith, buy and sell shares of its own stock " Republic Life Ins Co. v Swigert, 25 N E Rep., 680 (Ill, 1890), First, etc., Bank r Salem, etc, Co, 39 Fed Rep, 89 (1889) An agreement of a corporation to accept its own stock in payment for land sold by it is not *per se* an *ultra vires* act Thompson r Moxey, 20 Atl Rep, 854 (N J, 1890) A corporation may purchase shares of its own stock, subject to the right of creditors to object thereto if the capital stock is impaired thereby Blalock r Kernersville, etc, Co, 14 S E Rep, 501 (N C, 1892) A corporation may issue stock to an employee on an agreement to buy it back in case he is discharged Yeaton z Eagle, etc, Co, 29 Pac Rep 1051 (Wash, 1892) Where the majority stockholders cause the directors to purchase stock of them for the corporation at a price higher than the market price the minority may cause the transaction to be set aside Woodroof z Howes, 26 Pac Rep, 111 (Cal, 1891)

dividend[1] The few cases which appear to uphold a contrary rule are found, upon close examination, to come within the exceptions given above[1] All of the American courts coincide in the view that a corporation may take shares of its own stock in payment of or security for antecedent debts due to the corporation[2] A corporation may take its own stock by way of gift[3] or bequest.[4]

§ 312 The objection usually made to allowing a corporation to purchase its own stock is that thereby the corporate funds are expended and no property is received by the corporation, except the right to resell In some cases, also, a statutory liability at-

[1] In Ohio the early case of Taylor v Miami Ex Co, 6 Ohio Rep, 166 (1833), held that a bank may receive from the stockholders transfers of stock in payment of debts previously contracted by them See, also, State of Ohio v Franklin Bank of Columbus, 10 Ohio Rep, 91, 97 (1840) But in Cappin v Greenlees, 38 Ohio St, 275 (1882), the court refused to enforce an executory contract for the sale to the corporation of its own stock, and said "The doctrine that corporations when not prohibited by their charters, may buy and sell their own stock, is supported by a line of authorities . . . But, nevertheless, we think the decided weight of authority, both in England and in the United States is against the existence of the power, unless conferred by express grant or clear implication The foundation principle upon which these latter cases rest is that a corporation possesses no powers except such as are conferred upon it by its charter, either by express grant or necessary implication" The proposed purchase was held to be invalid under the constitutional provision imposing a personal liability on all stockholders But see Morgan v. Lewis, 17 N E Rep, 558 (Ohio, 1888). *Quo warranto* does not lie against a corporation for purchasing its own stock. State v Minn, etc, Co, 41 N W. Rep, 1020 (Minn, 1889).

[1] Thus, in German Sav Bank v Wulfekuhler, 19 Kan, 60 (1877), the bank was insolvent when the stock was purchased by it. The purchase was declared illegal

In Bent v Hart, 10 Mo. App., 143 (1881), the corporation did not purchase its own stock. The stock was purchased by another corporation, and was sustained. In St Louis, etc., Co. v Hilbert, 1 R'y & Corp L J, 160 (Mo. Ct. of App, 1887), the stock purchased by the corporation was not paid-up stock. In State v. Building Assoc, 35 Ohio St., 258 (1880), the peculiar purposes and articles of association of a building association governed the decision. In Barton v. Port Jackson, etc, Co, 17 Barb, 397 (1854), the company mortgaged its road in order to raise money to buy the stock.

[2] The leading case is City Bank of Columbus v Bruce, 17 N. Y, 507 (1858), where a corporation received $133,000 of its own stock in payment of debts due the corporation, the court saying it is "not aware of any common-law principle which forbids it" See, also, Verplanck v Mercantile Ins. Co., 1 Edw. Ch, 84 (1831). State Bank of Ohio v. Fox, 3 Blatch, 431 (1856), where the stock was taken in payment of a debt due the corporation In Williams v. Savage Mfg Co, 3 Md Ch, 418, 451 (1851), the creditor who had given stock to a corporation in payment of a debt was allowed to deny the amount of the debt and to take back the stock upon payment of the amount actually due

[3] Lake Superior Iron Co v Drexel, 90 N. Y., 87 (1882), where its legality was assumed See, also, ch III, *supra*

[4] Rivanna Nav. Co v Dawsons, 3 Gratt, 19 (1846).

tached to the stock is thereby jeopardized The latter objection is
answered by the principle of law that the transferrer of stock to
the corporation is liable on the subscription and statutory liability
to the same extent as though no transfer to the corporation had
been made [1] The former objection is merely a limit to the power of
the corporation to purchase In Illinois, the state where the rights
of the corporation to make such purchases is most clearly and decisively established, the collateral principle that such purchases are to
be declared illegal and voidable at the instance of corporate creditors
who are injured thereby is distinctly stated and rigidly applied [2]
If the corporation is insolvent at the time of the purchase, it is
clearly an invalid transaction, and will be set aside [3] The rule
goes still further, and declares that if a corporation, by a purchase
of shares of its own capital stock, thereby reduces its actual assets
below its capital stock, or if the actual assets at that time are less
than the capital stock, such purchase may be impeached and set
aside, and the vendor of the stock rendered liable thereon at the
instance of a corporate creditor [4] In Massachusetts not even a
dissenting stockholder can complain.[5]

---

[1] See § 251, *supra*

[2] Clapp *v.* Peterson, 104 Ill 26 (1882),
Peterson *v.* Ill Land & Loan Co, 6
Bradw, 257 (1880) In Crandall *v.* Lincoln, 52 Conn, 73 (1884), where stock
was bought for the corporation by a corporate agent, the latter was held liable
to the receiver of the corporation for
the money so expended The court
said: "The statute forbidding the company to make dividends payable from
the stock, and to loan money upon a
pledge of its stock, by necessary implication forbids the company from purchasing its stock . As a rule,
to which there are few, if any, exceptions, when a stockholder conveys his
stock to the company and receives in
return a portion of the capital, he holds
the money so received subject to the
superior equities of creditors" But the
selling stockholder, not knowing that
his vendee buys for the corporation, is
not liable Johnson *v.* Laflin, 5 Dill,
65; 103 U S, 800

[3] Currier *v.* Lebanon Slate Co, 56 N

H, 262 (1875), Alexander *v.* Relfe, 74
Mo, 495 (1881) A purchase by an insolvent bank of shares of its own stock
from one who had just resigned as vice-
president is illegal, and he cannot collect a certificate of indebtedness given
him therefor *In re* Columbian Bank,
23 Atl Rep, 626 (Pa, 1892) So also of
a sale by the president, even though he
held the stock as executor of an estate
Id, 625 Where a corporation is insolvent and a stockholder knows that fact,
he cannot sell his stock to the corporation in exchange for corporate property,
and he will be compelled by the court,
in behalf of then existing creditors, to
return the property Commercial National Bank *v.* Burch, 31 N E Rep, 420
(Ill, 1892).

[4] Fraser *v.* Ritchie, 8 Bradw. (Ill), 554
(1881), holding that the right of the corporation to purchase its own stock is
subject to certain restrictions, "one of
which is that it shall not be done at such
time and in such manner as to take
away the security upon which the credit-

[5] Dupee *v.* Boston, etc., Co. 114 Mass,
37 (1873) See § 282 as to the power of a
corporation to purchase stock in order
to reduce its capital stock.

§ 313　Frequently statutes are passed expressly prohibiting a corporation from purchasing shares of its own stock.[1] The national banks in this country are prohibited from so doing by the statutes of the federal government[2]　In New York, by statute, both mon-

ors of the corporation have the right to rely for the payment of their claims, or in other words, so as not to diminish the fund created for their benefit. Each case must, therefore, depend upon and be determined by its own facts and circumstances" Gillett v Moody, 3 N. Y, 479 (1850)　Where directors and stockholders desire to sell the enterprise, and do so by paying for their stock out of the corporate funds, and then re-insuring all risks in another company, and turning over everything to the latter, a receiver of the company so sold out may hold a director liable for moneys so paid out　Guild v Parker, 43 N J L, 430 (1881)　A receiver of a corporation seeking to set aside a purchase of stock by itself must tender back the stock before suing to recover the money　Pierson v McCurdy, 33 Hun, 520 (1884)　In the case In re Republic Ins. Co, 3 Biss, 452 (1873), where the insolvent corporation had, some three years previously, when the corporation was solvent, purchased stock of various stockholders and still held it, the court held that these old stockholders were not liable for the unpaid subscription price thereof. In Farnsworth v Robbins, 36 Minn, 369 (1887), the receiver of an insolvent company recovered from a stockholder whose stock the company had purchased　A scheme whereby the corporation takes back the stock and issues certificates of indebtedness for it is invalid as against creditors　The latter are entitled to the assets in preference to the former.　Heggie v Building, etc, Assoc, 12 S E Rep, 275 (N C, 1890).　Although a company buys its own stock from a stockholder, subsequent creditors cannot complain　Rollins v Shaver, etc., Co., 45 N W Rep, 1037 (Iowa, 1890)

[1] See Part VII, infra

[2] R. S of U S, § 5201　See Johnson

v Laflin, 5 Dill, 65, 103 U. S, 800, holding that, if a stockholder in good faith and without notice sells his stock to one who purchases for the bank, the sale is valid so far as he is concerned, and he is not liable thereon　See, also, Bank v Lanier, 11 Wall, 369 (1870), holding that the bank cannot take its own stock in pledge

When the president of a bank buys its stock for the bank itself, taking title in his own name, he is liable as a stockholder　The purchase for the bank, however, is void　Bundy v Jackson, 24 Fed Rep., 628 (1885)　Although a national bank must sell its stock taken in payment of a debt within six months, it may sell on credit, taking a note in payment and the stock as collateral. Union Nat. Bank v Hunt, 76 Mo, 439 (1882)　Where a national bank receives its own stock in pledge at the time of making the loan, and sells the stock as collateral, on failure of the debtor to pay, the latter cannot complain that the statute has been violated. National Bank of Xenia v Stewart, 107 U S., 676 (1882)　See, also, Gold Mining Co v National Bank, 96 U S, 640 (1877), Shoemaker v National Mechanics' Bank, 31 Md, 396, O'Hare v Second National Bank, 77 Pa St., 96, Stewart v National Union Bank, 2 Abb (N S), 424 (1869)　Although a national bank is prohibited from taking its own stock as security, yet if it does so, the stock being taken in the name of the cashier, it may enforce the security. Only the government can object after the transaction has been completed　It is immaterial that the stock was transferred to the cashier individually and not "as cashier"　Walden Nat Bank v Birch, 130 N Y, 221 (1891)　A transfer of the stock of a national bank to the bank in payment of a debt will not be set aside at the

eyed[1] and railroad[2] corporations are prohibited from purchasing shares of its own capital stock

§ 314 *The stock is not merged.*—When a corporation buys shares of its own capital stock, the capital stock is not reduced by that amount, nor is the stock merged.[3] So long, however, as the corporation retains the ownership, the stock is lifeless, without rights or powers. It cannot be voted nor can it draw dividends, even though it is held in the name of a trustee for the benefit of the corporation[4] But at any time the corporation may resuscitate it by selling it and transferring it to the purchaser Such sale may be made upon the authority of the corporate directors[5] It may be sold at its market value, and need not be held for its par value, as is necessary in an original issue of stock[6]

instance of the vendor as being in violation of the statute Chapin *v* Merchants' Nat Bank, 14 N Y St Rep, 272 (1888). A national bank president and directors are not liable criminally for purchasing the stock of the bank for the bank itself United States *v* Britton, 107 U S, 192 (1882), id, 108 U S, 655 (1882).

[1] See Part VII, *infra* "The evident intention was to prohibit a division of the capital, or any portion of it, among the stockholders, by whatever instrumentality the powers of the corporation in doing the act might be exerted" Gillett *v* Moody, 3 N Y, 479, 487. See. also, United States Trust Co *v* United States Fire Ins Co, 18 N Y., 199, 226 (1858), Tracy *v* Talmage, 14 N Y, 162 (1856) But purchasers of the stock from a banking corporation that had purchased it in violation of the statute cannot complain They cannot impeach their own title Case of the Reciprocity Bank, 22 N Y, 9, 17 (1860) Nor can the vendor of the stock to the bank claim that the sale was invalid He is estopped United States Trust Co *v*. Harris, 2 Bosw, 75, 91 (1857)

[2] See Part VII, *infra* See, also, Barton *v* Port, etc, P R Co, 17 Barb, 397 (1854)

[3] State *v* Smith, 48 Vt, 266 (1876), Williams *v* Savage Mfg Co, 3 Md Ch,

418, 451 (1851), City Bank of Columbus *v* Bruce 17 N Y, 507 (1858), State Bank of Ohio *v* Fox, 3 Blatch, 431 (1856), the court saying "The stock was not extinguished or destroyed by the purchase thereof by the corporation," Vail *v* Hamilton, 85 N Y, 453 (1881), American R'y Frog Co *v* Haven, 101 Mass, 398 (1869), Commonwealth *v* Boston, etc, R R. Co. 2 New Eng Rep, 617 (Mass, 1886), *Ex parte* Holmes, 5 Cow, 426 (1826) See, also, §§ 282, 251

[4] See ch XXXVII, *infra*

[5] State Bank of Ohio *v* Fox, 3 Blatch, 431 (1856); State *v* Smith, 48 Vt., 266 (1876). See, also, § 282 Stockholders cannot enjoin the corporate officers from selling shares of its own stock which it has purchased Jefferson *v* Burford, 17 S. W. Rep, 855 (Ky, 1891)

[6] See ch III, *supra* It may be issued by way of a stock dividend See ch XXXII, *infra* Land scrip of a land company, that is, certificates issued allowing the holder to exchange the certificate for land at a specified price, after being bought up by the company may be issued as a scrip dividend to the stockholders. A scripholder whose scrip was not bought up by the company cannot object unless there was actual fraud Rogers *v* Phelps, 9 N Y Supp., 886 (1890)

§ 315 *Purchase by a corporation of stock in another corporation — Purchase by railroad* — It may be stated as a general rule,
with but few exceptions, that a corporation has no implied power
to purchase shares of the capital stock of another corporation.
Especially is this the rule as regards railroad corporations   It has
been firmly settled by well-considered cases that one railroad company cannot purchase shares of stock in another railroad company,
especially where the purchase is for the purpose of controlling the
latter by means of corporate elections [1]   In a few instances, particular corporations, by their charters, are given the power to invest

[1] See § 64   The most important case
is Central R. R. Co *v* Collins, 40
Ga , 582 (1869), where a stockholder in
one railroad obtained an injunction
against its purchase, for purposes of consolidation, of stock in a rival and competing railroad   The court declared the
purchase to be beyond the corporate
powers and contrary to public policy,
and says, " it is a general principle that
a railroad company, without express
authority given by the legislature to
make the purchase, cannot purchase
stock in another railroad company."
Angell & Ames, § 392   To same effect,
Hazelhurst *v* Savannah, G & N A R.
R. Co., 43 Ga , 13, 57 (1871), the court
saying "If one railroad may, at its option, buy the stock of another, it practically undertakes a new enterprise not
contemplated by its charter   This it
cannot do by any implication The power
so to do must be clear " In the case of
Elkins *v* Camden & Atlantic R. R. Co,
36 N J Eq Rep , 5 (1882), a similar
injunction was granted Such purchase
is not authorized by a power to lease
other lines, nor to build them   "The
purchase of a rival railroad is (not to
speak of public policy) foreign to the
objects for which the defendant was incorporated   . . As a purchase with
a view to extinguishing competition, the
transaction is clearly *ultra vires*." It is
immaterial that the complainant purchased stock for the purpose of obtaining the injunction Salomons *v* Laing,
12 Beav , 389, 353 (1850), Great Northern
R'y Co *v* Eastern Counties R'y Co , 21
L J (Ch ` 837 (1851), where the object
was to control the corporation. The
court said it was an "attempt to carry
into effect, without the intervention of
parliament, what cannot lawfully be
done except by parliament, in the exercise of its discretion with reference to
the interest of the public " Maunsell *v*
Midland Great Western R'y Co , 1 Hem.
& M , 130 (1863), relative to the power of
a railroad company to subscribe for the
stock of another railroad , Central R. R.
Co of N J. *v* Pennsylvania R R. Co.,
31 N. J Eq Rep , 473, 494 (1879), where
the defendant was enjoined from building another railroad by means of an independent corporation operated by "dummies " The court said · "A corporation
cannot in its own name subscribe for
stock or be a corporation under the general railroad law, nor can it do so by a
simulated compliance with the provisions of the law through its agents as
pretended corporators or subscribers for
stock." Pearson *v* Concord R. R. Co., 13
Am & Eng R. R. Cases, 102 (N H ,
1883), where a railroad had purchased
the controlling interest in the stock of a
connecting railroad and was managing
it in the interest of the former road. A
suit by a stockholder of the defrauded
road to enjoin such act was sustained
A foreign corporation cannot buy railroad stock for the purpose of uniting
competing lines, where domestic corporations are prohibited from so doing
Clarke *v* Central R. R., etc , 50 Fed.

in other railroad stocks, and in other instances general statutes to that effect prevail[1] Occasionally prohibitions against such purchases are placed in the constitution of a state[2]

Rep, 388 (1892) A railroad has no power to buy the stock of another railroad Hamilton v Savannah, etc., R'y, 49 Fed Rep, 412 (1892), Columbus, etc, R. R. v Burke, 19 Week Law Bull, 27 (Ohio, 1887), Mackintosh v Flint, etc, R. R., 34 Fed Rep, 582 (1888) See, also, Green's Brice's Ultra Vires, 91 (2d ed) Where a railroad company, in the name of one of its leased lines, contracted to purchase a majority of the stock of still another line, the vendor representing that the last line was unincumbered, the first-mentioned company may avoid the contract by proving that an incumbrance rested on the road to be sold Southwestern R'y Co. v Papot, 67 Ga, 675 (1881). A controlling stockholder in one railroad corporation may become the controlling stockholder in another railroad corporation. Havemeyer v. Havemeyer, 43 Super Ct. (N Y.), 506 (1878), 45 id, 464, aff'd, 86 N Y. 618, O'Brien v. Breitonbach, 1 Hilt, 304 A bondholder cannot object. Matthews v. Murchison, 15 Fed. Rep, 691 (1883) Where a railroad president uses its funds to purchase the stock of a construction company that has the stocks and bonds of a contemplated competing line which the construction company has agreed to build, the sale of the stock to such president may be attacked by parties who were defrauded by the party who sold the stock of the construction company Langdon v Branch, 37 Fed Rep, 449 (1888) A railroad corporation which is advancing money to another corporation may take the bonds and stock of the latter as security The West Virginia statutes do not prevent such act. County Court v Baltimore, etc, R. R., 35 Fed Rep, 161 (1888)

[1] Mayor v Baltimore & O R. R. Co, 21 Md, 50 (1863), Zabriskie v Cleveland, etc, R. R Co., 23 How, 381 (1859), as to the Ohio statute The case of White v

Syracuse & Utica R. R Co. 11 Barb, 559 (1853), held to be constitutional and valid a general law allowing any New York railroad to subscribe to the stock of the Great Western Railroad, Canada West Matthews v Murchison, 17 Fed Rep, 760 (1883), on the North Carolina act. As to the Kansas act allowing such purchases see Atchison etc, R. R. Co v Fletcher, 10 Pac. Rep, 596 (1886), Ryan v Leavenworth, etc, R'y Co 21 Kan, 365 (1879), Atchison, etc, R R. v Cochran, 23 Pac Rep, 151 (Kan, 1890). In the case of Kimball v Atchison, etc, R R, 46 Fed Rep, 888 (1891), the court held that the Atchison, Topeka & Santa Fe Railroad Company had power under its charter to buy a majority of the stock of the St. Louis & San Francisco Railway, a partially competing line Under the statutes of Pennsylvania it is legal for a railroad company to own all the stock of a mining company which owns land and such land does not escheat. Comm v New York, etc, R. R., 21 Atl Rep, 528 (Pa, 1891), id, 19 id, 290

[2] By the constitution of Pennsylvania any railroad corporation is forbidden to control any other railroad corporation owning or having under its control a parallel or competing line Under this provision the Pennsylvania Railroad Company was enjoined from purchasing a majority of the stock of the South Pennsylvania Railroad Company In this noted case (Pa R. R. Co v. Commonwealth, 7 Atl Rep, 368 — 1886), the court said that the ownership of a majority of the stock gave "control" in the sense of that word as used in the constitution Cf Pullman Pal Car Co. v Missouri Pac R R Co, 11 Fed Rep, 632 (1882), affirmed, 115 U S, 587 (1885), construing the word "control" differently in a contract whereby the defendant was to use the plaintiff's cars over

Where a railroad company has power to purchase, lease or consolidate with another railroad company, it may buy the stock of the latter company with a view to such consolidation, lease or sale.[1]

It is illegal for a railroad company to buy a controlling interest in another railroad for the purpose of electing the board of directors of the latter. A minority stockholder in the latter company may enjoin the former from voting the stock so purchased.[2]

A railroad company owning all the stock and bonds of another company does not own the property of the latter. It cannot sue on a cause of action belonging to the latter.[3]

roads under the defendants control The supreme court of Pennsylvania, in Pa R R Co v Commonwealth, 7 Atl Rep, 374 (Pa, 1886), also sustained an injunction enjoining a corporation, a majority of whose stock was owned by the Pennsylvania Railroad Company, from purchasing a majority of the stock of a road competing with the Pennsylvania Railroad Company The constitution of Georgia forbids and prevents one railroad from buying the stock and control of a competing railroad scheme, even though the railroad of the latter is not even commenced and there is no intention of building it Hamilton v Savannah, etc, Ry, 49 Fed Rep, 412 (1892)

[1] Where a railroad corporation has power to consolidate with another, it may purchase the stock of that other in contemplation of the consolidation. Hill v Nisbit, 100 Ind, 341 (1884) A railroad corporation may purchase the stock of another railroad with a view to buying the railroad itself where the sale of the railroad is authorized Dewey v Toledo, etc, Ry, 51 N W. Rep, 1063 (Mich, 1892). Where a railroad company has power to lease another company's road, it may buy all the stock of the latter instead of taking a lease Atchison, etc, R. R v Fletcher, 35 Kan, 236, 247 (1886) A railroad corporation having the power to buy or consolidate with other railroads may buy a controlling interest in the stock of another railroad Wehrhauer v Nashville, etc, R. R, 4 N Y. St Rep, 541 (1886)

[2] See ch XXXVII, infra; Millbank v. N Y., etc, 64 How Pr, 20 (1882) Cf. Great Western R'y Co v Metropolitan R'y Co, 32 L J (Ch), 382 (1863) Where a railroad buys a controlling interest in the stock of a competing railroad, it and its officers and dummies will be enjoined from voting such stock at the instance of a minority stockholder, it being clear that if allowed to control the latter corporation the former corporation can enhance its profits at the expense of the latter corporation, by diversion of traffic. Memphis, etc, R R. v. Wood, 7 S Rep, 108 (Ala, 1889). One railroad corporation has no power to acquire the bonds of another railroad corporation in order to control the elections of the latter, such bonds having a voting power State v McDaniel, 22 Ohio St., 354, 369 (1872) Eleven years' delay is fatal to a complaint that another corporation has purchased a majority of the stock of the corporation in which the complainant stockholder holds stock, and that such purchaser is diverting the traffic to its own line and is wrecking the corporation which it controls. Alexander v Searcy, 8 S E. Rep, 630 (Ga., 1889).

[3] Fitzgerald v Missouri P. R'y, 45 Fed. Rep., 812 (1891) Although one railroad company owns a majority of the stock of another railroad company, yet the identity of the two are separate as regards being parties to suits Jessup v. Ill, etc, R R, 36 Fed Rep, 735 (1888). A corporation which owns a majority of the stock of another corporation, and

§ 316. *Purchases of stock by banks and pledges to banks* — A banking corporation has at common law no power to purchase or invest in the stock of another corporation, whether that other corporation be itself a bank or of a different business[1] The bank is organized for the purpose of receiving deposits and loaning money, not for the purpose of dealing in stocks Any attempt to engage in such transaction is a violation of its charter rights and of its duty towards the stockholders and the public There can be no difference of opinion as to whether a pledge of stock, as collateral security for a loan made by the bank at the time of pledging the stock, is legal. Such a pledge of stock is valid and may be enforced[2]

As regards a pledge of stock to a bank to secure a debt previously contracted, its legality is unquestioned, and is as free from objections as a pledge made contemporaneous with the loan[3]

§ 317 *Purchases of stock by insurance, manufacturing and other companies* — An insurance company has no power or legal right to subscribe for stock in a savings bank and building association,[4] nor

buys goods of it, is not bound to see that the latter turns the funds over to a party who owned the goods and consigned them for sale Wheeler *v* New Haven, etc, Co, 16 Atl Rep, 397 (Conn, 1889). See on this subject § 6, *supra*, and chs 38, 39 and 43 *infra*

[1] Talmage *v* Pell, 7 N Y, 328, 347 (1852), Nassau Bank *v* Jones, 95 N Y, 115, 120 (1884), First Nat Bank *v* Nat. Exchange Bank, 92 U S, 122, 128 (1875), where, in reference to national banks, the court said "Dealing in stocks is not expressly prohibited, but such a prohibition is implied from the failure to grant the power" Tracy *v* Talmage, 14 N Y, 162 (1856), Royal Bank of India's Case, L. R., 4 Ch, 252 (1869), Franklin Co. *v* Lewiston Institution for Savings 68 Me, 43 (1877) The bank is not liable to the corporate creditors on the stock

[2] Royal Bank of India's Case, *supra* "Making advances upon shares in public companies is within the ordinary course of the dealing of bankers" The stock pledged was stock in another bank To same effect *Re* Barned's Banking Co, L R, 3 Ch, 105 (1867)

Shoemaker *v* Nat Mechanics Bank, 1 Hughes (Ct Ct Md), 101 (1869), as applicable to national banks, also National Bank *v* Case 99 U S 628 (1878). Such a pledge to a national bank is not prohibited by the statute that the bank shall not take a real-estate mortgage as security So held where the property of the corporation whose stock was pledged consisted of real estate Baldwin *v* Canfield, 1 N W Rep, 261 (footpaging), (1879) See, also Sistare *v* Best, 88 N Y, 527 (1882) *Contra*, Franklin Bank *v* Commercial Bank, 36 Ohio St, 350 (1881), where the legality of the pledge was denied, and the right of the pledgee to have the stock registered in its name not granted On a reorganization it is legal for a bank owning some of the bonds to take part in such reorganization and accept stock in the new company Deposit Bank *v* Barrett, 13 S. W Rep, 337 (Ky, 1890).

[3] First National Bank *v* National Exchange Bank, 92 U S, 122, 128

[4] Mutual Sav Bank & Bldg Ass'n *v* Meriden Agency Co, 24 Conn, 159 (1855), holding the insurance company not liable on the stock An insurance

to purchase stock in another insurance company [1] It is difficult to state any rule as regards the right of a manufacturing or trading corporation to purchase shares of the capital stock of another corporation. It has been held that neither a note-selling company [2] nor a lumber company [3] has power to invest in the shares of a bank, nor a steamship company to subscribe for stock in a dry-dock company.[4] On the other hand, it has been held that a steamboat company may purchase stock in another rival line, even though the evident purpose be to injure it [5] It is clearly legal for a manufacturing corporation to take the stock of another in payment of a debt.[6]

A corporation formed to manufacture and sell gas has no power to buy shares of stock in other gas companies [7]

A steel-spring company may use its surplus earnings to purchase shares of stock in an iron and steel company for the purpose of purchasing steel cheaply from the latter company, especially where there is a combination which has put up the price of steel.[8]

Where a corporation owns stock in another corporation and sells it and takes a note in payment, it is no defense to a suit on the note to set up the *ultra vires* of the above act.[9]

company cannot invest in the stock of a bank State v. Butler, 8 S W Rep, 586 (Tenn, 1888).

[1] *Re* Liquidators of the British Nation Life Assurance Association, L R, 8 Ch Div, 679 (1878), the court refusing to hold the former liable on a winding up, Berry z Yates, 24 Barb, 199 (1857)· Pierson r McCurdy, 33 Hun, 530 (1884)

[2] Joint-stock Discount Co. v Brown, L R, 8 Eq, 381 (1869)

[3] Sumner v Marcy, 3 W. & M, 105 (1847)

[4] New Orleans, F & H S. Co v Ocean Dry-dock Co., 28 La. Ann, 173 (1876) Although a corporation purchases stock in another corporation contrary to statute, yet a *bona fide* holder of a note given in payment therefor may collect the note Wright v. Pipe Line Co., 101 Pa. St, 204 (1882).

[5] Booth v Robinson, 55 Md, 419 (1880). This decision goes to the extreme length in allowing one corporation to invest in the stock of another A manufacturing corporation is not presumed to be incapable of purchasing stock in another corporation Parker v Bernal, 66 Cal, 112 (1884).

[6] Howe v Boston Carpet Co., 82 Mass, 493 (1860) Where an iron company sells iron to a railway company to be paid for in stock of the latter, the contract is void, and the iron company cannot, it seems, even recover the value of the goods delivered Valley R'y Co. v. Lake Erie Iron Co, 18 N. E Rep., 486 (Ohio, 1888) Where one telegraph corporation holds the bonds of another and exchanges the bonds for the stock of the latter corporation, a subsequent mortgagee of the first corporation cannot attack the validity of the bonds and mortgage on the property of the second corporation Boston, etc., Co v. Bankers', etc, Co, 36 Fed Rep, 288 (1888). This case was affirmed *sub nom.* United Lines Tel Co v Boston, etc, Co., 147 U. S, 431 The court said in regard to the method of issuing the stocks and bonds, "It violated no principle of law, and no rule of good morals."

[7] People z. Chicago Gas T. Co, 22 N E Rep, 798 (Ill, 1889).

[8] Laying v A French, etc., Co., Limited, 24 Atl Rep., 215 (Pa, 1892).

[9] Holmes, etc, Co. v Holmes, etc, Co, 53 Hun, 52 (1889); affirmed, 127 N.Y, 252.

A trust company has no power to hold as trustee and vote the majority of the stock of a great railroad system, especially where it is also the trustee in a trust deed of the company.[1]

One company may be enjoined from voting stock in a rival corporation where such vote controls and will render the second company subject to the first.[2]

Although the statutes of a state authorize incorporation for any legal purpose, yet it may be a question whether incorporation can be had for buying and selling shares of stock in other corporations. The state only, however, can raise this objection.[3]

Religious and charitable and other corporations, not for profit, have, it seems, implied power to invest their funds in stock of other corporations.[4] There has been some controversy whether one corporation could sell all its property to another corporation taking pay in stock of the latter, and dividing such stock among the shareholders of the selling corporation. The weight of authority holds that such a transaction is legal if all the stockholders

---

[1] Clarke v Central R. R, etc, Co, 50 Fed Rep., 338 (1892)

[2] See § 315, also ch XXXVII Where a consolidation is effected by one company buying all the stock of another company, and just before the transaction is completed the company whose stock is thus sold issues a dividend of interest-bearing securities in order to defraud the purchasing company, the latter may, by a bill in equity, have such securities canceled Bailey v Citizens', Gas, etc, Co, 27 N. J Eq., 196 (1876).

[3] A stockholder in the corporation cannot enjoin it from purchasing stock in accordance with its articles of incorporation Willoughby v Chicago, etc, Co, 25 Atl Rep 277 (N J, 1892). It is not for a creditor of the vendor of stock to raise the question whether the vendee — a corporation — had power to purchase the stock Kern v Day, 12 So Rep, 6 (La, 1893) Although the charter authorizes other corporations to hold the stock of a corporation, yet a subsequent general constitutional provision against one corporation owning the stock of another applies to it Clarke v. Central R. R, etc, 50 Fed Rep, 338 (1892) A corporation organized to deal

in the stock of a stock-yard corporation and hold personal and real estate may buy competing stock yards, also buy the stock of a contemplated competing company also buy, guaranty and sell the bonds of such competing company, also pay money to settle suits against the first-named stock-yard company, and to bind stock-yard men not to erect competing yards for a specified term of years, within a certain territory, and may sell any or all of the above property and right to the first-named company Ellerman v Chicago, etc, S Y. Co, 23 Atl Rep, 287 (N J, 1891).

[4] Pearson v Concord R R. Co, 13 Am & Eng R R Cases, 102 (N H, 1883) "Certain classes of corporations may rightfully invest their moneys in the stock of other corporations, such as religious and charitable corporations, and corporations for literary purposes The power is not expressly mentioned in their charters, but is necessarily implied, for the preservation of the funds with which such institutions are endowed, and to render their funds productive" To same effect, Hodges v New Eng Screw Co., 1 R I, 312 (1850)

assent, but may be prevented by any stockholder of the former corporation [1] Where a corporation owns stock in the name of a trustee for the corporation, it is obliged to indemnify such trustee for calls paid by him.[2] The stock owned by a corporation may be sold by its general business agent and financial manager and representative, he having apparent power to sell, and the governing body not objecting [3]

§ 318 *Infants as purchasers of stock.*— An infant is incompetent to purchase shares of stock. Most cases of this class arise upon a winding up of the corporation, when the infant is placed upon the list of contributories, and, in defense, infancy is set up.[4] An infant's purchase of stock is voidable and not void.[5] This seems to be the rule finally arrived at by the English courts, after some hesitation and difference of opinion   The transfer is similar to a deed, and passes an interest to the infant even when coupled with a liability, if it be for his benefit to accept it [6] Consequently an infant, upon coming of age, is bound to elect whether he will affirm or disaffirm a purchase of stock made by him while yet an infant [7] He may disaffirm while still an infant, and is then not liable on calls [8] The plea of infancy is a good defense,[9] but the plea must allege a disaffirmation within a reasonable time after becoming of age [10] Where a stockholder sells his stock through a stock-exchange jobber, and the sale is made to an infant, the jobber is liable to the vendor for calls paid by him in consequence of such

[1] See ch XL, *infra*

[2] Goodson's Claim, 28 W R., 760 (1880) Where one company takes shares of stock in another company and puts such stock in the name of its treasurer and president as ' trustees of the stockholders of the A Co.," and the treasurer afterwards sells the stock and converts the money to his own use, he may be compelled to account for the same. Murray v Aiken, etc, Co, 16 S. E. Rep, 143 (S C, 1892).

[3] Walker v Detroit Transit R'y Co, 47 Mich, 338 (1882). See, also, Sistare v. Best, 88 N Y, 527 That the corporate treasurer may sell the stock, see Holden v Metropolitan Nat'l Bank, 138 Mass., 48

[4] See §§ 67, 250

[5] Lumsden's Case, L R, 4 Ch, 31 (1868) A minor's sale of stock is voidable by him It is not void Smith v Nashville, etc., R R, 18 S W. Rep., 546 (Tenn, 1892).

[6] Id

[7] Where, however, the corporation becomes insolvent just before or just after the infant comes of age, he need not affirm or disaffirm, but may await the action of the corporation Mitchell's Case, L R, 3 Eq, 363 (1870) Where he is silent for two years after coming of age, and corporate insolvency then occurs, he is bound. Id. For other cases of ratification, see references in §§ 67, 250

[8] Newry & Enniskillen R'y Co. v. Coombe, 3 Ex, 565, 578 (1849)   ' He became a shareholder by contract during infancy, and during infancy, he disaffirmed the contract, therefore, in my opinion, he ceased to be a shareholder liable to be sued for calls."

[9] Birkenhead, L & C J R'y Co v. Pilcher, 5 Ex, 24 (1850).

[10] Dublin & Wicklow R'y Co. v Black, 8 Ex, 181 (1852).

infancy.[1] An infant's sale of stock, even by a transfer of the certificate, is not binding on him[2]

§ 319. *Married women as purchasers, owners or vendors of stock*
At common law a married woman's rights as regards shares of stock were the same as prevailed with reference to other personal property purchased or owned by her She had no material rights Modern statutes have, however, completely changed her rights of property and of contract. These statutes are so different in form and effect that, for the purpose of ascertaining the *status* of a married woman as a stockholder, it is necessary to consult the statute law of the state of her domicile, and also of the state of the corporation itself.[3] In England the severity of the common law has been but partially modified by statute.[4]

[1] Nickalls *v.* Merry, L. R., 7 H L, 530 (1875)

[2] Smith *v* Baker, 42 Hun, 505 (1886)

[3] The wife's capacity to transfer is determined by the law of her domicile Hill *v* Pine River Bank, 45 N H, 300 (1864) Dow *v* Gould & C. S M. Co, 31 Cal, 629 (1867), holds that in California a gift of stock from husband to wife is valid, and that, after such gift, he could not sell and transfer it as his own. Leitch *v* Wells, 48 N Y 585 (1872), The case of Stanwood *v* Stanwood, 17 Mass, 57 (1820), holds that where the husband does not have the stock transferred to himself on the corporate books, but declares it to be his wife's stock, there is no reduction of it to his possession. See, also, Wall *v* Tomlinson, 16 Ves, 413 (1809), to the effect that a transfer of the wife's stock to the husband as trustee is not a reduction to possession, also, Arnold *v* Ruggles 1 R I, 165 (1837), Wildman *v* Wildman,

9 Ves., 174 (1803), and Slaymaker *v* Bank of Gettysburg, 10 Pa St 373 (1819), to the effect that only a registry will reduce the wife's stock to the possession of the husband See, also, ch XXXII, *infra* The wife's stock, standing in her name at the time of and after marriage, is not subject to her husband's debts. Cochrane *v.* Chambers, Ambl, 79, n (1825). *Contra* Stamford Bank *v* Ferris, 17 Conn, 259 (1845) In Connecticut it is held that the wife is not liable in *assumpsit* to her husband's creditors, to whom she has pledged her stock, although she subsequently pledges it to another An express promise to pay on her part is necessary Platt *v* Hawkins, 43 Conn, 139 (1879) Curtis *v* Steever, 36 N J Law, 304 (1873), clearly and properly holds that the wife's stock, held by her as her separate estate, is not subject to her husband's debts See, also, Cornell's Case, 18 W N Cases, 289 (Pa, Nov, 1886),

[4] By 33 and 34 Vict., ch. 93, § 4, married women may purchase or take paid-up stock, or stock upon which there can be no liability, but if taken without the consent of her husband, he may apply to the court and have it turned over to himself Previous to this act the corporation might refuse to register her as a stockholder, but now the corporation must accept her the same as any other applicant for registry Regina *v* Carnatic R y Co, 42 L J (Q B), 169 (1873) Under this act she may transfer her stock only after it has been formally set aside by statutory authority as her separate property. Howard *v* Bank of Eng, L R, 19 Eq, 295 (1875) Where the corporation has allowed a transfer by a married woman, it cannot cancel the registry Ward *v.* Southeastern R'y Co., 2 El & El, 812 (1860).

§ 320. *Competency of miscellaneous parties.*— A sale of stock by a person *non compos mentis* is void. The corporation is bound absolutely to know of the lunacy of a transferrer, even though it allows a registry on his ordinary signature and transfer.[1] An assignee in bankruptcy or for the benefit of creditors takes only the interest and equitable rights of his assignor A previous unrecorded transfer of the insolvent's stock is protected[2] A partner may accept stock as collateral security for a loan from the firm,[3] and may sell and transfer partnership stock[4]

and §§ 66, 250, 308, Vandenheyden *v* Mallory, 1 N Y, 452 (1848), Voorhees *v* Bonesteel, 16 Wall, 16 (1872) A certificate issued to husband as trustee of wife constitutes her separate estate, where he pays dividends to her In Kentucky a resident married woman's power of attorney to convey stock is void Bank of Louisville *v* Gray, 2 S W Rep, 168 (Ky, 1886) Taking out a certificate in his own name by the husband reduces his wife's stock to his possession, and it passes by his will, even though he made a memorandum to the effect that he held it in trust for her Cummings *v* Cummings, 9 N E Rep., 730 (Mass, 1887) Where a husband uses his wife's money to purchase stock and takes title in his own name, but considers himself trustee for her, a creditor of the husband, who at the time of incurring the debt knew that the latter held the stock for his wife, cannot subject it to the payment of the debt. Porter *v* Bank of Rutland, 19 Vt., 410 (1847) Although a corporation errs in allowing a wife to transfer her stock to her husband, yet the statute of limitations runs against her right of action from the time of the transfer Chase *v* Hibernia Nat. Bank, 10 S. Rep, 379 (La, 1891) In Kentucky, by statute, a wife's bank stock goes to her heirs, and not to her husband, upon her decease Kent's Adm'r *v* Deposit Bank, 14 S W. Rep, 962 (Ky, 1890) Possession by the husband, as executor, of stock of his wife is not a reduction to possession Sowles *v* Witters, 39 Fed Rep, 403 (1889) A person taking stock

from a person in whose name it stands cannot hold the same as against the latter's wife, where the stock belonged to her separate estate and was not known to be by the person taking it Stickney *v* Stickney, 8 S. Rep., 568 (Ala, 1890). A married woman may give away or pledge her stock Walker *v* Joseph, etc, Co, 20 Atl Rep., 885 (N J, 1890). Where the wife authorizes her husband to sell her stock and use the proceeds in his business, he cannot sell the stock and assign the proceeds to another person The latter cannot collect such proceeds Deming *v* Bailey, 2 Rob, 1 (1864)

[1] Chew *v* Bank of Baltimore, 14 Md, 299 (1859). A sale of stock is not easily set aside on the ground of mental incapacity on the part of the vendor Perry *v* Pearson, 25 N E Rep., 636 (Ill., 1890)

[2] Dickinson *v* Central Nat. Bank, 129 Mass, 279 (1880); Purchase *v* New York Exchange Bank, 3 Rob (N Y), 164 (1865) *Contra*, Shipman *v* Ætna Ins Co, 29 Conn, 245 (1860), where the previous transferee delayed unreasonably in claiming ownership of the stock.

[3] Weikersheim's Case, L. R., 8 Ch., 831 (1873) In Comstock *v* Buchanan, 57 Barb, 127 (1864), however, where the stock was registered in both partners' names, a contrary rule was upheld.

[4] Quiver *v* Marblehead Social Ins. Co., 10 Mass., 476 (1813). *Cf* Sargent *v.* Franklin Ins Co, 8 Pick, 90 (1829) Stock may belong to a partnership although standing in the individual names of the partners in order to make them stockholders. Fairfield *v* Phillips,

A director of the corporation itself may buy and sell its stock like any other individual The information which he has of the affairs of the corporation, whereby he is enabled to buy or sell at an advantage over the person with whom he deals, does not affect the validity of the transaction He is entitled to the benefit of his facilities for information. There is no confidential relation between him and a stockholder, so far as a sale of the stock between them is concerned, and, so long as he remains silent and does not actively mislead the person with whom he deals, the transaction cannot be set aside for fraud [1]

It is illegal for the directors to issue to themselves, in exclusion of others, such part of the original or increased capital stock as has not been already issued, the issue being for the purpose of controlling an election and making a profit.[2]

49 N W Rep, 1025 (Iowa, 1891). Where one of the partners in the building of railroads, and in many owning stocks, bonds, etc, dies, and his executor by means of experts, etc, makes a settlement with the other partner, such settlement is binding although the other partner did not impart all the knowledge or information he might have given The subsequent rise in value of some of the securities is immaterial Colton v Stanford, 23 Pac Rep, 16 (Cal, 1890).

[1] Board of Com'rs of T County v Reynolds, 44 Ind, 509 (1873), Carpenter v Danforth, 52 Barb, 581 (1868) This case was disapproved by the commentator to Story's Eq Juris, 12th ed, 229 n, but the disapproval is omitted in the 13th ed. So, also, Grant v Attrill, 11 Fed Rep, 469 (1882), where the sale was induced by threat of assessments See, also, Johnson v Laflin, 5 Dill, 65, 83 (1878), Deaderick v Wilson, 8 Baxter (Tenn), 108 (1874); Gilberts Case, L R, 5 Ch, 559 (1870), § 351, infra. See, also, Heman v Britton, 14 Mo. App, 109, aff'd, 84 Mo, 657 (1883) In New York, by statute, a director is prohibited from selling stock 'short.' Laws 1884, ch 223. Where the president of a company advises a stockholder to sell his stock at a certain price to a certain person, and the sale is made, the president is liable

for the difference between that price and the market price, where the person purchased as the secret agent of the president Fisk v Budlong, 10 R I 525 (1873) A director may buy stock from a stockholder at less than its real value, and there is no fraud in the fact that the director knew the real value while the stockholder did not Crowell v Jackson, 23 Atl Rep, 426 (N J, 1891) Where the president sells stock for $120 per share after he has indorsed a false statement of the company's affairs, the stock being really worth but $70 per share, the vendee may have the sale rescinded Prewett v Trimble, 17 S W Rep, 356 (Ky, 1891) It would be "inequitable to permit the directors of a corporation to so manage its business, or to so deal with its property, as to lessen the value of its stock for the purpose of purchasing such stock for themselves at a low figure" But this relation does not exist between one director and another director Perry v Pearson, 25 N E. Rep, 636 (Ill, 1890). The purchaser of stock from the secretary of the company cannot rescind on the ground of fraud, the secretary having given at the time of the sale all the information which he had concerning the company No confidential or fiduciary relation exists Krumbhaar v Griffiths, 25 Atl Rep., 64 (Pa, 1892)

[2] See § 70, supra.

A joint owner of stock cannot transfer the interest of the other joint owner where the stock is registered in the name of both.[1] On the death of one, the survivor takes title to the whole stock.[2]

A drunken person's sale of stock may be set aside if an undue advantage was taken.[3] Where stock is purchased by one person in his own name by due authority for himself and another, the latter is a part owner, and has rights and liabilities as such.[4] The statute of frauds does not apply to such an arrangement.[5]

§ 321 *Sales, purchases and transfers by agents.* — Stock may be purchased by an agent, and in making such a purchase the agent is not permitted to make a secret profit, even though he acts without compensation.[6] The real owner of stock may compel the nominal owner to transfer the stock to him.[7] The corporation may

---

[1] Standing v. Bowring, L. R., 27 Ch. D., 341 (1884), Comstock v Buchanan, 57 Barb, 127 (1864) But if the other joint owner dies first, the previous transfer of the survivor is effective and conveys the whole Slaymaker v. Bank of Gettysburg, 10 Pa St, 373 (1849) Where two persons own stock in common, replevin will not lie by one as against the other for his part of the stock Barrowcliffe v Cummins, 66 Hun 1 (1892)

[2] Garrick v Taylor, 3 L. T. (N S.), 460 (1860), Hill's Case, L R., 20 Eq, 585 (1874)

[3] A sale of stock by a drunken person for an insufficient consideration will be set aside, and if, without his fault, he is unable to restore the amount received, it will be provided for in the final decree Thackrah v. Haas, 119 U. S, 499 (1886)

[4] Staver v Flack, 41 Barb., 162 (1862). Where several parties buy and sell a certain stock in the name of one of themselves and close the deal, a subsequent purchase of the same stock by that one does not inure to their common benefit. Kennedy v Porter, 109 N Y, 526 (1888) Where several parties agree to purchase land in the name of a corporation in exchange for stock to be taken in the name of one of them, the others may compel the latter to account for the stock. King v Barnes,

109 N. Y., 267 (1888). See, also, § 252, *supra.* A partnership or joint ownership of stocks between two persons may be shown by the acts and contracts of the parties and by the fact that the property clearly owned by them in common was used in the acquisition of the other property. Beardsley v. Beardsley, 138 U S, 262 (1891) Where several parties buy a certificate of stock in fixed proportions and the certificate is taken by one for the benefit of all, he is a bailee for the others and not a vendor. Coquard v. Weinse, 13 S. W Rep., 341 (Mo, 1890) Where one party loans money to another party to buy stock in a certain company, such stock to be delivered to the former party in pledge, and the latter party uses the stock for another purpose, the loan of the money is not a mere loan, but the money is impressed with a trust, and this trust follows the stock as against *bona fide* holders Barnard v. Hawks, 16 S. E. Rep., 329 (N C., 1892).

[5] See § 339, *infra*

[6] Kimber v Barber, L R., 8 Ch, 56 (1872), holding that, where a person offers to buy for another stock at a certain price, but buys it at a less price and keeps the difference, he is liable to the vendee for his gains Keyes v Bradley, 35 N W Rep, 656 (Iowa, 1887).

[7] Colquhoun v Courtenay, 43 L J (Ch), 338 (1874).

disregard the nominal holder and allow the real owner to sell and transfer the stock[1] The relation of an agent towards his principal in the purchase, sale or holding of stock exists where a "dummy" is used to shield the real owner from liability on the stock.[2] A stockholder may of course sell stock through an agent[3] But power to sell does not give power to pledge[4]

The principal and most difficult questions connected with an agency herein arise where the owner of stock indorses it in blank, and places it in the hands of an agent, and the agent in violation of his orders then sells the stock to a *bona fide* purchaser The law is clear that the *bona fide* purchaser is protected in his ownership of the stock[5]

§ 322 *Purchases of stock by guardians, executors and trustees* — In England, at an early day, the common-law rule was declared to be that guardians, executors and trustees had no right to invest the trustee fund in the stocks of private corporations, and that if they did so they themselves were personally liable for the moneys so invested[6] The rigor of this rule has been relaxed somewhat in England, by statute and by orders in chancery, so that such in-

---

[1] Sabin v Bank of Woodstock 21 Vt, 353 (1849), holding also that the nominal holder is not protected although he subsequently becomes the real owner of the stock

[2] See § 253 *supra*

[3] See ch XXV, on stock-brokers A person may assign stock to another with discretionary power to sell at any time the latter thinks best, and pay the former's creditors therefrom Appeal of Neilson, 13 Atl Rep. 943 (Pa. 1888) Where an agent to sell stock is to have any excess of price over a sum named to him by the vendor, and the agent finds a customer at an advanced price and the vendor refuses to sell, the agent may recover such profit as he lost thereby Mattingly v. Roach, 23 Pac. Rep, 1117 (Cal, 1891). An agent authorized to sell stock may sell part of it Ulster, etc, Inst. v Fourth, etc, Bank, 8 N Y Supp, 162 (1889)

[4] See § 326. A stockholder's power of attorney to his agent "to exchange old issues or certificates of stock and to receive new issues or certificates in lieu thereof" does not authorize the agent to sell or pledge the stock. The corpo-

ration is liable for allowing a transfer to a third person on such authority Quay v Presidio, etc, R R, 22 Pac Rep, 925 (Cal, 1889) Where a person gives to another a general power of attorney, covering the sale and transfer of all stocks etc, the attorney may, upon delivering up the certificate therefor to the corporation, transfer the stock of his principal into his own name The corporation is not bound to inquire further than the power of attorney, nor is it given notice by the fact that the attorney is one of its directors Tafft v Presidio etc, Co, 23 Pac Rep, 485 (Cal, 1889).

[5] See § 351, *infra*.

[6] Trafford v Boehm 3 Atk, 440 (1746), where the investment was in bank and South Sea stock Lewin on Trusts, 281 (7th ed, 1879), says that, "unless specially given power, it is settled in England that a trustee may not invest the trust fund in the stock of any private company, as South Sea stock, bank stock, etc., for the capital depends upon the management of governors and directors, and is subject to loss."

vestments may be made in the stock of the banks of England and
of Ireland and the East India Company.[1] In this country, aside
from a few *dicta* and a few decisions to the contrary, the English
rule, in its original integrity, is upheld and followed   The weight
of authority clearly holds that the investment of trust funds in the
stock of railroad, insurance, bank, manufacturing or other corporations is made at the peril of the trustees[2] The *cestui que trust*

---

[1] Lord St. Vincent's Act, 22 and 23
Vict, ch 35, § 32, 23 and 24 Vict.,
ch 38

[2] In New York the case of King *v*
Talbot, 40 N Y , 76 (1869), aff'g 50 Barb,
453, clearly enounces and sustains this
rule. See, also. Adair *v* Brimmer, 74 N
Y , 539, 551 (1878), where the trustees
were held liable for selling coal lands,
taking in pay coal stocks, they being
authorized by the will to invest in such
securities as they deemed safe   Mills *v*
Hoffman, 26 Hun. 594 (1882), reversed
in 92 N Y , 181, but not on this point
Ackerman *v* Emott, 4 Barb 626 (1848).
See, also, Berry *v* Yates, 24 Barb, 210
(1857) Brown *v* Campbell, Hopkins'
Ch (2d ed), 265 (1824). In Pennsylvania
the rule is the same   Nyce's Appeal, 5
Watts & Serg , 254 (1843), holding the
trustee liable for investment in United
States bank stock, although the guardian approved of the trustee's investment. Norris *v* Wallace, 3 Pa St., 319
(1846), where the investment was in the
stock of a suspended bank   Worrell's
Appeal, 9 Pa St. 508 (1848), navigation
stock not good, although dividends had
been accepted by the *cestui que trust*,
sustained on second appeal. 23 Pa St.
(1854) Rush's Estate, 12 Pa St , 375
(1849) stock in Lehigh Coal and Navigation Company not good   Hemphill's
Appeal, 18 Pa St. 303 (1852), United
States bank stock not good   Pray's Appeal, 34 Pa St , 100 (1859), manufacturing corporation stock not good, the
works being unfinished   Barton's Estate, 1 Pars , 24, doubted. Ihmsen's Appeal, 43 Pa. St . 431 (1862), railroad stock
not good   In New Jersey the rule is the
same. Gray *v*. Fox, 1 N. J. Eq. Rep , 259

(1831), Halsted *v* Meeker's Ex'rs, 18 N
J Eq Rep , 136 (1866), Ward *v* Kitchen,
30 N J Eq Rep , 31 (1878)   Also in New
Hampshire   Kimball *v* Reding, 31 N
H , 352 (1855), stock in contemplated
railroad not good , French *v.* Currier, 47
N H , 88, 99 (1866), unproductive stock
not good   In Massachusetts the tendency is to favor a contrary rule. "Trustees in this commonwealth are permitted
to invest portions of trust funds in divi-
dend-paying stocks and interest-bearing
bonds of private business corporations,
when the corporations have acquired,
by reason of the amount of their property and the prudent management of
their affairs, such a reputation that cau-
tious and intelligent persons commonly
invest their own money in the stocks
and bonds as permanent investments "
But where the trustee invested over a
fifth of the estate in Union Pacific Railroad stock and afterwards invested a
further amount in the same stock, he
was charged with the loss due to the
second investment. Dickinson's Appeal,
25 N. E. Rep., 99 (Mass., 1890)   In the
case of Harvard College *v.* Amory, 26
Mass., 446 (1830), express power was
given   In Lovell *v* Minot, 37 Mass., 116
(1838), the stock was taken as security.
Kinmouth *v* Brigham, 87 Mass , 270
(1862), and Brown *v.* French, 125 Mass.,
410 (1878), were not cases of investments
in stocks   Hunt, Appellant, 6 N E
Rep , 554 (Mass., 1886), is a *dictum.* Several of the southern states clearly uphold the rule that trustees, etc., may
invest the trust funds in stocks   Boggs
v Adger, 4 Rich Eq (S C), 408 (1852),
United States bank stock good , Washington *v.* Emory, 4 Jones' Eq. (N. C.),

may hold the trustee liable for the amounts so invested, together with interest upon the same. Where the trustee is authorized to purchase stock he is not liable for the embezzlements of an agent whom with due care he employs to make the purchase[1]

§ 323　*Sale or pledge of stock by trustee in breach of his trust* — It is the function and duty of a trustee to keep and preserve the trust property, and to apply the income according to the terms of the instrument creating the trust. As a general rule it is not his duty or his right to sell or change the investment. Unless the instrument creating the trust authorizes the sale of the trust property, it is a breach of trust for the trustee to make a sale[2]. In this respect the powers of a trustee differ widely from those of an executor or administrator, and the rule applies to a trustee holding in trust shares of stock. Moreover, under ordinary circumstances, a trustee cannot sell stock held in trust, although such sale be for the purpose of investing the proceeds in other stock or other property[3]

---

32 (1859), railroad stock good, Gray v. Lynch, 8 Gill (Md), 403 (1849) bank stock good, Smyth v Burns, 25 Miss 422 (1853), bank stock good Lamar v Micou, 112 U S, 452 (1884), and 114 U S, 218 (speaking for Georgia and Alabama), bank and railroad stock good, but not Confederate bonds. See, also on this subject, generally, 40 Am Dec, 515, notes An executor who is interested in a corporation, and gets a commission for selling its stock, is liable to replace funds which he induces the *cestui que trust*, a woman, to invest in such stock Appeal of Potter, 12 Atl Rep, 513 (Conn, 1888) Where all the stockholders assign stock to the president to sell to pay corporate debts, he may assign part of it to himself to pay a debt due to himself from the corporation Appeal of Patterson, 12 Atl Rep, 679 (Pa, 1888) Where the trustee is expressly authorized to invest in bank stock he is not liable to the estate for losses, though the investment is made in his individual name Appeal of Pensyl, 15 Atl Rep, 719 (Pa, 1888) As to statutory and constitutional provisions, see Part VII, *infra* In Kentucky the statutes authorize the retention by a guardian of an investment in good bank

stock Fidelity, etc, Co v Glover, 14 S W Rep, 343 (Ky, 1890)

[1] Speight v. Gaunt, L R, 9 App. Cases, 1 (1883)

[2] Bohlen's Estate, 75 Pa St. 312 (1874), Bayard v Farmers' & M Bank 52 Pa St, 232 (1866) Jaudon v National City Bank, 8 Blatch, 430 (1871), affirmed 15 Wall, 165 (1871) On the relations and duties of trustees generally in regard to stock, see, also, Perry on Trusts (3d ed), 539, 556

[3] Trustee selling stock for purpose of investing in real estate may be compelled to replace it Earl Powlet v Herbert, 1 Ves, 297 (1791) Cf Bohlen's Estate, 75 Pa St, 312 (1874), Peckham v Newton, 4 Atl Rep, 758 (R I, 1886). *Cestui que trust* may waive the objection Duncan v Jaudan, 15 Wall, 171 The case of Washington v Emory, 4 Jones' Eq, 32 (1858), holds that a change in the investment is allowable if there is good reason to believe that the estate will be benefited Trustees should sell the stock if depreciation is probable Ward v Kitchen, 30 N J Eq, 31 (1878) But not liable for failure to sell if in good faith and sound discretion Bowker v Pierce, 130 Mass, 262 (1881); Parker v Glover, 9 Atl Rep, 217 (N J, 1887), Appeal of

§ 324 Where a trustee improperly sells shares of stock belonging
to the trust estate, the *cestui que trust* has a right to elect to have
the stock restored or the amount received for it paid over, together
with interest from the time of the sale.[1] Were the rule otherwise
the trustee would profit by his own breach of trust in case there
was a decline in the value of the stock. The trust attaches to any
stock standing in the name of the trustee, and although the same
certificates are not retained, an equal amount of other similar stock
owned by the trustee may be applied to the trust.[2] And in all cases
where the trustee has sold stock belonging to the trust estate in
breach of his duties as trustee, he may be held liable in damages by
the *cestui que trust* or his representative for the value of the stock.[3]

Stewart, 6 Atl Rep., 321 (Pa., 1887) — the
last case holding, also, that the trustee
cannot sell the stock to himself, even at
the market price. Cannot change stock
bequeathed Murray *v* Feinour 2 Md
Ch , 418 (1851) Nor a good investment
to a stock investment. *In re* Warde, 2
Johns & H , 191 (1861), Waite *v* Whorwood 2 Atkyns, 159 (1741) A trustee of
an estate has implied power to sell railroad stock belonging to the estate in
order to reinvest the proceeds in securities which the law allows him to invest
in Toronto, etc , Co ? Chicago, etc ,
R. R. 64 Hun, 1 (1892) See, also, *Re*
Bennison, 60 L. T Rep , 859 (1889) In
the case Jones *v* Atchison, etc R R , 23
N E Rep , 43 (Mass., 1889), the court upheld a sale of stock made by the trustee
for the purpose of changing the investment. A trustee selling stock at a high
price and then replacing it at a lower
figure is liable to the *cestui que trust*
for the high price Snyder's Adm'r *v*
McComb's Ex'r, 39 Fed Rep., 292 (1889)

[1] Harrison *v* Harrison, 2 Atkyns, 121
(1740), Bostock *v* Blakeney, 2 Brown's
Ch R , 653 (1789); Pocock *v* Reddington, 5 Vesey, 800 (1801), Long *v.* Stewart, 5 Vesey, 809, note (1801) Hart *v*
Ten Eyck, 2 Johns Ch , 62, 117 (1816),
Re Masouberd's Settlement, 60 L T Rep.,
620 (1889)

[2] Pinkett *v* Wright, 2 Hare, 120
(1842) A trustee is liable for breach of

trust of co-trustee in regard to stock
where the former is negligent in keeping himself informed as to the transactions of the latter in the trust property
Bullock *v* Bullock, 55 L. T Rep , 703
(1886) Trust stock was pledged by a
trustee to secure his own debts in 1864,
the pledgee knowing that the stock was
trust stock , the stock was sold by pledgee
in 1867 , the *cestui que trust* learned
thereof in 1877 and commenced suit
against the executors of the surety for
the trustee , judgment was rendered in
1882, and executors commenced this
suit against the pledgee within three
years after 1882. *Held*, that no laches
or statute of limitations barred the suit.
Blake *v.* Traders' Nat'l Bank, 12 N. E.
Rep , 414 (Mass , 1887).

[3] A trustee authorized to sell stock,
but selling in breach of trust, is liable for
the value of the stock at the time of commencing suit against him, and interest;
also for dividends declared after the
breach of trust; or the *cestui que trust*
may demand the value of the stock at
the time of the breach of trust, and interest, or a replacing of similar stock
and dividends McKim *v.* Hibbard, 8
N E Rep , 152 (Mass , 1886) A trustee
to use stock to pay debts may assign a
part of the stock to pay a debt due to
himself, if in good faith and at a full
valuation Appeal of Patterson, 12 Atl.
Rep , 679 (Pa., 1888).

A specific performance in regard to a trust estate of stock may be decreed [1]

§ 325 *Transferee of stock from trustee — is protected when.* — A vendee or pledgee of stock, directly from a trustee, is or is not protected in his interest in the stock, according as he is or is not chargeable with notice of the fact that the stock belongs to a trust estate, and that the trustee is using it in breach of the trust Anything that is sufficient to put a party on inquiry is considered equivalent to actual notice, if inquiry be not made and reasonably satisfied The law imputes to a purchaser the knowledge of a fact of which the exercise of common prudence and ordinary diligence would have apprised him This is called constructive notice, and has the same effect as an actual notice of the trusteeship. The most common instance of a constructive notice that stock being sold belongs to a trust estate is where the words "trustee" or "in trust," either with or without the name of the *cestui que trust*, are written on the face of the certificate of stock after the name of the person in whose name it stands on the corporate books It is well established that such words, indicating a trustee ownership, are notice to the purchaser that his vendor is selling trust property, and that he must ascertain whether the trustee has any power to sell the stock [2]

---

[1] See § 338, n , *infra.*

[2] "A certificate for shares of stock running to 'A. B., trustee,' or to 'A B., in trust,' without disclosing the names of beneficiaries or the particulars of the trust, is notice to a purchaser of the shares that 'A. B.' does not hold them in his own right but as a trustee " Gerard v McCormick, 130 N Y , 261, 267 (1891); Shaw v. Spencer, 100 Mass , 382 (1868), the court saying that the word "trustee" means trustee for some one whose name is not disclosed, and that a custom of trade disregarding such words on certificates of stock is illegal and ineffectual to protect the purchaser. To same effect, Jaudon v National City Bank, 8 Blatch , 430 (1871), aff'd, 15 Wall , 165, 176, where the court says the purchasers "are chargeable with constructive notice of everything which, upon inquiry, they could have ascertained from the *cestui que trust* " Gaston v American Ex. Nat. Bank, 29 N J Eq Rep., 98 (1878); Walsh v. Stille, 2 Parsons' Sel. Cases in Eq (Pa.), 17 (1842).

Simons v Southwestern R R Bank, 5 Rich Eq 270 (1853) where a master in chancery held the stock in his own name officially, Loring v Brodie, 134 Mass , 453 (1883), Loring v Salisbury Mills, 125 id , 138 (1878) Sweeney v Bank of Montreal, 5 Canadian Law Times, 503 (1885), Budd v Monroe, 18 Hun, 316 (1879), Bank of Montreal v Sweney 36 L T Rep , 897 (1887) In California, however, it is held that, although the word 'trustee' on the face of the certificate, followed by the name of the *cestui que trust*, may give notice that it is trust property yet that where the word "trustee" is but a cloak for an agency, for the purpose of shielding the real owner from liability on his stock, and to conceal the fact that he is dealing in stocks the court will disregard it and will not protect the real owner against his agent's unauthorized sale of the stock Brewster v Sime, 42 Cal , 139 (1871), Thompson v Toland, 48 Cal , 99 (1874) Where a certificate of stock runs to a person absolutely and

There are many other facts which will prevent the vendee from claiming that he is a *bona fide* holder of the stock. Thus, if the stock is pledged to a bank by the trustee, who is a director of a bank, and the bank is prohibited from loaning to its directors, the bank is not a *bona fide* holder, though without notice or knowledge of the trusteeship.[1]

In England, the house of lords have decided that certificates of stock in railway companies are not negotiable in any respect, and that a *bona fide* transferee of the certificate is not protected until he has obtained registry in the corporate books[2]. In this country a different rule prevails, and it is accepted and assumed as elementary that a *bona fide* purchaser for value of stock belonging to a trust estate and sold in breach of trust is nevertheless protected in his purchase, although he has not registered the transfer on the corporate books. A *bona fide* purchaser through several mesne conveyances, starting from a trustee who sells the stock in breach of trust, is protected[3]

passes into *bona fide* hands, the corporation is not liable for allowing a transfer, even though such stock was held in trust and the corporation knew the fact so to be. No harm was done by the transfer, inasmuch as the certificate had already passed into *bona fide* hands. Smith v Nashville etc., R. R., 18 S. W Rep 546 (Tenn, 1892). A purchaser of certificates of stock need not look back of the last registry of transfer on the corporate books. A breach of trust back of that does not invalidate his title. Winter v Montgomery, etc. Co, 7 S Rep. 773 (Ala, 1890). Where stock standing in the name of a person as trustee is sold and the certificates are turned in for transfer without the purchaser seeing them, he takes good title even though there was a breach of trust, he not knowing of such breach, nor of the trusteeship. Stinson v Thornton, 56 Ga, 379 (1876). Notice to a person attending to the transfer is not notice to the transferee

[1] Albert v Savings Bank of Baltimore, 2 Md, 159, 171 (1852) A bank which receives trust stock as security for a loan, and afterward, on payment of the loan, transfers the stock to parties designated by the pledgor, is liable to the *cestui que trust* for aiding in the latter transfer Hatten v Russell, 58 L T Rep. 252 (1889)

[2] Shropshire Union Rys. & Canal Co. v Queen, L. R, 7 H L, 496 (1875). *Cf* Dodds v Hills, 2 H & M, 424 (1865). *Cf* §§ 378 380, 416. A *cestui que trust* of stock in England may defeat a *bona fide* purchaser's title to the stock by suing for the stock before a transfer is made on the corporate books. Roots v Williamson, 58 L T Rep, 802 (1888).

[3] Salisbury Mills v Townsend, 109 Mass, 115 (1871), Stinson v Thornton, 56 Ga, 377 (1876), Cohen v Grayun, 4 Md Ch, 357 (1848). Where however, the trustee has been removed by a court and another trustee appointed in the state of the corporation, a purchaser of the certificates held by the old trustee is not protected, his purchase being after the removal. Sprague v. Cachigo Mfg Co, 10 Blatch, 173 (1872). But in Holbrook v New Jersey Zinc Co., 57 N Y, 616 (1874), it was held that a successful suit in a state not the state of the corporation, to remove a trustee, does not affect a *bona fide* purchaser of the certificate from the trustee, the purchase being made pending the suit; and that the corporation allowing registry

§ 326 The mere fact that a purchaser of stock knows he is buying from a trustee, and that the stock belongs to the trust estate, puts the purchaser to no inquiry except that of ascertaining whether the trustee has power to sell the stock or vary the investment If he has such power the purchaser will be protected, although the trustee uses the money for his own private purposes, provided the purchaser has no notice of such an intent on the part of the trustee [1] The purchaser has a right to assume that the object of the sale is to invest the funds in a permanent investment or to discharge liabilities [2] Where, however, the purchaser knows that his vendor sells or pledges the stock as trustee, and also knows that the sale or pledge is for the private debts or purposes of the trustee, the purchaser is chargeable with knowledge of the breach of trust, and is not protected.[3] Nor is a pledgee of stock from a trustee, acting as trustee, protected where the trustee is authorized merely to sell the stock.[4] Power to sell does not confer power to pledge [5]

§ 327 *Rights and liability of the corporation allowing a transfer by a trustee in breach of his trust* — Where a corporation has notice that a stockholder holds his stock as trustee for another, and the means of ascertaining the character of that trust are within the power of the corporation, it is bound to refuse to allow a registry of the trustee's transfer until it is satisfied that the trustee has power to make the transfer [6] If the corporation allows the transfer and the trustee had no power to make it, the corporation is

of the new trustee as holder of the stock, and issuing new certificates to him, is liable in damages to the purchaser from the old trustee

[1] Perry on Trusts, § 225 3d ed (1882), Lewin on Trusts, 417, 7th ed (1879), Godefroi on Trusts, 125, 127 (1879)

[2] Ashton v Atlantic Bank, 85 Mass, 217 (1861), where the trustee sold land, took notes in payment and stock as collateral, and sold the notes with the collateral

[3] Jaudon v National City Bank, 8 Blatch, 430 (1871) affirmed, 15 Wall, 165, *sub nom* Duncan v Jaudon, Walsh v Stille, 2 Parsons' Sel. Cases in Eq (Pa) 17 (1842), White v Price, 29 Hun, 394 (1886), Simmons v Southwestern R. R. Bank, 3 Rich Eq 279 (1853), Shaw v Spencer, 100 Mass, 382 (1868), holding also that silence while the vendee pays an assessment is no waiver

[4] Loring v Brodie, 134 Mass, 453 (1883)

[5] Merchants' Bank of Canada v Livingston 74 N Y, 223 (1878), Manhattan Bank v Walker, 130 U S, 267 (1889), The power of an agent to sell does not authorize him to pledge First Nat'l Bank v Taliaferro, 19 Atl Rep, 364 (Md, 1890)

[6] Chapman v City Council, 6 S E Rep, 158 (S C, 1888), Bayard v Farmers' & Mechanics Bank, 52 Pa St, 232 (1866) where a refusal of the corporation to transfer until the terms of the trust were examined by its attorney and found to allow the trustee, was sustained The corporation cannot, however, retain the copies of the probate records used in investigating Bird v Chicago, I & N R. R. Co, 137 Mass, 428 (1884) In transfer of trust stock the corporation may very properly re-

liable to the *cestui que trust*. The fact that the certificate runs to
the holder as "trustee" is sufficient notice to the corporation.[1]
Notice to a board of directors is notice to all subsequent boards.[2]
The corporation is bound to see that the sale by the trustee is made
in accordance with the terms of the trust. Thus, it is liable if it
permits a sale and transfer by one trustee when there are two
trustees; and a general power of attorney by the other trustee authorizing sales will not protect the corporation in its registry of a
transfer signed by one only.[3] It is liable for allowing a registry of
a trustee's transfer when the trust is for an unmarried woman, to
take effect when she shall marry.[4] If there are several *cestuis que
trust*, the corporation is liable for allowing one of them to transfer
the whole interest in the stock, where by mistake of the corporation the stock had been registered in the name of that one, and not
in the name of the trustee.[5] If, however, the *cestui que trust* is
guilty of laches in taking steps to obtain his rights, the corporation
is discharged.[6] The remedy of the *cestui que trust* is in equity, not
at law.[7] A waiver of former breaches of trust is no waiver of the

fuse to allow a registry where the sale
is made by the trustee at a price far
below its market value Succession of
Boullemet, 3 S Rep, 401 (La, 1887)
Where stock is transferred to a trustee
by the executors, the corporation knowing of the trust, and the corporation
subsequently allows the trustee to transfer the stock to third persons the corporation is liable to the *cestui que trust* if
such last mentioned transfer is fraudulent and in breach of trust Marbury
v Ehlen, 19 Atl Rep, 648 (Md, 1890)
If the will gives the executrix power to
sell the stock, the corporation is protected in allowing transfers by the executrix and trustee even though it did
not know the contents of the will Although the transfer is to a bank, the
corporation is not bound to know that
the transfer is a pledge and not a sale
Peck v Providence Gas Co., 21 Atl Rep,
543 (R. I, 1891). Where, upon reorganization, the committee issue transferable
certificates exchangeable into stock of
the new corporation when it is formed,
the new corporation is liable for allowing an exchange by a person to whom
a trustee has illegally transferred the
certificates issued to him. Mobile, etc,

R. v Humphries, 7 S Rep, 522 (Miss,
1890)

[1] See § 325, *infra* In the case of
Stockdale v South Sea Co, Barnardiston's Ch (folio) 363 (1740), the court said,
however "These great companies are
only to consider the person in whose
name the stock is standing, unless the
trust of that stock is declared in their
books"

[2] Mechanics' Bank of Alex v Seton, 1
Pet., 299 (1828)

[3] Bohlen's Estate, 75 Pa. St., 312 (1874).
Nor where the signatures of the other
trustees are forged by one Cottam v
Eastern Counties R y Co, 1 J & H, 243
(1860). In England one executor or
trustee cannot assign railway stock All
must join Barton v North, etc, R'y
Co., 58 L. T Rep, 549 (1884)

[4] Magwood v R. R. Bank, 5 S C, 379
(1874)

[5] Farmers' & M Bank v Wayman, 5
Gill (Md), 336 (1847).

[6] Albert v Sav Bank of Baltimore, 1
Md Ch, 407 (1849), affirmed, 2 Md, 159
(1852).

[7] Loring v Salisbury Mills, 125 Mass.
138 (1878). In a suit by a stockholder
to hold a corporation liable for his stock

one complained of, and a judgment against the trustee himself is no bar to the suit against the corporation, except to the extent that satisfaction has been obtained [1] The corporation may be compelled by the court to purchase an equal amount of stock and register it for the benefit of the *cestui que trust* [2]

§ 328 *Sales of stock by a guardian* — At common law a guardian may sell the personal property belonging to him as guardian without obtaining any special license or authority, and a *bona fide* purchaser from him of such property is protected and is entitled to the property, even though the guardian misappropriates the proceeds of the sale [3] This rule applies to shares of stock [4] In most of the states, however, statutes have been passed requiring guardians to obtain the consent of a court before selling the personal property of his ward [5] If such a statutory permission to sell is required, and the vendee of stock has notice that his vendor sells as guardian, the vendee is bound to see that the requisite permission to sell has been given [6] An order of the court allowing the guardian to sell is not authority to him to pledge the stock, and the pledgee is bound to take notice of that fact [7] Where stock is sold by a foreign guardian according to the laws of the state of the guardianship, title passes and the purchaser is protected.[8]

§ 329 *Sales of stock by an executor or administrator* — It is the duty of an executor or administrator of an estate to collect the assets, pay the debts, and distribute the remainder according to the provision of the will or of the statute of distribution [9] In order

and dividends, by reason of its allowing a transfer by an unauthorized agent of the stockholder, the subsequent owners of the stock are not necessary parties. The defense of prescription may prevail St Romes *v* Cotton Press Co, 127 U S, 614 (1888)

[1] Id.

[2] Bohlen's Estate, *supra*.

[3] Field *v.* Schieffelin, 7 Johns Ch, 150 (1823), Ellis *v* Prop of E. M Bridge, 2 Pick, 243 (1824), holding that a *bona fide* purchaser from the guardian of a person *non compos mentis* is protected

[4] Lamar *v* Micou, 112 U S, 452 475 (1884), the court saying "He had the authority, as guardian, without any order of court, to sell personal property of his ward in his own possession, and to reinvest the proceeds" See, also, Bank of Va *v* Craig, 6 Leigh, 399, 432 (1835), to the same effect, and hold-

ing that the corporation is not liable for a breach of trust by the guardian in selling the stock The court said "If the guardian defrauds his ward, his sureties are responsible, if the purchaser combines in the fraud, he too is chargeable, but the bank cannot interfere and arrest the transfer of its stock by the legal holder of the scrip upon such pretenses It would trammel and embarrass such transactions so as to impede materially that transferable character, which is one of the most valuable attributes of stock "

[5] Mass R S, ch 79, § 21

[6] Atkinson *v.* Atkinson, 90 Mass., 15 (1864)

[7] Webb *v* Graniteville Mfg. Co, 11 S. C., 396 (1878), 130 U S, 267

[8] Ross *v* Southwestern R. R. Co, 52 Ga, 514 (1874).

[9] Keylinge's Case, 1 Eq. Cases Abr.,

to pay the debts the executor may sell the personal property of the estate. Accordingly, the rule has become established that the purchaser of personal property from an executor or administrator is not bound to ascertain whether the sale is necessary in order to pay the debts of the estate, nor to see that the proceeds of the sale are applied to the debts. If he buys in good faith and for value, he is protected. Such also are the rules applicable to an executor's or administrator's sales of stock.[1] The executors in the state of the decedent may transfer the stock of the estate, and convey a title which the corporation is bound to recognize, although the corporation itself is domiciled in another state.[2] The rule is otherwise, however, as regards executors appointed in jurisdictions out of the United States.[3]

An executor may pledge estate stock at his bank on a representation that the money is to be used for the estate, and the bank

239 (1702) holding that, where the executor holds the stock for several years and it declines in value, he is chargeable with its value one year after the death of the testator

[1] Leitch v Wells, 48 N Y, 585 (1872), holding that the *bona fide* transferee is protected, although the executors had previously set aside the same stock to apply to the payment of a certain amount chargeable by the will to the estate annually   Woods' Appeal, 92 Pa St , 379 (1880), holding that a *bona fide* transferee of the executor's transferee is protected, although the latter would not have been, even though the former was aware that his title came from an executor   The court held that letters of administration are always evidence of power to sell, and that an executorship differed widely from a trusteeship as regards the right to sell. Prall v Tilt, 27 N. J Lq , 393 (1876), affirmed, 28 N J Eq , 479 (1877), where the will authorized advances to the sons, and they represented to the transferee that the stock was so advanced to them by the executor   Lowry v Commercial & F Bank of Baltimore, Taney (U S. C. Ct.), 310 (1848)   In this case the purchaser had no knowledge or notice that the transferrer sold the stock as an executor.   Clark v. South

Metropolitan Gas Co , 54 L J (Ch), 259 (1885), sustaining a sale of stock by an administratrix of an administrator.   Re London, etc , Tel Co , L R , 9 Eq , 633 (1870), sustaining the title of a *bona fide* purchaser from the executrix as against an assignee in bankruptcy of the deceased, the assignee having delayed his application for five years

[2] Middlebrook v. Merchants' Bank, 3 Keyes (N. Y), 135 (1866), Luce v Manchester, etc , R. R. Co , 2 New Eng Rep., 263 (N. H , 1886), Hobbs v. Western Nat Bank, 8 Weekly Notes, 131 (U. S. C Ct., 1880).   An executor or administrator may transfer stock in a foreign corporation without taking out letters in the state incorporating the company. *In re* Cape, etc., Co , 16 Atl Rep., 191 (N J , 1889).

[3] Alfonso's Appeal, 70 Pa. St., 347 (1872), holding that, in Pennsylvania, executors of a decedent, whose domicile was in Cuba, have no authority, under letters testamentary in Cuba, to transfer stock in a Pennsylvania corporation   "Domestic creditors, legatees or next of kin should not be sent abroad in quest of property to answer their claims when the decedent left property within the jurisdiction of the state that can be applied to meet their demands."

will be protected although the note given by the executor is renewed several times, and the proceeds of the transaction were passed to the executor's private account.[1] So, also, a *bona fide* purchaser of stock from a life tenant, to whom the administrator improperly transferred it, is protected   The remainder-man's remedy is on the administrator's bond [2] But a pledge of stock by an executor does not protect the pledgee, where the pledgee does not rely on the executor's power, but requires other ineffectual precautions to be taken [3] Where the transferee of the executor knows that the transaction is not for the benefit of the estate, but is a breach of trust, he is not protected.[4] Frequently statutes are found requiring executors, when selling personal property of the estate, to sell the same at public auction. When such a statute exists a purchaser at private sale is not a *bona fide* purchaser, and is not protected, and is liable for the stocks and dividends paid thereon after his purchase [5] The *bona fide* transferee of such a

[1] Goodwin v American National Bank, 48 Conn , 550 (1881), Gottberg v United States Nat Bank, N Y L J , November 21, 1890. where the bonds were even registered in the names of both executors and were pledged by one Under the English act. where shares are registered in the names of two executors jointly, the signature of both to a transfer is necessary, and the company is liable if it permits a transfer by one Barton v. London, etc , R'y, 62 L T Rep , 164 (1889)

[2] Keeney v Globe Mill Co , 39 Conn , 145 (1872)

[3] Moore v American, etc , Co , 115 N. Y , 65 (1889).

[4] Prall v Hamil, 28 N J Eq , 66 (1877). The facts in this case differed from those in Prall v Tilt, *supra*, in that the transferee knew that the stock was still owned by the executrix White v Price, 39 Hun, 394 (1886), the court saying "A person who takes title from an executor in payment of the executor's personal debts is not a purchaser in good faith, and acquires no rights over the prior title or rights of other persons" Also, that a purchaser, buying with knowledge that the right of the executor to sell is denied and is

being contested, is not a *bona fide* holder Cf. Keane v Robarts, 4 Madd Ch , 332 (1819). where it was held that where the executor did business through an agent, the application of the proceeds from sale of the stock to the running account between the executor and his agent was legal A suit in equity lies to set aside an illegal sale of stock by an executor. White v Price, 108 N Y , 661 (1888) A pledgee with notice of stock held by an executor in breach of his duty may be compelled to give up the stock Odd. etc , Bank's Appeal, 16 Atl Rep 606 (Pa , 1889) A pledgee who takes with knowledge that the executor is giving the pledge in breach of trust cannot foreclose the pledge Bell v Farmers', etc , Bank, 18 Atl Rep , 1079 (Pa , 1890) If the administrator sells to himself through "dummies" he may be compelled to disgorge Carter v. Good, 10 N Y Supp , 647 (1890)

[5] Nutting v Thompson, 57 Ga , 418 (1876), the court saying also that factors or brokers acting for third persons are also liable. Nutting v Boardman, 43 Ga., 598 (1871), holding that the administrator's bondsmen are not proper parties to the suit, Weyer v. Second Nat.

purchaser, however, is protected[1] An executor may have the duties of a trustee to perform, and then become subject to the rules governing trustees in their transfers of stock.[2] While a corporation may, under ordinary circumstances, allow an executor or administrator to register a transfer of stock from himself to a purchaser from him, yet, when so long a time has elapsed between the taking out of letters and the transfer that the executor has become practically a trustee, then the corporation must use the same precautions as in sales by a trustee.[3]

§ 330. *Duty and liability of the corporation in sales by executors or administrators.*—There has been great difficulty in ascertaining the rights and duties of the corporation in allowing and refusing to allow a registry on the corporate transfer-book of a sale of stock by an executor or administrator. The Bank of England, at an early day, assumed the power to refuse to allow a registry of an executor's transfer of stock that had been specifically bequeathed, unless the executor satisfied the bank that the sale was necessary to pay the debts of the estate The courts, however, compelled it to allow registry without investigating specific legacies or the application of the proceeds of the sale.[4] In this country the question of the liability of the corporation has arisen on a different state of facts. The cases of Lowry v. Commercial & Farmers' Bank of

Bank of Franklin, 57 Ind, 198 (1877), holding the purchaser liable. If the executor uses the proceeds of sales of stock for his own personal purposes he is liable for the dividends declared after such sales up to time of accounting, and for market value of stock at time of accounting Person taking stock from him with knowledge of the breach of trust is also liable. McGeary's Appeal, 6 Atl Rep , 763 (Pa., 1886).

[1] Nutting v. Thomason, 46 Ga, 34 (1872).

[2] White v. Price, 39 Hun, 394 (1886); Prall v Tilt, *supra*

[3] Where an executor holds stock for nine years and then sells it in breach of trust, the purchaser is bound to take notice. The executorship becomes a trusteeship Peck v Bank of America, 19 Atl Rep., 369 (R. I , 1890). Where an executrix has power by the will to sell stock held in trust for heirs, the corporation is not liable for a transfer by her in breach of trust, the corporation having no knowledge thereof The fact that the stock is transferred to banks which have no power to purchase is not notice to the corporation The executorship in this case was merged into a trusteeship Peck v Prov. Gas Co , 23 Atl Rep , 967 (R. I , 1892).

[4] Pearson v. Bank of England, 2 Brown's Ch. Rep , 529 (1789), Bank of England v Moffat, 3 id , 260 (1791); Hartga v. Bank of England, 3 Ves , 55 (1796), Bank of England v. Parsons, 5 Ves , 665 (1800), Bank of England v Lunn, 15 Ves , 568 (1809), Austin v. Bank of England, 8 Ves , 522 (1803); Marryatt v Same, id , 524, n (1793); Aynsworth v Same, id , Franklin v. Same, 1 Russ Ch , 575 (1826), Churchill v Same, 11 M & W , 323 (1843), Humberstone v Chase, 2 Y & C Ex Rep , 209 (1836), where the executor represented that the specific legatee had died.

Baltimore,[1] and Stewart *v* Firemen's Ins Co ,[2] clearly establish the rule that, where the corporation has reasonable notice of the fact that the executor is committing a breach of trust, the notice arising from the fact that the transfer is made several years after the estate should have been wound up, the corporation is under obligation to refuse to allow a registry of the transfer, and, having allowed it, the corporation is liable to the parties injured thereby

Where, by statute, executors' sales are to be at public auction, the corporation is bound to ascertain whether the statute was complied with, and is liable for allowing a registry when the sale was a private one[3]   In general, a corporation has a right to assume that the executor is transferring the stock for the purposes of the estate.   It is not obliged to inquire into the purposes of the parties, nor to investigate whether the transaction is in good faith or is fraudulent,[4] nor to examine the will[5]

[1] Taney, U S. C Ct, 310 (1848)   The court said the corporation "not only enabled the executor to perpetrate the wrong by permitting the transfer, but co-operated in it by certifying that the title of transferee was good   Justice, therefore, requires that it should bear the loss."

[2] 53 Md , 564 (1880), holding also that the corporation was bound to take notice of the contents of the will — a position that is denied by the case of Hutchins' Adm'r *v* State Bank, 53 Mass , 421 (1847).   Where, however, the executrix has power given by the will to apply the stock to her own use in case of need, the corporation is not bound to ascertain whether such a state of need exists   Hutchins' Adm'r *v* State Bank, *supra*

[3] Weyer *v.* Second National Bank of Franklin, 57 Ind , 198 (1877)   A contrary view seems to be held in Southwestern R R Co. *v* Thomason, 40 Ga Rep , 408 (1869)   In Indiana, where an administrator cannot sell personal property except in a certain way, the corporation is liable to the estate if it allows a transfer of stock on its books under a sale by the administrator who has not complied with the law   The purchaser, however, who does not see the old certificates but takes new certificates issued by the corporation is protected   Citizens St R'y *v* Robbins, 26 N E Rep , 116 (Ind , 1891).   A sale of stock by an executor at private sale was sustained in Wilson *v* Proprietors of Central Bridge, 9 R I , 590 (1870), although the statute declares that executors should be liable for double the appraised value of the property if they sold at private sale

[4] Crocker *v* Old Colony R R. Co , 137 Mass , 417 (1884)   See, also, Carter *v* Manufacturers' Nat'l Bank, 71 Me , 448; Goodwin *v* American Nat'l Bank, 48 Conn., 550

[5] Although the administrator transfers the stock to the "heirs and distributees" the corporation is protected in issuing absolute certificates to such distributees, and is not bound to learn or know of a will to the effect that the distributee had only a life interest.   Smith *v* Nashville, etc , R. R., 18 S. W. Rep., 546 (Tenn., 1892).

CHAPTER XX.

SALES OF STOCK — THE FORMATION AND PERFORMANCE OF THE CONTRACT — GAMBLING SALES — FRAUDULENT SALES.

A. FORMATION AND PERFORMANCE OF CONTRACTS TO SELL STOCK.

§ 331 *Shares of stock are transferable* — That shares of stock in a corporation are transferable the same as other personal property is a principle of law coeval with the existence of stock itself. The few decisions holding that shares of stock were real estate were exceptional rulings, and are no longer considered to be good law [1] Courts of law and of equity have guarded jealously the facilities for the transfer of title to stock, and all unreasonable attempts to restrain the right or readiness of passing title have been declared void as against public policy. The right to transfer stock is of vital importance, since the two chief causes of the phenomenal growth of corporations in recent times are the limited liability of the members and the readiness of withdrawing from the corporation by a transfer of the interest a member has therein The common law regards shares of stock as personal property, capable

[1] See ch I.

446

of alienation or succession in any of the modes by which personal property may be transferred[1]

§ 332. *Restrictions on right to sell stock, and contracts against selling* — The right of a stockholder to sell and transfer his stock cannot be restrained by a by-law of the corporation[2] An agreement or contract, however, between the members, or a part of them, not to sell except on certain conditions, is valid, unless it amounts to an unreasonable restraint of trade[3] In New York a contract whereby stockholders of a corporation agree to deposit their certificates of stock with a trustee for six months, for the purpose of preventing any disposition of the stock during that time, is unenforceable and void, as contrary to the statute law of the state and against public policy[4] The right of transfer is sometimes limited by statute, as in New York, where stock in railroad or manufacturing corporations cannot be transferred until all calls

[1] Mobile Mutual Ins Co v Cullum, 49 Ala , 558 (1873), Cole v Ryan, 52 Barb., 168 (1868), Heart v State Bank, 2 Dev Eq , 111 (1831), Allen v Montgomery R. R. Co , 11 Ala , 437, 451 (1847), Boston Music Hall v Cory, 129 Mass., 435 (1880), Sargent v Franklin Ins Co, 8 Pick , 90 (1829) Chouteau Spring Co v Harris, 20 Mo , 382 (1855), Poole v Middleton, 29 Bear , 646 (1861) Brightwell v Mallory, 10 Yerg (Tenn). 196 (1836).

[2] Morgan v. Struthers, 131 U. S , 246, 252 (1889), Fechheimer v Nat'l Ex Bank, 79 Va , 80 (1884), where a by-law prohibiting transfers except with the consent of the directors was declared void, Bank of Attica v Manufacturers' & T Bank, 20 N Y , 501 (1859) Orr v Bigelow , 11 N Y , 556 (1856), Sargent v. Franklin Ins Co, 8 Pick , 90 (1829), Moore v Bank of Com , 52 Mo , 377 (1873) A by-law to the effect that a transfer of stock shall be allowed only upon consent of all the other stockholders is void as in restraint of trade In re Klaus, 29 N W Rep , 582 (Wis , 1886) As regards corporate liens herein. see ch XXXI, *infra* See, also as to the general policy of the law to discountenance restrictions on right to sell, Moffatt v Farquhar, L R . 7 Ch D . 591 (1878) In this case the directors were compelled to allow a transfer although the pur-

pose of the transfer was to multiply votes As already stated, a by-law that no stockholder shall transfer his stock except by the consent of all stockholders is void A secretary cannot refuse to register a transfer on account of the motive of the transferee In re Klaus *supra.*

[3] Griffith v Jewett. 15 Week L Bul, 419, and ch XXXII The foreclosure and sale of a pledge of stock in the Western Associated Press has been refused where it was shown that the stock merely entitled the holder to receive news , that no transfer was allowed except by consent of the association, and such consent had never been given, and the association was not made a party to the suit Metropolitan, etc , Bank v St Louis, etc , Co , 36 Fed Rep 722 (1888) In this case it is to be noticed that no profits or dividends could arise from the stock An agreement of the holder of a majority of the stock that he will retain control is no defense by the corporation to an action by the receiver of such stockholder to transfer the stock on the corporate books Weller v Pace Tobacco Co , 25 N Y Week. Dig , 531 (1886)

[4] Williams v Montgomery, 68 Hun, 416 (1893)

thereon shall have been fully paid.[1] Where the charter or a statute forbids transfers before the full capital stock is paid in, any transfer before such payment has been held to be void.[2]

In England sometimes express authority is given to the directors, by the articles of association, to refuse to permit a transfer unless the same is satisfactory to them.[3] They have this power, however, only by express authority, and it is not extended by implication.[4] The power must be reasonably exercised, and its exercise must be free from fraud, caprice and arbitrary power.[5] The corporation cannot refuse to allow a registry on the ground that there was no consideration for the transfer;[6] nor because a

[1] See Part VII, *infra*

[2] Merrill *v* Call, 15 Me, 428 (1839). The case of Quiner *v* Marblehead Ins Co, 10 Mass, 476 (1813), holds that nevertheless, such a transfer rests in the transferee all the transferrer's interest in the stock *Cf* Cohn *v* Bank of St. Joseph, 70 Mo, 262 (1879) The statutes of a state cannot restrict or interfere with the transferability of certificates of stock in national banks Doty *v* First Nat'l Bank of Larimore, 53 N W. Rep, 77 (N Dak, 1892).

[3] Shortridge *v*. Bosanquet, 16 Beav, 84 (1852), Bargate *v* Shortridge 5 H L Cases, 297 (1855). *In re* Joint-stock Discount Company, Shepherd's Case, L. R., 2 Eq Cas, 564 (1866)

[4] Weston's Case, L R, 4 Ch App., 20 (1868), Gilbert's Case, L R, 5 Ch App, 559 (1870), Chappell's Case, L R, 6 Ch. App, 902 (1871), *Re* Stranton Iron & Steel Co, L. R., 16 Eq, 559 (1873), Moffatt *v*. Farquhar, *infra*, Slee *v* International Bank, 17 L T. Rep, 425 Judge Dillon, in Johnson *v* Laflin, 5 Dill, 65, 78, affirmed, 103 U S, 800 (1878), says. "Such a power is so capable of abuse and so foreign to all received notions and the universal practice and mode of dealing in these stocks, that it cannot. in the absence of legislative expression, be held to exist." See, also, Farmers' & M Bank *v* Wasson, 48 Iowa, 336 (1878), the court holding that a by-law that transfers of stock shall not be valid unless approved by the board of directors cannot restrain transfers. "Its enforcement would operate as an infringement upon the property rights of others, which the law will not permit. It would, besides, operate as a restraint upon the disposition of property in the stock of the corporation, in the nature of restraint of trade, which the courts will not tolerate."

[5] They cannot refuse to allow any transfers. Robinson *v*. Chartered Bank, L R 1 Eq, 32 (1865) And an objection, not to the transferee, but to the purpose of the transferrer in respect to voting, is not sufficient. Moffatt *v* Farquhar, L R., 7 Ch D. 591 (1878) But the board may refuse to give its reasons for refusing to allow the transfer, and in that case it will be presumed to have had sufficient reason for the refusal *Ex parte* Penny, L R. 8 Ch, 446 (1872). If misrepresentations are made in inducing the directors to allow transfer, they, having discretion, may avoid the same Payne's Case, L R., 9 Eq, 223, Master's Case L R. 7 Ch, 292, Bishop's Case, L R., 7 Ch, 296 Although a transfer is rejected by the directors the transferee is nevertheless entitled to dividends and the title to the stock Poole *v* Middleton, 29 Beav, 646 (1861). Where the company may accept or reject a transferee and rejects him, the transferee cannot recover back from the transferrer the consideration of the transfer London, etc., Ass'n *v* Clarke, 59 L T Rep, 93 (1888).

[6] Helm *v* Swiggett, 12 Ind, 194 (1859).

claimant of the stock notifies it not to make the registry [1] In this country no such power is given to the directors A person who purchases stock is entitled to a transfer on the books

§ 333 *"Pools," "corners" and combinations in stock* — The courts will not aid either party in carrying out an agreement for advancing the price of stock by means of fictitious dealings designed to deceive others concerning the real value of such stock [2] Where both the vendor and vendee of stock know that the purpose of the vendee is to control the corporation and illegally issue corporate paper, the sale is illegal and void [3] An agreement to make a "corner" in stock, by buying it up so as to control the market and then purchasing the future deliveries, is illegal [4] It is not necessarily unlawful to form a "pool" for the purpose of dealing in a particular stock [5] An agreement to hold stock and sell together is valid [6]

[1] *Ex parte* Sargent, L. R., 17 Eq 273 (1873). *Cf* § 387, *infra*.

[2] Livermore *v* Bushnell, 5 Hun. 285 (1875) See, also, in general, § 445, note and ch XXXVII, *infra*

[3] Town Council, etc., *v* Elliott 5 Ohio St., 113 (1855)

[4] Sampson *v* Shaw 101 Mass 145 (1869), Raymond *v* Leavitt, 13 Cent L J, 110 (1881), Morris Run Coal Co *v* Barclay Coal Co 68 Pa St 173 (1871), Arnot *v* Pittston, etc, Coal Co 68 N Y, 558 (1877) Kemer *v* Kent (N Y Sup Ct, Gen T), Daily Reg, March 15 1887 *Cf* Petrie *v* Hannay, 3 Term R, 418 (1789) No suit lies against a broker for fraud in carrying out a pool or combination to "corner" and advance the price of lard Leonard *v* Poole, 114 N Y, 371 (1889) See, also, §§ 445 476 A person making a "corner" in stocks is not subject to a criminal prosecution therefor Raymond *v* Leavitt, 46 Mich 447 (1881) It is not fraud for the owner of the larger part of the capital stock of a corporation to "corner" the market, that is, to enter into contracts with various parties to purchase stock of the corporation, although he knew that such contracts could not be fulfilled by such parties by reason of the fact that he himself held such stock, and it could not be obtained elsewhere The same rule prevails although such person offered the stock for public subscription and purchased the greater part of it himself Salaman *v*. Warner, 64 L T Rep, 598 (1891) *Cf* Barry *v* Croskey, 2 J & H, 1 (1861) holding that the victim of the 'corner' may file a bill in equity to recover back the money lost.

[5] Quincey *v* White 63 N Y 370, 383 (1875), modifying Quincey *v* Young 5 Daly 32 (1873) Where several parties buy a certificate of stock in fixed proportions and the certificate is taken by one for the benefit of all, he is a bailee for the others and not a vendor Coquard *v* Wernse, 13 S. W Rep, 311 (Mo, 1890) The general rule that an action

[6] Havemeyer *v* Havemeyer, 11 J & S (N Y), 507 (1878), S C 13 id, 464, aff'd, 86 N Y., 618; Griffith *v* Jewett, 15 Week Law Bull, 419 — an important case But an agreement not to sell except by concurrent consent of all signers to the agreement is void as in restraint of trade and against public policy Fisher *v* Bush, 35 Hun, 651 (1885) See, also, § 320, *supra* For a full discussion of this subject, see ch XXXVII, *infra* For an interesting statement of the *modus operandi* of a "corner,' see "An Investor s Notes on American Railroads," by Swann, ch XII (1886) See ch XXXVII, relative to purchases for the purpose of affecting corporate elections

A contract by which a shareholder in a corporation agrees to secure to the purchaser of his stock a corporate office at a stated salary, and in case of his removal to repurchase the stock, is void as against public policy and as a fraud on other stockholders, unless it is proved that the transaction is not for the private benefit of the vendor, or that it was consented to by the other stockholders [1]   But a contract to convey a majority of the stock of a corporation, and to procure the resignation of the corporate directors, thereby enabling the vendee to elect directors satisfactory to himself, is a valid and legal agreement [2]   One railroad company cannot purchase a controlling interest in another railroad company for the purpose of managing or absorbing the latter, but this rule grows out of the fact that such purchases are beyond the powers of the corporation [3]   It is immaterial that a vendee already controls one railroad company, and that the stock contracted to be sold will give him the control of another.   He is entitled to the stock [4]   An agreement to contribute stock towards a common undertaking is enforceable, the consideration being the mutual obligation [5]   But the common undertaking must be a legal one [6]

affecting a joint enterprise for the purchase, upon speculation, of certain mining stocks must join all the parties who enter the "pool" does not necessitate the joinder of one who is out of the jurisdiction Angell t Lawton, 76 N Y, 540 (1879)   The representative of a syndicate after selling the stock cannot modify the contract He is liable to the others if he does so Kountz v Gates, 47 N. W. Rep., 729 (Wis., 1891) Where there is a joint operation in stocks, a "pool," the transactions being carried on in the name of one only, the others may have specific performance leading to a division of the stocks Johnson r Brooks, 46 N Y Super Ct., 13 (1880), Thornton r St. Paul. etc, R'y, 45 How Pi 416 (1873), S C dismissed, 6 Week Dig, 309

[1] Guernsey r Cook, 120 Mass., 501 (1876), Noyes v Marsh, 123 Mass, 286 (1877).

[2] See ch XXXVII, Barnes v Brown, 80 N Y, 527 (1880) Contra, Jacobs v. Miller, 15 Alb L J, 188 (1877), Fremont v Stone, 42 Barb, 169 (1864) Where the agreement was to keep the vendor in a professorship the court will not aid the parties The agreement is against public policy Jones v Scudder, 2 Cin Sup Ct., 173 (1872)

[3] See § 315.

[4] Havemeyer r Havemeyer, supra, O'Brien r Breitenbach, 1 Hilt, 304 (1857). Cf. § 315. n

[5] Conrad r La Rue, 52 Mich, 83 (1883) Where the stockholders enter into a contract by which they give a certain amount of their stock to a person who agrees to do certain work for the corporation in consideration of the stock, the remedy for a breach of contract on his part is an action for damages unless by the contract the stock was to be returned in case of non-performance Gillett v. Bowen, 23 Fed Rep, 625 (1885) If the action is to recover back the stock the corporation is a proper party in order to obtain a transfer Johnson r Kirby, 65 Cal, 482 (1884). See, also, in general, Cates v.

[6] If the purpose is to rob a railroad and bribe a judge, the court will aid no one. Tobey v. Robinson, 99 Ill, 202 (1881).

§ 334 *Contract for sale of stock may be valid without delivery or specific time for delivery* — Generally a sale of stock is attended with an immediate delivery of the certificates therefor, or it is agreed that the certificates shall be delivered at some specified time in the future. If, however, the vendor offers to sell his stock and the vendee accepts the offer, the contract is complete and binds both parties, although nothing has been said as to the time when the certificates of stock shall be delivered. The law implies that the contract will be performed by a delivery of the certificates immediately or within a reasonable time, and either party may insist upon carrying out the contract[1] Where the vendor says, in his

Sparkman, 11 S W Rep. 846 (Texas, 1889). For the construction of a contract by which the owners of all the stock of a mining company turned it over in pledge to parties who would furnish the money to carry on the mine, see Newton v Van Dusen, 50 N W Rep, 820 (Minn, 1891) For the construction of an agreement whereby a stock and bondholder deposits all his stock and bonds as security to another person who advances money to carry on the business, see Appeal of Huston, 18 Atl Rep., 419 (Pa, 1889). Where a stockholder owning a majority of the stock, transfers it to a person under a contract by the latter to do certain work for the corporation, and make a loan to the former and retain the former as president, but the stockholder endeavors to sell out to another party, his bill in equity to set aside the transfer as obtained by fraud will fail Healey v Loveridge, 19 Atl Rep, 921 (Md, 1890) Where, for the purpose of forwarding a corporate enterprise, one of its chief promoters contracts to give and sell to a third person certain bonds, etc, if the latter will do certain acts, the former cannot, after part performance by the latter, rescind and recover back the bonds, etc, unless he recompenses the latter for his part performance, nor can he rescind at all unless he can recompense the latter His remedy is for damages So though defendant is charged with fraud in refusing complete performance. Snow v. Alley, 11 N. E. Rep,

764 (Mass, 1887) In a joint operation in stocks no bill for an accounting will lie where by mutual consent the joint operation was ended and one sold his stock while the other held his Keller v Swartz, 20 Atl Rep, 627 (Pa, 1890)

[1] "The performance of a contract, or the tender of performance, is no part of the contract. The making of a contract is one thing, but the performance thereof, or the tender of performance, is another and quite different thing The contract set up in the paragraph in question is an executory one, by which the plaintiff agreed to sell to the defendant the shares of stock, and the defendant agreed to pay him therefor the sum of $2,500 No time was fixed for the performance, the law will imply, therefore that it was to be performed immediately, or perhaps within a reasonable time Had a future day been agreed upon for the performance of the contract on each side, there could have been no doubt as to its validity, or the right of either party to enforce it he having done all he was required to do on his part The fact that no time was agreed upon for performance does not change the character of the contract. The contract did not pass any title to the stock, but it was, nevertheless, a valid contract and one which either party can enforce, he having been in no default himself" Bruce v Smith 44 Ind, 1 (1873), Kerchuer v Gettys, 18 S C, 521 (1882), Cheale v Kenward, 3 De G. & J, 27 (1858) Usage

451

contract, " I have sold " certain stock, deliverable at seller's option.
within a specified time, a sale *in præsenti* is made, and the vendor
assumes to have the stock and to hold it for the benefit of the purchaser until delivery.[1]   An agreement to purchase stock when the
corporation is created is enforceable only after a complete and
legal incorporation is effected [2] A sale of stock with an agreement
to take it back whenever the vendee desires is an enforceable contract.[3]

Great difficulty often arises in determining whether a contract
of sale of stock is an executed or is merely an executory contract
of sale.   There are a few general rules on this subject,[4] but each

may determine what is a reasonable time
for delivery Seven days held reasonable.
Stewart r Cauty, 8 M & W, 160 (1841)
In a contract by which one "agrees to
deliver" to the other certain stock at a
certain price, performance is to be
within a reasonable time, and the vendor
may tender the stock and then sue for
the price Boehm *v.* Lies, 18 N. Y. Supp.,
577 (1892). Specific performance of a
contract to sell stock will not be enforced, where the time of performance
and of payment is not fixed, and where
five years have elapsed, and where the
vendee, the corporate secretary, misrepresented the value of the stock to
the vendor Diamond, etc, Co. *v*
Todd, 14 Atl Rep, 27 (Del, 1888). An
agreement to transfer stock at any time
to a trustee, for creditors, is not enforceable against the insolvent estate
of the deceased stockholder Chafee
v Sprague, 13 Atl Rep, 121 (R. I,
1888) An offer to sell stock with a
statement that the stock could probably
be sent with a draft, even when accepted
with a direction to send it on, does not
make a binding contract. Topliff *v.*
McKendree, 50 N. W. Rep, 109 (Mich,
1891). Where stock is sold on condition
that the vendee shall be "in a position
to take up the stock," the condition is
fulfilled if the vendee accepts the stock
and acts as a director, and holds the
stock for five months. Wills *v* Fisher,
17 S E Rep, 73 (N C, 1893)

[1] Currie *v* White, 45 N Y, 822 (1871)
When the option is exercised the time

of delivery as fixed is as though that
time had been specified in the original
contract Kelley *v* Upton, 5 Duer, 336
(1866), holds otherwise where the contract has also the words "at buyer's option in ninety days" Such a contract
is executory as to time of passing title,
and tender is necessary.

[2] Childs *v.* Smith, 55 Barb,, 45 (1869).
If stock is sold conditionally, and the
condition does not happen, the sale is
void Mitchell *v* Wedderburn, 11 Atl
Rep, 760 (Md, 1887)

[3] See § 339

[4] A contract of sale of stock was
worded as follows

"I hold of the stock of the Washington and Hope Railway Company $33,250
or 1,350 shares, which is sold to Paul F
Beardsley (the appellee), and which,
though standing in my name, belongs
to him, subject to a payment of $8,000,
with interest at same rate and from
same date as interest on my purchase of
Mr Alderman's stock "

The court held that this was an executed contract, by which the ownership
of the stock passed to the purchaser,
with a reservation of title, simply as
security for the purchase-money — an
equitable mortgage The court pointed
out the difference between an executed
and executory contract of sale as follows

"If an agreement to sell, the moving
party must be the purchaser If a sale,
an executed contract with reservation
of security, the moving party is the

contract for the sale of stock is construed and enforced by the courts according to the intent of the parties as manifested by the written terms and conditions of the contract itself. Various contracts relative to the sale of stock are explained and referred to in the notes below[1]. Many cases are also referred to in the notes

vendor, the one retaining security. If an agreement to sell, the moving party, the purchaser, must within a reasonable time tender performance or make excuse therefor. If an executed contract, a completed sale, then the moving party is the vendor, the security holder, and he assumes all the burdens and risks of delay

. . . "It is not always easy to determine whether an instrument is a contract of sale or one to sell, yet certain rules of interpretation have become established

. 'Where the buyer is by the contract bound to do anything as a consideration, either precedent or concurrent, on which the passing of the property depends, the property will not pass until the condition be fulfilled, even though the goods may have been actually delivered into the possession of the buyer." Beardsley v. Beardsley, 138 U. S., 262 (1891).

[1] An offer to sell stock, open to acceptance after January 1st, must be accepted before July 9th. Park v. Whitney, 19 N. E. Rep., 161 (Mass., 1889). An agreement of a party to sell bonds for another party at a certain price may be enforced by the party who is to give the bonds to the other party to sell. Plumb v. Campbell, 18 N. E. Rep., 790 (Ill., 1888). The vendor may guaranty that the stock will be at par within a certain time. Suit lies if it is not at par within that time. Hill v. Smith, 21 How., 283 (1858). The fact that the corporation loses a large amount of money after a partner agrees to take stock as a part of his share of the partnership assets does not allow him to decrease the price which it was estimated to be worth. Donahue v. M'Cosh, 30 N. W. Rep., 14 (Iowa, 1886). Only a *de facto*

corporation need be proved. Reynolds v. Myers, 51 Vt., 444 (1879). A contract guarantying a certain dividend over and above certain corporate expenses does not include payment of salaries etc. Central etc. Assoc. v. James, 7 S. E. Rep., 862 (Ga., 1888). A guaranty upon the sale of stock that certain dividends will be declared is enforceable against the guarantying firm, even though they acted as agents for an undisclosed principal. Their obligation is primary, and not that of guarantors for the company. Kernochan v. Murray, 111 N. Y., 306 (1888). The memoranda of the contract together with the certificates of stock, are sufficient presumptive evidence of the existence of the corporation and the legal issue of the stock. Mann v. Williams, 9 N. E. Rep., 807 (Mass. 1887). See also, Lindley on Partnership, pp. 719, etc. 4th edition (Callaghan & Co., 1881). Where stock is issued to a person for construction work and he sublets the contract and agrees to divide the stock with others who are to share the expense of construction they all are liable to the subcontractor. M'Fall v. M'Keesport, etc., Co., 16 Atl. Rep., 478 (Pa., 1889). An option to purchase stock within three years is enforceable though one party has an option which the other has not. Seddon v. Rosenbaum, 9 S. E. Rep., 326 (Va., 1889). When a subscriber to stock agrees to sell $5,000 worth of the same at its "original cost," such cost is the cost to the subscriber and not the par value, nor the cost including loans by the subscriber to the corporation. Eagan v. Chisbey 13 Pac. Rep. 430 (Utah, 1887). Where a person sells goods to a corporation and agrees to make payment in stock, he must take the stock at par, even though its actual and market value

below relative to the contracts and rights of agents, promoters and partners in the purchase or sale of stock.[1]

§ 335. *Remedies for breach of a contract to sell stock.* — A person who is under contract to sell and deliver shares of stock may fulfill

is much less than par Tilkey v Augusta, etc, R. R., 10 S. E. Rep., 448 (Ga., 1889) A contract calling for "original ground floor or treasury stock" means any of the stock that is issued, where the statutes prohibit fictitious stock All the stock is then presumed to be "ground floor" stock and to represent at par the actual value received Williams v Searcy, 10 S Rep, 632 (Ala, 1891) A contract by a corporation that it will issue its stock for one-fifth of its par value is void under the Alabama constitutional prohibition The subscriber having sold his contract to another person cannot collect on such sale. Williams v. Evans, 6 S. Rep, 702 (Ala, 1889). See ch III An agency to sell the stock of a company refers to the stock then issued by the company. Gates v National, etc, Union, 49 N W. Rep, 232 (Minn, 1891) An executory contract to purchase stock is not such a claim against the estate of an insolvent vendee as to be provable against the assignee *In re* Ives, 11 N Y. Supp, 650 (1890) A vendor of the stock of a street railway company may collect damages for breach of the contract of the vendee to construct the street railway to certain land owned by the vendor, even though the corporation, the stock of which was sold, had agreed to acquire certain rights of way and had not done so. Blagen v Thompson, 31 Pac. Rep, 647 (Ore, 1892) Where a vendor of stock, in addition to the price received, is to have an additional sum equal to the highest price paid to any others for their stock, he cannot recover such additional price by proof that the vendee, in order to stop a stockholder's suit, paid a higher price for other stock Stewart v. Huntington, 124 N Y. 127 (1890).

was to divide with the vendor the amount for which the stock should be resold by the vendee, see Jones v Kent, 80 N Y, 585 (1880). An agreement to divide the profits on stock in consideration of information to be furnished is enforceable Parsons v. Robinson, 15 N Y Supp, 138 (1891), aff'd, 133 N Y, 537 A contract whereby an agent, one of the partners, is to have half of what he could sell partnership shares of stock for, is legal and enforceable by him Wright v Wood, 85 N Y, 402 (1881) A promoter who has brought about the sale of a large plant to new parties who have agreed to organize a new corporation and give the promoter a certain amount of stock therein, cannot, upon the ground that he is being defrauded of his commissions, enjoin the parties from closing the transaction irrespective of the promoter, nor can he have specific performance of the contract to incorporate a company and deliver the stock. There is no fiduciary relation between the parties, the value of the stock can be estimated in damages, there was no allegation of defendant's insolvency, and the promoter has ample remedy at law for damages Avery v Ryan, 43 N. W Rep, 317 (Wis, 1889). The question of whether a sale or pledge was involved in the relations between a contractor and the party who financiered the matter for him was involved in Griggs v Day, 11 N Y Supp, 885 (1890). The fact that a vendee makes out a check to a person and delivers it to him in payment for stock does not prove that the latter is the vendor and liable for misrepresentations. Aron v De Castro, 131 N Y. 648 (1892). For a breach of an agreement to give a certain quantity of stock in payment for services to be performed, the person entitled to the stock may sue for damages. Alford v Wil-

[1] For a sale of stock where the vendee

454

the obligation on his part by tendering to the vendee certificates of stock duly indorsed by himself, and containing a power of attorney authorizing the vendee to obtain a registry of the transfer on the corporate books[1] It has been held, however, and evidently

son, 20 Fed Rep, 96 (1884) The corporation is not liable for the breach of an agreement among the organizers as to the distribution of stock Summerlin v Fronteriza, etc, Co, 41 Fed Rep, 249 (1890) Nothing is more common than for the promoters of a company to agree to sell property to the company in consideration of a certain number of paid-up shares and it is certainly difficult to see why such a contract if valid and binding on both parties, should not be enforced, indeed, there is authority for specific performance in such a case See Fyfe v Swabey, 16 Jur, 49 M R Where a party to a contract relative to an incorporation and division of the stock sues to recover his interest according to the contract. the court will decree a proper division of the stock all parties being allowed the amounts invested by them in forwarding the enterprise. Bates v Wilson, 24 Pac Rep, 99 (Colo, 1890) Where the owner of a patent agrees to convey it to a corporation for stock, and then to divide the stock with others, he may be compelled to perform his agreement But where the patentee does not convey the patent to the corporation, but conveys to another corporation the latter is protected in its title, though some of its incorporators and directors knew all the facts. Davis, etc, Co. v Davis, etc., Co 29 Fed Rep, 699 (1884) Where a patentee agrees with a promoter to sell the patent to the corporation for stock, and divide the stock with the promoter, but the patentee after obtaining the stock sells the certificates to a *bona fide* purchaser the latter is protected though the transfer is not registered on the corporate books The purchaser may come into a suit instituted by the promoter against the corporation to compel a transfer Thurber v Crump 6 S W Rep, 145

(Ky 1887) Where a person holds property in trust or as agent for others and conveys that property to a corporation for its shares of stock the persons who had an equitable interest in the property may compel this agent or trustee to transfer to themselves such stock But all of the principals or *cestuis que trust* must be made parties to the suit O Conner v Irvine, 16 Pac Rep. 236 (Cal, 1887) Where there is a joint operation in stocks a "pool," the transactions being carried on in the name of one only the others may have specific performance leading to a division of the stocks Johnson v Brooks, 46 N Y Super Ct, 13 (1889) Thornton v St Paul, etc, Ry, 45 How Pr, 416 (1873), S C, dismissed 6 Week Dig, 309 Equity has jurisdiction to compel the transfer of stock as between parties Thus where stock is issued in payment for property and the party to whom the certificate is issued refuses to divide it among the owners of the property as provided by contract, a court of equity may compel the division and may enjoin any election of the corporation until such division is made Archer v American etc, Co, 24 Atl Rep, 508 (N J 1892) It is a question of fact whether a person selling stock is an agent or vendee of the person from whom he obtained the stock and whether the latter is liable on misrepresentation made by such person Henneberger v Mather, 50 N W Rep, 369 (Mich, 1891), Florida, etc, Co v Merrill, 52 Fed Rep, 63 (1892) A party selling stock is not liable for the false representations of the vendee to another person to whom the vendee is reselling the stock Masterton v Boyce, 6 N Y Supp 65 (1889)

[1] When certificates of shares are given to a purchaser they are analogous to the sale of chattels, and the assign-

with good reason, that if the vendee objects to the tender, on the ground that he wishes a registry of the transfer to be made on the corporate books, the vendor must cause such registry to be made in order to render his tender complete [1] A tender of a certificate indorsed in blank, not by the vendor but by some previous owner, is insufficient The vendee is not obliged to trace his vendor's title from the name appearing on the certificate [2] In England, where a transfer of shares is to be made by a deed, it is the duty sometimes of the vendor,[3] and sometimes of the vendee,[4] to furnish the necessary deed, according to the custom of the market in which the sale is made If, after the vendee accepts a tender of the certificates, the corporation refuses to allow a registry and transfer on the corporate books, the vendor is liable to him, since the registry is held to have been guarantied [5] The vendee may decline to accept the certificates if the stock has been attached.[6] But the vendee cannot decline the tender on the ground that the corporation has issued stock at a discount, nor because it has mortgaged its property [7] A contract whereby stock is sold to be paid for in the future is not forfeited by mere failure to pay as agreed upon [8]

---

ment and delivering of the certificate is a symbolical delivery of the shares themselves." Noyes t Spaulding, 27 Vt., 420 (1855), Merchants' Nat'l Bank t Richards, 6 Mo App, 454 (1879), Eastman v Fiske, 9 N H, 182 (1838), Munn v Barnum, 24 Barb, 283 (1857), Bruce v. Smith, 44 Ind, 1 (1873) Cf Moore v Hudson River R. R. Co, 12 Barb 156, 21 N E Rep, 242 (Mass, 1889), 5 N Y Supp, 937, 940

[1] White, Executor, t Salisbury, 33 Mo, 150 (1862)

[2] Hare v Waring, 3 M & W, 362 (1838), per B. Parke "The party is to convey and deliver certificates showing either on the face of them or from the indorsements that the title is in the person conveying."

[3] Stephens v. De Medina, 4 Q B., 422 (1843)

[4] Shaw v. Rowley, 16 M. & W, 810 (1847)

[5] Wilkinson t Lloyd, 7 Q B., 27 (1845)

[6] Eastman v Fiske, 9 N H, 182 (1838)

[7] Noyes t Spaulding 27 Vt, 420 (1855) See, also, § 349, etc, infra

[8] Chater v San Francisco Sugar Refining Co, 19 Cal, 219 (1861), where payment was made in notes and labor, and the notes were not paid Subsequent dividends on the stock are to be applied to the payment of such notes when the dividends have been received by the vendor A sale of stock to take effect when a note given in payment is paid does not enable the vendee to claim the stock long subsequently, the note not having been paid Davison v Davis, 125 U S 90 (1888) Where, however, two parties, one owning stock, the other bonds contract to exchange the same, delivery being in escrow at once, and absolutely after the performance of certain things, a failure of one party to perform on his part enables the other to have the contract canceled by a court of equity Wilson v Roots, 10 N E Rep, 204 (Ill, 1887) Where fifty shares of stock are sold but only twenty-five shares are delivered, and the vendor declines to deliver the balance, a suit by the vendor on the ground of fraud and a rescission will fail Matthews v. Cady,

A person who is under contract to purchase stock cannot defeat that contract by the fact that the corporation was insolvent, even at the time the contract was entered into [1] An agreement to deliver stock free and clear of all incumbrances does not refer to incumbrances against the corporation.[2] The legality of the sale of stock is governed by the law of the state within which it is made [3] It is no defense to a contract to buy stock for the vendee to allege that the directors have committed an *ultra vires* act in issuing more stock at a discount [4]

§ 336 Difficulty is often experienced in determining what the measure of damages is for breach of a contract relative to the sale of stock In certain cases, where the stock has been delivered or tendered, the measure of damages is the purchase price fixed by the contract itself [5] The vendor may tender the stock to the vendee

61 N Y, 651 (1875) Although a party to whom bonds and stock have been sold or issued to be paid for in installments has paid in part and is unable to pay the remainder, the vendor cannot rescind and demand back the securities unless he returns the money already paid American Water-works Co v Venner, 18 N Y Supp , 379 (1892). Where the owner of a majority of the stock sells it, the purchase price being only paid in part, and retains the stock in his own name until the full price is paid, he cannot be compelled to deliver the stock or to refrain from ousting the vendee from the presidency of the corporation where the vendee fails to meet the other payments, even though the vendee has proceeded to improve the property Stockton v Russell, 54 Fed. Rep. 224 (1892)

[1] Rudge v Bowman, L R 3 Q B, 689 (1868), Gordon v Parker, 10 La Rep , 56 (1836), where the question of whether fraud was involved was submitted to the jury See § 349 *et seq* Crubb v Miller, 19 W R , 519 (1871), where by reason of a winding up a transfer on the corporate books was no longer possible, Kerchner v Gettys, 18 S C , 521 (1882), holding that a loss by the corporation of its property is no defense Damages cannot be recovered for the breach of an executory contract to pur-

chase stock, if at the time of making the contract the corporation had been dissolved and the purchaser was not aware of that fact. Kip v Monroe 29 Barb 579 (1859).

[2] Williams v Hanna, 40 Ind , 535 (1872)

[3] Dow v Gould & S C M Co 31 Cal . 629 (1867)

[4] Faulkner v Hebard, 26 Vt 152 (1854) Fraud is a defense, see §§ 349-357

[5] Where the stock is sold to be delivered thereafter, and the vendee refuses to accept the stock, the vendor may tender the stock and then sue for the contract price The court said "The court refused to instruct the jury that it was necessary for Morgan to sell the stock on the market for the best price he could get, and that the measure of damages would be the difference between the price thus obtained and the contract price, and this refusal is assigned for error Of course, the seller would be at liberty, after tender and refusal, to adopt this course, but it was not essential to his right of action The measure of damages was the difference between the market price of the stock at the time of the breach and the contract price This is the ordinary rule, but there was evidence that the stock had no value, and there is no certainty — indeed no proof — that upon a resale any price could have been obtained for

and sue for the price, or may sell after notice to the vendee and then sue for the difference, or may retain the stock and sue for the

the stock, or that it had any market value when Parker finally refused to take Under these circumstances we see no reason why the price agreed to be paid should not be adopted as the measure of damages, if that was the only mode by which full compensation could be made for the breach of the contract by the purchaser ' Mobley v Morgan, 6 Atl Rep, 604 (1886) "In the absence of special circumstances in an action for conversion of personal property as well as one for failure to deliver it in performance of a contract where consideration has been received, the value of the property at the time of such conversion or default, with interest, is the measure of compensation" Barnes v Brown, 130 N Y , 372 (1892) As to the remedies for a breach, see, also, Benjamin on Sales §§ 428–498 For the measure of damages, see chapter XXXV, infra As regards the pleadings in an action by a vendor of stock to recover damages against the vendee for refusal to accept and pay for stock which the latter had agreed to accept at a stated price, one year from date, if the former desired to sell, see Strothers v Drexel, 122 U S, 487 (1887) The vendor may claim damages for a breach in that the vendee does not pay the contract price and take the stock, or he may bring an action "in effect for the specific performance thereof," in which case he must allege readiness to deliver the stock Corning v Roosevelt, 11 N Y Supp , 758 (1890) The court will compel the vendee to take and pay for stock where it would compel the vendor to deliver the stock if he defaulted on the contract to sell. Bumgardner v Leavitt, 13 S E Rep., 67 (West Va , 1891) Where the vendor gets judgment for the price of the stock sold but not delivered the court will order him to deposit the stock with the court or lose his judgment McKeever v Dady, 18 N Y Supp, 439

(1892) In the case Penn v. McGibben. 53 Fed Rep, 86 (1892), the court granted specific performance of a contract to sell stock in behalf of the vendor and against the vendee. The court said: "The agreement was in form a contract to buy all the shares of stock in the incorporated companies The language of the contract shows that the real agreement was to buy certain real estate, together with the personal property connected with its use for milling and distilling purposes Without discussing the question whether the sale of shares of stock can be specifically enforced in equity, it is sufficient to say that the sale here was in fact a sale of real estate, and the circumstance that personally was included in the sale would not affect the power of a court of equity to afford relief by requiring specific performance" The measure of damages for breach of a contract to purchase stock is the difference between the contract price and the market value of the stock at the time and place of delivery with interest. Corser v Hale et al, 21 Atl Rep, 285 (Pa, 1892). Where a vendee refuses to carry out an executory contract for the sale of shares, the measure of damages is the difference between the price as fixed by the contract and the value of the stock at the time of tender and refusal of the vendee to fulfill See Barned v Hamilton, 2 Rail & Canal Cas, 624 (1841), Tempest v Kilner, 3 C B, 249 (1846), and Stewart v Cauty, 8 Mees & W., 160 (1841) In Shaw v Holland, 15 Mees. & W., 136 (1846), the proper measure of damages is said to be the difference between the contract price and the market price on the day when the contract was broken If a person sells and conveys property to a company to be paid for in stock, and the vendee refuses to deliver, he may recover the value of the stock Humeston v Tel Co, 20 Wall, 20 (1873)

difference between the contract and market price.[1] The statute of limitations may be a bar to the action [2]

The vendee's remedy for a failure on the part of the vendor to deliver is an action for damages [3] or a bill in equity to obtain spe-

Where an agent to sell stock is to have any excess of price over a sum named to him by the vendor and the agent finds a customer at an advanced price and the vendor refuses to sell, the agent may recover such profit as he lost thereby Matting v Roach, 23 Pac Rep., 1117 (Cal, 1891) See, also, as to agents, § 334, *supra*

[1] The vendor's remedies for a breach of a contract to buy stock are (1) To hold the stock for the vendee and require payment of the entire price, (2) to sell after notice to the vendee and sue for the difference between the contract price and selling price, (3) to retain the stock and sue for the difference between the contract price and the market value price *In re* Ives, 11 N Y Supp, 650 (1890) No tender is necessary when the suit is for damages and the vendor intends to retain the stock Nyce v ander v. Lowman, 24 N E Rep, 355 (Ind, 1890) When suit is brought to recover the price of stock sold a delivery or tender must be shown Holmes, etc, Co v Morse, 53 Hun, 58 (1889) Where a party is sued on a note he may recoup by setting up that the note was given to plaintiff on plaintiff's agreement to assign and deliver certain shares of stock, which was not tendered until eight months after the time agreed upon Hill v Southwick, 9 R I, 299

[2] Williams v Meyer, 41 Hun, 545 (1886). The statute of limitations runs against a receipt reciting a first payment of stock ' standing in my name but owned by him, and he remaining responsible for the balance of the instalments when called in," there being no agreement as to the future disposition of the stock and of dividends Cone v Dunham, 20 Atl Rep, 311 (Conn, 1890) A sale of a certificate to the effect that when stock is issued a

specified amount will be issued to the holder is a valid sale and is not defeated by the statute of limitations Meehan v Sharp 24 N E Rep, 907 (Mass, 1890) Where certain owners of stock place it in the hands of a trustee for sale and the trustee invites subscriptions thereto, the subscription contract providing for payment of one-third down and the balance when called for, the statute of limitations is no bar to an action for the two-thirds, although six years have elapsed since the first payment was made Williams v Taylor, 120 N Y, 244 (1890)

[3] A person entitled by contract to purchase stock of another may collect damages against the latter for failure to comply Rand v Wiley, 29 N W. Rep 814 (Iowa, 1886) Where a person is paid for stock and fails to deliver the measure of damages for a breach of the contract is what it would cost the party to purchase the stock which he is entitled to If he cannot purchase it, then the par value of the stock is the measure of value, inasmuch as he would have had to pay that to the corporation in order to have had the stock issued to him Barnes v Seligman, 55 Hun, 339 (1890) Where a vendor of stock in a corporation which has a franchise, but nothing else is entitled to two thousand shares of full-paid stock at a later date, according to the contract of sale, his measure of damages for failure of the vendee to deliver the two thousand shares is nominal damages where there was no market or actual value for the stock Barnes v Brown, 130 N Y, 372 (1892) Where the vendor of stock is unable to obtain the stock for delivery by reason of an injunction against the corporation the vendee may sue for the return of the purchase-money Rose v Foord, 30 Pac Rep., 1114 (Cal, 1892)

cific performance[1] In almost all cases, however, his remedy is an action for damages only, inasmuch as specific performance of a sale of personalty is rarely granted

§ 337. *Specific performance as a remedy for breach of a contract to sell stock.* — It frequently happens that the person who has contracted to purchase stock is particularly anxious to procure that stock, and that, under the circumstances of the case, the stock is worth to him a value not to be compensated for by mere money damages. This cannot happen in the case of a contract to sell securities issued by the government, since they may be easily purchased in the market. Accordingly it is well established, both in England and America, that a contract for the sale of government securities will not be specifically enforced by a court of equity, but the vendee may sue the vendor in an action at law for damages for breach of contract[2]

§ 338. An entirely different rule prevails as regards contracts for the sale of stock of private corporations If the stock contracted to be sold is easily obtained in the market, and there are no particular reasons why the vendee should have the particular stock contracted for, he is left to his action for damages. But where the value of the stock is not easily ascertainable, or the stock is not to be obtained readily elsewhere, or there is some particular and reasonable cause for the vendee's requiring the stock contracted to be delivered, a court of equity will decree a specific performance and compel the vendor to deliver the stock

This rule, as applicable to contracts for the sale of railway stock, was clearly established in England in 1841, in the case of Duncuft v Albrecht[3] Contracts for the sale of stock in mining and other

---

[1] See next section

[2] Ross v Union Pacific Ry Co, 1 Woolw, 26, 32 (1863) Cud or Culdee v Rutter, 1 P Wms Rep, 570 (1719), 5 Viner's Abr, 538 (1715), Dorison v Westbrook, 5 Viner's Abr, 540 (1722), Cappur v Harris, Bunbury's Rep, 135 (1723), Colt v Netterville, 2 P Wms., 304 (1725), Buxton v Lister, 3 Atk, 383 (1746). Cf Daloret v. Rothschild, 1 Sim & S, 590 (1824)

[3] Duncuft v Albrecht, 12 Sim, 189 (1841), Parish v Parish, 32 Bear 207 (1863), granting also an accounting of dividends, Poole v Middleton, 29 Bear, 646 (1861), Turner v May 32 L T (N S), 56 (1875), Beckitt v Billsbrough, 8 Hare, 188 (1850), *dictum Contra, dictum* in

Ross v Union Pacific R'y Co, 1 Woolw 26, 32 (1863), per Miller, J In Cheale v. Kenward, 3 De G & J, 27 (1858), the court said "There is no doubt that a bill will lie for a specific performance of an agreement to transfer railway shares. This was set at rest by Duncuft v Albrecht.' In the case of Leach v Fobes, 77 Mass, 506 (1858), specific performance of a contract to convey land and stock was granted chiefly because of the land part of the contract. Todd v Taft, 89 Mass, 371 (1863), decreed specific performance of contract to convey railway shares, also Baldwin v Commonwealth, 11 Bush, 417 (1875), Ashe v Johnson's Administrator, 2 Jones' Eq (N C) 149 (1855) As to

460

private corporations will also be specifically enforced under like circumstances [1]

Specific performance is often granted as between several parties each of whom is entitled to a certain part of stock which is re-

when specific performance of a contract to sell stock will be specifically enforced, see, also, White & Tudor s Leading Cases in Equity, vol I, pp. 914–923, etc. As to possibility of mandatory injunction in any case, see authorities in Hilliard on Injunction, p. 7, note *a*

[1] Treasurer *v* Commercial Coal Min Co, 23 Cal, 390 (1863). See, also, Frue *v.* Houghton, 6 Col, 318 (1882) As applicable to manufacturing corporations, see Chater *v* San Francisco S R Co, 19 Cal 200 (1861) Granted in towboat association in White *v* Schuyler, 1 Abb Pr (N S), 300 (1865) Refused in the case of stock in a land association Jones *v* Newhall, 115 Mass, 244 (1874). And in a paper company Noyes *v.* Marsh, 123 Mass., 286 (1877). See Cushman *v* Thayer Mfg Co, 76 N Y, 365 (1879) "While the general rule is for courts of equity not to entertain jurisdiction for a specific performance on the sale of stock this rule is limited to cases where a compensation in damages would furnish a complete and satisfactory remedy" This case, however, is not a case of specific performance of a sale of stock, but of compelling the corporation to register a transfer See, also, in general, Austin *v* Gillaspie, 1 Jones' Eq, 261 (1854), Nutbrown *v* Thornton, 10 Vesey, 160 (1804), Shaw *v* Fisher, 5 De G., M. & G., 596 (1855), Wynne *v* Price, 3 De G & Sm, 310 (1849), Wilson *v* Keating, 7 W R, 484 (1859), Oriental Co. *v* Briggs, 2 J. & H, 625 (1861), Paine *v* Hutchinson, L R, 3 Eq, 257 (1866); Shepherd *v* Gillespie, L R, 5 Eq, 293 (1867), Birmingham *v* Sheridan, 33 Beav, 660 (1864): Strasburg *v* Echternacht, 21 Pa St, 220 (1853); Fallon *v* Railroad Co, 1 Dill, 121 (1871) In regard to a specific performance of a trust of stock, see Ferguson *v* Paschall, 11 Mo, 267 (1848), Cowles *v*

Whitman, 10 Conn, 121 (1834). Clark *v* Flint, 22 Pick, 231 (1839), Mechanics' Bank *v* Seton, 2 Peters, 299 (1828) Specific performance of a contract to sell stock will be decreed where the stock has no recognized market value, and cannot be bought in the market Appeal of Goodwin, etc, Co, 12 Atl Rep. 736 (Pa, 1888) Specific performance was refused in Eckstein *v* Downing, 9 Atl Rep, 626 (N H 1887), there being no evidence that the vendee had any wish or reason for wishing to own that particular stock or stock in that particular corporation See also, Cruse *v* Paine, L R, 6 Eq 641 Where a stockholder, who is also a director, contracts to give a person a certain amount of stock if he will do certain work for the corporation, and the board of directors, including this director discharge such person without cause, and thus prevent completion, a court of equity will compel a delivery of the stock Price *v* Minot, 107 Mass, 49 (1871). In suits in equity to compel a transfer of stock, parties interested by a purchase from the defendant should be brought in O Connor *v* Irvine, 16 Pac Rep, 236 (Cal, 1887) Specific performance of a contract to sell stock will be decreed where the property of the corporation is real estate — a brewery — and the real transaction is a sale of the entire property Megibben's Adm'rs *v* Penn, 49 Fed Rep, 183 (1892). Specific performance will not be decreed where there is doubt as to the contract actually being made and doubt as to the consideration, one party being dead Hibbert *v* Mackinnon, 49 N W Rep, 21 (Wis 1891) Where a debtor agreed to transfer stock as collateral security for a debt, and died insolvent before doing so, the court refused to enforce specific performance of the agreement to the injury of other

ceived by or held in the name of one of them   A court will compel him to distribute the stock in accordance with the contract   Such cases arise often in "pools" of stock, and in selling property

creditors.   City, etc, Ins Co. *v.* Olmstead, 33 Conn, 476   In general, see, also, Stevens *v* Wilson, 3 C E. Green, 447   An alleged vendee's suit for a dividend is *res judicata* as to a suit for the stock   Shepard *v* Stockham, 25 Pac. Rep, 559 (Kan, 1891)   The corporation is a proper but not a necessary party to an action by one person to compel another person to transfer stock to him in accordance with the contract   Sayward *v* Houghton, 23 Pac Rep 120 (Cal, 1890).   Where a citizen of Wisconsin claims stock in a Wisconsin corporation as against a citizen of Illinois in whose name the stock stands on the corporate books, the corporation is a necessary party defendant and the case cannot be removed to the federal courts   Rogers *v* Van Nortwick, 45 Fed Rep, 513 (1891).   The corporation is a proper party defendant.   Kendig *v* Dean, 97 U S, 423, Budd *v* Monroe, 18 Hun, 316, Crump *v.* Thurber. 115 U S, 56   The reason of this rule is that complete possession of the stock can be obtained only by obtaining a transfer of that stock on the corporate books to the plaintiff.   Where a person claims that he has a contract for the purchase of stock which the stockholder vendor is about to sell or has already sold to others, and the first-named person brings a suit in equity to obtain the stock, he must show, first, that it is a case for specific performance, and second, that the stock was impressed with a trust and that the last purchaser took with notice of that trust.   See White & Tudor's Leading Cases in Equity vol I, pp. 914, 919, and Pooley *v* Rudd, 14 Beav, 34, 43, 44

Lindley on Company Law states the rule as follows   "A contract for the sale of shares by one individual to another is distinguishable in many respects from a contract for the allotment and accept-

ance of shares in a company, and Lord Romilly refused to decree specific performance of a contract of this kind, on the ground that the decree would be ineffectual, as the shares might be transferred immediately after the contract was performed   Sheffield Gas, etc, Co *v* Harrison, 17 Beav, 294, Bluck *v* Mallalue, 27 Beav, 398, Columbine *v* Chichester, 2 Ph, 27   In this last case there were circumstances to show that specific performance was impossible.   In order that specific performance of an agreement to take or deliver shares in a company may be decreed, it is necessary that the agreement should be concluded and binding (which it was not in Oriental Steam Nav Co. *v* Briggs, 4 De G, F & J, 191), and be untainted by fraud (which was not the case in New Brunswick & Canada Rail Co *v* Muggeridge, 4 Drew, 686, and 1 Drew & Sm, 363, or in Maxwell *v* Port Tennant Co, 24 Beav, 495), or unfairness (as to agreements between co-directors, see Flanagan *v* Great Western Rail Co., 7 Eq, 116), and be capable of being performed by the defendant (Ferguson *v* Wilson, 2 Ch, 77, Columbine *v* Chichester, 2 Ph, 27) and not involve any breach of trust (Fry on Spec Perf, p 177, 2d ed, and see Flanagan *v* Great Western Rail Co, 7 Eq, 116), or performance by either party of obligations the performance of which a court cannot practically enforce (Flanagan *v* Great Western Rail Co., 7 Eq 116, Stocker *v* Wedderburn, 3 K & J, 393)   An action will lie for specific performance of a contract for the purchase and sale of shares, if it is capable of being performed (see as to this, Bermingham *v* Sheridan, 33 Beav, 660, and compare Poole *v* Middleton, 29 Beav, 616), and the purchaser will be compelled to pay the price, although it may have been expressed to be paid in the deed of transfer, if, in fact, it was not

to the company in consideration of stock and in buying stock in the names of other persons or agents.[1]

Specific performance may also be said to be granted where a corporation is ordered by a court to issue certificates of stock to its stockholders.[2]

Specific performance will not be granted, however, where the purpose of the purchaser of stock is to obtain control of a national bank, when the change in management would probably be to the detriment of the bank.[3] Where the vendor's contract is to deliver stock and construct a railway, the court will not decree specific performance, since part of the contract is never the subject of such compulsory performance.[4] If the vendor is not in possession of the desired stock, specific performance will not be granted,[5] except to the amount of stock which he has.[6] Although a court of equity

thus paid (Wilson v Keating, 27 Beav, 121, and 4 De G & J, 588. This case seems, at first sight, to have been a hard one upon the defendant, but the deed stated that he had paid the money, and this he knew was not the fact. He could not, therefore, be treated as having been misled by the plaintiff or by the contents of the deed), and will be compelled to accept a transfer of the shares he has bought and to indemnify the seller from all liabilities accruing subsequently to the same (Wynne v Price, 3 De G & S, 310. As to the right of a mortgagee of shares to an indemnity from his mortgagor see Phene v Gillan, 5 Ha, 1), and the seller will be compelled to account for any moneys he may have received from an improper subsequent sale to another person (Beckitt v Bulbrough, 8 Ha, 188). The court has however, refused to compel a purchaser of scrip to accept shares, and indemnify the seller from calls upon them (Jackson v Cocker, 4 Beav, 59. Compare this with the last case), and to compel an allottee of shares to accept them, and to execute the company's deed in respect of them (Sheffield, etc, Gas Co. v. Harrison, 17 Beav, 294), and to compel the promoters of a company to deliver shares to a subscriber to the company (Columbine v Chichester, 2 Ph 27. In this case, however, the pro-

moters did not appear to have any shares which they could allot). Neither will the court interfere to compel the completion of a gratuitous and intended transfer (see Milroy v Lord, 4 De G, F & J, 264)"

[1] See §§ 333, 334, supra, and § 705, infra

[2] See ch IV

[3] Foll's Appeal, 91 Pa St, 434 (1879) the court saying "I know of no instance in this state in which a court of equity has decreed specific performance of a sale of stock"

[4] Ross v Union Pacific R'y Co, 1 Woolw, 26 (1863), per Miller, J Court will not decree specific performance of a contract of a company to deliver its stock to a constructor of its road, even though the latter, the complainant, is willing to perform. The court cannot compel the latter to perform and hence will not tie up the stock of the former Peto v Brighton, etc, R'y Co, 1 H & M, 468 (1863)

[5] Columbine v Chichester, 2 Phil Ch, 27 (1846) Specific performance as to issuing stock is not decreed when performance is impossible Summerlin v Fronteriza, etc, Co, 41 Fed Rep, 249 (1890) An injunction against a transfer in the meantime may be granted Ruttman v Hoyt, N Y L J, July 19, 1890

[6] Turner v May, 32 L. T. (N. S.), 56 (1875).

refuses to grant specific performance, yet it will not always send the party to a court of law, but in some of the states will grant him damages.[1] Laches may constitute a bar to the bill in equity to enforce specific performance [2]

§ 339. *Seventeenth section of statute of frauds as affecting sales of stock.* — In England the rule is firmly established that the seventeenth section of the statute of frauds, relating to contracts for the sale of "goods, wares and merchandise," does not apply to sales of stock No delivery, payment of earnest money or memorandum in writing is necessary in order to render the contract of sale valid This principle of law was doubted in the early cases[3] but was determined by the case of Humble v Mitchell, in 1839.[4] In 1838 this question arose in this country, apparently for the first time, and it was decided in Tisdale v. Harris,[5] chiefly on the authority of the early English cases, that a contract for the sale of stock was within the seventeenth section of the statute of frauds This decision has been uniformly followed in America.[6]

[1] Wonson v Fenno, 129 Mass , 405 (1880), Austin v Gillespie, 1 Jones' Eq (N. C.), 261 (1854)

[2] Seven years' delay in bringing suit for specific performance is a bar York v Passaic, etc., Co, 30 Fed Rep, 471 (1887). Five years' delay held fatal where "the relations of the parties have changed and the stock has greatly appreciated in value" Mundy v Davis, 20 Fed Rep , 353 (1884) Where a person sells and delivers stock to be delivered within a reasonable time, and receives the money for it, and soon after announces his inability to perform by reason of an injunction, the statute of limitations begins to run from the date of this notice The two years' statute on verbal promises applies. Rose v Foord, 28 Pac. Rep, 229 (Cal, 1891).

[3] Mussell v Cooke, Finch's Prec. in Ch , 533 (1720), holding that the statute applied but was not properly pleaded; Pickering v Appleby, 1 Comyn's Rep. 353 (1721), not decided, the judges being divided six and six; Colt v Netterville, 2 P Wms., 306 (1725), not decided, the lord chancellor saying it was too difficult to decide on a demurrer; Crull v. Dodson, Sel Cas in Ch. temp. King (fol 41, 1724), statute held to apply.

[4] 11 A & E, 205, followed in Duncuft v Albrecht, 12 Sim., 189 (1841), the court saying that the statute applies only to goods capable of part delivery, Hibblewhite v McMorine, 6 M & W, 201, 214 (1840), Tempest v Kilner, 3 C. B., 249 (1846); Heseltine v Siggers, 1 Ex., 856 (1848).

[5] 37 Mass. (20 Pick), 9.

[6] Baltzen v. Nicolay, 52 N Y, 467 (1873), rigidly applying the rule; North v Forrest, 15 Conn , 400 (1843), where the court say. "Such contracts fall clearly within the mischiefs which the legislature by the statute intended to remedy There is as much danger of fraud and perjury in the parol proof of such contracts as in any other " Pray v Mitchell, 60 Me , 430 (1872), Fine v Hornaby, 2 Mo App, 61 (1876), Colvin v Williams, 3 Har. & Johns. (Md), 38 (1810), Sherwood v. Tradesman's Nat'l Bank, 16 N. Y. W Dig . 522 (1883, Supreme Ct.), French v Sanger, N. Y. L J., July 22, 1892 Cf Brownson v. Chapman, 63 N Y, 625 *Contra, dictum*, Vawter v Griffin, 40 Ind , 593, 602 (1872). See Reed on Statute of Frauds, § 234, Hagar v King, 38 Barb., 200 (1862), holding that the sale of railroad bonds is within the statute. A sub-

A broker, however, as a common agent, may make the memorandum for both parties.[1] A subsequent part payment of the consideration makes the contract valid,[2] and a payment in property[3] or services[4] suffices The statute does not apply as between partners for the purpose of buying stock[5] A contract for the sale of stock in a corporation not yet incorporated has been held not to be within the statute[6] The statute must be pleaded in order to be effectual as a defense[7] The assignee of a contract for the sale of stock, void by the statute of frauds, takes nothing by the assignment.[8] An agreement by the vendor of stock to take it back at any time is not affected by the statute, and such an agreement is a part of the executed sale[9]

---

scription for stock is not a contract for the sale of goods, etc, within the meaning of the statute of frauds Webb v Baltimore, etc, Co, 26 Atl Rep, 113 (Md, 1893). In Florida the statute applies, the word personal property being used Southern Life Ins Co v Cole, 4 Fla, 359, 378. See, also, Mason v Decker, 72 N Y, 595, affirming 10 J & S., 115, Johnson v Mulry, 4 Rob. (N Y), 401 (1867), holding that the New York Stock Jobbing Act (Laws N Y. 1858, ch 134) did not affect the application of the statute of frauds The statute is not sufficiently pleaded by alleging that the contract of sale of stock "was void in law and not binding upon him" Vaupell v. Woodward, 2 Sand Ch, 143 The question of whether there was a delivery sufficient to take a case of sale of stock out of the statute of frauds was submitted to the jury in Hinchman v. Lincoln, 124 U S., 38 (1887), discussed in N Y Daily Reg, January 28, 1888 Contract to sell stock at the vendee's option within three years is not void by statute of frauds, since the option may be exercised within a year Seddon v Rosenbaum, 9 S. E. Rep, 326 (Va, 1889) Without a memorandum in writing a contract for the sale of stock is not enforceable although made in the Stock Exchange, whose rules provide that the contract shall be enforceable Ryers v Tuska, 14 N Y Supp, 926 (1891).

[1] Calvin v Williams, 3 Harr & J, 38 (1810)

[2] Thompson v Alger, 53 Mass. (12 Metc), 428 (1847)

[3] Eastern R. R. Co v. Benedict, 76 Mass (10 Gray) 212 (1857)

[4] White v Drew, 56 How Pr, 53 (1878), holding that the furnishing of reliable information is sufficient

[5] Tomlinson v Miller, 7 Abb. Pr. (N S), 364 (1869) Nor as between persons, one of whom buys stock in his own name for the joint benefit of both Stover v Flack, 41 Barb, 162 (1862)

[6] Gadsden v Lance, 1 McMull Eq (S. C), 87 (1841), Green v Brookins, 23 Mich, 48, 54 (1871), where a person was induced to subscribe on parol contract that a purchaser for the stock would afterwards be found In Massachusetts, on similar facts, except that a certain person agreed to purchase, a contrary decision was rendered Boardman v Cutter, 128 Mass, 388 (1880).

[7] Porter v Wormser, 94 N. Y., 431, 450 (1884)

[8] Mayer v Child, 47 Cal, 142 (1873)

[9] Fitzpatrick v Woodruff, 96 N. Y. 561 (1884), Thorndike v Locke, 98 Mass, 340 (1867), Fay v Wheeler, 44 Vt, 292 (1872), Bank of Lyons v Demmon, Hill & Denio, Supp, 398 (1844) An agreement by promoters with a subscriber for stock that they would take the stock from him within a certain time, if he desired, is valid and enforceable Meyer

So, also, the agreement of third parties to take the stock, or to protect from loss the party buying it, is enforceable if founded on a sufficient consideration [1]

§ 340. *Other sections of statute of frauds as affecting sales of stock.* — The provision of the statute of frauds relative to answering for the debts, defaults or miscarriages of another does not apply

[1] Blair, 109 N Y., 600 (1888), Morgan *i* Struthers, 131 U S, 246 (1889) An agreement to take back bonds if the vendee desires to return them is valid and enforceable Johnston *v* Trask, 116 N Y, 136 (1889) A guaranty that a vendor will take back the stock sold if the vendee desires is enforceable, even after the company sells out to another company for its shares of stock, the vendee not assenting Richter *i* Frank, 41 Fed Rep., 859 (1890) An agreement of the vendor to buy back the stock is enforceable Graham *v* Houghton, 26 N E Rep, 876 (Mass , 1891). The agreement of the vendor of stock to buy it back at the price paid, and one per cent a month in addition, is not usurious as a matter of law Phillips *i* Mason, 66 Hun, 580 (1893) Where the vendor agrees to refund the money upon the return of the stock sold, the vendee cannot sue for the money unless he returns the stock Henderson *i* Wheaton, 28 N E Rep , 1100 (Ill , 1891) Where stock is sold with a contract on the part of the vendor that he will repurchase it if desired "at the end of one year," the time may be extended by oral agreement. Weld *v* Barker, 26 Atl Rep , 239 (Pa , 1893) The vendee in enforcing the contract of the vendor to take the stock back must make and allege a tender Taylor *v* Blair, 13 N Y Supp , 154 (1891)

[1] Where a stockholder subscribes for an increased capital stock on the agreement of parties to take the stock if the subscriber does not want it, the latter may hold the former liable for the difference between what the latter pays for the stock and what he is able to sell it for Herd *et al v* Thompson, 24 Atl Rep , 282 (Pa , 1892) A guaranty

that the vendee of stock shall not lose money by the purchase may be enforced by the vendee when he proves that the stock has no market value and that he has tried to sell it but has failed Phipps *v.* Sharpe, 21 Atl Rep , 901 (Pa , 1891). A statement of a party who is endeavoring to sell stock for another, that he will see the latter whole in the matter, creates no liability on the part of the former Willis' Appeal, 18 Atl Rep . 987 (Pa , 1890) A person who writes to a party when the latter subscribes for stock that the former will pay the subscription if the road is not completed within a certain time is a surety and may be held liable Allison *v* Wood, 23 Atl Rep., 550 (Pa , 1892) An agreement of a stockholder that another stockholder shall be made "whole" for any loss due to not selling stock is without consideration and void Martin's Estate, 4 R'y & Corp L J , 449 (Orphans' Ct. Phil , 1888) A person induced to subscribe by an agreement of a third person to purchase the stock at par at any time may collect from the latter the difference between the price at which the former sells and the par value, the latter having declined to perform Lewis *v* Coates, 5 S. W Rep , 897 (Mo , 1888) See, also, § 334 A memorandum "We agree to pay A Rampacker the par value of this stock . . upon the surrender of this certificate" indorsed on the back of the certificate enables him to tender the stock and collect the par value, even though there was no consideration for the promise Wheaton *v* Rampacker, 26 Pac. Rep., 912 (Wyo , 1891) An agreement of persons holding a majority of the stock, they being directors also, that a person purchasing stock from them shall be

to a guaranty that there will be a certain dividend on stock purchased,[1] nor to a broker's relation towards his client[2] The provision of the statute relative to transfers of land does not apply to stock,[3] since shares of stock are personal property[4] A transfer of stock for the purpose of defrauding the transferrer's creditors is void, and a court of equity will set it aside,[5] or the stock may be attached or sold under execution the same as though no attempt at transfer had been made[6]

B. GAMBLING SALES OF STOCK.

§ 341 *What are wager stock sales* — Executory contracts for the sale of stock may be made with an intent to actually deliver the stock, or they may be made with an intent not to deliver it, but to pay in cash the amount lost or won by the rise or fall of the market price of the stock A sale with the former intent is, at common law, legal and valid.[7] A sale with the latter intent is a gambling

general manager and may at the end of two years sell the stock back to them at a stated price is contrary to public policy and void The vendors need not repurchase The arrangement is unfair to the corporation Wilbur *v* Stoepel, 46 N W Rep, 724 (Mich, 1890).

[1] Moorehouse *v* Crangle, 36 Ohio St, 130 (1880).

[2] Genin *v* Isaacsen, 6 N Y Leg Obs, 213 (1845); Rogers *v*. Gould, 6 Hun, 229 (1875)

[3] Watson *v* Spratley, 10 Ex 222 Powell *v* Jessopp, 18 C B. 336 (1856), Walker *v* Bartlett, 18 C B, 845 (1856), Ashworth *v* Munn, L R 14 Ch D, 363, 368 (1880)

[4] See ch I

[5] Skowhegan Bank *v* Cutter, 49 Me, 315 (1860), State *v* Warren F & M Co, 32 N J Law Rep, 439 (1868), Bayard *v* Hoffman, 4 Johns Ch, 450 (1820), Hadden *v* Spader, 20 Johns Rep., 554 (1822), Scott *v* Indianapolis Wagon-works, 48 Ind, 75 (1874), Moore *v* Metropolitan Nat'l Bank, 55 N Y, 41 (1873) The fraudulent transferee must be made a party defendant Hyatt *v* Swivel, 52 N Y. Super Ct 1 (1885). See, also ch XXVII But the fraudulent transferee is not liable unless he has accepted the stock. Skowhegan Bank *v* Cutler,

49 Me, 315 (1860), Cartmell's Case L R, 9 Ch, 691 (1874) Acceptance is a question of fact Pim's Case, 3 De G & S 11 (1849) But he cannot plead the statute of frauds himself Smith *v* 49 and 56 Quartz M Co, 14 Cal, 242 (1859)

[6] Beckwith *v* Burrough, R I, Feb. 9, 1884 See §§ 482, 484, *infra*

[7] Irwin *v* Williar, 110 U S, 499, 508 (1883), the court saying "The generally accepted doctrine in this country is that a contract for the sale of goods to be delivered at a future day is valid, even though the seller has not the goods nor any other means of getting them than to go into the market and buy them, but such a contract is only valid when the parties really intend and agree that the goods are to be delivered by the seller and the price to be paid by the buyer, and if under guise of such contract the real intent be merely to speculate in the rise or fall of prices, and the goods are not to be delivered, but one party is to pay to the other the difference between the contract price and the market price of the goods at the date fixed for executing the contract, then the whole transaction constitutes nothing more than a wager, and is null and void And this is now the law in England by force of the statute of 8 and

or wager contract, and is not enforceable [1] The essential difference
between a wager contract and a contract not a wager is whether
there is an intent to deliver the property sold.[2]

9 Vict. ch 109, § 18, altering the common law in that respect." In England
it is held that although the parties may
have contemplated that, as a whole,
there would be a mere payment of differences between them, yet, inasmuch as
the actual contracts entered into involved the liability for the actual delivery of the stock dealt with, they were
not gaming or wagering transactions
Universal Stock Exch v Stevens, 66 L.
T Rep, 612 (1892; It may be speculation, nevertheless it is valid   Clark v
Foss, 7 Biss., 540 (1878), Smith v Bouvier, 70 Pa St., 325 (1872), Kirkpatrick
v Bonsall, 72 Pa St, 155 (1872), where
the court say "We must not confound
gambling, whether it be in corporation
stocks or merchandise, with what is
commonly termed speculation   Merchants speculate upon the future prices
of that in which they deal, and buy and
sell accordingly" Hatch v. Douglas, 48
Conn, 116 (1860), Flagg v Baldwin, 38
N. J Eq Rep., 219 (1884), Kent v Miltenberger, 13 Mo App, 503 (1883) A
corporation organized to act as a broker
in buying and selling grain is subject to
the same rule as regards gambling contracts that individuals are. Peck v
Doran, etc, Co, 57 Hun, 343 (1890) Concerning this subject of stock gambling

see Cook on The Corporation Problem,
pp 67-73

[1] "Wagers at common law are valid
and enforceable in the courts;" and,
with certain exceptions growing out of
the peculiar subject of the wager, they
have been held to be valid contracts.
Dewey on Contracts for Future Deliv-
ery and Commercial Wagers (1886), 10
To same effect Good v Elliott, 3 Term
R., 693 (1790), Gilbert v Sykes, 16 East,
150 (812), Atherford v Beard, 2 Term
R., 610 (1788), Morgan v Pebrer, 4 Sco.,
230 (1837), Hussey v Crickitt, 3 Camp.,
693, Grant v Hamilton, 3 McLean, 100
(1842), Campbell v Richardson, 10
Johns., 406 (1813), Bunn v Riker, 4
Johns, 426 (1809), Johnson v. Fall, 6
Cal, 359 (1856), Johnson v. Russell, 37
Cal, 670 (1869), Dewees v. Miller, 5
How, 347 (1848), Porter v. Sawyer, 1
How, 519 (1832), Griffith v. Pearce, 4
Houston, 209 (1869), Richardson v Kel-
ley, 85 Ill, 491 (1877), Petillon v. Hipple,
90 Ill, 420 (1878), Trenton Ins. Co v.
Johnson, 2 Zab, 526 (1854), Dunman v
Strother, 1 Tex, 89 (1846), McElroy v
Carmichael, 6 Tex, 454 (1851); Wheeler
v Friend, 22 Tex, 683 (1859), Monroe v.
Smelley, 25 Tex, 486 (1860) Contra
In Pennsylvania — Edgell v. McLough-
lin, 6 Whart, 176 (1841), Phillips v. Ives,

[2] Roundtree v Smith, 108 U S., 269
(1882), In re Hunt, 26 Fed Rep, 739
(1886) Dewey, in his recent work on
Contracts for Future Delivery and
Commercial Wagers, states the rule accurately as follows 'Where the parties to a contract in the form of a sale
agree expressly or by implication at the
time it is made that the contract is not
to be enforced, that no delivery is to be
made, but the contract is to be settled
by the payment of the difference between the contract price and the market price at a given time in the future,

such a transaction is a wager," citing
many cases If there is an intent to deliver, then the transaction is legal,
though the parties "exercise the option
of settling the difference in price, rather
than make delivery of the property"
Ward v Vosburgh, 31 Fed Rep, 12
(1887) As regards sales and margins,
see § 457, infra A note given in New
York to settle a gambling cotton debt is
governed by New York laws as to its
legality Soudheim v Gilbert, 18 N. E.
Rep, 687 (Ind, 1888).

§ 342 *Statutes prohibiting wager contracts, and also certain stock contracts* — There are two classes of statutes affecting stock sales as regards their speculative character. One class does not specify sales of stock, but declares in general terms that all gaming and wagering contracts shall be void, thereby rendering actions for the recovery of money won on such wagers unsustainable Such statutes exist in England[1] and New York[2] The second class of statutes is more explicit, and prohibits specified transactions in stock, irrespective of whether such transactions be wager contracts or not. Statutes affecting speculative sales of stock exist in many of the states. In Massachusetts short sales are prohibited,[3] in Pennsylvania, sales for future delivery,[4] in Ohio, sales of stock for future delivery, where the vendor has not on hand or the vendee the

1 Rawle, 86 (1828), Bruas' Appeal, 55 Pa St., 294 (1867), in Vermont — Collamer v Day, 2 Vt., 144 (1829), Tarlton v Baker, 18 Vt, 9 (1843), in New Hampshire — Clark v Gibson, 12 N H, 386 (1841), Winchester v Metter, 52 N H, 507 (1872), in Maine — McDonough v Webster, 68 Me, 530 (1878), Gilmore v Woodcock, 69 Me, 118 (1879), Missouri — Waterman v. Buckland, 1 Mo App, 45 (1876), and Massachusetts — Ball v Gilbert, 12 Met, 399 (1847) Babcock v Thompson, 3 Pick, 446 (1826), Sampson v. Shaw, 101 Mass, 150 (1869) The supreme court of the United States say, in Irwin v Williar, *supra* " In England it is held that the contracts, although wagers, are not void at common law, . . . while generally, in this country, all wagering contracts are held to be illegal and void as against public policy," citing Dickson's Executor v. Thomas, 97 Pa St, 278 (1881), Gregory v Wendell, 40 Mich, 432 (1877), Lyon v Culbertson, 83 Ill, 33 (1876), Melchert v American U. Tel Co, 3 McClary, 521 (1882), 11 Fed. Rep., 193, Barnard v. Backhaus, 52 Wis., 593 (1881), Love v Harvey, 114 Mass, 80 (1873), Embrey v Jemison, 131 U S, 336 (1889)

1 8 and 9 Vict, ch. 109, § 18, Grizewood v Blanc, 11 C B, 526 (1851) Agreements between buyers and sellers of stock to pay or receive the differences between their prices on one day and then prices on another day are gam-

ing and wagering transactions within the meaning of the statute. Thacker v. Hardy, L R, 4 Q B D 687 (1878) The statute does not necessarily affect "corners" in stocks Barry v Croskey, 2 J & H, 1 (1861) As to the application of this statute, see, also, Heinman v Hardie, 12 Ct of Ses., 406 (Sc, 4th series, 1885)

2 1 R. S of N Y, 662, § 8 (vol III, p 1962, 7th ed) As applied to stock cases, see Kingsbury v Kirwan, 77 N Y, 612 (1879) Story v Saloman, 71 N Y, 420 (1877), Harris v Tumbridge, 83 N Y, 92 (1880), Yerkes v Saloman, 11 Hun, 471 (1877)

3 Gen Stat. Mass, ch 105, § 6 For cases arising under this statute, see Howe v Starkweather, 17 Mass 243 (1821), Sargent v Franklin Ins Co, 25 id, 98 (1829), Barrett v Mead, 92 id, 337 (1865), Brigham v Mead, 92 id, 245 (1865), Barrett v Hyde, 73 id, 160 (1856), Durant v Burt, 98 id, 161 (1867), Brown v Phelps, 103 id, 313 (1869); Price v Minot, 107 id, 49 (1871) Colt v Clapp, 127 id, 476 (1879), Rock v Nicholls, 85 id 312 (1862), United States v Vaughan, 3 Binn, 391 (1811), Wyman v Fiske, 85 Mass, 238 (1861), Pratt v. American Bell Tel Co, 5 N E Rep, 307 (1886), following the decisions under the New York statute from which the statute in question was copied

4 Laws of Pa, 1841, p 398, § 6 This statute has been repealed For decisions,

means to pay,[1] in Illinois, all options are made gambling contracts, and are void [2] in Georgia, short sales cannot be enforced.[3]   In New York, the statute of 1812,[4] re-enacted in the Revised Statutes of 1828,[5] prohibiting short sales, was repealed by implication by the statute of 1858, declaring the sale to be valid though there be no consideration or payment of consideration, or no ownership by the vendor of such stock at the time of the sale   Various other states have statutes on this subject [6]   In England the statute of 1734,[7] prohibiting gambling in the public funds, was repealed in 1860 [8]   It is evident from the history of these statutes against stock gambling

see Krause v Setley, 2 Phil Rep. 32 (1856), Chillas v Snyder, 1 id , 289 (1850)

[1] Ohio Laws, May, 1885   Gambling contract in grain, Lester v Buel, 30 N E Rep, 821 (Ohio, 1892)

[2] Revised Stat. of Ill , § 178   For decisions, see Wolcot t Heath, 78 Ill 433 (1875), Pickering t Cease, 79 Ill, 328 (1875), Pixley t Boynton, 79 Ill, 351 (1875), Sanborn t Benedict, 79 Ill, 309, Cole v Milmine, 88 Ill , 349 (1878). This statute is restricted by the decisions to cases where the transaction is to be "adjusted only by differences"   But see Ward t Vosburgh 31 Fed Rep 12 (1887)   In Illinois by statute an option to buy coal at a future time is void Osgood v Bauder, 39 N W Rep, 887 (Iowa, 1888   A sale with an agreement of the vendor to take the stock back at the same price and interest within a certain time if the vendee desired is not a gambling contract under the Illinois statute   Richter t Frank, 41 Fed Rep, 859 (1890)   Concerning an indictment under the Illinois law for keeping a "bucket shop   see Soby v People 25 N E. Rep, 109 (Ill , 1890)   In Illinois by statute a "put ' is void   Schneider v Turner 22 N E Rep, 497 (Ill, 1889).

[2] Georgia Code, § 2638.

[4] 2 R. L., 187, § 18

[5] 1 R S , p. 710, § 6   For cases coming under this statute, see Dykers v Townsend, 24 N Y, 57 (1861), disapproving Stebbins t Leowolf, 3 Cush , 143 (1849) See, also, Thompson t Alger, 13 Mass , 428 (1847), on the New York statute, Staples v Gould, 9 N Y, 520 (1854),

(criticising Gram v Stebbins, 6 Paige, 124 — 1836), Frost v Clarkson, 7 Cowen, 24 (1827), Cassard v Heinmann, 14 How. Pr , 84 (1856), affirmed, 1 Bosw , 207. In New York a director is prohibited from selling "short '   L. 1884, ch 223   In Arkansas a broker and others are liable criminally for doing business in futures. Fortenbury t State, 1 S. W Rep, 58 (1886).

[6] A promissory note is void under the Tennessee act against gambling in futures where such note was given therein   Snoddy v American Nat'l Bank, 13 S W Rep, 127 (Tenn, 1890). The California constitution renders void a transaction wherein a broker buys stock for the customer with the broker's money and holds the stock as security and charges the customer interest and commissions Cushman t Root, 26 Pac Rep 883 (Cal, 1891)   Gambling stock transactions are void under the Kentucky statute   Lyons v Hodgen, 13 S W Rep., 1076 (Ky , 1890)

[7] 7 Geo II , ch 8, and 10 Geo. II , ch 8 For cases under this statute, see Hewett v Price, 4 Man , & Gr 355 (1842), Fisher v Price, 11 Beav , 194 (1848), Mortimer v McCullon, 6 M & W, 69 (1840), Ellsworth v Cole, 7 M & W , 30 , Byles on Bills, 194 , 2 Kent's Com , 468, note (6). The statute did not apply to stock in private corporations   Hibblewhite v. McMorine, 5 M & W , 462 (1839), overruling Bryan t. Lewis, R. & M , 386 (1826).

[8] 23 and 24 Vict., ch. 28

that it is a difficult and delicate task to frame a statute that will cure the evil. The great danger is that any statute will interfere with the legitimate transactions — transactions which for many years have been building the railways and developing the material resources of the country [1]

§ 343 *Test of legality of stock transactions* — Although, as already stated, stock sales, where no delivery but merely a settlement of gain or loss is intended, are wagers, and although such wagers are void by the statutes of some states and by the rules of public policy in others,[2] yet difficulty is experienced in determining whether the parties really intended to deliver the stock or to pay differences The question of intent is always difficult of ascertainment and of positive proof It is pre-eminently a question for the jury. It is accordingly found in most of the cases involving the question whether the transaction was stock gambling, that the court submitted to the jury whether an actual delivery of the stock was intended or not If not, then, as a matter of law, the transaction was a wager If a wager, it is, by statute in some states, by public policy in others, a void transaction, and the parties have only the rights given them on void contracts [3]

§ 344. *When intent to deliver is question for the jury and when not.*— The question whether the parties to an executory sale of stock intended to actually deliver the stock, or merely to pay and receive the gain or loss, is for the jury [4] In the application of this rule, however, great care is to be exercised in submitting the ques-

[1] Dos Passos on Stock Brokers and Stock Exchanges (1882), p 405, says, "The history of these stock-jobbing acts seems to prove conclusively that they have never been effective in preventing speculations in stocks In almost every instance in which they have been adopted, after lingering for years on the books, scorned and violated by the 'unbridled and defiant spirit of speculation,' despite the earnest efforts of the courts to enforce them, they have finally been repealed It is, perhaps, better to allow the evil to correct itself, as it surely does, than to bring the administration of justice into contempt by filling the books with useless laws, which are at all times openly violated and laughed at, and which seem hardly more effective to prevent the practice at which they are aimed than legislation against the laws of nature "

[2] Particularly in Pennsylvania are such stock wagers void by public policy Worth t. Phillips, 89 Pa. St., 250 (1879), Fareira t Gabell, 89 Pa. St., 89 (1879), Ruchizky t De Haven, 97 Pa St., 202 (1881), Dickson's Executor t Thomas, 97 Pa St., 278 (1881), Brua' Appeal, 55 Pa St., 294 (1867)

[3] See §§ 345, 346 See, also, Greenhood on Public Policy, pp 230-237

[4] Whitesides v. Hunt, 97 Ind., 191 (1884), Gregory t Wendell, 39 Mich., 337 (1878) And all the circumstances are to be taken into consideration. Beveridge v Hewitt, 8 Bradw, 467 (1881); Hawley t Bibb, 14 Reporter, 172 (1881); Brand t Henderson, 107 Ill, 141 (1883), Barnard t Backhaus, 52 Wis, 593 (1881), Kirkpatrick v. Bonsall, 72 Pa. St, 155 (1872).

tion and charging the jury. Thus, an "option," "put," "call," "straddle," or other similar stock exchange contract, may be made with an intent to actually deliver the stock, and, if so, are unobjec tionable and are enforceable [1] The parties may be asked directly whether they intended that a delivery should be made [2] If one party intended to have a delivery the transaction is valid, even though the other party intended otherwise [3] As between a party and his broker, however, greater difficulty arises, and in some juris dictions the intent between them governs their relations, irrespect-

---

[1] For definitions of these terms, see § 415, n A "put" is not *per se* conclusive evidence of an intent not to deliver Bigelow *v* Benedict, 70 N Y, 202 (1877). A "straddle" follows the same rule The parties may have intended to deliver the stock Harris *v* Tumbridge, 83 N Y, 92 (1880), Story *v* Salomon, 71 N Y, 420 (1877) *Cf Ex parte* Young, 6 Biss, 53 (1874); Webster *t* Sturges, 7 Bradw, 56 (1880); Tenney *v* Foote, 4 Bradw, 594 (1879); Lyon *v* Culbertson, 83 Ill, 33 (1876); Gilbert *v* Gouger, 8 Biss, 214 (1878). A short sale is not *per se* a wager, nor is it presumed to be Maxton *v* Gheen, 75 Pa St, 166 (1874), Huss *v* Rau, 95 N Y, 359 (1884), Knowlton *v* Fitch, 52 N Y, 288 (1873), White *v* Smith, 54 N Y, 522 (1874), Cameron *v* Durkheim, 55 N Y, 425 (1874), Third Nat'l Bank *v* Harrison, 10 Fed Rep, 243 (1882). A sale, delivery to be in twelve months, or if vendor wishes before then, is not a gambling contract Wolffe *v* Perryman, 9 S Rep, 148 (Ala, 1891) These decisions rest upon the principle of law laid down in Stanton *v* Small, 3 Sandf (N. Y), 230 that "a contract for the sale of goods, to be delivered at a future time, is not invalidated by the circumstances that, at the time of the contract, the vendor neither had the goods in his possession, nor has entered into any contract to buy them, nor has any reasonable expectation of becoming possessed of them at the time appointed for delivery otherwise than by purchasing them after making the contract." There are many cases to the same effect See

Noyes *v* Spaulding, 27 Vt., 420 (1855); Shales *v* Seigmoret, 1 Ld Raymond, 440 (1691), Frost *t* Clarkson, 7 Cow, 25 (1827), Dewey on Contracts for Future Delivery. 97, Thacker *v* Hardy, L R., 4 Q B D, 685 (1878), holding that, if the intent at the time of buying was to deliver, it is not a wager, even though that intent be afterwards changed As to the legality of a "corner," see § 333 Where there is evidence of some intent to deliver, the transaction is not gambling Mitchell *v.* Hartley, 16 N. E Rep., 645 (Ind, 1888).

[2] Yerkes *v* Saloman, 11 Hun, 471 (1877), Cassard *v* Hinman, 6 Bosw., 14 (1860); First Nat. Bank *v* Oskaloosa, 23 N W Rep, 255 (1885); *Ex parte* Young, 6 Biss., 53 (1874) In the case of Porter *v* Viets, 1 Biss, 177 (1857), the court refused to admit parol evidence that the contract was gambling for the reason that it varied a written contract

[3] Wall *v.* Schneider, 17 Reporter, 700 (1884), Irwin *v* Williar, 110 U S, 499 (1884), Whitesides *v* Hunt, 97 Ind, 191 (1884), Pixley *v.* Boynton, 79 Ill, 351 (1875), Ward *v* Vosburgh, 31 Fed Rep, 12 (1887), Powell *v* M'Cord, 12 N. E. Rep, 262 (Ill, 1887), Lehman *v* Strassberger, 2 Woods (C. C.), 554 (1873), Conner *t* Robertson, Louisiana Sup Ct (1886) *Contra*, Fareira *v* Gabell, 89 Pa St, 89 (1879); Beveridge *v* Hewitt, 8 Bradw, 467 (1881). In Tennessee, by statute, dealing in futures is gambling, if either party does not intend to deliver. See McGrew *v* City Produce Exchange, 4 S. W. Rep, 88 (Tenn, 1887).

ive of the intent of the party dealing with them [1] The fact that stock transactions were carried on by "margins" is no evidence that they were gambling contracts,[2] excepting in Pennsylvania and New Jersey In these states this fact alone seems to be sufficient evidence of a wager.[3] A wager contract is not proved by the fact that the party selling stock to be delivered at a future time intends to purchase that amount of stock in time for the delivery, or *vice versa*[4] "An executory contract for the sale of goods for future delivery is not infected with the quality of a wager by reason of the fact that at the date of the contract the vendor had not the goods, had not entered into any arrangement to provide them, and had no expectation of purchasing them, unless by a subsequent purchase in the market"[5] The financial responsibility of the parties,[6]

[1] See §§ 345, 346

[2] Sawyer v Taggart. 11 Bush, 727 (1879), Wall v Schneider, 17 Rep, 700 (1884), Bartlett v Smith, 13 Fed Rep., 263 (1882), Whitesides v Hunt, 97 Ind. 191 (1884), Union Nat Bank v Carr, 15 Fed Rep., 238 (1883). Hatch v Douglas, 48 Conn, 116 (1880) Many other cases do not directly pass on this question, but assume that the deposit of a margin, as a security to the broker, does not prove an intent not to have a delivery of the stock

[3] Ruchizky v De Haven, 97 Pa St, 202 (1881), Dickson v Thomas 97 Pa St., 278 (1881), Farenn v Gabell, 89 Pa St, 89 (1879) Maxton v Green, 75 Pa St, 166 (1874) North v Phillips, 89 Pa St, 250 (1879), Flagg v Baldwin, 38 N J Eq Rep, 219 (1884); Justh v Holliday, 11 Wash L Rep, 418 (1883)

[4] In the case of Ashton v Dakin, 7 W. R., 384 (1859), the court held it not to be a wager contract to order a broker to buy stock, "and let the bargain be so as to day of payment that you may have an opportunity of reselling it for me by such a day, when I expect the market will have risen, and then you will pay the seller for me with the money you receive from the purchaser, and I shall receive the gain from you, if any, or pay you the loss" So, also, Smith v Bouvier, 70 Pa. St., 325 (1872), holds that stocks bought and sold upon speculation are not necessarily wager contracts

A person may sell without owning the stock, and at time of delivery buy to deliver, and yet the transaction be not a wager, where the jury finds that there was an intent to deliver in both the selling and buying See, also, Thacker v Hardy, L. R., 4 Q B Div, 685 (1879). Sawyer v Taggart, 14 Bush, 727 (1879) A purchase of corn may be legal although made to fill certain sales which the party had made previously A mortgage given to a broker for advancements made in the transaction is valid Douglas v Smith, 38 N W Rep, 163 (Iowa, 1888)

[5] Conner v Robertson, 37 La Ann, 813 (1885), the court saying also that Larymer v Smith (1 B & C. 1) has been repeatedly overruled. See, also, *supra* page 472, note 1.

[6] Kirkpatrick v Bonsall, 72 Pa St, 155 (1872), First Nat'l Bank v Oskaloosa P Co, 66 Iowa. 41 (1885), *In re* Green, 7 Biss, 338 (1877). Beveridge v Hewitt, 8 Bradw, 467 (1881), Justh v Holliday, 11 Wash Rep, 418 (1883). North v Phillips, 89 Pa St, 250 (1879) Patterson's Appeal, 16 Rep, 59 (Pa. 1883). Flagg v Baldwin, 38 N J Eq, 219, Colderwood v McCrea, 11 Bradw, 543 (1882) The fact that one of the parties is already under obligation to other parties to purchase cotton several times greater in value than his fortune is evidence of an intent to gamble Beadles v McElrath, 3 S W Rep, 152

and their other transactions in the same line,[1] are admissible as evidence as to whether there was an intent to deliver the stock or merely to pay the gain or loss   The burden of proving that a stock transaction is a gambling contract is upon him who affirms it.[2]

§ 345   *Gambling stock contracts as affecting the relations between the principal and his broker* — A broker is but an agent of his principal   As such he may hold the principal liable for commissions and for losses paid on stock transactions where those stock transactions are legitimate and legal   Where, however, the stock contracts are of a wager or gambling nature, a more difficult question arises, and the decisions are irreconcilable   In England, in 1878, Judge Lindley, in Thacker v Hardy,[3] a carefully-considered case, held that, where the principal has been carrying on gambling transactions, he cannot escape or repudiate his liabilities to his broker in those transactions, even though the latter knew of the gambling character of the business   The principal is liable to his broker as though the transactions were free from such objections. This is the well-established rule in England.[4]

§ 346   In this country an opposite rule prevails for the most part.

(Ky, 1887) The fact that a party is financially unable to pay for property is evidence that the contract is gambling Myers v Tobias, 16 Atl Rep., 641 (Pa, 1889)

[1] Kirkpatrick v. Bonsall, 72 Pa St, 155 (1872), Beveridge v Hewitt, 8 Bradw, 467 (1881), Irwin v Williar, 110 U S, 499 (1884) *Contra*, Tomblin v Callen, 28 N W Rep., 573 (Iowa, 1886) The jury in passing upon the defense to a note that it was given in a stock-gambling operation may consider all the acts and accounts and the actual dealings. Gaw v. Bennett, 25 Atl Rep, 1114 (Pa, 1893) As to the competency of evidence herein, and that evidence of custom of settling by differences is incompetent, see Scofield v Blackman, 4 Atl Rep, 208 (Pa, 1886).

[2] Dewey on Contracts, etc, p. 207, says "All the cases except Barnard v Backhaus, 52 Wis, 503 (1881), Cobb v Prell, 15 Fed Rep, 774 (1883), Beveridge v Hewitt, 8 Bradw, 467 (1881), Stebbins v Leowolf, 3 Cush, 137 (1849), and possibly Chandler's Case, *Ex parte* Young, 6 Biss, 53, hold that these contracts are presumed to be *bona fide*, and

in order to show them to have been used as covers for wagers, an agreement to that effect must appear to have been made According to these excepted cases option contracts are presumed to be invalid, and proof must be made that they are *bona fide*" See, also, Dewey, p 46

[3] L. R., 4 Q B. D, 685 In Illinois the burden of proof is on the defendant to prove a gambling intent on the part of both parties In Wisconsin a contrary rule seems to prevail. See Ward v Vosburgh, 31 Fed Rep, 12 (1887)

[4] *Re* Hart, Weekly Notes, 85 (1870), Cooper v Neil, 13 Weekly Notes, 128 (1878), *Ex parte* Rogers, L. R., 15 Ch. D, 207 (1879), Fairuey v. Reynons, 4 Burr, 2069 (1767), Jessopp v Lutwyche, 10 Ex, 614 (1854), Knight v Cambers, 15 C B, 562 (1855), Knight v. Fitch, 15 C B, 566 (1855), Lyne v. Siesfield, 1 H & N, 278 (1856), Rosewarne v Billing, 15 C. B. (N. S), 316 (1863), Pidgeon v Burslem, 3 Ex., 465 (1849) *Contra* Byers v Beattie, 16 Weekly Rep, 279 (1868, Ex., Irish).

The great weight of authority holds that, where the broker has knowledge of the purpose to gamble in stocks and aids in carrying out that purpose, he cannot recover for services rendered or losses incurred and paid by himself[1] A few cases hold to the same effect as the English rule[2] Many cases which seem to favor the English rule do so only by *dicta*, inasmuch as the transactions involved in such cases are held not to be wager contracts[3] In Pennsylvania and New Jersey the American rule is rigidly enforced   The broker is held to be dealing as a principal, not as an agent, in all stock-gambling transactions[4] He cannot recover commissions nor losses[5] If his principal is an infant the broker is liable to such infant for all sums received by way of margins[6] If, however, the parties do

---

[1] Irwin v Williar, 110 U S., 499, 510 (1883), Flagg v Gilpin, 19 Atl Rep, 1084 (R I, 1890), McClean v Stuve, 15 Mo App, 317 (1884) per Thompson, J ; Ream v Hamilton, 15 Mo App 377 (1884) *Cf* Kent v Miltenberger, 13 Mo App, 503, 511 (1883) See, also, as supporting above rule, Everingham v Meighan, 5 Wis Leg News, 25 (1882), *In re* Green, 7 Biss, 338 (1877), Bartlett v Smith, 13 Fed Rep, 263 (1882), Tenney v Foote, 4 Bradw, 594 (1879), affirmed, 95 Ill, 99 (1880), defeating a note given to the broker, Calderwood v McRae, 11 Bradw, 513 (1882), Webster v Sturges, 7 Bradw, 56, Barnard v Backhaus, 52 Wis, 593 (1881), defeating notes, Beveridge v Hewitt, 8 Bradw, 467 (1881), Whitesides v Hunt, 97 Ind, 191, 203 (1884), Melchert v American U Tel Co, 11 Fed Rep, 193 (1882), First Nat'l Bank of Lyons v Oskaloosa Packing Co (Iowa), 23 N W Rep, 255 (1885), holding a note void, Stewart v Garrett, 4 Atl Rep, 399 (Pa, 1886), Stewart v Schall, 34 Alb L J, 98 (Md, 1886) Suit by broker against customer for moneys lost in purchase of grain for the customer. Mohr v Miesen, 49 N W Rep, 862 (Minn, 1891) Brokers are bound to know that banks have no power to purchase cotton futures on margins Cannot recover commissions and losses The *ultra vires* contract was not executed, inasmuch as the corporation received no property Jennison v Citizens' Sav Bank, 44 Hun, 412 (1887) A

broker may recover commissions, etc, from his principal when the former knew nothing of the latter's intention to gamble Lehman v Feld, 37 Fed Rep, 852 (1889) Broker may recover from principal though latter intended a gambling contract Edwards v Hoeflinghoff, 38 id, 635 (1889) Boyd v Hanson, 41 id, 174 (1890)

[2] Brown v Speyers, 20 Gratt (Va), 296 (1871), Wyman v Fiske, 85 Mass, 238 (1861), on the ground that the note sued on was a voluntary payment to the broker, Warren v Hewitt, 45 Ga, 501 (1872), Marshall v Thurston 3 Lea (Tenn), 741 (1879), where also a note had been given, Jackson v Foote 12 Fed Rep, 37, also a note case, the court saying that, as between the broker and his principal the decision probably would be different *Cf.* Tinsley's Case, 10 Fed Rep, 249

[3] Lehmann v Strassberger, 2 Woods, 554 (C C, 1875), Rumsey v Berry, 65 Me, 570 (1876), Sawyer v Taggart, 14 Bush, 727 (1879), Durant v Burt, 98 Mass, 161 (1867) Williams v Carr, 80 N C, 294 (1879)

[4] Ruchizky v De Haven, 97 Pa St., 202 (1881).

[5] North v Phillips, 89 Pa St 250 (1879), Flagg v Baldwin, 38 N J Eq Rep., 219 (1884), Farena v Gabell, 89 Pa St, 89 (1879), holding that notes given to the broker are void

[6] Ruchizky v De Haven, *supra* An infant gambling in stocks on a margin

not raise the question of the legality of the transaction, the court cannot[1] In Ohio it is held that the broker may be made to account for profits, even though the transaction was a gambling one[2] A note and mortgage given to the broker in settlement of a gambling transaction will not be interfered with[3] The broker is not liable for a sale of the stock on failure of margin, without notice to the principal, where the business is gambling[4]

§§ 347, 348 *Gambling stock transactions as affecting notes, bonds, mortgages, etc, growing out thereof.*— The penalty of engaging in a stock-gambling operation is that, in case the transaction is declared by a court of justice to be illegal as a wager contract, the court declines to aid either party[5] As a general rule all liability on the part of either party is unenforceable Money paid by the principal cannot be recovered back[6] Neither principal can collect the gains of the transaction, and neither is liable for a loss[7] Notes given in settlement are void and not collectible,[8] even in the hands

may recover from the brokers all that he deposited with them Mordecai v Pearl, 63 Hun, 553 (1892).

[1] Gheen v Johnson, 90 Pa St., 38 (1879), Williams v Carr, 80 N C, 294 (1879)

[2] Norton v Blinn, 39 Ohio St. 145 (1883) Where gambling stock transactions are closed and the account settled, and the balance due the customer is left on deposit with the broker, the latter must pay it over Peters *et al* v Grim, 24 Atl Rep, 192 (Pa, 1892)

[3] Clark v Foss, 10 Chicago Legal News (U. S. D Ct, 1878). *Cf* Tantum v West (N J), Central Rep, March 23, 1886

[4] North v Phillips, 89 Pa. St., 250 (1879).

[5] Reese v Fermie, 13 W R., 6 (1864), holding that the court will not aid one who has been tricked in gambling in stocks

[6] Gregory v Wendall, 39 Mich, 337 (1878) · Id, 40 Mich, 432 (1879); Wyman v Fiske, 85 Mass, 238 (1861) *Cf* Norton v Blinn, 30 Ohio St., 145 (1883) In Tennessee, by statute, a contrary rule prevails. McGrew v City Produce Exchange, 4 S. W Rep., 38 (Tenn, 1887), Dunn v Bell, id, 41 (Id), holding, also, that where there are several partners or co-conspirators who take the principal's

money they are liable therefor jointly and severally Under the New York statute money paid by a customer to a broker on gambling speculations may be recovered back Peck v Doran, etc, Co., 10 N Y Supp 401 (1890). Where a gambling contract is illegal by statute, a customer who gave money to the broker to gamble with, according to orders, cannot recover it back. Sale deliverable in a certain month, on a day to be fixed by seller, is not a gambling contract White v Barber, 123 U S, 392 (1887); 17 Atl Rep, 791 Certificate of deposit given to broker in gambling transactions may be recovered back. Dempsey v Harm, 12 Atl. Rep, 27 (Pa, 1887).

[7] Grizewood v Blane, 11 C. B. 526 (1851). Webster v. Sturges, 7 Bradw, (Ill), 560 (1880); *Ex parte* Young, 6 Biss, 53 (1874); Thompson v. Cummings, 68 Ga, 124 (1881); Yerkes v. Solomon, 11 Hun, 471 (1877) A partner, however, may have contribution for losses paid at the express request of the other member of the firm Pettie v Hannay, 3 Term Rep, 418 (1789).

[8] Barnard v Backhaus, 52 Wis, 593 (1881), Farcira v Gabell, 89 Pa St, 89 (1879), Lowry v Dillman, 18 N. W Rep, 4 (Wis, 1884), Davis v Davis, 21 N E.

of *bona fide* purchasers[1]   Bonds and mortgages given in payment
are void[2]   Due-bills,[3] acceptances[4] and guaranties[5] of notes are
not valid or enforceable   If a part of the consideration is void
the whole contract and all securities given thereunder are void[6]

C FRAUD AS AFFECTING A SALE OF STOCK.

§ 349 *Extent of subject treated herein* — In a previous chapter
of this treatise the effect of fraud and fraudulent representations
on a subscription for stock was fully treated   There is little dif-

Rep , 1112 (Ind , 1889), Justh v Holliday, 17 Central L J 56 (1883), 11 Wash
L Rep , 418, Cunningham v Third. etc ,
Bank of Augusta, 71 Ga., 400 (1883),
Tenney v Foote, 4 Bradw , 595 (1879),
affirmed, 95 Ill , 99   Cf Wyman v
Fiske, 85 Mass , 238 (1861)   Person loaning money and taking notes therefor
cannot be defeated in suit on notes by
evidence that he knew the loan was to
be used in gambling operations   Defendant must prove, also, that plaintiff
intended that the money should be so
used   Waugh v Beck, 6 Atl Rep , 923
(Pa , 1886)   Checks, notes, etc , in gambling contracts are void   Kahn v Walton, 20 N. E Rep , 203 (Ohio, 1889),
Embrey v. Jemison, 131 U S , 336 (1889)

[1] Barnard v. Backhaus, 52 Wis , 593
(1881), Steers v Lashley, 6 Term Rep,
61 (1794); Tenney v Foote, 4 Bradw
(Ill), 594 (1879); Cunningham v National
Bank of Augusta, 71 Ga , 400 (1883),
Lowry v. Dillman, 18 N W Rep , 4
(1884)   *Contra*, Crawford v Spencer, 4
S. W. Rep , 713 (Mo , 1887), citing Third
National Bank v Harrison, 10 Fed Rep.,
243, also, *contra*, Lilley v Rankin, 55
L. T Rep , 814 (1886)   An accommodation indorser to the note may set it up
Justh v Holliday, 17 Cent L. J , 56
(1883), 11 Wash L Rep , 418   Note to
bank is valid, though the proceeds
were to pay a stock-gambling debt and
the bank knew that fact.   Marshall v
Thurston, 3 Lea (Tenn), 741 (1879)   Cf
Cannon v Bryce, 3 B & A 179 (1819)

[2] Amory v Merryweather, 2 B & C ,
573 (1824), Flagg v Baldwin, 38 N J

Eq Rep , 219 (1884), Griffiths v Sears,
112 Pa St , 523 (1886), Barnard v.
Backhaus, 52 Wis , 593 (1881)   A judgment entered by confession on a bond
given for a gambling debt may be set
aside   Everitt v Knapp, 9 Johns , 331
(1810), Beveridge v Hewitt, 8 Bradw ,
467 (1881)   A court of equity will enjoin the transfer of a note and will
decree the cancellation of a mortgage
given by a married woman in payment
of her husband's stock-gambling debts
Tantum v West, 6 Atl Rep , 316 (N J,
1886)   But will not where given by the
party himself to his brokers   Clark v
Foss, 10 Chicago Legal News (1878)
A mortgage to a broker to pay losses on
gambling speculations is void and not
enforceable   Walters v Comer, 5 S E
Rep , 292 (Ga , 1888)   But see Crawford v Spencer, 4 S W Rep , 713 (Mo ,
1887)

[3] Rudolf v Winters, 7 Neb , 125 (1878)

[4] Steers v Lashley, 6 Term Rep , 61
(1794)   Rawlings v Hall, 1 Carr & P ,
11 (1823), holds that the broker on the
witness stand need not admit that the
consideration was a gambling debt,
since it would subject him to a common-
law criminal prosecution

[5] Tenney v Foote 95 Ill , 99 (1880).

[6] Tenney v Foote, *supra*   See, also,
Farena v Gabell 89 Pa St , 89 (1879)
But where, upon the close of a successful "corner," which is illegal by statute, one of the parties leaves his share
of the profits with the other party to
invest, the latter must account for it
when called upon so to do.   Where,

ference in the principles of law governing fraud as affecting sales of stock from fraud as affecting subscriptions for stock   Most of the cases assume that the same principles apply to both kinds of transactions. Consequently the questions of what constitutes fraud herein, what remedies the defrauded person has, and the general principles governing this branch of the law, will be fully understood only by a comparison of these two parts of this work.[1]

§ 350 *What has been held to constitute a fraud herein.*— It is difficult to lay down rules as to what does and what does not amount to fraudulent misrepresentations The courts, consequently, let each case stand upon its own facts. Certain states of fact have, however, been passed upon as constituting fraud, and as such they aid in coming to a conclusion on facts in somewhat similar cases   Thus, it has been held to be a fraudulent representation to make false statements as to the location, explorations and developed state of a mine,[2] or that a patent owned by the company was of great value, and that certain other persons were owners of stock,[3] that the company was prosperous, when in fact large overissues of stock had been made,[4] or that the corporate property was free from incumbrance,[5] or that the corporation would guaranty certain dividends,[6] or any false statement or general fraudulent act, or fraudulent concealment of a material fact

upon the close of an unsuccessful "corner," the parties losing settle among themselves, but one of them fraudulently overstates the losses, he is liable to account for the amount fraudulently allowed him   Wells ɪ McGeoch, 34 N. W Rep., 769 (Wis, 1888).

[1] See ch IX. In the important case of Western Bank v Addie, L. R., 1 H L (Sc) 145 (1867), part of the shares had been subscribed for and part purchased The court applied the same principle to both

[2] Morgan ɪ Skiddy, 62 N. Y, 319 (1875)

[3] Miller v Barber, 66 N Y, 558 (1876)

[4] Cazeaux v Mali, 25 Barb, 578 (1857) False representations as to solvency and financial condition of the corporation are material, and the purchaser may testify that he would not have purchased the stock except for the representations Pridham v. Weddington, 12 S. W Rep, 49 (Tex, 1889) It is fraud to state falsely that the company is

prosperous, that there was no stock for sale, and that defendant was selling stock of others and not his own   Miller ɪ Curtiss, 13 N Y Supp, 604 (1891).

[5] Southwestern R. R Co v. Papot, 67 Ga, 675, 692 (1881), the court saying "It is, we think, sufficient to show that the misrepresentation or suppression of fact was of such a nature as to prove that the property purchased was of no value to the purchaser for the purpose for which it was bought, or that it would be reasonable to suppose that the purchaser would not have contracted for it had he had knowledge of the existence of this defect." It is fraudulent to make misstatements to the effect that the corporation is out of debt and is making certain profits It is no defense that the defendant might have ascertained the facts from the corporation. Redding v Wright, 51 N W Rep, 1056 (Minn, 1892)

[6] Gerhard ɪ Bates, 20 Eng L & Eq, 129 (1853)

whereby the purchaser is induced to complete the sale of stock [1] It may or may not be a fraudulent representation to state that the stock is worth a certain sum [2]

It is a fraud on the vendee of stock to sell him as paid-up stock that which is not paid up, although issued as paid up, the vendor having participated in the issue [3]   It is fraud in the vendor to rep-

[1] See further illustrations in chapter IX   Declaring a dividend in good faith and sound discretion is not fraud by reason of its turning out to have been ill-advised. Burnes ι Pennell, 2 H of L. Cases, 497 (1849)   A representation that the stock ' is good property of investment and is about to make a dividend ' is a false representation when untrue, and where the person taking the stock as executor from a preceding executor objected to receiving it on account of his doubt or ignorance as to its character   Lawton ν Kittredge, 30 N. H, 500 (1855)   Representations that a corporate property is valuable and one of the best properties in Colorado, when in fact the company was a bubble company, raises a question of fraud for the jury to pass upon   Bradley ν Poole, 98 Mass, 169 (1867)   The payment of an excessive and speculative price for stock is not fraud and is no ground for setting the sale aside   Moffat ι Winslow, 7 Paige Ch, 124 (1838)   The vendor warrants the title to the stock, but not its quality or value   Allen ι Pegram, 16 Iowa, 163 (1864)   A sale of stock in a company formed to purchase a railroad cannot be set aside merely because its title to the railroad fails   State ι North La & T R. R. Co. 34 La Ann, 947 (1882).   In the case of Wright s Appeal 99 Pa St, 425 (1882), it was held that the corporation was not liable for the conversion of stock by its president, who obtained the certificates indorsed in blank from the owner on false representations that the corporation wished to use them   Newlands ν National, etc, Association, 53 L T (N. S), 242 (1885), March ι Eastern R R. Co, 43 N H, 515 (1862), holding that the fact that the earnings were not distributed by divi-

dends until after a sale of stock does not constitute fraud   A confidential agent who uses his position to obtain stock of which the principal has been deprived wrongfully must turn it over to the principal   Hardenburgh ι Bacon, 33 Cal 356 (1867).

[2] That it is not, see Union Nat'l Bank ν Hunt, 76 Mo, 439 (1882)   A false representation that the stock sold is worth eighty cents on the dollar — it being worth but forty cents — will not sustain an action for deceit. Ellis ι Andrews, 56 N Y 83 (1874). It is fraudulent to represent that the stock is worth par when in fact it is worthless   If the vendor persuades the vendee to make no inquiries, the latter may recover although he made none   The measure of damages is not the value of the land given for the stock, but the difference between the actual and the represented value of the stock. Nysewander ι Lowman, 24 N E Rep, 355 (Ind, 1890)   False representations may consist of statements that the stock is worth a certain price and is sold to plaintiff at a reduced price in order to obtain his services   Maxted ν Fowler, 53 N. W Rep. 921 (Mich 1892)

[3] Sturges ι Stetson 1 Biss, 246 (1858) holding that the vendee is not liable on a note given in payment thereof   Fosdick ι Sturges 1 Biss, 255 (1858) holding that the vendee may recover back money paid   Reeve ι Dennett 11 N E Rep 938 (Mass 1887), where the capital of $1 000,000 was issued for a worthless patent   holding also that the misrepresentations may invalidate also a second and subsequent purchase of stock, even though in the meantime the vendee has become a director in the corporation

resent that property is to be turned in by him to the corporation at a certain price and then to refuse to carry out the latter contract.[1] Where the vendor agrees to sell at a value to be ascertained by an examination of the corporate books and affairs, it is fraud in the vendee to cause false memoranda to be made by the employees of the corporation[2] It is not fraud, however, for a director or other corporate officer to buy or sell stock at a profit due to his official knowledge of the condition of the corporation,[3] nor to obtain the stock by a threat of a call.[4] The fact that a check given in payment for stock is not honored, although the money is in bank, is not fraud where payment was refused because of other frauds of the vendor,[5] nor is it fraud to issue certificates before anything has been paid thereon, there being no participation by the vendor.[6] It is fraud, however, to represent the company as having a full-paid capital stock when in fact the stock was wholly issued in payment of a worthless mine. The person making such representation is liable to the vendee[7]

There are various facts which constitute fraud herein, and various principles of law applicable to the remedy to be pursued Many cases are occurring constantly, and the decisions on this subject are becoming of great importance.[8]

---

[1] Seaman z Low, 4 Bosw , 337 (1859)

[2] Hagar z Thompson, 1 Black, 80 (1861).

[3] Board of Com'rs of T Co. v Reynolds, 44 Ind , 509 (1873) Where one of the partners in the building of railroads, and in owning stocks, bonds, etc , dies, and his executor, after an examination of all the assets by means of experts, etc , makes a settlement with the other partner, such settlement is binding although the other partner did not impart all the knowledge or information he might have given The subsequent rise in value of some of the securities is immaterial Colton v Stanford, 23 Pac. Rep., 16 (Cal , 1890). The purchaser of stock from the secretary of the company cannot rescind on the ground of fraud, the secretary having given at the time of the sale all the information which he had concerning the company No confidential or fiduciary relation exists Krumbhaar v. Griffiths, 25 Atl. Rep , 64 (Pa., 1892) And see § 320

[4] Grant v. Attrill, 11 Fed Rep, 469 (1882). As to other cases of fraud by the vendee, see Johnson v. Kirby, 65 Cal , 482 (1884), Hemppling v. Burr, 26 N W Rep., 496 (Mich , 1886).

[5] Comins v Coe, 117 Mass., 45 (1874)

[6] Woodruff v McDonald, 83 Ark , 97 (1878)

[7] Cross v Sackett, 2 Bosw. (N. Y.), 617 (1858) See, also, §§ 40, 48, supra. But an assertion that the capital stock is a certain amount is not an assertion that it has been all paid in Colt v. Wollaston, 2 P Wms , 154 (1723). When a promoter misrepresents to a subscriber the price paid by the promoter for property conveyed by him to the company, the subscriber may sue him for damages Teachout v. Van Hoesen, 40 N. W Rep., 96 (Iowa, 1888). A sale or pledge of stock stamped "non-assessable" when in fact it was not legally paid up, renders liable for false representations the president and secretary who made such sale or pledge and who knew that it was not paid-up stock Windram z French, 24 N. E. Rep., 914 (Mass , 1890)

[8] Where a debtor turned over to his

Fraud in the sale of stock frequently arises in the organization of the company The parties who cause the company to be organized are called the "promoters" of it As such they are disqualified from making a profit by selling property to the company at a

creditor, as trustee, the controlling stock of a corporation, for the latter to manage, and the latter afterwards, by threats of abandoning the enterprise, forced the debtor to sell him the stock outright, a court of equity will set aside such sale and hold the creditor liable as a trustee Ryle v Ryle, 7 Atl Rep., 484 (N J, 1886). Failure of vendor to state that the company is a joint-stock association and not a corporation is not fraud avoiding the sale of the stock Curtiss v Hurd, 30 Fed Rep, 729 (1887) Director selling stock cannot be defeated in his action for the price by reason of fraudulent representations of the corporate treasurer inducing defendant to purchase Doane v King, 30 Fed Rep, 106 (1887). Question for the jury whether it was fraud in representing that stock was paid up, when in fact first payment only had been made, and balance had been paid by dividends. Kryger v Andrews, 35 N. W Rep, 257 (Mich, 1887) Fraud may be by directors in fraudulently making dividends See ch XXXII, *infra.* Where, after an agreement to sell land for stock, the owner of the stock attends a corporate meeting and votes to sell all corporate property at sixty cents on the dollar, which is done, the purchaser of the stock may have the land returned. Harris v. Piatt, 31 N. W. Rep., 135 (Mich, 1887). Cases of fraud on the part of the vendee sometimes occur, where the vendee is given a majority of the stock, and then uses his control of the corporation to defraud the vendor in the execution of his contract to pay for the stock. Hardenburgh v. Bacon, 33 Cal, 356 (1867). Jury decided it to be fraud on part of corporate officers representing that the company was without debt. They are liable in damages for false representations. Favill v. Shehan, 26 N W. Rep, 131 (Iowa,

1885). Fraud may be by agent's representations as to cost of mining the coal, of transportation and of market price Booth v Smith, 7 N E. Rep, 610 (Ill, 1886). On a question of testimony by the defendant, see Reeve v Dennett, 6 N E Rep, 378 (Mass, 1886) Defendant entitled to bill of particulars as to when and by whom the misrepresentations were made Blanco v Navarro, N Y. Daily Reg, April 2, 1887, p. 640. It has been held that one who was induced by fraud to purchase stock in an insolvent corporation may bring suit to have his part of the corporate assets ascertained, to the exclusion of a debt due from the corporation to the person inducing him to purchase Poole v West, etc, Co, 30 Fed. Rep, 513 (1887) The person making sales of stock by false representations may be indicted for obtaining money by false representations. Commonwealth v Wood. 8 N. E. Rep, 432 (Mass, 1886). The statute of frauds as to the answering to the debt, defaults, etc, of another person has no application to a sale of stock herein. The fact that the corporate property sold several years later for a small amount is immaterial and not admissible. French v. Fitch, 35 N. W. Rep, 258 (Mich, 1887) Where a stockholder sells a controlling interest to a person who is to pay therefor by improving the corporate property, but who elects a board of directors and defrauds the vendor, the latter's remedy is a difficult one Cates v Sparkman, 11 S. W. Rep., 846 (Texas, 1889). The fraud or mistake must have been such that the agreement would not have been made in its absence, where a rescission of the contract is sought by decree Means v. Rees, 26 Fed. Rep, 210, 216 (1886). Where an agent to sell a mine induces his principals to place in his name all their stock,

much larger price than they gave for the property. The promoters act in a fiduciary capacity. Hence, when they have made a profit at the expense of the company they may be compelled to turn over that profit to the company, or, if they have sold stock

and he sells the propert and accounts to them for part only of the price, and refuses to return the stock, they may sue him for an accounting without previously tendering back the amount they received or demanding the stock Wooster z Nevills, 14 Pac Rep, 390 (Cal, 1887) False representations as to corporate property, business and prospects, and use of corporate prospectus which the vendee knows contains false statements, sustains rescission of transfer of land for stock Person purchasing land with full knowledge of fraud is not protected Certificates may be filed with clerk of court awaiting retransfer of land Ormsby z Budd, 33 N W Rep, 457 (Iowa, 1887). Vendee of stock cannot rescind or collect damages on ground that the corporation was not legally incorporated If it is a *de facto* corporation the vendor is not liable Hartei v Eltzroth, 111 Ind, 159 (1887) It is fraud for a person to sell as stock of another that which belongs to himself Maturin v Tredinnick, 2 New Rep., 514 (1863). Vendee of stock for which he gave real estate may have a reconveyance of the real estate decreed, where the sale of stock was induced by fraudulent representations Gray v Robbins, 11 Atl Rep, 860 (N J, 1887). For a case of misrepresentations, see, also, N Y Daily Reg March 21, 1888 A managing director who buys stock on credit and then aids in levying an attachment on the stock against the vendor and conceals the same from the vendor, and buys in the stock at a low price, and then repudiates his debt to the vendor, is guilty of fraud Young z Fox, 37 Fed Rep, 385 (1888) Where the president in selling stock makes false representations the vendee is not bound to investigate them He may defeat a note given in payment. Wannell v Kern, 57

Mo, 478 (1874). A representation that a bond is an "A No. 1" bond is not a material representation Deming v Darling, 20 N E Rep, 107 (Mass, 1889) See, also, instances in § 334, *supra* The vendee fails in his suit for damages if he does not contradict the defendant's testimony that the plaintiff vendee knew all the facts at the time of the sale. Nelson v Louling, 62 N Y, 645 (1875), aff'g 4 J. & S. 544

A statement that the last dividend was seven per cent and that the fiscal year ended on January 1 is a fraudulent suppression of the truth where the last dividend was a year prior to the past June 1 Tyler v Savage, 143 U S., 79 (1892) Where the contract of sale contains express warranties, parol representations as warranties are not admitted to prove false representations. Humphrey z Merriam, 49 N. W. Rep, 199 (Minn, 1891) A statement filed with the state commissioner as required by statute, in regard to the amount of the paid-up stock, is not such a representation as will sustain an action for damages for fraudulent representations inducing a person to take the notes of the company. Hunnewell v Duxbury, 28 N E Rep 267 (Mass, 1891). The fact that statements as to the affairs of the company are not filed as required by statute does not amount to fraud in the sale of stock, nor do representations that the stock will pay twenty per cent. dividends amount to fraud The question as to the validity of stock having once been litigated cannot be again raised in an action for deceit in the sale of the stock The mere act of conspiracy is not sufficient to sustain the action unless damage is shown Robinson v Parks *et al* 24 Atl Rep, 411 (Md, 1892). A representation as to the amount of water that can be obtained on water com-

of the company, the purchasers of the stock from them may rescind the purchase and hold them personally liable therefor [1]

It may be fraudulent for the directors to issue to themselves shares of the company's unissued stock in order to control elections or to make a profit [2]

An agent is not liable for misrepresentations made by his principal, but it may be a question of fact whether the vendor is a principal or agent [3]

§ 351 *Fraudulent sale by agent, etc., in breach of trust.* — A *bona fide* purchaser for value and without notice of stock from a vendor who delivers the certificates therefor indorsed in blank by another, or indorsed by the vendor himself, is protected and entitled to the stock, although it afterwards transpires that the agent was selling as agent of another and had been guilty of a breach of trust [4]

pany stock is material. A tender of the certificates is sufficient where there has been no transfer on the books   Hill v Wilson, 25 Pac Rep 1105 (Cal, 1891) Expressions of opinion as to the future, although exaggerated, are not representations Columbia Elec Co v Dixon, 49 N W Rep, 241 (Minn, 1891)   Notes given in the purchase of stock in a corporation whose sole business is to carry on an infringing telephone business are without consideration and void Clemshire v Boone, etc, Bank, 14 S. W Rep, 901 (Ark, 1890)   Where stock is issued to several persons for a patent and they return part of it to a trustee for the company to sell for working capital, and a subscriber to the company's stock gives his note to the company and the company indorses the note to one of the first-named parties who turns out his own stock to fill the subscription, the latter may recover on the note, and is not liable for false representations of one of his associates and an agent of the company   King v. Doane, 139 U S, 166 (1891)   A sale of stock will not be set aside on the ground of inadequacy of price unless so gross as to shock the conscience and give decisive evidence of fraud   Perry v Pearson, 25 N E. Rep, 636 (Ill, 1890)   It is not sufficient to prove that defendants managed the manufacturing business of the company, to sustain an action for fraud in stating that the company was doing a good business and making ten per cent., it appearing that the business was new, and defendants did not state that they knew of the financial condition   Hatch v Spooner, 13 N Y Supp, 642 (1891)   A vendor of stock may collect the price although the stock was worthless and known so to be by the vendor   Hunting v Downer, 23 N E Rep, 832 (Mass, 1890)   Statement that drill holes in coal fields showed certain results are material, and not matters of opinion   Martin v Hill, 43 N W Rep, 337 (Minn, 1889)

[1] See ch XLIII. §§ 705–708

[2] See § 70 *supra*

[3] See §§ 335 336, *supra*

[4] The case of McNeil v Tenth National Bank, 46 N Y, 325 (1871), is not only the leading case on the estoppel of the principal from repudiating the sale or pledge of his stock by his agent whom he intrusted with the certificates indorsed in blank, but it is one of the leading cases on the law of the *quasi*-negotiability of stock   Honold v Meyer, 36 La Ann, 585 (1884)   Strange v Houston & T C R R Co, 53 Tex, 162 (1880)   Dovey's Appeal, 97 Pa St., 153 (1881)   Where certificates of stock are deposited with the broker, duly transferred in blank, a *bona fide* holder

483

But the transferee is not protected where he is not a *bona fide* purchaser.[1] Where the same person acts as agent for both the transferrer and the transferee, and absconds with the purchase price after the certificates have been delivered, but before registry on the corporate books. the transferee is protected.[2] Where the corporation knows that the vendor is selling as the agent of the stockholder, who has given to the agent the certificates indorsed in blank, it must see to it that the agent has full power to sell the stock, and is liable for allowing a registry where the agent has not such power.[3] If the principal authorized the sale or ratified it, he of course can-

of such certificates from the broker is protected as against the real owner Ryman v. Gerlach, 26 Atl Rep., 302 (Pa , 1893); and see many cases in chapter on Stock Brokers, where this principle of law is often involved The case of Taylor v Great. etc , R R. Co , 4 De G & J , 559 (1859), to the contrary, turns on the English doctrine that transfers in blank are not valid The case of Donaldson v Gillet, L R , 3 Eq, 274 (1866), where the pledgee of one who held the certificate indorsed to himself was not protected, since the pledgor had purchased as agent and had fraudulently taken title in his own name, would not be good law in this country, where the failure to have the transfer registered has no effect on the pledgee's rights under such circumstances. Rumball v. Metropolitan Bank. L R, 2 Q B D, 194 (1877), where a broker committed a breach of trust The court said the stockholder "is in the position of a person who has made a representation, on the face of his scrip, that it would pass with a good title to any one on his taking it in good faith and for value, and who has put it in the power of his agent to hand over the scrip with this representation to those who are induced to alter their position on the faith of the representation so made" Moodie v Seventh Nat. Bank, 3 Weekly N C., 118 (1876), holding that if the purchaser takes partly for an antecedent debt he is not a *bona fide* holder to that extent. Dovey's Appeal, 97 Pa. St , 153 (1881). The books are full of cases wherein an

agent has committed a breach of trust in the sale of stock. For many instances of this kind of fraud and the various principles of law applicable thereto, see chs. 19, 22, 24 An assignee in insolvency of the agent does not take the stock. See § 320 An agent to collect dividends who loans the stock at a profit is liable for its loss, even 'though he informed the owner of the loan and she did not object. Persch v. Quiggle, 57 Pa St., 247 (1868) A *bona fide* purchaser from the agent is protected. State Bank v. Cox, 11 Rich. Eq , 344 (1860); West. etc., Co.'s Appeal, 81 Pa St., 19 (1870): Otis v Gardner, 105 Ill., 436 (1883); Gulick r Markham, 6 Daly, 129 (1875); Martin v Sedgwick, 9 Beav., 333 (1846); Appeal of Linnard, 6 E. Rep, 877 (Pa , 1886)

[1] Talmage v Third Nat. Bank, 91 N. Y , 531 (1883), Crocker v Crocker, 31 N. Y , 507 (1865), Weaver v Borden, 49 N. Y., 286 (1872), where the agent fraudulently bought in his own name and then fraudulently sold, Williamson v Mason, 12 Hun, 97 (1877). Purchaser from agent with notice of fact that he held as agent, and that he had sold to himself, is not protected. Bank of Louisville v. Gray, 2 S. W. Rep., 168 (Ky , 1886).

[2] *Ex parte* Shaw, L R, 2 Q. B. D., 463 (1877)

[3] Woodhouse v Crescent Mutual Ins. Co , 35 La. Ann , 238 (1882), holding also that the transferee who is charged with receiving with notice may be joined as a party defendant; St. Romes v. Cotton Press Co , 127 U. S , 614 (1888).

not afterwards complain.[1] Where an agent to sell is able to sell
for more than he accounts for to his principal, the latter cannot
recover the difference unless the sale was actually made.[2] Although
a customer may rescind a purchase of stock made for him by his
broker, when he discovers that the broker sold him stock owned
by such broker, yet if the customer has exchanged such stock for
reorganization stock he must tender back the reorganization stock.[3]
In England the courts do not protect a purchaser of certificates of
stock unless the latter has not only purchased but has obtained a
registry on the corporate books.[4]

An agent's power to sell stock does not authorize him to pledge
it.[5] A person who knows, or has the means of knowing, that
another person holds stock as an agent only, cannot take such stock
in pledge from the agent, although the latter represents that the
money is to be used for his principal. The principal may recover the stock if he has not authorized the pledge.[6] A *bona fide*
purchaser of certificates of stock from a pledgee is similarly protected.[7]

§ 352. *Fraud may be by corporate reports or prospectus* — A report of corporate officers to the stockholders, setting forth the condition of the affairs of the corporation, is deemed to be a statement to
the public also, and it may be relied upon by any one in purchasing
shares. This principle of law was first clearly established in Eng-

---

[1] As to the admissibility in evidence
of receipt showing that agent was authorized to sell by order of the principal's brother, see Dwyer v Fuller, 11 N.
E. Rep., 686 (Mass., 1887) Pledge of
stock by agent is not a conversion,
where the principal receives without
objection and retains a receipt from the
agent setting forth such pledge. Metcalf v. Williams, 11 N. E. Rep., 700
(Mass., 1887).

[2] Edison v. Gilliland, 42 Fed. Rep., 205
(1890).

[3] Mayo v. Knowlton, 10 N. Y. Supp.,
230 (1890).

[4] In England it is held, even in regard
to American certificates of stock, that a
bona fide purchaser of certificates of
stock, duly indorsed, from an agent
selling in breach of faith, is not protected until registry is obtained Colonial Bank v Hepworth, 57 L. T. Rep.,
148 (1887). But see Williams v. Colonial
Bank, 57 L. T. Rep., 188 (1887), and see

Easton v. London, etc., Bank, 55 L. T.
Rep, 678 (1886). Even in England, if a
broker transfers stock in breach of trust
to a bank, and the bank afterwards at
his request transfers the stock to another
person, the bank, being ignorant of his
agency, is not liable to the principal for
the value of the stock. Marshall v Nat l,
etc, Bank of Eng, 66 L. T. Rep, 525
(1892). See also, §§ 378, 379

[5] Merchants' Bank of Canada v Livingston, 74 N Y, 223 (1878). See §§ 321,
326

[6] Fisher v. Brown, 104 Mass., 259
(1870).

[7] A bank taking a pledge of negotiable bonds in good faith may hold
them though it turn out that the
pledger was not the owner of them but
held them as security that a mortgage
would be canceled Saloy v. Hibernia,
etc, Bank, 1 S Rep, 657 (La, 1887). As
to sales by trustees, etc, see ch. XIX,
supra.

land in 1860, in the case of Davidson v Tulloch[1] It was there held that there need be no privity between the officers issuing the report and the person purchasing shares of stock from third persons If such purchaser made his purchase relying upon material statements in corporate reports which were false, he has his remedy against all persons who knowingly made or issued the report[2] The leading case in this country on the liability of corporate directors for fraudulent representation as to the condition of the company, not made to a purchaser of stock personally, but to the public generally, is Cross v. Sackett,[3] decided in 1858, where fraudulent dividends and representations based thereon were made. ·

[1] 6 Jur (N S.) 543, S. C., 3 Macq (H. of L), 783

[2] Scott v Dixon, 29 L J. (Ex) 62, n (1859), explained in Peck v Gurney, L R , 6 H L , 398 (1873) as follows "The report, though originally made to the shareholders, was intended for the information of all persons who were disposed to deal in shares, and the representation must be regarded as having been made not indirectly, but directly to each person who obtained the report from the bank where it was publicly announced it was to be brought in the same manner as if it had been personally delivered to him by the director" Gerhard v Bates, 20 Eng L. & Eq. 129 (1853), Cullen v Thompson, 6 L T (N S.), 870 (1862), holding that, where directors of a joint-stock company issue false and fraudulent reports to the public and the manager, secretary and other officers of the bank supply the detailed statements for such report, knowing them to be false and that they are to be used for purposes of deceit, and a third party, acting on such reports, purchases shares in the company and suffers loss thereby, each of the officers of the company who knowingly assisted in the fraud is personally liable to such third party for the loss caused by such misrepresentation in the report, though the report was signed only by the directors and not by the subordinate officers

[3] 2 Bosw, 617, 6 Abb Pr, 247, 16 How. Pr 62, the court saying "When an instrument is made to deceive the public generally, and is adapted as well as intended to deceive some portion of the public, and as well one person as another, and was used as it was designed it should be, and fraudulently induces some one to act to his prejudice by acting in the mode it was intended to influence them to act who might be deceived by it, the person who made the instrument and caused it to be thus fraudulently used is liable to the person who has been defrauded by it In such a case the person injured has been subjected to damages by his fraudulent acts, and the fraudulent wrong-doer is liable for the consequences " Cazeaux v. Mali, 25 Barb, 578 (1857). ' It is not essential that the reference should be addressed directly to the plaintiff, if it were made with the intent of its influencing every one to whom it might be communicated, or who might read or hear of it, the latter class of persons would be in the same position as those to whom it was directly communicated, but they must have come to a knowledge of it before their purchase." Morse v Swits, 19 How. Pr, 275 (1859), holding a bank officer liable for false statements in a report published in accordance with the requirements of a statute The court said "Being published, the public or any individual of the public has a right to believe it And if, believing it, any one of the public acts on that belief, the makers and publishers of this falsehood are to be held liable for the conse-

§ 353. A somewhat different rule prevails in England as to false statements contained in a prospectus of a corporation. A prospectus is issued for the purpose of inducing persons to subscribe for stock. Its object is not to promote the sale of that stock. Accordingly it was decided in Peek v. Gurney,[1] in 1873, that "the purchaser of shares in the market, upon the faith of a prospectus which he has not received from those who are answerable for it, cannot, by action upon it, so connect himself with them as to render them liable to him for the misrepresentation contained in it as if it had been addressed personally to himself." In New York a directly opposite rule prevails. In the case of Morgan v. Skiddy,[2] in 1875, the court of appeals held that, "if the plaintiff purchased his stock relying upon the truth of the prospectus, he has a right of action for deceit against the persons who, with knowledge of the fraud and with intent to deceive, put it in circulation. The representation was made to each person comprehended within the class of persons who were designed to be influenced by the prospectus, and when a prospectus of this character has been issued, no other relation or privity between the parties need be shown except that created by the wrongful and fraudulent act of the defendants in issuing or circulating the prospectus, and the resulting injury to the plaintiff."

§ 354 *Remedies for the fraud.*—There are three methods by which a person who has been fraudulently induced to buy or sell stock may remedy the wrong.[3] He may bring an action at law

---

quences they have caused '(citing cases) See, also, Salmon v. Richardson, 30 Conn., 360 (1862), Fenn v. Curtis 23 Hun, 384 (1881), holding corporate secretary liable to purchaser of shares from an individual, the secretary having signed the certificate of stock and also a circular stating that the corporation was a corporation when in fact it was not. And see §§ 40, 48, *supra.* A person buying stock in what was supposed to be a corporation, but is a partnership, cannot recover back his money from all of the participants Perry v. Hale, 19 N. E. Rep., 174 (Mass., 1887). A corporation is not liable for misrepresentations of the president in selling stock belonging to himself. Prosser v. First Nat'l Bank, 106 N. Y. 677 (1887). Where stockholders in an apartment house corporation are entitled to rent apartments at a rental to be fixed by a majority vote of the stockholders, an increased rental

so voted is legal. The by-laws providing for such a vote override a general statement in a prospectus to the contrary, the stockholders knowing of the by-law. Compton v. Chelsea, 128 N. Y. 537 (1891).

[1] L. R., 6 H. L., 377, overruling Seymour v. Bagshaw 18 C. B. 903 (1856), and Bedford v. Bagshaw, 4 H. & N., 538 (1859), explaining Scott v. Dixon, 29 L. J. (Ex.), 62, n (1859), and Gerhard v. Bates, 2 El. & Bl. 476 (1853), and itself explained in Cargill v. Bower, L. R., 10 Ch. D., 502 (1878). In Bellairs v. Tucker, L. R, 13 Q. B. D, 563 (1884), the court seems to have assumed a different position, and to have treated the prospectus the same as any other method of misrepresentation

[2] 62 N. Y., 319

[3] "A person who has been induced by fraudulent representations to become the purchaser of property has upon dis-

for the consideration, or an action at law for damages for the deceit, or he may file a bill in equity to have the transaction set aside. The second remedy is the most difficult and the last the most easy to maintain.

In special cases other remedies are open to the purchaser. He may compel the defrauding party to abide by the statements that were made [1] If the contract is executory it may canceled by mutual agreement [2] The pleadings in enforcing the remedies which the vendee has vary, of course, according to the remedy which is pursued [3]

covery of the fraud three remedies open to him either of which he may elect. He may rescind the contract absolutely and sue in an action at law to recover the consideration parted with upon the fraudulent contract. To maintain such action he must first restore, or offer to restore, to the other party whatever may have been received by him by virtue of the contract.

"He may bring an action in equity to rescind the contract and in that action have full relief. Such an action is not founded upon a rescission, but is maintained *for* a rescission, and it is sufficient, therefore, for the plaintiff to offer in his complaint to return what he has received and make tender of it on the trial Lastly, he may retain what he has received and bring an action at law to recover the damages sustained. This action proceeds upon an affirmance of the contract, and the measure of the plaintiff's recovery is the difference between the article sold and what it should be according to the representations." Vail *v.* Reynolds, 118 N Y., 297 (1890) Where the sale of stock has been induced by fraud the vendee may follow the money paid by him and recover it back if the identity of the fund can be shown Moore *v.* Williams, 63 Hun, 55 (1891).

[1] Where an apartment house corporation induces by prospectus subscriptions on representations that certain subscriptions entitle the holder to a perpetual leasehold in the apartments selected by the subscriber, he cannot afterwards be evicted on the ground that

the building cost more than was expected and further rent must be paid Compton *v.* Chelsea, 8 N Y Supp., 622 (1890), aff'd, 128 N Y, 537. Where a person organizes a railroad corporation and takes a contract for its construction, and causes all the stock and a large quantity of bonds to be issued to himself, and then sells these stocks and bonds and has knowledge of representations made by corporate officers to his vendee that the company owes nothing except the bonds, he cannot afterwards enforce a claim for doing extra work under a contract, where such contract did not appear on the books of the company The transaction is a fraud on his part. Chicago, etc., R'y *v.* Miller, 51 N W Rep, 981 (Mich, 1892). Although a purchaser of stock cannot rescind, he having been guilty of delay, yet he may sue the vendor upon a warranty that the stock will be worth more than what it was sold for Maxted *v.* Fowler, 53 N W Rep, 921 (Mich, 1892)

[2] A subscription may be canceled by and with the consent of the directors when fraud is involved Four years afterwards corporate creditors cannot attack it. McDermott *v.* Harrison, 9 N Y Supp., 184 (1890) See ch X. If there has been a mutual mistake in regard to what the stock really represented in property, an action for money had and received or a suit to cancel the sale will lie. Norton *v.* Bohart, 16 S. W. Rep., 598 (Mo., 1891).

[3] In the case of Smith *v.* Tracy, 36 N. Y., 78 (1867), the vendee sued the vendor

§ 355. *Action for deceit* — In order to sustain an action for damages for deceit, whereby plaintiff was induced to buy or sell shares of stock, it is necessary for the plaintiff to prove that statements were made or acts done which were fraudulent, that the person guilty of them knew that they were fraudulent, and that the plaintiff acted on such statements or acts in buying or selling the stock.[1] In England a statement made recklessly, or without regard as to whether it is true or untrue, may constitute a fraudulent intent.[2]

for a breach of warranty, alleging that the vendor's agent made certain representations as to the condition of the corporation The action failed on the ground that the vendor did not authorize the agent to make a warranty In the case of Ayers *v* French, 41 Conn., 142 (1874), the court held that fraud, in ducing the owner of stock to part with it, may be remedied by the action of trover with a count in case for a fraudulent procurement and conversion of the stock. In the case of National Exchange Co *v.* Drew, 2 Macq (H. of L.), 103 (1855), it was held that where a person is induced by the fraudulent reports and representations of corporate officers to purchase stock, and the corporation loans him money to do so, it cannot recover back the money loaned. See Lightfoot *v.* Creed, 8 Taunt , 267 (1818), holding that the vendee should declare not for money paid, but specially on the contract.

[1] Arkwright *v.* Newbold, L. R., 17 Ch. D., 301 (1881), Arthur *v* Griswold, 55 N. Y., 400, 410 (1874), the court saying "The rules of law require a reasonable degree of certainty as to each requisite necessary to constitute the cause of action, viz., representations, falsity, *scienter*, deception and injury."

[2] In the important case of Derry *v* Peek, 61 L. T Rep, 265 (1889) the House of Lords decided that in order to sustain an action of deceit there must be proof of fraud, and nothing short of that will suffice. Fraud is proved when it is shown that a false statement has been made (1) knowingly , (2) without belief in its truth; (3) recklessly. But if a

man make a false statement honestly believing it to be true, it is not sufficient to support an action of deceit to show that he had no reasonable grounds for his belief. The directors of a tramway company issued a prospectus in which they stated that they were authorized to use steam power, and that by this means a great saving in working would be effected. At the time of making this statement they had not in fact obtained authority to use steam power, but they honestly believed that they would obtain it as a matter of course *Held* (reversing the judgment of the court below), that they were not liable in an action of deceit brought by a shareholder who had been induced to apply for shares by the statement in the prospectus. In an action for deceit by a misrepresentation in a prospectus as to the net profit on the capital employed, the action being against one who was a promoter, and also one of the vendors, and whose name appeared in the prospectus and who became a director, the plaintiff must prove (1) that the defendant's statement was untrue , (2) that it was dishonest , (3) that he believed it to be untrue. Glasier *v.* Rolls, 62 L. T. Rep., 133 (1889), reversing 60 id , 591, and following the House of Lords in Derry *v.* Peek, 61 id , 265 Peek *v.* Gurney, L R , 6 H. L., 377 (1873), the court saying: "It is said that the prospectus is true as far as it goes, but half a truth will sometimes amount to a real falsehood " See, also, ch IX, § 147. In Bellaires *v* Tucker, L. R., 13 Q. B D , 563 (1884), however, the court say "The action is one for deceit. It is necessary

In New York the rule is more stringent. The case of Wakeman v. Dalley[1] applies to this class of cases the rule that "an action founded upon the deceit and fraud of the defendant cannot be maintained in the absence of proof that he believed, or had reason to believe at the time he made them, that the representations made by him were false, and that they were for that reason fraudulently made, or that he assumed or intended to convey the impression that he had actual knowledge of their truth, though conscious that he had no such knowledge."

This case held that a director is not liable for false representations on the company's printed business cards, of which he was ignorant, even though his name was attached thereto. In California it is held that the purchaser of stock who has given a note in payment cannot defeat an action on the note by setting up that the purchase was induced by fraud. He must first disaffirm the contract and return the certificate, and such return must be made before the trial.[2] But where the purchaser brings an action for deceit he need not return the consideration nor rescind the contract.[3] His injury is to be duly measured, and credit may be given for the real value of the stock.[4] A director is not liable for the

not only to prove that the statements in a prospectus or any other document are not true, but it must be proved that they are fraudulently put forward with intent to deceive."

[1] 51 N. Y., 27 (1872); Nelson v. Luling, 4 N. Y. Sup. Ct., 544 (1873); aff'd, 62 N. Y., 645; Schwenck v. Naylor, 102 N. Y., 683 (1886). The case of Holmes v. Moffat, 120 N. Y., 159 (1890), was an action for false representations and deceit in the sale of stock, but the decision turned upon technical rules relative to the trial. See, also, Clark v. Edgar, 80 Mo., 106 (1884); Gee v. Moss, 68 Iowa, 318 (1886). The action for deceit does not lie against the corporation, at least where no fraudulent intent is proved. Pinedo v. Germania, etc., Co., N. Y. Daily Reg., July 29, 1885. See, also, § 157. In an action of tort for deceit against a director for inducing a person to purchase stock, "the plaintiff must prove representations of material facts which are false, and which induce him to act; and either that the defendant knew them to be false, or that the facts being facts susceptible of knowledge,

he represented as of his own knowledge that they were true, when in fact he had no such knowledge." Cole v. Cassidy, 138 Mass., 437 (1885). In an action for fraud inducing the purchase of stock *scienter* must be proved. It is sufficient that the defendant had no good reason to believe that material representations made by him were true. A statement that $1,500,000 worth of ore was lying on the ground around the mine is a material representation. Brandt v. Frederick, 47 N. W. Rep., 6 (Wis., 1890). In Wisconsin, in a suit by a vendee of stock against the vendor for damages for obtaining money and property by false and fraudulent representations, the defendant may be arrested. Warner v. Bates, 43 N. W. Rep., 957 (Wis., 1889), giving the complaint and affidavit.

[2] Gifford v. Carhill, 29 Cal., 589 (1866).

[3] Miller v. Barber, 66 N. Y., 558, 564 (1876); Newberry v. Garland, 31 Barb., 121 (1860).

[4] See ch. XXXV. In an action for false representations inducing the purchase of stock, the defendant may show

misrepresentations and frauds of his co-directors, unless he has expressly authorized or tacitly permitted commission thereof [1] The mere fact of being a director ' is not *per se* sufficient to hold a party liable for the frauds and misrepresentations of the active managers of a corporation Some knowledge of and participation in the act claimed to be fraudulent must be brought home to the person charged " [2] Where, however, proof is given tending to show that the defendants were jointly engaged in a common scheme to defraud the plaintiff, the acts and declarations of one are admissible in proof against all; [3] and frauds of a similar nature, at or near the same time as the one complained of, may be shown [4] The fraud practiced need not have been the sole inducement to the purchase [5] A party may be liable herein although he was neither a corporate officer nor the vendor of the stock. If, with intent to cheat and defraud the vendee, he induces him, by fraudulent means, to purchase stock for value which he knows to be worthless, he is liable for the damage sustained, although the purchase is actually made from another [6] A sale of stock does not transfer a right of action for damages caused by false representations made to the vendor by the party from whom the vendee purchased [7] In an action by a purchaser of stock against the company and two di-

that the stock was worth as much as it would have been had the representations been true Doran v Eaton, 41 N W Rep , 244 (Minn , 1889)

[1] Weir v Barnett, L R , 3 Ex D , 32

[2] Arthur v Griswold, 55 N Y , 400, 406 (1874), Morgan v Skiddy, 62 N Y, 319 Where a party purchases stock relying on a prospectus which states that reports had been prepared for the directors by the engineers, and giving extracts from the reports, the directors are not personally liable in an action for deceit, even if it is shown that the reports were not prepared on instructions from the directors, but were prepared on instructions from the vendors to the company It is necessary to prove that the reports were untrue Angus v Clifford, 65 L. T. Rep., 274 (1891), reversing 63 L. T. Rep , 684 (1890)

[3] Miller v Barber, 66 N. Y., 558 567 (1876)

[4] Id

[5] Morgan v. Skiddy, 62 N. Y., 319, 328 (1875), *Ex parte* Carling, 56 L T Rep ,

115 (1887) Plaintiff need not prove that he relied solely upon the misrepresentations Hatch v Spooner, 13 N Y, Supp. 642 (1891).

[6] Hubbell v Meigs, 50 N Y, 480 490 (1872) Upon the effect of false and fraudulent representations on an action for damages, see Tockerson v Chapin 52 N Y Super Ct, 16 (1885) It is no defense to such an action that the original conversion was by some one else Kuhn v McAllister, 1 Utah, 275 (1875), S C, *sub nom.* McAllister v Kuhn, 95 U S., 87 (1877)

[7] Kennedy v Benson, 54 Fed Rep , 836 (Iowa, 1893) Where fraudulent representations are made inducing a party to sell his stock, and then the purchaser wrecks the corporation, the vendor may hold the latter liable for damages The assignee of the cause of action may sue in *trover* for conversion, but cannot sue for damages for fraudulent representations, inasmuch as the latter cause of action is not assignable Smith v Thompson *et al*, 54 N. W. Rep., 168 (Mich., 1892).

rectors for deceit, the verdict may be against one or more of the defendants and may be sustained by one or more of the misrepresentations alleged.[1] Several persons defrauded of their contract whereby they were to receive stock cannot sue jointly. Each must sue separately.[2] The measure of damages for fraud inducing the purchase of stock "is the difference between the value of the stock at the time it was purchased and the price paid for it." [3]

§ 356. *Remedy in equity.* — A court of equity has concurrent jurisdiction with a court of law in enabling a purchaser of stock to recover back money paid, where the purchase was induced by fraud chargeable to the vendor.[4] The remedy in equity, for a sale or purchase of stock induced by fraud, is by a bill to set aside the

---

[1] Lare *v.* Westmoreland, etc., Co., 25 Atl. Rep., 812 (Pa., 1893), holding, also, that the party purchasing the stock may rescind or may retain the stock and sue for damages.

[2] Summerlin *v.* Fronteriza, etc., Co., 41 Fed. Rep., 249 (1890).

[3] Redding *v.* Godwin, 46 N. W. Rep., 563 (Minn., 1890). See, also, § 581. In an action for damages for fraud inducing the plaintiff to purchase stock, the measure of damages is "not the difference between the contract price and the reasonable market value if the property had been as represented to be, even if the stock had been worth the price paid for it; nor, if the stock were worthless, could the plaintiff have recovered the value it would have had if the property had been equal to the representations. What the plaintiff might have gained is not the question, but what he had lost by being deceived into the purchase." The defendant "was bound to make good the loss sustained, such as the moneys plaintiff had paid out and interest, and any other outlay legitimately attributable to defendant's fraudulent conduct; but this liability did not include the expected fruits of an unrealized speculation." Smith *v.* Bolles, 132 U. S., 125 (1889).

[4] Where a person is induced to subscribe for stock on the fraudulent representations of the president that the company is in a prosperous condition, the person may file a bill in equity to recover back the money, and equity has jurisdiction on the grounds of discovery, account, fraud, misrepresentation and concealment. Both the company and the president individually were made defendants and held liable. Tyler *v.* Savage, 143 U. S., 79 (1892). See, also, Hill *v.* Lane, L. R., 11 Eq., 215, where the court say: "It is so well settled that this court will entertain jurisdiction in such cases that it would be a misfortune, indeed, to the public if there were any sufficient ground for considering that the jurisdiction is doubtful. . . . Although courts of common law may have jurisdiction in some such cases, there is clearly concurrent jurisdiction in this court," doubting Ogilvie *v.* Currie, 37 L. J. (Ch.), 541 (1868); Campbell *v.* Fleming, 1 Ad. & El., 40 (1834). A bill in equity is a proper remedy for fraud inducing a sale of stock. Andriessen's Appeal, 16 Atl. Rep., 840 (Pa., 1889).

Where the president sells stock for $120 per share after he has indorsed a false statement of the company's affairs, the stock being really worth but $70 per share, the vendee may have the sale rescinded. Prewitt *v.* Trimble, 17 S. W. Rep., 356 (Ky., 1891). In a suit to rescind for fraud the plaintiff must prove that the stock was not worth what he paid for it or could not be sold for that sum. Aron *v.* De Castro, 13 N. Y. Supp., 372 (1891); affirmed, 131 N. Y., 651. In an action in equity to rescind a

whole transaction.[1]   This remedy follows the rules usually prescribed in such suits.   It is not necessary for the complainant to prove a fraudulent intent.   Innocent acts or misrepresentations

sale of stock for fraud the corporation is not a necessary party   The value of the stock need not be shown, and the amount paid with interest may be recovered   But six years' delay after discovering the fraud is a bar.   Higgins v Crouse, 63 Hun. 134 (1892).   In an action to rescind for fraud the defrauded subscribers need not join as plaintiffs, although they all purchased at the same time and on the same terms.   Moore v. Robertson, 11 N. Y. Supp, 798 (1890).   Where the vendors represent that the money will be used to buy a secret process, and they pay over the money to the company for that purpose, and it is mingled with other funds and is not used to purchase the process because the process is a fraud the vendees may rescind as to the vendors but cannot make the receiver of the company pay over the money   Id   The vendor may tender back the stock and file a bill in equity to cancel the sale on the ground that he was induced to purchase by false statements that the corporation owned the secret process; that a patent had been applied for, that it was ready to commence business, and that complainant would be made president and manager.   Benton v. Ward, 47 Fed. Rep., 253 (1891).   An equitable suit does not lie to rescind a sale of worthless bonds.   A suit at law is the proper remedy. United States Bank v Lyon County, 47 Fed Rep, 514 (1891).   A purchaser of stock who was induced to purchase by fraud cannot maintain a suit in equity when he fails to show more than

a right to pecuniary damages for misrepresentations   Whitney v. Fairbanks, 54 Fed. Rep, 985 (Vt., 1893)   A creditor holding an unpaid promissory note cannot by bill in equity bring in the directors to hold them liable for false representations and also claim that the company was not duly incorporated, and also bring in a subsequent corporation that took all the assets of the first, and also bring in those persons who finally obtained such assets — all in one bill brought to collect the debt.   National Bank v Texas, etc Co., 12 S W. Rep, 101 (Tex, 1889)   See, also, to the effect that a court of equity has jurisdiction, London, etc, Co. v Central T. Co, (N Y L J. June 12, 1891).   Where bank stock is sold by fraudulent and false representations. the bank being aware thereof and receiving indirectly the money paid for the stock, the sale may be rescinded and the money recovered back from it even though it is insolvent.   Florida, etc, Co v Murrill, 52 Fed. Rep, 63 (1892).   Several subscribers who have been induced by the same misrepresentations contained in a prospectus to subscribe for stock may join in a suit in equity for the benefit of themselves and others similarly deceived to set aside their subscriptions   Bosher v Richmond, etc, Co., 16 S. E. Rep, 360 (Va., 1892)   Several purchasers of stock may contribute to the bringing of a test case to decide whether representations inducing the purchase were fraudulent   Davies v Stowell 47 N W Rep. 370

---

[1] Stainbank v Fernley, 9 Sim., 556 (1839), where a sale by a director who has issued false reports and declared illegal dividends was set aside. The corporation is a proper party to such actions, if a registry has been obtained by the person who has obtained the stock by fraud, since a retransfer on the corporate books is asked for. See, also, Bradley v. Luce, 99 Ill, 234 (1881)   A judgment creditor of a foreign corporation cannot enjoin it from transferring stock and bonds owned by it.   The remedy sought must be something in addition to the injunction.   Rogers v. Michigan, etc., R. R., 28 Barb., 539 (1859).

suffice for this purpose, although they would be insufficient to sustain an action for deceit.[1]

Where, however, the fraud is chargeable to the corporate officers or third persons, and the vendor of the stock is innocent, the vendee cannot rescind the sale, unless such corporate officers or third persons acted as agents for the vendor[2]

Equity will sometimes compel the vendor to make good his representations Thus, where the vendor represented that the corporate property was unincumbered, equity will at the instance of the purchaser of stock enjoin the vendor from enforcing a lien which he has on such property[3] The right to rescind the contract for fraud is waived by taking a bond of indemnity against liability on the stock, such bond being taken upon discovery of the fraud.[4] Laches also is a bar[5] The purchaser repudiating the transaction must tender back the stock received by him[6]

(Wis, 1890) Where negotiable bonds are stolen from the owners and they pass into *bona fide* hands, and then the thief obtains them by force from such *bona fide* hands and returns them to the first owner, the latter is entitled to keep them London, etc, Co v London, etc, Bank, 6t L T Rep, 37 (1889) In England this remedy by bill in equity is held to be ' precisely analogous to the common-law action for deceit ' in that damages may be awarded Peek v Gurney, L R, 5 H L, 377, 390 (1873), the court saying also "There can be no doubt that equity exercises a concurrent jurisdiction in cases of this description, and the same principles applicable to them must prevail both at law and in equity "

[1] Arkwright v Newbold, L R, 17 Ch D, 301 (1881) A suit in equity lies to rescind a sale of stock induced by fraudulent representations Intent to defraud need not be proved Martin v Hill, 43 N W Rep, 337 (Minn, 1889)

[2] Moffat v Winslow, 7 Paige, 124 (1838) Benjamin on Sales, 4th Am ed, § 467a says "the only remedy of a shareholder in a joint-stock company, who has been induced to purchase shares by the fraud of the agent of the company, is rescission of his contract and *restitutio in integrum*."

[3] Jones v. Bolles, 9 Wall., 364 (1869)

[4] Bridge v Penniman, 51 Superior Ct. (N Y), 183 (1885) Where the vendee of stock becomes a director and has access to the books, and complains of fraud in the sale, and then takes a sum of money from the vendor in settlement, he cannot again complain upon the failure of the company Powell v Adams, 12 S W Rep 295 (Mo, 1889)

[5] A year's delay by the vendor of stock after being advised by his attorney that he had a good case of fraud is fatal Perry v Pearson, 25 N E Rep, 636 (Ill, 1890) Delay of six years after knowledge of fraud inducing a purchase of stock is fatal Andriessen's Appeal, 16 Atl Rep, 840 (Pa, 1889) Three years' delay in tendering back the bonds is not fatal, nor is the fact that the vendee resold the bonds on the same terms, and the sub-vendee returned them to the first vendee. Wooster v Sage, 67 N Y, 67 (1876); aff'd, 6 Hun, 285, Mayo v. Knowlton, 134 N Y, 250 (1892).

[6] In order to rescind a fraudulent sale of stock, the stock and also all other property received must be tendered back Wainwright v Weske, 23 Pac Rep, 12 (Cal, 1889). Francis v. New York & B. El R R Co., 108 N Y, 93 (1888), 17 Abb. N C., 1, holding, also, that where the vendee has transferred

If the person fraudulently obtaining stock has transferred it to another party, or is about to transfer it, an injunction may be obtained[1] The corporation should then be made a party[2]

§ 357. *Fraud in selling stock may amount to a conspiracy* — A combination of persons to fraudulently raise the price of a stock by misrepresentations and fraudulent practices may amount to a

said stock to another his action fails Defrauded vendee must tender back the stock unconditionally If he has used the stock in another transaction, even with the vendor, his right to rescind for fraudulent representations is barred Bridge *v* Penniman, 105 N Y, 642 (1887) But where the vendee has sold part of the stock he cannot maintain a suit in equity to collect money damages for loss occasioned by misrepresentations inducing him to purchase His remedy is at law No cancellation of the contract is involved White *v* Boyce, 21 Fed Rep 228 (1884) Selling some of stock before repudiating purchase for fraud is no bar to repudiation 1 R'y & Corp L. J , 434 Rescission is not barred although the vendee has lost the stock by forfeiture, the vendor having knowledge thereof Maturin *v* Tredinnick, 4 New Rep , 15 (1864) If the party selling the stock states that he is selling stock owned by the corporation, when as a matter of fact he is selling his own stock, the vendee upon discovering the fraud may rescind the sale, and recover back the purchase price paid He need not tender the same stock which he received inasmuch as stock has no "ear mark" If he has exchanged the stock for the stock of another company into which his company has been merged, he may borrow stock of the first company and make a tender of that He must, however, rescind promptly upon the discovery of the fraud Although he does not discover the fraud for four years he may then rescind Mayo *v* Knowlton, 134 N Y, 250 (1892) A suit to cancel a sale of stocks and bonds, on the ground of fraud on the part of the purchaser,

will not lie where the money paid at the sale has not been returned or tendered, even though the seller spent the money before he discovered the alleged fraud, and is unable to obtain the amount of money necessary for a tender Such is the rule even though the amount to be distributed will be due to the plaintiff in case he succeeds in the suit Rigdon *v* Walcott, 31 N E Rep 158 (Ill , 1892).

[1] See §§ 361, 362

[2] Although the party seeking the stock of which he has been deprived by fraud makes the party complained of and the corporation itself parties defendant, yet if the certificates are not obtained from the party holding them the court will not order the corporation to issue new certificates The outstanding certificates may pass into the hands of a *bona fide* purchaser Joslyn *v* St. Paul, etc , Co, 46 N W Rep, 357 (Minn 1890) Where a citizen of Wisconsin claims stock in a Wisconsin corporation as against a citizen of Illinois, in whose name the stock stands on the corporate books, the corporation is a necessary party defendant, and the case cannot be removed to the federal courts Rogers *v* Van Nortwick, 45 Fed Rep , 513 (1891) Where stock is deposited with a trustee for purposes of reorganization, and transferable certificates are issued therefor by the trustee, a claimant of stock which another person has deposited, and for which such other person has the trustee's certificate cannot compel the trustee to deliver up the stock until the trustee's certificate is returned, even though the party holding it is a party defendant Bean *v* American L. & T. Co , 122 N Y , 622 (1890).

criminal conspiracy.   In England, in 1858, the directors of a joint-stock bank were found guilty of a conspiracy to defraud, where, knowing the bank to be insolvent, they issued a balance sheet showing a profit, and declared a dividend, and issued advertisements inviting the public to invest on such representations.[1]

[1] Regina v Brown et al., 7 Cox's Criminal Cases, 442 (1858); Regina v. Esdaile, 1 F & F., 213 (1858), Queen v. Gurney   See Durrell & Hyde on Directors and Officers, 115, Queen v. Stewart, id, 119; Queen v Murch, id., 118, Burnes v. Pennel, 2 H. L. C., 479 There cannot be such an offense against the United States by the directors of a national bank, since the offense is not recognized by statute. United States v. Britton, 108 U S, 199 (1883). It is difficult for a corporate creditor to seek collection by making out a conspiracy. Brackett v. Griswold, 13 N. Y. Supp, 192 (1891).

CHAPTER XXI.

SALES OF STOCK — SALES WHILE SUITS ARE PENDING AFFECTING THAT STOCK; FORGERY; LOST AND STOLEN CERTIFICATES OF STOCK; CONFISCATION OF STOCK.

A. PURCHASES WITHOUT A CERTIFICATE OF THE STOCK.

§ 358. *Rights of a purchaser of certificate of stock where the corporation has registered transfer to another without surrender of certificate.*— It has often happened that an owner of stock, after selling his stock and delivering to the vendee the certificate therefor indorsed in blank, has gone to the corporation before such transfer is registered, and by misrepresentation or other fraudulent means induced the corporation to issue to another purchaser a new certificate of stock without a surrender of the old one. It is the duty of the corporation to refuse to register a transfer unless the old certificate is delivered up. The outstanding certificate is a continuing affirmation by the corporation that no registry of a transfer of the stock represented by that certificate will be allowed until the certificate itself is presented and surrendered. This affirmation is sometimes declared in a by-law,[1] and sometimes it is printed

---

[1] Bridgeport Bank *v.* New York, etc., R. R. Co., 30 Conn., 231 (1861); Strange *v.* Houston, etc., R. R. Co., 53 Tex., 162 (1880); New York, etc., R. R. Co. *v.* Schuyler, 34 N. Y., 30 (1865).

on the face of the certificate itself[1] The obligations of the corporation, however, to require a surrender of the old certificate upon obtaining a registry is the same whether there is a by-law, or a statement on the certificate, or neither of these. It exists without any express declaration[2]

§ 359 *Liability of the corporation herein* — It is the duty and right of a corporation to refuse to allow a registry of a transfer of stock unless the outstanding certificate representing the stock is delivered up and canceled And it is a duty which the corporation is bound to fulfill If it allows a transfer to be registered without the old certificate being produced and surrendered, it is liable to any person who, without notice, purchases or has purchased the outstanding certificate[3] This rule is well established, and is based

---

[1] Cushman z Thayer Mfg Co, 76 N Y, 365 (1879)

[2] Factors' & T Ins Co z Marine D D & S Co, 31 La Ann, 149 (1887). As regards the English rule herein, see 2 Ry & Corp L J, 577 and 625

[3] Id, where a pledgee recovered damages against the corporation for issuing new certificates without a surrender of the one which the plaintiff held, Smith v American Coal Co, 7 Lans, 317 (1873), where an unrecorded transferee recovered damages against a corporation for issuing certificate to purchaser at execution sale on attachment against the transferrer See, also, § 486 *et seq* Cushman v Thayer Mfg Co, 76 N Y, 365 (1879), Bank v Lanier, 11 Wall, 369 (1870), the court saying: "It is equally clear that the bank, in allowing this stock to be transferred to other parties while the certificates were outstanding in the hands of *bona fide* holders, was guilty of a breach of corporate duty," and is liable New York & N H R R Co v Schuyler, 34 N Y, 30, 81 (1865); Holbrook v New Jersey Zinc Co. 57 N Y, 616 (1874), the court saying: "It cannot be denied that, if a corporation having power to issue stock certificates does in fact issue such a certificate, in which it affirms that a designated person is entitled to a certain number of shares of stock, it thereby holds out to persons who may deal in good faith with

the person named in the certificate that he is an owner and has capacity to transfer the shares. This proposition does not rest on any view of the negotiability of stock, but on the general principles appertaining to the law of estoppel" Moores v Citizens' Nat'l Bank, 111 U S, 156 (1883) where the court seem to hold that the person receiving new certificates without requiring a surrender of the old ones is not such a *bona fide* transferee of stock as may hold the corporation liable Brisbane v Delaware L & W R R Co, 94 N Y, 204 (1883), affirming 22 Hun, 538, and holding that until the purchaser of the outstanding certificates presents them, the corporation is protected in paying dividends to the transferee without the old certificates If no certificate has been issued the rule does not apply First Nat'l Bank v Gifford, 47 Iowa, 575 (1877). The unregistered holder of the certificates is protected, since, if he were obliged to notify the corporation at the time he purchases the stock, the value of these certificates as a basis of credit would be greatly impaired, particularly where the pledge is made at a distance from the domicile of the corporation" Smith v Crescent City, etc, Co, 30 La Ann, 1378 (1878) See also Bridgeport Bank v New York & N H R R Co. 30 Conn, 231 (1861) the court saying "The *bona fide* holders of such

on the usages and requirements of trade, and on a wise public policy which favors the protection of those who invest their money in certificates of stock, relying upon the corporation to protect the holder of such certificates.[1] Thus the corporation has been held liable where seventeen years have elapsed since a new certificate was obtained, the latter having been obtained on the ground that the outstanding certificate has been lost.[2] The corporation need

certificates had a right to rely on the certificate, under the circumstances, as securing to them the stock which they represented against all other parties." Strange v. Houston & T. C. R. R. Co., 53 Tex., 162 (1880), to the same effect, on the ground that the non-production of the original certificate "is notice to the company that a superior title may be in a third party." If a corporation allows a transfer to be made on its books without the transfer on the old certificate being signed, it is liable to the owner of the old certificate, even though the old certificate is delivered up and the attorney in fact of the owner shows his power of attorney at the time of the transfer on the books. Taft v. Presidio, etc., Co., 24 Pac. Rep., 436 (Cal., 1890). Lee v. Citizens' Nat. Bank, 2 Cin. Sup. Ct., 298 (1872), holding that the holder of the old certificates is entitled to have the illegal registry canceled. In England there seems to be no decision directly in point. A *dictum*, however, in Shropshire U. R'y & Canal Co. v. Queen, L. R., 7 H. L., 496, 509 (1875), does not support the rule which prevails in this country. The court said: Whether a transfer of shares in a company can or cannot be made without the production of the certificates of the shares is "entirely within the discretion of the directors. They were not bound to permit a transfer without the production of the certificate; but though not bound to permit a transfer, I apprehend they would not be in any way answerable if the transfer should be in any case made without the production of the certificates of the shares." The case of Hart v. Frantino, etc., Gold Min. Co., L. R., 5

Ex., 111 (1870), holds, however, that where the corporation cancels the stockholdership of one who purchased after registry without a surrender of the old certificates having been obtained, he may hold it liable in damages. As between two unrecorded transfers, one having the certificates, and the other — a subsequent purchaser — not having it, the former prevails. Societe Gen. v. Tramways Union Co., L. R., 14 Q. B. D., 424 (1884). See, also, cases in § 351.

[1] Factors' & T. Ins. Co. v. Marine D. D. & S. Co., 31 La. Ann., 149 (1879), the court saying: "We think that, by thus making stocks transferable by mere delivery of the certificate, the law has intended to interdict corporations from transferring stocks on their books, except upon surrender of the certificate or upon proof of its loss or destruction. These certificates of stock have become such important factors in trade and credit that the law has intended to surround those who take them with the safeguards it accords to the holders of the other great agencies of commerce — bills, notes, bills of lading, etc."

[2] Cleveland & M. R. R. Co. v. Robbins, 35 Ohio St., 483 (1880). But is not liable for dividends paid in the meantime. It was held, further, that a by-law allowing such issue of new certificates in case of loss had no effect as regards the plaintiff, and that the statute of limitations ran against the plaintiff only from the time he had notice of the new certificate. By statute, in New York, the person claiming to have lost his certificate may be compelled to give a bond of indemnity to the corporation before obtaining new certificates, and a holder

not assume any risk, but may refuse to permit a registry on its books of the transfer unless the old certificate is produced and surrendered [1] Where, however, the corporation is compelled to make the registry by legal proceedings, as in case of execution sales, it cannot be held liable to the holder of the outstanding certificate.[2] The corporation, when sued by the holder of the old certificate, is required either to replace the stock which has wrongfully been taken from the plaintiff, or it is obliged to compensate him in damages.

§ 360 *Rights of purchaser of stock without certificates.* — A purchaser of stock who does not receive the certificates of the stock he has purchased, but who nevertheless obtains a registry on the corporate books, and receives new certificates without a surrender of the old, and who sells the new certificates, is not liable in damages to the holder of the old certificates.[3] The remedy of the latter is

of the old certificates may have the benefit of this bond New York Session Laws, 1873, ch 151 See § 370 Such a subrogation was refused in Greenleaf v Ludington, 15 Wis, 558 (1862).

[1] The corporation may refuse to issue stock to the heirs of a stockholder unless they surrender the old certificates. State v New Orleans & C R R Co, 30 La Ann, 308 (1878), National Bank of New London v Lake S & M S R R Co, 21 Ohio St., 221 (1871), where the corporation refused to allow registry by a purchaser at an execution sale, although it was quite plain that the judgment debtor's sale of the certificates had been in fraud of creditors As between two unregistered transferees, the one with the certificate is entitled to the stock, especially where he purchased first. Maybin v Kirby, 4 Rich Eq (S. C), 105 (1851), Societe Generale de Paris v Walker, L. R. 11 App, 20 (1885), aff'g L. R, 14 Q B D, 424 So, also, as between a *bona fide* purchaser, to whom the certificates are transferred, and a third party, to whom the vendor had given the stock previous to the sale the vendee with the certificates is protected Crawford v Dox, 5 Hun, 507 (1875). In Wilson v Atlantic, etc, R R Co, 2 Fed Rep, 459 (1880), where an assignee in bankruptcy applied for registry, the

bankrupt having fled with the certificates, it was held that the corporation was bound to allow transfer and to issue new certificates upon a bond of indemnity being given It has been held, however, that a sale of a certificate of stock to a *bona fide* purchaser is to be upheld, even as against a receiver who has been appointed and been given legal ownership of the registered stock. Dudley v Gould, 6 Hun, 97 (1875).

[2] Friedlander v Slaughter-house Co., 31 La Ann, 523 (1879) See, also, ch XXII, § 388 Where stock is deposited with a trustee for purposes of reorganization and transferable certificates are issued therefor by the trustee, a claimant of stock which another person has deposited and for which such other person has the trustee's certificate cannot compel the trustee to deliver up the stock until the trustee's certificate is returned, even though the party holding it is a party defendant. Bean v American L. & T. Co, 122 N. Y., 622 (1890)

[3] Baker v Wasson, 53 Texas, 150 (1880). Unless he obtained registry with knowledge that his vendor had already sold the old certificates to another Scripture v Francestown Soapstone Co, 50 N. H, 571 (1871).

against the corporation, or he may sue the corporate officer who allowed the transfer.[1] The purchaser of the stock may insist on the old certificate being produced and surrendered at the time of registration, but if he waives this right, and a registry is made, he cannot afterwards refuse to accept the stock on that account.[2] The corporation is not liable to the person who is registered as a stockholder without a surrender of the old certificate at least not where the registry is by the secretary, without special authority from the board of directors.[3] Where, however, the purchaser of stock without the certificates obtained registry on the corporate book, the corporation cannot afterwards remove his name in favor of the purchaser of the old certificate. The former may compel the corporation to replace his name.[4] A pledge made by a separate written assignment of the stock, the certificates remaining in the pledgor's possession and continuing to stand in his name on the corporate books, is not good as against the pledgor's receiver who takes possession of the certificates.[5]

B SALES OF STOCK WHILE SUITS ARE PENDING AFFECTING THAT STOCK.

§ 361. *Legal proceedings as affecting sales of outstanding certificates of stock* — It is a well-established principle of law that shares of stock may, for certain purposes, have a *situs* at two separate places at the same time. For the purposes of suits concern-

[1] Baker *t* Wasson, 59 Texas, 140 (1883)

[2] Boatmen's Ins. & Trust Co *v* Able, 48 Mo., 136 (1871). A bank cashier may transfer bank stock standing in his name in the stock register even though he does not turn back the certificates. Finn *v* Brown, 142 U S., 56 (1891). In Indiana, where an administrator cannot sell personal property except in a certain way, the corporation is liable to the estate if it allows a transfer of stock on its books under a sale by the administrator who has not complied with the law. The purchaser, however, who does not see the old certificates, but takes new certificates issued by the corporation, is protected. Citizens' St R'y *v* Robbins, 26 N. E Rep., 116 (Ind 1891)

[3] Hall *v* Rose Hill & E. Road Co, 70 Ill, 673 (1873), Houston & T. C R'y Co *v* Van Alstyne, 56 Texas, 439 (1882), holding that the corporation is not bound to recognize as a stockholder one who

obtains registry without a surrender of the old certificates, a regular registry with a surrender of such certificates having previously been obtained by another. Cf Hart *t* Frantino, etc, Co, 22 L T (N S) 30

[4] Cady *v*. Potter 55 Barb, 463 (1869) In Platt *v* Birmingham Axle Co, 41 Conn, 255 (1874), the corporation was protected by its lien, and the fact that it bought the stock without the certificates was not the essential point of the case The corporation cannot interplead after it has allowed the transfer Cady *v* Potter, *supra*. Mt. Holly L. & M T Co. *v* Ferric, 17 N J Eq, 117 (1864) But it may interplead if it has refused to transfer to any one Merchants' Nat'l Bank *v* Richards, 6 Mo App, 454 (1879). See, also, § 387

[5] Atkinson *v*. Foster, 25 N E Rep., 528 (Ill, 1890)

ing rights to its title, for taxation, and for a few other purposes, shares of stock follow the domicile of the stockholder.[1] On the other hand, it has at the same time a *situs* where the corporation exists, and this *situs* may be for the purposes of suits concerning the title to the stock, for attachment and execution, and for various other similar purposes. Great difficulty arises in many instances of legal proceedings affecting the title to stock by reason of the fact that, where the defendant has in his possession the certificates of stock and is not enjoined from transferring them, he may transfer them, either before or after suit has been commenced against him to obtain possession of the stock represented by such certificates or to subject it to his debts. The question then arises whether the *bona fide* transferee of such certificate is to be allowed to retain the stock, or whether the successful plaintiff in the suit against the defendant who has transferred the stock may follow such stock and take it from the transferee. This conflict of right between the purchaser of the outstanding certificates and the purchaser whose title is based on judicial proceedings arises most often in cases of attachment or execution issued against shares of stock at the domicile of the corporation. In such cases the better rule seems to be that transferees of the certificate held by the defendant are protected and entitled to protection at the hands of the corporation, if their purchase is made before the attachment or execution is levied; but that transfers made after the levy are utterly void so far as the corporation and the plaintiffs to the suit are concerned, provided the suit itself is successful.[2] The same difficulty and conflict of rights arise in suits to reclaim stock which has been taken from the plaintiff by fraud, or by the torts of an agent or pledgee, or by the breach of trust of an executor, administrator, guardian or trustee.[3] The plaintiff seeking to recover his stock, certificates for which are in the hands of the defendant, seems to have but two modes of procedure whereby he may prevent the defendant from transferring the certificates. The suit should be

[1] It is important here to distinguish shares of stock from the certificates for those shares. Certificates of stock have no situs or domicile. They cannot be attached or subjected to execution. The stock itself does not follow the certificate representing it. Winslow v. Fletcher, 4 Atl. Rep., 250 (Conn., 1886). Though prevented by injunction from transferring the corporation must preserve the rights of a party who notifies it of his rights. Purchase v. N. Y. Exchange Bank, 3 Rob., 164 (1865). As regards the rights and duties of the corporation herein when stock is sold under an execution or is attached, see § 488.

[2] Smith v. American Coal Co., 7 Lans., 317 (1873), Smith v. Crescent City, etc., Co. 30 La. Ann., 1378 (1878), and ch. XXVII.

[3] Holbrook v. New Jersey Zinc Co., 57 N. Y., 616 (1874); Leitch v. Wells, 48 N. Y., 585 (1872).

brought in the state of the domicile of the corporation and attachment against the stock issued,[1] or, when the defendant is sued in another state, an injunction restraining the defendant from transferring the stock should be obtained   It is true that, after judgment has been obtained and the decree of the court executed, any subsequent transfer of the certificates by the defendant is null and may be disregarded by the plaintiff and by the corporation[2]   But while the suit is pending the defendant may transfer the certificates and the *bona fide* transferee takes a good title to the stock   The latter is not affected by or bound to take notice of a *lis pendens* in that suit   If no temporary injunction is obtained, a transfer made on the corporate books pending suit is good, and the corporation cannot be made liable although a party defendant[3]   Although the party seeking the stock of which he has been deprived by fraud makes the party complained of and the corporation itself parties defendant, yet, if the certificates are not obtained from the party holding them, the court will not order the corporation to issue new certificates   The outstanding certificates may pass into the hands of a *bona fide* purchaser.[4]

§ 362 *Lis pendens as affecting a purchase of stock.* —A purchaser of certificates of stock is not chargeable with constructive notice that a suit is pending in which his vendor is defendant, and the plaintiff is endeavoring to obtain possession and title to the stock which the purchaser is buying   The doctrine of *lis pendens* has no application to sales of shares of stock. The purchaser is bound to know that a judgment or decree has been rendered and executed affecting the certificates he is buying, if such a judgment or decree exists; but he is not bound to know that a suit is pending in which judgment has not yet been rendered   That a *lis pendens* in a suit involving shares of stock does not affect a purchaser of the certificate representing those shares, the purchase being made while the suit is pending, was clearly established by the court of appeals of New York in the case of Holbrook v New Jersey Zinc Company.[5]

---

[1] Quarl v Abbett, 13 Am. & Eng Corp. Cases, 27 (Ind, 1886).

[2] Sprague v Cacheco Manuf Co, 10 Blatch, 173 (1872)

[3] Hawes v Gas Consumers, etc, Co, 12 N Y Supp. 924 (1891)   See also editorial N Y L J, March 29, 1890.

[4] Joslyn v St Paul, etc, Co, 46 N W Rep., 337 (Minn, 1890), Bean v. American L T Co, 122 N Y, 622 (1890)

[5] 57 N Y, 616 (1874), following Leitch v Wells, 48 N Y, 586 (1872). See Dovey's Appeal, 97 Pa St, 153 (1881), where the court refused to pass upon this question, also, Bank of Va. v Craig, 6 Leigh (Va), 399, 435 (1885), holding that a *lis pendens* in a suit by sureties to restrain guardian from selling stock is not notice to the corporation to refuse to allow him to register a transfer

C FORGERY

§ 363. *Forgery as affecting a sale of stock.*— An owner of shares of stock cannot be deprived of his property by a forgery through which his certificates of stock pass into the hands of innocent purchasers He may be deprived of his stock, but has in lieu thereof the right to collect the value of that stock, either from the corporation or from parties who have held the stock. The rights and remedies of the stockholder who has lost possession of certificates of stock by forgery vary according to the extent to which his certificate has been transferred This remedy may be against the transferees of the certificate before a registry has been obtained, or it may be against the corporation for allowing a registry, or it may be against the person obtaining the registry The forgery itself may consist of any writing on the certificate of stock, whereby, with intent to defraud, it is falsely and materially so made or altered as to have an apparent legality.[1] Generally the forgery is of the name of the stockholder to the transfer on the back of the certificate[2] The forgery may, however, be committed by changing the number of shares of stock which the transferrer has written out in the certificate,[3] or by inserting the numbers of shares of stock of one corporation in a blank transfer duly signed by the stockholder, but signed for the purpose of transferring shares of stock in another and different corporation[4]

The subject of forgery by one or more corporate officers, whereby spurious and overissued stock is issued, there being no old certificates returned to the company at that time, is considered elsewhere.[5]

The subject now under consideration is where the name of a stockholder is forged to an assignment of the certificate or the certificate itself is modified.

---

[1] See Bouvier's Dictionary, vol I, p 679; 2 Bishop's Criminal Law, § 523

[2] Nearly all of the cases in the several following sections are cases of a forgery of the stockholder's name to a transfer. It is forgery for one trustee to write in the names of the other trustees without authority Cottam v Eastern Counties R'y Co., 1 J & H., 243 (1860), Sloman v. Bank of England, 14 Sim , 475 (1845) Or for one partner to write in the name of the other partner without authority. where the stock stood in their joint names. Midland R'y Co. v Taylor, 8 H L. Cases, 751 (1862), affirming Taylor v

Midland R'y Co, 29 L J (Ch.), 731 (1860).

[3] Matthews v. Massachusetts National Bank, 1 Holmes, 396 (1874); Sewall v. Boston Water-power Co., 86 Mass., 277 (1862), where the alteration was treated as a forgery so far as legal rights were concerned, although the alteration was due to an innocent misunderstanding of a clerk

[4] Swan v North Bristol Co., 7 H. & N., 603 (1862), practically overruling Ex parte Swan, 7 C B. (N S), 400.

[5] See §§ 291–298.

§ 364. *Rights and liabilities of transferees of forged certificates of stock, there being no intervening registry on corporate books* — The position of a transferee of a certificate of stock which is invalid by reason of forgery depends largely on whether there has been an intervening registry of transfer on the corporate books after the former owner was deprived of his stock by the forgery The forger himself is of course liable, not only to the real stockholder, but also to any other person who has been injured by the forgery. If the purchaser of stock from one who has forged a transfer of the same sells the same after being notified by the real owner that the latter claims the stock and has been deprived of it by forgery, the real owner may recover damages in trover for the value of the stock from the person who so sells, although he purchased in good faith and without notice of the forgery [1] If the forgery is committed by a member of a firm, the real owner may sue the firm for money had and received, and may recover the value of the stock and dividends [2] Where the forger has sold the stock to a purchaser without notice, and the latter has sold to another purchaser without notice, and the latter is deprived of his apparent ownership on account of the forgery, the second transferee may hold the first transferee liable.[3] This principle grows out of the well-established rule of law that, in a sale of chattels, there is an implied warranty of title, unless the circumstances are such as to give rise to a contrary presumption. The broker or auctioneer of stock which passes through their hands cannot, it seems, be held liable, though it turns out that on account of a forgery there was no title to the stock in the party whom they represented [4] The transferee whose title is based on a forgery has no rights as against the corporation, where there has been no registry on the corporate books after the forgery. He cannot compel the corporation to allow him to register his transfer. If the corporation has already registered him as transferee, it may repudiate its registry so far as *he* is concerned, and refuse to recognize him as a stockholder or as having the right to transfer the stock.[5] Such

---

[1] Monk t. Graham, 8 Mod , 9 (1721)

[2] Marsh v Keating, 1 Bing New Cases, 198 (1834); Marsh v. Stone, 6 B & C, 551 (1827)

[3] Matthews v Mass. Nat. Bank, 1 Holmes, 396 (1874) This was an extremely harsh case, involving a rigid application of the principle, since the defendant's name appeared on the back of the certificate of stock as a transferrer, when in fact it had only been a

pledgee, and on payment of the pledge had retransferred the stock As to the liability of brokers for the forgery of their employee in delivering spurious stock to a customer, see Andrews v. Clark, 20 Atl Rep., 429 (Md , 1890).

[4] Machinists' Nat. Bank v. Field, 126 Mass., 345 (1879)

[5] Simon v Anglo-American Tel Co., L R, 5 Q B D, 188 (1879), Whitewright v American Tel & Cable Co.,

a registered transferee has no right of action against the corporation by reason of its rescission of his registry,[1] although the rule may be different if he purchased by reason of the fact that he was allowed such registry on the corporate books[2]   On the other hand, it is the transferee obtaining registry who warrants the validity of his title and right to transfer, and if the corporation is compelled to pay damages to the real owner on account of allowing such registry it may have recourse to and collect the same damages from the transferee who obtained the registry, however innocent the latter may have been[3]   The person who first obtains a registry after a forgery has deprived the real owner of his stock cannot retain the new certificates as against the real owner of the old ones.[4]

§ 365   *Liability of corporation to real owner of stock for allowing registry of forged transfer.*—It is the duty of a corporation to prevent and refuse a registry of transfer of stock where that transfer has been forged   If the corporation fails to detect the forgery it is liable to the real owner of the stock who has been deprived of it by the forgery[5]   It has been held that the owner of the stock may compel the corporation to cancel the illegal registry and re-

N Y Daily Reg. Aug 6, 1886 (Superior Ct)   Waterhouse v London & S W R'y Co, 41 L T (N S), 553 (1880), Hambleton v Central O R R. Co, 44 Md, 551 (1876)   Brown v Howard Ins. Co., 42 Md, 384 (1875)   Hildyard v South Sea Co, 2 P Wms, 76 (1722)   Cf Ashby v Blackwell 2 Eden. 299 (1765) holding the corporation liable not only to the real owner, but also to the transferee obtaining registry   See § 367 for rights of transferee of the first registered holder.

[1] Id

[2] Metropolitan Sav Bank v Mayor, etc, of Baltimore, 63 Md, 6 (1884)   In this case the plaintiff took the forged certificates in pledge from the forger   Afterwards, upon the forger's applying for a further loan on the same pledge of stock, the corporation refused unless the stock was registered in its name, which was accordingly done   Held that the bank lost the first loan, but had recourse to the corporation for the second loan

[3] Boston & Albany R R. Co v Richardson, 135 Mass, 423 (1883), the court saying also, in a *dictum*, that the de-

fendant has a remedy over against the parties that sold to him

[4] Johnston v Renton, L R, 9 Eq Cas, 181 (1870)

[5] Pratt v Taunton Copper Mfg Co., 123 Mass, 110 (1887), Sewall v Boston Water-power Co, 86 Mass, 277 (1862), Pratt v Boston & Albany R. R. Co, 126 Mass, 443 (1879), Johnston v Renton, L R, 9 Eq, 181 (1870), Cottam v Eastern Counties R'y Co, 1 J & H., 243 (1860), Midland R'y Co v. Taylor, 8 H L Cases. 751 (1862), aff'g Taylor v. Midland R'y Co, 29 L J (Ch), 731 (1860), Davis v Bank of Eng, Bing, 393 (1824), Swan v North British Aus Co, 7 H & N, 603 (1862), substantially overruling same case in court of law; Ex parte Swan, 7 C. B (N S), 400 (1859), Pollock v National Bank, 7 N. Y., 274 (1852), Day v American Tel & Cable Co, 52 N Y Sup. Ct, 128 (1885), Dalton v Midland R'y Co, 12 C B., 458 (1852), Mayor, etc, of Baltimore v Ketchum, 57 Md, 23 (1881), Coates v London & S W R'y Co, 41 L T (N S), 553 (1880), Blaisdell v Bohr, 68 Ga, 56 (1891), Sloman v Bank of Eng, 14 Sim, 475 (1845), Telegraph Co v Davenport, 97

store the name of the plaintiff[1] The better rule, however, is that, inasmuch as a *bona fide* transferee of the illegally *registered* transferrer is entitled to retain the stock, the former owner of the stock in suing the corporation should demand relief in the alternative, that the stock be restored to him, or that he be given damages in lieu thereof[2] Or he may demand that the corporation replace the stock by going into the market, if necessary, and purchasing similar stock[3] If the stockholder sues the corporation for a dividend on stock which by a forged assignment has been registered in the name of another person, the corporation cannot interplead[4] A court of equity has concurrent jurisdiction with law in remedying a forged transfer of stock[5] The corporation, the co-conspirators and the transferees of the forged certificate are all proper parties to the suit,[6] but the only necessary party is the corporation itself[7]

U S 369 (1878), where the court say "Upon the facts stated there ought to be no question as to the right of the plaintiffs to have their shares replaced on the books of the company and proper certificates issued to them, and to cover the dividends accrued on the shares after the unauthorized transfer, or to have alternative judgments for the value of the shares and the dividends Forgery can confer no power nor transfer any rights The officers of the company are the custodians of its stock-books, and it is their duty to see that all transfers of shares are properly made, either by the stockholders themselves or persons having authority from them If upon the presentation of a certificate for transfer they are at all doubtful of the identity of the party offering it with its owner, or if not satisfied of the genuineness of a power of attorney produced, they can require the identity of the party in the one case, and the genuineness of the document in the other, to be satisfactorily established before allowing the transfer to be made In either case they must act upon their own responsibility Neither the absence of blame on the part of the officers of the company in allowing an unauthorized transfer of stock, nor the good faith of the purchaser of stolen property, will avail as an answer to the

demand of the true owner" A corporation is liable to the owner of stock allowing a transfer of the stock to be made to a transferee who forged the owner's name to the transfer on the back of the certificate of stock Pennsylvania Co, etc, v Philadelphia etc, R Co, 25 Atl Rep, 1043 (Pa, 1893)

[1] Johnston v Renton, *supra*, Cottam v Eastern Counties R y Co *supra*, Sloman v Bank of Eng, *supra*

[2] This is the usual prayer for relief in this country

[3] Pratt v Boston & Albany R R Co, 126 Mass, 443 (1879)

[4] Dalton v Midland R R Co, 12 C B, 458 (1852)

[5] Blaisdell v Bohr, 68 Ga, 56 (1881)

[6] Id As to a statutory criminal liability of an officer forging and issuing stock, see State v Haven, 9 Atl Rep, 841 (Vt, 1887)

[7] Mayor, etc., of Baltimore v Ketchum, 57 Md, 23 (1881), Pratt v Boston & Albany R R Co, 126 Mass, 443 (1879). The statute of limitations in behalf of the corporation begins to run against a cause of action for forged transfer only from the time when the corporation denies its liability therefor Barton v North. etc, R'y Co, 58 L T Rep, 549 (1888) In a stockholder's action to compel the corporation to retransfer stock to them which has been transferred on the cor-

Where the corporation is sued by the real owner of the stock for allowing the registry of a transfer based on forgery, it cannot institute an independent action bringing in all the parties interested and enjoining the action of the owner of the stock.[1] The latter is entitled to his action at law without delay and without involving or settling the respective rights of others

§ 366 The right of the rightful owner of the stock to complain of the forgery whereby his certificate has passed into the possession of another may be barred by estoppel or ratification Formerly it was held that the negligence of the owner of the stock would be a bar to his remedy[2] Later decisions, however, have firmly established the rule that "there must be either something that amounts to an estoppel or something that amounts to a ratification in order to make the negligence a good answer"[3] Accordingly, the rightful owner of the stock is held not to be barred of his remedy by the fact that the stockholder, a corporation, allowed its corporate seal to be in the possession of its secretary, whereby he sold the stock owned by the corporation,[4] or by the fact that the owner delayed several months, during which time the forger escaped,[5] or that he transferred on the back of the certificate only part of the shares specified in the certificate,[6] or that he gave his address wrong, and thereby a letter of inquiry did not reach him,[7] or that he allowed his clerk, the forger, to have access to his papers, and gave him blank transfers duly signed to use in transferring other stock,[8] or that the guardian of the plaintiff was negligent.[9]

§ 367 *Rights of transferees who purchase after a registry has been obtained* — It has already been shown that the transferees of a certificate of stock which has been put in circulation by forgery are not allowed to retain such stock where there has not been, at some time subsequent to the forgery, a transfer registered on the corporate books It has also been shown that he who applies to

porate books by forgery, the holders of the new certificates are not allowed to come in and defend Barton r London, etc, R y, 59 L. T. Rep., 122 (1888)

[1] American Tel & Cable Co r. Day, 52 N. Y Superior Ct, 128 (1885).

[2] Coles r Bank of England, 10 Ad & E, 437 (1839), where the continuous receipt of dividends on a less quantity of stock than she was entitled to was held a bar, though the stockholder was old and infirm

[3] Bank of Ireland r Trustees of Evans Charities. 5 H L Cases, 389 (1855).

[4] Id, and Merchants', etc, r Bank of England, 56 L. T. Rep., 665 (1887), where the preceding case was reluctantly followed

[5] Davis r Bank of England, 2 Bing, 393 (1824)

[6] Sewall r Boston Water-power Co., 86 Mass., 277 (1862).

[7] Johnston r. Renton, L R, 9 Eq, 181 (1870)

[8] Swan t North British Aus. Co, 7 H & N, 603 (1862), substantially overruling *Ex parte* Swan, 7 C. B. (N. S), 400 (1859)

[9] Telegraph Co. v Davenport, 97 U. S., 369 (1878).

the corporation for a registry of transfer, such registry being the first one since the forgery was committed, is not allowed to retain the stock An entirely different rule prevails as regards all subsequent *bona fide* holders of the new certificate obtained by the first registry The person who obtains the first registry has no rights except as against his transferrer But all subsequent purchasers without notice are fully protected. They cannot be compelled to give up the stock, either to the corporation or to the person who lost it by forgery[1] This rule arises, not from the law of negligence, but from the law of estoppel operating against the corporation It is in accord with the demands of trade and the constant tendency of the law to protect *bona fide* purchasers of certificates of stock

D. STOLEN OR LOST CERTIFICATES.

§ 368 *Stolen or lost certificates of stock indorsed in blank.* — One of the most important elements of the negotiability of promissory notes is that, if the holder of such note loses it or it is stolen from him when it is indorsed in blank, a subsequent *bona fide* purchaser of such note is protected as against the person who lost it A different rule seems to prevail as regards certificates of stock indorsed in blank and then lost or stolen In this respect certificates of stock are not negotiable. It has been clearly held that a purchaser from a thief of certificates of stock indorsed in blank is not protected, nor is any subsequent purchaser of that identical *certificate* allowed to claim the stock. The real owner of the certificate may compel the corporation which has refused to recognize the thief's transferee's title to register the stock as his, or he may have damages against a *bona fide* transferee of the thief where such transferee

---

[1] Machinists' Nat'l Bank *v* Field, 126 Mass, 315 (1879); *Re* Bahia & San Francisco R'y Co, L. R, 3 Q. B, 584 (1868), where, however, the corporation, having canceled all the registries made subsequent to the forgery, was held liable in damages to a purchaser subsequent to the first registry The court said the giving of a certificate "is a declaration by the company to all the world that the person in whose name the certificate is made out and to whom it is given is a shareholder in the company and it is given by the company with the intention that it shall be so used by the person to whom it is given, and acted upon in the sale and transfers of shares " A purchaser of certificates of stock need not look back of the last registry of transfer on the corporate books A breach of trust back of that does not invalidate his title Winter *v* Montgomery, etc, Co, 7 S Rep, 773 (Ala, 1890) A corporation cannot refuse to transfer stock on the ground that the vendor fraudulently induced the company to issue the stock to him where the company has been guilty of laches in not seeking a remedy before the transfer The vendee in this case was a director American, etc, Co *v* Bayless, 15 S. W. Rep, 10 (Ky, 1891)

has sold the stock[1] In Nevada it is held that the purchaser and
vendor of the stolen certificate is liable in damages to its real owner,
although the former acted as a broker and without notice[2] The
bona fide purchaser of a stolen certificate of stock indorsed in blank
cannot compel the corporation to register him as a stockholder[3]
The person stealing certificates of stock is guilty of larceny, and
may be convicted for the same[4] The corporation cannot obtain
an injunction against a possible action by the purchaser of stolen
certificates who has applied for registry and been refused it.[5]

§ 369 Where, however, certificates of stock indorsed in blank
have been stolen, and the thief or his transferee has obtained a registry on the corporate books and obtained new certificates of stock,

[1] Barstow *v* Savage Min Co, 64 Cal,
388 (1883) substantially overruling Winter *t* Belmont Min Co, 53 Cal, 428
(1879). Anderson *v* Nicholas, 28 N Y,
600 (1864), where the purchaser of the
stolen certificate was not a *bona fide*
purchaser The court said that even if
he had been a *bona fide* purchaser he
would not be protected *Cf* Aull *v*
Colket, 33 Leg Intel, 44 (Pa, 1876),
where the question of negligence was
submitted to the jury The mere fact
of losing it is no proof of negligence
Biddle *v* Bayard, 13 Pa St., 150 (1850).
The purchaser of a certificate indorsed
in blank and stolen is not protected
Given's Appeal, 16 Atl Rep, 75 (Pa,
1888). The *bona fide* purchaser of a certificate of stock indorsed in blank, but
which was stolen from the owner, is not
protected Fast, etc, Co *v* Dennis, 5
R'y & Corp L J, 296 (Ala, 1889) A
stockholder is liable to the owner for
the value of mining shares received for
sale from one who had stolen them, although he acted in good faith, without
notice, and paid the proceeds to the
thief, relying on his representations of
ownership Swim *v* Wilson 27 Pac
Rep, 33 (Cal, 1891)

[2] Bercich *v* Marye, 9 Nev, 312 (1874),
Barstow *v* Savage Mining Co, 64 Cal,
388 According to the California decision the same rule would be applied to
negotiable instruments In another
case, where a broker innocently sold
for a principal a stolen negotiable gov-

ernment bond, the broker was held
liable to the true owner Kimball *v*
Billings, 55 Me, 147 The court expressly refused in this case, to place the
broker in the same position as an innocent purchaser for value In the case of
Zulick *t* Markham, 6 Daly, 129, it was
sought to extend this doctrine to the
sale of certificates of stock which had
only been misapplied Here a broker
had innocently sold for a fraudulent
principal indorsed certificates of stock,
which had not been stolen from the
owner, but delivered to him by the
principal who fraudulently sold them
through an innocent broker The New
York court held the broker in this case
to stand on the same footing as an innocent purchaser and not liable to the
owner for the proceeds, but no opinion
was expressed as to the rule of liability
if the stock had been stolen instead of
misapplied

[3] Sherwood *v* Meadow Valley M Co,
50 Cal, 412 (1875) Although two persons have a safety-deposit box in common, and one of them steals therefrom
a certificate of stock owned by the other
and indorsed in blank by the latter, yet
a purchaser even in good faith of such
stolen certificate is not protected Bangor, etc, Co *v* Robinson, 52 Fed Rep,
520 (1892)

[4] People *v* Griffin, 38 How Pr, 475
(1869)

[5] Buffalo Grape Sugar Co *v* Alberger,
22 Hun, 349 (1880)

and these new certificates have been sold, the purchaser is protected in his possession of the stock.[1] In Michigan this is held to be the rule even though such purchaser took the stock with full knowledge of all the facts[2] It is to be hoped that this rule will be generally sustained, since it is in accordance with the general rule that the rights and equities of all holders of stock back of the registry and issue of the certificates in existence are not allowed to affect the stockholdership or rights of purchasers of these new certificates

§ 370. *Owner of a lost certificate of stock may obtain new certificate* — An owner of a certificate of stock who has lost it or had it stolen from him may, by taking proper proceedings or by giving proper security to the corporation. have new certificates issued to him In Louisiana it is held that, upon satisfactory proof of the loss of certificate of stock, a writ of *mandamus* will issue to compel the corporation to issue new certificates, and that no bond of indemnity need be given[3] But the better rule seems to be that, except in cases of the clearest proof of loss, the corporation shall not be required to issue new certificates unless a bond of indemnity against its liability to possible legal holders of the lost certificate shall be given[4] In New York, by statute, security may be required in all such cases.[5] It would seem reasonable that a bond of indemnity should be given to the corporation, since, in case the old certificate has not been lost, but has been sold by its owner, the corporation is liable in damages or to replace the stock to the purchaser for issuing new certificates without a surrender of the old[6] Where certificates of stock have been lost, and a party turns

[1] Mandlebaum v North Am Min Co 4 Mich, 465 (1857). A purchaser of certificates of stock need not look back of the last registry of transfer on the corporate books A breach of trust back of that does not invalidate his title Winter v Montgomery, etc., Co, 7 S. Rep, 773 (Ala, 1890).

[2] Id

[3] State v New Orleans Gas Light Co, 25 La Ann, 413 (1873)

[4] Galveston City Co v Sibley, 56 Texas, 269 (1882), where one who became a stockholder in 1841 died in 1865, and his heirs applied for a new certificate in 1878, Societe Generale de Paris v Walker, L R, 11 App Cas (H of L), 20, affirming L R, 14 Q B D, 424, Butler v Glen Cove Starch Co 25 Hun.

47 (1879) A corporation need not issue new certificates of stock in place of those which are lost unless a bond of indemnity be given Guilford v Western U Tel Co, 46 N W Rep, 70 (Minn, 1890)

[5] This statute does not give a remedy to a purchaser of stock at a receiver's sale If he is unable to obtain the outstanding certificates his remedy is otherwise *In re* Biglin v Friendship Ass'n N Y Daily Reg Dec 5 1887

[6] See §§ 358-360 Persons receiving a duplicate certificate on the ground of loss of the original may be compelled by the company to return it where the original turns up in another person's hands. the certificate having been sold to the latter by the former owner New

up with them and applies for transfer on the corporate books, the
real owner may enjoin a transfer of the certificate, and also any
transfer by the corporation on its books, *pendente lite.*[1]

E. CONFISCATION OF STOCK.

§ 371 During the late Rebellion, acts of confiscation were passed,
both by the United States government and by the Confederate
government, and shares of stock owned by parties in one section
of the country in corporations domiciled in the other section were
confiscated   The result of the war having established that the
Confederate government was an illegal one, all its acts of confiscation became null and void, and all transfers and registers of stock
thereunder were held to be void utterly   The whole line of transactions based on the confiscation fell with the confiscation itself.[2]
The corporation was held not liable to purchasers whose title was
based on the confiscation, since it acted under compulsion of a
power temporarily greater than the law itself[3] If the corporation
neglects to remedy the confusion and claims growing out of the
illegal confiscation of stock, any stockholder may institute an action in its behalf for that purpose[4] The stock is to be restored to
the owner against whom the confiscation proceedings were had;
and if the corporation, during the Rebellion, voluntarily paid dividends to the illegal holders of the stock, it must pay the same to
the plaintiff, even though it would have been compelled to pay
such dividends to the southern holder if it had not done so voluntarily[5] On the other hand, proceedings for the confiscation of
stock under the confiscation acts of the United States government,
passed by reason of the late Rebellion, are held to have been effective it in accordance with established rules of procedure   Where,
however, no notice of the proceedings was given to the defendant,
and her name and the stock were not accurately described, the
proceedings were void, and the corporation, having obeyed the
illegal judgment of confiscation, was held liable in damages to the
southern owner of the stock.[6]

York Cen , etc R. R. v Stokes, N Y
Law Journal, Nov 16, 1888 In the
case Keller v Eureka. etc , Co., 9 R'y
& Corp , L J . 123 (St. Louis, 1890), the
court held that the corporation need not
issue an ordinary certificate in place of
one that was lost, but might write upon
the new certificate the word "duplicate"
[1] Sierra Nevada, etc , Co v Sears, 10
Nev , 346 (1875)
[2] Dewing v Perdicaris, 96 U S , 193
(1877)

[3] Id ; also Central R. R. & Banking
Co v Ward, 37 Ga., 515 (1868)
[4] Perdicaris v Charleston Gas-light
Co , Chase's Dec , 435 (1869), affirmed,
sub nom Dewing v Perdicaris, *supra.*
[5] Keppels Adm v. Petersburg R. R.
Co , Chase's Dec , 167 (1868).
[6] Chapman v Phœnix National Bank,
85 N Y , 437 (1881), reversing S C , 12
J & S, 340, Avil v Alexander Water
Co., 1 Hughes, 408 (1877).

CHAPTER XXII.

SALES OF STOCK — FORMAL METHOD OF TRANSFERRING CERTIFICATES AND REGISTRY THEREOF

§ 372. *Subject treated herein.*— Having considered the competency of parties to enter into a contract of sale of stock,[1] also of the legality, enforceability and character of that contract,[2] also the rights of third parties as affecting the contract between the transferrer and transferee,[3]— it is now necessary to discuss certain formalities whereby the title to stock is transferred These formalities are peculiar to sales of stock The only analogy to them is perhaps that arising from the making of a deed of real estate, and a registry of the same at a recorder's office In many respects, however, this analogy does not apply. Thus, the corporation itself

[1] Ch XIX
[2] Ch XX.

[3] Ch XXI.

(33)   513

has many rights and duties herein which a register of deeds has not. The principles of law governing the formalities of transfer of stock have occasioned great difficulties and much litigation. The rules given herein have arisen for the most part out of the necessities and demands of business as sanctioned by the courts They have been gradually formed, and still bear the imprints of the transition stage of a newly-created law.

§ 373 *The two usual steps in perfecting a transfer of stock.*—
To transfer a share of stock there are generally two distinct steps to be taken First, the certificate is assigned by the transferrer to the transferee, and second, that assignment and transfer are perfected and completed by delivering the assigned certificate to the corporation, obtaining an entry on the corporate transfer book to the effect that the transferee has purchased the stock of the transferrer, and taking from the corporation new certificates of stock certifying that the newly-recorded stockholder owns a specified amount of stock

§ 374 *Omission of either or both steps.*—Either and even both of these two steps in the complete transfer of stock may be omitted; and yet, where the facts estop the various parties from denying that a transfer has been made, it will be held to be complete Thus, it has been held that an owner of stock may transfer his stock to another by a delivery of the certificate without any assignment [1] This happens when a registry of transfer is made without any surrender of the old certificate [2] So far as the transferrer is concerned such a method of transfer is effectual Such cases also arise where the corporation has never issued certificates of stock The stockholder may then transfer his stock without assigning a certificate.[3]

A METHOD OF TRANSFERRING THE CERTIFICATE.

§ 375 *Usual forms of assignment and powers of attorney whereby the transferrer assigns the certificate of stock to his transferee.*—A certificate of stock is a paper issued by the corporation to a stockholder, stating that the person specified therein is the owner of a certain number of shares of its capital stock. The assignment of this certificate is made, it seems, in three different ways First, it has been held that it may be made by a simple delivery of the certificate without any writing [4] Again, it may be

---

[1] See §§ 308, 465, note.

[2] See § 360

[3] First Nat. Bank v Gifford, 47 Iowa, 575 (1877), Brigham v Mead, 92 Mass, 245 (1865). See, also, § 382

[4] See § 308, where a delivery of a certificate of stock *causa mortis* was held good, without any writing assigning the certificate, and § 465, note See, also, Fraser v Charleston, 11 S C., 486 (1878).

made by a formal instrument of assignment duly signed by the transferrer. This instrument may be separate from the certificate of stock, but generally is printed in blank on the back of it. In either case, in order to make the transfer complete by a registry of it on the corporate books, it is necessary for the transferrer to go to the office of the corporation and sign the transfer in the corporate transfer book, whereby the transfer is recorded   The third and most usual method of assigning a certificate of stock is by a formal instrument of assignment, similar to the one explained above, united with a power of attorney authorizing a person, whose name is generally left blank, to be subsequently filled in, to sign the corporate transfer book, whereby the transfer is recorded. This instrument of transfer and the power of attorney are generally printed in blank on the back of the certificate of stock   It enables the transferee to obtain a registry without the presence of the transferrer, provided the corporate registry agent is satisfied with the signature and intent of the transferrer to assign the stock   The blank power of attorney is generally filled in by the transfer clerk, who inserts his own name and thereby becomes the attorney [1]   This power of attorney is not revoked by the death of the transferrer before it is used [2]   A general power of attorney to sell land and build houses does not justify a sale of stock [3]   A general power of attorney authorizing an agent to sell and transfer stocks, etc authorizes him to sign the stockholder's name to a transfer [4]   Per-

---

Cf Sitgreaves v Farmers', etc, Bank, 49 Pa St, 359 (1870) Davis v Bank of England, 2 Bing, 393 (1824) Burrall v Bushwick R. R Co, 75 N Y, 211 (1878), Dunn v Com Bank of Buffalo, 11 Barb, 580 (1852). A deed of release of shares of stock is a sufficient transfer Hastings v Blue Hill, etc Corp'n, 26 Mass, 80 (1829) If a corporation allows a transfer to be made on its books without the transfer on the old certificate being signed, it is liable to the owner of the old certificate, even though the old certificate is delivered up and the attorney in fact of the owner shows his power of attorney at the time of the transfer on the books Taft v Presidio, etc, Co., 24 Pac. Rep, 436 (Cal, 1890)

[1] The fact that the officer of the corporation fills in his own name as agent to transfer does not make him the agent of the stockholder as regards notice of the agent's frauds, Allen v South Boston R. R., 22 N E Rep, 917 (Mass, 1889)

[2] Fraser v Charleston 11 S C, 486 (1878), Leavitt v Fisher, 4 Duer (N Y), 1 (1854), United States v Cutts, 1 Sumner, 133 (1832)

[3] Camden, etc, Assoc v Jones, 21 Atl Rep, 458 (N J, 1891) holding also that the corporation is liable for allowing a transfer of stock where the stockholder did not sign the transfer nor authorize another to transfer it

[4] Tafft v Presidio, etc Co, 22 Pac Rep 485 (Cal, 1889) Where a person gives to another a general power of attorney covering the sale and transfer of all stocks, etc, the attorney may, upon delivering up the certificate therefor to the corporation, transfer the stock of his principal into his own name The corporation is not bound to inquire further than the power of attorney, nor is it given notice by the fact that the

mitting, without inquiry, a transfer under a power of attorney thirteen years old is not proper vigilance on the part of a corporation [1]

§ 376. *Questions which arise herein* — The assignment of a certificate of stock by the transferrer to the transferee, considered apart from the actual registry of such assignment on the corporate books, involves the question whether such an assignment should be under seal, whether, after the assignment, the transferrer can claim any rights of ownership as against the transferee, even though there be no registry of the transfer, and whether a transfer and power of attorney duly signed by the transferrer, but left in blank as to the name of the transferee and attorney, are legal and may pass from hand to hand until some holder cares to fill up the blanks.   These and incidental questions are discussed in the following sections

§ 377. *A seal is not necessary to a transfer of stock* — In America an assignment or transfer of a certificate of stock need not be under seal [2] Formerly it was the custom to have all such transfers made by deed, duly sealed   As the nature of stock and certificates of stock, however, came to be understood more clearly, it became a rule of law that a transfer of the certificate, like the transfer of choses in action, did not require a seal.   Not even the presence of the seal gives the transfer the character of a sealed instrument. The seal is a superfluity and is disregarded.[3]

In England, on the other hand, transfers of railway stocks are generally required by charter to be under seal   This is held to give the instrument the character of a deed, and hence, in accordance with the ancient technical rule of law that a deed must be filled out as to the grantee and other essential particulars before it is sealed in order to be valid, it has been held in England that a transfer of a certificate of stock, duly signed and sealed, but with

attorney is one of its directors Id A stockholder's power of attorney to his agent "to exchange old issues or certificates of stock, and to receive new issues or certificates in lieu thereof," does not authorize the agent to sell or pledge the stock. The corporation is liable for allowing a transfer to a third person on such authority Quay *v.* Presidio, etc, R. R., 22 Pac Rep, 925 (Cal, 1889)

[1] Pennsylvania R R. Co's Appeal, 86 Pa St, 80

[2] Quiner *v* Marblehead Social Ins. Co,

10 Mass, 476 (1813), Atkinson *v* Atkinson, 8 Allen, 15 (1864). If, however, the by-laws require it, the transfer must be under seal Bishop *v.* Globe Co, 135 Mass, 132 (1883), holding, also, that the word "seal" is insufficient.

[3] German Union B. Ass'n *v.* Sendmeyer, 50 Pa St., 67 (1865); Commercial Bank *v* Kortright, 22 Wend, 348 (1839), McNiel *v* Tenth Nat'l Bank, 46 N Y, 325 (1871) Bridgeport Bank *v.* N Y & N H R R. Co, 30 Conn, 231, 274 (1861), Easton *v* London, etc., Bank, 55 L. T Rep., 678 (1886).

the name of the transferee in blank, is void absolutely[1]   In those
English companies, however, whose charters do not require transfers to be sealed, the transfer may be by an ordinary instrument in
writing, and the presence of a seal will be disregarded[2]

§ 378 *The assignment of the certificate of stock estops the transferrer from claiming any further title in the stock as against subsequent bona fide transferees, although such assignment be not
registered*[3]— There is no case which denies this principle of law
On close examination of the cases which seem to militate against
it, it will be found that the issue involved was whether the unregistered transferee was protected against third persons who claimed
title back of the transferrer. The transferrer himself is not allowed to impeach his unregistered transferee's title   Even in Connecticut, where at an early day the court held that the registry
was the originating act of the title of the transferee, the court was
considering the rights of third persons, and not the rights of the

[1] Hibblewhite *v* McMorine, 6 M &
W , 200 (1840), per Parke, B , Taylor *v*
Great Indian P R y Co , 4 De G & J,
559 (1859), Societe Gen *v* Tramways
Union Co, L R., 14 Q B D, 424 (1884),
where transfer was to be by deed,
affirmed, L R., 11 App , 20. *Cf* §§ 325,
380, 416

[2] *Re* Tees Bottle Co , 33 Law Times
(N S), 834 (1876), Walker *v* Bartlett, 36
Eng L & Eq, 369 (1856) *Re* Barned's
Banking Co., L R. 3 Ch, 105 (1867)
Ex parte Sargent, L R , 17 Eq , 327
(1873); Ortigosa *v* Brown, 47 L J
(Ch), 168 (1878). Transfer of certificates
in England must be under seal *Re*
Balkis, etc , Co , 58 L T Rep , 300
(1889). The American cases incline to
the opinion that, even though a seal
were required, the sealed transfer
would not be void because of the blanks
left in it Bridgeport Bank *v* New
York, etc , R R. Co , *supra*, Com Bank
v Kortright, *supra*, Matthews *v* Massachusetts Nat'l Bank, 1 Holmes, 396, 107,
(1874), McNiel *v* Tenth Nat'l Bank,
supra

[3] Scott *v* Pequonnock Bank (U S C.
Ct), 15 Rep , 137 (1883), Brown *v* Smith,
122 Mass , 589 (1877), Fitchburg Sav
Bank *v.* Torrey, 134 Mass , 239 (1883),
Duke *v* Cahawba Nav Co , 10 Ala , 82

(1846) Chouteau Spring Co *v* Harris,
20 Mo 382 (1855), St Louis P Ins Co
v Goodfellow, 9 Mo, 149 (1845), Gil-
bert *v* Manchester Iron Manuf Co, 11
Wend , 627 (1834) Sargent *v* Essex
Manuf Co , 26 Mass 202 (1829), Nesmith
v Washington Bank, 23 Mass ,324 (1829),
Sargent *v* Franklin Ins Co , 8 Pick , 90
(1829), Conant *v* Reed, 1 Ohio St., 298
(1853), Baltimore City P R'y Co *v*
Sewall, 35 Md , 238 (1871) Bank of
America *v* McNiel, 10 Bush, 54 (1873),
United States *v* Vaughan, 3 Binn (Pa),
394 (1811), Beckwith *v* Burroughs, 13
R I , 291 (1882), Farmers' & M Bank *v*
Wasson, 48 Iowa, 336 (1878), Carroll *v*
Mullanphy Sav Bank, 8 Mo App 249
(1880), B way Bank *v* McElrath 13 N
J Eq , 24 (1860), Smith *v* Crescent City,
etc , Co , 30 La Ann , 1378 (1878), People's Bank *v* Gridley, 91 Ill , 457 (1879)
Nor can the transferrer avoid the assignment before registry on the ground
that no consideration passed Hall *v*
United States Ins Co , 5 Gill (Md), 484
(1847), Cushman *v* Thayer Mfg Co , 76
N Y , 365 (1879) Such an assignment
satisfies a contract to sell stock White
v Salisbury, 33 Mo , 150 (1862), Merchants' Nat'l Bank *v* Richards, 6 Mo
App 454 (1879) The fact that the corporation subsequently **refuses to regis-**

transferrer himself.[1] That the transferrer cannot question the completeness of his transfer of title is a rule binding not only on himself, but also upon his assignees in bankruptcy or insolvency.[2] The transferrer is estopped also from attacking the assignment of the certificate on the ground of informalities in the transfer.[3]

§ 379. *Effect of charter provision requiring registry.* — This rule prevails even though the certificate or by-laws, or charter itself, declares that a transfer shall not be legal or complete or effectual until it is registered on the corporate books.[4] As between the transferrer and transferee, the unregistered assignment is complete and effectual in contradiction of such declarations. The courts construe these provisions of the certificate or by-laws or charter to be intended, not to affect the rights of the transferee as against the transferrer, but to affect the rights of the transferee as against attaching creditors of his transferrer and other third parties claiming an interest in the stock, and also to affect his right to claim dividends, the privilege of voting, and other rights of a stockholder.[5]

ter the transfer does not prevent title passing, as between transferrer and transferee   Crawford v Provincial Ins Co, 8 Upper Can, C P 263 (1859)

[1] Northrop v Newtown & B T Co, 3 Conn, 552 (1821) Fisher v Essex Bank, 5 Gray, 373 (1855), the rights of attaching creditors being involved

[2] *Ex parte* Dobson, 2 Mont D & D, 685 (1812) Dickinson v Central Nat'l Bank, 129 Mass, 279 (1880), Morris v Cannon, 8 Jur (N S) 653 (1862), Sibley v Quinsigamond Nat'l Bank, 133 Mass, 515 (1882)

[3] Holyoke Bank v Goodman Paper Mfg Co, 9 Cush, 576 (1852) Maguire's Case, 3 De G & S, 31 (1849), Sheffield A & M R'y Co v Woodcock, 7 M & W, 574 (1841), Cheltenham & G W N R'y Co v Daniel, 2 Q B 281 (1841), Home Stock Ins Co v Sherwood, 72 Mo 461 (1880) The legal sufficiency of the instrument of transfer cannot be questioned by the transferrer   Chew v Bank of Baltimore, 14 Md, 299 (1859)

[4] Johnson v Laflin, 103 U S, 800, 804 (1880), affirming 5 Dill, 65 (1878), Noyes v Spaulding, 27 Vt, 420 (1855) where the court say "That provision is similar to the statute in this state in relation to the transfer of real estate, under which

it has uniformly been held that the title passes to the grantee as between the parties to the conveyance, though the deed is unrecorded   .   .   The object of having the transfer recorded on the books of the corporation is notice, and that is the only object. For that reason the transfer, though unrecorded, is good against the party and all those who have notice in fact of the transfer" United States v Cutts, 1 Sumner, 133 (1832), First Nat'l Bank v Gifford, 47 Iowa 575 (1877). The same provision was involved in nearly all the cases cited in preceding sections. See, also, Johnson v Underhill, 52 N Y, 203 (1873), Bank of Utica v Smalley, 2 Cowen, 770 (1824), Baldwin v Canfield, 26 Minn., 43 (1879), where the court say that charter "provisions of this kind are intended solely for the protection and benefit of the corporation, they do not incapacitate a shareholder from transferring his stock without any entry upon the corporation books"

[5] Continental Nat'l Bank v Eliot Nat'l Bank, 7 Fed Rep, 369 (1881), Merchants' etc, Bank v Richards, 6 Mo App, 654 (1879), and cases cited *supra*, and § 465, *infra.*

§ 380. *Certificate of stock may be assigned with the name of the transferee left blank.* — By a commercial usage, which has been repeatedly recognized as valid by the courts, certificates of stock may be assigned by a transfer duly signed by the transferrer, but with the name of the transferee left blank.[1] Generally the combined instrument of transfer and power of attorney on the back of the certificate is signed by the stockholder and delivered to the purchaser, with the names of the transferee and of the attorney left blank   Such a certificate of stock, transferred in blank, may be sold and passed from hand to hand, and each purchaser of it is entitled to the same rights against his transferrer or previous transferrers as he would have if the names of the successive holders appeared on the certificate itself. Any purchaser of the certificate, duly signed but transferred in blank, may fill up the blanks and insert his own name[2] He may fill in his own name as transferee, and the name of an agent as the attorney to make the registry, or he may leave the latter blank and allow the registry clerk to fill in his own name, as is frequently done.

B METHOD OF REGISTERING A TRANSFER OF STOCK

§ 381 *Registry an important part of a transfer of stock* — The effect of obtaining a registry or of neglecting to obtain a registry of the transfer on the corporate books, immediately after purchas-

[1] Walker v Detroit Transit R y Co, 47 Mich, 338 (1882), Pennsylvania R R Co's Appeal 86 Pa St 80 (1878), Cutting v Damerel, 88 N Y 410 (1882), German Union B Ass'n v Sendmeyer, 50 Pa St, 67 (1865), *Ex parte* Sargent, L R, 17 Eq 273 (1873), Ortigosa v Brown, 47 L J (Ch), 168 (1878), *Re* Barned's Banking Co, L R, 3 Ch, 105 (1867) *Cf* §§ 325, 377 *supra* § 416 *infra* "Even in the absence of such usage, a blank transfer on the back of the certificate, to which the holder has affixed his name is a good assignment, and a party to whom it is delivered is authorized to fill it up by writing a transfer and power of attorney over the signature ' McNiel v Tenth Nat'l Bank, 45 N Y, 325, 331 (1871) "There is no force in the suggestion that the power of attorney in the present case was incomplete, because there were blanks for the number of shares and for the name of the attorney Any holder might fill up the blanks and constitute himself the attorney   These points are too well settled to need discussion " Holbrook v New Jersey Zinc Co 57 N Y 616 623 (1874) As to the English rule where the charter requires transfers to be under seal, see § 377 See also Colonial Bank v Hepworth, 57 L T Rep 118 (1887), Williams v Colonial Bank id, 188 (1887), Nanney v Morgan 57 id, 48 (1887)

[2] Broadway Bank v McElrath, 13 N J Eq, 24 (1860), Matthews v Mass Nat'l Bank 1 Holmes, 396 (1874), Bridgeport Bank v N Y & N H R R Co, 30 Conn 231 (1861), Kortright v Buffalo Com Bank, 20 Wend 91 (1838) affirmed 22 Wend, 348 (1839), Otis, Adm'r, v Gardner, 105 Ill, 436 (1883), Mount Holly L & M T Co v Ferrie, 17 N J Eq, 117 (1861), Prall v Tilt, 28 N J Eq 479 (1877), Leavitt v Fisher, 4 Duer, 1 20 (1854)

ing the same from the vendor, has given rise to much litigation and much apparent confusion. A registry of the transfer is important in two respects. First, as regards the rights of the purchaser in reference to the corporation; second, in regard to the rights of the purchaser as regards third persons who are either creditors of the old registered stockholders or have claims upon the stock in question. So far as the corporation is concerned, it is bound to recognize only the registered stockholder.[1] To him is accorded the right to vote, draw dividends, and exercise the general rights of stockholdership. The unregistered purchaser of stock cannot claim such rights. All the cases agree in this result of a neglect to register a transfer. As regards the rights of third persons, however, the courts of the different states vary widely in their opinions. Generally the question arises by reason of an attachment or execution levied by a creditor of the transferrer against the stock standing on the corporate books in the name of the transferrer, who has already sold and assigned the certificate of stock to another. As a general rule, it may be said that a purchaser of a certificate of stock is usually protected as fully without a registry on the corporate books as he would be by a registry, so far as subsequent attachments and most other possible equities against the stock are concerned.[2] This is the rule in New York and most of the states. In Connecticut, Illinois and a few other states a contrary rule prevails. In Massachusetts and New Hampshire a late statute has changed the old rule so that it now accords with that of New York.[3]

§ 382. *Formalities of making registry.* — The customary method of registering a transfer of stock on the corporate books is simple. The registered stockholder, or his attorney in fact, whose name is written in the blank power of attorney, applies to the corporate officer having charge of the transfer books, and requests a registry of the transfer to a person designated by a name written in the form of transfer. Books of transfer are kept for purposes of registering, and upon such an application and a surrender of the old certificate the old stockholder or his attorney makes the registry and a new certificate is issued.[4]

Any suitable registry or stock-list, or formal entry on the corporate books, suffices. No special book need be kept for that purpose.[5] Where the company does not keep a transfer book the

---

[1] Registry herein means not only an actual registry, but also a request to the corporation to allow registry where improperly refused by it. See § 382.

[2] These various questions are considered in chs XXI and XXVII.

[3] This statute is given in full in § 490.

[4] Burrall v. Bushwick R. R. Co., 75 N. Y., 211 (1878), Green, etc, Co. v Bulla, 45 Ind 1 (1873).

[5] "All that is necessary, when the transfer is required by law to be made upon the books of the corporation, is that the fact should be appropriately

transfer of stock is complete when the owner of stock transfers the certificate on the back and delivers it to the secretary in order that a new certificate may be issued to the transferee [1] The demand for registry should be made upon the principal officer or clerk at the office of the corporation   When so made it is sufficient [2] The method of registry may be regulated by the by-laws of the corporation   Thus, a by-law that the stock shall be transferable by indorsement in writing, made in the presence of the cashier or two other witnesses, has been sustained as valid, and is complied with only by the presence and signature of the cashier or of the wit-

recorded in some suitable registry or stock-list, or otherwise formally entered upon its books   For this purpose the account in a stock ledger, showing the names of the stockholders, the number and amount of the shares belonging to each, and the sources of their title, whether by original subscription and payment or by derivation from others, is quite suitable, and fully meets the requirements of the law "   National Bank v Watsontown Bank, 105 U S, 217 (1881)

[1] Chemical Nat'l Bank v Colwell, 132 N Y, 250 (1892)   A stockholder is liable by statute on stock where he has merely transferred the certificate and no effort has been made to complete the transfer on the corporate books   Where there is no transfer book, but certificates are merely canceled and new ones issued, this is sufficient to effect a transfer on the corporate books   Plumb v Bank of Enterprise, 29 Pac Rep, 699 (Kan, 1892) Where the corporation keeps a stock certificate book but no transfer book, a transfer on the back of a certificate, which is then canceled and pasted back in the certificate book, and a new certificate issued to the transferee, is a sufficient transfer to constitute a transferee a stockholder   He may vote at elections, and an assignment by the corporation on the direction of officers elected by such a transferee is valid   Such a transfer is valid also although a by-law provided that before selling his stock a stockholder must offer it to other stock-

holders for purchase   American Nat'l Bank v Oriental Mills, 23 Atl Rep, 795 (R I, 1891)

[2] ' It is sufficient for him to apply at the bank during the usual hours of business, and make his demand upon the officers and clerks who may be in attendance there, and, in case they are not authorized to transact that particular business, they must either refer him to the proper officer in the bank or procure the attendance of such officer or of the board of directors, if necessary without any unreasonable delay In the absence of any proof to the contrary, it may be fairly presumed that the principal officer or clerk in attendance at the bank, during the usual hours of business, is authorized to permit such a transfer when proper " Com Bank of Buffalo v Kortright, 22 Wend, 348, 351 (1839), Case v Bank 100 U S, 446 (1879), where application to the cashier was held to be proper McMurrich v Bond H H Co, 9 U C (Q B), 333 (1852), where the application was to the secretary, Re Goodwin v Ottawa & P R y Co., 13 U C (C P), 254 (1863), where an application to secretary and treasurer was sustained, Green Mount. & S L T Co v Bulla (1873), supra, where the application was to the president   Presentation of the certificate of stock duly indorsed to the person in charge of the office of the corporation is a sufficient demand of transfer   Dunn v Star etc, Ins Co, 19 N Y Week Dig, 531 (1884)

nesses[1] So, also, of a by-law requiring registry in the presence of
the president and secretary of the company[2] But a by-law requiring the assent of the president of the corporation to the registry
of a transfer would be in restraint of trade and void.[3] A delivery
of certificates to the corporation, and a mere request to the corporate officers to make the transfer, is not a registry until the entry
is actually made[4]

The fact that the registry clerk marks on the instrument of transfer the words "received for record" does not constitute a registry.[5]
A memorandum on the stock book that the stock has been transferred as collateral security is sufficient to give the transfer precedence over an attachment.[6] It has been held that, where the
corporation has a branch registry office in another state, a registry
in the branch office is not an effectual registry until it has been
reported and entered in the books of the main office of the corporation[7] If the corporation does not keep books for the registry of
transfers of stock, a mere notice to the corporation that a transfer
has been made constitutes a registry[8] But if the statute or charter requires a transfer to be made on the corporate books, no registry is possible until such books are obtained and opened[9] If
the corporation never issues certificates of stock, the stockholder
cannot demand them[10] If the corporation cannot allow the registry on account of an injunction, it is nevertheless bound to respect the rights of a transferee who gives notice to it of the trans-

---

[1] Dane i Young, 61 Me, 160 (1872)

[2] Planters' & M M Ins Co. v Selma
Sav Bank 63 Ala, 585 (1879)

[3] Sargent v Franklin Ins Co, 8 Pick,
90 (1829)

[4] Brown v Adams 5 Biss, 181 (1870)
Nor will a mere entry of credit to the
transferee, on the treasurer's books,
suffice Marlborough Mfg Co. i Smith,
2 Conn, 579 (1818) Cf § 258

[5] Northrop v Curtis, 5 Conn, 246 (1824)
But a memorandum entered on the stub
in the stock book opposite to the certificate issued, that that certificate has
been transferred, is a sufficient registry
as against attaching creditors of the
transferrer Fisher v Jones, 3 S Rep,
13 (Ala, 1887) A mere letter from the
transferee to the corporation that he
has purchased the certificate is insufficient, even though such letter is pinned
to the transfer book Newell i Williston, 138 Mass, 240 (1885)

[6] Moore i Marshalltown, etc, Co., 46
N W Rep, 750 (Iowa, 1890).

[7] Pinkerton i Manchester & L R R.
Co, 42 N H, 424 (1861)

[8] Crawford i Prov. Ins. Co, 8 U C
(C P), 263 (1859), Agricultural, etc., v
Wilson 24 Me, 273 (1844), holding that a
transfer on the books of a corporation
of stock for which certificates had not
been issued is sufficient to pass the property in the stock, and a valid consideration for a note given in payment

[9] McCurry i Suydam, 10 N J Law,
245 (1828) Where the corporation keeps
no stock ledger, a transfer is sufficiently
registered when the old certificate is surrendered, a new one issued, and the new
name entered on the subscription list.
Stewart i Walla Walla, etc, Co, 20
Pac Rep, 605 (Wash Ter, 1889)

[10] Thorp i Woodhull, 1 Sandf. Ch., 111
(1844) See §§ 60, 192.

fer.[1] The issue of a new certificate of stock is not essential to the completeness of a registry of the transfer[2] If the corporation delays unreasonably in allowing a registry it is liable in damages to the applicant for registry[3]

The instrument of transfer must be in proper form[4] Unless the old stockholder or his duly authorized attorney offers to make the registry, the corporation may refuse to allow it[5] The power of attorney must run from the previous registered stockholder, and not from an intermediate unregistered transferee of the certificate[6] Transfers under bankruptcy or insolvent laws are to be registered like voluntary transfers[7] In England a written acceptance of the stock by the transferee is required[8]

A mere notice to the corporation that an assignment has been

[1] Purchase v New York Exchange Bank, 3 Rob, 164 (1865).

[2] First Nat Bank v Gifford, 47 Iowa 575 (1877) Chouteau Spring Co v. Harris, 20 Mo, 382 (1855)

[3] Sutton v Bank of England, 1 C & P, 193 (1824), where the bank delayed longer than one day, the customary time, and refused to give any reason therefor, Catchpole v Ambergate. N, etc, R'y Co, 1 El & B, 111 (1852), where, by reason of the delay the stock was forfeited, notice of forfeiture going to the old stockholder See, also Healey on Law and Pr of Companies, p 81 Although the directors are entitled to reasonable time to decide whether to make a transfer, yet if they have already made up their minds, the measure of damages for refusal is the price of the stock on the day when the application was made Re The Ottos, etc, Mines, 68 L T Rep, 138 (1892).

[4] Queen v General Cemetery Co 6 E & B, 415 (1856) holding that the deed of transfer, where a deed is necessary, must be properly drawn See, also Societe Generale, etc, v Walker, L R, 11 App, 20 (1885).

[5] Mechanics' Banking Ass'n v Mariposa Co, 3 Rob (N Y) 395 (1865)

[6] Dunn v Commercial Bank, 11 Barb, 580 (1852).

[7] Dutton v Connecticut Bank 13

Conn, 493 (1840), State v Ferris, 42 Conn 560 (1875).

[8] Ortigosa v Brown, 47 L J (Ch), 168 (1878) The Joint-stock Company's Act of 1856 required such an acceptance The act of 1862, repealing the act of 1856, prescribed that transfers should be made as was customary, unless the by-laws prescribed otherwise Hence, in the absence of by-laws, the written acceptance is held to be customary and necessary In England, where a transfer of stock is made by first applying to the company, and having the company certify that the certificate of stock had been lodged with the company, and then the money is paid, it is held that the party purchasing the stock on the faith of this certificate of the company cannot hold the company liable although it turns out that the vendor was not entitled to the stock, and consequently the whole capital stock being already issued that the transfer could not be made The court held that the certification was ultra vires and hence not enforceable Bishop v The Balkis etc Co Limited 63 L T Rep 316 (1890) affirmed id 601 (1891) the court, however dissenting from the view that the certification was ultra vires but holding that the certification did not warrant the title nor the validity of the various documents.

made need not be considered by the corporation.[1] Where, however, the transferee giving such notice does not obtain registry
because the corporation refuses, for any reason, to make the registry, the mere notice must be borne in mind by the corporation,
and the rights of the applicant preserved by it, as regards future
registries.[2]

§ 383 *Formalities of registry may be waived by the corporation.*—
The corporation may waive the formalities connected with a registry of transfer, and when it does so the transferee becomes a stockholder as completely as though registry had been regularly made.[3]
Frequently the waiver arises by placing the transferee's name on
the list of stockholders, although no formal registry has been had.[4]
Even a charter requirement that the consent of the directors to a
registry of transfer shall be obtained may be waived by the corporation.[5] The corporation, by paying dividends to an unregistered
transferee of stock, thereby waives the formalities of registry.[6]
When the corporation refuses to allow a registry for reasons other
than those connected with the mere formalities of registry, or for
reasons not given to the applicant, it waives its right to insist on
them, and cannot afterwards claim that the appellant did not conform to such technicalities.[7] A failure, however, on the part of the

[1] Stockwell v St Louis M Co, 9 Mo
App. 133 (1880)

[2] See p 523 note 1 See, also § 532

[3] Richmondville Mfg Co v Prall, 9
Conn, 487 (1833), Clowes v Brettell, 11
M & W, 461 (1843) Sadler's Case, 3
De G & S, 36 (1849) Chambersburg
Ins. Co v Smith, 11 Pa St, 120 (1849)
Walter's Case, 3 De G & S 149 (1850),
Bauie v Whitehaven etc, Ry Co,
3 H L C, 1 (1860), Wills v Murray,
4 Ex, 843 (1850), Yelland's Case, 5
De G & Sm, 395 (1852), Powers v
Harding, 1 C B (N S), 533 (1857),
Henderson v Royal British Bank, 26 L
J (Q B), 112 (1857), Daniell v Same, 1
H & N 685 (1857), East G R'y Co v
Bartholomew, L R, 3 Ex, 15 (1867),
Ind's Case, L R, 7 Ch, 485 (1872),
Weber v Fickey 52 Md 500,516 (1879)
Home Stock Ins Co v Sherman 72
Mo, 461 (1880), Isham v Buckingham,
49 N Y, 216 (1872) See, also, §§ 258,
260, 262

[4] Upham v Burnham, 3 Liss, 431, 520
(1873).

[5] *Ex parte* Walton, 26 L J (Ch), 545
(1857). Likewise where the by-laws
contain such a provision Chambersburg Ins Co v Smith, 11 Pa. St., 120
(1849) holding also that an oversight
whereby the attorney who makes the
registry omits to sign the registry is immaterial

[6] Cutting v Damerel, 88 N Y, 410
(1882)

[7] Townsend v McIver, 2 S. C., 25
(1870), Bond v Mt. Hope Iron Co., 99
Mass, 505 (1868), holding that the corporation must put the refusal on the
ground of non-conformity with formalities at the time of the application, and
cannot afterwards raise such Chouteau etc, Co. v Harris, 20 Mo, 382
(1855), Robinson v Nat'l Bank of New
Berne, 95 N Y, 637 (1884), where the
court say "The requirement of a registry, existing only for its own protection and convenience, must be deemed
waived and non-essential when it
wrongfully refuses to obey its own
rule."

corporation to notify the transferee of a refusal to allow registry is no waiver of such registry.[1]

§ 384 *Either the transferrer or the transferee may apply to the corporation for a registry of transfer* — A person who appears on the corporation books as the holder of stock, but who in fact has sold the stock, has a right to have his transfer recorded on the corporate books, thereby releasing him from liability on the stock[2] The vendor may request the corporation to register the transfer, and the corporation may make it at his request. If he refuses so to do, the vendor may bring suit in a court of equity to compel the corporation to register the transfer[3] It has been held, also, that an intermediate vendor of the stock, whose name has never appeared on the corporate books, may likewise compel a registry to be made[4] After an ultimate vendee has been registered, the original vendor cannot have an intermediate vendee and vendor registered as the stockholder[5] The corporation may register the transfer, even against the wishes of the transferee.[6] The transferee also has a right to apply for and compel a registry of the transfer of stock to himself[7]

C. RIGHTS AND DUTIES OF THE CORPORATION IN ALLOWING OR REFUSING REGISTRY

§ 385 *Corporation may require proof of identity; also of genuineness of signature, etc.*— When a transfer of stock is presented to the corporation for registry, if the corporation is in doubt as to the identity of the person presenting it, whether he be the stock-

[1] Gustard's Case, L. R., 8 Eq, 438 (1869)

[2] "The purchase was in itself authority to the vendor to make the transfer. . A court of equity will compel a transferee of stock to record the transfer, and to pay all calls after the transfer . If so, it is clear that the vendor may himself request the transfer to be made." Webster v Upton, 91 U S, 65, 71 (1875) "If a subsequent transfer of the certificate be refused by the bank, it can be compelled at the instance of either of them." Johnston v Laflin, 103 U S., 800, 804 (1880).

[3] Wynne v Price, 3 D & S, 310 (1849), Birmingham v Sheridan 33 Beav, 660, Eustace v Dublin T C R'y Co, L. R., 6 Eq, 182 (1868).

[4] Paine v. Hutchinson, L R, 3 Ch, 388 (1868)

[5] Shaw v. Fisher, 5 De G, M & G, 596 (1855)

[6] Upton v Burnham, 3 Biss., 520, 525 (1873)

[7] Norris v Irish Land Co., 8 E & B, 512 (1857), Daly v Thompson, 10 M. & W, 309 (1842), Johnston v Laflin, 5 Dill, 65 (1878), 103 U. S, 800, Hill v Pine River Bank, 45 N H, 300 (1864) Presbyterian Con v Carlisle Bank, 5 Pa St, 345 (1847), Mechanics' Bank v Seton, 1 Peters, 299 (1828), Arnold v Suffolk Bank, 27 Barb, 424 (1857), Sargent v Franklin Ins Co, 8 Pick, 90 (1829), Cushman v Thayer Mfg Co, 76 N Y, 365 (1879) But the complaint must be full and accurate in its averments Edwards v. Sonoma Bank, 59 Cal, 136 (1881)

holder already registered on the books or the attorney of such, the corporation may require proof of such identity [1] If it is in doubt as to the competency of the transferrer to sell the stock,[2] legal proof of such competency must be given [3] If the applicant for registry applies as the attorney of the registered stockholder, the corporation may require satisfactory evidence of the genuineness of the latter's transfer, or may require the presence of the stockholder himself [4]

§ 386 *Corporation cannot refuse registry on account of the motive of the transferrer or transferee in the transaction.*—The corporation has nothing to do with the motive or purpose of the vendor or vendee of the stock [5] It can refuse a registry only when there is doubt as to the legal right of the applicant to have such registry It cannot refuse on the ground that the transfer would injure the corporation, nor on the theory that the object of the transfer is to increase the votes of the transferee [6] In England often the directors are by charter given a discretionary power to refuse a transfer [7]

[1] Telegraph Co v Davenport 97 U S, 369 (1878) Davis v Bank of England, 2 Bing, 393 (1824), where the court say the corporation "may take reasonable time to make inquiries, and require proof that the signature to a power of attorney is the writing of the person whose signature it purports to be" Bayard v Farmers' & M Bank, 52 Pa. St., 232 (1866).

[2] See §§ 318, 319.

[3] Id.

[4] *Supra*, note 1, and see §§ 363-367

[5] Townsend v McIver, 2 S. C, 25 (1870), People v Paton, 5 N Y St Rep, 316 (1887) But a transfer, merely nominal, to obtain for the transferee certain special privileges, such as free admission to a place of amusement, may be a fraud on other stockholders and will be set aside. Appeal of Academy of Music, 108 Pa. St., 510 (1885). Equity will not compel a corporation to register a transfer of stock when the purpose of the transfer is to obtain the control of the corporation and wreck it. Gould v Head, 41 Fed Rep, 243 (1890) In an action to compel the unincorporated Standard Oil ' trust ' to transfer on its books trust certificates which the plaint-

iff has purchased, the defendants, who allege that the plaintiff is a competitor of the trust and purchased the certificates in order to break up the trust and compel it to buy the plaintiff out, may be compelled to give a bill of particulars. Rice v Rockefeller, N Y Daily Reg, May 29, 1888 The plaintiff in this case finally succeeded. See 134 N Y, 174 (1892).

[6] Moffatt v. Farquhar, L R, 7 Ch D, 591 (1878).

[7] See Healey on Law and Practice of Companies. 79 Where the directors are authorized by the articles of incorporation to reject a transfer of stock on the ground that they do not approve of the transferee, "the discretionary power is of a fiduciary nature, and must be exercised in good faith, that is, legitimately for the purpose for which it is conferred It must not be exercised corruptly, or fraudulently, or arbitrarily, or capriciously, or wantonly It may not be exercised for a collateral purpose. In exercising it the directors must act in good faith in the interest of the company and with due regard to the shareholder's right to transfer his shares, and they must fairly consider the question

§ 387   *Corporation may interplead between two claimants to stock.*
The task imposed upon a corporation in determining whether to
refuse or to allow a registry of stock is a difficult and dangerous
one.   It is easy to avoid the risk of forgery or of failure of the
applicant to identify himself   But circumstances frequently are
such that the corporation dare not allow registry to either of two
parties, each of whom claims to be the sole and absolute owner of
the stock, and each of whom claims the right of registry or notifies
the corporation not to register the other claimant as a stockholder
These cases arise on various occasions but most often where the
stock has been attached or sold on execution by the transferrer's
creditors before the transferee had obtained registry, or where by
the fraud of the old stockholder's agent, the certificate has passed
into the hands of a *bona fide* purchaser, or where by a breach of
trust, an executor or administrator, or trustee or guardian has sold
the trust stock and appropriated the proceeds   or under other states
of fact wherein there are two claimants of the stock, each having
rights which can be clearly ascertained only by litigation.   It is
not incumbent on the corporation to decide between these conflicting parties and rights[1]   Such a requirement would expose
it to unreasonable risks and compel it to assume the functions of a
court.   Where there is a reasonable doubt as to the facts involved
or as to the respective rights of the claimants of the stock, and the
corporation is sued by one of the claimants for refusing to allow a
registry by him, the corporation may interplead, and thus compel
the claimants to ascertain their rights through the medium of a
court of justice.[2]   A similar interpleader may be made where the

of the transferee's fitness at a board
meeting   It is not a sufficient reason
that the transferee is not a member of a
particular family, and the directors will
be ordered to make the transfer   *Re*
Bell Bros, Limited, 65 L. T Rep 215
(1891)

[1] The discussion of the duty of the
corporation in various circumstances is
given under chapters devoted to them

[2] Mechanics Bank v Richards 6 Mo
App, 454 (1891), aff'd 74 Mo, 77   State
Ins Co v Gennett, 2 Tenn Ch 100
Leavitt v Fisher 4 Duer (N Y) 1
(1854)   If the court decides that the interpleader is properly filed by the corporation herein, it generally on a motion
dismisses the proceeding with costs to
the corporation, and the court also de-

cides between the defendants if the case
is ready as between them   If not ready,
it directs an action or an issue, or a reference to a master, to ascertain contested facts, as may be best suited to
the nature of the case   or the court
may leave it to the defendants to pre-
pare the case between them as they may
be advised which would be the effect
of a general order to interplead   State
Ins Co v Gennett, 2 Tenn Ch, 100
(1874) citing as cases on above rules of
practice East & West. etc.. Co v Littledale, 7 Hare 62 (1848)   Martinius v
Helmuth 2 V & B. 412 (1814), note,
Horton v Baptist Church 34 Vt., 317
(1861)   Rowe v Hoagland, 7 N J Eq,
131 (1848), Crawford v. Fisher 1 Hare,
441 (1842)   Condit v King, 2 Beas Ch,,

corporation is sued for dividends which are claimed by two opposing parties[1] An interpleader is proper, however, only after suit has been actually commenced against the corporation[2]

There is some doubt and considerable difficulty in laying down rules as to when a corporation may safely claim a right to refuse to act, and to compel the claimants to litigate between themselves before it allows a registry to either   The policy of the law doubtless is to go very far in allowing the corporation to refuse to incur responsibility by taking action   Where, however, the rights of one claimant are reasonably clear, the corporation should suspend action for a reasonable time within which the contesting party may apply to the courts, and if no such action is brought, it should allow a registry by the first-named claimant[3]   Any other rule would enable any person to practically deprive a stockholder of the possession of his stock temporarily, by simply notifying the corporation that he claims the stock[4]   Where, however, the corporation has allowed one claimant to register his transfer, or has recognized him as a stockholder, the right of the corporation to interplead is gone.[5] It

383 (1861); Hendrickson t Decow, Sax. 595 (1802) City Bank t Bangs, 2 Paige, 570 (1831), Angell v Hadden. 16 Ves 202 (1809) The case of State Ins Co v. Gennett, 2 Tenn Ch, 82 (1874), says- "The law is that the mere pretext of a conflicting claim is not sufficient. The court must be able to see from the facts stated that there is a question to be tried " See, also Norton v Union Trust Co, N Y Daily Reg, April 18, 1887, p 744 In England, by section 35 of the Companies Act, 1862, a corporation may interplead between two claimants of stock, and need not pay costs. Re Edie, etc 58 L T Rep, 305 (1888). An interpleader was sustained in Bangor, etc. Co v Robinson, 52 Fed Rep, 520 (1892)

[1] Salisbury Mills v Townsend, 109 Mass, 115 (1871); Diamond etc, Co. v Todd, 14 Atl Rep, 27 (Del, 1888). Quere, as to whether an action for dividends can be maintained before the right of the claimant to the stock is established. Hughes t. Vermont Copper Mn Co, 72 N. Y, 207 (1878) See ch XXXII

[2] Buffalo Grape Sugar Co v Albeiger, 22 Hun, 349 (1880). A corporation cannot interplead as between stockholders

for the purpose of determining the ownership of stock, there having been no claim made upon it in regard to registry or in regard to dividends. It must be shown also that the company has not acted in a partisan manner as between the different claimants. Hinckley v Pfister, 53 N W Rep, 21 (Wis, 1892). If the corporation allows a transfer to be made during the pendency of a suit between two claimants therefor, and the corporation has notice, it is liable to the successful party, who is thereby deprived of the stock. Hawes v. Gas etc, Co., N. Y. L J, March 29, 1890. See, also, the editorial on that day.

[3] Townsend v McIver, 2 S. C. (N S.) 25 (1870)

[4] Re Tahiti Cotton Co, L. R., 17 Eq, 273 (1874), Ex parte Sargent, L. R., 17 Eq, 273 (1873)

[5] Dalton v. Midland R'y Co, 12 C B, 458 (1852), Cady t Potter, 55 Barb, 463 (1869); Mt Holly, L & M T Co. v Ferrie. 17 N J Eq, 117 (1864). If the party has favored one of the two parties, as by voluntarily agreeing with the sheriff to recognize an execution, an interpleader will not lie. Cromwell v American, etc., Co, 11 N. Y. Supp, 144 (1890). A

cannot afterwards remove the name of the registered stockholder, especially where such stockholder has acted in reliance upon such registry.[1]

§ 388. *Corporation must obey mandate of court ordering registry and issue of new certificates.*— The authorities on this proposition of law are few in number, but they are decisive in protecting the corporation from liability where it proceeds under mandate of a court. Thus, where a decree is obtained commanding the corporation to register a transfer, the corporation is protected in obeying the decree, even though it is reversed on appeal, there having been no stay of proceedings [2] Cases herein may arise also where the registered stockholder alleges that he has lost his certificate, and the court compels the corporation to issue to him a new one,[3] also where an attachment or execution has been levied, the old certificate of stock being outstanding.[4] There is a limit, however, to the power of courts in these matters If the whole capital stock has been issued and the certificates therefor are outstanding, a court cannot order the issue of other certificates, unless the decree at the same time practically nullifies a corresponding outstanding certificate [5]

§ 389. *Remedies of a transferee of stock against the corporation for refusal to allow registry.*— Where, for any reason, the corporation refuses to allow the registry of a transfer of stock, when it is

corporation cannot refuse to transfer stock on the ground that the vendor fraudulently induced the company to issue the stock to him where the company has been guilty of laches in not seeking a remedy before the transfer The vendee in this case was a director American, etc Co r Bayless, 15 S W Rep., 10 (Ky , 1891).

[1] Ward v Southeastern R'y Co , 6 Jur (N S), 890 (1860), Hart v Frontino, etc , Co., 23 L T (N S), 30 (1870), Cohen v Gwynn, 4 Md Ch , 357 (1848) Unless there clearly is a clerical mistake and the issue is to the wrong party Smith v North Am Min Co, 1 Nev , 423 (1865) The corporation is liable for such mistakes Harrison v Pryse, Barnardiston (Fol), Ch , 324 (1740).

[2] Chapman v New Orleans G L & Banking Co , 4 La Ann , 153 (1849). See, also, Purchase v. N. Y Exchange Bank, 3 Rob , 164 (1865). But when the court directs the corporation to issue a

certificate to the life tenant of stock, the corporation is still bound to notify a purchaser of that certificate that it represents a life interest only , otherwise the corporation is liable to the remainder-man Caulkins v Memphis, etc Co, 4 S W Rep 287 (Tenn , 1887) A corporate officer is guilty of contempt if he refuses to obey an order of court requiring him to make certain transfers of stock upon the surrender of the old certificates King v Barnes, 113 N Y., 476, 655, 656 (1889).

[3] See §§ 368-370

[4] See § 488.

[5] See § 284 Where stock is deposited with a trustee for purposes of reorganization and transferable certificates are issued therefor by the trustee, a claimant of stock which another person has deposited, and for which such other person has the trustee's certificate, cannot compel the trustee to deliver up the stock until the trustee's certificate is

the duty and obligation of the corporation to allow it, the transferrer or the transferee who applies for registry may, in general,
pursue one of three remedies. He may apply to a court of law for
a *mandamus* to the corporation to compel it to open its books and
allow the registry; or he may bring a suit in equity, praying that
the corporation be decreed to allow the registry, or to pay him
damages if registry is impossible; or he may sue the corporation
at law for damages, on the ground that by its refusal it has been
guilty of a conversion of his stock

§ 390 *Remedy by mandamus* — The authorities are in irreconcilable conflict on the question whether a *mandamus* lies to compel a
corporation to allow a registry on its books of a transfer of stock.
The weight of authority holds very clearly that the *mandamus* will
not lie under such circumstances [1] This rule is based largely on the

returned, even though the party holding it is a party defendant Beau *v*
American L. & T. Co, 122 N Y, 622
(1890).

[1] The leading case in this country is
Shipley *v* Mechanics' Bank, 10 Johns,
484 (1813), where the court say   "The
applicants have an adequate remedy, by
a special action on the case, to recover
the value of stock if the bank have
unduly refused to transfer it. There is
no need of the extraordinary remedy by
mandamus in so ordinary a case It
might as well be required in every case
where trover would lie It is not a
matter of public concern, as in the case
of public records and documents; and
there cannot be any necessity or even a
desire of possessing the identical shares
in question ' *Ex parte* Firemen's Ins.
Co, 6 Hill, 243 (1843); People *v.* Parker
Vein Coal Co, 10 How. Pr, 543 (1854),
State *t* Rombauer, 46 Mo, 155 (1870),
State *t* St Louis, etc. Co, 21 Mo App,
526 (1886), King *v* London Assurance
Co, 1 Dowl & R, 510 (1822), Stackpole
t Seymour, 127 Mass., 104 (1879) King
v Bank of England, 2 Doug, 524 (1780);
Curry *v* Scott, 54 Pa. St, 270 276
Gray *r* Portland Bank, 3 Mass, 364,
381, State *r* Guerrero, 12 Nev, 105
(1877), People *v* Miller, 39 Hun, 557
(1886), Baker *v* Marshall, 15 Minn, 177
(1870), where the stock had already been

issued to another, Wilkinson *v.* Providence Bank, 3 R. I., 22 (1853); Kimball
v Union Water Co, 44 Cal, 173 (1872),
Birmingham Fire Ins. Co. *v,* Com, 92
Pa. St, 72 (1879), where the court says
that, even if the "courts were inclined
to enlarge the remedy, it could not be
done in a case where the right is disputed, where no public interest is involved, where no reason is shown for a
transfer of a specific and favorite thing,
and where the remedy by action is fully
adequate" Townes *v* Nichols, 73 Me,
515 (1882), where the court vigorously
says   "All the authorities declare that
the remedy by *mandamus* cannot be resorted to in a case like this, unless the
legal right of the petitioner to the possession of the thing sought for is clear
and unquestionable. If there be doubt
as to what his legal right may be, involving the necessity of litigation to
settle it, *mandamus* must be withheld
Mandamus is the right arm of the law.
Its principal office is not to inquire and
investigate, but to command and execute It is not designed to assume a
part in ordinary lawsuits or equitable
proceedings It is properly called into
requisition in cases where the law has
been settled, or in cases where questions
of law or equity cannot properly and
reasonably arise Its very nature implies that the law, although plain and

historical origin of the writ of *mandamus*, and on the theory that the stock of a private corporation has no peculiar value and may be readily obtained in open market or fully compensated for in damages.   It is doubted, however, whether these reasons will be sufficient to restrain the manifest tendency to enlarge the scope of this writ, particularly with reference to stock transactions.   There is a strong line of decisions which holds that a *mandamus* lies to compel a corporation to allow a registry of a transfer of stock, particularly where the corporation has no good and sufficient reason for refusing the registry.[1]   Perhaps the strongest argument

clear, fails to be enforced and needs assistance " See, also, Rex *v* Worcester Nav Co, 1 Mon & R, 529 (1828), Queen *t* Liverpool & M, etc., Ry Co, 21 L. J. (Q B.) 284 (1852), Murray *v* Stevens, 110 Mass, 95 (1872), where the court say, in refusing a *mandamus* to compel a registry of stock   "Without undertaking to lay down an invariable rule on the subject, we think it must be said that this process was not intended and is not well adapted for the trial of mere questions of property.' State *t* Warren Foundry & M Co, 32 N J L, 439 (1868), where a previous transfer had been registered, although possibly in fraud of creditors, Freon *t* Carriage Co, 42 Ohio St, 304 (1884), refusing a *mandamus*, although it is said "that this stock has no market value, that the corporation is doing a growing and profitable business, that its good-will enhances the value of the stock and that by reason of these things damages will not be an adequate remedy   These facts do not change the rule   They are elements in assessing damages which may be fully ascertained in an action at law " See, also, Pomeroy on Eq Juris, § 1412, State *t* Peoples Bldg, etc, Association, 43 N J L, 389 (1881), State *v* Timken, 2 Atl Rep, 782 (N J, 1886), Tobey *v* Hakes, 7 Atl Rep, 551 (Conn, 1886), refusing a *mandamus* on the corporate secretary, Bank *t* Harrison, 66 Ga 696   See, also, Lindley on Partnership, pp. 143, 520, 1036   *Mandamus* does not issue to compel a corporation to transfer stock when there

is no written transfer of the certificate, and another party claims it. Burnsville, etc, Co *t* State, 20 N E Rep, 121 (Ind, 1889)   *Mandamus* does not lie to compel a corporation to transfer stock People *t* Brandis, etc, Co N Y L J, Dec 11, 1889   *Mandamus* does not lie against the Bank of England to compel it to register a transfer of stock to an individual and a corporation jointly   Law Guarantee, etc, Soc *t* Bank of England, 62 L T Rep, 496 (1890)

[1] People *t* Goss Mfg Co, 99 Ill 375 (1881), State *v* First Nat'l Bank, 89 Ind 302 (1883), Green, Mount, etc, Co *t* Bulla, 45 Ind, 1 (1873), People *v* Crockett, 9 Cal, 112 (1858), Townsend *v* McIver, 2 S C, 25 (1870), State *v* Cheraw, etc, R R Co, 16 S C, 524 (1881), Cooper *v* Swamp, etc, Co, 2 Murph (S C), 195 (1812), Norris *t* Irish Land Co, 8 El & Bl, 512 (1857), Regina *t* Carnatic R'y Co, L R, 8 Q B, 299 (1873), Crawford *t* Prov Ins Co, 8 U C (C P), 263 (1859), Goodwin *t* Ottawa & P R'y Co, 13 U C (C P), 254 (1863), holding also that the *mandamus* may run to the corporation itself without specifying any officers, and that an evasive answer by them is equivalent to a refusal to register   It has been held that *mandamus* will issue to aid the sheriff in transferring stock sold on an execution sale   This rule, however would work harshly in states where the purchaser of the outstanding certificate may have some rights   Where such a possibility exists the *mandamus* should be denied   State *v* First Nat'l Bank,

against granting a *mandamus* for this purpose lies in the fact that by a bill in equity not only can a registry be specifically decreed and ordered by the court, but the rights of the corporation and any other claimant can be fully and finally heard and disposed of

§ 391 *Remedy by suit in equity* — This is, it seems, the surest, most complete and most just remedy for compelling a corporation to register a transfer of stock, and for adjusting the various conflicting rights or claims of other parties [1] It is a remedy applicable

---

supra, Bailey z Strohecker 38 Ga , 259 (1868). Durham *v* Man , etc , Co , 9 Oreg , 41 (1880) *Mandamus* will lie to compel the corporation to transfer the stock on its books where any other record would be inadequate because there is no market value for the stock, and because the company has fraudulently transferred its property for the purpose of injuring the value of the stock The *mandamus* will lie although a suit is pending in equity to accomplish the same purpose Slemmons z Thompson, 31 Pac Rep , 514 (Oreg , 1892).

[1] Cushman *v* Thayer Mfg Co , 76 N Y , 365 (1879), Walker *v* Detroit Transit R'y Co , 47 Mich , 338 , Iasigt z Chicago, B & Q R R Co , 129 Mass , 46 (1880), Mechanics' Bank z Seton, 1 Peters, 299 (1828), Wilson *v* Atlantic, etc , R R Co., 2 Fed Rep , 459 (1880), Middlebrook *v* Merchants' Bank, 3 Abb Ct of App, 295 (1866), Buckmister z Consumers' Ice Co , 5 Daly, 513 (1874). In the case of Rice z Rockefeller *et al*, 134 N Y , 174 (1892, reversing 9 N Y Supp , 866), a court of equity compelled the trustees of a trust to transfer on their books trust certificates which had been purchased in open market by a person who then applied to the trustees for a transfer The court based its decision on the similarity of such trust certificates to stock certificates, and said "The denial of the right to transfer upon the books is not consistent with the transferable quality of the shares, which imports that the purchaser taking an assignment of them in a duly formal manner has the right to become a transferee within the meaning

of the agreement upon which the trust was formed .   .   In such case it is within the equitable power of the court to compel such transfer to be made " The court held, also, that it was immaterial that the purchaser who applied for the transfer was hostile to and a competitor of the trust The court said that although it would have been legal in the beginning to have vested a discretion in the trustees as to allowing transfers, yet that, such discretion not having been reserved, it could not be exercised by the directors. Suit in equity lies, White z Price, 39 Minn , 395 (1886), 108 N Y , 661 (1888), Iron R R Co z Fink, 41 Ohio St , 321 (1884), the court saying that the power of equity to decree a registry is well settled As regards the pleadings, see Burrall *v*. Bushwick R R Co, 75 N Y , 211 (1878). See, also, § 579 Suits herein frequently arise wherein a complainant claims stock which is registered in the name of another The chief defendant is that other party But it is necessary also that the corporation be made a party defendant, in order that transfer may be decreed on corporate books For equitable action to compel a corporation to issue stock to a purchaser of the same from one of the parties defendant, see Tanner *v* Gregory, 37 N. W. Rep , 830 (Wis , 1888), Kendig *v* Dean, 97 U S., 423 (1878), Build *v* Munroe, 18 Hun, 316 (1879), the latter case holding also that the corporation may recover costs against a co-defendant who is defeated in the suit, Johnson *v* Kirby, 65 Cal , 482 (1884) In such cases the corporation is but nominally concerned in

to almost all cases arising under a refusal of the corporation to allow a registry of transfer. The case will be decided on equitable principles, however, and a transfer will not be decreed if it involves bad faith.[1] The relief usually demanded is in the alternative, being either for a registry of the transfer or damages in lieu thereof.[2] If all the stock has already been issued, equity has no power to compel a further issue.[3] Laches or the statute of limitations may also be a bar.[4]

the result of the suit It cannot appeal from the judgment when both of the real parties in interest are satisfied and do not appeal Board of L v New Orleans Water-works Co, 1 S. Rep, 445 (La, 1887) If the complainant is a citizen of the same state as the corporation, one of the parties defendant another defendant cannot remove the case into a United States court Crump v Thurber, 115 U S, 56 (1883) In an action against the secretary of a corporation to compel him to register a transfer of stock the corporation is not a necessary party. Gould v Head, 41 Fed Rep, 242 (1890). The federal courts have jurisdiction of a suit in equity brought by a citizen of one state to compel a corporation of another state to transfer on its books certain shares of stock which the complainant purchased from a citizen of the same state as the complainant Jewett v Bradford, etc., Co 45 Fed Rep 801 (1891) If the holder of a certificate of stock has applied for transfer and been refused, he may sue for the dividend before bringing a suit in equity to obtain a transfer of his stock Hill v. Atoka, etc, Co, 21 S. W Rep, 508 (Mo, 1893). An agreement of the holder of a majority of the stock that he will retain control is no defense by the corporation to an action by the receiver of such stockholder to transfer the stock on the corporate books Weller v Pace Tobacco Co, 25 N Y Week Dig, 531 (1886). A pledgee of a certificate of stock is not bound by an agreement of all the stockholders to surrender to the corporation a part of their stock, which part is to be then considered preferred

stock and is to be sold by the corporation for the purpose of paying corporate debts Although all the other stock has had this agreement stamped on the certificates yet the corporation cannot insist that the purchaser of the stock so pledged shall allow the same agreement to be stamped on the new certificate issued to such purchaser The court will order a transfer free from the agreement Campbell v. American, etc. Co, 122 N Y 455 (1890)

[1] Regina v Liverpool, etc, R'y, 21 L J (Q B), 284 Cf Rice v Rockefeller. 134 N Y, 174 (1892)

[2] "A bill in equity may be maintained by a bona fide purchaser of stock against the corporation to compel a transfer of the stock upon the corporate books.' The bill may be in the alternative for a transfer of the stock or for damages, and if the company has already issued its whole capital stock, damages will be granted Birmingham Nat'l Bank v Roden, 11 S Rep, 883 (Ala, 1892) Where a corporation refuses to issue the stock to a subscriber, he may file a bill in the alternative to compel the issue of the shares or the payment of their value with damages If during the pendency of the suit the company becomes insolvent the court can give him damages payable pro rata out of the assets of the corporation In re Reading Iron Works, 24 Atl Rep, 202 (Pa, 1892) See § 61, supra

[3] Smith v North Am Min Co, 1 Nev. 423 (1865), and see § 284

[4] In New York the ten-year statute of limitations runs against an equitable action against the corporation for a transfer of the certificates on its books,

§ 392 *Remedy by an action for damages* — An action at law for damages is an old and well-established remedy of a stockholder who has applied to the corporation for a registry of a transfer and has been refused.[1] The form of the action is not definitely fixed, and in different states different forms seem to have been passed upon without any question being raised as to their technical nature.[2] The measure of damages is substantially the same as in other cases of conversion of stock.[3] The statute of limitations runs only from the time when a demand for registry was made.[4]

from the time when the outstanding certificate was issued Ryder ɪ Bushwick R. R, 10 N. Y Supp, 743 (1890) In the case Ware ɪ Galveston City Company, 146 U S, 102 (1892), the bill of a claimant of stock against the company to hold it liable for allowing a transfer of the stock in fraud of his rights was barred by laches the suit having been brought thirty-five years after the cause of action had accrued The holders of full-paid stock cannot be assessed on such stock even under a reorganization agreement of the majority of the stockholders Where, however, for four years the stockholder does not object, and then applies for a transfer of his stock, a court of equity may refuse to grant the transfer and give him damages for the value of his stock at the time of the demand of transfer, together with interest. Gresham ɪ Island, etc, Bank, 21 S W Rep, 556 (Tex, 1893)

[1] Hussey ɪ Manufacturers' & M. Bank, 27 Mass., 414 (1830), Helm v Swiggett, 12 Ind, 194 (1859). Cases supporting this rule abound in all the states They will be found together with others in chapter XXXV If the corporation illegally refuses to allow a registry, but afterwards does allow it, the corporation is not liable in damages for the decline of the market value of the stock in the meantime. Skinner v. City of London M Ins Co, L R, 14 Q B D 882 (1885) Even in England if the company has completed a transfer upon its books and then repudiates the transfer on the ground that it had prior to that time transferred the same stock to others, the company is liable in damages to the party to whom the last transfer was made Tomkinson ɪ. Balkis, etc., Co 64 L. T. Rep, 816 (1891). A corporation is liable in damages for refusing to allow a transfer of the stock where such refusal is unjustifiable Doty v First Nat Bank of Larimore, 53 N W Rep, 77 (North Dak, 1892). If the company illegally refuses to transfer stock it is a conversion Rio Grande, etc, Co. ɪ Burns, 17 S. W Rep., 1043 (Tex, 1891) The appropriate remedy of a purchaser to compel a corporation to register a transfer to himself is an action on the case wherein the measure of damages is the value at the time of refusal to transfer German Building Ass n ɪ Sandemeyer, 14 Wright (Pa), 67, Waln ɪ Bank 8 S. & R., 73, Presbyterian Church v Bank, 5 Pa. St., 345.

[2] See ch XXXV.

[3] Id.

[4] Cleveland R. R. Co v Robbins, 35 Ohio St., 483, Iron R. R. Co *v.* Fink, 41 Ohio St, 321 (1884).

CHAPTER XXIII.

RULES FOR CORPORATIONS IN REGARD TO REFUSING OR ALLOWING REGISTRIES OF TRANSFERS OF STOCK.

§ 393. *Purpose of the chapter.*— It is proposed in this chapter, as a continuation of the last, and as a recapitulation of the various rights, liabilities and duties of the corporation in refusing or allowing a registry of a transfer of stock, to state briefly the rules which prevail herein. The stand-point taken is that of the corporation. The minute and particular application of the general rules governing this subject are not stated here at length; but an effort has been made to give, in systematic order, certain directions which will enable a corporation, when in doubt as to whether to allow or refuse a registry, to decide the question intelligently and safely.

§ 394. *Right to refuse until the transferrer pays the unpaid subscription price.*[1]— A corporation cannot refuse to register a transfer of stock merely because the subscription price has not been fully paid in, unless the charter or the statutes of the state expressly give that right. Nor can it refuse registry, even though a call for part of the subscription price has been made, is due, and remains unpaid. It must allow a registry, but may continue to hold the transferrer liable for the call. The corporation has no lien on the stock for the subscription price, nor has it a right to restrict transfers until calls or parts of the subscription price not yet called are paid. The policy of the law is to favor the right of transfer, and no impediments by the corporation are allowed to re-

---

[1] See chapter XV.

strict that right   As regards parts of the subscription not yet called in, the transferrer is released from liability and the transferee assumes the liability.   As regards calls made before the application for registry but not yet due, the transferrer is liable, but, it seems, not the transferee.   As regards calls made before the application and due before such, the transferrer and not the transferee is liable. As regards calls made after the application the transferee alone is liable.   In Pennsylvania, however, a different rule prevails, and by statute the transferrer, if he is the original subscriber, is liable until the whole subscription is paid.   In New York, by statute, both railroad and manufacturing corporations may refuse to allow registry of transfers until unpaid calls have been paid

§ 395. *Whether the corporation may refuse to register a transfer to an irresponsible transferee.*[1] — Greater difficulty is experienced in finding a working rule on this subject.   On one point, however, all the authorities agree   If the corporation is insolvent, or in such a state of decline that insolvency seems inevitable, the corporation may refuse to allow a registry of transfer from a responsible to an irresponsible insolvent transferee   The policy of the law is to protect corporate creditors, even at the expense of restricting the right of transfer   The above rule applies not only where the subscription is unpaid, but also where it has been paid and only a statutory liability exists.   Where, however, the corporation is solvent and a stockholder applies for a registry of transfer from himself to an irresponsible transferee, it seems that the corporation cannot refuse to make the registry.

§ 396   *Corporation may refuse to register as transferees persons who are incompetent to contract.*[2] — If the transferee of a certificate of stock is an infant or person of unsound mind, the corporation may refuse to register such transferee as a stockholder.   The reason of the rule is that such persons would not be obliged at law to respond to the obligations of a stockholder, and consequently are not entitled to its privileges   With married women at the present day the law is different   At common law they were incompetent to become a stockholder, the same as an infant is at the present time. But the statutes of all the states have substantially removed these disabilities, and enabled a married woman to transact business as a *feme sole*, so far as her separate estate is concerned.   She may become a stockholder in a corporation, but cannot bind her husband's estate for the liabilities of such stockholdership.

§ 397   *Trustees, executors, guardians, agents, pledgees.*[3] — In registering transfer to a trustee, executor or guardian, the corporation

---

[1] See chapter XV.
[2] See chapter XIV.
[3] See chapter XIV.

may be required to register the transferee as holder in his official capacity. A trustee who purchases or receives stock to hold in trust for the benefit of another may, it seems, require the corporation to register the transfer and issue new certificates to himself in his own name as "trustee" In England the rule appears to be different The reason of this rule is that the liability of a trustee on stock is in many of the states different from that of a complete owner of the stock, and also because where stock is held by a trustee as trustee, it is the duty of the corporation to refuse to allow the trustee to sell and register a sale of the stock unless the instrument creating the trust authorizes such sale So also an executor or administrator or guardian may compel the corporation to place his official title after his name in the stock registry Pledgees, however, and agents, have not this right The corporation need not write the word "pledgee" after the transferee's name either in the stock registry or on the certificate Such is the rule, for the reason that the corporation is not obliged to protect the rights of the pledgor, nor to recognize the pledgeeship of the transferee The same rule applies to transferees who take as agents of the transferrer.

§ 398 *Sales of stock by executors or administrators* [1]— A corporation may with safety, and in fact is obliged to, allow an executor or administrator to register a transfer of the sale of stock belonging to the estate upon presentation by the executor or administrator of the letters testamentary or letters of administration The executor or administrator may then register a transfer of the stock to himself, or directly from the name of the deceased to a purchaser from the executor; or from the deceased to the executor, and then from the executor to the purchaser. One executor may sell and register a transfer of the stock. The corporation is not bound to inquire whether it is necessary that the sale be made in order to pay the debts of the estate, nor to see to it that the executor actually applies the proceeds of the sale to that purpose. Where, however, the corporation has actual knowledge through its officers that a breach of trust is contemplated by the executor, it is bound to refuse registry, and will be liable to the estate for neglecting so to do So also, where such a long time has elapsed between the taking out of the letters and the sale by the executor that the latter has become practically a trustee, the corporation must use the same precaution as in sales by a trustee In the case of specific legacies of stock, the corporation need take no notice of them, but must allow the executor to transfer the stock into his

[1] See chapter XIX.

own name, since he may need it to pay debts, and the corporation is not bound to investigate such questions.

§ 399 *Sales by trustees*[1]— A trustee who holds stock belonging to the trust estate has no right to sell and transfer such stock unless he is expressly authorized so to do by the instrument creating the trust. Consequently the law imposes upon the corporation the duty of refusing to allow a trustee to transfer the stock unless he clearly has a right so to do. If the corporation neglects this duty it is liable to the trust estate, and, in case of a breach of trust by the trustee, may be compelled to replace the stock or pay damages. If the trustee has an express power given to him to sell, the corporation may allow him to make the transfer. If no such power is given, the corporation must refuse. The trustee is bound to reasonably satisfy the corporation of his right, but the corporation cannot permanently retain the papers submitted to it for that purpose.

§ 400 *Sales by guardians*[2]— A guardian has a right to change the investment of the funds in his charge, and consequently has a right to sell stock held by him in his official capacity. Accordingly, the corporation may allow him to register a transfer of stock held by him as guardian, and cannot require the guardian to obtain an order or decree from a court authorizing such transfer. An order or decree is often obtained by the guardian, however, for his own protection, and is to be commended. In New York the rights and duties of guardians are regulated by statute, and other states have similar statutes.

§ 401 *Forgery of transfer.*— A corporation is bound and required to detect a forgery whereby the name of the owner of a certificate of stock is signed to it and a transfer made which the corporation is requested to register. The stockholder in whose name the old certificate was made out, and whose name was forged to the transfer, may hold the corporation liable if it fails to detect the forgery and allows a registry of the forged transfer. He may compel it to replace the stock or pay damages. This rule is due to the fact that the corporation is a custodian of the books whereby a stockholder obtains his rights of stockholdership, and it cannot deprive him of these rights by allowing others to take them from him by the aid of the corporation and without his consent. It is in the power of the corporation to require the presence of the transferrer at the time of registry, or at least clear proof that the signature is genuine. The corporation, however, has recourse over against the person who applied for registry on the forged transfer, however inno-

[1] See chapter XIX.   [2] See chapter XIX.

cent the latter may be   He is held to have impliedly represented that the transfer was genuine.

§ 402   *Corporation must require a surrender of the outstanding certificate.*[1]—If a corporation permits a registry of a transfer of stock, and issues new certificates to the transferrer without requiring a surrender of the old certificate, it assumes a dangerous position and one which it is not obliged to assume   If the certificate which is not delivered up is in the hands of a *bona fide* purchaser for value and without notice, he may hold the corporation liable for allowing a registry of transfer to another without requiring a delivery of the certificates.   It is negligence and a breach of duty on the part of the corporation to allow a registry without a surrender of the old certificate   It generally refuses to do so as is its duty, and is sustained by the law in its refusal   There are occasions, however, where the law compels the corporation to register the transfer without a surrender of the old certificate   When so compelled to do, the corporation cannot be held liable by the purchaser of the outstanding certificate, but he must seek his remedy against others.   Such compulsory registry, excusing the corporation. may exist in cases of alleged loss of the old certificate, a decree of a court compelling the registry, and, under the latter, an attachment or execution against the stock [2]

§ 403.   *Alleged loss of the old certificate.*[3]— According to the rule of nearly all the states a corporation is not obliged to issue a new certificate of stock to the owner of an old one, which he alleges he has lost, unless such person gives to the corporation a sufficient bond of indemnity to protect it against liability in case it turns out that the old certificate was not lost, but was sold and passed into *bona fide* hands   In New York this rule is fixed by statute.   The corporation is liable to the holder of the outstanding certificate, if it is outstanding, and consequently should be protected against that liability by a bond from the applicant for registry.   In Louisiana a statutory advertisement is made and a bond of indemnity dispensed with   But in the other states the court compels the loser to give a bond, varying in amount according to the amount of the stock and the clearness of the proof of loss.

§ 404   *Attachment or execution.*[4]— Nearly all the states have laws whereby shares of stock are rendered subject to levy of attachment and to sale on levy of execution   Such attachment or execution can be levied only at the domicile of the corporation, since the certificates are mere evidences of title, and the *res* itself of the stock exists only where the corporation is created.   When, there-

---

[1] See chapter XXI.
[2] But see § 488.

[3] See chapter XXI
[4] See chapter XXVII.

fore, an execution sale, or an attachment followed by an execution
sale, takes place where the corporation exists, the purchaser at
such sale generally has not the outstanding certificate, but nevertheless demands registry of himself as stockholder in accordance
with the law authorizing the attachment and execution.   In the
meantime the judgment debtor whose stock is thus attached or
sold under an execution generally has sold or will sell his certificate of stock to a *bona fide* purchaser for value.   If it happens that
both parties claim the stock, the duty and privilege of the corporation is plain.   It may refuse to decide between them, and when
sued by either may interplead and compel the claimants to settle
the right between them in the courts   But frequently it happens
that the corporation does not know whether the judgment debtor
has sold the outstanding certificate or not.   By the law of most of
the states, if such certificate was sold before the attachment or execution was levied the purchaser would be protected, and the corporation would be liable to him for registering as a stockholder
the purchaser at the execution sale   Accordingly, in that case, it is
the duty of the corporation to refuse to register the purchaser at
the execution sale   It cannot afford to take the risk, and is not
obliged to take it.   If the court then compels it to make the registry of transfer to the execution purchaser, the court will also, probably, compel such purchaser to give a bond of indemnity to protect
the corporation   If such a bond is not required by the court the
corporation must nevertheless obey the decree   What rights the
purchaser of the outstanding certificate would then have, has not
as yet been passed upon by the courts

§ 405. *Decree of a court that certificates be issued.*[1] — A corporation must of course obey the decree of a court that it issue a certificate of stock to a specified person.   But a court will rarely resort
to such an extreme remedy where it is probable or possible that
there may be an outstanding certificate in the hands of an innocent holder representing the same shares.   As a principle of law
the court has no power to decree such an issue ordinarily, since the
whole capital stock has been issued, and its decree amounts practically to an order to make an overissue of stock.   Generally the
court decrees damages to be paid, or directs the corporation to purchase stock for the purpose of re-issuing it to the specified party.
This occurs frequently where the corporation has unjustly deprived
a person of his stock.   A different class of cases arises where the
corporation has refused to allow a registry because the outstanding
certificate is not surrendered   Such cases include those of alleged
loss of certificate, an execution sale of the stock, and, possibly, a

[1] See chapter XXII.

suit in equity at the domicile of the corporation to recover from another stock which the complainant claims A decree in such a suit in most states would be ineffectual to deprive of his rights one who purchased from the defendant his certificate of stock before the decree was rendered. It would accordingly be a harsh decree that compelled the corporation to register the successful complainant as a stockholder The corporation should not be compelled to assume the risk of being sued by the purchaser of the outstanding certificate The complainant should be compelled to give a bond of indemnity, or else be contented with a personal judgment against the defendant. The demands of trade and of an investing public require that the safety of a purchaser of a certificate of stock should be assured, except against attachments, execution sales or decrees duly obtained and notified to the corporation before the *bona fide* purchaser received the certificate of stock

§ 406. *Theft of certificates indorsed in blank.*[1] — The corporation has a duty to perform as regards certificates of stock which have been stolen from the owner who held them indorsed in blank

If the owner notified the corporation of the theft it must refuse to register a transfer to a purchaser of such stolen certificate Since the owner's negligence may have estopped him from reclaiming the stock, the corporation may refuse to recognize either party as a stockholder, where there is a reasonable question of negligence, and when sued by either may interplead If the corporation allowed a registry before it was notified of the theft, it is difficult to see on what principle it is to be held liable to the owner. Such a case seems not yet to have arisen. If notified of the theft before anything is learned concerning the whereabouts of the certificate, the case is to be treated the same as when the certificate is alleged to have been lost.

§ 407 *Interpleader by the corporation.*[2] — Whenever there are two or more conflicting claims made to stock and demands are made on the corporation to allow registry, it is the privilege of the corporation, if there is a reasonable legal doubt as to the rights of the parties, to refuse to register either party, and when sued by one to interplead and compel the parties to contest the matter between themselves in the courts The law does not oblige the corporation to turn itself into a court of justice and decide the rights of the parties. The corporation, however, cannot interplead if it has already committed itself by registering one of the claimants as the stockholder. Nor can the corporation resort to an interpleader where one of the claimants is clearly wrong The right of interpleader and the power of the corporation to refuse to register a

[1] See chapter XXI.   [2] See chapter XXII

transfer until compelled to do so by the courts, where an outstanding certificate is not surrendered, constitutes the two most effective safeguards of the corporation in allowing or refusing registry.

§ 408. *Restrictions by corporation on stockholder's right to sell or transfer.*[1] — The law has uniformly and decisively discountenanced and overruled all attempts of a corporation to prevent the sale and transfer of its stock by the stockholder. Such attempted restrictions are generally made by means of by-laws. Thus, a by-law requiring the consent of the directors or other corporate officers to a transfer, or a by-law requiring the stockholder when he sells to sell his stock to specified persons, is null and void. Restrictions may be created by a contract mutually agreed to by the stockholders, but cannot be imposed upon them by the majority of the stockholders nor by the board of directors. When, however, such restrictions are created by the charter, they are valid, since they arise with the corporation and stock itself. Thus, in England, the charter frequently authorizes the directors to refuse a registry unless the transferee is satisfactory to them. Even here, however, the directors must be reasonable in the use of their discretion. In this country the most frequent restriction created by charter is that of a lien for debts due to the corporation from the transferrer.

§ 409. *Lien of the corporation.*[2] — The charters of many corporations contain an express provision that the corporation may refuse to allow a stockholder to register a transfer of his stock until he has paid any and all debts which he may at that time owe to the corporation. Such a lien need not be stated in the certificate of stock. While it may not be created generally by a by-law, yet certain phrases in charters have been held to uphold a lien that is declared and made effectual by a by-law. Where the lien exists the corporation may refuse to allow a registry of transfer of any stock owned by the debtor until all debts due from him to the corporation are paid, whether due or not due, including, it seems, unpaid subscriptions. It does not apply, however, to debts due from a transferee of the certificate who never obtained registry or appeared as a stockholder on the corporate books. Nor does it apply to debts due from the registered stockholder, but incurred after the corporation was given notice that he had sold his stock to another. The corporation may waive its lien and allow registry without the debts of the old stockholder being paid. A registry without requiring payment is a waiver in itself.

§ 410. *Formalities of registry which the corporation may insist upon.*[3] — Where, as is ordinarily the case, the owner of stock has

---

[1] See chapter XX.   [3] See chapter XXII.
[2] See chapter XXXI.

sold it by signing the transfer and power of attorney on the back of the certificate, leaving the names of the transferee and of the attorney blank, the corporation may require the names of the transferee and of the attorney to be filled in before it allows a registry. If it is in doubt as to the genuineness of the signature of the former owner of the certificate, it may require his presence or reasonable proof that he actually made the signature. It cannot compel the transferrer to be present, but may require the presence of the attorney authorized to make the registry. The registry itself is generally made by the corporate officer, but he may require the attorney to make it. A surrender of the old certificate is required, and new certificates in the name of the transferee are issued. The by-laws may prescribe that the registry shall be in the presence of certain corporate officers. A mere request to register is not registry, although the old certificate is left with the clerk, together with the transfer, and he marks "received for record" on the same. If the corporation does not keep a transfer book or stock book, a surrender of the old certificate and the issue of a new one is sufficient to constitute a transfer and registry. The applicant may inquire of the corporate officer in charge for the registry clerk, and is not bound to ascertain the individual himself. Registry at a branch office may not be a legal registry until entered at the main office. The corporate registry may be on its ledger without any issue of certificate. If it keeps no registry at all, mere notice to it of a transfer constitutes a legal registry. The corporation has no right to delay registry unreasonably for the purpose of obtaining advice or for any other reasons. It may require that the power of attorney run directly from the former registered stockholder and not from an intermediate one. A written acceptance of the stock by the transferee cannot be insisted on by the corporation. The formalities of registry may be waived by the corporation, and any act which indicates that it considers a transferee to be a stockholder is effectual to make him such so far as the corporation is concerned, though no registry was had.

Either the transferrer or the transferee or an intermediate unregistered transferee may apply to the corporation for the purpose of obtaining a registry. The corporation cannot refuse it merely because of the motive of the transferrer or of the transferee in making the sale and transfer. Whenever the corporation refuses to allow a registry the applicant may sue it for damages, or he may go into a court of equity and ask that the corporation be decreed to allow registry or to pay damages in lieu thereof. A few cases hold that he may compel registry by a *mandamus* against the corporation, but the weight of authority holds otherwise.

CHAPTER XXIV.

NON-NEGOTIABILTY OF STOCK AND DANGERS INCURRED IN THE PURCHASE OF CERTIFICATES OF STOCK.

A. NON-NEGOTIABILITY.

§ 411 *Nature and kinds of negotiable instruments* — Negotiable instruments at the present day are promissory notes, bills of exchange, checks, bank-notes, bonds of the United States, of states, of foreign governments, of cities and counties and municipalities generally, certificates of deposit, interest coupons and bonds of corporations.[1] Bills of lading have only a *quasi*-negotiability.[2] These different instruments, however, are not necessarily negotiable, but are so only when in writing, when containing an unconditional promise or order to pay, when the payment is to be in money only; when the amount is certain, when it is payable to a specific person, and not in the alternative, when it is payable at a certain time; when it contains words such as "to A or order," or "to bearer," or their equivalent, and when delivery has been duly made.[3] If the instrument is lacking in any one of these qualities it falls back into the category of non-negotiable — that is, merely assignable — instruments. Again, a holder of one of the above-named negotiable instruments can have the benefit of its negotiability only when he has purchased it in good faith, for value, before the instrument was due, and without notice of the equitable rights of previous holders or makers, that is, he must be a *bona fide* holder. When all these elements of negotiability and ownership co-exist, the advantage of negotiability over non-negotiability is this that the holder of the instrument is entitled to the face value thereof, and his right cannot be affected, decreased or defeated by any facts or equities between previous holders which would defeat the security as between them, unless it be void for usury or other similar cause.

§ 412. *Certificates of stock are not negotiable instruments.* — It is very clear, and it is well established, that certificates of stock are not negotiable instruments.[4] A certificate of stock is not a prom-

---

[1] Daniel on Negotiable Instruments, 3d ed, book VI, Dos Passos on Stock Brokers, ch IX. As to bonds of corporations see ch XLVI

[2] Id. See, also, Bank of Batavia *v* N Y., etc, R. R. Co, 33 Hun, 589 (1884)

[3] Id.

[4] Certificates of stock are not negotiable. Hammond *v* Hastings, 134 U. S, 401 (1890). "Certificates of stock are not securities for money in any sense, much less are they negotiable securities." Mechanics' Bank *v* New York & N. H R. R. Co, 13 N Y, 599, 627 (1856), Barstow *v* Savage M Co 64 Cal, 391 (1883), Clark *v.* American Coal Co, 53 N W Rep, 291 (Ia., 1892) Weaver *v* Barden, 49 N Y, 286, 288 (1872), says that a certificate of stock has none of the qualities of com-

mercial or negotiable paper. Leitch *v* Wells, 48 N Y, 585, 613 (1872), says "Since the decision of the case of McNeil *v* Tenth National Bank . . . certificates of stock, with blank assignments, and powers of attorney attached, must be nearly as negotiable as commercial papers" Weyer *v* Second Nat'l Bank, 57 Ind, 198, 208 (1877), says "The difference between a promissory note and a certificate of bank stock is so wide and marked that a rule of law governing the transfer of the former is by no means applicable to the latter" Sewall *v* Boston Water-power Co, 86 Mass, 277 (1862), says "The authorities cited show that a certificate of stock is not a negotiable instrument and without any authorities it is apparent that it has not

ise or order to pay money, nor has it any of the essentials of a negotiable instrument　Moreover, it has been repeatedly decided by the courts that a certificate of stock is not negotiable, and no custom of trade or of brokers can give to it that character

§ 413　*The term "quasi-negotiability," as applied to certificates of stock, throws little light upon the subject*[1]—It is little satisfaction to the court, the practitioner, the student or the owner of stocks to be told that certificates of stock have a *quasi*-negotiability　The term itself has been coined to describe the character of certain things which can be understood only by a study and knowledge of the characteristics of the thing described　Especially is this true of certificates of stock　The information sought is not whether the certificate is *quasi*-negotiable, but whether the holder of it is protected under different states of fact and circumstances.　He who intends to purchase such certificates wishes to know what dangers or risks he incurs by the purchase　The practitioner is interested, not in the general character of the instrument, but in the law as applicable to his particular case　Many of the cases concede to certificates of stock a *quasi*-negotiability, but it is extremely doubtful whether such discussions do not confuse the understanding of the character of such an instrument more than they explain it.

§ 414　*The distinction between the "legal" and the "equitable" title in the transfer of certificates of stock is unsatisfactory.*— Many of the cases involving the rights of a transferee of stock discuss and treat the subject from the point of view that the transferee is pro-

---

a negotiable character '　To same effect, Mandlelaum v North Am Min Co, 4 Mich　465 473 (1857), holding, however that by statute in that state certificates of stock are practically negotiable　Shaw v Spencer, 100 Mass 382 (1868), says ' It is clear that a certificate of stock transferred in blank is not a negotiable instrument　.　No commercial usage can give to such an instrument the attributes of negotiability '　Sherwood v Meadow Valley M Co　50 Cal, 412 (1875), Bridgeport Bank v New York & N H R R Co, 30 Conn, 231, 275 (1874), holding that "the certificate accompanied by the assignment and power of attorney thus executed in blank has, perhaps, a species of negotiability, although of a peculiar character, but one necessary to

the public convenience"　In Bank v Lanier, 11 Wall, 369 377, the court say that although certificates of stock "neither in form nor character are negotiable paper, they approximate to it as nearly as practicable "

[1] Daniel on Negotiable Instruments, § 1708 says ' The phrase 'quasi-negotiability' has been termed an unhappy one and certainly it is far from satisfactory, as it conveys no accurate, well-defined meaning　But still it describes, better than any other short-hand expression, the nature of those instruments which, while not negotiable in the sense of the law merchant are so framed and so dealt with as frequently to convey as good a title to the transferee as if they were negotiable "

tected in his ownership when the legal title passes to him, but is not so protected when only the equitable title passes. Unfortunately it happens that, under the same state of facts, one court will hold that only the equitable title passes, another that the legal title passes, and a third court will hold that both the legal and equitable passes. The result is confusion, doubt and difficulty, with little light as to the real *status* of certificates of stock.[1]

[1] Such also seems to be the view taken in Lowell on Transfer of Stock (1884), p. 105, where the learned authors say "It is often supposed, for example, that the right of a creditor to seize stock which has been sold before it is transferred upon the books depends upon the passing of the legal title, but we shall attempt to prove that the legal title has in reality no effect upon the matter." The same authority shows the confusion resulting from this distinction of the legal from the equitable title in the following note to page 105 : That the legal title passes before the transfer on the books. In the following cases this is made part of the *ratio decidendi* Ross v. Southwestern R Co., 53 Ga. 514, 532, Merchants' Nat Bank v. Richards, 6 Mo App. 454, 463, S C., 74 Mo 77. Carroll v. Mullanphy Savings Bank, 8 Mo App. 249, 252, McNeil v. Tenth Nat. Bank, 46 N Y. 325, Leitch v. Wells 48 N Y, 585, Smith v. American Coal Co., 7 Laus, 317, Noyes v. Spaulding 27 Vt, 420, Cherry v. Frost, 7 Lea, 1. In the following cases the same principle was laid down *obiter* State v. Leete 16 Nev, 242 250, Eastman v. Fiske, 9 N H, 182 New York, etc, R. v. Schuyler, 34 N Y, 30, 80, Grymes v. Home 49 N Y, 17, Johnson v. Underhill, 52 N Y, 203, Holbrook v. New Jersey Zinc Co., 57 N Y, 616 Cushman v. Thayer Mfg Co, 76 N Y 365 and see Purchase v. Exchange Bank, 3 Rob., 164. That the legal title does not pass until transfer on the books. In the following cases this principle is made part of the *ratio decidendi* Union Bank v. Laird, 2 Wheat, 390, Lowry v. Commercial

Bank, Taney, 310, Brown v. Adams 5 Biss 181, Williams v. Mechanics' Bank, 5 Blatch, 59, Becher v. Wells Flouring Mill Co. 1 Fed Rep 276 Marlborough Mfg Co v. Smith, 2 Conn, 579, Northrop v. Newton & Bridgeport Turnpike Co., 3 Conn, 544 Oxford Turnpike Co v. Bunnell, 6 Conn, 552 Dutton v. Connecticut Bank, 13 Conn 493 ; Vansands v. Middlesex Co Bank, 26 Conn, 144 Coleman v. Spencer, 5 Blackf 197, Helm v. Swiggett, 12 Ind. 194 (*semble*): Weyer v. Second Nat Bank of Franklin 57 Ind, 198, Fisher v. Essex Bank 5 Gray, 373, Boyd v. Rockport Steam Cotton Mills 7 Gray, 406, Blanchard v. Dedham Gas Co, 12 Gray, 213 McConny v. Suydam, 5 Halst, 245,

Stebbins v. Phœnix Ins Co, 3 Paige, 350, Mechanics' Bank v. New York, etc, R. Co 13 N Y, 599, New York, etc, R Co v. Schuyler, 38 Barb, 534, Lockwood v. Mechanics' Nat. Bank, 9 R I, 308 331, 335 In the following cases the same doctrine is laid down *obiter* Black v. Zacharie 3 How, 483, United States v. Cutts, 1 Sumner 133 (this was, however, a case of government debt, not of corporate stock) Planters' & Merchants' Ins Co v. Selma Savings Bank, 63 Ala, 585, Otis v. Gardner, 105 Ill, 436 (*semble*), and see Kellogg v. Stockwell, 75 Ill, 68. People's Bank v. Gridley, 91 Ill, 457, Bruce v. Smith 44 Ind, 1, State v. First Nat Bank of Jeffersonville, 89 Ind 302, Shaw v. Spencer, 100 Mass, 382 Sibley v. Quinsigamond Nat. Bank, 133 Mass 515, White v. Salisbury, 33 Mo, 150, Boatmen's Ins Co v. Able, 48 Mo 136, . . Conant v. Seneca Co. Bank, 1

§ 415 *The only method of treatment of the subject seems to be by inquiring under what facts the holder or purchaser is protected —* The court, the practitioner, the purchaser or the holder of certificates of stock wishes to know what liability and what dangers are incurred by the purchase and ownership of a certificate of stock It becomes important for him to ascertain whether forgery or theft, or improper registry by the corporation, or breach of trust by a trustee, executor or agent formerly holding that particular stock or fraud whereby a former owner was deprived of that same stock, or legal proceedings, such as attachment, execution, *mandamus* and decrees of the court, or any other fact or equitable right between former owners of the stock which he purchases, can affect him, a *bona fide* purchaser for value and without notice of those rights These questions cannot be solved or answered by any general rules or theories, since certificates of stock have a law, an origin and a nature different from other kinds of securities The fact that a registry of transfer is required to be made on the corporate books adds further complication to the rights of a holder General rules formed from and applicable to other instruments or securities cannot, with any certainty, clearness or satisfactory results, be applied to certificates of stock They should be treated of by themselves The future character and *status* of certificates of stock will be much clearer, better and more satisfactory to the investing public if the law governing them be formed on its own basis

§ 416 *The particular rules protecting a bona fide purchaser of certificates of stock are based on estoppel —* Nearly all if not all of the rules whereby a purchaser of stock is protected against the rights of previous holders grow out of the fact that such previous holder or holders have enabled persons to sell the stock, and consequently are estopped from claiming that they did not intend so to do[1] This law of estoppel protects the purchaser against not only the rights of previous holders, but against the claims of the

Ohio St. 298 United States v Vaughan, 3 Binn 394 (*semble*), Bank of Commerce s Appeal, 73 Pa St, 59, Fraser v Charleston 11 S C 486 (*semble*) "

[1] Wood's Appeal 92 Pa St., 379, 390 (1880), McNeil v Tenth Nat'l Bank, 46 N Y., 325, 329 (1871), Weaver v Barden, 49 N Y, 286, 287 (1872), Moore v Metropolitan Nat'l Bank, 55 N Y, 41, 47 (1873), Mount Holly, etc Co v Ferrie, 17 N J Eq, 117 (1864), Walker v Detroit Transit R'y Co, 47 Mich, 338, 347 (1882) See, also, Fatman v Lobach, 1 Duer 354 (1852); Moodie v Seventh Nat'l Bank, 3 W. N. C, 118 (1881) Matthews v Mass. Nat'l Bank, 1 Holmes, 396 (1884) The agreement of a stockholder to surrender his stock in liquidation of an unpaid assessment is without consideration and does not bind a purchaser of the certificate. Hill v. Atoka, etc., Co., 21 S W Rep., 508 (Mo, 1893).

corporation itself Indeed, to such an extent has the law of estoppel been applied to protect a *bona fide* purchaser of stock that he is protected now in almost every instance where he would be protected if he were purchasing a promissory note or other negotiable instrument. The courts are steadily extending the application of the law of estoppel herein, and in the course of time it is possible that certificates of stock may become more negotiable than negotiable instruments themselves.

In England an entirely different rule prevails Certificates of stock in that country are merely evidences of ownership of stock, and this muniment of title is not negotiable nor *quasi*-negotiable The purchaser of it is not protected against equities involved in the title of prior owners of the certificate Only a transfer on the corporate books shuts off those equities Indeed, this rule is insisted upon in England so rigidly that not even the certificates of stock issued by American corporations and held by Englishmen are given the *quasi*-negotiability of the American law [1]

[1] The English courts refuse to follow the American rule in regard to the practical negotiability of certificates of stock transferred in blank, although such certificates of stock are issued by an American corporation Hence, where the English owner of such certificates delivered them to a broker to forward to America for a transfer, and the broker fraudulently sold them for his own purposes to other persons, it was held that no title was conveyed to such other persons, and that the American law did not apply. The court said, however, that there was sufficient in the case to put the purchasing party upon notice Colonial Bank *v* Cady, 63 L T Rep , 27 (1890) As between the trustee in bankruptcy of a defaulter and the party to whom the defaulter has transferred shares of stock without a transfer on the corporate books, the latter is entitled to the stock Re Dodds, 64 L T Rep , 476 (1891) In England the deposit of the certificates with the company for transfer, and the acceptance of them by the company, does not constitute a full transfer on the corporate books, and the real owner of the certificates may reclaim them before the complete

transfer is made Moore *v* North, etc , Bank 64 L T Rep , 456 (1891) In the case of Simmons *v* The London etc . Bank, 63 L T Rep. 789 (1890) affirming 62 id 427 the court held that a bank to whom a broker had pledged stocks belonging to his customer was not a *bona fide* purchaser under the facts in that case, and consequently was not protected even though a *bona fide* purchaser might have been Although in England an unregistered transferee of stock is not protected against another transfer which is registered yet he is protected where he lodged his transfer with the corporate secretary, and the latter accepted it for transfer before the second transfer was made Nanney *v* Morgan, 85 L T Rep , 228 (1887) In England an American certificate of stock indorsed in blank gives no more rights to a *bona fide* purchaser than to a *mala fide* purchaser Until a registry is made, the registered owner may claim his property and set up all equities to regain possession Williams *v* London etc , Bank, 59 L T Rep , 643 (1888), Dodds *v* Hills, 2 H & M., 424 (1865), Roots *v* Williamson, 5 L T Rep , 802 (1888) In England certificates of stock

B DANGERS INCURRED IN PURCHASING STOCK

§ 417　*Liabilities, risks and rights of one who owns or purchases a certificate of stock* — It is proposed to state separately and in detail the liabilities on the subscription price and by statute incurred by one who owns or purchases a certificate of stock, also the risks or dangers incurred by a purchase of stock as affected by the rights of previous holders of that stock, also a few of the rights of an owner or purchaser of a certificate of stock as regards the general incidents appertaining to stockholdership　These subjects are discussed in full in other parts of this work, and consequently the authority for rules laid down herein must be sought for in those parts The purpose here is to state succinctly and in language free from technical phraseology the position occupied by a *bona fide* purchaser of a certificate of stock

§ 418　*Liability on unpaid par value, that is, the unpaid subscription price of the stock* [1] — In general the purchaser of a certificate of stock is immediately liable on the subscription price of the stock so far as it has not been paid by previous holders of the stock purchased and has not been called by the corporation. The transferrer is bound to pay all calls made before the transferee purchases　If the transferee does not immediately register his transfer on the corporate books he is liable to pay to the transferrer such calls as are made after the transfer and which the corporation compels the latter to pay　The transferee, it has been held, is not liable for uncalled and unpaid parts of the subscription, even though the certificate is silent as to whether the par value of the stock has been paid in or not　Where, however, the certificate states that the stock is paid-up stock, or the transferee before purchasing inquires of the corporation and is told that the stock is paid up, he may purchase in reliance thereon, and cannot afterwards be held liable, even though the stock turns out not to have been fully paid up

§ 419　*Forfeiture for non-payment of calls* [2] — Where the corporation is given by its charter or by statute the right to forfeit and

indorsed in blank convey title by estoppel to a *bona fide* purchaser when the transfer need not be by deed under seal Rumball *v* Metropolitan Bank, L R, 2 Q B D, 194 (1877), *Ex parte* Sargent, L R, 17 Eq, 273 (1873)　But this is generally not the case　Ortigosa *v* Brown, 47 L J (Ch), 168 (1877)　Donaldson *v* Gillott, L R, 3 Eq, 274 (1866), and the late case of France *v* Clark

L R, 22 Ch D, 830 (1883), gives no protection to the *bona fide* purchaser until he is registered　See, also, Shropshire, etc, Co *v* Queen, L R, 7 H L, 496 (1875), Briggs *v* Massey, 42 L T 49 (1880). See, also, §§ 325, 377, 380, *supra*

[1] See ch XV.
[2] See ch VIII.

sell stock for non-payment of the subscription price when called in by the corporation, a notice to the stockholder of the intended forfeiture is always required This notice, however, is given always to him who appears by the corporate registry to be the stockholder Accordingly a transferee or owner of stock who has not obtained a registry of his transfer on the corporate books is liable to lose his stock by a forfeiture for non-payment of calls, and may lose it without knowledge of the call or forfeiture unless he appears on the registry of the corporation as the owner of the stock

§ 420 *Statutory liability* [1] — The liability by statute of a purchaser of certificates of stock to corporate creditors, in addition to the subscription price which is treated of above, exists in a great many cases. In the first place this liability may not exist at all against any one, either transferrer or transferee It rarely exists in the case of railroad corporations Where the statutory liability exists the liability of a purchaser of stock is as follows If the transferee immediately registers his transfer on the corporate books he becomes at once liable by statute for debts of the corporation contracted after such registry, and the transferrer is not liable thereon The transferee may or may not be liable on corporate debts contracted before he purchased, according to the words of the statute creating the liability. The transferrer is liable on corporate debts contracted after he sold the stock but before the transfer was registered In the latter case the transferrer has recourse to the transferee

§ 421 *Liability where the purchaser has the transfer made to a nominal holder* [2] — Where a person purchases stock and takes it in the name of a "dummy," the stock never having been registered in the name of the real owner, the latter is not liable on such stock, according to the English rule In America a contrary rule prevails, and the courts hold him liable on the ground that he is a principal, and as such is liable as an undisclosed principal for the acts of his agent, the "dummy."

§ 422 *No liability for assessments after the par value of the stock has been paid in* [3] — By well-established principles of law stockholders are liable on their stock only to the extent of the unpaid par value of the stock, unless the statute expressly provides otherwise Neither the directors, nor all the other stockholders combined, in corporate meeting assembled or otherwise, can compel a dissenting stockholder to pay any more money into the corporation or subject him to further liability on his stock. Nor can the

[1] See ch XII
[2] See §§ 253, 265

[3] See ch XIII.

legislature, subsequently to his purchase of the stock, pass a law increasing his liability, unless the power to alter or amend the charter is reserved to it, in which case such a law would be constitutional

§ 423 *Liability when stock was issued for property* [1]— Shares of stock may be issued under an agreement that payment is to be made in labor, services, material or contract work If so issued, and the labor or material received by the corporation is fairly equal in value to the par value of the stock, the transferee of such stock takes it as full-paid stock, and cannot be held liable for any further amount, even though the value of the property turns out subsequently to have been overestimated, but was made in good faith Where, however, the property is intentionally overvalued and stock is issued for it, the persons receiving the stock are liable to have the transaction set aside. the value of the property or work done credited to them, and the real value of the stock, not necessarily the par value, charged to them, or be compelled to return the stock. As to transferees the case may be different. If they purchased with notice of the fraud they are not protected, but if they purchased without notice or knowledge that the property was intentionally overvalued, but supposed that the stock was issued as paid up by payment in property or work taken at a *bona fide* value, or if they have no knowledge of how the stock was paid, but take it as paid-up stock, they may retain the stock, and are not liable for any further amount thereon

§ 424 *Liability as partners by reason of defective incorporation or for other reasons.* [2]— Where a supposed corporation has not been duly incorporated, owing to a failure of the incorporators to comply with the statutory requisites, or because a corporation for that business is not provided for, the supposed corporation has been held to be but a partnership, and all the stockholders held liable as partners A failure to file the articles of association, or to sign and publish them, or the omission from them of any of the essential facts required to be stated, however, does not ordinarily defeat the attempted incorporation and render the stockholders liable as partners Again, the stockholders are, in some jurisdictions, liable to be held to be partners, as regards creditors of the enterprise, where the corporation organizes in one place and proceeds to do all its business in another place In most cases, however, the corporation has been recognized and upheld, and the stockholders protected in their limited liability The latter class of decisions is the stronger, and certainly more to be commended and followed In any case a transferee is not liable for

[1] See chs. II and III.   [2] See ch XIII.

all precedent debts of the concern, but only for those incurred subsequently to the registry of his transfer.

§ 425. *Danger of corporate lien.*[1] — Frequently corporations are given by charter or statute a lien on a stockholder's stock for debts due from him to the corporation. When such lien exists a purchaser of the certificate in open market buys subject to the risk that the one from whom he buys owes the corporation a debt, and that the corporation will not allow the transferee of the certificate to obtain a registry until such debt is paid. In many of the states the lien of the corporation cannot be created by by-law. Generally it exists by reason of a provision of the charter. When it does legally exist it extends to all debts owed by the last registered stockholder, whether the debt be due or not due, and includes uncalled parts of the subscription price of the stock. It does not, however, apply to debts due from one who has bought and sold the certificate without appearing on the registry as a stockholder. The corporation may waive the lien, and a registry without insisting on the lien is such a waiver. The lien of the corporation extends to debts incurred by the transferrer after the transfer but before the corporation is notified thereof.

§ 426. *Overissued stock.*[2] — The capital stock of a corporation is fixed by statute. There is no power in the corporation itself to increase that amount. It can be done only by a legislative enactment. Accordingly, if the corporation issues certificates of stock when the whole capital stock has already been issued, the new issue, if an equivalent amount of outstanding certificates is not surrendered, is an overissue, and is void. Any issue of stock in excess of the amount of the capital stock as fixed by the charter is null and void. The purchaser of such certificates, however, is not without his remedy. His certificate is so much waste paper, and he is not a stockholder; but he may sue the corporation for damages, and recover to the extent of his injury. The purchaser may also sue the corporate officers who participated in the issue of the spurious stock, and may recover damages. He cannot, however, hold an innocent transferrer liable. The latter, if he knew nothing of the overissue, is not to be held as a guarantor of the validity of the stock which he sells.

§ 427. *Danger that transferrer or previous holder is an infant, married woman or lunatic.*[3] — A purchase of stock from an infant is a dangerous investment. When the infant comes of age he may elect to disaffirm, and may hold the transferee liable for the stock,

[1] See chapter XXXI.   [3] See §§ 65, 66, 250, 308, 318, 319, 310
[2] See chapter XVII.

There is less danger, however, in accepting a transfer of stock from an infant who has previously purchased the stock which he sells This previous purchase, and also his sale of the stock, are technically voidable acts; but after the stock has passed from his control the law disregards the doubtful medium of title, and considers the purchaser from the infant as the legal stockholder. As regards married women, the common law allowed the husband to sell her stock after he had reduced it to possession by registering it in his own name on the corporate books In modern times, however, the right of a married woman to hold and convey personal property as though unmarried has been established in most states by statute. Her right to sell shares of stock owned by herself exists where she may sell other personal property similarly owned, and this right depends upon the law and statutes of her domicile. A purchase of stock from a lunatic is void.

§ 428 *Purchase of stock by or from a corporation.*[1]— In England a corporation cannot purchase shares of its own capital stock. In this country there is a difference of opinion as to the law. The statutes governing the corporation, however, sometimes prohibit such purchases Such is the case with national banks, and in New York with railroad and banking corporations. In any case, however, whether the corporation purchased the stock legally or illegally, a purchaser of the same stock from the corporation itself is not affected by the invalidity of the title of the corporation. Again, it is a general rule, both in England and America, that one corporation has no right to purchase stock in another corporation. Sometimes the statutes allow such purchases, but more often expressly provide to the contrary by prohibiting them. Nevertheless, whatever rule applies to a purchase by a corporation of stock in another corporation, the law is very clear that a purchaser of such stock from the corporation is protected in his purchase. The unauthorized act of the corporation in purchasing has no effect upon the legality of its sale of the stock.

§ 429 *Purchase from joint owners, partners and agents.*[2]— One joint owner cannot sell stock standing in the name of two or more as joint owners. One partner may sell and convey stock standing in the partnership name. As regards purchases of stock from agents, greater difficulty occurs. If the purchaser does not know that the vendor is selling as an agent, but supposes he is buying stock owned by the person with whom he is dealing, the purchaser is always protected. The same rule, after considerable doubt and discussion, has been established, even though the purchaser knows that the agent is selling as agent. The sale is valid, and the pur-

---

[1] See chapter XIX.   [2] See chapter XIX.

chaser is protected, provided he has no reason to suspect that the agent is selling in fraud of the owner's rights or in contradiction of his orders.

§ 430 *Purchase of stock at sheriff's execution sale, or from assignee in bankruptcy, or for benefit of creditors.*[1] — A purchase of stock at an execution sale by the sheriff is a dangerous investment Almost always the judgment debtor has already sold and transferred his certificates of stock to a *bona fide* purchaser. If such *bona fide* purchaser has registered the transfer on the corporate books before the attachment or execution is levied, the purchaser at the execution sale gets nothing. If no such registry has been made, but the judgment debtor sold and transferred the certificate before the levy of attachment or execution, in most of the states, including New York, such a purchaser takes title and the execution purchaser none. In Connecticut, New Hampshire and a few other states a contrary rule prevails If, however, the judgment debtor sells the certificate after the attachment or execution is levied, the purchaser takes no title — the execution purchaser is entitled to the stock A purchaser of stock from an assignee in bankruptcy or insolvency, or for the benefit of creditors, takes a good title if he obtains the certificates of stock. If, however, the insolvent has sold such certificates to another, the latter is entitled to the stock.

§ 431 *Purchase from a pledgee.*[2] — A pledgee of stock has no right to sell or repledge the stock held as collateral by him, unless the pledgor intended that he should do so If, however, the pledgee sells or repledges the stock to one who takes it in good faith, for value, and without notice of the fact that he is dealing with a pledgee of the stock, such a *bona fide* purchaser is protected. He is protected absolutely, and can keep the stock if he purchased it. If, however, he merely took it in pledge from the pledgee, he is obliged to give up the stock to the real owner, where the latter tenders to the repledgee the amount of the debt owed by the pledgee to the repledgee, for which the stock was given as security. Where, however, a person buys or takes in pledge stock from one who makes known the fact that he is holding the stock as pledgee, the former is not a *bona fide* purchaser. Moreover, he is not a *bona fide* holder where he would not be a *bona fide* holder of a promissory note transferred under similar circumstances, as, for instance, where he loans the money at an usurious rate of interest; or where he knows that the person with whom he is dealing is but an agent, and is pledging his principal's stock In all these cases, where the purchaser or pledgee of stock is not a *bona fide* holder, the real owner and original pledgor of the stock may reclaim his stock from the

[1] See chapter XXVL   [2] See chapters XIX, XXVL

repledgee, or purchaser from the pledgee, where the original pledgor could recover it from the first pledgee.   The repledgee or purchaser from the pledgee stands in the shoes of the first pledgee, and has no better rights than the latter

§ 432. *Pledgee is protected in the same way as purchaser of stock.*[1] The rules contained in this chapter explain the rights, dangers and liabilities incurred by the purchaser of stock.   The same rules prevail for the most part in favor of one who receives stock in pledge. A purchaser and a pledgee are treated in the cases as being similarly protected or similarly not protected.   There is, however, one important exception to this rule.   If a person who is about to take stock from another knows that the latter is disposing of the stock as an agent, the former may purchase the stock and be protected, but cannot take it in pledge and be similarly protected.   An agent to sell is not an agent to pledge   Another exception to the similarity of position of a vendee and pledgee of stock is that by statute, frequently, the latter is not liable on stock where the former is liable.

§ 433. *Danger of purchasing from an executor, administrator or guardian.*[2]—There is practically little danger incurred in purchasing stock from any one of these.   It is the duty and right of the executors or administrators to sell the personal property and convert it into money.   As regards guardians they have the right to change the funds from one investment to another unless a statute prescribes otherwise   Accordingly a purchaser of stock from any one of those is protected in his purchase, even though he knows that his vendor is selling in his official capacity.   If, however, the vendee knows that a breach of trust is involved or contemplated, he is not a *bona fide* purchaser and is not protected.   All the executors or administrators need not join in a sale of the stock owned by the estate.   A sale and transfer by one is sufficient.

§ 434. *Purchase from a trustee.*[3]—An entirely different rule prevails as regards stock held by a trustee as trustee.   A purchaser of stock which he knows the vendor holds as belonging to a trust estate is bound to ascertain whether, by the instrument creating the trust, the trustee has a power to sell.   If he has no such power, and the vendee knows that he is buying trust estate stock, the latter is not protected, but is a party to any breach of trust that may be involved by the sale   If, however, the purchaser has no notice or knowledge that his vendor is selling trust stock, the former is a *bona fide* purchaser to that extent.   He is not bound to know that the stock is trust estate stock, and consequently he is protected in his

[1] See chapter XIX, XXVI.   [3] See chapter XIX.
[2] See chapter XIX.

purchase. Any facts that would put an ordinarily intelligent man on inquiry as to whether the stock belongs to a trust estate is notice, and prevents the purchaser from claiming to be a *bona fide* purchaser. Thus, such a notice is held to be given by the fact that on the face of the certificate of stock, and following the name of the stockholder, the word " trustee " or equivalent words are written. In California, however, the mere word "trustee" conveys no notice

§ 435 *Sale by vendor to another purchaser without delivery of certificate of stock.*[1] — A purchaser of certificates of stock has no reason to fear that the vendor can sell the stock to another person and thereby defeat the rights of the purchaser with the certificates If the purchaser without certificates does not obtain registry on the corporate books, he obtains nothing as against the purchaser with the certificates, even though the latter's transaction was subsequent in time to the former. If, however, the former obtains registry on the corporate books, the corporation is at fault, and is liable to the purchaser with the certificates The corporation must either issue new certificates to the latter or pay damages.

§ 436 *Danger of forgery*[2] — Forgery cannot be the source of a good title to any chose in action, whether a promissory note, bond and mortgage, or a certificate of stock. Consequently a purchaser of stock takes the risk that some previous owner of the stock, whose name appears on the certificate either as the registered owner or as transferee, was deprived of his title by forgery. If the forgery has been made, the purchaser cannot claim or hold the stock, although he had no actual knowledge of the forgery. He, however, has recourse to his vendor, and may compel him to repay the amount paid for the stock. Where, however, the forgery was committed prior to the last *registered* transfer of that stock, a *bona fide* purchaser from or subsequent to the last *registered* holder of that stock is protected. All rights and equities to particular shares of stock are cut off by a registry and sale of the new certificates. The party whose name was forged has recourse then only to the corporation, or to the party obtaining registry, or to previous holders. This limitation to the dangers incident to the purchase of stock extends to other rights and wrongs as well as to a case of forgery, and is of great importance in protecting a *bona fide* purchaser of stock.

§ 437. *Loss or theft of certificates indorsed in blank.*[3] — It is extremely doubtful whether a purchaser of a certificate of stock which was indorsed in blank, and which has been lost by the owner

---

[1] See chapter XXI.   [3] See chapter XXI.
[2] See chapter XXI.

and found by another who sells it. or which has been stolen by the latter, would be protected in his purchase, even though he buys in good faith In a case of negotiable paper, such a purchaser would, of course, be protected But probably the purchaser of the certificate of stock would not be. No case holds that he would be protected, while many hold that he would not. If the real owner was guilty of gross negligence, perhaps the purchaser from the thief or finder of the certificate indorsed in blank would be protected In one case this question of negligence was submitted to the jury. Again, sometimes a person sells stock without delivering the certificate - the vendor telling the vendee that the certificates have been lost. Such a title is very precarious The purchaser should refuse to buy until new certificates are issued by the corporation to the vendor — an issue which the corporation will make upon a suitable bond of indemnity being given to it by the person who alleges a loss If the purchaser does not take this precaution, he buys subject to having his title defeated by another purchaser who obtained the certificates which are alleged to have been lost.

§ 438. *Danger that a previous holder has been deprived of that same stock by fraud.*[1]— Shares of stock are the same as other kinds of property, in that a person who has been deprived of his stock by fraud cannot follow the stock and take it from the hands of a *bona fide* purchaser for value. The remedy of the defrauded person is for damages against the person defrauding him, or for a re-transfer of the stock, if the latter still holds it, together with an injunction against the transfer of the latter. But if the person obtaining the stock by fraud sells it, even in violation of an injunction, the *bona fide* purchaser for value and without notice is protected The defrauded party may, however, sue the person defrauding him in the state of the corporation, and, by an attachment or execution, obtain the stock if it has not passed into *bona fide* hands. Such a danger, however, is the ordinary danger of an attachment or execution. A *lis pendens* of a suit involving stock never charges the vendor of the stock with notice, as is the case of a *lis pendens* affecting real estate. Cases of fraud in the sale of stock frequently arise in cases of sales by agents and an appropriation of the proceeds; also when fraudulent representations are made to the vendor.

§ 439. *Statute of frauds.*[2]—The statute of frauds requires that sales of personal property exceeding in value a certain amount, generally fifty dollars, shall be valid and enforceable only when the property is partly or wholly delivered, or partly or wholly paid for at the time of the sale, or the terms of the sale are reduced to writ-

---

[1] See chapter XX. [2] See chapter XX.

ing In this country a sale of stock must conform to this statute. Generally the sale is made by a delivery of the certificate indorsed in blank Such a sale constitutes a delivery, and is legal, and is not void by the statute of frauds The statute applies both to sales of stock which are considered as completed and to sales which are to be completed in the future

§ 440. *Gambling sales of stock.*[1]— A gambling sale or contract to sell stock is void absolutely, and cannot be enforced As a matter of practical experience, however, it is difficult to prove that a stock sale is a gambling sale. It is such only when both the vendor and vendee intend, not to actually have a delivery of the stock, but to wait and see whether the stock rises or falls in the market, and then to settle the contract by the loser paying the loss. An intent by one of the parties that there shall be no delivery will not make the sale a gambling one It must be the intent of both.

§ 441 *Method of assigning a certificate of stock.*[2]— A certificate of stock is generally assigned by the owners signing the blank transfer and power of attorney on the back of the certificate The transfer gives title to him whose name is afterwards filled into the blank transfer thus signed. The blank power of attorney is for an entirely different purpose It enables the person whose name is filled in to register the transferee as a stockholder in the corporate books Generally the power of attorney is filled in with the name of a clerk or agent of the transferee, or a clerk of the corporation who has charge of the registry books. After the registered holder has signed the transfer, leaving the transferee's name in blank, the certificate passes from hand to hand until some holder cares to fill his name into the blank He may then obtain registry, or he may execute another transfer and sell the certificate. Transfers need not be under seal in this country. In England, by statute, they generally are required so to be.

§ 442. *Registry of transfer.*[2]— A registry of transfer is made by surrendering an old certificate of stock to the corporation, making an entry of the transfer on the corporate registry, and taking from the corporation a new certificate issued in the name of the transferee The entry is generally made by a corporate officer, but he may insist on its being made by the person applying for transfer. The object of obtaining the registry is to obtain a right to vote, to receive dividends, and various other incidental stockholders' rights, also to cut off corporate liens and the rights of third parties who may attach or claim the stock If there is a reasonable legal doubt as to the right of the applicant to obtain registry, the corporation may refuse it, and thus obtain the protec-

---

[1] See chapter XX. [2] See chapter XXII.

tion of being compelled to make it by legal proceedings. If two
parties claim the stock, each denying the right of the other, the
corporation may interplead, provided there is a reasonable legal
doubt as to who is entitled to the stock. If the corporation improperly refuses to register a transfer when requested, the applicant
may have his remedy in damages, but in most states cannot have a
mandamus.

§ 443 *Purchaser not affected by rights of holders of that stock
back of the last registry.*[1]— This rule is peculiar to stock certificates,
and cuts off rights even of a former owner who has been deprived
of the stock by forgery In this respect certificates of stock are
more negotiable than negotiable paper itself. The person who
obtains registry first, after the illegal act has been done, is not protected by this rule. But his *bona fide* purchaser of the new certificates and all subsequent purchasers are protected, and cannot be
compelled to give up the stock to the prior owner who was deprived of it illegally.

§ 444 *Summary* — It will be seen, by a review of the sections of
this chapter, that the dangers of loss incurred by the purchase of a
certificate of stock are not serious or numerous; and it is well that
such is the result Perhaps the most striking industrial feature of
modern times is the accumulation of personal property, and the investment of that property, not in landed estates, but in the stocks
and bonds of corporations. Such investments are made, not alone
by capitalists, but by thousands whose savings have no other satisfactory mode of disposition The constant tendency of the statutes
and of the decisions of the courts to protect *bona fide* purchasers
of certificates of stock is to be commended and aided. Beyond all
question, the surplus wealth of the future will be invested in corporate bonds and stocks. It is well, then, in these days of the formative period of the law governing stock, that the principles governing
the transfer of certificates should be formed for the protection and
security of an investing public, and should be against secret liens,
attachments, claims and negligence of both the corporation and
third persons.

[1] See §§ 367, 369.

PART III.

MISCELLANEOUS RIGHTS OF STOCKHOLDERS

CHAPTER XXV.

STOCK-BROKERS AND THEIR CONTRACTS

§ 445 *Definitions and scope of the subject* — By far the greater part of purchases and sales of stock is made both in this country and in England, through organizations specially formed for that purpose and called stock exchanges. A stock exchange is a place of business where those who make up the membership of the exchange buy and sell stocks and bonds. These persons are called stock-brokers. A stock-broker is one who buys and sells stock as the agent of another, the latter being called a customer of the stock-broker[1] Accordingly, in an ordinary purchase of stock through stock-brokers, there are, generally, at least four persons

---

[1] In Sibbald v. The Bethlehem Iron Company, 83 N. Y., 378 (1881), Finch, J., favors the definition from Pott v. Turner, 6 Bing., 702, 706, where a broker is defined as "one who makes a bargain for another and receives a commission for so doing." Story on Agency, § 28 (9th ed.) says "The true definition of a broker seems to be that he is an agent employed to make bargains and contracts between other persons in matters of trade, commerce or navigation, for a compensation commonly called brokerage."

involved — the two brokers and their respective customers. Stock-brokers have a language of their own They have coined and put into general circulation certain phrases and terms descriptive of their business These terms have become so closely identified with the subject of stock and transactions in stock that the courts have defined their meaning and explained their application [1]

[1] A "bull" is a dealer who endeavors to make the price of stocks go higher A "bear" is a dealer who endeavors to make the price of stocks go lower A "short" sale is a sale of stocks which the seller does not possess, but which he expects to purchase later on at a lower figure, thus fulfilling his contract and making profit by the decline In the meantime the broker generally borrows the stock from other parties to deliver to the vendee, and to be returned to the person loaning the stock at the end of the transaction The broker is bound to continue the transaction for a reasonable time The customer deposits with the broker a small amount of money as security, called a margin, and he is bound to keep the margin good Hess v Rau, 95 N Y, 359 (1884), White v Smith, 54 N Y, 522 (1874), Knowlton v Fitch, 52 N Y, 288 (1873), Appleman v Fisher, 54 Md, 540 (1871), Sistare v Best, 88 N Y, 527, 533 (1882) A "long" purchase of stock is a purchase in the expectation that the stock will rise in value

Stock options are of three kinds — puts, calls, and straddles A "put" is a contract whereby a person has the privilege of requiring another person to take from the former certain specified stock at a specified price at any time within a specified period of time, the former not being bound to sell See Bigelow v Benedict, 70 N Y, 202 (1877) A "call" is a contract whereby a person has the privilege of requiring another person to sell or deliver to the former certain specified stock at a specified price at any time within a certain specified period, the former not being bound to purchase. A "straddle"

or "spread-eagle" is a combination of a put and a call It gives a person the double privilege of delivering to or demanding from another person certain stock at a certain price within a specified time Harris v Tumbridge, 83 N. Y. 92 (1880), Story v Salomon, 71 N. Y. 420 (1877) A "corner" exists where the "bears" have sold a large quantity of stock "short," and cannot borrow the stock to fill their contracts, but must buy it from those who have cornered the market on that stock See Cameron v. Durkheim, 55 N Y, 425, 438 (1874). As to the legality of these various transactions, see §§ 341–348, especially § 344, n It is not fraud for the owner of the larger part of the capital stock of a corporation to "corner" the market, that is, to enter into contracts with various parties to purchase stock of the corporation, although he knew that such contracts could not be fulfilled by such parties by reason of the fact that he himself held such stock, and it could not be obtained elsewhere The same rule prevails although such person offered the stock for public subscription and purchased the greater part himself Salaman v Warner, 64 L. T Rep., 598 (1891)

A "loan" of stock is still another transaction The initiated do not require to be told that when a man sells stock on the exchange he must deliver it, and if he does not own any he must borrow it of some one who does When he borrows the stock, he advances the market price of it to the lender, who pays interest on this money The transaction is really a call loan The lender of the stock can call for his stock at any time, and the borrower can call for his

This chapter treats of the rights, duties and liabilities of stock-brokers.[1] There are various incidental subjects, however, which enter largely into brokers' contracts, such as pledges of stock[2] and gambling sales of stock[3] These subjects are fully treated elsewhere

§ 446 *Who may be a broker and customer.*— Any person may be a stock-broker who may make a contract, but it is beyond the power of a national bank to act as a broker[4] Strict rules prevail as to who may be a customer An infant is not bound by his contracts with or through a stock-broker any more than he is bound by his other contracts. Moreover, if the broker carries on stock transactions for an infant he is liable to the latter for all moneys lost thereby.[5] Again, a broker who sells or buys stock in the name of an infant is himself liable to the other party in case the contract is not completed by reason of such infancy[6] On the other hand, if the broker's customer hands in the name of a third person, an infant, as the seller or purchaser, such customer is liable to the broker for liabilities thereby incurred by the latter[7]

§ 447 *Facts making person a broker or customer unintentionally* The relationship of broker and customer may be established and exist although one of the parties is personally ignorant of such a relationship[8] A broker also may be liable as such in transactions

money When a strong bearish feeling is running, and too much short selling has been indulged in, stocks become scarce, and those who have them will only lend at a concession, either at less than current interest rates, or "flat," that is, without interest, or actually at a premium, according to the urgency of the demand.

[1] See, also, on this subject, Lindley on Partnership, 721, etc

[2] Ch XXVI

[3] See ch XX

[4] First Nat'l Bank of Allentown *v.* Hock, 89 Pa St, 324 Weckler *v* First Nat'l Bank, 42 Md, 581 (1879) But Williamson *v* Mason, 12 Hun, 97 (1877), holds that a bank has power to take stock from a customer and agree to sell it and credit customer with the proceeds, and that the bank is liable for the conversion of such stock by its cashier

[5] Ruchizky *v* De Haven, 97 Pa. St., 202 (1881) The transactions in this case were held to be gambling contracts Heath *v.* Mahoney, 12 Week. Dig, 404

(1881) The broker himself may be an infant and may repudiate his obligations See 4 Law Notes, 314

[6] Nickalls *v* Merry, L R, 7 H I, 520 (1875), Heritage *i* Paine, 34 L. T, 947 (1876), Maxted *i* Paine, L R, 4 Ex, 81 (1869) The first case holds him liable although ignorant of the infancy of his customer See same case, Merry *v* Nickalls 41 L J (Ch), 767 (1872) Broker is liable although the name of the infant was passed to him by another broker Dent *i* Nickalls, 29 L T, 536 (1873) It is no defense to the broker that the infant's father was the real customer Nickalls *v* Eaton, 23 L T, 689 (1871) See, also § 250 *supra*, as to liability to the corporation

[7] Peppercorne *i* Clinch, 26 L T, 656 (1872)

[8] Thus the customer may be bound by the acts of his clerk Webb *v* Challoner, 2 F & F, 120 (1860) So also where the firm does a broker business through its agents, the transactions by the agents on their own private ac-

where he had no intention of incurring any liability.[1] A broker is nothing more nor less than an agent for a special purpose The agency may arise by the acts of the parties without any specific agreement.

§ 448. *Broker must obey specific orders of customer* — A broker is bound to obey and carry out strictly the orders of his customer in the purchase or sale of stock. This rule is rigidly insisted upon by the courts The orders of the customer may be such as he wishes to give, and when given they must be obeyed, or liability will be incurred by the broker [2] When the customer fixes a limit at which the broker may purchase. the latter cannot bind the customer by a purchase at a higher figure.[3] Frequently the customer gives to the broker a "stop order," which is an order to sell or buy, as the case may be, at a certain specified figure, or upon a specified contingency Under this order the broker must sell or buy when the price or contingency occurs, but not until after it occurs If the market changes too quickly for him, he must sell or buy at the market price immediately after the fixed price or contingency arises [4] The customer may leave it in the discretion

counts, but ostensibly for the firm, will bind the firm Wells, Fargo & Co. *v* Welter, 15 Nev, 276 (1880) *Cf* 6 N Y Supp, 665

[1] As where he continues to allow his name to remain in the firm name after its dissolution Hixon *v* Pixley, 15 Nev, 475 (1880). Also where one of the firm is a trustee and defaults therein, the firm having charge of the trust estate's stocks De Ribeyre *v* Barclay 23 Beav, 107 (1856) As a silent partner he cannot prevent a customer from setting off against a liability a debt personal to the ostensibly sole broker Read *v* Jaudon 35 How Pr, 303 (1868). A stock-broker is bound to obey orders promptly Galigher *v* Jones, 129 U S, 193

[2] Parsous *v* Martin, 77 Mass, 111 (1858) Thus, where the customer authorizes a sale if the stock goes down to 51, but the broker sells when it goes down to 52, he is liable for an unauthorized sale Clarke *v* Meigs 10 Bosw. 337 (1863) *Cf* Whelan *v* Lynch, 60 N Y 469 (1875) Jones *v.* Marks, 40 Ill, 313 (1866) But the broker may correct a palpable error in the order given him

by his customer. Luffman *v.* Hay, 13 N. Y. Week Dig, 324 (1881).

[3] Whether a limit was fixed is a question for the jury, if the facts are disputed *Cf* Smith *v* Bouvier, 70 Pa St, 375 (1872) The customer may ratify the unauthorized purchase Genin *v* Isaacson, 6 N Y. Leg Obs, 213 (1848). If the power to sell depends on the construction of writings it is a question of law only Davis *v* Gwynne, 57 N Y, 676 (1874), S C, 4 Daly, 218 (1871) But the written order may be subsequently modified by parol Burkitt *v* Taylor, 86 N Y, 618 (1881), Clarke *v* Meigs, 10 Bosw, 337 (1863) Or be waived Hope *v* Lawrence, 50 Barb., 258 (1867)

[4] Porter *v* Wormser, 94 N. Y, 431 (1884), Bertram *v* Godfrey, 1 Knapp s Rep P C, 381 (1830) The latter case involved an absolute order to sell should the stock reach a certain price Where a broker is carrying a "short" sale on a "stop order," and purchases before the price of the "stop order" is reached, and the customer a week later then orders the broker to purchase, the purchaser may recover the profit that a purchase at the latter date would

of the broker as to the best time for buying or selling [1] When
this is done the broker must exercise such discretion in good faith
and with reasonably good judgment and care [2]

§ 449 *Must act in good faith and in reasonable time* — The
broker must make the purchase or sale in good faith on the best
terms possible, and must give the customer the advantage of the
transaction as actually made   Any material failure to do this, or
to make the sale or purchase as directed, will release the customer
from the transaction, although it was reported to him as made in
accordance with orders [3] The broker is allowed a reasonable time
within which to make the sale or purchase [4]

---

have netted   Campbell *r* Wright, 118
N Y , 594 (1890)   Brokers cannot disregard a "stop order," and act before that
price is reached, even though prices are
fluctuating rapidly   Id   See, also,
§ 459

[1] Such discretion when given is revoked only by clear notice of revocation,
Davis *r* Gwynne, 4 Daly 218 (1871)

[2] Harris *r* Tumbridge, 83 N Y , 92
(1880)

[3] Where the broker buys in his own
name at a price less than the price reported to the customer, sells without
notice, and subsequently pretends to
sell again, the whole transaction is void
as to the customer   Levy *r* Loeb, 85
N. Y , 365 (1881), 89 id 386   So, likewise, where he purchases an option instead of cash purchase, and reports a
higher price than that paid   Voris *r*
McCready, 16 How Pr , 87 (1856)   So,
likewise, where the broker varies the
order from a cash purchase to an option, he himself taking the risk of the
option   Dey *r* Holmes, 103 Mass 306,
Pickering *r* Demeritt. 100 Mass. 416
(1868)   A broker who sells bonds and
then reports no sale, but loans money
to the customer on the bonds as collateral, may be held liable to account for
the sale   Bischoffsheim *r* Brown, 34
Fed Rep , 145 (1888).

[4] Fletcher *r* Marshall, 15 Mees & W ,
755 (1846)   Cf Dickinson *r* Lilwal, 1
Starkie, 128 (1815), which holds that
the transaction must be carried out on
the day of the order   The broker is en-

titled to his commission although his
customer fails before the transaction is
made   Inchbald *r* The Western Coffee
Co , 43 L J (C P.) 15   The contract
is to be carried out within a reasonable
time   A broker s custom is evidence as
to what is reasonable time   Stewart *r*
Cauty, 8 Mees & W , 160 (1840)   A few
hours' notice held insufficient   Johnson
r Mulry, 51 N Y , 631 (1872).   Usually the broker is entitled to a fair and
reasonable opportunity to perform his
obligation, subject of course to the right
of the seller to sell independently   But
that having been granted him, the
right of the principal to terminate his
authority is absolute and unrestricted
except only that he may not do it in
bad faith and as a mere device to escape the payment of the broker s commissions'   Sibbald *r* The Bethlehem
Iron Co , 83 N Y , 378 384 (1881)   A
customer is under no obligation, when
he learns that his broker has not sold
stock as ordered to notify the broker
that he abandoned any claim to the
stock and held the broker responsible
for their value   Nor is he obliged to redeem the stock from the sub-broker
Allen *r* McCombe, 124 N Y , 342 (1890)
In this case the court allowed as damages against a broker who delayed selling when ordered to sell, the difference
between the price when the order was
given and the price when the sale was
actually made   Where for four years
both the broker and the customer have
apparently abandoned an alleged pur-

§ 450 *Cannot purchase from or sell to himself* — A broker cannot, in behalf of his customer, buy or sell with himself as the other principal   The law will not allow him to act both as agent and as principal at the same time   Such an act is a constructive fraud on account of his fiduciary relation, and will be set aside [1] Custom or usage cannot legalize such a transaction [2] The broker may, however, show by parol evidence that he did not deal with himself, though writings indicate otherwise [3] And there is no rule which prevents the broker from acting as agent both for the selling and the buying customer. [4]

§ 451 *Duties and liabilities of customer towards broker.* — A stock-broker is but the agent of his customer   As such he may bind his customer by acts within the scope of his authority, and compel the customer to respond to his liability   Thus, the broker may proceed to close the transaction paying out his own money as though it was his own business and may then compel the customer to repay to him the money so expended in the customer's behalf. [5]

chase of stock on a margin it is a question for the jury whether there was an abandonment or whether the customer continued to be liable   Seligman t Rogers 21 S W Rep 94 (Mo 1893) A broker ordered to purchase stock on a margin need not actually purchase at once   It is sufficient if he is ready to fulfill when called upon so to do at the price on the day of the giving of the order Ingraham t Taylor 20 Atl Rep 601 (Conn 1890)

[1] Mayo t Knowlton 134 N Y 250 (1892) Conkey t Bond 36 N Y 427 Brookman t Rothschild 3 Sim 153 (1829) Mirye t Strouse 5 Fed Rep. 483 (1880) Robinson t Mollett L R 7 H L 802 818 826 (1874) Even though the purchase was in good faith and at a lower figure than the market price Taussig t Hart 58 N Y 425 (1874), Gillett t Peppercorne 3 Beav 78 (1840) In Bryan t Baldwin 33 N Y 232 (1873) the court say   The plaintiff being pledgee of the stock and in that character exposing it for sale could not become the purchaser unless the defendant assented to such purchase Story on Bailments § 319 Torry t Bank of Orleans 7 Paige, 649 (1842), Hawley r Cramer, 4 Cow , 736 (1825) This sale to

the plaintiff was not void but voidable at the election of the defendant Edwards on Bailments, 260 The defendant was at liberty to ratify the sale, and had he done so it would have been valid for all purposes The ratification would have made it lawful, and relieved it from any imputation of being tortious as to him   . But the defendant has not done this, but has elected to treat the purchase by the plaintiff as illegal This avoids the sale, and that being avoided by the defendant, the parties are remitted to their rights the same as though no sale had been attempted

[2] Commonwealth t Cooper, 130 Mass., 285 (1881) The custom of brokers to buy in large quantities and sell in small quantities is illegal Robinson r Mollett L R 7 H L, 802 (1874).

[3] Potter t Wormser 94 N. Y, 431 (1884)

[4] Knowlton t Fitch, 52 N. Y., 288 (1873)

[5] Bayley t Wilkins 7 C B. 886 (1849), Whitehouse t Moore 13 Abb. Pr, 142 (1861) Dails t Lloyd, 12 C. B, 531 Cf Ex parte Neilson, 3 De G , M. & G, 556 (1853).

Or, if his customer refuses to carry out the transaction, the broker may settle with the opposite party by paying the loss incurred by buying or selling the stock elsewhere, and may then sue his customer for the differences thus paid.[1]   He may also recover his disbursements, commissions and interest.[2]   The customer is liable to the broker for stock purchased, although the stock turns out to be spurious or unauthorized.[3]   If the broker, however, seeks to recover the full value of the stock, he must first tender the stock to the customer,[4] or he must sell it after due notice to the customer, and thus accurately ascertain the loss.[5]   If he is seeking to recover for differences paid the opposite broker in settlement, *assumpsit* is his remedy.[6]   He must clearly prove that the customer authorized the order.[7]

§ 452. *Duties and liabilities of a broker towards customer.*— The broker also owes certain duties and incurs certain liabilities in his

[1] Durant v. Burt, 98 Mass., 161 (1867); Bayliffe v. Butterworth, 5 Railw. Cas., 283, per Parke, B.; Marten v. Gibbon, 33 L. T., 561 (1876); Biederman v. Stone, L. R., 2 C. P., 504 (1867).

[2] Where the commissions and interest were paid to other brokers, it may be charged to the customer. Robinson v. Norris, 51 How. Pr., 442 (1874). Even though that interest be usurious. Smith v. Heath, 4 Daly, 123 (1871). On commissions, see Inchbald v. Western Coffee Co., 43 L. J., C. P., 15. Excessive expenses will not be allowed, although customary. Marye v. Strouse, 5 Fed. Rep., 483 (1880). But the broker is entitled to commissions only when he has rendered some service to the customer. Sibbald v. The Bethlehem Iron Co., 83 N. Y., 378 (1881); Hoffman v. Livingston, 46 N. Y. Super. Cr., 552 (1880). The case of Hatch v. Douglas, 48 Conn., 116 (1880), holds that the broker's customary monthly charges and interest thereon are not usurious. Cf. Robinson v. Norris, 6 Hun, 233 (1875). The broker may recover from the principal the purchase price of stocks bought by the broker, but not delivered, before the corporation became insolvent. Chapman v. Shepherd, L. R., 2 C. P., 225. Members of a syndicate are jointly liable to a broker employed by them.

Sternberger v. Bernheimer, 121 N. Y., 194 (1890).

[3] See Adamson v. Jarvis, 4 Bing., 66 (1827); Peckham v. Ketchum, 3 Bosw., 506 (1859). So, also, for spurious stock innocently given to the broker to sell. Westropp v. Solaman, 8 C. B., 345 (1849).

[4] Merwin v. Hamilton, 6 Duer, 244 (1856); Bowlby v. Bell, 3 Com. B., 284 (1846). But after once tendering it he need not continually keep it on hand. Wynkoop v. Seal, 64 Pa. St., 361 (1870).

[5] Monroe v. Peck, 3 Daly, 128 (1869). In Rosenstock v. Tormey, 32 Md., 169, the necessary allegations were held to be a purchase of stock according to an order, at fair market price, which was paid, and the customer notified and payment demanded; willingness to deliver the stock; refusal of customer to pay; notice of sale; a proper sale and loss.

[6] Pollock v. Stables, 12 Q. B., 765 (1848). Contra, Child v. Morley, 8 Term R., 610 (1800).

[7] Ward v. Van Duser, 2 Hall (N. Y.), 167 (1829). In White v. Baxter, 71 N. Y., 254 (1877), the court held that a customer's contract with his broker to protect the latter against loss by expulsion from the stock exchange for non-compliance with its rules is a valid and enforceable contract.

relations towards his customer   It is said that he cannot sell on
credit, since that is not the usual course of his business [1]   He is
liable in damages for failure to buy or sell in accordance with his
express orders [2]   Where the customer fails to carry out the transaction, but the broker does carry it out at a profit, the profit belongs to the customer [3]   But the customer is not entitled to stock
held for him by the broker until he pays the broker all his reasonable disbursements thereon [4]   The broker may deposit a margin
with the opposite broker, according to custom, and not be responsible to his customer if it is lost,[5] although the rule may be otherwise as to a delivery of the stocks themselves [6]   The broker is
required to exercise reasonable diligence and care and no more [7]
The broker has a lien on the customer's property in his hands for
all debts due to the former [8]   But he has no such lien if he knows
that the customer is acting as agent for another [9]   It is a question
of doubt whether a broker who has received in good faith commissions from a person guilty of embezzlement is liable to pay over
to the persons injured by his customer commissions so received [10]
A broker may, by bill of discovery, be compelled to disclose acts

[1] 2 Kent's Com , 622 (b) 12th ed
[2] Speyer v Colgate 4 Hun, 622 (1875),
Whelan v Lynch, 60 N Y, 469 (1875)
the case of a wool-broker   See also,
Jones v Marks 40 Ill, 313 (1866). The
damages may sound in tort, thus preventing a release in bankruptcy from
barring the action   Parker v Crol 5
Bing, 64 (1828)   Under the New York
code he may be arrested if he does not
use the money for the purpose designated   Dubois v Thompson, 1 Daly 309.
And in England he is liable criminally
Regina v Cronmire, 54 L. T. Rep, 580
(1885)
[3] Fowler v N Y, Gold Ex Bank, 67
N Y, 138 (1876)
[4] See McEwan v Woods 11 Q B. 13,
where the broker paid calls made on the
stock after its sale
[5] Gheen v Johnson, 30 Pa St., 38
(1879)
[6] Brown v Boorman, 11 Cl & F, 1
(1844)
[7] Phillips v Moir, 69 Ill, 155 (1873).
Gheen v Johnson, 90 Pa St, 38 (1879)
As to the construction of a contract
wherein the broker invests the customer's money as the broker sees fit,

and the broker guaranties the return of
the capital and interest and all profits
made, see In re Assignment of Vermilye, 10 Atl Rep, 605 (N J 1887) As
to the liability of stock-brokers and job-
bers and vendees towards the vendors,
see, also, White & Tudor s Leading
Cases in Equity, vol I pp. 922-929
[8] Jones v Peppercorne, 5 Jur (N S.),
Pt. 1 p 140
[9] Fisher v Brown, 104 Mass, 259 (1870).
Pearson v Scott, L R, 9 Ch D, 198
(1878)
[10] See Butler v Finck, 21 Hun, 210
(1880)   The case of Taft v Chapman,
50 N Y, 445 (1872), seems to hold that
the broker is not liable where he acted
without knowledge of his customer's
acts   See, also, S C under name Brownson v Chapman, 63 N Y, 625 (1875)
See also, Porter v Parks, 49 N Y, 564
(1872), § 350, n   The case Kissam v Anderson 145 U S, 435 (1892), reversed
the decision below (Anderson v Kissam,
35 Fed Rep, 699, holding the broker
liable) on the ground that it was for the
jury to say whether the bank, whose
funds were used by the president to pay
the broker, had notice of payment by

amounting to misconduct.[1] The question of the broker's liability, where the stock delivered by him to his customer is forged or stolen stock, is considered elsewhere[2]

§ 453 *Method of completing a broker's contract.*— The formalities and method of completing a stock-broker's contract are governed largely by the usages of the stock exchange. It is well established law that, when a man sells or buys shares through his broker on the stock exchange, he enters into an implied contract to sell or buy according to the custom and usages prevalent in that body[3] These usages and customs are to be found, for the most part, in the rules of the stock exchange, so far as the formalities of completing the contracts are concerned Occasionally, however, such formalities are reviewed and sanctioned by the courts[4]

§ 454 *Privity of contract between broker and opposite parties* — A broker who buys or sells stock does so subject to certain liabilities towards the parties to whom he sells or from whom he buys. If he does not send in the name of his customer, he is liable on the transaction as though he were the principal himself[5] He has been held liable for a forgery perpetrated by his customer.[6] Where, however, the broker hands in the name of his customer, and that name is accepted, the broker is thereby discharged,[7] unless, of course, the name is unauthorized, or is that of an infant[8] Upon the disclosure by the broker of his customer's name, the opposite

the broker to the president A broker who takes money as a margin, knowing that the money comes from a trustee and is trust estate money, is liable to the estate for money lost thereby Leake ? Watson, 20 Atl Rep., 343(Conn , 1890)

[1] Green v Weaver 1 Sim , 404 (1827). See Rawlings v Hall, 1 Carr & P , 11 (1823)

[2] See ch XXI, also, see Andrews v Clark, 20 Atl Rep , 429 (Ind , 1890)

[3] See § 462

[4] Thus, a usage by which the ultimate purchaser s name is handed to the seller for the purpose of having the latter execute a transfer to the former is upheld Sheppard ? Murphy, 16 W R., 948 (1868) The custom of giving the seller time to investigate and object to a purchaser may be insisted on by the seller Sumner v Stewart 69 Pa St , 321 (1871) The purchaser may be compelled, by a bill

in equity, to register the transfer made through brokers Paine v Hutchinson, L R , 3 Eq Cas , 257 (1866)

[5] Wynne v Price, 3 De G & Sm , 310 (1849)

[6] Royal Exchange Ins Co v Moore, 11 Week Rep , 592 (1863) The broker herein sold in his own name, but the opposite party knew he acted as a broker

[7] Maxted v Paine (2d action), L R , 6 Ex , 132 (1871), holding that the broker does not guaranty his customer's responsibility nor that he is the real purchaser So also of the stock-jobber Grissell v Bristowe, L R., 4 C P , 36 (1868) Contra, Cruse ? Paine, 37 L J (Ch), 711 (1868)

[8] See § 446 Broker handing in the name of a customer without authority is himself liable Maxted v Norris 21 L T , 535 Cf Shepherd v Gillespie, L R , 5 Eq Cas , 293 (1867)

party has the option of holding either the broker or his customer responsible, but cannot hold both.[1]

§ 455. *Privity of contract between the opposite customers.*—When the broker of one customer has agreed with the broker of another customer on the terms of a purchase and sale of stock, there immediately arises a privity of contract between the two customers. The purchasing customer is liable to the selling customer for all calls and liabilities arising on the stock after the broker's contract is made, if the selling customer is obliged to pay such liabilities by reason of his being the registered stockholder.[2] So also the purchasing customer may hold the selling customer responsible for the carrying out of the contract[3] It has been held that the remedy may be an action at law[4] or in equity[5] The right of set-off for other debts applies as between the two customers,[6] but not for debts due from one of the brokers to the opposite customer.[7]

§ 456 *Intervening sub-brokers and sub-customers* —Where a customer's broker employs another broker to transact the business, the customer cannot compel the second broker to complete the contract as he might compel the first broker[8] The second broker cannot claim a lien on the stock for debts due him from the first broker[9] If the first broker merely introduces the parties he can-

[1] Watson v Miller, 11 Week Notes, 18 (1876) . A custom or usage releasing the broker from this liability is void Magee v Atkinson, 2 Mees & W, 440 (1837) Cf Jones v Littledale, 1 Nev. & Per , 677 (1837), the sale being of hemp Also Thomson v Davenport, 9 Barn & Cr , 78 (1829), holding that the purchaser's option remains open until the *name* of the undisclosed principal is given It is for the jury to say which one the opposite customer gave credit to irrespective of a stock exchange custom Mortimer v. McCallan, 6 Mees & W 58 (1840)

[2] Hawkins v Maltby, L R , Ch App , 200 (1869), affirmed, S C , L. R., 6 Eq, 505. Evans v Wood, L. R.. 5 Eq Cas , 9 (1867), Hodgkinson v Kelly, L R, 6 Eq. Cas, 406 (1868), 37 L J (Ch), 837, Remfrey v Rutter, 1 Ell , Bl & Ell , 887 (1858), Allan v Graves, 39 L. J , 157 (1870) A stock exchange custom, making the broker a principal, does not prevent the customer suing as principal Langton v Waite, 16 W. R., 503 (1868)

Refusal of directors to register the sale does not enable the purchasing customer to recover back the purchase price. Stray v Russell, 1 Ll & El, 888 (1859)

[3] Even though the selling customer did not authorize the use of his name, but knew of it and did not object Shepherd v Gillespie, L R., 5 Eq Cas , 293 (1867)

[4] Street v Morgan, L R , 4 Ex , 384 See, also Davis v Haycock, L R., 4 Ex , 373 (1869)

[5] Sheppard v Murphy, 16 W. R., 948 (1868)

[6] Carr v Hinchliff, 4 Barn & Cr., 547 (1825)

[7] Fish v Kempton, 7 C. B., 687 (1849). See, also, Sweeting v Pearce, 7 C. B. (N S) 449 (1859) Unless, possibly, where the customer supposed the opposite broker was the principal See Kelley v Munson, 7 Mass , 318 (1811)

[8] Booth v Fielding, 1 Week. Notes, 245 (1866)

[9] Fisher v Brown, 104 Mass , 259 (1870).

not charge a commission therefor, although custom allows it [1]   The real customer may hold an intermediate customer liable   A sub-broker or correspondent broker is not obliged to ascertain the relations and agreements between the chief broker and the customer   The sub-broker may hold all stocks as security for all accounts between himself and the chief broker, there being no notice given of the customer's rights   If there is any surplus after the sub-broker's debt is paid, a customer who placed his own stock in the chief broker's hands to sell is preferred to another customer who had purchased on a margin and left the stock as security [2]   If brokers in New York take orders through a local broker in another place, they are liable for false and fictitious orders given to them by him in the name of a customer [3]

§ 457 *Purchases or sales on margins — Broker as a pledgee —* By far the larger part of a stock-broker's business consists of purchases and sales of stock on what is called a "margin." [4] The customer deposits with the broker, as security, a sum of money equal to but a small part of the value of the stock involved. This sum of money is the "margin." If the customer's order is to purchase, then the broker keeps both the margin and the purchased stock as security against loss in the final closing of the transaction. If the customer's order is to sell, then the broker sells, but, having no stock to deliver, he borrows the same from other parties and delivers it to the purchaser, the broker still keeping the margin as security   Frequently no stock passes, nor is intended to pass, but merely the ultimate profit or loss called "differences" is paid, the losing customer loses the whole or part of his margin, the winning customer getting back his margin and also the profits, less commissions   This is a gambling contract, and, like all gambling contracts, whether in or out of a stock exchange, is not enforceable [5] But a purchase or sale of stock on margins, where there is no proof

[1] Gibson v Crick, 1 Hurl & C 142 (1862) He may hold the intermediate customer or agent liable for set-off due from the latter to the broker   Jaycox v Cameron, 49 N Y, 645 (1872)

[2] Willard v White, 56 Hun, 581 (1890) See, also, § 460 A sub-broker who knows that the stock deposited as collateral with the chief broker belongs to the customer is liable in damages for conversion where he receives such stock on further orders and it transpires that such use of the stock was unauthorized   Ryman v Gerlach, 25 Atl. Rep. 1031 (Pa , 1893)

[3] Caswell v Putnam, 120 N Y, 153 (1890)

[4] A margin ' means, in the broker s lexicon additional collateral security against loss to the broker while he is

carrying stock for his employer "   McNeil v Tenth Nat Bank of N Y, 55 Barb, 59 (1869)

[5] McBurney v Martin 6 Conn , 502 A broker cannot recover commissions or disbursements from his customer, where the transactions were gambling and intended so to be by both   Harvey v Merrill, 22 N E Rep, 49 (Mass, 1889)

of an intent not to actually deliver the stock, is legal.[1] The relation between a customer and his broker, in cases where the broker buys for his customer and retains the stock as security, is the relation of a pledgor towards a pledgee, the customer being the pledgor, the broker being the pledgee, and the stock being the article pledged.[2] Some of the most important questions connected with brokers' contracts arise out of this pledgee relationship. This subject, however, is fully treated in the following chapter. Like

[1] See chapter XX, where the character, effect and non-enforceability of a broker's gambling contracts are fully treated. A "margin" transaction is not necessarily gambling and invalid. The important case of Hatch v. Douglas, 48 Conn., 116 (1880), clearly sets out the legality of such contracts. The court said "It is pretty evident that the parties did not contemplate that the stock should be actually transferred to the defendant. The defendant [customer], through his agents the plaintiffs, actually purchased the stock, and there was an actual delivery — not to the principal, but to the agents for the principal." The brokers knew "that the defendant was speculating, and that they advanced him money for that purpose. But that was neither illegal nor immoral . . . No case has been decided which declares such a contract illegal. If we should so hold, it would be difficult if not impossible to draw the line between legal and illegal transactions." The California constitution renders void a transaction wherein a broker buys stock for the customer with the broker's money and holds the stock as security and charges the customer interest and commissions. Cusham v. Root, 26 Pac. Rep., 883 (Cal', 1891). A broker holding as pledgee stock purchased for a customer on margin need not keep that identical stock on hand, and it is sufficient if he keeps an equal quantity on hand over and above stock of the same kind held by him for other customers. Caswell v. Putnam, 120 N. Y., 153 (1890). In Massachusetts it is held that a broker carrying stocks on a mar-

gin is not a pledgee. Covell v. Loud, 135 Mass., 41 (1883). A broker holding stock as collateral security on a margin does not hold the stock in a fiduciary capacity. McBurney v. Martin, 6 Rob., 502, Lambertson v. Van Boskerk, 49 How., 256, 4 Hun, 628. In England the carrying of stock by a broker on a margin is called "contango," and the broker is held to be the owner of the stock. In the case of Bentinck v. The London, etc., Bank, 68 L. T. Rep., 315 (1893), the court said "In all these transactions, therefore, where money is borrowed by a stock-broker in this way on contango or continuation, whether it is got from the dealer, whether it is got from other stock-brokers, or whether it is got from the bankers, the result is the same; that the arrangement is one by which he becomes, as between himself and his client, the owner of the security in question, although he is under a contract to provide similar stock at a future date."

[2] Markham v. Jaudon, 41 N. Y., 235 (1869), Baker v. Drake, 66 N. Y., 518 (1876). The broker is bound to keep constantly on hand the amount of stock so held on margin, i. e., pledged. Taussig v. Hart, 58 N. Y., 425 (1874), Rogers v. Gould, 6 Hun, 229 (1875). See, also, § 169, infra. In fact, the broker is obliged to conform to the rules governing pledges of stock — a subject treated in ch. XXVI. The customer as pledgor may claim his stock from the broker's assignee for the benefit of creditors if the customer can identify it. Chamberlain v. Greenleaf, 4 Abb. N. C., 178 (1878). See Boylan v. Huguet, 8 Me., 345 (1873).

an ordinary pledgee of stock, the broker may have the stock transferred into his own name,[1] he is not allowed to repledge the stock,[2] and he can put his customer in default only by tendering the stock and demanding payment for their whole value less the margin[3] A broker or pledgee need not sell the stock held as collateral before bringing an action against the pledgor for the amount due, and a brokers' custom cannot compel it[4]

§ 458 *Broker's rights and duties on failure of margin.*— When the "margin" which the customer deposits with his broker happens to become exhausted by the fluctuations of the market adversely to the customer, difficult questions arise as to the several rights and duties of the broker and of the customer. If the broker

[1] Horton v Morgan, 19 N Y 170

[2] Dykers v Allen, 7 Hill, 497 Where it was understood between a firm of brokers and its customers, for whom and on whose order it bought stocks on the security of a margin that the firm might, according to the usual course of business pledge or hypothecate as security for loans to the firm the stocks thus bought, held, that a mere pledge of such stocks would not be of itself a conversion Chamberlain v Greenleaf, 4 Abb N C, 178 (1878). See, also, Lawrence v Maxwell, 58 Barb, 511 (1873), 6 Laus, 469 53 N Y, 19 In Wood v Hays, 15 Gray, 375 (1860), it was held that "a broker who advanced money to buy stock for another, and held it in his own name, might, so long as he had not been paid or tendered the amount of his advances, pledge it as security for his own debt to a third person, without making himself liable to an action by his employer, and this upon the ground that the contract was conditional to deliver the shares upon the payment of the money" Approved in Covell v Loud, 135 Mass. 41 (1883), where it was held that, where the customer was unable to advance further margin and tells the broker to do the best he can, he may sell without notice. The decided weight of authority, however, holds that, unless the power is expressly given to the broker to repledge the stock, he cannot legally repledge it See ch. XXVI.

This, however, does not affect the rights of a repledgee or a purchaser of the stock from the broker A *bona fide* transferee absolutely or in pledge from a broker holding his customer s stock in pledge is protected to the extent of the transfer, the transferee having no notice of the fact that the stock was held in pledge by the broker Thompson v Toland, 48 Cal. 99 (1874), McNeil v Tenth Nat Bank of N Y, 46 N Y, 325 (1871) Zulick v Markham, 6 Daly, 129 (1875), and see many cases in § 321 These cases apply equally whether the person transferring contrary to law is an agent or a pledgee, and equally also, whether he sells or only repledges Where a broker, a gratuitous bailee of corporate stock, delivers the same to the company without authority, and the stock is converted to the use of the company, the bailee is liable for its value, irrespective of what his intentions were in the premises. In such case the bailor may recover the value of the stock at the time of conversion, with all dividends paid from the time of delivery, together with interest on the value of the stock from date of conversion, and on the dividends from date of respective payments Hubbell v Blandy, 49 N W Rep., 502 (Mich:, 1891)

[3] Read v Lambert, 10 Abb. Pr (N. S.), 428 (1871)

[4] De Cordova v. Barnum, 130 N. Y, 615 (1892).

is under orders to close the transaction when the margin becomes exhausted, he of course is obliged to do so[1] But, otherwise, the rule is that the broker cannot summarily close the transaction, even though he has fear of greater loss, involving a loss by himself. He is obliged to demand further margin from his customer, at the same time notifying him that the previous margin is exhausted, also that, in case the margin is not made good, he will close the transaction, holding the customer liable for the loss, also stating the time and place of such threatened sale.[2] The notice must be given a reasonable time before such closing of the transaction, and notice may be sent by mail[3] If the broker fails to comply with these rules and sells, he is guilty of conversion of the stock[4] Where

[1] See § 148.

[2] In the usual short sale of stock through a broker on a margin, the brokers " were bound to carry the stock until plaintiff directed them to close the transaction, so long as he complied with the terms of the contract on his part, and to give the plaintiff reasonable notice of the want of sufficient margin, and of their intention to buy in the stock and cover his short account if the margin was not made good, in accordance with the terms of the notice" Rogers v. Wiley, 131 N. Y., 527 (1892) Where a customer who is selling on a margin desires to close the transaction, but his broker dissuades him by promising to carry the stock, the broker cannot close the transaction without notice Id Brokers before selling a customer's stock which they hold as pledges, the stock having been purchased on a margin, are bound to demand further margin and give notice of intent and time and place of sale. If they fail to do so, but sell and then sue the customer for the loss, they cannot recover anything. They cannot claim that their loss has been greater than defendant's loss due to their conversion Gillett v. Whiting, 120 N Y, 02 (1890), Markham v Jaudon, 41 N Y, 235 (1869), overruling Hanks v Drake 49 Barb, 186 (1867), and Sterling v Jaudon, 48 Barb, 459 (1867) See, also, Kenheld v Latham 2 Cal Leg Rec 235 (1879) and § 461 Cf. Worth-

ington v. Tormey, 34 Md, 182 (1870); and see ch XXVI Leaving notice at office held insufficient where it did not reach the customer. Bryan v Baldwin, 52 N Y, 232 (1873) A formal demand for further margin is insufficient where, subsequently to that demand, the broker negotiates with the customer and tells him that he will consider what to do McGinnis v Smythe, 4 N. E. Rep, 759 (N Y 1886) The broker's telegrams and conversations with his customers may amount to a waiver of his right to demand further margin Rogers v Wiley, 14 N Y Supp, 622 (1891) When called upon for further margin, a customer may make a "stop-order," the price fixed in such "stop-order" being within the margin already furnished Campbell v Wright, 118 N Y, 594 (1890). The giving of a note to a broker pledgee does not extend the time within which the pledgor was to deposit further margin Gould v. Trask, 10 N Y Supp 619 (1890).

[3] Worthington i Tormey, 34 Md, 182 (1870). Two days' notice held sufficient. Stewart v. Drake, 46 N Y, 449 (1871). See, also, in general § 477, infra A notice after the sale is insufficient, and the question of whether a notice was given is for the jury if it is denied Gillett v Whiting, 120 N Y, 402 (1890).

[4] Baker i Drake, 66 N Y, 518 (1876) Cf Gregory v Wendall, 40 Mich, 432 (1879), involving a purchase of corn.

the broker is merely authorized to sell he is not bound to sell [1] If a broker sells illegally without giving due notice he cannot recover anything from his customer [2]

§ 459. *What will excuse notice and demand for more margin.*— All these rights of the customer to notice of failure of margin, demand of more margin, notice of intent to sell, and of time and place of sale, may be waived , and brokers generally require their customers to sign written contracts to that effect [3] It is doubtful whether the death of the customer will authorize the broker to close the transaction without notice [4] A custom of brokers to dispense with

Stocks alone, in brokers' transactions, give rise to the relation of pledgor and pledgee Where the broker closes the transaction without notice, and later the customer gives an order which, if the transaction had not been closed, would have yielded a profit, the customer may recover damages to the amount of that profit. Rogers *v* Wiley, 131 N Y , 527 (1892)

[1] Robinson *v* Norris, 51 How Pr 442 (1874). Esser *v* Linderman, 71 Pa St., 76 (1872) *Cf* Harris *v* Tumbridge, 83 N Y , 92 (1880) On a short sale of grain the broker is not bound to sell as soon as the principal refuses to advance more margin Penn *v* Parker, 18 N E. Rep , 747 (Ill , 1888)

[2] See note 2, p 574

[3] Thus, a written authority to the brokers "to sell at their discretion, at public or private sale without any notice whatever, the stocks or gold which they might be carrying for the plaintiff, whenever the margin should fall below " a certain figure, waives all the customer's rights herein Wicks *v* Hatch, 62 N Y , 535 (1875) See, also Cameron *v* Durkheim, 55 N Y , 425 (1874) The customer may waive his rights after the broker has made the unauthorized sale. Stewart *v* Drake, 46 N Y , 449 (1876), Milliken *v* Dehon, 27 N Y , 364 (1863) But authority "to close the account, without notice, by purchase or sale, at public or private sale," does not waive right to notice of failure of margin and demand for more Stenton *v* Jerome, 54 N Y , 480 (1873), Kenfield *v* Latham,

2 Cal Leg Rec , 235 The demand for further margin may be waived and waiver may be inferred from the negotiations and proposition Harris *v* Pryor, 18 N Y Supp , 128 (1892) A common form of the contract which the broker requires the customer to sign is the following

"—— hereby agree to maintain with you at all times a margin of —— per centum of the par value of all stocks and bonds against which you have made or may hereafter make advances to ——, and a like margin on stocks or bonds which —— have borrowed or may hereafter borrow through you to make deliveries on sales made for —— account or otherwise

"In case —— margin should become impaired and the same is not promptly made good in response to personal notice or notice sent by wire or letter and directed to —— usual address, you are authorized in your discretion to buy or sell at the New York Stock Exchange or at public or private sale without further notice, such securities as may be necessary to place the account in condition satisfactory to you or to close the same entirely, as you may prefer

"In case of my decease you are hereby authorized to close my account by purchase or sale of securities as the same may require ——"

[4] The broker will be protected in continuing the transaction until personal representatives are appointed Hess *v* Rau, 95 N Y , 359 (1884) *Cf* Lacey *v* Hill, L. R., 8 Ch App , 921 (1873).

these notices is void, and not binding on the customer.[1] The fact that a panic occurs, or unusual fluctuations of the market happen, does not excuse a broker from giving such notice.[2]

§ 460 *Customer's remedies and damages herein* — For an unauthorized sale by a broker of stock held upon a margin, the customer has ample remedies. He may claim the benefit of the sale or may claim the value of the stock.[3] Or the customer may require the broker to replace the stock, and upon his failure so to do, the customer may replace it himself and charge the broker with the loss.[4] Or the customer may recover the advance in the market price from the time of the sale up to a reasonable time to replace the stock after notice of the sale.[5] The unauthorized sale by the broker herein is not necessarily a fraudulent sale.[6] The suit should be at law,[7] and demand and tender need not be alleged.[8]

Where a broker buys or sells stock on his customer's account in violation of the terms of his contract, and thereby makes a profit, the customer has his option either to repudiate the transaction altogether and sue for damages, or he may adopt it and claim for himself the benefit made by his agent.[9] It has been held that,

[1] Markham v Jaudon, 41 N Y 235 (1869) Taylor v Ketchum, 35 How Pr, 289 (1861). S C, 5 Robt., 507 *Contra*. Appleman v Fisher, 34 Md, 540 (1871), a case of a gold-broker, also Colbert v Ellis, 10 Phil, 375 (1875), where both parties were brokers and knew the custom. If the customs are expressly made a part of the contract, insolvency of the customer authorizes sale without notice, such being the custom Lacy v Hill, L. R., 18 Eq, 182 (1874)

[2] Markham v. Jaudon, 41 N Y, 235 (1869), Brass v. Worth, 40 Barb, 648 (1863), Ritter v Cushman, 7 Robt. 294 (1867) See, also, § 448.

[3] Taussig v Hart, 58 N Y, 425 (1874), Caswell v Putnam, N Y Daily Reg, March 7, 1887, Strong v Nat'l, etc, Ass'n, 45 N Y., 718 (1871)

[4] Baker v Drake 53 N Y, 211, 217 (1873), Colt v Owens, 90 N Y, 368 (1882).

[5] Colt v Owens, 90 N Y, 368 (1882), holding that prices within thirty days after the sale is a reasonable rule See, also, Gruman v Smith, 81 N. Y, 25 (1880), Capron v. Thompson, 86 N. Y.,

418 (1881) *Cf* Andrews v Clerke, 3 Bosw, 585 (1858)

[6] Stratford v Jones, 97 N. Y., 586 (1885)

[7] Delevan v Simonson, 3 J. & S, 243 (1873). In the case of Butts v Burnett, 6 Abb Pr (N S), 302 (1869), involving the arrest of a broker who had sold the pledge before the note was due, the court said "It is very questionable, I think, whether a demand after default in payment of the debt for which property is pledged as security will render a refusal to deliver the pledged property a tortious conversion of it No doubt the pledgor can redeem upon a tender of the debt, or he may recover the difference between the value of the pledge and the debt But to lay the foundation for an action for commission, I am of opinion that an offer and demand must be made on the day, and is not sufficient if made after the day on which the debt has become payable."

[8] Clark v Meigs, 22 How. Pr, 240 (1873), 13 Abb Pr, 467

[9] Kimber v Barber, L. R., 8 Chan, 56 (1872), Marsh t Keating, 1 Bing. N. C., 198 (1834), Taussig v Hart, 49 N. Y., 301

where the broker fails to buy according to the instructions of his customer, and the customer suffers a loss by reason of the failure, the object of the purchase being to cover a short sale, the measure of damages is the difference between the price at which the stock was sold short and the market price upon the day when the order was given to the broker to buy in In other words, the plaintiff may in such a case recover the profits which he would necessarily have made had his order been properly executed [1] And the rule is the same when the loss to the customer results from the failure of the broker to sell as instructed, or where the broker sells at an improper or manifestly unfavorable time [2] A customer who owns

(1872); S C, 58 N Y, 425 (1874), Pickering v Demeritt, 100 Mass, 416 (1868) Day v Holmes, 103 id, 306 (1869) For the measure of damages where a broker converts his customer's securities, and then is unable by reason of his insolvency to replace them, see Chamberlain v Greenleaf, 4 Abb New Cas, 92, 178 Sometimes an advance in the price of the stock, within a reasonable time after notice of the conversion is received, is allowed Gruman v Smith, 81 N. Y., 25 (1880) See § 460 And what is a reasonable time in such a case is a question for the jury Baker v Drake, 66 N Y, 518 (1876), Stevens v Hurlbut Bank, 31 Conn, 146 (1862), Stewart v Cauty, 8 Mees. & W, 160 (1841), Field v Lelan, 6 Hill & N, 617 (1861) Cf Allen v Dykers, 3 Hill, 593 (1842), 6 N Y. Supp, 137

[1] In an action to recover damages, where a firm of stock-brokers sold for a customer, upon his order and for his account, three hundred shares of stock, short, at 186, and subsequently without the customer's order or knowledge bought in stock to cover the sale, and then a few days later, the stock having declined several points, the customer ordered them to cover their sale, to which order no attention was paid, it was held that the proper measure of damages was the difference between the price at which the stock was sold short and the market price upon the day when the order was received to purchase, with interest, deducting commissions, etc White v Smith, 54 N Y, 522 (1871) See Magee v Atkinson, 2 Mees & W, 440 (1837). In Allen v. McCombe, 124 N Y, 312 (1890), the court allowed as damages against a broker who delayed selling when ordered to sell, the difference between the price when the order was given and the price when the sale was actually made

[2] In Harris v Tumbridge 83 N Y, 92 (1880), it appears that the plaintiff purchased through the agency of the defendant a stock option, a privilege known as a "straddle," upon which the defendants guarantied that the fluctuations in the stock during the pendency of the contract should amount to eight per cent On the next day after the purchase defendant sold the stock short, which resulted in a loss to the plaintiff, who had at the time of the purchase authorized defendant, as her agent to exercise the option As to the measure of damages the court say "An objection is taken to the rule of damages It is insisted that, as plaintiff never gave any directions to 'put' or 'call' the stock, she should not have recovered as if she had But in the absence of such directions it was defendant's duty, under the circumstances of this case, as we have already said, to have closed the 'straddle' contract by exercising the option at the most favorable time, and to have acted for her in that respect with reasonable care and skill As he did not do so, she is entitled to recover what she has lost by

particular certificates of stock and pledges them with his broker may reclaim such certificates from the broker's assets upon the insolvency of the latter, but he cannot claim any particular stocks which the broker has purchased for him, even though he is able to identify them as being the ones which were purchased for him, inasmuch as his equities are no better than the equities of other customers[1] Where a party telegraphs to sell a certain stock, the sale to be "short" and speculative, the damages for failure of the telegraph company to deliver the message are too remote and speculative even though the stock goes down on the market.[2]

§ 461 *Brokers' remedies and damages herein.*— If a broker sells out his customer's stock without notice, he cannot recover any loss from the customer, even though the broker's loss is greater than the customer's usual measure of damages for the conversion.[3] But where the broker's act is strictly according to law, he is of course entitled to recover from his customer any loss that has been sustained in excess of the margin[4]

It is a well-settled rule that if a broker, acting in good faith and without default, incurs personal loss or damage in the course

his neglect, and the price of the stock from day to day during the running of the option having been shown, it was for the jury to determine that amount." *Cf* Speyer *v* Colgate, 4 Hun, 622 (1875) Where a broker sold stock for his customer without authority and in violation of an agreement not to sell, and it appeared that for thirty days after notice was given to the customer of the sale the stock could have been purchased in the market for the price at which it was sold or even for less, it was held, in an action to recover damages, that the customer, having had a reasonable time after he was notified of the sale of his stock to replace it at the same or a lower price, was entitled only to nominal damages Colt *v* Owens, 90 N Y, 368 (1882) *Cf.* Randall *v* Albany City National Bank, 1 N Y State Rep, 592 (Sept 1886). See, also, McArthur *v* Seaforth, 2 Taunt., 257 But when the action of the broker is fraudulent the customer may, upon obtaining knowledge of the facts repudiate the whole transaction and recover back the money paid Levy *v* Loeb, 89 N Y, 386 (1882), reversing S C, 15 Jones &

Spencer, 61 *Cf* Stewart *v* Drake, 46 N Y, 449 (1871) In Baker *v* Drake, *supra*, where a broker unauthorized to do so sold stock which he was carrying for his customer, it was held, in an action for damages, that the measure of damages was the advance in the market price from the time of the sale up to a reasonable time to replace it after notice of sale

[1] Sillcocks *v* Gallaudet, 66 Hun, 522 (1892) As to sub-brokers or correspondent brokers, see § 456.

[2] Cahn *v* W U Tel Co., 48 Fed Rep, 810 (1891), 46 id, 40 The measure of damages for error in the delivery of telegraph messages to buy stock is the "difference between the market value of the shares at the time when the dispatch should have been delivered and the sum paid for them in the market on the receipt of the message" Pearsall *v* Western U Tel Co, 124 N. Y., 256 (1890)

[3] Gillett *v* Whiting, 120 N Y., 402 (1890) *Contra*, Gruman *v* Smith, 81 N Y, 25 (1880) See, also, Capron *v*. Thompson, 86 N Y, 418 (1881), and § 458

[4] Schepeler *v* Eisner, 3 Daly, 11 (1869).

of transacting the business of his agency, or in following the instructions of his principal, he may recover from the principal full
compensation therefor [1]   Accordingly, where a broker buys stock
upon his customer's order and pays for it, and upon a decline in
value the customer refuses to accept it, the broker may recover the
price paid by him, and not merely the difference between that
price and the market value on the day of his demand [2]

§ 462 *Brokers' customs and usages* — It has been a greatly disputed question as to how far and when a custom or usage among
stock-brokers or at stock exchanges may enter into and govern
stock-brokers' contracts   At an early day the rule was laid down
by the English courts, that he who buys or sells stock through a
stock-broker must be considered as dealing with him according to
the usages of the market in which he deals, and the customs which
prevail in relation to that species of business [3]   The American rule

[1] Sedgwick on Damages (7th ed), 86,
Lindley on Partnership (4th ed), 731,
where the English authorities upon the
right of a stock-broker to indemnity
from his principal, and the measure of
damages in such cases, are collected
and fully considered, citing Sutton *v*
Tatham, 10 Ad & E, 27 (1839)   Bayliffe *v* Butterworth, 1 Exch, 425,
Bowlby *v* Bell, 3 C B 284, Bayley *v*
Wilkins, 7 id, 886 (1849)   McEwen *v*.
Woods, 2 Car & K 330, Taylor *v*
Stray, 2 C B (N S), 175   Stray *v* Russell, 1 El & El, 888, Chapman *v* Shepherd, L R, 2 C P, 228, Biederman *v*
Stone, id, 504   Mollett *v* Robinson, L R,
7 H L, 802; S. C, 7 C P 84   5 C P,
646; Pollock *v* Stables, 12 Q B, 765,
Lacey *v* Hill, 8 Chan, 921, Dos Passos
on Stock-brokers 123 802

[2] Giddings *v* Sears, 103 Mass, 311
Cf Field *v* Kinnear, 4 Kan, 476
Where there is a rescission of a contract
for the sale of stock, the measure of the
damages is the value of the stock at the
time and place of the proposed delivery
White *v*. Salisbury, 33 Mo 150 (1862),
Vance *v* Tourne, 13 La, 225

[3] In the case of Biederman *v* Stone,
L. R., 2 Com Pl, 504 (1867), the court
says "It has been held in a great number of cases that persons buying or selling stock or shares through members of
the stock exchange are bound by the
rules which govern the transactions of
that body"   To the same effect, see
Bayliffe *v* Butterworth, 5 Railw Cas.,
283, per Parke, B, Mitchell *v* Newhall,
15 Mees & W, 308 (1846), Maxted *v*
Paine (2d action), L R, 6 Ex 132 (1871).
Grissell *v* Bristowe, L R, 4 C P 36, 47
(1868), Appleman *v* Fisher, 34 Md, 540
(1871), Coles *v* Bristowe, L R, 4 Ch
App. 3, Stray *v* Russell, 1 El & El,
888 (1859), Davis *v* Maycock, L R 4 Ex,
373 (1869), Nickalls *v* Merry, L R 7
H L, 530 (1875)   Cf Pollock *v* Stables,
12 Q B, 765 (1848)   Taylor *v* Stray, 2
C B (N S), 197 (1857), Morrice *v* Hunter, 14 L T, 897, Kingsbury *v* Kirwin,
43 Super Ct, 451 (1878), 77 N Y, 612
But the usage must not be illegal   Robinson *v* Mollett, L R, 7 H L, 802, 818,
826 (1874), Hodgkinson *v* Kelly, 37
L. J (Ch), 837 (1868), Taylor *v* The
Great Indian Peninsular R y Co, 4 De G
& J, 559, 573 (1859).   Nor be the custom
established by that one transaction
Westropp *v* Solaman, 8 C B, 345 (1849).
It must be reasonable   Goldschmidt *v*
Jones, 32 L T (N S), 220   The usage
may show how the business is to be
transacted, but must not be unreasonable   Rosenstock *v* Tormey, 32 Md, 169
(1869), holding also that the broker s
correspondence with his city broker is
not competent to prove purchases and
sales.   A usage that is contrary to an

is more guarded, and allows usages of brokers to interpret the language of the contract, and where it is obscure to ascertain its nature and extent, but not to vary its terms, introduce new conditions or authorize acts contrary to its provision[1] The customer may, however, by express agreement, waive his common-law rights and allow usage to govern the transaction[2]

act of parliament, requiring the broker to notify his customer of the particular numbers of the shares purchased on his account. is void. Perry v Barnett. L. R., 15 Q B D, 388 (1885) Cf Seymour v Bridge, L. R., 14 Q B D, 460 (1885).

[1] Parsons v Martin, 77 Mass, 111 (1858) Hopper v Sage, 112 N Y, 530 (1889), Lombardo v Case, 39 How Pr, 117 (1865), 1 Add Contr (4th Amer, 8th Eng, ed, 1883), marg p 60, c 2, 21 Am L Reg (N S), 176 Cf Winans v Hassey, 48 Cal, 634 (1874) The case of Baker v Drake 66 N Y, 518 (1876), holds that stock-brokers' usage cannot add to or make part of the contract. Cf Horton v Morgan, 19 N Y, 170 (1859), Peckham v Ketchum, 5 Bosw, 506 (1859), Whitehouse v Moore, 13 Abb., 142 (1861) If there is doubt as to the existence of the usage the question is for the jury Dent v Nickalls, 29 L T, 636 (1873). Upon the effect of usage in other transactions, see Corn Ex Bank v Nassau Bank, 91 N Y, 74 (1883), Richmond v Union Steamboat Co, 87 N. Y, 240 (1881), Walls v Bailey, 49 N. Y, 464 (1872), Vail v Rice, 5 N Y, 155 (1851), Delafield v State of Illinois, 26 Wend, 192 (1841), Dawson v Kittle, 4 Hill, 107 (1843), Boardman v Gaillard, 1 Hun, 217 (1874), Minnesota C R'y Co. v Morgan, 52 Barb., 217 (1868), Sipperly v Stewart, 50 Barb, 62, 68 (1867), Duguid v Edwards, 50 Barb, 288 (1867), Haskins v Warren, 115 Mass, 514, 536 (1874), Dickinson v Gay, 89 Mass, 29, Parrott v Thatcher, 26 Mass, 426 (1830), Greenleaf v Moody, 13 Allen, 363 (1866), Tilley v County of Cook, 103 U S, 155 (1880), National Bank v Burkhardt 100 U S, 686 (1879), Vermilye v Adams Ex. Co., 21 Wall, 138 (1874), Forrester

v Boardman, 1 Story, 43 (1839); Oelrichs v Ford, 23 How, 49 (1859); Renner v. Bank of Columbia, 9 Wheat, 582 (1824); Cape v. Dodd, 13 Pa. St., 33 (1850); Corbett v. Underwood, 83 Ill, 324 (1876); Phillips v Moir, 69 Ill, 155 (1873), Bissell v Ryan, 23 Ill, 566 (1860), Williams v. Gilman, 3 Maine, 276 (1825), Partridge v Forsythe, 29 Ala, 200 (1856), Halwerson v Cole, 1 Spear (S. C), 321 (1843); Hagg v Snaith, 1 Taunton, 347 (1808), Gibson v Crick, 1 H. & C., 142 (1862), Fleet v Murton, L. R, 7 Q B., 126 (1871). Brokers' usages cannot vary fixed principles of law Hopper v Sage, 20 N E Rep, 350 (N. Y, 1889).

[2] Van Brunt, J, in Robinson v Norris, 51 How Pr, 442 (1874), says, in his clear and decisive diction· "It has been settled by our court of appeals that no custom among brokers can deprive parties of rights which the law gives them, but they have not decided that these rights may not be waived by agreement I think it perfectly clear that, if the broker informs his customer of the terms upon which he will act for him as his broker, and in view of that notice the customer gives an order, he is bound by the terms on which the broker proposed to act for him" See, also, Baker v Drake, 66 N Y, 578 (1876). See, in general, Colket v Ellis, 32 Leg Int., 82 (1875), Sutton v Tatham, 10 Ad. & El, 25 (1839); Bayley v Wilkins, 18 L J (C P), 273 (1849), Duncan v Hill, L R, 6 Ex, 255 (1871); Sheppard v Murphy, Ir L R, 2 Eq, 569 (1868), Bowring v Shepherd, L. R, 6 Q. B, 309 (1871), Evans v. Waln, 71 Pa. St., 69 (1872), Sweeting v. Pearce, 7 C. B. (N S), 449 (1859), Shaw v. Spencer, 100 Mass, 382 (1868), Day v. Holmes, 103 Mass, 306 (1869).

CHAPTER XXVI.

PLEDGES AND MORTGAGES OF STOCK

§ 463 *Definition of pledge, mortgage and lien.* — A pledge may be defined to be a delivery of personal property as a security for some debt or engagement A mortgage of personalty, on the other hand, is a sale with the condition attached, that, if the mortgagor performs some act, the sale shall be void. In a pledge the title remains in the pledgor, and the pledgee has a special property in the thing pledged[1] In a mortgage the title passes to the mortgagee, subject to being revested in the mortgagor upon payment of the debt In pledges the thing pledged must be delivered to the pledgee. In mortgages, generally, the possession of the thing mortgaged remains with the mortgagor.

A pledge differs also from a lien A pledge, by implication, gives the pledgee a power to sell on due notice, in case the debt is not paid at maturity, while a lien gives merely the power of detention until the debt is paid[2]

§ 464 *Mortgages and pledges of stock* — Shares of stock may be the subject of a mortgage or pledge[3] A mortgage of stock, how-

---

[1] See Parsons on Contracts, I, p. 569, II, p 113, III, p 272

[2] Donald v Suckling, L R, 1 Q B, 604

[3] "Nothing is better settled than that shares in the capital stock of a corporation are the subject of pledge." Dayton

ever, is not often made, and, unless there is a clear intent to the contrary, the courts will treat the transaction as a pledge rather than a mortgage[1] In fact, it is difficult to ascertain from the cases how shares of stock may be mortgaged, and a few early decisions, which held certain transactions to be mortgages, would to-day be held to be pledges[2] There are but few clear cases of a mortgage of stock

Nat l Bank r Merchants' Nat'l Bank, 37 Ohio St, 208 (1881) "It was formerly doubted whether it [stock] could be the subject of a pledge, but it is now held that it can be" Newton r Fay, 92 Mass 505 (1865). The pledge may be for a running liability, and is not released by an extension of any particular debt Merchants' Nat l Bank r Hall, 83 N Y, 338 (1881) Stock may be given by the debtor to his creditor to sell for the benefit of the creditor and the surplus to be returned to the debtor Beckwith r Burrough, 13 R I, 294 (1881) This probably makes the creditor the agent of the debtor The pledge may be to secure the carrying out of a contract. Vaupell r Woodward, 2 Sandf Ch 143 (1844) If the loan secured by the pledge of stock is usurious the pledgor may recover back the stock without payment The pledge is void Cousland r Davis, 5 Bosw, 619 (1859) If stock is pledged to secure an usurious note, the pledgor may under the New York law sue to recover back the stock without paying the debt. Dickson r Valentine 6 N Y Supp 540 (1889), also § 466 The pledge of stock may provide that, for part payments of the debt, the pledgor may withdraw part of the stock pledged First Nat l Bank r Root, 8 N E Rep, 105 (Ind, 1886) If a person agrees to deposit stock to secure the debt of another and fails to do so, he is liable, not for the debt, but for the value of the stock Appeal of American, etc., Co, 12 Atl Rep, 270 (Pa, 1887). As to pledges to secure parties who advance money to the company, see ch XX and § 76

[1] Newton r Fay, supra Nabring r Bank of Mobile, 58 Ala, 204 (1877) Mer-

chants' Bank r Cook, 4 Pick, 405 (1826), Mechanics', etc, Association r Conover, 14 N J Eq, 219 (1862), Doak r Bank of the State, 6 Ired L, 309 (1846) In England security is given by a process called a sale with a contract of repurchase The court holds that this is not a pledge 'An essential term of a pledge is that on fulfillment by the pledgor of the conditions of the bargain, commonly called redemption, the pledgee is bound to hand back to the pledgor the very thing deposited with him " Whereas in a sale and contract of repurchase, the identical property in numbers, etc need not be returned Simmons r Joint, etc, Bank, 62 L T. Rep, 427 (1890)

[2] Thus, in Huntington r Mather, 2 Barb, 538 (1848), the court say "There are two leading considerations to be regarded in determining whether the transaction is a pledge or a mortgage, namely, the title and the possession If it is a mortgage, the legal title passes to and is vested in the creditor With a pledge it is different, the legal title, until a sale on default of payment or redemption, continuing in the pledgor .   The essential difference as to matter of right is that in one the title passes and in the other it does not But the difference in substance and fact is that, in the case of a pawn or pledge, the possession must pass out of the pawnor, but in the case of a mortgagor it need not " The court, however, influenced probably by the equities of the case, held the transaction to be a mortgage, and that the right of the debtor to redeem was barred by the ten-year statute of limitations In the case of Smith r 49 and 56 Quartz Min Co., 14 Cal,

to be found It seems that a formal instrument of chattel mortgage of stock, duly executed and registered at the municipal clerk's office, as required by law in case of chattel mortgages, would not constitute an effectual mortgage of stock, and the mortgagee would not be protected where he does not receive the certificate of stock from the mortgagor, or does not obtain a registry of transfer on the corporate books [1] Where a railroad company owns shares of

242 (1859), the court held the transaction to be a mortgage rather than a conditional sale of the stock The question of pledge was not considered Manns v Brookville Nat'l Bank, 73 Ind, 243 (1881), speaks of the transaction as a mortgage, and Williamson v New Jersey Southern R. R. Co, 26 N J Eq, 398 (1875), says that such a mortgage need not be recorded in the municipal clerk's office as required by the chattel mortgage act. In both cases the transaction might better have been treated as a pledge. In Adderly v Storm, 6 Hill, 624 (1844), the court said "I have already said that this was not a pawn or pledge of the stock neither was it strictly a mortgage" At the present day it would be held to be a pledge Wilson v Little, 2 N Y, 443 (1849); Hasbrouck v Vandervoort, 4 Sand, 74 (1850) In the case of Brewster v Hartley, 37 Cal, 15 (1869), the court say "The transfer in writing of shares of stock not only does not prove that the transaction is not a pledge, but the stock, unless it is expressly made assignable by the delivery of the certificates, cannot be pledged in any other manner In the case of Thompson v. Holladay, 14 Pac Rep, — (Oreg, 1887), a chattel mortgage on shares of stock was involved. It was declared void because it was given to a receiver who previously held the stock as receiver Sometimes a chattel mortgage of stock arises where a railroad mortgage covers not only real estate, but also all personal property, bonds and stock which are or shall be owned by the mortgagor corporation

[1] The clearest and most satisfactory

case is Spalding v Paine's Adm'r, 81 Ky, 416 (1883), where a chattel mortgage of a share of stock was duly recorded in the proper county, the mortgagor retaining the certificate of stock The mortgagor subsequently sold and transferred the certificate of stock to a *bona fide* purchaser The court held that the recording of the mortgage was of no avail, that there could be no mortgage of choses in action, and that the *bona fide* transferee took the stock Pryor, J, well says Much of the business of the country is conducted on the faith of the pledge of such stock as collaterals, and to adjudge that the holder of the stock by transfer on the books of the corporation, or by indorsement and delivery by the owner, is subordinate in his claim to the mortgagee, upon the doctrine of constructive notice, would paralyze trade and open a wide field for the fraudulent disposition of such valuable interests at the expense of honest and confiding purchasers" Cf Manns v Brookville Nat'l Bank, 72 Ind, 243 (1881), Foster v Potter, 37 Mo., 525, Vowell v Thompson, 3 Cranch, 428 (1859) See, also, Holyoke v McMurtry, 50 N W Rep, 767 (Neb, 1891) A mortgage of stock is valid as between mortgagor and mortgagee without a transfer of certificates The mortgagee after foreclosure may compel the corporation to transfer without making the transferee a party. Tregear v Etiwanda, etc, Co, 18 Pac Rep, 658 (Cal, 1888). Stock may be mortgaged and no delivery of the certificates need be made Though a foreclosure is made irregularly, the mortgagor may ratify it, or may be barred by the six-year statute

stock in an elevator company, such stock is not subject to the general mortgage executed by the railroad company.[1] A pledge of stock without a delivery is not strictly and legally a pledge. It "may have amounted to a mortgage, but it could amount to nothing more, and if a mortgage, it did not place the mortgagee in possession, but gave him merely a naked right to have the property appropriated and applied to the payment of his debt."[2] A mere direction to the corporation cannot constitute a pledge.[3] But where no certificate has been issued to the stockholder he may pledge the stock by an instrument in writing.[4] Where, on the other hand, the certificate of stock is delivered to the creditor as security, it is evident that possession of the property is given to

of limitations. Campbell v Woodstock Iron Co, 3 S Rep, 369 (Ala, 1887)

[1] Humphreys v McKissock, 140 U S, 304 (1891) A chattel mortgage does not include shares of stock, although broad enough in its terms to do so, where both parties testify that it was not the intent to include the stock, and the mortgagee allowed the mortgagor's assignee to take away the stock Younkin v Collier, 47 Fed Rep, 571 (1891)

[2] Christian v Atlantic, etc, R. R. 133 U S, 233, 242 (1890). A pledge to secure the debt of another is not waived by temporarily allowing that other to have the pledge for a short time Wing v Holland T Co, 5 N Y Supp., 382 (1889). An agreement that certain bonds in the possession of a third party shall be held in pledge is not a good pledge Actual delivery is necessary to constitute a pledge Seymour v Hendee, 54 Fed Rep, 563 (Vt., 1893). Where stock is placed in a trustee's hands and a trustee's certificate is taken therefor a pledge of the trustee's certificate is not a pledge of the stock sufficient to cut off subsequent attachments of the stock Bidstrup v Thompson, 45 Fed Rep, 452 (1891) Where one party loans money to another party to buy stock in a certain company, such stock to be delivered to the former party in pledge, and the latter party uses the stock for another purpose, the loan of the money is not a

mere loan, but the money is impressed with a trust, and this trust follows the stock except as against *bona fide* holders. Barnard v Hawks, 16 S. E Rep, 329 (N C, 1892) A pledge made by a separate written assignment of the stock, the certificates remaining in the pledgor's possession and continuing to stand in his name on the corporate books, is not good as against the pledgor's receiver who takes possession of the certificates. Atkinson v. Foster, 25 N E. Rep, 528 (Ill, 1890).

[3] Cumming v Prescott, 2 Y. & C (Ex), 488 (1837), Lallande v. Ingram, 19 La Ann, 364 (1867), the court saying "In all cases of pledge, the pledgee must be put in possession of the thing pledged, and, if it be a claim, the evidence of the obligation must be transferred and delivered Shares in stock cannot be pledged unless they be evidenced by certificates which must be transferred and delivered to the pledgee." But see § 465

[4] First Nat. Bank v. Gifford, 47 Iowa, 575 (1877), where such a pledgee was protected against a third person who had advanced the money to the pledgor to purchase the stock See, also, Brigham v Mead, 92 Mass, 245 (1865); Thorp v Woodhull, 1 Sand Ch, 411 (1844) Unissued stock may be pledged by the person entitled to it. When issued, it at once becomes a pledge Appeal of Harris, 12 Atl. Rep., 743 (Pa, 1888).

the creditor, but that the debtor still considers the stock to be his
Such a transaction is a pledge and a mortgage, and consequently,
since the giving of stock certificates as security is almost invariably
effected by a delivery of the certificates, a mortgage of stock may
be said to be possible, but not probable or even sensible. The delivery of a certificate of stock with a blank power of attorney, as
collateral security, constitutes a pledge and not a mortgage,[1] and
the same rule prevails even though an absolute transfer or registry
is made on the corporate books[2]

§ 465 *How a pledge of stock arises or is made —* A pledge of
stock is generally made by a delivery of the certificates of stock
indorsed in blank to the pledgee, and a memorandum in writing
to the effect that the stock is held in pledge is generally signed and
given to the pledgor, and a copy thereof attached to the certificates
of stock   In a few cases a mere delivery of the certificate without
a written transfer has been held sufficient to constitute a pledge[3]
A mere delivery of the certificate of stock indorsed in blank, however, is sufficient to constitute a pledge, without any memorandum
in writing to that effect, and without a registry of the same being
made on the corporate books[4] Not even a provision of the charter or a by-law of the corporation to the effect that transfers are
not valid until registered on the corporate books can prevent a
pledge of stock being made by a mere delivery of the certificates
indorsed in blank, or indorsed to the pledgee, without such registry[5] The provision requiring such registry would seem not to

---

[1] Mechanics' B. & L. Association v
Conover, 14 N J Eq, 219 (1862), Lewis
v Graham, 4 Abb Pr, 106 (1857) But
see Greene v Dispean, 14 R I, 375
(1884)

[2] Nabring v Bank of Mobile, 58 A'a,
204 (1877) Wilson v Little, 2 N Y, 443
(1849) The question of whether a sale
or pledge was involved in the relations
between a contractor and the party who
financed the matter for him was discussed in Griggs v. Day, 11 N Y. Supp,
885 (1890).

[3] See Brewster v Hartley, 37 Cal, 15,
Jarvis v Rogers, 13 Mass, 105, Robinson v. Hurley, 11 Iowa, 410, but see
Lollande v Ingram, 19 La Ann, 364
(1867), United States v Cutts, Sumner,
133 *Contra,* Nisbit v Macon, etc Co,
12 Fed Rep, 686 (1882) See, also, § 375,
infra A pledge of the certificates of
stock is effective without notice to the

corporation Crescent, etc, Co v De-
blieux, 3 S Rep., 726 (La, 1888)

[4] Mount Holly, etc, Co v Ferree, 17
N J Eq 117 (1864); Finney s Appeal,
59 Pa St, 398 (1868), Blouin v Liqui-
dators, etc, 30 La Ann, 714 (1878)
Merchants' Nat'l Bank v Richards, 6
Mo App, 454 (1879), aff'd, 74 Mo, 77,
Broadway Bank v McElrath, 13 N J
Eq, 24 (1860), Cornick v Richards, 3 Lea
1 (1879), Baldwin v Canfield, 26 Minn, 43
(1879), Pitot v Johnson, 33 La Ann,
1286 (1881), New Orleans Nat'l Banking
Ass'n v Wiltz, 10 Fed Rep, 330 (1881),
Continental Nat'l Bank v Eliot Nat'l
Bank, 12 Rep, 35 (1881) *Cf* State v
First Nat'l Bank, 89 Ind, 302 (1883) The
pledgor may, by word of mouth, extend
stock already pledged to further ad-
vancements by the pledgee Van Blarcom
v Broadway Bank, 9 Bosw, 532 (1862)

[5] McNeil v Tenth Nat'l Bank, 46 N. Y.,

concern the pledgee in any way, except that he could not claim the dividends without the registry, and in a few states, where an attachment of the stock for the pledgor's debts would cut off a previous unregistered vendee's or pledgee's rights, he by not registering encounters that risk[1] A transfer of stock, whether registered on the corporate books or not, may be shown to be a pledge, and parol evidence is admissible to prove that fact.[2]

325 (1871) Dickinson i Central Nat l Bank 129 Mass, 279 (1880), Fraser r Charleston. 11 S C, 486 (1878), Factors' & T Ins Co i Marine D D Co, 31 La Ann. 149 (1879), Pitot r Johnson 33 La Ann 1256 (1881), Continental Nat'l Bank i Eliot Nat l Bank, *supra*, Lowry r Com Bank, Taney, 310 (1848), Blouin r Liquidators etc, 30 La Ann, 714 (1878) Lightner's Appeal 82 Pa St, 301 United States i Cutts 1 Sumn, 133 (1832), Leitch i Wells 48 N Y, 585 (1872), Commercial Bank of Buffalo i Kortright, 22 Wend, 348 (1839), aff g 20 Wend, 91, Otis i Gardner, 105 Ill, 436 (1883) As regards such provisions requiring registry, a pledge of stock stands on the same footing as a sale of stock See, also § 379, *supra* The unregistered pledge is protected against the pledgor s assignee in bankruptcy *Re* Shelly, 34 L J (Bankr), 6 (1865)

[1] Thus, in states where an attachment has precedence over not only transfers without registry made after the attachment is levied, but over unregistered transfers made before the levy of attachment, a pledge, like a sale of stock is protected against attachment on the pledgor s debts only by registry. Weston i Bear R. & A. Co, 5 Cal, 186 (1855), Williams r Mechanics' Bank, 5 Blatchf, 59 (1862) State Ins Co r Sax, 2 Tenn Ch, 507 (1875), State i First Nat'l Bank. 89 Ind, 302 (1883), Shipman i Ætna Ins Co. 29 Conn, 245 (1860) Pinkerton r Manchester, etc, R R. Co, 42 N H, 424 (1861), Oxford Turnpike Co i Brund, 6 Conn, 552 (1827). *Cf* Strout r Natoma W & M Co, 9 Cal, 78 (1858). But the purchaser at the execution sale is not protected

against the pledgee, if he purchased with notice Weston r Bear R. & A Co 6 Cal, 425 (1856) And if notice of the pledge is given to the corporation, the pledgee is protected against attachments, although no registry is had State Ins Co i Gennett, 2 Tenn. Ch, 100 (1874 See, also, § 486 *et seq* As regards the ordinary rights of stockholdership, it is no object to the pledgee to obtain registry. Even if registered he cannot vote nor have a voice in corporate meetings. See § 468 As to the dividends, however, he is entitled to them as against the pledgor, but of course can obtain them from the corporation only by obtaining registry

[2] Brick i Brick 98 U S, 514 (1878), Wilson i Little, 2 N Y, 443 (1849); Ginz i Stumph, 73 Ind, 209 (1880), Newton i Fay, 92 Mass, 505 (1865), McMahon r Macy, 51 N. Y, 155 (1872); Becher r Wells Flouring Mill Co, 1 Fed Rep, 276 (1880), Burgess r Seligman, 107 U S, 20 (1882), Pinkerton v. Railroad Co, 42 N H, 424; Butman r Howell, 10 N E Rep., 504 (Mass, 1887). An apparent sale of stock is not proven to be a pledge on the evidence of plaintiff contradicted by defendant, when the full value of the stock was paid and a receipt therefor given by the plaintiff Travers i Leopold, 16 N E Rep, 902 (Ill, 1888). A pledgor may bring a suit for an accounting and to establish the fact that the transfer of stock was a pledge, and he may restrain a suit by the pledgee against the corporation for the stock McDowell's Appeal, 16 Atl Rep, 753 (Pa, 1889); 5 N Y. Supp, 650.

A corporation may pledge its unissued stock,[1] but there is a difference of opinion as to whether the pledgee is liable as an absolute stockholder on such stock[2] The question of usury in the note secured by a pledge of stock may affect the pledge itself[3] A *bona fide* pledgee of stock is protected against claims of former owners of that stock to the same extent that an absolute purchaser of the stock would be protected The *quasi*-negotiability of certificates of stock protects a pledgee and a vendee alike[4] The negotiability of a note is not destroyed by a provision that certain bonds are given as collateral security for its payment[5]

§ 466 *Pledgee may have the stock registered in his own name or the name of another* — Where certificates of stock indorsed in blank are delivered to a person in pledge as collateral security for a debt or for any other purpose, the pledgee may fill in the blanks and have the stock registered in his own name on the corporate books[6]

[1] Fisher t Seligman 7 Mo App 383 (1879) Griswold t Seligman 72 Mo 110 (1880) Burgess t Seligman, 107 U S, 20 (1882). Melvin t Lamar Ins Co, 80 Ill, 446 (1875) Protection Ins Co r Osgood, 93 Ill 69 (1879) *Contra* Brewster t Hartley 37 Cal 15 (1869) Where a corporation pledges its own stock the pledgee may sell that stock for nonpayment of the debt at less than par This rule prevails even though the charter provides that the stock shall not be sold below par Peterborough etc, R R Co t Nashua etc, R R Co, 59 N H, 385 (1879) Unissued stock may be issued by the corporation as a pledge to secure a loan, and the corporation cannot set up that it was issued at less than par in violation of the constitution The issue is good in the hands of the pledgee to the extent of the loan Casquet t Crescent City B Co, 49 Hun 496 (1892). Where the company issues its stock as collateral security to notes given to it by its subscribers in payment for such stock and then sells the notes the stock follows the notes and may be subjected to the payment of judgments on the notes If the corporation has issued the stock to others it must pay the judgments Houston etc, R y t Bremond 18 S W Rep, 448 (Tex, 1886). A mortgage is valid as against the corporation giving it although the officers give to the mortgagee their individual notes as additional security and cause the corporation to issue stock to themselves without payment, which they deposit also as collateral with the mortgagee The giving of the mortgage is not an increase of indebtedness such as is prohibited by the Pennsylvania constitution Powell s Appeal 19 Atl Rep 559 (Pa 1890) Questions relative to the pledge by a company of its own bonds are considered elsewhere See ch XLVI

[2] See §§ 138 247, 474

[3] See Little t Barker t Hoff Ch, 487 (1840) and cases on p 581, n 3 *supra*, and see Frost t Stokes 55 N Y Sup Ct 76 (1887), holding that the New York statute of 1882 allows any interest if the debt is over $5,000 and stock is pledged

[4] See § 432. *supra*

[5] Valley Nat'l Bank t Crowell, 23 Atl Rep 1068 (Pa, 1892)

[6] Hubbell t Drexel 11 Fed Rep, 115 (1882), *Re* Angelo 5 De G & S, 278 (1852), Horton r Morgan 19 N Y 170 (1859), Union & P Bank t Farrington, 13 Lea (Tenn), 333 (1884) Hiatt t Griswold, 5 Fed Rep, 573 (1881) holding also that a surety is not thereby discharged. Smith r Traders' Nat'l Bank 17 S W Rep, 779 (Tex, 1891); Day t. Holmes, 103 Mass, 306 (1869),

or the pledgee may have the stock registered in the name of another person, in order that he may protect his special property in the stock and at the same time not be liable thereon [1]

§ 467. *Stock-broker purchasing stock for a customer on a margin is a pledgee of the stock* — It has been well established that, where a stock-broker purchases stock on an order from his customer, and the customer does not pay for the stock, but deposits with the broker a sum of money called a "margin," to protect the broker against loss, the broker is bound to have on hand the stock so purchased during the entire time of the contract, and has the rights, duties and liabilities of a pledgee, with the customer as a pledgor [2] The broker under such circumstances must conform to all the rules governing a pledgee's attitude towards a pledgor He cannot repledge nor sell without due notice, unless such rights be waived by the customer, the pledgor [3]

§ 468 *Miscellaneous rights of pledgee and pledgor.* — Dividends declared during the continuance of the pledge belong to the pledgee, even though the latter is not registered as owner on the corporate books [4] The pledgee is entitled to the dividends on the stock, but must account for them when the pledge is redeemed.[5] A pledgee may surrender his certificate to the corporation and take a new certificate for a larger number of shares where the corporation has decreased the par value of the stock.[6] Where the pledgor pledged

Fitchburg Sav Bank *v* Torrey, 134 Mass , 239 (1883), also holding that a release of the stock by the pledgee releases a surety , Fay *v* Gray, 124 Mass , 500 (1878). *Cf.* State *v* Smith, 15 Oreg , 98, 114, but see p 132 (1887). The pledgee may sue to have the pledge transferred to himself and determine the rights of other claimants Newcombe *v* Lottimer, 12 N Y Supp , 381 (1890). Corporation must allow the registry. Cornick *v* Richards, 3 Lea (Tenn), 1 (1879)

[1] Day *v* Holmes, *supra*, Heath *v* Griswold, 5 Fed Rep , 573, Anderson *v*. Philadelphia Warehouse Co , 111 U. S, 479 (1884) See, also, § 470

[2] Baker *v*. Drake, 66 N Y , 518 (1876), Markham *v* Jaudon, 41 N Y , 235 (1869), and see ch XXV. A broker holding stock as collateral security on a margin does not hold the stock in a fiduciary capacity McBurney *v* Martin, 6 Rob, 502 , Lambertson *v* Van Boskerk, 49 How , 266, 4 Hun, 628.

[3] See ch XXV

[4] Herriman *v*. Maxwell, 47 Super. Ct., 347 (1881). And the pledgor who collects them holds them in trust for the pledgee. Hill *v* Newichawanick Co , 8 Hun, 459; affirmed, 72 N. Y , 599 (1887). In Central Nebraska, etc , Bank *v*. Wilder, 49 N W. Rep , 369 (Neb , 1891), it was held that not only was the pledgee entitled to the dividends, but was entitled to them although the stock stood on the corporate books in the name of the pledgor, where the officers knew all about the pledge Where a pledge of stock is renewed and a new note given, dividends accruing before the renewal go to the pledgor Fairbank *v* Merchants', etc , Bank 22 N E. Rep , 524 (Ill , 1889)

[5] Isaac *v* Clarke, 2 Bulst , 306 (1858); Hasbrouck *v* Vandervoort, 4 Sandf , 74 (1850), Edwards on Bailments, 300.

[6] Donnell *v* Wyckoff, 7 Atl. Rep., 672 (N J., 1887).

the stock to secure the debts of another at a bank and renewals thereof, the pledge continues though the pledgor dies [1] As against the pledgor a pledgee has not the right to vote on the pledged stock, even though he is registered as a stockholder [2] If so registered the pledgor may compel him, by legal proceedings, to give a proxy for voting purposes [3] A pledgee is not bound to protect the stock from forfeiture for non payment of calls [4] A pledgee of certificates of stock is protected against further sales or pledges of the same stock by the pledgor, such other sales or pledges being without the delivery of any certificate, the same as the vendee of a certificate of stock is protected against another sale of the stock to a purchaser who takes without any certificate [5] The possession of the certificate protects the pledgee herein The pledgee is not liable for a loss of the pledge by theft, there being no negligence on his part.[6]

A pledgee of a certificate of stock is not bound by an agreement of all the stockholders to surrender to the corporation a part of their stock, which part is to be then considered preferred stock and is to be sold by the corporation for the purpose of paying corporate debts [7] The stockholders of a corporation may together with the directors cause the corporate property to be sold to a new corporation in exchange for the stock of the latter. A pledgee of stock in the former corporation cannot after the sale undo it, nor hold the latter corporation liable His remedy is against the pledgor and the first corporation.[8] Although the pledgor of

---

[1] Cotton v Atlas Nat'l Bank, 12 N E. Rep, 850 (Mass, 1887)

[2] Baldwin v Canfield, 26 Minn, 43 (1879) See, also, Merchants' Bank v Cook, 4 Pick, 405 (1826), Ex parte Willcock, 7 Cowen, 402, McDaniels v Flower, etc., Co, 22 Vt. 274 (1850), Laws of N Y, 1850, ch 140, § 5 Butterworth v Kennedy, 5 Bosw, 143 (1859) The pledgor may cause the corporate property to be leased at a rental which will not yield any dividends, and yet the pledgee cannot attack the validity of the lease Gibson v Richmond, etc, R R. Co, 37 Fed. Rep, 743 (1889)

[3] See ch XXXVII

[4] Southwestern R R. Bank v. Douglas, 2 Spear (S C.), 329 (1844).

[5] Maybin v Kirby, 4 Rich Eq, 105 See § 321. The cases therein cited are partly cases of pledge and partly of sale of certificates of stock The rule applies

equally to both A person to whom a pledgor fraudulently transfers his equity and who redeems the stock cannot be compelled to turn it over to creditors except upon repayment of the amount so paid by him Hamilton Nat'l Bank v Halsted, 9 N Y Supp, 852 (1890)

[6] Fleming v Northampton Nat'l Bank, 62 How Pr, 177 (U S C C, 1881)

[7] Although all the other stock has had this agreement stamped on the certificates, yet the corporation cannot insist that the purchaser of the stock so pledged shall allow the same agreement to be stamped on the new certificates issued to such purchaser The court will order a transfer free from the agreement. Campbell v American, etc, Co, 122 N Y, 455 (1890).

[8] Leathers v Janney, 6 S Rep, 884 (La, 1889) In the case of Allis v Jones, 45 Fed Rep, 148 (1891), it is intimated

stock votes the stock in favor of a lease of the corporate property on such terms that no dividends on the stock are possible, yet in the absence of fraud the pledgee is bound[1] A pledgee is not bound to prosecute suits to protect the pledge, nor to sell, and a provision that the pledgee may claim repayment of any sums expended in the prosecution of claims is not an agreement of the pledgee to prosecute[2] If a note is secured by collateral, an accommodation indorser is not liable if the collateral is withdrawn from being security for the note[3] A pledge for any "note or claim against me" applies to a claim against the pledgor's firm[4]

§ 469 *Pledgee need not retain or return to the pledgor the identical certificates or shares of stock which were pledged, but must have equal quantity always on hand* — One share of stock does not differ from another share of the same capital stock Each is but an undivided interest in the corporate rights, privileges and property. Accordingly, it is held that a pledgee of stock need not retain in his possession the identical shares of stock which were pledged to him, but that the rights of the pledgor are fully preserved if similar stock is retained by the pledgee until the termination of the pledge[5] The pledgee must have on hand at all times the full amount of the stock pledged, whether the debt secured is due or not, since the law will not allow the pledgee to speculate or deal with the stock of another as though it were his own[6] It is not

that a pledgee has not the same right to attack an *ultra vires* corporate debt that the pledgor has, especially where the stock is worthless

[1] Gibson t Richmond, etc, R R, 37 Fed Rep, 743 (1889)

[2] Culver t Wilkinson, 145 U S, 205 (1892). The pledgee may claim credits for defending the pledge against attacks by law suits, and in some cases for adding to its value by aiding the subject of the pledge Cridge's Appeal, 18 Atl Rep, 1010 (Pa, 1890)

[3] Smith t Traders' Nat'l Bank, 17 S W Rep, 779 (Tex, 1891).

[4] Hallowell t Blackstone etc, Bank, 28 N E Rep, 281 (Mass. 1891)

[5] Caswell v. Putnam, 120 N Y, 153 (1890), Nourse v Prince, 4 Johns Ch, 490 (1820), S C, 7 Johns Ch 69 (1823), Horton v Morgan, 19 N Y, 170 (1859), Barclay v Culver, 30 Hun, 1 (1883), Noyes v Spaulding, 27 Vt. 420 (1855), Atkins t Gamble, 42 Cal, 86, Price t

Grover 40 Md, 102 (1874), Gilpin v. Howell, 5 Pa St, 41 (1816), Haidenburgh t Bacon, 33 Cal, 356 (1867), Taylor t Ketchum, 35 How Pr, 289 (1867), Langton t Waite, L R, 6 Eq, 165 (1868), Thompson v Toland 48 Cal, 99 (1874) Le Cray v Eastman 10 Mod, 499 (1735). Hubbell v Drexel, 21 Am L Reg (N S), 452 (1882) S C, 11 Fed Rep, 115 Baylin t Huguet, 8 Nev, 345 (1873) In the case of Dykers v Allen, 7 Hill, 497 (1844), the pledgee at one time seems to have had no stock on hand. In selling the pledgor s stock on notice for non-payment of the debt, the pledgee need not sell the identical stock pledged Berlin t Eddy 33 Mo, 426 (1863). In the case Mayo v Knowlton, 134 N Y, 250 (1892). the court said "The stock had no ear-mark, one share was the same as another and could not be identified or distinguished therefrom"

[6] *Ex parte* Dennison, 3 Ves, 552 (1797), Taussig t. Hart, 58 N Y., 425 (1874),

enough that he can at once procure the stock from one to whom it is loaned,[1] or that he had sufficient on hand for the plaintiff pledgor, but not enough for all the pledgors whom he had at any particular time.[2] The law requires him to set aside as much stock as has been pledged to him.

§ 470. *Pledgee's liability on subscription and statutory liability on stock.*[3]—A pledgee who has obtained registry on the corporate books appears to third parties as a full stockholder. Accordingly, in case the corporation becomes insolvent, the registered pledgee is held liable on his stock, as though he were an absolute stockholder. In order to avoid this danger the law allows the pledgee to have the pledged stock registered on the corporate books in the name of a nominee of the pledgee.[4] Where such a registry is obtained the pledgee has the advantage of a control of the stock, and at the same time escapes the danger of liability as a stockholder.

§ 471. *Pledgee has no right to sell or repledge the stock, even temporarily, except upon notice, unless the debt is assigned with the stock.* — "Equity will not tolerate a separation of the pledge from the debt, and they must stand together, and will force upon a wrong-doer the character of a trustee, and thus compel him to do justice." Such is the language of the New York court of appeals.[5] In no other way can the pledgee legally part with the possession of such stock by a sale or repledge of it. If he does so he is guilty of a conversion.[6] In Pennsylvania it is a penal offense for the pledgee

Thompson v. Toland, 48 Cal., 99 (1874). Hubbell v. Drexel, 21 Am. L. Reg. (N. S.), 452 (1881). The pledgor may waive this restriction by express agreement. Ogden v. Lathrop, 65 N. Y. 158 (1875).

[1] Dykers v. Allen, 3 Hill, 593; 7 id. 497 (1844). *Ex parte* Dennison, *supra*.

[2] Fay v. Gray, 124 Mass., 500 (1878).

[3] See ch. XIV, § 247.

[4] Newry, etc., R'y Co. v. Moss, 14 Beav., 64 (1851). See § 466.

[5] Bennett v. Austin, 81 N. Y., 308, 322 (1880). *Cf.* Easton v. Hodges, 18 Fed. Rep., 677 (1883).

[6] Goss v. Hampton, 16 Nev., 185 (1881). The case of *Ex parte* Sargent, L. R., 17 Eq., 273 (1874), contained a *dictum* giving a contrary rule, but the case of Franco v. Clark, L. R., 22 Ch. Div., 830 (1883), disapproves such *dictum* and says: "As a general rule the pawnee of chattels has no right to sell them, unless a time was originally fixed for their re-

demption, and that time has expired, or unless he had made a demand upon the pawnor for the payment of what is due to him." Fay v. Gray, 124 Mass., 500 (1878), holds that the pledgee has no right to sell, lend or repledge the stock. A broker has no right to repledge the stocks held by him as collateral to advances to a customer, especially so after the customer has repaid the advances. Van Voorhis v. Rea, 25 Atl. Rep. 800 (Pa., 1893). In the notes contained in 21 Am. Law Reg. (N. S.), 454, a contention is made that the pledgee should be allowed to repledge, but it is admitted that the weight of authority holds otherwise. The following cases are cited: Bank v. Trenholm, 12 Heisk. (Tenn.), 520 (1873); Bank v. Bryce, 19 Am. Law Reg. (N. S.) 563 (1880); Taussig v. Hart, 58 N. Y. 425 (1874); Work v. Bennett, 70 Pa. St., 484 (1872); Wood v. Hayes, 15 Gray, 375 (1860); Thompson v. Patrick,

to repledge the stock [1] Although, apparently, the pledgor would not be injured by the pledgee's separating the stock from the debt and by transferring to another the stock pledged as collateral security, yet the law rigidly protects the interests of the debtor and pledgor, and will not compel him to submit to the danger of such transfers by the pledgee. There may, of course, be an express agreement or understanding to the contrary [2]

A pledgee may assign the principal debt to a third person and "give him the benefit of the collateral securities to secure the payment of the principal debt. So long as nothing is done to deprive the pledgor of the right to redeem, on payment of the amount due on the principal debt, the pledgor is not injured." [3]

---

[4] Watts (Pa), 414 (1835), and see § 469 In Lawrence v Maxwell, 53 N Y, 19 (1873), the court say "Ordinarily, and in the absence of an agreement or assent by the pledgor, the pledgee would have no right to use the thing pledged, and a use of it would be illegal But, under special circumstances, depending somewhat upon the nature of the pledge, and in all cases with the assent of the pledgor express or implied the property pledged may be used by the pledgee in any way consistent with the general ownership and the ultimate rights of the pledgor."

[1] Act of May 25, 1878 (Purdon's Digest, 2107), modified as to purchases by broker on margin by act of June 10, 1881 (P L, 1881, 107).

[2] Choteau v Allen, 70 Mo, 290 (1879)

[3] Chapman v Brooks, 31 N Y 74, 84 (1865), Duncomb v New York, etc, R. R. 84 N Y, 190, 208 (1881) The pledgee may assign his interest in the pledge and transfer the pledge to such assignee Overton on Liens, §§ 168, 172, Schouler on Bailments (2d ed), § 218, etc Story on Bailments § 324, says the pawnee "may sell or assign all his interest in the pawn, or he may convey the same interest conditionally, by way of pawn, to another person, without in either case destroying or invalidating his security" See, also, Talty v Freedman's Sav, etc, Co, 93 U S. 321 (1876), 2 Kent's Com, 579, Jarvis v. Rogers, 13 Mass, 105, 15 id. 389, 408,

Mores v Conham, Owen, 123 (1854); Ratcliffe v Davis, 1 Buls., 29 (1857); Anon, 2 Salk, 522 The right of the pledgee to repledge may exist by force of a custom understood by both parties. Chamberlain v Greenleaf, 4 Abb N. C, 178 (1878), Oregon, etc Co. v Hilmers, 20 Fed Rep. 717 (1884) In the case of Lewis v Mott, 36 N Y, 394 (1867), where, after the debt was due and unpaid, the pledgee turned over the debt and security to another without a foreclosure or sale on notice, the court held that the latter could hold the collateral stock until the pledgor tendered the amount of the debt The latest English cases hold that, although the repledge may be wrong, yet that the pledgor cannot reclaim the stock from the repledgee until the former pays the debt for which the pledge was made. Donald v Suckling, L. R., 1 Q B., 585 (1866), Halliday v. Holgate, L. R., 3 Ex, 299 (1868) Where a broker, holding stock in pledge on a margin, repledges it without the consent of his customer, it has been held that he can recover the value of the stock from the customer on a tender of the certificate Clarkson v. Snider, 5 Canadian Law Times, 587 (1885). In Langton v Waite, L. R., 6 Eq, 165 (1868), the court say: "The law is clear that, in the absence of express contract to the contrary, a pawnee cannot sell without the express permission of the owner, and that if he does, the owner can charge him with the excess

§ 472. *Purchasers or pledgees of stock from pledgee with notice are not protected.*— A person who purchases or takes in pledge stock which he knows is held in pledge by the person from whom he takes it is not a *bona fide* holder of such stock, and is not entitled to the rights of such. At the best he stands merely in the place of the pledgee from whom he receives the stock. He must restore the stock to the owner in case the pledgee would be obliged to restore it, had no second sale or pledge been made. The second pledgee or vendee, with notice that he was taking pledged stock, has no rights which the first pledgee has not. He is but an equitable assignee of the latter, and can be compelled by the owner to deliver the stock in any case where the first pledgee could be so compelled[1]. The same rule applies whether the pledgee assigns or repledges both the debt and the stock or the stock alone[2]

§ 473. *Bona fide repledgees or purchasers of pledged stock are protected* — Where, however, a pledgee of certificates of stock indorsed in blank takes the certificates and sells or pledges them to another, who takes such certificates in good faith and for value and without notice that his vendor or pledgor held them as a pledge, the purchaser or pledgee from the pledgee is as fully protected in his rights as though the person with whom he dealt was the absolute owner of the stock.[3] This rule arises, not on the ground

---

of the price over the loan" The court, however, seemed to think that the pledgee could repledge the stock In Gould *v.* Farmers' Loan & Trust Co., 23 Hnn, 322 (1880), the court said that the pledgee might repledge the stock so far as he had an interest in it

[1] Any fact, such as usury in the second transaction, which prevents the second pledgee or purchaser from being a *bona fide* purchaser, applies to a repledgee of stock. The repledgee is not protected. Felt *v* Heye, 23 How Pr., 359 (1862), Little *v.* Barker, 1 Hoff Ch, 487 (1840) So, also, where the repledgee takes in consideration of a pre-existing indebtedness Ashton's Appeal, 73 Pa St., 153 (1873) A bank receiving a collection with collateral is not entitled to the latter where it becomes insolvent before the collection is remitted. Coin Exchange Bank *v* Blye, N Y Daily Reg, Sept 9, 1886 In general, see also Duncan *v* Jaudon, 15 Wall, 165 (1872), Shaw *v* Spencer, 100

Mass., 382 (1868), Ellis' Appeal, 8 Weekly Notes of Cases (Pa), 538, Porter *v.* Parks, 49 N Y, 564 (1872), Chouteau *v* Allen, *supra*

[2] Felt *v* Heye, *supra* (1862) Nor can the repledgee claim the benefit of the debt not assigned to him See, also, Talty *v* Freedman's, etc., Co, 93 U. S., 321 (1876).

[3] The important case of McNeil *v* Tenth Nat'l Bank, 46 N. Y., 325 (1871), was on the rights of a *bona fide* repledgee of stock, and fully sustains the general rule See, also, Fatman *v* Lobach, 1 Duer, 354 (1852), Wood's Appeal, 92 Pa St., 379 (1880), Wood *v* Smith, 8 Week Notes, 441, Goss *v.* Hampton, 16 Nev, 185 (1881), Mount Holly, etc., Co *v* Ferree, 17 N J. Eq, 117 (1864); Otis *v* Gardner 105 Ill, 436 (1883), *Ex parte* Sargent, L R, 17 Eq, 273 (1874), Cherry *v* Frost, 7 Lea (Tenn), 1 (1881), the court saying that in general a pledgee of personal property cannot convey a good title to another, but "if the owner in-

that the certificate of stock is negotiable, but for the reason that the owner is held to have enabled his pledgee to sell the stock as the pledgee's own, and that as between the owner and the *bona fide* purchaser or pledgee from the pledgee the owner must bear the loss. The law of estoppel prevents his denying the right of his pledgee to sell or pledge as against a *bona fide* purchaser or pledgee from the pledgee   So, also, this principle arises under the well-established rule that, where one of two innocent parties must suffer from the fraud of a third, the loss must fall upon him who enabled the third party to perpetrate the fraud.   If the pledgee has repledged the stock the owner can obtain the stock only by paying to the repledgee the amount of the latter's advancement to the first pledgee [1]   The pledgor of stock, under these rules, has practically no protection as to his stock except the honesty and responsibility of his pledgee.   The *bona fide* purchaser or pledgee from the pledgee is equally protected whether the certificates of stock are indorsed by the pledgor or vendor, or are indorsed in blank by some previous holder [2]   The repledgee or vendee is held to be a *bona fide* holder only where he would be held so to be in cases of promissory notes and other similar cases [3]   If the repledgee has also other

trusts to another not merely the possession of the property, but also written evidence over his own signature of title thereto and of unconditional power of disposition over it, the case is vastly different "   Thus a pledgee, without notice, of bonds from a pledgor, who turns out to have held the bonds as securities for the cancellation of a mortgage, is protected in his pledge   Saloy r Hibernia, etc, Bank, 1 S. Rep., 657 (La, 1887).   In New York a pledgee is not *bona fide* when he takes bonds in pledge for a precedent debt.   Duncomb t N. Y, etc, R. R. Co, 84 N Y, 190 (1881).   In the case of Ortigosa v. Brown, 47 L. J (Ch) 168 (1878), the court, following the English doctrine that an unregistered transferee of certificates of railway stock has no more rights than his transferer, refused to protect the unregistered repledgee of stock.
[1] Wood s Appeal, 92 Pa. St., 379 (1880), Fatman t Lobach, 1 Duer, 354 (1852), *Ex parte* Sargent, L. R., 17 Eq, 273 (1874), Cherry t Frost, 7 Lea (Tenn), 1 (1881), holding, however, that payments on the subscription by the owner subse-

quently to the repledge do not inure to the benefit of the latter   See, in general, Donald r Suckling, L. R., 1 Q B, 585 (1866), Moore t Conham, Owen, 123 (1856), Ratcliffe t Davis, Yelv, 178 (1710), Johnson t Cumming, Scott's C B (N. S), 331 (1819); Jarvis, Adm'r, t. Rodgers, 15 Mass., 369 (1819).
[2] Goss t Hampton, 16 Nev, 185 (1881).
[3] In California the peculiar doctrine is sustained that the word "trustee" on the face of the certificate is no notice, and does not deprive the pledgee of his character of being a *bona fide* holder   Brewster t Sime, 42 Cal, 139 (1871); Thompson r Toland, 48 Cal, 99 (1874).   If the repledgee receives the stock as security for an antecedent indebtedness he is not a *bona fide* holder   Gould t Farmers' Loan & Trust Co, 23 Hun, 322 (1880).   A pledgee is not *bona fide* when the name of another pledgee in the certificate is erased and his own inserted.   Denny t Lyon, 38 Pa. St., 98 (1860).   Where a party receives from his debtor certain stock as security for the purchase of other stock and holds it for the old debt, and sells it after being no-

collateral for his debt, a court of equity will marshal the assets and compel resort to such other collateral first, where it is equitable so to do[1]

§ 474 *Pledges by agents, trustees, executors, etc, legally and in breach of trust* — It is within the power of an executor or administrator to pledge shares of stock belonging to the estate, and the pledgee is protected even though he knew that the executor pledged it as an executor.[2] A trustee, on the other hand, has no implied power to pledge or sell corporate stock belonging to the trust[3] An agent's pledges of his principal's stock follow the same rules as where a pledgee repledges the stock given to him in pledge A *bona fide* holder for value and without notice is protected, while one who takes with notice is not protected Where, however, the

tified that it belongs to another party, he is liable to the latter party for conversion Niles v Edwards 27 Pac Rep, 159 (Cal, 1891)

[1] If the repledgee has other collateral also. it will be applied to the debt before the repledged stock is applied Gould v Farmers' Loan & Trust Co, 23 Hun, 322 (1880). The assets applicable to the debt will be marshaled Hurbert v Mechanics' Bldg & Loan Ass'n. 17 N J Eq, 497 (1864) Where the pledgee repledges the stock illegally with other stock. the first pledgor may enjoin the second pledgee from selling the stock until the other stock of the pledgee is sold and an account rendered and notice of intent to sell the remainder given. Myers v Merchants Nat'l Bank, 16 N. Y. Supp, 58 (1891) Where a broker pledgee with the assent of the pledgor has repledged the stock. the second pledgor, having no notice of who the first pledgor is, may hold all stocks until all debts from the second pledgor to him are paid A person who gave stock to the first broker to sell is preferred to one who purchased stock on a margin Willard v White, 56 Hun, 581 (1890). Where pledged stock is repledged and sold out by the repledgee together with various other stock held as collateral by the repledgee a court of equity will marshal the assets. Smith v Savin. 9 N Y Supp 106 (1890). Where the pledgee sells the securities

and has a surplus he cannot interplead between two claimants where he is sued by one of them for more than he admits the surplus amounts to Dodge v. Lawson N Y. L J, April 20, 1892. A pledgee need not resort to the pledge in order to obtain payment, but if the pledgor becomes insolvent the court will marshal the assets. Chemical Nat'l Bank v Armstrong, 50 Fed Rep, 798 (1892). See, also, § 476, *infra*

[2] Goodwin v American Nat'l Bank, 48 Conn, 550 (1881). Wood s Appeal. 92 Pa St, 379 (1880). Carter v Mfs. Nat'l Bank, 71 Me, 418 (1880), § 329 Manhattan Bank v Walker, 130 U S, 267 (1889). A pledgee from an executor is protected. Gottberg v United States Nat'l Bank 13 N Y. Supp, 841 (1891). A pledge of stock by an executor is illegal and the pledgee is not protected where the pledgee not trusting to the executor's power as executor, causes the stock to be transferred first to a legatee Moore v American, etc, Co, 115 N Y, 65 (1889) Where an executor pledges stock for his own debt, the pledgee knowing the fact so to be, the latter becomes trustee and the statute of limitations does not run against redemption until after the pledgee has notified the *cestui que trust* of the estate that he holds the stock adversely *In re* Marshall's Estate, 22 Atl Rep, 24 (Pa 1891)

[3] See ch XIX, §§ 323-327, Shaw v Spencer, 100 Mass., 382 (1868), § 465.

one taking stock in pledge from an agent knows that the latter is acting as agent, he is bound to inquire whether the principal has authorized his agent to pledge the stock, since a power to pledge cannot be presumed from a power to sell [1] The right of corporations and persons to give and take stock in pledge is considered elsewhere [2]

§ 475 *Pledgor's remedies*.—Where the pledgee of stock has been guilty of a conversion of it, the pledgor's remedy against him is generally by an action at law for damages He need not tender to the pledgee the amount of the debt secured by the pledge, since the pledgee may recoup to that extent and thus decrease the damages of the pledgor.[3] The pledgor's damages are measured by the market value of the stock at the time of the conversion, together with interest and subsequent damages.[4] The pledgor may be barred from his action for damages by a waiver of the particular act of conversion by the pledgee.[5] He has the option, however, of ratifying the transaction and claiming the proceeds, or he may repudiate the sale and sue for conversion.[6] This remedy at law may

[1] See ch XIX, § 321.

[2] See ch XIX.

[3] Allen v Dykers, 3 Hill, 93 (1842), 7 id, 497, New York, L E & W. R. R Co v Davies, 38 Hun, 477 (1886), Work v Bennett, 70 Pa. St., 484 (1872), Fisher v Brown, 104 Mass, 259; Neiler v Kelly, 69 Pa. St., 403 (1871), Langton v Waite, L. R., 6 Eq, 165 (1868), Felt v Heye, 23 How Pr, 359 (1862), Lewis v Graham, 4 Abb Pr, 106 (1857), Cortelyou v Lansing, 2 Caines' Cas, 200 However, a later case in Massachusetts — Cumnock v Institution for Sav, 142 Mass, 342 (1886) — holds that a tender of payment of a debt is necessary to enable a pledgor to maintain trover for a conversion of property pledged, unless the lien created by the pledge has been otherwise discharged "After the sale by the pledgee, the pledgee need not make a tender of the amount due nor a demand of the securities before bringing his action A formal tender of the amount of the notes would have been a useless ceremony, such as the law never requires" Fletcher v Dickinson, 7 Allen, 23. A pledgor's vendee may tender the amount of the debt and demand the stock as a condition of payment Trover lies for a refusal of pledgee to deliver. The pledgee is liable for depreciations of stock after such tender An attachment of stock against the pledgor, but after sale by him, is no defense to the pledgee. Loughborough v M'Nevin, 14 Pac. Rep., 869 (Cal., 1887). An assignee of the pledgor of stock may tender the amount due and demand the stock The pledgee cannot refuse, because the stock has been attached, the assignee not being a party thereto. Tender is sufficient without paying the money into court Id., 15 Pac Rep, 773 (Cal, 1887) See, also, Thompson v. St. Nicholas, etc, Bank, 113 N. Y., 325 (1889).

See ch XXXV. In Fowle v. Ward, 113 Mass., 548 (1873), the court said the damages should be "a sum of money which would enable him to purchase seventeen new shares to replace those which have been taken from him, with such additional sum as would indemnify him for the dividends which he has lost since the sale, and also an equitable allowance for interest."

[5] Child v Hugg, 41 Cal., 519 (1871). See, also, sub.

[6] Atkins v Gamble, 42 Cal., 86, 91

596

be on contract or in tort.[1] The pledgor may, if he prefers, begin suit in a court of equity, when the pledgee has converted the stock, and compel him either to replace the stock or give compensation in damages. The jurisdiction of a court of equity in such a case has been denied,[2] but has been sustained on the ground that only

(1871) If there are several pledgors, and the pledge is redeemed, and the pledgee, at the request of one of the pledgors, transfers the stock to third parties, the pledgee is liable to the other pledgors for loss incurred thereby Magnus v Queensland, etc, Bank, 57 L. T Rep., 136 (1887)

[1] The form of a complaint or declaration in an action by a pledgor against a pledgee for the conversion of the stock held in pledge may be in tort or in *assumpsit* but not in both Stevens v Hurlbut Bank, 31 Conn, 146 (1862) It is a conversion for the pledgee to retain the stock after the principal of the debt is paid, nothing being said about interest Kullman v Greenebaum, 28 Pac Rep, 674 (Cal, 1891). A complaint which, after stating that shares of stock had been pledged to defendant, avers that "defendant, in consideration of the premises, then and there undertook and promised plaintiff" to hold the stock only as pledge, but that, in violation of its promise, defendant sold and converted the stock to its own use, without giving plaintiff notice of the sale, and in which plaintiff seeks to recover as damages the full value of the shares alleged to have been converted, though informal, is good as a complaint in case Sharp v National Bank, 7 S Rep., 106 (Ala, 1888) This case discussed also the difference between *assumpsit* and in case in such an action In the case of Butts v Burnett, 6 Abb Pr (N S), 302 (1869), involving the arrest of a broker who had sold the pledge before the note was due, the court said "It is very questionable, I think, whether a demand after default in payment of the debt for which property is pledged as security will render a refusal to deliver the pledged property a tortious conversion of it. No doubt the

pledgor can redeem upon a tender of the debt, or he may recover the difference between the value of the pledge and the debt But to lay the foundation for an action for conversion, I am of opinion that an offer and demand must be made on the day, and is not sufficient if made after the day on which the debt has become payable ' As to the complaint in action by pledgor against pledgee for not returning goods pledged, see 2 Chitty on Pleading, 69, Stanton v. Collier, 3 El & Bl, 274 An answer is not good where it merely denies the conversion and does not deny the possession by the defendant of certain stocks belonging to the plaintiff, nor the tender of the balance due, nor the demand for such stocks, nor the non-delivery of the same Dubois v Sistare, N Y L J, Dec 9, 1890 Where the repledgee converts the stock the remedy for conversion is with the first pledgee, not with the first pledgor Thompson v Toland, 48 Cal 99 (1871). *Contra*. Smith v Savin, N Y L J, June 21, 1893 A pledge of stock to secure future liabilities does not secure past liabilities If the pledgee refuses to surrender the stock on demand and tender, the pledgor may recover the value of the stock on that day, less the amount tendered Presdt, etc, of Franklin Bank v Harris, 26 Atl Rep, 523 (Md, 1893)

[2] Lacombe v Forstall's Sons, 123 U S, 562 (1887), Genet v Howland, 45 Barb, 560 (1866) Remedy of pledgor is at law after a tender, not by bill in equity to redeem. Doak v Bank of the State, 6 Ired L, 309 (1846) Where the pledgee has sold the stock, the pledgor cannot compel him to restore it by a bill in equity, even though he alleges that the sale was to a person who holds the stock as trustee for the pledgee The pledgor's

a court of equity can compel a retransfer of the stock or an accounting of the dividends declared while the pledge was running, or an
accounting by third persons to whom the pledgee has assigned the
debt and pledge, or enjoin an illegal transfer of the stock[1] An

remedy is at law Hinckley v Pfister.
53 N W Rep., 21 (Wis., 1892). A bill in
equity does not lie for damages due to
an illegal sale of stock by a pledgee
Henry v Travelers', etc, Co, 45 Fed
Rep 209 (1891) A pledgor cannot file
a bill in equity to hold the pledgee liable
for selling the stock in violation of the
pledge, there being no disputed accounts Roland v Lancaster, etc, Bank,
19 Atl Rep, 951 (Pa, 1890), Augus v
Robinson's Adm'r, 19 Atl Rep, 993
(Vt, 1890) "It is well settled that a
bill in equity will not ordinarily lie to
redeem property from a pledge Kemp
v Westbrook, 1 Ves, 278, Story, Eq
Juris, § 1032 The reason is obvious
The legal title to the thing pledged does
not pass to the pledgee, as it does to a
mortgagee in possession in the case of a
mortgage The pledgor retains the legal
title and parts only with possession and
a special property Jones on Pledges,
§ 552. He has therefore a legal right
to redeem, and upon tendering the
amount due to the pledgee he may bring
replevin for the collateral or an action
to recover its value It is only when
his legal remedies are insufficient that
the pledgor can come into equity Jones
on Pledges, § 556, and cases cited If,
for instance, the collaterals consist of
shares of stock which have been transferred into the pledgee's name upon the
books of a corporation, an action in
equity will lie, for the reason that such
an action is necessary to secure the retransfer of the shares So equity may
be invoked where an accounting or a
discovery is needed or where the pledgee
has assigned the pledge." Stokes v
Stokes, N Y L J, Nov 15, 1892

[1] Bryson v Raynor, 25 Md, 424 (1866),
Conyngham's Appeal, 57 Pa St, 474
(1868), Hasbrouck v Vandervoort, 4
Sand, 74 (1850), Koons v First Nat l

Bank, 89 Ind, 178 (1883). The pledgee
must return the stock and stock dividends and account for money dividends.
Vaughan v Wood, 1 M & K., 403 (1833).
A court of equity has power to decree
the return of pledged stock and money
deposited as collateral. Post v. Simmons, 9 N Y Supp, 112 (1890); Brown
v Runals, 14 Wis, 693 A pledgor may
file a bill in equity to have a surplus delivered up and the notes for which the
collateral was given delivered up also
Cahoon v Bank of Utica, 7 N. Y, 486
(1852), reversing 7 How Pr, 134 In
case of a wrongful repledge the pledgor
may claim the proceeds or redeem the
stock from the second pledgee Chamberlain v Greenleaf 4 Abb. N C., 178
(1878). Where the second pledgee has
sold the stock for non-payment of his
debt the first pledgor may claim the excess, the amount retained by the repledgee being more than the first
pledgor s debt. Re Bonner, 8 Daly, 75
(1878). See, also, Fowle v Ward, 113
Mass, 548 (1873). An action to redeem a
pledge of stock is to be tried without a
jury, even though the defendant sets up
a counter-claim of false representations
Lynch v Macdonald, 58 L. T. Rep, 293
(1888) Where the pledgee is about to
sell the stock and denies the pledge,
the pledgor may enjoin the sale
Thielens v Dialogue, 19 Atl. Rep., 970 (N
J, 1890) For other cases sustaining the
jurisdiction on the ground that an injunction was proper, see Hower v
Weiss etc, Co., 55 Fed Rep., 356 (1893);
Myers v Merchants', etc, Bank, N. Y. L
J, Sept 1, 1891 The pledgor cannot
enjoin a sale by the pledgee on the
ground that the sale will be at a sacrifice Park v Musgrave, 2 T. & C, 571.
Where a purchaser of stock agrees to
give a long-time note with the stock as
security, and subsequently, for the ac-

unreasonable delay or laches on the part of the pledgor will bar his remedy against the pledgee [1] In New York a contrary rule prevails [2]

commodation of the vendor, a short-time note with the stock as security is delivered to a third person named by the vendor, and the vendor then obtains possession of the stock and note, and after the short-time note becomes due, proposes to collect the note and sell out the stock, the pledgor may enjoin the sale of the stock In this case the stock was of uncertain value, and represented a controlling interest in the company, and damages for its conversion would not have been an adequate remedy The court held that an action for replevin was not adequate, inasmuch as in order to bring replevin the pledgor would have to tender the debt, which, according to the original agreement, was not yet due. Hower v. Weiss, etc, Co, 55 Fed Rep, 356 (1893)

[1] Eight years' delay by pledgor in complaining of refusal of pledgee to deliver up the stock on tender of the debt, the stock having subsequently declined in value, held fatal under the facts of this case. Murriam v. Childs, 5 S. W Rep, 615 (Mo, 1887). Where the pledgor's executor for value received sells the pledgor's interest to the pledgee, long lapse of time after full knowledge of the facts by all parties will raise a presumption in favor of the pledgee's complete ownership. Lockwood v Brantly, 103 N Y, 680 (1886) Equity has jurisdiction to ascertain the amount due on a pledge and to decree that the pledgor may redeem. As to the statute of limitations, see Maynard v Tilden, 28 Fed. Rep, 688, 703 (1886); Child v. Hugg, supra. In Greene v. Dispean, 14 R. I, 575 (1884). a pledge of stock was treated as a mortgage, and the right to redeem was held to be barred six years after the date of the mortgage Pledgor waives informality of notice, where, after the sale, he, as an officer of the corporation, enters a transfer of the

stock to the one who purchased at the sale Downing v Whittier, 11 N. E. Rep 585 (Mass, 1887) Four years' delay in complaining is fatal Receiving the benefit of the sale is a waiver of objections. M'Dowell v Chicago Steel Works, 16 N E Rep, 854 (Ill, 1888). Although the pledgee gives no public notice of the sale, and although he purchases the stock at the sale, yet the pledgor ratifies the sale by acquiescing and by negotiating to buy the stock Hill v Finigan, 19 Pac Rep., 494 (Cal, 1888). The statute of limitations is no bar to an action to redeem a pledge of stock, unless the statute was set running by demand of payment and notice of intent to sell Gilmer v Morris, 35 Fed. Rep., 682 (1888) See S C, 80 Ala, 78. In the case of a pledge of stock to secure future advances the statute of limitations begins to run against the right of the pledgor to redeem from the time when the pledgee, by some positive act, repudiates the pledge and claims the property as his own or improperly disposes of it Gilmer v Morris, 43 Fed. Rep, 456 (1890). If the pledge is recognized by extension to other debts, the statute of limitations runs from the latter date Gilmer v Morris, 46 Fed. Rep, 333 (1891) The statute of limitations runs against a receipt reciting a first payment on stock "standing in my name but owned by him, and he remaining responsible for the balance of the instalments when called in," there being no agreement as to the future disposition of the stock and of dividends. Coxe v. Dunham, 20 Atl Rep, 311 (Conn, 1890). A pledge is not legally abandoned although no demand is made for it during a long lapse of time. Cridge's Appeal, 18 Atl Rep, 1010 (Pa, 1890) Redemption, laches, etc, see Schouler on Bailments (2d ed), § 250

[2] Bailey v Chamberlain, N. Y. Daily Reg, July 23, 1888 See Miner v Beek-

A pledge of stock to secure another person's debt is released by an extension of that debt.[1] A pledgor cannot compel his pledgee to sell the stock and apply the proceeds to the debt by a notice to make such a sale[2] When the pledgee causes the stock to be sold the pledgor is entitled to the surplus proceeds of the sale remaining after the debt and the expenses of the sale have been paid[3] In certain cases a pledgor may defeat an action by the pledgee on the debt by showing that the pledgee has converted the pledge.[4]

§ 476 *Pledgee's remedies when debt secured is not paid* — Where shares of stock are pledged as collateral security for a debt and the debt is not paid, and the pledgee wishes to apply the stock to the payment of the debt, he has the right to pursue either one of two remedies: he may file a bill in equity for the foreclosure and sale of the pledge,[5] or he may give notice to the pledgor of an

man, 50 N Y, 337 Pledgee cannot claim that he has held the stock, adversely to the pledgor, for a time more than sufficient to give him title to it under the statute of limitations. He is not allowed to assert that he holds the stock adversely Cross v Eureka, etc, Co, 73 Cal, 302 (1887)

[1] Price v Reed, 15 N E. Rep, 754 (Ill, 1888)

[2] Lawrence v Maxwell, 53 N Y, 19, Robinson v Hurley, 11 Iowa, 412, O'Neill v Whigham, 88 Pa St., 394; Rozet v. McClellan, 48 Ill, 345; Smouse v Bail, 1 Grant, 397; Taggard v Curtenius, 15 Wend, 155, Fisher v Fisher, 98 Mass., 303, Napier v Central, etc, Bank, 68 Ga, 637, holding, however that where the pledgee does not sell, because he and others were "bearing" the market, there may be an element of fraud which gives a cause of action The pledgor cannot by request compel the pledgee to sell Minneapolis. etc, Co v Betcher, 44 N W. Rep, 5 (Minn, 1889).

[3] And the pledgor's assignee for the benefit of creditors may claim it. The pledgee bank has no banker's lien on the surplus for other debts Brown v New Bedford Inst. for Sav, 137 Mass, 262 (1884) A pledgee bank cannot refuse to deliver back the stock to pledgor who tenders the amount due, on the ground that the pledgee owes it still

another debt. McIntire v Blakeley, 12 Atl Rep, 325 (Pa, 1888). If the officers of a pledgee bank refuse to deliver back the pledged stock upon a tender of the debt they are liable personally in damages to the pledgor McIntire v Blakeley, *supra*. If pledgee has also other security, an unsecured creditor of the pledgor may compel the pledgee to resort to such other security first. Bishop, etc, Assoc v Kennedy, 12 Atl Rep, 141 (N. J., 1887) Pledgee on sale of pledge cannot apply the excess to another debt due him from the pledgor, who died before the sale was made. Peters v. Nashville Savings Bank, 6 S. W Rep, 133 (Tenn, 1887).

[4] See §§ 461, 478, note In an action by the pledgee for the debt, the pledgor may set up a conversion of the stock pledged Donnell t Wyckoff, 7 Atl. Rep, 672 (N J, 1887)

[5] Vaupell v Woodward, 2 Sand. Ch., 143 (1844). The pledge may be made to secure the carrying out of a contract, and a court of equity will foreclose it although the damages are unliquidated. Robinson v Hurley, 11 Iowa, 410, from which it seems that where the pledge was made without a written transfer of the certificate this is the only remedy. See, also, Merchants' Nat'l Bank v Hall, 83 N Y, 338 (1881), Smith v. Coale, 34 Leg Intel, 54, Blount v. Liquidators,

intent to sell the stock, and may so sell it without any judicial proceedings, and apply the proceeds to the payment of the debt[1] No
express power to sell need be contained in the memorandum of

etc., 30 La Ann., 714 (1878), Johnson v
Dexter 2 MacArthur, 530 A person
holding and carrying stock for himself
and others may file a bill in equity to
bring about a sale and an adjustment
of the accounts Goodwin v Evans, 19
Atl Rep., 49 (Pa, 1890) An action lies
for judgment on a note and for a sale of
the collateral and the application to the
judgment of the amount realized on
such sale Farmers', etc, Nat l Bank v
Rogers, 1 N Y. Supp, 757

[1] Story on Bailments, 9th ed. (1877),
§ 310, saying "The law as at present
established leaves an election to the
pawnee He may file a bill in equity
against the pawnor for a foreclosure
and sale, or he may proceed to sell *ex
mero motu*, upon giving due notice of
his intention to the pledgor In the
latter case, if the sale is *bona fide* and
reasonably made, it will be equally obligatory as in the first case" The leading case, allowing this remedy of the
pledgee against the pledge, is Tucker v
Wilson, 5 Bro Par Cases, 193 (1714),
rev'g 1 P. Wms., 261 In Brown v Ward,
3 Duer, 660 (1854), the court say "Since
the time of the case of Hart v Ten
Eyck [2 Johns. Ch Cas, 180], before
Chancellor Kent, the right of the
pledgee to sell after the debt is due,
upon reasonable notice, has been unquestioned, and a custom has grown up
and has been sanctioned by the courts
of selling stocks at the Merchants' Exchange" To same effect, Diller v · Bru-
baker, 52 Pa St., 498 (1866), Finney's
Appeal, 59 Pa St., 398 (1866), Easton v
German, etc, Bank, 127 U S , 532 (1888),
Mount Holly, etc, Co v Ferrec. 17 N J.
Eq, 117 (1864), where the court say "A
sale of a pledge by the pawnee where
reasonably and *bona fide* made, and
after notice to the pawnor, is equally
obligatory as if made by judicial pro-

cess" 2 Kent's Com, 582, saying that the
pledgee "may file a bill in chancery
and have a judicial sale under a regular
decree of foreclosure, . . . and he
may sell without judicial process, upon
giving reasonable notice to the debtor to
redeem" Sitgreaves v Bank, 49 Pa St.,
359, Stearns v Marsh, 4 Denio, 227
(1847), Markham v Jaudon, 41 N Y,
235, 241 (1869), Drury v Cross, 7 Wall,
299 (1868) The parties may provide for
any manner of disposing of the pledge
to satisfy the claim upon it which is not
in contravention of statute, against
public policy or fraudulent. McNeil v.
Tenth Nat. Bank, 46 N Y, 325, 334,
says "The distinction between a lien
and a pledge is said to be that a mere
lien cannot be enforced by sale by the
act of the party but that a pledge is a
lien with a power of sale superadded"
Pledgee's power of attorney to sell is
coupled with an interest and is not
revocable Renshaw v Creditors, 3 S
Rep, 403 (La, 1888). Person secured by
pledge of stock in another's name may
sue latter for the amount received by
latter on a sale of the stock Maynard v.
Lumberman's Nat. Bank, 11 Atl Rep,
529 (Pa., 1887) Although the pledgee
has not advanced all that he agreed to,
yet, where he ceased advances after the
pledgor's default in paying the part already advanced, the pledgee may proceed to sell the pledge after notice.
Midland R'y v Loan, etc, Co, N Y L
J, May 24, 1890 The pledgee cannot
be enjoined from selling the pledge
on notice, merely because by legal proceedings he has injured the value of the
pledge Id A pledgee who has
brought an action to foreclose his
pledge may nevertheless abandon the
suit and resort to his remedy of a sale
after notice Id. A sale by a pledgee
will not be enjoined merely because the

pledge in order to authorize the latter remedy.   It exists by force of law

The pledgee, however, is not bound to pursue either remedy merely because the debt is due and unpaid [1] He need not sell the stock upon the maturity of the note secured, nor is he liable because the stock declines in value.[2] He may sue on the debt without tendering back the stock [3] The pledgor cannot compel him to sell by merely giving him notice so to do.[4] Nor is the pledgee bound to sell on non-payment of the debt, although the memorandum of pledge expressly authorizes a sale, but he may file a bill in equity to foreclose instead of pursuing the other remedy.[5] The pledgee's remedy by attaching the stock and selling it at an execution sale [6] is his remedy as a creditor and not as a pledgee of the person indebted to him.   A pledgee may prove his entire claim against the

corporation is in insolvency proceedings in another state and the sale has been enjoined by courts of that state Union Cattle Co v International, etc, Co, 21 N E Rep, 963 (Mass, 1889).

[1] O'Neil v Whigham, 87 Pa. St, 394 (1878), Rezet v McClellan, 48 Ill, 345 (1868), Palmer v Hawes, 40 N W Rep, 676 (Wis, 1888)

[2] Simonton v Kelly, 122 U S, 220 (1887), Palmer v Hawes, 40 N W Rep, 676 (Wis, 1888)

[3] Taylor v Cheever, 6 Gray, 146; Butman v Howell. 10 N E Rep, 504 (Mass., 1887). A broker or pledgee need not sell the stock held as collateral before bringing an action against the pledgor for the amount due, nor does a broker's custom compel it De Cordova v Barnum, 130 N. Y, 615 (1892). Pledgee having sold the stock, and there still being a balance due him from the pledgor, may sue for such balance, and need not allege that the sale was on due notice and demand Wallace v Berdell, 24 Hun, 379 (1881). Where stock pledged to secure a note is to be transferred as payment in case the note is not paid, the pledgee may sue on the note if the pledgor has not transferred the stock Fullerton v Mobley, 15 Atl Rep, 856 (Pa, 1888) As to the duties of the pledgee towards an indorser of the note, see Payne v Com

Bank, 14 Miss, 24 (1846) Misrepresentations by pledgee of stock as to the value of the stock made after its pledge are no defense for the pledgor when sued on the debt. Palmer v. Hawes, 40 N. W Rep., 676 (Wis, 1888). The fact that stocks are deposited as collateral security to a note does not prevent the statute of limitations running against the note In re Hartranft's Estate, 26 Atl Rep, 104 (Pa, 1893). Although the debt is barred by the statute of limitations, the pledgee may compel the corporation to transfer the stock to him on the books. Miller v Houston, etc, Co., 55 Fed Rep., 366 (1893)

[4] See § 475

[5] Cornick v Richards, 3 Lea (Tenn), 1 (1879); Coffin v. Chicago & N, etc., Co, 4 Hun, 625 (1875).

[6] Lee v Citizens' Nat. Bank, 2 Cin. Super Ct, 298 (1872). His remedies as a pledgee are not released or affected by his pursuit of other remedies. See Sickles v. Richardson, 23 Hun, 559 (1881). Judgment on the debt does not release the stock pledged   "Until the debt is paid, the pledgor, under the terms of the bailment, has no right to have the pledge given up to him" Donnell v. Wyckoff, 7 Atl Rep, 672 (N. J, 1887). See, also, Hill v Beebe, 13 N Y., 556, 563, 567

insolvent estate of the pledgor, and obtain his proportionate part thereof.[1]

§ 477　*Notice of sale of stock by pledgee to apply to debt secured — Waiver of notice* — In case the pledgee pursues the remedy of selling the stock without any judicial proceedings, he must give the pledgor reasonable notice of the intent to sell and of the time and place of sale.[2] A sale without a notice is a conversion of the stock.[3] The pledgee must demand payment of the debt secured by the pledge of stock, and a waiver of notice of sale is not a waiver of a right to have such a demand made.[4] A notice of intent to sell, however, is equivalent to a demand of payment.[5] A broker's custom to the effect that no notice is necessary is illegal and void.[6] The time and place of the proposed sale must be specified in the notice.[7] The time between the service of the notice and the time

[1] People v. Remington, 121 N Y, 328 (1890). The pledgee may prove his entire claim against the insolvent pledgor's estate without first resorting to surrendering or accounting for the pledge. In re Ives, 11 N Y Supp., 655 (1890) See, also, § 473 supra Where stock is pledged to secure several debts, some of which are secured in other ways, the pledgee may apply the proceeds of the pledge to those debts which are not secured by indorsements Fall River Nat Bank v Slade, 26 N E Rep, 843 (Mass, 1891) In a suit to foreclose a pledge of stock where the pledgee has other securities also, the court will not compel the pledgee to sell the other securities first. Work v Ogden, N Y L J, May 20, 1890.

[2] "To authorize the defendants to sell the stock purchased, they were bound, first, to call upon the plaintiff to make good his margin, and, failing in that, he was entitled, secondly, to notice of the time and place where the stock would be sold, which time and place, thirdly, must be reasonable." Markham v Jaudon, 41 N Y, 235, 243 (1869) See, also, Stratford v Jones, 97 N Y., 586 (1885), Baker v Drake, 66 N. Y., 518 (1876), Conyngham's Appeal, 57 Pa St, 474, Stearns v Marsh, 4 Denio, 227 (1847), Neiler v Kelley, 69 Pa St., 403 (1871), Cushman v Hayes, 46 Ill, 145

(1867). A joint owner is entitled to notice Clark v Sparhawk, 2 Weekly Notes, 115 (1875).

[3] Fowle v Ward, 113 Mass 548 (1873), Hemppling v Burr, 26 N W Rep, 496 (Mich, 1886), 21 N E. Rep, 510 (Ill, 1889)

[4] Lewis v Graham, 4 Abb. Pr, 106 (1857) Brass v Worth, 40 Barb, 59 (1863), Wilson v Little, 2 N Y. 443 448 (1849), saying "It is well settled that where no time is expressly fixed by contract between the parties for the payment of a debt secured by a pledge, the pawnee cannot sell the pledge without a previous demand of payment, although the debt is technically due immediately" Genet v Howland, 45 Barb., 560 (1866)

[5] Nabring v Bank of Mobile, 58 Ala., 204 (1877). So, also, of notice of intent to foreclose Howe v Bemis, 2 Gray, 203 Demand of payment may be made by long urging for payment, even though the word "demand" is not used Carson v Iowa, etc, Co, 45 N W Rep, 1068 (Iowa, 1890) The giving of a note to a broker pledgee does not extend the time within which the pledgor was to deposit further margin Gould v Trask, 10 N Y Supp., 619 (1890).

[6] Markham v Jaudon, 41 N Y, 235 (1869).

[7] Conyngham's Appeal, 57 Pa St,

when the sale is to take place must be reasonable in length, so as to give the debtor on opportunity to obtain money to pay the debt.[1] In Massachusetts, by statute, sixty days' notice must be given.[2] A notice by a newspaper advertisement is insufficient.[3] It must be served personally, and it seems that it cannot be served on one who has charge of the pledgor's office for the transaction of business.[4]

By an express agreement the pledgor may waive his right to notice of the time and place of the sale.[5] Such contracts are fre-

474 (1868); Genet v. Howland, *supra;* Canfield v. Minn., etc., Ass'n, 14 Fed. Rep., 801. See Schouler on Bailments, 206–212. It has been held in Maryland that a notice of the place is unnecessary. Worthington v. Tormey, 34 Md., 182 (1870). But such decision would be unsafe, and probably would not be followed elsewhere. In New York, the place of sale formerly, by custom, was at the Merchants' Exchange, No. 111 Broadway, but is now both there and at the Real Estate Exchange in Liberty street.

[1] In Maryland, etc., Co. v. Dalrymple, 25 Md., 242, a week's notice was held sufficient. Lewis v. Graham, 4 Abb. Pr., 106 (1857), holding that thirty-four days, where the pledgor resides in Illinois and the sale is to be in New York, is sufficient; Bryan v. Baldwin, 7 Lans., 174 (1872); affirmed, 52 N. Y., 232, holding that two days was sufficient; Stevens v. Hurlbut Bank, 31 Conn., 146 (1862), holding that a sale on the same day is unreasonable and the notice insufficient. See other cases in ch. XXV, §§ 457, 458; Willoughby v. Comstock, 3 Hill, 389 (1842), where two days was held sufficient. Edwards on Bailments, 285. As to place of sale, see ch. XXV, §§ 458, 476.

[2] Gen. Stat., ch. 151, § 9.

[3] Lewis v. Graham, *supra;* and see § 119.

[4] Bryan v. Baldwin, 52 N. Y., 232 (1873). *Cf.* Milliken v. Dehon, 27 N. Y., 364 (1853).

[5] Maryland Fire Ins. Co. v. Dalrymple, 25 Md., 242 (1866); Genet v. Howland, *supra;* and see ch. XXV, §§ 459,

462; Milliken v. Dehon, 27 N. Y., 364; Stevens v. Hurlbut Bank, 31 Conn., 146; Hyatt v. Argenti, 3 Cal., 151; Wheeler v. Newbould, 16 N. Y., 392; Stenton v. Jerome, 54 N. Y., 480; Wicks v. Hatch, 62 N. Y., 535; Butts v. Burnett, 6 Abb. Pr. (N. S.), 302 (1869). Pledgor of stock may, by the terms of the agreement creating the pledge, waive his right to notice of sale for non-payment of the debt. Appeal of Jeanes, 11 Atl. Rep., 862 (Pa., 1887). Formerly the validity of a waiver was doubted. Campbell v. Parker, 9 Bosw., 322; Wilson v. Little, 2 N. Y., 443. 448; Gilpin v. Howell, 5 Pa., 41; Hanks v. Drake, 40 Barb., 186; Sterling v. Jaudon, 48 id., 459. Authority to the pledgee to sell "at public or private sale, at his discretion," thirty days after notice, waives notice of sale. McDowell v. Chicago, etc., 16 N. E. Rep., 854 (Ill., 1888). Notice may be waived. Chouteau v. Allen, 70 Mo., 290 (1879). In the case of Huiskamp v. Wise, 47 Fed. Rep., 236, 249 (1891), where the pledgee was authorized to sell before maturity and without notice if the security became insufficient, the court held that "the pledgee could not make sale of the collateral until after the default in the payment of the note, without notice and demand of payment to the pledgor." In the case of Williams v. United States Trust Co., 14 N. Y. Supp., 502 (1891), a provision that the pledgee might sell without notice and at the exchange or at public or private sale, and that the note should become due at once if the security depreciated a certain amount, was upheld. The pledgor may, subsequently to the

quently entered into with stock-brokers by customers buying stock on a margin. But an express power to the pledgee to sell the pledge on certain contingencies is not a waiver of a right to notice.[1]

§ 478 *Formalities of sale* — A sale of stock on notice by a pledgee, for the purpose of applying the proceeds to the pledgor's debt, must be at public auction.[2] A private sale is unauthorized

making of the pledge, release his right to redeem. He may agree that the pledgee may sell the pledge at any time at private sale and that the proceeds shall, after repayment of the amount loaned, be divided equally between the pledgor and pledgee. Rutherford v Mass M., etc., Ins Co., 45 Fed Rep., 712 (1891). The fact that the pledgee, under a waiver of notice, of demand and public sale, sells the stock and debt to an enemy of the corporation does not invalidate the sale. Carson v Iowa, etc., Co., 45 N W Rep., 1068 (Iowa, 1890). Although the pledgor agrees that the pledgee may sell part of the pledge without notice upon default, this does not release the remainder of the pledge from being additional security for the debt. Bank of Africa v Salisbury, etc., Co., 66 L. T Rep., 237 (1892). Where the pledgees are given power to sell "in such manner as they, in their discretion, may deem proper, without notice," a sale without notice after the maturity of the loan is legal. Williams v United States Trust Co., 133 N Y, 660 (1892).

An approved form of a note and waiver is as follows:

"$——　NEW YORK, ——, 18—.

"—— after date —— promise to pay to the order of ——, —— dollars, at —— for value received, with interest at the rate of —— per cent. per annum, having pledged to the said —— —— the under-mentioned securities (with authority to sell the same on non-performance of this promise, in such manner as they, in their discretion, may deem proper, without notice, either at any brokers' board or at public or private sale and to apply the proceeds thereon). viz ——

"In case of depreciation in the market value of the security hereby pledged,

or which may hereafter be pledged, for this loan, a payment is to be made on account on demand, so that the said market value shall always be at least —— per cent. more than the amount unpaid of this note. In case of failure to do so, this note shall be deemed to be due and payable forthwith, anything hereinbefore expressed to the contrary notwithstanding, and the —— —— may immediately reimburse —— —— by sale of the security. It is understood and agreed that if such sale be by public auction, the said —— —— shall be at liberty to purchase for —— own account any property offered at such sale, and it is further agreed and understood that the above-mentioned securities, or substitutes therefor, or additions thereto, shall also be held as collateral and be applicable to any other note or claim held against —— —— by said —— ——, and that in case the proceeds of the whole of the collaterals shall not cover principal, interest and expenses, —— hold —— —— bound to pay on demand any deficiency.

"Due ——　　　　—— ——."

[1] Stevens v Hurlbut Bank, 31 Conn., 146 (1862), Lewis v Graham, 4 Abb Pr, 106. See, also, Wilson v. Little, 2 N Y, 443, Genet v Howland, 30 How Pr 360, Stenton v Jerome, 54 N Y, 480. Cf Milliken v Dehon, 27 N Y, 364 (1863). But an express power to sell on a specified day is held to waive right of notice. Bryson v Raynor, 25 Md, 424 (1866).

[2] Conyngham's Appeal, 57 Pa St, 474 (1868), Rankin v McCullough, 12 Barb, 103 (1851), Genet v Howland, 45 Barb, 560 (1866), Ogden v Lathrop, 65 N Y, 158 (1875). An express power to

and illegal, even though the utmost market price is obtained.[1] The pledgee cannot have the sale made at a broker's board or in a stock exchange, since only the members of the association are allowed to bid for stocks sold therein, while the law requires that the public shall be allowed to bid at a pledgee's sale[2] Frequently a special agreement is made between the pledgor and pledgee, especially between a customer and his stock-broker, whereby the pledgee is allowed to sell at a broker's board[3] Such an agreement, however, does not authorize a private sale at a broker's board[4] A sale is valid though the stock is sold for only a small part of its value.[5]

§ 479 *Pledgee himself cannot purchase at the sale* — It is a well-established rule that, where a pledgee pursues the remedy of selling the stock upon notice, the pledgee himself is disqualified from purchasing the stock[6] The rule is based on the principle that the law carefully protects the interest of the pledgor, and will not open the

sell has been held to authorize a private sale Bryson v Raynor, 25 Md, 424 (1866) Or a sale at a broker's board Id

[1] Castello v City Bank of Albany, 1 Leg Obs, 25 (1842), Willoughby v Comstock, 3 Hill. 389 (1842), Cf Nabring v Bank of Mobile 58 Ala, 205 (1877) The pledgee's right to object is waived by long delay Hayward v National Bank, 96 U S, 611 (1877)

[2] Brass v Worth, 40 Barb, 648 (1863), Rankin v McCullough, 12 Barb, 103 (1851) A sale in New York is legal King v. Texas, etc, Ins. Co, 58 Texas, 669 (1883)

[3] Wicks v Hatch, 62 N Y, 535 (1875) In Maryland a contrary rule prevails. Maryland Fire Ins. Co. v. Dalrymple, 25 Md, 242 (1866) See ch XXV

[4] Allen v Dykers, 3 Hill, 503, 7 id, 497

[5] A *bona fide* purchaser at a pledgee's sale is protected, though he purchased for less than the real value of the stock, and though a receiver had previously been appointed of the pledgor's property and it had been transferred to the receiver Dudley v Gould, 6 Hun, 97 (1875)

[6] Easton v German, etc, Bank, 127 U S, 532 (1888); Bryan v Baldwin, 52 N. Y., 432 (1873), the court saying "The plaintiff being the pledgee of the

stock, and in that character exposing it for sale, could not become the purchaser unless the defendant assented to such purchase. This sale to the plaintiff was not void, but voidable, at the election of the defendant" Maryland Fire Ins Co v Dalrymple, 25 Md, 242 (1866). Nor can he buy where the pledge is being sold on a forfeiture sale for non-payment of calls. Freeman v Harwood, 49 Me, 195 (1859) See, also, Sickles v Richardson, 23 Hun, 559 (1881), where the sale of the property pledged was on an attachment. The pledgor's silence may constitute a ratification of the pledgee's purchase Carroll v Mullanphy Sav Bank, 8 Mo App, 249 (1880). If the pledgee is a corporation, its president cannot purchase for it. Star Fire Ins. Co v Palmer, 41 Super. Ct., 267 (1876) Lewis v Graham, 4 Abb. Pr, 106 (1857), holds that a special partner of the pledgee firm may purchase. And see ch XXV, § 450 Cf Finney's Appeal, 59 Pa. St., 398 (1868). Where a pledgee bank having a right to sell at private sale and without notice sells the pledge through its president, who buys the pledge himself, and the president openly pays the bank for it, long delay on the part of the bank in complaining is fatal. Raymond v. Palmer, 6 S. Rep, 692 (La, 1889).

door to possible devices of the pledgee for purchasing the stock for himself at a low price. The pledgee cannot purchase, either directly or indirectly, in his own name or in the name of another [1] The effect of a purchase by the pledgee for himself is that the whole proceeding of the pledgee for subjecting the pledge to the payment of the debt is utterly futile, and voidable at the election of the pledgor The pledgor cannot claim that the pledgee has converted the stock by purchasing at the sale,[2] but he may disregard the notice and sale and whole proceeding as being ineffectual and voidable The pledge relationship continues as though no attempt had been made by the pledgee to subject the pledge to the payment of the debt [3] Where, however, the pledge is foreclosed by legal proceedings similar to those for the foreclosure of chattel mortgages, either party may bid at the public judicial sale [4] The pledgor may authorize the pledgee to purchase at the sale and retain the pledge [5] Stock held in pledge to secure a debt cannot be sold before the debt is due.[6] The pledgor may release his equity to the pledgee.[7]

[1] Minnesota Assoc v Canfield, 121 U. S., 295 (1887)

[2] Bryan v Baldwin, 52 N. Y., 232 (1873). If the pledgee buys it in there is no conversion The pledge continues Terry v Birmingham, etc , Bank, 9 S Rep , 299 (Ala , 1891)

[3] Bryson v Raynor, 25 Md , 424 (1866), Middlesex Bank v Minot, 45 Mass , 325 (1842), Hestonville, etc , R. R. Co v Shields, 3 Brews (Pa), 257 (1869) If the pledgee purchases at the sale the pledge continues The pledgor does not waive his rights by settling in ignorance that the pledgee purchased Sharpe v National Bank, 7 S Rep , 106 (Ala , 1888)

[4] Pewabic Min Co v Mason, 145 U. S , 349 (1892) In Newport, etc , Bridge Co. v Douglass, 12 Bush (Ky), 673, 720 (1877), the pledgee of bonds from the company issuing them obtained a foreclosure of the pledge by suit, and bought the bonds in and was then held to be the absolute owner of them.

[5] Chouteau v Allen, 70 Mo , 290 (1879). A pledgee cannot himself purchase the stock at the sale, but the pledgor may lawfully contract so as to allow the pledgee to purchase at such sale, or may ratify such purchase after it has been made If there is no such contract or ratification, however, the sale is void and the parties remain in the same position as though no sale had taken place Appleton v Turnbull, 24 Atl Rep , 592 (Me , 1891))

[6] National Bank v Baker, 21 N E Rep , 510 (Ill , 1889).

[7] Small v Saloy, 7 S Rep , 450 (1890). A pledgor may sell the securities pledged, and the sale may be to the pledgee The sale may be oral and will be upheld, the debt being canceled thereby Brown v Farmers', etc , Co , 117 N Y , 266 (1889) Cf Ryle v Ryle, 41 N J Eq , 582 Receiving the surplus in ignorance of illegality is no waiver Allen v American, etc , Ass'n, 52 N W Rep , 144 (Minn 1892).

§ 480 *An execution at common law could not reach shares of stock.* — A share of stock is in the nature of a chose in action, and at common law a chose in action could not be reached by or made subject to a levy of execution Consequently it has been uniformly held by the courts that at common law a levy of execution could not be made on shares of stock Unless, therefore, the process of execution has been extended by statute so as to reach such property. the stock of a judgment debtor cannot be subject to the payment of his debts by means of an execution.[1] An attachment,

---

[1] Van Norman v. Jackson County Circuit Judge, 45 Mich, 204 (1881), Goss v. Phillips, etc., Co, 4 Bradw, 510 (1879) Blair v Compton, 33 Mich, 414 (1876), Slaymaker v Bank of Gettysburg, 10 Pa. St., 373 (1849), Foster v Potter, 37 Mo, 525 (1866), Howe v Starkweather, 17 Mass, 240 (1821), Nabring v Bank of Mobile, 58 Ala, 204 (1877), Denton v Livingston, 9 Johns, 96 (1812), per Chancellor Kent, Nashville Bank v Ragsdale, Peck (Tenn), 296 (1823) Even where the stock is held to be real estate. Cooper v. Canal Co, 2 Murph (N. C.), 195 (1812). *Cf.* Gue v Tide-water Canal Co, 24 How. (U S), 257 (1860) At an early day, when the nature of stock was little understood, an attachment was attempted on the corporate property for the debts of a stockholder It failed. Williamson v. Smoot, 7 Mart. (La.), 31 (1819) Stock cannot be taken on a tax warrant. Barnes v Hall, 55 Vt. Rep., 420 *Cf* M'Neal v Mechanics', etc, Assoc, 3 Atl Rep, 125 (N J, 1885), Smith v

being entirely statutory, can be levied on shares of stock only when the words of the statute declare that an attachment may be levied on such property [1]

§ 481. *Nor, it seems, could a court of equity subject stock to the payment of debts.* — There is some doubt whether a court of equity has power to subject a judgment debtor's choses in action to the payment of his debts, where the only ground for the interference of the court is that, unless it does interfere, such property cannot be reached by the judgment creditor. In New York, previous to the statutes regulating this subject, the jurisdiction of a court of equity therein was emphatically denied in one case,[2] and with equal emphasis declared to exist in another case.[3] The English authorities are quite uniform in holding that a court of equity has no such jurisdiction [4] And in America, for the most part, a similar conclusion is arrived at [5] Where, however, the debtor has conveyed away his stock for the purpose of defrauding his creditors, a court of equity will aid the judgment creditor, inasmuch as it has jurisdiction in all matters involving fraud, trust or accident, or other ingredient of similar character.[6]

Northampton Bank, 4 Cush, 1 (1849). A tax collector cannot levy on and sell stock under the law relative to attachments. Kennedy v Neary, etc, R'y, 9 S Rep, 608 (Ala, 1891), and § 566 Execution against a corporation cannot be levied on stock owned by the corporation itself, such stock having been purchased by it under statutory authority at a forfeiture sale for non-payment of calls. Robinson v Spaulding, etc, Co, 13 Pac. Rep, 65 (Cal, 1887) An attachment of stock does not prevent a sale of property by the corporation. Gottfried v Miller, 104 U S, 521 (1881). The question of whether an execution may be levied on a seat in an exchange is considered in ch XXIX.

[1] Plimpton v Bigelow, 93 N Y 592, 602 (1883), Merchants' Mut. Ins Co v Brower, 38 Tex, 230 (1873)

[2] Donovan v Finn. Hopk Ch, 67, 91 (1823). See, also, Daniell's Ch Pr, vol. II, p 1037, note

[3] Storm v. Waddel, 2 Sand. Ch, 495, 511 (1845)

[4] Dundas v Dutens. 1 Ves, 196 (1790), Bank of England v Lunn, 15 Ves, 569 (1809), Grogan v. Cooke, 2 Ball & B.

(Ir Ch), 230 (1812), Nantes v Corrock, 9 Ves, 183 (1803), McCarthy v Gould, 1 Ball & B (Ir Ch), 387 (1810), applying the same rule to dividends. In King v Dupine, 2 Atk, 603. note (1744), a court of equity subjected to the payment of a debt the debtor's reversionary interest in an annuity In Horn v Horn, Ambl, 79 (1749), the court refused aid, inasmuch as the debtor had been imprisoned under a *cap satis*

[5] Williams v Reynolds, 7 Ind, 622 (1856) Disborough v Outcalt, Saxton's Ch (N J), 298, 306 (1831) McFerran v Jones, 2 Litt. (Ky), 219 (1822), Erwin v. Oldman, 6 Yerg, 185 (1834) *Contra, dictum,* Watkins v Dorsett, 1 Bland's Ch, 530 (1828) In Brightwell v Mallory, 10 Yerg (Tenn) 198 (1836), the proceeding was statutory

[6] See §§ 339, 340, on Statute of Frauds, also Taylor v Jones, 2 Atk, 600 (1743), holding that the debtor's transfer of stock in trust was in fraud of creditors, Hadden v Spader, 20 Johns (N Y), 554 (1822), Scott v Indianapolis Wagon Works, 48 Ind, 75 (1874), Van Norman v Jackson Circuit Judge, 45 Mich, 204 (1881), Lathrop v McBurney, 71 Ga,

§ 482 *By statutory provisions executions are generally sufficient to reach the debtor's stock — Strict compliance necessary — Levy on stock fraudulently conveyed away.* — Nearly all of the states of the Union have enacted statutes extending the scope of executions so as to render subject to them all choses in action, including shares of stock in a corporation   Frequently special provisions are made applicable to stock, and prescribing the steps which are necessary in rendering the execution levy effectual   Where an execution is levied in accordance with such statutes its provisions must be substantially complied with, and if not complied with the sale is not merely voidable, but is wholly unauthorized and void[1]   It is fatal to the levy and sale if the sheriff fails to give to the corporation the notice that is generally required by statute,[2] or if the sale by the sheriff is not made promptly as advertised in accordance with the statute[3]   The sale itself is not complete until the sheriff gives the proper instruments of title to the purchaser, and until then the corporation is not obliged to recognize the latter as having any rights.[4]

815 (1883), Gillett v Bate 86 N Y 87, State Bank v Gill, 23 Hun, 410 (1881), and §§ 482, 484

[1] Blair v Compton, 33 Mich. 414 (1876), holding that, where the sheriff sold without knowing or stating how many shares of stock the debtor owned, and which were being sold, the sale was void   See, also, People v Goss, etc., Mfg Co. 99 Ill, 355 (1881), reversing Goss, etc, Mfg Co. v People, 4 Bradw, 510   The procedure in levy of execution on stock, as laid down by the charter of the corporation, supersedes the procedure of a previous general statute   Titcomb v Union Marine, etc., Ins Co 8 Mass. 326 (1811)   And vice versa, Howe v Starkweather, 17 Mass, 240 (1821)   The sheriff need not sell the stock in parcels, but may sell the whole at once   Morris v Conn, etc, R. R. Co (Montreal Ct of Appeal, September, 1886)   An execution sale of stock will be set aside where it was made with an intentional concealment of the sale from the stockholder, the execution debtor Voorhis v Terhune, 13 Atl Rep, 391 (N J., 1888)   If no notice is given to the debtor of the levy on his stock, a sale under the attachment is not good   Commercial Nat. Bank v Farmers', etc,

Bank, 47 N W Rep., 1080 (Iowa, 1891) A levy and sale of "all the shares" which defendant owns is not good   The number of shares must be ascertained and stated   Keating v J Stove, etc, Co, 18 S W Rep, 797 (Tex, 1892).

[2] Princeton Bank v Crozer, 22 N J Law, 383 (1850), where no notice was given, but the stock was merely mentioned in the inventory returned by the sheriff   Oral notice by the sheriff to the corporation that stock has been attached is insufficient.   Moore v. Marshalltown, etc, Co, 46 N W Rep, 750 (Iowa, 1890)

[3] Titcomb v Union Marine, etc, Ins Co, 8 Mass, 326 (1811), and Howe v Starkweather, 17 Mass, 240 (1821), where the sale was made after the proper day, without a re-advertisement, and consequently was held to be void   The court said   "The sale of them upon execution not being justifiable at common law, the statute must be strictly pursued to give any property to the purchaser"   An execution sale of stock at 9 o'clock at night when few are present, is void. McNaughton v McLean. 41 N W. Rep, 267 (Mich, 1889).

[4] Morgan v Thames Bank, 14 Conn., 99 (1840)

A court of equity will not compel a corporation to allow a transfer of stock by a purchaser at an execution sale where the price paid at such sale is so small as to shock the conscience of the court.[1]

Whether or not an execution can be levied on stock which has been fraudulently transferred away by the judgment debtor depends upon the wording of the statute allowing the levy of execution on stock. If it allows a levy on all interests of the debtor, whether legal or equitable, then the fraudulent transfer may be disregarded and the stock seized as though still standing in the name of the judgment debtor.[2] If, however, the statute does not expressly provide for a levy on an equitable interest, the judgment creditor's remedy is not an execution, but a suit in equity to set aside the fraudulent transfer.[3]

§ 483. *Attachment of stock as allowed by the statutes of the various states* — The states of the Union have quite generally passed statutes providing for the attachment of a debtor's property where the debtor is a non-resident or is guilty of a fraud, or where other facts exist which bring the case within the attachment statute. Inasmuch as in modern times a large part of the property of individuals consists of shares of stock in corporations, the attachment statutes generally provide specially for the attachment of stock, and give specific directions in reference to the steps necessary to be taken in making such attachment.[4] In New York an attach-

---

[1] Mississippi, etc., R. R. *v.* Cromwell 91 U S, 643, Randolph *v.* Quidnick Co, 135 U S, 457 (1890). Inadequacy of price is not sufficient cause for setting aside an execution sale of stock. Conway *v.* John, 23 Pac. Rep, 170 (Cal, 1890).

[2] Scott *v.* Indianapolis Wagon Works, 48 Ind, 75 (1874). *Cf.* State *v.* Warren Foundry, etc, Co, 32 N J L., 439 (1868). See, also, § 484, *infra,* relative to attachments on stock that has been fraudulently conveyed away.

[3] Van Norman *v.* Jackson County Circuit Judge, 45 Mich, 204 (1881). See § 481.

[4] California, Code of C Proc § 5141, Colorado, Code of C Proc., § 97. Connecticut, Gen Stat (1875), § 6, Georgia, Code of 1882, §§ 3289-3291, Indiana, R S (1881), § 933, Iowa, McClain's Annotated Stat., 1880, § 2967, Maine, R S 1884, ch 81, § 27, Maryland, R Code of 1874, § 20, Massachusetts, Public Stat 1882, ch. 161, §§ 71-73, Michigan, How-

ell's Annotated Stat, 1883, Minnesota, Gen Stat. 1878, § 156, Missouri, R S 1879, § 417, Nebraska, Common Laws 1881, ch 3, § 201, Nevada, Gen Stat. 1885, ch 4, §§ 3149, 3150, New Hampshire, Gen L 1878, ch 224, § 13, New York, Code of Civil Proc., § 647, also § 649, as amd by L 1879, ch 541, also §§ 650, 651, 708 (2), Ohio, R S 1880, title 1, div 6, ch 2, § 5521, Pennsylvania, Brightley's P Dig, § 71, South Carolina, Code of C Proc, ch 1, §§ 256, 258, Wisconsin, R S 1878, § 2738. Where both an attachment and an execution on stock are allowed by statute, the former is said to be the preferable remedy when the corporation has a lien on the stock or there is a claimant to the stock. Weaver *v.* Huntingdon, etc, Coal Co, 50 Pa St, 314 (1865), Lex *v.* Potter, 16 Pa St, 295 (1851). An attachment of stock covers the dividends also. Upon vacating the attachment damages may be recovered. Jacobus *v.*

ment of stock is provided for; but an execution without a previous
attachment is not allowed [1]   It has been held that shares of stock
may be attached under the general provisions of an attachment
law which does not specify shares of stock as being subject to an
attachment.[2] The formalities prescribed by the statute must be
complied with fully as in the case of a levy of execution upon
stock [3]

Mononagahela etc, Bank, 35 Fed Rep.,
395 (1888). Decrease in value of stock
while subject to attachment does not
render the sureties on the undertaking
liable therefor Miller v Ferry, 50 Hun,
256 (1888) An attachment bond should
not be increased merely because the
price of the stock may go down Id.
In New York shares of stock cannot be
levied on under a writ of execution, although they may be attached and subsequently sold by execution in that suit.
Code of Civil Procedure, §§ 647, 649-651
See 4 Wait's Pr, 36, J Stock may be
reached, however, by proceedings supplementary to execution See, in general, Barnes v Morgan, 3 Hun, 703
(1875); O Brien v. Mechanics' & T Ins
Co, 56 N. Y, 52 (1874), Smoot v Heim,
1 Civ. Proc. Rep, 208 (1891) — cases
arising under the attachment law. The
statute may provide for the sale of
stock at the place where the corporation exists, in case the taxes upon such
stock are not paid A purchaser of the
outstanding certificates after the assessment has been made takes subject to
the tax and tax seizure Parker v Sun
Ins Co, 8 S Rep, 618 (La, 1890) Under the English statute, 1 and 2 Vict.,
ch 110, § 14, and 3 and 4 Vict., ch 82,
§ 1, stock in any public company standing in the name of any person against
whom judgment shall have been obtained, whether "in his own right or
in the name of any person in trust for
him," may be charged by a judge's order with the payment of the amount of
the judgment The statute says "The
interest of any judgment debtor,
whether in possession, remainder or
reversion, and whether vested or con-

tingent," may be so reached Cragg v.
Taylor, L. R, 2 Ex, 131 (1867), Baker
v Tynte, 2 Ell & E, 897 (1860).
[1] See preceding note.
[2] Chesapeake & O R R Co. v Paine,
29 Gratt. (Va), 502 (1877), where stock
was held to be included under the word
"estate," and the procedure prescribed
for garnishment was followed and upheld So also, Curtis v. Steever, 36
N J L Rep, 304 (1873), where an attachment of stock was upheld though
the statute merely allowed attachment
of "rights and credits." In Haley v
Reid, 16 Ga, 437 (1854), however, an attachment of stock was not allowed
where the statute allowed levy "upon
the estate both real and personal." See,
also Merchants' M Ins Co v Brower,
38 Tex, 230 (1873) It has been held
that there can be no attachment of
stock under a statute which allows an
attachment of "real and personal property" Foster v Potter, 37 Mo., 525
Shares of stock are "personal property"
subject to attachment, although the statutes provide only for levy of execution
upon them Union Nat'l Bank v. Byram,
22 N E Rep, 842 (Ill, 1889). The ordinary attachment statute authorizing
the attachment of shares of stock is not
applicable to shares of stock in a club
organized for lawful sporting purposes
and being more of the nature of a statutory joint-stock association than a corporation Lyon v Denison, 45 N W
Rep, 358 (Mich, 1890)
[3] Stamford Bank v Ferris, 17 Conn,
259 (1845), where the attachment failed
because the sheriff did not leave a copy
of the writ, duly indorsed, with the corporation, even though the cashier of

§ 484. *Attachment of stock held in pledge or by trustee and of stock which the debtor has fraudulently transferred away* — As has been said in the case of an execution levied on shares of stock, an attachment may be levied on the same when the words of the attachment statute are so broad as to render subject to the attachment all equitable interests of the debtor whose stock is attached Thus, it has been held in Ohio and New Jersey that, although the debtor has transferred his stock for the purpose of defrauding his creditors, an attachment of the stock will lie nevertheless.[1] An attachment may be levied upon stock although the stock has been mortgaged or pledged, and the attaching creditor is seeking to reach merely the equity of redemption[2] An attachment is not the best remedy for a pledgee who wishes to subject the pledge to

the corporation was absent. A transfer subsequent to such irregular attachment is valid and carries title See, also, § 484.

[1] National Bank of N L, *v* Lake Shore & M S R R Co, 21 Ohio St, 221 (1871), holding also that the attachment is good, even though the corporation deny that the defendant owns any stock therein, Curtis *v* Steever 36 N J L. Rep., 304 (1873) the court saying that the attachment is good, since the fraudulent transfer is void, and holding that the transferee may bring a suit for trespass, and that the attaching creditor may then set up the fraud in defense *Cf* State *v* Warren Foundry, etc, Co, 32 N J. L., 439 (1868) See, also, § 482 *supra*. Where an insolvent debtor transfers all his property to trustees for the benefit of creditors, excepting certain shares of stock which are transferred to them in trust in order not to render the trustees liable thereon, and ten years later a creditor levies on the equity in such stock, causes its sale and purchases it at a nominal figure, equity will not compel the corporation to transfer the stock to such creditor on the corporate books Randolph *v* Quidnick Co, 135 U S, 457 (1890)

[2] Edwards *v* Beugnot, 7 Cal., 162 (1857), holding also that, if the mortgage is recorded on the corporate books,

notice must be served on the mortgagee also, and that, where one attachment was served on the corporation and another on the mortgagee, the latter attachment prevails and takes the surplus Norton *v* Norton, 43 Ohio St, 509 (1885), holding that the court will order the stock to be sold, the pledgee paid and the balance held under the attachment. See also, Vantine *v* Morse, 104 Mass, 275 (1870), New England, etc, Co. *v* Chandler, 16 Mass, 275 (1820) *Cf* Cooke *v* Hallett, 119 Mass, 148 (1875) A garnishment for the surplus is ineffectual Kyle *v* Montgomery, 73 Ga 337 (1884), Seehgson *v* Brown, 61 Texas, 114 (1884) Mechanics', etc, Ass'n *v* Conover, 14 N J Eq, 219 (1862), Foster *v* Potter, 37 Mo, 525 (1866), Mauns *v* Brookville Nat'l Bank, 73 Ind, 243 (1881), Nabring *v* Bank of Mobile, 58 Ala, 204 (1877) If a purchaser at an execution sale purchases merely a nominal equity of redemption and pays a fair price for the same, the court will order the corporation to allow a transfer to him in order that he may so redeem See *dictum* in Randolph *v* Quidnick Co, 135 U S, 457 (1890) Stock held as collateral is property subject to garnishment under the statutes of Texas Smith *v* Traders' Nat'l Bank, 12 S W Rep, 113 (Texas, 1889) See, also, §§ 340, 491.

the payment of the debt [1] His remedy is by foreclosure or a public sale on notice to the pledgor. Dividends on the stock which is attached follow the stock, and are covered by the attachment.[2] An attachment on stock standing on the books in a debtor's name is not good where it is shown that in fact he held the stock as trustee for another.[3] An attachment will lie in Rhode Island for stock which is registered in the name of a person other than the defendant, the transfer by the defendant having been in fraud of creditors [4] Where the corporation has a lien on stock for debts due from the stockholder to the corporation, it may enforce the lien by an attachment.[5]

§ 485 *Stock can be attached only in the state creating the corporation* — Shares of stock in a corporation are personal property, whose location is in the state where the corporation is created [6] It is true that, for purposes of taxation and some other similar purposes, stock follows the domicile of its owner, but, considered as property separated from its owner, stock is in existence only in the state of the corporation All attachment statutes provide for the attachment of a non-resident debtor's property in the state, and generally, under such statutes, the stock owned by a non-resident in a corporation created by the state wherein the suit is brought may be attached and jurisdiction be thereby acquired to the extent of the value of the stock attached [7] But under no circumstances can a defendant's shares of stock be reached by levy of attachment in an action commenced outside of the state wherein the corporation is incorporated For purposes of attachment, stock is located where the corporation is incorporated and nowhere else.[8] The

---

[1] Lee v Citizens' Nat'l Bank, 2 Cin Super Ct., 298, 312 (1872) See § 476

[2] Moore v Gennett, 2 Tenn Ch , 375 (1875)

[3] Mowry v. Hawkins, 18 Atl Rep., 784 (Conn , 1889) Execution or garnishee process cannot be levied on stock held by an individual as trustee, where the debt is his individual debt Nor can it be levied on the dividend from such stock So held where stock was owned by a city in trust for the citizens Hitchcock v Galveston W. Co., 50 Fed Rep., 263 (1890).

[4] Beckwith v Burroughs, 14 R. I. 366 (1884) And the purchaser at the execution sale may file a bill in equity to clear the title to the stock. Cf. S. C., 13 R. L, 294 (1881)

[5] Sabin v Bank of Woodstock, 21 Vt , 353 (1849).

[6] Evens v Monet, 4 Jones' Eq (N. C), 227 (1858)

[7] National Bank of N. L. v. Lake Shore & M. S. R R. Co, 21 Ohio St , 221 (1871), Chesapeake & O. R. R. Co. v Paine, 29 Gratt. (Va.), 502 (1877). An attachment and sale of stock made on a debt not justly due will be enjoined as regards registry on the corporate books, and the sale declared void Seligman v. St. Louis, etc., R. R. Co., 22 Fed. Rep., 39 (1884),

[8] Winslow v Fletcher, 13 Am. & Eng Corp Cas, 39 (Conn , 1886), the court saying that "stock in a corporation for the purposes of an attachment has its *situs* where the corporation is located "

shares owned by a non-resident defendant in the stock of a foreign corporation cannot be reached and levied upon by virtue of an attachment, although officers of the corporation are within the state engaged in carrying on the corporate business[1] Nor can such an attachment be levied although the foreign corporation has a branch registry office in the state where the attachment is levied, and although the certificates of stock are also in such state[2] Certificates of stock are not the stock itself — they are but evidence of the stock, and the stock itself cannot be attached by a levy of attachment on the certificate[3] As was well said by the supreme court of Pennsylvania, stock cannot be attached by attaching the certificate any more than lands situated in another state can be attached by an attachment in Pennsylvania levied on the title deeds to such land.[4] There can be no attachment of stock as the property of an

Under the statutes of Tennessee, however, requiring a foreign corporation doing business in that state to file its articles of incorporation with the secretary of state, it was held that it became a domestic corporation sufficiently to authorize an attachment of stock in that state Young v South etc Iron Co. 2 S W Rep 202 (Tenn, 1886) Bonds which are pledged by a non-resident cannot be attached by serving a notice on the pledgee Tweedy v Bogart 15 Atl Rep, 874 (N J, 1888)

[1] Plimpton v Bigelow, 93 N Y, 592 (1883), reversing 29 Hun, 362, the court saying "We do not doubt that shares for the purpose of attachment proceedings may be deemed to be in the possession of the corporation which issued them, but only at the place where the corporation by intendment of law always remains, to wit, in the state or country of its creation. . . Manifestly the *res* cannot be within the jurisdiction, as a mere consequence of a legislative declaration, when the actual locality is undeniably elsewhere" To same effect, Preston v Pangburn, N Y L J, March 7, 1892 Garnishment proceedings also will not apply The defendant may move to have the attachment levy set aside. Martin v Mobile & O R R Co, 7 Bush (Ky), 116 (1870), holds that a statute authorizing a foreign

corporation to exercise certain powers does not make it a domestic corporation Certificates of stock in a corporation of another state cannot be subjected to the payment of the stockholders' debts, either by attachment or a bill in equity Morton v Grafflin, 13 Atl Rep, 341 (Md, 1888)

[2] Christmas v Biddle, 13 Pa St, 223 (1850), approved in Childs v Digby 24 Pa St, 23 (1854) In this case the attachment was levied in Pennsylvania on certificates of stock in Pennsylvania, but belonging to a citizen of Mississippi and the corporation was created by the laws of Mississippi Certificates of stock in a corporation cannot be attached anywhere except in the state where the corporation is incorporated Armour, etc., Co v Smith, 20 S W Rep, 690 (Mo, 1892).

[3] Christmas v Biddle, *supra*, Moore v Gennett, 2 Tenn Ch, 375 (1875)

[4] Christmas v Biddle, *supra* In Winslow v Fletcher, 13 Am & Eng Corp Cas, 39 (Conn, 1886), the court well says "While the certificates are in themselves valuable for some purposes and to some extent may properly be regarded as property, yet they are distinct from the holders' interest in the capital stock of the corporation, and are not goods and effects within the meaning of the statute relating to foreign at-

unregistered holder through whom title has passed to another.[1] This rule is peculiar to certificates of stock.

§ 486 *Rights of an unregistered transferee of a certificate of stock as against an attachment or execution levied on that stock —* The most difficult and unsettled question connected with an attachment or execution levied on stock is the question of how far a purchaser of the certificate of stock from the stockholder and debtor is protected in his ownership where such purchaser does not have his transfer registered on the corporate books before the attachment or execution is levied. The question is especially important, since it affects the rights of a *bona fide* purchaser of stock in the open market, and constitutes one of the greatest dangers incurred in the purchase of certificates of stock It has been held that if a stockholder whose stock has been already attached or sold on execution sells his certificate of stock after the levy of such attachment or execution, the vendee or transferee buys subject to such levy, even though he had no knowledge of it The stock, in contemplation of law, has already been seized by the levy, and the purchaser is bound to take notice of that fact[2] The only means of avoiding this danger in the purchase of stock is by an inquiry at the office of the corporation at the time of making the purchase.

A different question, however, presents itself when the stockholder against whose stock an attachment or execution is levied has already and before such levy sold and transferred his certificate of stock, but that transfer has not been registered on the corporate books. The courts of the different states are in irreconcilable conflict on this question of whether the unregistered transferee is protected in his purchase. The better rule, and the rule which ultimately will prevail, is that an unrecorded transfer of stock is in this respect like an unrecorded deed of land, and gives good

---

tachment They are no more subject to an attachment or a trustee process than a promissory note The debt is subject to attachment, but the note itself, which is simply evidence of the debt, is not So with stock That may be attached, but the certificate cannot be" Negotiable bonds held outside of the jurisdiction of the court cannot be attached by serving the attachment on the corporation which issued the bonds Von Hesse *v.* Mackaye, 55 Hun, 365 (1890), affirmed, 121 N Y, 691 An attachment cannot be levied on bonds in a foreign corporation, the bonds not being in the state Id Cf p. 615, note *supra*

[1] Lippett *v* American, etc., Co, 14 R I, 301 (1885). Thus, where A, the registered stockholder, transfers the certificate of stock to B and B transfers it to C, and C obtains registry directly from A there can be no attachment of the stock against B

[2] Chesapeake & O R R Co *v* Paine, 29 Gratt. (Va), 502 (1877), Shenandoah Valley R. R. Co. *v.* Griffith, 76 Va., 913 (1882). Cf Dudley *v* Gould, 6 Hun, 97 (1875)

title as against subsequent attachments or levies of execution, even though made in ignorance of the unrecorded transfer or deed.

§ 487 *Rule in New York, Pennsylvania, New Jersey, Minnesota, South Carolina, Texas, Louisiana and the federal courts* — The decided weight of authority holds that he who purchases for a valuable consideration a certificate of stock is protected in his ownership of the stock, and is not affected by a subsequent attachment or execution levied on such stock for the debts of the registered stockholder, even though such purchaser has neglected to have his transfer registered on the corporate books, thereby allowing his transferrer to appear to be the owner of the stock upon which the attachment or execution is levied. Such is the rule prevailing in the federal courts and in the courts of the above-named states [1] Frequently this rule is justified and explained on the

[1] *New York*. The case of Smith *v* American Coal Co, 7 Lans, 317 (1873), fully discusses and sustains this rule See, also, Comeau *v* Guild Farm Oil Co, 3 Daly, 218 (1870), where Van Brunt, J, says that the sheriff, "by the levy of such an attachment, could not acquire any better or greater title to the stock than a person would have done who had purchased this stock of the person in whose name it stood on the day of the levy of the attachment And the principle is well established in this state that such a purchaser would not acquire any interest whatever as against a prior purchaser for value." Where the corporation causes an attachment to be levied on the stock of a stockholder of record who has sold his certificates to another person and causes a sale to be made to deprive the latter of his stock, he may hold the corporation liable Sims *v* Bonner, 16 N Y Supp, 801 (1891) See also, in general, Dunn *v* Star, etc, Ins Co, 19 N Y Week Dig, 531 (1884). An assignment of the certificates to a receiver in another state takes precedence of an attachment against the stock at the home of the corporation The court will direct the corporation to register the transfer Weller *v* Pace, etc, Co, 5 R'y & Corp. L. J, 5 (N. Y Sup Ct, 1888)

Pennsylvania For Pennsylvania, see Eby *v.* Guest, 94 Pa. St., 160 (1880); Finney's Appeal 59 Pa. St., 398 (1868), Com-

monwealth *v* Watmouth, 6 Whart, 117 (1840), holding also that the sheriff need not levy on stock which he knows has already been sold to an unregistered transferee When the transferrer notifies the corporation of the transfer, a subsequent attachment of the stock as the property of the transferrer is not good, although the transfer was not recorded in the corporate book Tilford, etc, Co *v* Gerhab, 13 Atl Rep 90 (Pa, 1888), United States *v* Vaughan, 3 Binn, 394 (1811), where the unregistered transferees resided in foreign lands

Minnesota A sale and transfer of corporate stock, although not entered on the books of the corporation, is effectual as between the parties, and takes precedence of a subsequent attachment in behalf of a creditor of the vendor Lund *et al* *v* Wheaton, etc, Co, 52 N W Rep, 268 (Minn, 1892).

New Jersey Broadway Bank *v* McElrath 13 N J Eq, 24 (1860), S C, *sub nom* Hunterdon Bank *v* Nassau Bank, 2 C E Gr, 496, Rogers *v* Stevens, 8 N. J. Eq, 167 (1849).

South Carolina Fraser *v* Charleston, 11 S C, 486, 519 (1878).

Texas Seeligson *v* Brown, 61 Texas, 114 (1884)

Louisiana Pitot *v* Johnson, 33 La. Ann, 1286 (1881), Smith *v.* Crescent City, etc, Co, 30 La Ann, 1378 (1878). The attaching creditor of one who ap-

ground that registry and by-laws or charter provisions requiring
registry of transfers on the corporate books are not for the purpose of notifying the creditors of the old registered stockholder
that he no longer owns the stock, nor for any similar purpose, but
are for the purpose of protecting the corporation in paying dividends and allowing the stock to be voted   Another and stronger
reason is that the law favors the transfer of stock certificates, and
decreases, so far as possible. all secret dangers incurred in their
purchase

By protecting the purchaser against subsequent attachments and
executions the law removes one of the chief risks incurred by holding certificates of stock without a registry, and thereby increases
the safety and desirability of such investments   If the corporation
improperly refuses to allow the transferee of stock to register his

pears on the books of a corporation as
registered owner of shares of its stock
cannot hold the stock against the true
equitable owner, who holds the certificate of stock duly indorsed by the
debtor   Kern v Day, 12 S Rep, 6 (La,
1893)   Cf Bidstrup v Thompson, 45
Fed Rep., 452 (1891), where the pledge
had not been completed

Federal Courts In regard to stock in
national banks, the federal courts have
firmly established the rule that the unregistered transferee is protected against
a subsequent attachment or execution
Continental Nat'l Bank v Eliot Nat'l
Bank, 5 Fed Rep, 369 (1881), with a full
review of the authorities by Judge
Lowell, Scott v Pequonnock Nat'l
Bank, 15 Fed Rep, 494 (1883), where the
rule was applied, although the national
bank was in Connecticut, a state which
strongly favors the opposite rule. The
court said   "The tendency of modern
decisions is to regard certificates of
stock attached to an execution blank,
assignment, and power to transfer, as
approximating to negotiable securities,
though neither in form nor character
negotiable" Under the federal statutes.
the rights of a transferee of national
bank stock, under an unrecorded transfer, good at common law, are superior
to the rights of a subsequent attaching
creditor of the transferee without no-

tice   Doty v First Nat'l Bank of Larimore, 53 N W Rep, 77 (N Dak, 1892).
Even in Massachusetts, where the courts
upheld an opposite rule, the state courts
will follow the above rule when the
stock of a national bank is in question
Sibley v Quinsigamond Nat'l Bank, 133
Mass., 515 (1882), but see State v First
Nat'l Bank of J, 89 Ind, 302 (1883)
The statute of a state cannot restrict or
interfere with the transferability of certificates of stock in national banks
Doty v First Nat'l Bank of Larimore,
53 N. W Rep 77 (N Dak, 1892). Williams v Mechanics' Bank, 5 Blatch, 59
(1862), is not in accord with the other
federal decisions

Tennessee As regards Tennessee, compare Cornick v. Richards, 3 Lea, 1 (1879),
with State Ins Co. v Sax, 2 Tenn. Ch,
507 (1875).

Maryland In Maryland, by statute,
stock which is pledged cannot be attached   Morton v Grafflin, 15 Atl Rep,
298 (1888). But see Noble v. Turner, 18
id, 124

In England the creditor of a registered stockholder cannot subject the
stock to his debt as against the owner
of the certificates, who has allowed the
stock to remain in the name of the
debtor in order to qualify the latter as a
director   Cooper v Griffin, 66 L. T.
Rep, 660 (1892)

transfer, and the stock is afterwards attached by a creditor of the stockholder, the transferee may, if he chooses, hold the corporation liable in damages for its refusal to allow the registry.[1]

§ 488 *Rights and duties of the corporation in such cases* — The corporation has a dangerous duty to perform when stock has been attached or sold under levy of execution, and a registry is requested by the purchaser at such sale or by a purchaser of the outstanding certificate of stock If the purchaser of the certificate demands registry before registry has been allowed to the purchaser at the execution sale, and if the former claims to have purchased the certificate before the attachment or execution was levied, the right of the corporation is clear It may refuse to allow the registry, and when sued therefor may interplead and compel the claimants to litigate the matter between themselves.[2] But where the corporation does not know whether the outstanding certificate is in the hands of a purchaser or not, and a registry is demanded by a purchaser at an execution sale, the rights and duties of the corporation are not so clear It has two courses open to it [3] it may refuse to allow a registry until compelled to do so by a court, or it may allow registry without being so compelled The former is the safer course, since the corporation will probably be thereby protected from all liability to a possible purchaser of the outstanding certificate [4] The corporation, it seems, is protected in its obedience to the decree of a court [5] It is quite probable, also, that no court in any of the above-named states would require the corporation to issue new certificates of stock to a purchaser of stock at an execution sale unless such purchaser give to the corporation a bond of indemnity, whereby an unknown purchaser of the outstanding cer-

[1] Robinson v National Bank of New Berne, 95 N Y, 637 (1884) See also, Plymouth Bank v Bank of Norfolk, 27 Mass, 454 (1830).

[2] See ch XXII, § 387. The proper remedy for the purchaser from the judgment debtor to pursue under such circumstances is to enjoin the corporation and the purchaser at the execution sale from registering the latter as a stockholder Smith v Crescent City, etc, Co, 30 La Ann, 1378 (1878). If an attachment has been levied he should enjoin that Cheever v Meyer, 52 Vt 66 (1879).

[3] Robinson v National Bank of New Berne, 95 N, Y, 637 (1884).

[4] "Where a judicial tribunal of competent jurisdiction of last resort, after a fair contest in good faith by the corporation, orders the stock to be transferred to the purchaser under such seizure and sale, the corporation cannot be liable to the holder of the certificate who took no steps to protect himself" Friedlander v Slaughter-house Co, 31 La Ann, 523 (1879) Where, also, the unregistered transferee contested in the courts the right of the purchaser at the execution sale, and was defeated in the lower court, and appealed without staying the decree below, the corporation is not liable for obeying the decree of the lower court, although the appeal is successful Chapman v New Orleans Gas Light, etc, Co, 4 La. Ann., 153 (1849).

[5] See §§ 359, 388.

tificate may be protected [1] The other course open to the corporation, that of allowing a registry by the purchaser at the execution sale without being compelled to do so by a court, is pursued by the corporation at its peril If it afterwards transpires that the outstanding certificate had been purchased before the attachment or execution was levied, the corporation is liable in damages to such purchaser for allowing the registry,[2] but not unless such purchaser gave a valuable consideration for the certificate and alleges that fact in his pleading[3] Until such purchaser demands a registry from the corporation it may safely pay dividends to the execution purchaser.[4] These rules are complicated, but they protect all parties If the statute prescribes that the corporation shall register as a stockholder the purchaser at the execution sale, the writ of *mandamus* will lie to compel the corporation to make such registry,[5] but the relator must allege that he presented to the corporation the required papers, and was refused such registry[6] A court of equity will not compel a corporation to allow a transfer of stock by a purchaser at an execution sale where the price paid at such sale is so small as to shock the conscience of the court.[7]

[1] The supreme court of Ohio, in Nat'l Bank of N L t Lake Shore & M S R. R. Co, 21 Ohio St., 221 (1871), very properly and very distinctly refused to compel a registry, although conceding that the execution purchaser is entitled to dividends The court said ' Can it be that, because the defendant refused to assume the peril of deciding between the contending claimants by issuing other certificates for the same stock to the plaintiff upon demand, that it thereby became a wrong-doer and converted the plaintiff's stock to its own use, and rendered itself liable to respond in the full value of the stock to the claimant who could establish his right in a court of law? The very statement of the proposition refutes it." Where the attachment is on stock that the complainant alleges was transferred in fraud of creditors, *mandamus* will not lie to compel the corporation to allow a registry under the execution sale State v. Warren Foundry & M Co., 32 N J L., 439 (1868). As to the mode of pleading that the defendant company has been compelled to transfer the stock to a purchaser at an execution sale, see

Wyoming. etc., Assoc v. Talbott, 21 Pac Rep., 700 (Wyom, 1889).

[2] Smith v American Coal Co, 7 Lans. (N Y), 317 (1873). It the purchaser at the execution sale still has the certificates the purchaser of the old certificate may bring suit against him and the corporation to compel a retransfer. Rogers v Stevens, 8 N. J. Eq, 167 (1849). In a suit by a purchaser at an execution sale to cut off the rights of a judgment debtor the corporation is an indispensable party, since it alone can allow a transfer on the books St. Louis & San F. R'y Co v Wilson, 114 U S, 60 (1884). See, also, the late case of Hazard v Nat'l Ex Bank, 26 Fed Rep., 94 (1886), holding the corporation liable in damages to the purchaser of the outstanding certificate.

[3] Littell t Scranton Gas & Water Co., 42 Pa St., 500 (1862).

[4] Smith v American Coal Co, *supra*.

[5] Bailey v Strohecker, 38 Ga., 259 (1868) See, also, § 390

[5] Lippett t American Wood Paper Co. 14 R. I, 301 (1883)

[7] Mississippi, etc., R. R. v Cromwell, 91 U. S., 643, Randolph v Quidnick,

§ 489. *Rule in Connecticut, Maine, Vermont, Indiana, Iowa, Maryland, Wisconsin, Alabama and California.* — The courts of these states all hold that, where regulations exist requiring a transfer of stock to be registered on the corporate books in order to be effectual, an attachment or execution levied on stock standing in the defendant debtor's name will cut off the rights of a previous purchaser of the certificate who has not completed his transfer by registry[1] Sometimes these regulations requiring a registry are contained in the charter, sometimes only in the by-laws, and sometimes are merely printed on the face of the certificate of stock.[2] Even in these states, however, it is well established

135 U S., 457 (1890) Inadequacy of price is not sufficient cause for setting aside an execution sale of stock Conway v John, 23 Pac Rep, 170 (Cal., 1890)

[1] See note following

[2] Oxford Turnpike Co. v Bunnell. 6 Conn, 552 (1827), Dutton v Conn Bank, 13 Conn, 493 (1840), where the provision was in the by-laws, Skowhegan Bank v Cutler 49 Me, 315 (1860), Fiske v Carr, 20 Me, 301 (1841), Warren v. Brandon Mfg Co, cited in 52 Vt, 75 (1879), State v First Nat'l Bank of J, 89 Ind, 302 (1883) Coleman v Spencer 5 Blackf (Ind), 197 (1839), Fort Madison, etc, Co v Batavian Bank, 32 N W. Rep, 336 (Iowa, 1887), 43 id 331, *Re* Murphy, 51 Wis, 519 (1881). where the provision was by statute Also, under a statute, Weston v Bear River, etc., Min Co, 5 Cal, 186 (1855), Nagle v Pacific Wharf Co., 20 Cal, 529 (1862). *Cf* Supply, etc, Co v Elliott, 15 Pac Rep, 691 (Cal, 1887) In California an attachment takes precedence over an unrecorded prior transfer of the certificate, the by-laws providing for transfer of title by registry Conway v John, 23 Pac Rep., 170 (Cal, 1890). If the unregistered purchaser buys the judgment obtained under the attachment the latter is merged Strout v Natoma Water & Min Co., 9 Cal, 78 (1858) As to North Carolina, see Morehead v Western N. C. R. R. Co., 2 S E Rep, 247 (1887) The statutory law of Alabama on this subject is indicated in

Fisher v Jones, 3 S Rep., 13 (Ala, 1887) In Alabama by statute the attaching creditor takes title in preference to an unregistered transferee, and the same rule prevails where the registered holder is a mere "dummy" for another White v Rankin, 8 S. Rep, 118 (Ala., 1890) In Alabama the unregistered pledgee is not protected against attachments. Notice to the corporate officer of the attachment may be oral Abels v Mobile, etc, Co, 9 S Rep, 423 (Ala, 1891) Under the Alabama attachment statute the attachment takes precedence over a prior transfer of the certificates, where such transfer is not recorded on the corporate books within fifteen days Berney Nat'l Bank v Pinckard, 6 S. Rep, 364 (Ala, 1889). In Maryland a subsequent attachment precedes a pledge of the certificates Noble v Turner, 16 Atl Rep, 124 (Md, 1888) Where an agreement to sell is negotiated but before the certificate is transferred an attachment is levied on the stock, it is held in Tennessee that the attachment prevailed Young v South, etc, Iron Co, 2 S W Rep, 202 (Tenn, 1886) A sale of stock after an attachment suit has failed, and before that decision is reversed, gives the purchaser good title. Loveland v Alvord, etc, Co., 18 Pac. Rep, 682 (Cal, 1888) For a lurid and yet just invective against the decisions of California, Indiana, Colorado and other states allowing attachments in those states to have priority against a prior transfer of stock, see 12

that if the person who levies the attachment or purchases at the
execution sale has notice that the defendant debtor had transferred
his certificate before the attachment or execution was levied, the
purchaser of the outstanding certificate may have his remedy.   If
the attaching creditor has notice before the attachment is levied
the purchaser may obtain a perpetual injunction against the attachment [1] Moreover, if the purchaser at the execution sale has notice,
he may be prevented from obtaining registry and claiming the
stock [2] It is also held that where the unregistered transferee of
the certificate of stock has notified the corporation thereof and demanded registry, which is not granted, any attachment or execution
levied subsequently to the improper refusal by the corporation to
register does not take precedence over such purchaser.[3]   Where

R'y & Corp L J, 145 As to Illinois,
see People's Bank v Gridley, 91 Ill 477
(1879) The laws of 1883, p 110, changed
the rule for that state

[1] Cheever v Meyer, 52 Vt, 66 (1879),
Scripture v Francistown Soapstone Co,
50 N H, 571 (1871), Black v Zacharie,
3 How , 482 (1845) A purchaser at an
execution sale takes no title as against
a prior purchaser of the certificate
where the former knew of the latter's
purchase when the execution sale took
place Wilson v St Louis, etc , R. R.,
18 S W Rep, 286 (Mo, 1891) If the
purchaser at the execution sale buys
with knowledge that the judgment
debtor does not own the stock at the
time of the sale he takes no title to the
stock. Blakeman v Puget Sound Iron
Co, 13 Pac Rep, 872 (Cal, 1887).

[2] People v Elmore, 35 Cal, 653 (1868);
Weston v Bear River, etc, Min Co., 6
Cal, 425 (1856), Van Cise v Merchants'
Nat Bank, 33 N W. Rep, 897 (Dak,
1887), Farmers' Nat. Gold Bank v. Wilson, 58 Cal, 600 (1881), holding, also,
that the execution sale will not be enjoined, since the claimant may attend
and give notice of his claim, Newberry
v Detroit, etc, Iron Co, 17 Mich, 141,
158 (1868), per Cooley, J Where the
plaintiff bought for itself at the execution sale and had notice it is liable in
tort to the unregistered purchaser of
the old certificates. Bridgewater Iron

Co. v Lissberger, 116 U. S, 8 (1885).
But Jones v Latham, 70 Ala , 164, seems
to hold that, if the execution is levied
without notice of an unrecorded transfer, a subsequent notice before the sale
to the purchaser at the sale is ineffectual,
and does not affect the latter.

[3] Merchants' Nat Bank v Richards, 6
Mo App. 454 (1879); aff'd, 72 Mo, 77,
Colt v Ives, 31 Conn 25 (1862), State
Ins. Co v Gennett, 2 Tenn Ch. 100
(1874), Plymouth Bank v Bank of Norfolk, 27 Mass, 454 (1830), Sargent v.
Franklin Ins Co., 25 Mass., 90 (1829).
Contra, Fiske v Carr, 20 Me, 301 (1841).
But not if the transferee merely sends a
letter to the corporation requesting a
transfer, without sending the evidences
of his title and the old certificate Newall v Williston, 138 Mass., 240 (1885).
The corporation is liable in damages if
it levies the attachment under such circumstances Sargent v Franklin, etc,
Co, supra Where registry is allowed
it cuts off a subsequent attachment
even though the transferee has not
formally accepted the stock as required
by statute Woodruff v Harris, 11
U. C, Q. B, 490 (1854) A memorandum
on the stock book that the stock has
been transferred as collateral security is
sufficient to give the transfer precedence
over an attachment. Moore v Marshalltown, etc., Co, 46 N W Rep, 750 (Iowa,
1890)

the unregistered purchaser is cut off by an attachment he cannot compel his vendee to pay for the stock which is made valueless by the attachment [1]

§ 490 *Rule in Massachusetts and New Hampshire* — The courts of Massachusetts were the first to lay down the rule which places an attachment or execution levy ahead of an unregistered purchaser of the certificate of stock The evil consequences of the rule, however, seem to have become apparent to her courts; and it was held that, although the unregistered purchaser was not protected where the charter of the corporation required registry,[2] yet, where only the by-laws or the certificate itself created such a requirement, the unregistered purchaser was protected and took precedence over the attachment or execution [3] The legislature of Massachusetts seems to have had a still clearer perception of the demands of trade and of the interests of those who invest in certificates of stock, and, in 1884, enacted a statute which probably will be construed to make an attachment or execution levied on stock no more effective than in New York state [4] A similar statutory change has been made in New Hampshire.[5]

---

[1] Rock r Nichols 85 Mass , 342 (1862)

[2] Fisher r Essex Bank, 71 Mass , 373 (1855), Newall z Williston, 138 Mass , 240 (1885), Central Nat'l Bank r Williston, 138 Mass , 244 (1885) Boyd r Rockport Steam Cotton Mills, 78 Mass 406 (1856), Blanchard z Dedham Gas Light Co , 78 Mass , 213 (1858)

[3] Sargent r Essex M R'y Co. 26 Mass , 202 (1829), Boston Music Hall r Cory, 129 Mass 435 (1880), holding that a delay of four years was not fatal to the unregistered purchaser's rights

[4] "The delivery of a stock certificate of a corporation to a *bona fide* purchaser or pledgee for value together with a written transfer of the same, signed by the owner of the certificate, shall be a sufficient delivery to transfer the title as against all parties, but no such transfer shall affect the right of the corporation to pay any dividend due upon the stock, or to treat the holder of record as the holder in fact until such transfer is recorded upon the books of the corporation, or a new certificate is issued to a person to whom it has been so transferred" Act of May 9, 1884 The enactment of a similar statute is respectfully recommended to the states mentioned in § 489 Since the first edition of this work was printed several states have enacted a statute similar to this Massachusetts statute Where a father delivers stock to his son in order to qualify the latter as director, and the son transfers the certificate back to his father, the creditor of the son cannot attach the stock as against the father although the stock stands on the corporate books in the name of the son Andrews r Worcester, etc Co , 33 N E Rep , 1109 (Mass , 1893)

[5] Formerly in New Hampshire an attaching creditor took precedence over an unrecorded transferee Pinkerton r Railroad Co , 42 N H 424 (1861), Buttrick r Nashua, etc , R R , 62 N H , 413 (1882). But in 1887 the legislature passed an act to the effect that the delivery of a certificate of stock to a *bona fide* purchaser or pledgee should transfer the title as against all parties (Ch. 16, L. 1887)

§ 491 *Shares of stock cannot be subjected to the payment of the stockholder's debts by the process of garnishment* — The process of garnishment is proper only where a debt is due from a third person to the defendant debtor It is not a proper remedy for reaching shares of stock owned by the debtor [1] The corporation owes the stockholder no debt, and by no fiction of law can it be held to be a debtor of the defendant debtor Consequently, where the sheriff levies an attachment, not according to the procedure governing attachments, but according to the procedure of garnishment, the whole proceeding is void, and a subsequent transfer of the stock by the defendant debtor is valid.[2]

[1] Planters & M Bank v Leavens, 4 Ala (N S). 753 (1843), Ross v Ross, 25 Ga , 297 (1858), where the court say "Is stock in this railroad such a debt ('indebtedness') of the railroad to the stockholder that a garnishing creditor of the stockholder can enter up judgment for it against the railroad? It is not, it is a debt which the railroad does not pay, even to the stockholder himself The road may pay him *dividends* on it, but that is all" See, also, Foster v Potter, 37 Mo , 525 , § 484, n , *supra* Stock held as collateral is property subject to gar-

nishment under the statutes of Texas. Smith v Traders' Nat l Bank, 12 S. W. Rep , 113 (Tex , 1889).

[2] Mooar v Walker, 46 Iowa, 164 (1877) *Cf* Chesapeake & O R R Co v Paine, 29 Gratt (Va), 502 But see Harrell v Mexico, etc , Co , 11 S W Rep., 863 (Texas, 1889) Garnishee process must conform to the statute relative to attachments, and if served on the holders of the certificates instead of on the corporation it is ineffectual Younkin v. Collier, 47 Fed. Rep , 571 (1891).

CHAPTER XXVIII.

CONSTITUTIONALITY OF AMENDMENTS TO CHARTERS — RIGHT OF A STOCKHOLDER TO OBJECT

§ 492 *A corporate charter is a contract between three parties — the state, the corporation and the stockholders.*— The charter of a corporation having a capital stock is a contract between three parties, and forms the basis of three distinct contracts [1] The charter is a contract between the state and the corporation, second, it is a contract between the corporation and the stockholders, third, it is a contract between the stockholders and the state

§ 493 *The charter as a contract between the corporation and the stockholders —* That the charter is a contract between the corporation and the stockholders has within the last fifty years been firmly established, and is now unquestioned law The cases of Natusch

---

[1] See State Bank of Ohio v Knoop, 16 How , 369 (1853), Port Edwards etc , R'y v Arpin, 49 N W Rep , 828 (Wis 1891), Northern R. R. Co v Miller 10 Barb , 260 (1851), Cooley on Constitutional Limitations (5th ed) p 337 where the learned author says· "Those charters of incorporation, however, which are granted not as a part of the machinery of the government, but for the private benefit or purposes of the corporators stand upon a different footing. and are held to be contracts between the legislature and the corporators, having for their consideration the liabilities and duties which the corporators assume by accepting them, and the grant of the franchise can no more be resumed by the legislature, or its benefits diminished or impaired without the consent of the grantees. than any other grant of property or valuable thing, unless the right to do so is reserved in the charter itself "

v Irving [1] in England, and Livingston *v* Lynch [2] in this country, followed by a long line of supporting decisions, distinctly hold that the charter is a contract prescribing to the corporation that it shall not attempt to materially change, extend, alter or abandon the particular business which that charter authorizes the corporation to do Any attempt of the corporation to make such a change, extension, alteration or abandonment of that business is called an *ultra vires* act. It is an act which a single stockholder may prevent by injunction or set aside by a suit in equity. This subject, however, is fully treated in another part of this work [3]

§ 494 *Charter as a contract between the state and the corporation* — As between the state and the corporation the corporate charter is a contract, protected by that provision of the United States constitution which prohibits a state from passing any law which will impair the obligation of the contract [4] Hence it is beyond the power of the state to repeal or materially annul such a corporate charter, unless the power of amendment and repeal has been expressly reserved by the state, or unless all the parties to the contract consent to the change All the franchises, privileges and express and implied powers necessary and essential to carrying out the corporate purposes are protected by this contract [5] This

---

[1] This case decided by Lord Eldon in 1824, is reported in Gow on Partnership, 398, also 2 Cooper's Ch, 358

[2] 4 Johns Ch, 573 (1820) Thus in Clearwater *v* Meredith 1 Wall, 25 (1863), the court say "The relation between the corporation and the stockholders is one of contract. The stockholder subjects his interest to the control of the proper authorities to accomplish the object of the organization, but he does not agree that the purpose shall be changed in its character at the will of the directors, or a majority of the stockholders even The contract cannot be changed without the consent of both contracting parties '

[3] See ch XL

[4] This rule of law first enunciated in the case of Trustees of Dartmouth College *v* Woodward, 4 Wheat., 518 (1819), by Marshall, C J, has become thoroughly established As early as 1806 a court said "We are also satisfied that the rights legally vested in this or in any corporation cannot be controlled

or destroyed by any subsequent statute, unless a power for that purpose be reserved to the legislature in the act of incorporation " Wales *v* Stetson. 2 Mass, 143 (1806) In England the unwritten constitution is not superior to the powers of parliament, and consequently the rule is different In that country, as is said by Lord Coke, "the power and jurisdiction of parliament is so transcendental and absolute that it cannot be controlled or confined, either for causes or purposes within any bounds" Stevens *v* Rutland & Burlington R. R. Co, 29 Vt 545 (1854), Thorpe *v* Rutland & Burlington R R. Co, 27 Vt., 140 (1857), Trustees of Dartmouth College *v* Woodward, 4 Wheat., 518, 643 (1819) Consequently, the English authorities are of little use in this chapter.

[5] State Bank of Ohio *v* Knoop, 16 How, 369 (1853), Thorpe *v* Rutland & Burlington R. R. Co, 27 Vt., 140 (1857), per Redfield, J The latter case discusses the nature of the privilege thus protected.

branch of the law is important to stockholders in cases where the corporation neglects or refuses to protect itself against legislative amendments or repeals violating the charter contract between the corporation and the state. In such cases the stockholder may enjoin or remedy the wrong by bringing an action in place of and on behalf of the corporation, making it a party defendant, together with the parties who, under the authority of the state, have violated the contract.[1] A stockholder's action to prevent the payment of a tax levied upon the corporation in violation of a statutory exemption from taxation is an action of this character.[2] Corporate charters, however, are subject to constitutional provisions enacted subsequently to the granting of the charters unless there is a clear contract to the contrary.[3]

§§ 495, 496. *Charter as a contract between the state and the stockholders.* — As between the state and the stockholders, also, the corporate charter is a contract protected by the United States constitution.[4] In consequence thereof the state cannot materially amend the charter, except by the unanimous consent of the stockholders, unless the power of amendment is expressly reserved by the state

[1] Greenwood v. Freight Co., 105 U. S., 13 (1881). The character of such an action, also the parties, pleadings and rules of relief are explained in Part IV.

[2] Dodge v. Woolsey, 18 How., 331 (1855), State Bank of Ohio v. Knoop, 16 How., 369 (1853). See, also, Wilmington R. R. v. Reid, 13 Wall., 264 (1871), Delaware R. R. Tax, 18 Wall., 206 (1873). See also, § 562.

[3] Pennsylvania R. R. v. Miller, 132 U. S., 75 (1889).

[4] "A charter of incorporation granted by a state creates a contract between the state and the corporators which the state cannot violate." This has been held so often by this court that "it is supererogation to repeat it." Wilmington R. R. v. Reid, 13 Wall., 264 (1871). It "has been the settled law of this court since the Dartmouth College case." Delaware R. R. Tax, 18 Wall., 206 (1873). To the same effect, see Zabriskie v. Hackensack & N. Y. R. R. Co., 18 N. J. Eq., 178 (1867), Lothrop v. Stedman, 42 Conn., 583 (1875). Stevens v. Rutland & Burlington R. R. Co., 29 Vt., 545 (1854). "An act granting corporate privileges to a body of men is, when accepted, a contract between the state and the corporators.... It is sustained by everything that we are bound to regard as authority" — by the courts, by the opinion of the legal profession and by the acquiescence of the people. Erie & Northeast R. R. v. Casey, 26 Pa. St., 287 (1856) per Jeremiah Black, J. See, also, Sinking Fund Cases, 99 U. S., 700 (1878). "That an act of incorporation is a contract between the state and the stockholders is held for settled law by the federal courts and by every state court in the Union. All the cases on the subject are saturated with this doctrine. It is sustained not by a current but by a torrent of authorities. No judge who has a decent respect for the principle of *stare decisis* — that great principle which is the sheet-anchor of our jurisprudence — can deny that it is immovably established." "If anything is settled it is this rule of construction that a corporation takes nothing by its charter except what is plainly, expressly and unequivocally granted." Per Black, J. Bank of Pennsylvania v. Commonwealth, 19 Pa. St., 144 (1852).

at the time of granting the charter　It is this contract which constitutes the subject of the present chapter.

§ 497. *Charter amendments imposed upon the stockholders.*—The right of the legislature to amend a charter against the will of the stockholders has been the subject of much litigation.　Such amendments are clearly divisible into two kinds.　The first are those which, by their terms, are absolute and compulsory, and become a part of the charter irrespective of the action or willingness of the corporation or the stockholders to accept them　Such amendments are unconstitutional and void, unless made under a reserved power to amend [1]　Of such a kind are amendments repealing an exemption of stockholders from taxation [2]　So, also, a statute passed subsequent to the granting of a charter, and increasing the liability of a stockholder on his stock for the debts already incurred, is unconstitutional and void unless the legislature has reserved the right to alter or amend the charter. [3]　Under such a reservation the

[1] Such as an amendment changing the route and terminus　Ames v Lake, etc, R R 21 Minn. 241 (1875)　Amendment under reserved right cannot affect rights of previous creditors against the corporation　Bank of Old Dominion v McVeigh, 20 Gratt. 457 (1871)　A corporate charter right to take certain rate of interest is a contract and is protected against subsequent legislation　Hazen v Union Bank of Tennessee 1 Sneed. 115 (1853)　See, also, *dictum* in Phil, etc, Co s Appeal, 102 Pa St, 123 (1883). that an amendment to a charter which enlarges it without imposing any new or additional burden upon it is a mere license and may be revoked, citing Johnson v Crow, 6 Norris, 184, Christ Church v Philadelphia, 24 How, 300　May subsequent to charter authorize sale of corporate franchises, etc. to pay debts. Louisville, etc., T R. Co v Ballard, 2 Metc (Ky), 165 (1859)

The case of Cross v Peach Bottom Ry Co, 90 Pa St, 392 (1879), holds that "the legislative reservation is in the nature of a police power, designed for the protection of the public welfare, and where such protection becomes necessary, the law-making power may act without consulting either the interests or will of the company, and in such case

it may well be that not only the company but its stockholders must submit . . . The reservation . . . was only intended to enable the legislature to act without the consent and against the will of the corporation"　Under its reserved power to amend, the legislature may require several railroads to acquire, build to and use a union depot. Mayor, etc. v. Norwich, etc., R. R, 109 Mass, 103 (1871).

[2] Thus, in a case of a statute authorizing the taxation of stock which by the corporate charter is exempt, the statute is unconstitutional　Gordon v Appeal Tax Court, 3 How, 133 (1845), Farrington v Tennessee, 95 U S, 679 (1877). An exemption from taxation which is a gift may be repealed　Philadelphia v Contributors, etc, 19 Atl Rep, 490 (Pa., 1890)　See § 568.

[3] It certainly is as regards corporate debts already incurred　Commonwealth v Cochituate Bank, 3 Mass., 42; Wheeler v Frontier Bank, 23 Me, 308　And has been held to be so as regards future corporate debts. Ireland v Palestine, etc, Turnpike Co, 19 Ohio St., 369 (1869)　*Contra*, Stanley v Stanley, 26 Me, 191 (1846), Coffin v Rich, 45 Me, 507 (1858), Shufeldt v. Carver, 8 Ill. App., 545 (1881); Fogg v. Sidwell, 8 Ill. App., 551

statute is legal and binding [1] The limits of this reserved power of the legislature are stated elsewhere in this chapter

A statute imposing additional liability upon the shareholders cannot be repealed so as to affect those who were corporate creditors previously to the repeal [2] But, whenever the statute imposing

(1881), Child v Coffin 17 Mass, 64 (1820), *dictum*, Gray v Coffin. 63 Mass, 192, 200 (1852), Stanley v Stanley, 26 Me, 191 (1846), Hanthorne v Calef, 53 Me, 471 (1866) See Wedenger v Spruance, 101 Ill, 278 (1881) And it is said that a stockholder may restrain by a proper proceeding the acceptance by the corporation of an unconditional amendment to the charter by which the liability of the shareholders is increased Owen v Purdy, 12 Ohio St, 73 (1861), Fry's Ex'r v Lexington, etc, R R Co, 2 Metc (Ky), 314 (1859) *Cf* Bailey v Hollister, 26 N Y 112 (1862), Thompson v Guion, 5 Jones' Eq (N C), 113 (1859), Mowrey v Indianapolis, etc, R R Co, 4 Biss, 78 (1866); Lauman v Lebanon Valley R R. Co, 30 Pa St, 42 (1858), Hamilton, etc Ins Co v Hobart, 2 Gray, 543 (1854), Gardner v Hamilton, etc, Ins Co 33 N Y, 421 (1865) Where the incident of individual liability was repealed by an amendment to the state (Missouri) constitution after the debt accrued, but before the increase of stock was issued the holders of the new stock were not held liable under the former constitution Ochiltree v Railroad Co 21 Wall, 249 (1874)

[1] Frequently, and now almost universally, the legislature has a reserved power to alter, amend or repeal the charters of corporations granted by it New York Const of 1846 art 8, §§ 1 and 2, Matter of New York Elevated R R Co. 70 N Y, 327 (1877), Johnson v Hudson River R R Co, 49 id, 455 (1872), Bank of Chenango v Brown 26 id, 467 (1863), Ashuelot R R Co. v Elliott, 58 N H, 451, 454 (1878) Under this reserved power the legislature, it is held, may impose a statutory liability, in addition to the liability at common law, upon stockholders after they have

been incorporated and gone into business under a charter which does not impose such liability The exercise of this power by the legislature in such a case is held to be only a repeal of part of the corporate franchises South Bay Meadow Dam Co v Gray, 30 Me, 547 (1849) Sleeper v Goodwin 31 N W Rep, 355 (Wis, 1887) *Cf* Close v Glenwood Cemetery, 107 U S, 466 (1882) See §§ 212, 289 *supra* So, also, it is said that under this reserved power the legislature may impose a statutory liability for the future debts and obligations of the corporation Sherman v Smith 1 Black 587 (1861), Matter of Lee's Bank of Buffalo, 21 N Y, 9 (1860) Matter of the Empire City Bank, 18 id, 199 (1858) *Cf* Bailey v Hollister, 26 N Y, 112 (1862), Sinking Fund Cases 99 U S, 700 (1878), Oldtown, etc, R R Co v Veazie, 39 Me, 571 (1855), Green v Biddle 8 Wheaton, 1, 84 (1823), Gardner v Hope Ins Co 9 R I, 194 (1869) Such increased liability may be imposed by a new constitution of the state *Re* Reciprocity Bank, 22 N Y, 9 (1860), *Re* Empire Bank 18 N Y, 199 (1858), *Re* Lee's Bank of Buffalo 21 N Y, 9 (1860), affirmed *sub nom* Sherman v Smith, 1 Black, 587 (1861) In The Consolidated Ass'n v Lord. 35 La Ann 425 (1883), the court refused to uphold an amendment which imposed further liability on the stockholder

[2] Hawthorne v Calef, 2 Wall, 10 (1864), Conant v Van Shaick, 24 Barb, 87 (1857), Norris v Wrenschall, 34 Md, 492 (1871) Provident Savings Institution v Jackson Place, etc, Co., 52 Mo., 552 (1873) St Louis R R etc, Co v Harbine, 2 Mo App, 134 (1876) Central, etc, Mechanical Association v Alabama etc, Insurance Co, 70 Ala, 120 (1881), Woodruff v Trapnall, 10 How.,

the liability is penal in its nature, a repeal of it, even so as to affect existing debts, is constitutional at any time before the corporate creditor obtains judgment on his claim [1] An important exception to the general rule stated above exists in regard to amendments under the police power of the state The state may amend the charter of a railroad corporation by reducing its traffic charges, requiring it to build fences, and in various other ways for the protection of the public.[2]

§ 498 *Charter amendments offered to the stockholders* — The second class of amendments to a charter — the amendments which occur most frequently and give rise to many difficulties — are those which allow the corporate directors or a majority of the stockholders in corporate meeting assembled to engage in a new or different or more extensive or more contracted business than that authorized by the original and unamended charter

§ 499. *Auxiliary and incidental amendments are constitutional, though some of the stockholders dissent* — An amendment made to a corporate charter is either a material and fundamental change from the original plan, or it is an auxiliary and incidental change, consistent with the carrying out of the original plan.[3] The latter

190 See, also Story *v* Furman, 25 N Y, 214 (1862), Rochester *v* Barnes, 26 Barb, 657 (1858), Sinking Fund Cases, 99 U S, 700 (1878) *Cf* Jerman's Adm'r *v* Benton, 79 Mo, 148, Woodhouse *v* Commonwealth Ins Co, 54 Pa St, 307 (1867), *Re* State Insurance Co., 14 Fed Rep 28 (1882), S C, 11 Biss, 301, Palfrey *v* Paulding, 7 La Ann, 363 (1852), *Re* Telegraph Construction Co L R, 10 Eq, 384 (1870), Cooper *v* Frederick, 9 Ala, 742 (1846), *In re* Credit Foncier of England, L R, 11 Eq, 356 (1871), Coffin *v* Rich 45 Me, 507, 5 S Rep, 120 (Ala, 1888) A statutory liability of stockholders cannot be repealed as regards corporate creditors who are such at the time of the repeal McDonnell *v* Ala, etc, Ins Co, 5 S Rep, 120 (Ala 1888) Registered transferees are liable the same as their transferrers even though before the transfer the statutory liability was decreased by statute The liability to old creditors follows the stock Nat'l Com Bank *v* McDonnell 9 S Rep, 149 (Ala, 1891) A statute giving the corporation a summary remedy against a stockholder for non-payment of calls

may be repealed *Ex parte* Northeast, etc, R R Co, 37 Ala, 679

[1] Breitung *v* Lindauer, 37 Mich, 217 (1877) Union Iron Co *v* Pierce, 4 Biss, 327 (1869), Gregory *v* German Bank, 3 Col, 332 (1877), Cooley's Constitutional Limitations (5th ed), 444, 474 See § 223.

[2] See § 675, *infra*

[3] The general principle of law governing this branch of the subject is well expressed in Woodfork *v* Union Bank, 3 Coldw (Tenn), 488 (1866). "The contract of charter, after acceptance, is inviolable between the state and the corporation, as it is also between the corporation and stockholders Neither the one nor the other can disregard its obligations or alter its essential franchises without the unanimous concurrence of the stockholders . . . If the alterations proposed in the charter of a private corporation by legislative enactment are merely auxiliary and not fundamental, they may be accepted by a majority of the corporators, and when so assented to they are binding on the whole, but it is otherwise . . . when the alterations are fundamental, radical

class of amendments are constitutional and valid   The acceptance of an auxiliary amendment should be by the stockholders in meeting assembled instead of by the board of directors[1] But acceptance may arise from user,[2] and hence it generally happens that an incidental or auxiliary amendment to a charter is deemed to have been accepted by user and a vote of acceptance by the directors or by user alone[3] An amendment may be said to be auxiliary and incidental when it merely grants new powers or authorizes new methods and new plans for the purpose of carrying out the original plan and effecting the real object of that plan   The individual motives and interests of a stockholder are disregarded   Whatever is for the benefit of the corporation is conclusively presumed to be for the benefit of each stockholder. A change immaterial to the corporation is immaterial to each and every stockholder[4]

Whether an amendment materially changes the corporate plans or not is a question of law for the court[5] Accordingly each case is to be decided according to the peculiar circumstances of that case, and no general rules can be laid down which will apply to all cases.[6]

and vital   The acceptance must then be unanimous"

[1] Marlborough Mfg Co v Smith, 2 Conn, 579 (1818), Brown v Fairmount Mine Co, 10 Phil, 32 (1873) Cf Venner v Atchison, etc , R. R , sub

[2] See § 640

[3] Illinois, etc , R. R. v Zimmer 20 Ill, 658 (1858) See, also Blatchford v Ross 5 Abb Pr (N S), 434 (1869) Re Excelsior Co, 16 Abb. Pr , 14 (1862) In Venner v Atchison, etc , R R, 28 Fed Rep, 581 (1866), it is held that the directors are the proper persons to accept an amendment.

[4] Supervisors of Fulton County v Miss & Wabash R. R. Co, 21 Ill , 338 (1859), Delaware R R. Co v Tharp, 1 Hous. (Del), 149 (1856), Irvine v Turnpike Co., 2 Penr & W , 466, Ill Riv R R. Co v Zimmer, 20 Ill , 654 (1858) Sprague v. Ill. River R R. Co, 19 Ill , 174, Banet v Alton & Sangamon R R Co, 13 Ill , 504 (1851) Cf Hester v Memphis & Charleston R R Co 32 Miss , 378 (1856), Witter v Miss, Ouachita & Red River R R Co, 30 Ark , 463 (1859). The cases of Zabriskie v Hackensack & N. Y R. R Co, 18 N J

Eq , 178 (1867), Dayton & Cincinnati R. R Co v Hatch, 1 Disney, 84, and Central R R Co v Collins, 40 Ga , 617, repudiate the distinction between the material and immaterial changes All changes are held to be equally material

[5] Winter v Muscogee R. R Co, 11 Ga , 438 (1852), Witter v Miss, Ouachita & Red River R. R. Co, 30 Ark , 463 (1859) Memphis Branch R R Co v Sullivan, 57 Ga , 240 (1876) Cf Southern Pa Iron & R R Co v Stevens, Ex'r, 87 Pa St , 190 (1878)

[6] Certain changes in the route of a railroad have been held to be immaterial, Wilson v Willes Valley R R Co 33 Ga 466 (1863), Johnson v Pensacola & Ga R R. Co, 9 Fla, 299 (1860), Peoria & Oquawka R R. Co v Elting, 17 Ill , 429 (1856) Banet v Alton & Sangamon R. R Co, 13 Ill , 504 (1851), building branch lines, Peoria & Rock Island R R Co v Preston, 35 Iowa, 115 (1872), Greenville & Columbia R. R Co v. Coleman, 5 Rich Law (S. C), 118 (1851), issuing preferred stock, Everhart v West Chester & Phila R R. Co, 28 Pa St , 339 (1857), Rutland & Burlington R R Co v Thrall, 35 Vt , 536 (1863).

§ 500 *Material amendments offered to the stockholders can be accepted only by a unanimous vote* — On the other hand, a material and fundamental change in the charter by an amendment to that charter is an unconstitutional violation of the contract rights of any stockholder who does not assent to such an amendment Considerable difficulty is experienced in determining what is a

Curry v Scott, 54 Pa St, 270 (1867), or more common stock, City of Cov v Cov & Cin Bridge Co, 10 Bush. 69 (1873), Buffalo, etc. R. R. v Dudley, 14 N Y, 336 (1856), Joslyn v Pacific, etc, Co, 12 Abb Pr (N S), 329 (1872). Cf Hughes v Antietam, etc, Co, 34 Md, 316 (1870), extending the time for completing the road. Agri. Branch R. R. Co v Winchester 13 Allen, 29 (1866), Poughkeepsie, etc, Co v Griffin, 24 N Y, 150 (1861) Bailey v Hollister 26 N Y, 112 (1862), power to amend being reserved, Taggart v Western R R Co, 24 Md, 563 (1866), Union Hotel Co v Hersee, 79 N Y 454 (1880), Danbury, etc. R R Co v Wilson, 22 Conn 435 (1853) consolidations that take the place of part of the line as laid out Sprague v Ill Riv R. R. Co, 19 Ill, 174 (1857), Hanna v Cin & Fort Wayne R R Co, 20 Ind, 30 (1863) change of corporate name, Bucksport & Bangor R. R Co v Buck, 68 Me 81 (1878), Clark v Monongahela Nav Co, 10 Watts (Tenn), 364 (1840), changing the terminus, Pacific R R v Renshaw 18 Mo, 210 (1852), Ross v Chicago, etc, R R Co, 77 Ill, 134 (1875), reduction of capital stock and shortening of the road, Troy & Rutland R. R. Co v Kerr, 17 Barb, 588 (1854). Cf Oldtown, etc. R. R v Veazie, 39 Mo, 571 (1855), or enlarging the capital stock and extending the road such changes not appearing on the record to be detrimental, Peoria & Oquawka R R Co v Elting, 17 Ill, 420 (1856), Rice v Rock Island R. R Co, 21 Ill, 93, and minor changes in general, Union Agri & Stock Ass'n v Mill 31 Iowa, 95 (1870), also extensive changes, Ill River R. R Co v Zimmer, 20 Ill.

674 (1858), such as extending the road, Cross v Peach Bottom R'y Co, 90 Pa St, 392 (1879), purchasing another railroad Venner v Atchison, etc, R. R. Co, 28 Fed Rep, 581 (1886), or increasing the number of directors, Mower v Staples 32 Minn 284 (1884). See, also Gray v Coffin, 9 Cush, 192 (1852), Child v Coffin 17 Mass, 64 (1820) Langley v Little, 26 Me, 162 (1846), Payson v Withers, 5 Biss, 269 (1873), Joy v Jackson etc, Co, 11 Mich, 155 (1863); Bank v Richardson, 1 Me, 79, Greenville, etc, R R Co v Johnson, 8 Baxt, 332, Fall River Iron Works v Old Colony R. R Co 5 Allen 221 An amendment may authorize the directors to change the location of toll gates Bardstown, etc. Co v Rodman 13 S W. Rep, 917 (Ky), 1890 In the case of Atchison, etc, R. R Co v Fletcher, 10 Pac Rep 596 (Kan, 1886) an amendment authorizing a corporation to buy the stock of another railroad corporation and to guaranty its bonds was held to be valid The court said It is settled that the legislature may authorize a body of corporators to exercise new powers or franchises without impairing those previously granted, and, if the new powers can be exercised without a departure from the original compact between the corporators, there is no reason why they should not be accepted and exercised on behalf of the company by a majority of the stockholders . No franchises are diminished, no contract impaired. At most its powers are enlarged to carry out successfully the object of its incorporation So to speak, auxiliary powers are added, but its charter not violated or the benefits thereby granted infringed

material and fundamental change   Each case is decided upon its own facts, and consequently the best light as to the spirit of what constitutes a material change is obtained by a study of the facts of cases which have been decided.[1]

[1] Under the circumstances of the cases it has been held a material change to shorten and vary the route Winter v Muscogee R R Co, 11 Ga, 438 (1852), to vary the route. Middlesex Turnpike Corporation v Locke, 8 Mass, 268 (1811), Same v Swan, 10 Mass, 384 (1813), Hester v Memphis & Charleston R R Co, 32 Miss, 378 (1856): Witter v Miss, Ouachita & Red River R R. Co, 20 Ark, 463 (1859), Champion v Memphis, etc, R R Co, 35 Miss, 692, Simpson v Denison, 10 Iare, 54, changing a terminus, Manheim, etc, Co v Arndt, 31 Pa St, 317 (1858), Marietta, etc, R R Co v Elliott, 10 Ohio St, 57 Middlesex, etc, Co v Locke, 8 Mass., 267, Same v Swan, id, 385, Thompson v Guion, 5 Jones' Eq, 113, permitting a railroad to go into water transportation business, Hartford & New Haven R R Co v Croswell, 5 Hill, 383 (1843), a leading case, Marietta & Cin R R Co v Elliott, 10 Ohio St 57 (1859), shortening the line, Bank v City of Charlotte, 85 N C, 433 (1881), allowing business to be commenced before the full capital stock is subscribed, Memphis Branch R R Co v Sullivan, 57 Ga, 240 (1876), dividing the line and forming two or more corporations, Leed & Evensburg Turnpike Road Co v Phillips, 2 Pen & Watts (Pa), 184 (1830), Supervisors of Fulton County v Mississippi & Wabash R R Co, 21 Ill, 338 (1859), Carlisle v Terre Haute & Richmond R R Co, 6 Ind, 316 (1855), transferring a railroad subscription from one railroad to another Pittsburg, R R v Gazzam 32 Pa St, 340 (1858), making the charter perpetual and increasing power to hold property, Prop of the Union Lock & Canals v Towne, 1 N H, 44 (1817), allowing a life insurance company to insure against fire and marine loss, Ashton v Burbank, 2 Dill, 435, extending the line, Stevens v Rutland & Burlington R. R. Co, 29 Vt, 545 (1857) See, also, Noesen v Town of Port Washington, 37 Wis, 168 (1875) where there was an amendment authorizing the purchase of a railroad running at right angles to the old, but a release was upheld, increasing the par value of the stock, Mahon v Wood, 44 Cal, 462 (1872) consolidating the corporation with another corporation, Illinois Grand Trunk R R Co v Cook, 29 Ill, 237 (1862). McCray v Junction R R Co, 9 Ind, 358 (1857), Shelbyville & Rushville Turnpike Co v Barnes 42 Ind, 498 (1873), Booe v Junction R R Co, 10 Ind, 93 (1857), New Orleans, Jackson & Great Northern R R Co v Harris, 27 Miss, 517 (1854), Clearwater v Meredith 1 Wall, 25 (1863), Knoxville v Railroad Co, 22 Fed Rep, 758, Kean v Johnson, 1 Stock (9 N J Eq), 401 (1853), Black v Delaware & Raritan Canal Co 24 N J Eq, 455 (1873), criticised in Mowrey v Ind & Cin R R Co, 4 Biss, 78 Cf Lauman v Lebanon Valley R R Co 30 Pa St, 42 (1858), Fry's Executor v Lexington, etc, R R Co, 2 Metc (Ky), 314 (1859), the court saying "Each shareholder in an incorporated company has a right to insist on the prosecution of the particular objects of the charter   He cannot be deprived of his rights and privileges without his assent. Such alterations of the charter as are necessary to carry into effect its main design may be made without his consent. But an alteration which materially and fundamentally changes the responsibilities and duties of the company, or which superadds an entirely new enterprise to that which was originally contemplated, may be resisted by the stockholders, unless such alterations are provided for in the charter

§ 501. *Amendments under the reserved power of the state to alter, amend or repeal the charter.*— The extent of the power of the legislature to amend a charter, where it has reserved that power, is not yet fully settled, and is full of difficulties. There is a strong

itself, or in the general laws of the state in force at the time the act of incorporation was passed" Until, however, the corporation accepts such amendment the stockholders cannot complain To same effect Delaware, etc, R R Co z Irick 23 N J L., 321 (1852). Amendments which have not been acted upon do not release the subscriber. Gravely v Commonwealth, 10 S E Rep 431 (Va, 1889). See, in general Pearce v Madison R R Co, 21 How, 441, Tuttle v Michigan An Line Co, 35 Mich, 217 (1877), New Jersey, etc, R R Co z Strait, 35 N J L, 322 (1872) In all these cases neither a mandatory statute, nor a vote of the directors, nor a majority of the stockholders, can compel a dissenting stockholder to accept the change It would be unconstitutional The stockholder may say "I have agreed to become interested in a railroad company, and I have contracted in view of the profits to be expected and the perils and losses incident to that description of business, but I have not agreed that those to be intrusted with the capital I contribute shall have power to use it in a business of a different character, and attended with hazards of a different description ' Marietta, etc, R R Co z Elliot, 10 Ohio St, 57 (1859). Even though the legislature, after a turnpike corporation is organized, authorizes it to issue stock in payment for another turnpike, yet a dissenting stockholder may prevent the purchase by showing that it decreases the value of his stock. Shaw v Campbell, etc, Co, 15 S W Rep, 245 (Ky, 1891) Acts relative to a corporation may be so radical as to constitute a new charter instead of amendments to the old one. Youngblood z Georgia Imp Co, 10 S E Rep, 124 (Ga 1889) Where a municipality has subscribed for stock and

issued its bonds indorsed by the railroad company to raise money to pay the subscription, the legislature cannot authorize the company to apply its assets to the payment of such bonds A stockholder may enjoin it. Hill v Glasgow R R., 41 Fed Rep., 610 (1890). The legislature cannot, in the amendment itself authorize the majority to bind the minority herein New Orleans, etc, R R Co z Harris, 27 Miss, 517 (1854). An amendment cannot deprive the members of the corporation of the privilege of electing its directors The legislature cannot arbitrarily name and appoint trustees of an educational corporation, the charter providing that vacancies shall be filled by the remaining trustees. Sheriff z Lowndes, 16 Md., 357 (1860) It cannot give to the city of Louisville the power to elect the trustees of the University of Louisville, an educational corporation City of Louisville v President, etc, 15 B Mon, 642 (1855). It cannot vest the government of an incorporated academy in a new board of trustees Norris v Trustees, etc, 7 Gill & J, 7 (1834) On the right of a dissenting stockholder in general, see, also, Goodwin v Evans, 18 Ohio St., 150, 166 (1868), Railway Co. z. Allerton, 18 Wall, 233, 235 (1873), Printing House z Trustees, 104 U S, 711 (1881), Roberts' Appeal, 92 Pa St., 407, Buffalo, etc, R R Co v Potter, 23 Barb, 21 (1856), Hoey v Henderson, 32 La Ann, 1069, Waring v Mayor, etc, of Mobile, 24 Ala, 701 (1854), Miss, etc, R R Co v Cross, 20 Ark, 443 (1859), Clinch v Financial Co., L R, 4 Ch, 117 (1868), Dougan s Case, L R, 8 Ch, 540, Barrett v Alton. etc., R R Co, 13 Ill, 504 (1857). See, also, Gray z Monongahela Nav Co 2 Watts & S, 156 (1841), Currie v Mut. Ass Soc, 4 Hen & M, 315 (1809), Zabriskie v Cleveland, etc, R.

tendency in the decisions, and a tendency which is deserving of the highest commendation, to limit the power of the legislature to amend a charter under this reserved power It should be restricted to those amendments only in which the state has a public interest Any attempt to use this power of amendment for the purpose of authorizing a majority of the stockholders to force upon the minority a material change in the enterprise is contrary to law and the spirit of justice Under such reserved power the legislature has only that right to amend the charter which it would have had in case the Dartmouth College case had decided that charters were not contracts [1] In other words, by this reserved right the restraint of the federal constitution is done away with The power, however, to make a new contract for the stockholders is not thereby given

The power to make amendments and to repeal and alter charters has been reserved in most of the states of the Union [2] It is clearly established that the legislature cannot, under this reserved power, amend the charter so as to change the whole character of the enterprise and compel the corporation to proceed under the amended

R. Co, 23 How, 381 (1859), Cincinnati, etc, R R. Co v Cole, 29 Ohio St, 126 (1876), St Mary's Church 7 Serg & R, 517, Lyons v Orange, etc, R R Co, 32 Md, 18 (1869); Ill Riv R. R Co v Beers, 27 Ill, 185 (1862), Hope Ins Co v Beckman, 47 Mo, 93 (1870) Same v Koeller, 47 id, 199 (1870), Wetumka & Cooso R R Co v Bingham, 5 Ala, 657 (1843) Palfrey v Paulding, 7 La Ann, 363 (1852), State v. Sibley, 25 Minn, 387 (1879), Bangor, etc, R R Co v Smith, 47 Me, 34 (1859), Shields v Ohio, 26 Ohio St., 86 (1875), S C, 95 U S. 319, State v Maine, etc, R. R Co, 66 Me, 488, S C, 96 U S, 499, New Jersey v Yard, 95 id, 104, 113 (1877), S C, contra, 37 N J L., 228, Smead v Indianapolis etc, R R Co, 11 Ind 104 (1858), Sumrall v Mut Ins Co, 40 Mo, 27 (1867), Kenton Co. Court v Bank Lick Turnp Co, 10 Bush, 525 (1874), Regents v Williams, 9 Gill & J. 365 (1839), S C, 31 Am Dec, 72, St John's College v Purnell, etc, 23 Md., 629 (1865), White v Syracuse R R Co, 14 Barb 560 (1853) Schenectady etc Plank R Co v Thatcher, 11 N Y 102

(1854), Caley v Philadelphia, etc, R R Co, 80 Pa St, 363 (1876) See, also Burlington, etc, R. R. Co v White, 5 Iowa, 409 (1857). South Georgia etc, R R Co v Ayres, 56 Ga, 230 (1876), where, however, a sale of the road was made without legislative authority

[1] County of San Mateo v Southern Pacific R R Co, 8 Sawyer, 238, 279 (1882), Detroit v Detroit & Howell Plank-road Co, 43 Mich, 110 (1880)

[2] Constitution of Alabama, XIII, 1 Arkansas, V, 48, California, IV, 31 1879, XII, 1, Colorado, 1876, XV, 3 Delaware, II 17, Iowa, VIII, 12, Kansas, XII, 1, Maine, Laws of 1831, Massachusetts, St 1830, ch 81, R. S, ch 44, § 23 Gen St., ch 68, § 41, Maryland, III, 48, par 2, Michigan, XV, 1, 8, Missouri, VIII 14, New Jersey, Amend IV, 7, par 11, ch 11 New York, VIII 1, R S, pt I, ch XVIII, title 3, §§ North Carolina, VIII, 1, Nebraska, 1875, XI, Nevada, VIII.'1, Ohio, XVIII 2 Oregon, XI, 2 Pennsylvania XVI 10, South Carolina, XII 1, Tennessee, XI, 8, Texas, 1875 XII, 5, 7, Wisconsin, XI, 1

charter[1]   The restrictions of the state constitution still exist, and individuals cannot be forced by the state into new contracts[2]   An amendment under the reserved power cannot change the character of the enterprise, nor take away rights already acquired under the charter   It must not be foreign to the purposes and objects of the original charter.[3]

[1] In Pennsylvania it is held that the reserved power, when used so as to make an amendment compulsory on the corporation, "is in the nature of a police power, designed for the protection of the public welfare" Cross v Peach Bottom Ry Co, 90 Pa St. 392 (1879) "The power of amendment was never reserved with reference to any question between the corporation and its stock subscribers, but solely with reference to questions between the corporation and the state, where the latter desired to make compulsory amendments against the will of the former " The corporation cannot be compelled to proceed All the state "can do is to grant it the power, and then it is for the corporation to accept it or not, as it pleases" Under its reserved power to amend, the state may give a remedy against a mill-dam corporation for injuries by flood Monongahela Nav Co v Coon, 6 Pa. St 379 (1847), holding, also, that by accepting an amendment which is granted on condition that the reserved power to amend shall apply to the corporation it is subject to such power Kenosha, Rockford & Rock Island R. R. Co. v Marsh, 17 Wis., 13 (1862), Troy & Rutland R. R. Co v Kerr, 17 Barb, 581 (1854) In The City of Knoxville v Railroad Co, 22 Fed Rep, 758 (1884) the court say "It was not competent for the legislature to do more in this respect than to waive the public rights It could not divest or impair the rights of the shareholders, as between themselves, as guarantied by the company's charter, without their consent It was upon the faith of the stipulations contained in the said charter that the shareholders subscribed to the capital stock, and thereby made themselves members

of the corporation ' In the case, also, of Orr v Bracken County, etc, 81 Ky, 593 (1884), an amendment under the reserved power, changing the method of voting, was decided to be of no effect until the stockholders accepted it. The court said "The right to amend the charter may be expressly reserved, but that right does not confer the favor of taking from the corporators the control of the corporate property" See, also, ch XXXVII. as to amendments affecting the right to vote Query, whether a mandatory consolidation would be legal Mowrey v Ind & Cin R. R. Co, 4 Biss, 78 (1866) When legal, a mandatory change does not require acceptance by the stockholders. Zabriskie v Hackensack & N Y R R. Co, 18 N. J Eq, 178 (1867) But when the mandatory amendment goes beyond the legal limits, it must be accepted by the corporation as though it were made optional with the corporation Kenosha, Rockford & Rock Island R. R. Co v. Marsh, 17 Wis. 13 (1863) See, also, § 497, supra.

[2] Cooley on Constitutional Limitations (5th ed), 454 As to repeals of charters under this reserved power, see ch XXXVIII

[3] This power has its limits. "It can repeal or suspend the charter; it can alter or modify it, it can take away the charter but it cannot impose a new one and oblige the stockholders to accept it.   The power to alter and modify does not give power to make any substantial additions to the work" Zabriskie v Hackensack & N Y R R Co 18 N J Eq, 178 (1867). "The power of alteration and amendment is not without limit, the alterations must be reasonable, they must be made in good faith, and be consistent with the

It may, however, go to any extent in authorizing the corporation itself, by a unanimous vote of the stockholders, to make fundamental changes.   The latest and best view taken of this reserved
power of the state is that under it a fundamental amendment to
the charter does not authorize a majority of the stockholders to
accept the amendment and proceed, but that unanimous consent
of the stockholders is necessary [1]

The constitutionality of various amendments to charters in which
the legislature reserved the right to amend or repeal is considered
in the notes below [2]

scope and object of the act of incorporation   Sheer oppression and wrong
cannot be inflicted under the guise of
amendment or alteration"   Shields v
Ohio, 95 U S, 325 (1877), Spring Valley Water-works v Board of Supervisors of San Francisco, 61 Cal, 3 (1881)
The amendment must "not defeat or
subsequently impair the object of the
grant, or any rights vested under it '
Close v Glenwood Cemetery, 107 U S,
466 (1882)   See, also, Miller v State 15
Wall, 478 (1872), Mayor, etc, of Worcester v Norwich & Worcester R. R.
Co, 109 Mass, 103 (1871)   The motives
of the legislators cannot be inquired
into   Northern R R Co v Miller 10
Barb, 260 (1851), Matter of Elevated R R
Co, 70 N Y, 327, 351   See 113 N Y, 111

[1] Mills v Central R R Co, 41 N J
Eq, 5 (1886), where a statute subsequent
to the charter authorized the consolidation of railroad companies   The court
said, "The legislature did not intend to
affect the rights of stockholders inter
sese, and the act does not do so, either
expressly or by implication. . . .
After shareholders had entered into a
contract among themselves, under legislative sanction, and expended their
money in the execution of the plan
mutually agreed upon, the plan could
not, even by virtue of legislative enactment, be radically changed by the majority alone, and dissentient stockholders be compelled to engage in a new and
totally different undertaking, because
such action would impair the obligation
of the dissenting stockholders' contract

with their associates and the state '
The court said also that, under its reserved power to amend a charter, the
state cannot give "a power to one part
of the corporators as against the other
which they did not have before"   It
has been held, however, that, under its
reserved power, the legislature may
authorize a road to lease to another
Durfee v Old Colony & Fall River R R.
Co, 87 Mass, 230 (1862)   A consolidation thereunder has been held legal
Bishop v Brainerd, 28 Conn, 289 (1859),
Durfee v Old Colony, etc, R. R, 87
Mass, 230 (1862)   Also not legal   Kenosha, Rockford & Rock Island R R
Co, v Marsh 17 Wis, 13 (1862), Mowrey v Ind & Cin R. R Co, 4 Biss, 78
(1866).   Authorizing one railroad to subscribe for stock in another railroad has
been held legal   White v Syracuse &
Utica R. R Co, 14 Barb, 559 (1853)
Also borrowing money and building
branches.   Northern R. R Co v Miller,
10 Barb, 260 (1851)   Also reducing capital stock.   Joslyn v. Pacific Mail Steamship Co, 12 Abb Pr. (N S), 329
(1872)   See, also, White Hall & Platts-
burgh R R Co v Myers, 16 Abb Pr
(N S), 34 (1872).   State v Accommodation Bank of La, 26 La Ann, 288 (1874)
Kenosha, Rockford & Rock Island R R
Co, v. Marsh, 17 Wis, 13 (1863).   The
extension of the line from six to seventeen miles was held to require a unanimous acceptance in Zabriskie v Hackensack & N Y R. R. Co, 18 N. J Eq,
178 (1867)

[2] The case of Commissioners, etc., v.

§ 502 *Dissenting stockholder's remedy against an illegal amendment.*—Where an unauthorized and illegal amendment has been accepted by a corporation and is about to be acted upon, a stockholder has two remedies   If he has not paid his subscription, he

Green, etc , Co . 79 Ky , 73, holding that the right to take tolls cannot be abolished where the company has maintained and kept in repair the rivers, relying upon the right to take toll, is referred to in Louisville Water Co v Clark, 113 U S , 1 (1892) Concerning this subject, see Part VI, *infra* In the case of Ohio & M Ry v People, 123 Ill , 467 (1888), the court referred to but did not decide the question whether a state could withdraw its consent to a consolidation after the consolidation had been made Under the reserved power to amend or repeal a charter the legislature may amend the charter of an agricultural college, which has private stockholders but to which the state contributes funds so that instead of the state having four directors out of eleven, the state shall have seven out of twelve Jackson v Walsh, 23 Atl Rep , 778 (Md , 1892) Where a gas company has an exclusive right to supply gas to a city, subject to the right of the legislature to alter or revoke the same, the legislature may authorize the city to construct its own gas works A municipal ordinance is not such a contract as is protected by the constitution of the United States in regard to impairing the validity of contracts It is a contract that is protected in the same way as contracts of individuals Hamilton, etc , Co v Hamilton City, 146 U. S , 258 (1892) Where an amendment exempts the company from taxation and provides that it shall furnish the city with water free of cost, a repeal of the exemption repeals the obligation as to water Louisville Water Co. v Clark, 143 U S , 1 (1892) An exemption from taxation may be repealed under the reserved right to amend etc. Wagner, etc , Institute's Appeal, 19 Atl. Rep , 297 (Pa , 1890) Under the reserved power to amend or repeal a char-

ter the legislature may compel it to pay wages weekly to its employees. State v Brown, 25 Atl Rep , 246 (R I , 1892) Under the reserved right to amend the charter the legislature may amend so as to confine the road to a particular route, and outstanding contracts of the company do not prevent such an amendment Macon, etc , R R v Stamps, 11 S E Rep , 442 (Ga , 1890) Where, subsequently to the incorporation of a company, a general act reserves to the legislature the right to amend or repeal any and all charters, the legislature may repeal any amendments to the charter, so far as such amendments are passed after the general act, where the amendments do not expressly waive the legislative right of amendment or repeal. But any amendment should be "saving, whenever that power was exerted all rights previously vested" An exemption from taxation may be repealed under the reserved power (Approving Tomlinson v Jessup, 15 Wall, 454, and Railroad Co v Maine, 96 U S , 499) Creditors stand upon the same footing in this respect Louisville Water Co. v. Clark, 143 U S , 1 (1892) In regard to the question as to the constitutionality of a radical amendment to a charter under the reserved right to amend, see Railroad Co v Maine, 96 U S , 499; Sinking Fund Cases, 99 U S , 700; Commonwealth v Essex Co , 13 Gray, 253; Commonwealth v Bonsall, 3 Whart., 559, Pennsylvania College Cases, 13 Wall , 190 , State v Miller, 15 Wall , 478, Spring Valley Water-works v Shottler, 110 U S , 347, Close of Glenwood Cemetery, 107 U S , 466, Jackson v Walsh, 23 Atl Rep , 778, Sage v Dillard, 15 B Monroe, 357, State v Adams, 44 Mo , 570, Allen v. McKean, 1 Sumner, 276.

may consider himself released from his liability to pay the subscription, or he may begin suit in equity to obtain an injunction against or to set aside any action by the corporation under the amendment [1] If the stockholder has already paid his subscription, then his only remedy is an injunction or a suit to set aside [2] In

[1] This rule is recognized and applied in most of the cases of this chapter See, also, Clearwater v Meredith. 1 Wall, 25, holding that the stockholder was released, and saying "Clearwater could have prevented this consolidation had he chosen to do so" Nugent v Supervisors, 19 Wall, 241 (1873) A change of the termini under an amendment to the charter releases previous subscribers, there being no reserved right to make such amendment Snook v Georgia Imp. Co, 9 S E Rep, 1104 (Ga., 1889). A subscriber is released by an amendment changing the termini, the original charter not providing for such changes Youngblood v Georgia Imp Co, 10 S E Rep, 124 (Ga., 1889) A fundamental change in the corporation releases subscribers Greenbrier, etc, Exposition v Rodes, 17 S E Rep., 305 (W. Va, 1893). A change in the plan of organization so as to have a larger capital stock than was originally intended releases a subscriber Norwich, etc, Co v Hockaday, 16 S E Rep, 877 (Va, 1893), Champion v Memphis, etc, R. R. Co, 35 Miss, 692 (1858) A charter amendment enlarging the corporate objects from fire and accident to fire marine and inland insurance releases dissenting stockholders Ashton v Burbank 2 Dill, 435 (1873). In England cases generally arise releasing the subscriber when the memoranda of association vary from the prospectus Stewart s Case, L R, 1 Ch, 574 (1866). Webster s Case, L. R., 2 Eq. 741 (1866) Ship s Case, 2 De G J & S., 544 (1865), Dawes v Ship, L R., 3 H of L, 343 (1868), Cf Nixon v Brownlow, 3 H & N, 686 (1858), Norman v Mitchell, 5 De G, M & G, 648 (1854). See, also, Dorris v Sweeney, 60 N Y, 463 (1875) After a winding-up has commenced there can be no release here n Oakes v Turquand. L. R. 2 H L, 325 (1867) In opposition to this rule of law there are some decisions holding that the subscribers' only remedy is an injunction Were it not that the great weight of authority holds otherwise this view would be commended as the only logical result of the law There is no reason why a stockholder who has not paid his subscription should be better off than he who has met that obligation See § 187, also Hays v Ottawa, etc, R R Co 61 Ill, 422 (1871), Pacific R R v Hughes 22 Mo., 291 (1855), Martin v Pensacola R R Co, 8 Fla, 389 (1859), Ware v Grand, etc, R'y Co, 2 Russ & M, 470 (1831) Bank v Charlotte, 85 N C, 433 (1881) The plea of release must allege acceptance by the corporation, and injury to the defendant sued on his subscription Hawkins v Miss & Tenn R R Co, 35 Miss, 688 (1858) An increase of the capital stock as allowed by the charter does not release subscribers Port Edwards, etc, Ry v Arpin, 49 N W Rep, 828 (Wis, 1891) Where the statutes under which the company is organized allow the objects of the company to be changed on a vote of the stockholders, a dissenting stockholder is not released from his subscription by such change Mercantile Statement Co v Kneal 53 N W Rep, 682 (Minn, 1892)

[2] This remedy also is supported by a large number of the cases in this chapter See Stevens v Rutland & Burlington R R Co, 29 Vt, 545 (1855), Black v Del & Raritan Canal Co, 24 N. J Eq, 455 (1873), Mowrey v Ind. & Cin R R Co, 4 Biss, 78 (1866) The stockholder cannot enjoin parties from applying to the legislature for the amendment. Story v Jersey, etc, Co., 16 N J. Eq, 13 (1863), reviewing the cases,

Pennsylvania it has been held that the stockholder may have an injunction herein, but only until the corporation shall have purchased his interest in the corporation[1] This decision, however, has been doubted, and hardly seems consistent with well-established principles protecting persons in their rights to retain their property except as taken from them under the power of eminent domain.[2]

§ 503 *Assent and acquiescence as a bar to the stockholder's remedy* — A stockholder may be estopped from objecting to an amendment by his express or implied acquiescence therein. Any acts indicating an acceptance by him of the amendment bind him and bar his suit.[3] Acquiescence may sometimes grow out of his silence or delay, under circumstances that called on him to dissent if he so intended[4] His assent, however, is not to be presumed, but must be

Stevens v Rutland, etc. R. R. Co. 29 Vt, 545 (1855)

[1] Lauman v Lebanon Valley R. R. Co, 30 Pa St, 42 (1858), approved in State v Bailey, 16 Ind, 46 (1861) Cf Ship v Crosskill, L R., 10 Eq, 73 (1870) Stewart v Austin, L R, 3 Eq, 299 (1866), holding that the recovery back cannot be in a court of equity

[2] Mowrey v Ind & Cin R R Co, 4 Biss, 78 (1866) Changes and amendments as to the route do not release the subscriber where he took part therein Owenton, etc Co v Smith, 13 S. W Rep, 426 (Ky, 1890).

[3] Bedford R R. Co v Bowser, 48 Pa. St., 29 (1864) Long delay may constitute a ratification herein Gifford v New Jersey R R Co, 10 N J Eq, 171 (1854), Bangor, etc, R R Co v Smith, 47 Me, 34 (1859), State v Sibley, 25 Minn, 387 (1879). Hope, etc. Ins Co v. Beckman, 47 Mo. 93 (1870), Hope, etc, Ins Co. v Koeller, 47 Mo, 129 (1870), Covington v Covington, etc, Co, 10 Bush, 69 (1873), Kenton, etc, Court v Bank, etc, Co, 10 Bush 529 (1874), Sumrall v Sun, etc, Co, 40 Mo, 27 (1867) Smead v. Indianapolis, etc, R R, 11 Ind, 104 (1858) Cf Pingry v Washburn, 1 Aiken (Vt.), 264 (1826) See, in general, Memphis, etc, R R Co v. Sullivan, 57 Ga, 240, Houston v Jefferson College, 63 Pa. St., 428, Danbury, etc, R. R. Co. v. Wilson,

22 Conn, 435, Vermont, etc., R R Co v Vermont Cent R R Co, 34 Vt, 2, Hayworth v Junction R R Co, 13 Ind, 348 (1859), Mills v Central R. R. Co, 41 N J. Eq, 1 (1886); Zabriskie v Hackensack, etc, R R Co, 18 N. J Eq, 178; Ex parte Booker, 18 Ark, 338, Upton v. Jackson, 1 Flipp, C C, 413; Goodin v. Evans, 18 Ohio St, 150, and ch XLIV. If the stockholder subscribed after the amendment was made he cannot complain Eppes v Miss, etc, R. R. Co, 35 Ala. (N S), 54 (1859), McClure v People's Freight Co, 90 Pa. St, 269 (1879) If a stockholder does not object to an amendment, it is not for a person whose land is being taken under eminent domain proceedings to object Ames v. Lake Superior, etc, R R, 21 Minn, 241, 291 (1875)

[4] Commonwealth v Cullen, 13 Pa. St, 133 (1850), Martin v. Pensacola & Ga. R R Co, 8 Fla, 370 (1869); Owen v Purdy, 12 Ohio St, 73 (1861). Contra, Hamilton Mutual Ins Co. v Hobart, 2 Gray 543 (1854) Although a stockholder may enjoin a consolidation of his company with another under a statute passed after the incorporation, the object of the consolidation being different from that of the original corporation, yet where the stockholder delays applying to the court for nearly a year and in the meantime the consolidated com-

proven [1] A court of equity will go far to aid a dissenting stockholder, where he applies promptly and before large investments and many changes are made on the faith of the acts complained of But laches will not be tolerated by the courts, especially where important interests are involved.[2]

pany has borrowed money and given mortgages, and such mortgages are about to be foreclosed, the complaining stockholder is guilty of laches and his remedy is barred   Rabe v Dunlap, 25 Atl Rep , 959 (N. J , 1893). A consolidation of railroads under an amendment to the charter may be prevented by a single stockholder. But several years delay in complaining is fatal The stockholder then can only recover the value of his stock and past dividends. Deposit Bank v. Barrett, 13 S. W. Rep , 337 (Ky , 1890). Where stockholders in a college exchange their stock for scholarships, a removal of the college to another location under an amendment to the charter, such amendment having been made twenty-five years prior to such removal, will not be enjoined   Bryan v Board, etc., 13 S W. Rep., 276 (Ky , 1890)

[1] March v. Eastern R. R. Co , 43 N H , 515 (1862) , Prop , etc., Union Lock & Canals v Towne, 1 N H , 44 (1817); Ireland v Palestine, etc., Turnpike Co , 19 Ohio St., 369 (1869).

[2] See ch. XLIV.

(41)   641

CHAPTER XXIX.

"TRUSTS" AND UNINCORPORATED JOINT-STOCK ASSOCIATIONS.

§ 503a. *Definition and legality of a "trust"* — The word "trust" was first used to mean an agreement, between many stockholders in many corporations, to place all their stock in the hands of trustees and to receive therefor trust certificates from the trustees. The stockholders thereby consolidate their interests and become trust certificate-holders. The trustees own the stock, vote it, elect the officers of the various corporations, control the business, receive all the dividends on the stock, and use all these dividends to pay dividends on the trust certificates The trustees are periodically elected by the trust certificate-holders The purpose of the "trust" is to control prices, prevent competition and cheapen the cost of production. The Standard Oil Trust, the American Cotton-Seed Oil Trust and the Sugar Trust were examples of this method of combination.[1]

[1] The committee of the house of representatives at Washington, in their report, explain the nature of the Standard Oil Trust and Sugar Trust very clearly The committee reports "that there exist a certain number of corporations organized under the laws of the different states and subject to their control, that these corporations have issued their stock to various individuals, and that these individual stockholders have surrendered their stock to the trustees named in the agreements creating these trusts, and accepted in lieu thereof certificates issued by the trustees named therein The agreements provide that the various corporations whose stock is surrendered to the trustees shall preserve their identity and carry on their business." See 4 Ry & Corp L J, 98. Mr S. C T Dodd, the general solicitor and originator of the Standard Oil Trust, defines a trust as "an arrangement by which the stockholders of va-

642

But the word "trust" has a wider and more popular use It is used to designate any combination of producers for the purpose of controlling prices and suppressing competition In this sense of the word, all contracts, agreements and schemes whereby those who were competitors combine to regulate prices are "trusts"

During the past five years these trusts have come into great prominence They multiplied rapidly and extended into many branches of business They became the object of great popular opposition and their legality was fiercely assailed, both in the courts and by means of prohibitory statutes

The courts have held with great uniformity that these combinations are illegal if their purpose is to restrict production, raise prices or restrain trade The law is clear that any combination of competing concerns for the purpose of controlling prices, or limiting production, or suppressing competition, is contrary to public policy and is void This principle of law has been applied with great rigor to trusts, the recent combinations in trade Many cases showing the different circumstances under which this rule has been applied are given in the notes below [1]

nous corporations place their stocks in the hands of certain trustees and take in lieu thereof certificates showing each shareholder's equitable interest in all the stock so held. The result is twofold , 1 The stockholders thereby become interested in all the corporations whose stocks are thus held. 2 The trustees elect the directors of the several corporations." See 7 Ry & Corp L J 236

[1] The state will at the instance of the attorney-general forfeit the charter of a corporation whose stockholders have entered into a "trust' with the stockholders of competing corporations for the purpose of forming a monopoly in and raising the price of sugar People i North R S Rep Co, 121 N Y 582 (1890) This case broke up the 'Sugar Trust" and drove it into transferring all its property to a New Jersey corporation organized for that purpose The next important case was State i Standard Oil Co, 30 N E Rep, 279 (Ohio, 1892) This case declared illegal the Standard Oil Trust That trust is now in process of liquidation These two cases are now the leading authorities on this subject Various other decisions

on this subject arranged in the order of the states are as follows

California A contract whose effect is to give a monopoly in bags by the vendor agreeing to sell to one party exclusively is illegal, and no damages can be collected Pacific, etc Co i Adler 27 Pac Rep 36 (Cal, 1891) Although the state is prosecuting a suit to forfeit the charter for entering into a combination yet a sale of part of the corporate property to a stockholder pending the suit is legal and the receiver cannot follow the property A writ of prohibition will issue against him Havemeyer i Superior Court, 24 Pac Rep 121 (Cal 1890 Where all the manufacturers of lumber at a certain point contracted to sell to a corporation all the product of the mills so far as such product was sold in four counties and the mills agreed not to sell to any other parties in those counties except upon a forfeit to the corporation the court held that any one of the mills could repudiate the contract In a suit brought by the corporation against one of the mills for refusing to live up to the contract the court held that the

These cases indicate the complicated questions and important litigation that have arisen by reason of the trusts. It is believed, however, that the volume of such litigation will decrease rather than increase in the future. Most of the great trusts have been

corporation could not recover Santa Clara etc., Co t Hayes, 18 Pac Rep, 391 (Cal , 1888)

Illinois Although the general statute authorizes incorporation for any "lawful purpose," yet an incorporation to buy a majority of the stock of each of four competing gas corporations in a city is illegal where the purpose is to create a monopoly The state may by suit have the charter forfeited People t Chicago Gas T Co, 22 N E Rep, 798 (Ill 1889) All gas companies owe a duty to the public An agreement of two companies in one city to keep out of each other's territory is void Chicago etc, Co v People's, etc, Co, 13 N E Rep, 169 (Ill , 1887) In Illinois all the grain dealers in a town secretly combined and made contracts by which they controlled the price of grain and the local store-house accommodations The parties succeeded, but disagreed in their division of the profits An action for an accounting was brought by one against another The court refused to aid either party. The law will leave the guilty conspirators as it finds them. Craft v McConoughy, 79 Ill , 346 (1875)

Kansas Insurance business is not interstate business Foreign insurance companies that combine to control and increase the rates of insurance on property inside the state violate the statute against trusts, and their local agents are subject to prosecution therefor State v Phipps, 31 Pac. Rep , 1097 (Kan , 1893).

Kentucky The agreement of two rival boats to divide their earnings in a certain proportion, and if either owner sells he shall not go into the business again for a year, is void The party who has sold and then returned at once to the business is not liable in damages Anderson v Jett, 12 S W Rep, 670 (Ky., 1889)

Louisiana A stockholder cannot hold a director liable for the stock becoming worthless by reason of the fact that the director and others sold their stock amounting to three-fourths of the stock to the Cotton Seed Oil Trust. and that the trust then dissolved the corporation by a three-fourths vote as allowed by statute, although the directors as such voted for the dissolution Trisconi v. Winship. 9 S Rep., 29 (La , 1891) A pooling contract between two railroads competing for business between the same points is void as against public policy The court will leave the parties where they are The arrangement in this case was for a division of earnings. Texas, etc , R'y v Southern Pac. R'y, 6 S Rep., 888 (La , 1889) In Louisiana, where several firms owned a large quantity of Indian bagging, and combined and agreed not to sell except upon the consent of a majority of these who were parties to the agreement, the court refused to uphold the agreement, and refused to enjoin one of the parties from violating his compact. India Bagging Association v. Kock, 14 La Ann , 168 (1859).

Massachusetts The combination of two parties who each claim a patent on an article not a prime necessity nor a staple commodity in the market is legal and may be specifically enforced Gloucester, etc , Co. v Russia, etc , Co., 27 N E Rep., 1005 (Mass., 1891). In Commonwealth v Smith, 9 N. E. Rep , 629 (Mass, 1887), where certain shade-roller manufacturers formed a corporation to sell their product, the court enjoined one of the parties from repudiating the agreement, but said "The agreement does not refer to an article of prime necessity, nor to a staple of commerce, nor to merchandise to be bought and sold in the market . . . It does not look to

driven from their original mode of organization and have reorganized by conveying all their property to a corporation organized for the purpose of taking over the property. Such has been the case with the Sugar Trust and the Cotton-seed Oil Trust. The decisions of

affecting competition from outside — the parties have a monopoly by their patents — but only to restrict competition in price between themselves .
When it appears that the combination is used to the public detriment, a different question will be presented from that now before us."

Michigan. In ascertaining the market price of articles sold, the price as fixed by a combination in the trade will not be considered. Lovejoy *v*. Michels, 49 N. W. Rep., 901 (Mich., 1891). A contract of a concern not to manufacture a certain line of articles in some states for five years is void. Western, etc., Ass'n *v*. Starkey, 47 N. W. Rep., 604 (Mich., 1890). Where three persons interested in a match factory agreed to unite their property with that of their competitors in one large corporation, a monopoly — the Diamond Match Company — the courts will not enforce the contract between these three persons which specifies the proportion in which each of the three was to participate in the profits coming to them jointly from the monopoly. The history, character and purpose of the match monopoly are fully stated in this decision. Richardson *v*. Buhl, 43 N. W. Rep., 1102 (Mich., 1889).

Minnesota. By-laws of an exchange restricting the freedom of members to reduce prices and establish offices for selling are void. Kolff *v* St. Paul, etc., Exchange, 50 N. W. Rep., 1026 (Minn., 1892).

Missouri. See Skrainka *v* Scharringhausen, 8 Mo. App., 522 (1880), upholding a pooling contract of certain owners of stone quarries located in St. Louis, on the ground that the restraint was local in its effect.

Nebraska. Where the stockholders of a distilling corporation transfer their stock to trustees, for the purpose of entering into a trust, such trustees being the holders of the stock of various other corporations engaged in the same business, and trust certificates are issued by them in place of the stock, the state, at the instance of the attorney-general, will cause the charter to be annulled on the ground of misuser, the corporation being no longer engaged in a lawful business. Although the corporate property was transferred just before judgment, the court will not allow its decree to be evaded. State *v* Nebraska Distilling Co., 46 N. W. Rep., 155 (Neb., 1890).

New Jersey. Where a contract between a domestic railroad company and a foreign railroad company is declared illegal and void by the court on the ground that it seeks to create a monopoly in the coal business, and the court orders the domestic railroad company to cease complying with such contract, the court will appoint a receiver of such company if it attempts to evade the decree, but on proof that no evasion has been attempted, the court will refuse to appoint a receiver. Stockton, Att'y-Gen'l, *v* Central R. Co. of N. J., 25 Atl. Rep., 912 (N. J., 1893). It is not illegal for one stockyard company to buy out another stockyard company. Willoughby *v* Chicago, etc., Co., 25 Atl. Rep., 277 (N. J., 1892), Ellerman *v* Chicago, etc., S. Y. Co., 23 Atl. Rep., 287 (N. J., 1891).

New York. See People *v* North River, etc., Co., *supra*. Where several carbon manufacturers have formed a combination by leasing their several concerns to a trustee and also assigning to him their orders for carbons, and subsequently one of them withdraws the withdrawing concern cannot sue for and claim the amount due upon one of the orders assigned to and filled by such trustee.

the New York court of appeals against the Sugar Trust and of the supreme court of Ohio against the Standard Oil Trust have convinced the trusts that their original mode of organization was illegal and must be abandoned. The result has been that the trusts for the

The defendant having interpleaded, the trustee takes the money. Pittsburg C. Co. v McMillan, 119 N. Y., 46 (1890). Where a manufacturer of a peculiar kind of machinery under a patent agrees with a trustee for several corporations that he, the manufacturer, will sell his machinery to them alone, and they agree to give him a percentage of their profits, the agreement is legal and may be enforced by him. Good v Daland, 121 N. Y., 1 (1890). A combination of coal dealers for the purpose of preventing the solicitation of business, and for the purpose of regulating the retail price, is a conspiracy, and is punishable as a criminal offense under the New York law. People v Sheldon, 66 Hun, 590 (1893). Where many manufacturers under various patents form a corporation and convey to it the patents and take back licenses under which the corporation regulates the price, and they agree not to use any new patents and not to manufacture any new kind of harrow the combination is illegal. Any one of the parties may by suit in equity be relieved from its terms. Strait v National Harrow Co, 18 N. Y. Supp., 224 (1891). It is established "that no contracts are void as being in general restraint of trade where they operate simply to prevent a party from engaging or competing in the same business." Hence, an agreement of one steamship company to pay another company a certain sum for withdrawing its line of boats was upheld as against the dissent of a stockholder in the former company. Leslie v Lorillard, 110 N. Y., 519 (1888). A large number of the proprietors of boats on the canals made a combination. The income from every boat, over and above a certain amount allowed to the boat for expenses for wear and tear, was turned into the "pool".

At certain times the fund in the 'pool" was to be divided among the parties according to the number of their boats. In an action to enforce payment under the agreement the court held that the whole arrangement was illegal, void and not enforceable. Stanton v Allen, 5 Denio, 434 (1848). The proprietors of five lines of boats engaged in canal transportation agreed to combine and do business at certain rates for freight and passage. The net earnings were to be divided among themselves in a fixed proportion. One of the parties sued another to compel him to make payment. The court held that the combination was void under the statutes of New York and said: "It is a familiar maxim that competition is the life of trade. It follows that whatever destroys or even relaxes competition in trade is injurious if not fatal to it." Hooker v Vandewater, 4 Denio, 349 (1847). A coal company bought coal from several corporations upon their contract not to sell to any other parties in that locality. The purpose was to enable the purchaser of the coal to have a monopoly of the market. The party which purchased the coal did not pay for it. The coal company which had sold brought suit for the price, but the court held that the suit must fail. The company had taken part in an illegal contract and combination. In such cases the parties are outside of the pale and protection of the law. The courts will not aid either party. Arnot v Pittston, etc., Coal Co., 68 N. Y., 558 (1877). Many salt manufacturers in New York state combined to limit the production and control the price of salt. They formed a corporation, and each of the parties leased to the corporation his manufactory of salt. Each of the parties was, however, to continue the manufacture of salt in his

most part have reorganized and reappeared in the form of gigantic corporations. How far the law will interfere with this class of corporations remains to be seen In the Chicago Gas Company case the supreme court of Illinois forfeited the charter of the company

manufactory, but only to a limited extent, and was to sell the product to a corporation at a fixed price. The agreement was carried out. One of the parties could not collect from the corporation the price for the salt delivered to it, and accordingly he brought suit. But the court decided that he could not collect. He lost his salt, and also the price of it. The law declares such combinations illegal, and will not aid any of the parties. Clancy v Onondaga Fine Salt, etc, Co., 62 Barb 395 (1862) The agreement of the various members of the "Wire Trust" not to sell at less than a certain price is void A forfeit cannot be recovered back by one of the parties De Witt, etc., Co v N J, etc , Co, 9 Ry. & Corp L J, 314 (N. Y. C, 1891). The receiver of one of the corporations forming a "trust" may enjoin it from reorganizing in the shape of one large corporation Gray v. De Castro, etc, Co, 10 N. Y Supp., 632 (1890). Although the charter of one of the corporations whose stock is held by a "trust" is forfeited, yet the receiver cannot have a receiver appointed of the "trust" property This would amount to a receivership of all the property of a stockholder in an insolvent corporation Gray v North River, etc., Co, N. Y. Law J, June 6, 1890 The receiver of the company whose charter is forfeited has no right to an accounting from the other corporations as partners. He is confined to the property of his own company. Gray v Oxnard, etc, Co, 11 N. Y. Supp., 118 (1890), affirmed in 59 Hun, 387 (1891), on the ground that an illegal contract cannot be enforced A receiver of an insolvent corporation may recover money due it from an illegal "trust," though the corporation was a party to the "trust." Pittsburgh, etc., Co v McMillan, 6 N Y Supp, 433

(1889) A contract between two corporations whereby the stockholders of the former were to buy only from the stockholders of the latter and the stockholders of the latter were to sell only to the stockholders of the former was upheld in Live-Stock Assoc, etc. v Levy, 3 N. Y St Rep, 514 (1886) A trust being illegal, a certificate-holder may have a receiver appointed of all the stock and assets held by the trustees, and may have an accounting by the trustees. Cameron v Havemeyer, 12 N Y. Supp, 126 (1890) Where a "trust" passes into a receiver's hands by reason of insolvency, the receiver may recover debts due the "trust" from the constituent corporations Pittsburgh, etc, Co v McMillan, 6 N Y. Supp, 433 (1889) The purchaser of a trust certificate issued by the trustees, the certificate being in a form similar to that of certificates of stock, may compel the trustees to transfer the same to him on their books, although he is a competitor of the trust and has opposed it in all ways possible. Rice v Rockefeller et al, 134 N Y, 174 (1892) In this case the court, speaking of the nature of a trust, said "The agreement constituted not a partnership, but a trust in behalf of the beneficiaries And while it is not a corporation, it, by the agreement, took some of the attributes of a corporation in so far that, through its trustees, certificates of shares in the equity to the property held by them were issued, and were transferable in like manner apparently as are those of corporations ' The case of Diamond Match Co v Roeber, 106 N. Y, 473 (1887), was not a "trust" case, and is no authority on the subject.

Ohio The Candle Manufacturers unincorporated association, formed to control prices, etc, is illegal A member cannot recover his share of the profits.

on the ground that it was formed to bring about an illegal combination. New Jersey, on the other hand, grants broad charters to the combinations and receives a heavy toll for the privileges and immunities granted.

Emery v Ohio Candle Co, 24 N E. Rep., 660 (Ohio, 1890). Many salt manufacturers formed a "trust," by agreeing to sell all their product to an unincorporated joint-stock association The latter was composed of, and its directors were elected by, the manufacturers The purpose of the combination was to have the association buy the salt from the manufacturers and sell it to the public. Competition would thereby be prevented The court held that the combination was void, and refused to enjoin one of the parties from breaking his contract with the association Central Ohio Salt Co v Guthrie, 35 Ohio St., 666 (1880)

Pennsylvania Five Pennsylvania coal corporations, which together controlled a certain kind of coal, combined and agreed that sales should be made through a committee and a general agent, and that thereby prices should be fixed, freights made, and sales and deliveries adjusted If any company sold more than a fixed proportion it was to pay a certain amount to the others. The combination was made and carried out in New York In the course of time one of the companies sued another to recover its proportion of the amount which the latter was to pay for the excess of coal sold by it. The Pennsylvania court held that it could not recover, that the combination was illegal and void, and that it was a conspiracy under the New York statute against the commission of any act by two or more persons "injurious . . to trade or commerce." Morris Run Coal Co v Barclay Coal Co, 68 Pa. St, 173 (1871). The courts will refuse a charter to a company whose business is to be "to promote the business of such retail dealers as become members thereof, and to protect them," etc, the intent being

to combine the retail coal dealers Matter of Richmond Retail Coal Co, 9 R'y, & Corp L J., 31 (Phil, 1890).

Tennessee It is illegal for an Ohio corporation to purchase a majority of the stock of a Tennessee corporation for the purpose of controlling the latter, even though they are engaged in a similar business, the object being to form a monopoly Hence the purchasing company cannot enforce the contract as to certain things which were to be done by the vendor of the stock. Buckeye, etc, Co v Harvey, 20 S. W. Rep., 427 (Tenn, 1892) A combination of four cotton-seed oil corporations by an agreement that the possession and use of all their property should be turned over to certain persons to run is a partnership, and contrary to the rule of law that a corporation cannot become a partner. One of the four corporations sued and recovered repossession of its property. Mallory v Hanover, etc, Works, 8 S. W. Rep, 346 (Tenn, 1888).

Wisconsin See Kellogg v. Larkin, 3 Pin (Wis.) 123 (1851).

The United States Courts Where a car manufacturing corporation leases all its property to another corporation for a term of years and agrees not to engage in business during that time, "the contract between the parties is void, because in unreasonable restraint of trade, and therefore contrary to public policy." Central Trans Co. v Pullman's Car Co., 139 U S, 24 (1891), quoting from and approving of Alger v Thacher, 19 Pick., 51 In the case United States v. Trans-Missouri Freight Assoc., 53 Fed Rep., 440 (1892), the court held that an agreement between several competing railway companies, that an association be formed for the purpose of maintaining just and reasonable rates, preventing unjust discriminations by furnishing

In more recent times, in England, the genuine "trust" has been used for legitimate investment purposes The trustees are authorized to invest the funds of the "trust" in the stocks and bonds of

adequate and equal facilities for the interchange of traffic between the several lines, without preventing or illegally limiting competition, is legal and is not in violation of the federal statute against trusts The court said ' The rule of law which recognizes the rights of the public to have the benefit of fair and healthy competition and to require that equal facilities and reasonable rates shall be secured to all, does not condemn a contract between railway companies operating competing lines, which is made for the sole purpose of preventing strife, and preventing financial ruin to one or the other, so long as the purpose and effect of such an agreement is not to deprive the public of its right to have adequate facilities and fixed and reasonable prices . The object and purpose of the agreement and the formation of the association thereunder was to maintain just and reasonable rates, and to prevent unjust discriminations, in compliance with the terms of the act regulating commerce by furnishing equal facilities for the interchange of traffic between the several lines " A copy of the agreement itself was given in this report It is an agreement to regulate rates, but does not provide for a division of the traffic A contract by a manufacturing company not to manufacture for a certain period if it is paid a certain percentage on sales made by others is illegal and void Oliver v Gilmore, 52 Fed Rep, 562 (1892) It is no defense to an infringement suit that the complainant has formed a monopoly of all patents bearing upon the matter Strait v National Harrow Co, 51 Fed. Rep, 819 (1892) An assignment of patents by one of several parties to a corporation formed to unite various patents in a certain business is absolute and cannot be revoked, even though the party was by agreement to have a salary

of $6,000 per year and this salary has not been paid Bracher v Hat Sweat Mfg Co, 40 Fed Rep, 921 (1892) A person who has sold his bakery to a corporation which is a 'trust,' taking stock in the corporation in payment, may tender back the stock and retake possession of his bakery The act of congress against combinations applies. American, etc, Co v Klotz, 44 Fed Rep, 721 (1891) Where the stockholders of a corporation enter into a contract for and in behalf of the corporation and for its benefit and the corporation accepts that benefit the latter is bound and affected by the contract and subject to the liabilities of the contract the same as though it had directly entered into it Hence it is that a corporation is guilty of entering into a "trust" in a case where its stockholders enter into the "trust" American P Trust v Taylor, etc, Co, 46 Fed Rep, 152 (1891) In this case the court held that the trustees were agents, and that the corporations were among the principals, and that it was ultra vires of the corporations to purchase stocks bonds and various properties through these agents, the trustees Hence one of the corporations cannot be enjoined from breaking the contract Where, in order to enter into a combination one of the corporations assigns all its property to its stockholders, and they assign it to the new consolidated and absorbing corporation, and also agree with that corporation not to compete with it in business, the first-named corporation may be started in the business anew and will not be enjoined American Preservers Co v Norris 43 Fed Rep, 711 (1890) In controversies between a certificate-holder and the trustees the court will not consider the legality of the "trust" Gould v Head, 41 Fed Rep, 240 (1890) A certificate-holder cannot

miscellaneous corporations   Generally, however, they are limited
in the amount which they may invest in any one direction.   That
which is lost in one investment is expected to be made up by large

enjoin an *ultra vires* or illegal act of the
trustees where he obtains service on only
four out of the nine trustees.   Each
trustee is liable personally for past
breaches of trust, but an injunction
against future acts can only be where
all the trustees are made parties   Wall
v Thomas 41 Fed Rep, 620 (1890)   Various decisions have been made under
the act of congress against monopolies
A combination of coal dealers to regulate prices and provide for the division
of prices with the miners of the coal is
contrary to the act of congress, where
the coal mining companies operate
chiefly in one state and the contract is
made and carried out in a city in another state   United States v Jellico,
etc, Co 46 Fed Rep, 432 (1891)   A suit
for damages, based on the federal anti-
trust law, failed in Bishop v American
Preservers Co, 51 Fed Rep, 272 (1892)
The statute applies to illegal trusts of
stock to unite competing railroads
Clarke i Central R R, 50 Fed. Rep,
338 (1892)   In the case United States i
Patterson, 54 Rep, 1005 (Mass, 1893) the
federal statute was held to apply in certain particulars, and not to apply in
others   The act of congress relative to
monopolies does not authorize an injunction except on the part of the government.   Blindell v Hagan, 54 Fed
Rep 40 (1893)   An indictment of a
number of lumbermen for raising the
price of lumber fifty cents a thousand
feet will not lie under the federal statute.   United States v. Nelson, 52 Fed
Rep. 646 (1892)   Indictment under the
federal law against monopolies quashed.
In re Corning, 51 Fed Rep, 205 (1892),
In re Terrell, id, 213, *In re* Greene, 52
Fed Rep 104 (1892).

England   The house of lords, the
highest court in England, in 1891 affirmed the decisions of the courts below
in the case Mogul Steamship Co v Mc-

Gregor (66 L. T. Rep., 1, affirming 61 id.,
820 and 59 id, 514), and held that an action of conspiracy would not lie against
a company that gave lower rates of
freight to parties who shipped exclusively by them, there being in the transaction no desire to injure others and no
ill-will   The defendant shipping companies and owners had combined together and formed a "conference" or
"ring," and their agents in China had
issued circulars to shippers there to the
effect that exporters in China who confined their shipments of goods to vessels
owned by members of the "conference"
should be allowed a certain rebate, payable half-yearly, on the freight charged
The court held that the "conference,"
being formed by the defendants with
the view of keeping the trade in their
own hands, and not with the view of
ruining the trade of the plaintiffs, or
through any personal malice or ill-will
towards them, was not unlawful, and
that no action for conspiracy was maintainable   Lord Coke, in the great and
leading "Case of the Monopolies," 11
Coke, 84 (1711), declared that a monopoly
was illegal and void   Lord Coke said
that a monopoly led to three results an
increase in price, a decrease in quality,
and the impoverishment of artisans and
others   An agreement of manufacturers that one shall not employ the discharged hands of any other except
upon the written consent of the latter
is void   Mineral Water, etc, Co. v.
Booth, 57 L. T Rep 573 (1887)   A company which is organized in violation of
a statute cannot collect debts which are
due to it   Jennings v Hammond, 51
L. J (Q B), 492 (1882), the company in
this case being organized in violation of
a statute which prohibited more than
twenty persons uniting in an association or partnership except under certain
conditions.   In another case many man-

profits in another. It is a mode of investment on a large scale, and is made on the principle of an average gain and loss [1]

The American "Car Trust." is practically an agreement of several owners of cars to place them in the hands of an agent to sell on the instalment plan, the agent having the power to issue certificates representing an interest in the instalments [2]

§ 503b. *Further inquiry as to the legality of a "trust"* — There are other things to be considered in determining whether or not a "trust" is legal Does it vest personal property or real estate in a trustee for a longer period than is allowed by law? Is the formation of a trust for the purpose of carrying on business authorized by law? Is the shifting of the parties interested — that is, the certificate-holders — allowed in cases of trusts? These questions will be considered in the order named

It is the policy of the law to limit the time during which a person may tie up his personal property or real estate Generally this time is fixed as the life time of the survivor of any two persons then living and designated by the person creating the trust Each state, by its statutes, generally provides and names the time during which property may be tied up by a trust, and if a trust is formed for a period longer than that allowed by statute the trust itself is void [3] There is little doubt that merchandise, land and shares of stock may be placed in trust The law is clear that "every kind

---

ufacturers, in consequence of troubles between themselves and their employees, entered into an agreement and gave a bond that they all would abide by the rates of labor, hours of work and other regulations which a majority of those who entered into the combination should decide upon The court held that the compact was in restraint of trade, that it was illegal and void, and that the bond could not be enforced Hilton v Eckersley, 6 E! & Bl, 47 (1856) *Cf* Ontario Salt Co v Merchants' Salt Co, 18 Grants Ch, 540 (1871), where a Canadian "pool" on salt was sustained, Wicken v Evans, 3 G J, 318 (1829) The word "monopoly" originally meant an exclusive privilege granted by the crown The courts held that the crown could not grant it See Case of Monopolies, *supra*, Mitchell v Reynolds, 1 P Williams, 181, 187 Concerning the subject of trusts and monopolies and exclusive privileges in

general, see Cook on The Corporation Problem, ch V, and pp 111-116

[1] See Healey on Company Law and Practice, p 191 For the form of articles of agreement of this kind of a "trust,' and for a detailed statement of the various provisions that are made, varying according to the character of the enterprise and the purposes of the participants, see Sykes v Beadon, L. R., 11 Ch D, 170 (1879), Smith v Anderson, L R, 15 Ch D, 247 (1880), Wigfield v. Potter, 45 L T, 612 (1882), Credit Mobilier v Commonwealth, 67 Pa St, 233 (1870) the last case being a "trust' created to construct a railroad, the *cestui que trust* being the stockholders of a designated corporation

[2] See ch L, *infra*

[3] Gerard s "Titles to Real Estate," p 228 Moreover, if the time is to be measured by the life of a person then living, a trust which is to exist for a fixed period, however short, without

of valuable property, both real and personal, that can be assigned at law may be the subject-matter of a trust." [1]

A different question arises, however, in determining whether a trust may be created to carry on business and trade, or to control a concern which carries on business [2]

At common law the placing of personal property in trust for the purpose of carrying on business in the name and under the management of the trustees is legal and allowable [3] The statutes of the various states, however, must be consulted in reference to this point [4]

reference to the life of a person then living is void Id , pp 228, 229 In New York the suspension can be for only two lives in being and, in certain cases twenty-one years thereafter 2 R. S., 723, § 15 (p 2176, 7th ed) This statute applies equally to real and personal property Gerard on Titles to Real Estate, 235 Howe v Van Schaick, 7 Paige, 221 (1839), Bean v Bowen, 47 How Pr , 306 Holmes v Mead, 52 N Y 332, 344 1873) The statutory prohibition against the accumulation of the income of trust property, except in the case of infants applies both to real estate and personalty Gerard's "Titles to Real Estate," p 238

[1] Perry on Trusts, § 67

[2] Under the statutes of New York a trust of property consisting of *real estate* is void, unless the purpose of the trust is to sell the land for the benefit of creditors, or to sell, mortgage or lease it for the benefit of legatees or for satisfying a lien on the land, or to receive the rent and use it for the support of a certain person, or to accumulate the rent for a certain person See 2 R S of N Y, 728, § 55 (p. 2181, 7th ed.). Accordingly a modern "trust," whose property consists of real estate in New York, would be void But as to personal property the law is generally different

[3] For decisions at common law to the effect that property may be vested in trustees for the purpose of carrying on business, see *Ex parte* Garland, 10 Ves., 110 (1883) Scott v Izou, 34 Beav , 434

(1865) In the case of Holmes v Mead, 52 N Y , 332 (1873), the court said "A trust in personal property, which is not in conflict with the statute regulating the accumulation of interest and protecting the suspension of absolute ownership in property of that character, is valid when the trustee is competent to take, and a trust is for a lawful purpose well defined, so as to be capable of being specifically executed by the court. . . Trusts of personal property are not affected by the statute of uses and trusts, which applies only to trusts in real property " In Gott v Cook, 7 Paige, 521, 534 (1839), the chancellor said: "The Revised Statutes have not attempted to define the objects for which express trusts of personal property may be created, as they have done in relation to trusts of real estate Such trusts, therefore, may be created for any purposes which are not illegal " See, also, Graff v. Bonnett, 31 N Y, 139 (1865) In Power v Cassidy, 79 N Y , 602, 613 (1880), the court said . "The law does not limit or confine trusts as to personal property except in reference to the suspension of ownership, and they may be created for any purpose not forbidden by law " To same effect, Bucklin v. Bucklin, 1 Keyes (N Y), 141 (1864); Yoebel v Wolf, 113 N Y , 405 (1889)

[4] Many of them, including Michigan, Wisconsin, Minnesota, California, Dakota, North Carolina, Georgia, Pennsylvania, Connecticut, Kentucky and Vermont, have statutes expressly specifying the objects for which a trust may

There is little difficulty in determining the question whether it is allowable in law to create a trust where the *cestuis que trust* — that is, the certificate-holders — change and fluctuate in their identity. The law does not require the *cestui que trust* to remain continuously one and the same person   He is not indefinite, even though by transfer of interest his identity may change.[1]

A more formidable objection to the legality of "trusts" is that they are similar to an unincorporated joint-stock association, and that the latter are illegal, inasmuch as they assume the powers, privileges and name of a corporation   It was on this ground that the decision in Louisiana declared that the American Cotton Oil Trust was illegal, and was disqualified to do business within that state   The court held that, under the statutes of Louisiana, an unincorporated joint-stock association is illegal, that a "trust" was one kind of an unincorporated joint-stock association, and consequently that it was illegal and void.[2]

But this view of the law would not be sustained elsewhere in this country, nor would it be sustained under the old common law of England.   Unincorporated joint-stock companies have existed for years and are common throughout all the other states of the Union They are legal methods of carrying on business.[3]

§ 503c. *Liability of trustee and certificate holders* — The law is clear that a trustee who carries on any kind of business is liable personally, and to the entire extent of his private fortune, for all the debts incurred in the management and execution of the trust.[4]   It

be created   See Stimson's American Statute Law, § 1703.

[1] See Harrison *v* Harrison, 36 N Y, 543 (1867), affirming 32 Barb, 162, Holmes *v* Mead, 52 N Y, 332, 343 (1873), Conkling *v* Washington University, 2 Md Ch, 497 (1849), Perry on Trusts, § 66   In regard to this matter, a "trust" is legal on the same principle that it is legal for a bondholder secured by a railway trust deed or mortgage to sell and transfer his interest to another

[2] State of Louisiana *v* American Cotton Oil Trust, 1 R'y & Corp. L, J, 509 (1887), the court saying · "A joint-stock company is not known to the laws of Louisiana."

[3] See § 504, *infra*.   In England there formerly was doubt upon this subject, but this doubt was due to the "Bubble Act."   This statute was passed in 1720 for the purpose of suppressing unin-

corporated companies   At that time they were regarded as "dangerous, mischievous and, in short, public nuisances"   But the statute was repealed in 1826, and Lindley, the great English judge and jurist, says of it   "Juster views of political economy and of the limits within which legislative enactments should be confined have led to the repeal of the statute in question, which, though deemed highly beneficial half a century ago, probably gave rise to much more mischief than it prevented"   Lindley on Partnership 193 -- the great English work on corporations   Moreover, a careful examination of the English authorities up to the present day shows conclusively that at common law an unincorporated joint-stock association is legal and valid   Id, 192, 196 *Cf* 21 N. E Rep, 605 (Ill, 1889)

[4] Thompson *v* Brown, 4 Johns Ch,

is possible, however, that the use of the words "as trustee," in the contract entered into, will protect him against this liability[1] And there is little doubt that the creditors of the trust may collect their debts from its property. This has been a doubtful point, but is now reasonably well settled It matters not whether the trustees have expressly bound the trust property to pay the debts. Where the trustee is insolvent, a creditor of the trust may proceed against its property to procure payment of a debt incurred in the execution of the trust.[2]

But a different rule prevails as regards the *cestui que trust*, the beneficiary The *cestui que trust* cannot be held liable for the debts created by the trustees or for debts incurred in the execution of the trust This question has arisen chiefly in cases where trustees have carried on the business of an insolvent person for the benefit of the creditors of the latter.[3] And the same conclusion is reached in cases where an executor, administrator or trustee carries on a business for the benefit of a beneficiary.[4]

619 (1820), Wild v Davenport, 7 Atl Rep., 295 (N J., 1887), Stephens v James, 3 S L. Rep, 160 (Ga 1887), Rogers v Wheeler, 43 N Y, 598 (1871), Jones v Seligman, 81 N Y, 190 (1880)

[1] Contracts entered into by the trustees of a trust deed for many shareholders bind the latter but not the former personally, where the trustees were authorized to make the contracts and did so as trustees It is immaterial that the contracts are under seal. Cook v Gray, 133 Mass, 106 (1882) But see Stephenson v Pold, 32 N W Rep, 340 (Iowa, 1887), 1 Parsons on Contracts (6th ed), *122 As to the mode of compelling payment of a debt incurred by a trustee who has issued scrip to represent the property, see Mayo v Moritz, 24 N E Rep., 1083 (Mass., 1890), holding that the remedy is not for a receiver to wind up the trust

[2] Cater v Everleigh, 4 Desaus, 19 (1809), James v Mayrant, 4 Desaus, 691 (1815), Montgomery v Everleigh, 1 McCord Ch, 267 (1826), Magwood v Patterson, 1 Hiles Ch, 228 (1833), Gaudy v Barrit, 56 Ga, 640 (1876), Tennant v Stoney 1 Rich Eq, 222, 243 (1845), Wylly v Collins, 9 Ga, 223 (1851), Frost v Shackleford, 57 Ga, 261 (1876), Ferrin v. Myrick, 41 N Y, 315 (1869) *Contra,*

Worral v Harford, 8 Ves. Jr, 8 (1802), Mulhall v Williams, 32 Ala, 489 (1858), Jones v Dawson, 19 Ala., 672 (1851) See, also, New v Nicoll, 73 N Y, 127 (1878), Noyes v. Blakeman, 6 N. Y., 567 (1852).

[3] Storrs v Flint, 14 J. & S. (N. Y), 498 (1880), Cox v Hickman, 8 H. L. Cases, 268 (1860), Re Stanton Iron Co., 21 Beav, 164 (1855), Selwyn v Harrison, 2 J & H. 334 (1862). See Bingaman v Hickman, 8 Atl Rep, 644 (Pa, 1887)

[4] In the case of *Ex parte* Garland, 10 Ves, 110 (1803), where a testator directed that a certain sum be used to carry on a business, and the executor so used it, and the business became insolvent, *held,* per Lord Eldon, that no other part of the testator's property was liable for the debts thereby incurred, overruling Hankey v Hammond, 1 Cooke s Bank Law, 67 (1786) Lord Eldon further said: "On the other hand, the case of the executor is hard. He becomes liable as personally responsible, to the extent of all his property, though he is but a trustee. But he places himself in that position by his own choice" In the case of *In re* Johnson, L R, 15 Ch D, 548 (1880), the cases are reviewed Lord Eldon's

It has been held also that the trustee cannot render the *cestui que trust* liable, even though the trustee contracts with the creditor to that effect [1]

There is little doubt that these old principles of law are applicable to "trusts." The courts of England have decided that a modern "trust" is not a partnership or mere association, but is similar to an old common-law trust estate. This conclusion was reached in construing an English statute which prohibits certain partnerships or associations from doing business.[2]

decision that it is not the general estate of the testator which is liable, but only so much as he has authorized to be employed in the business, is stated to be still the law. See, also, Strickland *v* Symons, L. R., 26 Ch. D., 245 (1884). An estate is not liable for debts created by a partnership continued by order of the will. Stewart *v.* Robinson, 115 N. Y., 328 (1889).

[1] Stanton *v* King, 8 Hun (N. Y.), 4 (1876), affirmed, 69 N. Y., 609. See 15 Am. L. Rev., 456; Burch *v* Breckenridge, 16 B. Mon., 488; New *v* Nicoll, 12 Hun, 431 (1877), affirmed, 73 N. Y., 127.

[2] In England a statute exists which forbids any company, association or partnership consisting of more than twenty persons from carrying on any business for the acquisition of gain, unless it is registered as a company under the Joint-stock Company's Act, and complies therewith as regards reports, etc. It has been held that a "trust" is not a "company, association or partnership," and consequently is not affected by this statute. Wigfield *v* Potter, 45 L. T., 612 (1882), Crowther *v* Thorley, 32 W. R., 330 (1884), *In re* Siddall, L. R., 29 Ch. D., 1 (1885); Smith *v* Anderson, L. R., 15 Ch. D., 247 (1880). The last case cited was an action to have the "trust" dissolved on the ground that it was a partnership, and was doing business in violation of the statute. The court refused to grant the relief desired, and said that the certificate-holders were not partners and did not form an association. "There

has never been anything creating any mutual rights or obligations between these persons. They are from the first entire strangers, who have entered into no contract whatever with each other, nor has either of them entered into any contract with the trustees or any trustee on behalf of the other, there being nothing in the deed pointing to any mandate or delegation of authority to act for the certificate-holders as between themselves, and nothing, as it appears to me, by which any liability could ever be cast upon the certificate-holders either as between themselves or as between themselves and anybody else . . . If there is any business at all, it is to be carried on by the trustees. Whatever is to be done is to be done by the trustees." And Cotton L. J., said, "The trustees here are the only persons who are dealing with the investments, and they are dealing not as agents for some principal, but as trustees in whom the property and the management of it are vested, and who have the power of changing the investments and securities. That is just like the case which often occurs where the executors or trustees of a will are directed to carry on a business. The fact that they are to account to others for the profits made is a matter utterly immaterial as between them and those with whom they deal. They deal with those persons as the only persons contracting and hold themselves out as personally liable. These persons have no right whatever as against the persons beneficially entitled." This case was one involving a

Such being the case, it seems to be clear that the trustees and the property of a modern "trust" are liable for all debts incurred by it, but that the holders of the trust certificates are not in any way liable therefor, unless they have expressly agreed to assume that liability.

§ 503*d* *Qualifications, powers, rights and duties of the managers and certificate-holders of a "trust"*— Any person may serve as a trustee, provided that person is competent to take the legal title to the property.[1]

The trustees of a "trust" correspond somewhat to the directors of a corporation. They generally are elected annually by the certificate-holders in a regularly called meeting of themselves. The instruments creating the "trust" usually provide for the election of trustees, and for their succession and term of office. There is nothing in the old law of trust estates which forbids this change of trustees[2]

Where, by the trust deed, a majority of the *cestuis que trust* have power to fill a vacancy caused by the incapacity or inability of the

"trust" See, also, *dicta* to the same effect in Credit Mobilier *v* Commonwealth, 67 Pa St., 233 (1870)

[1] Perry on Trusts, § 39

[2] "The person who creates the trust may mould it into whatever form he pleases, he may therefore determine in what manner, in what event and upon what condition the original trustees may retire and new trustees may be substituted All this is fully within his power, and he can make any legal provisions which he may think proper for the continuation and succession of trustees during the continuation of the trust." Perry on Trusts, § 287 In England, under the vesting acts, the court held that it had power to vest the estate of a modern "trust" in new trustees where one of the old trustees was dead, another was insane, and under the trust agreement the certificate-holders had elected new trustees. *In re* Siddall, L. R., 29 Ch. D, 1 (1885) A similar power was given to trustees of personal property in New York by ch 185, L. 1882 As regards the common-law rules and powers of the courts herein, see Perry on Trusts, § 356 *et seq* At common law, upon the death

of the surviving trustee, his executor or administrator became the trustee. Boone *v* Citizens' Bank, etc., 84 N. Y., 83, 87 (1881) De Peyster *v* Beekman, 55 How Pr Rep, 90 (1877) In the Cost-book Company Case of Johnson *v.* Goslett, 18 C B, 729 (1856), the following provision appears· "The trustees of the said lease shall, when and if required by the directors, execute a deed declaring that they hold the said mine under and by virtue of such lease as trustees for the benefit of the shareholders in the said company, according to their respective shares and interests therein; and if any or either of the said trustees or any future trustees shall resign or die or become incapable or unwilling to act, then new trustees or a new trustee may be appointed by any of the general meetings of shareholders hereinafter provided for, in the place of the trustees or trustee so resigning or dying or becoming incapable or unwilling to act as aforesaid, and the said premises shall be forthwith assigned to and vested in the said new trustee or trustees jointly with the continuing trustee or trustees, or in such new trustees only, as the case may

trustee, they may substitute a new trustee when the old trustee removes to and becomes a resident of a foreign country [1]

The extent of the powers of the trustees of a "trust" is a matter of great interest to the public and the certificate-holders. Especially is this the case since the extent of the trustees' powers is kept a secret from all except the favored few Often the certificate-holders are not allowed to examine and know the contents of the trust instrument which defines the powers of trustees It is true that the law guards jealously against any assumption of powers by the trustee beyond those which are expressly conferred by the trust instrument [2]

The trustees who hold the stock in the various corporations which make up the "trust" are trustees and not vendees of the stock.[3] The trustee ordinarily has no power to sell the stock [4]

There are other incidents which explain the position of the trustee He may sue and be sued in his own name on all matters and contracts pertaining to the trust.[5]

He is not liable to the *cestui que trust* for losses incurred by his management of the property of the trust. He is bound merely to exercise ordinary discretion and to obey the directions of the instru-

require, at the expense of the said company."

[1] Farmers' Loan & Trust Co. v Hughes, 11 Hun, 130 (1877) In this case the deed of trust provided that the trustees or their survivor might be removed by the vote of a majority in interest of the holders of the bonds referred to in the trust deed at any meeting called for that purpose, and further, by a separate and distinct provision, that in case of the death, removal, resignation, incapacity or inability of both or either of said trustees to act in the execution of the trust, then a majority of the holders of such bonds might designate and select, in writing, one or more competent persons to fill the vacancy so occurring The property may be made to vest in new trustees without transfer, if the trust instrument is so drawn Perry on Trusts, § 284

[2] Perry on Trusts, §§ 451, 460

[3] People v North River S. Rep. Co., 121 N Y., 582 (1890)

[4] See ch. XIX. The trustees of the American Cattle Trust cannot sell shares of stock which they hold Gould v Head, 38 Fed. Rep, 886 (1889), Id, 41 Fed Rep, 242 (1890)

[5] In this respect the trustee is not the same as the director of a corporation "A trustee is a man who is the owner of the property, and deals with it as principal, as owner and as master, subject only to an equitable obligation to account to some persons to whom he stands in the relation of trustee, and who are his *cestuis que trust* .
The office of director is that of a paid servant of the company A director never enters into a contract for himself, but he enters into contracts for his principal, that is, for the company of whom he is a director and for whom he is acting He cannot sue on such contracts, nor be sued on them unless he exceeds his authority That seems to me to be the broad distinction between trustees and directors" Smith v. Anderson, L. R., 15 Ch D., 247 (1880).

(42)

ment creating the trust. It is only for a breach of trust that he may be made to account to the *cestui que trust*.[1]

In the case of the modern 'trust" it has been doubted whether the consent of all the trustees is essential to its contracts and acts, as is the case with the old common-law trust[2] But, in general, these matters are regulated and provided for by the instrument which creates the "trust."

The compensation of the trustee is usually fixed by the trust deed If not, it falls within the provisions of the statutes, or a reasonable compensation is allowed by the common law.[3]

The property of the "trust" cannot be seized for the individual debts of the trustee,[4] but the interest of the certificate-holder may be reached so as to subject it to the payment of his debts.[5] In this respect the certificates resemble shares of stock

The trust property, where it consists of personal property in the nature of bonds. stocks, notes or evidences of indebtedness, or corresponds to the capital stock of a corporation, may be taxed at the place where the main office or place of business of the "trust" exists The extent of the taxation depends, of course, upon the statutes of the state wherein the tax is laid.[6]

There is more difficulty in determining whether a certificate-holder may terminate his interest in the "trust" and demand his proportion of the property In certain "trusts," whose property consists of shares of stock, he undoubtedly may.[7] But in general a single certificate-holder cannot have the whole "trust" dissolved

---

[1] Simonton v Sibley, 122 U. S, 220 (1887) Where a railroad construction contract is assigned to trustees to be carried out and the profits to be paid to the stockholders of a designated corporation, the stockholders may compel the trustees to pay over such profits. The trustees cannot set up that they were also directors of the railroad Hazard v Dillon, 34 Fed Rep, 485 (1888)

[2] Mills v Hurd, 29 Fed Rep, 410 (1887)

[3] Perry on Trusts, § 917

[4] Gibson v Stevens, 7 N H, 352 (1834), where a trustee was authorized to continue the testator's business The property was held not subject to the trustee's personal debts

[5] It can be reached, doubtless, just as the bonds of a bondholder under a railroad mortgage or trust deed may be reached As to the rule at common law,

see 2 Albany L Journal, 261, 288. In New York, by statute, all transfers of personal property made in trust, for use of the person making the same, are void as against his creditors, existing or subsequent 2 R. S, 135, § 1 (7th ed, p 2327, and cases there cited). See, also, Graff v Bonnett, 31 N Y, 1, 14, 18.

[6] Ricker v American Loan & Trust Co, 140 Mass, 346 (1885) See, also, People v Assessors, etc, 40 N. Y., 154 (1869), In re County of Washington v. Estate of Jefferson, 28 N. W Rep, 256 (Minn, 1886), citing many cases on this subject It is well settled in New York state that under its statutes no shares of stock in either domestic or foreign corporations are subject to taxation except shares of stock in national banks. See § 565, *infra*

[7] See § 503b.

and wound up before the time fixed by the trust agreement for its dissolution has arrived.[1]

If the "trust" itself is forbidden by the statutes of the state wherein it exists, it never will be wound up by the courts The law will not compel a trustee to account for property or transactions which grow out of a contract which is prohibited by statute The courts leave the parties where they are found. They are outside of the protection of the law.[2]

If, however, the "trust" is legal it may be terminated at any time by a decree of a court, upon the consent of all the parties who are interested in it[3] But a "trust" will not be dissolved and wound up merely because the trustees have been guilty of a breach of trust. The remedy in such a case is to enjoin or remove the trustees[4] Where, however, the trust is insolvent and incapable of proceeding, a dissolution and winding up of its business will be decreed by a court.[5]

B. UNINCORPORATED JOINT-STOCK ASSOCIATIONS

§ 504 *Definitions — Joint-stock companies, clubs, exchanges, etc.— Ownership of land* — A joint-stock company may be defined to be an association of persons for the purpose of business, having a capital stock divided into shares, and governed by articles of association which prescribe its objects, organization and procedure, and the rights and liabilities of the members, except that the articles cannot release the members from their liability as partners to the creditors of the company.[6]

[1] Smith v Anderson, L R., 15 Ch D., 247 (1880) The same rule prevails in unincorporated joint-stock associations. See Smith v Virgin, 33 Me, 148 (1851). See, also, Waterbury v Mercantile, etc , Ex Co, 50 Barb, 157 (1867), holding that such company will not be wound up merely because the directors have been guilty of a breach of trust

[2] *In re* Padstow, etc , Co., L. R., 20 Ch D, 137 (1882).

[3] Perry on Trusts, § 920

[4] Id., §§ 816–853.

[5] See Baring v Dix, 1 Cox, 213 (1786); Bailey v. Ford, 13 Sim , 495 (1843), Jennings v Baddeley, 3 K & J , 77 (1856), where insolvent copartnerships were wound up, though the time for which they were to exist had not yet expired See, also, Seighortner v Weissenborn,

20 N. J Eq , 172 (1869), Howell v. Harvey, 5 Ark , 270 (1842) Van Ness v Fisher, 5 Lans , 236 (1871), Brien v Harriman, 1 Tenn Ch , 467 (1873), Halladay v Elliott. 8 Oreg , 84 (1879), Bagley v Smith, 10 N Y, 489 (1853). In Sibley v Minton, 27 L J (Eq), 53 (1858), the court held that in an action by an adventurer in a cost-book mining company to wind up the company and adjust the losses, all the co-adventurers were necessary parties

[6] In Hedge & Horne's Appeal, 63 Pa St , 273 (1869), it is defined to be "a partnership whereof the capital is divided or agreed to be divided into shares, and so as to be transferable without the express consent of all the copartners." In the statutes of Massachusetts the words "joint-stock company" are used

A joint-stock company lies midway between a corporation and a copartnership. It is, however, to be distinguished from them,[1] and

to mean a corporation organized under the general incorporation act of the state. Attorney-General v. Mercantile Ins Co., 121 Mass., 524 (1877) But this is not an accurate use of the term · The articles of association of an unincorporated joint-stock company bear the same relation to it that the charter bears to an incorporated company They regulate the duties of the officers and the duties and obligations of the members of such a company among themselves, they specify the capital, limit the duration and define the business of the company " Bray v Farwell, 81 N Y, 600 (1880), per Earl, J. See also, White v Brownell, 42 Abb Pr (N S), 162, 193 (1862). In Robbins v Butler, 24 Ill, 387, 426, 432 (1860), it is said that joint-stock companies "have none of the rights and immunities of . a regularly incorporated company These stock companies are nothing more than partnerships, and every member of the company is liable for the debts of the concern, no matter what the private arrangements among themselves may be " To the same effect, see Moore v Brink, 4 Hun, 402 (1875), Skinner v Dayton, 19 Johns, 513 (1822); Wells v Gates, 18 Barb, 554 (1854), Keasley v Codd, 2 Carr. & P, 408 (1826) · The term joint-stock company appears to have originated in England in comparatively recent times. Joint stock companies may be said to be partnerships or individuals associated for some specified purpose under a designated name or description, to which, by some general or special statute, when they have been formed or composed in a specified manner, some of the powers or proper attributes of a corporation have been given " Dayton, etc, R. R. Co. v Hatch, 1 Disney, Cin Super Ct, 84, 90 (1855) Factors', etc, Insurance Co. v Harbor, etc., Co., 37 La. Ann., 233, 239 (1885), speaks of a joint-stock company as "a nondescript organization, composed of the owners of certificates showing the proportion of their respective interests in its assets and liability for its obligations, and who are co-owners or proprietors in common As no one is bound to own property in indivision, it follows that such owners who wish a division have a right to have that property sold, and after a liquidation of the affairs of the concern to have the residue distributed ratably among themselves." At common law a partnership or joint-stock association may do business under any name that it chooses. See § 233, note; Preachers', etc Soc. v Rich, 45 Me., 552, 2 Perry on Trusts, § 730, Swasey v. American Bible Soc, 57 Me., 523; Cory, etc., Soc. v Beatty, 27 N J. Eq 570.

[1] It differs from a corporation in that a joint-stock company has no limited liability as regards its stockholders; and it cannot sue or be sued in the name of the association It differs from a copartnership in that it is not dissolved by a transfer of stock, and each member has not the same powers of transacting business and disposing of the assets as in a partnership. See Cox v. Bodfish, 35 Me, 302 (1853) A company organized under the statutes of Pennsylvania and having mixed characteristics of a partnership and corporation, is a corporation so far as removal to the federal court is concerned. Bushnell v Park Bros & Co, 46 Fed Rep, 209 (1891) The ordinary attachment statute authorizing the attachment of shares of stock does not apply to a club organized for lawful sporting purposes and being more of the nature of a statutory joint-stock association than a corporation Lyan v Denison, 45 N. W. Rep., 358 (Mich, 1890) In Illinois it is a criminal offense for individuals or an incorporated association to use a name · that implies incorporation. Hazelton,

also from clubs,[1] from social, benevolent[2] and mutual aid[3] organizations, and from associations formed for business purposes, but without a capital stock,[4] especially in respect to the right of ex-

etc., Co. v Hazelton, etc, Co, 30 N. E Rep. 339 (Ill. 1892)

[1] Park v Spaulding, 10 Hun, 128 (1877), Ridgely v Dobson 3 Watts & S, 118 (1842), Loubat v Le Roy, 40 Hun, 546 (1886), Fleming v Hector, 2 Mees. & W, 172 (1836), Re St James Club, 2 De G, M & G, 383 (1852), Ewing v Midlock, 5 Port. (Ala), 82 (1837), Todd v Emly, 8 M & W, 505 (1841), Raynell v Lewis, 15 M & W, 517 (1846), Wood v Finch, 2 F. & F, 447 (1861), Cross v Williams, 10 W R, 302 (1862), Cockerel v Aucompe, 5 W R, 633 (1857), Koehler v Brown 31 How, 235 (1866), Waller v Thomas, 42 How, 337 (1871), Hopkinson v Marquis of Exeter, 16 W R, 266 (1869), Gardner v Frunatte, 19 W R, 256 (1870), Delauney v Strickland, 2 Stark. 416, Coldicott v Griffiths, 8 Ex, 898, Ebbinghousen v Worth Club 4 Abb N C, 300.

[2] Penfield v Skinner, 11 Vt, 296 (1839), Beaumont v Meredith, 3 Ves & B, 180 (1814) See, also, Thomas v Ellmaker, 1 Parsons' Sel Eq Cases, 98 (1844) On Masonic lodges See Ash v Gnie, 97 Pa. St, 493 (1881) See, also, Cohn v Borst, 36 Hun, 562 (1885), Goodman v Jedidjah Lodge, 9 Atl Rep, 13 (Md, 1887), Schmidt v Abraham, etc, Lodge. 2 S. W Rep, 150 (Ky., 1886) By-law of benevolent society that for non-payment of dues, name shall be dropped, is legal and self-executing. Rood v Railway, etc, Ass n, 31 Fed Rep., 62 (1887). See McCalhon v Hibernia, etc Soc, 12 Pac Rep., 114 (Cal, 1886), involving a secession from a benevolent association Benevolent associations are not necessarily copartnerships Brown v Stoerkel, 41 N W Rep., 921 (Mich 1889)

[3] Lafand v. Deems, 81 N Y, 507 (1880), Fitts v Muck, 62 How Pr, 69 (1881), Pipe v Bateman, 1 Iowa, 369 (1875). Cf Thomas v Ellmaker, 1 Parsons' Sel. Eq Cases, 98 (1844), Olery v

Brown, 51 How Pr, 92 (1875) See, also, Boone on Corporations, § 338.

[4] Such as stock exchanges See White v Brownell, 4 Daly, 162 Clute v Loveland, California (1885), Leech v Harris, 2 Brews, 571 (1869), Slate v Chamber of Com, 20 Wis., 63 (1865), Weston v Ives, 97 N Y, 222 (1884), relative to sale of a seat by the exchange to pay the member's debts See, also, Platt v. Jones, 96 N Y., 24 (1884). As to a levy of execution on a seat in an exchange, see Bowen v. Bull, 12 N. Y. Supp, 325 (1890), Powell v. Waldron, 89 N Y, 328, Ritterband v Baggett, 4 Abb N C, 67, Landhenn v White, 67 How. Pr, 467 A seat in the exchange is property which may be reached by creditors But if an assignee in bankruptcy refuses to take it and pay the dues, the bankrupt who pays them may retain the seat. Sparhawk v Yerkes, 142 U. S., 1 (1891) A stock exchange may expel a member who does not fulfill his contracts made within the exchange, due notice, etc, being given to him in the matter Lewis v Wilson, 121 N. Y., 284 (1890). Seat of a member of an exchange may be reached, though by-laws contra. Habenicht v Lissak 20 Pac Rep., 874 (Cal, 1889) Stock exchanges cannot expel members for carrying case into courts instead of arbitrating People v N Y Cotton Ex, 8 Hun, 216 (1876) As to power of board of trade to expel member, see Pitcher v Board of Trade of Chicago, 13 N. E Rep, 187 (Ill, 1887). Expulsion from unincorporated associations Otto v Journeymen, etc, Union, 17 Pac. Rep, 217 (Cal, 1888). See, also, § 700b, infra. For improving a water-power Troy Iron & Nail Factory v Corning, 45 Barb, 231 (1884) For building a school-house Maustin v Durgin, 51 N H, 347 (1874) For protecting business interests Caldicott v Griffiths, 8 Ex, 898 (1853) See, also, Tenney v.

661

pulsion[1] A joint-stock company, although it exercises the power to issue stock, the same as a corporation, yet when organized for the purpose of transacting any lawful business is itself a lawful mode of carrying on business[2]

New Eng Protection Union, 37 Vt., 64 (1864) Abels v McKean, 18 N J Eq, 462 (1867), Heury v. Jackson, 37 Vt, 431 (1865), Frost v. Walker, 60 Me, 468 (1865) Building associations. Strohen v Franklin, etc, Ass'n, 8 Atl Rep., 843 (Pa. 1887), Quern v Smith, 108 Pa St, 325 Jackson v Cassidy, 4 S. W Rep, 511 (Tex, 1887), Auld v Glasgow, etc, Society 56 L T Rep, 776 (1887) A building association has power to borrow money and give security for it. North. etc, Assoc v First Nat'l Bank, 47 N W Rep, 300 (Wis, 1890) A building and loan association can foreclose a mortgage irrespective of payments by the mortgagor on his stock in the association Peoples', etc, Assoc v Furey, 20 Atl Rep, 890 (N J 1890) For a full explanation of the character and mode of business of a mutual benefit building association or corporation, where regular dues are paid and the money loaned to the members on mortgages without interest see People v Lowe, 117 N Y, 175 (1889) As to the stockholder's right in a building association to withdraw and sue for his payments under a by-law providing therefor to the extent of one-third of the funds in the treasury, see Texas. etc, Assoc v Kern, 13 S. W. Rep, 1020 (Tex, 1890) Concerning a building association, stock complication and the rights of creditors of a stockholder, see Wilson v Schoenlaub, 12 S W Rep, 361 (Mo., 1889) In Pennsylvania by statute the law against usury does not apply to building co-operative associations. See Albright v Lafayette, etc, Assoc., 102 Pa St, 411 (1883), Winget v Quincy, etc, Assoc, 21 N E Rep, 12 (Ill, 1889) In a Michigan co-operative savings and loan corporation if a member sells his stock to the company, he cannot afterwards redeem or sell it It is not a loan as other authorities have

held Michigan Bldg, etc, Assoc v. McDevitt, 43 N W Rep, 760 (Mich, 1889) See Atwood v Dumas, 21 N. E. Rep, 236 (Mass, 1889).

[1] An action is not maintainable to compel an unincorporated voluntary political association to admit a person to membership McKane v Adams, 123 N Y, 609 (1890) A member of a union cannot bring a suit in equity to declare void and illegal a by-law that members shall be fined for accepting employment in connection with non-union persons, and to enjoin the infliction of a fine upon himself His remedy is at law or by application to the attorney-general Thomas v Musical, etc, Union, 121 N. Y, 45 (1890) A by-law that the members of a news association shall not publish news furnished by other associations in the same territory is valid The penalty for violation may be suspension Matthews v. Associated Press, 61 Hun, 199 (1891) See, also, notes supra Where a member of a lodge was expelled for entering into a conspiracy to blackball applicants for admission, the court refused to restore him by mandamus, and said that such a case was different from one where property rights or money demands are involved State v Grand Lodge, 22 Atl Rep, 63 (N J, 1891) Where the expelled member has the right by by-law to appeal from the decision to a corporate meeting, the courts will not interfere until such appeal is taken. Screwman s etc, Assoc v Benson, 13 S. W. Rep, 379 (Tex, 1890) Expulsion from a club under a by-law. Commonwealth v Union League, 19 Atl. Rep, 1030 (Pa, 1890)

[2] "It is too late to contend that partnerships with transferable shares are illegal in this commonwealth. . . . The grounds upon which they were

The earlier cases declaring that joint-stock companies were illegal were so decided largely because of the Bubble Act, existing from 1720 to 1726.[1]

Very high English authority, after a thorough review of the English cases, gives the opinion that at common-law joint-stock associations are legal[2]

In Louisiana and Illinois a contrary conclusion has been arrived at[3]

formerly said to be illegal in England, apart from statute, have been abandoned in modern times." Phillips v Blatchford, 137 Mass 510 (1884) "These companies, being consonant with the wants of a growing and wealthy community, have forced their way into existence, whether fostered by the law or opposed to it" Greenwood's Case, 3 De G. M. & G, 459, 477 (1854), Townsend v Goewey, 19 Wend, 423 A laboring men's association for the purpose of opposing capitalists has been upheld Snow v Wheeler, 113 Mass., 179 (1873)

[1] Enacted, 6 Geo 1. ch 18, § 18, repealed, 6 Geo 4, ch 91 Lindley says of this act 'Juster views of political economy and of the limits within which legislative enactments should be confined have led to the repeal of the statute in question, which, though deemed highly beneficial half a century ago, probably gave rise to much more mischief than it prevented."

[2] Lindley on Partnership, 192 In a thorough and exhaustive note on this subject the learned author refers to Rex v Dodd, 9 East, 406 (1808), holding that a company with a prospectus limiting the liability of subscribers is illegal, as a trap to ensnare the unwary. Josephs v Pebrer, 3 B & C., 639 (1825), holding that unincorporated companies with transferable shares are illegal, and Buck v Buck, 1 Campb, 547 (1808) R. v Stratton, id, 549, n, to same effect That Kinder v Taylor, Coll on Partn, 917, 2d ed (1810), Duvergier v Fellows, 5 Bing, 248; affirmed, 10 B. & C, 826, and Blundell v Winsor, 8 Sim., 601, contained dicta only so far as they passed on the legality of these compa-

nies. The following cases clearly establish the legality of joint-stock associations Harrison v Heathorn, 6 Man & Gr, 81 (1843), Garrard v Hadley, 5 Man & Gr, 171, Ex parte Barclay, 26 Beav, 177; Ex parte Aston 27 Beav, 474, Ex parte Griswood, 4 De G & J, 544, Sheppard v Oxenford, 1 K & J, 491, R. v Webb, 14 East, 516, Walburn v Ingilby, 1 M & K, 61 and see Pratt v Hutchinson 15 East 511 Ellison v Bignold, 2 J & W, 510, Nockels v Crosby, 3 B & C, 814 Kimpson v Saunders, 1 Bing, 5, Brown v Holt, 4 Taunt, 587 And the learned jurist comes to this conclusion ' The case of Blundell v Winsor, always relied upon as an authority by those who contend that such a company is illegal has never met with approbation from the bench, nor has it ever been followed Upon the whole therefore, it appears that there is no case deciding that a joint-stock company with transferable shares, and not incorporated by charter or act of parliament, is illegal at common law that opinions have nevertheless differed upon this question, that the tendency of the courts was formerly to declare such companies illegal, that this tendency exists no longer and that an unincorporated company with transferable shares will not be held illegal at common law unless it can be shown to be of a dangerous and mischievous character, tending to the grievance of her majesty's subjects The legality at common law of such companies may therefore be considered as finally established"

[3] See § 503b, supra, 21 N E Rep, 605 (Ill, 1889)

The real estate of an unincorporated joint-stock association is generally held in the names of trustees for its benefit.[1] The English cost-book mining companies were organized on this principle.[2]

[1] Where the association holds land in the name of trustees for the benefit of certificate-holders, the latter are an equitable lien on the proceeds from the sale of the land and even a consolidation with another association does not disturb this lien Crawford v Gross 21 Atl Rep, 356 (Pa 1891) A conveyance of land to certain individuals as trustees for the members of an unincorporated association is not void by the statute of uses and trusts. Turner v Cntona an, etc, Co, 43 N W Rep, 1062 (Mich, 1889). In matters of deeds usage and long lapse of time may validate deeds made out by an unincorporated association as a corporation Braeder v Jennings, 40 Fed Rep, 199 (1889) Where an unincorporated association owns land which is held in trust for it by individuals it may, upon becoming incorporated compel the trustees to deed to it the land Organized Labor Hall v Gebert 22 Atl Rep, 578 (N J, 1891). A deed to a corporation not in existence is void Provost v Morgan s, etc., S Co, 8 S. Rep 584 (La, 1890). If a trustee who holds land for the benefit of a corporation commits a breach of trust, any stockholder may cause him to be removed Fisk v Patton, 27 Pac. Rep, 1 (Utah, 1891) A new unincorporated association cannot claim the land of the one which it succeeds where the members are not the same Allen v Long, 16 S W Rep 43 (Tex 1891) Although the association has been dormant for many years yet a new association formed of part of the members of the old cannot convey the land of the old one Allen v Long, 16 S W Rep., 43 (Tex 1891) A deed to an unincorporated association vests title in it as soon as it is incorporated Clifton etc, Co v Randall, 47 N W Rep, 905 (Iowa, 1891) A deed to a corporation not in existence is void Provost v. Morgan's,

etc, S Co, 8 S Rep., 584 (La., 1890) Cf. ch XLI infra

[2] These mining companies existed in the counties of Cornwall and Devonshire They were first heard of in the courts about the year 1830 Their plan of organization and operation arose from custom Their organization and mode of business were as follows: Many persons, desirous of working a mine, would cause the title or lease thereto to be taken in the names of one or more persons called trustees. The business was then carried on by an agent called a "purser" or by a board of managers elected by the participants, who were called the "adventurers." The latter, of course, were the beneficiaries of the "trust" Any adventurer had a right to transfer his interest to a transferee There was no fixed capital stock Calls for money were made on the adventurers, according to their shares as often as it was needed. For a full statement of the character of these mining companies, see Kittow v. Liskeard Union, L R, 10 Q B D (1874) See, also, In re Bodwin, etc, Co, 23 Beav, 370 (1857), holding that the court would not take judicial notice of the nature of a cost-book mining company, Hybart v Parker, 4 C B (N S), 209 (1858), holding that the purser could not sue at law on an unpaid call; In re Wrysgan, etc, Co, 28 L J (Ch), 894 (1859), as to right to relinquish shares, also describing the functions of the purser and managing directors, Johnson v Goslett, 18 C. B, 728 (1856), affirmed in 3 C B (N S), 569 (1857), giving the full terms of the articles of agreement, Thomas v. Clarke, 18 C B, 662 (1856), where the court said "Every partnership has a right to make its own regulations as to the mode of transferring shares or interests therein" In re Prosper, etc, Co, L R, 7 Ch, 286 (1872),

§ 505 *Statutory joint-stock company.*—There is an essential difference between a joint-stock company as it exists at common law and a joint-stock company having extensive statutory powers conferred upon it by the state within which it is organized. The lat-

relative to rights upon a resignation, Mayhew's Case, 5 De G , M & G 837 (1854), holding that by a transfer of his share "the liability of the transferrer is entirely divested from him and passes to the transferee," *In re* Wrysgan Co 5 Jur. (N. S), 215 (1859), where the court said: "The various phases of absurdity which these joint-stock companies display are such that the marvel in my mind is daily increasing how any man can become a member of a joint-stock company," Northey *v* Johnson, 19 L T , 104 (1852), holding that after transfer the transferrer is not liable for the debts incurred

It is clearly established that the adventurers in a cost-book mining company are personally and individually liable as partners for the debts incurred in the enterprise Peel *v* Thomas, 13 C B , 714 (1855), Newton *v* Daly, 1 F & F , 26 (1858), Harvey *v* Clough, 8 L T (N. S.), 324 (1863), Tredwen *v* Bourne, 6 M. & W , 461 (1840), Ellis *v* Schmoeck, 5 Bing , 521 (1829); Lanyon *v* Smith, 3 B. & S., 938 (1863), holding a transferrer liable for debts incurred previous to the transfer To same effect, Teake *v* Jackson, 15 W R , 338 (1867). They are liable, also, to indemnify the directors or trustees *Ex parte* Chippendale, 4 De G , M & G 19, 52 (1854) See, also, Bach's Case, 2 De G & J , 10 (1857), and Fenn's Case, 4 De G., M & G., 285 (1854), where the members who had exercised their right to withdraw were held not liable In Hart *v.* Clarke, 6 De G , M & G , 232 (1855), an adventurer compelled the company to account to him for his share of the profits. The adventurers have no interest in the land, and consequently a transfer of their shares is not a transfer of an interest in land Sparling *v.* Parker, 9 Beav, 450, Powell *v* Jessopp, 18 C

B , 336 (1856), Hayter *v* Tucker, 4 K & J , 243 (1857) The cost-book mining company was frequently spoken of as a species of joint-stock company *In re* Wrysgan Co, *supra*, Teake *v* Jackson, 15 W R , 338 (1867), Watson *v* Spratley, 10 Ex , 222 (1854) See Watson *v.* Spratley, *supra*, where the court said: "The interest of the shareholder in the great incorporated joint-stock companies and in the smallest mine conducted upon the cost-book principle, is, in its essential nature and quality, identical For an American mining case applying similar principles see Treat *v.* Hiles, 32 N W Rep , 517 (Wis , 1887) It is well settled that the shareholders in an unincorporated association cannot convey or dedicate to the public any land that may be held by trustees for its benefit Ward *v* Davis, 3 Sandf. Rep (N Y.), 502 (1850). The interest of one of the *cestuis que trust* of such a trust, consisting of real estate, is personalty, and descends as such upon his death Mallory *v* Russell, 32 N W Rep , 102 (Iowa, 1887) As to the effect of a deed, grant or bequest of real estate to an unincorporated association. see Webb *v* Weatherhead, 17 How , 576 (1854), Gerard's Titles to Real Estate, p 490 (2d ed), Owens *v* Missionary Soc of the M E Church, 14 N Y , 380 (1867) Washburn on Real Prop, vol III, p 264 (4th ed), Holmes *v* Mead, 52 N Y , 332 (1873), Goesele *v* Bimeler, 5 McLean, 223 (1851), German Land Association *v* Scholler, 10 Minn , 331 (1865), Peabody *v* Eastern Methodist Society in Lynn, 87 Mass , 540 (1857), Towar *v.* Hale, 46 Barb , 361 (1866); Dart on Vendors and Purchasers, vol I, p. 21 (5th ed), Chapin *v* First, etc, Soc , 74 Mass , 582 (1857)· African, etc, Church *v* Conover, 27 N J Eq , 157; Leonard *v.* Davenport, 58 How Pr ,

ter kind of joint-stock companies are found in England and in the state of New York   To such an extent have these statutory powers been conferred on joint-stock companies that they differ from corporations only in not having a seal, and in the members not being exempt from liability as partners for the debts of the company. Accordingly, joint-stock companies, both those of England and New York, have been held to be corporations in many respects although expressly declared by statute not to have that character.[1]

384, Sherwood v American Bible Soc, 4 Abb App, 227, McKeon v Kearney, 57 How Pr, 349, Gibson v McCall, 1 Rich 174, Byam v Beckford, 140 Mass, 31 (1885), holding that, although a deed to the association is ineffectual, yet that it passes title to the members of the association   They cannot take by devise in New York   White v Howard 46 N. Y 144 (1871). Trustees, etc, v Hart's Ex'rs, 4 Wheat, 1 (1819).

[1] See Thomas v Dakin, 22 Wend, 9 (1830), Warner v Beers, 23 Wend, 103, Parmley v Tenth Ward Bank, 3 Edw, 395 (1838) People v Watertown, 1 Hill, 616 (1841), Bank of Watertown v Watertown 25 Wend, 686 (1841); Willoughby v Comstock 3 Hill, 389 (1842), Leavitt v Yates, 4 Edw, 134 (1840), Leavitt v Tyler, 1 Sandf Ch, 207, People v Niagara, 4 Hill, 20 (1842), Boisgerard v New York Banking Co, 2 Sandf Ch, 231 (1844), Matter of Bank of Danville, 6 Hill, 370 Gifford v Livingston, 2 Den, 380 (1845), Case v Mechanics' Banking Ass n, 1 Sandf, 693, Leavitt v Blatchford, 17 N Y, 521 (1842), 5 Barb, 9, Culver v Sanford, 8 Barb, 225 (1850), Gillett v Moody, 3 N Y 478 (1850), Talmage v Pell, 7 N Y, 328 (1852), Tracy v Talmage, 18 Barb, 456 (1854); Gillett v Phillips, 13 N Y 114 (1855), Falconer v Campbell, 2 McLean, 195 (1840), Duncan v Jones, 32 Hun, 12 (1884) The English joint-stock company is much the same ' The company has a name as an association, maintaining the identity of the body through all changes of its members, its property is divided into transferable shares, and it has conferred

upon it the legal capacity to sue and be sued in the name of one of its officers, and such a suit   . . may be brought by or against a member as well as a third person" It is a corporation though the English statute declares it is not Oliver v Liverpool & London Life & Fire Ins. Co, 100 Mass, 531 (1868), affirmed, sub nom Liverpool Ins. Co. v Massachusetts, 10 Wall, 566 (1870) So also, with the New York joint-stock companies. Fargo v Louisville, New Albany & Chicago R'y Co., 6 Fed Rep, 787 (1881), Sanford v Board of Supervisors of N Y 15 How Pr, 172 (1858), Waterbury v Merchants' Union Ex Co, 50 Barb, 157 (1867). As regards the liability of the members for the debts of the company, it is held to be a copartnership Boston & Albany R R Co v Pearson, 128 Mass, 445 (1880): Oliver v Liverpool & London Life & Fire Ins Co, ubi supra The refusal of the legislature to call them corporations is important as cutting off the exemption of the members from liability to creditors an exemption which, at common law, belongs to all corporations. Joint-stock companies in England have always been largely statutory See Van Sandau v Moore, 1 Russ, 391 [*441] (1826). In the state of New York the English decisions on these companies are doubtless good authority, since they exist under statutes which are much alike A New York joint-stock association cannot sue as such in the federal courts. Chapman v Barney, 129 U S., 677 (1889) In New York the statutes relative to taxation of corporations do not apply to joint-stock com-

§ 506 *Joint-stock companies may arise by implication of law.*—
Joint-stock companies are generally formed by the mutual agreement and direct intent of the parties They may, however, arise
by implication of law. Thus, an ineffectual attempt at an incorporation may make the parties members, not of a corporation, but of
a joint-stock company [1] In like manner, after the charter of a corporation expires and the parties continue to do business, they do
so as a joint-stock company.[2]

§ 507 *How a person becomes a member — Transfers.*— A person
becomes a member of a joint-stock company by any act which indicates an intent to become a member on his part, and a consent
or acquiescence therein by the company itself.[3] He may also become a member by a transfer made to him of another member's
interest, unless the articles of association restrict the right of
transfer [4]

§ 508 *Liability of members to creditors and to the company* —
A joint-stock company is, in regard to the liability of its members
to creditors of the company, a partnership,[5] its members are liable
as partners,[6] and the ordinary rules of partnership exist between

panies They are not corporations
People v Coleman, 133 N Y, 279 (1892),
Hoey v Coleman, 46 Fed Rep, 221
(1891) An unincorporated joint-stock
association is legal in New York
Under the statutes of that state such
associations are corporations for many
purposes People v Wemple, 117 N Y,
136 (1889)

[1] *Re* Mendenhall, 9 Bankr. Reg, 497,
Whipple v Parker, 29 Mich, 369, 380
(1874), and see ch XIII *Cf* Foster v.
Pray, 29 N W. Rep, 155 (Minn, 1886).

[2] National Bank of Watertown v London 45 N Y 410 (1871)

[3] The formalities need be no greater
than in forming an ordinary partnership National Bank v Van Derwerker,
74 N. Y 234 (1878), Pettis v Atkins,
60 Ill, 454 (1871), Machinists' Bank v
Dean, 124 Mass., 81 (1878). *Cf* Volger
v Ray, 131 id, 439 (1881) It is not necessary that certificates of the stock be
issued in order to constitute membership. Dennis v Kennedy, 19 Barb, 517
(1854); Boston & Albany R R. Co v
Pearson, 128 Mass, 445 (1880) Evidence
of subscription and payment of an assessment is sufficient, Frost v. Walker,

60 Me, 468 (1872). But not of subscription without any participation Hodge
& Horne's Appeal 63 Pa St, 273 (1869)

[4] Transfer of the certificate of stock
has such effect although not registered in the stock-book Butterfield v
Beardsley, 28 Mich, 412 (1874) Transfer may be before the certificates are
issued Butterfield v Spencer, 1 Bosw,
1 (1856) But if the articles of association prohibit transfer, the transferee
takes only the right to profits not as a
partner but as an assignee Harper v
Raymond 3 Bosw, 29 (1858) So also
where transfer is allowed only on consent of certain officers who refuse
Kingman v Spurr, 7 Pick, 234 (1828)
A transfer does not carry dividends already declared Harper v Raymond,
ubi supra If a transfer is improperly
allowed, the company is liable to the
party injured Cohen v Gwynn, 4 Md
Ch, 357 (1848) As to the liability of
the transferee see next section.

[5] Kellogg Bridge Co. v United States,
15 Ct of Cl, 111, Allen v. Long, 16 S
W Rep, 48 (Tex, 1891). *Cf* Chandler
v Brainard, 31 Mass, 285 (1833).

[6] Westcott v. Fargo, 61 N. Y., 542

the members themselves,[1] including the right to contribution as between themselves,[2] and also between a member and third persons.[3] The question whether a stockholder may limit his common-law or

(1875), Witherhead v Allen, 3 Keyes, 562, Cross i Jackson, 5 Hill, 478 (1843), Skinner v Dayton, 19 Johns, 513 (1822), Wells v Gates, 18 Barb, 554 (1854), Boston & Albany R. R. Co. v Pearson, 128 Mass, 445 (1880). Taft v Ward, 106 Mass, 518 (1871), S C., 111 Mass, 518 (1873), Bodwell v Eastman 106 Mass, 525 (1871), Tappan v Bailey, 45 Mass., 529 (1812), Cutter v Estate of Thomas, 25 Vt, 73 (1852), Frost v Walker, 60 Me, 468 (1872), Kramer v Arthurs, 7 Pa. St, 165 (1847), Gott v Dinsmore, 111 Mass, 45 (1872), Newell v Borden, 128 id, 31 (1879) See, also, § 504 Contra, Irvine v Forbes, 11 Barb., 587 (1852). Livingston v Lynch, 4 Johns Ch 573 (1820), overruled as dicta by Townsend v Goewey, 19 Wend, 423 (1838), Ridenour v Mayo, 40 Ohio St, 9 (1883) In Frost v Walker, 60 Me., 468 (1872), the court said "An unincorporated joint-stock company is a mere partnership, and each member is per-

sonally liable for all its debts It is important for the public to know that if persons connect themselves with a company of this description they are every one of them liable to pay the demands upon it." The officers who enter into a contract for the company are liable thereon personally "It is immaterial whether they be so held because they held themselves out as agents for a principal that had no existence, or on the ground that they must, under the contract, be regarded as principals, for the simple reason that there is no other principal in existence" Lewis v. Tilton, 64 Iowa, 220 (1884), Fredenhall v Taylor 26 Wis, 286 (1870) A lease to an unincorporated association binds personally all members assenting to it Reding v Anderson, 31 N W Rep, 300 (Iowa, 1887) Members of co-operative trading associations are liable as partners for the debts of the concern Davison v Holden, 10 Atl Rep., 513 (Conn., 1887).

[1] Bullard v Kinney, 10 Cal, 60 (1858) The remedy of one member against another is in equity Huth v Humboldt, etc, 23 Atl. Rep., 1084 (Conn, 1892). One member cannot sue another at law for his part of the profits of the business, which is under control of the latter. Myrick v Dame, 63 Mass., 248 (1852), Duff v Maguire, 99 Mass, 300 (1868), Whitehouse v. Sprague, 7 Atl Rep, 17 (Conn, 1886). Person induced to put money into an enterprise on false representations that it is a joint-stock company may recover back his money Libby v Ahrens, 2 S E Rep., 387 (S C, 1887) Director of an unincorporated association who contracts for it is not liable personally Abbott v Cobb, 17 Vt, 593 (1845), Alexander v. Worman, 6 H. & N, 100 (1860).

[2] Morrissey v Weed, 12 Hun, 491 (1878); Skinner v. Dayton, 19 Johns.,

513 (1822). Ray v Powers, 134 Mass., 22 (1883), Witman v Porter, 107 Mass., 522 (1871), Tyrrell v Washburn, 88 Mass, 466 (1863) But not if the expense was incurred contrary to the articles of association Danforth v. Allen, 8 Metc, 334 (1844), Clark v Reed, 28 Mass., 446 (1831). One stockholder cannot sue another at law for his part of the assets Whitehouse v. Sprague, 7 Atl. Rep., 17 (1886).

[3] His interest cannot be reached by execution Kramer v. Arthurs, 7 Pa St., 165 (1847). But see Lindley on Partn (2d ed). 696. Acquiescence in the dealings of other members with third persons binds a member. Penn Ins Co v Murphy, 5 Minn, 36 (1860), Wells v Yates, 18 Barb, 554 (1854). For the liability as affected by the transfer of stock see Smith v. Virginia, 33 Me., 148 (1851).

statutory liability by an express contract with the company's creditors to that effect is discussed elsewhere.[1] The member's subscription may be enforced by a suit at law.[2]

And sometimes are liable also for debts contracted after they have sold their stock See Shamburg v Abbott, 4 Atl. Rep. 518 (Pa., 1886) The members of an unincorporated association to enforce the liquor laws are not liable to an attorney for services in prosecuting cases McCabe v Goodfellow, 133 N Y, 89 (1892). The vice-president and the treasurer of an unincorporated fair association are liable for premiums offered Murray v Walker, 48 N W Rep, 1075 (Iowa, 1891) Members of a joint-stock company are personally liable for the debts of the company Durham etc, Co. v Clute, 17 S. E Rep., 419 (N C., 1893) The members of a joint-stock company are liable for its debts People v. Coleman 133 N Y, 279 (1892). In the case of Seacord v Pendleton, 55 Hun, 579 (1890), the court reviewed the authorities and decided that the stockholders in a bank which was not incorporated were not liable to depositors, there being no allegation that the stockholders had any articles of association or partnership, or had performed any act, or had knowledge of the business or consented thereto. A subscription agreement prior to incorporation in which the parties state the number of shares taken and in which they agree to pay the contractors who are parties to the contract, a specified sum is a joint undertaking on the subscriber's part. The contractors may hold them liable as partners, the agreement not limiting their liability to the number of shares taken by each An immaterial alteration after a part have signed does not release any one The agreement of the contractors to hold each subscriber liable only on his subscription if he would pay that is without consideration and void Any subscriber could expressly limit his liability to his subscription. Davis v. Shafer, 50 Fed. Rep, 764

(1892) If proof is given by plaintiff that a copartnership existed and the defense is that it was a corporation, the defendant must prove that fact. Although the company had a president and secretary, this in itself does not raise a presumption of a corporation Clark v Jones, 6 S. Rep, 362 (Ala, 1889) A notice to stockholders that they will be held liable under a statute is not served on the members of an unincorporated association by serving such notice on the chief officer of such association Wells v Robb, 23 Pac Rep, 148 (Kan, 1890) Where a creditor of a bank sues the stockholders as partners the burden of proof is on him to prove that no corporation existed, it being shown that the bank always acted as a corporation and held itself out as such and was supposed so to be by the stockholders Hallstead v Curtis, 22 Atl Rep, 977 (Pa, 1891) The supposition or belief of the members that they are not liable beyond the par value of their stock does not protect them from liability Farnum v. Patch, 60 N H, 294, and see § 233, note

[1] See § 216. supra.

[2] If the subscription runs to the trustees personally they may sue thereon Otherwise all must join as plaintiffs Cross v Jackson, 5 Hill, 478 (1843). Townsend v. Goewey, 19 Wend., 423 (1838) It seems that a subscription to a voluntary association is enforceable by a corporation which took the place of the proposed voluntary association, where the subscriber knew of the change of plan and did not object. City Sav Bank v Whittle 63 N H, 587 (1885) Subscription to its stock is collectible the same as subscriptions to stock of corporations Bullock v Falmouth, etc, Co, 3 S. W. Rep., 129 (Ky, 1887).

In enforcing the liability of members of a joint-stock company by a suit in equity, if the parties are very numerous or unknown they need not all be joined as defendants.[1] Suits by or against unincorporated associations must be brought in the name of all the members[2] A member who transfers his interest is nevertheless liable for precedent debts of the association[3] A purchaser of stock in an unincorporated association is not liable for debts contracted before he became a member[4] The rights and liabilities of a member depend upon the law of the place of the domicile of the company itself[5] The rules applicable to stockholders in corporations are, by analogy, applied to members in these companies, especially as regards their defenses to subscriptions[6] and meetings of the company[7] These associations cannot be taxed on a franchise, as corporations may be[8]

[1] Manderville v. Riggs, 2 Pet., 482 (1829), reversing Riggs v Swann. 3 Cr, 183 See, also, Phipps v. Jones, 20 Pa St., 260 (1853); Dennis v Kennedy, 19 Barb, 517 (1854), Wood v Draper, 24 Barb., 187 (1857), Smith v Lockwood, 1 Code Rep (N S), 319 (1851), Birmingham v Gallagher, 112 Mass., 190 (1873), Snow v Wheeler, 113 Mass., 179 (1873), Pipe v Bateman, 1 Iowa, 369 (1855), Marshall v Loveless, Cam & N, 217 (1801), Lloyd v Loaring, 6 Ves., 773 (1802), Deems v Albany, etc, Line, 14 Blatch, 471 (1878). As regards the practice in bringing actions against members of an unincorporated association, see Kneeland on Attachments, ch XVI.

[2] Williams v Bank of Mich, 7 Wend, 542 (1831), Detroit, etc, Bank v Detroit, etc, Verein, 44 Mich, 313 (1880), Mears v Moulton, 30 Md, 142 (1868), McGreary v Chaudler, 58 Me, 537 (1870) One or more members of an unincorporated association may sue for the benefit of all Liggett v. Ladd, 21 Pac. Rep, 133 (Oreg, 1888).

[3] Morgan s Case, 1 De G & Sm, 750 (1849) Tyrrell v Washburn, 88 Mass., 466 (1863)

[4] Stockdale v Moginn, 19 Atl Rep, 205 (Pa, 1890) Transferee of a share in an unincorporated company is liable for all debts existing at the time of or after the transfer Taylor v Ifill, 1 N R., 566

(1863). Although a stockholder purchased his stock from the association which was insolvent at the time, yet he cannot offset this as capital contributed by him Barndollar v. De Bois, 21 Atl Rep, 988 (Pa, 1891).

[5] Cutler v Estate of Thomas, 25 Vt, 73 (1852).

[6] That the full capital stock must be subscribed before any subscription is collectible, see Bray v Farwell, 81 N Y, 600 (1880). Contra, Tappan v. Bailey, 45 Mass., 529 (1842); Boston & Albany R. R. Co v Pearson, 128 Mass, 445 (1880), Pitchford v Davis, 5 Mees. & W, 2 (1839) Forfeiture of stock releases the member only as to subsequent debts. Skinner v Dayton, 19 Johns, 513 (1822).

[7] Notice of the time and place must be given Irvine v Forbes, 11 Barb, 587 (1852) The members cannot act except in meeting assembled The majority do not rule Livingston v. Lynch, 4 Johns. Ch, 573 (1820), Irvine v Forbes, ubi supra But the articles may provide otherwise Waterbury v. Merchants' Union Ex. Co., 50 Barb, 157 (1867).

[8] Hoadley v County Com'rs, 105 Mass, 519 (1870), Gleason v McKay, 134 Mass., 419 (1878), holding the statute to be unconstitutional Cf § 505.

§ 509 *Actions by members against officers and the company* — The members may bring an action to remedy the fraud,[1] *ultra vires* acts[2] and negligence[3] of the trustees In New York a member may, by statute, sue the company, in the same manner that a stock-holder in a corporation may sue the corporation [4]

§ 510 *Dissolution.*— Where the term of existence of a joint-stock company is fixed by its articles of association, it cannot be dis-solved at the instance of a member before the expiration of that time.[5] It may be dissolved where the enterprise becomes wholly

[1] The other members are not proper parties Boody v Drew, 46 How Pr, 459 (1874) An officer may be enjoined but not removed The suit must not be in the interest of a rival company Waterbury v Merchants' Union Express Co, 50 Barb, 157 (1867) Trustees receiving gifts are liable therefor to the company In re Fry, 4 Phil Rep, 129 (1860) Cannot sell to the company Robbins v Butler, 24 Ill, 387 (1860) Treasurer may be compelled to pay over funds belonging to the company Sharp v Warren, 6 Price, 131 (1818) The trustees are liable in tort for their frauds on the company Dennis v Kennedy, 19 Barb 517 (1854) A committee to build may be made to account where they secretly contract with themselves, though the contract is nominally with other persons Whitman v Bowden 2 S E Rep, 630 (S C, 1887)

[2] A member cannot be compelled to accept the stock of another company for his interest, a consolidation of the two having been made Frothingham v Barney 13 Hun, 366 But he may not be able to prevent the consolidation McVicker v Ross 55 Barb, 247 (1869) An *ultra vires* act may be enjoined Abels v McKean, 18 N J Eq, 462 (1867) The members need not make good to the officers debts paid by the latter, growing out of *ultra vires* acts Crum's Appeal, 66 Pa St, 474 (1878) But the officers themselves are liable to third persons Sullivan v Campbell, 2 Hall (N Y) 271 (1829) And possibly the members Id If a member has not participated or acquiesced in the

ultra vires act he is not liable thereon Roberts' Appeal, 92 Pa St, 407 (1880) Cf Van Aernam v Bleistein, 102 N Y, 355 (1886) holding the members liable for a libel, aff'g 32 Hun, 316

[3] *In re* Fry 4 Phil Rep 129 (1860).

[4] Code of Civil Procedure § 1919 Westcott v Fargo 61 N Y, 542 (1874) Saltsman v Shults, 14 Hun, 256 At common law the name is not recognized and the suit would fail Habicht v Pemberton 4 Sandf, 657 (1851), Pipe v Bateman, 1 Iowa 369 (1855), Ewing v Medlock, 5 Port (Ala), 82 (1837) Schmidt v Gunther 5 Daly, 452 (1874).

[5] Von Schmidt v Huntington 1 Cal, 55 See, also, Smith v Virgin, 33 Me 148 (1851) Cf Lindley on Partn, 234 Lafond v Deems 81 N Y, 507 (1880) The minority cannot force a dissolution as in the case of partnership Equity will not aid, unless there be good reason for dissolution Hinkley v Blethen, 3 Atl Rep, 655 (Me, 1886) Minority of an Odd Fellows lodge cannot compel sale of property and distribution Robbins v Waldo, 7 Atl Rep, 540 (Me 1887), and see Bagley v Smith 10 N Y 489 A court will wind up a partner-ship even before its fixed time of exist-ence has expired, if it is insolvent or unprofitable or incapable of proceeding Jennings v Baddeley, 3 K & J, 78 Baring v Dix, 1 Cox, 213 Bailey v Ford, 13 Sim 495, Holliday v Elliott 8 Oreg, 84, Seighortner v Weissen-born 20 N J Eq, 172, Brien v Har-riman, 1 Tenn Ch, 467, Howell v Har-vey 5 Ark, 270, Van Ness v Fisher, 5 Lans 236 The death of a member does

impracticable or its attainment impossible, but not always because of the misconduct of its officers.[1]   The death of a member does not dissolve it,[2] nor does a transfer of one's interest[3]   The dissolution of one of the subordinate unincorporated organizations by the general organization does not vest in the latter the property of the former.[4]   The incorporation of the association by a part of the members does not dissolve the association[5]   Upon dissolution the trustees of the company are bound to convert the property into cash and distribute it[6]   In proceedings for a dissolution all the members need not be made parties[7]

not dissolve it   Phillips v Blatchford 137 Mass, 510 (1884)

[1] Waterbury v Merchants' Union Express Co, 50 Barb, 157 (1867)   *Contra*, Mills v Hurd 32 Fed Rep, 127 (1887)

[2] McNeish v Hulless Oat Co. 57 Vt, 316   *Cf* Walker v Wait, 50 Vt, 668 The death of a stockholder does not dissolve the association, nor release his estate from subsequently incurred debts Phillips v. Blatchford, 137 Mass, 510 (1884).

[3] A transfer of his stock by a member does not dissolve a joint-stock association under the Pennsylvania law   *In re* Globe Refining Co, 25 Atl Rep, 128 (Pa, 1892).

[4] Wicks v Monihan, 130 N Y, 232 (1891).   The withdrawal of a charter by a higher body from one of its branches does not affect the right of the latter to its property   Wells v. Monihan, 13 N. Y. Supp, 156 (1891)

[5] A part of the members of an unincorporated association cannot proceed to incorporate it against the objections of the others.   Rudolph v. Southern, etc, League, 23 Abb. N C. 199 (1889).   Where an unincorporated association appoints a committee to incorporate, and they do so, and then proceed to run an opposition business, the association cannot enjoin them from so doing   Paulino v. Portuguese Ben. Ass'n, 26 Atl Rep, 36 (R. I, 1893).

[6] Frothingham v Barney, 13 Hun, 366, Butterfield v Beardsley, 28 Mich, 412 (1874)   Upon the expiration of the time for which the company was organized it becomes dissolved, and the assets must be distributed if any one of the members insists thereon   Mann v Butler, 2 Barb Ch, 362 (1847)   Distribution of funds of incorporated association. Aston v Dashaway, 22 Pac Rep, 660, aff'd in 23 id, 1091 (1890).   As to the land, see § 504, *supra*.   As to the rules governing the distribution of the assets of a mutual benefit building corporation, see People v Lowe, 117 N Y, 175 (1889).

[7] Such as non-residents who cannot be reached   Angell v Lawton, 76 N Y, 540 (1879).   The complainant may bring the proceeding in behalf of himself and others having a common interest with him   Mann v Butler, 2 Barb, Ch, 362 (1847).

CHAPTER XXX.

§ 511. *Common-law rights.*— The stockholders of a corporation had, at common law, a right to examine at any reasonable time any one or all of the books and records of the corporation.[1] This

[1] Stockholders "have the right, at common law, to examine and inspect all the books and records of the corporation at all seasonable times, and to be thereby informed of the condition of the corporation and its property." Per Redfield, J., in Lewis *v.* Brainard, 53 Vt., 519 (1881). In the case of Commonwealth *v.* Phœnix Iron Co., 105 Pa. St., 111 (1884), the court said: "In the absence of agreement, every shareholder has the right to inspect the accounts — a right subject to the necessities of the company, yet existing." Also, "The doctrine of the law is that the books and papers of the corporation, though of necessity kept in some one hand, are the common property of all the stockholders." The right exists although "its exercise be inconvenient to the book-keepers and managers of the partnership business." In the case of Huylar *v.* Cragin Cattle Co., 40 N. J. Eq., 392 (1885), the court said: "Stockholders are entitled to inspect the books of the company for proper purposes at proper times, and they are entitled to such inspection though their only ob-

ject is to ascertain whether their affairs have been properly conducted by the directors or managers. Such a right is necessary to their protection." Deaderick *v.* Wilson, 8 Baxt. (Tenn.), 108. Mr. Simon Sterne, in the Cyclopædia of Political Science, Political Economy and United States History, vol. III, p. 526, says: "Another problem presented by the existing condition of the railways in the United States is that which arises from secrecy of management. This evil must be dealt with radically. One of the prime motives for secrecy of management is the enormous advantage which at the present day it gives to the managers in the maintenance of their power. They alone know where the stockholders are to be found, and can therefore control votes by the knowledge of how to reach or buy them, thus perpetuating their control. Another motive is the advantage thus afforded for stock speculations. The board of managers, by keeping unto themselves the knowledge that their property is losing heavily in comparative traffic, can sell their own holdings

rule grew out of an analogous rule applicable to public corporations and to ordinary copartnerships, the books of which, by well-established law, are always open to the inspection of members.[1]

A director has an absolute right to examine all the books of the company,[2] even though he is hostile to the corporation.[3] But in Connecticut a contrary rule is laid down where he is seeking information in order to organize a rival company.[4]

A creditor of the corporation or any person who is a stranger to it can obtain access to its records by a bill in equity for discovery.[5]

§ 512 *Common-law action for damages for refusal.*— The legal right of a stockholder of a corporation to examine the corporate books is a right which gives him a cause of action at law for damages against the corporate officers if they refuse to allow the inspection.[6] The plaintiff is entitled to nominal damages, and to

and go short of the market under circumstances which will yield them an absolute certainty of profit on the transaction This gives them an enormous advantage over the community by depleting the pockets of the unwary, who find themselves saddled with stocks at high prices, bought months in advance of the public announcement that the road is in difficulties The knowledge of rapid gains in the development of business likewise gives, so long as it can be kept secret, a like advantage in purchase of stock This advantage has been exploited to such a degree in the United States that the investing public has become inspired with a general distrust for railroad stock investment."

[1] Commonwealth r Phoenix Iron Co , *supra*

[2] People r Throop 12 Wend , 181 (1834), Charlick r Flush, etc , R R , 10 Abb Pr , 130 (1860), *In re* Ciancimino, N Y L J, Dec 23 (1890)

[3] People r Throop, *supra*

[4] A director who is actively organizing a rival company has no right to examine the letter files of the former in order to aid the latter The secretary may forcibly take them from him Hemingway r Hemingway, 19 Atl Rep, 766 (Conn , 1890).

[5] Bill of discovery lies at instance of corporate creditors in courts of one state to compel corporate officers to give names of stockholders of corporation in another state with view to enforcing statutory liability in latter state Post r Toledo, etc , R R Co., 11 N. E. Rep, 540 (Mass , 1887), 144 Mass , 341 As to the remedy by subpœna, etc., see § 519, *infra* As to the general right of a stockholder to examine the books of a corporation and the recognition of such right in equity by discovery, see Gresley s Eq Ev , 116, 117 Kynaston r East India Co , 3 Swanst., 249 Bolton v. Liverpool, 3 Sim , 467, 1 Myl & K , 88, Brace r Ormond, 1 Meriv , 403

[6] Lewis r Brainerd, 53 Vt , 510 (1891) As to the right to inspection and to take copies of records in a county clerk's or register s office, see Randolph r State, 2 S Rep ,714 (Ala , 1887), Hanson v Eichstaedt, 35 N W Rep, 30 (Wis , 1887); Brewer r Watson, 71 Ala , 299, Phelan v. State, 76 Ala 49, Webber v Townley, 43 Mich , 534, Diamond Match Co. t Powers, 51 Mich , 145, People t Cornell, 47 Barb , 329, People r Reilly, 38 Hun, 429, People t Cady, 99 N Y , 620. A stockholder has the legal right to inspect the books of the corporation of which he is a member, but the company is not liable for a refusal of the secretary to allow a stockholder to examine the books. Legendre r. New Orleans, etc., Ass'n, 12 S. Rep , 837 (La., 1893).

such further damages as he may prove   He need not allege or prove any special reason or purpose of his desire and request to examine the books [1]

§ 513 *Mandamus is the preferable remedy* — But an action for damages is generally totally inadequate as a remedy [2]   The stockholder wishes to inspect the corporate books and does not wish damages or a lawsuit   Accordingly, in certain cases, upon the application of a stockholder who has been denied the privilege of examining the corporate records, it has been the practice of the courts to issue a *mandamus* to the corporate officers commanding them to allow a specified stockholder to examine the books of the corporation [3]

§ 514. *Not granted as a matter of course unless the right is statutory* — The writ of *mandamus*, however, does not issue herein as a matter of course   It is an extraordinary remedy to be invoked only upon special occasions   The courts do not grant the *mandamus* until it has taken into careful consideration all the facts and circumstances of the case   The condition and character of the books, the reasons for refusal by the corporation, the specific purpose of the stockholder in demanding inspection, the general reasonableness of the request, and the effect on the orderly transaction of the corporate business in case it is granted, are all considered in granting or refusing the writ.   It is granted only in furtherance of essential justice [4]

[1] Lewis v Brainerd, 53 Vt 510 (1881)

[2] In Cockburn v Union Bank, 13 La Ann., 289 (1858), the court said a suit for damages "might last for a long time and petitioner suffer great loss by being debarred from an examination" of the books   "He does not ask for damages, but for the exercise of a right If he has the right he ought to have the exercise of it as soon as possible, for the deprivation of his right cannot, perhaps, be accurately estimated in damages   It may be many years before the amount of the damage can be known "

[3] 'It would seem, from the weight of authority and in reason, that a shareholder is entitled to *mandamus* to compel the *custos* of corporate documents to allow him an inspection and copies of them at reasonable times for a specified and proper purpose upon showing a refusal on the part of the *custos* to allow it, and not otherwise " Commonwealth v Phœnix Iron Co, *supra*, S C, 6 Atl Rep, 75 (1886), explaining the method of procedure, and holding that the applicant need not apply to a court of equity   The old rule that *mandamus* will issue only for a public purpose is no longer a rule of law so as to prevent its use herein   Commonwealth etc *supra*, questioning King v Bank of England, 2 B & Ald, 620 (1819), and King v London, etc, Co, 5 B & Ald, 899 (1822)   See, also, King v Clear, 4 Barn & C, 899 (1825), 6 S Rep, 88 (Ala 1889)

[4] The application is addressed to the sound discretion of the court.' The reasons for granting it "should be clear and cogent.   .   .   To hold that every person who shows himself to be a holder of stock is at liberty to demand an examination of the transfer books when and as often as he pleases, and if re-

Where a statute gives to stockholders the right to examine corporate books, *mandamus* seems to be granted as a matter of right.[1]

§ 515. *When it will and will not be granted* — It will not be granted to satisfy curiosity, nor to aid the stock-market speculations of the stockholders[2] Either some property rights of the

fused to apply for a writ of *mandamus* to enforce an absolute right, would be to establish a rule highly prejudicial to the interests of all corporations and their stockholders . . The power of the court should be exercised in such cases with great discrimination and care" People v Lake Shore & M S R R Co, 11 Hun, 1 (1877), affirmed, *sub nom Re* Sage, 70 N Y, 220 (1877). See, also, People *ex rel* Field v Northern Pac R R Co, 50 N Y Super Ct., 456 (1884), S C, 18 Fed Rep, 471. ' Discretion in these matters should be exercised in a reasonable manner and subject to precedent." Reg v Wilts. & Berks Canal Nav., 29 L T, 922 (1874) A reference may be ordered by the court to determine the truth of the allegations in the affidavits used to obtain a *mandamus* People v St. Louis, etc, R y Co, 44 Hun, 552 (1887) *Mandamus* is the preferable remedy Legendre v New Orleans, etc., Ass n 12 S Rep, 837 (La, 1893)

[1] Under the Wisconsin statute authorizing a stockholder to examine the stock books and accounts, a *mandamus* may be issued to the officer having the books in charge State v Bergenthal, 39 N W Rep, 566 (Wis, 1888). Under a constitutional right to see the list of stockholders, a stockholder has no absolute right to take a list of them Empire P R'y Appeal, 19 Atl Rep, 629 (Pa, 1890) *Mandamus* lies to enforce the statutory right of inspection People v Pacific Mail Steamship Co, 50 Barb, 280 (1861). *Mandamus* lies to compel the resident agent of a foreign corporation to open its transfer books to a stockholder as required by statute. People v Paton, 20 Abb. N C, 195 (1887). *Mandamus* will lie in behalf of the wife of a deceased stockholder, who

holds the certificates made out in his name, to compel the corporation to allow her to examine the transfer books in order that she may vote intelligently at a coming election. People v. Eadie, 63 Hun, 320 (1892). *Mandamus* lies to open for the inspection of a stockholder and for taking memorandum therefrom such corporate books as the statute prescribes shall be opened to him. Matter of Martin, 62 Hun, 557 (1891). *Mandamus* lies to allow inspection as required by the statute, and the fact that the applicant holds a certificate of stock is sufficient. Martin v. Williams, etc., Co, 25 Abb N C, 350 (1890) Where there is a state statute allowing stockholders to examine the corporate books, a national bank in the state is subject thereto and *mandamus* will issue. Winter v Baldwin, 7 S Rep, 734 (Ala., 1890). Under a statute to the effect that "the stockholders of all private corporations have the right of access to, of inspection and examination of the books, records and papers of the corporation, at reasonable and proper times," a stockholder has the "right to examine the books at any and all reasonable times," and "when this right is claimed and refused, he is entitled to a *mandamus* on the averments that he is a stockholder of the corporation; that he has demanded the right of inspection; that the time was reasonable and proper, and that the right was denied him" He may make the examination through an agent. Foster v White, 6 S. Rep, 88 (Ala, 1889)

[2] The writ will not be "granted to enable a corporator to gratify idle curiosity" People v Walker, 9 Mich, 328 (1861). "The interests of all the corporators require that the writ shall not go at the caprice of the curious or suspi-

stockholder must be involved, or some controversy exist, or some specific and valuable interest be in question, to settle which an inspection of the corporate records becomes necessary.[1] *Mandamus* will be granted in order to enable the applicant to ascertain who

cious." Commonwealth *v* Phœnix Iron Co, *supra* 'Courts should guard against all attempts by combinations to use its writ of *mandamus* to accomplish their personal or speculative ends" People *v* Lake Shore & M S R R. Co, *supra*. Nor will the court grant 'a mere wrecking petition to ruin a going concern" *In re* West Devon, etc, Mine, L R, 27 Ch D, 106 (1884). Mere suspicion is not enough, even though the applicant stockholder intends to bring suit against the directors. Central, etc, R R Co *v* Twenty, etc, R'y Co, 53 How Pr, 45 (1877)

[1] Thus, where there had been no dividends for nine years, and the officers were partners in a competing concern, and refused to allow inspection, it was granted in order to enable the applicant to ascertain whether the real facts justified an action for fraud on the part of the officers Commonwealth *v* Phœnix Iron Co, *supra* Granted also to allow applicant to ascertain whether a by-law existed entitling him to an office by promotion Reg *v* The Saddlers' Co, 10 W. R, 77 (1861). Mismanagement and intent to bring suit need not be alleged "Oftentimes frauds are discoverable only by examination of the books by an expert accountant' Huyler *v* Cragin Cattle Co, *supra* It is granted also to a stockholder who has a suit or controversy with a party other than the corporation itself Mayor of Southampton *v* Graves, 8 T. R., 590 (1800), Rex *v* Newcastle, 2 Strange, 1223 (1737) It has been granted to enable a stockholder to see the discount book, although there is no suit between him and the corporation and no intent to bring one Cockburn *v* Union Bank. 13 La Ann, 289 (1858) At an early day, however, it was held that "the members have no right, on speculative

grounds, to call for an examination of the books and muniments in order to see if, by possibility, the company's affairs may be better administered than they think they are at present If they have any complaint to make, some suit should be instituted, some definite matter charged   . or there should be some particular matter in dispute between members, or between the corporation and individuals in it, there must be some controversy, some specific purpose, in respect of which the examination becomes necessary" King *v* The Merchant Tailors' Co, 2 Barn & Ad, 115 (1832). The applicant must allege the extent of his interest, also wherein his object of inspection is just and useful Hatch *v* City Bank of New Orleans, 1 Rob (La), 470 (1842) The case of State *v* Bienville Oil Works, 28 La Ann, 204 (1876), states that the two preceding cases "failed through want of precision and definiteness in stating some well-defined purpose, some reasonable cause, and showing that they had some interest in the matter " A charter provision that the corporate powers "shall be exercised by a board of directors" is immaterial herein Id Where a reduction of capital stock is contemplated, a large stockholder has a right to inspection to ascertain whether the business is being "prudently and profitably" carried on Id Not granted to allow applicant, a director to inspect and make entries Rosenfeld *v* Einstein, 46 N J L, 479 (1884) General purpose of ascertaining "the condition of the company " held insufficient. People *v* Walker, 9 Mich, 328 (1861) The stockholder may take memoranda or a list of the stockholders Commonwealth *v* Phœnix Iron Co, 105 Pa St, 111 (1884), Cotheal *v* Brower, 5 N Y, 562 (1851), affirming Brower *v.* Cotheal, 10 Barb, 216 (1850), Hide *v.*

are stockholders, with a view to canvassing their votes for an election.[1] *Mandamus* will not be granted to allow a stockholder to make a list of the stockholders where the object is to combine them in attacking a lease made by the corporation.[2]

§ 516. *Allegation and form of writ* — The writ should run to the person or officer who has control of the records.[3] The stockholder may make the inspection through an agent, and may have the aid of an interpreter, attorney or expert.[4] The request to inspect the books, for refusal of which the *mandamus* is asked, must be alleged to have been made at a proper time and place, and of the proper person, and to have been refused.[5] The application should also state what information the applicant needs, and what books of the corporation he wishes to inspect.[6] "The order should be so drawn

Holmes 2 Molloy, 372. In the case of Stettaner v. New York, etc., Co., 6 Atl. Rep., 303 (N. J., 1886), where a stockholder filed a bill in equity to compel corporate officers to allow himself and his accountant to examine the corporate books, its business having been closed and distribution of assets made but a statement of its affairs refused, the court held that the bill would not lie, since no fraud or insufficient distribution of assets were alleged. *Mandamus* is the proper remedy. Swift v. State, 6 Atl. Rep., 856 (Del., 1886), holds that *mandamus* will issue to the officers of a foreign corporation to exhibit its books then in the state and allow copies of records to be taken by a stockholder who intends to commence suit against a pledgee of his stock, the controversy turning on the question of the earnings and expenses of the corporation. *Mandamus* to open the stock-ledger was denied in a case where the owner of four shares of stock alleged that little or no dividends were paid, and the stock was depreciating, no mismanagement being charged. A by-law authorizing inspection of books of account does not authorize inspection of stock-ledger. Lyon v. American, etc., Co., 17 Atl. Rep., 61 (R. I., 1889).

[1] *Mandamus* was granted in People v. Eadie, N. Y. L. J., Dec. 30, 1891, to open the stock books to a stockholder who wished to ascertain who were stock-holders in order to confer with them for the purpose of changing the board at an approaching election. *Mandamus* was granted to a stockholder who wished to persuade other stockholders not to appeal a suit in which he was interested adversely to the corporation, the defeated party. Reg. v. Wilts & Berks. Canal Nav., 29 L. T., 922 (1874). See, also, People v. Lake Shore & M. S. R. R. Co., 11 Hun, 1 (1877).

[2] Empire P. Ry. Appeal, 19 Atl. Rep., 629 (Pa., 1890), and note. See criticism on this case in N. Y. L. J., Oct. 13, 1890.

[3] "The writ shall be directed to him who is to do the thing required to be done." A director may demand inspection though hostile to the corporation. People v. Throop, 12 Wend., 181 (1834).

[4] May inspect through his duly-authorized agent. State v. Bienville Oil Works Co., 28 La. Ann., 204 (1876). See, also, § 519.

[5] The stockholder must first apply to the proper corporate officer having authority to grant inspection. King v. Proprietors of the Wilts. & Berks Canal Nav., 3 Ad. & El., 477 (1835). And must state to him the reason why he desires inspection. Id., also King v. Clear, 4 Barn. & Cr., 899 (1825), People v. Walker, 9 Mich., 328 (1861).

[6] Morgan's Case, L. R., 28 Ch. D., 620 (1884). This case also states that in England it is customary for many banking companies to insert in their constitu-

as not to inconvenience the transaction of business."[1] Technical objections to the writ are not favored by the courts. Nevertheless the substantial allegations must be made.

§ 517 *Right to inspect minutes of meetings of directors* — It would take a strong case to induce a court to issue a *mandamus* commanding the corporate officers to allow a stockholder to inspect the minutes of the meetings of the directors.[2] The success of the corporate enterprise depends frequently upon the secrecy of the plans of the directors. In connection with litigations the rule, of course, is different, but, aside from this, it seems that a stockholder is not entitled as a matter of right to a *mandamus* to allow him to inspect the minutes of the directors' meetings. The same rule would seem to apply to miscellaneous questions asked of the directors at stockholders' meetings.

§ 518 *Statutes giving right of inspection* — The right to inspect corporate records is frequently given to stockholders by statutory provisions. Sometimes this statutory right extends only to the corporate transfer book.[3] Sometimes it includes all corporate rec-

tions a provision forbidding the inspection of customers' accounts by shareholders or creditors. Irrelevant parts of the books may be sealed up. Jones *v* Andrews, 58 L. T. Rep. 601 (1888) Earp *v* Lloyd 3 K. & J. 549 Napier *v* Staples, 2 Moll. 570 Hill *v* Great W R y Co, 10 C B (N S) 148 Clifford *v* Taylor 1 Taunt 167, Gerard *v* Penswick, 1 Swanst. 533, Dias *v* Merle, 2 Paige, 494, Titus *v* Cortelyou, 1 Barb, 444, People *v* Pacific Co. 50 Barb 280, Pynchon *v* Day (Ill.), 22 Reporter, 234 But if such irrelevant matter cannot be separated, the party must produce the whole Carew *v* White 5 Beav 172

[1] Duffy *v* Mutual Brewing Co N Y L J, Oct. 3, 1892, p 18. approving of text

[2] "It is highly proper that an inspection of the books containing the proceedings of the directors should be obtained on special occasions and for special purposes, . but the proposed daily and hourly inspection and publication of all their proceedings would be tantamount to admitting the presence of strangers at all their meetings, and would probably ere long be

found very prejudicial to the shareholders." Queen *v* Mariquita Mining Co 1 Ell & Ell. 289 (1858) "A private stockholder of an incorporated company has no right to have access to the minutes of the proceedings of the directors unless that right is expressly given by the charter, and consequently and of necessity he must remain ignorant of their action until they choose to make that action known" (*dictum*) Ala & Fla. R. R. Co *v* Rowley 9 Fla 508 514 (1861) See, also, Lindley on Partn (4th ed). 809

[3] In New York, see 1 R S. ch XVIII title 4 § 1. applying to all corporations Construed in Cotheal *v* Brower 5 N Y, 562 (1851) People *v* Pacific Mail Steamship Co, 50 Barb 280 (1867) Kennedy *v* Railroad Co 14 Abb N C 326, People *v* Mott 1 How Pr 247, Kelsey *v* Pfaudler, etc, Co 3 N Y Supp, 723 (1889), 1 R S ch XVIII title 2, § 45 for moneyed corporations applied in People *v* Throop 12 Wend. 183 (1834) Laws 1842, ch 165 for transfer agents in this state of foreign corporations construed in People *v* Lake Shore & M S. R R Co 11 Hun, 1 (1877), People *ex rel* Field *v*

ords[1] *Mandamus* lies to enforce this right.[2] Frequently the charter itself states that the stockholder shall have certain rights of inspection. In England the Companies Act regulates specifically the stockholders' right of inspection, and provides for a committee of investigation in behalf of the stockholders whenever an investigation is desired by them[3]

§ 519. *Orders to corporation to allow inspection — Subpœna duces tecum — Bill of discovery.* — An inspection of corporate records is often desired in connection with an action which is pending in the courts, and it has been the practice of the courts to grant applica-

Northern Pacific R. R. Co, 50 N Y Super Ct, 456 (1884), S. C, 18 Fed Rep., 471, Kennedy v Chicago, etc, R. R., 14 Abb N C, 326 (1884), People v U S, etc, Co., 20 Abb N C, 193, People v Peyton, id, 196, *In re* Commerford v Williams, etc, Co, N Y L J, Oct. 7, 1890, Laws of 1848, § 25, for manufacturing corporations. For New Jersey, see Revision of 1877, p 183, § 36, Huylar v Cragin Cattle Co, 40 N J Eq, 392 (1885) S C, 7 Atl Rep, 521 (1887). Ind R S (1881), §§ 3010 3011 Connecticut. see Pratt v Meriden Co, 35 Conn, 36, Sykes' Case, 10 Beav, 162, Ervin v Oregon R Co, 22 Hun, 566; Cain v Pullen, 31 La. Ann, 511 A delay of one day in allowing the inspection, owing to the absence of the person having charge of them, does not cause the penalty to attach Kelsey v Pfandler, etc, Co., 41 Hun 20 (1886)

[1] Rev Stat of Ohio (1880), § 3312, California Civil Code, §§ 377, 378, Penal Code, 565, Rhode Island Pub St., ch 153, § 21, and ch 158, § 24 (1882), Michigan Gen St, § 3173, for banks See, also, Colorado Gen St. (1882), § 249, Missouri R S. (1879), §§ 720, 721, Vermont R Laws (1880), §§ 3294, 3295, Mass. 1860, ch 68, § 10, Illinois R S (1874), ch. 32, § 13 The pleading in a cause of action arising under a statute herein must clearly bring the case within the statute Lewis v Brainerd, 53 Vt, 510 (1881) That the officer had notice of plaintiff's stockholdership must be alleged Williams v College Corner & Richmond Gravel Road Co,

45 Ind 170 (1873) The purpose of the inspection need not be stated to the officer Lewis v Brainerd, 53 Vt, 510 (1881). *Cf* Queen v Undertakers of the Grand Canal, 1 Ir L R, 337. The common-law right of inspection remains. although a special statutory right is also given People v. Lake Shore & M S R R. Co, *supra* Under the statutes of New Jersey the court will order the books of the company to be brought within the state on the petition of the president and a director. A person having a right to examine the books of the company may do so through an attorney It is immaterial what the motive of the applicant may be Mitchell v Rubber, etc, Co., 24 Atl Rep, 407 (N J, 1892).

[2] See § 514, *supra*

[3] 25 and 26 Vict., ch 89, Table A, No. 78 and Nos 60 and 86 In England, under a statute allowing a stockholder to inspect the corporate rights of stockholders, etc, an injunction lies to restrain corporate officers from refusing this right. Holland v Dickson, 58 L T Rep., 845 (1888). Under the English statute a stockholder may inspect the transfer book and take copies, even though he is acting in the interest of a rival company Mutter v Eastern, etc, R'y, 59 L T Rep., 117 (1888), also 36 W R. 401 A stockholder suing to set aside a fraudulent contract may have inspection even of privileged matters between the company and its attorney Gourand v. Edison, etc., Co, 59 L. T. Rep., 813 (1888).

tions for this purpose.[1] The order to allow an inspection may be made at any stage of the action. A stockholder has this right to aid him in suits with strangers, and his right herein is more extensive than the rights of the other party to the action. In fact, a person who

[1] The evidence sought must be directly material to the cause. Rex *v.* Newcastle, 2 Strange, 1223 (1737), Rex *v.* Babb, 3 Term R, 579 (1790). Mayer, etc., *v.* Graves, 8 T R, 590 (1800), holding that a stranger has no more right to have an inspection here than in a case where he sues a copartnership. See Central Nat Bank *v.* White, 5 J. & S. 297 (1874) holding that in New York the inspection is proper if the evidence is material and cannot otherwise be obtained, Clinch *v.* Financial Co, L. R., 2 Eq, 271 (1866), where a director was compelled to produce. In the federal courts an inspection will not be granted in order to frame a complaint. Paine *v.* Warren 33 Fed Rep, 357 (1888)

In a bill alleging fraud on the part of the directors, whereby complainant, a stockholder, has been injured, he may obtain such inspection. Walburn *v.* Ingilby, 1 Myl & K, 61 (1832) Stanton *v.* Chadwick, 3 Macn & G, 575 (1851) See Bassford *v.* Blakesley, 6 Beav, 131. On a verified petition by a single shareholder stating that a mine owned by the company is being worked at a loss, an inspection of the company's books will be granted. West Devon, etc., Case, L R, 27 Ch Div, 106 In a suit to hold the directors of a life insurance company personally responsible for large losses alleged to have been caused by moneys improperly paid on policies, an inspection has been allowed, although plaintiff was said to have but a trifling interest in the company and was desirous of injuring it, and had published prejudicial statements in regard to the matter. Williams *v.* Prince of Wales Ins. Co, 23 Beav, 338. Where a company was being wound up an application on behalf of twenty-four out of eight hundred and fifty-six shareholders, who

had associated themselves together for an investigation into the company's affairs, was allowed, with permission to employ an accountant to carry on the examination of the books. Joint-stock Discount Co's Case, 36 L J, Eq, 150 See Emma Silver Mining Co Case, L. R., 10 Ch App, 194, People *v.* Lake Shore Road, 11 Hun, 1 (1877), 70 N Y, 220, *Ex parte* Buchan, 36 L J, Ch, 150 (1867). Not granted to fish out a defense. Birmingham Co *v.* White, 1 Q B, 282 (1841), Imperial Gas Co *v.* Clarke, 7 Bing 95 (1830). See Hoyt *v.* Amer Ex Bank, 1 Duer, 652 (1853). Shoe and Leather Ass'n *v.* Bailey, 17 Jones & S (N Y), 385 (1883) Nor to furnish materials to the other side for a new trial. Pratt *v.* Goswell, 9 C P (N S), 706 (1861) Nor to ascertain whether petitioner might better accept with the other shareholders, what was offered her for her holding in an old company, which was being wound up instead of proceeding with an arbitration. Glamorganshire Banking Co, L. R., 28 Ch Div, 620 Nor to establish a justification in an action against the petitioner for libel, imputing insolvency to the company. Metropolitan Co *v.* Hawkins, 4 H. & N, 146 (1859) See Finlay *v.* Lindsay, 7 Irish C L, 1, Collins *v.* Yates, 27 L J, Exch, 150 (1858), Opdyke *v.* Marble, 44 Barb, 64 (1864) Nor to examine all the books of the company for fifty years back, because petitioner alleges that he is dissatisfied with the management of the company and with the accounts, besides other grounds. Reg *v.* Grand Canal, 1 Irish Law Rep 337 (1839) Nor where the petition does not specify the particular books asked for, nor the object of the petitioner in making the application to the officers and to the court. Reg. *v.* London and St. Cathe-

is not a stockholder has no more right to an inspection of the corporate books than he has to inspect the books of a copartnership. This is the rule even though he is suing or being sued by a stockholder.[1] If a stockholder, and sometimes a third person, is suing or being sued by a corporation, he is entitled to the usual right of a notice to produce documents,[2] or by an order,[3] or by compelling

ines Docks Co, 44 L. J. Q. B. 4 (1874) See Hunt v Hewitt, 7 Exch., 236 (1852), Pepper v Chambers, 7 Exch. 226 (1852), New England Iron Co v N. Y. Loan Co, 55 How. Pr. 351 (1878), Central R. R. v Twenty-third St. R., 53 How. Pr., 45 (1877), Comm'rs v Lemley, 85 N. C., 311 (1881), Walker v Granite Bank, 44 Barb, 39 (1865) The court may direct the *manner* of the examination Williams v Prince of Wales Ins Co, 23 Beav, 338 (1857) An appeal may be taken from an order granting a party leave to inspect and examine the books of a corporation the appellant Thompson v Erie R Co, 9 Abb Pr (N S), 212 (1870), Lancashire Co v Greatorex, 14 L. T. (N S), 290 (1866), Cummer v Kent, 38 Mich, 351 (1878), Comm'rs v Lemley, 85 N C, 311 (1881) See Saxby v Easterbrook, L. R., 7 Exch, 207 (1872), Bustros v White, L. R, 1 Q B Div, 423 (1876), Clyde v Rogers 24 Hun, 145 (1881), Met argo v Crutcher, 27 Ala, 171 (1855), Sage's Case, 70 N Y, 221 As to the costs of an inspection see Hill v Philp, 7 Exch, 232 (1852), Davey v Pemberton 11 C B (N S), 629 (1862) Gardner v Dangerfield 5 Beav, 389 (1842) Stockholders obtaining inspection may be ordered not to disclose the information received In re Birmingham, etc, Co 36 L J, Ch, 150 (1867), Williams v Prince, etc, Co, 23 Beav, 340 (1857) May examine through an attorney Williams v Prince, etc, Co, 23 Beav, 338 (1857) Professional accountant may be used Bonnardet v Taylor 1 J & H, 386 (1861), 1 Greenl on Ev, § 474 Inspection of stock-ledger allowed People v Pacific etc. Co. 50 Barb, 280 (1861) Of discount book Cockburn v Union Bank, 13 La. Ann, 289

(1858), People v Throop, 13 Wend., 183. Of by-laws Harrison v Williams, 3 B. & C, 162 (1824), Reg v Saddlers' Co., 10 W R, 77 (1861). See, also, Walburn v Ingleby, 1 Myl & K, 61 (1832), where the order was to a third person having charge of the books. "The courts of common law may also make an order for the inspection of writings in the possession of one party to a suit in favor of the other" Greenleaf's Ev, vol. I, § 559 An article of the company taking away the right of inspection does not prevent a rule issuing requiring its allowance in pending litigation Hall v Connell, 3 Younge & Col, 707 (1840) The rule applies to joint-stock companies Woods v De Figaniere, 1 Rob, 681 In the federal courts the right is statutory U S R S, § 724

[1] Strangers have no more right to demand inspection of the books of a corporation during litigation in which the corporation is not interested than they have to demand a similar right of any other person Mayor of Southampton v Graves, 8 T R., 590 (1800), overruling earlier cases. See, also, Opdyke v Marble, 44 Barb, 64 (1864), Morgan v Morgan 16 Abb Pr (N. S), 291 (1874). A corporation will not be compelled to open its records for the purposes of a litigation in which it is not a party. Henry v Travelers' Ins Co, 35 Fed Rep, 15 (1888).

[2] See Wait on Insolvent Corporations, § 519 See, also, § 714, *infra*

[3] King v Travannion, 2 Chitty, 366 (1818) Swansea Vale R'y Co v Budd, L. R, 2 Eq Cas 274 (1866), Macintosh v Flint, etc, R R. Co, 1 R'y & Corp. L. J 384 (Mich, 1887), a stockholder's case Where a stockholder files a bill to obtain an accounting, and charges

the corporate officers to swear to the pleading of the corporation, where the facts sought for are brought out by that pleading[1] or by a bill of discovery.[2]

misappropriation, and makes a motion that he be allowed to examine the books, the court will wait until the corporation pleads or answers before granting the motion Ranger v Champion, etc, Co, 51 Fed Rep, 61 (1892) A corporation may appeal from an order for the examination of one of its officers Sherman v Beacon, etc, Co, 11 N Y Supp, 369 (1890) Under the statutory practice in Rhode Island the court may order the production of the record book of the corporation in court or for an inspection Arnold v Pawtuxet, etc, Co, 26 Atl Rep, 55 (R I 1893) By examination before trial may ascertain whether defendants are proper defendants or whether they are a corporation Sweeny v Sturges, 24 Hun, 162 The affidavit to obtain the order must show that the information sought is essential

Imperial Gas Co v Clarke, 7 Bing, 95 Williams v Savage, etc, Co 3 Md Ch, 418, 428 (1851) See Lindley on Partn 809 The officers may be orally examined by the court with reference to where the books are Lacharme v Quartz Rock Mariposa Gold Min Co, 1 Hurl & Colt, 134 (1862) They may be required to make affidavits. Ranger v Great etc, R R Co, 4 De G & J, 71 (1859), Re Barton, 31 L J, Q B, 62 (1861) Such inspections may be through agents Bonnardet v Taylor, 1 J & H, 383 (1861) Draper v Manchester, etc, R R Co, 7 Jur (N S), pt 1, 86 (1861) But see In re West Devon, etc Mine L R 27 Ch D, 106 (1884), Bank of Utica v Hilliard, 6 Cowen, 62 In an action against a corporation the plaintiff is entitled to inspect all the minutes and entries in the company's books having

[1] Formerly in equity suits it was the practice to make as co-defendants with the corporation such officers as could answer under oath such matters as the complainant desired to know See § 738 infra, Glasscott v Copper etc, Co, 11 Sim, 305 (1840), In re Barnets, etc, Co, L R, 2 Ch, 350 (1867), French v First Nat'l Bank, 7 Ben, 488 (1874) This rule prevails because the corporation itself cannot be convicted of perjury McKim v Odom, 3 Bland Ch (Md), 407, 420 (1828), Wych v Meal, 3 P Wms, 311 (1734), Bevans v Dingman's, etc, 10 Pa St, 174 (1849) The corporation itself may be compelled to answer fully See Gamewell, etc, Co v Mayor, etc, 31 Fed Rep, 312, citing cases.

[2] A bill lies in equity to compel a corporation to discover, in aid of a suit at law, for damages for infringement of patent. Colgate v Compagnie, etc, 23 Fed Rep, 82 (1885) See, also, as to a bill of discovery, McComb v Chicago etc, R R, 19 Blatch, 69 (1881), Costa

Rica v Erlanger, 1 Ch D, 171 (1875) Glasscott v Copper, etc, Co, 11 Sim, 305 (1840), Moodalay v Morton, 1 Bro C C, 469 (1785), Colgate v Compagnie etc, 23 Fed Rep, 82 Stettauer v New York, etc Co, 42 N J Eq, 46 (1886), French v First Nat'l Bank, 7 Ben 488 (1874) But a bill of discovery will not lie against one who is merely a witness Fenton v Hughes, 7 Ves, 288 (1802), Dummer v Corporation, etc, 14 id, 245 (1807) As to the difference between a bill of discovery and other bills see McIntyre v Trustees, etc, 6 Paige, 239 (1837), Many v Beekman, etc, Co, 9 Paige, 188 (1841) Where discovery is sought from an officer he should be made a party defendant Virginia, etc, Co v Hale, 9 S Rep, 256 (Ala, 1891) A discovery will not be granted where there is no allegation that information is refused or that the party cannot examine the books or that a mandamus was inadequate Wolf et al v Underwood et al, 11 S Rep, 344 (Ala, 1892)

A bill of discovery may be brought to discover the names of stockholders in order to enforce their statutory liability [1] Sometimes a subpœna *duces tecum* may be issued in behalf of a stockholder or of a third person [2]

reference to the subject in litigation. Hill v. Great Western R. Co, 10 C. B (N S), 148, Harrison v Williams, 3 B & C, 162; Burton & Saddlers' Co, 31 L J, Q B, 62 Sinclair v Gray, 9 Fla., 71. See Hill v Manchester Co., 5 B & Ad, 866, Rex v Buckingham, 8 B. & C., 375, Imperial Gas Co v Clarke, 7 Bing, 95 It includes the agent, solicitor, counsel or expert of the party asking the inspection Hyde v Holmes, 2 Moll, 372, Blan v Massey, L. R., 5 Irish Eq, 623 Joint stock Discount Co 's Case, 36 L J, Eq. 150; Bonnardet v Taylor, 1 Johns & H, 383, Attorney-General v Whitwood, 40 L J (Ch Div), 592, Lindsay v Gladstone, L. R., 9 Eq, 132, Williams v. Prince of Wales Ins. Co, 23 Beav, 338, State v Bienville Co, 28 La Ann, 204, Ballin v Feist, 55 Ga 546. But see Bartley v Bartley, 1 Drew, 233, Summerfield v Pritchard, 17 Beav, 9. Draper v Manchester R. R., 3 De G, F & J, 23, West Devon Mine Case, L. R., 27 Ch Div, 106 And a shareholder who is also the solicitor of opposing litigants is nevertheless so entitled Reg v Wilts Co, 29 L T (N S), 922, Kingsford v Great Western R'y Co, 16 C B, (N S), 761 But see Hutt's Case, 7 Dowl Pr, 690, Herschfield v Clark, 11 Exch, 712 See, also, notes *supra* Manner of inspection must be gentlemanly. Williams v. Prince, etc, Co, 23 Beav, 338 (1857). The plaintiff may have inspection of corporate minutes in a suit by a superintendent against the corporation Hill v. Great, etc., R y. 10 C. B (N S), 148 (1861). Or in a suit by a claimant of office *In re* Burton, etc, Co, 31 L. J (Q B), 62 (1861) See, also, § 714, *infra* An order will not be granted for the purpose of fishing out a defense Birmingham, Bristol & Thames Junction R'y Co v White, 1 Q B., 282 See, also, Credit

Co. v Webster, 53 L T Rep, 419 (1885). In New York the right of inspection by order is regulated by statute. Code of Civil Proc, §§ 803-809 See Boorman v Atlantic & Pacific R. R. Co, 78 N. Y., 599 (1879), Ervin v Oregon R'y & Nav Co, 22 Hun, 566 (1880), holding that where the books are in use only sworn copies can be required, Johnson v. Consol Silv. Min Co, 2 Abb. Pr (N S.), 413, Walker v Granite Bank, 19 Abb, 111, Thompson v. Erie R'y Co, 9 Abb (N S), 230, N Y Daily Reg, October 22, 1887, January 31, 1888, January 26, 1888 So, also, is the right to subpœna a corporation Code of Civil Proc, §§ 868, 869, 872, 873. See N. Y, etc, R. R. Co. v Carhart, 36 Hun, 288 (1885), Richman v Manhattan Co, 26 Hun, 433 (1882), ch 536, L. 1880, Fenlon v Dempsey, 50 Hun, 131 (1888), Russell v. Manhattan R'y Co. Daily Register, Dec. 8 1887, People v Mutual Gas, etc, Co., 74 N. Y, 434 (1878), N Y Daily Reg, Dec 17, 1887 The transfer-book may be thus examined See Fenlon v Dempsey 50 Hun, 131 (1888).

[1] Post v Toledo, etc, R. R., 144 Mass., 346 (1887).

[2] The right of a stockholder to compel a corporation to produce in court the corporate records has been the subject of some controversy. It has been held that a subpœna *duces tecum* will not always lie herein, but that an order to the corporation to allow an inspection is the proper remedy La Farge v La Farge Fire Ins. Co, 14 How Pr, 26 (1857) Central Nat'l Bank v. White, 37 N Y Super Ct, 297 (1874). In Iowa a corporate servant who is required by a subpœna to produce the corporate books, which show that the corporation has violated the liquor laws, need not do so if the books are not in his possession But otherwise he is guilty of con-

Most of the states have statutes regulating this subject, and these statutes frequently displace the common-law procedure.

tempt. United States Ex. Co *v.* Henderson, 28 N E Rep., 426 (Iowa, 1886) See, also, preceding notes. The president may be compelled by subpœna *duces tecum* to produce drawings owned by the company in a suit in which it is a party Johnson, etc, Co. *v.* North. etc. Co, 48 Fed. Rep, 195 (1891). Stock exchange books as evidence must be proved by the secretary. Terry *v.* Birmingham, etc, Bank, 9 S Rep, 299 (Ala., 1891)

CHAPTER XXXI.

LIENS OF THE CORPORATION ON STOCK FOR THE STOCKHOLDER'S DEBTS TO THE CORPORATION

§§ 520-521 *No lien at common law* — Corporations, both in this country and in England, frequently possess and exercise a lien on a shareholder's stock for debts due from that shareholder to the corporation In this chapter it is proposed to consider the origin of the lien, the extent to which it may be exercised and enforced; the waiver of it by the corporation, and its effect generally upon the transfer of shares

It is clear that at common law a corporation has no lien upon the shares of its stockholders for debts due from them to the company.[1]

[1] Gemmel v Davis, 23 Atl Rep, 1032 (Md, 1892), Massachusetts Iron Co v. Hooper, 61 Mass., 183 (1851); Bates v. New York Insurance Co, 3 Johns Cas., 238 (1802), Steamship Dock Co. v Heron's Adm'x, 52 Pa St., 280 (1866), Merchants' Bank v Shouse, 102 id, 488 (1883), Fitzhugh v Bank of Shepherdsville, 3 Monroe, 126 (1825), Williams v Lowe, 4 Neb., 382, 398 (1876), Dana v Brown, 1 J. J. Marsh, 304 (1829); Heart v State Bank, 2 Dev Eq (N C), 111 (1831); Farmers', etc, Bank v Wasson, 48 Iowa, 336 (1878), People v Crockett, 9 Cal, 112 (1858) Sargent v. Franklin Insurance Co, 25 Mass., 90 (1829), Neale v Janney, 2 Crauch C. C., 188 (1819), McMurrich v Pond Head Harbor Co, 9 U C, Q B, 333 (1852). Cf Weston's Case, L R., 4 Chan, 20 (1868). See, also, Gibson, Assignee of Evans, v. Hudson's Bay Company, MS Rep. Michael, 12 Geo I. (1726), 7 Viner's Abridgment (2d London ed), 125, Pinkett v. Wright, 2 Hare's Chan, 120 (1842); Byrne v. Union Bank of Louisiana 9 Rob. (La), 433 (1845), Hussey v Manuf. & Mech. Bank, 27 Mass., 415 (1830), Bryon v. Carter, 22 La Ann, 98 (1870). In New York the rule that there is no lien at common law is applied to banking corporations. Bank of Attica v Manuf, etc., Bank, 20 N Y, 501 (1859). And to corporations formed under the General Manufacturing Companies Act Driscoll v West Bradley, etc., Manuf'g Co., 59 id., 96 (1874).

The policy of the common law has always been to discountenance secret liens, inasmuch as they hinder trade and restrict the safe and speedy transfer of property It is upon this ground that the courts refuse to enforce a lien upon stock when such lien is not created by charter or by by-law.

§ 522 *A lien may be created by statute, by charter, or possibly by by-law or contract — Notice of the lien* — Such a lien as this in favor of the corporation may be created by statute,[1] by charter,[2] and the weight of authority holds that it may be created by by-law.

With respect to the right of a corporation to enact a by-law creating such a lien, it is held in many jurisdictions that such a by-law is valid and binding upon all persons who buy or transfer the shares[3] There is nevertheless strong authority for the rule that such a by-law cannot create a lien on the stock so as to bind a *bona fide* purchaser, or other person into whose hands the shares may

[1] Pittsburg, etc, R. R Co v Clarke, 29 Pa St. 146 (1857). First National Bank v Hartford, etc, Ins Co, 45 Conn, 22 (1877), Presbyterian Cong v Carlisle Bank 5 Pa, St. 345 (1847), Rogers v Huntington Bank, 12 Serg & R, 77 (1824), National Bank v Watsontown Bank 105 U. S, 217 (1881) In New York a statute gives railway corporations which operate railroads in foreign countries a lien upon the stock for the amount of the unpaid calls. New York Sess Laws, 1881 ch 468 § 12.

[2] Bradford Banking Co v Briggs, L R, 31 Chan Div, 19 (1885), S C 53 L T Rep (N S), 816, reversing S C, L R, 29 Chan Div, 149 (1885). Union Bank v Laird, 2 Wheat, 390 (1817). Stebbins v Phœnix Fire Ins Co, 3 Paige, 350 (1832). Reese v Bank of Commerce, 14 Md, 271 (1859), Brent v Bank of Washington, 10 Peters, 596 (1836), German Security Bank v Jefferson, 10 Bush (Ky), 326 (1874), Arnold v Suffolk Bank, 27 Barb., 424 (1857), Leggett v Bank of Sing Sing. 24 N Y, 283 (1863), Bank of Utica v Smalley, 2 Cowen, 770 (1824), Farmers' Bank of Maryland v Iglehart, 6 Gill, 50 (1847), Bohmer v City Bank, 77 Va, 445 (1883), Hodges v. Planters' Bank, 7 Gill & J, 306 (1835), Sabin v. Bank of Woodstock,

21 Vt, 353 (1849), Cross v Phenix Bank, 1 R I, 39 (1840)

[3] Knight v Old National Bank, 3 Clifford, 429 (1871), McDowell v Bank of Wilmington. 1 Hair (Del), 27 (1832), Bank of Holly Springs v Pinson, 58 Miss, 421 (1880), St Louis Perpetual Ins Co v Goodfellow, 9 Mo, 119 (1845), Mechanics' Bank v Merchants' Bank 45 Mo, 513 (1870), Spurlock v Pacific R R Co, 61 Mo 319 (1875), *In re* Bachman, 12 Nat Bank Reg, 223 (1877), People v Crockett, 9 Cal, 112 (1858), Pendergast v Bank of Stockton, 2 Sawyer, 108 (1871), Lockwood v Mechanics' National Bank, 9 R I, 308 (1869), Cunningham v Alabama, etc, Trust Co, 4 Ala (N S), 652 (1843), Geyer v Western Ins Co, 3 Pittsb, 41 (1867), *In re* Dunkerson, 4 Biss, 227 (1868) Young v Vough, 23 N J Eq, 326 (1873), Brent v Bank of Washington, 10 Peters 565, 615 (1836), Child v Hudson Bay Co, 2 P Wms, 207 (1723), Planters', etc, Ins Co v Selma Savings Bank, 63 Ala., 585 (1879) *Cf* Heart v State Bank, 2 Dev Eq (N C), 111 (1831), Farmers', etc, Bank v Wasson, 48 Iowa, 336, 340 (1878) In Tuttle v Walton, 1 Ga, 43 (1846), it was said that as between the corporators themselves such a by-law will be held valid

come, to whom actual knowledge of the by-law cannot be imputed

Such is the rule in New York,[1] Louisiana,[2] Massachusetts,[3] Alabama,[4] Pennsylvania,[5] California,[6] Mississippi[7] and, it seems, in some other states[8]   It is also the rule declared by the supreme court of the United States in cases that involve the right of the national banks to enact such by-laws[9]

Upon the whole it may be said that the question whether a corporation may, by by-law, create a lien in its own favor upon the shares of its stockholders for debts due by them to the corporation is not settled.   The weight of authority in this country is against the validity of the by-law, and such would seem to be a result most in accord with a wise and broad public policy.

[1] Driscoll v West Bradley, etc., Co., 59 N Y, 96 (1874), Bank of Attica v Manufacturers' Bank, 20 id, 501 (1859), Rosenback v. Salt Spring National Bank, 53 Barb, 495 (1868), Conklin v Second National Bank, id., 512 (1868), S. C, aff'd, 45 N Y, 655 (1871). In the case last cited it was held that not even where the certificate of stock contained a provision that the stock was not transferable until all the liabilities of the stockholder to the bank were paid did the bank acquire a lien upon the shares for the subsequent indebtedness of the share-owner   And all the New York decisions proceed upon the broad ground that the policy of the law is to protect a *bona fide* vendee of shares of stock against secret or equitable claims thereto   Cf Leggett v Bank of Sing Sing, 24 N Y, 283 (1862), McCready v Rumsey, 6 Duer, 574 (1857); Arnold v Suffolk Bank, 52 Barb, 424 (1857).

[2] Bryon v. Carter, 22 La. Ann, 98 (1870); Pitot v Johnson, 33 id, 1286 (1881)   Cf New Orleans National Banking Association v Wiltz, 4 Woods, 43 (1881), S C, 10 Fed Rep, 230.

[3] In Nesmith v. Washington Bank, 23 Mass, 324 (1828), the court doubted whether a by-law could under any circumstances create a lien on the shares as against the creditors of the share-owner, but did not decide the point. In Sargent v. Franklin Ins. Co., 25 Mass.,

90 (1829), there is a somewhat decided ground taken against the validity of any by-law which tends to limit the free transfer of shares. In Plymouth Bank v Bank of Norfolk, 27 Mass., 454 (1830). Chief Justice Shaw seems to doubt the validity of a by-law giving the bank a lien on its own stock.

[4] Planters', etc., Mutual Ins. Co. v. Selma Savings Bank, 63 Ala, 585 (1879).

[5] Steamship Dock Co. v. Heron's Adm'x, 52 Pa. St., 280 (1866), Merchants' Bank v. Shouse, 102 Pa. St, 488 (1883).

[6] Anglo-Californian Bank v Grangers' Bank, 63 Cal, 359 (1883).

[7] Bank of Holly Springs v. Pinson, 58 Miss, 421 (1880).

[8] Carroll v Mullanphy Savings Bank, 8 Mo. App., 249 (1880); Evansville National Bank v. Metropolitan National Bank, 2 Biss, 527 (1871); Lee v. Citizens' National Bank, 2 Cin. Super. Ct., 298 (1872)   Cf. Neale v Janney, 2 Cranch C C, 188 (1819). A lien of the corporation on stock is prevented by a statutory provision that the company should not loan money on the security of its own stock   Nicollet National Bank v. City Bank, 35 N W. Rep., 577 (Minn, 1887).

[9] Bank v. Lanier, 11 Wall 369 (1870); Bullard v. Bank, 18 id., 589 (1873). *Vide* § 533, *infra.*

§ 523 In Pennsylvania it is the statutory law that the transfer of shares of stock in a railway corporation can be made only upon payment of any indebtedness that may exist on the part of the shareholders who seek to transfer, unless the lien is waived by the corporation[1] In New Hampshire liens upon shares are forbidden by statute.[2]

When a lien is expressly given to the corporation by its charter or by statute, all persons dealing with the corporation are affected by it and must take notice of it[3] A statutory lien need not be set out in the certificate in order to give notice to the transferee[4] And where the lien is not authorized by the charter or by statute, the mere declaration of its existence in the certificate will not avail against a *bona fide* purchaser[5]

§ 524. It is a salutary rule that a lien created by by-law can bind only those who take the stock with notice of the by-law. This is because by-laws do not of themselves impart or convey notice.[6] So,

[1] Pittsburgh, etc, R. R. Co t. Cluke, 29 Pa St., 146 (1857); Rogers t. Huntingdon Bank, 12 Serg & R., 77 (1824) Cf Everhart v. West Chester R. R. Co, 28 Pa St., 339 (1857).

[2] Hill v. Pine River Bank, 45 N. H., 300, 309 (1864)

[3] Bishop v. Globe Company, 135 Mass, 132 (1883), Union Bank of Georgetown v. Laird, 2 Wheat., 390 (1817), Bohmer v. City Bank of Richmond, 77 Va., 445 (1883), Downer's Adm't v. Zanesville Bank, Wright (Ohio), 477 (1833), Grant v. Mechanics' Bank, 15 Serg & R, 140 (1826), St. Louis Perpetual Life Insurance Co v. Goodfellow, 9 Mo, 149 (1845), Bank of Utica v. Smalley, 2 Cowen, 770 (1824), Rogers t. Huntingdon Bank, 12 Serg & R., 77 (1824), Sewall t. Lancaster Bank, 17 id, 285 (1828) Cf Stebbins v. Phœnix, etc, Insurance Co, 3 Paige, 350 (1832)

[4] McCready v. Rumsey, 6 Duer 591 (1857), Reese t. Bank of Com, 14 Md, 271 (1859), First Nat'l Bank v. Hartford, etc, Ins. Co, 45 Conn, 22 (1877) A lien on stock created by statute gives the corporation a prior right in the stock as against a subsequent pledgee and purchaser at the pledgee's sale, even though the certificate of stock gives no intimation of a lien Hammond v. Hastings,

134 U S, 401 (1890) But where the by-law under which the lien is claimed directs that notice of the lien should be given in the certificate of stock, this provision must be regarded as meaning that the lien should not be asserted against a person not having notice by the certificate And the issuance of certificates not containing this notice is a waiver of the lien contemplated by such by-law Bank of Holly Springs v. Pinson, 58 Miss, 421 (1880)

[5] Conklin v. Second National Bank, 45 N Y, 655 (1871) But in Vansands v. Middlesex County Bank, 26 Conn, 144 (1857) it is held that a statement on the face of the certificate of stock that it is issued subject to all debts due from the owners to the corporation will bind a transferee as a qualification or restriction of the transferrer's title, and that, too, although no charter provision or by-law authorizes such a lien on the stock So, also, 21 Pac Rep., 852 (Cal, 1889).

[6] Driscoll v. West Bradley, etc, Co, 59 N Y, 96, 109 (1874), Bank of Holly Springs v. Pinson, 58 Miss, 421, 435 (1880), Anglo-Californian Bank t. Grangers' Bank, 63 Cal, 359 (1883) See, also, People ex rel Krohn v. Miller, Treas, 39 Hun, 557 (1886), con-

too a by-law enacted subsequently to a transfer, although the transfer has not been recorded on the corporate books, cannot affect the rights of the parties as to that transfer[1] By-laws creating liens on stock have been, however, held valid and enforceable as against the assignees in bankruptcy or in insolvency.[2]

A clause in a charter declaring that debts due from the stockholders must be paid before a transfer will be allowed is sufficient to create a lien on the stock without other action on the part of the corporation.[3] And so, also, a power conferred by the charter upon the directors to refuse a transfer so long as the shareholder who wishes to transfer is indebted to the corporation, when exercised by the corporate management, supports the lien.[4]

A lien may be created by special agreement among the shareholders[5] And even a mere usage of a corporation not to transfer shares while the owner is indebted to the corporation is sufficient to create a lien on stock, valid between the corporation and its shareholders, and one which will bind a shareholder who borrows money with knowledge of it[6]

§ 525 *What phrases in charters or statutes will or will not authorize the corporation to create or enforce a lien on stock* — The question sometimes arises whether or not the corporation, by the charter or the statute under which it acts, has authority to enact a by-law creating a lien upon its stock in favor of the corporation for debts due it by the shareholders. It has been held that, where the directors are authorized to make "regulations" as to

cerning the validity and effect of by-laws regulating the sale and transfer of seats or membership in the commercial exchanges, and the enforcement of the liens created thereupon by such by-laws in favor of other members of the corporation

[1] People v Crockett, 9 Cal, 112 (1858).

[2] Morgan v Bank of North America, 8 Serg & R. 73 (1822), S C, 11 Am Dec, 575. Vansands v Middlesex Co. Bank 26 Conn, 144 (1857), *In re* Bigelow, 1 Nat Bank Reg. 632, 667 (1868)

[3] Farmers' Bank of Maryland Case, 2 Bland's Chan, 394 (1830), Kenton Ins. Co. v Bowman, 1 S W. Rep, 717 (Ky, 1886).

[4] Arnold v Suffolk Bank, 27 Barb, 424 (1857)

[5] Vansands v Middlesex County Bank, 26 Conn, 144 (1857) By inserting in the certificate of stock that the corpo-

ration has a lien on it for debts due to the corporation, a purchaser takes subject thereto It is a contract lien. Jennings t Bank of Cal, 21 Pac. Rep., 852 (Cal, 1889) By consent of all, a lien given to the corporation for debts due to it by the stockholders is valid and the method of foreclosing it may also be so prescribed. The statute of limitations does not run against it. Reading, etc, Co v Reading, etc., Works, 21 Atl Rep, 170 (Pa., 1891)

[6] Waln's Assignees t Bank of North America, 8 Serg & R., 73, 88 (1822), S. C, 11 Am Dec., 575 *Cf.* Vansands v. Middlesex Co Bank, 26 Conn, 144 (1857). So in Bryon v Carter, 22 La. Ann, 98 (1870), it is held that a by-law creating a lien, while it may be valid as between the parties if it be brought to their knowledge, is not binding on the judgment creditors of the shareholders.

transfers, they may make a by-law creating a lien[1] So various other phrases have been held sufficient to confer this power[2]

§ 526 *The lien, when established, covers all the stockholder's shares and dividends* — A valid lien in favor of the corporation, when regularly established, attaches to all the shares and dividends of the indebted stockholder. Thus, it attaches to all the shares the stockholder owns, although the debt be for calls due and unpaid upon only a part of them[3] The lien attaches not only to the stock itself but to dividends declared on the stock.[4] It is accordingly held that a corporation may lawfully retain dividends, and apply them to the payment of a debt due to it from the shareholder, since in an action by the shareholder to enforce payment of his dividends the corporation may plead the debt by way of set-off[5]

---

[1] Cunningham v Alabama, etc, Trust Co., 4 Ala (N S.), 652 (1843). Spurlock v Pacific R. R. Co, 61 Mo 319 (1875); Pendergast v Bank of Stockton 2 Sawyer, 108 (1871) Cf Tuttle v Walton, 1 Ga, 43 (1846)

[2] Bryon v. Carter. 22 La. Ann. 98 (1870), Brent v Bank of Wash, 10 Peters, 596, 611 et seq (1836), Pendergast v Bank of Stockton, 2 Sawyer, 108 (Cal, 1871) Except when such power is expressly given to the directors it can only be exercised by vote of the stockholders. Carroll v Mullanphy Sav Bank, 8 Mo App, 249 (1880) A charter power given to the directors of a corporation "to make all by-laws not inconsistent with any existing law of the state for the management of its property, the regulation of its affairs and the transfer of its stock," has been held in Missouri to include the power in question Mechanics' Bank v Mech Bank, 45 Mo, 513 (1870) But in New York the same language used in the general statute was held not to include it Driscoll v West Bradley, etc, Co, 59 N. Y., 96 (1874) See, also, Perpetual Ins. Co v Goodfellow, 9 Mo, 149 (1845), Vansands v Middlesex Bank, 26 Conn, 144 (1857); Bank of Attica v Manuf, etc, Bank, 20 N. Y, 501 (1859). For a discussion of this question as applied to national banks, see § 533

[3] Stebbins v. Phœnix Fire Ins Co., 3 Paige, 350 (1832). Cf. Brent v Bank of Washington, 2 Cranch C C, 517 (1824). In Virginia, however, it seems that there can be no lien on wholly paid up shares to secure the payment of an unpaid subscription to other shares Shenandoah Valley R R Co. v Griffith, 76 Va, 913 (1882) Cf. Va Code, 1887, §§ 1127, 1128, 1130 ; Petersburg Savings, etc, Co v Lumsden, 75 Va, 327 (1881) And in England a lien on stock for unpaid calls is a lien only on those particular shares upon which the calls is made and not on other shares Hubbersty v Manchester, etc, R'y Co, L R, 2 Q B, 471 (1867)

[4] Thus it attaches to the dividends even though only "shares and stock" be specifically named in the statute or charter as subject to the lien (Hague v. Dandeson, 2 Exch, 147 — 1848), and though, in the absence of express provision, it is held that no such lien impliedly exists Sargent v Franklin Ins Co, 25 Mass., 90 (1829), Bates v N Y Ins Co, 3 Johns Cas., 238 (1802) So, in Hagar v Union Nat'l Bank, 63 Me, 509 (1874), it was held that the terms of the act of 1864 which are inconsistent with the existence of a stock lien do not preclude a lien on dividends

[5] Hagar v Union National Bank, 63 Me, 509 (1874), Sargent v Franklin Ins Co, 25 Mass., 90 (1829), Bates v New York Ins Co., 3 Johns Cas., 238 (1802).

But dividends declared after the death of the stockholder are not
subject to a lien for his debts.[1] The lien attaches to the shares
even after a liquidation or dissolution of the company[2] It attaches
not only to valid stock, but to spurious stock obtained by forgery.[3]
So also the lien attaches to trust stock for debts due from a trustee
who holds stock in trust, but in his own name, and without any indication of the trust[4] Where a *cestui que trust* owes the corporation a debt, the lien attaches to his stock though held for him in
the name of a trustee[5] And stock standing on the corporate books
in the name of a fictitious person is subject to a lien for the indebtedness of the real owner[6]

§ 527 *The lien protects the corporation as to all the debts due to
it from the shareholder* — It is a general rule that a lien upon stock
is a lien for all debts of the shareholder due to the corporation;[7]
and it is not necessary that the debt be due and payable at the
time when the lien is sought to be enforced. It covers debts which
are not due as well as those that are due, and all indebtedness to
the corporation, whether payable presently or at a future time.[8]

Cf Merchants' Bank *v* Shouse, 102 Pa
St., 188 (1883), S C 16 Rep, 442, Brent
v Bank of Washington, 2 Cranch C C,
517 (1824). See, also, § 545, *infra*

[1] Brent *v* Bank of Washington, *supra*,
Merchants' Bank *v* Shouse, *supra*

[2] *In re* General Exchange Bank, L R,
6 Chan, 818 (1871)

[3] Mt Holly Paper Co's Appeal, 99 Pa
St. 513 (1882)

[4] New London & Brazilian Bank *v*
Brocklebank, L R., 21 Chan Div, 302
(1882), Young *v* Vough, 23 N J Eq,
325 (1873), Burns *v*. Lawrie's Trustees,
2 Scotch Ct. of Sessions Cas (2d series),
1318 (1840), otherwise cited, 2 Dunlap,
Bell & Murray, 1348.

[5] Stebbins *v* Phoenix Fire Ins. Co, 3
Page. 350 (1832)

[6] Stebbins *v* Phoenix Fire Ins Co, 3
Page, 350 (1832), where the president of
a corporation with fraudulent intent
procured shares to be recorded in a fictitious name, and, having himself become
indebted to the corporation, procured an
assignment of the shares to another
creditor, who sought to have the transfer recorded *Held*, that the lien still
attached for the debts of the original
holder.

[7] Union Bank of Georgetown *v* Laird,
2 Wheat, 390 (1817), Mobile Mutual Ins.
Co. *v* McCallum, 49 Ala, 558 (1873);
Cunningham *v* Ala, etc, Trust Co., 4
Ala (N S), 652 (1843), Rogers *v.* Hunt-
ingdon Bank, 12 Serg. & R., 77 (1824),
Ex parte Stringer, L R, 9 Q B. Div,
436 (1882), *In re* Peebles, 2 Hughes, 394
(Va, 1875), Planters', etc, Mutual Ins.
Co *v* Selma Savings Bank, 63 Ala., 585
(1879)

[8] Pittsburg, etc, R R. Co. *v* Clarke,
29 Pa. St, 146 (1857), *In re* Bachman,
12 Nat. Bank Reg, 223 (1875), Downer's Adm'r *v* Zanesville Bank, Wright
(Ohio), 477 (1833), Brent *v* Bank of
Washington, 10 Peters, 596 (1836), Grant
v Mechanics' Bank, 15 Serg & R., 140
(1826), Rogers *v* Huntingdon Bank, 12
id, 77 (1824), Sewall *v* Lancaster Bank,
17 id, 285 (1828), McCready *v.* Rumsey,
6 Duer. 574 (1857), St. Louis Perpetual
Insurance Co *v* Goodfellow, 9 Mo., 149
(1845), Cunningham *v* Ala, etc, Trust
Co., 4 Ala (N S.), 652 (1843); Hall *v*
United States Ins. Co, 5 Gill (Md.), 484
(1847) Leggett *v* Bank of Sing Sing,
24 N Y, 283 (1862), *In re* Stockton Mal-
leable Iron Co, L R, 2 Chan. Div., 101
(1875). In Grant *v* Mechanics' Bank,

The lien also will continue for the benefit of the corporation although the debt be barred by the statute of limitations [1] The lien attaches whether the stockholder's debt to the corporation accrued before or after he became a stockholder.[2] It also secures debts for which the shareholder is liable only as surety,[3] and debts due from a partnership in which the stockholder is a partner [4] So, also, it secures the corporation for unpaid calls upon the original subscription.[5] But the lien does not attach until a call is made [6]

supra, it was held that a bank organized under the Pennsylvania law of March 21, 1814, might lawfully refuse to permit the transfer of the stock of a shareholder who was the drawer of a bill discounted by the bank, but not payable at the time the transfer was demanded — both the shareholder and his indorser having, since the discount of the paper, become insolvent. So, also, Downer's Adm'r v Zanesville Bank, supra. But where the lien is expressly made a security for debts "actually due and payable," it will be held to cover only debts due and payable Reese v Bank of Commerce, 14 Md, 271 (1859) Cf Downer's Adm'r v Zanesville Bank, supra.

[1] Farmers' Bank of Md. v Iglehart, 6 Gill (Md), 50 (1847); Geyer v Western Ins Co, 3 Pittsb, 41 (1867), Brent v Bank of Washington, 10 Peters, 596, 617 (1836)

[2] Schmidt v Hennepin, etc, Co, 35 Minn, 511 (1886).

[3] McLean v Lafayette Bank, 3 McL, 587 (1846); Leggett v Bank of Sing Sing, 24 N. Y., 283 (1862), Union Bank of Georgetown v Laird, 2 Wheat, 390 (1817), McDowell v Bank of Wilmington, 1 Harr. (Del), 27 (1832), Brent v Bank of Washington, 10 Peters, 596, 615 (1836), St. Louis Perpetual Ins Co. v Goodfellow, 9 Mo, 149 (1845) Cf Miles v. New Zealand, etc, Co., 54 L. T Rep., 582 (1886), West Branch Bank v Armstrong 40 Pa. St 278

(1861). A corporation on discounting a bill or note, may take security from one of the parties and also hold the shares of another party as security for the same loan Union Bank v Laird, supra. Cf Conant v Seneca Co Bank, 1 Ohio St., 298 (1853), Helm v Swiggert, 12 Ind, 194 (1859), Dunlop v Dunlop, L R, 21 Chan Div, 583 (1882), holding that where the corporation has other security it is not obliged to resort to the lien

[4] In the Matter of Bigelow, 2 Benedict, 469 (N Y, 1868), Geyer v Western Ins. Co, 3 Pittsb, 41 (1867), Arnold v Suffolk Bank, 27 Barb 424 (1857) Planters', etc, Ins Co v Selma Savings Bank, 63 Ala, 585 (1879).

[5] Spurlock v Pacific R. R. Co 61 Mo, 319 (1875), McCready v. Rumsey, 6 Duer, 574 (1857), Regina v Wing, 33 Eng L. & E, 80 (1855), Ex parte Littledale, L. R., 9 Chan, 257 (1874); Companies Clauses Consolidation Act, 1845 (8 Vict, ch 16, § 16), Shaw v Rowley, 5 Eng R'y & Canal Cas 47 (1847), Ex parte Tooke, 6 id, 1 (1849) Cf. Newry, etc, R'y Co v Edmunds, 2 Exch, 118 (1848) Ambergate, etc, R'y Co v Mitchell, 4 id, 540 (1849) Great North of Eng R'y Co v Biddulph, 7 Mees & W, 243 (1840), Pittsb, etc, R. R. Co v Clarke 29 Pa St. 146 (1857). Rogers v Huntingdon Bank 12 Serg & R., 77 (1824), Petersburg Sav, etc, Co v Lumsden 75 Va 327 (1881). Cf Hall v U S Ins Co, 5 Gill (Md),

[6] A director transferring his shares before the call avoids the lien although he knew the call was to be made The call is made when the date of payment is fixed and not by a mere general resolution Re Cowley, etc, Co, 61 L. T. Rep, 601 (1889).

Whether the lien will avail to protect the corporation as to instalments on the stock not called seems not to be settled. Whether it does or not will depend upon the wording of the provision authorizing the lien Generally no such lien exists[1] The lien also attaches to the stock of a depositor who has overdrawn his account[2]

§ 528 *Right of lien as against miscellaneous parties* — The lien of a corporation on shares of stock as security for the payment of debts due to the corporation from the owner is a lien only as to the indebtedness of duly recorded shareholders.[3] There is no lien on the stock as to debts of an intervening unrecorded owner of the stock[4]

§ 529 *The lien can be enforced for the benefit of the corporation only.* — The right of a corporation to a lien on the stock of its shareholders as security for the payment of their debts to the corporation is a right to be enforced only by the corporation and exclusively for its own benefit Accordingly, it is held that the corporation cannot become the assignee of the claim of some third person against one of its shareholders in order to enforce payment of that claim for the benefit of the third person by a recourse to the corporate lien on the shareholder's stock.[5] Neither can the corporation be compelled, for the benefit of sureties as to a part of the shareholder's indebtedness, to apply the proceeds of the sale of the stock to the liquidation of that part of their claim which is secured.[6] The lien is for the benefit of the corporation, and it may

---

481, 499 (1847), holding that instalments not called in constituted no such indebtedness as was contemplated in the statutory provision for the lien Such a construction "would be to render its stock wholly untransferable until the par amount of it had been paid up, although the requisite instalments for that purpose had never been called in "

[1] Hall z United States Ins Co , 5 Gill (Md) 484 (1847), *Cf In re* Bachman, 12 Nat Bank Reg , 223 (1875); Pittsburgh, etc , R. R. Co r Clarke, 29 Pa St., 146 (1857)

[2] Reese r Bank of Commerce, 14 Md , 271 (1859)

[3] *Cf* §§ 526, 532 Where the legal title to shares can only be acquired by a transfer made in a prescribed mode, yet a complete equitable title may be other-

wise acquired, and the lien may attach thereto

[4] Helm r Swiggert, 12 Ind , 194 (1859).

[5] White's Bank r Toledo, etc , Ins. Co., 12 Ohio St., 601 (1861) To the point that this lien is one exclusively for the benefit of the corporation, see Bank of Utica r Smalley, 2 Cowen, 770 (1824).

[6] Cross r Phenix Bank, 1 R. I, 39 (1840) But see Kuhns v. Westmoreland Bank, 2 Watts (Pa.), 136 (1833), where it is said that "the principle that a surety is entitled to the benefit of all the creditor's securities is of such universal application that it would require strong evidence of legislative intention to make the present case an exception to it." *Cf* also Klopp v Lebanon Bank, 46 Pa St, 88 (1863), Petersburg Savings Co v Lumsden, 75 Va., 327, 340 (1881)

apply the proceeds of the sale of the stock in such a way as best to subserve its own interest [1]

§ 530 *Methods of enforcing the lien.* — When a corporation has a lien upon the stock of those of its shareholders who are indebted to it, it may refuse to allow a transfer of the stock until the debt is paid or secured to its satisfaction   This is the usual method of enforcing the lien.[2]   And the corporation may insist upon its lien and hold the stock even against a *bona fide* purchaser [3]   It may, moreover, hold the whole amount of the shareholder's stock, although the amount of the debt be less than the value of the shares   It cannot be compelled to transfer so much of the stock as is in excess of the amount of the debt [4]   But the corporation can enforce its lien against the transferee only by a refusal to allow the transfer or by a suit to foreclose   It cannot elect to make the transferee personally liable for the debt

The corporation may, however, proceed by an attachment of the stock [5]   So, also, upon non-payment of the debt, the corporation may make an application to a court of chancery and have the shares sold in the usual way, as in other cases of property held under a lien [6]   A decree authorizing the sale of stock for the payment of

[1] Planters', etc., Ins Co v Selma Sav. Bank, 63 Ala. 585 (1879), Mt. Holly Paper Co.'s Appeal, 99 Pa St, 513 (1882), Anglo Cal Bank v Grangers' Bank 63 Cal, 359 (1883), Bishop v Globe Co, 135 Mass, 132 (1883)

[2] Reese v Bank of Commerce, 14 Md, 271 (1859); Brent v Bank of Washington, 10 Peters, 596 (1836), First National Bank of Hartford v Hartford, etc, Ins Co, 45 Conn, 22 (1877), Vansands v Middlesex County Bank, 26 Conn, 144 (1857), Farmers' Bank of Maryland v Iglehart, 6 Gill (Md), 50 (1847), McCready v. Rumsey, 6 Duer, 574 (1857), Tuttle v. Walton, 1 Ga, 43 (1846); Sewall v Lancaster Bank, 17 Serg & R., 285 (1828), Rogers v Huntingdon Bank, 12 id, 77 (1824); Grant v Mechanics' Bank, 15 id. 140 (1826)   *Cf* Sabin v Bank of Woodstock, 21 Vt, 353 (1849), West Branch Bank v Armstrong, 40 Pa. St, 278 (1861). In Bishop v Globe Co, 135 Mass, 132 (1883), the rule is declared that if by the law of the state under which a corporation is organized the corporation has a lien on the stock of any shareholder for a debt due from him to the corporation that the lien is a good defense to an action in another state against the corporation by a person to whom the shareholder has transferred his stock, but in whose name, by reason of the lien, the corporation has refused to register the transfer

[3] Newbury v Detroit, etc, R R Co., 17 Mich, 141 (1868), Titcomb v Union, etc., Ins Co., 8 Mass., 326 (1811), Rogers v Huntingdon Bank, 12 Serg & R, 77 (1824); Grant v Mechanics' Bank, 15 id, 140 (1826), Sewall v Lancaster Bank, 17 id, 285 (1828), West Branch Bank v Armstrong. 40 Pa St, 278 (1861), Mechanics' Bank v Merchants' Bank, 45 Mo, 513 (1870), St Louis Perpetual Life Ins. Co v Goodfellow, 9 id., 149 (1845), Tuttle v Walton, 1 Ga, 43 (1846)

[4] Sewall v Lancaster Bank, 17 Serg. & R, 285 (1828), Pierson v Bank of Washington, 3 Cranch C. C, 363 (1828).

[5] Sabin v Bank of Woodstock, 21 Vt, 353 (1849).

[6] *In re* Morrison, 10 Nat'l Bank Reg, 105 (1874), Farmers' Bank of Maryland's Case, 2 Bland's Chan (Md), 394 (1830),

the debt need not give the shareholder the right of redemption. An absolute and valid title may pass to the purchaser immediately upon the sale.[1] A valid lien in favor of a bank upon shares of stock in the bank belonging to the estate of a deceased person will not yield to a prior claim against the estate in favor of the government.[2] But an unwarranted claim of lien by a corporation, and a consequent refusal to register a transfer until the debt as to which the lien is asserted is paid, is a conversion of the shares, and the transferrer may have his action against the corporation therefor[3] In order, however, to put the corporation in the wrong for a refusal to transfer where it claims more than is due, the shareholder must tender what he admits to be due[4] A corporation is liable in damages for selling the stock of a stockholder for non-payment of dues where such sale was irregular and illegal[5]

§ 531 *The corporation may waive its lien.*— A corporation which has a lien upon its stockholders' stock for debts due to it from them need not necessarily depend upon or insist upon its lien for the collection of the debt. It has two remedies — one to enforce the lien, the other to collect the debt as though there was no lien[6] Hence

Brent i Bank of Washington. 10 Peters, 596 (1836) Under the California code a corporation may by suit foreclose a lien which it has on its stock Mechanics', etc , Assoc v King, 23 Pac. Rep , 376 (Cal , 1890)

[1] Reese v Bank of Commerce, 11 Md , 271, 284 (1859). In one case the lien was held to be equivalent to a pledge, and it was held that, after giving due notice to the delinquent shareholder, the corporation might sell at public auction without filing a bill to foreclose. Farmers' Bank of Maryland's Case, *supra* In this case it is also held that, where the corporation neglects or refuses to sell the stock of a deceased shareholder who is in arrears, the administrator may file a bill and obtain an order of sale directed to the corporation

[2] Brent v Bank of Washington, 10 Peters, 596 (1836)

[3] Bank of America v McNeil, 10 Bush, 54 (1873) Cf Dickinson v Central National Bank, 129 Mass , 279 (1880) , Case v Bank, 100 U. S., 446 (1879) , Skinner v City of London Co , 53 L T , 191 (1885), holding, also, that only nominal dam-

ages could be recovered where the terms of the transfer were secret.

[4] Pierson v Bank of Washington, 3 Cranch C C , 363 (1828). In German Security Bank v. Jefferson, 10 Bush, 326 (1874), it was held that, where the stock sold under the lien realized a sum insufficient to satisfy the corporate debt, the unpaid balance of the claim of the corporation could not be paid until there had been a proportionate payment of the claims of other creditors of the shareholder out of his general assets. Cf In re Peebles, 2 Hughes, 394 (1875).

[5] The sale here was contrary to the requirements of the by-laws The corporation bought the stock itself at such sale The fact that a surplus realized at the sale was sent to the stockholder by check, and was received by him, did not bar his remedy, he being in ignorance of the illegality Allen v. American Building, etc , Ass'n et al., 52 N. W Rep., 144 (Minn , 1892)

[6] A subscriber for stock cannot avoid liability to the corporation by setting up that the corporation has a lien on the stock therefor and may enforce it.

it is that the lien of a corporation on stock may be asserted and enforced, or in the discretion of the corporation it may be waived [1]

Where the corporation has other security it is not obliged to resort to the lien.[2] Cases may arise where the intervening rights of other creditors of the shareholder render it inequitable for the corporation to waive its lien on the stock,[3] but in general the right of the corporation to waive the lien at its option is absolute

Accordingly, where a note discounted for a shareholder was protested for non-payment, it was held that the bank might waive its lien on the stockholder's shares in the bank and proceed directly against the indorser[4] And the corporation, by waiving the lien, does not discharge a surety unless the surety has given the corporation express notice not to waive the lien[5] The corporation will not be held to have waived its lien upon the stock of its debtor merely because it has taken other or additional security for the debts,[6] nor because it assents to a general assignment by the shareholder for the benefit of creditors.[7] And the corporation may allow the transfer of a portion of a shareholder's stock without waiving its lien on the rest[8] But a waiver of the lien for a limited time is fatal, provided the stock is transferred during that time[9]

A waiver which will bind the corporation may, in the absence of something to qualify the power, be made by the cashier of a bank, acting by virtue of an express or implied authority, for the board

Lankershim, etc, Co v Herberger, 23 Pac Rep, 134 (Cal, 1890)

[1] National Bank v Watsontown Bank, 105 U. S, 217 (1881); S C, sub nom Cecil National Bank v Watsontown Bank, 21 Am Law Reg (N S.), 545 Hodges v Planters' Bank, 7 Gill & J, 306 (1835), Hall v United States Ins Co., 5 Gill (Md), 484 (1847); In re Hoy Lake R'y Co, L R., 9 Chan., 257, 259 (1874). But see Conant v Seneca Co Bank, 1 Ohio St., 298, 301 (1853); In re Bigelow, 1 Nat Bank Reg, 667 (1868). A waiver is the intentional relinquishment of a known right. It is not to be inferred and imputed to a corporation in the absence of proof of it, and a mere failure to assert the lien is not equivalent to a relinquishment or waiver of it First National Bank of Hartford v. Hartford, etc., Ins. Co, 45 Conn, 22, 44 (1877)

[2] Dunlop v Dunlop, L. R., 21 Ch D, 583 (1882)

[3] In re Bachman, 12 Nat. Bank Reg, 223 (1875).

[4] Cross v. Phenix Bank, 1 R. I, 39 (1840)

[5] Perrine v Fireman's Ins Co, 22 Ala, 575 (1853).

[6] Union Bank of Georgetown v Laud, 2 Wheat, 390 (1817)

[7] Dobbins v Walton, 37 Ga., 614 (1868)

[8] First National Bank of Hartford v Hartford, etc, Insurance Co, 45 Conn, 22 (1877) But cf Presbyterian Congregation v Carlisle Bank, 5 Pa St. 315 (1847).

[9] Thus, if within such time the stock is pledged for a debt, the right of the corporation, after the expiration of the time to acquire its charter lien, is subordinate to the right of the pledgee until the debt is paid or the pledge is released Bank of America v McNeil, 10 Bush (Ky), 54 (1873).

of directors,[1] or the secretary of an insurance company,[2] or the general manager or properly-qualified general agent of the corporation, especially if that is a general custom of the company.[3] Accordingly, where one buys shares on the faith of a representation of the corporate officers that the stock is unincumbered, he is entitled to the shares free from any corporate lien[4]

And where the corporate officers allow a transfer to be registered and a new certificate to be issued, there is a waiver of the corporate lien as to the debts of the transferrer.[5]

It is held that a failure to recite the lien on the face of the certificate is not a waiver of the lien,[6] and that a statement in the certificate that the holder is entitled to a certain number of shares, transferable upon presentation and surrender thereof, is not a waiver of the lien, though there be no assertion of the lien, but is a mere indication of the manner in which the shares are to be transferred[7] When the lien is given to the corporation by the charter or the articles of association, or by statute, there is constructive notice to all persons dealing with the corporation that they must at their peril, without reference to what the certificate recites or fails to recite, inform themselves as to any debts to the corporation that may affect the shares they propose to buy. If there is a lien they are held to have known it, whether the certificate declares it or not. As already explained, where the lien is created by a by-law it is something of which purchasers of the shares cannot be held to have had constructive notice. In such a case, if the certificate does not disclose the lien, and actual knowledge of it be shown, a *bona fide* purchaser would be protected. But the rule is otherwise where the lien is created by statute or the charter of the corporation[8]

---

[1] National Bank v Watsontown Bank, 105 U S, 217 (1881) So, also, the refusal of the cashier to permit a transfer is the act of the bank, for which it may be charged. Case v. Bank, 100 U. S, 446 (1879)

[2] Chambersburg Ins Co v Smith, 11 Pa. St. 120 (1849) *Cf* Kenton Ins Co v Bowman, 1 S. W. Rep, 717 (Ky., 1886)

[3] See Bishop v Globe Company, 135 Mass, 132 (1883), Young v Vough, 23 N. J Eq, 325 (1873)

[4] Moore v Bank of Commerce, 52 Mo, 377 (1873)

[5] Hill v Paine River Bank, 45 N H, 300 (1864), Higgs v Assam Tea Co, L.

R., 4 Exch, 387 (1869), *In re* Northern Assam Tea Co, L. R, 10 Eq, 458 (1870) So, also, a by-law requiring the consent of the board of directors to a transfer by one indebted to the corporation is held to be repealed where a custom of disregarding it has been shown, it appearing also that the secretary had been allowed to exercise his own discretion about such transfers without consulting the directors In such a case the consent of the secretary to the transfer is a waiver of the lien Chambersburg Ins Co v Smith, 11 Pa. St., 120 (1849).

[6] See § 523

[7] See § 523.

[8] Bank of Holly Springs v. Pinson,

§ 532 *The lien as affected by transfers and notice* — Upon a transfer of stock the title thereto passes absolutely as between transferrer and transferee, even though the corporation, in the assertion of a lien upon the stock for the indebtedness of the transferee, refuses to register the transfer until a certain debt is paid or secured [1] But of course the assignee or transferee, or whoever succeeds to the rights of the shareholder in the stock, takes it subject to the lien of the corporation [2] And when the stock is sold by the corporation to pay the debts of the transferrer, the transferee is entitled to the surplus, if any there be, which remains after the claim of the corporation is satisfied [3]

The corporation cannot, after it has been regularly notified of the transfer, assert a lien upon the stock to secure an indebtedness of the transferrer contracted subsequently to the notice [4] A mere notice to the bank is, in such a case, sufficient to protect the transferee. It is immaterial that the transfer was not registered [5] And in a case where the transfer was registered but no certificate had been issued, it was held that a pledgee was protected [6] But where

58 Miss, 421 (1880), Anglo-California Bank v Grangers' Bank. 63 Cal, 359 (1883) See § 523.

[1] National Bank v Watsontown Bank, 105 U S, 217 (1881), Johnson v Laflin, 103 id, 800 (1880), Fitzhugh v Bank of Shepherdsville, 3 Mon (Ky) 126 (1825), St. Louis Perpetual Life Ins Co v Goodfellow, 9 Mo, 149 (1845) Commercial Bank of Buffalo v Kortright, 22 Wend, 348 (1839), S C, sub nom Kortright v Buffalo Commercial Bank, 20 id, 91 (1838), Bank of Utica v Smalley, 2 Cowen, 770 (1824), McNeil v Tenth National Bank, 46 N Y, 325 (1871), People ex rel Krohn v Miller, 39 Hun, 557, 563 (1886) Cf Dunn v Commercial Bank of Buffalo, 11 Barb, 580, Merchants' Bank v Livingston, 74 N Y, 223 (1878), Pittsburgh, etc, R R Co v Clarke 29 Pa St, 146 (1857), Sargent v Essex Marine R y Corp, 26 Mass, 202 (1829), Carroll v Mullanphy Savings Bank, 8 Mo App, 249 (1880) Corporations having a statutory lien on stock for debts, nevertheless must allow transfer to one who takes subject to the corporate lien for part of the unpaid subscription Heidegen v Cotzhausen 36 N W Rep, 385 (Wis, 1888) The lien

attaches when a call is made and not when it becomes due Queen v London-derry, etc, R y, 13 Q B, 998 (1849)

[2] Mobile Mutual Ins, Co v Cullom, 49 Ala, 558 (1873), New Orleans National Banking Association v Wiltz, 4 Woods, 43 (1881), S C, 10 Fed Rep, 330

[3] Weston v Bear River, etc, Mining Co, 5 Cal, 186 (1855), Tuttle v Walton, 1 Ga (1846), Foster v Potter, 37 Mo, 325 (1866), West Branch Bank v Armstrong, 40 Pa St, 278 (1861).

[4] Conant v Seneca County Bank, 1 Ohio St 298 (1853), Nesmith v Washington Bank, 6 Pick, 324 (1828) The same rule applies where the stock is pledged Bradford, etc, Co v Briggs, 56 L T Rep, 63 (1886) But where the shareholder transfers his stock, and subsequently, without notifying the corporation of the transfer, borrows money from the corporation in regular course of business, the corporation may refuse to register the transfer and may insist upon the lien Platt v Birmingham Axle Co, 41 Conn, 255 (1874)

[5] Bank of America v McNeil, 10 Bush, 54 (1873)

[6] Cecil National Bank v. Watsontown

there is neither a register of the transfer nor notice of it served
upon the corporation, the stock may properly be subjected to a corporate lien for the indebtedness of the transferrer incurred subsequently to the transfer.[1] A pledgee who is duly registered on the
corporate books as a shareholder, but to whom no certificate has
been issued, is nevertheless protected against liens upon his shares
for the indebtedness of the pledgor.[2] But a pledgee who neglects
to notify the corporation that he holds the stock in pledge, or to
take the proper steps to secure title to the stock in his own name,
will not be protected against the lien of the corporation upon the
stock to secure the payment of an indebtedness contracted to the
bank by the pledgor in the meantime and subsequently to the
pledge of the shares[3] A corporate lien will not attach to stock
for the debts of a legatee unless the legatee accept the shares[4]

Where one pays a debt as surety for a shareholder, he is entitled
to be subrogated to the rights of the corporation by way of lien
on the shareholder's stock[5] And where the transferee pays the
transferrer's debt to the corporation in order to obtain a registry
of the transfer, he of course may have his action to recover back
from his transferrer the amount so paid[6]

Bank, 21 Am Law Reg (N S), 545
(1881), S C, sub nom National Bank
v Watsontown Bank, 105 U S, 217.

[1] Platt v Birmingham Axle Co, 41
Conn, 255 (1874) In England the rule
has been recently settled, after much
contest, that a provision in the articles
of association creating a paramount lien
on shares in favor of the corporation
gives the company priority over a mortgagee of the shares, or over one whose
claim is an equitable one, of whose
charge upon the shares the company
had notice before the specific liability
of the shareholder toward the company
has been incurred Bradford Banking
Co v Briggs, L R, 31 Chan Div, 19
(1885), S C, 53 L T Rep (N S), 846,
reversing S C, L R, 29 Chan. Div, 149
(1885). See, also, Miles v New Zealand
Alford Estate Company, 54 L J, Chan,
1035 (1885), S C, Week Notes (1885),
page 142, S. C, 53 L T Rep (N S),
219, Re Dunlop, 48 L T Rep (N S),
89 (1883), Societe Generale de Paris v.
Tramways Union Co, L R, 14 Q B.
Div, 424 (1884), New London & Brazilian Bank v Brocklebank, L R, 21

Chan Div, 302 (1882). In England,
however unrecorded transferees of
stock have few if any rights as against
the corporation; and this is the reason
for these decisions. Contra, Pitot v.
Johnson, 33 La. Ann, 1286 See § 377,
infra

[2] National Bank v Watsontown Bank,
105 U. S, 207 (1881)

[3] Platt v Birmingham Axle Co, 14
Conn, 255, 264 (1874), 21 Pac. Rep, 852
(Cal, 1889), Gemmell v. Davis, 23 Atl.
Rep., 1032 (Md, 1892)

[4] Farmers' Bank of Maryland v Iglehart, 6 Gill (Md), 50 (1847).

[5] Young v Vough 23 N J Eq, 325
(1873); Hodges v Planters' Bank, 7 Gill
& J, 306, 310 (1835), West Branch Bank
v Armstrong, 40 Pa. St, 278 (1861),
Klopp v Lebanon Bank, 46 id, 88 (1863).
Cf Higgs v Assam Tea Co, L R, 4
Exch, 387 (1869). In re Northern Assam
Tea Co, L. R. 10 Eq, 458 (1870); Na-
tional Exchange Bank v. Silliman, 65
N Y, 475 (1875).

[6] Bates v New York Ins. Co., 3 Johns.
Cas, 238 (1802). See, also, § 262, supra.

Where the company has a lien upon the stock of a shareholder, the latter may compel the company to assign their lien to a third person who will advance the money, and to whom the shares are at the same time transferred [1]

§ 533 *Liens on national bank stock* — National banks were formerly held to have power to enact by-laws creating a lien on stock in the bank for debts owed by its owner to the bank [2] But the supreme court of the United States, when the question came before it, refused to enforce such a by-law, and decided that its enactment was not within the spirit of those provisions of the National Banking Act of 1864 which confer power upon the management of a national bank to regulate the business of the bank and to conduct its affairs [3] In the present state of the law, therefore, no national bank can, by any by-law, create any lien upon shares of stock in the bank to secure the payment of any indebtedness which the owner of the shares may contract to the bank [4] This conclusion is in accord with the well settled policy of the federal courts to protect purchasers of certificates of stock against all secret dangers.

[1] Everitt v The Automatic, etc., Co, 67 L T Rep., 349 (1892).

[2] The leading case was Knight v The Old National Bank, 3 Clifford, 429 (1871), upholding the lien To the same effect see Lockwood v Mechanics' National Bank, 9 R I, 308 (1869), *In re* Dunkerson, 4 Biss, 227 (1868), Young v Vough, 23 N J Eq, 235 (1873)

[3] Bullard v. Bank, 18 Wall, 589 (1873) See, also, Bank v Lanier, 11 id, 369 (1870), Case v Bank, 100 U S, 446 (1879) The reason for denying this power to national banks is that they are prohibited from loaning money to stockholders on the security of their stock The decisions, therefore, do not militate against the general doctrine as above set forth

[4] Delaware, etc, R R Co v Oxford Iron Co 38 N J Eq, 340 (1884), Myers v Valley National Bank, 18 Nat Bank Reg, 34 (1878), Hagar v Union National Bank, 63 Me, 511 (1874), New Orleans National Bank v Wiltz, 10 Fed Rep, 330 (1881), S C, 4 Woods, 43, Goodbar v City Nat'l Bank, 14 S L

Rep, 851 (Tex, 1890), Second National Bank of Louisville v National State Bank of New Jersey, 10 Bush, 367 (1874); Lee v Citizens' National Bank, 2 Cin, 298, 306, Evansville National Bank v Metropolitan National Bank, 2 Biss, 527 (1871) In the case last cited, which upon appeal was affirmed by the supreme court of the United States, it was held that such a by-law was in its operation the same thing as though a loan were made by the bank upon the security of the stock — a transaction forbidden by the thirty-fifth section of the National Banking Act. Conklin v Second Nat'l Bank, 45 N Y, 655 (1871) Cf National Bank of Xenia v Stewart. 107 U S, 676 (1882), Rosenbach v Salt Springs National Bank, 53 Barb, 495 (1868) This accords with the more general rule in New York, which holds all such by-laws of any corporation in that state invalid See §§ 522, 525 A bank, however, may attach the stock of one of its stockholders for debts due from him to it Hagar v Union Nat'l Bank, *supra*.

CHAPTER XXXII.

DIVIDENDS.

§ 534 *Definition of a dividend and the four kinds of dividends.*— A dividend is a corporate profit set aside, declared and ordered by the proper corporate authorities to be paid to the stockholders on demand or at a fixed time[1] Until the dividend is declared these corporate profits belong to the corporation, not to the shareholders, and are liable for corporate indebtedness[2]

A corporation may, in general, make four different kinds of dividends namely, a dividend payable in cash, in stock, in bonds or scrip, or in property.

Dividends are declared by the directors and not by the stockholders[3] A division of profits without the formality of declaring a dividend is equivalent to a dividend[4]

---

[1] Lockhardt v Van Alstyne, 31 Mich 76 (1875), Chaffee v Rutland R. R. Co, 55 Vt., 110, 129 (1882), Hyatt v Allen, 56 N Y, 553 (1874).

[2] Goodwin v Hardy, 57 Me, 143, 145 (1869), Rand v Hubbell, 115 Mass, 461, 474 (1874), Minot v Paine, 99 id, 101 (1868), Hyatt v Allen *supra*, Mickles v Rochester, etc, Bank. 11 Paige, 118 (1844), holding that stockholders are

neither tenants in common nor copartners of corporate property

[3] See § 545, *infra*.

[4] Rorke r Thomas, 56 N Y, 559 (1874), Reading etc, Co. i Reading etc., Works, 21 Atl Rep, 170 (Pa, 1891); McKusick i Seymour, etc, Co, 50 N. W. Rep., 1116 (Minn, 1892) Where a fixed per cent is paid annually to stockholders instead of dividends and charged

Numerous cases on the definition of the word "dividend" have arisen in connection with the taxation of corporations.[1]

§ 535. *Scrip dividends, property dividends and bond dividends.—* A scrip dividend is a dividend of certificates giving the holder certain rights which are specified in the certificate itself. These dividends are usually declared when the company has profits which are not in the shape of money, but are in other forms of property, and the company wishes to anticipate the time when the property may be sold for cash, and the cash distributed by a money dividend The certificate sometimes entitles the holder to a sum of money payable with interest at a certain time after date, or at the option of the company, or when the company shall have accumulated sufficient surplus to pay the certificates in full. Sometimes the certificates are certificates of indebtedness and are made convertible at the option of the holder into bonds or stocks,[2] and sometimes the certificate entitles the holder to exchange the cer-

to them and the stock held in pledge for the same, such a payment to the life tenant does not create a valid lien on the stock as against the remainderman Reading, etc, Co. t Reading, etc, Works, 21 Atl Rep, 169 (Pa, 1891)

[1] A tax upon the receipts of a railroad is not a tax upon dividends Comm'rs, etc, v Buckner, 48 Fed Rep, 533 (1891) Profits applied to betterments are not ' dividends earned " within the meaning of a statute imposing taxation State v Comptroller 23 Atl Rep, 122 (N J, 1891) Where all the shares are reduced in par value from $50 to $38 and the $12 difference is paid to the stockholders in cash, this is a reduction of capital stock and not a dividend and cannot be taxed as a dividend Commonwealth v Central T Co, 22 Atl Rep, 209 (Pa, 1891) Where a tax is levied on dividends the officers cannot defend on the ground that the dividend was illegal Central Nat'l Bank v United States, 137 U S, 355 (1890). In Commonwealth t Pittsburg, etc, R'y, 74 Pa St., 83 (1873), a lessor company having twelve per cent. dividends guarantied on its stock declared a stock dividend so that the guarantee should be seven per cent on the stock thus increased The court held that such a dividend did not subject the com-

pany to a tax based on dividends In Louisiana taxes are assessed on franchises, the value of which is ascertained from the earning capacity of the corporation Crescent City R Co v City of New Orleans et al, 11 S Rep, 681 (La, 1892) New Orleans, etc, Co v City of New Orleans et al, 11 id, 687 (La., 1892); New Orleans City, etc, Co v City of New Orleans et al, 11 id, 820 (La., 1892)

[2] Chaffee t Rutland R R Co., 55 Vt., 110 (1882), State v Baltimore, etc., Co, 6 Gill (Md), 363 (1818) In the case of Rogers v New York, etc. Land Co, 134 N. Y., 197 (1892), land had been sold to the company for a certain amount of preferred stock and also a certain amount of "land scrip," such scrip entitling the holder to exchange them for land so conveyed at a price to be thereafter determined The company had the right to pay off the scrip and retire it. The company sold part of the land, and then proceeded to make a scrip dividend of the scrip so taken up by it A dissenting scripholder brought suit to undo the transaction on the ground that the scrip taken up by the company should be canceled The court sustained his action, and held that from the original contract it was clear that the land

tificate for lands of the corporation to an amount equivalent in value to the face value of the certificate; or to receive from the corporation any other benefit or advantage which the corporation may lawfully confer   Sometimes the certificate so far partakes of the character of a certificate of stock as to entitle the holder to dividends [1]   Where the corporation, having a large surplus, issues

was received as a trust fund to ultimately pay off the scrip   See, also, Rogers t Phelps, 9 N. Y Supp., 886

In the case of Brown v Lehigh, etc , Co. 49 Pa St., 270 (1865), a dividend of scrip had been declared, the scrip being as follows

"No ——   SCRIP   Shares.

"This is to certify that ——, —— heirs or assigns, will be entitled, upon the surrender of this certificate to —— shares in the capital stock of the Lehigh Coal and Navigation Company as soon as the present funded debt of the company has been paid off, or adequate provision made for its discharge when due and payment demanded, and will also be entitled to a *pro rata* share of any future distribution of scrip, but not to any cash dividend until this certificate has been converted into stock, as above provided

"Or, this certificate may, at any time, at the option of the holder thereof, be converted into stock upon payment by said holder, either in cash or in the six per cent loans of the company, of the par value of said stock, and the surrender of this certificate

‘ This certificate is transferable only at the office of the company.

"Witness, etc "

Several years after the issue, the mortgage being paid off, the scripholders claimed that they were entitled to back dividends equal to past dividends paid on the stock.   The court held, however, that the terms of the contract did not give any such right, and that dividends commenced only from the time the scrip was converted into stock.

The holder of a certificate of indebtedness convertible into stock cannot claim an interest in a stock dividend until he has converted the scrip into stock   Miller v Ill Central R. R., 24 Barb., 312 (1857), Brundage v Brundage, 63 Barb. 397 (1873), affirmed, 60 N. Y, 544 (1875), holding that assignable "interest certificates" representing earnings spent for improvements, and payable out of future earnings with dividends, or convertible into stock at the company's option, did not pass with a bequest of a life interest in certain shares of the stock   See, also, Butler v. Glen Cove, etc Co , 18 Hun, 47 (1879).   See § 283   Cf Bailey t Citizens' Gas Light Co., 27 N. J Eq, 196 (1876).   The court in this case, speaking of a dividend of interest-bearing securities, said: "That the company had no lawful authority for issuing the certificates cannot be doubted."

[1] Bailey t Railroad Co., 22 Wall., 604 (1874)   Cf Brundage v Brundage, 60 N Y, 544 (1875).

The character of the scrip in this case is shown by the resolution authorizing it, as follows

"Whereas, this company has hitherto expended of its earnings for the purpose of constructing and equipping its road, and in the purchase of real estate and other properties with a view to an increase of its traffic, moneys equal in amount to eighty per cent of the capital stock of the company, and whereas, the several stockholders of the company are entitled to evidence of such expenditure, and to reimbursement of the same at some convenient future period:

"Now, therefore, resolved, that a certificate signed by the president and treasurer of this company be issued to the stockholders severally, declaring that such stockholder is entitled to

such certificates, they are held not to transfer the title to that surplus from the corporation to the holders of the certificates [1] In general the issue of scrip dividends may be entirely lawful, and they are upheld by the courts; but when they are declared in fraud of the rights of third parties they may be set aside [2]

Scrip is practically the same thing as shares of stock, except that it has no voting power. It is issued sometimes because the company cannot issue any more capital stock, the whole capital stock

eighty per cent of the capital stock held by him payable ratably with the other certificates issued under this resolution, at the option of the company, out of its future earnings, with dividends thereon at the same rates and times as dividends shall be paid on the shares of the capital stock of the company, and that such certificates may be, at the option of the company, convertible into stock of the company, whenever the company shall be authorized to increase its capital stock to an amount sufficient for such conversion" This was the famous scrip dividend made by the New York Central R R Co under the management of Commodore Vanderbilt

The form of the certificate was as follows:

' THE NEW YORK CENTRAL RAILROAD COMPANY

"No. —— Interest Certificate

"Under a resolution of the board of directors of this company, passed December 19th, 1868, of which the above is a copy, the New York Central Railroad Company hereby certifies that A B., being the holder of —— shares of the capital stock of said company is entitled to —— dollars, payable ratably with the other certificates issued under said resolution, *at the pleasure of the company out of its future earnings*, with dividends thereon at the same rates and times as dividends shall be paid upon the shares of the capital stock of said company.

"This certificate may be transferred on the books of the company on the surrender of this certificate

"In witness whereof, the said company has caused this certificate to be signed by its president and treasurer, this 19th day of December, 1868

"—— ——,   President.
Treasurer "

At the foot of each certificate there was a form of transfer in blank

"For a valuable consideration I, A. B, do hereby sell, assign and transfer all interest in the above certificate to C D, and do hereby irrevocably appoint E F attorney, to execute a transfer thereof on the books of the railroad company therein mentioned "

See Bailey v Railroad, 22 Wall., 608. This dividend was declared although the company by its charter was limited to ten per cent. dividends

A dividend of scrip — i e, a paper entitling the holder to dividends equal to dividends thereafter declared on the capital stock — is practically a stock dividend, except that the scrip cannot vote and provision is generally made for taking it up in some manner Such a dividend was involved in Gordon's Ex'rs v Richmond, etc, R R, 78 Va, 501 (1884).

[1] People v Board of Assessors, 76 N Y, 202 (1879), affirming S C, 16 Hun, 196 In this case it was held that the issue of these certificates could not operate to relieve the corporation from their obligations to pay their tax upon the surplus, because the surplus remained in the hands of the company, and as such was liable to assessment and taxation See, also, Bailey v Railroad Co, 22 Wall. 604 (1874)

[2] While negotiations were pending between two gas companies for their con-

being already out, sometimes to avoid taxes, and sometimes to increase the transferable shares without giving to the new shares a voting power If the interest or dividends are payable only from the profits, the issue of the scrip is legal whenever a stock dividend would be legal, that is, whenever the property of the company is equal in value to the capital stock plus the scrip dividend

A property dividend is where property is divided instead of that property being sold for cash and the cash then used to pay a dividend A property dividend occurs where a corporation sells all its property to another corporation and takes in payment thereof the stock and the bonds of the purchasing corporation and then makes a distribution of the same among its stockholders. Any one of its stockholders may object and insist on payment of his shares in cash[1] This, however, is practically a dissolution of the company and a distribution of its assets, a subject which is considered elsewhere[2]

A dividend or distribution of the company's bonds among its stockholders is legal, if the capital stock is not thereby impaired and if corporate creditors existing at that time do not object.[3]

In the absence of a special provision to the contrary, dividends will be presumed to be payable in cash, and in lawful or current money[4] But where the dividend is paid in depreciated currency, a stockholder cannot insist that he shall be paid any more than what the depreciated currency is worth in regular currency.[5]

§ 536. *Stock dividends* — A stock dividend, as the name imports, is a dividend of the stock of the corporation Such a dividend is lawful when an amount of money or property equivalent in value

solidation by one company buying the stock of the other, upon a certain basis of capital and indebtedness, one of them without the knowledge of the other passed a resolution declaring a scrip dividend of ten per cent on its capital stock, thus increasing its indebtedness by that amount The certificates were accordingly issued, but after the consolidation, upon a bill filed for that purpose, the scrip was declared void Bailey v Citizens' Gas Light Co., 27 N J Eq. 196 (1876).

[1] See § 667, *infra*

[2] See § 548, *infra*

[3] See ch XLVI, *infra*.

[4] Ehle v Chittenango Bank, 24 N Y., 548 (1862).

[5] Back dividends may be recovered on stock which has been illegally confiscated; but where the dividends to other stockholders were paid in Confederate currency, the back dividends paid after the war to a northern stockholder are a sum equal in value to the Confederate currency when the dividends were declared Keppel's Adm'r v Petersburg R. R., Chase's Dec., 167 (1868), Scott v Central Railway, etc Co, of Georgia, 52 Barb, 45 (1868) In this case two of the three judges held that though the dividends were declared without specifying how they should be paid, yet where they were paid as a matter of fact in depreciated Confederate currency, a northern stockholder could not after the war, claim the same dividends payable in United States currency.

to the full par value of the stock distributed as a dividend has been accumulated and is permanently added to the capital stock of the corporation   Corporations frequently make a dividend of this character when improvements of the corporate property or extensions of the business have been made out of the profits earned   It is also made when the corporate plant has increased in value and it seems better to issue new stock to represent the excess of value than to sell the increase and declare a cash dividend.   In this country these dividends are frequently made and are constantly sustained by the courts.[1] The shareholders, having voted to declare such a dividend, may, at any time before the certificates are issued, reconsider the matter and revoke the dividend [2] Preferred stockholders are entitled to share in the distribution of stock by a stock dividend according to the terms of their preferred stock [3] In some of the states a stock dividend is prohibited by statute or constitutional provision [4]

§ 537 *Interest-bearing stock* — It has already been shown that a corporation may issue stock and make a contract with the subscriber that the company will pay interest upon the sums paid in by the subscriber [5] Such a contract is legal, however, only

---

[1] Williams v Western Union Telegraph Co 93 N Y, 162 188 *et seq* (1883), City of Ohio v Cleveland, etc, R. R. Co, 6 Ohio St, 489 (1856), Howell v Chicago, etc, R. R. Co, 51 Barb, 378 (1868), Clarkson v Clarkson, 18 id 646 (1855), Simpson v Moore, 30 id, 637 (1859), Gordon's Executor v Richmond, etc, R R Co, 78 Va, 501, 521 (1884), Minot v Paine, 99 Mass, 101 (1868), Boston etc, R. R. Co v Commonwealth, 100 id, 399 (1868), Deland v Williams, 101 id, 571 (1869), Rand v Hubbell, 115 id, 461, 474 (1874), Gibbons v Mahon, 4 Mackey, 130 (1885), Jones v Morrison 31 Minn, 140 (1883), Earp's Appeal, 28 Pa St, 368 (1857), Wiltbank's Appeal, 64 id, 256 (1870), Commonwealth v Pittsburgh, etc, R R Co, 74 id, 83 (1873), Brown v Lehigh Coal & Nav Co, 49 Pa St, 270 (1865), Commonwealth v Cleveland, etc, R R, 29 id, 370 (1857), Parker v Mason, 8 R I, 427 (1867), State v Baltimore, etc, R. R. Co, 6 Gill (Md), 363 (1847) See Harris v. San Francisco, etc, 41 Cal, 393 (1871), holding that one who is entitled to and receives a stock dividend cannot claim also a part of the cash profits which are used for improvements, even though a contract calls for cash See, also § 51, *supra*, and ch XXXIII. *infra* In England a stock dividend has been declared to be *ultra vires* so far as dissenting stockholders are concerned It cannot be forced upon a stockholder Hoole v Great Western R'y, L R, 3 Ch 262 (1867) In the case Re The Eastern etc, Co, 68 L T Rep, 321 (1893), a stock dividend was involved, but its legality was not passed upon It is discretionary with the directors as to whether they will declare a stock or a cash dividend Howell v Chicago etc, R'y, 51 Barb 378 (1868)

[2] Terry v. Eagle Lock Co, *supra* After cancellation there is no statutory liability on such stock Hollingshead v Woodward, 35 Hun, 410 (1885).

[3] Gordon's Executors v Richmond, etc., R. R. Co, 78 Va., 501 (1884). See, also Phillips v Eastern R R Co, 138 Mass., 122 (1881) See, also, ch XVI

[4] See §§ 51, 287, *supra*.

[5] See ch XVI, *supra*.

when the interest is to be paid from the net profits of the enterprise, and not from the capital stock Unless net profits have been earned the stipulated interest cannot legally be paid Consequently there is little difference between interest-bearing stock and preferred stock.

§ 538 *To whom the corporation is to pay the dividend* — The question as to whom a dividend shall be paid after it has been regularly declared is one which sometimes involves the corporation in considerable difficulty. It is not always easy to decide which one of two or more claimants is entitled to the dividend.

The general rule is that the corporation may pay the dividend to the person in whose name the stock stands registered upon the corporate stock book at the time the dividend is declared[1] It may do so without inquiring whether he has transferred the stock, and without requiring the production of the certificate.[2] Moreover, it is a well-settled rule that the corporation is protected in paying dividends to a recorded shareholder, although he may have transferred his shares, no notice of the transfer having been given to the company[3] But after notice of a transfer the corporation may pay the dividend to the transferee, although no registry has been made[4] And between two claimants of the dividend, one

[1] Brisbane v Delaware, etc, R. R. Co., 94 N Y 204 (1883), affirming 25 Hun, 438 (1881), Jones v. Terre Haute, etc R R. Co 29 Barb, 358 (1859), affirmed, 57 N Y, 196, Northrup v Newton, etc, Turnpike Co, 3 Conn, 544 (1821) *Cf* Manning v Quicksilver Mining Co, 24 Hun, 360 (1881), in regard to the assignment of dividends The guaranty accumulations of an insurance company conducted both on the mutual and stock principle belong to the stockholders and not to the policy-holders Traders', etc, Ins Co. v Brown 112 Mass, 403 (1886) As to dividends on a tontine insurance policy, see Pierce v Equitable Life Assurance Co, 115 id, 56 (1887) As to a dividend by way of redeeming stock in a building association, see Appeal of Mechanics, etc, Ass n, 7 Atl Rep, 728 (Pa, 1887).

[2] Brisbane v Delaware etc, R R Co, 94 N. Y, 204 (1883), affirming 25 Hun, 433, Cleveland, etc R. R. Co v Robbins, 35 Ohio St, 483 (1880)

[3] Bank of Commerce's Appeal, 73 Pa St., 59 (1873), where a distribution of assets was made, Bell v. Lafferty, 1 Pa Sup Court, 454 (1881), where the assignee of a dividend without a certificate obtained payment, and the court held the company not liable to an unrecorded pledgee, Bank of Utica v Smaller, 2 Cowen, 770 (1824), Smith v American Coal Co, 7 Lans, 317 (1873); Jones & Cleveland, etc, R. R. Co v Robbins, 35 Ohio St., 483 (1880), the corporation not having been notified

[4] Id The corporation is liable to a transferee for dividends declared after a registry has been requested and improperly refused Robinson v National Bank, 95 N Y, 637 In Central Neb., etc, Bank v Wilder, 49 N W. Rep, 369 (Neb., 1891), it was held that not only was the pledgee entitled to the dividends, but was entitled to them although the stock stood on the corporate books in the name of the pledgor, where the officers knew all about the pledge. The corporation is liable to a pledgee to whom the stock has been transferred on

being the *cestui que trust* and the other a *bona fide* transferee, the corporation may interplead [1]

The right to dividends does not, however, depend upon the issue of the certificate, and the owner of shares may claim his dividends though no certificate has ever been issued by the corporation [2] The corporation is protected if it pay dividends to the administrator without notice of a transfer by him [3]

With respect to the dividends on the stock of a married woman, the corporation must pay them to the husband or not, according to the law of the domicile of the corporation, and not according to the law of the domicile of the married woman.[4] The husband by collecting dividends on his wife's shares does not thereby reduce the stock to possession.[5]

Even though the corporation closes its transfer-book several days before a dividend is declared, nevertheless those are entitled to the dividend who apply for registry on or before the day of the declaration of the dividend [6]

If the holder of a certificate of stock has applied for transfer and been refused, he may sue for the dividend before bringing a suit in equity to obtain a transfer of his stock [7]

the books for dividends paid to the pledgor The acceptance of part payment, etc, by the pledgee from the pledgor does not waive his cause of action against the company Boyd v Conshohocken Worsted Mills, 24 Atl Rep. 287 (Pa., 1892)

[1] Salisbury Mill v Townsend, 109 Mass, 115 (1871), Cross v Eureka, etc, Co, 73 Cal, 302 (1887), a case between pledgor and pledgee. See, also, § 387 Cf Stowe v Reed, 25 N E Rep., 49 (Mass, 1890), where a corporate creditor sued the treasurer for distributing property among the stockholders A corporation cannot interplead as between stockholders for the purpose of determining the ownership of stock, there having been no claim made upon it in regard to registry or in regard to dividends It must be shown also that the company has not acted in a partisan manner as between the different claimants. Hinkley v. Pfister, 63 N W Rep, 21 (Wis, 1892).

[2] Ellis v Proprietors of Essex Merrimack Bridge, 19 Mass., 243 (1824)

[3] Brisbane v. Delaware, etc., R. R. Co, 94 N. Y, 204 (1883) The heirs of a stockholder must, in order to entitle themselves to dividends, procure a transfer of their ancestor's shares into their own names on the corporate books where the certificates have been pledged and the company notified State v. New Orleans, etc, R R Co, 30 La Ann, 308 (1878)

[4] Graham v First Nat'l Bank of Norfolk, 84 N Y, 393 (1881) affirming S C, 20 Hun 325 As to the rule in California, see Dow v Gould & Curry Silver Mining Co, 31 Cal, 629 (1867)

[5] Burr v. Sherwood 3 Bradf (N Y Surrogate) 85 (1854) Cf Harcum v Hudnall 14 Gratt, 369, 382 (1858), Searing v Searing, 9 Paige, 283 (1841). A receipt of dividends by the husband only reduces the dividends into possession and not the stock See § 319

[6] Jones v Terre Haute, etc R R. Co, 57 N Y, 196, 205 (1874) Robinson v. National Bank, supra Frequently, however, the charter or statutes provide otherwise

[7] Hill v Atoka, etc, Co, 21 S W Rep. 508 (Mo, 1893).

§ 539　*To whom the dividend belongs* — As between the vendor and vendee of shares of stock, it is a settled rule that the vendee is entitled to all the dividends on the stock which are declared after the sale of the stock. Even though the transfer has not been recorded the transferee has a right to the dividends as against the transferrer The law, moreover, refuses to investigate the question when the dividend was earned In contemplation of law the net profits are earned at the instant the dividend is declared This rule is just, inasmuch as the accrued profits and expected dividends enter into the value and price at which the stock is sold [1]

A transfer of stock passes, of course, all dividends declared subsequently to the transfer, although the dividend was earned before the transfer was made [2]

[1] Jermain t Lake Shore, etc R. R. Co, 91 N Y, 483, March t Railroad Co, 43 N H, 515, 520 (1862), Ryan r Leavenworth etc R R Co, 21 Kan, 365, 403 (1879) Foot t Worthington, 39 Mass, 299 (1839) Jones r Terre Haute, etc, R R Co, 57 N Y, 196 (1874), Currie r White, 45 id, 822 (1871), Brundage r Brundage, 65 Barb, 397, 408 (1873), affirmed, 60 N Y, 544. Goodwin t Hardy, 57 Me 143 (1869) Hill t Newichawanick Co 8 Hun, 459 (1876), affirmed, 71 N Y, 593 (1877) Bates t McKinley, 31 L J, Chan 389 (1862) King r Follet 3 Vt, 385 (1831), Abercrombie t Riddle 3 Md Ch, 320 (1850) See, also, ch XXXIII Cf Kane t Bloodgood 7 Johns Ch, 90 (1823) A person who guaranties to another a dividend and is obliged to pay it himself cannot claim a subsequent dividend by way of reimbursement. Parks r Automatic, etc, Co (Super Ct) N Y Daily Reg, May 12, 1888 A dividend declared after the certificates have been sold belongs to the transferee as against the transferrer Gemmell r Davis, 23 Atl Rep 1032 (Md, 1892), approving the text herein Where stock is sold at auction on August 1 and a deposit paid, the balance to be paid August 29 a dividend declared on August 24 belongs to the purchaser Black t Homersham, L R 4 Ex D, 24 (1878) Where a company purchases shares of its own stock and subsequently uses it to declare a stock divi-

dend, a stockholder who sold part of his stock in the interim is entitled to the dividend on only such stock as he owned when the dividend was declared Coleman t Columbia Oil Co, 51 Pa. St, 74 (1865) Where defendant purchased stock for the plaintiff and accounted therefor, but refused to account for dividends received while he held the stock, the defendant is guilty of conversion Shaughnessy r Chase, 7 State Rep, 293 Although the purchaser of stock is entitled to a dividend declared after the contract of sale is made, even though the contract has not yet been carried out, yet the purchasers cannot insist on the vendor's giving an order on the corporation for such dividends. The vendee should collect without such order. He rescinds the sale by insisting on such order Phinizy r Murray, 10 S E. Rep, 358 (Ga, 1889) An alleged vendee's suit for a dividend is res judicata as to a suit to the stock Shepard r Stockham, 25 Pac Rep 559 (Kan, 1891)

[2] Kane t Bloodgood 7 Johns Ch, 90 (1823), by Chancellor Kent, Goodwin r Hardy 57 Me, 143 (1869); March r Eastern R R Co, 43 N H, 515 (1862), Phelps r Farmers' & Mechanics' Bank, 26 Conn, 269 (1857), Brundage r Brundage, 1 Thomp & C, 82, aff'd, 60 N Y, 544 (1875), Jones v Terre Haute, etc., R R Co, 57 N Y, 196 (1874), Currie v. White, 45 id., 822 (1871) And a purchaser of stock at a tax sale, if the pro-

When a dividend is made payable on a day subsequent to the day on which it is formally declared, it belongs to the stockholder who owns the shares on the day the dividend is declared, and not to the owner at the time it is payable.[1]

Where stock is bought deliverable at the seller's option, the dividends declared between the day of the purchase and the delivery belong to the purchaser.[2] But a contract to sell on demand entitles the vendor to dividends declared before the demand is made.[3] But of course any agreement between vendor and vendee, modifying or changing this rule, will be upheld. It is a proper subject for a contract, and a valid contract may be made in reference to it.[4]

A legatee of shares takes the stock as it was at the time of the testator's death. All dividends declared previous to that event go to the administrator.[5]

ceedings are legal and regular, is entitled to a certificate and to dividends subsequently declared. Smith *z* Northampton Bank, 58 Mass, 1 (1849).

[1] Wheeler *v* Northwestern S Co, 39 Fed Rep, 347 (1889), Wright *z* Tuckett, 1 Johns & H, 266 (1860), De Gendre *z* Kent, L R, 4 Eq 283 (1867), Hill *v* Newichawanick Co 71 N. Y, 593 (1877), affirming S C 8 Hun, 159, 48 How Prac, 427 (1874). Spear *z* Hart, 3 Robertson, 420 (1865). Bright *z* Lord, 51 Ind, 272 (1875), where an option had been given. *Cf* Hopper *v* Sage, 112 N Y, 530 (1889), Manning *v* Quicksilver Mining Co, 24 Hun 360 (1881), Boardman *z* Lake Shore, etc, R R Co, 84 N Y, 157, 178 (1881), *Re* Kernochan, 104 N Y, 618 (1887), Clive *z* Clive, Kay (Eng Chan), 600 (1854). *Contra* Burroughs *z* North Carolina R. R. Co, 67 N C, 376 (1872). The transfer of stock does not transfer past stock dividends which have been declared, even though the stock dividend has not been actually delivered. City of Ohio *z* Cleveland etc, R R, 6 Ohio St, 489 (1856). See, also, ch XVI. Where a pledge of stock is renewed and a new note given, dividends accruing before the renewal go to the pledgor. Fairbank *v* Merchants', etc., Bank, 22 N E. Rep, 524 (Ill, 1889).

[2] Currie *v* White, 45 N Y, 822 (1871),

Black *r* Homersham, L R, 4 Ex D 24 (1878). Under a contract of a person to buy certain stock within a certain time if the other party desired to sell (a "put"), the first person reserving all dividends "declared during the time," a dividend declared before but payable during the time of the option belongs to the seller. Hopper *z* Sage, 112 N Y, 530 (1889). *Contra*, Harris *r* Stevens, 7 N H 454 (1835).

[3] Bright *r* Lord, 51 Ind, 272 (1875).

[4] Brewster *z* Lathrop, 15 Cal, 21 (1860), Hyatt *v* Allen, 56 N Y, 553 (1874), Union Screw Co *v* Amer, etc Co, 11 R I, 569 (1877), affirmed 13 R I, 673 (1880), in which it was held that where a contract between two corporations for the purchase of the stock of one of them on a certain day was by agreement postponed to a later day, a dividend declared in the interval belonged to the purchaser. Where the vendor of stock reserves "one-half of whatever price the same should be sold for, when sold, over and above that sum," he is not entitled to an account of dividends, or other income received by the vendee from or on account of the stock. Jones *v* Kent, 80 N Y., 585 (1880).

[5] Brundage *r* Brundage, 60 N Y, 544 (1875), *Re* Kernochan, 104 N. Y., 618

The question of whether a dividend is apportionable is considered elsewhere [1]

A person who claims to be the owner of stock cannot establish his rights in a court by suing the party in possession of the stock for the dividends declared and paid [2]

§ 540 *Dividends must be equal and without preferences* — Dividends among stockholders of the same class must be always *pro rata*, equal and without preference   If the company has issued preferred stock, the holders thereof constitute a class for themselves, and shareholders of that class will be entitled, as a class, to dividends in preference to holders of the common stock.   But as between shareholders of the same class there can be no discrimination, and profits set aside for dividends must be evenly divided among the stockholders according to the amount of stock each one owns [3]   Accordingly there can be no lawful discrimination in the division of dividends, although the subscription price of part of the

(1887), where it was payable after the testator's death   Cf Johnson r Bridgewater Iron Mfg Co, 14 Gray 274 (1859), § 301.   The profits and surplus funds of a corporation whenever they may have accrued are, until separated from the capital by the declaring of a dividend a part of the stock itself, and will pass under that name in a transfer or bequest   Phelps r Farmers' & Mechanics' Bank, 26 Conn, 269 (1857)   Cf Clapp r Astor, 2 Edw Chan, 379 (1834)   In regard to the rights of a life tenant of stock as against a remainder-man, see chapter XXXIII

[1] See § 558, *infra*

[2] Peckham r Van Wagenen, 83 N Y, 40 (1880)   Conversion lies for an unauthorized sale of stock and also for dividends received thereon   Shaughnessy v Chase, 7 State Rep, 293 (Supr Ct 1887).

[3] Luling r Atlantic Mutual Ins. Co, 45 Barb, 510 (1865), where part were paid in gold, Jones r Terre Haute etc, R. R. Co, 57 N Y, 196 (1874), affirming 29 Barb., 353 (1859)   Morgan r Great Eastern R'y, 1 Hem & M, 500 (1863), Ryder r Alton, etc, R. R Co, 13 Ill, 516 (1851), a case of preferred stock, State v Baltimore, etc, R. R. Co, 6 Gill, 363 (1847), where some were paid in

cash and others were offered part cash and part stock, Atlantic, etc, Telegraph Co r Commonwealth, 3 Brewster (Pa.), 366 (1870), where a tax was levied on the assumption of an equal dividend to all   Hale r Republican River Bridge Co 8 Kan 466 (1871), where by mistake a stockholder got more land scrip than was his share, Jackson's Adm'rs v Newark Plank road Co., 31 N J Law, 277 (1865)   Cf Chase r Vanderbilt, 62 N Y, 307 (1875)   Holder of receipt under re-organization, entitling him to preferred stock in the new company, is entitled to dividends declared before he obtains the certificates.   Ellsworth v. New York etc R. R., 33 Hun, 7, aff'd, 98 N Y, 618.   See, also, Coey v. Belfast, etc, R'y Co (Irish Rep.), 2 C L, 112 (1866), Harrison r Mexican R'y Co., L. R., 19 Eq, 358 (1875), preferred stock cases.   As to preferred stock, see ch XVI   Although dividends are guaranteed to a certain date and are paid, the stock is entitled to participate in all subsequent dividends.   Parks r Automatic, etc, Co, 14 N Y St Rep, 710 (1888).   If a stockholder by accepting the benefits assents to a change in the privileges which pertain to his stock, he cannot afterwards object thereto   Compton v. Chelsea, 13 N. Y. Supp., 722 (1891).

stock is due and unpaid,[1] or because the contract work has not
been done,[2] nor can there be a discrimination between the large
and small stockholders of a company as to the manner of payment
of dividends[3] After paying a dividend to a part of the shareholders the corporation cannot refuse to pay the rest upon the
ground that by so doing the capital stock will be impaired,[4] or
that all the surplus earnings have been either paid out as dividends
or invested in permanent improvements[5]

A bill in equity may be maintained by a stockholder to prevent
an unequal or unfair distribution of the profits of the company,[6]
and for an injunction to restrain a dividend when stock has been
fraudulently overissued, until a true list of the holders of genuine
stock can be obtained[7]

§ 541. *A dividend when declared is a debt due absolutely to the
shareholder* — When a dividend out of the earnings of the company
has been regularly declared and is due it becomes immediately the
individual property of the shareholder. There is, *eo instanti*, a

---

[1] Oakbank Oil Co *t* Crum L R, 8
App, 65 (1882) Where a subscription
for stock is paid up, the stockholder is
entitled to his stock and past dividends,
even though for thirty years he has
slept upon his rights Kobogum *v*
Jackson Iron Co, 43 N W Rep, 602
(Mich, 1889), Bedford County *t* Nashville, etc, R. R., 14 Lea (Tenn), 525
(1884).

[2] Although stock is issued to contractors before they are entitled to it, yet
they are entitled to the dividends on
such stock unless there was some agreement to the contrary Central R. R.,
etc, *v.* Papot, 59 Ga, 342 (1877), S C,
sub nom Southwestern R. R. *v* Papot,
67 Ga, 675 690 (1881)

[3] Accordingly where a dividend was
declared, viz, to all stockholders owning less than fifty shares, cash, but to
all of fifty shares and over part cash
and part in interest-bearing bonds of
the corporation, the discrimination was
held invalid and unlawful State *v*
Baltimore, etc. R. R. Co, 6 Gill, 363
(1848), Jones *t* Terre Haute, etc R. R.
Co, 57 N Y, 196 (1874) So, also, where
a part of the authorized capital stock
remained untaken, and a resolution of
the directors was carried into effect, by

which the untaken portion of the stock
was issued to those shareholders not in
arrears upon shares previously taken,
to the exclusion, as to the new shares,
of those in arrears upon the original
issue, it was held an invalid discrimination and an unlawful imposition of a
penalty upon those in arrears Reese *t.*
Bank of Montgomery County, 31 Pa St,
78 (1857).

[4] Stoddard *t* Shetucket Foundry Co,
34 Conn, 542 (1868). The validity of a
dividend cannot be called into question
by a bank in a suit to collect taxes on
such dividend. Central Nat l Bank *v.*
United States, 137 U S, 355 (1890).

[5] Beers *t* Bridgeport Spring Co., 42
Conn, 17 (1875).

[6] Luling *v* Atlantic Mutual Ins. Co.,
45 Barb, 510 (1865) The minority may
bring the officers to an accounting for
an unfair distribution of the bonds, etc,
owned by a construction company
Meyers *v* Scott, 2 N Y Supp, 753
(1888) Or the stockholder may sue at
law for an equal dividend. See § 542.

[7] Underwood *v* New York, etc., R. R.
Co, 17 How Prac, 537 (1859), a case
growing out of the Schuyler frauds in
New York.

severance, for the use and benefit of the members of the corporation, of so much of the accumulated earnings as are declared; and the dividend thereafter exists as a separate fund, distinct from the capital stock or surplus profits. It then becomes the absolute property of the stockholders [1]

Accordingly, whenever a dividend is regularly declared and credited to a depositor it becomes his property, to which he is entitled in preference to the creditors of the corporation [2] If the funds to pay a dividend are placed by the corporation on deposit at a bank or elsewhere, the deposit is made and remains at the risk of the corporation and not of the shareholders, until a reasonable time after actual notice is given to the latter.[3] But it cannot be withdrawn and reclaimed either by the corporation or a receiver of the corporation, since the shareholders acquire, by virtue of the declaration of the dividend, a lien in equity upon the deposit [4] And the shareholders' right to a dividend regularly declared, and to the fund set apart by the corporation to pay the dividend, is not affected by the subsequent insolvency of the corporation [5] But where no specific fund has been set aside, a shareholder not having claimed or received his dividend has, upon the insolvency of the corporation, merely a claim of debt against the corporation, and must come in and fare as the other creditors do.[6] A dividend is

---

[1] Van Dyck r McQuade, 86 N Y, 38 (1881), Jermain r Lake Shore, etc, R. R. Co, 91 id, 483 (1883), Keppul's Adm'r r Petersburg R R. Co, Chase s Dec, 167 (1868), King z Paterson, etc, R R Co, 29 N J Law, 82, 504 (1860), Hill r Newichawanick Co. 71 New York Rep, 593 (1877), affirming S C, 8 Hun, 459 (1876), Brundage r Brundage 60 N Y, 544 (1875), affirming S C, 65 Barb, 397 (1873), Spear r Hart, 3 Robertson. 420 (1865), Manning r Quicksilver Co, 24 Hun, 360, Bloodgood r Kain, 7 Johns Ch, 90, Beers r Bridgeport Spring Co, 42 Conn, 17 (1875), Fawcett r Laurie, 1 Drew & Sm, 192 (1860), Matter of Le Blanc, 14 Hun, 8 (1878). Upon the latter point compare People r Merchants' and Mechanics' Bank, 78 N Y, 269 (1879) Dividends on life insurance policies when once declared cannot be varied by the company subsequently Heusser r. Continental, etc, Ins Co, 20 Fed Rep, 222 (1884). Execution or garnishee process cannot be levied on stock held by an individual as trustee, where the debt is his individual debt. Nor can it be levied on the dividend from such stock So held where stock was owned by a city in trust for the citizens. Hitchcock z Galveston W Co, 50 Fed Rep, 263 (1880).

[2] Van Dyck v. McQuade, 86 N Y, 38 (1881), Peckham r Van Wagener, 83 N Y, 40 A dividend declared and ordered deposited to the order of the stockholders and so held until the further order of the court is legal and the amount cannot be taxed as belonging to the bank Pollard v. First Nat'l Bank, 28 Pac Rep, 202 (Kan, 1891).

[3] King r Paterson, etc, R R Co, 29 N J Law, 82, 504 (1860)

[4] Matter of Le Blanc, 14 Hun, 8 (1878); aff'd, 75 N Y, 598, Beers v. Bridgeport Spring Co, 42 Conn, 17 (1875)

[5] Le Roy r Globe Insurance Co, 2 Edw. Chan, 657 (1836).

[6] Lowne v. American Fire Insurance

something distinct and separable from the fund upon which it is declared, and it may be the subject of assignment by a shareholder before it is received from or declared by the corporation.[1] So it is held that a dividend must be made payable within a reasonable time after it is declared, and when once declared cannot be be revoked[2] But where the fact that a dividend has been voted by directors is not made public, or communicated to the stockholders, and no fund is set apart for payment, the vote may be rescinded.[3] Not only must the time of payment be reasonable, but a reasonable place of payment must be designated, and the entire transaction must be in good faith[4]

§ 542 *It is a debt which may be collected by legal proceedings* — The debt which the corporation owes its shareholders, when a dividend is declared and the day of payment arrives, is one which may be collected by the usual action at law. A suit to enforce the declaration of a dividend must be in equity but when the dividend is not paid after it has been regularly declared, the shareholder's action is at law, and he may sue in *assumpsit* for the amount due him by the resolution declaring the dividend,[5] or he

Co, 6 Paige, 482 (1837), Curry v Woodward, 44 Ala, 305 (1870)

[1] Marten v Gibbon, 33 L. T Rep (N S), 561 (1875) Cf Jermain v Lake Shore, etc, R R Co, 91 N Y, 483 (1883) Bargains in prospective dividends are transactions which, by rule 61 of the stock exchange, the committee will not recognize or enforce The contract is, however, one which is not contrary to law, and it is good between the parties Marten v Gibbon, *supra*

[2] Beers v Bridgeport Spring Co, 42 Conn, 17 (1875).

[3] Ford v Easthampton, etc., Co, 32 N E Rep, 1036 (Mass, 1893)

[4] King v Paterson, etc, R R Co, 29 N J Law, 82 (1860).

[5] Jackson's Adm'rs v Newark Plankroad Co, 31 N J Law, 277 (1865), West Chester, etc, R R Co v Jackson, 77 Pa St, 321 (1875), Coey v Belfast, etc, R'y Co, Irish Rep, 2 C L, 112 (1866), King v Paterson, etc, R R Co. 29 N J Law, 504 (1860), Stoddard v Shetucket Foundry Co. 34 Conn, 542 (1868), Hall v Rose Hill, etc, Co, 70 Ill, 673 (1873), City of Ohio v Cleveland, etc R R Co, 6 Ohio St, 489 (1856), Marine Bank of Baltimore v Biays, 4 Har & J, 338 (1818) State v Baltimore, etc, R R Co, 6 Gill, 363 (1847), Kane v Bloodgood, 7 Johns Chan, 90 132 (1823), Jones v Terre Haute, etc, R R Co., 57 N Y, 196 (1874), Fawcett v Laurie, 1 Drew & Sm, 192 202 (1860), Dalton v Midland Counties R'y Co, 13 C. B, 474 (1853), Scott v Central Railroad, etc, Co of Georgia, 52 Barb, 45 (1868) See Beers v Bridgeport Spring Co, 42 Conn, 17 (1875), sustaining a remedy in equity But if a shareholder is not entitled to share in the dividend according to the terms of the resolution declaring it, he cannot have his action of *assumpsit* State v Baltimore, etc, R R Co, 6 Gill, 363 (1848) In suing for a dividend the plaintiff must allege that the dividend has been declared Hill v Atoka, etc, Co, 21 S W Rep 508 (Mo, 1893). Where a dividend has been paid to all stockholders except one, he may collect his by a suit Southwestern, etc, R'y v Martin, 21 S. W. Rep., 465 (Ark., 1893)

may file a bill in equity for an accounting[1]　But *mandamus* is not a proper remedy in such a case[2]

§ 543. A contract of directors to pay a dividend as a debt at fixed intervals, being in reality a preferred dividend. cannot be enforced either at law or in equity, except out of net profits lil o other dividends.[3] A demand is necessary before the action at law by the shareholder can be maintained[4]

It has been held, however, that the commencement of the suit constitutes in itself a sufficient demand[5] Under ordinary circumstances interest is not recoverable upon dividends which have been declared, but which the shareholder has not claimed. The right to interest arises only upon a demand and a refusal to pay.[6] The statute of limitations begins to run only after demand[7]

[1] Keppel's Adm'rs r Petersburg R R. Co Chase's Dec. 167 (1868) This is the usual remedy where preferred stockholders sue to have a dividend declared See ch XVI

[2] Van Norman r Central Car, etc, Co, 41 Mich 166 (1879) But see *dicta* in King r Paterson, etc, R R, 29 N J L, 504 (1861), and Ie Roy t Globe Ins Co, 2 Edw Ch, 677

[3] Painesville, etc, R R. Co t King 17 Ohio St., 534 (1867) See, also, ch XVI, *supra*

[4] Hagar r Union National Bank, 63 Me, 509 (1874) Scott r Central R R & Banking Co of Ga, 52 Barb, 45 (1868), State r Baltimore, etc, R R Co, 6 Gill, 363 (1847), King t Paterson etc, R R, Co, 29 N J Law, 504 (1866) A mere letter of inquiry has been held under this rule an insufficient demand Scott r Central R R & Banking Co of Ga, *supra* A demand while the shares are under and subject to an attachment by the corporation is not such a demand as this rule contemplates Hagar r Union National Bank, *supra*

[5] Robinson r National Bank of New Berne, 95 N Y, 637 (1884), Keppel's Adm r r Petersburg R R Co, Chase's Dec, 167 (1868) This accords with the settled theory of the law as to demand in similar cases See East New York, etc, R R Co t Elmore, 5 Hun, 214 (1875); Delamater v. Miller, 1 Cowen, 75

(1823), Everett t Coffin, 6 Wend, 603 (1831), Walradt t Maynard, 3 Barb, 584 (1848), Carroll r Cone, 40 Barb, 220 (1862), Ayer r Ayer, 16 Pick., 327 (1835)

[6] Keppel's Adm'r v Petersburg R R. Co, *supra*, Boardman r Lake Shore, etc, R R. Co, 84 N Y, 157, 187 (1881), State t Baltimore, etc, R R. Co, 6 Gill, 363, 387 (1847), Phil, etc, R R Co r Cowell 28 Pa St, 329 (1857); Bank of Louisville t Gray, 2 S W. Rep, 168 (Ky, 1886) As to interest on preferred dividends, see ch XVI

[7] The statute of limitations begins to run against a stockholder's suit to collect dividends only after a demand and refusal, or notice to a shareholder that his right to dividends is denied Phil, etc, R R r Cowell, 28 Pa St., 329 (1857), Bank of Louisville r Gray, 84 Ky, 563 (1886) The statute of limitations does not begin to run against the collection of a dividend until it is demanded. A charter provision of a new charter into which the old company is merged, applying a three-year statute of limitations to dividends does not affect dividends on old stock which has not come into the reorganization Airmant r New Orleans, etc, R R, 7 S Rep, 35 (La, 1889); Kobogum r. Jackson Iron Co, *supra;* Bedford Co v. Nashville, etc, R R, *supra.*

The action at law for the payment of a dividend which has been declared should be against the corporation, and not against the corporate officers.[1] But where the treasurer of an incorporated company withheld a dividend belonging to one of the stockholders on the ground that he himself owned the stock, an action of *assumpsit* against him individually was sustained.[2] And in a case where a stockholder had been unjustly deprived of his stock it was held that he could not sue an individual shareholder to recover a dividend which should have been paid to him, but that his action was properly against the corporation.[3] In actions on the part of shareholders to enforce the payment of dividends the validity or legality of the dividend cannot be questioned by the corporation.[4] But when a corporation is sued for a dividend by two claimants therefor it may support a bill of interpleader between them.[5]

§ 544. *Right of the corporation to apply dividends to the payment of debts due to it by the shareholder.*—It is well settled that if, at the time a dividend becomes payable, the stockholder owes the corporation any debt, the dividend due that shareholder may be applied in liquidation of the indebtedness; and if the corporation is sued for the dividend it may set up the debt by way of set-off or counter-claim.[6] This, however, amounts to a corporate lien on the

[1] French *v.* Fuller, 40 Mass., 108 (1839); Smith *v.* Poor, 40 Me., 415 (1855); S. C., 3 Ware. 148 (1858).

[2] Williams *v.* Fullerton, 20 Vt., 346 (1848).

[3] Peckham *v.* Van Wagenen, 83 N. Y., 40 (1880).

[4] Stoddard *v.* Shetucket Foundry Co., 34 Conn., 542 (1868).

[5] Salisbury Mills *v.* Townsend, 109 Mass., 115 (1871). See, also. § 387. In England the rule was formerly otherwise. Dalton *v.* Midland R'y Co., 12 C. B., 458 (1852). Where a corporation is sued by a stockholder for a dividend declared by the directors, and all the other stockholders have received their dividends and retained them, the company cannot be allowed to set up its defense to the suit that the dividend has not been earned, and that its payment would withdraw a part of the capital of the company. Stoddard *v.* Shetucket Foundry Co., *supra.*

[6] Hagar *v.* Union National Bank, 63

Me., 509 (1874); Phil., etc., R. R. *v.* Cowell, 28 Pa. St., 329 (1857); King *v.* Paterson, etc., R'y Co., 29 N. J. Law, 504 (1860); Sargent *v.* Franklin Ins. Co., 25 Mass., 90 (1829); Bates *v.* New York Ins. Co., 3 Johns. Cas., 238 (1802). See, also, § 526, *supra.* But a contrary rule prevails as to a deceased stockholder, upon a winding up of the company and a distribution of its assets. See Merchants' Bank, etc., *v.* Shouse, 102 Pa. St., 488 (1883); Brent *v.* Bank of Washington, 2 Cranch C. C., 517 (1824). See, also, *contra,* in general, *Ex parte* Winsor, 3 Story C. C., 411 (1844). By agreement a dividend may be applied to an unpaid call. Kenton, etc., Co. *v.* McAlpin, 5 Fed. Rep., 737 (1880). For a contract of a corporation to sell to its superintendent shares of its stock at his option, and to allow him to pay for the stock by the dividends, see Appeal of Goodwin, etc., Co., 12 Atl. Rep., 736 (Pa., 1888). The only right that a corporation has to retain a dividend from a stockholder who owes

stock so far as dividends are concerned, and it is not upheld where the registered stockholder has sold and transferred his certificate of stock before the dividend is declared

§ 545 *The courts very rarely compel the directors to declare a dividend* — It is for the directors, and not the shareholders, to determine whether or not a dividend is to be declared [1]

When, therefore, the directors have exercised this discretion and refused to declare a dividend, there will be no interference by the courts with their decision, unless they are guilty of a wilful abuse of their discretionary powers or of bad faith or of a neglect of duty It requires a very strong case to induce a court of equity to order the directors to declare a dividend, inasmuch as equity has no jurisdiction unless fraud or a breach of trust is involved. There have been many attempts to sustain such a suit, yet, although the court did not disclaim jurisdiction, it has quite uniformly refused to interfere.[2]

it money is based on set-off Gemmell v Davis, 23 Atl Rep 1032 (Md , 1892). This set-off is not good on a debt against the transferrer where the certificates were sold, although not transferred on the books, before the dividend was declared Id A pledgee of stock, even though not recorded as a stockholder, is entitled to dividends declared after the pledge was made as against a claim of the corporation against the pledgor as an offset Id

[1] "The directors of a corporation, and they alone, have the power to declare a dividend of the earnings of the corporation and to determine its amount ' Hunter v Roberts etc , Co., 47 N W Rep , 131 (Mich , 1890) See also, the various cases in this and succeeding sections

[2] New York, etc , R R t Nickalls, 119 U S , 296 (1886), rev'g 15 Fed Rep , 575 Ely v Sprague, Clarke's Chan (N Y), 351 (1840), Williams v Western Union Telegraph Co , 93 N Y , 162 (1883), Park v Grant Locomotive Works, 40 N J Eq 114 (1885), Barnard v Vermont, etc , R R Co., 7 Allen, 512 (1863), Chaffee v Rutland R R Co. 55 Vt, 110, 133 (1882), Smith v Prattville Manuf'g Co , 29 Ala , 503 (1857); Barry v Merchants' Exchange Co., 1 Sandf

Chan 280 (1844), The King v Bank of England, 2 Barn & Ald , 620 (1819), where the court refused to grant a *mandamus* for an examination of the accounts with a view to compelling a dividend The directors are bound to distribute as profits only such part of the net income as they think proper ; and their judgment of what is proper is conclusive upon the stockholders. State v Baltimore, etc , R R Co., 6 Gill, 763 (1848) Cf Dent v London, etc , Co , L R , 16 Ch D , 344 In Park v Grant Locomotive Works, 40 N J. Eq , 114 (1885), the court said , "In cases where the power of the directors of a corporation is without limitation and free from restraint they are at liberty to exercise a very liberal discretion as to what disposition shall be made of the gains of the business of the corporation Their power over them is absolute so long as they act in the exercise of an honest judgment They may reserve of them whatever their judgment approves as necessary or judicious for repairs and improvements, and to meet contingencies, both present and prospective " In the above case, however, a contract that all the net profits should be divided annually varied these rules. The court refused to order a dividend.

Accordingly the directors may, in the fair exercise of their discretion, invest profits to extend and develop the business, and a reasonable use of the profits to provide additional facilities for the

In State of Louisiana v Bank of Louisiana, 6 La , 745 (1834), the court refused to order a bank to declare a dividend although it had profits on hand of about one-tenth of its capital The court said "If the board honestly err in these matters we are not ready to say the courts possess the power to rectify its mistakes." The remedy is in the elections Courts will not order a dividend to be declared unless the directors "refuse to declare a dividend when the corporation has a surplus of net profits which it can, without detriment to its business, divide among its stockholders and when a refusal to do so would amount to such an abuse of discretion as would constitute a fraud or breach of that good faith which they are bound to exercise towards the stockholders" A dividend will not be ordered when the profits are invested in the plant and in long-time notes Hunter v Roberts, etc , Co , 47 N W Rep. 131 (Mich , 1890) In the case of Smith v Prattville, etc , Co , 29 Ala , 503 (1857), the court refused to order a dividend inasmuch as the charter expressly vested discretion as to that matter in the board of directors

Where large dividends are made by a manufacturing company it is entirely within the fair and honest discretion of the directors whether the remaining profits shall be passed to surplus or used for dividends McNab v McNab, etc , Co , 62 Hun, 18 (1891) The fact that a manufacturing company extended its business so as to include iron pipe as well as brass, and loaned money, which loans, however the president was willing to take up, and had owned government bonds, is not sufficient to entitle a stockholder who has acquiesced therein to demand that all profits be paid out in dividends Id Although the road was leased and the floating debt was only $1,000 and the

bonded debt, $70,000, was due in seventeen years, and the other expenses only $6,000, while the company had $36,000 on hand and the regular rental for its road coming in, yet the court refused to order a dividend in Karnes v Rochester etc R R , 4 Abb Pr (U S), 107 (1867), the court holding also that a demand must first be made and that the directors instead of the company, are the proper parties defendant See ch XVI In the case of Barnard v Vermont, etc , R R., 89 Mass , 512 (1863), there was a contract to pay dividends, and it was upon this contract that the court based its right to pass upon the ability of the company to declare a dividend The court refused to order a dividend In Richardson v Vermont, etc R R 44 Vt , 613 (1872), the court decreed the payment of what was substantially a dividend to the stockholders, but stated that an accounting must first be had to ascertain whether there was available for that purpose "a fund adequate, not only for the payment of the claims of the plaintiffs in the cause, but for the payment of all stockholders having like claims, and there must be a surplus fund over and above what is requisite for the payment of the current expenses of the business, for discharging its duties to creditors and over and above what reasonable prudence would require to be kept in the treasury to meet the accidents, risks and contingencies incident to the business of operating the railroad ' In the case of Dent v London Tramways Co , L R , 16 Ch D 344 (1880), the court compelled the company to pay a dividend on the preferred stock, where there were profits available, but the common stockholders proposed to use all the profits for long neglected repairs, the real reason being that there were profits sufficient for a dividend on the preferred but not on

business cannot be objected to or enjoined by a minority of the stockholders [1]

Profits may also be set aside for the payment of indebtedness, though it is not yet due [2] The free exercise of the directors' discretion cannot be interfered with by the contracts of promoters or original incorporators as to the disposition of corporate profits [3]

Nevertheless the discretion of the directors in the matter of declaring or refusing to declare a dividend is not absolute, and where there is a clear abuse of power in refusing to declare the dividend, a court of equity will, at the instance of any shareholder, compel the proper authorities to declare and pay the dividend [4] Laches on the

both the common and preferred The court said that profits meant the "surplus in receipts after paying expenses and restoring the capital to the position it was in on the first of January in that year" Where a bill in equity, filed for the purpose of obtaining an accounting and the declaration of a dividend, does not clearly make out the existence of a surplus which the directors ought to distribute, the suit will fail A discovery will not be granted where there is no allegation that information is refused or that the party cannot examine the books, or that a *mandamus* was inadequate Wolf *et al* v Underwood *et al*, 11 S Rep. 344 (Ala, 1892)

[4] Where a corporation having a large surplus proposed, with the concurrence of a majority of the shareholders to employ the surplus in extending the business, although such extension was opposed by a minority of the shareholders, it appearing that the proposed enlargement of the corporate enterprise was clearly *intra vires*, it was held on a bill brought by the dissenting minority for an injunction against the proposed use of the surplus, and praying a distribution of it among the shareholders, that the facts were not such as to require the interposition of the court on behalf of the minority, Pratt v Pratt, 33 Conn., 446 (1866), the court saying "On a question of this sort much must necessarily be left to the discretion of the managing directors, and so long as they keep within the ob-

jects contemplated by the articles of association and the expenditure is not unreasonable in reference to the amount of their capital, a court of equity ought very seldom to interfere with them"

[2] Karnes v Rochester, etc, R. R. Co, 4 Abb Prac (N S) 107 (1867).

[3] The agreement of the promoters and preliminary subscribers to the stock of the proposed company as to the division and disposition of the net profits does not bind the company unless it has expressly agreed to such agreement. Coyote, etc, Co v Ruble, 8 Oreg, 284 (1880) But if expressly ratified by the company it is binding Richardson v. Vermont, etc, R R, 44 Vt, 613 (1872), where an agreement to pay annual interest to the stockholders out of the net profits was considered

[4] Where for seven years a stockholder who owned a majority of the stock elected himself and two of his dummies as directors of the company, and caused the board to vote a large salary to himself as president and manager, and had leased to the company his property at a large rental the salary and rental are illegal and void Where the company had failed to pay its dividends by reason of such acts a court of equity, upon the suit of another stockholder, ordered the president to account, and appointed a receiver of the company and directed that its affairs be wound up Miner v. Belle Isle Ice Co, 53 N W Rep, 218 (Mich, 1892). Where a town lot corporation consisted of but three stockhold-

part of the shareholders in failing to commence their suit to compel the payment of a dividend until the corporation becomes insolvent is fatal[1] And the court will also consider that the aggrieved shareholders may, if a majority, refuse to re-elect the directors at the next election, or may sell their shares[2]

§ 546 *Dividends can be made only from profits — What are profits which may be used for dividends —* A dividend can lawfully be made only out of profits The payment of it must leave the capital stock of the company intact and unimpaired, or the dividend itself will be held fraudulent and void.[3]

In view of the rule that dividends can be made only from profits, it becomes important to ascertain what part of the income of a corporation constitutes "profits" which may be used for a dividend. This question has caused the courts considerable difficulty. There have been various definitions, explanations and different states of facts involved in the cases which have come before the courts. A general idea of what constitutes profits available for dividends can be obtained only by a study of the cases themselves[4]

ers, and two of them control the company and refuse to declare dividends although there is a large surplus in the treasury, and although the corporation is free from debts, and further sales are being made, and cash being paid in on account of them, the court ordered a dividend to be declared paid of all the cash on hand, and even intimated that a division of the property itself might be ordered by way of a dividend, the two stockholders in control having been guilty of fraud in the management. Fougeray v Cord *et al*, 24 Atl Rep, 499 (N J, 1892) In this case the directors had voted to themselves large salaries and had restored the same upon the order of the court. The court ordered a distribution of the money by way of dividends Brown v Buffalo, etc, R R Co, 27 Hun, 342 (1882) See, also, Park v Grant Locomotive Works, 40 N J Eq, 114 (1885) In this case there was a contract that the net profits should be divided annually Scott v Eagle Fire Ins. Co., 7 Paige, 198 (1838), Pratt v Pratt, 33 Conn, 446 (1866); Beers v Bridgeport Spring Co., 42 id, 17 (1875) Upon a sale of all the property of the corporation the direct-

ors may be compelled to declare a dividend Cramer v Bird, 6 Eq, 143 (1868) A stockholder cannot sue for profits until a dividend is declared Beveridge v New York, etc, R. R. Co., 112 N. Y, 1 (1889)

[1] Scott v Eagle Fire Ins Co., *supra*

[2] Barry v Merchants' Exchange Co, 1 Sandf Chan, 280 (1844)

[3] Lockhardt v Van Alstyne, 31 Mich, 76 (1875), Hughes v Vermont Copper Mining Co, 72 N Y, 207, 210 (1878) See, also, ch XVI, and cases in notes to this section. See, also, as to what constitutes a payment of dividends out of capital, 3 R'y & Corp L J, 409, reviewing recent English decisions. For a valuable note on this subject by Judge Thompson, see 36 Cent. L J, 455

[4] "Net earnings are, properly, the gross receipts, less the expenses of operating the road to earn such receipts. Interest on debts is paid out of what thus remains, that is, out of net earnings Many other liabilities are paid out of the net earnings When all liabilities are paid, either out of the gross receipts or out of net earnings, the remainder is the profit of the shareholders, to go towards dividends, which in

There are some general principles connected with this subject which have been established by the adjudications   It is not necessary for a railroad or other corporation to use its profits to pay its funded or bonded debt instead of using those profits for a dividend   Such bonded debt is practically though not theoretically

that way are paid out of the net earnings" St. John v Erie R'y Co , 10 Blatch , 271, 279 (1872), S. C, aff'd, 23 Wall, 136 (1874), Warren v King, 108 U. S, 389 (1882), Van Dyck v McQuade, 86 N Y , 38, 47 (1881) "Popularly speaking, the net receipts of a business are its profits" Eyster v Centennial Board of Finance, 54 U S , 506 (1876) "Surplus earnings" are said to be the moneys available for dividends Williams t Western Union Telegraph Co , 93 N Y , 162, 191 (1883) "Net earnings" is a term synonymous with "net income," and also "net income" as used in the statute under consideration Phillips v Eastern R R Co , 138 Mass , 122 (1884). In Belfast, etc , R R Co v Belfast, 77 Me , 415 (1885), it is said that the term 'net earnings" does not imply that the company is wholly out of debt. The profits mean "the clear gains of any business venture, after deducting the capital invested in the business, the expenses incurred in its conduct, and the losses sustained in its prosecution" Bills receivable are counted as part of the assets or net profits, but are not to be considered as the basis of a dividend unless they can be sold without material loss Park v Grant Locomotive Works, 40 N J Eq , 114 (1885) In the following cases the term "net profits," or an equivalent phrase, is defined Coltness Iron Co v Black, 51 L J (Q B Div), 626 (1881); New York, etc , R R Co v Nichols, 119 U S , 296 (1886). In Richardson v Buhl, 43 N. W Rep , 1102, 1107 (Mich , 1889), the court approved of the following statement· "That the first thing to be done by any manufacturer, who would ascertain his net earnings during the preceding year, is to take a careful inventory of what he has left, including his plant and machinery,

and then make just and full allowances for all losses and shrinkages of every kind that he has suffered in his property during the year, and for all expenses of every kind, ordinary or extraordinary, that have occurred during the year , and, having made such inventory, and deducted such losses and shrinkage of every kind, his net earnings will be the difference between all his investments in his business and all his expenses of every kind on the other hand, and this new inventory, with the deductions properly made, and all that he has received of every kind on the other hand ; and if his books are properly kept and proper deductions made, these net earnings will finally appear on the balance sheet to the credit of the profit and loss account." In Gratz v Redd 4 B Mon 178, 187 (1843), it is held that capital paid in on stock which is afterwards forfeited does not thereby become profits and liable to be distributed as a dividend Money paid in as capital must remain and be treated and expended as capital, whether the stock that represents it is forfeited or not. To distribute such money as profits is to squander and dissipate the capital stock. "Gross earnings" include earnings of the railroad through a transfer company operated by it. Dardanelle, etc., R'y v. Shinn, 12 S W Rep., 183 (Ark., 1889) "The assets, resources and funds of the corporation must consist of cash on hand and other property, and, if such assets exceed the liabilities, a dividend can be lawfully declared , in other words, a profit exists." Hubbard v. Weare, 44 N W. Rep., 914 (Iowa, 1890); Miller v Bradish, 69 Iowa, 278 See, also, McDougall v Jersey, etc., Co , 2 Hem & M , 528 (1864), Phillips v Eastern R R., 138 Mass., 122 (1884);

a part of the capital of the company.[1] But it is necessary to pay the interest on such bonded debt before any dividend is declared[2]

The floating debt should be paid or funded before a dividend is declared[3] But outstanding and disputed claims need not be first paid.[4]

[1] A company has power to and does raise its capital both by stock and by borrowing "They expend that money in executing the works, and the works having been executed, the capital of the company remains in the shape of the station houses, the permanent way, the warehouses and everything else which requires expenditure of capital The shareholders . . are not to be told that all those things are to be paid for before they are to have any dividend out of the income" Mills v Northern R'y, L R, 5 Ch, 621 (1870) For a learned and very satisfactory discussion of when net earnings are to be retained for the purpose of accumulating a fund to pay a corporate debt not yet due, see Hazeltine v Belfast, etc, R. R. Co, 10 Atl Rep, 328 (Me, 1887) All interest must be paid out of profits and should not be charged to construction account. The court said also that a sinking fund should also be provided and an annual contribution made to it out of the profits. Gratz v Redd, 4 B Monroe, 178, 188 (Ky, 1843)

[2] Gratz v Redd, supra A dividend cannot properly be based on a statement which includes accrued interest with no allowance for interest on liabilities, outstanding accounts with no allowance for bad debts; and expense for perfecting a machine, it not being a success Hubbard v Weare, 44 N. W Rep, 914 (Iowa, 1890) Whether the interest on debentures can be legally charged upon the capital account of the company, the revenue available for dividend being thereby increased, was not decided in Bloxam v Metropolitan R'y Co, 3 Ch, 337, 344, 350 (1868), but a preliminary injunction against the dividend was granted

[3] The funded debt need not be paid before dividends are declared but "any

debts which have been incurred and which are due from the directors or the company, either for steam-engines, for rails, for completing stations, or the like, which ought to have been and would have been paid at the time, had the defendants possessed the necessary funds for that purpose, those are so many deductions from the profits, which, in my opinion, are not ascertained till the whole of them are paid." Corry v Londonderry, etc, R'y, 29 Beav, 263, 273 (1860) However in the case of Stevens v South Devon R y, 9 Hare, 313 (1851), a stockholder failed in his suit to enjoin dividends until the floating debt was paid The court said. "I am of opinion that the court ought not, upon this ground, to interfere by injunction

I think, also, that the question upon this third point is one of internal management, with which the court cannot interfere." Net earnings are the gross receipts less the expenses of operating the road to earn such receipts, also less the interest on the bonded, funded, permanent or standing debt, also floating debts "which it is not wise and prudent to place in the form of a funded debt or to postpone for later payment;" also an annual contribution to a sinking fund to pay the funded debt when the condition of the company renders it expedient, as where the company will at some future time earn only its operating expenses As to whether the floating debt should be paid and a contribution be made to a sinking fund "depends upon the financial resources and abilities of the corporation and the prospects of its road ' The cost of construction may be charged to the capital stock account. Belfast, etc, R. R. v Belfast, 77 Me, 445 (1885)

[4] The court will not enjoin a dividend

A proper sum must first be expended or set aside for repairs and reconstruction to replace depreciation due to wear and tear.[1] But in the case of a mining company or a company whose produce when once used can never be replaced, it is not necessary to set aside funds for the purpose of purchasing a new mine.[2]

where the company shows that it has the necessary profits, even though there are outstanding claims on illegally issued stock Carpenter v N. Y. & N. H R R, 5 Abb Pr, 277 (1857) Where the company denies that the complainant is a stockholder, a preliminary injunction falls Blatchford v Id, id, 276 Directors are not liable to replace dividends declared (by reason of a statute making them so liable if the dividends are not "from the surplus profits"), although dividends were declared while the company, being engaged in mining, assumed a mortgage debt in buying additional property, a sinking fund being begun to meet that liability gradually, and although the money to pay the dividend was borrowed, money to that amount having been put into improvements, and although losses due to an injunction against using a stream of water were not at once charged up to operating expense. Excelsior, etc, Co v Pierce, 27 Pac. Rep, 44 (Cal, 1891)

[1] In the case Davison v Gillies, L. R. 16 Ch D, 347, note (1879), the court, at the instance of a stockholder, enjoined the declaration of a dividend on the ground that the street railway tracks of the company had become worn out, and needed very expensive repairs, for which no provision had been made by the company, and that this capital so used up must be restored before a dividend was declared The by-laws prohibited dividends except from the capital stock The court said "A tramway company lay down a new tramway Of course the ordinary wear and tear of the rails and sleepers, and so on, causes a sum of money to be required from year to year in repairs. It may or may not be desirable to do the repairs all at once, but if at the end of the first year the line of tramway is still in so good a state of repair that it requires nothing to be laid out on it for repairs in that year, still, before you can ascertain the net profits, a sum of money ought to be set aside, as representing the amount in which the wear and tear of the line has, I may say, so far depreciated it in value as that sum will be required for the next year or next two years. . . I should think no commercial man would doubt that this is the right course — that he must not calculate net profits until he has provided for all the ordinary repairs and wear and tear occasioned by his business . . . That being so, it appears to me that you can have no net profits unless this sum has been set aside. When you come to the next year, or the third or fourth year, what happens is this as the line gets older the amount required for repairs increases. If you had done what you ought to have done, that is, set aside every year the sum necessary to make good the wear and tear in that year, then in the following years you would have a fund sufficient to meet the extra cost." See, also, as to construction account, Mackintosh v. Flint, etc, R. R., 34 Fed Rep., 583.

[2] A company owning a mine, lease or patent may declare dividends out of its net proceeds, although the necessary result is that that much is permanently taken away from the substance of the estate Excelsior, etc, Co v Pierce, 27 Pac Rep., 44 (Cal, 1891). In the case Lambert v Neuchatel Asphalte Co., 51 L. J. (Ch), 882 (1882), a stockholder sought to enjoin a dividend on the ground that the beds of asphalte belonging to the company were being consumed by the company, and that funds sufficient to replace this consumption

In estimating the profits for a year for the purpose of declaring a dividend, it is not correct to take into account the increase or decrease in the value of the assets of the company prior to that year. The fact that in a year prior to the declaration of the divi-

should be set aside before any dividend was declared   Otherwise the capital would gradually be entirely used up   The court refused the injunction, inasmuch as the by-laws of the company gave absolute discretion to the stockholders to determine the net profits   No creditors' rights were involved in the case

A very full and careful discussion of the right to declare dividends out of a mining property is to be found in Lee v Neuchatel Asphalte Company, 61 L. T Rep. 11 (1889) In that case however, the mines were at the time of the litigation more valuable than at the time when the company was formed, and it is to be noticed that the rules laid down expressly assumed that enough property existed to pay all creditors after declaring the dividend The court said, per Lindley, J

"It is obvious with respect to such property, as with respect to various other properties of a like kind, mines and quarries, and so on, every ton of stuff which you get out of that which you have bought with your capital may, from one point of view be considered as embodying and containing a small portion of your capital and that if you sell it and divide the proceeds you divide some portion of that which you have spent your capital in acquiring It may be represented that this is a return of capital All I can say is, if that is a return of capital it appears to me not to be such a return of capital as is prohibited by law

"As I pointed out in the course of the argument, and I repeat now, suppose a company is formed to start a daily newspaper, supposing it sinks £250,000 before the receipts from sales and advertisements equal the current expenses, and supposing it then goes on, is it to be

said that the company must come to a stop, or that it cannot divide profits until it has replaced its £250,000, which has been sunk in building up a property which if put up for sale, would, perhaps, not yield £10 000? That is a business matter left to business men. If they think their prospects of success are considerable, so long as they pay their creditors there is no reason why they should not go on and divide profits. so far as I can see, although every shilling of the capital may be lost It may be a perfectly flourishing concern and the contrary view I think is to be traced to this, that there is a sort of notion that the company is debtor to capital In an accountant's point of view it is quite right, in order to see how you stand, to put down company debtor to capital But the company do not owe the capital What it means is simply this· that if you want to find out how you stand, whether you have lost your money or not, you must bring your capital into account somehow or another . . .

"If a company is formed to acquire and work a property of a wasting nature, for example a mine, a quarry or a patent, the capital expended in acquiring the property may be regarded as sunk and gone, and if the company retains assets sufficient to pay its debts, it appears to me that there is nothing whatever in the act to prevent any excess of money obtained by working the property over the cost of working it from being divided amongst the shareholders, and this, in my opinion, is true, although some portion of the property itself is sold, and in some sense the capital is thereby diminished . . .

"But it is, I think, a misapprehension to say that dividing the surplus after payment of expenses of the produce of

dend some portion of the capital of an incorporated company has been lost and not made good affords no ground for restraining the payment of a dividend out of profits subsequently earned [1] A dividend may be declared although the company has not yet completed its works [2] In the case of railroads the cost of additional rolling stock and improvements may be charged to capital account and need not be paid before a dividend is declared.[3]

Insurance companies cannot declare dividends out of unearned premiums.[3] Banks cannot declare dividends out of interest not yet received [4] The question of what constitutes profits applica-

your wasting property is a return of capital in any such sense as to be forbidden by the act."

The court held consequently that the stockholder's suit to enjoin the dividend must fail

[1] Hence where in 1882 $350,000 was charged off for bad debts, but this was offset by credit for $350,000 for increase in the value of land owned by the company, this transaction was not to be considered in 1885 in ascertaining the profits of 1885   It is immaterial whether the alleged increase in the value of the land was correct or not   Bolton v. The Natal Land, etc , Co , 65 L T Rep , 786 (1891) Though the capital stock has been impaired in time past, it has been held that dividends may be declared out of profits subsequently earned without setting them aside to restore the lost capital   Healey on Companies Law and Practice, 122 See, also, cases in last note   Where a bank sells its business for a certain sum, and subsequently buys back a portion of it for another sum, it may declare the dividend of the surplus that remains after deducting from the first-mentiond sum the second-mentioned sum, and also the capital stock Lubbock v British Bank, etc., 67 L T Rep, 74 (1892)

[2] In Browne v Monmouthshire R'y, 13 Beav , 32 (1851), the court refused to enjoin a company from declaring a dividend, the only ground of complaint being that the company had not yet completed its works.

[3] Rolling stock may be carried to cap-

ital account instead of being charged to operating expense   Mills v. Northern R'y, L R, 5 Ch App , 621 (1870) For a definition of " net earnings" as used in the federal statutes in regard to the government's claims on the Pacific Railroads, see Union Pacific R R v. United States, 99 U S, 402 (1878); United States v Central Pac. R R , id , 449, United States v Kansas Pac R R , id , 455, United States v Sioux City & Pac R R , id , 491. Although ordinarily from the gross earnings there should be deducted " a reasonable amount for betterments and improvements, rendered necessary by the gradual increase of traffic, the better discharge of business, and the public accommodation," in arriving at the net earnings, under the Thurman act, relative to the Pacific railroads, no such deductions are to be made United States v Central Pac. R R, 138 U S, 84 (1891).

[3] Unearned premiums received by an insurance company, on which the risks are still running, are not surplus profits out of which dividends can legally be made, there not being a sufficient surplus on hand in excess of the capital stock to meet the probable losses on risks not yet terminated. De Peyster v American Fire Ins Co , 6 Paige, 486 (1837) See, also, Scott v. Eagle Fire Ins Co , 7 id , 198 (1838), Lexington, etc., Ins Co v Page, 17 B Mon, 412 (1856).

[4] " Money earned as interest, however well secured, or certain to be eventually paid, cannot in fact be distributed as

ble to dividends arises often in connection with preferred stock [1] Profits earned and invested in times of prosperity may properly be paid out as dividends subsequently and at a time when no dividends have been earned [2] When the company has used profits for improvements, it may lawfully borrow an equivalent sum of money for the purpose of a dividend [3] And it may properly borrow money to pay a dividend if, upon a fair estimate of its assets and liabilities, it has assets in excess of its liabilities and capital stock equal to the amount of the proposed dividend [4] The subsequent insolvency of the corporation does not invalidate a dividend declared when there were net profits [5] And even though the business is a hazardous one, money need not be set aside for possible disasters [6]

Upon a reduction of the capital stock the surplus funds over and above the full amount of the capital stock as reduced may be divided among the stockholders, the only restriction being that such a distribution must leave the reduced capital stock entire and unimpaired A stockholder may insist upon a division of such a surplus [7]

---

dividends to stockholders, and does not constitute surplus profits" People v. San Francisco Sav. Union, 72 Cal, 199 (1887). In Iowa it has been held that where a bank with a capital of $106,860; assets of $156,904; liabilities of $56,065, declares and pays a dividend of ten per cent., i. e, $10,686, the corporate creditors could not compel the stockholders to return the dividend. Miller v Bradish, 69 Iowa, 278 (1886)

[1] See ch XVI

[2] Mills v Northern Railway of Buenos Ayres Co, L. R., 5 Ch, 621 (1870); Hoole v Great Western R'y Co, L. R., 3 Ch, 262 (1867); Beers v. Bridgeport Spring Co, 42 Conn, 17 (1875); In re Mercantile Trading Co, L. R., 4 Ch, 475 (1869)

[3] Mills v Northern Railway of Buenos Ayres Co, L. R., 5 Chan, 621 (1870); Stringer's Case, L. R., 4 Ch, 475, 492 (1869).

[4] Stringer's Case, L. R., 4 Ch, 475 (1869). See, also, § 539, supra. "A company is quite as competent to declare dividends out of property which is invested for the time being in buildings, or anything else, as it is out of cash in hand, and it is not at all necessary that a company, any more than an individual, should have cash at the bank on which

he can draw in order to declare dividends ' Municipal, etc, Co, Limited, v. Pollington, 63 L. T Rep., 238 (1890)

[5] Reid v. Eaton Iron Mfg Co, 40 Ga., 98 (1869); Le Roy v Globe Ins. Co., 2 Edw. Ch, 657 (1836). In deciding whether a dividend was rightfully made the transaction must be viewed from the stand-point of that time and not in the light of subsequent events. Notes or overdrafts by persons then considered abundantly good, included among the corporate assets when the dividend was declared and paid, should not be regarded as losses sustained by the corporation because they afterwards proved to be unavailable Main v. Mills, 6 Biss., 98 (1874) Cf Flitcroft's Case, L. R., 21 Ch D, 519 (1882), where the directors figured in what they knew were bad debts

[6] A balance sheet sustaining a dividend is upheld where the business is extra hazardous, such as blockade running, and such dividend need not be refunded even though the blockade runners are lost and other assets turn out to be worthless. In re Mercantile Co., Ld, 4 Ch App, 475 (1869)

[7] Seeley v. New York National Exchange Bank, 8 Daly, 400 (1877), S C.,

The question of dividends where one road is consolidated with another is considered elsewhere [1]

§ 547. *A stockholder may enjoin an illegal dividend* — A court of equity will, upon the application of a stockholder, enjoin an attempt to distribute in dividends any part of the capital stock.[2] But the courts will not lightly review the decision of the board of directors in regard to whether the necessary profits actually exist [3] If the dividend has been declared but not paid, all the stockholders must be joined as parties [4] The court will not interfere, however, if neither the stockholders nor the corporate creditors can be injured by the dividend [5] The courts of one state will not enjoin a corporation created by another state from declaring a dividend unless a fraud is being perpetrated on citizens of the first-mentioned state.[6] A corporate creditor has no standing in court to enjoin a dividend, even though it will impair the capital stock.[7]

Thompson Nat'l Bank Cas, 804, aff'd, 78 N Y 608 (1879), Strong v Brooklyn Crosstown R. R Co, 93 N Y, 426, 435 (1883), Parker v Mason, 8 R. I, 427 (1867) See, also § 548, Eyster v Centennial, etc 94 U S., 500

[1] See ch XVI.

[2] Macdougall v Jersey Imperial Hotel Co, 2 Hem & M, 528 (1864), Bloxam v Metropolitan R'y Co, L R, 3 Ch, 337 (1867), Salisbury v Metropolitan R'y Co, 38 L J, Ch, 249 (1869), Carlisle v Southeastern R'y Co, 1 Macn & G, 689 (1850), Ward v Sittingbourne, etc, R'y Co, L R, 9 Chan, 488 (1874), Davison v Gillies, L R, 16 Ch D, 347, n (1879) See, also, cases in preceding section

[3] Where the directors declare a dividend after a proper investigation of the financial position of the company, the court will not lightly interfere with the payment thereof, but where they declare it without proper investigation or professional assistance and it is called in question, the burden of proof is upon them to show that it is to be fairly paid out of net profits *In re County M Ins Co*, L R, 6 Ch, 104 (1870), Hoole v Great Western R'y Co, L R, 3 Ch, 262

[4] A stockholder may file a bill in behalf of himself and other stockholders to enjoin the declaration of dividends where there are no net profits, but where he has not joined all the stock-holders as parties he cannot enjoin the payment of a dividend already declared, even though the time of payment has not yet arrived Fawcett v Laurie, 1 Dr & Sm, 192 (1860) To same effect, Carlisle v Southeastern R'y, 1 Macn & G, 689 (1850) See Browne v Monmouthshire R'y & Canal Co., 13 Bear, 32 (1851), Coates v Nottingham Water-works Co, 30 id, 86 (1861)

[5] "Equity would not interfere with a dividend unless it appeared that somebody in particular was hurt or liable to be injured It would not interfere after all danger had passed, and for the sake of vindicating general principles." In the case of Chaffee v Rutland R. R, 55 Vt 110, 133 (1882), the court stated and acted upon the principle of law stated above

[6] Howell v Chicago, etc, R. R. Co, 51 Barb, 378 (1868) In Massachusetts no equitable relief can be granted against a foreign corporation, which has neither officers nor place of business in that state, to compel the company to declare and pay dividends according to the stipulations of their certificates of preferred stock Williston v Michigan Southern, etc, R R. Co, 95 Mass, 400 (1866), Berford v N Y, etc, Co, 4 N Y Supp, 836 (Super Ct, 1889)

[7] Mills v Northern R'y, L R, 5 Ch, 621 (1870) See, also, ch XLV.

§ 548 *Dividends which impair the capital stock are illegal, and may be recovered back from the stockholders — Dividends on dissolution —* As already shown, a dividend can be lawfully declared only when sufficient net profits have been earned to pay that dividend. Accordingly, a dividend paid wholly or partly from the capital stock is illegal, and subjects the corporation and the shareholders who are parties to it to serious liability   It is the well-determined doctrine of the courts of this country that the capital stock is a trust fund to be preserved for the benefit of corporate creditors [1] Hence the rule has been firmly established that, where dividends are paid in whole or in part out of the capital stock, corporate creditors, being such when the dividend was declared, or becoming such at any subsequent time, may, to the extent of their claims, compel the shareholders to whom the dividend has been paid to refund whatever portion of the dividend was taken out of the capital stock.[2] In this country shareholders are bound to take notice of the true character and condition of the capital stock, and they cannot escape liability by reason of their ignorance.

[1] See § 199, *supra.* Goodwin v McGehee, 15 Ala , 232, 217, holding that a corporation cannot give away its effects to the prejudice of creditors, and any arrangement made by it with its stockholders to defeat the claims of creditors will be held void both in law and in equity, and that a stockholder cannot buy up claims against the company as an offset to his subscription

[2] Curran v State of Arkansas, 15 How , 304 (1853), Railroad Company v Howard, 7 Wall , 392 (1868), Osgood v Laytin, 48 Barb , 463 (1867), affirmed, 3 Keyes, 521, Johnson v Laflin, 5 Dill , 65, 86, note (1878); Hastings v Drew, 76 N Y , 919 (1879), Sagory v Dubois, 3 Sand Ch , 466 (1846), Wood v Dummer, 3 Mason, 308 (1824), Gratz v Redd, 4 B Mon , 178 (1843), Bank of St Marys v St John, 25 Ala , 566 (1854); Bartlett v Drew, 57 N Y , 587 (1874), Heman v Britton, 88 Mo., 549 (1886), Story's Equity Juris (13th ed , 1886), § 1252 A stockholder who receives an illegal dividend is liable for it even though he has paid it over to another person to whom the stock belonged Finn v Brown, 142 U. S., 56 (1891) Where the stockholders distribute the assets among themselves a creditor may follow the assets Panhandle, etc , Bank v Stevenson, 16 S W. Rep., 23 (Tex , 1890) The shareholders of a corporation have, in Louisiana no right to appropriate any part of its assets to pay large salaries to themselves as officers of the company, until all creditors who are not stockholders have been paid Cochran v Ocean Dry Dock Co , 30 La Ann , 1365 (1878) In Lexington Life, etc , Ins Co v Page, 17 B Mon , 412 (1856), it is held that the action to recover the dividend in such a case may be maintained by the company or its assigns where the dividend had been paid by mistake See, also, in general, Skramka v Allen, 7 Mo App , 434 (1879), Ward v Sittingbourne, etc , R R Co., L R , 9 Ch , 488 (1874) Clapp v Peterson, 104 Ill , 26, holding that the property so withdrawn was liable for the creditor's whole debt and not merely for a *pro rata* share thereof If a fixed per cent is drawn out by stockholders instead of a dividend and this per cent exceeds the profits, a stockholder, upon the insolvency of the corporation, must pay back the excess received by him Reading etc Co v Reading, etc., Works, 21 Atl Rep. 170 (Pa., 1891)

If a dividend has been paid out of the capital stock the stockholders are conclusively presumed to have known it, and are liable to an action for a repayment. They cannot claim to hold the position of innocent or *bona fide* holders [1]

A stockholder may by bill in equity compel a return of the dividend paid out of the capital stock.[2] A stockholder who receives dividends wrongfully declared cannot then, as a corporate creditor, hold other stockholders liable on a statutory liability for wrongfully declaring dividends [3] In Massachusetts at an early day it was held that an action at law would not lie to reach dividends paid out of the capital stock [4]

A corporate creditor may compel stockholders to refund the amount received by them on a distribution of the corporate assets upon dissolution or a sale of all the assets of the company, to the extent that his claim has not been paid after he has exhausted his remedy against the corporation itself.[5] But aside from this it is legal for the stockholders to dispose of the assets.[6]

Creditors may reach shares of stock that the corporation which becomes insolvent has distributed without a dividend McKusick *v* Seymour, etc , Co, 50 N W Rep., 1116 (Minn , 1892)

[1] A stockholder must turn back illegal dividends, although he knew nothing of the illegality Finn *v* Brown, 112 U. S , 56 (1891), *In re* Denham & Co , L R., 25 Ch D 752 (1883).

[2] Holmes *v* Newcastle, etc., Co, 15 L. J , Ch , 383 (1875).

[3] Thompson *v* Bemis, etc , Co, 127 Mass , 595 (1879)

[4] Vose *v* Grant, 15 Mass., 505, 517 (1819), Spear *v* Grant, 16 id , 9, 15 (1819); Paschall *v* Whitsett, 11 Ala., 472 (1847).

[5] See ch XL

[6] See ch XL Where three persons have formed a corporation and transferred a patent to it for all its capital stock and are the sole stockholders, there being no creditors, they may purchase the patent back and give the corporation their note for the par value of the whole capital stock Although the corporation subsequently becomes insolvent the transaction cannot be impeached Skinner *v* Smith, 56 Hun, 437 (1890) A debt of a stockholder to be paid from "dividends" must be paid from the dividends of assets, if the company dissolves Cozad *v.* McKee, 18 Atl Rep , 618 (Pa , 1889). Distribution of funds of incorporated association Aston *v* Dashaway, 22 Pac Rep, 660, aff'd in 23 id , 1091 (1890). It is legal for a coal corporation with the assent of all its stockholders to sell all its property to its president, and for him to pay therefor in cash and by a mortgage on the property so purchased, he also agreeing to pay all the debts of the company Payment was made directly to the stockholders and they transferred their stock to him in addition to the transfer of the property A subsequent creditor of the company who knew all of the facts cannot complain Parke, etc., Co. *v.* Terre etc , Co., 26 N. E. Rep , 884 (Ind , 1891). Where all the property of a telegraph company is sold and the proceeds distributed among the stockholders, a creditor of the company may by a bill in equity compel the stockholders to pay the claim against the corporation, the proceeds being a trust fund. Baltimore, etc , Co *v.* Interstate, etc., Co., 54 Fed Rep., 50 (1893) After dissolution has been decreed it is too late for a corporate creditor to bring an action to hold the directors liable for declaring divi-

The distribution of the assets among the stockholders upon dissolution is made upon equitable principles [1]

§ 549. *Proceedings to recover back such a dividend* — It is in general the practice, where dividends have been paid out of the capital stock in prejudice of the rights of corporate creditors, for a judgment creditor, upon the return of his common-law execution against the corporation wholly or partly unsatisfied, to commence an action in equity on behalf of himself and all other creditors who may come in, in the nature of a creditors' bill, against the stockholders to whom the dividend was unlawfully paid, to recover back so much thereof as was paid out of the capital stock [2]

It is a necessary condition precedent to the right to bring this action that a valid judgment shall have been obtained against the corporation, and that execution thereon shall have been returned wholly or partly unsatisfied, and this judgment is conclusive as to the merits of the creditor's claim.[3] If the treasurer is sued he can-

dends out of the capital stock no fraud in obtaining the dissolution being alleged Coxon v Gorst, 64 L T Rep, 444 (1891)

[1] Where the original stock is paid for in cash at par and then increased stock is paid for at the rate of $3 on $10, and upon the winding up of the company a large surplus exists for distribution, the court ordered that the original stock should first receive $7 on each $10, and then that the remaining assets should be distributed *pro rata* on all the stock *Re* Weymouth, etc, Co, 63 L T Rep, 445 (1890), aff'd, id, 686 (1891) On a dissolution and winding up, where part of the stock is paid up and part not, each class of stockholders is repaid the amount paid upon that class of stock, and then the surplus is divided proportionately *Re* Wakefield, etc, Co, 67 L T Rep, 83 (1892) On a winding up if it turns out that the profits had been systematically overestimated for many years, thereby depriving common stockholders of the dividends, an account would be taken and such dividends would be then paid *Re* Bridgwater, etc, Co, 64 L T Rep, 576 (1891)

[2] Hastings v Drew, 76 N Y, 9 (1879), Bartlett v Drew, 57 N Y, 587 (1874), McLean v Eastman, 21 Hun, 312 (1890), Gratz v. Redd, 4 B Mon, 178 (1843)

Curran v State of Arkansas, 15 How, 304 (1853) See, also United States v, Globe Works, 7 Fed Rep, 530 (1881), Brewer v Michigan Salt Association, 58 Mich, 351 (1885) See, also, § 548 And see Vose v Grant, 15 Mass, 505 (1819) where it was held that an action as for tort could not be maintained by a creditor against an individual stockholder who had received dividends Spear v Grant, 16 Mass, 9, 15 (1819), holding that an action at law will not lie An action on the case for fraud lies for a conspiracy, the stock having been sold back to the corporation bank and the bank then closed Bartholomew v Bentley, 15 Ohio, 659 (1846)

[3] Sturgis v Vanderbilt, 73 N Y, 384 (1878) In this case there was no recovery against a director who had sold his stock and ceased to participate in the company's affairs five years before the dissolution Dudley v Price's Adm'r, 10 B Monroe, 84 (Ky, 1849), Andrew v Vanderbilt, 37 Hun, 468 (1885), Hastings v Drew, 76 N Y, 9 (1879), where this liability was enforced against one who had become a purchaser of stock after the cause of action arose upon which the judgment was secured, the shares being by the terms of the transfer subject to all claims against it. In

not interplead[1] A receiver may institute the suit.[2] He represents the creditors as well as the corporation and stockholders As an officer of the court he may sue and is not estopped by the acts of the corporation

In the creditor's suit all the stockholders who can be reached should be made parties defendant, and as to those unknown or insolvent or beyond the jurisdiction there should be a proper averment in the bill[3] The corporation also should be made a party defendant to the bill[4]

The shareholder who is compelled to pay more than his equitable proportion of any unpaid corporate debt may, in a proper proceeding, resort to his associates for contribution[5] A transferee of stock against which creditors have this claim at the time of transfer is not liable to respond in a creditor's suit therefor[6] The statute of

New York the receiver of an insolvent corporation may maintain an action for the benefit of the creditors against the shareholders to recover the sums received by them as dividends at the time the company was insolvent, and in such an action the creditors of the corporation are proper parties defendant for the purpose of restraining them from proceeding individually against the shareholders separately to recover the unlawful dividends. Osgood v Laytin 3 Keyes, 521 (1867) See also, Lexington Life, etc, Ins Co v Page, 17 B Mon, 312 (1856), holding that an assignee of the company for the benefit of the company might sue But a receiver's suit cannot in such a case be brought for the benefit of the stockholders. Butterworth v O'Brien, 39 Barb, 192 (1863) Cf McLean v Eastman, 21 Hun, 312 (1880).

[1] A treasurer cannot interplead between the stockholders and a corporate creditor who is seeking to reach bonds received by the corporation in payment for its property Stone v Reed, 25 N E Rep, 49 (Mass., 1890)

[2] A receiver of the corporation is the proper party to sue to recover back any dividends which were paid from the capital stock Corporate creditors cannot sue for these after the receiver goes in It is doubtful whether the corporation itself could complain of such dividends. A sale of the assets by the receiver does not carry this cause of action Minnesota, etc, Co v Langdon, 46 N W Rep, 310 (Minn, 1890).

[3] Wood v Dummer, 3 Mason, 308 (1824), Bartlett v Drew, 57 N Y, 587 (1874) In the case last cited — a leading authority in New York — it is held that the creditor is not required to bring his suit on behalf of other creditors who may choose to come in, but may sue alone and for his own benefit exclusively, and that he need not make all the stockholders parties but may pursue one, any or all as he may elect, upon the theory that with the equities between the stockholders themselves he has nothing to do unless he choose to intervene to settle them Brewer v Michigan Salt, etc 58 Mich, 351 (1885) See. also, Pacific R R Co v Cutting. J, 27 Fed Rep. 638 (1886); Williams v Boice, 38 N J Eq, 364 (1884).

[4] First National Bank of Hannibal v Smith, 6 Fed Rep., 215 (1879), followed in Dormitzer v Illinois, etc, Bridge Co, 6 Fed Rep., 217 (1881) Where all the assets have been distributed, an action against the stockholders to recover back damages for a tort committed by the corporation must include the corporation as a co-defendant. Swan, etc, Co v Frank, 39 Fed Rep, 456 (1889).

[5] Bartlett v Drew, supra

[6] Hurlbut v Tayler 62 Wis., 607 (1885).

limitations runs in favor of shareholders who receive such dividends in good faith and without actual notice from the time they are declared as against the corporation and its creditors [1]

§ 550 *The liability herein of the corporate officers* — The liability of the corporate officers as to dividends paid out of the capital stock is not definitely determined That they are liable for the amount of any such dividend that they themselves receive as shareholders cannot, however, be questioned [2]

Some cases go to the full extent of holding the directors liable absolutely for all dividends paid out of capital stock. But the better rule is that when the directors declare a dividend in good faith and without negligence, they are not to be held liable merely because the dividend turns out to have impaired the capital stock [3]

---

[1] Lexington Life, etc , Ins. Co *v* Page, 17 B Mon , 412, 446 (1856). See, also, Mammoth Copperapolis, etc , Co., 50 L J (Ch), 11 (1880), Dudley *v* Price's Adm'r, 10 B Monroe, 84 (Ky , 1849)

[2] Main *v.* Mills, 6 Biss , 98, and the note (1874), where a dividend paid to the president, but not legitimately earned, was recovered from the president of a bank by the assignee in bankruptcy , Rance's Case, L R., 6 Ch , 104 (1870), which was the case of a marine insurance company, where the directors declared a bonus on the shares of stock without making out a profit and loss account, and it was held that a director who had received such bonus on a balance sheet thus carelessly drawn up should, in consequence of his neglect of duty, repay the amount to the liquidator It was the gross neglect of the directors which militated so strongly against them, and both the lord justices declared the court would not have so held had there been *bona fides* and regularity in the declaration of the bonus In re Denham & Co , L. R., 25 Ch D , 752 (1883) Here it was held that an innocent director was not personally responsible for the fraudulent reports and balance sheets and the dividends paid under them, and that — having regard to the extraordinary powers vested by the articles in the chairman, and to the fact that the books had been kept and audited by duly authorized officers, and that the director sought

to be charged had no reason to suspect any misconduct — he was not liable to repay any of the dividends so received by him, although they were in fact paid out of the capital

[3] Excelsior Petroleum Co *v* Lacey, 63 N Y , 422 (1875) In Stringer's Case, L R., 4 Ch 475 (1869), it was held, in accordance with this view, that where the action of a board of directors in making a dividend was *bona fide*, they are not liable for errors of judgment in preparing a balance sheet showing the assets of the concern In this case it appears that the directors included among the corporate assets a debt due the company by the government of the Confederate States , some cotton owned by the company but stored within the limits of the Confederacy , and certain merchant ships engaged in running the blockade, all which were estimated at their full value These assets being subsequently destroyed and lost to the company, its bankruptcy followed Osgood *v* Laytin, 3 Keyes (N Y), 521, was an action by a receiver to recover dividends improperly declared The court said "Ignorance of facts that it was the duty of the *managers* to know — not to know which was gross ignorance — cannot excuse the *managers* and impart any virtue or validity to acts otherwise clearly illegal, and which were a palpable fraud upon the creditors" But the directors of a bank

Where the directors negligently or wilfully and knowingly declare and pay a dividend out of the capital stock, they are personally liable to refund that dividend.[1]　Frequently also, when a dividend

are not liable for dividends declared in good faith, even though it subsequently turns out that debts to the bank which they considered good were found to be bad　Witters ı Sowles, 31 Fed Rep, 1 (1887). However, the court in *Re* Oxford, etc, Society, 55 L T Rep. 598 (1886), say it is settled that "directors who improperly pay dividends out of capital are liable to repay such dividends personally upon the company being wound up," that the company or a creditor or a liquidator may enforce it; that the acquiescence of the stockholders does not affect creditors, that the statute of limitations does not apply, and that the innocent intent of the directors is no defense

[1] In order to ascertain profits the directors should have a revaluation　If they employ persons whom they reasonably believe to be competent and adopt their conclusions they are not liable for mistakes　Where, however, the directors take no active, intelligent, guiding part in the affairs of the company, and really did nothing except as suggested by the secretary, and do not examine the accounts at all, and cause the stockholders to declare dividends on a statement which omits large liabilities so that dividends are really paid out of the capital stock, such directors are personally liable to corporate creditors for such dividends. The secretary also is liable, he being the active manager of the company　The six-years statute of limitations, however, applies, and only those dividends which have been declared within six years must be repaid　Interest, however, will be allowed　Municipal, etc. Co., Limited, ı Pollington, 63 L. T Rep, 238 (1890), *In re* National Funds, etc, Co, L. R, 10 Ch D, 118 (1878); Gratz *v* Redd, 4 B. Mon, 178 194 (1843); Hill ı Frazier, 22 Pa St, 320 (1853), *In re* Alexander Palace Co, L. R,

21 Chan Div, 149 (1882), Salisbury *v.* Metropolitan R'y Co., 22 L. T. (N S.), 839 (1870), where the suit was by a non-participating stockholder, Flitcroft's Case, L. R., 21 Ch D, 519 (1882); Evans *v* Coventry, 8 De G, M. & G, 835 (1857); Turquand *v* Marshall, L. R, 4 Chan, 376 (1869), denying this remedy to the stockholders as a body.　In Burnes *v* Pennell, 2 House of Lords Cases, 497, 531 (1849), Lord Brougham said · "I beg to be understood as going with those who view with the greatest severity the conduct of railway directors in declaring dividends which can only be paid out of capital, because I consider that that is of itself a most vicious and fraudulent course of conduct.　It is telling the world that their profits are large when it may be that their profits are *nil*, or that their losses are large with no profits.　It is a false and fraudulent representation by act and deed much to be reprobated; and I go to the full length of what my noble and learned friend has laid down, that it would be a just ground, if a course of conduct of this sort were pursued, coupled with such circumstances as clearly to show a fraudulent intent, for proceedings of a graver nature against these parties '　The payment of a dividend out of the capital stock is *ultra vires*, and incapable of ratification by the shareholders.　Accordingly, where the directors mislead the shareholders by representing in the reports and balance sheets as good debts which they know to be bad, and thus knowingly pay dividends which in fact impair the capital stock, it is not a defense that the shareholders, relying in good faith upon the representations and reports of the directors, pass resolutions declaring the dividends at regular meetings of the corporation, and an action will lie on behalf of creditors to compel the direct-

is paid out of the capital stock, the directors are made liable therefor by statute without reference to any fraud or fraudulent intent on their part.[1]

Under certain circumstances, in the absence of actual fraud, the directors who have been compelled to pay the claims of corporate creditors may in turn recover what they have paid in an action against the shareholders[2] But a director from whom a recovery is had under the Pennsylvania statute,[3] as a wrong-doer, has no right of subrogation as against the corporation[4] And claims against directors who are made liable by statute in these cases may, in the absence of actual fraud on their part, be barred by laches[5]

ors to refund In such an action the directors cannot set off any money due from the company to them, nor have they recourse to the shareholders who took the dividends *bona fide* In re Exchange Banking Co., L. R., 21 Chan Div., 519 (1882); *In re* County Marine Ins. Co., L. R., 6 Chan, 104 (1870). See, also, Scott *v.* Eagle Fire Ins Co, 7 Paige 198 (1838). In Kentucky it is doubted whether directors are liable to creditors, the courts of that state seeming to incline to hold them liable only to the corporation or the stockholders Lexington, etc, R. R. Co *v* Bridges, 7 B. Mon, 556, 559 (1847)

[1] In Massachusetts officers of a corporation can be charged, under the statute in force upon the subject in that state (Stat. 1862, ch 218, § 3, Stat 1870, ch. 224, §§ 40, 42), with corporate debts after a judgment against the corporation, and after a demand and return upon the execution Chamberlin *v* Huguenot Manufacturing Co, 118 Mass, 532, 536 (1875), Priest *v* Essex Manufacturing Co, 115 id, 380 (1874) So, in New Jersey, directors are similarly liable by statute Rev of N J. (1877), p 178; Williams *v*. Boice, 38 N J Eq, 364 (1885) And in New York, 1 Rev Stat. ch XVIII, tit 2 art 1, §§ 1, 10 Dividing the property is equivalent to declarations of dividend so far as the directors are concerned Roike *v* Thomas, 56 N Y, 559 (1874) In Massachusetts the liability of the directors has been held to be enforceable by cor-

porate creditors only Smith *v* Hurd, 12 Metc, 371 (1847), and the cases *supra*

[2] Salisbury *v* Metropolitan R'y Co., 22 L T (N S), 839 (1870), *In re* Alexandria Palace Co, L. R, 21 Chan Div, 149 (1882) *Cf.* § 548, *supra* A director who with knowledge of the insolvency of the company loans money to the corporation for the purpose of declaring a dividend is not entitled, upon an assignment of the corporate effects, to repayment of any part of the loan so made until the claims of stockholders are satisfied Kisterbock's Appeal, 51 Pa. St., 483.

[3] Act of 7th April, 1849, § 9.

[4] Hill *v* Frazier, 22 Pa. St, 320 (1853). In this case it was held that, in the creditor's suit against the director, the corporation itself is not a necessary codefendant.

[5] *In re* Mammoth Copperopolis of Utah, 50 L J, Chan 11 (1880) The acquiescence of stockholders does not bind creditors, and the statute of limitations does not apply *Re* Oxford. etc, Society, *supra* That the statute of limitations does not apply, see, also, Flitcroft's Case, L. R, 21 Ch D, 519 (1882) The statute of limitations does not commence to run against an officer of the corporation who has paid dividends to himself out of the capital stock, until the fraud is discovered Main *v* Mills. 6 Biss, 98 (1874), Where the directors paid out dividends from the organization of the company in 1868 until 1878, and were then stopped at the instance

§ 551. *Guaranty of dividends by contract.*—A guaranty of dividends is often made by the corporation itself that issues the stock. The stock is then called guarantied or preferred stock. This class of stock is fully considered elsewhere.[1]

A guaranty of dividends frequently is made by a third person. Such a guaranty is often made when one person sells stock to another and guaranties that the corporation will pay certain dividends thereon. It often arises also where one company buys out another or leases the property of another corporation and guaranties dividends on the stock or the interest on the bonds of the latter. This subject, also, is considered elsewhere.[2]

ot the board of trade, and the company was wound up in 1886, and in 1890 the receiver brought suit to hold the directors liable, it was held that there was not such delay as to bar the remedy, since the defendants had not been prejudiced by the delay. Masonic, etc., Co. *v.* Sharpe, 65 L. T. Rep., 76 (1891); affirmed, 65 id., 806.

[1] See ch. XVI.
[2] See ch. XLVI.

CHAPTER XXXIII.

LIFE ESTATES AND REMAINDERS IN SHARES OF STOCK.

§ 552. *The subject* — Where shares of stock are held by an estate and the income of the estate is to go to a life tenant for life and the remainder to another party, the question of whether the life tenant or the remainder-man is entitled to a stock dividend or extraordinary cash dividend is a perplexing one. The stock dividend or extraordinary cash dividend may represent profits which were earned or accumulated before the life tenancy began. In that case it is clear that in justice the remainder-man should receive it. If, however, it was earned after the life tenancy began, it is clear that the life tenant should have it. If it was earned partly before and partly after the life tenancy began, then it is apparent that in justice some apportionment should be made if possible.

The courts, however, differ widely in laying down rules on this subject. These differences form the subject of this chapter.

§ 553. *The three rules in regard to stock or extraordinary cash dividends* — When a stock or extraordinary cash dividend is declared upon shares held in trust, or owned in such a way that one person has an estate therein for life and another person the remainder over, there at once arises a contest between life tenant and remainder-man. Their interests necessarily conflict, because, if such dividend is held to be income, it belongs to the tenant for life, whereas if it is held to be a part of the *corpus*, or principal, it inures to the benefit of the remainder-man's estate. There are three well-defined rules upon this subject, which may be denominated respectively the American or Pennsylvania, the Massachusetts, and the English rule. They lead to essentially contrary conclusions and will be considered in order.

§ 554 *The American or Pennsylvania rule* — This rule, inasmuch as it obtains in nearly every state in the Union, may well be called the American rule. It proceeds upon the theory that the

court, in disposing of stock or property dividends, as between life
tenant and remainder-man, may properly inquire as to the time
when the fund out of which the extraordinary dividend is to be
paid was earned or accumulated If it is found to have accrued
or been earned before the life estate arose, it is held to be principal, and, without reference to the time when it is declared or made
payable, to belong to the *corpus* of the estate, and not to go to the
life tenant. But when it is found that the fund out of which the
dividend is paid accrued or was earned, not before but after the
life estate arose, then it is held that the dividend is income, and
belongs to the tenant for life.[1] This salutary rule prevails not only
in Pennsylvania, where it seems to have first been clearly declared,
but also in many other jurisdictions.[2]

§ 555 *The Massachusetts rule* — This rule, which prevails in
Massachusetts, Georgia and Rhode Island, is sometimes called "the
rule in Minot's Case" It regards cash dividends, whether large
or small, as income, and stock dividends, whenever earned and

---

[1] Earp's Appeal, 28 Pa. St., 368 (1857),
Wiltbank's Appeal, 64 Pa St, 256 (1870)
See, also, the following later Pennsylvania cases in point Moss' Appeal, 83 Pa.
St., 264 (1877), Biddle's Appeal, 99 id,
278 (1882), S C. 3 Am Prob. Rep.,
442, Vinton's Appeal, 99 Pa St., 434
(1882) S C, 3 Am Prob Rep., 231,
In re Thompson's Estate, 11 Week
Notes Cas, 482 (1882) *Cf* Roberts Appeal, 92 Pa St., 407 (1880), Thompson's
Appeal, 89 id, 36 (1879) A scrip dividend converted into stock belongs to
the life tenant Philadelphia, etc. Co.'s
Appeal, 16 Atl Rep., 734 (Pa, 1889) A
large dividend in cash, owing to a sale
of part of the property of an unincorporated association is income, and goes
to the life tenant Appeal of Merchants'
Fund Assoc 20 Atl Rep 327 (Pa, 1890).
Money received by the corporation from
new stock issued to obtain funds to replace profits which had been used for
improvements is capital and not income, and does not go to the life tenant.
Smith's Appeal 21 Atl Rep., 439 (Pa.,
1891) Where the company in which
the trustee holds stock gives to its stockholders the option to subscribe to the
stock of another company, the premium
at which the trustee sells this option is

principal and not income *In re* Thompson's Estate, 26 Atl Rep., 652 (Pa, 1893).

[2] *Connecticut* A stock dividend based
upon the profits actually invested in the
business is not income or dividends such
as pass to the life tenant Spooner r
Phillips *et al*, 24 Atl Rep., 524 (Conn,
1892). In Connecticut it is held that
where an estate is merged into a corporation, the life tenant of the real estate
cannot claim that a part of the capital
stock represents past increase of value
and that she is entitled absolutely to that
part of the stock Hotchkiss r. Brainerd, etc, Co, 19 Atl Rep., 521 (Conn,
1889)

Kentucky As between a life beneficiary in corporate stock and the remainder-man, a stock dividend will be
treated as income if it in fact represents
a profit A privilege given by a corporation to its stockholders to take additional stock at par is appurtenant to the
old stock, and does not belong to the life
beneficiary. Aite r Hite, 20 S W Rep,
878 (Ky, 1892), S. C below, 2 R'y &
Corp. L J, 568

Maine For the rule in Maine, see
Richardson v. Richardson, 75 Me, 570
(1884) A stock dividend of a company
purchased by an issue of its bonds be-

however declared, as capital, and the rule, accordingly, is a simple one. Cash dividends belong to the tenant for life and stock dividends to the *corpus*[1] There is little doubt, however, that this rule works great hardship and injustice in many cases.

The court in deciding whether the distribution is a stock or a cash dividend may consider the actual and substantial character of the transaction, and not its nominal character merely.[2]

longs not to the life estate but to the body of the estate. Gilkey *v.* Paine, 14 Atl. Rep., 205 (Me, 1888)

New Hampshire Lord *v* Brooks, 52 N H, 72 (1872), Wheeler *v* Perry, 18 N H, 307 (1846), Pierce *v* Burroughs, 58 N H, 302 (1878)

New Jersey Van Doren *v* Olden, 19 N J Eq, 176 (1868), Ashurst *v* Field's Adm'r, 26 id, 1 (1875)

New York Riggs *v* Cragg, 89 N Y., 479 (1882), *In re* Kernochan, 104 N Y, 618 (1887), Riggs *v* Cragg, 26 Hun, 89 (1881), Clarkson *v* Clarkson, 18 Barb, 646 (1855); Simpson *v* Moore, 30 Barb, 637 (1859). Estate of Woodruff 1 Tucker (New York Surrogate Ct.), 58 (1865), and Goldsmith *v* Swift, 25 Hun 201 (1881) *Cf* Cragg *v* Riggs, 5 Redf, 82 (1880); Scovil *v* Roosevelt, 5 id, 121 (1881) Profits upon the sale of stock are principal and not income in New York Whitney *v* Phœnix, 4 Redf, 180 (1880) In Hyatt *v* Allen, 56 N Y, 553, 557 (1874), the court of appeals intimated plainly its disapproval of the rule prevailing in England upon this subject. Farwell *v* Tweddle, 10 Abb. N C, 94, Estate of Prime, N Y. L J, March 6, 1891, reviewing the authorities. A dividend arising from the sale of part of the assets of the company belong to the remainder-man *In re* Curtis, N Y L J, January 24, 1890 Money received from stock upon the winding up of the corporation belongs to the remainder-man. *In re* Skillman's Estate, 9 N Y Supp, 469 (1890) Where the capital is reduced and returned to the stockholders with a surplus, the surplus goes to the life tenant. *In re* Warren's Estate, 11 N. Y Supp, 787 (1890)

South Carolina Profits and income existing when the trust is created are *corpus*, but subsequent profits and income are income Cobb *v* Fant, 14 S E Rep, 959 (S C, 1892) For articles on "Right to dividends as between life tenant and remainder-man," American Law Review, February, 1892. and 24 Am Rep, 169 Concerning the question as to the rights of the life tenant and remainder-man where trustees buy securities at a premium or sell them at a premium, see Scovil *v* Roosevelt, 5 Redf, 121, Townsend *v* U S Trust Co, 3 id, 220, Ducios *v* Benner, 5 N Y Supp, 734, Farwell *v* Tweddle, 10 Abb N C, 94, Whittemore *v* Peekman, 2 Dem, 275, Appeal of Hele, 19 Atl Rep, 362 See note in 18 Abb. N. C, 185

[1] Minot *v* Paine, 99 Mass, 101 (1868) In this case the principle is thus stated, "A simple rule is to regard cash dividends, however large, as income, and stock dividends, however made, as capital" In subsequent cases this rule has been affirmed and elaborated Daland *v* Williams, 101 Mass, 571 (1869), Leland *v*. Hayden, 102 id, 542 (1869), Heard *v* Eldridge, 109 id, 258 (1872) Rand *v* Hubbell, 115 id, 461 (1874); Gifford *v* Thompson, 115 id, 478 (1874), Hemenway *v* Hemenway, 134 id, 446 (1883), New England Trust Co *v* Eaton, 140 Mass 532 (1886) See. also, Harvard College *v* Amory, 9 Pick, 446 (1830), Balch *v* Hallet, 10 Gray, 402 (1858), Atkins *v* Albree, 94 Mass, 359 (1866)

[2] Thus, in Daland *v* Williams, 101 Mass, 571 (1869), where the directors, having voted to increase the capital stock by three thousand shares, declared

The supreme court of the United States has held that a life tenant of stock does not take a stock dividend declared during the life tenancy [1]

In Rhode Island the courts have adopted a rule somewhat like "the rule in Minot's Case," without the modification ingrafted upon it by the subsequent decisions of the Massachusetts courts   It is a rule which in general prefers the remainder-man to the life tenant.[2]

a cash dividend of forty per cent, and authorized the treasurer to receive that dividend in payment for two thousand eight hundred of the shares the remaining two hundred shares to be sold, the court held that the transaction was virtually a stock dividend, and that the shares must go to the remainder-man's fund   Cf Rand v Hubbell, 115 Mass, 461 (1874) In Leland v Hayden, 102 Mass, 542 (1869), where it appeared that the company had invested its surplus earnings in its own stock and subsequently declared a dividend of that stock, the life tenant was held absolutely entitled to it. The life tenant takes the dividend where it is in cash, although the cash is derived from increased stock which is offered to the old stockholders for subscription, the profits having been used for improvements This is not a stock dividend   Davis v Jackson, 25 N E Rep. 21 (Mass, 1890) See also, Balch v Hallett 10 Gray, 402 (1858), Reed v Head, 6 Allen, 174 (1863), Harvard College v Amory, 9 Pick, 446 (1830), Gifford v Thompson, 115 Mass, 478 (1874) Heménway v Heménway, 134 Mass, 416 (1883) In New England Trust Co v Eaton 140 Mass, 532 (1886), it was held, in an elaborate opinion by Devens, J, that the gain or loss arising from the sale of stock held in trust is the gain or loss of the *corpus*, and that the sum received constitutes a new principal Accordingly, a trustee who has invested in bonds at a premium may retain annually from the income payable to the life tenant such sums as will restore to the fund at its maturity what was taken therefrom at the time of the investment. See, also, the dissenting opinion

of Mr Justice Holmes in this case; and cf Bowker v Pierce, 130 Mass, 262 (1881), Dodd v Winship, 133 id, 359 (1882), Wright v White, 136 id, 470 (1884), Parsons v Winslow, 16 id, 361 (1820), Lovell v Minot, 20 Pick, 116 (1838) The court will take into consideration, in determining the question as between life tenant and remainder-man, the whole character of the transaction, and the nature and source of the property distributed, with due regard to all the facts preceding, attending and resulting from the declaration of the dividend In Heard v Eldridge, 109 Mass, 258 (1872), it is said "The suggestion that the intention of the directors shall determine the question whether the dividend is capital or income cannot be correct. .   It is more safe to look at the character of the property and the transaction " See three interesting and valuable little pamphlets, by a layman, wherein the merits of the question are fully and learnedly discussed, published by G P Putnam's Sons, New York, and entitled respectively "Common Sense *versus* Judicial Legislation," "Stock Dividends, the Rule in Minot's Case Restated, with Variations by the Supreme Judicial Court of Massachusetts," and "A Third Chapter on the Rule in Minot's Case " See 5 Am Law Rev, 720 (July, 1871), Perry on Trusts (3d ed), §§ 544 545 and the notes. In Georgia the code is construed so as to follow the Massachusetts rule Millan v Guerrard, 67 Ga, 284 (1881); Code of Georgia, § 2256

[1] Gibbons v Mahon, 132 U. S, 549 (1890)

[2] Parker v Mason, 8 R. L, 427 (1867);

§§ 556-557. *The English rule* — In England an ordinary, regular, usual cash dividend or stock or property dividend belongs to the life tenant, while an extraordinary cash or stock or property dividend belongs to the *corpus* of the trust [1] This rule was established in 1799 in England.[2]

Busbee *v.* Freeman, 11 R. I. 149 (1875), Petition of Brown 14 R. I., 371 (1884) A stock dividend is capital and not income Greene *v.* Smith. 19 Atl Rep, 1081 (R. I, 1890)

[1] The courts, perhaps uniformly, insist upon this distinction Extraordinary dividends may be either of cash or stock, and appear under a variety of names, such as ' participations,' "distributions," or, more commonly, ' bonuses" See Witts *v.* Steere, 13 Vesey, 363 (1807), Norris *v.* Harrison, 2 Madd, 268 (1817), Hooper *v.* Rossiter, McClelland, 527 (1824), Bates *v.* MacKinley, 31 Beav 280 (1862) To the point that regular dividends, though increased in amount, go as income to the owner of the life estate, see Barclay *v.* Wainewright, 14 Vesey, 66 (1807), Price *v.* Anderson, 15 Sim, 473 (1847) To the point that "extra" or unusual dividends, whether of cash or shares, go to augment the principal of the trust fund, see Irving *v.* Houstoun, 4 Paton's H of L Cases, 521, 1803 (a stock dividend), Hooper *v.* Rossiter, McCleland 527, 1824 (a stock dividend) *In re* Barton's Trust, L. R, 5 Eq 238, 1868 (a stock dividend), Paris *v.* Paris, 10 Vesey, 185, 1804 (a cash dividend), Clayton *v.* Gresham, 10 Vesey, 288, 1804 (a cash dividend), Witts *v.* Steere, 13 Vesey, 363, 1807 (a cash dividend), Price *v.* Anderson, 15 Sim, 473, 1847 (a cash dividend), Bates *v.* MacKinley, 31 Beav, 280 1862 (a cash dividend). *Cf* Gill *v.* Burley, 22 Beav, 619 (1856), Straker *v.* Wilson, L R., 6 Chan, 503 (1871)

[2] Brander *v.* Brander, 4 Vesey, 800 (1799), Paris *v.* Paris, 10 Vesey, 185 (1804), Irving *v.* Houstoun, 4 Paton's H of L., 521 (1803), Preston *v.* Melville, 16 Sim, 163 (1848), Barclay *v.* Wainewright, 14 Vesey, 66 (1807), Murray *v.*

Glassee, 17 Jur, 816 (1852), Johnson *v.* Johnson, 15 Jur 714 (1850), Witts *v.* Steere, 13 Vesey, 363 (1807), *In re* Barton's Trust, L. R, 5 Eq. 238 (1868), Plumbe *v.* Neild, 6 Jur (N S), 529 (1860) Hollis *v.* Allen, 12 Jur (N S), 638 (1866), Hooper *v.* Rossiter 13 Price, 774 (1824), Bates *v.* MacKinley, 31 Beav, 280 (1862) See, also. *In re* Hopkins Trust, L. R, 18 Eq, 696 (1874), Scholefield *v.* Redfern, 32 L. J, Chan, 627 (1863) Hartley *v.* Allen 4 Jur (N S), 500, Lock *v.* Venables, 27 Beav, 598 (1859), holding to the effect that a specific bequest of " the dividends interest and proceeds ' of shares will not pass a bonus on the shares In Alcock *v.* Sloper, 2 Mylne & K, 699 (1833), the "income of the testator's long annuities' was given to the life tenant Wildey *v.* Sandys, L. R, 7 Eq 455 (1869). In Lane *v.* Loughnan, 7 Vict L. R, Eq, 19 (1881), it was held that the premium on a lease of part of a trust estate belonged to the tenant for life and not to the *corpus* An executor may plainly transfer the stock to pay the decedents debts although it is bequeathed for life with remainder over Franklin *v.* Bank of England 1 Russ. 575 (1826) In Clive *v.* Clive Kay (Eng Chan) 600 (1854), by the terms of the deed of settlement the net profits of the concern were to be divided ratably to such an amount as should be declared at the semi-annual meetings, and were to be paid within twenty-one days thereafter and it was provided that a shareholder was not to receive any dividend after the period at which he ceased to be a proprietor of shares, but the dividends on such shares were to continue in suspense until some other person should become proprietor of them When a shareholder died sixty-nine

There are, however, recent cases in England to the effect that extraordinary cash dividends may be decreed to belong to the life tenant [1] There, of course, is no question that ordinary cash dividends belong to the life tenant [2] This rule applies even though it may be shown that the dividend in question was earned, wholly or in part, before the commencement of the life estate [3]

Where it is shown that dividends have been fraudulently retained in prejudice of the rights of the life tenant, and subsequently a bonus is paid upon the shares, it belongs, as income deferred, to the tenant for life, even though it be called a bonus [4]

days after a half-yearly meeting at which a dividend had been declared, but before notice had been given that such dividend was payable, having by his will bequeathed the interest and annual income arising from all his shares to one for life, and then in remainder to others, it was held that this dividend belonged to the legatee for life, and not to the general personal estate of the testator See, also, Title to Dividends, 19 Am Law Rev 571 (1885) Bostock r Blakeney, 2 Brown's Chan, 653 (1788) Re Willoughby, 53 Law Times Rep, 926 (1886), 2 Perry on Trusts, §§ 544 547 Mr Monk's note, 31 Eng Rep, 328, 332, Browne r Collins, L R, 12 Eq, 586 (1871) is to the effect that profits of a partnership accrued and earned before, but not set aside qua profits until after the death of the testator, belong to the corpus of the estate, and that profits accruing after his death go to the tenant for life as income See, also the recent and important review of the whole subject in Bouche r Sproule, 57 L T, 345 (H of L, 1887), reversing the court below, Bouche r Sproule, 29 Ch D 635 (1885)

[1] In the case of Sugden r Alsbury, 63 L T Rep, 576 (1890), the court held that the life tenant was entitled to an extraordinary dividend payable in cash The dividend was called a bonus, but was nothing more nor less than a large dividend, being a division of accumulated profits In the case of Ellis r Barfield, 64 L T Rep, 625 (1891), the court held that a large dividend was income

and belonged to the life tenant, although it was used by the trustee to pay up the stock in full, and also to purchase new shares which he immediately sold, but the excess for which he sold the stock at a profit belongs to the remainder-man

[2] A cash dividend of profits which have been earned since the last preceding dividend, such last preceding dividend having been made in a regular and reasonable time previously, belongs to a life tenant of stock, and not to the remainder-man Barclay v Wainewright, 14 Ves, 66 (1807); Norris v. Harrison, 2 Madd, 268 (1817); Clive v. Clive, Kay, 600 (1854), Murray r Glasse, 17 Jur, 816 (1853), Preston v Melville, 16 Sim, 163 (1848), Cuming r. Boswell, 2 Jur (N S), 1005 (1856) Cf Ware v McCandlish, 11 Leigh (Va), 595 (1841), Price r Anderson, 15 Sim, 473 (1847); Witt r Steere, 13 id, 563 (1807). As will be seen hereafter, in England a different rule prevails if the cash dividend is made from long-accumulated profits.

[3] Bates r MacKinley, 31 Bear 280 (1862) Jones r Ogle, L R, 8 Chan, 192 (1872)

[4] Maclaren r Stainton, L R, 11 Eq, 382, S C, 3 De G, F & J, 202 (1861), reversing S C, 27 Bear, 460 (1859); Edmondson r Crosthwaite, 34 Bear, 30 (1864), Dale r Hayes 40 L J, Chan, 244 (1871), S C, 24 L T (N S), 12, 19 W R, 299 Cf Lean r Lean, 33 L T, (N S), 305 S C, 23 W R, 484, Lambert r Lambert, 29 L T (N S), 878 (1874) S C, 22 W R, 359 In re Tinkler, 45 L J (Chan Div), 135

In all cases, however, the intent of the grantor or testator is the pole-star, and will be carried out by the courts [1]

§ 558 *The apportionment of dividends* — When a life tenant dies before the date at which a dividend is declared, the question arises whether the dividend declared next after his death ought or ought not to be apportioned between the reversioner or remainder-man and the estate of the life tenant for the period of time partially covered by the life estate   It is, in general, the rule in such a case that the dividend is not apportionable, but belongs entirely to the *corpus* of the trust fund [2]   But where a tenant for life dies after the dividend is declared, but before the dividend becomes due, his estate will be entitled to the whole of that dividend [3]   In England, however, under the statute known as the Apportionment Act of 1870, dividends are apportionable in these cases between the estate of the life tenant and the *corpus;* [4] and in this country at common

---

[1] *In re* Bouch, L. R., 29 Chan Div, 635 (1885), *In re* Hopkin's Trusts L R, 18 Eq , 696 (1874), Jones v Ogle. L R. 14 Eq, 419 (1872), *Re* Box's Trusts, 9 L T (N S), 372 (1863). *Cf* Read v Head, 6 Allen, 174 (1863), Clarkson v Clarkson. 18 Barb., 646 (1855) Millen v Guerrard, 67 Ga , 284 (1881), Thomson's Appeal, 89 Pa St 36 (1879)

[2] Pearly v Smith, 3 Atk , 260 (1745) Sherrard v Sherrard, id , 502 (1747). Wilson v Harman 2 Vesey, Sen , 672 (1755), Hartley v Allen 4 Jur (N S) 500 (1858), *In re* Maxwell's Trusts 1 Hem & M , 610 (1863) Scholefield v Redfern. 2 Drew. & Sm , 173 (1863), Foote, Appellant, 22 Pick , 299 (1839) Granger v Bassett, 98 Mass , 462 (1868), Clapp v Astor, 2 Edw Chan 379 (1834) *Cf* Hyatt v Allen 56 N Y . 553 (1874), Brundage v Brundage 60 id 544, 551 (1875), Perry on Trusts, § 556 , 1 Williams on Executors § 836 note *m* But in Massachusetts it has been held that sometimes dividends declared after the life tenant's death will, nevertheless, go to his estate   Thus a life tenancy in stock for the support of the testator's widow and children was held to entitle the widow's estate to a dividend declared after her death but for a period which expired before that event Johnson v Bridgewater Mfg Co 14

Gray, 271 (1859)   See, also, Ellis v Proprietors of Essex Merrimack Bridge, 2 Pick , 243 (1824) Gifford v Thompson, 115 Mass , 478 (1874) *Cf* King v Follett, 3 Vt , 385 (1831), in which the residuary legatee claimed from the legatee of certain stock the share of dividends earned in the life-time of his testator, but declared after his death , the court holding that a sale or gift of stock carries with it all dividends declared after it takes effect, whether earned before or not.

[3] *Wright* v Tuckett, 1 J & H, 266 (1860), Paton v Sheppard, 10 Sim , 186 (1839)

[4] 33 and 34 Vict, ch 35 § 2 Pollock v Pollock, L R., 18 Eq , 329 (1874), qualifying or explaining Whitehead v Whitehead, L R, 16 Eq , 528 (1873), Beavan v Beavan, 53 L T Rep, 245 (1885)   *Cf* Capron v Capron, L R.. 17 Eq 288 (1874) and see Banner v Lowe 13 Ves 135 (1806), Hay v Palmer 2 P Wms , 501 (1727) The statute applies only to dividends upon the stock of corporations, strictly speaking, and not to those upon the shares in private trading corporations Jones v Ogle, L R S Chan , 192 (1872) And does not apply to stock dividends Hartley v Allen 4 Jur (N S.), 500 (1858)

law, in one or two jurisdictions, there is a tendency to hold that dividends are apportionable [1]

§ 559 *The right to subscribe for new shares as between life tenant and remainder-man* — The right to subscribe for new shares at par upon an increase of the capital stock, which is an incident of the ownership of the stock, does not belong as a privilege to the life tenant, but such an increment must be treated as capital, and be added to the trust fund for the benefit of the remainder-man This is equally the rule whether the trustee subscribes for the new stock for the benefit of the trust or sells the right to subscribe for a valuable consideration In either event the increase goes to the *corpus* [2] The subsequent income, however, of such increase belongs, during the continuance of the life tenancy, to the life tenant as income, the new shares are part of the *corpus*, and the life tenant, being entitled to the income from the *corpus*, takes the income from the accretions thereto. [3]

§ 560 *Miscellaneous questions herein* — The life tenant must pay calls which are made [4] and taxes levied [5] during the continuance of

---

[1] In *Ex parte* Rutledge, 1 Harper s Eq (S C), 65 (1824), S C. 14 Am Dec, 696, a dividend was apportioned between life tenant and remainder-man This is regarded a leading case in favor of apportionment. In Pennsylvania the interest on municipal bonds and on the bonds of private corporations is apportionable, but *quere* whether or not the interest on government bonds would be Wilson s Appeal, 108 Pa St, 344 (1885), overruling Earp's Will 1 Parson's Eq Cas, 556 But in Massachusetts the statute of apportionment is held not to apply to dividends upon the stock of corporations Granger v Bassett, 98 Mass, 362, 469 (1868), construing Gen Stat of Mass, ch 97, § 24 In New York an apportionment is provided for by Laws of 1875, ch 542 See Goldsmith v Swift, 25 Hun, 201 (1881)

[2] Atkins v Albree 94 Mass, 359 (1866) Brinley v Grou, 50 Conn, 66 (1882) Biddle's Appeal, 99 Pa St, 278 (1882), Moss' Appeal, 83 Pa. St, 264 (1877), Vinton's Appeal, 99 Pa St, 434 (1882), Goldsmith v Swift, 25 Hun, 201 (1881) Sanders v Bromley, 55 L T (N S), Chan. Div. 145 (1886) Profit upon the sale of stock is *corpus*, and not income for the life tenant Whitney v Phoenix, 4 Redf (N Y Sur), 180 (1880) Cf Leith v Wells, 48 N Y, 585 (1872), Hemenway v Hemenway, 134 Mass, 446 (1883), New England Trust Co v Eaton, 140 Mass, 532 (1886), S. C, 4 Am Prob Rep., 368 Sometimes certificates of new stock are not stock dividends. Chicago, etc, R. R. Co v Page, 1 Biss, 461 (1864) In Londesborough v Somerville, 19 Beav, 295 (1854), where consols were sold just before a dividend day and the proceeds invested in realty, a tenant for life was held entitled to be paid, as income on the consols, the difference between the price obtained and the value exclusive of the next dividend See, also, in general § 286, *supra*

[3] Moss' Appeal, 83 Pa St, 264 (1877), Biddle's Appeal, 99 Pa St, 278 (1882), and the cases generally cited in the preceding note, *In re* Bromley, 55 L T (N S), Chan Div, 145 (1886)

[4] *Re* Box's Trusts, 9 L T (N S), 372

[5] Webb v Town of Burlington, 28 Vt, 188 (1856), Citizens' Mutual Ins Co v Lott, 45 Ala., 185 (1871). Cf Nat Albany Exchange Bank *v.* Wells, 18 Blatch, 478 (1890),

his estate upon shares held in trust for his benefit   And where stock to produce a fixed income is bequeathed for life, a subsequent increase in the earnings from that stock inures to the benefit of the life tenant [1] But the enhanced price for which stock sells by reason of dividends earned but not declared belongs entirely to the remainder.[2] A life tenant is not entitled to have the stock transferred to him on the corporate books [3] But the corporation, if it had notice of the trust, may be held liable for transferring shares in prejudice of the rights of the life tenant [4] And an administrator who permits an irregular transfer in fraud of the life tenant's rights makes himself personally liable [5] A dividend declared before but payable after the testator's death belongs to the estate [6] A claim of the company against the life tenant for dividends paid cannot be enforced against the remainder-man's interest.[7]

(1863), Day v Day, 1 Dr & Sm, 261 In case of a life estate, followed by a life estate, followed by a remainder to the nominees of the first life tenant, the estate of the first life tenant is liable for calls made after the remainder commences   Hobbs v Wayet, 57 L T Rep, 225 (1887) If a call becomes due the day after the testator dies it is the duty of the executor to pay it from the general fund   Emery v Wason, 107 Mass, 507 (1871)

[1] Russell v Loring, 3 Allen, 121 (1861) But when a fixed income is bequeathed and the income fails or falls short, the principal must be resorted to   Bonham v Bonham, 33 N J Eq, 476, Haydel v Hulck, 72 Mo, 253 The opposite rule, however, prevails in New York   Delaney v Van Aulen, 84 N Y, 16 (1881), reversing S C 21 Hun, 274. Cf Crawford v Dox, 5 Hun, 507 (1875) See, also, § 304.

[2] Scholefield v Redfern, 32 L J, Chan, 627 (1863), Abercrombie v Riddle 3 Md Chan, 320 (1850), Van Blarcom v Daget, 31 N J. Eq, 783 (1879) Cf Londesborough v Somerville, 19 Beav, 295 (1854), Matter of Stutzer, 26 Hun, 481 (1882), Re Accounting of Gerry, 103 N Y, 445

[3] Collier v Collier, 3 Ohio St, 369 (1854) Cf State v. Robinson 57 Md,

186 (1881) If the corporation transfer the stock to the life tenant, even by orders of the court, but issues a certificate not stating the facts of life tenancy, and tells a purchaser of the certificate that it is all right, the corporation is liable to the remainder-man   Caulkins v Memphis, etc., Co, 4 S. W Rep, 287 (Tenn, 1887) See, also, Lindley on Partnership, p 1079, etc

[4] Stewart v Fireman's Ins Co, 53 Md, 564 (1880)

[5] Keeney v Globe Mill Co, 39 Conn, 145 (1872) See, also, Ames v Williamson, 17 West Va., 673 (1881)

[6] De Gendre v Kent, L R, 4 Eq, 283 (1867) Cf Browne v Collins, L R 12 Eq 586, 591, Locke v Venables 27 Beav, 598 (1859) See also, Cogswell v Cogswell, 2 Edw Chan, 231 (1831), Abercrombie v Riddle, 3 Md Chan 320 (1850), Wright v Tuckett 1 Johns & Hem, 266 (1860), Furley v Hydes, 42 L J. Ch, 626

[7] Where a fixed per cent is paid annually to stockholders instead of dividends and charged to them and the stock held in pledge for the same, such a payment to the life tenant does not create a valid lien on the stock as against the remainder-man   Reading, etc., Co. v Reading etc, Works 21 Atl Rep, 169 (Pa, 1891).

CHAPTER XXXIV.

TAXATION OF SHARES OF STOCK AND OF CORPORATIONS.

§ 561 *The four methods of taxing corporate interests —* There are, in general, four methods of taxing corporate interests. These are, first, by a tax on the franchise, second, on the capital stock; third, on the real estate and personal property of the corporation; fourth, by a tax on the shares of stock in the hands of the stockholders[1] There is another mode of taxation which is sometimes adopted — a tax on corporate dividends, but since this is generally construed to be only a method of valuing the franchise or capital stock, it can hardly be called a fifth method of taxing corporate interests[2]

It is entirely within the discretion of the legislature to say which one of these four methods of taxation shall be adopted, where the matter is not regulated by the state constitution Not only this, but it is also within the discretion of the legislature to tax the corporation in two or more of these ways — to levy a double tax on the corporate interests, and even to levy a treble or quadruple tax thereon

[1] Redfield on Railways, vol II (3d ed), Ill, 556 (1876), Louisville, etc., R. R. Co p. 453, Ottawa Glass Co v McCaleb, 81 v State, 8 Heisk (Tenn), 663, 795
[2] See § 572a.

746

A. TAXATION OF SHARES OF STOCK

§ 562 *Relation of stockholders to the first three methods of taxation* —The stockholders in a corporation have very little to do directly with any of the first three modes of taxing corporate interests   The tax is levied directly against the corporation, and is paid by the corporate officers out of the treasury of the corporation   If the tax is unauthorized or illegal, or improperly assessed, or is based on too high a valuation, it is ordinarily the duty of the corporate officers to rectify or oppose such tax   The stockholders have nothing to do with the ordinary transaction of corporate business, of which this forms a part.   Where, however, the corporate officers refuse, upon request of one or more stockholders, to oppose or decline to pay an unauthorized tax levied in any one of the three methods mentioned above, the stockholder himself may bring a suit in a court of equity, in behalf of and for the protection of the corporate interests, to enjoin the payment and collection of such unauthorized tax [1]

§ 563. *Tax on shares of stock as distinguished from the other methods* —A tax on shares of stock is clearly different from a tax upon the franchise, the corporate property or the capital stock   Especially is it important to distinguish a tax on shares of stock from a tax on the capital stock.[2]   The latter is always taxed against

---

[1] Dodge *v* Woolsey, 18 How   331 (1855), State Bank of Ohio *v* Knoop, 16 id , 369 (1853); Wilmington R. R Co *v* Reed, 13 Wall , 264 (1871), Delaware R. R. Tax, 18 id , 206 (1873), Greenwood *v* Freight Co, 105 U S, 13 (1881), Paine *v*. Wright, 6 McClain, 395 (1855), Foote *v*. Linck, 5 McClain, 616 (1853), holding also that the corporation is a necessary party, and that if the complainant is a non-resident he may bring the suit in the United States circuit court, Davenport *v* Dows, 18 Wall , 626 (1873), also holding that the corporation is a necessary party defendant, Bailey *v* Atlantic, etc , R R Co , 5 Dill , 22 (1871), Parmley *v* Railroad Cos, 5 Dill , 13, 25 (1874)   But the stockholder must allege actual tender of the amount of tax conceded to be due   Allegation of readiness to pay is insufficient.   Huntington *v* Palmer, 8 Fed Rep , 449 (1881)   See, also, Trask *v* Maguire, 18 Wall , 391 (1873), Wood *v* Draper, 24 Barb , 187

(1857), London *v* City of Wilmington, 78 N C, 190 (1878), § 494   The case of State *v* Flavell, 21 N J L, 370 (1854), denies this right   A stockholder's injunction against a tax in corporate property falls when the property is subsequently sold under execution   Secor *v* Singleton, 35 Fed Rep 376 (1888)   The general character of such a suit as this comes under the principles of law set forth in Part IV, *infra*

[2] In the case of Porter *v* Rockford, R. I, etc   R. R Co , 76 Ill, 561 (1875), the court clearly recognized this distinction, and said   The legal property of the shareholder is quite distinct from that of the corporation, although the shares of stock have no value save that which they derive from the corporate property and franchise, and a tax levied upon the property of the one is not, in a legal sense, levied upon the property of the other"   See, also, Bradley *v* Bauder, 36 Ohio St , 28 (1880)   *Cf.* Dela-

the corporation, is paid by the corporation, and is based on a valuation which does not necessarily depend on the value of the shares of stock   A tax on the shares of stock is generally levied directly against the stockholders themselves at their place of residence, is based on the market value of the stock, and is entirely distinct from the location, interests, property or taxes of the corporation itself.   There are, however, some instances of taxation herein which are on the border-line between the two   Thus, a statute expressly laying a tax on the shares of stock, but requiring the corporation to pay that tax from the corporate funds, has been held to be a tax not on the shares of stock but on the capital stock.   In other jurisdictions it has been held to be a tax on the shares of stock. Taxes on shares of stock in national banks are frequently so levied and collected and are held to be upon the shares of stock and not on the capital stock.[1]   A tax laid on shares owned by non-residents

ware R. R. Tax, 18 Wall, 206, 230 (1873); Farrington ι Tennessee, 95 U S., 679 where the distinction is clearly drawn, Quincy Bridge Co ι Adams Co, 88 Ill, 615 (1878)   In the case of North Ward National Bank ι City of Newark, 39 N J L, 380 (1877), the court said   'The moneyed capital of a bank is an entirely different thing from its capital stock   The former is the property of the corporation   It may consist of cash or bills discounted or be in part invested in real estate or in the securities of federal government.   In whatever form it is invested, it is owned by the bank as a corporate entity and not by the stockholders.   The stock or shares represent the interests of the shareholders, which entitle them to participate in the net profits of the bank in the employment of its capital, and is a distinct and independent interest or property in the shareholders, held by them like other property "   The case of Porter ι Rockford, etc, R. R. Co, *supra*, holds also that a tax on the "capital stock" means the property of the corporation and not the aggregate of the shares of stock   See, also, State v Hamilton, 5 Ind, 310 (1854) where the word "stock" was construed to mean the tangible property of the corporation   But see Trask v Maguire, 18 Wall, 391 (1873).   And even though the

value of the capital stock is estimated by the aggregate value of the shares, it is still a tax on the capital stock   New O, etc, R. R. Co ι Board of Assessors, 32 La Ann, 19 (1880)   See, also, State Bank of Va ι City of Richmond, 79 Va, 113   So, also, where the franchise is valued in that manner for taxation   Commonwealth ι Hamilton Mfg Co, 91 Mass, 298 (1866), Att'y-Gen ι Bay State Min Co, 99 Mass, 148 (1868)   Hamilton Co v Massachusetts, 6 Wall 632 (1867), holds that a tax on the excess of the market value of the stock over the value of the corporate realty and machinery is a franchise tax   In Indiana it is held that a tax on the shares of stock is the proper mode of taxation unless the statute provides otherwise   Whitney v. City of Madison, 23 Ind, 331 (1864).   *Cf.* Wright v Stolz 27 Ind, 333 (1866). The mere fact that the corporation is compelled to pay the tax does not prevent its being considered a tax on the shares. National Bank ι Commonwealth, 9 Wall, 353, 360 (1869), per Miller, J. Stockholders are liable for taxes levied on a distillery where the statute levies the tax on "persons interested in the use of the distillery "   United States v Walters, 46 Fed Rep., 509 (1891).

[1] See § 570, *infra.*

of the state which creates the corporation and which levies the tax is a tax on the shares of stock and not on the capital stock, even though the corporation is required to pay it and to collect the same from the owners of those shares

§ 564 *Tax on stockholders residing in the state creating the corporation* — The right of the state to tax resident stockholders of a resident corporation on their shares of stock is undoubted, and has been unquestioned except where double taxation would result therefrom and is prohibited, or where a constitutional provision restricts this mode of taxation.[1] Generally such a tax on resident stockholders is levied on them, not in the municipality where the corporation is, but in the cities, counties or towns where the stockholders respectively reside This is always the rule if the statute is silent, and is the rule unless the statute expressly provides otherwise[2]

Controversies sometimes arise as to the power of a municipality to tax stockholders living in the state, but not in the municipality which levies a tax on their shares of stock, the corporation itself being located within that municipality. The law plainly is that such a tax is unauthorized, illegal and not collectible unless the municipality is authorized by statute to levy the tax[3] A mere

[1] In Illinois, under the act of 1872 taxing railroad corporations, resident stockholders in domestic corporations are not taxed Porter v Rockford, etc., R R. Co., 76 Ill , 561 (1875). In Iowa stock is taxed under section 813 of the code. See Cook v City of Burlington, 59 Iowa, 251 (1882); Henkle v Town of Keota, 27 N. W. Rep, 250 (1886) *Cf.* National State Bank v Young, 25 Iowa, 311 In Iowa, where deductions for debts are allowed to persons taxed on their "credits," no deduction is allowed from the tax on shares of stock. They are not "credits" Bridgman v. City of Keokuk, 33 N W. Rep., 355 (Iowa, 1887) As to the valuation of the shares of stock, see St Charles, etc., R R. Co v Assessors, 31 La. Ann , 852 (1879) If the corporation owns shares of its own stock it is taxable the same as though owned by another. Richmond, etc', R. R. Co. v Alamance Co , 84 N C, 504 (1881)

[2] City of Evansville v Hall, 14 Ind , 27 (1850). A pledgor is the proper person to be assessed on stock which has been pledged Tucker v Aiken, 7 N H , 113 (1834) A pledgee of stock is not subject to a tax levied on the shares of stock held by him Waltham Bank v Waltham, 51 Mass , 334 (1845) In Massachusetts shares held by executors or administrators are taxed in the town of which the deceased was an inhabitant at the time of his death, and shares held by trustees are taxed in the towns in which the *cestuis que trust* respectively reside Revere v Boston, 123 Mass , 375 (1877) As to the legal remedy in Massachusetts for an unjust valuation of stock for taxation, see Boston Mfg Co v Commonwealth, 12 N E Rep , 362 (Mass , 1887) As to taxation of stock under the Vermont law, see Willard v Pike, 9 Atl Rep., 907 (Vt , 1887)

[3] Stetson v City of Bangor, 56 Me , 274 (1868), the court saying "Municipalities can tax shares of stock only when authorized so to do by some law of the state They are the creatures of

general authority to the municipality to tax all property within its
boundaries will authorize a tax by it of shares of stock owned by
persons living within it.[1] But such authority does not sustain a
tax on stockholders residing out of the municipality, although
within the state. The location of such shares of stock, as property
for purposes of taxation, is not where the corporation is located,
but where the stockholder lives[2] The statutes of the state may
change this *situs* of the stock so as to render it taxable where the
corporation is; but unless there is a statute to that effect such a
tax by a municipality is unauthorized and void.

§ 565 *Tax on resident stockholders in a non-resident or foreign
corporation* — It is undoubtedly within the constitutional power of
the legislature of a state to enact a statute that persons residing in
that state, who are stockholders in a corporation created by another state, shall be taxed on their shares of stock at their residence within the former state[3] This principle of law is based on
the fact that shares of stock are personal property, that they are
distinct from the corporate property, franchises and capital stock,
that they follow the domicile of their owner like other personal
property, and that consequently he may be taxed therefor wherever
he may reside. It accordingly is a question of policy and expediency with a state whether or not it will tax its citizens who are

state law, and derive their powers in
this respect solely from state enactments" Griffith v. Watson, 19 Kan,
23 (1877), City of Evansville v. Hall 14
Ind, 27 (1859), Conwell v Town of Con-
nersville, 15 Ind, 150 (1860). Such a
tax may be levied under a general
power of the municipality to tax property Gordon's Ex'rs v. Mayor, etc, 5
Gill (Md), 231 (1847). Cf. Richmond v
Daniels, 14 Gratt, 385, Augusta v. National Bank, 37 Ga., 620 (1868). Markoe
v Hartranft, 6 Am L Reg (N S), 487
(1867), holds that in Pennsylvania such
a tax is unconstitutional, and that a tax
must be levied where the stockholder
resides. See, also, Craft v. Tuttle, 27
Ind, 332 (1866).

[1] But a municipality can levy a tax
only when specially authorized so to do,
and can tax only such property as the
statute permits it to tax. Cooley on
Taxation (2d ed.), 678. Hence power to
a municipality to levy a tax for watch-
men purposes will not authorize a tax

on shares of stock Bank of Georgia v
Savannah, Dudley (Ga.), 130 (1852).

[2] See § 566.

[3] Worthington v Sebastian, 25 Ohio
St, 1 (1874), Bradley v Bauder, 36 Ohio
St, 28 (1880), holding it valid, although
the corporation is taxed in the state
where it exists. To same effect, Seward
v City of Rising Sun, 79 Ind, 351 (1881);
Dyer v Osborn, 11 R. I., 321 (1876);
McKeen v County of Northampton, 49
Pa. St., 519 (1865), Dwight v. Boston,
12 Allen, 316 (1866), Whitesell v Same,
id, 526, Great Barrington v County
Com'rs, 33 Mass., 572 (1835), Worth v
Com'rs, 82 N C, 420 (1880), S C., 90
N C., 409 (1884) In Illinois, also, resi-
dent stockholders in foreign corporations are taxed on their shares of stock.
Porter v Rockford, etc, R. R. Co., 76
Ill., 561 (1875), Cooley on Taxation
(2d ed.), 57, 221, Holton v Bangor, 23
Me, 264, Smith v. Exeter, 37 N. H, 556
(1859).

stockholders in foreign corporations A few of the states[1] levy such taxes But New York pursues the more broad and liberal policy that shares of stock should not be taxed where the corporation is already taxed, that the state which furnishes facilities to the corporation for the earning of dividends should have the sole benefit of taxes on such corporate interests. that a tax on resident stockholders in non-resident corporations would generally result

[1] State v Hannibal & St J R R Co, 37 Mo, 265 (1866), Ogden v City of St. Joseph, 3 S W Rep, 25 (Mo 1887), Sturges v Carter. 114 U S, 511 (1884), upholding such a tax in Ohio, Newark City Bank v Assessor, 30 N J L, 1 (1862) See, also, Webb v Burlington, 28 Vt., 188 (1856). See Pa Act of April 29, 1844, Lycoming County v Gamble, 47 Pa St, 106 (1864) See, also, *In re* Short's Estate. 16 Pa St, 63 (1851), where a decedent who died a resident of Pennsylvania left a fortune in stocks of non-resident corporations The stocks were held subject to a collateral inheritance tax In 1879, however, Pennsylvania adopted in large part the system of taxation that prevails in New York for the taxation of corporations See Hunter's Appeal, 10 Atl Rep, 429 (Pa, 1887) By the still later statute of 1885, manufacturing corporations are specially favored in the way of taxation. MacKellar, etc, Co v Commonwealth. 10 Atl Rep, 780 (Pa, 1887) In New Jersey now there is no tax on shares of stock except in banks See Newark B Co v Newark, 121 U S, 163 (1887) Shares of stock owned by residents in foreign corporations are not taxable if a tax is paid by the corporation itself. State v Ramsey, 24 Atl. Rep, 445 (N J, 1892) In Texas shares of stock are not taxed where the capital or property of the corporation is taxed Gillespie v Gaston, 4 S W Rep, 248 (Tex, 1887) California made a wise resolution when, in 1881, it repealed § 3640 of its political code taxing shares of stock, and added the following (§ 3608) to the code "Shares of stock in corporations possess no intrinsic value over and above the actual value of the property of the corporation which they stand for and represent, and the assessment and taxation of such shares and also of the corporate property would be double taxation Therefore all property belonging to corporations shall be assessed and taxed but no assessment shall be made of shares of stock, nor shall any holder thereof be taxed therefor" Sustained and applied in Burke v Badlam, 57 Cal, 502 Spring Valley W W v Schottler 62 Cal, 69, 118 (1882) But the temptation to tax stockholders in non-resident corporations was yielded to See San Francisco v Fry, 63 Cal, 470 (1883), Same v Flood, 64 Cal., 504 (1884) As to Ohio, see R. S 1886, §§ 2737, 2739 2744, construed in Jones v Davis, 35 Ohio St, 474 (1880) See, also, Worth v. Com'rs of Ashe County, 90 N C., 409 (1884), Seward v City of Rising Sun, 79 Ind, 351. As to taxation of shares of stock in foreign corporations under the Michigan statutes, see Graham v St Joseph, 35 N W Rep., 808 (1888). Shares of stock may be taxed although the corporation is also taxed The corporation may be compelled to pay the tax on the shares of stock by deducting it from dividends South, etc, R. R. Co v Morrow, 11 S W Rep, 348 (Tenn, 1889). In Ohio resident stockholders in foreign corporations may be taxed on their stock Lee v Sturges, 19 N E Rep, 560 (Ohio, 1889) Under the Connecticut statutes shares of stock owned by residents in foreign express companies are taxed even though such companies are not incorporated Lockport v. Weston, 23 Atl. Rep, 9 (Conn., 1891)

in a double taxation of stockholders not residing in the state creating the corporation; and that interstate comity, interests and financial investments are promoted best by taxing corporations directly, and not levying a tax on either resident stockholders in non-resident corporations or resident stockholders in resident corporations where the corporation itself is subject to taxation [1] The injustice of a tax on resident stockholders in foreign corporations is at once apparent when it is considered that the state creating the corporation nearly always taxes the corporation itself or all its stockholders, resident and non-resident, and that if stockholders residing elsewhere are taxed again where they reside, they are taxed both in the state of the corporation, directly or indirectly, and also directly in the state where they reside   No reduction need be allowed in the latter state for taxes levied upon the corporation in another state [2]

§ 566 *Tax on non-resident stockholders in resident or domestic corporation — Mode of collecting —* When it is determined by a state that it prefers to levy a tax on shares of stock rather than on the franchises, capital stock or tangible property of the corporation, or to levy a tax on both, there is no doubt as to its right to tax the stockholders residing within the state   But more difficulty

---

[1] R. S. of N Y, ch XIII, title 1, § 7 (p 982, 7th ed), provides as follows "The owner or holder of stock in any incorporated company liable to taxation on its capital shall not be taxed as an individual for such stock " See, also, People r. Com of Taxes, 4 Hun, 595 (1875), aff d. 62 N Y, 630 holding that residents of this state, owning shares of stock in a corporation created under and by the laws of this state or of any foreign state, are not subject to be personally assessed and taxed thereon under the laws of this state   Also People r Com'rs. 5 Hun, 200 (1875), *In re* Euston's Estate, 21 N E Rep, 87 (N Y, 1889)   For the purpose, however, of making the taxation of moneyed corporations correspond to taxation of shareholders in national banks, and for the purpose of taxing the latter, stockholders in banks incorporated under the laws of New York are now taxed on their shares of stock, under the following statutes. Laws of 1866, ch 671, Laws of 1880, ch 110, Laws of 1880, ch. 596, Laws of 1881, ch 477, Laws of 1882, ch. 410, § 848. The tax generally levied on corporations in New York is held to be a tax on their franchises. See People *v* Home Ins Co, 92 N Y, 328 (1883), Same r McLean, 80 N Y., 254 (1880), Same t Ferguson, 38 N Y, 89 (1868), Same *v* Williamsburgh Gas Light Co, 76 N Y, 202 (1879), Laws of 1880, ch 542, as am'd by Laws of 1881, ch. 361; also Laws of 1883, ch 359 See People t New York, etc, Co, 92 N Y, 497 (1883); Same t Davenport, 91 N. Y, 574 (1883); Nassau, etc, Co t City of Brooklyn, 89 N Y, 409 (1882), Oswego, etc., Factory *v* Dolloway 21 N Y, 449 (1860); People r Com'rs, 95 N Y, 554 (1884); Valle r Ziegler, 84 Mo, 214 (1884); People t Bradley, 39 Iowa, 130 (1866). *Cf.* Bank of Republic r County of Hamilton, 21 Ill, 54 (1858). See, also, Smith *v* Exeter, 37 N. H, 556 (1859), and Jersey City Gas Light Co r Jersey City, 46 N J. L, 194 (1884).

[2] See §§ 566, 567.

occurs as to the right of the state to tax non-resident stockholders in corporations created by the state. This right has been strenuously denied on the ground that shares of stock are not located at the domicile of the corporation, but follow the domicile of the stockholder.

It is the well-established rule, however, that although shares of stock have at common law no *situs* except the domicile of the shareholder, yet that a statute enacted by the state creating the corporation may give to the shares of stock a *situs* at the location of the corporation; that such a statute may thus determine the *situs* of shares of non-resident stockholders without changing the *situs* of shares of resident stockholders, and that consequently, under a statute expressly authorizing such a tax, non-resident stockholders in a resident corporation may be taxed thereon in the place where the corporation has its domicile [1] The method of enforcing the

---

[1] In the case of Ottawa Glass Co v McCaleb, 81 Ill, 556 (1876) the court said that the legislature might "require the taxes to be paid by the corporation and collected by them of the shareholder, by deducting the amount from his dividends or otherwise ' State v Mayhew, 2 Gill (Md), 487 (1845), where the corporation was to pay the tax from dividends if declared, and from profits if no dividends were declared, St. Albans v National Car Co 57 Vt., 68 (1884), holding that the statute giving shares of stock a *situs* at the location of the corporation may be passed after the incorporation, and that *mandamus* lies to compel the corporation to pay the tax. In the case of Tappan v Merchants' Nat l Bank, 19 Wall, 490, 499 (1873) the court said "Personal property, in the absence of any law to the contrary, follows the person of the owner, and has its *situs* at his domicile But, for the purpose of taxation, it may be separated from him, and he may be taxed on its account at the place where it is actually located See, also, Whitney v. Ragsdale, 33 Ind, 107 (1870), Tallman v Butler Co, 12 Iowa, 531 (1861) Faxton v McCarter id , 527 (1861), Mayor, etc , of Baltimore v Baltimore, etc , R'y Co 57 Md, 31 (1881). The last case holds that stock

in street railways in Maryland may be taxed, although by statute stock in steam railways cannot be Cf City of Richmond v Daniel, 14 Gratt. (Va), 385 (1858), also the case of Oliver v Washington Mills, 93 Mass , 268 (1865), which holds such a tax to be unconstitutional The common-law rule is well expressed in Union Bank v State, 9 Yerg (Tenn), 490 (1836), where the court say ' The power to tax non-resident stockholders is denied, and we think correctly ; from its very nature it must be a tax *in personam* and not *in rem* Stock is in the nature of a chose in action and can have no locality, it must, therefore, of necessity follow the person of the owner

Bank stock is not a thing in itself capable of being taxed on account of its locality, and any tax imposed upon it must be in the nature of a tax upon income, and of necessity confined to the person of the owner and if he be a non-resident he is beyond the jurisdiction of the state, and not subject to her laws" See, also, Minot v Railroad Co., 18 Wall , 276, Davenport v Miss , etc , R R , 12 Iowa, 539 (1861), Howell v Cassopolis, 35 Mich , 471 (1877) In Bradley v Bauder, 36 Ohio St 28 (1880), the court said · that shares of stock may be separated from the person of the owner by statute, and given

payment of this tax may be by compelling the corporation to pay it and giving it a lien therefor on the stock, or authorizing it to deduct the tax from the non-resident stockholders' dividends; or, if the statute is silent as to the mode of collection, a tax warrant or an attachment and execution therefor may be levied on the shares of stock [1] In New York, where neither resident nor non-resident

a *situs* of their own, was held in Tappan *v* Merchants' Nat'l Bank, 19 Wall, 490 But when not so separated, that this *situs* follows and adheres to the domicile of the owner, is supported by a great weight of authority ' See State Tax on Foreign-held Bonds 15 Wall, 300 (1872) See, also Jenkins *v* Charleston 5 S C, 393 (1874) In Nat'l Com Bank *v* Mobile 62 Ala, 284 (1878), the court well say ' It may be made the duty of a bank to pay for its shareholders the tax legally assessed against their respective shares, whether the stockholders reside in the state of Alabama or not Contestations upon these points have been made time and again sometimes by the banks and sometimes by the shareholders to avoid this liability But it is established by repeated adjudications and ought to be considered definitely settled" And in First Nat'l Bank *v* Smith 65 Ill, 44 (1872), the court say " The separation of the *situs* of personal property from the domicile of the owner for the purposes of taxation is familiar doctrine of the courts of this country and has been sanctioned by this court in various cases. The act of congress itself contemplates a severance of the *situs* of such shares from the person of their owner by providing that they should not be taxed except in the state where the bank is established But, apart from this, it is really much more reasonable to fix the *situs* of shares at the place where the bank is located, and where it must continue to do its business or wind up its affairs, than to separate by legislation tangible personal property from the person of its owner " In the case of St. Louis Nat'l Bank *v* Papin, 4 Dill, 29 (1876), the following statute was sus-

tained "The taxes assessed on shares of stock embraced in such list shall be paid by the corporations respectively, and they may recover from the owners of such shares the amount so paid by them or deduct the same from the dividends accruing on such shares, and the amount so paid shall be a lien on such shares respectively, and shall be paid before a transfer thereof can be made.' And again, in American Coal Co. *v* County Comm'rs. 59 Md, 185 (1882), the court say ' The state may give the shares of stock held by individual stockholders a special or particular *situs* for purposes of taxation, and may provide special modes for the collection of the tax levied thereon ' But where the statute merely made the bank the agent to pay the tax and to deduct it from the dividends, the bank is not liable if there have been no dividends Hershire *v* First Nat'l Bank, 35 Iowa, 272 Non-resident stockholders in Virginia banks are taxed Stockholders *v* Board of Supervisors 13 S E Rep, 407 (Va, 1891). Concerning the *situs* of stock, see, also, an article in 45 Alb L J, 330

[1] In Farrington *v* Tennessee 95 U S, 679, 687 (1877), the court say "The bank may be required to pay the tax out of its corporate funds or be authorized to deduct the amount paid for each stockholder out of his dividend " And, in general, under the act of congress allowing taxation of shares of stock in national banks, a *situs* is given by statute to the shares so as to locate them where the bank is located, even though the shareholders be non-resident But collections cannot be enforced against the corporation unless the statute specially authorizes it First Nat'l Bank *v.* Fancher, 48 N Y, 524 (1872) Collec-

stockholders in either foreign or domestic corporations, excepting banking corporations, are taxed on their shares of stock, these interstate complications, hardships and jealousies do not arise [1]

§ 567　*Double taxation* — The most objectionable feature of a tax levied on shares of stock is that almost inevitably it operates to impose a double tax on a part or all the stockholders [2]　Such a

tion by execution, see Gordon's Ex'rs v Mayor, etc, 5 Gill (Md), 231 (1847), Weld v City of Bangor, 59 Me, 416　But a levy of execution on stock can only exist when the statute allows stock to be so taken　Barnes v Hall 55 Vt, 420 (1883)　Or under a tax warrant McNeal v Mechanics etc, Ass'n (N J 1885)　But if the stockholder pays the tax, even under protest, he cannot recover back the money paid　Sowles v Soule, 7 Atl Rep 715 (Vt, 1887)　See, also, § 480　In the case of State v. Thomas, 26 N J L, 181 (1857), the court refused to compel the corporation to pay the tax on stock of nonresidents, and said　"It has been decided by this court that the bonds and stocks of corporations in this state held by non-residents are not liable to taxation, though they are clearly within the letter of the act."　A state may collect a non-resident stockholder's tax from the corporation and give it a lien therefor on his stock　North Ward Nat'l Bank v City of Newark, 39 N J L, 380 (1877), but see Raleigh, etc, R R Co. v Connor, 87 N C, 414　A tax collector cannot levy on and sell stock under the law relative to attachments　Kennedy v May, etc, R y, 9 S Rep, 608 (Ala, 1891)　The statute may provide for the sale of stock at the place where the corporation exists, in case the taxes upon such stock are not paid　A purchaser of the outstanding certificates after the assessment has been made takes subject to the tax and tax seizure　Parker v Sun Ins Co, 8 S Rep, 618 (La 1890) It is clear, where shares of stock are sold under a tax warrant, that the corporation is not obliged to oppose the sale　McNeal v Mechanics' Building, etc., Ass'n, 12 Am. & Eng Corp Cas,

131 (N J, 1885)　Cooley on Taxation (2d ed), 433 clearly upholds the rule that the state may levy a tax on shares of stock and compel the corporation to pay it citing Maltby v. Reading R. R. Co, 52 Pa St, 140 (1866)　Haight v Railroad Co 6 Wall, 15 (1867), National Bank v Commonwealth, 9 Wall, 353 (1869), United States v Railroad Co 17 Wall, 322 (1872), Minot v Railroad Co, 18 Wall, 206 (1873)　Ottawa, etc v McCaleb, 81 Ill, 556 (1876)　New Orleans v Saving, etc, Co, 31 La Ann, 826 (1879)　Baltimore v City Passenger R Co, 57 Md, 31 (1881), St. Albans v National Car Co, 57 Vt, 68 (1884)　American Coal Co v Allegany County, 59 Md, 185 (1882)　Barney v State 42 Md 480 (1875)　McVeagh v Chicago 49 Ill 318 (1868)　First Nat'l Bank v Fancher 48 N Y 524 (1872), Leonberger v Rowse, 43 Mo, 67 (1868)　Relfe v Life Ins Co 11 Mo App, 374 (1882).

[1] See § 565, note

[2] In Ohio such double taxation is advocated and recommended　In Frazer v Seibern 16 Ohio St, 614 (1866), the court said that an equitable system of taxation "is best attained in case of a corporation or joint-stock company by taxing the stockholders, the persons who own the property, upon the full value of their shares therein, including, of course, their interest in the franchise or privilege, and in all tangible property owned by the company, and by taxing the corporation also upon the value of such tangible property　The stockholder is thus taxed, as all other individuals who own tangible and intangible property are sometimes unavoidably taxed, once upon all he is worth, and a second time upon that part of his property which is tangible'

double tax exists where either the corporate realty or personalty or franchise or capital is taxed, and a tax is also levied on the shares of stock without any deduction for the former taxation.[1] There has been some controversy as to the right of a state to levy a double tax on property. Sometimes the state constitution prohibits such taxation[2] But aside from constitutional restrictions it unquestionably is within the power of the state to levy, not only a double tax, but even a treble or quadruple tax, if it so chooses.[3] The injustice of such taxation, however, generally prevents its occurrence The courts also do their utmost to prevent double taxation, and will construe a taxation statute so as to avoid such a result, and sometimes even in opposition to the plain words of the statute itself.[4]

---

[1] This is practically the result In the case of Farrington v Tennessee, 95 U S, 679, 687 (1877), however, the court says in a dictum "The capital stock and the shares may both be taxed, and it is not double taxation" See, also, New Orleans v Houston, 119 U S, 265, 277 (1886) Cf Ryan v Com'rs, 30 Kan , 185 (1883).

[2] County Com'rs v Farmers' Nat'l Bank, 48 Md , 117 (1877), the constitution saying that each person shall pay a tax "according to his actual worth in real or personal property" See, also, City of San Francisco v Mackey, 21 Fed Rep , 539 (1884), Burke v Badlam, 57 Cal , 594 (1881) relative to the California constitution, art XII, § 1, that "all property shall be taxed in proportion to its value"

[3] Salem Iron, etc. Co v Danvers, 10 Mass 514 (1813), where corporate realty was taxed although the shares of stock were also taxed See, also, Belo v Com'rs of Forsyth, 82 N C, 415 (1880). In the remarkable case of Toll Bridge Co v Osborn, 35 Conn , 7 (1868), it seems that the realty, capital stock and shares of stock of a corporation were taxed, and that the chief stockholder, a railroad, was taxed on its capital stock and shares of stock, making four or five taxations of the same property Evidently corporations were not popular in Connecticut in 1868, except for

taxation purposes. Cf Jones, etc., Co v Commonwealth, 69 Pa. St , 137. See, also, Cook v City of Burlington, 59 Iowa, 251 (1882), State v Branin, 23 N J L, 484 (1852), Same v Bentley, id , 532, City of Memphis v. Ensley, 6 Bax (Tenn) 553 (1873), Prov , etc R. R. Co. v Wright, 2 R. I , 459, 464 (1853), holding that a tax on the stock does not raise a presumption that a municipality is thereby prevented from taxing the corporate realty See, also, Hannibal, etc. R. R. Co. v Shacklett, 30 Mo , 550, 560 (1860) Although by the charter a tax is levied on the capital stock, a tax may also be levied on the shares of stock. State v Home Ins Co , 19 S W. Rep., 1012 (Tenn , 1892). A tax on the bonds which are issued by a corporation does not constitute double taxation although there is also a tax on the franchises of the corporation Commonwealth v. New York, etc , R Co , 24 Atl Rep., 609 (Pa., 1892). Where the stock is not taxable if the tangible property is taxed, the stock may nevertheless be taxed for such part of its value as the capital stock exceeds in value the tangible property. Hyland v Central Iron, etc., Co , 28 N. E. Rep , 308 (Ind , 1891)

[4] Thus, in Illinois, in cases where the capital stock is taxed by the state, the shares of stock are held to be free from taxation Republic Life Ins. Co. v. Pollak, 75 Ill , 292 (1874). See, also, County

§ 568. *Exemptions from taxation as affecting tax on shares of stock* — An exemption of shares of stock is a contract protected by that provision of the constitution of the United States which prevents a state from passing a law which will impair the validity of contracts [1] This provision has frequently been construed and applied in cases involving the taxation of the corporate franchises, capital stock or tangible property. Aside from questions of this nature there are two classes of cases of exemptions from taxation which affect the taxation of shares of stock. The first class involves the question whether an exemption of the corporate property, franchises or capital stock from taxation exempts also the shares of stock from any tax, the second, whether an exemption of the shares of stock from taxation exempts the corporate property, franchises and capital stock   As regards the former exemption, the effect thereof depends largely on the words used in the statute or charter granting the exemption   The question has given rise to a difference of opinions   In the federal courts, New Jersey,

of Lackawanna *v* First Nat'l Bank, 94 Pa St, 221 (1880), holding that under the act of March 31, 1870, releasing corporations from all other taxes if they pay a one per cent tax on the par value of the stock, the corporate realty cannot be taxed after such one per cent. has been paid   State *v* Hannibal & St. J R R. Co, 37 Mo, 265 (1866), Jersey City, etc., Co *v* Jersey City, 46 N J L, 194 (1884), Cheshire, etc, Telephone Co. *v* State 63 N H, 167 (1884), Valle *v* Zeigler, 84 Mo, 214 (1884), Tax Cases, 12 G & J. (Md), 117 (1841), Prov Inst for Sav *v*. Gardiner. 4 R. I, 484 (1857), Mechanics' Bank *v* Thomas, 26 N J L, 181 (1857), American Bank *v* Mumford, id, 478 (1857), State *v* Tunis, 23 N J L., 546 (1852), Smith *v*. Burley, 9 N H, 423 (1858); Frazer *v* Siebern, 16 Ohio St, 614 (1866)   Savings Bank *v* Nashua, 46 N H 389 (1866), the court saying "It is a fundamental principle in taxation that the same property shall not be subject to a double tax payable by the same party, either directly or indirectly   and where it is once decided that any kind or class of property is liable to be taxed under one provision of the statutes, it has been held to follow as a legal conclusion that the legislature could not

have intended the same property would be subject to another tax, though there may be general errors in the law which would seem to imply that it was to be taxed a second time '   In Michigan where shares of stock in savings banks are taxed, a reduction being allowed for realty, which is taxed separately, the courts held that no other tax can be levied against the corporation   Lenawee, etc, Bank *v* City of Adrian, 33 N W Rep, 304 (Mich, 1887). The Kentucky tax statutes are so construed that a corporation need not pay a tax on its property in addition to the tax on the stock   Louisville, etc Co *v* Barbour, 9 S W Rep, 516 (Ky, 1888), Com *v* St Bernard Coal Co., id, 709   The Pennsylvania acts are construed so as to prevent double taxation   Penn Co, etc., *v* Com, 15 Atl Rep, 456 (Pa 1888)

[1] Farrington *v* Tennessee, 95 U S, 679 (1877)   See, also, § 497   An exemption of the stock of a railroad company does not exempt stock issued for constructing branch roads of that company, such construction being subsequent to a constitutional provision prohibiting exemptions   Chicago, etc, R. R. Co. *v* Guffey, 120 U. S, 569.

Indiana and Kentucky, it has been decided that an exemption of the corporation from taxation on one or more of the first three methods of taxation exempts by implication the shares of stock.[1] But in Tennessee, North Carolina and Maryland a contrary rule prevails.[2]

As regards the second class of exemptions, it seems to be established by the great weight of authority that an exemption of the shares of stock from taxation exempts also, by implication, the corporate franchises, capital stock and tangible property from any

[1] State v Branin, 23 N J L, 484 (1852) Same v Bentley, id, 532; Johnson v Commonwealth, 7 Dana (Ky), 3d (1838) King v City of Madison, 17 Ind, 48 (1861), holding that an exemption of the capital stock exempts shares of stock Gordon v Appeal Tax Court, 3 How, 133 (1845) held that an exemption prohibiting any "further tax or burden upon them," the banks, exempted the shares of stock Again, where the charter provided that "the capital stock of said company shall be forever exempt from taxation, the shares of stock cannot be taxed . Each share is a part of the whole, and, as the whole is exempt from taxation, it follows that each part or share must also be exempt." State of Tenn v Whitworth, 22 Fed Rep, 75 (1884). And the purchaser and successor of a railroad taking by statute all its rights and privileges, is also exempt in same manner Id 81, aff'd, 117 U S, 139 (1886) An exemption of the corporation exempts it from a tax upon the shares of shareholders, which the company is required to pay irrespective of any dividends or profits payable to the shareholder since this is substantially a tax on the corporation itself New Orleans v Houston 119 U S, 265 (1884) Cf United States v Railroad Co., 17 Wall, 322 An exemption of shares of stock from taxation is waived by the acceptance of subsequent statutes imposing a tax Hannibal & St J R R Co v Shacklett, 30 Mo, 550 (1860), Cooley on Taxation (2d ed), 212

[2] Union Bank v State, 9 Yerg (Tenn), 490 (1836) holding that an exemption of the capital stock did not exempt shares of stock To same effect, City of Memphis v Farrington, 8 Baxter (Tenn), 539 (1876), the court saying "The capital stock and shares of stock are two distinct properties, and an exemption of the one does not thereby necessarily exempt the other, nor the taxation of the latter operate as a tax on the former, so as to interfere with its exemption from such burdens' Belo v Com'rs of Forsyth, 82 N C, 415 (1880), holding that an exemption of the corporate realty does not exempt the shares of stock, Appeal Tax Court v Rice, 50 Md, 302 (1878), Tax Cases, 12 G & J. (Md), 117 (1841) In the case of County Com'rs v Annapolis, etc, R R Co, 47 Md, 592 (1877), the court say "To make out the claim to this exemption from the taxing power of the state so essential to the support of its government, it is incumbent upon corporations to show that the power to tax has been clearly relinquished by the state and if this has not been done in clear and explicit terms, or by necessary implication, the question whether or not the exemption has been granted must be resolved in favor of the state ' Citing Prov Bank v Billings, 4 Pet, 514 (1830), Wilmington R. R. Co. v Reid, 13 Wall, 264, Phil & Wilmington R. R Co v State, 10 How, 376 (1850) But a clear exemption of the shares of stock is a contract which is protected by the United States constitution State v Baltimore & O R R Co, 48 Md, 49 (1877). A charter provision, however, that a certain tax shall be paid by the

tax.[1] Exemptions, however, have no effect and are of no avail beyond the boundaries of the state granting them, and accordingly a non-resident stockholder, who is taxed on his stock in the state where he resides, cannot defeat that tax by reason of exemptions enjoyed within the state creating the corporation.[2]

B TAXATION OF NATIONAL BANK STOCK

§ 569 *General rules.*-- It is one of the established principles of constitutional law in this country that the instruments of government by the United States shall not be taxed by any state, and also that those of a state shall not be taxed by the United States. Accordingly, the bonds issued by the United States government cannot be taxed by any state.[3] So, also, when the old United States bank was in existence, it was held that neither the bank nor its capital stock could be taxed by a state. But it was

corporation does not prevent a subsequent change in that tax Delaware Railroad Tax, 18 Wall 206 (1873) And an exemption by the state has been held not to exempt the shares from taxation by a municipality Gordon's Ex'rs r Mayor, etc 5 Gill (Md), 231 (1847).

[1] In the case of Tennessee r Bank of Com, 53 Fed Rep 735 (1892) it is held that a provision imposing a tax on each share of stock ' which shall be in lieu of all other taxes ' exempts the property of the company as well as the stock from further taxation Scotland Co r Mo, Iowa etc, R'y Co, 65 Mo, 123 (1877), the court saying "It is clear that a tax on the property represented by the stock is substantially a tax on the stock ' See, also, County Com'rs r Annapolis, etc, R R Co 47 Md, 592 (1877), where the court say "It is settled by repeated decisions of this court, which we are not disposed to distub, that the exemption of the shares of the capital stock operates as an exemption of the property of the corporation, or so much of it as the corporation is fairly authorized to hold for the proper exercise of its franchises and this upon the principle that the shares of the stock in the hands of the shareholders represent the property held by the corporation."

Bank of Cape Fear r Edwards 5 Ired Law (N C), 516 (1845), where the charter said ' The said bank shall not be liable to any further tax." Mayor, etc, of Baltimore r Baltimore & O R R Co, 6 Gill (Md) 288 (1848), Tax Cases 12 G & J (Md), 117 (1841) Gordon's Ex'rs r Mayor, etc, of Baltimore, 5 Gill (Md), 231 (1847) In the case, however, of Wilmington & W R R Co r Reid, 64 N C 226 (1870), it was held that an exemption of shares of stock does not exempt the corporate franchise from taxation Raleigh etc, R R r Reid, id 155 (1870) And in State r Petway, 2 Jones' Eq (N C), 396 (1856), it was held that a charter provision that the shares of stock should be taxed a certain amount did not prevent a tax on dividends

[2] Appeal Tax Court r Patterson, 50 Md, 354 (1878), Same r Gill, id, 377 See also, Railroad Co. r Pennsylvania, 15 Wall, 300 (1872)

[3] Cooley on Taxation (2d ed), 84, 85. Formerly government bonds were called stock both in England and in this country The use of the term, however, has become practically obsolete See Bank of Commerce r New York, 2 Black, 620 (1862) Weston r City, etc, of Charleston 2 Peters, 449 (1829)

also held that, inasmuch as the interest of the stockholders in the
bank was different from the franchises, property, capital stock and
the United States bonds held by the bank, such interest of the
shareholder could be taxed by a state, and that such taxation
would be constitutional and legal[1] The same rules apply to the
present national banks   A state tax on the capital stock of the
bank is illegal and void.[2] But a tax on its real estate or on its shares
of stock is upheld as legal and enforceable[3]   This is the law, although a large part or all of the bank's capital stock is invested in

[1] McCulloch v State of Maryland, 4
Wheat, 316, 436 (1819), Bulow v City
of Charleston, 1 Nott & McCord (S C),
527 (1819) See, also, Berney v Tax
Collector, 2 Bailey (S C), 654 (1831), National Bank v Commonwealth, 9 Wall,
353 (1869), per Miller, J

[2] Bank of Omaha v Douglas County,
3 Dill, 298 (1873), Collins v Chicago, 4
Biss., 472, Salt Lake, etc, Bank v Gold-
ing, 2 Utah, 1 (1876), Mayor, etc of
Macon v First Nat'l Bank 59 Ga, 648
(1877), Bradley v Illinois, 6 Am L
Reg (N S), 466, Bank of Commerce v
N Y City, 2 Black, 620, reversing People v Com'rs of Assessments, 23 N Y,
192, S C, 32 Barb, 509, and declaring
unconstitutional the New York statutes
under which the national banks were
taxed New York has been exceedingly
unfortunate in its efforts to tax national
banks. After the decision in Bank of
Commerce v N Y City, supra, came
Bank Tax Case, 2 Wall, 200 (1864), declaring unconstitutional the New York
statute of 29th April, 1863, for the taxation of national banks, the tax still being on the capital stock Next came
Van Allen v The Assessors, 3 Wall,
573 (1865) (reversing City of Utica v
Churchill, 33 N Y 161 See, also, First
National Bank v Fancher, 48 N Y, 524
1872), declaring unconstitutional the
New York statute of 9th March, 1865,
taxing the shareholders in national
banks, because the act did not prescribe
expressly that the tax should be no
greater than the tax on other shares of
stock, and because taxes in New York

on other corporations were not on shares
of stock but on the capital stock. New
York then passed the act of 23d April,
1866, which was sustained in People v.
Com'rs 4 Wall, 244 (1866) Still later
came the case of People v Weaver, 100
U S, 539 (1879), reversing 67 N Y, 516,
overruling People v Dolan, 36 N Y,
59, and declaring void the New York
tax of national bank stock, for the reason that the New York court of appeals
construed the New York taxation statute to allow persons taxed on ordinary
securities a deduction for debts, while a
similar deduction was not allowed to
stockholders in banks state or national.
Supervisors v Stanley, 105 U S, 305
(1881) [see People v Dolan, 36 N Y, 59,
1867], practically modified the preceding case, however, by holding that a
stockholder who owed no debts could
not complain, and that those who did
owe debts were entitled not to a release from the tax altogether, but only
to the extent of what the state ought to
have allowed as a deduction The last
case in New York was decided by Judge
Wallace in November, 1886. States cannot tax national bank currency Horne
v Greene, 52 Miss, 452 Cf Ruffin v.
Board of Com'rs, 69 N C, 498, Lily v
Com rs, 69 N C, 300, Bond of Com'rs
v Elston, 32 Ind, 27 (1869.

[3] Austin v Boston 96 Mass, 359 (1867),
First Nat l Bank v Douglas County, 5
Dill, 330 (1874), upholding the Nebraska
statute herein of 27th of February, 1873;
Stetson v City of Bangor, 56 Me, 274
(1868).

United States bonds [1]   The authority of a state to tax shares of stock in national banks is expressly conferred by the statutes of the United States which create and regulate these banks.[2] The only questions of importance that are still unsettled turn upon the meaning and application of that statute, and, accordingly, the law is stated most clearly when it is connected with the various provisions of these statutes

§ 570 *Place in which shares of national bank stock may be taxed* — The Revised Statutes of the United States expressly declare that non-resident stockholders in a national bank are to be taxed at the place where the bank is located [3] Under this statute a non-resident of the state within which the bank is situated can be taxed on his stock only where the bank is located [4] The state where he resides cannot also tax him on such stock   As regards residents of the state within which the bank is located, the state itself determines where the tax is to be levied [5] If the state statute requires

---

[1] Van Allen v Assessors, 3 Wall, 573 (1865), People v Com rs, 4 Wall, 244 (1866) See, also, Home Ins Co v New York, 119 U S 129 (1886) In taxing the stock no reduction is allowed for bonds held by the corporation Home Ins Co z Board, etc, 8 S Rep, 481 (La, 1890), Parker v Sun Ins Co, id, 618

[2] R S U S, § 5219 (taken from act of 3d June, 1864, as amended by act of February 10, 1868) The case of People v. Weaver, 100 U S., 539, 543 (1879), says that the effect of the act of congress, as regards the taxation of national banks, is that congress says to the states "You may tax the real estate of the banks as other real estate is taxed, and you may tax the shares of the bank as the personal property of the owner to the same extent you tax other moneyed capital invested in your state It was conceived that by this qualification of the power of taxation equality would be secured and injustice prevented" Wasson v First Nat'l Bank, 8 N E Rep, 97 (Ind, 1886) New shares cannot be taxed until the increase has been approved by the comptroller of the currency   Charleston z People's Nat'l Bank, 5 S C, 103

[3] Such was the effect of the amendment of 1866. Previous to that time

there was controversy herein as to the meaning of the act of 1864. See Austin v Boston, 96 Mass 359 (1867).

[4] See McIver v Robinson, 53 Ala, 456; Weaver v Weaver, 75 N Y, 30, Kyle v Fayetteville, 75 N C, 415 National Bank v Commonwealth, 9 Wall, 353, Lionberger v Rowse, 9 Wall, 468

[5] Austin v Aldermen, 7 Wall, 694 (1868) The tax may be levied on resident stockholders in the city, county or town where they reside   Austin v Boston, 96 Mass, 359 (1867) And the cashier of the bank may be required by statute to send to the clerks of the various towns the names of such stockholders as reside in those towns Waite v Dowley, 94 U S, 527 (1876) As to the taxation of national bank stock in Iowa, see First Nat'l Bank of Albia *et al* v City Council of Albia, 52 N W Rep, 334 (Ia, 1892). As to the assessment of bank stock in West Virginia, see Bank of Bramwell v County Court of Mercer County, 15 S E. Rep, 78 (W Va, 1892) Concerning the taxation of national bank stock in Nevada, see First Nat'l Bank, etc, v Kreig, 32 Pac Rep, 641 (Nev, 1893) National bank stock in Delaware may be taxed by the state First Nat'l Bank v Herbert, 44 Fed. Rep., 158 (1890).

that the whole tax shall be paid in the city, county or town where
the bank is located, even though some of the stockholders reside
in other counties or cities, the statute must be obeyed [1] Generally,
however, the statute requires that stockholders residing in the state
shall be taxed at their place of residence on stock owned by them
in a national bank within that state [2] If the statute is silent herein,
then the state statutes regulating the taxation of stockholders in
other corporations are to apply to stockholders in national banks
situated within the state.   The statute may require the bank to retain from dividends the tax on the shares of stock, such tax being
determined by the amount of dividends.[3]   The collection of a tax
on national bank stock may be enforced by the same procedure
through which taxes on other personal property are collected.[4]

§ 571 *The tax must not be greater than that imposed on other
" moneyed capital "*— The most difficult, unsettled and litigated
questions connected with the taxation of shares of stock in national
banks arise from the meaning and application of that provision of
the statutes of the United States requiring that the taxation of national bank shares of stock shall not be at a higher rate than the

[1] National Bank *v* Commonwealth, 9
Wall, 353 (1869), Tappan *v* Merchants'
Nat'l Bank, 19 Wall, 490 (1873), Prov
Inst. *v* City of Boston, 101 Mass, 575
(1869), McLaughlin *v* Chadwell, 7 Heisk
(Tenn), 389 (1872) Craft *v* Tuttle, 27
Ind , 332 (1866), holds that if a munici-
pality has no power to tax shares in
state banks, it cannot tax national bank
shares

[2] Clapp *v* City of Burlington, 42 Vt,
579 (1870) See Trustees of Eminence
v Deposit Bank, 12 Bush, 538 (1877),
Farmers Nat'l Bank *v* Cook, 32 N J L,
347 (1867) *Cf* State *v* Hart, 31 N J.
L , 434 (1866), State *v* Haight, 31 N. J
L , 399 (1866)—objectionable and unfortunate decisions in all respects The
decision in Tenth Ward Nat'l Bank *v*.
City of Newark, 39 N J L, 380 (1877),
however, placed New Jersey among the
states which levy the tax in the most
approved manner, residents being taxed
where they reside, non-residents being
taxed at the domicile of the corporation
See, also, Kyle *v* Mayor, etc, 75 N C,
445 (1876), Buell *v* Com'rs of Fayetteville, 79 N C, 267 (1878), Austin *v* City
of Boston, 96 Mass, 359 (1867), First

Nat'l Bank *v* Smith, 65 Ill, 44 (1872),
Baker *v* First Nat'l Bank, 67 Ill, 297
(1873), Clapp *v* City of Burlington, 42
Vt , 579 (1870); Howell *v* Cassopolis, 35
Mich 471 (1877) *Cf* Mintzer *v* County
of Montgomery, 54 Pa St , 139 (1867)
For taxation of national bank stock
under the Alabama act, see Maguire *v*
Board of Revenue 71 Ala . 401 (1882).

[3] Central Nat'l Bank *v* United States,
137 U S, 355 (1890). *Cf* First Nat'l
Bank *v* Richmond, 39 Fed Rep., 309
id , 877 The taxation of the capital
stock of a national bank against the
bank *in solido* is invalid It may be collected from the bank but should be
assessed against the stockholders Deductions should also be allowed when
allowed on other similar property First
Nat'l Bank *v* Fisher, 26 Pac. Rep., 482
(Kan , 1891).

[4] Palmer *v* McMahon, 133 U S, 660
(1890) A tax on national bank stock to
be collected in the first instance from
the bank cannot be collected from the
receiver of the bank, the bank being insolvent City of Boston *v* Beal, 51 Fed.
Rep, 306 (1892).

taxation of other " moneyed capital " within the state. The words " moneyed capital " have been construed to mean " not only bonds, stocks and money loaned, but all credits and demands of every character in favor of the tax-payer " [1] This has been the subject of much controversy, however, and the latest decisions go very far in upholding the tax, if substantial justice has been done.[2]

The method of taxing shares of stock need not correspond to that followed in taxing other corporations in the state.[3] The ma-

[1] Wasson v First Nat'l Bank, 8 N E Rep, 87 (Ind, 1886), Boyer v Boyer, 113 U S, 689 (1884) Shares of stock in banks are other moneyed capital, but shares of stock in other corporations are not necessarily so ' Moneyed capital " means money put out by way of loan, discount, etc. or invested in stocks of banks, etc, which put out money by way of loan, discount, etc Trust companies are different from banks herein Mercantile Bank v New York, 121 U S, 138 (1887), affirming 28 Fed Rep, 776 A tax on national bank stock is legal although stock in state and savings banks is not taxed directly, but the corporation itself is taxed in another way Richards v Town, etc, 31 Fed Rep, 505 (1887) See, also, Hepburn v. School Directors, 23 Wall, 480 (1874) Other moneyed capital means capital employed in banking or loaning, and not in business Talbott v Silver Bow Co, 139 U S, 438 (1891)

[2] People v Commissioners, 4 Wall, 256, Adams v Nashville, 95 U S, 19 (1877) A recent case in New York — In re McMahon, 102 N Y, 176 (1886) — holds that shares of stock in railroads, manufacturing and other corporations are not " moneyed capital " in the sense in which these terms are used in the act of congress See, also, First National Bank v Waters, 19 Blatch, 242 Prov Inst v City of Boston, 101 Mass, 575 (1869), holds that the comparison is to be made with other moneyed capital in the same town or city where the tax is levied See, also, People v Moore, Idaho, 504 (1873) Subject to this rule the shares of national banks may be as-

sessed at their value even above par Hepburn v School Directors, supra (1874), People v Commissioners, etc, 94 U S, 415 (1876), S C, 67 N Y, 516 (1876), affirming 8 Hun, 536, St Louis Nat'l Bank v Papin, 4 Dill, 29 (1876), the court saying, also, that the assessors may ascertain that value by including ' all reserve funds, profits, earnings and other values " when the intent of the statute is to base the tax "upon an inquiry, inter alia, into the actual value of the property of the banks so far as this imparts or confers a value upon the shares." Stockholder cannot enjoin the tax unless he first pays such part of it as he admits is legal Rosenburg v Weekes, 4 S W Rep, 899 (Texas, 1887). The stock is listed against the stockholder, not against the bank Miller v First, etc, Bank, 21 N E Rep, 860 (Ohio, 1889). The statute may authorize taxation for years past State v Simmons, 12 S Rep, 477 (Miss, 1893)

[3] Davenport Bank v Davenport, 123 U S, 83 (1887) "There is no reason to suppose that congress cared at all about the mode the states might adopt for the collection of their taxes A tax imposed on the capital or property of a corporation falls as effectually on the capital of the shareholder represented by his shares as does a tax upon the shares directly, and although, in legal discrimination, a tax upon the former is not a tax upon the latter, practically and substantially taxation of the capital of the corporation is taxation of the capital of the shareholder" Tax on national bank stock upheld, though all other stock except bank stock is ex-

terial point is that national bank stock must not, as a result, be taxed higher than other moneyed investments. If this rule is observed, it is of little consequence whether the tax on national bank stock is levied and assessed in the same way as other corporations are taxed

If the state laws allow a deduction to a person taxed on bonds, notes and similar property for debts due from him to others, a similar deduction must be allowed to stockholders taxed on their shares in a national bank.[1] If the statute does not allow the same

empt, the tax being on capital stock Mercantile Nat l Bank v New York, 28 Fed Rep., 776-785 (1886), Wallace, J ; affirmed, 121 U S., 138 The mode of collection need not be the same The state may compel the bank to pay the tax National Bank v Commonwealth, 9 Wall, 353, 363 (1869), per Miller, J But if the assessment is illegal, in that no notice and opportunity is given to the shareholder to appear and resist the tax, it cannot be enforced   Albany City Nat'l Bank v Maher, 20 Blatch, 341 (1882) In general cf Van Allen v Assessors. 3 Wall, 573, Bradley v People, 4 Wall, 459 (1866), Hubbard v Johnson County, 23 Iowa, 130 (1867), People v Assessors, 29 How Pr, 371 (1865), Wright v Stelz, 27 Ind, 338 (1866), overruling Whitney v Madison, 23 Ind, 231, on certain points, Cooley on Taxation (2d ed) 390 Contra, People v Bradley 39 Ill, 130 (1866) See, also, Frazier v Siebern, 16 Ohio St. 614, Smith v First Nat'l Bank, 17 Mich, 479, Van Slyke v State, 23 Wis, 656, Boynoll v State, 25 Wis, 112 Where a state and also a local tax are levied on shares of stock in a state bank, and the local tax is declared illegal, the same local tax is illegal as regards shares in national banks. City Nat'l Bank v Paducah, 2 Flippin 61 (1877)

[1] Evansville Bank v Britton, 105 U S, 322 (1881), affirming 8 Fed Rep, 867. But a deduction to individuals for United States bonds held by them will not invalidate a tax on the national bank stock without a deduction for bonds held by the bank. Bressler v Wayne County, 41 N. W. Rep, 356 (Neb, 1889), People v Commissioners, 4 Wall, 244 (1866) In the recent case of Wasson v First Nat'l Bank, 8 N. E. Rep. 97 (Ind, 1886), the court held that the deduction allowed to others is fatal to a tax on national bank shares without that deduction only when it is "material and serious," and that that depends on the proportion of moneyed capital which is allowed the deduction to that moneyed capital which is not allowed it If material, the national bank share tax is to be allowed a similar deduction National bank stock cannot be taxed at a higher valuation on its actual value than other moneyed property is valued at Deductions allowed to other moneyed capital must also be allowed on national bank stock Whitbeck v Mercantile, etc., Bank, 127 U S, 193 (1888).

Where a tax on stock is not illegal except in that the assessors have proceeded in a wrong manner, the court will not enjoin its collection unless the plaintiff stockholders pay in such a tax as would have been legal Frazer v Seibern, 16 Ohio St., 614 (1866), Cummings v Merchants' Nat'l Bank, 101 U. S., 153 (1879), Supervisors v Stanley, 105 U S, 305 (1881), S. C, sub nom. Stanley v Supervisors, 121 U. S, 535 (1887), holding that the stockholder cannot recover back the excess of tax where he has not attempted to have the tax remedied, Hills v. Exchange Bank, 105 U S, 319 (1881), reversing National Albany Exchange Bank v. Wells, 18 Blatch, 478 (1880); 5 Fed. Rep, 248. In

to the latter, and the courts of the state refuse to allow the deduction, then the tax is illegal. Such was the result of a tax in New York on national bank stock.[1]

consequence of this escape of the stockholders from taxation, a special statute was passed levying a back tax   See N Y Laws, 1883, ch 311   Such a statute is constitutional   See McVeigh v Loomis, 49 Ill, 318 (1868)   The legislature may cure any defects in the levy of taxes in past years, provided such defects could have been so modified before the levy was made   Williams v Supervisors of Albany, 122 U S, 154 (1887), sustaining ch 345 Laws of 1883   Cf City Nat'l Bank v Paducah, 2 Flippin, 61 (1877)   And a deduction to other moneyed corporations for their real estate must be allowed in taxing national bank shares.   Pollard v State, 65 Ala, 528 (1880); overruling McIver v Robinson, 53 Ala, 456, and Sumbre County v National Bank, 62 Ala, 464   In general see, also, Ruggles v City of Fond du Lac, 53 Wis, 436 (1881), Miller v Heilbron, 58 Cal, 133 (1881), St. Louis Nat'l Bank v Papin, 4 Dill, 29 (1876), Covington, etc, Bank v Covington, 21 Fed Rep, 484 (1884).   Deduction for debts, if allowed to persons taxed, generally must be allowed national bank stockholders who are taxed on their stock.   McAden v Commissioners, etc, 2 S E Rep, 670 (N C, 1887)   Deductions are to be allowed the national bank stockholder for debts due from him to others where the state statute permits its citizens to deduct their debts from the valuation of their personal property.   Richards v Town, etc, 31 Fed Rep, 505 (1887), Peavey v Town, etc, 9 Atl Rep, 722 (N H, 1887)   As regards deductions for surplus funds which are already taxed, see Strafford Nat'l Bank v Dover, 58 N H, 316 (1878).   Cf. North Ward, etc, Bank v City of Newark, 39 N J L, 380 (1877), First Nat'l Bank v Peterborough, 56 N H., 38 (1875)   As regards its realty, see Com'rs of Rice County v Citizens' Nat'l Bank,

23 Minn, 280 (1877)   In Indiana the national bank stockholder may recover back such part of the tax as should have been deducted by reason of his indebtedness.   City of Indianapolis v Vajen, 12 N E Rep., 311 (Ind. 1887).   Exchange Nat'l Bank v Miller, 19 Fed Rep, 372 (1884).

[1] People v Weaver, 100 U S, 539 (1879)   The New York court held that " the effect of the state law is to permit a citizen of New York who has moneyed capital invested otherwise than in banks to deduct from that capital the sum of all his debts, leaving the remainder alone subject to taxation, while he whose money is invested in shares of bank stock can make no such deduction "   The supreme court of the United States declared the tax on the national bank shares to be invalid   But the case of Supervisors v Stanley, 105 U S., 305, 315 (1881), holds that the tax is not void absolutely   Deduction allowed to individuals for national and state securities, but not allowed on national bank stock, invalidates a tax on the latter   Whitney Nat'l Bank v Parker, 41 Fed Rep, 402 (1890)   If the stockholder owed no debts he is not injured, and even if he owes debts he cannot defeat the tax altogether, but is allowed a similar deduction   No discrimination, although the state taxes banks and nothing else   Gorge's Appeal 79 Pa St, 149 (1875).   No discrimination, though a deduction for debts is allowed to those whose property consists of debts due them, but no deduction otherwise   First Nat'l Bank v St. Joseph, 46 Mich, 526 (1881)   The exemption of all capital which is wholly invested in mining is not a discrimination   Board of Com'rs v Davis, 12 Pac Rep, 688 (Mont, 1887).   Exemption of savings banks, municipal bonds and shares of stock in all foreign and domestic corporations other than

A refusal to allow a deduction to stockholders in national banks similar to a deduction allowed on a tax levied on other "moneyed capital" was held to be a discrimination in contravention of the statute. Special exemptions, however, of certain stocks or other forms of "moneyed capital" do not require that a similar exemption should be made on national bank stock.[1]

Again, the national bank act cannot be evaded by an unfair assessment of the shares in national banks as compared with the assessment of other moneyed capital It is a well-known fact and an understood matter in nearly all localities that no kinds of property are valued at their actual selling worth in making the valuation for taxation purposes Consequently, if other moneyed capital is valued in the assessment rolls at a certain proportion of the actual value, and national bank stock at a higher proportion, the tax is illegal and cannot be collected [2]

---

banks from taxation does not invalidate tax on shares of stock in national banks Mercantile Bank v New York, 121 U S, 138 (1887), Newark, etc, Co v Newark, 121 U S 163 (1887), Bank of Redemption v Boston 125 id 60 (1888) No discrimination exists in taxation of national bank stock in territory where the shares of stock in corporations paying taxes on their property or capital stock are exempted from taxation County of Silver Bow v Davis, 12 Pac Rep. 689 (Mont, 1887) In Nebraska the owner of national bank stock, in listing his shares for taxation, is not entitled to deduct his *bona fide* indebtedness from the value of such shares of stock The decision on the former hearing of the case, reported in 25 Neb. 468, 41 N W Rep, 356 is overruled Bressler v Wayne County, 49 N W Rep, 787 (Neb, 1891) National bank shares in Massachusetts are taxed at their actual value, and the bank may petition for a reduction of the tax Nat'l Bank of Com v New Bedford 29 N E Rep., 532 (Mass, 1892)

[1] Thus, a special contract exemption of a few state bonds from taxation will not exempt the national bonds. Lionberger v Rowse, 9 Wall, 468 (1869), Hepburn v School Directors 23 Wall, 480 (1874), where an exemption of mortgages, judgments and contracts to sell

land were immaterial herein See, also, Adams v Nashville. 95 U S, 19 (1877), Supervisors v Stanley, 105 U S, 305, 317 (1881), *In re* McMahon. 102 N Y, 176 (1886). McLoughlin v Chadwell, 7 Heisk (Tenn), 389 (1872), Boyer v Boyer, 113 U S, 689, Everitt's Appeal 77 Pa. St., 216 Albany, etc, Bank v Maher, 19 Blatch 175 (1882) See, also, City of Richmond v Scott, 48 Ind, 568 (1874), Mercantile Nat'l Bank v City of New York, 28 Fed Rep, 776, 785 (1886)

[2] Pelton v National Bank, 101 U S., 143 (1879) the court saying that "any system of assessment of taxes which exacts from the owner of the shares of a national bank a larger sum in proportion to their actual value than it does from the owner of other moneyed capital valued in like manner does tax them at a greater rate within the meaning of the act of congress." Where, however the assessors assess ordinary securities at three-fifths of their actual value, and assess bank stock at its full actual value, and such method of unequal assessments is contrary to the constitution of the state, the court will relieve the stockholders only upon payment by them of such a tax as would have been legal Cummings v Merchants' National Bank of Toledo, 101 U. S, 153 (1879, Supervisors v. Stanley,

§ 572. *The bank may bring suit to restrain illegal tax on its stockholders.*—There has been some doubt as to whether a national bank could bring suit to restrain an illegal tax on its stockholders. Ordinarily a corporation cannot do so. Each stockholder must protect his own interests. But where, as in the case of national banks, the tax is paid by the bank itself and collected by it from its stockholders, if the latter refuse to pay the bank or recognize its payment as legal, many suits would result. Accordingly, in order to avoid a multiplicity of suits, it is now well established that the bank itself may file a bill in equity to prevent and enjoin the collection of an illegal tax on its stockholders.[1]

105 U S, 305 (1881). When the national bank stock is assessed too low, the fact that another bank is assessed still lower will not invalidate the tax against the former. People v. Assessors, etc., 2 Hun, 583 (1874). In the recent case of First National Bank of Toledo v. Treasurer, 25 Fed. Rep., 749 (1885) where ordinary moneyed capital was assessed at six-tenths of its actual value, while shares in national banks were assessed at a higher proportion of the real value, the collection thereof was enjoined upon the complainant paying the tax admitted to be due. As to the pleadings, see National Bank v. Kimball, 103 U S, 732 (1880). Lower valuation of other property has been held to be immaterial. Wagoner v. Loomis 37 Ohio St. 571 (1881). As regards taxation of national banks, a custom of assessing property at fifty per cent of its value is not proved by a few examples. Engelke v. Schlender, 12 S. W Rep, 999 (Tex, 1890). If, as a matter of fact, personal property and capital of individuals escape taxation and little effort is made to tax such capital then a tax on national bank stock cannot be enforced. If such stock is assessed at two-thirds of its actual value, and other personal property at one-half then their value the assessment is illegal. First Nat'l Bank v. Lindsay, 45 Fed Rep, 619 (1891).

[1] City Nat'l Bank v. City of Paducah, 2 Flippin, 61 (1877), where the court say "The bank is so far the trustee of the stockholders and the custodian of the dividends, that it is entitled to maintain the bill. It might be subjected to great annoyance by stockholders who denied the legality of the tax and gave the bank notice that it would pay at the peril of being sued by them. It is certainly no hardship to permit the whole question to be litigated in a single action." This case holds also that an injunction against the collection of the illegal tax will be granted. In general see, also, Albany City Nat'l Bank v. Maher, 20 Blatch, 341 (1882). North Ward Nat'l Bank v. Newark, 40 N J L, 558 (1878). Cf. Dows v. City of Chicago, 11 Wall, 108 (1870), Tappan v. Merchants Nat'l Bank, 19 Wall, 490 (1873), Pelton v. National Bank, 101 U S 143 (1879), Cummings v. National Bank 101 U S, 153. *Contra,* First Nat'l Bank of Hannibal v. Meredith, 44 Mo, 500 (1879). See, also, Union Nat'l Bank v. Chicago, 3 Biss, 82 (1871). As to the rule in New York see People v. Wall Street Bank, 39 Hun, 525, People v. Coleman, 41 Hun 344. The same rule does not apply to a corporation which brings suit to prevent the levy upon and sale of a non-resident stockholder's stocks for non-payment of his tax. Waseca Co. Bank v. McKenna, 32 Minn, 468 (1884). The case of Farmers' Nat'l Bank v. Cook, 32 N J L, 347 (1867), denies the right of the bank to bring the action, and says : "The corporation is not the agent of the stockholders for any such purpose." A national bank may file a

C. OTHER METHODS OF TAXING CORPORATIONS

§ 572a General principles.— A state may tax corporations. The rate of taxation may be greater or less than or equal to the rate at which individuals are taxed[1] The method of assessing taxes upon corporations varies in the different states[2]

Where a company is really located in a city and does all its business there, but its articles of incorporation state its principal place of business as being in an adjacent town, the sole object being to evade taxation, the court will hold that for taxation purposes its principal place of business is in such city[3] Where the capital stock is invested in patent rights it cannot be taxed by the state[4] A state may compel corporations to pay taxes for years past[5]

bill to restrain the imposition of a tax on stock, the bank having to pay the tax Whitney Nat'l Bank v Parker, 41 Fed Rep , 402 (1890) But the injunction against collection of the tax is granted only as to the excess of tax Id The bank cannot file a bill in the federal court unless the tax involved is over $2,000 Sioux Falls Nat'l Bank v Swenson, 48 Fed Rep , 621 (1892)

[1] It is constitutional to tax corporations without taxing individuals Singer Manuf Co v Wright, 33 Fed Rep 121 (1887), State R R Tax Cases 92 U S, 575 Cf The Railroad Tax Cases, 13 Fed Rep , 722 (1882), Santa Clara Co v Railroad, 18 id 355, S C , 118 U S , 396 (1885) Concerning the general problem of how corporations should be taxed, see Cook on The Corporation Problem, pp 102-107

[2] See Part VII, infra

[3] Milwaukee, etc , Co v City of Milwaukee, 53 N W Rep , 839 (Wis 1892). Where the actual place of business of a corporation is at one place, but its nominal place of business is fixed elsewhere in order to evade taxation, the actual place of business is the place where the company will be taxed under the Michigan statutes Detroit, etc Co v. Board of Assessors, 51 N W Rep , 978 (Mich., 1892), distinguishing the New York cases. In regard to a corporation being taxed in another place in the state from the place where its principal office is

located, see also Matter of McLean; Lough v Outerbridge, 66 Hun, 122 (1892) It must be the principal place or places of business for the purposes of taxation and service of process; and in New York under somewhat similar statutes it is held that the certificate is conclusive as to this Western Transportation Co v Scheu, 19 N. Y., 408 A domestic corporation will not be allowed to deny that it has a place of business in the state Chapman v Doray, 26 Pac Rep, 605 (Cal , 1891).

[4] Commonwealth v Westinghouse, etc., Co , 24 Atl Rep 1107 (Pa , 1892) Where the stock is issued in payment for the exclusive right to use certain patented articles within certain territory, it is not invested in patent rights so as to be exempt from taxation by reason of the acts of congress Commonwealth v Central, etc , Tel Co , 22 Atl Rep, 841 (Pa , 1891) Id v Brush, etc , Co , id , 844

[5] An attempt of the state to make a railroad corporation pay $1,250,000 back taxes, not levied under an alleged mistaken view of the law by former state officials, failed in Commonwealth v Penn. Co , 23 Atl Rep., 549 (Pa , 1892). Where the charter provides for "a tax not exceeding twenty-five cents per annum per share on each share of the capital stock whenever the annual profits thereof shall exceed six per cent.," the legislature may compel the company to pay such tax and to pay it for twenty-five

A tax on the capital stock based upon the amount of dividend declared cannot be evaded by distributing profits without declaring a dividend   But a stock dividend does not come within the tax statute[1]   A corporation claiming that it is taxed too much cannot enjoin collection unless it offers to pay the amount it admits to be due[2]   Where taxes are based on the aggregate value of all the shares of stock, unissued stock should not be considered even though ten per cent has been paid thereon[3]

In ascertaining the actual value of capital stock for taxation the price at which the stock is selling is not taken as the actual value, where the market value is due to speculation and market influences.[4]   Bonds of domestic corporations held by non-residents are

years past, during which time the company had evaded payment   State v. Seaboard, etc, R. R, 52 Fed Rep, 450 (1892)   See, also, § 572   A tax on a gas company on gross receipts and on dividends by way of license for the right to act as a corporation is not a tax upon the property or corporate franchises, but is a license fee   Jersey City G L. Co v United G, etc, Co, 46 Fed Rep., 264 (1891).   Generally, the statutes prescribe that a corporation shall be taxed where its principal office or place of business is located   People v McLean, 17 Hun, 204 (1879), Pelton v Northern Trans Co., 37 Ohio St, 450 (1882), Baltimore v Baltimore City Pass R'y Co, 57 Md, 31 (1881), Western Transportation Co v Stevens, 19 N Y, 408 (1859), Glaize v. South Carolina R R, 1 Strobh, 70 (1816), holding that a corporation may have a special or constructive residence extending to the territorial limits of the jurisdiction which granted its charter for purposes of taxation

[1] Lehigh, etc, Co v Commonwealth, 55 Pa St., 448 (1867), Commonwealth v Pittsburg, etc, R'y, 74 Pa St, 83 (1873). See State of Ohio v Franklin Bank, 10 Ohio, 91 (1840); People v Home Ins Co., 92 N Y, 328 (1883)   Where the dividends declared during the year were partly earned during prior years, the latter portion are not taxable under the Pennsylvania statute taxing the capital stock according to the dividends. Commonwealth v Brush, etc., Co, 22 Atl Rep.,

844 (Pa, 1891)   Where all the shares are reduced in par value from $50 to $38 and the $12 difference is paid to the stockholders in cash, this is a reduction of capital stock and not a dividend, and cannot be taxed as a dividend   Commonwealth v Central T Co, 22 Atl Rep, 209 (Pa, 1891)   A tax upon the receipts of a railroad is not a tax upon dividends. Com'rs, etc., v Buckner, 48 Fed Rep, 533 (1891)   A dividend declared and ordered deposited to the order of the stockholders and so held until the further order of the court is legal, and the amount cannot be taxed as belonging to the bank. Pollard v First National Bank, 28 Pac. Rep, 202 (Kan, 1891).   Profits applied to betterments are not "dividends earned" within the meaning of a statute imposing taxation   State v Comptroller, 23 Atl Rep., 122 (N J, 1891)

[2] Smith v Rude, etc, Co, 30 N. E. Rep, 917 (Ind, 1892).   See, also § 572.

[3] Boston, etc, Co. v Commonwealth, 31 N E Rep., 696 (Mass, 1892)   The whole capital stock may be taxed under a city charter, although only a part of it has been paid in   Shelby, etc, Co v Board, etc, 16 S W Rep, 460 (Ky, 1891)

[4] Commonwealth v Phil, etc, R R, 22 Atl Rep, 235 (Pa, 1891)   In Louisiana the corporation may sue to reduce or annul taxation of the shares of stock   The value of the stock may be ascertained from various sources, including that of the stock for which it has been

(49)

not taxable by the states creating the corporations[1] A railroad cannot be taxed to aid in paying a municipal subscription to its construction.[2] The franchise to build and operate a street railway is subject to taxation A license fee may be imposed on the railway, although, under its franchise, it is also bound to pay other taxes annually.[3] The taxation of unincorporated associations is considered elsewhere[4] Where a railroad company of one state is consolidated with companies of other states the consolidated company is considered, for the purposes of taxation, to be a corporation of each state to the extent that its property is in that state. It is taxed in the state on the capital stock of the company which it absorbed[5]

§ 572*b* *Exemptions from taxation.*— A state, if not restricted by its constitution, may exempt the property of a corporation from

exchanged Planters', etc, Co. *v.* Assessor, 6 S Rep, 809 (La , 1889)

[1] Railroad Co *v.* Jackson, 7 Wall , 262 (1868), State tax on Foreign-held Bonds, 15 Wall , 300 (1872), Davenport *v* Mississippi & Missouri R. R. Co , 12 Iowa, 539 (1861); Commonwealth *v* Chesapeake & Ohio R. R Co , 27 Gratt, 344 (1876), People *v.* Eastman, 25 Cal , 603 (1864), where the same principle was applied between counties in the same state *Contra,* Maltby *v.* Reading & Columbia R. R. Co , 52 Pa St , 140 (1866) As to the rule where part of the capital stock is used out of the state, see Commonwealth *v* Standard Oil Co , 101 Pa. St , 119 (1882), State Treasurer *v.* Auditor-General, 46 Mich , 224 (1881); People *t* Equitable, etc., Co , 96 U. S, 387 (1884) A statute making the corporation liable for taxes on bonds which it neglects to withhold, and the interest is paid on such bonds, is constitutional. Commonwealth *v* Delaware, etc., Canal Co , 24 Atl Rep., 599 (Pa , 1892) The Pennsylvania system of taxing against corporations all bonds issued by them and owned by citizens of the state, and compelling the corporation to pay the tax and deduct it from the interest on the bonds, is constitutional Bell's Gap R. R *v* Pennsylvania, 134 U. S, 232 (1890)

[2] Louisville, etc , R. R. *v.* Commonwealth, 12 S W Rep 1064 (Ky , 1890).

[3] New Orleans, etc., Co *v.* New Orleans, 143 U S., 192 (1892).

[4] See ch XXIX.

[5] Ohio & Mississippi R. R. Co. *v.* Weber, 96 Ill , 443 (1880), Chicago & N W. R'y Co *v* Auditor-General, 53 Mich , 79 (1884), Railroad Co. *v.* Vance, 96 U S, 450 (1877) In this case a railroad corporation of Indiana which had been recognized by an act of the Illinois legislature as a corporation of that state was held for taxes upon the capital and franchises of a road leased by it in Illinois and assessed to the lessor company, but charged to the lessee company and to be collected from it. Quincy R. R. Bridge Co. *v* County of Adams, 88 Ill , 615 (1878), where a bridge company originally incorporated by two states and consolidated by articles which were confirmed by the legislature of one of them (Illinois) was held to be a corporation of that state for purposes of taxation. *Quære,* whether the formation of an interstate railroad corporation by the consolidation of separate corporations in two states creates a new corporation. An incorporating fee cannot be imposed on the whole consolidated capital. People *v* New York, etc , R. R., 129 N. Y., 474 (1892) The state may constitutionally charge a large fee as a condition of granting a charter. Edwards *v.* Denver, etc., R. R., 21 Pac Rep., 1011 (Colo , 1889).

taxation. Such an exemption constitutes a contract between the state and the corporation, which cannot be repealed or changed by subsequent legislation, unless the right to alter or repeal it has been reserved by the state [1]

[1] An exemption from state taxation is a contract between the state and the corporation which cannot be impaired by a subsequent legislative enactment. Such exemption, however, will not be extended to branch lines thereafter constructed   Wilmington, etc., R R. v Alsbrook, 146 U S, 279 (1892), Tomlinson v Branch, 15 Wall, 460 (1872), Home of the Friendless v Rowse, 8 Wall, 430 (1869), Wilmington R R. v Reid, 13 Wall, 264 (1871), Mobile & Ohio R. R. Co v Moseley, 52 Miss, 127 (1876), Jefferson Bank v Skelley, 1 Black, 436 (1861), where the charter provided for the payment of six per cent. of the bank's profits in lieu of taxes, Livingston Co. v Hannibal & St J R R Co, 60 Mo, 516 (1875), where, however, an exemption from county taxes was held not to include a school tax which originated after the charter was granted, Hannibal & St Joseph R R Co r St Joseph, 39 Mo, 476 (1867), holding that an exemption from county taxation will not prevent taxation by a city   A contract between the state and a railroad, that the latter shall pay a certain tax and no more, is not repealable by the state   State v Morris, etc., R. R., 7 Atl Rep, 872 (N J, 1886)   Though a charter may be repealable, yet an amendment giving an exemption from taxation may be irrepealable, since the latter may be a contract and not a franchise   Ibid. A bonus to the state on increase of capital stock cannot apply to previous charters having charter right to increase   Commonwealth v. Erie, etc, Co., 107 Pa St, 112 (1884), Railroad Companies v Gaines, 97 U S., 698 (1878), holding that a new corporation invested with the powers and privileges of, and subject to the obligations of the charter of, another corporation, does not take an exemption from taxation   To

same effect, Railroad Co v Commissioners, 103 U S, 1 (1880), Dauphin & Lafayette R'y Co v Kennerly, 74 Ala, 583 (1883)   But see East Tennessee, V. & G R. Co v Pickerd, 24 Fed Rep., 614 (1885), The Delaware Railroad Tax, 18 Wall, 206 (1873), Dartmouth College v Woodward, 4 Wheat, 518 (1819), Providence Bank v Billings, 4 Pet., 514 (1830), The Binghamton Bridge, 3 Wall, 51 (1865), Humphreys v Pegues, 16 Wall, 244 (1872), Pacific R R. v. Maguire, 20 Wall, 36 (1873); North Mo. R R Co v Maguire, 20 Wall, 46 (1873), People v Soldiers' Home, etc., 95 Ill, 561 (1880); University v People, 99 U. S. 309 (1878), holding void a statute limiting a general exemption previously conferred to property in immediate use by a corporation, Farrington v. Tennessee, 95 U. S., 679 (1877); Railway Co v Philadelphia, 101 U. S. 528 (1879), Hoge v Railway Co., 99 U S, 348 (1878), Dodge v Woolsey, 18 How, 331 (1855), holding that the adoption of a new constitution declaring that corporate property shall be taxed will not be allowed to impair the contract, Mobile & Spring Hill R R Co v Kennerly, 74 Ala, 566 (1883), City of Richmond v Richmond & Danville R. R. Co, 21 Gratt, 604 (1872), holding, also, that an exemption of corporate property in a city from taxation, which conflicts with the charter of the city previously granted, is not unconstitutional if the city has remaining ample means of taxation to meet its needs, Commonwealth v Fayette R. R Co, 55 Pa St, 452 (1867), holding that, where power to alter or repeal the exemption is reserved, the exercise of the power is no impairment of the contract, State v Miller, 30 N J L., 368 (1863), holding that the repeal may be made by a general law, State v. Commissioners of

Where a corporation whose property is exempt from taxation is merged into or consolidated with another, the question of whether the exemption from taxation passes with its property to the lessee,

Taxation, 37 N J L, 240 (1874), holding that where a general exemption from taxation is granted to a corporation without reserving the power to alter or repeal it, and there is a provision for a special mode of assessing its property, it may consent to another mode of assessment without surrendering or altering its exemption from general taxation, East Tennessee, V & G R Co. *v* Pickerd, 24 Fed Rep, 614 (1885), Temple Grove Seminary *v* Cramer, 98 N. Y, 121 (1885), holding that an incorporated academy does not waive or forfeit its exemption from taxation by reason of having leased its building for a boarding-house during vacations. Elizabethtown & P R R *v* Elizabethtown, 12 Bush (Ky), 233 (1876), holding that an exemption of railroad property from taxation precludes any imposition of taxes by the state, whether for state or local purposes In Mott *v* Penn R R Co, 30 Pa St, 9 (1858), a sale of a railroad and canal by the state on terms exempting the vendee from future taxes was enjoined. The exemption was held to be unconstitutional. County Com'rs *v.* Woodstock Iron Co, 82 Ala, 151 (1886), holding that an exemption of private corporations from taxation made by a general law was not a contract, but only a legislative bounty, subject to be repealed

The act by which the exemption from taxation is made must be clear and unequivocal, the intent to confer the immunity must be beyond reasonable doubt. Ohio, etc, Trust Co *v* Debolt, 16 How 416 (1853), The Delaware Railroad Tax, 18 Wall, 206 (1873), North Missouri R R Co *v* Maguire, 20 Wall, 46 (1873), Mobile & Spring Hill R R Co *v* Kennedy, 74 Ala, 566 (1883), holding that a reasonable doubt is to be construed against the exemption, Dauphin & Lafayette R'y Co *v* Kennedy, 74 Ala, 583 (1883), City of Richmond *v.* Richmond & Danville R R Co, 21 Gratt, 604 (1872). An exemption of a corporation from taxation upon payment of a fixed annual tax on the capital stock is not voidable. State *v* Butler, 8 S. W. Rep, 586 (Tenn, 1888) A particular mode of taxation may be changed under the reserved right to amend the charter Detroit St R'ys *v.* Guthard, 51 Mich, 180 (1883) See, also, Bank of Republic *v* County of Hamilton, 21 Ill, 53 (1858), Mayor, etc., *v.* Twenty, etc, R R Co, 113 N. Y, 311 (1889). A specific rate of taxation prescribed in the charter raises no implication of a legislative contract to impose no further burdens by way of taxation. Iron City Bank *v* City of Pittsburgh, 37 Pa. St, 340 (1860) A constitutional prohibition as to exemptions from taxation does not apply to railroad corporations, they being *quasi*-public. Yazoo, etc, R R *v* Board, etc, 37 Fed. Rep, 24 (1888) A charter exemption from all taxation upon payment of a certain tax is legal Franklin, etc. *v.* Deposit Bank, 9 S W Rep, 212 (Ky, 1888). An exemption from taxation which is a gift may be repealed Philadelphia *v.* Contributors, etc, 19 Atl Rep, 490 (Pa, 1890). An exemption from taxation may be repealed under the reserved right to amend, etc Wagner, etc, Institute Appeal, 19 Atl Rep, 297 (Pa, 1890) An exemption from all other taxation is an exemption from local as well as state taxation People *v* Coleman, 121 N Y, 542 (1890) A railroad may give up its exemption from state taxation and still retain its exemption from county taxation State *v.* Hannibal, etc, R R 11 S W Rep., 746 (Mo, 1889) A railroad that is divided by the legislature with the consent of the stockholders does not lose its exemp-

vendee or consolidated company is a question which turns largely on the words granting the exemption.[1]

Where a consolidation is effected after the adoption of constitutional provisions prohibiting the legislature from exempting the

tions Louisville, etc, R R v Commonwealth, 12 S. W Rep, 1064 (Ky, 1890) An exemption from taxation is not a franchise Hence *quo warranto* does not lie to oust the corporation from such exemption International, etc, R'y v. State, 12 S W. Rep, 685 (Tex, 1889)

The decision of the state court that an exemption does not apply to certain property is not an impairment of a contract. St. Paul, etc, Ry z Todd County, 142 U S, 282 (1892) Where a contract of exemption from taxation between a state and a water-works company is declared unconstitutional by the highest court of the state, there is no impairment of the contract by subsequent legislation which assumes the old contract to have been invalid New Orleans z N O, etc., Works, 142 U S, 79 (1891). In the case of Citizens' Bank z Board of Assessors, 54 Fed Rep, 73 (1893), an exemption from taxation was held to apply to extensions of the original charter. Although the charter provides that the real and personal property of the company shall be taxed the same as that of individuals this does not exempt the capital stock from taxation State v Simmons, 12 S Rep, 477 (Miss, 1893) An exemption from taxation does not pass to a company that buys out the company which is exempt Commonwealth v Nashville, etc, Co, 20 S W Rep, 383 (Ky, 1892) An exemption from local taxation is not an exemption from state taxation Wilkesbarre, etc, Bank v Wilkesbarre, 24 Atl. Rep, 111 (Pa, 1892) An exemption from taxation does not apply to assessments for improvements Illinois Cent R. R. v Mattoon 30 N E. Rep. 773 (Ill, 1892). Concerning exemptions from taxation and the Dartmouth College case in connection therewith, see Cook on the Corpora-

tion Problem, pp 105-107. A company to generate and sell electric power is not a manufacturing company as regards taxation Commonwealth v. Northern, etc, Co, 22 Atl Rep, 839 (Pa, 1891), Commonwealth z Brush, etc, Co, id, 844 Exemption of manufacturing corporations from taxation construed to exempt merely such of their property as was invested in manufacturing Appeal of Commonwealth, 18 Atl Rep, 133 (Pa, 1889), Commonwealth v Mahoning, etc, Co, id, 137 Where subsequently to the incorporation of a company a general act reserves to the legislature the right to amend or repeal any and all charters, the legislature may repeal any amendments to the charter, so far as such amendments are passed after the general act, where the amendments do not expressly waive the legislative right of amendment or repeal Amendment should be worded "saving whenever that power was exerted, all rights previously vested" An exemption from taxation may be repealed under the reserved power (Approving Tomlinson v Jessup, 15 Wall, 454, and Railroad v Maine, 96 U S., 499) Creditors stand upon the same footing in this respect. Louisville Water Co. v. Clark, 143 U. S, 1 (1892).

[1] An exemption from taxation pertains to the franchise as a corporation, and does not pass with the sale of the franchise to operate the road Chesapeake & Ohio R'y Co v Miller, 114 U S, 176 (1885), Memphis R. R. Co v Com'rs, 112 U S, 609 (1884), Tomlinson v Branch, 15 Wall, 460 (1872), Branch v Charleston, 92 U S, 677 (1875), Central R. R Co v Georgia, 92 U S, 665 (1875), reversing S C, 54 Ga, 401, Chesapeake & O R. R. Co v Virginia, 94 U S, 718 (1876); The Delaware Railroad Tax, 18 Wall, 206 (1873). See,

property of corporations from taxation, the consolidated company is looked upon as a new corporation, which is not entitled to exemptions from taxation possessed by the companies of which it is composed.[1]

If the franchises and property of a corporation be transferred by a sale in foreclosure, an exemption from taxation does not accompany the transfer. The exemption is a personal privilege and not a franchise.[2] A statute exempting the property of a corporation from being taxed does not prevent the taxation of land held by it merely for convenience and not necessary to its operation.[3] In

also, cases in preceding note   Where by statute "all rights" of a railway are to pass to another, an exemption from taxation passes   Atlantic, etc, R R r Allen, 15 Fla, 637 (1876)   It certainly will not be extended to the property of other corporations consolidated with it   Philadelphia, W & B R R Co r. Maryland, 10 How, 376 (1850), Chesapeake & O R. R. Co r Virginia, 94 U S, 718 (1876), The Delaware Railroad Tax, 18 Wall, 206 (1873)   See, also, Wait on Insolvent Corporations, 381   An exemption of a corporation may not exempt also its timber lands   County of Todd r St. Paul, etc, R'y, 36 N. W. Rep, 109 (Minn, 1888)   An exemption of railroad lands from taxation may pass to the grantee railroads thereof and of the franchises.   *In re* County of Stevens, 31 N W Rep, 912 (Minn, 1887)   Consolidation in Missouri destroys exemption from taxation   Keokuk, etc, R R r County Court, etc, 41 Fed Rep., 305 (1890)   A consolidated company under the Missouri statutes relative to railroads meeting at the state line is a new corporation, and the old one is dissolved   An exemption from taxation of the old corporation is thereby lost.   State r Keokuk, etc, R. R., 12 S W Rep, 290 (Mo., 1889)   Although an exemption from taxation is to pass to a consolidated company, yet this is a gratuity to the new company and may be repealed   Wilmington, etc, R R r Alsbrook, 14 S E Rep, 652 (N C, 1892)

[1] Memphis & Little Rock R R Co r Berry, 112 U. S, 609 (1884), St. Louis,

Iron Mt. & S. R. R. Co, v. Berry, 113 U S, 465 (1885), Chesapeake & Ohio R. R. Co r Miller, 114 U S, 176 (1885). Where the legislature ceded to a company to be formed "all the right, interest and privileges of whatever kind" of a defunct railroad company, it was held that an exemption from taxation conferred on the old company was not vested in the new one   Railroad Co. r Georgia, 98 U S, 359 (1878). In this case the restriction upon granting exemptions was in a statute instead of a constitutional provision.

[2] Morgan r Louisiana, 93 U. S., 217 (1876); Louisville & N R. R. Co. v. Palmer, 109 U S, 224 (1883), Wilson v. Gaines, 103 U S, 417 (1880), where the transfer was under proceedings to enforce a statutory lien of a state; Arkansas Midland R. R. Co. r Berry, 44 Ark, 17 (1884)   See, also, 130 U S, 637, and cases *supra*   Where the exemption is as to all the property of a railroad its franchise is included   Wilmington R. R. r Reid, 13 Wall, 264 (1871).

[3] State r Commissioners, etc, 23 N J Law, 510 (1852); State r Collectors, etc, 25 N J Law, 315 (1855). In these cases lands owned by a railroad and occupied by dwellings for employees, car and locomotive works, coal mines, etc, were held to be subject to taxation   See, also, Toll-bridge Co, v Osborn, 35 Conn, 7 (1868), where lands held for wharves by a bridge company by authority of law were held taxable as real estate — a provision in its charter that all its property should be consid-

general, an exemption from taxation by the state is not an exemption also from municipal taxation for local purposes,[1] nor from assessments for improvements.[2]

§ 572c. *Taxation of foreign corporations* — Any state may tax foreign corporations doing business within its borders.[3]

ered personal property and be divided into shares being construed to relate to the property of the stockholders as represented by the shares; *In re* Swigert, 119 Ill., 83 (1886), holding that a railroad exemption did not exempt its elevator.

[1] Elizabethtown & P R R *v* Elizabethtown, 12 Bush (Ky), 233 (1876); Roosevelt Hospital *v* Mayor of New York, 84 N. Y, 108 (1881), where real estate exempted from state taxation was held to be subject to assessment by a city for the construction of a sewer. *Cf* Applegate *v* Ernst, 3 Bush (Ky), 648 (1868), where a tax by a county upon a railroad to obtain money to pay a county subscription for the purpose of completing the road was held to be unlawful. See, also, p 771, n. 1, *supra*.

[2] New Jersey, etc., R. R *v*. Jersey City, 42 N J. L, 97 (1880)

[3] Liverpool Ins. Co *v* Massachusetts, 10 Wall, 66 (1870), S. C. Oliver *v* Liverpool, etc, Co, 100 Mass, 531 (1868). Goods in New York for sale, also many on deposit in New York; also other property in the state, form the proper basis for taxation of such part of the capital stock of foreign corporations as is employed in the state. Taxation for such part of the capital stock as sales in New York bear to all the sales is unjust; since many sales may be by sample. People *v* Wemple, 133 N Y, 323 (1892). A tax on foreign manufacturing corporations to the extent of the business which they do in the state is constitutional and enforceable. People *ex rel* S. Cotton Oil Co. *v*. Wemple, 131 N Y, 64 (1892). The New York statute taxing foreign corporations doing business in the state on the same basis as domestic corporations is constitutional. Horn Silver, etc, Co *v* New York, 143 U S, 305 (1892). The New York tax upon the

business of all foreign and domestic corporations doing business in the state is a tax on the right to be a corporation and to do business, and is not a tax upon the franchise, even though the tax is measured by the dividends declared. The tax is legal although the corporation owns United States bonds. Home Ins. Co *v* New York, 134 U. S., 594 (1890). Where foreign corporations are required to report stock, bonds, etc, owned by residents for taxation, it need report only such as its books disclose and is not to be held liable further. Commonwealth *v* N Y, etc., R. R., 22 Atl Rep, 236 (Pa, 1891). *Cf*. Commonwealth *v*. American B T Co., 18 Atl Rep., 122 (1889). Foreign corporations doing business in New Jersey are subject to taxation. State *v* Berry, 19 Atl Rep., 665 (N J, 1890). Where a parent corporation of Massachusetts owns stock in a branch corporation of New York and collects royalties, etc, from the latter, the parent corporation is not subject to taxation in New York. People *v* American Bell T Co, 117 N Y, 241 (1889). Debts due to a foreign corporation from residents cannot be taxed in Louisiana. Barber, etc, Co *v*. New Orleans, 6 S. Rep, 794 (La, 1889). The New York statute levying a tax on foreign corporations doing business in the state, the tax being upon "the amount of capital stock employed within the state," is legal, and a New Jersey corporation is liable to taxation for maintaining a sales agency and office and bank account in New York city, even though its factories, books of account, etc, are in other states. Southern Cotton Oil Co *v* Wemple, 44 Fed Rep., 24 (1890)

The Pennsylvania statute imposing a quarter of a mill license tax on the capital stock of foreign corporations having

A state may impose on foreign insurance companies a tax equal to the tax levied by the state creating the foreign corporation on corporations foreign to the latter state [1] Where a railroad corporation is incorporated by the United States, a state cannot tax its franchises, it may tax the tangible property, but not the franchise [2] Where an assessment of taxes against a railroad company has been affirmed by the supreme court, *mandamus* may be used to compel payment of them if there is no other adequate remedy.[3]   The tax

an office in the state, and prohibiting such offices unless the tax is paid, the act applying to all foreign corporations except insurance companies, is constitutional   A state may exclude or impose conditions upon foreign corporations unless they are engaged in interstate or foreign commerce, or are employed by the government   Pembina Min Co v Pennsylvania, 125 U S., 181 (1888), Blackstone Manuf Co v Blackstone, 13 Gray. 488 (1859), State t Lathrop, 10 La. Ann. 402 (1855), State v Fosdick, 21 La Ann, 434 (1869); Tatem v Wright, 23 N J L, 429 (1852), State v Western Union Tel Co., 73 Me, 518 (1882), Commonwealth v Western Union Tel Co, 98 Pa St, 105 (1881), Norfolk, etc, R. R. v Commonwealth, 114 id, 256 (1886); Commonwealth v Milton, 12 B M, 212, 218 (1851), Boston Loan Co v Boston, 137 Mass., 342 (1884), Singer Manuf Co. v County Comm'rs, 139 Mass, 266 (1885), Att'y-Gen v Bay State, etc, Co, 99 Mass, 148 (1868); Commonwealth v Texas & Pac R. R. Co, 98 Pa. St, 90 (1881), holding, however, that a corporation created by the United States congress is not a foreign corporation within the revenue act of Pennsylvania, Commonwealth v Gloucester, etc, Ferry Co, 98 id, 105 (1881), People v. Equitable Trust Co, 96 N Y, 387 (1884), holding that a tax may be imposed upon the business done by a foreign corporation in New York, but not upon its property in other states, nor upon its franchise   For the New York act which applies to foreign corporations, see Parker Mills v Commissioners, etc, 23 N Y, 242 (1861), People v. Horn, etc,

Co, 105 id, 76 (1887). They are to be taxed where their principal offices in the state are situated   People, etc., v. McLean, 17 Hun, 204 (1879).   A corporation chartered by the federal government is not such a foreign corporation as is obliged to pay a license fee under the Pennsylvania statutes.   Commonwealth v Texas, etc, R. R. Co, 98 Pa St, 90 (1881)   Unless a statute otherwise provides, a lien upon corporate property for state taxes attaches in preference to pre-existing judgments or decrees; it has been held that a sale under a judgment or decree will not avoid such a lien.   Osterburg v. Union Trust Co, 93 U S., 424 (1876)   In New York it is held that the rolling stock of a railroad is subject to seizure and sale for taxes.   Randall v Elwell, 52 N. Y, 521 (1873).   But not so in Kentucky   Elizabethtown & P R. R. v. Elizabethtown, 12 Bush, 233 (1876).

[1] Home Ins Co v Swigert, 104 Ill, 653 (1882), Phila Fire Ass'n v New York, 119 U S, 110 (1886)

[2] California v Pacific R R. Co., 127 U S, 1, 40 (1888)   A county ordinance requiring a railroad chartered by the United States to take out a license is void   San Benito, etc, v. Southern P. R. R. Co, 19 Pac Rep, — (Cal, 1888)

[3] Person v Warren R. R. Co, 32 N J L, 441 (1868), Silverthorn v Warren R. R. Co, 33 N J L, 173 (1868).   And the party making return to an alternative *mandamus* must show that he has complied with the order to the extent of his ability, want of funds is not a sufficient return where it is the result of the voluntary act of the party.

lien on a railroad may by delay be rendered subordinate to a mortgage[1]

§ 572d. *Taxation must not interfere with interstate commerce.*—
A state cannot tax corporations so as to interfere with interstate
commerce   The Pennsylvania license fee which all foreign corporations keeping an office in the state are required to pay, with a
few exceptions, is unconstitutional as regards a foreign railroad
corporation which owns a railroad in the state, such railroad being
part of an interstate system of railroads[2]   But a state may levy a
tax on the capital stock of a foreign sleeping-car company which
runs its cars through the state, the tax being on such part of the
capital stock as the number of miles over which its cars run in the
state bears to the whole number of miles over which its cars run
in all the states.[3]

A tax on interstate telegraph messages is unconstitutional[4]   A
state cannot prohibit the agents of foreign express companies from
doing business in the state except upon obtaining a license.   Such
a law is an interference with interstate commerce[5]   A tax may be
levied based on the gross receipts, and if the road is but partly in
the state on a proportion of the gross receipts determined by a
mode prescribed by statute[6]   A state may tax a railroad on business that passes out of the state into another state and back into
the first state again[7]   Various other decisions on taxation in its
bearings upon interstate commerce are given in the notes below[8]

[1] Cooper v Corbin, 105 Ill , 224 (1883),
Parsons v East, etc., Co , 108 Ill , 380
(1884)

[2] Norfolk, etc , R R. v. Penn, 136 U S ,
114 (1890)

[3] Pullman's Car Co v Penn, 141 U S ,
18 (1891), the court holding that a tax
on the capital stock on account of the
property owned is a tax on the property
itself.   A similar decision was made
concerning a tax on the capital stock of
a foreign telegraph company, the capital stock being valued at the aggregate
value of all its shares of stock and the
proportion of its lines within the state
to those outside of it being the basis of
taxation   Massachusetts v Western U
Tel Co , 141 U. S , 40 (1890).

[4] Western U T. Co v Alabama, 132
U S , 472 (1889)

[5] Crutcher v. Kentucky, 141 U. S , 47
(1891).

[6] Maine v Grand Trunk, etc , R'y, 142
U S , 217 (1891).

[7] Lehigh Val R R v Penn, 145 U S.,
192 (1892)

[8] A tax on sleeping-car companies may
be illegal as interfering with interstate
commerce   State v Woodruff, etc , Co.,
15 N. E Rep , 514 (Ind , 1888)   A state
tax on interstate railroad earnings is
unconstitutional.   Fargo v Michigan,
121 U S , 230 (1887), Phila , etc , Co v.
Pennsylvania, 122 U S , 326 (1887), Delaware, etc , Co v Commonwealth, 17 Atl.
Rep , 175 (Pa , 1888), Northern, etc , R'y
Co v Raymond, 40 N. W Rep , 538
(Dak , 1888)   A state may tax a foreign
telegraph company on such a proportion of its capital stock as its lines in
the state bear to all of its lines , but the
state cannot enjoin the operation of the
telegraph until the tax is paid   Western,
etc , Tel Co v. Massachusetts, 125 U S.,

There has been a large number of decisions by the supreme court of the United States on this subject, and the efforts of various states to tax interstate commerce directly or indirectly are being constantly overthrown by that court.

530 (1888), Erie R'y Co. v. New Jersey, 31 N. J L., 531 (1864), holding that a state tax upon foreign corporations transporting passengers and freight through the state graduated by the number of passengers and weight of the goods is in violation of that clause of the United States constitution giving congress the right to regulate commerce between the states, Indiana v American Express Co., 7 Biss. 227 (1876), where a tax upon transportation through a state was held to be an interference with interstate commerce and unconstitutional So held, also, of a tax upon locomotives, cars, etc., of a foreign railroad company in Minot v Philadelphia, Wilmington & B. R. R. Co, 2 Abb. (U. S C. C.), 323 (1870). As to an interstate bridge, see Anderson v. C. B., etc., R. R., 117 Ill, 26 (1886). Pullman cars operated wholly within the state may be taxed as a privilege. Gibson County v Pullman, etc., Co., 42 Fed. Rep, 572 (1890) A foreign corporation's rolling stock used in interstate commerce is not taxable by the state Bain v Richmond, etc., R. R., 11 S. E. Rep, 311 (N. C, 1890) Interstate express companies may be taxed on the business which they do within the state. Pacific Ex Co. t. Seibert, 44 Fed. Rep, 310 (1890). As to telegraph companies, see, also, Western Union Tel. Co. v. Lieb, 76 Ill, 172 (1875); Western Union Tel. Co. v Mayer, 28 Ohio St., 521 (1876).

CHAPTER XXXV.

FORMS OF ACTIONS AND MEASURE OF DAMAGES WHERE A STOCK-HOLDER HAS BEEN DEPRIVED OF HIS STOCK.

§ 573 *Pleading and practice in actions relative to stock.*— When an owner of stock who is out of possession brings an action for its recovery, or for the recovery of the certificate, or for damages for the detention or conversion of either the stock or the certificate, it is important to determine what action will lie, in what court the action is to be prosecuted, and what is the measure of damages. Similar questions arise when suits are brought for breach of contract to subscribe for stock, or of contracts to sell and convey stock. There are certain well-settled rules as to the form of the action in these cases which are deduced from the older common-law pleading and practice. These rules, even in the code states, where forms of action are little regarded, and where the old actions have been abolished in name, are still at least partially applicable. Some knowledge, therefore, of the procedure at common law in stock cases is necessary.

§ 574 *Assumpsit.*— An action of *assumpsit*, or *indebitatus assumpsit* at common law, lies against a corporation for unjustly refusing to register a transfer, or for refusing to issue a certificate to one entitled to it.[1] So, also, *assumpsit* lies for breach of contract

[1] The King v Bank of England, Doug., 524 (1780); Kortright v Buffalo Commercial Bank, 20 Wend, 90 (1838); Arnold v Suffolk Bank, 27 Barb, 424 (1857), Wyman v American Powder Co, 8 Cush, 168 (1851), Sargent v Franklin Ins Co, 8 Pick, 90 (1829), Hayden v Middlesex Turnpike Co., 10 Mass, 397 (1813); Pinkerton v Manchester, etc., R. R. Co., 42 N H, 424 (1861), Hill v Pine River Bank, 45 id, 300 (1864). *Cf* Foster v Essex Bank, 17 Mass, 479 (1821), Eastern R. R Co. v Benedict, 10 Gray, 212 (1857) *Assumpsit* does not lie against a corporation for refusal to register a transfer of stock Action on the case is the remedy Telford, etc., Co v Gerhab, 13 Atl Rep, 90 (Pa., 1888).

to return borrowed bank stock on demand.[1] But *mandamus* is not a proper remedy in these cases, and it will not lie to compel a corporation to transfer[2] The form of a complaint or declaration in an action by a pledgor against a pledgee for the conversion of the stock held in pledge may be in tort or in *assumpsit*, but not in both[3] A corporation may sue in *assumpsit* its treasurer who has illegally issued excessive stock and converted the proceeds to his own use[4]

§ 575 *Trespass on the case* — An action of trespass, or an action of trespass on the case, may also be brought against the corporation for a denial to a stockholder of a certificate of stock,[5] and an action on the case lies for a conversion of shares of stock[6]

§ 576 *Trover* — It is a very generally-accepted rule that trover will lie for the conversion of shares of stock[7] This is the favorite

[1] McKenney v Haines, 63 Me, 74 (1873)

[2] See § 390

[3] Stevens v. Hurlbut Bank, 31 Conn, 146 (1862).

[4] Rutland R. R. v Haven, 19 Atl Rep 769 (Vt, 1890)

[5] Bank of Ireland v Trustee of Evans' Charities, 5 H of L Cas, 389 (1855), The King v Bank of England, Doug, 524 (1780), Davis v Bank of England, 2 Bing, 393 (1824), Coles v Bank of England, 10 Ad & Ells, 437 (1839), Gray v. Portland Bank, 3 Mass, 364, 381 (1807), North American Building Association v Sutton, 35 Pa St, 463 (1860), Webster v Grand Trunk R'y Co., 3 Lower Can Jur, 148 (1859); S C, 2 id, 291 (construing the judicature act, 12 Vict., ch 38, § 87), Protection Life Ins Co v Osgood. 93 Ill, 69 (1879), Baker v Wasson, 53 Texas, 150 (1880), Smith v Poor, 40 Me, 415 (1855), Catchpole v. Ambergate, etc, R'y Co., 1 Ellis & B, 111 (1852), Daly v Thompson, Sec'y, etc, of the Anti-Dry-Rot Co., 10 Mees. & W, 309 (1842) Cf Swan v. North British Australasian Co, 7 Hurl & N, 603 (1862), Kortright v Buffalo Commercial Bank, 20 Wend, 90 (1838) Tort with a count in contract for refusal to transfer Bond v. Mount Hope Iron Co, 99 Mass, 505 (1868)

[6] Daggett v Davis, 53 Mich, 35 (1884),

Ayres v French 41 Conn, 142 (1874); Bank of America v McNeil, 10 Bush, 54, Parsons v Martin, 11 Gray, 111 (1859), Boylan v Huguet, 8 Nev, 345 (1873), Nabring v Bank of Mobile, 58 Ala, 204 (1877) A complaint which, after stating that shares of stock had been pledged to defendant, avers that "defendant, in consideration of the premises, then and there undertook and promised plaintiff" to hold the stock only as pledgee, but that, in violation of its promise, defendant sold and converted the stock to its own use, without giving plaintiff notice of the sale, and in which plaintiff seeks to recover as damages the full value of the shares alleged to have been converted, though informal, is good as a complaint in case. Sharpe v National Bank, 7 S Rep, 106 (Ala, 1888). This case discussed also the difference between *assumpsit* and in case in such an action.

[7] Payne v Elliot, 54 Cal, 339 (1880); Kuhn v McAllister, 1 Utah 273 (1875); S C, 96 U S, 87 (1877), Bank of America v McNeil, 10 Bush, 54; Boylan v. Huguet, 8 Nev, 345 (1873), Nabring v. Bank of Mobile, 58 Ala, 204 (1877); Morton v Preston, 18 Mich, 60 (1869); Jarvis v Rogers, 15 Mass, 389 (1810) — a case where trover was held to lie for the value of Mississippi scrip, representing one hundred and fifty thousand

remedy when the shareholder has been unjustly deprived of his stock; and it is nowhere denied, except in Pennsylvania,[1] that this form of action is proper But even there, for the conversion of a certificate of stock, trover will lie [2] For the maintenance of the action of trover there must be title in the plaintiff to the subject of the action, and an actual conversion by the defendant. If either of these elements is wanting the action will not lie Thus, trover will not lie for the conversion of a certificate where the title to the shares is divested [3]

acres of land; Anderson v Nicholas, 28 N Y, 600 (1864), Freeman v Harwood, 49 Me., 195 (1859), Ayres v French, 41 Conn, 142 (1874), Connor v Hillier, 11 Rich Law, 193 (1857), Sturges v Keith, 57 Ill, 451 (1870), Budd v Multnomah Street R R Co, 12 Oregon, 271 (1885), S C, 22 Am & Eng R. R. Cas, 27 (1885) Cf Atkins v Gamble, 42 Cal, 86, 100 (1871), Maryland Fire Ins Co v Dalrymple, 25 Md, 242, 267 (1866) Trover and arrest lie for conversion of certificates of stock Barry v Calder, 48 Hun, 449 (1888) The action for conversion lies, even though the plaintiff uses the term "shares of stock" and "certificates of stock" interchangeably Godfrey v. Pell, 49 N Y Sup. Ct., 226 (1883) A party whose stock has been converted may sue for damages instead of following the stock Moore v Baker, 30 N E Rep., 629 (Ind 1892). For the allegations in an action for the conversion of a bond, see Saratoga, etc, Co v Hazard, 55 Hun, 251 (1889), aff'd, 121 N Y, 677 Where defendant purchased stock for the plaintiff and accounted therefor, but refused to account for dividends received while he held the stock, the defendant is guilty of conversion Shaughnessy v Chase, 7 N Y State Rep, 293 There are many cases in the lower courts of New York on this subject As to refusal to return pledge after payment is a conversion, see Roberts v Berdell, 52 N Y, 644, S C, 15 Abb Pr (N S) 177 As to arrest for conversion, replevin thereby being waived, see Chappel v Skinner, 6 How Pr, 338, Person v Civer, 29 How Pr,

432; rev'g 28 id, 139; Niver v Niver, 43 Barb, 411, 19 Abb Pr, 14; 29 How Pr, 6, Dubois v Thompson, 1 Daly, 309, 25 How Pr, 417, Causland v Davis, 4 Bosw, 619, Schoeppel v Corning, 6 N Y, 107 Conversion of railway shares in a foreign country Northern R'y v Carpenter, 13 How Pr Rep, 222 In the case Butts v Burnett, 6 Abb Pr (N S), 302 (1869) involving the arrest of a broker who had sold the pledge before the note was due, the court said "It is very questionable, I think, whether a demand after default in payment of the debt for which property is pledged as security will render a refusal to deliver the pledged property a tortious conversion of it. No doubt the pledgor can redeem upon a tender of the debt, or he may recover the difference between the value of the pledge and the debt But to lay the foundation for an action for conversion I am of opinion that an offer and demand must be made on the day, and is not sufficient if made after the day on which the debt has become payable"

[1] Sewall v Lancaster Bank, 17 Serg & R, 285 (1828), Neiler v Kelley, 69 Pa St, 403 (1871)

[2] Biddle v Bayard, 13 Pa St, 150 (1850) Cf Aull v Colket, 2 Week Notes Cas, 322 (1875) So in Michigan Daggett v Davis, 53 Mich, 35 (1884)

[3] Broadbent v Farley, 12 C. B (N S), 214 (1862) Trover does not lie against a person to whom stock is given to sell and use the proceeds to start in business. Borland v Stokes, 14 Atl Rep,

And, upon the other hand, withholding possession of a certificate of stock cannot amount to a conversion of the stock itself so long as the certificate is not indorsed, but it may amount to a technical conversion of the certificate.[1] It is well established that a refusal of a corporation to register a transfer in the name of one entitled to the stock is a conversion of the shares.[2] And likewise a failure or refusal by the corporation to issue a certificate to an original subscriber when by the terms of the contract of subscription it ought to be issued may be treated as a conversion[3] So, also, a failure to deliver stock according to a contract for delivery,[4] or to return borrowed stock on demand, or at the time when by agreement it ought to be returned;[5] and an unauthorized sale of stock by a pledgee in violation of the terms of the contract of bailment,[6]

61 (Pa., 1888). Where several shareholders mutually agree to contribute a number of shares each, to be sold for the benefit of the corporation, one of them cannot, after the rest have contributed their proportion, refuse to allow his shares to be sold as agreed; and if the corporation takes them under the agreement and sells them he cannot have an action of trover. Conrad v La Rue, 52 Mich, 83 (1883) In trover for a certificate of stock, the acceptance by the plaintiff of the certificate ends the suit and nothing further can be recovered Collins v Lowry, 47 N W. Rep, 612 (Wis, 1890)

[1] Daggett v Davis, 53 Mich, 35 (1884). Cf Morton v Preston, 18 id, 60 (1869) Where an administrator sells stock pledged to the deceased in his life-time as security for a loan of money and receives the proceeds and properly accounts to the estate, this is not a conversion of the shares, and the pledgor cannot have an action of trover If any action lies it is for money had and received Von Schmidt v Bourn, 50 Cal, 616 (1875) For an example of an insufficient complaint in trover for shares, in that there was no sufficient averment of a conversion or of facts from which a conversion might be inferred, see Edwards v Sonoma Valley Bank, 59 Cal., 136 (1881), and see, also, Cunnock v. Inst for Sav., 7 N. E. Rep., 869 (Mass, 1886).

[2] Allen v. American Building, etc, Ass'n, et al, 52 N. W. Rep. 144 (Minn, 1892); North America Building Assoc v Sutton, 35 Pa. St, 463 (1860), West Branch, etc, Canal Co's Appeal, 81* Pa. St. 19 (1870), Baltimore City, etc., R'y Co. v Sewell, 35 Md, 238 (1871); McMurrich v Boud Head Harbour Co, 9 Upp Can (Q B.), 333 (1852)

[3] See § 60

[4] Huntington, etc, Coal Co v. English, 86 Pa. St., 247 (1878); North v. Phillips, 89 id, 250 (1879), Noonan v. Ilsley, 17 Wis, 314 (1863); Pinkerton v. Manchester, etc, R. R. Co, 42 N. H, 424 (1861)

[5] McKenney v. Haines, 63 Me, 74 (1873), Fosdick v Greene, 27 Ohio St., 484 (1875), Forrest v Elwes, 4 Ves, 492 (1799) Where a person loans stock to another to borrow money upon, conversion does not lie for a failure to return the stock Barrowcliffe v Cummins, 66 Hun, 1 (1892). Where bonds are loaned to use temporarily upon an agreement to return them when called for, and the member of the firm to whom they are delivered uses them for his own purposes, he converts them. Birdsall v Davenport, 43 Hun, 552 (1887)

[6] Maryland Fire Ins Co v Dalrymple, 25 Md, 242, 267 (1866). Freeman v Harwood, 49 Me, 195 (1859), Fisher v Brown, 104 Mass, 259 (1870). For refusal of pledgee to return property, the action of pledgor may be in tort or con-

or by a broker in violation of his contract,[1] are examples of conversion of stock   In a late case in Oregon it is said that any interference subversive of the right of the owner of stock to enjoy and control it is a conversion.[2] In New York a transferee may try his right to registry in an action for dividends,[3] but not after commencing an action for conversion.[4] Where there are conflicting interests in and contending claimants for the same stock, the corporation is not liable for conversion at the suit of one of them in tort, because it may refuse to transfer, pending the contest between the claimants[5] Trover will not lie by a trustee on stock which stands in the name of the *cestui que trust* against a person taking title from a co-trustee. A suit in equity is the proper remedy[6]

§ 577. *Detinue and replevin* — The common-law action of detinue will lie for the recovery of a certificate of stock unlawfully detained[7] In this action the judgment is conditional, either to restore the thing detained, or pay the value and damages for the detention. The more modern action of replevin or its equivalent will doubtless lie for the recovery of a certificate, as for any other tangible personal property.

§ 578 *Money had and received.* — A pledgor whose stock has been wrongfully sold by the pledgee, in violation of the contract of bailment, may have an action against the pledgee for money had and received.[8]

tract. International Bank v. Monteath, 39 N. Y, 207 Conversion lies for an unauthorized sale of stock and also for dividends received thereon   Shaughnessy v Chase, 7 N. Y State Rep , 293 (Supr Ct., 1887)

[1] See ch. XXV, *supra*, Sadler v. Lee, 6 Beav , 324 (1843).

[2] Budd v Multnomah St R'y Co , 12 Oregon, 271 (1885).

[3] Robinson v National Bank of New Berne, 95 N. Y , 637 (1884).

[4] Hughes v Vermont Copper Mining Co , 72 N. Y , 207 (1878).

[5] National Bank of New London v Lake Shore, etc., R. R. Co , 21 Ohio St., 221, 232 (1871) See, also, § 387, *supra* In trover the goods ought to be set out with some degree of certainty of description , but the same certainty is not required as in detinue and replevin, damages being recovered in trover, the very articles in detinue and replevin Neiler v. Kelley, 69 Pa. St., 403 (1871).

[6] Onondaga, etc., Co. v Price, 87 N. Y , 542 (1882) , S C , in a court of equity, as White v Price, 39 Hun, 395 (1886); 108 N Y , 661 (1888).

[7] Williams v Peel, etc , Co. 55 L T Rep , 689 (1886), Williams v. Archer, 5 C B, 318 (1847); S C , 5 Railway & Canal Cas , 289, where it was held that detinue lay to recover two hundred and fifty scrip certificates, Peters v Heywood, Cro. Jac , 682 (21 Jac 1, 1621). where detinue was allowed for a bond detained. As to replevin in cepit for bonds wrongfully received in pledge from a pledgee, see Thompson v St Nicholas Nat'l Bank 113 N. Y , 325

[8] Von Schmidt v Bourn, 50 Cal , 616 (1875), Marsh v. Keating, 1 Bing N C., 198 (1834) *Cf* Jones v Brinley, 1 East. 1 (1800), The King v Churchwardens, etc , of the Parish of St John Maddermarket, 6 id , 182 (1805) In an old case a contrary rule is laid down Nightingal v Devisme, 5 Burr , 2589 (1770).

§ 579 *Bill in equity* — A bill in equity may be maintained by a *bona fide* purchaser of stock against the corporation to compel a transfer of the stock upon the corporate books.[1] A bill in equity may be filed also to relieve a stockholder from an unauthorized forfeiture,[2] to rescind a subscription obtained by fraud,[3] to compel a specific performance of an agreement to sell stock,[4] to remedy a purchase, sale or transfer of stock induced by fraud,[5] and to redeem stock held in pledge[6] A preliminary injunction against transferring stock is also frequently granted[7] A bill in equity is the proper remedy to obtain possession of shares of stock[8]

§ 580 *Pleading under the codes* — In general, a pleading under the code is not a safe pleading, unless it conforms substantially to the rules of pleading at common law. Some verbiage may be omitted, but the relief granted by the various common-law actions cannot be obtained even under the code without the necessary averments entitling the plaintiff to that relief

The crucial test under the code is whether the facts alleged are sufficient to entitle the plaintiff to relief. It is the allegation of the facts, and not the method of alleging them, that constitutes a sufficient pleading under the code.[9]

In a suit for profits received by defendant as agent for plaintiff in buying and selling stock, the value of the stock need not be alleged with any particular definiteness Herlich v McDonald, 22 Pac. Rep., 298 (Cal, 1890) Where a corporation repudiates a pledge of stock made by its treasurer, it cannot sue the pledgee for the money received by the pledgee upon a sale of the stock by the latter Holden v Metropolitan, etc, Bank, 23 N. E. Rep, 733 (Mass, 1890).

[1] See § 391, *supra*
[2] See § 131, *supra*
[3] See §§ 155, 156, *supra.*
[4] See § 338, *supra*
[5] See § 356, *supra* *.-*
[6] See § 475, *supra* —
[7] Heck v Bulkley, 1 S W, Rep., 612 (Tenn, 1886), holding, also, that a violation of the injunction is a bar to damages upon a dissolution of it. The preliminary injunction, being an equitable remedy, is not granted if only legal relief is sought by the action See McHenry v Jewett 90 N Y, 58 (1882) A principal who is suing an agent to obtain shares of stock may enjoin the agent from transferring the same *pendente lite* Chedworth v. Edwards, 8 Ves., 46 (1802) Where a proposed consolidation is attacked by a stockholder, a preliminary injunction, granted so as not to render useless the whole suit in case it is successful, will not be disturbed by the court of appeals. Young v Rondout, etc, Co, 129 N. Y, 57 (1891).

[8] This rule of law has frequently been applied in actions by a pledgor to obtain from a pledgee the stock which has been pledged The rule itself is well established White v. Price, 39 Hun, 394, 108 N Y, 661, Hasbrouck v Vandevoort, 4 Sand. Rep, 74, Bryson v Raynor, 25 Md 424, Conyngham's Appeal, 57 Pa St, 474; Koons v. First Nat'l Bank, 89 Ind, 178.

[9] Brisbane v Delaware etc, R. R. Co., 94 N Y, 204 (1883), Burrall v Bushwick R. R. Co, 75 id, 211 (1878). *Cf.* Tackerson v Chapin, 53 N Y Super. Ct., 16 (1885) In Nevada there is a statutory action of claim and delivery. Bercich v Marye, 9 Nev, 312 (1874). See Webster v Grand Trunk R'y of Canada, 3 Lower Can Jur, 148 (1859);

§ 581. *The measure of damages* — (*a*) *The first rule* — Great difficulty has been experienced in determining what shall be the measure of damages for the conversion of stock   As the manner and conditions of the conversion vary, so also will the measure of damages vary from nominal damages to the highest value of the stock with dividends and interest, and also any special damages which the plaintiff can establish   In general, the courts incline to the rule that the true measure of damages is the value of the stock at the time of the conversion,[1] or a reasonable time

S C, 2 id, 291, for a construction of that provision of the judicature act [12 Vict., ch 38, § 87] which governs actions of this nature in the Canadian provinces   In Kuhn ι McAllister 1 Utah, 275 (1875), it is held that the language used in the pleadings in these actions is not material, or that the language is that of one form of action or another or of no form, but that the question is whether the facts entitle the plaintiff to recover   A declaration in an action for the wrongful conversion of the shares of the capital stock of a corporation is sufficient for the purposes of pleading if it states the ultimate facts to be proven   The circumstances which tend to prove those facts may be used for the purpose of evidence, but they have no place in the pleadings   McAllister ι Kuhn, 96 U S 87 (1877), affirming Kuhn ι McAllister 1 Utah, 275 (1875)   As to a misjoinder of causes of action under the California code where the plaintiff sues to recover certain stock see Johnson ι Kirby, 65 Cal, 482 (1884)   Upon the question of what is, in New York a sufficient pleading in an action to compel delivery of stock, see Burrall ι Bushwick R R Co, 75 N Y, 211 (1878)   See, also, Chitty on Pleadings vol 2 p. 618, Lowell on Transfers, § 11

[1] *In re* Bahia & San Francisco R'y Co 3 Q B, 584 (1868), Williams ι Archer, 5 Rail & Canal Cas, 289 (1847), S C, 5 C B, 318, 17 L J (C. P), 82, Tempest ι Kilner, 3 C B, 249 (1849), Shaw ι Holland, 15 Mees & W, 136 (1846), Pott ι Flather, 5 Rail & Canal Cas,

85 (1847), Davidson ι Tulloch, 6 Jur (N S), 543 (1860), Wells ι Abernethy 5 Conn, 222 (1824), O'Meara ι North American Mining Co, 2 Nev, 112 (1866) Baker ι Drake, 53 N Y 211 (1873), S C, 66 N Y, 518 (1876), Colt ι Owens, 90 N Y, 368 (1882), Gruman ι Smith, 81 id, 25 (1880), Ormsby ι Vermont Copper Mining Co, 56 id, 623 (1874), Pinkerton ι Manchester, etc, R R Co, 42 N H, 424 (1861), McKenney ι Haines, 63 Me, 74 (1873), Sturges ι Keith, 57 Ill, 451 (1870), Noonan ι Ilsley 17 Wis, 314 (1863) Bull ι Douglas, 4 Munf (Va), 303 (1814), Enders ι Board of Public Works, 1 Gratt. 364 (1845) White ι Salisbury 33 Mo, 150 (1862), Connor ι Hilber, 11 Rich Law, 193 (1857) Nabring ι Bank of Mobile, 58 Ala 204 (1877), Eastern R R Co ι Benedict, 10 Gray, 212 (1857) Boylan ι Huguet 8 Nev, 345 (1873), Bercich ι Marye, 9 id, 312 (1874) Sargent ι Franklin Ins Co 8 Pick 90 (1829), Fisher ι Brown, 104 Mass 259 (1870), Wyman ι American Powder Co, 8 Cush, 168 (1857), North ι Phillips, 89 Pa St, 250 (1879), Huntington, etc, Coal Co ι English, 86 id, 247 (1878), Neiler ι Kelley, 69 id, 403 (1871); Randall ι Albany City National Bank, 1 N Y State Rep., 592 (Sept., 1886), Douglas ι Merceles, 25 N J Eq, 141 (1874) See, also, Eicholz ι Fox 12 Phila., 382 (1878), Larrabee ι Badger, 45 Ill, 440 (1867), Barned ι Hamilton, 2 Rail & Canal Cas, 624 (1841), Blyth ι Carpenter L R, 2 Eq, 501 (1866) *Cf* Moody ι Caulk, 14 Fla, 50 (1872), Kent ι, Ginter, 23 Ind, 1 (1864), Orange, etc,

(50)

after.[1] By the term the value of the stock is usually to be understood the market value.[2] The fact that the shares of stock have no known market value will not prevent recovery where the actual value is ascertainable in an action to recover damages The value may be shown by showing the value of the property and business of the corporation.[3] The question of what was the market value

R R. Co. v Fulvey, 17 Gratt., 366 (1867), Jefferson v Hale, 31 Ark, 286 (1876), Third National Bank v Boyd. 44 Md, 47 (1875), Thomas v. Sternheimer, 29 id, 268 (1868)

[1] Colt v Owens, 90 N Y, 368 (1882); Douglas v Merceles, 25 N J Eq, 144 (1874), Brewster v Van Liew, 8 N E. Rep, 842 (Ill, 1886), Budd v Multnomah St R'y Co, 15 Pac Rep, 65 (Oreg, 1887). Upon what is reasonable time herein in transactions on the stock exchanges, see Stewart v Cauty, 8 Mees. & W, 160 (1841); Field v Lelean, 6 Hurl & N, 617.

[2] By the "market value of stock" is meant the actual price at which it is commonly sold. That price may be fixed by sales of the stock in market at or about a given time If no sales can be shown on the precise day, recourse may be had to sales before or after the day, and for that inquiry a reasonable range in point of time is allowable. Douglas v Merceles, 25 N J Eq, 144 (1874) Cf Stewart v Cauty, 8 Mees. & W, 160 (1841), Sturges v Keith, 57 Ill, 451 (1870), Seymour v Ives, 46 Conn, 109 (1878). The measure of damages for non-delivery of stock at a certain date is presumptively the par value The defendant is obliged to prove differently if this price is incorrect Appeal of Harris, 12 Atl Rep, 743 (Pa, 1888) If there is no market value of stock, proof of a few sales is competent. Brown v Lawton, 6 N. Y. Supp, 137 (1889)

[3] In actions for conversion of personal property, such as these shares are, the damages are not limited to the market value of the stock. Its actual value to be determined under all the circumstances, such as the dividend-making capacity, the good-will, etc, etc., is the measure of damages " Freon v. Carriage Co. 42 Ohio St, 30, 38 (1884). In Hitchcock v McElrath, 14 Pac Rep, 305 (Cal, 1887), the court allowed evidence to be given showing the market value of all the property of the corporation, there being no other method of ascertaining the value of the stock See, also, McGuffey v Humes, 1 S W. Rep, 506 (Tenn, 1886). The value of stock may be shown by showing the value of the property of the corporation, the amount of capital stock and the amount of debts. It may be shown, also, by proving how much could be borrowed on the stock, at the place where the company's headquarters were. Smith v Traders' Nat'l Bank, 17 S. W Rep., 779 (Tex, 1891). In the case of Riker v Campbell (U S. C C., S. D. of N Y ; see Mss), Judge Wallace held that the value of stock might be shown by proving the value of the corporate property See, also, Simkins v Law, 4 N. Y, 179 Where a vendor of stock in a corporation which has a franchise, but nothing else, is entitled to two thousand shares of full-paid stock at a later date, according to the contract of sale, his measure of damages for failure of the vendee to deliver the two thousand shares is nominal damages where there was no market or actual value for the stock Barnes v Brown, 130 N. Y., 372 (1892). The value of stock may be shown by the value of its assets where there is no known market value. Redding v. Godwin, 46 N. W. Rep, 563 (Minn, 1890). The president and managing agent renders his corporation liable for a bonus of stock in another corporation which he gives secretly and corruptly to the agent of the latter corporation in

at the time of the conversion is generally a question for the jury,[1] and it may be shown by tables of prices current published in the newspapers or otherwise at the time of the conversion, and these may be read in evidence[2]

A conversion arises at the time when the stockholder, being entitled to the immediate possession or delivery of the stock or the certificate, makes a demand for it which is refused. Accordingly in this class of cases the measure of damages is the value of stock on the day of the demand and refusal[3]

order to get a contract for the former corporation Grand Rapids, etc., Co *v* Cincinnati, etc., Co., 45 Fed Rep, 671 (1891), holding the former corporation liable for the par value of the stock, inasmuch as it was the original issue of that stock Not the nominal but the true value of the shares is what the plaintiff is entitled to recover Bull *v* Douglas, 4 Munf (Va), 303 (1814) Enders *v* Board of Public Works, 1 Gratt, 364 (1845) Where a railroad is sold to be paid for in bonds a failure to deliver the bonds enables the vendor to recover their par value from the vendee Texas, etc, R'y *v* Gentry, 8 S W. Rep, 98 (Tex, 1888).

[1] 1 Sedgwick on Damages (7th ed), 585, and cases cited; Dos Passos on Stock-brokers 801 See Cameron *v* Durkheim, 55 N Y. 425 (1874), Fowler *v* New York Gold Exchange Bank, 67 id, 138 (1876); Harris *v* Tumbridge, 83 id, 92 (1880), and notes *supra* Where there is no evidence that the stock is worthless, the question of value should be submitted to the jury, the rule of damages in a case for fraud as to representations as to the value of the stock being the difference between the par value of the stock as represented and what it was in fact worth Maxted *v* Fowler, 53 N W Rep, 921 (Mich, 1892)

[2] Chiquot's Champagne, 3 Wall. 114 (1865) S. P, Whelan *v* Lynch, 60 N Y, 469 (1875) A price current or market report is admissible in certain cases to prove the fluctuations and value of stock. Seligman *v* Rogers, 21 S W. Rep, 94 (Mo., 1893).

[3] So when stock held as collateral is improperly sold by the pledgee, the value on the day when the pledgor pays his debt and demands his stock is to be taken Fisher *t* Brown, 104 Mass, 259 (1870) In Freeman *v* Harwood, 49 Me, 195 (1859) shares of stock standing in the name of the defendant as collateral security for a debt which had been paid were sold for non-payment of an assessment and bought by defendant It was held that the defendant was liable in *trover* for the value of the shares at the time of the sale, with interest, and all dividends received thereon, deducting the amount of the assessment and the expenses of the sale. In Sturges *v* Keith, 57 Ill, 451 (1870) it is held that where the demand and refusal constitute the conversion or afford presumptive evidence of it, the date of such demand and refusal is the proper time for estimating the value Again, where the corporation wrongfully refuses to register a transfer and to issue a certificate the measure of damages is the value of the stock on the day when the transfer was demanded and refused Wyman *v* American Powder Co, 8 Cush, 168 (1851), Eastern R. R. Co *v* Benedict, 10 Gray, 212 (1857), West Branch, etc. Canal Company's Appeal, 81* Pa St, 19 (1870), Baltimore City, etc, R R. Co. *v* Sewell, 35 Md, 238 (1871), McMurrich *v* Bond Head Harbour Co, 9 Up. Can (Q B), 333 (1852), where it is said that while the rule as announced above is the proper one, yet, when the jury allows a larger sum, the question of the measure of damages not having been

Where the pledgee of stock wrongfully sells it the injured party may recover the highest market price between the time of notice of sale and a reasonable time within which he might have bought the stock elsewhere [1]

The New York court of appeals after many variations has settled on the rule that "in the absence of special circumstances in an action for conversion of personal property as well as one for failure to deliver it in performance of a contract where consideration has been received, the value of the property at the time of such conversion or default, with interest, is the measure of compensation "[2]

§ 582 (b) *The second rule* — In another line of cases the true measure of damages in these actions is said to be the value of the stock on the day of the trial [3] In an English case it is said that

pressed at the argument, the court will not reduce the verdict. So, also, where there is a failure to return borrowed stock on demand, or according to the terms of the bailment, the value on the day of demand, or on the day when the stock ought by contract to have been returned, is the measure of damages McKenney v Haines, 63 Me, 74 (1873); Fosdick v Greene, 27 Ohio St, 484 (1875), S C, 22 Am Rep, 328, McArthur v. Seaforth, 2 Taunt, 257, Day v Perkins, 2 Sandf Chan, 359 Cf Cortelyou v Lansing, 2 Caines' Cas in Error, 200 (1805), West v Wentworth 3 Cowen, 82, Clark v Pinney, 7 id 681, Wilson v Matthews, 24 Barb, 295, 2 Sedgwick on Damages (7th ed), 141, 365, n In an old case where borrowed stock was not returned the plaintiff was allowed to recover the value at the time of the transfer to the borrower, no account being taken of an increase in value Forrest v Elwes, 4 Ves, 492 (1799). See, also, McKenney v. Haines, 63 Me, 74 (1873) Upon a failure to deliver stock according to contract or on demand, the value at the time of the demand is the value to be taken Noonan v Ilsley, 17 Wis., 314 (1863), Pinkerton v Manchester, etc., R. R. Co, 42 N. H, 424 (1861), North v Phillips, 89 Pa St., 250 (1879), Huntington, etc, Coal Co. v. English, 86 id, 247 (1878) Cf. Pott v. Flather,

5 Rail & Canal Cas, 85 (1847), Barned v. Hamilton, 2 id, 624 (1841); Shaw v. Holland, 4 id, 150 (1846); S C, 15 Mees & W., 136, Tempest v. Kilner, 2 C. B., 300, S. C., 3 id, 249, Gainsford v. Carroll, 2 Barn & C, 624 Williams v. Peel, etc., Co, 55 L T Rep., 689 (1886), holds that suit for damages for wrongful detention lies against a party who has wrongfully obtained possession of stock, and that the measure of damages, where the defendant afterwards abandons his claim, is the intervening fall in the value of the stock Bankers of trustees wrongfully sold out stock, and applied the proceeds to their own purposes. The measure of their liability is the amount paid in replacing the stock Sadler v. Lee, 6 Bear, 324 (1843). As to damages in cases of trust, see Story's Eq (13th ed), §§ 1263, 1264.

[1] Wright v Bank of Metropolis, 110 N Y, 237 (1888), Galigher v Jones, 129 U S, 193 (1889), the court saying in the latter decision that the measure of damages is "the highest intermediate value of the stock between the time of its conversion and a reasonable time after the owner has received notice of it to enable him to replace the stock "

[2] Baines v Brown, 130 N. Y., 372 (1892)

[3] Owen v. Routh, 14 C B. 327 (1854); Shepherd v. Johnson, 2 East, 211; Ber-

this is a sound rule in the ordinary cases of conversion of stock, but that in cases of failure to deliver stock the true measure of damages is the value when the demand is made and refused [1] This second rule has found little favor, and there is believed to be no sound reason for its adoption

§ 583. (c) *The third rule.* — It has been held in still another class of decisions that the measure of damages for the conversion of stock is the highest market value of the stock between the date of the conversion and the day of the trial. This is the rule in California in some cases [2] So, also, in South Carolina,[3] Georgia,[4] and it was formerly the rule in New York [5] and Pennsylvania [6] The

cich v Marye, 9 Nev , 312 (1874) *Cf* Williams v Archer, 5 C B 318 (1817) S. C, 5 Rail. & Canal Cas, 289, 17 L J (C P), 82, and see Wilson v Little, 2 N Y, 443, 450 (1849), wherein there is a *quere* as to whether this may not be the better rule In Fowle v Ward, 113 Mass, 548, S. C , 18 Am Rep, 534 (1873), it is held that the measure of damages is the value of the stock upon the day when the bill in equity is filed, it being an equitable action by a pledgor against a pledgee The measure of damages in England is the price at which the defendant sold the securities if already sold and if not sold then the amount of depreciation in value since plaintiff demanded them, together with intervening dividends Simmons v Joint. etc, Co, 62 L T Rep , 427 (1890)

[1] Shaw v Holland, 15 Mees & W , 136, 145 (1846), S C , 4 Rail & Canal Cas, 150 , 15 L J, Exch , 87

[2] Code of California, § 3336, is as follows "The detriment caused by the wrongful conversion of personal property is presumed to be 1 The value of the property at the time of the conversion, with interest from that time, or, where the action has been prosecuted with reasonable diligence, the highest market value of the property at any time between the conversion and the verdict, without interest, at the option of the injured party" This is held to apply to the conversion of the shares of stock Fromm v Sierra Nevada Silver Mining Co, 61 Cal , 629 (1882), Dent v

Holbrook, 54 id , 145 (1880) *Cf* Thompson v Toland, 48 Cal , 99 (1874). The courts have held that this section of the code applies to the conversion of shares of stock, but they have not worked out a very consistent rule on the subject In Douglass v Craft, 9 Cal , 562 (1867), the "highest value" rule is adopted but in later cases the court seems to incline toward the modern New York rule Hamer v Hathaway, 33 Cal , 117, Page v Fowler, 39 id , 412, Dent v. Holbrook, 54 id , 145 (1880), Tully v Tranor, 53 id , 274, Thompson v Toland, 48 id , 99 (1874), Fromm v Sierra Nevada Silver Mining Co, 61 Cal , 629 (1882)

[3] Kid v Mitchell, 1 Nott & McCord, 334 (1818)

[4] Central R R & Banking Co v Atlantic, etc R. R. Co , 50 Ga , 444 (1873)

[5] Markham v Jaudon, 41 N Y, 235 (1869), Romaine v Van Allen, 26 id , 309 (1863) In an action to recover damages for the unlawful conversion of a quantity of grain the rule in New York was held to be the highest price up to the time of the trial is the proper measure of damages Lordell v Stowell, 51 N Y, 70 (1872) To same effect, Kent v Ginter, 23 Ind , 1 (1864) See 1 Sedgwick on Damages (7th ed), 578, and note (a) *Cf* Burt v Dutcher, 34 N Y , 493 (1866), Scott v Rogers, 31 id , 676 (1864), Devlin v Pike, 5 Daly (N Y), C P , 85 For the modern rule in New York see § 581, *supra*

[6] Bank of Montgomery v Reese, 26

courts of the two latter states have, however, in later cases wholly receded from this position, and in both the rule is now established in such actions that the measure of damages is not the highest price of the stock, but the value at the date of the conversion [1].

§ 584 *Interests, dividends and special damages* — It is settled law that, in addition to the value of the stock at the date of conversion, the plaintiff may recover legal interest upon such valuation from the date of the conversion to the day of the trial   It follows as of course that, if the plaintiff has been damaged in an ascertained sum, he may, in an action for damages, recover not only that sum, but interest thereon for the time during which he has been wrongfully deprived of his stock.[2]   In addition to interest

Pa St., 143 (1856), Musgrave *v* Beckendorff, 53 id, 310 (1866), Reitenbaugh *v* Ludwick, 31 id. 131, 141 (1858).   In Pennsylvania where one was accountable for stock as trustee, and converted it, he was held chargeable with the highest market value   Reitenbaugh *v* Ludwick, 31 Pa St., 131 (1858), North *v.* Phillips, 89 Pa. St., 250 (1879)   *Cf.* Bates *v* Wiles, 1 Handy (Ohio), 532 (1855).   It is now held in Pennsylvania that where a corporation, through innocent mistake, permits a transfer on its books of shares of stock under a forged power of attorney, the owner's measure of damages is the value of the stock at the time of the transfer, with interest from the date of the verdict, and not the highest price reached by the stock between the date of the conversion and the time of bringing suit, with the dividends since declared   Pennsylvania Co, etc, *v* Philadelphia, etc, R. Co, 25 Atl Rep, 1043 (Pa., 1893)   But where upon a re-organization an old stockholder is wrongfully refused his stock in the new, he may recover the highest market price of the same up to the time of the insolvency of the corporation   Reading, etc, Co. *v* Reading, etc, Works, 21 Atl Rep, 169 (Pa., 1891).

[1] North *v* Phillips, 89 Pa. St., 250 (1879).   Huntington, etc, Coal Co *v* English, 86 id 247 (1878), Work *v* Bennett, 70 id, 484 (1872)·   Neiler *v* Kelley, 69 id., 403 (1871).   *Cf* Wilson *v* Whittaker, 49 id, 114 (1865).   So, also, in the later New York cases.   Baker *v* Drake, 53 N Y, 211 (1873), S C, 66 N Y, 518 (1876), White *v* Smith, 54 id, 522 (1874), Harris *v.* Tumbridge, 83 id, 92 (1880), Colt *v* Owens, 90 id, 368 (1882), Randall *v* Albany City Nat'l Bank, 1 N. Y State Rep, 592 (Sept, 1886).   *Cf* Suydam *v* Jenkins, 3 Sandf. Super Ct., 614 (1850), Matthews *v.* Coe, 49 N Y, 57 (1872), Bryan *v* Baldwin, 52 id, 236 (1873)   See, also, Seymour *v.* Ives, 46 Conn, 109 (1878), McGuffey *v.* Humes, 1 S W Rep, 506

[2] O'Meara *v* North American Mining Co, 2 Nev, 112 (1866); Boylan *v.* Huguet, 8 id, 345 (1873); Fisher *v.* Brown, 104 Mass, 259 (1870), Sargent *v* Franklin Ins Co., 8 Pick, 90 (1829), Seymour *v* Ives, 46 Conn, 109 (1878), McKenney *i* Haines, 63 Me, 74 (1873), Freeman *v* Harwood, 49 id, 195 (1859); Ormsby *v* Vermont Copper Mining Co, 56 N Y, 623 (1874); White *v* Smith, 54 id, 522 (1874), Sturges *v* Keith, 57 Ill, 451 (1870); Baltimore City, etc, Ry Co *v* Sewell, 35 Md, 238, 257 (1871); Pinkerton *v* Manchester, etc, R. R. Co., 42 N H, 424 (1861), North *v* Phillips, 89 Pa. St., 250 (1878); Huntington, etc. Coal Co *v* English, 86 id, 247 (1878); North American Building Ass'n *v.* Sutton, 35 id., 463 (1860), Noonan *v* Illsley, 17 Wis, 314 (1863).   Forrest *i* Elwes, 4 Ves, 492 (1799), *In re* Bahia & San Francisco R'y Co., 3 Q B, 584 (1868), Blyth *v.* Carpenter, L. R., 2 Eq., 501 (1866);

the plaintiff may recover also all accretions to the property made during the time when he was deprived of it. He is, therefore, entitled to judgment for all dividends paid upon the stock between the date of the conversion and the day of the trial[1] The reason why the plaintiff recovers dividends in addition to the value of the stock and interest is that often the dividends involved were earned, wholly or in part, before the conversion, but that such net earnings were distributed by dividends declared after the conversion, and that the market value does not always represent fully the undistributed profits   The plaintiff may also recover any special damages which legitimately arise out of matters in existence at the date of conversion, and which he has sustained by reason of the detention of his stock[2]

§ 585. *Nominal damages* — In certain cases, where the plaintiff has been guilty of laches, or where the stock is of no actual value, or where the stock could, for a reasonable time after the conversion, have been purchased in the market for the same or a lower price, or in any other case where the plaintiff has suffered only a technical conversion without any actual pecuniary loss, only nominal damages can be recovered[3]   Thus, the measure of damages for

McMurrich z Bond Head Harbour Co., 9 Upp Can (Q B), 333 (1852) In the civil code of California, § 3336 interest in these cases is expressly provided for Fromm z Sierra Nevada Silver Mining Co, 61 Cal, 629 (1882), 2 Sedgwick on Damages (7th ed), 391

[1] Bull v Douglas, 4 Munf (Va.), 303 (1814) Baltimore City, etc, R y Co v Sewell, 35 Md, 238 (1871), Bercich v Marye, 9 Nev, 312 (1874), Bank of Montgomery v Reese, 26 Pa. St., 113 (1856). Cf. Boston, etc, R. R Co z Richardson, 135 Mass, 473, 477 (1883) Where a broker, a gratuitous bailee of corporate stock, delivers the same to the company without authority, and the stock is converted to the use of the company, the bailee is liable for its value, irrespective of what his intentions were in the premises In such case the bailor may recover the value of the stock at the time of conversion, with all dividends paid from the time of delivery, together with interest on the value of the stock from date of con-

version, and on the dividends from date of respective payments   Hubbell z Blandy, 49 N W Rep 502 (Mich, 1891)

[2] Boylan z Huguet, 8 Nev 345 (1873), 2 Sedgwick on Damages (7th ed), 391, Bodley z Reynolds, 8 Ad & El (N S), 779 (1846), Davis z Oswell, 7 Car & P, 804 (1837). Cf Seymour v Ives, 46 Conn, 109 (1878).

[3] Thus, where a borrower of shares fails to return them until after the corporation is dissolved, the lender having made no demand during the existence of the company, the measure of damages in an action to recover the shares will be the market value of them at the time the cause of action accrued, that is, at the time of demand   And if at that time the stock is worthless, only nominal damages are recoverable   Fosdick z Greene, 27 Ohio St., 484 (1875), S C, 22 Am Rep., 328. See Cameron v Durkheim, 55 N Y, 425 (1874), Hope z Lawrence, 50 Barb, 258 (1867) In an action by a vendee on a contract for the sale of specific stock, which, with-

the conversion of a mere certificate of stock cannot be placed at the value of the shares themselves which the certificate represents if the ownership of the shares is not affected [1]

§ 586 *Damages for failure to complete a purchase of stock and for fraud inducing a purchase of stock* — The measure of damages for the failure of a purchaser of stock to complete his contract is considered elsewhere [2] The measure of damages for fraud inducing the purchase of stock "is the difference between the value of the stock at the time it was purchased and the price paid for it." [3]

out the knowledge of the vendor, had already been sold to another by his agent, the plaintiff can recover only nominal damages. Wilson v Whitaker, 49 Pa St, 114 (1865), Skinner v City of London, etc, Ins Corporation, L. R., 14 Q B Div, 882 (1885) See Fowler v New York Gold Exchange Bank, 67 N Y, 138 (1878)

[1] Daggett v Davies, 53 Mich, 35 (1884), by Cooley, C J

[2] See ch XX, *supra*

[3] Redding v Godwin, 46 N W Rep, 563 (Minn, 1890). In an action for damages for fraud inducing the plaintiff to purchase stock, the measure of damages is "not the difference between the contract price and the reasonable market value if the property had been worth the price paid for it, nor if the stock were worthless, could the plaintiff have recovered the value it would have had if the property had been equal to the representations. What the plaintiff might have gained is not the question, but what he had lost by being deceived into the purchase" The defendant "was bound to make good the loss sustained such as the moneys plaintiff had paid out and interest, and any other outlay legitimately attributable to defendant's fraudulent conduct, but this liability did not include the expected fruits of an unrealized speculation" Smith v Bolles, 132 U S, 125 (1889) The measure of damages in an action by a vendee for fraud in the sale of stock is the difference between the selling price and the real value at the time of the sale.

High v Berret, 23 Atl Rep, 1004 (Pa, 1892) In an action for damages for deceit inducing the plaintiff to purchase stock the measure of damages is 'a sum of money equal to the difference between the value of the property as it was in fact and the value as it would have been if the representations had been true" In this kind of action no tender of the stock is necessary or proper Testimony as to the value of the property of the corporation and of a sale of stock by a witness is admissible. Vail v Reynolds, 118 N Y, 297 (1890) As to the measure of damages where worthless stock is sold for land and fraudulent misrepresentations are made and the company fails see Titus v Poole, 14 N Y Supp 678 (1891) Where one has been induced by fraudulent misrepresentations to buy or subscribe for shares of stock, the measure of damages in an action against the vendor is the difference between the value of the stock as represented and the actual value Miller v Barber, 66 N Y, 558, 568 (1876); Hubbell v Meigs 50 id, 480, 491 (1872). The measure of damages in an action for deceit against directors who issued a false prospectus inducing subscription is the difference between the subscription price and the real value of the stock, and evidence that the stock subsequently proved to be worthless is admissible Peek v Derry, 59 L T Rep., 78 (1888). And where one with intent to cheat and defraud induces another, by false and fraudulent representations, to purchase shares for value which he knows

§ 587. *Damages in actions between stock-brokers and their customers* — This subject is considered elsewhere [1]

to be worthless, he is liable for the damages sustained whether the purchase was made from him or from another at his instance   Hubbell v Meigs, *supra*

[1] See §§ 460, 461, *supra.*

CHAPTER XXXVI.

STOCKHOLDERS' MEETINGS — CALLS, TIME, PLACE AND CLASSES OF MEETINGS.

§ 583. *Introductory* —The stockholders of a corporation constitute the origin, existence and continuance of the corporation itself. They elect its officers, control its general policy, and within the charter limits may prolong or dissolve its existence at their pleasure All these vital powers of the stockholders can be exercised by them only in corporate meetings, duly convened and properly organized for the transaction of business Accordingly, the method of calling together a corporate meeting, the time and place of that meeting, the notice to be given to the stockholders and the various incidents relative to a proper convening of the members of the corporation, are of great importance. They constitute the subject of this chapter.

§ 589. *The place of meeting of stockholders must be within the state creating the corporation* —The first and most general rule as to the place where stockholders may hold corporate meetings is that the place of meeting should be within the boundaries of the state which created the corporation Through its agents, of course, the corporation may make contracts, carry on business, sue and be sued and buy and sell property in another state.[1]

But there is a difference of opinion as to the effect of business transacted at a stockholders' meeting held beyond the borders of the state creating the corporation Upon the one hand, it is held that all the acts and proceedings of such a meeting are wholly in-

---

[1] See chs. 13 and 41.

valid and void; that the corporation is not bound thereby, and that the meeting is as though it had never been [1]

But it is the sounder view to regard the votes and proceedings at such a meeting as voidable rather than void The corporation itself cannot allege that such proceedings are void. It is estopped from so doing [2] So, also. are the stockholders who participate in the meeting. [3] As to the creditors of the corporation the author-

[1] Directors elected at a stockholders' meeting held out of the state and to which all did not agree are not directors The old board holds over Hodgson v Duluth, etc, R. R., 49 N W Rep., 197 (Minn, 1891), Miller v Ewer, 27 Me, 509 (1847), where a mortgage executed by the authority of directors who were elected at the organization meeting of corporators held outside of the state which granted the charter was declared void. Cited and followed in Freeman v Machias Water, etc, 38 Me, 343 (1854) where a forfeiture of stock was declared illegal, Ormsby v. Vermont Copper, etc., 56 N Y, 623 (1874), where it was held that a forfeiture of stock by authority of a by-law adopted by stockholders of a Vermont corporation at a meeting held in New York was not valid Mitchell v Vt Copper Co, 40 N Y Super Ct, 406 (1876), aff'd, 67 N Y, 280, Smith v Silver Valley Mining Co, 64 Md, 85 (1885), the organization being held out of the state, Camp v Byrne, 41 Mo., 525 (1867), to the same effect, Mitchell v Same, 40 Super Ct, 406 (1876). In the case Copp v Lamb, 12 Me, 312 (1835), thirty years' user was held to have cured any defect A Virginia corporation cannot be organized by an organization meeting in New York Nor can the charter be assigned by a blank assignment after an organization in Virginia The assignment must be of the stock. The corporation is neither *de facto* nor *de jure* Suits against it fail Welch v Old Dominion, etc, Ry, N Y L J, June 12, 1890

[2] Heath v Silverthorn Lead Mining, etc, Co, 39 Wis, 146 (1875), holding that the corporation may be estopped to deny the validity of acts done outside the state when the rights of third parties intervene, even though that meeting was the organization meeting The legislature may validate the acts passed at such a meeting Graham v Boston, Hartford & Erie R. R. Co 118 U S, 161, 178 (1886), affirming S C, 14 Fed. Rep, 753 (1883) *Cf.* Grenada Co v Brogden, 112 U S, 261 (1884), and the various cases of municipal subscriptions, ch VI, § 94, n

[3] A *bona fide* holder of a note given by a stockholder in payment of his subscription may enforce it even though the organization and all other meetings of the company were held out of the state Camp v Byrne, 41 Mo., 525 (1867) In the case of Ohio & M R R v McPherson, 35 Mo 13 (1864), the charter declared the directors to be the corporation They met out of the state and organized and made a call on subscriptions. The court upheld the call But the mere neglect on the part of a shareholder who did not attend a meeting of this kind, or a mere failure to take affirmative action for a period of time short of that prescribed by the statute of limitations, will not deprive that shareholder of his right to attack the proceedings as irregular and in fraud of his rights Ormsby v Vermont Copper Mining Co, 56 N Y, 623 (1874). Directors elected at a stockholders' meeting held out of the state and to which all did not agree are not directors The old board holds over Hodgson v Duluth, etc, R. R., 49 N W Rep, 197 (Minn, 1891) By-laws enacted by a board of directors of a Texan corporation at a meeting of stockholders held

ities differ.[1] If the corporation has been incorporated in two or more states, it is lawful to hold meetings of the stockholders in either state[2] And proceedings at a meeting in any one of the states are valid in respect to the property of the corporation in all of them without the necessity of the repetition of the meeting in any other of those states[3]

§§ 590-591 *First meeting under a special charter.* — Where an act incorporates three specified persons and their "associates," those three alone organize the company and are entitled to subscribe the capital stock or to allow others to subscribe.[4]

Statutory provisions as to notice of the first meeting are directory. They need not be observed if the stockholders acquiesce[5]

Where several persons, their associates and successors, are declared to be a corporation, one of them with new parties may meet, organize, adopt by-laws, etc, without the capital being first subscribed and without the others if they do not object[6] As to an over-subscription for stock the rules that govern the subject are considered elsewhere[7]

§ 592 *Directors' meetings.* — The various questions connected with directors' meetings, the place where such meetings may be

in Paris are void and a stockholder may disregard them, although he was represented by proxy at the meeting The directors are not even *de facto* Franco-Texas Land Co *v* Lagle, 59 Texas, 339 (1883) A special charter must be accepted before the corporation exists, and such acceptance cannot be at a meeting held out of the state Hence a bill by a stockholder to set aside a forfeiture of his stock was dismissed by the court. Smith *v* Silver, etc, Co. 20 Atl Rep, 1032 (Md, 1885) A stockholders' meeting out of the state is "irregular if not void" Mack *v* De Bardelaben, etc, Co, 8 S Rep, 150 (Ala, 1890) A stockholders' meeting held outside of the state cannot be attacked by those who participate in it or receive the benefits of it. A statute against holding elections out of the state does not prevent stockholders' meetings for other purposes. Handley *v* Stutz, 139 U S, 417 (1891) An increase of capital stock which is voted at a stockholders' meeting held out of the state is valid if all the stockholders assent. "No valid objection can be made to a stockholders' meeting held

in a foreign jurisdiction, provided all the shareholders give their consent to such meeting or ratify its action." Id, 41 Fed Rep, 531 (1890)

[1] Where a meeting of stockholders other than the first organization meeting is held out of the state and directors are elected the acts of those directors cannot be attacked by corporate creditors on the ground that the election was illegal Wright *v* Lee, 51 N W. Rep, 706 (S D 1892) For cases to the contrary see notes *supra*

[2] Graham *v* Boston, Hartford & Erie R. R. Co, 118 U. S., 161 (1886); Covington, etc, Bridge Co *v* Mayer, 31 Ohio St., 317 (1577) See, also, Ohio, etc, R'y *v* People, 123 Ill., 467 (1888), and ch 53, *infra*

[3] Same cases

[4] Lechmere Bank *v* Boynton, 65 Mass., 369 (1853). See, also, p. 313, note, also; p 797, note 6.

[5] Braintree, etc, *v* Braintree, 16 N. E. Rep, 420 (Mass, 1881).

[6] McGinty *v* Athol, etc, Co., 29 N. E. Rep, 510 (Mass, 1892)

[7] See §§ 57, 58, *supra*.

held, the notice that is required. the question of whether the directors may act without meeting, and the requirements as to a quorum, are discussed elsewhere [1]

§ 593 *By whom meetings are to be called — Mandamus — Fraud in the call* — Where the time and place of a meeting and the business to be transacted at that meeting are not fixed by charter or otherwise, so that the stockholders are bound to take notice of them, it is necessary that the meeting be called by a properly-authorized corporate authority [2]

In the absence of any special authority to any particular person to call meetings, it has been held that the general agent of the corporation may make the call,[3] but that the secretary cannot [4] The board of directors may always call a meeting of the stockholders [5]

Statutory provisions as to who shall call the meeting, whether it be the first and organization meeting, or a subsequent one, may be waived by unanimous consent of the incorporators or stockholders [6]

---

[1] See § 713a, *infra*

[2] Evans *v* Osgood, 18 Me , 213 (1841), holding that, where a proprietors' meeting could be called "by a petition signed by twelve of them at least,' it was not a legal call if eleven signed, although they owned twelve shares, Congregational Soc of Bethany *v* Sperry. 10 Conn , 200 (1834), State of Nevada *v* Pettineli, 10 Nev , 141 (1875), where the by-laws of a corporation provided that meetings of the stockholders should be called by the trustees, and it was held that any other mode of calling, such as by the president, was insufficient Angell & Ames on Corp., § 491, to effect that ' want of authority may be waived by the presence and consent of all who have a right to vote" Johnston *v* Jones, 23 N J Eq 216 (1872) Here the charter provided for annual elections, but no by-laws had been made fixing the time The authority to call an election being in the directors, it was held not sufficient for a majority of these to sign the notice without stating that it was given by order of the board, and without designating themselves as directors. See, also, Stevens *v* Eden Meeting-house Soc , 12 Vt , 688 (1839), holding that notices of meetings could not be proved by parol where there was

a by-law requiring the clerk to post written notice

[3] Stebbins *v* Merritt. 64 Mass , 27 (1852)

[4] The secretary and a person holding proxies on stock owned by the state cannot call a meeting to elect officers, nor can a statute order an election in a brief time Cassell *v* Lexington etc , Co, 9 S W Rep , 502 (Ky., 1888), id , 701

[5] Cassell *v* Lexington, etc , Co , *supra* The board of directors may fix the time if the charter or by-laws do not Commonwealth *v* Smith, 45 Pa St., 59 (1863)

[6] See § 234 notes, *supra*, also § 599. *infra* Although the charter prescribes that the commissioners who receive the subscriptions shall call the first meeting by publishing a notice yet this call may be waived and the stockholders may meet and organize without a call, if all assent Judah *v* American, etc , Ins Co 4 Ind , 333 (1853), Chamberlain *v* Painesville, etc , R R Co , 15 Ohio St , 225 (1864) where the statute provided that, as soon as ten per centum on the capital stock should be subscribed, the persons named in the certificate of incorporation or any three of them, might give notice of an election of directors It was held simply directory,

If, upon the organization of a corporation, a majority of the sub-scribers refuse to proceed in calling a meeting, the minority may call it, and bind the corporation [1]

Where the statute requires due notice to be given, it need not be given by any particular person nor in any particular form [2]   A charter provision or by-law authorizing the calling of a meeting in a certain way does not necessarily prevent the meeting being called in a different way, but unless waived the rule is otherwise where the charter or by-law is peremptory.[3]

Although the time of a meeting is fixed by charter, nevertheless the meeting may be held at a subsequent time and be valid [4]   The officers or agents of a corporation whose duty it is to call meetings may, in case they neglect or refuse to issue the call, be compelled

and not indispensable to an election, that the notice be so given   In New-comb v Reed, 94 Mass, 362 (1866), the court declared the purpose of such stat-utes to be to avoid such difficulty as would arise where two parties should attempt to organize separately under the same charter   It was there held that persons elected officers at a meet-ing held in variance with such statu-tory direction were directors neverthe-less, and were subject to the statute liability for corporate debts   Where three persons are appointed to make a call, and one of them calls the meeting of incorporation, the other two making no objection, the organization of the company at the meeting so called is valid.   Walworth v. Brackett, 98 Mass., 98 (1867); Hardenburgh v. Farmers', etc, 3 N. J. Eq, 68, holding that if the call for the meeting to elect the first directors be signed by the commission-ers authorized to make the call individ-ually, and not by virtue of a formal order of the commissioners, or if their names be signed to such a call by the secretary without objection by them, these irregularities will not affect the validity of the proceedings at the meet-ing.   Although the charter runs to cer-tain persons and associates and assigns, they need not have associates or assigns. Hughes v. Parker, 20 N H , 58 (1849).

[1] Busey v. Hooper, 35 Md., 15 (1871).

[2] West, etc., Cong v Ottesen, 49 N. W Rep., 24 (Wis , 1891)

[3] Where a by-law provides that special meetings may be called by the presi-dent, or in his absence by the secretary, on application made by ten members in writing, the directors may call a special meeting without such an application. Citizens' Mutual Fire Ins. Co. v. Sout-well, 90 Mass., 217 (1864   But where a by-law authorizes the trustees to call a meeting, a meeting called by the presi-dent is irregular.   State of Nevada v Pettineli, 10 Nev , 141 (1875).   When the by-laws require a call to be posted in writing, a call by parol is insufficient. Stevens v Eden Meeting-house Society, 12 Vt , 688 (1839)   The manner of mak-ing the call may be prescribed by by-law , and when so prescribed, provided the by-law is reasonable, calls made in that way are valid even though the charter said that three stockholders might call a meeting   Taylor v. Gris-wold, 14 N J L., 222 (1834)

[4] People v. Cummings, 72 N. Y, 433 (1878), Hughes v Parker, 20 N H , 58. Failure to hold an election at the pre-scribed statutory time does not prevent an election at any later time.   Beardsley t Johnson, 1 N Y Supp, 608 (1888). Elections need not be held on the day fixed by the by-laws.   They may be held at any subsequent time.   Beards-ley v. Johnson, 121 N. Y , 224 (1890).

by *mandamus* to call a meeting at the instance of a shareholder who is injured by reason of their failure[1]   Courts have no power to call corporate meetings except by *mandamus*[2]

If there is any fraud in the calling of the meeting, the proceedings of the meeting may be attacked in the courts   The fraud may consist in concealing the notice,[3] or in changing the time of the meeting,[4] or in the unreasonable time in which it is called,[5] or in misstating the business.[6]

[1] People v Cummings, 72 N Y , 433 (1878); State of Nevada v Wright, 10 Nev., 167 (1875), People v Board of Governors of Albany Hospital, 61 Barb , 397 (1871); McNeely v Woodruff, 13 N J Law, 352 (1833), Regina v Aldman, etc , Insurance Society, 6 Eng' L & Eq , 365 (1851)   The court will not order the directors to call a meeting for business other than an election when they or a certain proportion of the stockholders may call it   MacDougall v Gardiner, L R , 10 Ch App., 606 (1875)   In Goulding v. Clark, 34 N H , 148 (1856), it is held that, where there is no officer competent to call a meeting, there is no way of convening except by a reorganization of the company or a published notice given under the statutes   All the stockholders of course could convene and thereby waive notice   See § 599   The proper officer may be commanded by *mandamus* to send out notices of the annual election   People v Hart, 11 N Y Supp , 671 (1890)   id , 673   *Mandamus* lies to compel a meeting of vestrymen   People v. Winans, 9 N Y Supp , 249 (1890)   Where those who have the right to call a meeting of the shareholders refuse to exercise that right, for the express purpose of preventing the shareholders from duly assembling, the court will, if necessary, interfere to protect the shareholders against an abuse of power on the part of those intrusted with the management of the affairs of the company   Foss v Harbottle, 2 Ha , 461 ; Isle of Wight Rail Co v Tahourdin, 25 Ch D. 320   *Mandamus* lies to compel annual election of entire body of directors or trustees.   Com v. Kenn,

38 Leg Int., 32   The People v Town of Fairbury, 51 Ill , 149   *Dictum* that *mandamus* lies to compel election   *In re* Union Ins Co   22 Wend , 591 (1840).

[2] The fact that foreclosure proceedings are pending and a receiver is in possession does not give the court jurisdiction to call a stockholders' meeting to hold an election   Taylor v Phil , etc R. R., 7 Fed Rep , 381 (1881).

[3] See § 596, *infra*

[4] In a stockholder's suit to enjoin a consolidation the court will consider the legality of an election, the time of holding which was illegally changed by the board of directors   Nathan v. Tompkins, 82 Ala., 437 (1886)

[5] Where directors give notice that a meeting will be held on a day when they know that a large number of shareholders will not be in a position to vote, the court will interfere and restrain such an abuse of power   Cannon v Trask, 20 Eq , 669

[6] If directors convene a meeting to pass resolutions favorable to themselves on questions in which the interests of the directors are opposed to those of the shareholders, by a circular which is misleading, and which contains statements calculated to obtain proxies in their favor without giving the shareholders the information necessary to enable them to form a just judgment as to who are the proper persons to whom to intrust their votes, the court will grant an injunction to restrain the holding of the meeting or to restrain the directors from laying such resolutions before the meeting.   Jackson v. Munster Bank, 13 L. R., I1 , 118.

§ 594 *When the stockholders are entitled to notice of corporate meetings* — If the time and place at which a corporate meeting is to be held and the business to be transacted are distinctly fixed in the charter or by a by-law, this is of itself sufficient notice to all the stockholders, and no further call or notice of that meeting is necessary unless the by-laws require it [1] But a by-law which fixes the day of meeting without also fixing the hour is insufficient as a notice of the meeting [2] It is a general and settled rule of law that notice, in some way or other, must be given to every person entitled to be present at a corporate meeting.[3] When, therefore, no sufficient notice is given by charter or statute or by-law, each stockholder is entitled to an express notice of every corporate meeting [4] No usage can operate to excuse a failure to give such a notice.[5] These rules are based on the necessity of protecting the rights of stockholders, and especially of the minority.

[1] Warner v. Mower. 11 Vt., 385. 393 (1839) State v Bonnell, 35 Ohio St., 10, 15 (1878)

[2] The fact that one of the by-laws of the corporation fixes the day upon which the annual meeting of the corporation shall be held is not of itself a sufficient notice of the hour and place at which the meeting is to be held There must be an express notice of the hour and place of meeting Otherwise, unless all the stockholders are present and consent, either in person or by proxy, the meeting cannot legally be held San Buenaventura Commercial, etc, Co v Vassault, 50 Cal, 534 (1875). Though the by-laws of a corporation fix the date of the annual meeting, that of itself will not be notice of the meeting Notice must be given of the place of the meeting, and a provision of the charter for the calling of all meetings is a mandatory provision, applicable alike to general and special meetings United States v McKelder, 8 Rep, 778 (Sup Ct Dist. of Col, 1879)

[3] "To support the validity of corporate acts, each member must be actually summoned" Angell & Ames on Corp., § 492 A member who is expelled at a meeting of which he had no notice may cause the proceedings to be set aside Medical, etc, Soc v. Weatherly,

75 Ala., 248 (1883) "Due notice of the time and place of a corporate meeting is, by the English law, essential to its validity, or its power to do any act which shall bind the corporation" Dillon on Munic Corp, § 200

[4] Stow v Wyse 7 Conn, 214 (1828), the court saying, in a *dictum*. "If no particular mode of notifying the stockholders be provided either in the charter or in any by-law, yet personal notice might be given, and this, in such case would be indispensable" Wiggin v Freewill Baptist Church, 49 Mass, 301 (1844), a *dictum*, Jackson v Hampden, 20 Me, 37 (1841), Rex v. Langhorn 4 Ad & El, 538 (1836), S C, 6 Nev & M, 203 (1836), Smyth v. Darley, 2 H of L Cas., 789 (1849), the last four cases being municipal corporation cases. See, also. Stebbins v Merritt, 64 Mass, 27 (1852) where a meeting called by a general agent in the absence of a statute or by-law was upheld though one member was mentally incapable of receiving notice.

[5] Wiggin v Freewill Baptist Church, 49 Mass. 301 (1844), The King v. Hill, 4 Barn & C, 426 (1825), where an ancient custom of calling a meeting for an election of burgesses by ringing a bell was held to be no sufficient notice.

§ 595 *The essential elements of a notice of a meeting are time, place and business.*— The contents of the notice depend upon the character of the meeting There are three matters concerning every corporate meeting of which the members are entitled to notice, namely: the time, the place and the business proposed to be transacted. Some or all of these may be known to him by virtue of a charter provision or a by-law or a statute. But if any one of them is not known in that way, the stockholders are entitled to an actual notice thereof Accordingly, it is the rule that, in the absence of other valid notice, the call must specify the time and place of meeting and the business to be considered The precise hour at which the meeting is to be held must be stated in the notice [1]

In general, the notice need not specify the business to be considered where the meeting is one prescribed by charter, or where the business is prescribed by charter or statute or by-law; and no unusual business is to be transacted [2] But if the meeting is to be held at a time not provided by the charter, or if unusual business is to be transacted, the call must specify particularly the time and it seems also the unusual business [3] Thus, at a meeting called to

---

[1] San Buenaventura Commercial, etc , Co. v. Vassault, 50 Cal , 534 (1875).

[2] Notice need not be given of special business to be transacted at the regular annual meeting of the stockholders Chicago, etc., R'y v. Union Pac R'y, 47 Fed Rep., 15 (1891); Sampson v Bowdoinham Steam-mill Co, 36 Me , 78 (1854), holding that the notice of the annual meeting need not specify that the officers are to be elected, even though the by-laws require the notice to state the business Warner v Mower, 11 Vt., 385 (1839), where a provision of the by-laws relating to notices was considered as not affecting those for stated meetings, and holding that a notice of a stated annual meeting need not specify the business to be transacted, there being nothing in the by-laws limiting or specifying the business. It is believed, however, that the rights of stockholders will be best preserved by requiring notice to be given of any extraordinary business that may come before an annual meeting

[3] *In re* Bridport Old Brewery Co.,

L R, 2 Ch , 191 (1866), *In re* Silkstone Fall Colliery Co, L. R., 1 Ch D, 38 (1875) *Cf* Wright's Case, L. R., 12 Eq , 335, n , 345 n (1868), Tuttle v Michigan Air Line, etc , 35 Mich , 247 (1877), holding that at common law all notices of meetings for special or exceptional purposes were required to state the object of the call Citing Ang & A , § 492 A meeting to organize and elect directors is invalid where no notice of the business is given *In re* London, etc , Co, L. R., 31 Ch D , 223 (1885), Shelby R. R., etc., v. Louisville, etc , R. R., 12 Bush (Ky), 62 (1876), in which a sale of a railroad was set aside because authorized at a meeting of stockholders called by a notice not sufficient in point of time and defective in not stating the object of the meeting Zabriskie v Cleveland, etc , R. R. Co , 23 How , 381, 400 (1859), holding that though the notice was insufficient, yet one who was represented by proxy cannot object, especially where he delayed a long time in complaining A notice of a meeting of a benevolent society called to dis-

alter the by-laws and transact other business, an election cannot lawfully be held.[1] Nor can an assessment be levied at a special meeting when the stockholders were not duly notified that that matter would come up for consideration[2] At a special meeting which has been called for a particular purpose, only the business specified in the call can lawfully be transacted[3] The transaction, however, of business other than that for which the meeting was called will not invalidate the entire proceedings at that meeting. There is only an invalidity *pro tanto.*[4]

The notice of the business to be transacted must " be a fair notice, intelligible to the minds of ordinary men. . . . The court does not scrutinize these notices with a view to excessive criticism to find out defects, but it looks at them fairly."[5]

§ 596 *Service of the notice* — If the particular form of the notice or the manner in which it shall be served is prescribed by charter or by-law or by statute, the notice must be given in that manner, unless notice is waived by unanimous consent; otherwise, all the proceedings of the meeting are invalid.[6] In the absence of

solve must state the object of the meeting St. Mary's, etc, Ass'n v Lynch 9 Atl Rep, 98 (N H, 1887). A resolution passed at an extraordinary meeting, upon a matter for the consideration of which it was not avowedly called, or which was not specified in the notice convening the meeting, is altogether inoperative Imp. Bank of China v Bank of Hindustan, L. R., 6 Eq, 91, Anglo-California Gold Mining Co v Lewis, 6 H & N, 174, Stearic Acid Co., 9 Jur. (N S), 1066 Notice of a meeting to consider the giving of a mortgage is sufficient to enable the meeting to authorize a mortgage. Evans v Boston, etc, Co. et al, 31 N E Rep, 698 (Mass., 1892). One and the same meeting may be both ordinary and extraordinary; ordinary for the purpose of transacting the usual business of the company, and extraordinary for the transaction of some particular business of which special notice may have been given See Cutbill v Kingdom, 1 Ex, 494; Graham v Van Diemen's Land Co., 1 H & N, 541

[1] People's Insurance Co v. Westcott, 80 Mass, 440 (1860) Nor an amotion made. Rex v Town of Liverpool, 2

Burr, 723 (1759); Rex v. Doncaster, id, 738

[2] Atlantic Delaine Co v Mason, 5 R. I, 463 (1858).

[3] Warner v Mower, 11 Vt, 385 (1839).

[4] *In re* British Sugar Refining Co., 3 Kay & J, 408, 413 (1857), *In re* Irrigation Co. of France, L. R., 6 Ch, 176 (1871). But it is held that at a special meeting, all the members being present and consenting, business other than that specified in the call may lawfully be transacted. The King v Theodorick, 8 East, 543 (1807).

[5] Henderson v Bank of Australasia, 62 L. T Rep, 869 (1890), South School District v Blakeslee, 13 Conn., 227 (1839). A notice that in case certain things happen a meeting will be held is not good It is conditional and not absolute. Alexander v. Simpson, 61 L. T. Rep., 708 (1889)

[6] Shelby R. R. Co v Louisville, etc., R. R. Co, 12 Bush, 62 (1876) where there was no such publication as was required by statute and there was no waiver. Tuttle v Michigan Air Line, etc., R. R., 35 Mich, 247 (1877), where a consolidated company sued a subscriber to stock in one of the old companies and

an express provision as to the manner of making a call it is the
common-law rule that each member of the corporation is entitled
to notice, either personal or by writing, which he receives [1] The
physical or mental incapacity of one of the stockholders will not
excuse a failure to give him notice of a meeting, but it is very clear
that the meeting may lawfully convene and transact business, although one of the members is incapable, by reason of imbecility,
of receiving the notice [2] The absence of a stockholder from home
does not excuse a failure to leave the notice [3] And where one of
the stockholders dies after notice of a meeting but before the meeting convenes, and no administrator is appointed in time to act at
that meeting, there is on this account no ground to impeach the
regularity of the meeting [4] A pledgee of shares is not entitled to
a notice of corporate meetings if the pledgor receives notice,[5] since
the pledgor is entitled to vote upon the stock until his interest has
been closed out by a sale or foreclosure [6] Where stock is owned
by a firm, notice to one of the firm is sufficient.[7] If the notice is
fraudulently concealed from the owner of a majority of the stock,

he defeated the action by showing that
the statutory notice of the proposed
consolidation had not been given Reilly
v Oglebay, 25 W Va 36 (1884), where a
notice by *the secretary*, when the statute required it to be given by the board
of directors or by stockholders holding
one-tenth of the capital, was held insufficient although it was shown that he
had the authority from stockholders
holding the required amount of stock,
Stevens v Eden Meeting-house Society,
12 Vt., 688 (1839), holding that where a
by-law required notice to be posted,
parol proof of such posting was incompetent unless the written notice was
shown to have been lost, Swansea Dock
Co v Levien, 20 L J, Exch 447 (1851),
where a notice was held bad because
the statute declared it should be printed
in a newspaper circulating in the district of the principal place of business,
while in this case there was no proof
that the paper selected ever circulated
there   Hence the removal of directors
at such a meeting was illegal   Id   As
to waiver, see § 599 *infra*

[1] Notice to non-residents by letter was
upheld in Stebbins v Merritt, 64 Mass,
27 (1852)   For *dicta* to the effect that

the notice must be personal, see Tuttle
v Michigan Air Line R R Co, 35 Mich,
247 (1877), Stow v Wyse, 7 Conn,
214 (1828)   See, also, § 592, *supra*, as to
the kind of notice required of directors'
meetings.   See, also, § 594, *supra*, and
notes

[2] Stebbins v Merritt, 64 Mass 27 (1852)

[3] Jackson v Hampden, 20 Me, 37
(1841)   In Porter v Robinson, 30 Hun,
209 (1883), it is held that notice need not
be given to a member of a board of
school trustees, the board being a body
corporate, who is absent from the state
and cannot attend the meeting, and
that a failure to notify such a member
will not render the proceedings at the
meeting irregular or invalid   Members
of English joint-stock companies residing abroad are not entitled to any notice
of corporate meetings   *Ex parte* Union
Hill Company, 22 L T Rep, 400 (1870)

[4] Freeman's National Bank v Smith,
13 Blatch, 220 (1875)

[5] McDaniels v Flower Brook Mfg Co,
22 Vt, 274 (1850)

[6] See §§ 612, 468.

[7] Kenton, etc Co v McAlpin, 5 Fed.
Rep, 737, 747 (1880).

even where the notice is published in accordance with the statute, the election will be set aside [1]

§ 597 *Notice must be served a reasonable time before the meeting* — The notice must be served upon the stockholders a reasonable or customary time before the day of the meeting [2] Where by statute it is provided that thirty days' notice shall be given of certain corporate meetings, that length of time applies to notices of other meetings of the same corporation [3]

§ 598 *The division of meetings into ordinary and extraordinary* — Corporate meetings of stockholders are frequently divided, both by the judges and the text-writers, into two classes — the first being special or extraordinary, and the second being ordinary, regular, stated or general   By reason of this attempt at classification much confusion has been introduced into the law without any corresponding advantage   The terms employed to distinguish the various kinds of meetings are used in different senses by different writers, so that it is difficult to define them in such a way as to avoid confusion.

§ 599 *Waiver of notice* — The stockholder may, in general, waive his right to have a notice of a corporate meeting duly served upon him [4]

---

[1] Where in addition to irregularities the notice of the election at a deferred day, which is published in accordance with the charter, is concealed from the leading stockholder, the court will set the election aside   Johnston v Jones, 23 N J Eq, 216 (1872)

[2] In the Matter of the Long Island R. R. Co, 19 Wend, 37 (1837) *Cf* Covert v Rogers, 38 Mich, 363, where a similar rule is declared as to notice to directors of their meetings. The legislature cannot unreasonably shorten the time of the next meeting Cassell v Lexington, etc, Co, 9 S. W Rep, 502 (Ky, 1888), id 701 A reorganization under the English statute will not be sustained as against American stockholders, where the entire business of the English company is to own and work American mines, and the by-laws of the company provide for a longer notice than is specified in the English statute The notice of the meeting to reorganize not having reached the American stockholders in time to attend the meeting, the American courts will not sustain the reorganization Brown v Republican, etc, Mines, 55 Fed Rep, 7 (Col, 1893).

[3] Shelby R. R. Co v Louisville, etc, R. R. Co, 12 Bush, 62 (1876).

[4] The acts of a meeting are valid, though held without notice, if all are present or subsequently ratify and approve of the action Stutz v Handley, 41 Fed Rep, 531 (1890), affirmed as to this point, but reversed as to others, in Handley v Stutz, 139 U S, 417 (1891) A party accepting the benefit of a contract for a long time cannot repudiate it on the ground that the calls for the meetings of the executive committee and of the stockholders which authorized the contract were insufficient, nor can he set up in such a case that the directors had not authorized the contract Union Pac R y v Chicago, etc, R'y, 51 Fed Rep, 309 (1892) Objections to the regularity of the notice which was given are waived if all are present at the meeting and do not object to such irregularity Stebbins v Merritt, 64 Mass, 27

Greater difficulty has been encountered where by statute or by charter the notice must be published or must be given a specified length of time before the meeting is held. This question arises often in regard to the first and organization meeting of the company, or in regard to a meeting to increase the capital stock, or to issue bonds, or to give a mortgage, or to effect a consolidation The rule, however, is now well established that such statutory notice is for the benefit of the stockholders themselves, and if they are willing and do waive it, the meeting and all the proceedings are as valid as they would be had the full statutory notice been given [1]

(1852), Richardson v. Vermont, etc, 44 Vt, 613 (1872), holding that objections to the proceedings of a meeting called on a notice which did not state what its object was had been waived by a ratification at a later meeting, Jones v Milton & Rushville Turnpike, 7 Ind, 547 (1856), where the stockholders not notified appeared and voted by proxy, Kenton Furnace v McAlpine, 5 Fed. Rep, 737 (1880) See, also, § 606, infra. Where several persons, their associates and successors, are declared to be a corporation, one of them with new parties may meet, organize, adopt by-laws, etc, without the capital being first subscribed and without the others, if they do not object. McGinty v Athol etc., Co, 29 N E. Rep, 510 (Mass, 1892) Notice may be waived People v Twaddell, 18 Hun, 427 (1879)

[1] Although the statutes of Montana require that a mortgage may be given only after a stockholders' meeting convened by publication of notice, etc, has voted it, yet all the stockholders, by voting therefor, waive the required notice and no one can complain The mortgage is valid Campbell v Argenta, etc, Co, 51 Fed Rep. 1 (1892). Although the constitution provides that there shall be sixty days' notice of the meeting to authorize the issue of bonds, yet where all the stockholders assemble and authorize the issue without any notice and the bonds pass into bona fide hands they may be enforced The absence of a nominal stockholder whose

stock is really owned by one of those present is immaterial Wood v Corry, etc, Co, 44 Fed Rep, 116 (1890) A constitutional provision in regard to notice being given of a meeting for increasing the stock or bonds of a corporation is for the benefit of the stockholders and may be waived by them or the omission of it may be ratified by them Nelson et al v Hubbard, 11 S Rep., 428 (Ala., 1892) The voluntary dissolution of a company under the statute, but without the ten days' notice required by the statute, is not such a dissolution as to prevent creditors from attaching the property of the company as though no dissolution had been had Cleveland, etc, Co v Taylor, etc, Co., 54 Fed Rep, 82 (1893) But the dissolution cannot be enjoined by creditors in the absence of fraud. Id, 85 To same effect, Appeal of Columbia Nat'l Bank. 16 Weekly Notes Cas (Pa), 357, Hardware Co v Phalen 128 Pa St. 110, Kenton Furnace Co v McAlpine, 5 Fed Rep, 737 (1880). where no notice was given, although prescribed by the charter and by-laws It was held to have been waived by the presence of all the stockholders at the meeting and their participation in its action, In re British Sugar Ref Co, 3 Kay & J, 408 (1857). where it was adjudged that a shareholder who had received a circular notice of the meeting and was present could not question the legality of the meeting on the ground that the charter required, in addition to the circular,

Thus participation as an officer in issuing the call is a waiver by him of informalities as to that call,[1] and recognition of an agent appointed at a certain meeting, by dealing and offering to deal with him as the agent of the company, is a waiver of the right to notice of that meeting[2] One stockholder cannot avail himself of the neglect of the corporate officers to give due notice to another stockholder who does not himself complain[3] But the waiver of all

publication in a newspaper, which was not made A person who takes part in a meeting cannot object that it was held on five days' notice instead of fourteen as required by the charter Bucksport, etc, R R v Buck, 68 Me, 81 (1878), Chamberlain v Painesville, etc, R R, 15 Ohio St, 225 A failure to give the statutory notice of the first meeting is immaterial where all but one stockholder was present and he afterwards ratified all that was done Babbitt v East, etc, Co (N J, 1876), Stew Dig, p 208, § 13 To same effect, § 234 note supra, and § 593, also § 288 A stockholder who knows of and approves of a proposed sale of a railroad by a stockholders' vote as allowed by statute cannot have the sale set aside on the ground that he was not notified of nor present at the meeting voting such sale, but he must be paid the value of his stock Young v Toledo, etc, R R, 43 N W Rep, 632 (Mich, 1889) The constitutional provision that bonds or stock shall not be increased except in a certain way does not apply to an original issue of bonds Union etc, Co v Southern etc, Co, 51 Fed Rep, 840 (1892) Directors elected at a meeting called on thirteen days' notice instead of fourteen as required by statute may make calls where their election has been confirmed by a subsequent annual general meeting Briton, etc, Ass'n v Jones, 61 L T Rep, 384 (1889), People v Peck, 11 Wend, 604 (1834) holding that a failure to comply with a statutory requirement regarding notice will not affect the proceedings of a meeting of a religious corporation where there is no claim that every voter was not present,

or that evil resulted from the omission, and no fraud was involved If all parties attended, they thereby admitted notice See, also, Stebbins v. Merritt, 64 Mass, 27 (1852), The King v. Chetwynd, 7 Barn & C, 695 (1828), where the election of a burgess at a meeting of which no notice was given was held valid, because it appeared that all the members of the electing body were present, The King v Theodorick, 8 East, 343 (1807) Cf United States v McKelden, 8 Rep, 773 (1879), where it was held that, although the date for the annual meeting is fixed by a by-law, the notice by publication provided for by the charter is necessary See, also, In the Matter of Long Island R R Co, 19 Wend, 37 (1837), in which it was said in a dictum that a notice regulated by statute of course cannot be modified or dispensed with "

[1] Bucksport etc, R R Co v Buck, 68 Me, 81 (1878), Schenectady, etc, Plank-road Co v Thatcher, 11 N. Y., 102 (1854)

[2] Bryant v Goodnow, 22 Mass, 228 (1827)

[3] Schenectady, etc, Plank-road Co v Thatcher, 11 N Y, 102 (1854). In this case the court said "The court rejected the offer of the defendant to prove that no notice had been given of the first election of directors I think this was properly rejected on the ground that the defendant could not avail himself of a neglect to give notice to any other stockholder The defendant himself was present at that meeting and voted, and was elected a director He has not suffered by an omission to serve notice, and he is not in a situation to object as

the stockholders is essential in order to validate an election held at a meeting not properly called [1]

§ 600. *Notice is presumed to have been regularly given.*— It is a presumption of law that proper and valid notice of a corporate meeting has been duly given to every stockholder, and that the meeting itself was regularly and lawfully held   The burden of proof is therefore upon him who alleges want of notice or insufficiency of notice, or attacks the regularity and validity of the proceedings.[2]

§ 601 *Adjourned meetings.*— An adjourned meeting is but a continuation of the meeting which has been adjourned, and when that meeting was regularly called and convened and duly adjourned, the shareholders may, at the adjourned meeting, consider and determine any corporate business that might lawfully have been transacted at the original meeting [3]

---

to others " A stockholders' meeting held without notice or call cannot be objected to by those who participate or receive the benefits of it. Handley v Stutz, 139 U S, 417 (1891)   A stockholder who takes part cannot object that another stockholder had no notice. *Re* Union Hill, etc, Co, 22 L. T Rep., 400 (1870), *In re* British, etc, Co, 8 Kay & J, 408 (1857)   A party who did not attend the meeting cannot object that the inspectors were not sworn   In the Matter of the Election of Directors of the Mohawk & Hudson R. R. Co, 19 Wend, 135 (1835)

[1] State of Nevada v Pettineli, 10 Nev, 141 (1875)

[2] McDaniels v Flower Brook Manuf Co, 22 Vt, 274 (1850), Porter v Robinson, 30 Hun, 209 (1883), Sargent v Webster, 54 Mass., 497 (1847), South School, etc, v Blakeslie, 13 Conn, 227, 235 (1839), Lane v Brainerd, 30 Conn, 565 (1862), Pitts v Temple, 2 Mass, 538 (1807), Wells v Rodgers, 27 N W Rep, 671 (Mich, 1886), holding that notice is presumed, and the burden of proof in attacking the legality of the meeting is on the plaintiff   See, also, § 606, *infra*   All the stockholders are presumed to have had notice of a meeting that has been held   Beardsley v Johnson, 121 N Y, 224 (1890). *Cf.* Wiggin v Free-

will, etc, Church, 49 Mass, 301, 312 (1844).

[3] Granger v Grubb, 7 Phila 350 (1870), Farrar v Perley, 7 Me, 404 (1831), Scadding v Lorans, 3 H of L. Cas, 418 (1851). *Cf.* People v Batchelor, 22 N Y, 128 (1860), where the New York city board of aldermen appointed a day for the election of a city officer   At a subsequent stated meeting this resolution was rescinded, and then an election was thereupon held   *Held,* that the election was void, as some members were absent from the former meeting and had no notice of the election   A board of aldermen cannot elect an assessor and then at an adjourned meeting reconsider and elect some one else   State v Phillips, 10 Atl Rep., 417 (Me, 1887)   See, also, Hardenburgh v Farmers', etc, Bank, 3 N J Eq, 68 (1834), where the stockholders at the first meeting proceeded to an election in spite of an adjournment by the commissioners and the election was upheld   A meeting adjourned for want of a quorum may at the adjourned meeting proceed to business, if a quorum is present, and no notice of the adjourned meeting is necessary where the charter or by-laws provided for such adjournment   Smith v Law, 21 N Y, 296 (1860), involving a meeting of the board of directors.

But where there is an absence of good faith, and an adjourned meeting is held in such a way as to prevent certain of the stockholders from knowing of it, the proceedings are invalid.[1] Where the original meeting was duly called and convened, the stockholders are not entitled to any other notice of the adjourned meeting than that which is implied in the adjournment[2] But nothing can, without notice, be transacted at an adjourned meeting except the unfinished business of the first meeting.[3]

---

[1] State r Bonnell, 35 Ohio St., 10 (1878) Where an election is held, after many adjournments, and a minority are present and elect directors, who repudiate a contract which exists with the holder of a majority of the stock, the latter being ignorant of the intent to elect officers, equity will enjoin the repudiation of the contract. New York, etc., Co. v. Parrott, 36 Fed. Rep , 462 (1888).

[2] Smith v. Law, supra, Warner v.

Mower, 11 Vt., 385 (1839). Cf. United States v. McKelden, 8 Rep , 778 (1879), where it was held that the proceedings of an original meeting being invalid by reason of insufficient notice, the adjourned meetings were invalid also, they being merely continuations of the original To same effect, Wiggin v. Freewill, etc., Church, 49 Mass, 301 (1844).

[3] R. v. Grimshaw, 10 Q. B., 747.

CHAPTER XXXVII.

ELECTIONS AND OTHER CORPORATE MEETINGS

§ 602 *Scope of the subject* — The business which the stockholders of a corporation in meeting assembled have the power to transact is not extensive, but it is of great importance   It elects the directors, passes upon amendments to the charter, checks any *ultra vires* acts, determines whether any increase of the capital stock shall be made, makes the by-laws, and dissolves or continues the corporation.   These constitute the chief functions of a stockholders' meeting.   They are extraordinary in their character, and although they are exercised at long intervals are of vital importance   This chapter treats of the business which may be transacted at stockholders' meetings and of the methods of its transaction.

§ 603. *Elections are to be by the stockholders and may be compelled by mandamus* — At common law the directors of a corporation are to be elected by the stockholders in corporate meeting assembled[1] Generally this is declared to be the law by charter or statutory provisions. The president, vice-president, secretary, treasurer and agents of the corporation are usually elected or appointed, not by the stockholders, but by the directors. All these matters, however, are generally regulated by the charter or a statute

At common law *mandamus* lies to compel an election of corporate officers[2]

All corporations for profit have power to elect a board of directors[3]

The legislature may amend the charter so as to increase the number of directors,[4] but it cannot deprive the members of the corporation of the privilege of electing its directors[5]

Although the corporation is not a going concern, nevertheless it may have an election of directors.[6]

§ 604 *The meeting must be held at the prescribed hour, which must be reasonable.* — The particular time at which corporate meetings shall be held is often prescribed in the charter or a statute or

[1] Stockholders cannot fill vacancies in the board of directors at a special meeting, when elections can only be at annual meetings Moses *v* Tompkins, 84 Ala, 613 (1888) The by-laws, however, may and generally do give this power to the directors And see *dictum* in *In re* Union Ins. Co, 22 Wend, 591 (1840)

[2] See § 593, *supra*

[3] A bank may have directors though the statute does not provide for them All private corporations may have directors Hurlbut *v* Marshall, 62 Wis., 590 (1885) "The power inheres in the corporation to hold an election," where the charter or statutes are silent Wright *v* Commonwealth, 109 Pa St., 560 (1885). "The power of electing both officers and members is an incident to every corporation It is not necessary that such a power should be expressly conferred by the charter ' Commonwealth *v* Gill, 3 Whart. (Pa), 228, 247 (1837).

[4] Mower *v* Staples 32 Minn, 284 (1884) See, also, Gray *v* Coffin, 9 Cush, 192 (1852), Child *v* Coffin, 17 Mass., 64 (1820), Langley *v* Little, 26 Me, 162 (1846), Payson *v* Withers, 5 Biss, 269 (1873), Joy *v* Jackson, etc, Co, 11 Mich, 155

(1863), Bank *v* Richardson, 1 Me., 79; Greenville, etc, R. R. Co. *v* Johnson, 8 Baxt, 332, Fall River Iron Works *v.* Old Colony R. R. Co., 5 Allen, 221

[5] The legislature cannot arbitrarily name and appoint trustees of an educational corporation, the charter providing that vacancies shall be filled by the remaining trustees. Sheriff *v.* Lowndes, 16 Md, 357 (1860) It cannot give to the city of Louisville the power to elect the trustees of the University of Louisville, an educational corporation City of Louisville *v* President, etc., 15 B. Monr, 642 (1855). It cannot vest the government of an incorporated academy in a new board of trustees. Norris *v* Trustees, etc , 7 Gill & J, 7 (1834). Under the reserved power to amend or repeal a charter, the legislature may amend the charter of an agricultural college which has private stockholders, but to which the state contributes funds, so that instead of the state having four directors out of eleven, the state shall have seven out of twelve Jackson *v* Walsh, 23 Atl. Rep., 778 (Md , 1892)

[6] Beardsley *v.* Johnson, 121 N. Y., 224 (1890).

in the by-laws of the corporation When not so prescribed it is fixed by the officers who call together the corporate meeting But, in whatever way it is decided upon, the meeting must be convened at the time decided upon or within a reasonable time thereafter [1] Accordingly, if the meeting is convened before the hour at which it is called and business is transacted, the proceedings will be invalid [2] In general, a court of equity will restrain the directors from fixing the time for an annual meeting at a date when many members are in the country, the purpose being to prevent them from exercising their right to vote [3]

Frequently the particular office or place for meeting within the state is specified in the charter or by-laws of the corporation In that event a meeting held at a different place will be irregular, and the proceedings at such a meeting void and ineffectual [4]

§ 605 *Inspectors of election — Conducting and closing elections.* Ordinarily a chairman and inspectors of election are elected or appointed by the stockholders The presiding officer at a stockhold-

[1] Where a meeting was held by a minority of the stockholders several hours after the time fixed in the notice, and an adjournment made until the following day, at which adjourned meeting, without the knowledge of the other members, an election was held the election was unfair and invalid State of Ohio v Bonnell, 35 Ohio St , 10 (1878) But a delay of an hour and five minutes after the time specified in the notice is not, as a matter of law, an unreasonable delay which will vitiate the proceedings South School District v Blakeslee, 13 Conn , 227, 235 (1839)

[2] So, where a meeting was called for 12 o'clock, but was called to order and organized fifteen minutes before 12, it was held to be a surprise and a fraud upon such of the stockholders as were not actually present at that hour, and that in consequence the proceedings were irregular and void People v. Albany, etc , R. R. Co , 55 Barb 344 (1869) Where commissioners, after calling a meeting of subscribers, ordered the election postponed, but the subscribers nevertheless refused to postpone and proceed with the election, the election is not void, unless, in the opinion of the court, a postponement was clearly

necessary Hardenburgh v Farmers' & Merchants' Bank, 3 N J Eq , 68 (1834) *Quere*, in this case, whether the election might not have been avoided if any considerable number of the shareholders were deprived of their election franchise by the failure to postpone See, also § 605

[3] Cannon v Trask, L R , 20 Eq , 669 (1875) A majority of the board of directors cannot shorten their term of office by merely changing the time of the annual meeting of the stockholders in violation of the stockholders' by-laws Nathan v Tompkins, 82 Ala , 437 (1886)

[4] Where the customary place of meeting of a corporation is abandoned and a new place fixed upon in a regular and lawful manner, a meeting at the old place is irregular, and the proceedings at such a meeting are invalid Miller v English, 21 N J. Law, 317 (1848) The meeting must be held at the usual place. American Primitive Society v Pilling, 24 N J Law, 653 (1855). *Cf* McDaniels v Flower Brook Manuf Co , 22 Vt. 274 (1850), holding that a meeting at a residence is good, if all assent, even though the statute requires the meetings to be at the counting room of the company.

ers' meeting need not be a stockholder,[1] and he need not be elected with any particular formality [2]

The inspectors of election need not be stockholders [3] If inspectors are provided for by the charter, and they do not act or are enjoined from acting, the stockholders may appoint others to take their place [4] The duties of the inspector are ministerial and not judicial Their discretion and powers of investigation are very limited [5]

A requirement that the election shall be by ballot does not invalidate an election by show of hand if no one objects.[6]

Where no time is specified by law during which the polls must be kept open it rests within the sound discretion of the inspectors to say when the polls shall close [7] So also it is held that holding the polls open after the hour specified in the notice for them to close will not, where the inspectors exercise a reasonable discretion, invalidate an election [8]

§ 606 *Conducting and closing meetings generally — Irregularities and informalities* — The form or mode of conducting an election is in general not material, provided it violates no positive provision of the charter or of a statute regulating it, is orderly and in good faith, and is conducted by authorized or proper persons [9] And as a general rule of law, where, in the election of cor-

---

[1] Stebbins v Merritt, 64 Mass , 27 (1852)

[2] Acquiescence in a person's assuming to act as chairman of a stockholders' meeting validates his acting as such *In re* Argus Printing Co , 48 N W. Rep , 347 (N D , 1891)

[3] People v Albany, etc . R R, 55 Barb , 344, 373 (1869). Although an inspector is required by by-law to be a stockholder, yet the election of one who is not a stockholder is voidable and not void Id An inspector may be a candidate for directorship *Ex parte* Willcocks, 7 Cowen, 402 (1827)

[4] People v Albany, etc., R R Co , 55 Barb , 344, 357 (1869) See, also, Matter of Wheeler, 2 Abb Prac (N S.), 361 (1866). The failure of the inspectors so appointed to take the prescribed oath will not invalidate the election *Re* Mohawk, etc , R R, 19 Wend , 135 (1838), *Re* Chenango, etc., Ins Co , id , 635 (1839) Where by statute an election is to have "inspectors" one inspector is insufficient. Matter of Lighthall, etc.,

Co, 47 Hun, 258 (1888); but see N. Y. L J , June 29, 1889

[5] See § 611, *infra*, *Re* Mohawk, etc , R. R., *supra* The office of the inspectors is ministerial rather than judicial. Commonwealth v Woelper, 3 Serg & R, 29 (Pa., 1817). Inspectors at elections having once accepted a vote and declared the result cannot then reject it and declare a different result. Hartt t. Harvey, 32 Barb , 55 (1860).

[6] Wardens of Christ Church v. Pope, 74 Mass., 140 (1857).

[7] In the Matter of the Chenango County Ins. Co , 19 Wend , 634 (1839).

[8] In the Matter, etc , of the Mohawk & Hudson R. R. Co., 19 Wend , 135 (1838). An election is not vitiated by the fact that the polls are kept open after the designated hour and votes received. Rudolph v Southern, etc , League, 23 Abb. N C., 199 (1889), People v Albany, etc , R. R. 55 Barb, 344, 356, 360 (1869).

[9] Fox v Allensville, etc., Turnpike Co , 46 Ind , 31 (1874).

porate officers, no particular mode of proceeding is prescribed by law, if the wishes of the corporators have been fairly expressed, and the election was conducted in good faith, it will not be set aside on account of any informality in the manner of conducting it [1]

It is a general rule that, in the transaction of the ordinary business of a corporation, no particular formalities are necessarily to be observed. The motions, however, must be put in an intelligible way and then voted upon [2]

The parliamentary usages are the same as in other bodies, and mere irregularities in the manner of conducting the business are immaterial if the sense of the meeting has been fairly expressed [3]

After the meeting is organized the majority cannot withdraw and organize another meeting [4]

Although the chairman refuses to poll the vote, but declares the

---

[1] Philips v Wickham, 1 Paige, 590 (1829).

[2] A motion must be plainly and clearly made, separate from a rambling speech, before the chairman can be held to be wrong in rejecting it. Henderson v Bank of Australasia, 62 L T Rep, 869 (1890) A general understanding or assent or want of dissent is not equivalent to a question being put and voted upon The statement by a minister of what salary he wished and the failure of members to object is not a sufficient expression of the meeting Lauders v Frank, etc., Church, 114 N Y., 626 (1889).

[3] Philips v Wickham, 1 Paige, 590 (1829), Matter of Wheeler, 2 Abb Pr (N S), 361 (1866); Downing v Potts 23 N J Law, 66 (1851), in which it was held that non-compliance with a statute requiring a list of stockholders entitled to vote to be made out ten days before an election will not of itself make void an election, such provision being only directory A motion may be put by the chairman, although it has neither been made nor seconded In re Horbury, etc., Co, L. R., 11 Ch D, 109 (1879). Although the meeting has voted down two motions to make calls it may then pass another motion for a larger one In re British, etc., Co. 3 Kay & J, 408 (1857). In England, by statute,

any five stockholders may demand a poll Phoenix, etc, Co, 48 L T Rep, 260 (1883), Hurrell & Hyde on Directors and Officers, 78 Even if on a poll demanded by five members each share has one vote, yet until such poll is demanded voting is by show of hands In re Horbury, etc, Co L. R., 11 Ch D, 109 (1879) In general see, also, Gorham v Campbell, 2 Cal, 135 (1852), Hardenburgh v Farmers', etc, Bank, 3 N J Eq, 68 (1834), People v Peck, 11 Wend, 604 (1834). See, also, § 605, supra In State of Nevada v Pettineli 10 Nev, 141 (1875), the court held that an election was illegal where there was no presiding officer and no inspectors. Although the notice of a special stockholders' meeting states that the resolution will be presented and passed upon, to give to each share one vote, provided such share has been held by the party for six months prior to an election, an amendment proposed at the meeting striking out the latter part of the resolution must be considered and put to vote by the chairman Henderson v Bank of Australasia, 63 L T Rep, 597 (1890)

[4] Their acts are void, but if the statute requires a majority in interest of the stock to elect, the election is invalid In re Argus, etc Co, 48 N W Rep, 347 (N D, 1891)

meeting adjourned, the courts will not necessarily interfere.[1] If any fraud, surprise or deceit has been practiced in conducting the meeting a different rule prevails[2] The right to object to an informality may be waived, and a failure upon the part of those members not present to protest promptly, upon learning of the informality, is a waiver.[3] The presumption is that all proceedings were regular and lawful.[4]

§ 607. *The quorum — A majority of the stockholders attending a meeting may transact business* — The right of the majority to rule in the management of the affairs of a private corporation is fully established[5] They may control the company's business, prescribe

[1] The courts will not interfere although the chairman of the meeting refused to poll the vote on a motion to adjourn, but declared the meeting adjourned on a *viva voce* vote and left. In regard to the right to be heard the court said the court would not sustain a bill "for the purpose of enabling one particular member of the company to have an opportunity of expressing his opinions *viva voce* at a meeting of the shareholders. MacDougall t Gardiner, L. R. 1 Ch D, 13 (1875)

[2] Johnson t Jones. 23 N J Eq. 216 (1872), People r Albany etc . R. R. Co, 55 Barb. 344 (1869), State of Nevada t Pettineli 10 Nev 141 (1875) Commonwealth t Woelper 3 Serg & R. 29 (1817). See, also. §§ 604. 605. *supra*, and § 596

[3] State r Lehre 7 Rich Law, 234 325 (1854). *In re* Mohawk, etc. R. R., 19 Wend, 135 (1838); The King t Trevenen, 2 Barn & Ald. 589 (1819) Shareholders who receive reports of what takes place at meetings and who do not object to what is being done, will be considered as acquiescing therein if what is done might have been validly sanctioned by them if present. but not if what is done is altogether illegal, and beyond the power of even all the shareholders. See Phœnix Life Assur Co's Case, 2 J & H., 441 Irvine t Union Bank of Australia, 2 App. Cas. 366 Compare Evans t Smallcombe, L. R., 3 H. L., 249; Spackman t Evans, id, 171; Houldsworth r Evans, id, 263, Phos-

phate of Lime Co. r Greene, L. R., 7 C P, 43

[4] Blanchard v. Dow, 32 Me, 557 (1851). where it was presumed that the election was by ballot · Ashtabula, etc., R. R. Co. r Smith. 15 Ohio St., 328 (1864), where it was presumed that the requisite amount of stock was subscribed before the election took place See, also, §§ 599, 600. *supra.* The corporate minutes may be signed after the meeting has been held Miles r Baugh, 3 Q. B., 845 (1842). Southampton, etc., Co. r. Richards, 1 M & Gr, 448 (1840); Lindley on Partn, 551 Concerning the mode of proving the corporate minutes, see § 714. *infra* A ratification by the stockholders of directors' acts cannot be made by a general resolution ratifying "all of the acts of the officers." Farmers' L. & T Co. t San Diego, etc., St. R'y Co 45 Fed Rep. 518 (1891).

[5] Durfee t Old Colony, etc, R. R. Co., 87 Mass. 230 (1862); City of Covington r Covington, etc. Bridge Co., 10 Bush, 69, 76 (1873), East Tennessee, etc., R. R. Co. t Gammon 5 Sneed (Tenn), 567 (1859); McBride t Porter, 17 Iowa. 203 (1864); Faulds t Yates 57 Ill, 416 (1870), Leo r Union Pacific R R Co 19 Fed. Rep., 283 (1884) S C 17 id, 273 (1883); Barnes t Brown 80 N Y, 527 (1880), Gifford r New Jersey R. R. Co, 10 N J Eq, 171 (1854), Dudley r Kentucky High School, 9 Bush (Ky). 576 (1873). See, also Livingstone t Lynch, 4 Johns. Ch , 573 (1820), in which Chancellor Kent clearly states that the right of the majority to

its general policy, make themselves its agents, and take reasonable compensation for their services[1] The minority, however, have a right to be heard and it is the duty of the majority to give a due consideration to their arguments and wishes concerning the management of the corporate business[2]

The question has arisen whether a meeting can be held and business transacted when a majority in interest of the stockholders are not present But the law is clear that those stockholders who attend a duly-called stockholders' meeting may transact the business of that meeting, although a majority in interest or in number of the stockholders are not present[3]

Of those who attend the stockholders' meeting a majority rule Their acts are as valid as though they constituted a majority of all

rule is one of the chief differences between a corporation and a partnership The majority rule at common law Commonwealth v Nickerson 10 Phil, 55 (1875) New Orleans etc R. R. Co v Harris. 27 Miss.. 517, 537 (1854) A majority of the stockholders control the policy of the corporation, and regulate and govern the lawful exercise of its franchise and business, even though the management may not seem to be wise The majority rule Wheeler v Pullman, etc. Co, 32 N E Rep, 420 (Ill., 1892) Where a statute requires a three-fourths vote in value for a reorganization of a company, the stock not voted is not counted to make up the three-fourths even though the trustees who represent the stock refuse to assent or dissent. Re The Neath etc, Co, 66 L T Rep 40 (1892) Where stockholders in an apartment-house corporation are entitled to rent apartments at a rental to be fixed by a majority vote of the stockholders an increased rental so voted is legal The by-laws providing for such a vote override a general statement in a prospectus to the contrary, the stockholders knowing of the by-law Compton v Chelsea 128 N Y, 537 (1891)

[1] Meeker v Winthrop Iron Co 17 Fed. Rep 48 (1883) S.C sub nom Winthrop Iron Co v Meeker, 109 U S, 180 (1883). See. also, § 662, infra.

[2] But see MacDougall v Gardiner, supra.

[3] Granger v Grubb, 7 Phil, 350 (1870, Craig v First, etc., Church, 88 Pa St. 42 (1878), where the principle is elucidated that this is the rule for a meeting composed of an indefinite number of persons, like stockholders but that where a definite number is involved as in a board of directors, then a majority must be present, Brown v Pacific Mail. etc, 5 Blatch, 525 (1867), Field v Field 9 Wend, 394 (1832), Gowen's Appeal, 10 Week Notes of Cas, 85 (Pa, 1880), Madison Ave., etc, Church v Baptist Ch, etc 5 Rob. (N Y), 649 (1867), Everett v Smith 22 Minn, 53 As to the rule concerning directors. see § 592. supra It has been held that one person cannot constitute a quorum, that at least two members are necessary to make a corporate meeting Sharpe v Dawes. 46 L J (Q. B) 104 (1876). In this case one stockholder met," did all necessary business, and then voted himself a vote of thanks In the case of In re Sanitary etc., Co, W N, 1877 p 223, where one stockholder having also proxies of the remaining three stockholders held a meeting, ' voted himself into the chair, proposed a resolution to wind up voluntarily, declared the resolution passed and appointed a liquidator the court reluctantly followed the preceding case and declared the "meeting" invalid.

the stockholders, or constituted a majority at a meeting in which a majority of the stockholders were present.[1] The presumption always is that a legal majority voted for any act or proceeding that appears to have been passed [2]

Two important limitations and exceptions to these principles are to be borne carefully in mind

First, the majority cannot bind the minority to submit to an act by the corporation where such act is beyond the express and implied powers of the corporation as given to it by its charter Such an act is *ultra vires*. A large amount of litigation has arisen from the attempt of the majority to carry out *ultra vires* acts. The minority may object, and even a single stockholder may have the *ultra vires* act enjoined or set aside.[3]

The second exception arises where the legislature amends the charter of the corporation, and the majority of the stockholders attempt to accept that amendment and act upon it. In such a case, if the amendment materially changes the scope and purpose of the enterprise, the minority may object and may prevent the acceptance of the amendment.[4]

The question of how far the majority rule when that majority are interested in a contract which the corporation has made, and which is being passed upon by a stockholders' meeting, is considered elsewhere [5]

§ 608. *The majority of votes cast shall elect.*— It is the well-settled rule in corporations having a capital stock divided into shares that a majority of the votes cast at any election shall elect.[6] And this majority, moreover, need not be an actual numerical majority of all the votes which all the stockholders have, but only a majority of the votes cast [7] Accordingly, a majority of the votes cast will elect, even though a majority of the shares of stock are not voted at all, and even though the owners are present at the meeting and refuse to vote.[8]

---

[1] Columbia, etc , Co v Meier, 39 Mo , 53 (1866), and same cases as in the preceding note , Gowen's Appeal, 10 Weekly Notes Cas , 85 (1881)

[2] Citizens' Mutual, etc , Ins. Co. v Sortwell, 90 Mass , 217 (1864)

[3] This subject is fully treated in Part IV, *infra*.

[4] See chapter XXVIII, *supra*.

[5] See chapter XXXIX, *infra*

[6] People v Albany, etc , R. R. Co , 55 Barb , 344 368 (1869), State v Fagan, 42 Conn , 32 (1875), a municipal corporation case. See, also, § 607, *supra*

[7] See § 607, *supra*, Craig v. First Pres Church, 88 Pa. St., 42 (1878); *In re* Union Ins. Co. 22 Wend , 591 (1840), holding also that a plurality elects. At a municipal corporation meeting only those who vote are counted Persons not voting at all are not counted Smith v. Proctor, 130 N Y , 319 (1891). In regard to voting in church elections in New York, see People v Keese, 27 Hun, 483 (1882)

[8] Appeal of Gowen, 10 Weekly Notes of Cases, 84 (1881) where the supreme court held that "those who voluntarily

Although less than the full number of directors to be elected receive a majority or plurality, yet those receiving such majority or plurality are elected, and another ballot or election may be had to elect the remainder [1]

§ 609. *Is every share of stock entitled to one vote?* — At common law, in public or municipal corporations, each qualified elector has one vote, and only one　This was a natural rule, since each duly-qualified citizen voted as a citizen and not as the holder of stock.　But the same rule should not apply to private corporations Stockholders are interested not equally, but in proportion to the number of shares held by them　Naturally and reasonably each share should be entitled to one vote　It must be conceded, however, that the decisions are otherwise, and it seems that at common

absent themselves from a meeting duly called for an election must recognize the validity of the election regularly made by those who do attend ' The question was whether an election held by a meeting of railroad stockholders at which a majority of all votes was not cast could be considered valid　State ı Green, 37 Ohio St　227 (1881)　This was a case of election of clerk by a city council, and it was held that, all being present and engaged in holding the election, half the members may not defeat an election by refusing to vote and then objecting because a quorum had not voted　Commonwealth ı Wickersham, 66 Pa St, 134 (1870), was the election of a county school superintendent which was required to be " viva voce by a majority of the whole number of directors present.' A person receiving exactly half that number could not be declared elected although one director refused to vote on the last ballot　"He remained, and being present was entitled to be counted." "The legal intendment [of his action] was that he voted for neither or for the minority candidate "
But, under a by-law requiring a majority of the stock to be present, it has been held that the majority must be a majority of the whole stock, and not merely of the stock subscribed for　Ellsworth, etc, Co ı Faunce, 79 Me, 440 (1887)
If the statute requires a majority of the

directors to elect a director or president, one who is present but does not vote must be counted　People ı. Conklin, 7 Hun 188　See, also, § 713a, *infra*, on this point.　Stockholders may vote for less than the whole number of directors to be elected　Vandenburgh ı Broadway R'y Co, 29 Hun, 349 (1883)　But where a meeting was called to elect three directors and a majority of the stockholders voted for five directors only a small minority voting for three the latter votes were held the only valid ones, and the three voted for were declared elected. State ı Thompson, 27 Mo 365, 369 (1858). Where twenty-three directors are to be elected, a vote electing twenty-two is effectual to elect those twenty-two　In re Union Ins. Co , 22 Wend , 591 (1840) A new election may be held to elect the remaining one　Id　This case holds also that a plurality is sufficient to elect.
[1] *In re* Union Ins Co , *supra*　Less than the full board may be elected The old board goes out, however, and none of them hold over　People ı Fleming, 13 N Y Supp , 715 (1891) Where five candidates receive a plurality and three others receive a less number, but the latter are a tie, the board being seven, the five are duly elected and may act as a board even though no second ballot is taken to vote off the tie Wright ı Commonwealth, 109 Pa. St, 560 (1885)　See, also, § 620.

law each stockholder had but one vote, irrespective of the number of shares held by him [1] Where the statutes are silent on the subject, a by-law may give to each shareholder one vote for each share up to ten, and may fix the proportion of votes which he may cast in excess of that number.[2]

Generally the charter or statutes prescribe that each share of stock shall be entitled to one vote [3] And a statutory or charter provision to this effect applies not only to elections, but also to all other questions that may come before the stockholders' meetings.[4]

§ 609a　*Cumulative voting* — In the constitutions of several of the states there are provisions for enabling a minority in interest of the stockholders to elect a minority of the directors This is effected by what is known as a system of cumulative voting By it each shareholder is entitled to as many votes for directors as equal the number of shares he owns multiplied by the number of directors to be elected Thus, if there are six directors to be elected, a stockholder who owns one hundred shares may poll six hundred votes; and these votes he may give entirely to one or two or more of the six candidates, as he may see fit. In this way any minority of the stockholders exceeding one-sixth part, acting together, may elect one member of a board of six directors, and thus secure a representation in that body A larger minority might secure the election of two members of such a board, the possibility of increasing the minority representation increasing as the minority increases, without it ever becoming possible for a minority upon a full vote to secure more than its equitable proportion of the representation The larger the number of directors the smaller would be the minority which would be able to elect one member of the board; and

[1] Taylor v. Griswold, 14 N. J Law, 222 (1834), declaring that a by-law to the contrary is void At common law stockholders voted by show of hands, and a large stockholder had no greater vote than a small one *In re Horbury* etc, Co, L. R. 11 Ch D, 109 (1879). Stockholders each have one vote; not even a special provision in the articles filed under a general act can change this rule Commonwealth v Nickerson, 10 Phil, 55 (1873). For an interesting statement of the origin of the practice of giving each stockholder one vote only, and of the gradual changes made in the rule, see Harvard Law Review, November, 1888, p 156 A by-law may limit the votes of a person who holds

stock in excess of ten shares. Detwiler v Commonwealth, 18 Atl Rep, 990 (Pa, 1890) See § 621, *infra.*

[2] Detwiler v Commonwealth, 18 Pa. St, 990 (Pa., 1890)

[3] Hays v Commonwealth, 82 Pa St, 518 (1876) Where by statute two-thirds of the stockholders are authorized to do an act, this is construed to mean two-thirds of the stock — at least long acquiescence therein has that effect. Fredericks v Pennsylvania Canal Co., 109 Pa. St., 50 (1885)

[4] *Re Rochester*, etc., Co., 40 Hun, 172 (1886), construing a statute which is applicable to all New York corporations.

the larger the minority the greater the representation possible to be secured.[1] Constitutional or statutory provisions which are designed to secure such a minority representation are found in California, Pennsylvania, Illinois, West Virginia, Missouri, Nebraska, Michigan and Kansas[2] These provisions, if designed to be retroactive, have been held unconstitutional and void They can only apply to corporations chartered after their enactment So far as they concern corporations chartered before the adoption of such a constitutional provision they impair the obligation of the contract between the corporation, the stockholders and the state, and infringe the vested rights of the stockholders[3] It is a serious ques-

[1] Cumulative voting given by the constitution is an absolute right, and does not require notice of the intent to so vote, nor any by-laws to give it efficacy By this provision, "if there are six directors to be elected, the single shareholder has six votes, and contrary to the old rule, he may cast these six votes for a single one of the candidates, or he may distribute them to two or more of such candidates as he may think proper He may cast two ballots for each of three of the proposed directors — three for two, or two for one, and one each for four others, or finally he may cast one vote for each of the six candidates Pierce v. Commonwealth 104 Pa. St, 150 (1883).

[2] A statutory provision to the same effect prevails in Michigan The California provision is construed in Wright v Central Cal, etc, Co 67 Cal 532 (1885), holding that this constitutional right as to voting could not be changed by a resolution of the directors The Pennsylvania provision is construed in Wright v Commonwealth 109 Pa St, 560 (1885), holding that part of the directors so elected by a plurality and declared elected may act although the remaining directors are not elected by reason of the vote as to them being a tie See, also, Commonwealth v Lintsman 6 Pitts. L J (N S), 122 The Ohio statute prescribing that each share shall entitle the owner to as many votes as there are directors to be elected does not authorize cumulative voting State

v Baumgardner 13 N E Rep 279 (Ohio, 1887) Where cumulative voting prevails and the statutes require three directors to be residents, and all the votes are cumulated on non-residents excepting thirty-two which are cast for three residents, the three residents are elected and the remaining directors are those of the non-residents who received the highest number of votes Horton v Wilder, 29 Pac Rep, 566 (Kan, 1892) As to the other states that provide for cumulative voting see Part VII, infra In Wright s Case, supra the court said that this provision conferred "upon the individual stockholder, entitled to vote at an election, the right to cast all the votes which his stock represents, multiplied by the number of directors to be elected, for a single candidate, should he think proper so to do   . or by distributing them, upon the same principle, among as many candidates for directors as he shall think fit "

[3] State v Greer, 78 Mo, 188 (1883), Hays v Commonwealth, 82 Pa. St, 518 (1876) Baker s Appeal, 109 Pa St 461 (1885) See, also, on this subject, ch XXVIII, supra Upon the question of the constitutionality of statutes providing for minority representation or cumulative voting in the election of public officers, a matter germane to the present subject, see People v. Kenney, 96 N Y, 294 (1884) People v Crissey, 91 id. 616 (1883), State v Constantine, 42 Ohio St. 437 In Michigan it has been decided that a statute providing for the cumula-

tion, however, whether such a statute or constitutional provision could not be applied to existing as well as future corporations, where the power to amend the charter has been reserved by the legislature [1]

The plan of cumulative voting is growing in popularity, and is fitted to protect the minority from the frauds of directors who are elected wholly by the majority [2]

§ 610 *Proxies* — At common law a stockholder has no right to cast his vote by proxy [3] This rule was evolved from the analogous

tive plan of voting in public elections is unconstitutional Maynard *t* Board, etc , 47 N W Rep , 756 (Mich , 1890).

[1] See § 501, *supra* In West Virginia it is held that where the legislature has the right to amend or repeal a charter, the statute giving the right to cumulate the votes applies to a corporation already existing as well as later corporations Cross *v* West Va., etc , R'y, 12 S E Rep., 1071 (W Va , 1891).

[2] Mr Simon Sterns, in the Cyclopedia of Political Science, Political Economy and United States History (vol III, p. 526), says ' The severest blow, however, which could be dealt to corporate mismanagement would be the rigorous introduction of minority representation in boards of direction, which would make secrecy of management as against the interest of shareholders substantially impossible, and would prevent the possibility of the recurrence of some of the worst abuses which characterize their administration Suppose twenty directors were to be elected, the reform would consist in allowing each section of one-twentieth of the stockholding-interest to elect one director by accumulating their votes upon a single name, or by distributing their votes for one or more, as they may see fit This is the cumulative plan Another is the preferential or list plan, in allowing each twentieth part of the constituency to elect one director by preferences indicated on a ballot in the order of the names as printed When the first name has a *quota* sufficient to elect him — *i. e*, one-twentieth of the votes cast — the bal-

lot is counted for the second name, and so forth The result of this system of minority representation would be to make of the board of directors a reduced photograph of the whole constituent body, and make it impossible to capture an organization like a railway from the actual owners thereof. Any one of the numerous plans suggested for securing minority representation, if applied to corporate management, would successfully accomplish that result. The objection which has been urged to minority representation in public representative bodies has no validity to corporate elections, as in corporations neither localities nor persons are supposed to be represented, but pecuniary interests only It would better secure fair representation than does the English system of diminished value of votes in proportion to stockholders' interest — *i e*, one vote for every share up to ten, an additional vote for every five others beyond the first ten, and one vote for every ten beyond one hundred shares· or the classification plan, by which only a few directors of the whole retire each year Minority representation would give permanency in management, and prevent the swamping of the interest of the smaller shareholders ''

[3] Taylor *v* Griswold, 14 N. J. Law, 223 (1834); Philips *v*. Wickham, 1 Paige, 590 (1829), Brown *v* Commonwealth, 3 Grant (Pa), 209 (1856), where the charter allowed only those *present* to vote; Craig *v*. First Presbyterian Church, 88 Pa. St., 42 (1878). Commonwealth *v* Bringhurst, 103 id , 134 (1883); People

rule governing municipal corporations, which requires all votes to be given in person. The right to vote by proxy is often given by the charter itself Even if not so given the right may be created by by-law.[1]

The ordinary proxy, being intended to be for an election merely, does not enable the proxy to vote to dissolve the corporation or to sell the entire corporate business and property, or to vote upon other important business, unless the proxy itself in general or special terms gives the proxy the power to vote on such questions.[2] The sale of proxies is forbidden by statute in New York.[3]

Directors may be enjoined from using the funds of the company to obtain proxies for themselves or their nominees.[4]

Where a will directs that of the three executors two shall give

v Twaddell, 18 Hun, 427, 430 (1879); Case of the Dean and Chapter of Fernes, Davies, 116, 120 (1608), Attorney-General v Scott, 1 Vesey, 413 (1749), Harben v Phillips, L R, 23 Ch D, 14, 22, 36 (1882) Where the statute allows citizens to vote by proxy, an alien is not within its terms, and cannot do so In re Barker, 6 Wend, 509 (1890)

[1] People v Crossley, 69 Ill, 195 (1873), Philips v Wickham, 1 Paige, 590, 598 (1829), State v Tudor, 5 Day (Conn), 329 (1812), 2 Kent's Commentaries, 294, 295 A contrary rule is laid down in New Jersey Taylor v Griswold 14 N J Law, 222 (1834) Where the charter authorizes voting by proxy at elections for directors and also empowers directors to make by-laws not inconsistent with the laws of the commonwealth a by-law adopted by the board of directors allowing voting by proxy at all stock elections was held valid Wilson v Academy of Music, 43 Leg Int. 86 A by-law may allow voting by proxy Detwiler v Commonwealth, 18 Atl Rep, 990 (Pa, 1890) Where the statute gives a right to vote by proxy, a by-law to the effect that only a stockholder can act as proxy is illegal and void Matter of Lighthall, etc, Co, 47 Hun, 258 (1888) A corporation as a stockholder may of course give a proxy where proxies are allowed In re Indiana, etc., Co, L R, 26 Ch D, 70 (1884)

[2] Abbot v American Hard Rubber Co, 33 Barb, 578, 584 (1861), Cumberland Coal Co v Sherman, 30 Barb, 553, 577 (1859), Matter of Wheeler, 2 Abb Pr (N S), 361 (1866), where the proxy, being authorized to vote for increasing the stock, voted also to issue the new stock in exchange for the stock of another company Marie v Garrison, 13 Abb N C, 210, 235 (1882) Where directors are authorized by charter to vote by proxy the proxy cannot authorize a borrowing of money — an *ultra vires* and void act in England Brown v Byers, 16 M & W, 252 (1847) A proxy to vote is not a proxy to demand a poll In re Haven, etc, Co, L R, 20 Ch D, 151 (1881), Reg v Gov Stock Co, L R, 3 Q B D, 442 (1878) See, also, Decatur, etc, Co v Neal, 12 S Rep, 780 (1893) A proxy for an election does not extend to an election four months later the first election not having been held, the proxy being by a director, the directors being authorized to vote by proxy Howard v Hull, 5 Ry & Corp L J 255 (Eng, 1888)

[3] See Part VII, *infra* It is illegal for a stockholder to sell his right to vote Hafer v New York, etc, R R, 14 Week L Bul 68 (1885)

[4] Studdert v Grosvenor, 55 L T Rep, 171 (1886).

proxies to the third on stock owned by the estate, a court of equity will compel the two to give the proxies although the third intends to use the proxy to continue himself as president, and the management of the company is alleged to be fraudulent and ruinous [1]

A proxy should be in writing, but it need not be in any particular form, it need not be acknowledged or proved, but it must be in such a shape as reasonably to satisfy the inspectors of election of its genuineness and validity [2] And to this end the corporate officers may insist upon reasonable evidence of the regularity and genuineness of the proxy before allowing it to be voted [3]

Where certificates of proxies are destroyed after use, parol evidence is admissible to prove their former existence and sufficiency.[4]

A member who signs a form of proxy in blank, and hands it over to another to be used in the ordinary way, impliedly authorizes that other to fill up the blank with his own name.[5]

A proxy is always revocable Even when by its terms it is made "irrevocable," the law allows the stockholder to revoke it. Frequently an attempt is made to permanently unite the voting power of several stockholders and thus control the corporation by giving irrevocable proxies to specified persons But the law allows the stockholder to revoke the proxy at any time [6]

[1] This case was affirmed on an even division of the court Lafferty v Lafferty, 26 Atl Rep 388 (Pa, 1893). Tunis v Hustonville, etc, R R, 24 Atl Rep, 88 (Pa, 1892).

[2] In the Matter of Election of St Lawrence Steamboat Co, 44 N J Law 529 (1882), In re Indian, etc Co, L R, 26 Ch D, 70 (1884) See the form of proxy in Marie v Garrison, 13 Abb N C, 210, 234 (1883) Proxies need not be acknowledged, proved or witnessed Matter of Cecil, 36 How Pr, 477 (1869) A proxy need not state the day upon which the election is to be held In re Townsend, 18 N Y Supp, 905 (1892). A proxy is good although the date when it is given is left blank and has not been filled in In Matter of St Lawrence, etc, Co, supra Where one gave a proxy to vote at an annual election, it was held prima facie evidence that he was a stockholder just before such election Harger v McCullough, 2 Denio, 119, 122 (1846) A proxy which had been exercised and voted upon for many years without renewal was sus-

tained in Mousseaux v. Urquhart, 19 La Ann, 482 (1867)

[3] In Matter of St. Lawrence, etc., Co., supra But the inspectors have no right to refuse a vote by proxy or to assume a judicial power to try its genuineness if it is apparently executed by the stockholder and is regular in form. Matter of Cecil, 36 How Pr, 477 (1869) Neither the stockholder nor his proxy can be compelled by a by-law to take an oath that the former is the owner of the stock People v Tibbits, 4 Cowen, 358 (1825) People v Kip, 4 Cowen, 382 (1822) The by-laws may require the proxies to be witnessed Harben v. Phillips, L R, 23 Ch D, 14 (1882).

[4] Haywood & Pittsborough Plankroad Co v Bryan, 6 Jones' L (N. C.), 82 (1858).

[5] Ex parte Duce, L R, 13 Ch D, 429; Ex parte Lancaster, L R, 5 Ch D, 911 As to whether a blank proxy may be filled in by the agent, see quære in Re White v N Y, etc, Soc, 45 Hun, 580 (1887), citing cases.

[6] Woodruff v Dubuque, etc., R R Co,

§ 611. *The transfer book as evidence of a right to vote* — The question who is entitled to vote upon a particular share of stock is, as a general rule, answered by a reference to the corporate transfer book. He who is there registered as the owner of the stock is entitled to vote upon it [1] It is not necessary that the owner of stock produce his certificate or even have a certificate in order to vote [2]

30 Fed Rep, 91 (1887) In this case the stock certificates were turned over to trustees to transfer to themselves, with power to vote, hold or sell the same "Trust" certificates were issued The court held that at any time previous to an actual sale by the trustees a certificate-holder might revoke his interest in the "trust" and demand back his part of the stock To same effect and on very similar facts, see Griffith v Jewett, 15 Weekly Law Bull, 419 Vanderbilt v Bennett, 2 Ry & Corp. L J, 409 (Pa, 1887) Such irrevocable proxies are not necessarily void as against public policy Brown v Pacific Mail Steamship Co, 5 Blatch, 525 (1867) It simply is revocable A proxy given for a valuable consideration may nevertheless be revoked if it is about to be used for a fraudulent purpose Reed v Bank of Newburgh, 6 Paige, 337 (1837) An agreement not to revoke a power which from its nature or by law is revocable is not binding People v Nash 111 N Y, 310, 315 (1888) A written contract not to vote by proxy, entered into by certain shareholders mutually for the purpose of preventing the board of directors from consummating a proposed sale of the franchises of the corporation, has been held a pernicious and unlawful compact Fisher v Bush 35 Hun, 641 (1885) An irrevocable proxy is prohibited by statute in New York It may be revoked even though coupled with an interest in this case being to a pledgee Matter of Germicide Co 65 Hun, 606 (1892) A proxy for five years given so as to unite enough stock to control the corporation, the holder of the proxy agreeing that the person giving the proxy shall have an office at a

salary of $2,500 a year, is void At the instance of the latter person a court of equity will enjoin voting thereunder Coues Ex'rs v Russell, 21 Atl Rep, 847 (N J, 1891)

[1] "The general rule is that, as between the corporation and the person offering to vote, the right follows the legal title, of which the certificates and stock books are the *prima facie* evidence By-laws may establish a different rule, and there may be special circumstances to change the equities as to individuals or even as to the corporation" Commonwealth v Dalzell, 25 Atl Rep, 535 (Pa), *Ex parte* Willcocks, 7 Cowen 402 (1827), stating, however, that in certain cases like that of stock held for the corporation itself, a different rule prevails, State v Ferris 42 Conn, 560, 568 (1875), sustaining a vote by a bankrupt, the court saying 'The party who appears to be the owner by the books of the corporation has the right to be treated as a stockholder and to vote on whatever stock stands in his name' Hoppin v Buffum 9 R I, 513 (1870) the court saying "In a case of a dispute as to a right to vote, the books of the corporation are the *prima facie* evidence at any rate, the corporation cannot be required to decide a disputed right Upon any other rule it could never be known who were entitled to vote until the courts had decided the dispute" Allen v Hill, 16 Cal, 113 (1860), *In re* St Lawrence, etc Co, 44 N J L. 529 (1882) See also, next section for various cases on the conclusiveness of the transfer book

[2] Beckett v Houston, 32 Ind, 393 (1869)

Neither will indebtedness for the subscription price prevent the stockholder from voting[1] So, also, it is immaterial that the person in whose name the stock is registered is merely the nominal holder, and that another person really owns the stock[2] A subscriber upon a condition not yet performed may vote upon the question whether that condition shall or shall not be performed.[3] And stock issued for construction, the work not having been performed, may nevertheless be voted.[4]

Persons who are not stockholders on the day an election is held cannot vote though they were stockholders on the day the election should have been held[5] The corporation may be compelled to register transfers made merely for the purpose of increasing the voting power of the stock, there being a limit to the number of votes one stockholder may cast[6] The holders of stock issued by a stock dividend are entitled to vote[7]

Where the corporation keeps a stock certificate book but no transfer book, a transfer on the back of a certificate, which is then canceled and pasted back in the certificate book, and a new certificate issued to the transferee, is a sufficient transfer to constitute a transferee a stockholder[8] If the stock book is lost the directors

[1] Birmingham etc. Ry Co ι Locke. 1 Q B., 256 (1841). Savage v Ball. 17 N J Eq, 142 (1861), People v Albany, etc, R. R. 55 Barb. 344, 386 (1869) Downing ι Potts, 23 N J Law, 66 (1851) So held in this case, even though the subscriber had paid nothing on his stock

[2] State of Nevada v Leete, 16 Nev, 242 (1881), where a man put stock in the name of his son in order to qualify him to serve as a director

[3] Greenville, etc, R. R. Co. ι Coleman, 5 Rich Law (S C), 118, 135 (1851).

[4] Savage ι Ball, 17 N J Eq. 142 (1861) Where a sale of bonds having a voting power is made subject to the ratification of another party, the vendor has the right to vote such bonds until the sale is so ratified State ι McDaniel, 22 Ohio St. 354 (1872) The registered stockholder may vote even though he has transferred his certificates to another In re Argus, etc, Co. 48 N W Rep., 347 (N D, 1891)

[5] Johnston v Jones, 23 N J Eq 216, 228 (1872).

[6] In re Stranton Iron & Steel Co, L R, 16 Eq, 559 (1873). Moffatt v Farquhar, L R, 7 Ch D, 591 (1878). See, also, § 618 But where valuable privileges other than voting attach to stock, a nominal transfer to obtain these privileges will not be sustained as regards them Appeal of the Academy of Music, 108 Pa St, 510 (1885), where free admission to a theatre was given to stockholders

[7] Bailey v Railroad Co, 22 Wall, 604, 637 (1874) But the rule is otherwise as regards the holders of a scrip dividend. Id, where the scrip was redeemable by the company in cash or convertible into stock

[8] He may vote at elections, and an assignment by the corporation on the direction of officers elected by such a transferee is valid Such a transfer is valid also, although a by-law provided that before selling his stock a stockholder must offer it to other stockholders for purchase American Nat'l Bank v Oriental Mills, 23 Atl Rep, 795 (R I, 1891)

may substitute a new one, filled out as accurately as is possible[1] Where the transfer book differs from the stock ledger the former governs.[2] A by-law authorizing the administration of an oath to examine the stockholders as to their title is illegal and void where the charter regulates the right to vote[3]

There are some exceptions, however, to the rule that the transfer book is conclusive on the question of who is entitled to vote Thus, the inspectors of election may inquire whether the stock which is about to be voted belongs to the corporation, and if it does they may reject the vote.[4] So, also, they may allow an administrator to vote, although the stock stands in the name of the deceased person[5]

In some courts this rule is carried still further, and it is held that the inspectors of election may allow the pledgor to vote, although the stock stands in the name of the pledgee on the books of the company,[6] and it has also been held that the purchaser of certificates of stock may vote thereon, although the stock stands on the books of the company in the name of the vendor[7]

[1] *Re Schoharie, etc., R. R.*, 12 Abb. Pr (N S.), 394

[2] *Downing v Potts*, 23 N J L., 66 (1851).

[3] *People v Kip*, 4 Cowen, 382, note (1822)

[4] See § 613, *infra*.

[5] See § 612, *infra*.

[6] See § 612, *infra*

[7] In the case *Allen v Hill*, 16 Cal, 113 (1860), the court said "It would seem, upon principle, that the real owner of stock should be entitled to represent it at the meetings of the corporation, and that the mere fact that he does not appear as owner upon the books of the company should not exclude him from the privilege of doing so." In Illinois it is held that the corporation must allow the real owner of the stock to vote whether he be the registered owner or not, where the corporation has no by-law requiring a registry of transfers, and the vendee produces his certificate of stock duly transferred on the back *People v Devin*, 17 Ill, 84 (1855). In a stockholder's vote ratifying the acts of directors, a stockholder has no right to vote stock which he has transferred to others, even though it still stands in his name on the books. *Graves v Mono etc. Co*, 22 Pac Rep, 665 (Cal, 1889). Where, however, the unregistered transferee did not challenge the right of his transferrer to vote and did not claim the right to vote, but attacked the election afterwards by *quo warranto*, his suit failed *People v. Robinson*, 64 Cal, 373 (1883) *State v Smith*, 15 Ore, 98, 118 (1887), contains a *dictum* that the purchaser of a certificate of stock cannot vote on the stock until it has been transferred into his name Where both the legal and equitable owners of stock agree as to how stock shall be voted, other stockholders cannot complain that the vote was not cast in accordance with law *State v. Ferris* 42 Conn, 560 (1875), where a bankrupt voted stock still standing in his name *State v Pettineli*, 10 Nev, 141 (1875) In this last case the registered holder had transferred the certificate but obtained it again and exhibited it at the meeting. If a vote is not challenged an objection to it afterwards may not meet with much favor In the Matter of Long Island R R, 19 Wend, 37, 44 (1837) See, also, § 620, *infra*

In New York, by statute, the corporate transfer book is made conclusive upon the question who may vote[1] There are various other statutory provisions in New York regulating voting[2]

§ 612 *The right of trustees, pledgees, administrators, etc, to vote* — It is the general rule that a person holding stock as trustee is entitled to vote upon the stock, not only where he is duly registered as a stockholder in that capacity, but also where he is registered absolutely as a stockholder upon the books of the corporation.[3] If the trustee, however, is disqualified from being trustee of the stock, as in the case of a trust company that represents conflicting interests, the courts will enjoin it from voting.[4]

[1] Vandenburgh v Broadway Railway Co, 29 Hun, 318, 355 (1883), In the Matter of the Long Island R R Co, 19 Wend, 37 (1837), In the Matter of the Mohawk & Hudson R R Co, id, 135 (1838) A registered stockholder is entitled to vote although he has assigned his certificate of stock Schoharie Valley R R Case, 12 Abb Pr (N S), 394 (1872).

[2] See § 619 *infra* Strong v Smith, 15 Hun 222 (1878), holding that the transfer book is conclusive upon the inspectors, but that the court has power to go back of the entries therein and inquire whether, as for instance in this case, a transfer of shares was an absolute sale or a pledge, and thus whether the transferer or transferee has the right to vote them, citing *Ex parte* Holmes, 5 Cow, 426, Matter of Long Island R R Co, *supra*, and see N Y L J, June 29 1880 Although only stockholders who still own their stock are allowed to vote, a person who has given an option on his stock is nevertheless entitled to vote on it *In re* Newcombe, 18 N Y Supp, 16 (1891) In New York, when for any reason the corporation fails to hold an election at the stated time as provided in the charter or by-laws, and the election is held subsequently, only those stockholders are entitled to vote who were qualified electors at the time when the election ought to have been held Vandenburgh v Broadway R R Co, 29 Hun, 348 (1883); People v Tibbets, 4 Cowan, 358 (1825).

[3] Widow Conant v Millaudon, 5 La Ann, 542 (1850), Wilson v Proprietors of Central Bridge, 9 R I, 590 (1870); Hoppin v Buffum, 9 id, 513 (1870), the court saying ' If the trust was of such a nature that the trustee has the control and management of the property, and is to exercise his discretion concerning it, he is the proper person to represent and vote upon it And the corporation cannot be required to examine into the nature of the trust with a view to decide as to the right to vote." *In re* Barker, 6 Wend, 509 (1831); In the Matter of the Mohawk & Hudson R R Co, 19 id, 135 (1838), In the Matter of the North Shore Staten Island Ferry Co, 63 Barb, 556 (1872), holding, also, that the administrator of the trustee may vote the stock, Pender v. Lushington, L R, 6 Ch D, 70 (1877). If the trustees disagree as to how the stock shall be voted the courts have power to direct them Wanneker v Hitchcock, 38 Fed Rep., 383 (1889).

[4] A trust company has no power to hold as trustee and vote the majority of the stock of a great railroad system, especially where it is also the trustee in a trust deed of the company. Clarke v. Central R R, etc, 50 Fed Rep., 338 (1892), the court saying "There are many situations in which stock may be so placed that it becomes inequitable or illegal for it to be voted The law places the voting power of pledged stock in the pledgor or mortgagor, even where there is no express stipulation to that

In California the real owner of stock may vote on it, although it stands on the books of the company in the name of a "dummy" as "trustee."[1]

A pledgor of stock is entitled to vote upon it in all cases where the stock continues to stand on the books of the company in the name of such pledgor[2] And even where the pledgee has caused the stock to be transferred into his own name, as by law he is allowed to do,[3] it has been held that the pledgor may demand the right to vote at elections, and that upon proof of the facts, the inspectors of election must allow the pledgor to vote the stock[4]

It must be conceded, however, that the established rule is to the contrary.[5] Nevertheless the pledgor may control the vote on his

effect. And where the pledgor or mortgagor is disqualified to vote the stock the disqualification extends as well to the pledgee or trustee '

[1] Under the California statute stock placed by the secretary in the name of a "dummy,' as trustee, cannot be voted by such dummy the real owners of the stock not having assented thereto, even though for business reasons they did not wish to have the stock issued to themselves Stewart z Mahoney Min Co, 54 Cal, 149 (1880) To same effect, *Ex parte* Holmes, 5 Cowen, 426 (1826). See, also, American Nat'l Bank z Oriental Mills, 23 Atl Rep, 795 (R. I, 1891), holding that the beneficial owners are entitled to say how the vote shall be cast. In this case the stock had been surrendered and new certificates issued, but no transfer book was kept

[2] *In re* Barker, 6 Wend, 509 (1831), *Ex parte* Willcocks, 7 Cowen 402 (1827), Matter of Cecil, 36 How Prac, 177 (1869), Schofield v Union Bank, 2 Cr C C, 115 (1815) Matter of Election of St Lawrence, etc, Co, 44 N J L, 529, 540 (1882), a *dictum* Although the pledgor of stock votes the stock in favor of a lease of the corporate property on such terms that no dividends on the stock are possible, yet in the absence of fraud the pledgee is bound Gibson v Richmond, etc, R. R, 37 Fed Rep, 743 (1889).

See § 466

[3] In Oregon it is held that at common

law the real owner of stock is entitled to vote it even though it stands on the corporate books in the name of his pledgee It is denied that the transfer book is binding upon the inspectors of election and the decisions to that effect in New York are stated to be based on the New York statutory law State v Smith, 15 Oreg, 98 (1887) See, also, Allen v Hill, 16 Cal, 119 (1860), to substantially the same effect.

[5] The pledgor and pledgee of stock may agree between themselves as to who should vote the stock If there is no agreement, the right to vote should follow the legal title, in other words, the title as it appears on the corporate books Even under a statute authorizing inspectors of election, upon a challenge, to determine whether the party who appears to be the owner is really the owner the pledgee is entitled to vote the stock standing in his name where there is no agreement to the contrary Commonwealth z Dalzell, 25 Atl Rep, 535 (Pa) A pledgee into whose name the stock has been transferred may vote it He is a "*bona fide*" stockholder as required by the statute The pledgor cannot appear at the meeting and vote the stock *In re* Argus Printing Co, 48 N W Rep, 347 (N D 1891) It is not a conversion for one who holds stock as pledgee to attend corporate meetings and vote upon the stock Heath z Silverthorn Lead Mining, etc, Co, 39 Wis, 146 (1875)

stock if he desires so to do   In many of the states there are statutes which give to the pledgor the right to vote the stock [1] And
even where there is no statute to protect the pledgor's right to
vote the courts will intervene.[2] By a bill in equity the pledgor
may compel the pledgee to give him a proxy to vote the stock.[3]
But in order to invoke the extraordinary powers of a court of
equity in this respect, the pledgor must show that the interests of
the company have been or will be prejudiced, or that the value of
the stock has been or will be impaired, and that the intervention
of the court is necessary to protect the pledgor's rights.[4]

An administrator or executor may vote on the stock of the deceased stockholder, even though such stock has not been transferred to the executor or administrator on the books of the company.[5] A partner may vote upon stock belonging to the firm and

[1] So in New York, see Part VII, infra
Also Strong v Smith, 15 Hun, 222 (1878)
Concerning a similar statute in Rhode
Island, see Sayles v Brown, 40 Fed Rep,
8 (1889) Under the Colorado statutes
an owner who has pledged his stock
may represent the stock at all meetings
of the stockholders and vote accordingly Miller et al v Murray, 30 Pac
Rep, 46 (Col, 1892)

[2] Schofield v Union Bank, 2 Cr C C,
115 (1815), State v. Smith 15 Oreg, 98
(1887) where the pledgor obtained an injunction against the pledgee voting the
stock and the pledgor was allowed by
the inspectors to vote

[3] Vowell v Thompson, 3 Cranch, C C,
428 (1829), Hoppin v Buffum, 9 R I,
513 (1870), holding that although the
pledgor may by a bill in equity compel
the pledgee, in whose name the stock
stands, to make a retransfer or to give
a proxy to the pledgor, yet where the
pledgor for many years allows the
pledgee to vote the stock and claims the
right at an election only after the ballots are cast and are being counted, the
court will not set the election aside

[4] McHenry v Jewett, 93 N Y, 58
(1882) Where the owner of a majority
of the stock has been fraudulently deprived of her stock by her pledgee, who
has thereby deprived her of the control
and claims the stock as his own, the

court will enjoin him from voting the
stock and will appoint a receiver of
such stock pendente lite Ayer v Seymour, 5 N Y Supp 650 (Com Pl, 1889).
Where a person pledges his stock as additional security to a corporate creditor
who has bonds of the company in pledge
for the same debt, such pledge of bonds,
however, being illegal, the pledgor of
the stock cannot compel the creditor to
resort to the bonds first, nor although a
fictitious sale of the stock is alleged can
he compel the transferee of the stock
to return the stock so that the pledgor
may vote it unless the pledgor pays the
amount due Hinckley v Pfister, 53 N.
W Rep, 21 (Wis, 1892)

[5] A foreign executor may vote stock
belonging to the estate even though the
stock stands in the name of the deceased
stockholder In re Cape, etc, Co, 16
Atl Rep, 191 (N. J, 1888), In the Matter of the North Shore Staten Island
Ferry Co, 63 Barb, 556 (1872), holding
that an administrator may vote upon
stock standing in the name of the deceased person, even though the latter
held the stock as trustee. Stock held
jointly by three executors cannot be
voted unless they all agree upon the
vote Tunis v Hestonville, etc, R. R.,
24 Atl Rep, 88 (1892) In a proceeding
to dissolve a corporation the administrator is the proper representative of

registered in the partnership name[1] Where stock is entered in the corporate books in the name of a person as an officer of another corporation, the successor in office of that person may vote the stock without a transfer on the corporate books[2] Where a corporation is authorized to hold stock in another corporation it is entitled to vote such stock[3] When a municipal corporation is a stockholder in a private corporation it is entitled to vote upon its stock in the same way as any other stockholder[4] The fact that the government or a single person owns all the stock of a company does not put an end to the corporate existence[5] Where joint owners of stock disagree as to its vote, the vote is to be rejected[6] A corporation as a stockholder may vote its stock by an agent[7]

A receiver who is in possession of shares of stock generally votes such stock without his right to do so being questioned Sometimes the courts upon appointing a receiver of stock expressly authorize him to vote the stock and sometimes direct him how to vote it.[8]

stock owned by the estate Wolfe v Underwood, 12 S. Rep, 234 (Ala, 1893). The administrator and not the heirs at law have the right to vote Schoharie Valley R. R. Case, 12 Abb Pr (N S.), 394 (1872).

[1] Kenton Furnace Railroad and Mfg Co v McAlpin, 5 Fed Rep, 737 (1880). In California he may vote such stock where the stock belongs to the firm but is registered in the name of the other partner who is dead Allen v Hill, 16 Cal, 113 (1860)

[2] Farmers', etc, Co v Chicago. etc, R'y Co 27 Fed Rep., 146, 156 (1886), Mousseaux v Urquhart, 19 La. Ann, 482 (1867) Contra, In the Matter of the Mohawk & Hudson R. R. Co, 19 Wend, 135, 146 (1838), holding that the word "cashier" attached to a stockholder's name does not authorize a succeeding cashier to vote the stock.

[3] Davis v U. S, etc, Co. 25 Atl Rep, 982 (Md., 1893). Cf § 616

[4] See § 99, supra Where stock in a railroad is owned by a part of a county, that part becomes a municipality for the purpose of owning and voting the stock. Hancock v Louisville, etc, R. R, 145 U. S, 409 (1892)

[5] The United States government, though the owner of all the stock of a canal company, may continue as a stockholder and keep up the corporate existence by allowing the directors to retain one share each as a qualification share United States v Louisville, etc Canal Co., 4 Dill, 601 (1873) See also, § 769, infra

[6] Re Pioneer Paper Co, 36 How. Pr, 111 (1865)

[7] State v Rohlffs, 19 Atl. Rep, 1099 (N J, 1890)

[8] A court may appoint a receiver to hold an election, etc. where the entire interests in the corporation, including the stock, belong to parties who have been defrauded King v Barnes, 51 Hun, 550 (1889), aff'd. 113 N Y. 655 See, also, dictum in Wanneker v Hitchcock, 38 Fed Rep, 333 (1889), where the trustees of stock disagreed as to voting, People v Albany, etc, R R, 55 Barb, 344, 371 (1869), where a receiver's vote was set aside, fraud being involved and the appointment being invalid, American Ins Co v Yost, 25 Abb N C, 274 (1890), where a receiver of stock was instructed how to vote, the action being to enforce an agreement to place stock

§ 613 *The corporation cannot vote upon shares of its own stock*
Shares of stock owned by the corporation itself cannot be voted
either directly by the corporate officers or indirectly by a trustee
of the corporation This is the established rule, whether the stock
is registered in the name of the corporation or not.[1]

Where the directors, just before the election, issue or sell stock
owned by the corporation, the purpose of such issue or sale being
to control the election, the courts will interfere at the instance of
other stockholders where an actual fraud is involved [2]

§ 614 *Injunction against elections and against voting particular
stock* — A court of equity has power to enjoin the holding of an
election by a corporation during the pendency of a suit.[3]

in the hands of trustees until the debts
of the company and chief stockholder
were paid

[1] *Ex parte* Holmes, 5 Cowen, 426
(1826), McNeely *v* Woodruff, 13 N J
Law, 352 (1833), American Railway
Frog Co *v* Haven, 101 Mass, 398 (1869),
State *t* Smith, 48 Vt., 266 (1876), Monsseaux *v* Urquhart, 19 La Ann 482
(1867), United States *v* Columbian
Ins. Co, 2 Cranch, C C., 266 (1821),
New England Mutual, etc, Ins. Co *v*
Phillips, 141 Mass, 535 (1880) where income bonds entitled to vote were held
to have lost that right when they were
paid, Brewster *v* Hartley 37 Cal, 15
(1869), where the company had pledged
its stock If all the stockholders consent the stock owned by the corporation may be voted Farwell *v* Houghton, etc, Works, 8 Fed Rep, 66 (1881).
Where a mortgage can be given only
upon the vote of the stockholders, stock
owned by the corporation cannot be
voted, but the pledgee of such stock
from the corporation was allowed to
vote. Vail *v* Hamilton, 85 N Y, 453
(1881) Directors elected by votes upon
stock owned by the corporation are illegally elected *Ex parte* Desdoity, 1
Wend, 98 (1828).

[2] See § 615, *infra*, on this subject.

[3] In the case of Walker *v* Devereaux,
4 Paige, 229, 247 (1833), Chancellor Walworth said "This court unquestionably
has the power to prevent their election
by an injunction operating upon the

commissioners, restraining them from
acting as inspectors of the election"
In Haight *v* Day, 1 John., 18 (1814),
Chancellor Kent dissolved the injunction but did not question the power of
the court to grant it. High on Injunc-
tions, sec. 1230, says. "While the propriety of equitable interference by
injunction with the election of officers
of private corporations has been frequently criticised, and with no incon-
siderable show of injustice, the jurisdiction itself, although sparingly exercised,
is too firmly established to be readily
shaken without the intervention of legislative authority The jurisdiction is,
however, almost entirely of American
growth, the English authorities affording few instances of its exercise" A
court of equity has jurisdiction on a bill
in equity to enjoin an election, although
the statute provides for a summary remedy by application to the court where
the relief asked for by the bill involves
also the transfer of stock. Archer *v.*
American, etc, Co, 24 Atl. Rep., 508
(N J, 1892) The court may enjoin the
company from receiving any votes at
an election unless the votes of the
plaintiff are received Brown *v* Pacific
Mail, etc, Co, 5 Blatch, 525 (1867). In
the latter case Judge Blatchford said:
"As to the character of the injunction
asked for, it is laid down in Judge Redfield's Treatise on the Law of Railways
(vol 2, sec. 221), that 'it has been common to produce a positive effect through

· A court of equity may also enjoin the voting of particular stock In order to obtain such an injunction, however, the complainant must show that the defendant intends to vote the stock, that he has no equitable right to do so that the effect of the vote will be to control the election, and that irreparable and permanent injury will come to the corporation or to the stockholders unless the injunction is granted [1]

an injunction out of chancery by means of a prohibitory order,' and that a mandatory order is in courts of equity, seldom denied unless the remedy at law is perfectly adequate" In this case Judge Blatchford enjoined the election inspectors from holding any election until the further order of the court, unless certain persons should first be permitted to vote certain stock, and also enjoined certain persons from voting any stock until after certain other persons had been afforded an opportunity to vote their stock In the case of Shelmerdine v Welsh 47 Legal Intell, 26 (Phil Com Pl, January, 1890) the court did not deny its power to enjoin the election, but said "The case is not sufficiently clear to warrant a preliminary injunction that would prevent an election on the day named in the charter and might cause the irreparable injury which such remedies are given to prevent." If the election is held in violation of an injunction, this fact will be considered in quo warranto proceedings People v Albany, etc, R R 55 Barb 344, 381 (1869) The injunction generally runs against the inspectors, president, directors, officers, agents, servants, etc Campbell v Poultney, 6 Gill & J (Md) 44 (1834) It has been held that an injunction permanently forbidding the holding of any election whatever is an interference with the management of corporate affairs, to which the courts will decline to be a party, and such an injunction would, if granted, be void People v Albany, etc, R R Co, 55 Barb, 344 (1869), holding that while an injunction forbidding inspectors to hold an election at all or to receive and count

the votes thereof is entirely void, since a court of equity has no power to restrain permanently an officer of a corporation from performing the ordinary duties of his office, yet they may be enjoined from holding an election until the further order of the court or from receiving the votes of certain stockholders until the votes of others are deposited But an injunction may be granted staying an election Scholfield v Union B, 2 Cr (C C), 115 (1815), where the inspectors denied the right of pledgors to vote

[1] Reed v Jones, 6 Wis, 680 (1858), holding that a preliminary injunction against a stockholder voting his stock cannot be granted on the ground that he had no title to the land which he conveyed in payment of the stock The stock had not been canceled by the company, and no action was pending to cancel it. McHenry v Jewett, 90 N Y, 58 (1882), where the preliminary injunction was denied, inasmuch as the complaint showed no equitable cause of action Where the owner of a majority of the stock has been fraudulently deprived of her stock by her pledgee, who has thereby deprived her of the control and claims the stock as his own the court will enjoin him from voting the stock and will appoint a receiver of such stock pendente lite Ayer v Seymour, 5 N Y Supp, 650 (Com Pl, 1889) An injunction against a stockholder's voting certain stock is not an injunction to ' suspend the general and ordinary business of a corporation" Reed v Jones 6 Wis, 608 (1858) An election is not such business 1J

Thus an injunction has been granted where there was a conspiracy to obtain on the eve of the election an injunction against the complainants from voting their stock,[1] also where the directors propose to postpone the election in order to prolong their term of office,[2] also where a stockholder has transferred part of his stock in order to increase the voting power of the stock, the charter limiting the number of votes one stockholder may cast,[3] also where a majority of stock is owned by a competing company which has acquired control for the purpose of diverting business to itself,[4] also where "trustees," who are mere agents, refuse to transfer the stock to their principals or to give proxies[5]

Where the owner of a majority of the stock sells it, the purchase price being only paid in part, and retains the stock in his name until the full price is paid, he cannot be compelled to deliver the stock or to refrain from ousting the vendee from the presidency of the corporation where the vendee fails to meet the other payments, even though the vendee has proceeded to improve the property.[6]

Equity has jurisdiction to compel the transfer of stock as between parties. Hence where stock is issued in payment for property, and the party to whom the certificate is issued refuses to divide it among the owners of the property, as provided by contract, a court of equity may compel the division and may enjoin any election of the corporation until such division is made.[7]

The general rule is that one stockholder has nothing to do with the motive of another stockholder. The injunction must be based

[1] Brown v Pacific Mail, etc , 5 Blatch , 525 (1867, in which the allegation was that the defendants contemplated, through improper means, to obtain an injunction preventing plaintiffs, who were large stockholders in a corporation, from voting at an approaching election, and that defendants were improperly obtaining proxies from other stockholders in order to control the election for their private purposes The complainant alleged that defendants intended to obtain control for the benefit of rival companies and intended fraudulently to prevent the complainants from voting. The court enjoined defendants from participating in any election unless plaintiffs' votes were received thereat, and from restraining plaintiffs in their right to vote.

[2] A stockholder may enjoin directors from postponing an annual election which comes in February, but which the directors by by-law have changed to October, thereby endeavoring to extend their term Elkins v. Camden, etc , R. R., 36 N J Eq , 467 (1883) See, also, Camden, etc , R. R v Elkins, 37 id , 274 (1883)

[3] Webb v Ridgely, 38 Md , 364 (1873), where stock had been colorably transferred without consideration for the purpose of controlling an election, there being a provision in the charter prohibiting a single stockholder from voting on more than twenty shares See, also, § 621

[4] See § 616

[5] See § 622.

[6] Stockton v Russell, 54 Fed. Rep., 224 (1892)

[7] Archer v American, etc., Co., 24 Atl Rep , 508 (N. J., 1892).

on damage reasonably certain to ensue.[1]   Accordingly, an injunction will not be granted upon the ground that the stockholders against whom the injunction is sought are likely to obtain control of the affairs of the company, and that then they will probably misuse their power.[2]   The form of the injunction order varies, of course, with the circumstances of the case.   The federal courts have sanctioned a form, which, while drastic in its terms, is effective in reaching the desired result, and is none too severe when the difficulties are considered.[3]

Where a party is enjoined from voting the court will enjoin his proxy from voting.[4]

The proxy may be enjoined although his principal is not made a party and is not served.[5]   But stockholders who are not made parties will not be enjoined.[6]   The injunction against certain persons voting certain stock does not prevent the election from taking place   On the contrary, the election goes on and is valid, even though it happen that what would have been a minority of the votes, had not the injunction issued, becomes, by reason thereof, a majority, and elects.[7]   Where the injunction is applied for at a time so near the election that the opposition will have no reasonable opportunity to be heard, the court may refuse the application on that ground.[8]   The practice of serving an injunction after the meeting has assembled is not looked upon with favor by the courts.[9]   Where an injunction has been obtained on false affidavits and bill to control an election, and the proceedings in court

---

[1] Ryder v Alton, etc, R R Co, 13 Ill, 516 (1851), where a subscriber failed in his defense against a subscription by attacking the policy of the majority in control

[2] Camden, etc, R. R. Co v Elkins, 37 N J Eq, 273 (1883). Cf Brown v Pacific Mail, etc, Co, supra

[3] See the form of injunction granted in Brown v Pacific etc, Co, 5 Blatch, 525   Approved in People v Albany, etc, R. R, 55 Barb, 344, 383 (1869).

[4] Clarke v Central R R, etc, 50 Fed Rep., 338 (1892)

[5] Brown v Pacific Mail, etc, Co, 5 Blatch, 525 (1867)

[6] Id

[7] Brown v Pacific Mail Steamship Co (1867), supra

[8] Where a bill was filed to restrain certain shareholders from selling or assigning their stock, or from voting upon

it at an ensuing election, which was to be held within three days from the date of the filing of the bill, the court held that inasmuch as the probable effect of the injunction would be to change the result of the election, and the consequent control of the affairs of the company, without allowing the shareholders sought to be restrained to be heard in their own defense, the injunction ought to be denied   Hilles v Parish, 14 N J Eq, 380 (1862)   It appears, however, that counsel stipulated for a new election in case the complainant succeeded and the court so ordered

[9] "The practice of procuring an injunction and serving it, after the meeting had assembled, is not to be commended, and should only be tolerated in cases where the right thereto is clearly established" In re Rochester, etc, Co, 40 Hun, 172 (1886)

are discontinued immediately after the election, the court will summarily vacate and set aside the election by reason of the abuse of the process of the court and the fraud on the rights of the stockholders [1] An appeal from an injunction against voting certain stock will be dismissed where the parties may, under a statute, apply to the court to review the election on affidavits.[2]

§ 615 *Issuing stock in order to carry an election* — Where the directors cause treasury stock to be sold to themselves at less than its real value and for the purpose of carrying an election, the court will set the transfer aside as fraudulent [3] In a proper case the court will enjoin the issue of the new stock.[4]

But an election is valid although it is carried by treasury stock of the corporation, which is sold by the directors just before the election in order to carry the election, so long as the sale is not attacked and set aside for fraud [5] Where the stock is not treasury stock, but is new increased capital stock, all the existing stockholders have a right to subscribe for their proportion of the new stock, and may protect that right by injunction [6]

§ 616 *Where one corporation owns a majority of the stock of a rival company, may it vote the stock and control the latter company?* It has been decided in several cases that where one corporation owns a majority of the stock of a rival company, the temptation to manage the latter company for the benefit of the former company will be so great that a minority stockholder of the latter company may enjoin the former company from voting the stock.[7]

[1] Putnam v Sweet, 1 Chandler (Wis), 286, 334 (1849)

[2] Where an injunction against postponing an election is granted, and the election is held, and the next day an appeal is taken from the injunction order, the appeal will be dismissed, inasmuch as the parties have the remedy under the statute of applying to the court to review the election   Camden, etc., R. R. v Elkins, 37 N. J Eq, 273 (1883).

[3] Hilles v Parish, 14 N J Eq, 380 (1862) See, also, p. 838, note.

[4] The court will enjoin the board of directors from issuing new stock on the verge of an election and for the sole purpose of carrying that election where the directors really represent a minority of the stock and where the power to issue the new stock is very doubtful   Such an injunction was granted

even though the charge was made that the complainant was interested in rival companies and was exercising control in their behalf. Fraser v. Whalley, 2 Hem & M, 10 (1864).

[5] State v. Smith, 48 Vt., 266 (1876). In the case of Taylor v Miami, etc., Co, 6 Ohio, 176, 223 (1833), a bill by a stockholder to compel a person to take back from the corporation certain stock which he had purchased of it just before the election, and had voted at the election, and then immediately sold again to the corporation, failed. The vote on these shares, however, did not affect the result.

[6] § 286, *supra.*

[7] In Memphis, etc., R. R. v. Woods, 88 Ala., 630 (1889), it was held that where one railroad company has acquired a majority of the stock of another railroad company, and has elected the board

The same principle of law was stated and applied in a lower court in New York[1] A contrary conclusion was reached in New Jersey[2] A federal court has held that where a corporation is organized to own and vote the stock of two competing railroads, the courts will enjoin the voting of the stock, the combination itself being forbidden by law.[3] It has been held in Ohio that one railroad corporation has no power to acquire the bonds of another railroad

of directors, and oppressed and defrauded such latter company by buying unnecessary rolling-stock, making unnecessary repairs at exorbitant charges, unduly apportioning the earnings as between the two roads, and in other ways increasing its own profits at the expense of the latter company, a minority stockholder in such latter company may enjoin the former company from voting such stock at an election A request to the company to bring the action was first made by the stockholder who brought the suit. A transportation company owning a majority of the stock of an ice company may be enjoined from voting the stock, if the former company intends to purchase ice from the latter company, but otherwise no such injunction will issue. American, etc, Co v Linn. 7 S Rep, 191 (Ala 1890). A stockholder in one mining and manufacturing company may enjoin another rival company from voting the majority of stock in the former company, such majority being owned by the latter company Mack v De Bardelaben, etc, Co, 8 S Rep. 150 (Ala, 1890) Where an electric light company purchases a majority of the stock of a competing electric light company in the same city, and elects the board of directors, and fraudulently uses its power to make the latter subservient to and as a feeder to the former, and intends to destroy the latter, the court, at the instance of a minority stockholder of the latter, will appoint a receiver of the company, but the proof of such intent must be clear The fact that the directors so elected are stockholders in the

controlling company is not sufficient. Davis v U. S, etc, Co of Baltimore City 25 Atl. Rep, 982 (Md, 1893) It is illegal for an Ohio corporation to purchase a majority of the stock of a Tennessee corporation for the purpose of controlling the latter, even though they are engaged in a similar business, the object being to form a monopoly Hence the purchasing company cannot enforce the contract as to certain things which were to be done by the vendor of the stock Buckeye, etc, Co v Harvey, 20 S W Rep., 427 (Tenn, 1892). See, also, 8 S. E Rep, 630 (Ga, 1889).

[1] In the case also of Milbank v N Y etc, R R, 64 How. Pr, 20 (1882), the court, at the instance of a minority stockholder, enjoined another railroad company from voting a majority of the stock in his company, although fraud and partiality in the management for the benefit of the majority stockholder was a fear of the future instead of a fact in the past. The court said: "It is against public policy to have or permit one corporation to embarrass and control another and perhaps competing corporation in the management of its affairs, as may be done if it is permitted to purchase and vote upon the stock '

[2] A stockholder will not be enjoined from voting on the ground that he is not a bona fide stockholder but that his stock was paid for by rival companies and that he intends to control the company for the advantage of those companies. Camden, etc, R R v Elkins, 37 N J Eq, 273 (1883)

[3] Clarke v Central R. R., etc, 50 Fed. Rep, 338 (1892).

corporation in order to control the elections of the latter, such bonds having a voting power [1]

The reasonable rule would seem to be that, where one company having no power to purchase the stock of another rival company [2] illegally purchases a controlling interest in such stock, or where one company having legally purchased the majority of the stock of a rival company has managed the latter company fraudulently in its own interest, a court of equity will enjoin it from voting the stock at the next election. But if the purchase of the stock was legal and there has as yet been no fraud in the management, such an injunction will not be granted.

§ 617 *Illegal or fraudulent elections — The remedy of quo warranto and mandamus.*— There are various ways in which an illegal or fraudulent election of directors or managers of an incorporated company can be investigated and remedied The natural and proper remedy in all cases is the old remedy of *quo warranto* to test the title to office. In England *quo warranto* does not lie to test the legality of the election of officers of a private corporation, but in this country a contrary rule prevails.[3] An information in the nature of a *quo warranto* is not allowed of course, but is a subject for the exercise of a sound discretion.[4] *Mandamus,* instead of *quo warranto,* lies when the title *de jure* has been adjudicated [5] In West Virginia *mandamus* is held to be the proper remedy to place a *de jure* director in the place of the *de facto* director, and service on the latter may be by publication,[6] and *mandamus* lies at the instance of a corporation to compel illegally-elected directors to turn over the books to the legally-elected directors [7]

---

[1] State *v.* McDaniel, 22 Ohio St., 354, 368 (1872)

[2] See §§ 315–317.

[3] Commonwealth *v* Arrison, 15 S & R., 127 (1827), a case of church trustees, Commonwealth *v* Graham, 64 Pa St, 339 (1870), the same, People *v* Tibbits, 4 Cow, 358 (1825), an insurance company, State *v* Ferris, 45 Mo., 183 (1869), college trustees, Creek *v* State, 77 Ind, 180 (1881), church trustees, State *v.* Kupersfolte, 44 Mo, 154 (1869), an insurance company, State *v* McDaniel, 22 Ohio St, 354 (1872), directors of a railroad; Commonwealth *v* Smith, 45 Pa. St, 59 (1863), High on Extraordinary Remedies, § 653, etc, Shortt on Informations, etc, 129 (Eng, 1887), Commonwealth *v* Gill, 3 Whart (Pa), 228 (1837), giving the pleadings herein,

People *v* Albany, etc, R. R. Co., 55 Barb, 314, 354 (1869) For a clear statement of the nature of an information in the nature of a *quo warranto* filed by a claimant for an office in the name of the attorney-general, see State *v.* Mayor, etc., 10 Atl Rep, 377 (N J, 1887). See, also, § 713, *infra,* concerning *de facto* officers.

[4] State *v* Lehie, 7 Rich Law (S. C), 234 (1854).

[5] State *v* Mayor, etc, 19 Atl. Rep., 780 (N J, 1890).

[6] Cross *v.* West Va, etc, R'y, 12 S. E. Rep., 1071 (W Va, 1891) Compare S. C., id, 765, and People *v* N. Y, etc., Asylum, 122 N. Y, 190 (1890).

[7] American Railway Frog Co. *v* Haven, 101 Mass, 398 (1869).

§ 618 *Illegal or fraudulent elections — The remedy by bill in equity and injunction* — A court of equity has no inherent power or jurisdiction to entertain a bill for the purpose of reviewing a corporate election and ousting the parties who claim to have been elected [1]

But where there has been a palpable fraud practiced in the election and usurpers are about to take possession of the property in violation of all justice, a court of equity will enjoin them from doing so [2]

[1] The title of *de facto* officers to their office cannot be tested by an injunction or bill in equity Quo *warranto* or a proceeding under the statute is necessary People *v* Albany, etc, R. R. Co, 57 N Y, 161, 171 No injunction against officers acting as such on ground of illegal election Quo *warranto* lies Hartt *v* Harvey, 32 Barb, 55 (1860) Equity has no power except as incidental to other relief to review an election Perry *v* Tuscaloosa, etc, Co, 9 S Rep, 217 (Ala, 1891), Hullman *v* Honcomp, 5 Ohio St, 237 (1855), New England, etc, Co *v* Phillips, 141 Mass, 535 (1886), where an injunction was sought to restrain persons from acting as directors who had been illegally elected Allen J "This course is open to the objection that suits to remove or to institute corporation officers do not belong to the original jurisdiction of chancery and that the right to be such officer cannot, in general, and in the absence of special legislation allowing this remedy, be tested by means of an injunction" Pom Eq I, § 171, id, III, § 1345 See, also, to same effect, Owen *v*. Whitaker, 20 N. J Eq 122 (1869), where the legality of the first election was the only thing involved, Hughes *v* Parker, 20 N H, 58 (1849), Johnston *v* Jones, 23 N J Eq, 216 (1872), Mickles *v* Rochester City Bank, 11 Paige, 118 (1844), Mechanics' National Bank of Newark *v* Burnet Mfg Co, 32 N J Eq, 236 (1880), where a third person suing the corporation sought to have its answer stricken out because the officers were not duly elected, Fadness *v* Braunborg, 41 N W Rep, 84 (Wis, 1889), a religious corporation case, Wandsworth, etc, Co *v* Wright, 18 W R, 728 (1870), where fraud was charged on the part of the inspectors, Davidson *v* Grange, 4 Grant's Ch (Up Can), 377 (1854), where the court refused an injunction, but said in a *dictum* that the election might be set aside on account of fraudulent voting of shares subscribed for by "dummies" to get control of the election on promise that subscriptions would afterwards be canceled Where by reason of an injunction against voting certain stock the meeting is not held at the time specified in the notice, but later in the day a minority meet and adjourn to the next day and conceal such adjournment from the majority and elect directors, the court will oust them from office. State *v* Bonnell, 35 Ohio St, 10 (1878) Self-constituted directors without a regular organized meeting have not a good title to their office, and where subsequently the incorporators elected other directors, the latter may cause to be stayed an action brought in the name of the company by the self-constituted directors. John Morley etc, Co *v* Barras, 64 L. T Rep, 856 (1891)

[2] Where the owners of the whole stock sell it and part of them resign and place the representatives of the vendee in possession, and those who remain in the board do so at his request but transfer to him their certificates of stock, and then subsequently, when the time for the annual meeting has gone by, they publish a notice of a meeting and conceal the notice from him and elect a

The *de facto* directors may enjoin the claimants to office from attempting to take forcible possession or exercising the duties of the office[1] So also if the validity of a corporate election arises incidentally in connection with a suit in equity the court will pass upon the election. This may occur where a bill is filed to enjoin a forfeiture of stock[2] or a consolidation of corporations.[3]

A court of equity may appoint a master to hold an election of a corporation when by reason of fraud, violence or unlawful conduct on the part of some stockholder a fair election cannot otherwise be held[4]

§ 619. *Illegal or fraudulent elections — Statutory remedy by petition to a court of equity* — In consequence of the delays and difficulties attending the remedy of *quo warranto*, statutes have been enacted in many of the states which give courts of equity the power to review corporate elections at the instance of the parties aggrieved[5] Such a statute is found in New York, New Jersey,

board and attempt to take possession, a court of equity will enjoin them Johnston v Jones 23 N J Eq, 216 (1872). Equity is not obliged ' to leave the corporation and its lawful directors to the remedy at law always taking at least months, and in the meantime suffer the road to be operated and perhaps ruined by the depredators, because they claim to be directors *de facto* or *de jure*." Id In the case Clarke v Central, etc, Co. of Georgia, 54 Fed Rep, 556 (Ga, 1893), it appeared that the board of directors having been illegally elected, "the voting power of the stock was enjoined, a new election ordered, and the court appointed receivers, not for the purpose of subjecting the properties to the claims of creditors but to protect and to preserve them until they could be turned over to a legally elected board of directors, as proper trustees, who would have the right under the law to take and operate the railroad in the interest of all concerned The court further directed that, when this new election should have taken place said new board of directors might apply to the court to have the property returned to the control of the properly constituted officers of the corporation " Where a corporation has an

authorized capital of $5 000, but only $2.500 are directed by the stockholders to be issued, it is illegal and fraudulent to issue the remaining authorized capital without giving the existing stockholders a prior right to subscribe to such increased capital *pro rata*. Directors elected by reason of such illegal issue would be enjoined from acting, where they are about to change the whole policy of the company Humboldt, etc., Ass n v Stevens *et al*, 52 N W Rep, 568 (Neb, 1892).

[1] Reis v Rohde, 34 Hun, 161 (1884).

[2] In an injunction suit brought by a stockholder to prevent the corporate officers from forfeiting stock, the court will pass upon the legality of an election of directors, but of course will not and cannot remove them Moses v. Tompkins, 84 Ala, 613 (1888); Garden, etc., Co v McLister, L R, 1 App, 39

[3] Where the directors are about to make an illegal consolidation and a stockholder files a bill to enjoin it, the court will pass also upon the legality of the election of the *de facto* directors. Nathan v Tompkins, 82 Ala, 437 (1887).

[4] Tunis v Hestonville, etc., R R, 24 Atl Rep, 88 (Pa, 1892). See, also, § 612.

[5] See Part VII.

California and other states[1] By these statutes the court, sitting as a court of chancery, is empowered to review corporate elections, and to grant such relief as the particular circumstances and justice of the case seem to require[2]

Such a statute has proven to be one of the wisest and best that a legislature ever enacted in regard to corporations. It furnishes a speedy, simple, just and effective remedy for all complaints, and is free from useless technicalities and expense. Various decisions under these statutes are given in the notes below[3]

[1] Id

[2] Brewster v Hartley, 37 Cal, 15 (1869), Wright v Central California Colony Water Co, 67 Cal, 532 (1885), In the Matter, etc, St Lawrence, etc, Co. 44 N J L 529 (1882), a case where proxies were illegally rejected For various cases in New York showing the wide powers exercised by the court under this statute, see Ex parte Holmes, 5 Cowen, 426 (1826). The Schoharie Valley R. R. Case, 12 Abb Prac (N S), 394 (1872). Re Desdoity 1 Wend ; 98, Vandenburgh v Broadway R. R. Co, 29 Hun, 318, Strong v Smith, 15 Hun, 222 (1878); Ex parte Willcocks, 7 Cow, 402 (1827) Mickles v Rochester City Bank, 11 Paige, 118, In the Matter of the Long Island R. R. Co, 19 Wend, 37 In this case an election was set aside because the directors had illegally declared certain shares forfeited for non-payment of instalments and refused to record an assignment thereof so as to entitle the assignee to vote Under these statutes an election may be declared void by reason of the conspiracy, frauds or trickery of a part of the stockholders. People v Albany, etc, R. R Co., 55 Barb 344 (1869).

[3] The statute authorizing a court of chancery to review elections and order new ones does not authorize the courts to issue a mandamus to the inspectors of election in regard to counting votes by proxy and amending the return People v Simonson 61 Hun 338 (1891) ‘ Surprise and fraud upon part of the electors is ground for avoiding an election.” People v Albany, etc, R. R., 55 Barb, 344, 363 (1869) Where the place of an election is filled by one party with roughs as proxies brought there for purposes of intimidation and for voting on viva voce votes and for crowding out the regular voters. Id., p 379 In this case under the New York statute, in an equitable suit brought by the state, the court appointed a receiver and issued an injunction pending the suit, and finally declared elected persons who would have received the most votes of all votes that had been legally cast, although there had been two elections held at the same time by the two parties at different places in the same town Under the New York statute making the transfer book conclusively binding upon the inspectors of election, the inspectors cannot exclude the vote of the registered stockholder although he holds the stock merely as pledgee, but under the New York statute allowing the courts to summarily review the election the court has power to go back of the transfer book and set the election aside where the statute gave the pledgor the right to vote Strong v Smith 15 Hun, 222 (1878. "Where no allegation of fraud or deceit is made, the court cannot interfere under the power vested in it by the Revised Statutes to nullify or set aside the will of the shareholders as expressed by their votes. In re Wellman, etc v. Ciancimino, etc, Co, N Y L J, May, 13, 1890, per Lawrence J The statutory power of the court to inquire into the legality of corporate elections does not apply to the appointment of a director by the board to fill a vacancy

§ 620 *Who may complain of an illegal election — A new election is not granted if the result will be the same* — Only a shareholder whose rights have been infringed and who is equitably entitled to complain may institute the proceedings   Accordingly, a transferee of one of the shareholders who participated in the fraud will not be heard to impeach the result of that fraud.[1] And in general the plaintiff, a relator seeking to set aside a corporate election, is barred of relief if he himself was guilty of misconduct or neglect, or if it appears that he has subsequently acquiesced with knowledge of the facts[2] It is a principle of law also that the legality of an election will not be inquired into upon the ground that illegal votes were cast, unless those votes were challenged at the election at the time when they were cast[3]

An election will not be set aside if it be shown that after throwing out the invalid votes the officers declared elected would still have, according to the return, a valid majority of the votes cast;[4]

due to a resignation Wickersham v Brittan, 28 Pac Rep, 792 (Cal, 1892) Nor does such a statute enable the director so "appointed" to settle the question of the legality of the election by applying to the court. Wickersham v Murphy, 28 Pac Rep, 793 (Cal, 1892) Nor does it apply to the legality of an election of the president by the directors In re Caguey, N Y L J, Sept 15, 1891 Although the inspectors admitted votes on insufficient evidence, yet if additional and sufficient evidence is presented to the court the election will stand Widow Conant v Millaudon, 5 La Ann, 542 (1850) The corporation itself may apply under the statute for an order to the effect that the persons declared elected were legally elected. Matter of Pioneer Paper Co, 36 How. Pr, 111 (1863). In attacking the validity of a vote the burden of proof is on him who attacks it. In re Indian, etc, Co, L R, 26 Ch D, 70 (1884)

[1] Matter of the Application of the Syracuse, etc, R R Co, 91 N Y, 1 (1883)

[2] Wiltz v. Peters, 4 La Ann 339 (1849), where a commissioner of election attacked the legality of votes which he himself had admitted as commissioner.

[3] In the Matter of the Chenango, etc, Ins. Co., 19 Wend, 635 (1839), wherein the court said "It is quite clear, generally speaking, that an illegal vote not challenged will not invalidate an election, nor will even be inquired into" See, also, The Schoharie Valley R. R. Case, 12 Abb. Prac. (N S), 394 (1872). A stockholder who attends the election and votes and does not object to others voting, although he knows that they are doing so in violation of a by-law, cannot himself afterwards object to the legality of the election State v. Lehre, 7 Rich Law (S C), 234 (1854). See, also, People v Robinson, 64 Cal, 373 (1883). In re Long I, etc, R R, 19 Wend, 37, 41 (1837)

[4] People v Tuthill, 31 N Y, 550 (1864); Ex parte Murphy, 7 Cowen, 153 (1827); In the Matter of the Chenango, etc, Ins. Co, 19 Wend, 635 (1839), State v Lehre, 7 Rich (Law), 234, 325 (1854) McNeeley v Woodruff, 13 N J Law, 352 (1833); First Parish in Sudbury v Stearns, 38 Mass., 148 (1838), Trustees of the School District v Gibbs, 56 Mass, 39 (1848); Wardens of Christ Church v. Pope, 74 Mass, 140 (1857). The court will not consider the legality or illegality of votes, where those votes will not change the result whatever the decision might

and a new election will not be ordered if after rejecting all the illegal votes, and after admitting the legal votes which were rejected, it still appears that the directors returned as elected had a majority of the votes [1]

The court may, in the exercise of its equity powers, declare a candidate elected who received only a minority of the votes actually cast, when such candidate plainly received a majority of all the legal votes cast [2] Where *quo warranto* proceedings are pur-

be Widow Conant v Millaudon, 5 La Ann, 542 (1850) Where the officers declared elected received a majority of the original stock as well as a majority of the alleged illegal increased stock, they will not be ousted Byers v Rollins, 13 Colo, 22 (1889) Where after rejecting all votes illegally cast by proxy there is still a majority for the persons who were declared elected, the court will not disturb the election Craig v First Pres Church, 88 Pa St, 42 (1878)

[1] McNeeley v Woodruff, 13 N J L, 352 (1833), *Ex parte* Desdoity, 1 Wend, 98 (1828).

[2] Where the whole number of votes is five hundred and ninety-three, and there were present five hundred and thirty-seven, and the candidates declared not elected received three hundred votes, one hundred and fifty of which were illegally rejected by the inspectors, the court under the New Jersey statute declared those candidates elected and did not order a new election Matter of Election of St Lawrence etc, Co, 44 N. J L, 529 (1882), Monsseaux v Urquhart, 19 La. Ann, 482 (1867); *Ex parte* Desdoity, 1 Wend, 98 (1828), Vandenbuigh v Broadway R'y Co, 29 Hun, 348 (1883); Downing v Potts, 23 N. J Law, 66, 84 (1851), where an election was set aside and a new one ordered because votes were illegally rejected on one side and illegally accepted on the other, which changed the result, but two directors who were on both tickets and received all the votes cast were held elected The court said that unless the legal votes rejected and the illegal votes received were sufficient to

change the result of the election, the election would not be set aside Hence where of two thousand three hundred and ninety-two votes for certain candidates seven hundred and ninety-nine were illegal and there were illegally rejected one thousand eight hundred and ninety-four votes for the defeated candidate, who received forty-six votes, the court ordered a new election In the case *In re* Long I R. R, 19 Wend, 37, where the votes illegally rejected would have elected other persons, the court set the election aside, and did not declare elected those who would have been elected if the rejected votes had been counted there being one thousand seven hundred votes not represented, and eleven thousand that were disqualified under the statute The court may declare part of the directors illegally elected, and order a new election as to them without affecting the title of the others to their offices People v Fleming, 59 Hun 518 (1891) In the case Monsseaux v Urquhart, 19 La Ann 482 (1867) the court ousted a director and declared elected another person in his stead Where the presiding officer illegally rejects certain votes, declares certain persons elected and adjourns the meeting, and the dissatisfied party continue the meeting and hold another election, the court will consider merely the question as to who received a majority of the votes which were legally offered to be cast State v Smith, 15 Oreg, 98 (1887) A court will not force upon the company directors who are technically entitled to be declared elected, certain proxies being irregularly

sued, the court can only oust the party who is in office. It cannot declare another person elected.[1]

§ 621 *Restrictions on the right to vote* — It is legal for a corporation upon issuing preferred stock or increased capital stock to impose a condition that such stock shall not have any right to vote.[2] It is legal also for the corporation with the assent of all stockholders to give to bonds a voting power.[3] There is no rule of public policy which forbids a corporation and its stockholders from making any contract they please in regard to restrictions on the voting policy. If the agreement is made by unanimous consent it is legal. Such restrictions, however, generally are and always should be printed on the certificates of stock so that a purchaser shall take with full notice. Thus, a by-law passed at the time of the organization of the company may limit the number of votes which a single stockholder may cast[4] All this is a mere matter of private contract.

executed, but will order a new election Harben v Phillips, L. R., 23 Ch D 14 A statute repealing the statutory remedy in chancery to review elections operates retrospectively as well as prospectively *In re N Y*, etc, Co, 23 Hun, 615 (1881) A late case holds that, if the illegally-rejected votes would have given the defeated candidate a majority of all the stock, the court will declare him elected, and will oust the one that was declared elected *In re Cape*, etc, Co, 16 Atl Rep, 191 (N J, 1888).

[1] State v McDaniel, 22 Ohio St, 354 (1872), where a number of legal votes were rejected which would have sufficed to elect certain directors who without such votes had only a minority of the votes cast The court held that persons cannot be declared elected and inducted into office upon a *quo warranto* information, People v. Phillips, 1 Denio, 388 (1845), making the same ruling as to a church corporation

[2] It is legal upon the issue of preferred stock to provide that it shall not vote at corporate elections. Such a provision will be upheld Miller v Ratterman, 24 N E. Rep, 496 (Ohio, 1890) See, also, ch XVI, *supra*.

[3] In the case of State v. McDaniel, 22

Ohio St, 354 (1872), the bondholders on a reorganization were given by contract the power to vote, and the court upheld such contract right. In the case of Phillips v Eastern R. R., 138 Mass., 122 (1884), the court passed upon a statutory scheme in which the creditors of a railroad company, by the terms of a mortgage, chose two-thirds of the directors and the stockholders chose one-third until the debt was reduced to a certain figure

[4] A by-law may provide that stockholders shall have one vote for each share held by them up to ten shares, and may fix the proportion which their votes shall bear to their shares above that number. Detwiler v Commonwealth, 18 Atl Rep., 990 (Pa, 1890). A by-law restricting the right of members of a church to vote as authorized by statute is void People v. Phillips, 1 Denio, 388 (1845) By-law restricting the right of electors in a town to vote is not good Rex v Spencer, 3 Burr., 1827 (1766), Rex v. Head, 4 Burr, 2515, 2521 (1770) See, also, § 700a, *infra*, People v Kip, 4 Cowen, 382, note (1822), holding that a corporation has no power, by a by-law, to demand an oath of a stockholder in order to test his qualifications as a voter. Where the charter author-

Where the charter limits the number of votes which one stockholder may cast, the provision cannot be evaded by transfers to various persons The courts will enjoin the voting of the stock [1]

A statute prohibiting a stockholder from voting " whose liability is past due and unpaid " refers to a subscription liability and not to a commercial liability [2]

§ 622 *Combinations and contracts as to elections — Voting trusts and pooling agreements —* Stockholders owning a majority of the stock have a right to combine and secure the election of the board of directors.[3] But a contract in regard to elections in private corporations is not legal if it provides that a lucrative corporate position shall be given to one or more of the parties to the contract Thus an agreement of a large stockholder holding a majority of

izes the depositors and stockholders to elect new members, the directors cannot by by-law exclude the former from elections and give a vote to stockholders only Commonwealth *v* Gill, 3 Whart (Pa) 228 (1837)

[1] Mack *v* De Bardelaben, etc , Co , 8 S. Rep., 150 (Ala , 1890) Where stock has been transferred in order to give it a vote, the transferrer having already all the stock that the charter allows one stockholder to vote, the transfer being merely nominal and for voting purposes only, an injunction will issue against its being voted Campbell *v* Poultney, 6 G & J , 94 (1834), Webb *v* Ridgely, 38 Md , 364 (1873) Although the charter limits each person to one hundred votes, yet a person voting a hundred votes in his own name may vote another hundred as proxy for his wife, if it is *bona fide* her property Widow Conant *v* Millaudon, 5 La Ann , 542 (1850) In England a contrary rule prevails It is not illegal to transfer or procure shares before a meeting so as to multiply votes at it nor can votes so obtained be disregarded They may be cast Pender *v* Lushington, L. R., 6 Ch D , 70 (1877), Stanton Iron and Steel Co , L R , 16 Eq , 559, Cannon *v* Trash, 20 Eq , 669, Moffatt *v* Farquhar L R , 7 Ch D , 591 (1878) and see Northwest Transportation Co *v* Beatty, L. R., 12 App Cas , 589 A statute which

confines the right to vote to stockholders who are citizens of the state by which the corporation is chartered cannot be evaded by colorable transfers of shares to residents of the state merely for the purpose of having them voted upon State *v* Hunton, 28 Vt , 594 (1856) Such a statute would now, however, probably be held to be unconstitutional See § 813, relative to statutes prohibiting citizens of other states from being trustees

[2] United States *v.* Berry, 36 Fed Rep , 246 (1888)

[3] Havemeyer *v.* Havemeyer, 43 N Y Super Ct , 506 513 (1878), affirmed, 86 N Y , 618 (1881), Faulds *v* Yates, 57 Ill , 416 (1870), where it was held that persons holding the majority of stock in a corporation could lawfully agree among themselves to vote as a unit to control an election, and that their agreement that their votes should be cast as should be decided by the majority of their own votes was not void as being against public policy "There is if I may say so, no obligation on a shareholder of a company to give his vote merely with a view to what other persons may consider the interests of the company at large He has a right, if he thinks fit, to give his vote from motives or promptings of what he considers his own individual interest " Pender *v* Lushington, L R , 6 Ch D , 70 (1877)

the stock that upon the purchase and absorption of plaintiff's business by the corporation the plaintiff should be engaged for a term of years as vice-president and general manager of the corporation at a specified salary is contrary to public policy and is void.[1]

A sale by a stockholder of his vote is illegal[2] Closely connected

[1] West *z* Camden, 137 U. S, 507 (1890)
A contract made by a stockholder for a consideration to vote for a particular person for manager of the company, and in the event of his election to vote for an increase of the salary attaching to that position, is illegal and cannot be enforced Woodruff *v* Wentworth 133 Mass 309 (1882) An agreement of persons holding a majority of the stock they being directors also, that a person purchasing stock from them shall be general manager and may at the end of two years sell the stock back to them at a stated price, is contrary to public policy and void The vendors need not repurchase The arrangement is unfair to the corporation Wilbur *z* Stoepel 46 N W Rep, 724 (Mich, 1890) A proxy for five years given so as to unite enough stock to control the corporation, the holder of the proxy agreeing that the person giving the proxy shall have an office at a salary of $2 500 a year is void At the instance of the latter person a court of equity will enjoin voting thereunder Cone's Ex'rs *v* Russell, 21 Atl Rep, 847 (N J, 1891) Where a stockholder in a railroad company is induced to take part in the formation of a land company and is to receive a certain sum of money when a depot is located on such land, he cannot enforce the agreement It is practically a sale of his vote Fuller *v.* Dame, 35 Mass, 472 (1836) A contract of the vendor of bank stock that he would make the vendee the cashier is illegal and void Noel *v* Drake, 28 Kan, 265 (1882) An agreement to vote in a particular way in consideration of some personal benefit, is illegal, for a vote ought to be an impartial and honest exercise of judgment. Elliott *z* Richardson, L R, 5 C

P, 744. See, also, Moffatt *v* Farquharson, 2 Bro C C., 338, Caird *v* Hope, 2 B & Cr, 661 Compare Bolton *v* Madden, L R, 9 Q B, 55, where an agreement between two subscribers to a charity to vote for each others nominees was held not to be illegal Directors have no power to contract with an outsider that he shall, upon purchasing certain stock, be made a director in the company Seymour *v* Detroit Copper, etc, Mills, 56 Mich, 117 (1885) But a sale of stock with an agreement that the vendee should be elected superintendent may be rescinded if the latter part of the agreement is not carried out Id Although a contract of certain stockholders to vote together is legal, yet a conspiracy to obtain an illegal injunction against others voting will not be countenanced by the court People *v* Albany, etc, R R Co, 55 Barb, 344, 368 (1869) A contract by which a shareholder in a corporation agrees to secure to the purchaser of his stock a corporate office at a stated salary, and in case of his removal to repurchase the stock, is void as against public policy and as a fraud on other stockholders, unless it is proved that the transaction is not for the private benefit of the vendor, or that it was consented to by the other stockholders Guernsey *v.* Cook, 120 Mass, 501 (1876), Noyes *v.* Marsh, 123 Mass, 286 (1877) Where the agreement was to keep the vendor in a professorship the court will not aid the parties The agreement is against public policy Jones *z* Scudder, 2 Cin Sup Ct, 178 (1872)

[2] Hafer *z* N Y, etc, R R, 14 Week. Law Bull, 68. See, also, Yale Law Journal, vol 1, p. 7

with this principle of law is the question whether a director or
stockholder may vote his stock in favor of a sale to or a purchase
from another corporation in which such director or stockholder is
interested as a stockholder. The general rule is that a contract
between two corporations having certain stockholders or directors
in common will be sustained by the courts if the contract is fair
towards the minority stockholders If it is not fair the courts will
set it aside upon the complaint of the minority stockholders[1] A
contract, however, by which the directors who own a majority of
the stock sell such stock and agree to substitute the vendees as
directors of the company, is legal[2] The vendor of stock may of
course agree to vote as the vendee wishes[3]

Restrictions on the right to vote stock, like restrictions on the
right to sell stock, are not favored by the courts These two classes
of restrictions are so closely allied that it is best to consider them
together. They both are due generally to a desire to so tie up the
stock or the voting power that the control will be permanently obtained and retained thereby It is an old problem in corporation
law how to compel parties to live up to their agreement in regard
to holding their stock and voting with other parties to the contract
in order to keep the control of the corporation Various devices
have been tried the object being to place the stock in such a position that no one of the parties can break his agreement to act with
the others. "Irrevocable" proxies to vote upon the stock have
been given by all the parties to a designated person, who acted as
their agent But the courts decided that these proxies were not
irrevocable, but might be revoked at any time[4]

Another plan was to place the stock of the various parties in the
hands of trustees with power to transfer the stock to themselves,

[1] See ch. XXXIX.

[2] A contract to sell one's stock in a
corporation and to resign a directorship
and the presidency, and having done so
to endeavor to induce other directors to
resign in order that the purchasers of
the stock may come in and take their
places and so control the management
of the company, there being no evidence
of fraud, has been held a contract not
void as against public policy Barnes v
Brown, 80 N Y 527 (1880) Specific
performance will not be granted of an
agreement of the vendors of stock that
they will resign as directors and substitute the vendee's representatives instead
Fremont v Stone, 42 Barb, 169 (1864)

the court stating that such a contract is
unfair towards the minority stockholders See, also, contra, Jacobs v Miller,
15 Alb L J, 188 (1877)

[3] An agreement by a vendor of stock,
which is to be delivered after an election, that he will vote as the vendee desires, is legal Mobley v Morgan 6 Atl
Rep, 604 (Pa, 1886 One corporation
contracting with another may agree
that the latter shall hold and vote the
stock of and in the former Tonawanda
etc, R R Co v N Y, etc, R R Co. 42
Hun, 496 (1886) This is but a mode of
issuing the stock

[4] See § 610, supra.

and to hold and vote the same. Trustees' certificates were then issued by the trustees to the various parties, specifying the amount of stock so deposited by them and their interest in the pool. But this plan failed. The courts held that any holder of a trustee's certificate might at any time demand back his part of the stock.[1]

Voting trusts of this kind are resorted to in forming "trusts," the combinations in trade. All the stock of various competing corporations are placed in the hands of trustees, who issue trustee certificates therefor. Such voting trusts as those are declared illegal because the monopolistic combination that is sought is illegal.

[1] Woodruff v Dubuque, etc, R. R., 30 Fed Rep, 91 (1887); Hafer v New York, etc R. R. Co (Ohio), 14 Week Law Bul, 68 (Cincinnati Sup. Ct., 1885). See Griffith v. Jewett (Ohio), 15 Week Law Bul, 419 (Cincinnati Sup Ct, 1886); Vanderbilt v Bennett, 2 R'y & Corp L. J, 409 (Pa 1887), Starbuck v Mercantile, etc., Co, 24 Atl Rep., 32 (Conn, 1891) See, also, an excellent article and careful review of the cases by Professor Baldwin in 1 Yale Law J, 1 (1891) A trust of stock for the benefit of both the bondholders and the stockholders cannot be broken up by one of the stockholders only Shelmerdine v. Welsh, 47 Legal Intell, 26 (Phil. Com. Pl, Jan, 1890) Although many stockholders transfer their stock to a trustee to hold and vote it for three years, and agree not to sell until they have offered to sell to each other, yet any one may sell to an outsider, and the latter may demand back his stock from the trustee Moses v Scott, 4 S Rep, 742 (Ala, 1888) The trustees are not purchasers and owners of the stock People v North River S. Ref Co, 121 N. Y., 582 (1890). An outside stockholder cannot object to other stockholders uniting their interests in a "trust," and thereby obtaining control of the corporation Zimmermann v. Jewett, 19 Abb. N C, 459 (Ohio, 1886). But he can object when the purpose of the "trust" is to work out some scheme which is illegal in itself Hafer v New York, etc, R. R. Co, 14 Week Law Bull, 68 (Ohio, 1886) A "trust" of stock was involved in Farmers' L. & T

Co. v Chicago, etc, R'y, 27 Fed Rep, 146 (1886), where Hugh J Jewett, president of the Erie railway, held as trustee the stock of the Chicago & Atlantic Railroad, the western connection of the former company. The court did not pass on the permanency of the trust. An agreement of the holder of a majority of the stock that he will retain control is no defense by the corporation to an action by the receiver of such stockholder to transfer the stock on the corporate books. Weller v Pace Tobacco Co, 25 N Y Week. Dig, 531 (1886). A contract to combine to control the majority of the stock of a railroad company may be violated by a party to it, although by its terms it is irrevocable Clarke v Central R. R, etc, 50 Fed. Rep., 338 (1892). Where stock is placed in a trustee's hands, and a trustee's certificate is taken therefor, a pledge of the trustee's certificate is not a pledge of the stock sufficient to cut off subsequent attachments of the stock. Bidstrup v Thompson, 45 Fed Rep, 452 (1891). Where stock is deposited with a trustee for purposes of reorganization, and transferable certificates are issued therefor by the trustee, a claimant of stock which another person has deposited, and for which such other person has the trustee's certificate, cannot compel the trustee to deliver up the stock until the trustee's certificate is returned, even though the party holding it is a party defendant. Beau v American L. & T Co., 122 N. Y, 622 (1890)

Hence the decisions concerning the "trusts" are not applicable to the questions now under consideration.[1]

Another device was tried. The parties contracted together not to sell their stock for a specified time, and agreed that if they did they would sell together or to a purchaser who would be agreeable to the old stockholders. But this plan also did not succeed. If it prohibited any sale whatsoever, and did not limit the time during which the agreement was to last, it was void as an illegal restraint of trade.[2] Moreover it constituted no check on the parties. At any time any one of the parties might sell his stock. The only remedy of the other parties against him then was a doubtful, difficult, protracted and expensive suit for damages.[3]

Another plan was to restrict by a by-law of the corporation the right to transfer stock. But such by-laws are illegal.[4]

Still another plan was tried. An unincorporated joint-stock association was formed to carry on the business. A provision was inserted in the articles of association of the company restricting the right of a shareholder to sell his stock. This provision was upheld by the courts. The purchaser of a certificate of stock, who sold in violation of the agreement, received no right to vote or participate in the company. He merely was entitled to the dividends on his stock.[5] But this device is not open to corporations. Their charters are generally obtained by filing a certificate in accordance with a general law. A special provision inserted in the certificate, limiting the right to transfer stock, would be ineffectual and void. All these various devices have proved to be impracticable.

It is legal, however, for stockholders to agree to place their stock in the hands of a trustee for a reasonable time, or until the debts of the company and of one of the parties are paid.[6] Such an

[1] See ch. XXIX, concerning "Trusts"

[2] Fisher v Bush, 35 Hun (N Y), 641 (1885).

[3] In the case Havemeyer v Havemeyer, 43 N Y. Super Ct., 506 (1878), aff'd, 86 N Y., 618, it was held that an agreement of several stockholders not to sell their own stock except in connection with that of the other parties to the contract was not in restraint of trade and was not contrary to public policy, as restricting the right of alienation, but the measure of damages for breach of such a contract is only the actual loss suffered by a decline in the value of the stock by reason of the breach

[4] See § 332, supra

[5] Harper v Raymond 3 Bosw (N Y), 29 (1858). See, Kingman v Spurr, 7 Pick, 234 (1828) See also, Taft v Harrison, 10 Hare, 489 (1853) as to liability after an offer to sell to the company

[6] An agreement by which various owners of stock place their stock in the hands of one person as trustee or agent to hold for a certain period of time, the parties agreeing not to sell their stock without having first offered to sell it to the rest of their associates at a price not above the then current market value, and in case of their declining to take it, without next offering it to the trustee,

agreement has to be supported, however, by something more than
the mere agreement of the parties.[1] It is legal for parties to
agree that certain persons shall be directors for a certain length
of time.[2]

It is legal for the stockholders to deposit their stock with a
depositary, to be transferred to such depositary and voted by him
as directed by a committee of the stockholders, such committee
being named, the object of the deposit being to effect an adjustment of differences between the common and preferred stockholders.[3]

Where, in order to prevent the foreclosure and sale of a railroad, a reorganization agreement is entered into by the creditors
and stockholders, whereby the claims of the creditors and the voting power of the stockholders are vested in trustees, the voting
power to be exercised by the trustees until certain debts were

but any one of the parties to be at liberty to withdraw at any time on those
terms, is not " contrary to public policy,
or any wise open to objection." Brown
v. Pacific Mail S. Co., 5 Blatch., 525
(1867). See, also, Griffith v. Jewett, 15
Week. L. Bull., 419. A contract
whereby stockholders of a corporation
agree to deposit their certificates of
stock with a trustee for six months, for
the purpose of preventing any disposition of the stock during that time, is unenforceable and void, as contrary to the
statute law of the state and against public policy. Williams v. Montgomery, 68
Hun, 416 (1893).

[1] Fisher v. Bush, 35 Hun, 641 (1885).
"There is no consideration whatever
between the trustees and the subscribers;
none is claimed or mentioned in the
agreement itself, and as between the
subscribers there is also none. The
mere fact that several or a majority
have signed does not furnish a supporting consideration. No one subscriber
acquired under the agreement any interest in any other one stock, or any undivided interest in the whole of the
stock represented by the subscribers.
No real and special consideration is
claimed, and without this the agreement
cannot be supported." Vanderbilt v.

Bennett, 2 R'y & Corp. L. J., 409 (Pa.,
1887).

[2] But a receiver will not be appointed
on account of a breach of the contract.
Baumgarten v. Nichols, N. Y. L. J., May
19, 1891. An agreement to elect a certain person president is waived if he
participates in electing others. American, etc., T. Co. v. Toledo, etc., R'y, 47
Fed. Rep., 343 (1890).

[3] The agreement did not prevent any
stockholder from demanding back his
stock whenever he saw fit. The court held
that this was not a " voting trust," and
that it was merely "a convenient method
by which distant and widely-separated
shareholders became enabled, indirectly,
to participate in the control and management of the company, and from
which each could recede at any time
and demand return of his stock without
violating any term of the agreement.
The depositary is a proxy required to
vote the stock as directed by the committee." The contract of deposit is
given in the report. The suit arose on
quo warranto proceedings to oust the
board of directors who were elected by
the vote of the depositary, but whose
title to office was denied by the company. Ohio, etc., Co. v. State, 32 N. E.
Rep., 933 (Ohio, 1892).

paid, the stockholders cannot withdraw from the agreement and claim the right to vote upon their stock.[1]

The most effective way in which a majority or all the stock of a company may be pooled or tied up seems to be by selling and transferring it to another corporation formed for that purpose Such corporations may be organized under the laws of many of the states   The objection to this plan is that it enables the directors of the second corporation to sell the stock at any time, and it involves not merely a temporary pooling of the stock but a permanent parting with the title and interest in it

§ 623. *Who may be a director or corporate officer* — In general, any one who may be an agent may be elected a director of a private corporation, and at common law it is not necessary that a director be a stockholder.[2]   A director need not be a citizen of the state by which the corporation is created.[3]   The constitutionality of a statute which prohibits the citizens of other states from being directors in a corporation may well be doubted.[4]

An alien may be a stockholder and director in a corporation if the statutes do not prohibit it.[5]   A married woman is not at common law qualified to act as an incorporator nor as treasurer,[6] but under the usual statutes conferring rights upon her, she is qualified to

---

[1] Mobile, etc , Co *v* Nicholas, 12 S Rep., 723 (Ala , 1893)   Not even the subsequent change in the agreement so as to issue first-mortgage bonds to take up some of the debt will enable the stockholders to claim the right to vote upon their stock before the debts specified above have been paid   Id

[2] State *v* McDaniel, 22 Ohio St. 354, 367 (1872), McDowall *v* Sheehan, 129 N Y., 210 (1891) Wight *v* Springfield, etc., R. R. Co 117 Mass , 226 (1875), In the Matter of Election of St Lawrence Steamboat Co , 44 N J Law, 529 (1882), Hoyt *v.* Bridgewater, etc , Co , 6 N J Eq 253, 274 (1847), *Ex parte* Stock, 33 L J , Chan , 731 (1864)   The charter or by-laws may, however, provide otherwise   Dispatch Line of Packets *v* Bellamy Mfg Co , 12 N H , 205 (1841), Bartholomew *v* Bentley, 1 Ohio St , 37 (1852), People *v* Northern R R Co , 42 N. Y , 217 (1870), Cammeyer *v* United, etc , Churches 2 Sand Ch , 186, 249 (1844), Hutchell & Hyde on Directors and Officers, 2 , State *v* Swearingen, 12

Ga 23 (1852) — a municipal corporation case   It is not necessary that the directors should be either subscribers to the stock or corporators.   Densmore Oil Co *v* Densmore, 54 Pa , 43 , *Re* British Provident Life Ass n, L R 5 Ch Div 306.

[3] Kerchner *v* Gettys, 18 S C , 521 (1883) A citizen of one state may be a stockholder and director in a corporation incorporated in another state   Detwiler *v* Commonwealth, 18 Atl. Rep 990 ,Pa , 1890)

[4] See § 813 to the effect that such a statute as regards trustees in a mortgage deed of trust is unconstitutional and void   A constitutional provision requiring directors to be stockholders does not apply to a consolidated railroad company existing as one corporation in two states   Ohio, etc., R y Co *v* People, 123 Ill 467 (1888).

[5] Robinson *v.* Hemingway 18 Atl Rep 992 (Pa , 1889).

[6] 9 R y & Corp. L J., 197

act as a director or officer.[1] An executor may be a director.[2]
If the charter or statutes require a director to be a stockholder, one
who holds stock transferred to him in trust for the express purpose
of qualifying him for the position may serve[3] And where a person
has the right to vote on stock as a stockholder, he is eligible to
any corporate office to which any stockholder is eligible, and accordingly may be elected a director even though an assignee in
bankruptcy has been appointed of his estate.[4] He may obtain stock
in any way and become thereby qualified[5] Although the charter
requires the directors to be stockholders, it has been held that the
transferee and holder of a certificate of stock is qualified, even
though the stock itself stands on the books of the company in the
name of his transferrer[6] It has been doubted whether the by-
laws of a company may require directors to be stockholders[7]

Votes cast for a person not eligible to the office cannot elect
him He is not even a *de facto* director, and he may be ousted by
legal proceedings[8] Such votes, however, are not to be ignored so

[1] People v Webster, 10 Wend, 554
(1833)

[2] In re Santa Clara etc, Co. N Y
Daily Reg June 19, 1888

[3] Budd v Monroe, 18 Hun 316 (1879).
Contra, Bartholemew v Bentley, 1 Ohio
St, 37 (1852)

[4] State v Ferris, 42 Conn., 560 (1875).

[5] A stockholder may have purchased
stock with a view of becoming a director or have obtained it by gift, or he
may hold it upon a trust, and be qualified to be a director He is qualified
unless the "title was put in him colorably, with a view to qualify him to be a
director for some dishonest purpose, in
furtherance of some fraudulent scheme
touching the organization or control of
the company or to carry into effect
some fraudulent arrangement with the
company " Matter of Election of St
Lawrence, etc. Co, 41 N J L, 529 (1882)
A person is qualified who buys stock in
his own name with his wife's money
and transfers the certificate to her, but
afterwards and before registry keeps
the stock for himself Id If the director has sufficient stock registered in
his name, it is immaterial that he does
not own it. Pulbrook v Richmond,

etc, Co, L R, 9 Ch D, 610, Bam-
bridge v. Smith 60 L T Rep, 879 (1889)

[6] State v Smith, 15 Oreg, 98 (1887). The
corporate books are not conclusive as to
the qualification of a person to act as a
director If he owns stock he is qualified, even though he does not appear as a
stockholder on the corporate books, and
vice versa The inspectors cannot reject votes on the ground that the candidate is not qualified Matter of Election of St. Lawrence, etc. Co, 44 N J
L, 529 (1882) Under the statutes of
North Dakota an unregistered holder of
stock is not qualified to be elected a director In re Argus, etc, Co, 43 N W
Rep, 347 (N D, 1891)

[7] People v Albany, etc, R R, 55
Barb, 344 373 (1869)

[8] The election of a person not qualified does not make him even a *de facto*
director In re Newcombe, 18 N Y
Supp, 16 (1891) Where cumulative
voting prevails, and the statutes require
three directors to be residents, and all
votes cast are cumulated on non-residents excepting thirty-two which are
cast for three residents, the three residents are elected, and the remaining
directors are those of the non-residents

as to elect a candidate who receives a minority of all the votes cast.[1]

Where a person not eligible to the office is declared elected and no stockholder objects or takes legal proceedings to test the right to the office, and such person is allowed to perform the duties of his office, he becomes an officer *de facto* As such his acts cannot be objected to on the ground that he was not a legally elected director. Neither corporate creditors, nor the corporation, nor the stockholders, nor the director himself are allowed to raise this objection in that manner The remedy is to oust him by *quo warranto* or to enjoin him as a usurper But after he is allowed to

---

who received the highest number of votes. Horton *v* Wilder, 29 Pac Rep, 566 (Kan, 1892) Where directors must be stockholders qualified to vote, a stockholder not qualified to vote by reason of not owning his stock for thirty days before the election is not qualified to be a director His election does not make him even a *de facto* director *In re* Newcombe *supra* Where an election is "conceived in fraud and conducted contrary to law," the call being insufficient, the notice concealed, the instigators having sold and transferred their certificates of stock the purpose of the election being to steal the control from one who really owned all the stock, and two of the alleged new directors not being stockholders as required by law, there are no directors *de facto*, even though they take possession and drive away the contractor who is building the road Johnston *v* Jones, 23 N J Eq, 216 (1872) In Barber's Case, L R, 5 Ch D, 963 (1877), arising under similar facts, the court said "Mr Barber was not qualified to be elected a director, and his election was absolutely null and void .   If he had acted as a director, there might have been an estoppel" The board of directors cannot, even under a by-law authorizing them to fill vacancies, oust a director on the ground that he was ineligible when elected, and then proceed to fill his place. Detwiler *v.* Commonwealth, 18

Atl. Rep., 990 (Pa, 1890) A director who is not a stockholder cannot sign a statutory notice of a meeting to increase the capital stock Matter of Wheeler, 2 Abb Pr (N S) 361 (1866) It formerly was held in England that the election of one not a shareholder as a director in a corporation in which it is required that the directors be owners of a certain amount of stock is valid, and such a person, upon acceptance of the directorship, is bound to take and pay for the required number of shares But the later decisions have established a contrary rule See § 52 The election of a disqualified person as director is voidable not void People *v* Albany, etc R. R., 55 Barb, 344, 373 (1869)

[1] Where the person declared elected received a minority of the votes he will be ousted even though the other candidate was not qualified to act as a director "Votes cast for a candidate who is disqualified for the office will not be thrown away, so as to make the election fall on a candidate having a minority of votes, unless the electors casting such votes had knowledge of the fact on which the disqualification of the candidate for whom they voted rested, and also knew that the latter was for that reason, disabled by law from holding the office" Matter of Election of St. Lawrence, etc, Co 44 N J L, 529 (1882), citing cases See also, People *v* Clute, 50 N Y, 451

become a *de facto* director his title to office cannot be attacked collaterally nor can his acts be repudiated on that ground [1]

Where the charter requires the director to be a stockholder he must continue to hold stock during his term of office. If he sells all his stock in the company he thereby becomes disqualified and ceases, *ipso facto*, to be a director.[2] He may, however, remain as

[1] Although a director is not qualified according to the by-laws, yet if he is elected and permitted to act, his election is valid so far as his acts as director affect third persons. Despatch Line, etc., v Bellamy, etc., Co., 12 N H, 205 (1841). See, also, § 713, *infra* The fact that a contract of a Pennsylvania company is made by its president and managers, who are non-residents and not residents as required by statute, does not enable the other party to the contract to raise that objection Delaware, etc., Canal Co v Penn Coal Co., 21 Pa. St., 131 (1853) The eligibility of a director who has acted with the consent of all cannot be questioned on an application to have the company dissolved under the statute *In re* Santa, etc., Co 4 N Y Supp., 173 (1889). Although the statutes require the directors to be residents of the state, nevertheless even though the directors are non-residents the incorporation is valid and the corporation is not dissolved, nor are the stockholders liable as partners. Demarest v Flack, 128 N Y. 205 (1891). The qualification of a director cannot be questioned by a creditor who is seeking to enforce a statutory liability of officers. Wallace v Walsh, 125 N Y. 26 (1890) One who assumes the duties of a director cannot say that he never was a director McDowall v Sheehan, 129 N Y, 200 (1891). The disqualified director is bound, he is liable as a director for breach of trust. Western Bank v Baird, 11 Cases in Ct of Sess, 3d series, 96, 121, Easterly v Barber, 65 N Y., 252 (1875) Cf Craw v Easterly, 54 N Y, 679 (1873) The principle of law that the acts of an ineligible but *de facto* officer may bind the corporation

arises often in municipal corporation cases State v Farrier, 47 N J. L., 383 (1885) aff'd, 48 id 613 Although the directors are not qualified, nevertheless the company cannot repudiate stock issued to a contractor in payment for work, where such work has been received, such contract being authorized by the disqualified directors. The company cannot accept the subscription, and at the same time repudiate the contract mode of payment. *Re* The Staffordshire, etc., Co., 66 L. T Rep., 413 (1892) Directors may act as such before they acquire qualification shares. *Re* International, etc., Co., 66 L. T Rep., 253 (1892)

[2] Where the statutes require the director to be a stockholder it follows "that as soon as a director parts with all beneficial interest in, and control over, the stock which he is required to hold, and causes the officers of the corporation to have knowledge of such fact by a request that a proper transfer be made on the books of the company, he no longer possesses the qualifications which the statute declares to be essential," and hence he ceases *ipso facto* to be a director and is no longer liable on a director's statutory liability. "The statute executing itself operated to divest him of title to the office." Chemical Nat'l Bank v Colwell, 132 N.Y., 250 (1892). *Contra*, Nathan v Tompkins, 82 Ala, 437 (1887), holding that he may be removed, but does not cease to be a director by the mere act of selling his stock. To same effect, Atlas Nat'l Bank v F B. Gardner Co., 6 Biss., 537 (1879). Where a trustee sells and delivers all his stock, he ceases to be an officer *de jure*, the statute requir-

a *de facto* director and bind the company by his acts, if allowed to continue in his position[1] The director does not become disqualified by reason of his pledging his stock.[2] The secretary, treasurer or other officer of a corporation need not be a resident or citizen unless the statute requires it.[3]

A corporation may pass a by-law prescribing the qualifications of its directors, and may prescribe that a person who is an attorney against it in a suit shall not be a director[4]

§ 624 *Acceptance and resignation of office and failure to elect officers — Removal of directors —* An acceptance of the office by one who is elected director is necessary to constitute him a director. Some direct and positive act of acceptance is necessary[5]

A director may resign, and no formal acceptance or entry thereof on the minute-book of the corporation is necessary to effect the resignation[6]

---

ing him to be a stockholder, and where the whole board of directors have sold their stock then acts as a board of directors are not binding on the corporation Ori, etc, Co v Reno Water Co., 30 Pac. Rep, 695 (Nev, 1882) "Can a director part with his qualification shares?" See on this subject, 8 R y & Corp. L J, 99 A person may purchase stock although such stock constitute the qualification shares of the vendor as a director. Kern v Day. 12 S Rep, 6 (La, 1893). A motion declaring the office vacant and electing another person before the director has really sold his stock is void Craw v Easterly. 54 N Y, 679 (1873)

[1] A director who sells his stock ceases to be a *de jure* director If he continues to and is permitted to act he is a director *de facto* Beardsley *v.* Johnson, 121 N Y, 224 (1890)

[2] Cumming v Prescott, 2 Y & C. Exch, 488 (1837). This was held in a case where the qualification shares were to be held by the directors in their own right Pulbrook *v* Richmond Consolidated Mining Co, 9 Ch D, 610

[3] Kerchner v. Gettys, 18 S. C. 521 (1882), McCall v Byram Manuf Co, 6 Conn, 428 (1827). But in Matthews *v* Trustees 2 Brews, 541 (1868), the court enjoined the company from compelling

its resident treasurer to turn over funds to a newly-elected non-resident treasurer

[4] Cross *v* West Virginia, etc, Co, 16 S E. Rep, 587 (W Va, 1892)

[5] Osborne, etc Co v Croome, 14 Hun, 164 (1878) aff'd, 77 N Y, 629, Cameron v Seaman, 69 N Y, 396 (1877) An 'honorary director" who sits with the board, makes up a quorum and accepts pay is subject to the disabilities and liabilities of a director as to being interested in contracts with the company There is no such thing in law as an "honorary director" *Ex parte* Stears, 29 L J (Ch), 43 (1859) Holding over may also arise from acting as a director Sanborn *v* Lefferts, 58 N Y, 179 (1874). It is a question for the jury whether a person accepted a directorship. The mere fact that as an advisor he met with the directors and made motions is not conclusive if he declined to accept Blake v Bayley, 82 Miss, 531 (1860) Acceptance is presumed Lockwood *v* Mechanics etc Bank 9 R I, 308 (1869) But may be disproved even though the person attended directors' meetings Blake *v* Bayley 82 Mass, 531 (1860)

[6] Movius v Lee, 30 Fed Rep, 301 Smith v Danzig, 64 How Pr, 320 (1883), Chandler v Hoag 2 Hun, 613 (1874), aff'd, 63 N Y, 624, Blake v Wheeler 18

A director may resign by an oral statement to that effect, and his resignation may be accepted in the same manner by the president [1] But a mere statement of a director that he will have nothing more to do with the office is not a sufficient resignation [2]

A resignation may be effectual even though it is not accepted, but it has been doubted whether all the directors can resign, thereby leaving the corporation helpless [3]

A director whose resignation has been accepted cannot afterwards vote at a meeting as a director. [4] The fact of the resignation need not be published or made known to corporate creditors. [5]

The resignation of a director must be presented to a meeting of the stockholders in order to be effective, unless the by-laws allow the directors to accept it. It is not sufficient to present the resignation to a meeting of the board of directors. Hence, although a resignation is sent in in the middle of the year, and is not accepted until the stockholders' meeting later in the year, the director continues to be such until such acceptance. [6] Such is the law as laid down in England, but in America the practice is different.

The insolvency of a director does not vacate his office. [7] A director does not lose his seat by absence [8] But the by-laws may provide otherwise [9]

Hun 496 (1879), aff'd 80 N Y., 128 A resignation to take effect on the termination of the term for which a director is elected is effectual, and he does not hold over though no successor is elected Van Ambuigh t Baker, 81 N Y., 46 (1880). A resignation releases a director if laid before the board of directors, and it is effective though not accepted, where it has been duly presented Maitland's Case, 1 De G, M & G, 769 (1853). Even though an officer resigns for the purpose of preventing service upon the company, yet if the resignation is accepted, service cannot be made upon him Sturgis t Crescent, etc, Co, 10 N Y Supp., 470 (1890) A director may resign after the company and officers have been enjoined from interfering with the corporate assets, and may then pursue his remedies as a corporate creditor Mexican, etc, Co t Mexican, etc., Co 47 Fed Rep., 351 (1891)

[1] Briggs v Spaulding, 141 U S, 132, 150 (1891).

[2] A mere statement by one director to another that he would have no more to do with the office is not a resignation. Kindberg v. Mudgett, 24 N Y Week. Dig, 239 (1886) A statement by a director to the secretary and treasurer at the time of transferring all his shares that he severed all connection with the company is not a resignation so far as corporate creditors' rights are concerned. Chemical Nat'l Bank t Colwell, 9 N. Y. Supp., 286 (1890), Id, 288, reversed on other grounds, 132 N Y, 250 Application to sue may be made to the president though he claims to have resigned. Averill v Barber, 6 N Y Supp., 255 (1889).

[3] Carnaghan v Exporters', etc, Co., 11 N Y Supp., 172 (1890).

[4] Wickersham v. Chittenden, 28 Pac. Rep, 788 (Cal, 1892)

[5] Bruce v. Platt, 80 N Y., 379 (1880).

[6] Municipal, etc, Co, Limited, v. Pollington, 63 L T. Rep, 238 (1890).

[7] Atlas National Bank v Gardner, 8 Biss., 537 (1879).

[8] Phelps v. Lyle, 10 A & E, 113 (1839).

[9] Wilson v. Wilson, 6 Scott, 540 (1838).

A director continues to be such until his successor is elected, even though he never attends meetings and is never consulted [1]

A reduction in the number of trustees may be valid although the statutory certificate is not filed, so far as corporate creditors are concerned [2]

The stockholders have no power to remove directors before the expiration of their term of office unless the charter or by-laws expressly give that power [3] Nor can they remove the president [4]

A failure to elect officers at the stated time does not work a dissolution of the corporation The old directors continue in office until their successors are duly elected [5] And even when the failure to elect has extended over a period of several years, and there are by reason thereof no directors in office, the old directors having wholly abandoned their trust, the stockholders may at any time in a lawful manner proceed to the election of a new board of directors [6] But if the majority fail or refuse to hold an election and the corporate property is thereby endangered, a court of equity may appoint a receiver to take charge of it, [7] and will in a proper case authorize a winding up [8]

A director is an "officer" of the corporation in the usual meaning of that term [9]

holding that an absconding director becomes "unable to act" within the meaning of the by-laws Sturges v Vanderbilt, 73 N Y, 384 11 Hun 136

[1] First National Bank v Lamon, 130 N Y, 366 (1891)

[2] Wallace v Walsh, 125 N Y, 26 (1890)

[3] See § 711, infra Concerning the advisability of allowing stockholders to remove directors at any time, see Cook on the Corporation Problem, pp 87 88 A director cannot be excluded from his duties as such nor can his election be declared invalid merely because of what he may contemplate doing is a director. Ohio, etc Co v State, 32 N E Rep, 933 (Ohio, 1892)

[4] Id A contract between a company and a person that he shall be the managing director for ten years does not prevent the corporation from dismissing him Bainbridge v Smith, 60 L T Rep, 879 (1889)

[5] State v Bonnell, 35 Ohio St 10, 17 (1878) in which an election of directors being held invalid, those previously in office were restored to office as being

entitled to hold until their successors were qualified Huguenot Bank v Studwell 6 Daly, 13 (1875) reversed on other grounds, 74 N Y, 621, and see § 631 Hold-over directors may hold meetings, fill vacancies in the board and vote to sell property the same as though regular elections had been held Kent County, etc Soc v Houseman, 46 N W Rep, 15 (Mich 1890)

[6] People v Twaddell 18 Hun 427 (1879) In Reilly v Oglebay 25 West Va, 36, 43 (1884), it is held that where there is no board of directors the shareholders themselves may lawfully assume and perform, pending a regular election the duties which ordinarily belong to a board of directors See ch XXXVI

[7] Lawrence v Greenwich Fire Ins Co 1 Paige 587 (1829)

[8] Brown v Union Ins Co, 3 La Ann, 177, 182 (1848) in which the neglect for nearly ten years to appoint officers being to the injury of creditors, the court appointed a manager to wind up the affairs of the company

[9] A director is an officer under a stat-

§§ 625-627 *Stockholders can act only at corporate meetings* — Stockholders can hold elections and transact the other business which they as a body are qualified to transact only at a corporate meeting duly called and convened   Consequently, all votes taken elsewhere than at such a meeting, and all separate consents, either oral or in writing, whereby the stockholders assume to bind the company, are invalid and void [1]

ute making officers liable for debts in certain cases Brand v Godwin 8 N. Y Supp, 339 (1890) The president and directors are "officers" within the meaning of a criminal statute Commonwealth v Wyman, 49 Mass, 217 (1844) So, also, of the treasurer Commonwealth v Tuckerman, 76 id, 173 (1857) In certain cases an "officer" is construed to mean merely an agent and not a director So held in regard to appointing a receiver of a foreign corporation Moran i Alvis, etc, Co, N Y Law Jour, Dec 5, 1891

[1] Commonwealth v Cullen, 13 Pa. St, 133 (1850), Finley Shoe, etc, Co v Kurtz, 34 Mich, 89 (1876), Peirce v New Orleans Building Co, 9 La, 397, 404 (1836), Livingston v Lynch, 4 Johns Ch, 573, 597 (1820), Torrey v. Baker, 83 Mass, 120 (1861), *Ex parte* Johnson, 31 Eng L & Eq, 430 (1854),

Short v Unangst, 3 Watts & S. (Pa), 45 (1841) *Cf* Graham v Boston, Hartford & Erie R. R. Co, 118 U S, 161 (1886), Granger v Grubb, 7 Phila, 350 (1870) For the rule relative to directors' meetings, see § 592, *supra* A lease authorized upon a two-thirds vote of the stockholders cannot be effected by two-thirds consenting thereto in writing without a meeting Reiff v Western, etc, Tel Co, 49 N. Y Super Ct, 441 (1883) The separate assent of stockholders to an act is not valid Their acts must be in meeting assembled. Duke v Markham, 10 S E. Rep., 1017 (N C, 1890) An actual meeting of the stockholders is not necessary if all consent even though the statutes require a meeting A subsequent creditor cannot complain Coe i East, etc, R R, 52 Fed Rep, 531 (1892).

CHAPTER XXXVIII.

DISSOLUTION, FORFEITURE AND IRREGULAR INCORPORATION.

§ 628. *Methods of dissolution.*— The dissolution of a corporation may be brought about by reason of (1) the forfeiture of its franchises by the adjudication of a court,[1] (2) the loss of its charter by a charter provision to that effect, in case the corporation fails to do certain things within a certain time,[2] (3) the repeal of its charter under the reserved power of the state,[3] (4) the voluntary surrender of the franchises by the stockholders; or (5) the expiration of the time limited for its existence in the charter.[4] Upon dissolu-

---

[1] See §§ 632-637, *infra*

[2] See § 638, *infra*

[3] This subject is considered in § 639, *infra*

[4] "The dissolution of corporations is or may be effected by expirations of their charters, by failure of any essential part of the corporate organizations that cannot be restored, by dissolution and surrender of their franchises with the consent of the state, by legislative enactment within constitutional authority, by forfeiture of their franchises and judgment of dissolution declared in regular judicial proceedings, or by other lawful means " Swan, etc, Co *v* Frank, 148 U S, 603, 611 (1893) In Michigan all charters except those of railroads, canals and turnpikes are limited by the constitution to thirty years "The evident intent of this section was to prevent the perpetuation of corporate power and corporate wealth so as to place it practically beyond the reach of the people or the legislature" It does not apply to a county fair corporation Kent County, etc, Soc *v* Houseman, 46 N W Rep, 15 (Mich, 1890). Where a special charter is granted and nothing is prescribed as to the duration of the corporation, the charter is perpetual State *v* Ladies, etc, 12 S W Rep, 293 (Mo, 1889) A corporation without limit of time in its charter as to duration is perpetual Snell *v* Chicago 24 N E Rep, 532 (Ill, 1890)

857

tion by any one of these methods the stockholders have certain rights in the corporate assets

§ 629. *Dissolution by the stockholders — A court of equity has no power to dissolve a corporation — Statutory dissolution —* It is an unquestioned rule that all the stockholders, by unanimous consent, may effect a dissolution of the corporation by the surrender of the corporate franchises.[1]

Greater difficulty is found in determining whether a majority of the stockholders may dissolve a corporation   It has been held that the majority in interest of the stockholders of a corporation may dissolve it by a voluntary surrender of its franchises, even though a minority of the stockholders are opposed to the dissolution.[2]

Such, undoubtedly, is the case where the corporation is insolvent or is doing a failing business, and is manifestly unable to accomplish the purposes of its organization   But where such is not the case, and where the term during which the corporation was to exist has not expired;[3] or where the dissolution is desired in order to obtain a new charter for a different object,[4] or where the dissolution is merely a device to effect a consolidation which otherwise would be *ultra vires*,[5] — it has been held that the majority cannot

[1] Mobile & Ohio R. R. Co v State, 29 Ala, 573, 586 (1857), Savage v Walshe, 26 id, 619 (1855), Attorney-General v Clergy Society, 10 Rich Eq, 604 (1859), Chesapeake & Ohio Canal Co t Baltimore & Ohio R. R. Co, 4 Gill & J, 1, 121 (1832), McIntyre Poor School v Zanesville Canal, etc. Co, 9 Ohio, 203 (1839), La Grange, etc, R. R. Co v Rainey, 7 Coldw. (Tenn), 420 (1870); Slee v Bloom, 19 Johns, 456 (1822), Webster v Turner, 12 Hun, 264 (1877); Houston v Jefferson College, 63 Pa St., 428 (1869), Denike v. New York, etc., Co., 80 N Y, 599, 606 (1880)   Although a stockholder has sued in the federal court to wind up a Connecticut corporation, nevertheless it seems that such corporation may dissolve voluntarily   Kessler v Continental, etc, Co., 42 Fed Rep, 258 (1890)

[2] Treadwell v Salisbury Manuf Co, 7 Gray, 393 (1756), Hancock v Holbrook, 9 Fed. Rep, 353 (1881) (reversed on another point, 112 U S, 229), Wilson v. Proprietors of Central Bridge, 9 R I, 590 (1870)   Compare, however, *dictum* in Denike v New York, etc., Co., 80 N.

Y, 599, 606 (1880), citing cases, and in Mobile, etc, Co t State, 29 Ala, 573, 586 (1857), citing New Orleans, etc., Co. v Harris, 27 Miss, 577 (1854). Ward v. Society, etc, 28 Eng Ch (1 Collier), 370 (1844), Angell & Ames on Corp, § 772; Barry v Broach, 4 S. Rep, 117 (Miss, 1888), where the business was a losing one   That the majority may not dissolve, see Zibriskie v Hackensack, etc., R. R. Co, 18 N J Eq, 168 (1867), Mowrey t Indianapolis, etc., R. R. Co., 4 Biss, 78 (1866), Lauman v Lebanon, etc., 30 Pa. St., 42 (1858), and cases in following notes

[3] Kean v Johnson, 9 N J, Eq, 401 (1853)   See, also, Van Schmidt v. Huntington, 1 Cal, 25 (1850)   Dissolution of a solvent corporation before its charter time has elapsed cannot be had except by unanimous consent of the stockholders.   Barton v Enterprise, etc., Ass'n, 16 N E. Rep., 486 (Ind., 1888)

[4] Ward v Society of Attorneys, 1 Coll, 370 (1844).

[5] Black v. Delaware, etc., Canal Co., 22 N J Eq, 403 (1871). See, also § 667, *infra.*

dissolve the corporation in opposition to the wishes of the minority [1] Stockholders owning only a minority of the stock cannot, at common law, compel a dissolution before the expiration of the time limited in the charter for the existence of the corporation [2] The directors of a corporation cannot dissolve it [3]

A court of equity has, in the absence of statutory power, no jurisdiction over corporations for the purpose of decreeing their dissolution and the distribution of their assets among the individual corporators at the suit of one or more of the stockholders [4]

[1] Polar Star Lodge v Polar Star Lodge, 16 La Ann, 53 (1861), Currien v Santini, id, 27 See, also, *dictum* in Mobile, etc, R. R. Co v State, 29 Ala, 573 (1857), and n 1, *supra*

[2] Denike v New York, etc, Co, 80 N Y, 599 (1880) (citing cases) Folger v Columbian Ins Co, 99 Mass, 267 (1868), Pratt v Jewett, 9 Gray, 34 (1857) where dissolution was denied, although the business was a losing one and the single person holding a majority of the stock was mismanaging the business, Croft v Lumpkin, etc, Min Co, 61 Ga, 465 (1878), where the corporation was solvent, but made no effort to transact business or proceed, Waterbury v Merchants', etc, Co, 50 Barb, 157 (1867), holding that misconduct of the corporate officers is no cause for dissolution at the suit of the minority To same effect, Belmont v Erie R'y Co, 52 id, 637 (1869). A stockholder has no right to bring an action for the dissolution of the corporation Byrne v New York, etc, Co., 16 Week Dig, 139 (1882)

[3] Lake Ontario, etc, Bank v Onondaga Bank, 7 Hun, 549 (1876), Jones v Bank of Leadville, 17 Pac Rep, 272 (Col, 1888), Ward v Sea Insurance Co, 7 Paige, 294 (1838), Abbot v American Hard Rubber Co 33 Barb, 578 (1861). *Cf* Bank of Switzerland v Bank of Turkey, 5 L T (N S), 549 (1862), where the directors repaid sums advanced to an abortive company

[4] United States T Co v N Y, etc, R. R., 101 N Y, 478 (1886), Verplanck v Mercantile, etc, Co, 1 Edw Ch, 84 (1831), Hardon v. Newton, 14 Blatch,

376 (1878), Fountain Ferry, etc, Co v Jewell, 8 B Mon, 140 (1848), Ferris v Strong 3 Edw Ch, 127 (1837). See. also, Strong v McCagg, 55 Wis, 624 (1882), Latimer v Eddy, 46 Barb, 61 (1864) But the court will appoint a receiver to preserve the corporate assets where the majority do not elect officers Lawrence v Greenwich Fire Ins. Co, 1 Paige, 587 (1829) Any person may be appointed receiver See § 864, *infra*. Where, upon voluntary dissolution, the stockholders appoint two of their number to administer the assets, the court will not displace them and appoint a receiver Follett v Field, 30 La Ann, 161 (1878) A single stockholder in an insolvent corporation cannot have it dissolved in a court of equity Merryman v Carroll, etc, Co, 4 R'y & Corp L. J, 12 (1888) A corporation cannot be dissolved except by judicial sentence or sovereign power A court of equity has no inherent power to decree dissolution A member cannot sue for his part of the assets until a dissolution is had Magee v Genesea Acad, 17 N Y St Rep, 221 (1888) A stockholder cannot have the corporation wound up in equity Hinckley v Pfister, 53 N W Rep, 21 (Wis, 1892) Where for seven years a stockholder who owned a majority of the stock elected himself and two of his dummies as directors of the company, and caused the board to vote a large salary to himself as president and manager, and had leased to the company his property at a large rental, the salary and rental are illegal and void Where the company had failed

In many of the states there are statutes regulating the dissolution of a corporation. These statutes generally specify what parties may bring suit for dissolution, on what grounds dissolution will be decreed, and what proceedings must be taken to obtain the decree   Such a statutory dissolution is hardly a voluntary dissolution, and yet it approaches that kind of dissolution more nearly than any other.[1]

to pay its dividends by reason of such acts, a court of equity upon the suit of another stockholder ordered the president to account, and appointed a receiver of the company and directed that its affairs be wound up   Miner v Belle Isle Ice Co, 53 N W Rep, 218 (Mich, 1892). "The power to declare a forfeiture of corporate franchises was originally in England vested in the courts of law, and was exercised in a proceeding brought by the attorney-general in the name of the sovereign. The court of chancery never assumed jurisdiction in such cases until it was conferred by act of parliament It declined until the power was conferred by statute to sequestrate corporate property through the medium of a receiver or to dissolve corporate bodies, or to restrain the usurpation of corporate powers." Decker v Gardner, 124 N Y., 334 (1890) In the absence of statutory authority, a court of equity has no jurisdiction to dissolve a corporation Wheeler v Pullman, etc., Co, 32 N E. Rep., 420 (Ill, 1892)

[1] Thus, in New York, elaborate provision is made The majority of the directors may apply for dissolution. See §§ 2419, etc, Code of C P As also may a creditor or stockholder §§ 1784, etc., id Under the New York statute the court will order the dissolution of a corporation where a majority of the directors and stockholders wish it, where the interests are discordant and a dissolution will be beneficial Matter of Importers', etc, Exchange, 132 N. Y. 212 (1892). Under the old statute, part of the stockholders might compel a dissolution where there had been a failure to

elect officers. Ward v. Sea Ins. Co, 7 Paige, 294 (1838). Where a majority of the directors and stockholders apply for dissolution the court will presume that it should be granted In re Niagara Ins. Co 1 Paige, 258 (1828). In general see, also. In re Pyrolusite, etc., Co., 29 Hun, 429 (1883), In re Boynton, etc., Co, 34 Hun, 369 (1884) In West Virginia one-third in interest of the stockholders may apply to the court for a dissolution. See Hurst v Coe, 3 S E. Rep., 564 (1887). Corporate creditors cannot, before judgment, apply for dissolution of corporation Cole v Knickerbocker, etc., Ins. Co, 23 Hun, 255 (1880); aff'd. 91 N. Y., 641 Where the statute provides that two-thirds of the stockholders may cause the corporation to be wound up, their right to do so is absolute and cannot be controlled by the court. Watkins v. National Bank, 32 Pac. Rep., 914 (Kan, 1893). The voluntary dissolution of a company under the statute, but without ten days' notice required by the statute, is not such a dissolution as to prevent creditors from attaching the property of the company as though no dissolution had been had. Cleveland, etc., Co. v Taylor, etc., Co, 54 Fed. Rep., 82 (1893) But the dissolution cannot be enjoined by creditors in the absence of fraud Id, 85 Statutes usually contain a provision that the corporate existence shall be continued for a fixed time, pending the proceedings for dissolution, so that suits may be brought by and against the corporation for the purpose of closing the business and disposing of the assets. Stetson v City Bank of New Orleans, 12 Ohio St. 577 (1861), McGoon v Scales, 9 Wall, 23 (1869), Mariners'

The courts of one state cannot dissolve a corporation created by another state,[1] but may appoint a receiver of the corporate assets within the jurisdiction.[2]

Bank v Sewall, 50 Me, 220 (1861), Muscatine Turn Verein v Funck, 18 Iowa, 469 (1865). Thornton v Marginal Freight R'y Co, 123 Mass, 32 (1877), Folger v Chase, 18 Pick, 63 (1836), Crease v Babcock, 10 Metc, 525, 567 (1846), Re Independent Ins Co, 1 Holmes 103, Franklin Bank v Cooper, 36 Me, 179 (1853); Nevitt v Bank of Port Gibson, 14 Miss, 513 (1846). The life of the corporation is frequently extended by these statutes for three years Herron v. Vance, 17 Ind 595 (1861), Foster v Essex Bank, 16 Mass, 245 (1819), Blake v Portsmouth, etc, R. R. Co., 39 N H, 435 (1859), Van Glahn v De Rosset. 81 N C, 467 (1879), Michigan State Bank v Gardner 15 Gray 362 (1860) Sometimes five years Tuskaloosa etc, Association v Green, 48 Ala, 346 (1872) Cf Lincoln, etc, Bank v Richardson, 1 Me, 79 (1820) Under statutes in some of the states an information in the nature of *quo warranto* may be filed at the relation of a shareholder against an illegally-existing corporation to compel a dissolution Albert v State, 65 Ind 413 (1879) Under the National Banking Act, see Kennedy v Gibson, 8 Wall, 498 (1869). Bank of Bethel v Pahquique Bank, 14 Wall, 383 (1870), Bank v Kennedy, 17 Wall, 19 (1872), In re Platt, Receiver, 1 Ben, 534 (1867) A resolution of two-thirds of the stockholders in a national bank to go into liquidation does not dissolve the corporation Merchants' Nat'l Bank v Gaslin, 43 N W. Rep, 483 (Minn, 1889)

Under the English act it has been held that the majority cannot insist upon dissolution though the business is a losing one In re Suburban Hotel Co, L. R., 2 Ch, 737 (1867) But the court may grant it under such circumstances even to a few stockholders Re Factage Parisien 34 L J, Ch, 140 (1865) In determining whether to order a winding up the court will not consider possible future profits In re European, etc, Society, L. R., 9 Eq, 122 (1869) For an application to have a winding up because business had not been commenced within a year, see In re Tumacacori, L. R., 17 Eq, 534 (1874). If the corporation has sold its property and ceased business the court will order a distribution of the assets Cramer v Bird, L R 6 Eq, 143 (1868) The mere fact that the company is losing money is not sufficient to have a winding up In re Joint-stock Coal Co., L. R., 8 Eq, 146 (1869) The court has a judicial discretion, and will not ordinarily order a winding up at the instance of one stockholder in opposition to all the others In re London Suburban Bank, L. R., 6 Ch, 641 (1871) But if the company is insolvent or is doing a ruinous business with no prospect of a change the court will order a winding up on the petition of a minority Re Great Northern etc, Min Co 17 W R, 462 (1869) A court has no jurisdiction to wind up a corporation where a company was never incorporated one of the requisite incorporators not having signed the articles of incorporation Re National, etc, Co 64 L T Rep 512 (1891), aff'g id, 229 See, also in general, under this winding-up act, Re Factage Parisien, 34 L J, Ch 110 (1865), In re Exmouth Docks Co. L. R., 17 Eq, 181 (1873), In re Sanderson's Patents Association, L. R 12 Eq, 188 (1871), In re Bradford Navigation Co, L. R., 10 Eq, 331 (1870), Princess of Reuss v Bos, L. R. 5 H of L, 176 (1871), In re Commercial Bank of India,

---

[1] Baker v Backus, 32 Ill, 79, 110 (1863).

[2] See ch. LL

Where a dissolution is being obtained or has been obtained by fraud and an inequitable overbearing of the rights of an innocent stockholder,[1] a court of equity will, at the instance of the latter, enjoin or set aside the dissolution [2]

§ 630 There has been some doubt whether a voluntary dissolution by all or a majority of the stockholders is completed by a mere vote of the stockholders, or whether a decree of a court is needed and is sufficient, or whether a legislative acceptance and confirmation of the dissolution is essential. The better opinion is that the resolution of the stockholders to dissolve will effect a dissolution only after the legislature has accepted it and ordained it, or a court duly authorized by statute to accept a voluntary dissolution has entered a decree to that effect [3]

L. R., 6 Eq., 517 (1868), *In re* London India Rubber Co, L. R., 1 Chan, 329 (1866). *In re* Pen-y-Van Colliery Co, L. R., 6 Chan Div, 477 (1877). *In re* United Service Co, L. R. 7 Eq, 76 (1868) *Re* German Date Cor Ltd, 46 L T Rep (N S) 327 (Ct of App, 1882), holding that where a company was organized and chartered to engage in manufacture and sale of goods under a certain patent, when in fact there was no patent such as was referred to, and an application for such a patent was refused, *held,* that the sub-stratum upon which the company was based or main object for which it was formed not being in existence, the company must be dissolved on petition of a shareholder, notwithstanding it was profitably engaged in the manufacture and sale of the commodity without any patent, and notwithstanding a very large majority of the company desired to have the company continue in business. To same effect, under somewhat similar circumstances, *Re* The Havana Gold Mining Co, 46 L. T. Rep, 322 (Ct. of App, 1882) Lender of money to benefit building society cannot petition to wind it up *Ex parte* Williamson, L. R., 5 Ch, 309 (1869). Mortgage bondholders cannot institute winding-up proceedings under the English act. *In re* Uruguay, etc., R'y Co, L. R., 11 Ch. D, 372 (1879). For many cases relative to where a court will order a winding

up and when not under the English statute see Healey's Companies Law and Practice, pp 446, etc.

[1] People *v* Hektograph Co., 10 Abb N C (N Y), 358 (1882).

[2] *In re* Beaujolais Wine Co, L. R., 3 Chan, 15 (1876). *In re* London & Mercantile Discount Co, L. R., 1 Eq, 277 (1865) In Stupart *v* Arrowsmith, 3 Sm. & G, 176 (1855), a bill filed by a shareholder on behalf of himself and others to set aside a dissolution, after three years' acquiescence, no fraud or imposition being alleged was dismissed with costs *Cf* Kent *t* Jackson, 2 De G, M & G, 49 (1852), Bailey's Appeal, 96 Pa St, 253 (1880), where certain stockholders procured the dissolution of a corporation by fraud They were held to be trustees *ex maleficio* for the *bona fide* stockholders, and as such liable to account to them for the assets of the company

[3] Portland Dry Dock, etc. Co. *v.* Trustees of Portland, 12 B. Mon, 77 (1851), La Grange & Memphis R. R. Co *v* Rainey, 7 Coldw. (Tenn), 420 (1870), Harris *v* Muskingum Mfg Co, 4 Blackf (Ind), 267 (1836), Town *v* Bank, etc, Raisin 2 Doug (Mich), 530 (1847); Currier *t.* Santini, 16 La. Ann, 27 (1861), Norris *v* Mayor of Smithville, 1 Swan (Tenn), 164 (1851), Bradt *v* Benedict, 17 N Y, 93, 99 (1858). Boston Glass Co. *v.* Langdon, 24 Pick, 49 (1834); Wilson *v.* Proprietors of Central Bridge, 9 R I,

§ 631. *Acts which do not constitute dissolution* —There are certain acts and facts which do not in themselves constitute a dissolution. A dissolution is not effected by a failure to elect officers,[1] nor by a sale or assignment of all the corporate property,[2] nor by

590 (1870) Penobscot Boom Corp v Lamson, 16 Me, 224 (1839). Enfield Toll Bridge Co v Conn River Co, 7 Conn, 28, 45 (1828), Mumma v Potomac, etc, 8 Peters, 281, 287 A mere resolution of the stockholders is ineffectual New York, etc, Works v Smith, 4 Duer, 362 (1855), Powell v Oregonian R y Co, 38 Fed Rep, 187 (1889) A notice of the resolution sent to the governor is ineffectual Merchants' Bank v Heard, 37 Ga, 401 (1867), Revere v Boston, etc, Co, 15 Pick, 351 (1834). By a statute the acceptance may be made by a proclamation Campbell v Miss Union Bank 7 Miss, 625, 681 (1842) The judgment of a court of law in such a case is ineffectual Chesapeake, etc, Co v Baltimore, etc, R R Co 4 Gill & J, 1, 107 (1832) In England the surrender at common law was to the king, and had to be accepted by him in order to work a dissolution. The King v Amery, 2 Term Rep, 515, 531 (1788), The King v Gray, 8 Mod Rep, 358 (1825) Cf Bruce v Platt, 80 N Y 379 (1880). Voluntary dissolution need not be accepted by the state Merchants', etc, Line v Wagoner, 71 Ala 581 (1882). The case of Webster v Turner 12 Hun 264 (1877), can be upheld only in connection with § 631, *infra* See, also, cases in notes *supra*, to effect that a court cannot decree a dissolution at the instance of stockholders Many states now have statutes expressly giving to courts such authority

[1] Rose v Turnpike Co, 3 Watts (Penn) 46 (1834) Lehigh Bridge Co v Lehigh Coal & Navigation Co, 4 Rawle (Penn), 8, 23 (1832), Commonwealth v Cullen, 13 Pa St, 133 (1850), Hoboken Building, etc, Association v Martin, 13 N J Eq, 427 (1861), Evarts v Killingworth Mfg. Co, 20 Conn, 447 (1850), Nashville

Bank v Petway, 3 Humph (Tenn), 522 (1842), Boston Glass Mfg Co v Langdon, 24 Pick, 49 (1834). Russell v McLellan, 14 id 63 (1833), Cahill v Kalamazoo, etc, Ins Co, 2 Doug (Mich), 124, 140 (1845). Harris v Mississippi Valley, etc, R R Co, 51 Mich, 602 (1875), People v Runkle, 9 Johns, 147 (1812), Philips v Wickham, 1 Paige, 590 (1829) Slee v Bloom, 5 Johns Chan, 366 (1821), S C, 19 Johns, 456 (1822) St Louis, etc, Loan Association v Augustin, 2 Mo App 123 (1876), Knowlton v Ackley, 8 Cush, 93 (1851), President & Trustees, etc, v Thompson, 20 id, 197 (1858). People v Wren, 5 Ill 269 (1843). Nor will a resignation of all the officers dissolve the corporation Muscatine Turn Verein v Funck, 18 Iowa, 469 (1865), Evarts v Killingworth Mfg Co 20 Conn, 447 (1850) The corporate rights and franchises are, in such a case, merely dormant until other officers are elected Philips v Wickham, 1 Paige, 590 (1829) Cf Lea v American Atlantic, etc, Canal Co, 3 Abb Prac (N S), 1 (1867)

[2] Barclay v Talman 4 Edw Chan 123 (1842) De Camp v Aylward, 52 Ind, 468 (1876), Richwald v Commercial Hotel Co, 106 Ill, 439 (1883), Rollins v Clay, 33 Me, 132 (1851) Kansas City Hotel v Sauer, 65 Mo, 279 (1877), Troy etc R R Co v Kerr, 17 Barb, 581 (1854), where a railroad corporation had leased the entire property to another corporation, State v Merchant, 37 Ohio St 251 (1881), Smith v Gower 2 Duvall, 17 (1865). To same effect State v Rives 5 Ired Law (N C) 297 (1849), Bruffett v Great Western R R Co, 25 Ill 353 (1861) The statutes may cause dissolution by the company s going out of business and selling all the property People v De Grauw, 63 Hun, 221 (1891).

the fact that one person owns all the shares of stock;[1] nor by a cessation of all corporate business and acts,[2] nor by the death of its stockholders,[3] nor by insolvency,[4] nor, in all cases, by a consolidation with another corporation under statutory authority.[5] Nor is it dissolved by the appointment of a receiver,[6] or the foreclosure of a mortgage,[7] nor by failure to file reports.[8] The fact that there are less stockholders than the charter requires does not invalidate the acts of the corporation[9] For certain purposes, however, such as rendering stockholders liable on their statutory liability,[10] or relieving directors from a penal liability,[11] dissolution is held to arise by some of these acts

[1] See § 709

[2] Attorney-General ι Bank of Niagara, Hopkins' Chan (N. Y), 403 (1825), Baptist Meeting-house ν Webb, 66 Me, 398 (1877), Rollins ν Clay, 33 Me, 132 (1851), Harris ν Nesbit 24 Ala, 393 (1854), Kansas City Hotel Co ν Sauer, 65 Mo, 279, 288 (1877), Simmons ν Tappan, 2 Sweeney (N Y), 652 (1870); Mickles ν Rochester City Bank, 11 Paige, 118 (1844), State ν Barron, 58 N H, 370 (1878)· Re Jackson Marine Ins Co, 4 Sandf Chan (N Y), 559 (1847), West ν Carolina, etc, Co 31 Ark, 476 (1876), Bache ν Horticultural Soc, 10 Lea (Tenn), 436 (1882), Brandon Iron Co ν Gleason, 24 Vt, 228 (1852), Atlanta ν Gate, etc, Co, 71 Ga, 106 (1883) Dissolution may exist by cessation, etc, so far as the reversion of property given to the corporation is concerned Stone ν Framingtou, 109 Mass, 303 (1872). A cessation of business with the understanding that the company is dissolved, the property having been transferred to the stockholders, does not work a dissolution Suits may be instituted against the company Carnaghan ν Exporters', etc, Co, 11 N. Y. Supp, 172 (1890) A foreclosure sale of all the property and franchises of a corporation will close out and foreclose the whole interest of the stockholders therein Vatable ν New York, etc, R R Co, 96 N Y, 49 (1884), Thornton ν Wabash R'y Co, 81

id, 462, 467 (1880). See, also, Sullivan ν Portland & Kennebec R R Co, 94 U S, 806 (1876). As to reorganizations, see ch LII infra

[3] Boston Glass Mfg Co. ν. Langdon, 24 Pick, 49, 52 (1834), Russell ν McLellan 14 Pick, 63, 69 (1833).

[4] Moseby ι Burrow, 52 Tex, 396 (1880); Valley Bank & Savings Institution ν. Sewing Society, 28 Kan, 423 (1882). Such is the case though a receiver has been appointed State ν Merchant, 37 Ohio St., 251 (1881), National Bank v. Insurance Co, 104 U. S, 54 (1881); Kincaid ν. Dwinelle, 59 N Y, 548 (1875).

[5] See ch LIII, infra

[6] The appointment of a receiver does not dissolve a corporation Nothing but the expiration of the charter or the judgment of a court can do that. Harselman ι Japanese, etc, Co., 27 N E Rep, 318 (Ind, 1891).

[7] Smith ι Gower, 2 Duv (Ky), 17 (1865); White, etc, R R ν White, etc, R R, 50 N H, 50 (1870)

[8] Failure to file a report does not work a forfeiture of charter State ν Brownstown, etc, Co., 22 N E Rep., 316 (Ind, 1889).

[9] Welch ν Importers', etc, Bank, 122 N Y, 177 (1890).

[10] See Slee ν Bloom, 19 Johns, 456 (1822), and § 219, supra Cf. Bradt ι Benedict, 17 N Y, 93 (1858).

[11] Losee ν. Bullard, 79 N. Y., 404 (1880).

§ 632 *Only the attorney general can institute a suit to forfeit a corporate charter.*— Such unquestionably is the law   It is for the state alone to withdraw the charter which the state has given   A stockholder cannot institute the suit,[1] nor a corporate creditor,[2] nor can the municipal authorities by reason of a change of route by a railroad,[3] nor can a person who is overcharged on a turnpike bring suit to forfeit the company's charter[4]   The state cannot even authorize the secretary of state to forfeit a charter[5]   The corporation is entitled to its day in court

§ 633. *Forfeiture for misuser — Acts which constitute a misuser*   The law is clear that, if a corporation misuses its powers, the state may by a suit withdraw the charter which it has given   Great difficulty, however, arises in determining what constitutes a misuser.   A clear idea can be obtained only by a study of the cases themselves.[6]

[1] North v State, 8 N E Rep, 159 (Ind, 1886), Baker v Backus, 32 Ill, 79 (1863), Commonwealth v Union Ins Co., 5 Mass, 230 (1809), State v Paterson & T Co., 21 N J L, 9 (1847), Murphy v Farmers' Bank, etc, 20 Pa St, 415 (1853), Rice v National Bank, etc, 126 Mass, 300 (1879), Folger v Columbian, etc, Ins Co, 99 Mass, 267 (1868), where the court refused to recognize a dissolution decreed by a New York court at the instance of a stockholder, Raisbeck v Oesterricher, 4 Abb N C, 444 (Com Pl, 1878), where the plaintiff claimed that the incorporation was irregular.

[2] Gaylord v Fort Wayne, etc, R R Co., 6 Biss., 286 (1875) A judgment forfeiting the charter of a private corporation, where the state is not a party to the suit, is a nullity Pickett v. Abney, 19 S W Rep, 859 (Tex, 1892)

[3] Moore v Brooklyn, etc, R. R., 108 N Y, 98 (1888)

[4] Commonwealth v Allegheny Bridge Co, 20 Pa St, 185 (1852), State v White's, etc, Co, 8 Tenn Ch, 164 (1876), where the bill purported to be in the attorney-general's name A shipper of freight cannot by bill in equity compel a canal company to repair and render its canal navigable Only the state can complain Buck, etc, Co v Lehigh

etc, Co, 50 Pa St, 91 (1865) The statutes of a state, however, sometimes change these rules of law

[5] The statute of West Virginia authorizing the secretary of state to declare corporate charters forfeited if its taxes are not paid is ineffectual for that purpose Forfeiture can be made only after a suit by the state brought for that purpose Greenbrier, etc, Co v Ward, 3 S E Rep, 227 (W Va, 1887)

[6] The state will, at the instance of the attorney-general, forfeit the charter of the corporation, whose stockholders have entered into a 'trust' with the stockholders of competing corporations, for the purpose of forming a monopoly in and raising the price of sugar The "trust" is not a joint-stock association It is of the character of a trust estate People v North R. S Ref Co., 121 N Y, 582 (1890) The state may forfeit a charter for a failure of the officers to file the annual report and of the stockholders to pay in the capital stock as required by statute It is immaterial that the state's action was induced by parties who were themselves responsible for the failure to comply with the statute People v Buffalo, etc, Co, 131 N Y, 140 (1892) It has been held to be a misuser to file a false certificate that the capital stock has been paid up,

§ 634 *Non-user as a cause for forfeiture.*— Non-user of its franchise is a cause for forfeiture where a corporation is possessed not

Eastern, etc, Co. v. Regina, 22 Eng L. & Eq, 328 (1853); or to establish a branch bank where the charter authorizes only a principal banking place, People v Oakland Co. Bank, 1 Doug (Mich), 282 (1844), or to keep its books and place of business out of the state, State v Milwaukee, etc, R'y Co, 45 Wis, 590 (1878), or for an insurance company to take risks which it cannot pay if required, Ward v. Farwell, 97 Ill, 593 (1881), or for taking 'grave-yard" insurance, State v Central, etc Assoc, 29 Ohio St. 399 (1876), the person receiving the insurance having no insurable interest in the person insured, or for not keeping tracks in a condition required by the charter. State v. Madison, etc, R'y Co, 40 N W Rep, 487 (Wis, 1888), or for a canal company to allow the canal to become out of repair, State v Penn, etc, 23 Ohio St, 121 (1872) or for a ferry company to be guilty of the same neglect. State v. Council Bluffs, etc, Co, 11 Neb, 354 (1881), or for filing false and fraudulent articles of association. State v Bailey, 16 Ind, 46 (1861), holding, also, that mere insolvency is no cause for forfeiture, or for accepting subscriptions by persons who are notoriously insolvent, Holman v State, 105 Ind, 569 (1885), Jersey City Gas Co v Dwight, 29 N J Eq, 242 (1878), or for a failure of a river improvement company to make an improvement as commanded by a statute, People v Improvement Co., 103 Ill, 491 (1882), or for a bank to loan to its directors in violation of a statute, Bank Com'rs v Bank of Buffalo, 6 Paige, 497 (1837), or for a charitable corporation to divide with a lobbyist an appropriation obtained from the legislature. People v Dispensary, etc, Soc, 7 Lans., 304 (1873), or for an insurance company to insure in a manner contrary to statute and to delay payments of losses, State v. Standard, etc, Assoc, 38 Ohio St., 281 (1882);

for a bank to contract debts beyond the charter limits, and to make dividends before resuming specie payments, State Bank v State, 1 Blackf (Ind), 267 (1823); or for persistently taking usurious interest, Commonwealth v Commercial Bank, 28 Pa St, 383 (1857), State v. Same, 33 Miss, 474 (1857), or for a mutual relief association to be run for the benefit of its officers only, State v People's, etc, Assoc, 42 Ohio St, 579 (1885); or for a bank to suspend specie payments, State v Bank of S. C., 1 Spears, L (S C), 433 (1841), Com Bank v State, 6 Sm & M (Miss), 599 (1846); but see State v New Orleans, etc., Co, 2 Rob. (La), 529 (1842), or for a turnpike company to allow its road to be out of repair, Washington, etc, T. Co. v. State, 19 Md, 239 (1862), Coon v Plymouth, etc, Co 32 Mich, 248 (1875), Darnell v. State, 3 S W Rep., 365 (Ark, 1887); State v Pawtucket, etc, Corp'n, 8 R. I, 182 (1865), where the company neglected a part of its road which it had sold to a municipality Not every neglect is fatal. The question is for the jury. People v. Woodstock T. Co, 11 Vt, 431 (1839). It is cause for forfeiture of its charter if a railroad company does not keep tracks in a condition required by its charter. State v Madison R'y Co, 40 N W Rep., 487 (Wis, 1888). And it is no defense to forfeiture for neglect that the road has been sold on an execution sale. Commonwealth v Tenth, etc, Co., 59 Mass, 509 (1850). Nor is it a defense that the state has authorized a competing line. Turnpike Co v State, 3 Wall, 210 (1865).

In the case of State v Essex Bank, 8 Vt, 489 (1836) the court refused to decree a forfeiture, since the public were not injured, though the corporation was clearly guilty of misuser. If a gas company is ordered by a municipality under a statutory power to reduce the price of gas, it may defend against forfeiture for non-compliance by asserting that the

only of its franchise to be a corporation, but also other franchises, such as a right of way, which the public are interested in having kept in active use [1]

municipality was fraudulently induced to act   State v Cincinnati, etc, Co, 18 Ohio St, 262 (1868)   If a company has incorporated under a general act, but for a purpose not authorized by it, a suit for forfeiture lies   State v Beck, 81 Ind, 501 (1882), where a turnpike company incorporated to *purchase* turnpikes, a purpose not authorized by the statute   The state may create causes for the forfeiture of insurance companies' charters   Chicago, etc, Ins Co v. Needles, 113 U S, 574 (1885)   Where the state sues to forfeit the charter of a railroad company which has leased its road, the latter cannot institute a suit to test the validity of that lease   Ogdensburgh, etc, R R Co v Vermont, etc, R. R. Co, 4 Hun, 712 (1875)   If *quo warranto* is brought for not making reports the corporation may offer to make the reports   State v Barron, 57 N H, 498 (1876)   By statute, forfeiture may be decreed where the court decides that a continuance of business by an insurance company will be hazardous to the community   Ward v Farwell, 97 Ill, 593 (1881)   The legislature cannot amend a charter by forfeiting the charter if specie payments are not made within a specified time   State v Tombeckbee Bank, 2 Stew (Ala), 30 (1829)   It can-

[1] Non-user is good ground for the forfeiture of franchises   People v Broadway R R, 126 N Y, 29 (1891)   A suit for forfeiture lies where a railroad company takes up part of its track   State v West, etc, R'y Co, 34 Wis, 197 (1879), S C, 36 id, 166 (1874)   Or where a railroad company constructs but part of its road, has no station or freight-houses and no passenger coaches but engages only in getting out coal from beds owned by those interested in the company   State v Railway Co, 40 Ohio St, 504 (1884)   But the suit does not lie on the ground that the company does not *intend* to complete its road   State v Kingan, 51 Ind, 142 (1875), State v Beck, 81 id, 501 (1882)   No forfeiture is decreed because a railroad company discontinues passenger trains over a branch line which is run at a loss by reason of horse-car competition   Commonwealth v Fitchburg R. R. Co 78 Mass, 180 (1858)   The lessee of a railroad is a proper party to a suit to forfeit franchises for non-user   People v Albany, etc, R. R. Co. 77 N Y, 232 (1879), State v Minn etc, R'y Co, 30 N W Rep, 816 (Minn, 1886)   An assignment of all corporate assets to others, thereby rendering the corporation incapable of continuing business, is cause for forfeiture   State v Real Estate Bank, 5 Ark, 595 (1843)   A bank which ceases to do business and to file statements and which makes improper loans to its directors, is liable to forfeiture of charter   State v Seneca Co. Bank 5 Ohio St, 171 (1856)   It is not a non-user for a county fair corporation to rent its grounds   Kent County etc, Soc v Houseman 46 N W Rep, 15 (Mich, 1890)   Where the statute prescribes that non-user for a year shall be cause for forfeiture, a non-user for a few days is insufficient   People v Atlantic, etc, R R., 125 N Y, 513 (1891)   A railroad which is leased to another company without statutory provisions to do so is subject to forfeiture at the instance of the state   State v Atchison etc R R Co, 38 N W Rep, 43 (Neb 1888)   As to a failure of a railroad corporation to complete its road see § 638 *infra*   The abandonment of the right of way by the railroad is no ground for an action of trespass by the former owner to recover it   Logan v Vernon, etc, R R, 90 Ind, 552 (1883).

But a more difficult question arises where a corporation, exercising no franchise except that of being a corporation, is guilty of

not provide that charters shall be forfeited for non-payment of corporate obligations, so far as corporations existing before the statute are concerned Aurora, etc, Co v Holthouse, 7 Ind, 59 (1855) But it may prescribe that the charter be repealed unless within certain time the company do certain things — here make good its capital Lothrop v Stedman, 42 Conn, 583 (1875) And may force the dissolution of insolvent insurance corporations or corporations whose continuance of business will be dangerous to the public Ward v Farwell, 97 Ill, 593 (1881), Chicago Life Ins Co v. Auditor, 101 Ill, 82 (1881) So also as to banks The remedy "for a violation of duty may be altered and changed by legislative provisions if the power of accomplishing the same objects by any means is within the legitimate scope of legislative authority" Commonwealth v Farmers', etc, Bank, 21 Pick, 542 (1839) Quo warranto does not lie against a corporation for ultra vires acts, such as issuing watered stock or purchasing its own stock "Acts in excess of power may undoubtedly be carried so far as to amount to a misuser of the franchise to be a corporation and a ground for its forfeiture" The courts refuse to define what ultra vires acts will and what will not sustain quo warranto proceeding They must be acts which "so derange or destroy the business of the corporation that it no longer fulfills the end for which it was created" State v Minn, etc, Co, 41 N. W Rep, 1020 (Minn, 1889)

The following acts and facts do not constitute a misuser There is no misuser of franchises by a corporation where the objectionable act was by a cashier in direct violation of orders given to him by the directors. State v Commercial Bank, 6 Sm & M (Miss).

218 (1846); or where a railroad or turnpike company has constructed its road over land without obtaining the right of way, State v Kile, etc, Co., 38 Ind, 71 (1871); People v Hillsdale, etc, T. Co, 2 Johns., 190 (1807), or where the company deviates slightly from its route, fails to file a map of the route, and neglects to elect new directors, Harris v Mississippi, etc, R. R. Co, 51 Miss, 602 (1875), or fails to file a statement of its condition as required by statute, the object of such filing having ceased, People v Improvement Co., supra, or where the public are compelled to open a draw-bridge for themselves, Commonwealth v Bried, 21 Mass, 460 (1827), or where a bank has assigned its assets to trustees to pay its debts, State v Commercial Bank, 13 Sm & M, 569 (1850), or for the insolvency of a bank, it having since then become solvent, People v Bank of Niagara, 6 Cow, 196 (1826), People v Washington, etc, Bank, 6 Cow, 212 (1826) (but the contrary has been held as regards a suspension of specie payments and a subsequent resumption, Commercial Bank v State, 6 Sm & M (Miss), 599 (1846) Planters' Bank v. State, 7 id, 163 — 1846), or where a bridge company gives reduced rates to constant patrons, and gives free passage in payment for land and fails to file required statements, Commonwealth v Alleghany, etc, Co., 20 Pa. St., 185 (1852); or that the corporation has incorporated also in another state Commonwealth v. Pittsburg, etc, R. R. Co, 58 Pa St, 26 (1868), or that required statements are not filed, State v Barron, 58 N H., 370 (1878). Though a corporation take more interest than allowed by charter it may recover. The only penalty is such as the usury law prescribes. Grand G. Bank v Archer, 16 Miss., 151 (1847) For a vigorous and interesting but futile effort to oust a going railroad company

a non-user. The weight of authority holds that *quo warranto* will lie[1]

§ 635. *Forfeiture for ultra vires acts and usurpation of franchises — Quo warranto and injunction at the instance of the state* — Frequently a corporation does acts which its charter does not authorize it to do, or which its charter or a statute expressly prohibits it from doing The question then arises, What is the remedy of the state? The right of a stockholder, or the corporation itself, or a person contracting with the corporation, to object to such acts is discussed elsewhere[2] But may the state object? Undoubtedly it may. It seems that the state has four remedies Its legislature may repeal the charter of the corporation under the re-

from its franchises for all kinds of misfeasances, malfeasances and non-feasances, see International, etc, R'y v State, 12 S W Rep, 685 (Tex, 1889), and for a successful case in the same line, see East, etc, R. R. v State, 12 S W. Rep, 690 (Tex, 1889) It is not for the state to institute an action to dissolve and wind up a mutual benefit and building corporation merely because some of the members are dissatisfied People v Lowe, 117 N Y, 175, 190 (1889) No *quo warranto* lies for using an abbreviated corporate name People v Bogart, 45 Cal, 73 (1872) The averments of misuser must be definite and certain Danville, etc, P' Co v State 16 Ind, 456 (1861) And the misuser must be wilful State v Columbia, etc, Co, 2 Sneed (Tenn.), 254 (1854), Baltimore v Connellsville, etc, R'y Co, 6 Phil, 190 (1866) Concerning the pleadings in *quo warranto*, see People v Stanford, 19 Pac Rep, 693 (Cal, 1888) An information in the nature of *quo warranto* to forfeit the charter of a temperance enterprise is not definite enough in its charges when it charges a perversion of funds People v Dashaway, 24 Pac Rep, 277 (Cal, 1890), containing also a discussion on the pleadings and practice

[1] The state may forfeit a charter for wilful non-user, although the corporation is a private one People v Milk Exchange, 133 N. Y, 565 (1892) See Attorney-General v Simonton, 78 N C

57 (1878), holding that the suit will not lie, although only five shares of stock were subscribed for and no other act done by the corporation State v Societe, etc, 9 Mo App, 114 (1880), holding the same, though the company was dormant. But the case of State v Pipher, 28 Kan, 128 (1882), forfeited the charter of an agricultural college for non-user for nineteen years And see *dicta* in Terrell v Taylor, 4 Cranch 43, 51 (1815), State v Commercial Bank, 13 Sm & M, 569 (1850) In New York by statute such a suit will lie Code of C P, § 1798 See, also, *In re* Jackson, etc, Ins Co, 4 Sand Ch, 559 (1817) Where a corporation has abandoned its authorized business and engaged in another it will be wound up This is different from a case where the directors have merely and incidentally committed *ultra vires* acts *Re* Crown, etc, Bank, 62 L T Rep, 823 (1890) An abandonment by a corporation of part of the purposes of its incorporation is no cause for dissolution Norwegian Titanic Iron Co 35 Beav, 223 (1865) where, its purpose being to purchase English and Norway mines, it sold the English mines. By the terms of a new constitution all corporations which have failed to organize before its adoption may be deemed to have forfeited their franchises thereby Chincleclamauch, etc, Co v Commonwealth, 100 Pa St, 438 (1882).

[2] See Part IV

served right of the state to repeal;[1] or the state may institute a suit at law to forfeit the charter for misuser of powers; or such suit may be only to oust the corporation from the exercise of the usurped powers, or, according to some authorities, the suit may be in equity for an injunction restraining the corporation from committing the *ultra vires* acts   It seems that the judgment in an ordinary *quo warranto* suit herein may be either a forfeiture of all the corporate franchises and of its charter, or may be a forfeiture only of the right to continue to do the illegal acts, and that it is in the discretion of the court to say which decree shall be made.[2] The nature of *scire facias, quo warranto* and information in the nature of a *quo warranto* is explained in the notes below [3]

[1] See § 639, *infra*

[2] State *v* People's, etc, Assoc, 42 Ohio St . 579 (1885), where only a discontinuance of the acts complained of was ordered, People *v* Improvement Co . 103 Ill , 491 (1882), where a complete forfeiture of charter etc, was decreed See, also, People *v* Utica Ins Co . 15 Johns , 357 (1818), where an insurance company had engaged in banking contrary to statute   In State *v* Building Assoc , 35 Ohio St , 258 (1879), the court said that where the corporation is guilty of an offense which by statute is cause for forfeiture of its franchise as a corporation, the court will decree that forfeiture, but where the cause of forfeiture is outside of those prescribed in the statutes, then the court may decree either a forfeiture of the franchise to be a corporation or an ouster from the powers and acts illegally assumed or done

[3] Professor Dwight explained these as follows

"*Scire facias* is resorted to where there is original defect in the charter, as if, e q , a grant obtained by fraud It may be used also in the case where the charter was valid but the powers of a corporation have been abused The distinction taken in England is this that a *scire facias* may be resorted to where a legal corporation in full possession of its powers abuses them, while a *quo warranto* is applicable where a corporation, from a defect in its constitution,

such as a loss of part of its members which are integral to its existence, becomes an imperfect body, but nevertheless continues to act as a corporation See Grant on Corpora , 296.

"*Writ of quo warranto* This is an ancient writ, employed by the king against any one who claims or usurps an office or franchise, or who, having had a right to the franchise, neglects to exercise it, to inquire by what warrant he still claims to exercise it. The theory of the writ is, there is an unlawful encroachment upon the royal prerogative, and being a dilatory proceeding and technical, it is not now so much employed as the succeeding remedy.

"*Information in the nature of a quo warranto* This is in form a criminal proceeding There were two proceedings in the criminal law for the conviction of criminals. One is termed an information and the other an indictment. They differ in this respect, that while an indictment is found by a grand jury, an information is simply the allegation of an officer who files it. In this case the attorney-general proceeds on twofold ground, both to punish the usurper and to prevent the unlawful exercise of its franchises In the case of a corporation the main object is to interfere with the exercise of the franchise The inquiry is the same as in the writ of *quo warranto*, that is, by what warrant the franchise is exercised. The reason why

Quo warranto or an information in the nature thereof is the proper remedy where the corporation has not been legally incorporated [1]

it is more resorted to is that it is easy and simple of application

"Under the New York code the proceeding is simply an action brought by the attorney-general, governed by the same general rules as an action at common law. If judgment goes against the corporation it is liable to be dissolved This proceeding in England was instituted in the great criminal court, the king's or queen's bench and in New York in the supreme court only, which represents the queen s bench"

In the case of State z Merchants', etc, Trust Co, 8 Humph (Tenn), 235 (1847) the court said "By the common law the forfeiture of a charter can be enforced in a court of law only, and the proceeding to repeal it is by a *scire facias* or an information in the nature of a writ of *quo warranto* A *scire facias* is the proper remedy where there is a legal existing body capable of acting, but which had been guilty of an abuse of the power intrusted to it, a *quo warranto* where there is a body corporate *de facto*, which takes upon itself to act as a body corporate, but from some defect in its constitution it cannot legally exercise the power it affects to use' Citing 8 Wheat, 483-4 In Pennsylvania, where the state filed an information to declare *ultra vires* a contract between a canal company and a coal company, whereby one-half of the canal facilities were monopolized by the latter, the court held that the information was a proper remedy, and that the court in its judgment in favor of the state might order the corporation to discontinue the unauthorized act, and that the judgment need not oust the corporation from its charter and franchises Commonwealth z Delaware, etc, Canal Co, 43 Pa. St. 295 (1862) For the ancient learning as to the *scire facias* in forfeiting charters, see State

v Moore, 19 Ala., 514 (1851). When the information has for its object to oust the defendants from acting as a corporation, and to test the fact of their incorporation, it must be filed against individuals When the object is to effect a dissolution of a corporation which has had an actual existence, or to oust such corporation of some franchise which it has unlawfully exercised, the information must be filed against the corporation People v Rensselaer, etc, R. R., 15 Wend, 113 (1836) Although the state proves the case, yet the court will not adjudge a forfeiture unless justice requires it. State v Essex Bank, 8 Vt., 489 (1836). Pleadings in *quo warranto* People v Stanford, 19 Pac. Rep., 693 (Cal, 1888).

[1] The state may forfeit a charter where the statute required five persons to sign and acknowledge the articles, but only four out of the five actually did acknowledge them People z Montecito, etc, Co, 32 Pac. Rep, 236 (Cal, 1893) In *quo warranto* proceedings on the ground that the company was not properly incorporated, the corporation itself is a necessary party defendant Id Under the statutes of Alabama in reference to watered stock *quo warranto* lies where $1 000 000 of stock is issued for the possibility of patents to be thereafter granted In such *quo warranto* proceedings stockholders need not be made parties. State v Webb, 12 S Rep, 377 (Ala, 1893). In an action by the state to forfeit a railroad charter the state must prove not only that a cause of forfeiture did exist but that it still continues to exist. Moreover some public interest must be involved in obtaining the forfeiture People z Ulster, etc, R. R. 128 N Y, 240 (1891) A charter of the company will be forfeited at the instance of the state where some of the parties who are al-

Quo warranto lies against foreign corporations doing business illegally in the state.[1]

The state by *quo warranto* may oust a railroad from discriminations in favor of oil shipped in tank cars[2]

An exemption from taxation is not a franchise Hence. *quo warranto* does not lie to oust the corporation from such exemption[3]

Although *quo warranto* can be only for acts committed within five years in Ohio, yet it serves to oust a company from exercising a power which it has not exercised continuously for twenty years[4]

It is very doubtful whether the state may file a bill in equity to enjoin a corporation from committing an *ultra vires* act The remedy of the state is *quo warranto* In England a bill has been

---

leged to join in the corporation did not so join, but their names were inserted without their sanction or authority. Such parties are not liable as stockholders La Banque d'Hochelaga *r* Murtay, 63 L. T Rep, 63 (1890) In a *quo warranto* proceeding to declare void an alleged charter the corporation is a necessary party defendant. People *r* Flint, 28 Pac Rep, 495 (Cal, 1883) After the attorney-general institutes *quo warranto* proceedings, and much testimony is taken and then the proceeding is discontinued and the company proceeds to expend money and make contracts the attorney-general will not be allowed to institute new proceedings. *In re* Equity Gas-Light Co, 10 N Y Supp, 801 (1890). In *quo warranto*, charging defendants with usurping a public franchise to operate a ferry, where they attempted to defend on the ground that they had a legal right to use the ferry, the burden was on them to show a valid title Gunterman *r* People, 28 N E. Rep, 1067 (Ill). Where an incorporation is for several objects, one of which is illegal, the charter will be forfeited, the objects not being clearly separable People *r* Chicago Gas T Co, 22 N E. Rep, 798 (Ill, 1889). The issuing of transferable certificates of stock is not assuming the functions of a corporation Rice *r* Rockefeller, 56 Hun, 517 (1890). A suit instituted by the state to

forfeit a charter cannot be removed to the federal court on the ground that a contract exists between the corporation and the state, and that such contract will be violated Commonwealth of Ky. *r* Louisville Bridge Co., 42 Fed. Rep, 241 (1890) The court may forfeit the charter of a railroad corporation for illegally leasing its road, and need not merely enjoin the continuation of the lease East Line, etc R. R., *r* State, 12 S W Rep, 690 (Tex, 1889). A corporation incorporated for an illegal purpose, such as buying a majority or all of the stock in each of four competing gas corporations, and thereby creating a monopoly, is subject to having its charter forfeited at the instance of the attorney-general People *t* Chicago Gas T Co, 22 N E. Rep, 798 (Ill, 1889).

[1] State *r* Western, etc, Soc., 24 N. E. Rep, 302 (Ohio 1890), State *v.* Fidelity, etc, Co, 41 N W Rep, 108 (Minn, 1888). *Quo warranto* against a foreign corporation illegally doing business in the state must be against the corporation as such and not merely against its officers and agents. State *r* Sowerby, 43 N. W. Rep, 689 (Minn, 1889).

[2] State *r* Cincinnati, etc, R R., 23 N. E. Rep, 928 (Ohio. 1890).

[3] International, etc., R'y *r* State, 12 S. W Rep, 685 (Tex, 1889).

[4] State *r* Standard Oil Co, 30 N E. Rep, 279 (Ohio, 1892)

sustained to restrain a railroad corporation from engaging in the coal business [1] It lies to enjoin a corporation, the same as an individual, from creating a public nuisance [2] In Wisconsin it is held that the attorney-general may enjoin railroad companies from taking greater rates than are prescribed by statute, [3] and in many of the states such a bill will lie by statute [4]

The decided weight of authority, however, is that the remedy of the state is by *quo warranto* and not by a bill in equity for an injunction [5]

[1] Attorney-General v Great Northern R'y Co, 1 Dr & Sm, 154 (1860). But the attorney-general cannot enjoin a corporate act merely because it is *ultra vires*. Some injury to the public must be involved Attorney-general's suit at instance of a manufacturer to enjoin one railroad from leasing rolling-stock to another failed Attorney-General v Great Eastern R'y Co., L R. 11 Ch D, 449 (1879) A court of equity cannot compel a corporation to cease collecting tolls, although it has not improved the stream as required by its charter Pixley v Roanoke, etc, Co., 75 Va, 320 (1881) In Attorney-General v Mid Kent R'y Co., L R, 3 Ch, 100 (1867), a mandatory injunction requiring the defendant to construct a bridge was granted

[2] Attorney-General v Jamaica, etc, Corp, 133 Mass, 361 (1882)

[3] Attorney-General v Railroad Cos, 35 Wis, 525, 553 (1874), reviewing many cases, but cf Strong v McCagg, 55 Wis, 624 A lease by a domestic railroad company of its railroad to a foreign railroad corporation is illegal, especially where it is expressly prohibited by statute The court will enjoin the lease upon the application of the attorney-general where the effect of the lease would be to create a combination in the transportation of coal and to destroy competition in production and sale Stockton, Att'y-Gen'l v Central R Co. of N J et al, 24 Atl Rep 964 (N J, 1892) A telegraph company has no power to sell and assign its lines unless such power is expressly given to it

The franchise is personal United States v Western U Tel Co 50 Fed Rep, 28 (1892), holding also that the government may file a bill in equity to set aside an illegal telegraph consolidation and need not resort to *mandamus* All of the corporations were state corporations in this case

[4] State v Merchants', etc, Co, 8 Humph. (Tenn), 254 (1874), where an insurance company was restrained from banking So, also, in New York Bank Com'rs v Bank of Buffalo, 6 Paige, 496 (1837), Brinckerhoff v Bostwick, 88 N Y, 52 (1882) explaining the difference between this class of cases and cases where other parties are complainants. Concerning the power of the state to object to an *ultra vires* act of a private corporation by any proceeding other than *quo warranto*, see People v Ballard, 134 N Y, 269 (1892), a carefully considered case

[5] Attorney-General v Utica Ins Co, 2 John Ch, 371 (1817). Attorney-General v Bank of Niagara, Hopk Ch, 354 (1825). But see People v Ballard, *supra* In Attorney-General v Tudor Ice Co, 104 Mass, 239 (1870), an injunction restraining an ice company from importing teas was denied Where a railroad leases its line in violation of a constitutional provision prohibiting the consolidation of parallel lines it is subject to forfeiture So, also, where it issues "watered stock" in violation of the constitution State v. Atchison, etc, R R 35 N W Rep, 43 (Neb 1888) A state creating a corporation has no visitorial power over it — i e, power to

§ 636. *The state may waive its right to forfeit a charter* — Various acts have been held to constitute such a waiver. "When a legislature has full power to create corporations, its act recognizing as valid a *de facto* corporation, whether private or municipal, operates to cure all defects in steps leading up to the organization, and makes a *de jure* out of what before was only a *de facto* corporation" There must, however, be a *de facto* organization upon which this recognition may act [1] Numerous instances of acts of the legislature which constitute a waiver are set forth in detail in the notes below.[2]

correct corporate abuses — except "(1) where municipal, charitable, religious or eleemosynary corporations, public in their nature, had abused their franchises, perverted the purpose of their organization or misappropriated their funds, and as they, from the nature of their corporate functions, were more or less under government supervision, the attorney-general proceeded against them to obtain correction of the abuse, or (2) where private corporations, chartered for private and limited purposes, had exceeded their powers and were restrained or enjoined in the same manner from the further violation of the limitation to which their powers were subject' Hence the United States as the creator of the Union Pacific Railroad cannot exercise visitorial power over it in respect to frauds in its management United States v Union Pacific R. R. Co, 98 U S, 569, 617 (1878). Cf Attorney-General t Wilson, 1 Cr & Ph. 1 (1840), holding that the court had jurisdiction over charitable corporations, and that when the trustees of them abused their trust the court would take notice of such abuse by reason of its visitorial powers. Also, on this point, Attorney-General v Foundling Hospital, 4 Bro Ch Rep., 165 (1793). For pleadings in *quo warranto* proceedings by the state to oust a corporation from usurped franchises and to forfeit a railroad charter, see People v Standford, 18 Pac Rep., 85 (Cal, 1888), holding also that the statute of limitations is no bar But see the Pennsylvania cases in § 315,

supra, where the state enjoined an illegal purchase of stock by a corporation.

[1] Comanche County v. Lewis, 133 U. S., 198 (1890)

[2] A legislative recognition of a charter cures any unconstitutionality in the statute creating it. Snell v. Chicago, 24 N E Rep., 532 (Ill, 1890). The extension of time to complete railroads applies so as to prevent forfeiture for noncompletion within the original time. State t Bergen, etc., R'y, 20 Atl Rep., 762 (N J, 1890). Although suit is brought to forfeit a street railway franchise for using electric power without authority, the legislature may cure the defect of power To forfeit for not commencing work within a year the pleading must allege when the work was commenced People t. Los Angeles, etc, R'y, 27 Pac. Rep., 673 (Cal, 1891) An amendment to a charter is a waiver of any forfeiture thereof due to not commencing business within the prescribed time. Farnsworth v Lime Rock R. R., 22 Atl Rep, 373 (Me, 1891). Although the act requires the certificate of incorporation to specify the termini, and the certificate merely says the termini are in a certain city, yet if the legislature subsequently by special act recognizes the company, the legality of its existence cannot be questioned Koch v North, etc, R'y, 23 Atl. Rep, 463 (Md, 1892). In this case the organization was under the general railroad law Under such a charter the route and its termini are to be determined by the mayor and city council ' under

§ 637 *Who may allege that forfeiture or non-incorporation or dissolution exists* — It has already been shown that no one but the

their general power of control and regulation of the streets "

A waiver may be express or by statutes recognizing its continued existence, *In re* New York El R. R. Co, 70 N Y, 327, 338 (1877) People v Manhattan Co 9 Wend, 352, 380 (1832), or requiring it to make alterations on its road, Att'y-Gen l v Petersburg, etc. R R. Co 6 Ired L. (N C) 470 (1846), or authorizing a transfer of its property and franchises to another corporation. Chesapeake, etc. Canal Co v Baltimore, etc. R R Co. 4 G & J (Md), 1, 127 (1832), or requiring a bank to resume specie payments by a certain date, Commercial Bank v State, 6 Sm & M (Miss) 599 622 (1846) But waiver as to terminus is not a waiver of an abandonment of part of the road, nor of a defect as to the width of the turnpike People v Fishkill etc. Co 27 Barb, 445 (1857) Waiver may arise by a statue extending the corporate powers, People v Ottawa etc Co 115 Ill, 281 (1885). Central etc R R Co v Twenty, etc R R Co 51 How Pr, 168 186 (1877), or by authorizing a change of route. State v Fourth, etc, Co, 15 N H, 162 (1844), or by expressly waiving the cause for forfeiture Lumpkin v Jones 1 Ga, 27 (1846) Legislature may expressly waive forfeiture arising by suspension of specie payments Atchafalaya Bank v Dawson, 13 La, 497 (1829) May waive by extending the time for completion La Grange, etc, R R Co v Rainey 7 Coldw (Tenn) 420 (1870) Amending charter, etc is a waiver Whites etc Co v Davidson County 3 Tenn Ch 396 (1877) An act reviving a corporation is a waiver even though the act was fraudulently passed *In re* Mechanics' Soc 31 La Ann, 627 (1879) The waiver protects the turnpike corporation from an indictment for obstructing the road State v Godwinsville etc

Co, 44 N J L, 496 (1882) But the waiver must have been clearly intended People v Kingston, etc, Co, 23 Wend, 193 (1840) The appointment of a corporate officer by the governor and senate is not a waiver People v Phoenix Bank, 24 Wend, 431 (1840) Long delay in bringing the *quo warranto* may be a waiver People v Williamsburgh etc Co 47 N Y 586 (1872), People v Oakland etc, Bank, 1 Doug (Mich), 282 *Dictum* that the state may waive Briggs v Cape Cod, etc, Co. 137 Mass, 71 (1884), citing cases. Special act amending charter waives defects in the articles of association as filed Basshor v Dressel, 34 Md, 503 (1871) Amendment to charter waives right of forfeiture for fraud non-user and misuser People v Ottawa etc Co, 115 Ill, 281 (1886) An amendment of the charter is a waiver Att'y-Gen l v Peter-burgh etc. R R Co 6 Ired L. 456 (1846), Charles River Bridge Co v Warren Bridge 24 Mass, 344 (1829) Waiver may be express State v Bank of Charleston 2 McMullan, 439 (1843) Enfield Bridge Co v Conn, etc, Co, 7 Conn, 28 (1828) Kanawha, etc, Co v Kanawha, etc Co 7 Blatch 391 (1870) Where the incorporation had been irregular the recognition of a corporation by the legislature is equivalent to a charter McAuley v Columbus, etc R y, 83 Ill, 348 (1876), Cowell v Colorado etc, Co 3 Col, 82 (1876), Mead v N Y, etc R R 45 Conn 199 (1877), Kanawha, etc, Co v Kanawha, etc Co, 7 Blatch, 391 (1870) St Louis R R v N W etc R'y 2 Mo App, 69 (1876), Atlantic, etc R R v St Louis 66 Mo 228 (1877), 11 S W Rep, 392 (Tex, 1889) *Contra* where charters must be granted by general laws, Oroville etc, R R v Supervisors 37 Cal, 354 (1869) But see Brent v State, 43 Ala, 297 (1869)

state can institute a suit to declare a forfeiture.[1] Also, that no one
can institute a suit in equity to dissolve a corporation[2] The question now arises whether the state or any person, either as plaintiff
or defendant, may allege forfeiture or dissolution or non-incorporation where there have been no *quo warranto* proceedings instituted
and prosecuted by the state to judgment With a few exceptions
such an allegation is not allowed. A creditor of a supposed corporation cannot ordinarily hold the stockholders liable as partners
although they did not legally incorporate[3] It is true, also, in certain cases where a stockholder is made liable to corporate creditors
upon the dissolution of the corporation, a dissolution is held to
exist where the corporation is hopelessly insolvent[4] And it is the
law that where a railroad corporation attempts to acquire a right
of way, the persons whose property will be affected thereby may
oppose the acquisition of the right of way by showing that the
company is not legally incorporated[5] But aside from these exceptions no one is allowed to assert that the corporation is dissolved,
or its franchise forfeited, or its incorporation illegal, until after
such a result has been decreed by a court in a proceeding instituted
for that purpose by the state Thus, a stockholder sued on his
subscription cannot, unless his subscription was made previous to
the incorporation, set up that the company was not legally incorporated[6]

The corporation is called a *de facto* corporation, and only the
state is allowed to question its existence There are many instances
where attempts have been made to avoid this rule of law by setting up that the charter has been rendered forfeitable at the instance of the state, but they have uniformly failed.[7]

---

[1] § 632, *supra*.

[2] § 629, *supra*

[3] See ch XIII, *supra*.

[4] See § 631, *supra*.

[5] *In re* Brooklyn, etc, R'y Co , 72 N Y,
245 (1878), *In re* N Y Cable Co v
Mayor, etc , 104 N Y, 1 (1887) In condemnation proceedings the incorporation may be attacked as not being *de
facto* Its *de jure* existence cannot be
so attacked Brown v Calumet, etc,
R y, 18 N E. Rep., 283 (Ill , 1888) An
adjacent owner cannot enjoin a street
railway company on the ground that its
charter is invalid, unless his property
rights are affected Nichols v Ann
Arbor, etc St R'y. 49 N W Rep., 538
(Mich , 1891) A person whose land a

corporation seeks to take under power
of eminent domain cannot set up that
the articles of incorporation had not been
filed with the secretary of state as required by the incorporating statute.
Portland, etc , Co v. Bobb, 10 S. W. Rep.,
794 (Ky, 1889) A railroad charter is
not good so far as the right to condemn
land is concerned, where the terminus
is stated to be on the state line in a certain county Atlantic, etc , R R v. Sul-
livant, 5 Ohio St. 276 (1855).

[6] §§ 183–186, *supra* Concerning the
question of who can complain of mistakes, irregularities and illegalities in
the corporation, see ch. I, *supra*

[7] Thus, a person sued for tolls cannot
set up that the corporation has not ren-

So, also, a party contracting with a corporation cannot defeat

dered required statements, and hence its charter is forfeitable Kellogg v Union Co., 12 Conn , 7 (1837) Nor that the charter was never legally vested or has been violated Dyer v Walker, 40 Pa St., 157 (1861) Where two railroad companies claim a right of way, one cannot allege that the other's charter is forfeitable Central, etc , R R. Co. v Twenty-third, etc , R R Co, 54 How Pr , 168, 185 (1877). A religious corporation suing for its real estate cannot be met by a plea of dissolution, there having been no decree Baptist House v Webb, 66 Me , 398 (1877) A corporation suing for personal property is not defeated by a plea that it was not legally organized or is dissolved by non-user Penobscot, etc , Corp v Lamson, 16 Me , 224 (1839) A grantee of a corporation's right to overflow land is not deprived of his right by dormancy and non-user of its franchises by the corporation Heard v Talbot, 73 Mass, 113 (1856) Attachment lies against the land of a foreign corporation though a receiver of it exists in the state creating it. Moseby v Burrow, 52 Texas, 396 (1880). One corporation cannot enjoin a competing corporation from proceeding on the ground that the latter has subjected its charter to forfeiture by misuser or non-user Elizabethtown G L. Co. v Green, 18 Atl Rep, 844 (N J, 1889). A county cannot seize a turnpike, although the company is guilty of misuser or non-user A judgment of forfeiture is first necessary Moore v Schoppert, 22 W. Va., 282 (1883). A city seeking to lay out a road on a right of way cannot claim that the railroad company's right is forfeited by non-user New Jersey R R. Co v Long Branch Com'rs, 39 N J L., 28 (1876) The corporation cannot avoid a tax on the ground that it has ceased business. Bank of U S. v Commonwealth, 17 Pa St , 400 (1851) A grantor of land to a corporation cannot reclaim it on the

ground of a dissolution, there having been no decree of dissolution Bohannan v Binns, 31 Miss , 355 (1856) Service on a corporation cannot be made by service on a stockholder on the ground that it has forfeited its charter by non-user Bache v Nashville, etc , Soc 10 Lea (Tenn), 436 (1882) A suit by the corporation on a bond is not to be met by a plea of forfeiture for non-user West v Carolina, etc , Ins Co , 31 Ark 476 (1876). Nor its suit on a note by the plea that it has abandoned its franchises John v Farmers', etc , Bank 2 Blackf , 367 (1830), East Tenn , etc , Co v Gaskell, 2 Lea (Tenn), 742 (1879), President, etc , v Hamilton, 34 Ind 506 (1870) The forfeiture can exist only after a decree to that effect. Chesapeake, etc , Co v Baltimore, etc , R. R. Co, 4 Gill & J (Md), 1 (1832) An agent sued for conversion of funds cannot allege that the corporation is guilty of a non-user of its franchises Elizabeth, etc , Acad v Lindsey 6 Ired L. (N C), 476 (1846) A railroad suing on a note cannot be defeated by the defense that it has forfeited its charter, there being no adjudication to that effect Toledo, etc , R R v Johnson, 49 Mich , 148 (1882) A squatter on corporate land cannot dispute the corporate title by alleging that it was not legally incorporated or organized Only the state can object East. etc , Church v Froishe, 35 N W Rep 260 (Minn , 1887) In a suit by a toll road to recover a penalty for refusal to pay toll, the validity of the company's organization and the condition of the road cannot be brought into the controversy by way of defense Canal St , etc , Co v Paas, 54 N W Rep 907 (Mich 1893) But a turnpike company cannot recover fares for the part of its road which is constructed beyond its chartered limits Pontiac etc , Co v Hilton, 36 N W Rep , 739 (Mich , 1888). Statutory provisions as to notice of the first meeting are directory They need

his obligation by showing that the corporation was never legally incorporated [1]

not be observed if the stockholders acquiesce Braintree, etc, *v* Braintree, 16 N E Rep, 420 (Mass. 1881). But the failure of a railroad to cause to be paid in a certain amount of its capital stock before incorporation may defeat municipal bonds which are given to it. Fainham *v* Benedict, 107 N Y, 159 (1887) Indorser sued by the corporation cannot claim that it has rendered its charter liable to forfeiture by suspension of specie payments Atchafalaya Bank *v* Dawson, 13 La., 497 (1839) Corporation cannot defeat its taxes by alleging failure to comply with conditions subsequent in its charter Baltimore, etc, R R. *v.* Marshall Co, 3 W Va., 319 (1869) Though the provision in the Kentucky statutes requiring publication of the charter is not complied with, yet the corporation is valid and complete, except that the state may proceed to annul the charter No other party can raise the objection Stutz *v* Handley, 41 Fed Rep, 531 (1890), Walton *v* Riley, 85 Ky, 413, 421, overruling Heinig *v* Manufacturing Co., 81 Ky, 300 Running a blockade is not a forfeiture *per se.* Importing, etc, Co *v* Locke, 50 Ala, 332 (1873).

[1] Commercial Bank *v* Pfeiffer, 108 N Y, 242 (1888) The maker of a note to a bank cannot question its incorporation Exchange National Bank *v* Hastings, 49 N W. Rep, 223 (Neb. 1891), Columbia Electric Co. *v* Dixon, 49 N W Rep, 244 (Minn, 1891) An officer cannot defend against an action to make him account, by setting up that the company was fraudulently organized Haacke *v* Knights, etc, Club, 25 Atl Rep., 422 (Md, 1892) In the case of Perine *v* Grand Lodge, etc, 50 N W Rep, 1022 (Minn, 1892), where an insurance policy was sued upon, the court held that it was immaterial that the defendant was not incorporated, inasmuch as it had held itself out as a

corporation Bou, etc, Co *v* Standard, etc., Ins. Co, 12 S E Rep, 771 (W Va, 1891) Where a corporation sues for the price of articles sold, the defendant cannot set up that the plaintiff sold the articles before its capital stock was fully paid up as required by statute Chasis, etc, Co. *v* Baston, etc, Co, 28 N E. Rep, 300 (Mass, 1891), McCord, etc, Co. *v.* Glen 21 Pac Rep, 500 (Utah, 1889) In a suit by a *bona fide* indorsee of a note from a corporation as indorser, the maker cannot set up that the company was not properly incorporated Buckley *v* Edwards, 30 N E. Rep, 708 (Ind, 1892) The defendant cannot allege that the corporation was for an illegal purpose — that of running blockades — the charter *not* showing that fact. Importing, etc, Co. *v* Lock, 50 Ala. 332 (1873). Where the suit is on a bond a stockholder cannot sue to have the corporation declared a copartnership by reason of irregular incorporation Baker *v* Backus, 32 Ill, 79 (1863). Nor can the maker of a note to a corporation defeat it by showing that the corporation was not duly incorporated Butchers', etc, Bank *v* McDonald, 130 Mass, 264 (1881), Jones *v* Bank of Tennessee, 8 B. Mon, (Ky), 122 (1847); Louisville Bank *v.* Willard 25 N. Y, 574 (1862), Nutting *v.* Hill, 71 Ga, 557 (1883) Irvine *v* Lumberman's Bank, 2 W & S (Pa), 204 (1841), Congregational Soc *v* Perry, 6 N. H, 164 (1833); Massey *v* Bldg Ass'n, 22 Kan, 624 (1879), Vater *v* Lewis, 36 Ind, 288 (1871); Smith *v* Miss, etc, R R. Co, 14 Miss., 179 (1846), where the maker of the note claimed that the corporation was fraudulently and illegally organized, Studebaker, etc, Co *v* Montgomery, 74 Mo., 101 (1881), Stoutimore *v* Clark, 70 Mo., 471 (1875); Blake *v.* Holley, 14 Ind, 383 (1860), Jones *v* Cincinnati, etc Co., 14 Ind, 89 (1860), holding also that the corporation need not prove even a *de facto*

A person who gives a bond to a corporation is not allowed to defeat the bond by alleging that the corporation was not duly incorporated,[1] nor can the corporation defeat its bonds by alleging its want of lawful incorporation.[2] A person who mortgages land to a supposed corporation cannot defeat a foreclosure of the mortgage by alleging that the mortgagee is not a corporation,[3] nor can

---

existence To same effect. Montgomery R R Co v Hurst, 9 Ala, 513 (1846) Cf White v Campbell, 5 Humph (Tenn), 38 (1844), where the remarkable decision was made that, if the corporation had been dissolved at the time the note was given, the maker was not liable and could have a mortgage which he gave as security set aside A *de facto* corporation, as indorsee of a note may enforce it. Wilcox v Toledo, etc., R R. Co, 43 Mich, 584 (1880) A corporation cannot be defeated in an action on a contract by the fact that twenty-four instead of twenty-five persons signed the articles of incorporation Buffalo, etc, R'y Co. v N Y, etc, R R. Co, 22 Alb L J, 134 (N Y, 1886) Proof of organization in fact and user meets a plea of *nul tiel corporation* by the maker of a note to the corporation Mitchell v Deeds, 49 Ill. 416 (1867), Smelser v Wayne, etc. T Co, 82 Ind, 417 (1882) But see Williams v Bank of Michigan 7 Wend, 540 (1831). The corporation itself, when sued upon notes which it has made, cannot set up any informality in its incorporation Kelley v Newburyport, etc, R R Co 141 Mass, 496 (1886), Empire Mfg Co v Stuart, 46 Mich, 482 (1881), where the corporation re-incorporated in order to cure the irregularity Estoppel as to corporate existence seems to mean that the corporation is obliged to prove only a *de facto* existence, and need not prove the details of incorporation Leonardsville Bank v Willard 25 N. Y, 574 (1862) A person taking water from an irrigation company under contract cannot defend against an action thereon by alleging that the company was not incorporated Fresno etc Co v Warner, 14 Pac. Rep 37 (Cal 1887)

In a suit by a corporation on a note the execution of the note to the corporation is *prima facie* proof of its incorporation A *de facto* corporation may enforce a note given to it. Hudson v. Green, etc, 113 Ill, 618 (1885), 5 S. Rep, 247 (Fla, 1888), 21 N E Rep, 12 (Ill 1889) That the corporation may ratify and enforce contracts entered into in its behalf by its promoters before incorporation, see § 705, etc, *infra*

[1] McFarland v Triton Ins Co 4 Demo. 392 (1847), City of St. Louis v. Shields, 62 Mo, 247 (1876). Loaners Bank v Jacoby, 10 Hun, 143 (1877), Commissioners, etc, v Bolles, 94 U S, 104 (1876), Henriques v Dutch West India Co, 2 Ld Raym, 1532 (1729), where a foreign corporation sued, and the general issue was not pleaded

[2] Independent etc, And v Paine, 14 N E Rep, 42 (Ill, 1887), Blackburn v Selma, etc, R R Co, 2 Flipp, 525 (1879), Racine etc R R v Farmers'. etc, Co 49 Ill, 331, 316 (1868) Later v Ozokerite Min Co, 27 Pac Rep 690 (Utah 1891), Allen v Town of Cameron, 3 Dill, 198 (1874), where a municipality set up this defense Empire etc. Mfg Co v Stuart, 46 Mich, 482 (1882), a promissory note case A corporation cannot defend against its contracts by alleging that it never published its articles of association as required by statute Wood v Wiley etc Co 13 Atl Rep 137 (Conn 1888) A corporation is liable for a tax even though it failed to file its articles of association with the secretary of state as required by statute Walton v Riley, 3 S W Rep, 605 (Ky, 1887)

[3] Peoples Sav Bank v Collins 27 Conn 142 (1858) West, etc Sav Bank v Ford, id, 282 (1858), and Hasenritter

In like manner the corporation itself is not allowed to defeat its contracts by such a plea.[1] But in suits where the party is not estopped from denying the incorporation of the other party, such a denial may of course be made.[2]

The mere fact that a person contracts with a party and designates the latter as a "company" will not estop the former from denying the incorporation of the latter. This is the law, and is reasonable, since many copartnerships do business and make con-

and the defendant alleges that it is doing all its business outside of the state incorporating it. Newburg, etc., Co v Weare, 27 Ohio St, 343 (1875). See, also, §§ 237-239, *supra* Or where a foreign corporation sues the sheriff for trespass Persse, etc., Works *v* Willett, 1 Rob (N Y), 131 (1863). Or where the company sues for tolls. Sinclair *v.* Wayne, etc, T Co, 82 Ind, 417 (1882). A *de facto* corporation exists where the company might have incorporated under the statutes and has acted as a corporation. Methodist, etc., Church *v.* Pickett, 19 N. Y, 482 (1859). But a person who agreed to and did convey property to a company to be incorporated may subsequently repudiate the corporation and his conveyance as against his associates who shared in the stock received therefor. Doyle *v.* Mizner, 42 Mich, 332 (1879). The case of Boyce *v* Trustees, etc, 46 Md, 359 (1876), allowed a corporation to deny its existence as against a director who sued it for moneys advanced to it. Welland Canal Co *v* Hathaway, 8 Wend, 480 (1832), allowed a contractor to deny the existence of a corporation which sued to recover back money which had been overpaid to him. A corporation receiving the stock of another corporation in consideration of certain agreements as to renting machines belonging to said latter company cannot, when enjoined from violating that agreement, set up that the latter company was not properly organized Automatic, etc, Co. *v.* North American, etc., Co., 45 Fed. Rep., 1 (1891) Although there are less stockholders and less directors than the stat-

ute or charter require, yet the acts of these are sufficient to sustain obligations incurred by the corporation with third persons Welch *v* Importers', etc, Bank, 122 N. Y, 177 (1890) It is no defense to a proceeding by a religious corporation to collect a legacy to allege that there were irregularities in its incorporation, and that there has been a non-user of its franchises. Matter of Congregational Church, etc., 131 N Y., 1 (1892). In order to constitute a *de facto* corporation "there must at least be an organization under some existing charter or law And such organization must be in good faith " Welch *v.* Old Dominion, etc., R'y, 56 Hun, 650 (1890). Where an attorney sues for his services the supposed corporation may set up that it is not a *de facto* nor *de jure* corporation. Id. The California code provides that the existence of a *de facto* corporation shall not be called in question in private suits. Lakeside, etc., Co *v.* Crane, 22 Pac. Rep., 76 (Cal, 1889); Golden, etc., Co *v.* Joshua, etc, Works, 23 Pac. Rep, 45 (Cal, 1890)

[1] Dooley *v* Cheshire Glass Co., 81 Mass., 494 (1860); Callender *v* Painesville, etc, R. R., 10 Ohio St, 516 (1860). See, also, Bommer *v* American, etc, Co, 81 N. Y., 468 (1880), where the corporation sought to escape royalties by alleging that it incorporated after the contract by it to pay them was made A corporation sued for work done cannot set up that it was not regularly incorporated. Merrick *v.* Reynolds, etc., Co., 101 Mass., 381 (1869).

[2] Carey *v.* Cincinnati, etc., R. R., 5 Iowa, 357 (1857), and the principles and cases *supra.* See, also, § 638, *infra.*

tracts under the name of "company."[1] Such, also, is the rule where a supposed incorporation is not even a *de facto* corporation[2] But where the party contracted with is a *de facto* corporation, then the rules given above apply. It is true, also, that a company which is supposed to be incorporated, but is not, may after incorporation ratify and enforce contracts made in its behalf[3]

§ 638 *Lapse of charter by failure to comply with conditions — Effect of failure to complete road within a specified time —* Frequently a charter of a railroad corporation requires it to complete its road or a certain number of miles of road within a certain time, and the charter expressly declares that for failure to comply with this requisite the corporate powers and existence shall cease. There is a strong line of decisions to the effect that such a provision as this forfeits the charter absolutely upon non-compliance, and that no decree of a court is necessary to effectuate that forfeiture[4]

---

[1] See §§ 233, 234, *supra*.

[2] Id

[3] See § 705, etc., *infra*.

[4] See Brooklyn, etc, Co. v City, 78 N. Y, 524 (1879); *In re* Brooklyn, etc, R. R. Co., 72 N Y., 245 (1878), id, 75 N. Y, 335 (1878); Commonwealth v Lykens, etc., Co, 110 Pa. St., 391 (1885), Farnham v Benedict, 107 N Y, 159 (1887). *Cf Re* Kings County El. R'y Co, 105 N Y, 97 (1887), rev'g 41 Hun, 415, People v Nat'l Sav Bank, 11 N E Rep., 170 (Ill, 1887), aff'd, 22 id, 283 (1889). A new state constitution may forfeit all charters previously existing, but which have not been used by the incorporators. Chincleclamonche Lumber, etc., Co. v. Commonwealth, 100 Pa. St., 438 (1882), holding also that a constitutional provision that charters under which no organization has been made and business has been commenced shall lapse forthwith is constitutional and self-enforcing In the case of Putnam v Ruch, 54 Fed Rep, 216 (1893), the court, in a *dictum*, said that the repeal of a charter by a constitutional enactment may be self-executing, but that in the case before the court the judgment of the court was necessary Where by its charter a street railroad is to be commenced within three years and completed within ten, but it does not even open books for subscriptions until nearly twenty years have elapsed, the corporation never came into existence, and an abutting property owner may enjoin the laying of tracks Bonaparte v Balt. etc, R. R., 23 Atl Rep. 784 (Md 1892) *Contra*, N Y, etc, R. R. v N Y, N H., etc, R R 52 Conn. 271, 284 (1884). *Cf* State v Bull, 16 Conn, 179 In Texas the statute is self-executing, the words used being the same as in the New York statute But the property rights survive for the benefit of creditors and stockholders Sulphur Springs, etc., Co. v St. Louis, etc, Co., 22 S W Rep, 107 (Tex, 1893). A provision that unless certain roads should be completed within a certain time, "its corporate existence and its powers shall cease, so far as it relates to that portion of said road then unfinished," is self-executing Mayor, etc. of City of Houston v Houston, etc, Co., 19 S. W. Rep., 786 (Tex, 1892) A subscriber, sued on his subscription for stock, may defeat the suit by showing that by statute the charter was to be void if no work was commenced within two years, and that such two years have elapsed and no work has been done Bywaters v. Paris, etc, R'y, 11 S. W Rep, 856 (Tex, 1889) Under the Virginia law requiring organization within

But this drastic and dangerous construction of charters does not commend itself to law and justice It adds one more to the perils which are attached to all great corporate enterprises. Even in New York, where the above doctrine seems to have had its origin, the courts are inclined to limit its application The New York courts have recently held that a provision in a charter, that unless certain things are done within a certain time the company should "forfeit the rights acquired," does not work a forfeiture *ipso facto*.[1]

It is good cause for forfeiture of a charter by judicial decree where a railroad company does not complete its road or does not complete it within a prescribed time.[2] And such a forfeiture at the instance of the state by reason of the failure of the corpora-

two years or else the charter is void, the charter becomes void, ' without legal proceedings of any kind, from mere operation of law " Welch v. Old Dominion, etc, Co., 10 N Y Supp, 174 (1890), Silliman v Fredericksburg, etc., R R, 27 Gratt (Va), 119 (1876) A provision in the general statutes to the effect that the powers of a corporation shall cease if it does not organize within one year does not apply to a special charter the terms of which indicate that organization might be after one year People v Bowen, 30 Barb, 24 (1859), affirmed on other grounds, 21 N Y, 517 *In the case of Bybee v. Oregon, etc. R. R., 139 U S, 663 (1891), the court reviewed the conflicting decisions on the question whether a corporate charter could be made by the legislature to lapse and cease *ipso facto* and without judicial action

[1] Consequently this is no defense to condemnation proceedings In re Brooklyn, etc, R R, 125 N Y, 434 (1891) A provision that if the road is not completed within a certain time "the charter shall be forfeited " is not self-executing Galveston, etc, R'y v State. 17 S W Rep, 67 (Tex, 1891). This principle is not applicable where the statute merely limits the term of existence of the corporation Elizabeth G L Co. v. Green, 78 Atl. Rep, 844 (N J, 1889).

[2] The failure of a railroad corporation to complete its line as laid down in the charter is ordinarily good cause for for-

feiture of its charter, but the state may waive it People v. Ulster, etc., R. R., 128 N Y, 240 (1891). See, also, N. Y., etc, R. R. v N Y. & N. H., etc, R. R., *supra* A railroad may construct its line long subsequently to the date of its charter, there being no limit in its charter as to time of construction Western, etc, R. R.'s Appeal, 104 Pa. St, 399 (1883), Union Canal Co. v Young, 1 Whart. (Pa.), 410 (1836). Failure to commence work within a time specified in the charter, and a penalty that therefor the company should be dissolved, does not effect dissolution. A judgment is necessary Day v. Ogdensburg, etc, R. R. Co, 107 N. Y., 129 (1887) If the time limited for the completion of the road has expired, this is a defense to eminent domain proceedings. Morris, etc, R. R. Co. v Central, etc., R. R, 31 N. J L., 205 (1865). *Cf.* § 637, *supra* The state may forfeit the charter where the road is not constructed within the time fixed by the charter and amendments; also where it abandons a part of its lines State v. Noncannah, etc., Co, 17 S W. Rep., 128 (Tenn. 1875). Where a railroad company mortgages such part of its road as is completed, and the mortgage is foreclosed, the purchasers are not bound to go on and complete the road Failure on their part to complete it is no defense to an action on a subscription. Chartiers R'y v. Hodgens, 85 Pa. St., 501 (1877).

834

tion to complete its enterprise as required by charter has often been decreed[1]　But forfeiture *ipso facto* is a doctrine of modern date　It is contrary to reason, justice and the weight of authority[2]

[1] People *v* Kingston, etc, T Co, 23 Wend, 193 (1810), where the road was not constructed as required, Thompson *v* People, 23 Wend, 537 (1840) reversing 21 id, 235, holding that an immaterial omission is not fatal, People *v* National Sav Bank, 11 N E. Rep, 170 (Ill, 1887), forfeiting for failure to complete subscriptions as required by charter, Eastern, etc, Co *v* Regina, 22 Eng L & Eq, 328 (1853), for failure to pay in capital stock as required by charter, People *v* City Bank, 7 Col, 226 (1883), to same effect　See People *v* Jackson etc, P Co, 9 Mich, 285 (1861), for a case of the construction of a road in sections　And where the charter prescribes that a certain number of miles shall be completed within a certain time, but does not prescribe that the effect of non-compliance shall be a forfeiture, then the only way of forfeiting the charter is by a suit and a decree of a court　Hughes *v.* Northern Pac R'y Co　18 Fed Rep, 106 (1883), Arthur *v* Commercial Bank, 17 Miss, 394, 430 (1848)　The fact that a corporation commences business in another state within a year suffices for a charter provision that it must commence business within a year　*Re* Capital, etc, Ins Co, 47 L T Rep, 123 (1882), The People *v.* Kankakee Improvement Co, 103 Ill, 491 (1882)　In this case the charter required the proposed improvements to be completed within eight years as far east as the state line　The company completed as far east as Kankakee City and claimed the right to exercise the option of making or not making further improvements between that point and the state line　The court say "The non-compliance with the requirements was *per se* a misuser, and a cause of forfeiture of the franchise as for condi-

tion broken " and "we can see here but one entire franchise for the improvement of these streams and that this obligation to make the improvements above Kankakee City was a condition annexed to this entire franchise We think the non-compliance with the requirement in question was a cause of forfeiture of the entire franchise" Briggs *v* Cape Cod Land Co, 137 Mass, 71 (1884)　In this case the charter of a corporation required it to deposit with the state treasurer within four months from its date the sum of $200,000 as security for certain purposes, among others for the payment of damages for taking land and the corporation did not deposit the $200,000 in cash but in bonds of the United States of the par value of $200,000, and of the market value of $230,000　*Held*, a sufficient compliance, as the object of the provision was to provide security to various interests Also held that the question whether a corporation has ceased to exist for non-compliance with charter provisions could only be judicially determined in a suit to which the commonwealth was a party　The corporation itself, when sued for taxes, cannot set up this defense　Baltimore, etc, R R *v* Marshall Co., 3 W Va, 319 (1869)　Where a charter, by its terms, is to be void unless the capital stock is subscribed within two years and business commenced, a failure to secure the whole subscription within that time renders the charter void though business was commenced　*Quo warranto* lies　People *v* Nat'l Sav. Bank, 11 N E Rep, 170 (Ill, 1887)　An owner of land which a railroad has taken cannot reclaim possession by reason of the failure of the company to complete its road within the time limited by charter　Cincin-

§ 639 *Repeals of charters — Right of stockholders to object.*— The repeal by the state of a charter before the expiration of the time it was to exist, or the repeal at any time where the charter is perpetual, is an unconstitutional breach of the contract between the state and the corporation and the stockholders[1] Where, however, the right of repeal is reserved by the legislature, then such reservation becomes a part of the contract, and the repeal of the charter rests in the discretion of the legislature[2] Upon a repeal the cor-

nati, etc, R. R. v. Clifford, 15 N. E. Rep, 524 (Ind., 1888), Bravard v Cincinnati, etc, R. R., 17 N E. Rep, 183 (Ind, 1888). The bondholders of the company take the risk of this forfeiture of the charter for non-compliance with conditions. Silliman z Fredericksburg, etc, R. R, 27 Gratt (Va), 119 (1876), where, however, the corporate officers were endeavoring to enforce fraudulent bonds Some of the English railway acts are plainly not obligatory but only enabling, and it is held that the evident intention of parliament was to permit the companies to complete their lines as far as possible or desirable before the limit of time set, and to abandon the remaining portion York & North Mall R'y Co r Queen, 1 Ellis & Bl, 878 (1853), reversing same case, id p 178, Great Western R'y Co r Queen id, 874, reversing same case, id, 253 Edinburgh, etc, R'y Co, r Philip 2 Macq (Scot. App in H of L) 514, 526 (1857). Scottish N E R v Co r Stewart 3 id, 382, 414 (1859). See, also, Rex r Birmingham Canal, 2 W Bl, 708 (1780), by Lord Mansfield, Bakemore r Glamorganshire Canal, 1 Myl & K, 162 (1832), by Lord Eldon, Queen r Eastern Counties R'y Co, 10 Ad & El, 531 (1839), Queen r Lancashire, etc, R'y Co, 1 El & Bl, 228 (1852)

[1] Greenwood r Freight Co, 105 U S, 13 (1881) "A grant of corporate privileges for a specified period cannot be resumed by the state within such period If the charter be without limitation as to time it is forever irrepealable" Erie & Northeast. R. R r Casey, 26 Pa. St, 287 (1856). The legislature cannot for-

feit a charter Forfeiture can be decreed only by the courts. It is not a legislative function unless reserved. Allen v. Buchanan, 9 Phil (Pa), 283 (1873). Congress may repeal a charter granted by a territory Mormon Church r United States, 136 U S, 1 (1890). A forfeiture of land by the government for non-compliance with the terms of the grant may be by legislative enactment. Farnsworth r Minn, etc, R. R, 92 U S, 49 (1875).

[2] Under a reserved power to repeal at the pleasure of the legislature the courts cannot question the necessity nor the legislative motives leading to a repeal. Greenwood r Freight Co, 105 U S, 13 (1881), Lothrop r Stedman, 13 Blatch, 134 (1875). See Sinking Fund Cases, 99 U S, 700, 720 (1878); Northern R. R. Co r Miller, 10 Barb, 260 (1851); Erie, etc, R. R Co r Casey, 26 Pa. St, 287, 302, Miners' Bank t United States, 1 Greene (Iowa), 553; Lothrop r Stedman, 42 Conn 583, McLaren t Pennington, 1 Paige, 102, Crease r Babcock, 23 Pick, 334, 341 If the power of repeal arises only upon an abuse of franchise the court may review the question whether there was an abuse. Erie & Northeast. R. R t Casey, *supra*, Mayor, etc, of Baltimore r Pittsburgh & Connellsville R. R. Co, 1 Abb. U S. Rep, 9 (1865). Hence the legislature cannot forfeit a charter merely because the corporation has been incorporated elsewhere and has brought suits in the federal courts. Commonwealth t Pittsburgh, etc, R. R, 58 Pa St, 26 (1868). See, in general, Flint, etc, Plank-road Co r. Woodhull, 25 Mich, 99 (1872), Montgomery r Mer-

porate property becomes a trust fund, to be applied first to the payment of the debts of the corporation, and the balance to be distributed among the stockholders[1]

§ 640 *Acceptance of a charter by the corporation arises from merely acting under it, and a want of formal acceptance is no defense to actions on its contracts* — It is an old principle of law that individuals cannot be compelled by the state to accept a charter to act as a private corporation   Accordingly an acceptance of the charter by them is necessary to the actual existence of the corporation   But there is no rigid rule of law requiring them to indicate such acceptance in a formal manner.   Any acts which prove an intent on the part of the corporators to proceed under the charter is a sufficient acceptance of it.   It has been frequently held that an acceptance may be shown by proof that corporate meetings and elections have been held and other corporate acts entered into.   Mere user of the right to act as a corporation is sufficient[2]

rill, 18 Mich , 338 (1869)   State v Noyes, 47 Me , 189 , Canal Co v Railroad Co , 4 Gill & J 122 , Regents v Williams, 9 Gill & J 365 , Cooley's Con Lim 106 , Mayor, etc , v Twenty, etc , 113 N Y 311   Under this reserved power the state may authorize one corporation to build its road on a route which a prior corporation has designated but not acquired   Re Cable R'y, 40 Hun 1 (1886)   A general statute or constitutional provision reserving the right to repeal, alter or amend charters enters into all charters granted subsequent thereto as much as if actually inserted in such charters Re Lee's Bank of Buffalo, 21 N Y, 9 (1860), Commissioners etc , v Holyoke Water-power Co , 104 Mass , 446 (1870), Delaware R R Co , v Tharp, 5 Harr (Del), 454   The repeal of a general incorporating act and the enactment of a new one does not repeal charters which have already been taken out under the old act   Freehold, etc , Assoc v Brown, 29 N J Eq , 121 (1878)   United, etc Assoc v Benshimol, 130 Mass , 325 (1881)   *Contra*, Wilson v Tesson, 12 Ind , 285 (1859)

[1] See § 641

[2] Acceptance of a charter is sufficiently shown by user under it   Demarest v Flack, 128 N. Y , 205 (1891), Androscog-

gin Bridge v Bragg, 11 N H , 102 (1840), Bank of Manchester v Allen, 11 Vt , 302 (1839), Talledega Ins Co v Landers, 43 Ala , 115, 136 (1869), Trustees, etc , v Gibbs, 56 Mass , 39 (1848), Gleaves v Brick, etc , Co , 1 Sneed (Tenn), 491 (1853), Perkins v Sanders, 56 Miss , 733 (1879), Mutual, etc , Ins Co v Stokes, 9 Phil , 80 (1872), Penobscot Boom Corp v Lamson, 16 Me , 224 (1839)   Sampson v Bowdoinham, etc , Corp , 36 Me , 78 (1853), Lincoln, etc , v Richardson 1 id , 79 (1820), Bow v Allenstown, 34 N H 351, 372 (1857), Jameson v People 16 Ill , 257 (1855), City of Covington v Covington, etc , Co 10 Bush (Ky), 69 (1873), People v Farnham, 35 Ill , 562 (1864), Middlesex, etc , v Davis. 44 Mass , 133 (1841), Commonwealth v Bakeman, 105 Mass , 53 (1870), Palfrey v Paulding 7 La Ann , 363 (1852), Trott v Warren, 11 Me , 227 (1834)   Building a part of the road is an acceptance of a special charter   St. Joseph, etc , R R v Shambaugh, 17 S W Rep , 581 (Mo , 1891)   Acceptance is sufficient where the grantees afterwards apply for an amendment to the charter   Farnsworth v Lime Rock R R , 22 Atl Rep , 373 (Me , 1891), and see cases in §§ 183-86 *supra*, holding that a subscriber cannot defeat an action to collect his subscrip-

§ 641 *The assets upon dissolution* — Upon the dissolution of a corporation all its property, both personal and real, is to be used to pay the debts of the corporation, and after the debts are paid

tion by alleging informalities in organization Formerly it was customary at the first meeting of the corporation to pass a formal vote accepting the charter This, however is not necessary. The fact of holding the meeting is a sufficient acceptance See same cases, also City of Atlanta v Gate City, etc., Gas Co, 71 Ga., 106 (1883), where a charter granted in 1868 was not acted on until 1877 It was held that the application for a charter constituted an acceptance in advance McKay v Beard, 20 S C, 156 (1883), holding that an acceptance existed though no meeting at all for organization was held, but the corporation proceeded to business Logan v McAllister, 2 Del Ch, 176 (1858), holding that irregularities in organization are immaterial, Russell v McLellan, 31 Mass, 63 (1833), where no notice was given of the first meeting, and a stockholder sued for a dissolution of the company as a copartnership The best evidence possible of the acceptance should be given Hudson v Carman, 41 Me, 84 (1856). Where subscription books are opened and then abandoned, and ten years later are secretly re-opened and subscriptions taken without giving the statutory notice to the public that they may subscribe, the charter is forfeitable State v Bull, 16 Conn, 179 (1844) So, also where a new charter is granted to an existing corporation, and it continues to act the jury are to say whether the corporation continued under the old charter or accepted the new one. Hammond v Straus, 53 Md, 1 (1879) As regards the acceptance of a charter amendment by simply acting under it, see State v Sibley, 25 Minn, 387 (1879), Sumrall v Sun, etc, Ins Co, 40 Mo, 27 (1867), King v Hughes, 7 B & C, 708 (1828), a municipal corporation case, Bangor, etc, R R Co v Smith, 47 Me, 34 (1859), Lyons v Orange, etc, R

R Co, 32 Md, 18 (1869); Wetumpka, etc, R R Co v Bingham, 5 Ala, 657 (1843) and many cases in ch XXVIII, *supra* Failure to organize under a special charter until after a constitutional amendment prohibiting special charters is fatal to it State v Dawson, 16 Ind, 40 (1861) Acceptance must be *in toto* or not at all Rex v Westwood, 4 Barn & C, 781 (1825). A person cannot be compelled to act as a corporator in a private corporation Ellis v. Marshall, 2 Mass, 269 (1807) Hence his acceptance must be proved by user at least Collin v Collins, 17 Me, 440 (1840). Organizing out of the state may not be legal, yet it suffices for an acceptance of the charter. Heath v. Silverthorn, etc, Co, 39 Wis, 146 (1875) A special charter must be accepted before the corporation exists, and such acceptance cannot be at a meeting held out of the state Hence a bill by a stockholder to set aside a forfeiture of his stock was dismissed by the court Smith v Silver, etc, Co, 20 Atl Rep, 1032 (Md, 1885). Acceptance of a new charter is not necessarily an abandonment of the old one Johnston v Crawley, 25 Ga, 316 (1858); Woodfork v Union Bank, 3 Cold, (Tenn), 488 (1866) A corporation cannot accept part of a special charter and reject the rest Matter of Metropolitan, etc, T. Co, 111 N Y, 588 (1888). Acceptance of the charter is not implied by accepting the benefits but performing none of the burdens imposed, as where a toll road was established over a highway Welsh v Plumas Co, 29 Pac. Rep, 720 (Cal, 1892). Acceptance must be within a reasonable time After ten years' delay before organizing, the state may object by an information in the nature of *quo warranto* State v Bull, 16 Conn, 179 (1844).

the remainder is to be distributed among the stockholders[1] Formerly it was held that the real estate of the corporation upon dissolution reverted to the grantor, its personal property to the state or sovereign, and the debts due to it and from it were forgiven and extinguished[2] But a contrary rule now prevails.[3]

[1] Krebs v. Carlisle Bank, 2 Wall (C. C.), 33 (1850), Heath v Barmore, 50 N Y, 302 (1872), Burrall v Bushwick R R Co, 75 N Y, 211 (1878) James v Woodruff, 10 Paige, 541 (1844), Frothingham v Barney, 6 Hun, 366 (1876), Wood v. Dummer, 3 Mason, 308, 322 (1824) *Cf. In re* Hodges Distillery Co, L. R., 6 Chan, 51 (1870), Nathan v Whitlock, 9 Paige, 152 (1841), Curran v State of Arkansas, 15 How, 304, 307 (1853), Hastings v Drew, 76 N Y, 9 (1879), affirming S C, 50 How Prac., 254 (1887) The same rule prevails where the charter is repealed by the legislature Lothrop v Stedman, 13 Blatch, 134 (1875), McLaren v Pennington, 1 Paige, 102 (1828), by statute, Detroit v Detroit & Howell Plank-road Co, 13 Mich, 140 (1880), County of San Mateo v Southern Pacific R. R. Co, 8 Sawyer, 238, per Field, J, holding that "the property of the corporation acquired in the exercise of its functions is held independently of such reserved power, and the state can only exercise over it the control which it exercises over the property of individuals engaged in similar business" (p 279) 111 N Y, 1 The legislature cannot repeal a charter granted by the constitution of the state New Orleans v Houston, 119 U. S, 265 (1886).

[2] Hightower v Thornton, 8 Ga., 486 (1850), Life Association of America v. Fassett, 102 Ill, 315 (1883) Commercial Bank v Lockwood, 2 Harr (Del), 8 (1835), State v Rives, 5 Ired Law (N C), 297 (1844), White v Campbell, 5 Humph (Tenn), 38 (1844), Fox v Horah, 1 Ired Eq (N C), 358 (1841), Malloy v Mallett 6 Jones Eq (N C) 345 (1863), holding also that the stockholders liability was extinguished, President, etc, of Port Gibson v Moore,

21 Miss., 157 (1849), Bingham v Weiderwax, 1 N Y, 509 (1848), Owen v Smith, 31 Barb, 641 (1860), State Bank v State, 1 Blackf (Ind), 267, 282 (1823), Acklin v Paschal, 48 Texas. 147 (1877), St Philip's Church v. Zion, etc, Church, 23 S. C., 297 (1885), Coulter v Robertson, 24 Miss, 278 (1852), Bank of Miss v Duncan, 56 Miss, 166 (1878), Hamilton v Accessory, etc, Co, 26 Barb, 46 (1857)

[3] Bacon v Robertson, 18 How (U S), 480 (1855), Heath v Barmore, 50 N Y, 302 (1872), Lum v Robertson, 6 Wall, 277 (1867), Robinson v Lane, 19 Ga. 337 (1856), Lothrop v Stedman, 13 Blatch, 134 (1875), Blake v Portsmouth, etc, R. R Co, 39 N H, 435 (1859), Matter of Woven Tape Skirt Co, 8 Hun, 508 (1876), Mumma v Potomac Co, 8 Peters, 281 (1834), Fox v Horah, 1 Ired Eq (N C), 358 (1841), Bingham v Weiderwax, 1 N Y, 509 (1848), Curry v Woodward, 53 Ala, 371 (1875), 2 Kent's Com, 307, n, Powell v North Mo R. R Co, 42 Mo, 63 (1867), Wood v Dummer, 3 Mason, 308 (1824). Statutes are frequently enacted to this effect. Nevitt v Bank etc, 14 Miss, 513 (1846), McCoy v Farmer, 65 Mo., 244 (1877) Owen v Smith, 31 Barb, 641 (1860) A deed of property to a railroad for fifty years or so long as its charter continued which by charter is fifty years, passes the land to a corporation which by legislative enactment succeeds to the rights of the first corporation Davis v. Memphis, etc, R. R, 6 S Rep, 140 (Ala, 1889) So far as land grants are concerned the consolidated company is the same as the old company United States v Southern P. R. R, 45 Fed Rep. 596 (1891) A consolidated company succeeds to land owned by one of the consolidating companies. Cushman v Brownlee, 27 N E

When the corporation owns a right of way or other franchise obtained from a municipality or by the exercise of the state's power of eminent domain, this right of way franchise is a corporate asset upon the dissolution of the corporation. It does not revert to the state or municipality.[1]

This is the natural and logical result of the principle of law that a railroad company may make a contract to run longer than its chartered existence,[2] may take a deed of land in fee, although the company's duration is limited,[3] and may acquire a perpetual right of way under the same circumstances.[4] On the dissolution of a cor-

Rep, 560 (Ind, 1891) An agreement that upon dissolution of the company the telegraph line should go to the railroad is binding Latrobe v Western Tel Co, 21 Atl Rep., 788 (Md, 1891) A corporation cannot deed land fter its charter has expired Marysville, etc, Co v Munson, 21 Pac. Rep, 977 (Kan, 1890) A deed duly authorized is good though executed after the corporation is consolidated with another Edison, etc, Co v New Haven, etc, Co, 4 R'y & Corp. L. J, 4 (1888).

[1] Where a legislature, under its reserved right of repeal, repeals a street railroad charter, the right to use the streets and operate the road does not revert to the state, but passes as property to the receiver for the benefit of the creditors and stockholders of the corporation People t O Brien, 111 N Y., 1 (1888). In Pennsylvania the franchise of the right of way of a railroad rests, upon its dissolution, in the state, and the state may grant it to another railroad Erie, etc, R. R Co. v Casey, 26 Pa St, 287 (1856) See, also, Platt v Cox, 43 Pa St, 486 (1862) In Ohio it seems that the right of way reverts to the owner of the fee. New York, etc, R R. Co v Parmalee, 1 Ohio C. C Rep., 239 (1885) See, also, as to the rule in New York, Heard t City of Brooklyn, 60 N Y, 242 (1875) People v White, 11 Barb, 26 (1851), Hooker v Utica & M I R. Co, 12 Wend, 371 (1834). There is no reversion of the right of way on the dissolution of the company after fifty years Davis v Memphis, etc, R R

Co, 6 S. Rep, 140 (Ala, 1889). A lottery grant cannot be repealed, when mortgaged by the corporation, until the mortgage is paid Gregory's Ex. v. Trustees, 2 Mete (Ky), 589 (1859). Cf., in general, Turnpike Co v Illinois, 96 U S, 63 (1877). Where the stockholders of an old plank-road company are still operating the road but under another charter, they cannot be ousted from the latter by an injunction suit against their operating under the former. The court stated that it did not favor such a confiscating suit. People v. De Grauw, 133 N Y, 254 (1892). Unused right of way does not revert to original owner McConihay v. Wright, 121 U.S, 201 (1887). The state may grant an unused street railway franchise to another company Henderson v Central, etc, R'y, 21 Fed. Rep., 358 (1884). No reverter where the railroad takes a fee. Yates t. Van De Bogert, 56 N. Y., 526 (1874) See, also, in general, Norton v Wallkill, etc, R. R Co, 42 How Pr, 228 (1871), States v. Rives, 5 Ired (N. C), 297 (1844), Hopkins v Whitesides, 1 Head, 31 (1859) Where a turnpike company is authorized to collect tolls only for fifteen years, the road is free after that date People v Anderson, etc., Co, 18 Pac. Rep, 308 (Cal, 1888).

[2] A corporation whose charter expires in forty years may nevertheless make a contract for nine hundred and ninety-nine years Union Pac R'y t Chicago, etc R'y, 51 Fed Rep, 309 (1892).

[3] Nicoll t Railroad, 12 N Y, 121

[4] Miner t N Y C, etc, R R, 123 N

poration having no stockholders the common-law rules of reverter and appropriation apply.[1] Upon dissolution the stockholders are entitled to an immediate settlement of the corporate debts and a distribution of the residue[2] They are not obliged to accept the stock of another corporation as payment upon a final distribution, but may demand that the distribution be in cash[3] The company by unanimous consent may distribute the assets without a dissolution provided all creditors are paid[4]

When corporate assets are placed in the hands of a corporate officer or other person for distribution, a stockholder may file a bill in equity for his part, but in such a suit the corporation is a necessary party.[5] The remedy in such a case is not at law.[6] The

Y., 242 (1890), Davis v Memphis, etc, R R 6 S. Rep, 110, Bailey v Platt, etc, Co, 21 Pac Rep, 35   Taft, J, reached a contrary conclusion in City of Detroit v Detroit Street R'y, 56 Fed Rep, 867 (1893), and held that a city ordinance granting street rights to a company for a longer period than the duration of the corporation was void.   Dissolution does not terminate a lease to a corporation People v Nat'l Trust Co, 82 N Y., 284 (1880).

[1] Upon the dissolution of a public or charitable corporation its property goes to the state and former owners, subject to the trust that the property shall still be used for similar purposes if those purposes be legal   Mormon Church v United States, 136 U. S., 1 (1890)   Upon the dissolution of an eleemosynary corporation having no stockholders or creditors, the title to its land reverts to the donor   Danville Seminary v Mott, 28 N E Rep, 54 (Ill, 1891).   A private corporation — a normal college — cannot by act of the legislature be converted into a public corporation and the property vested in the state   Bakewell v Board of Education, 33 N E Rep, 186 (Ill, 1893).   In California, on the dissolution of a corporation for literary purposes, its land goes to the state.   People v Pres., etc, 38 Cal, 166 (1869)   Upon dissolution of a mutual insurance com-

pany having no stockholders, its assets, after the payment of its liabilities, belong to the state   Titcomb v Kennebec, etc, Co, 9 Atl Rep, 732 (Me, 1887).   But where an insurance company is organized both on the stock and mutual plan, upon a dissolution of the stock part of the organization the guaranty accumulations belong to the stockholders   Traders', etc, Ins Co v Brown, 8 N E Rep, 134 (Mass, 1886)   Land reverts to the former owner   Mott v Danville Sem, 21 N E Rep, 927 (Ill, 1889).   Distribution of funds of incorporated association   Aston v Dashaway, 22 Pac Rep, 660, affirmed in 23 id, 1091, 1890   As to unincorporated associations, see ch XXIX, supra

[2] Frothingham v Barney, 6 Hun, 366 (1876)

[3] See § 667, infra

[4] Rorke v. Thomas, 56 N Y, 559 (1874).   Although the state is prosecuting a suit to forfeit the charter for entering into a combination, yet a sale of part of the corporate property to a stockholder pending the suit is legal and the receiver cannot follow the property   A writ of prohibition will issue against him   Havemeyer v. Superior Court, 24 Pac Rep, 121 (Cal, 1890).

[5] Young v Moses, 53 Ga, 628 (1875)   For the remedies and procedures when the directors on dissolution have di-

[6] Brown v Adams, 5 Biss, 181 (1870).   Cf Pacific R. R. Co v Cutting, 27 Fed   Rep, 638 (1886), Hodsdon v. Copeland, 16 Me, 314 (1839)

stockholders may insist on the statute of limitations as a bar to the claim of corporate creditors upon the assets[1] The rights of the stockholders in the assets upon a dissolution depend upon the law of the country creating the corporation.[2] And these rights cannot be taken from the stockholders by an act repealing the charter[3] It has been held that assets ought to be distributed in proportion as the subscriptions to the stock have been paid.[4]

Debts due from the stockholder to the corporation are in any event to be deducted from his interest in the assets[5] And an assignment or transfer of stock by a stockholder after the dissolution of the corporation is merely an equitable assignment of his interest in the assets of the concern as it may appear upon the settlement[6]

vided the assets fraudulently, see Horner v Carter, 11 Fed Rep. 362 (1882). The minority may bring the officers to an accounting for an unfair distribution of the bonds, etc , owned by a construction company Meyers v Scott, 2 N Y Supp , 753 (1888) The corporation may file a bill to distribute a specific fund only, and need not in that bill have a general distribution of all its funds. Pacific R. R. v Cutting, 27 Fed Rep, 638 (1886). If the directors who by statute are made trustees to wind up the corporation upon dissolution, delay in so doing the court will appoint a receiver Matter of Pontius, 26 Hun, 232 (1882) Although the charter is forfeited at the instance of the state, yet the directors are trustees to wind up the company under the statute, unless a receiver is appointed at the instance of a creditor or stockholder Havemeyer v Superior Court 24 Pac Rep, 121 (Cal, 1890). Although the fund upon dissolution is small and the number of stockholders large yet the directors cannot avoid their duty as to the distribution of the fund by turning it over to a court to administer In re Centennial Board of Finance, 48 Fed Rep, 350 (1891) If the directors are by statute authorized to administer the assets upon dissolution, but fail to do so the court will appoint a receiver. Re Pontius supra

[1] Johnston v. Talley, 60 Ga , 540 (1878).

On a bill to wind up an insolvent corporation the stockholder may prove that some claims against the company were not legally contracted Crutchfield v Mutual, etc., Co , 2 S. W. Rep., 678 (Tenn , 1886)

[2] Hamilton v Accessory Transit Co , 26 Barb , 46 (1857).

[3] Lothrop v Stedman, 13 Blatch., 134 (1875)

[4] Krebs v Carlisle Bank, 2 Wall (C. C) 33 (1850), Sheppard v Seinde, etc , R's Co , 56 L T Rep, 180 (1887); In re Hodges, etc Co , L. R. 6 Ch, 51 (1870). On winding up, stockholders who have advanced on the subscription price more than the calls required, under an agreement of repayment with interest, are entitled to repayment before a general dividend is made So held where full-paid stock was issued for property, but other stock for cash was not fully paid up Exchange, etc , Co , 58 L T Rep, 544 (1888) This is the rule by statute in New York upon the voluntary dissolution of a corporation 3 Rev. Stat, ch XVIII, art, 3, § 88

[5] James v Woodruff, 10 Paige, 541 (1844), Nathan v Whitlock, 9 Paige, 152 (1841), Paxton v New Orleans, etc , R R Co , 3 La Ann , 1032 (1848).

[6] James v Woodruff, 10 Paige, 541 (1844), S. C affirmed, 2 Denio, 574 (1845); Sewall v Chamberlain, 16 Gray, 581 (1860).

A person who conveys property to the corporation in payment for stock may contract that upon dissolution he shall receive back that property [1]

§ 642. *The liabilities upon dissolution, consolidation or sale —* As already seen, the old rule that upon dissolution all debts by or to the corporation are rendered unenforceable is no longer the law [2]

An important question arises in this connection where one corporation sells out all its property to another corporation leaving some of the debts of the former corporation unpaid. The rights and remedies of the creditors in such a case are fully considered elsewhere [3] So also it frequently becomes important to know whether a consolidated company is liable for the debts of the constituent companies,[4] and whether a purchaser at a foreclosure sale is liable for the debts of the foreclosed corporation [5]

The question of liability where the corporation is a mere "dummy" is considered elsewhere [6]

Another interesting and difficult question is whether a person or corporation which owns all the stock of another corporation is ever liable for the debts of the latter on the ground that the latter is a mere "dummy" for the former. This subject also is considered elsewhere [7]

At common law upon dissolution of a corporation all suits by or against it abate [8]

Suit does not lie against a corporation which has been dissolved [9]

---

[1] Fish z Nebraska, etc, Co, 25 Fed Rep, 795 (1885)

[2] See preceding section But a judgment declaring a corporation illegal, void and the association dissolved puts an end to a contract by it to pay certain parties its bonds and stock if they would build its road Vinal v Continental, etc, Co, 32 Fed. Rep, 345 (1887)

[3] See ch XL, *infra.*

[4] See ch LIII.

[5] See ch LII

[6] See §§ 6 and 663a, *infra.*

[7] See Id

[8] McCulloch v Norwood, 58 N Y, 562, *In re* Norwood, 32 Hun, 196 (1884), Greeley z Smith, 3 Story. C C, 657 (1845), Saltmarsh v Planters', etc, Bank, 17 Ala, 761 (1850), Merrill v Suffolk Bank, 31 Me., 57 (1849); Ingraham z Terry, 11 Humph (Tenn), 572 (1851), Life Association v Fassett, 102 Ill, 315 (1882), Platt v Ashman, 32 Hun, 230 (1884) An action for tort abates upon the expiration of the corporate charter. Grafton z Union Ferry Co, 13 N. Y Supp, 878 (1891). Corporate suits end when the charter expires. Logan v. Western, etc., R. R., 13 S E Rep, 516 (Ga., 1891) An action against a corporation may be continued against those who administer its assets where the corporation is dissolved pending the suit. Hepworth z. Union Ferry Co. 62 Hun, 258 (1891).

[9] Dobson v Simonton, 86 N C., 492 (1882) The legislature may provide for suits against corporations after dissolution, thus changing the common-law rule. Stetson v City Bank, etc, 2 Ohio St., 167 (1853), Foster z Essex Bank, 16 Mass., 244 (1819). A corporation may be sued as such for a tort committed by it after its charter has expired Miller z Newberg, etc, Co., 8 S E Rep., 600 (W Va, 1888). No action after dissolution. Gold v. Clyne, 58 Hun, 419 (1890).

A contract made by the officers after the charter has been forfeited does not bind the stockholders.[1]

A director who is a creditor of the corporation may share proportionately with other creditors in the assets.[2]

Where a company owing debts allows a foreclosure of a mortgage and buys in the property and holds it secretly in the name of a trustee, an execution may be levied on it by a judgment creditor of the company.[3]

Where an attorney brings suit in the name of a corporation that has been dissolved before the action he is liable for costs if beaten Attleboro Nat'l Bank v. Wendell, 64 Hun, 208 (1892) After dissolution has been decreed it is too late for a corporate creditor to bring an action to hold the directors liable for declaring dividends out of the capital stock, no fraud in obtaining the dissolution being alleged. Coxon v. Gorst, 64 L. T. Rep., 444 (1891) Upon dissolution, the directors becoming trustees by statute, the statute of limitations begins to run against claims against the secretary. Landis v Saxton, 16 S. W. Rep., 912 (Mo , 1891).

[1] Wilson v. Terson, 12 Ind., 285 (1859).

[2] Thompson v. Huron Lumber Co , 30 Pac. Rep., 741 (Wash , 1892).

[3] State v McBride, 15 S. W. Rep., 72 (Mo , 1891)

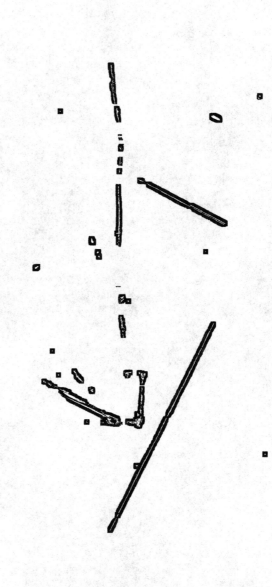

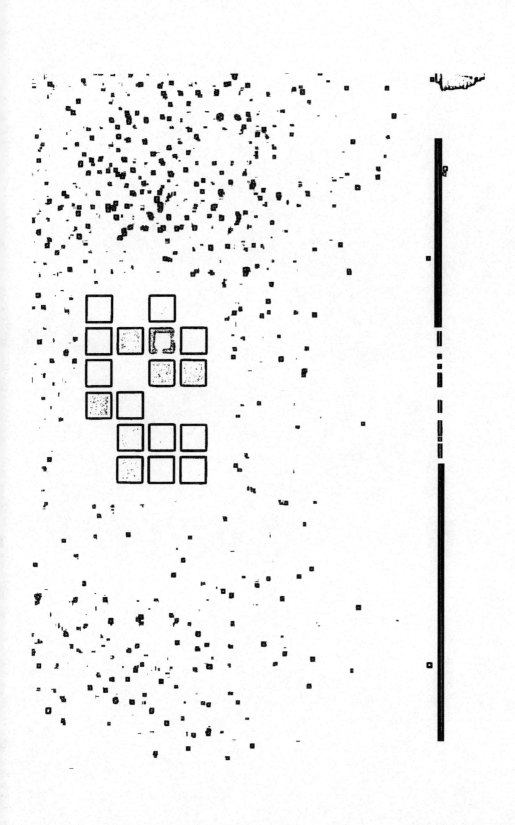